THE FACTS ON FILE
COMPANION TO THE

FRENCH
NOVEL

KAREN L. TAYLOR

☑® Facts On File

An imprint of Infobase Publishing

To Sacha, Nathalie, et Philippe

The Facts On File Companion to the French Novel

Copyright © 2007 by Karen L. Taylor

Facts On File, Inc.
An imprint of Infobase Publishing
132 West 31st Street
New York, NY 10001

ISBN-10: 0-8160-5405-3
ISBN-13: 978-0-8160-5405-3

Library of Congress Cataloging-in-Publication Data

Taylor, Karen L.
The Facts on File Companion to the French novel / Karen Taylor.
    p. cm
  Includes bibliographical references and index.
  ISBN 0-8160-5405-3 (hc : alk. paper)
  1. French fiction—History and criticism. I. Title: Companion to the French Novel. II. Title.
  PQ631.T39 2006
  843.009—dc22   2005036768

Text design by Joan M. Toro
Cover design by Cathy Rincon/Anastasia Plé

Printed in the United States of America

VB Hermitage 10 9 8 7 6 5 4 3 2 1

This book is printed on acid-free paper.

CONTENTS

INTRODUCTION

One of the most fascinating things about literature is the way in which writers make use of their creative powers to comment on society and the human condition. In France, as early as the 16th century, the works of humanist writers such as François Rabelais introduced into literature the notion of an independent subject, a necessary component for the rise of the novel as a literary genre. At the same time, Rabelais both revealed the complex levels of society and questioned its values in a rich and imaginative use of language.

In the 17th century, rather than offering a pointed critique of society, *précieuse* writers associated with the salons, such as Madeleine de Scudéry and Honoré d'Urfé, chose instead to draw from the tradition of the medieval romance and courtly love to create a utopian world in fiction that stood as a challenge to social reality. In contrast, contemporary burlesque writers such as Charles Sorel and Paul Scarron challenged the overly elaborate language of the *précieuses* as well as their idealized heroes in a style that blends comedy and realism.

A period characterized by socioeconomic and political transition, the 18th century witnessed the rise of new ideas about the relationship of the individual to society. The French Revolution marked a watershed in Western thought, as it not only brought about the fall of Old Regime society, but also sought to construct a new one based on principles associated with Enlightenment thought.

The Enlightenment represented emancipation from ignorance and superstition by reason. Enlightenment thinkers questioned traditional authorities, both civil and religious, while emphasizing the importance of human dignity and such basic rights as freedom of expression and freedom of religion. The notion of sovereignty based on representative government that developed in this period naturally reflects a heightened sense of individualism. The works of Voltaire and Montesquieu are particularly representative of Enlightenment principles.

Meanwhile, authors such as the marquis de Sade, Crébillon fils, Laclos, Restif de la Bretonne, and Nerciat used eroticism to promote a philosophy of militant rationalism. The primacy of nature and the notion of human as animal led them to emphasize the pursuit of physical pleasure. Nonconformist in morality, religion, and politics, the 18th-century libertine novel thus served as a philosophical reaction to the idealism of the previous century. Libertine novels are philosophical novels that promote materialism and rationalism. Like other 18th-century novels, they, too, signify an unwillingness to submit to authority that manifests itself in a more radical challenge to the social order.

As writers began to explore more deeply the subjective experience of the individual, new movements in literature arose. A particularly popular genre in the 18th century was the epistolary novel. A number of these works were written by men such as Jean-Jacques Rousseau, Montesquieu, and Laclos. Yet as women began to read and, increasingly, to write fiction, their first choice was often the novel in the form of letters.

Letter writing allowed women a public voice when they could not hold an official position in the public sphere. The letter is, by nature, a means of determining one's identity. It is also necessarily subjective.

Love was a common theme in 18th-century fiction, and it remained so with the epistolary novel. When such novels were written by women, marriage was a central topic. Because women were denied, for the most part, an existence independent from a male protector, the choice of a husband was an important one. The heroine of such novels is of a type: young, beautiful, virtuous; but there is rarely a precise description of her physical appearance. In contrast to the libertine novel, where the male figure is central to the narrative, in the epistolary novel, he is frequently observed from the female perspective. Male characters are often depicted as weak, indecisive creatures unworthy of a woman's constancy. To the 18th-century mind, the epistolary novel was suited to women because of its focus on the intimate, the domestic, the female sphere. In terms of themes and subject matter, the epistolary novel is closely tied to the sentimental novel. Rousseau, for example, serves as a transitional writer in the sense that he paved the way for the rise of the sentimental novel and romanticism.

The romantic movement was, in part, a reaction against the rigidity of Enlightenment thought, raising questions about the use of reason and rationality. The romantics opposed restrictions on the individual based on rationalism, be they civil, religious, or political. The concurrent rise of industrial society, a consequence of the application of empirical knowledge to daily life, only increased the romantics' belief that the modern era created heightened conditions for the individual's alienation and isolation in the material world.

The emergence of nationalism in the post-Napoleonic era (post-1815) gave rise to a conservative romanticism that focused on a definition of nature and culture derived from the nation-state. Stendhal's novel *The Red and the Black* depicts both the isolated romantic individual's struggle in society and the importance of nationalism to personal and cultural identity. The French Revolution reflected a belief that the state can be artificially constructed. In contrast, the romantic concept of the nation is not as the conscious joining of individuals but a natural union of people who share the same language, culture, and traditions.

The effects of industrialization and modernization on the European psyche caused some romantics to seek solace in an idealized past. Pastoral novels, such as those written by George Sand, thus represent the romantics' fascination with traditional, rural peasant life. Moreover, the romantic movement reflects a profound interest in the subjective human experience. If the Enlightenment espoused the power of human reason to improve society on the basis of accepted truths, romanticism emphasized instead feeling, intuition, and what we now call the subconscious as another basis of truth. Romanticism is revolutionary in the sense that it introduced into modern thought a sense of relativity.

The excesses of the French Revolution and the political turbulence of the 19th century combined with industrialization to create a disturbing sense of an often unjust modern world. The social tensions of the 19th century ultimately led writers such as Émile Zola and Honoré de Balzac to develop new literary movements such as naturalism and realism to grapple with social reality. Naturalism, for example, competed with science to represent nature. Like a doctor or scientist, the writer sought to observe the world carefully, examining man as a physical and chemical machine interacting with its environment. Zola argued that "the Naturalists take up a study of nature at its very sources, replacing metaphysical man with physiological man, no longer separating him from the environment that determines him."

Realists carried on the naturalist program as they, too, drew their themes from everyday life, especially from among the lower classes, hitherto ignored by most literary and artistic movements. Influenced by contemporary political movements, realists were primarily concerned with trends in modern life related to politics, economics, industry, and the rise of new social classes in the modern industrial age.

In contrast, the symbolists sought an autonomy in literature that some critics view as a reaction against the contemporary sociopolitical context. The development of a mass press contributed to the symbolists' desire to distinguish themselves from the crowd. Unlike the naturalists, symbolists such as Joris-Karl

Huysmans desired to create a completely different, exclusive literary movement that stood in opposition to the much acclaimed serial novel.

The origins of the serial novel lie in the 19th century with the rise of the press and mass production. Critics assailed this modern genre of "industrial literature." Alexandre Dumas took a journalist to court after being accused of running a "fiction factory." Those who opposed the serial novel did so on the basis of its aesthetic weakness, emphasis on emotion over style, theatrical effects, and melodrama. Eugène Sue's *Mysteries of Paris* is one of the best-known examples of the 19th-century serial novel, but nearly all the major novelists of the period wrote in serial form at one point or another.

As much as the 19th century was marked by profound social change, even more so the traumatic experience of World War I destroyed faith in traditional Western humanist values. Writers such as Roland Dorgelès and Louis Ferdinand Céline did not hesitate to depict the horrors of trench warfare in stark, compelling language. At the same time, the loss of faith in traditional values had a positive effect in the sense that a number of writers discovered a new creative freedom, and the interwar period consequently witnessed the rise of the Dada and surrealist movements.

Early French writers associated with Dada include the poet Paul Éluard, Louis Aragon, Philippe Soupault, and André Breton, along with other writers associated with the *Nouvelle revue française* (New French review). Surrealist writers soon eclipsed Dada, seeking to promote revolutionary ideas for the transformation of literature and life through innovations such as "automatic writing." Breton's *Nadja,* for example, evokes the power of surrealist literature to blend dreams with reality in an attempt to liberate the human spirit and its creative power.

The experience of World War II confirmed once more the uncertainty of the human condition and the relativity of truth. Artists and writers of Marxist orientation such as Aragon and Elsa Triolet promoted socialist realism, a movement obviously charged with political meaning. Like 19th-century naturalists and realists, socialist realist writers sought to depict reality accurately, but for a didactic purpose. After World War II, communist writers again promoted socialist realist literature in contrast to writers such as Jean-Paul Sartre, Albert Camus, and Roland Barthes, who argued in favor of "committed literature."

Existentialist writers such as Sartre and Simone de Beauvoir sought rather to articulate a new vision of the world in which the individual asserts his or her existence through deliberate choice and action. A number of writers followed their example in emphasizing the necessity of the writer's political engagement in the world. The novels of many such postwar intellectuals, not surprisingly, bear the influence of Marxist theory and reflect these authors' association with the Communist Party, either as members or as fellow travelers.

In the years following World War II, innovative writers such as Alain Robbe-Grillet, Nathalie Sarraute and Michel Butor among others developed still new approaches to the novel through the *nouveau roman* movement. These authors played with chronology and deliberately confused narrative voices. According to the *nouveau roman* writers, traditional narrative cannot truly apprehend reality. Sarraute, for example, explicitly rejected the idea that literature conforms to our sense of reality. The novel contains nothing and expresses only itself, nothing else. Moreover, it is constantly in the process of reinventing its own rules. In their laboratory for writing, *nouveau roman* writers frequently played with word games, metonymy, and metaphor.

Rather than focusing on the individual, an analogous literary movement, structuralism, emphasized the subject in such a way that even things that the individual experiences are formed by culture and are thus, on some level, collective. The self is socially constructed just like everything else. Consequently, structuralists were also interested in the subconscious as reflecting repressed signs prevalent in culture. Even reality is structured by codes and conventions made up of signs. Whether one considers the individual, the subconscious, or society, all are structured by the same signs.

In literature, philosophy, and the social sciences, the theory of postmodernism is the means of grappling with the conditions of the late 20th and early 21st centuries. Characteristics of the postmodern world are globalization, late consumer capitalism, mass media, and postindustrial service-oriented economies. In literature, postmodernism is associated with post-structuralism.

Poststructuralism and deconstruction reexamine the concept of the self in relation to the binary oppositions central to structuralist thought. The goal of poststructuralists is to reexamine the relationship between binary pairs, for example, good/bad, masculine/feminine, and light/dark. Poststructuralism tends to be political in its concern with hierarchy and power relations. Poststructuralist works challenge the values and experience of Western civilization manifest in phenomena such as colonialism, racism, sexism, and homophobia.

The rise of feminist and francophone literature in the second half of the 20th century continues today to explore and reveal the complexity of the human experience through female, lesbian, African, Caribbean, or French Canadian eyes. Writers such as Hélène Cixous, Monique Wittig, Tahar Ben Jelloun, Simone Schwarz-Bart, and Anne Hébert offer new possibilities of self-actualization and self-realization at the turn of the 21st century.

Feminist novels posit "writing" in contrast to traditionally male-dominated "literature." Rather than viewing women's artistic production within the confines of a male paradigm, feminist writers seek to define a particularly female domain. Catherine Clément, Julia Kristeva, and Xavière Gauthier, among others, have explored new, feminist-oriented interpretations of psychoanalysis in relation to women's creativity and artistic production.

Meanwhile, writers such as Cixous and Wittig began to reexamine the relationship of word and body. Drawing on one's own experience is perhaps only natural in a movement intended to reconstruct and reevaluate female identity in a manner that defies the myth of the "eternal feminine." Feminist writers seek to restore women to themselves on both a theoretical and a practical level as they redefine woman as an autonomous *subject*.

Francophone literature similarly grapples with questions of identity. Most frequently, the goal of francophone literature has been to express a separate cultural identity, often the product of cultural contact in an imperialist context, as something rich, distinct, and legitimate in its own right. In French Canada, the production and dissemination of literature written in French is an act of resistance. In the Antilles, writers such as Schwarz-Bart and Raphael Confiant have sought to reconcile their people with the past while unveiling the richness of Caribbean culture.

In Africa, the celebration of francophone literary expression in the negritude movement gave way to dissatisfaction and disillusionment. In North Africa, francophone literature of the first generation of Maghreb liberation writers such as Kateb Yacine and Mohammed Dib lay the foundation for postliberation writers whose works explore the complexity of Franco-Arab cultural contact. Literature thus becomes the means of questioning Arab culture as much as French colonization.

To explore the development of the French novel from its origins to the present is a rich and rewarding experience. The reader fully engaged in such a pursuit will pass through the principal intellectual movements that have marked the course of Western thought, as each historical period finds its reflection in the novel. Yet to envision a survey of the French novel in all its richness and breadth, from its origin to the present, is a daunting task. Naturally, not every novel could be included here, and certain selections may at times appear surprising. The reader will find entries, for example, on medieval romances and lays such as the *Song of Roland* and the writings of Chrétien de Troyes, works that introduced love and passion as central themes in French literature. Yet without reference to such works, it is impossible to understand their influence on subsequent works of fiction.

Most novels and authors traditionally included in the canon have been addressed in this work, as well as contemporary writers such as Michel Houllebecq. French titles are supplied when the English translation is not immediately evident. On occasion, the title remains in the original French if it is normally not translated into English. Particularly significant works have an entry of their own, while lesser-known novels are frequently addressed in the author entry. The most significant and familiar writers and their works are covered in the longest entries. At the same time, emphasis has also been placed on often under-represented works by women or francophone writers.

While scholars increasingly focus attention on feminist, francophone, and postcolonial works, general surveys up to now often ignored or glossed over texts that have since attained recognition from the reading public as significant contributions to the body of literature written in French. Nonetheless, even in these areas, there are many interesting and moving works that readers may go on to discover on their own. The suggestions for further reading found at the end of each entry as well as the selected bibliography at the end of the book should be helpful in this endeavor.

In preparing the entries, every attempt has been made to offer an outline of the basic plot, characters, and standard literary interpretations of the text or author in question, while simultaneously placing novels and authors within their broader historical, cultural, and intellectual context. The selection of terms and topics included is meant to aid the reader further in understanding the world out of which literature emerges.

A

***ABYSS* (L'ŒUVRE AU NOIR)** MARGUERITE YOURCENAR (1968)   In this novel, Yourcenar draws from historical figures such as Erasmus of Rotterdam, Michel Servet, Ambrose Paré, Leonardo da Vinci, Paracelsus, and Tommaso Campanella to create the character of Zeno. The novel traces Zeno's life from his illegitimate birth in Brussels to his suicide in prison 50 years later. In the intervening period, the many traumatic events of 16th-century Europe, religious and intellectual crises alike, come to life. The transformation of beliefs inherited from classical antiquity and medieval theology is represented in the French title as an alchemical experiment in the dissolution of forms, as Zeno tries to find a balance between the human and the divine that recalls Hadrian's philosophical quest (see MEMOIRS OF HADRIAN, THE).

This fictional biography re-creates the intellectual climate of 16th-century Europe, divided by religious strife and affected by the rise of modern scientific thought that coexisted for a time with ancient beliefs. Zeno, an alchemist, physician, and humanist interested in the human body, travels across Europe to escape persecution and to search for truth. At the end of the novel, he returns to his native Brussels under the false name of Sebastian Théus. He is arrested and tried for his writings, as well as for a crime he did not commit. Zeno ends by committing suicide in prison.

The novel reflects Zeno's spiritual quest, which, paradoxically, ends with his finally comprehending the union of body and spirit in death. Historically accurate, this well-researched novel differs significantly in its classical form and style from contemporary postwar novels. *Abyss* won the Femina Prize and along with *The Memoirs of Hadrian,* brought fame to its author. The novel was adapted to film in 1987 by André Delvaux.

FURTHER READING
Farrell, C. Frederick. *Marguerite Yourcenar in Counterpoint.* Lanham, Md.: University Press of America, 1983.

Horn, Pierre L. *Marguerite Yourcenar.* Boston: Twayne, 1985.

Howard, Joan E. *From Violence to Vision: Sacrifice in the Works of Marguerite Yourcenar.* Carbondale: Southern Illinois University Press, 1992.

Sarnecki, Judith Holland, and Ingeborg Majer O'Sickey, eds. *Subversive Subjects: Reading Marguerite Yourcenar.* Madison, N.J.: Fairleigh Dickinson University Press, 2004.

Savigneau, Josyane. *Marguerite Yourcenar: Inventing a Life.* Translated by Joan E. Howard. Chicago: University of Chicago Press, 1993.

Shurr, Georgia Hooks. *Marguerite Yourcenar: A Reader's Guide.* Lanham, Md.: University Press of America, 1987.

ADÈLE AND THÉODORE MADAME DE GENLIS (1782)   This lengthy pedagogical novel in epistolary form bears the influence of ROUSSEAU in its promotion of parental responsibility in the education of their children. Although Genlis later took Rousseau to task for his *ÉMILE,* his influence on her thinking is pervasive. *Adèle and Théodore* likewise echoes principles found in Madame d'Épinay's *Émilie's Conversations.* In fact, the

character Adèle is advised to read that work as a child. *Adèle and Théodore* also reflects elements of 18th-century sensibility.

The novel shows Genlis's concern with the education of both sexes. At the same time, she is particularly sensitive to a woman's position in society as she evokes the inescapable tensions in women's lives that arise from conflicting societal expectations. Moreover, while she recognizes the contemporary constraints on female education, Genlis nonetheless proposes a broad program for reform. The novel is consequently of interest to modern feminist scholars.

The principal character of the novel, the baroness d'Almane, speaks with Genlis's voice as she promotes moral values and common sense. The baroness is a model maternal figure who articulates Genlis's adherence to conservative Christian principles, something for which the author was criticized. *Adèle and Théodore* was, nonetheless, an enormous success in the genre of educational literature, popular not only in France but across Europe in the 18th century.

FURTHER READING

Harmand, Jean. *A Keeper of Royal Secrets; Being the Private and Political Life of Madame de Genlis.* London: E. Nash, 1913.

Schroder, Anne L. "Going Public Against the Academy in 1784: Madame de Genlis Speaks out on Gender Bias," *Eighteenth Century Studies* 32, no. 3, Constructions of Femininity (Spring 1999): 376–382.

Wyndham, Violet. *Madame de Genlis, a Biography.* New York: Roy, 1960.

ADOLPHE Benjamin Constant (1816) With this work, Constant proves himself the father of the modern psychological novel. The novel opens with a statement from the "editor" presenting the work as a manuscript found among the papers of Cerenza, a stranger whom he met at an inn. The manuscript contains the first-person narrative of Adolphe's story in which he expresses his thoughts about death and the veil of sadness that has been cast over his life.

In this introspective work the reader witnesses the autopsy of a love affair between Adolphe and his mistress Ellénore. Adolphe's feelings are marred by an inner failing that he describes as an insurmountable coldness and distance from his mistress and others. Overcome by a sense of alienation, Adolphe wishes to reestablish a connection with the world but is unable to do so.

Adolphe is not an entirely sympathetic character, but he is very human in his weakness and inner contradictions. Adolphe's confession reveals that the tragedy of his relationship with Ellénore lies in their mutual miscomprehension, a rather modern notion. The fundamental question Constant seems to ask is whether it is possible to commit oneself to another person.

Ellénore devotes herself to Adolphe in vain as he finds life with her monotonous and unsatisfying. Suffering from an arid heart, he ponders death. Ellénore's love brings him nothing. When she dies, rather than finding liberation, Adolphe realizes his disaffection from other human beings. He is incapable of love.

Adolphe's desire for independence is first directed toward his father, later his lover. Ellénore initially represents the forbidden fruit and Adolphe's goal is to seduce her away from her protector. By winning her over he theoretically liberates himself from social and familial expectations by allying himself with a woman of lesser status. In fact, he experiences no real liberation. As a result of his conquest, Adolphe is tied to his mistress. Following her to Poland, Adolphe becomes "a stranger in a foreign land," thus putting an end to his ambitions by cutting himself off from his own society. Adolphe's betrayal of his father (with whom he never reconciles) leads to his betrayal of Ellénore (resulting in her death).

Constant argued that he had written Adolphe out of pure artistry, intending to show that it is possible "to give interest to a novel concentrated on two characters whose situation never changes." In fact he draws from his own experience of being torn between an old mistress and a new love, warning against the falsity in human relations. Constant once described himself as "surrounded by I do not know what sort of barrier that others cannot penetrate."

Some critics have argued that Germaine de Staël is the model for Ellénore. Others cite an earlier liaison with an Irish woman named Anna Lindsay. It is certain that Constant drew from his own experience in writing this confessional novel. Ellénore's dying words, "This voice, it is the voice of the man who hurt me. This man killed me," are the last words of Constant's wife, Charlotte von Hardenberg.

Constant is not easy on himself in the character of Adolphe. He meticulously points to the pain he causes the woman he loves. While the novel may be autobiographical, it is also more than that, revealing something of the human character generally. Constant is not afraid to expose the more humiliating aspects of the human character to a harsh light. He described *Adolphe* as "a true enough story about the misery of the human heart." Along with FLAUBERT and PROUST, he presages 20th-century existentialism by unveiling the uncertainty of the human condition and its potential meaninglessness.

Adolphe is frequently referred to as an example of the romantic (see ROMANTICISM) hero who embodies the disease of romanticism (*mal du siècle*), along with CHATEAUBRIAND'S RENÉ and SENANCOUR'S OBERMANN. Constant wished to reveal the disease of his time by describing it as "this fatigue, this uncertainty, this lack of strength, this perpetual analysis that places a mental reservation before each feeling that corrupts them the moment they are born." The sufferer of this malady loses the will to act. For Constant, 19th-century man has lost a sense of duty that once gave meaning to life. Adolphe is disturbed by the meaninglessness of life, yet he is incapable of taking decisive action, a typically romantic failing. Despite the romantic themes, Constant writes in a dry style reminiscent of 18th-century classicism.

FURTHER READING

Call, Michael J. *Back to the Garden: Chateaubriand, Senancour, and Constant.* Saratoga, Calif.: Anma Libri, 1988.

Cruickshank, John. *Benjamin Constant.* New York: Twayne, 1974.

Fontana, Biancamaria. *Benjamin Constant and the Post-revolutionary Mind.* New Haven, Conn.: Yale University Press, 1991.

Heck, Francis S. *Spiritual Isolation in French Literature from Benjamin Constant and Senancour.* Madrid: Dos Continentes, 1971.

Wood, Dennis. *Benjamin Constant: A biography.* London, New York: Routledge, 1993.

ADRIENNE MESURAT JULIEN GREEN (1927)

Set in a small provincial town at the beginning of the 20th century, this novel tells the tragic story of a tormented young woman. Adrienne's mother has died and she lives with her frail sister and a senile father. When her sister leaves for life in a convent, Adrienne is left to suffer her father's dementia alone. Adrienne's only way of coping is to withdraw into herself until one day a single glance from the doctor Maurecourt gives birth to passion in Adrienne's heart. Increasingly obsessed, Adrienne begins to think of her father as an insurmountable obstacle to her love. One day she pushes him violently down the stairs and he dies. The question is, did she really mean to kill him?

Adrienne is overcome with remorse and guilt. Furthermore, the doctor rejects her declaration of love. Meanwhile, Adrienne is also menaced by a neighbor who suspects her crime. From then on, Adrienne sinks further and further into her own guilt, until she falls into madness.

Adrienne Mesurat is similar to Green's novel MOÏRA in its heavy and painful tone. In its descriptions, it also recalls the works of HONORÉ DE BALZAC, whom Green admired. Moreover, this novel is marked by the presence of evil, and thus reflects Green's concern with spiritual matters.

FURTHER READING

Burne, Glenn S. *Julian Green.* New York: Twayne, 1972.

Cooke, Gerard, Mother. *Hallucination and Death as Motifs in the Novels of Julien Green.* Washington, D.C.: Catholic University of America Press, 1960.

Dunaway, John M. *The Metamorphoses of the Self: The Mystic, the Sensualist, and the Artist in the Works of Julien Green.* Lexington: University Press of Kentucky, 1978.

Green, Julien. *The Apprentice Writer.* New York: M. Boyars, 1993.

Kostis, Nicholas. *The Exorcism of Sex and Death in Julien Green's Novels.* The Hague: Paris Mouton, 1973.

Newbury, Anthony H. *Julien Green: Religion and Sexuality.* Amsterdam: Rodopi; Atlantic Highlands, N.J.: Humanities Press, 1986.

O'Dwyer, Michael. *Julien Green: A Critical Study.* Portland Ore.: Four Courts Press, 1997.

Wildgen, Kathryn Eberle. *Julien Green: The Great Themes.* Birmingham, Ala.: Summa, 1993.

Ziegler, Robert. "From Writing to Scripture: The Character as Text in Julien Green's *Le Voyageur sur la terre*," *French Review* 63, no. 5 (April 1990): 819–826.

ADVENTURES OF GIL BLAS DE SAN-TILLANE (GIL BLAS DE SANTILLANE)

ALAIN RENÉ LESAGE (1715–1735)   Lesage worked on this novel for more than 20 years. As a result, the narrative reflects both historical developments and the author's own maturation as a writer. Like *The DEVIL UPON TWO STICKS,* this novel bears a Spanish influence. In fact, the story is set in Spain but the depiction of human nature, so appealing to contemporary readers, is universal. The main character, too, despite varied circumstances (he is at one time or another, a thief, adventurer, wayward traveler, social success) is also a universal man. Lesage draws from the tradition of the Spanish picaresque novel, much as the BURLESQUE NOVELS of SCARRON or FURETIÈRE before him.

Like his Spanish models, Gil Blas is an itinerant hero. He starts out as an honest, observant, and sensible young man of modest means who leaves his native town for Salamanca, where he will pursue his studies. As he travels from city to city and master to master, he undergoes a series of adventures. Along the way, Gil Blas meets a variety of characters from different social groups (priest, doctor, nobleman, actor), providing the panoramic perspective on society that contemporary readers found so engaging. Gil Blas's life is a series of ups and downs until he eventually becomes a master himself, gains a title, marries well, and becomes confidant to a government minister. This is when he decides to write his autobiography.

At the opening of the novel, Gil Blas is 17 years old when he is captured by bandits and forced to join them in their life of crime. Along the way, he saves a wealthy woman who offers to reward him, and so begins his adventures. The journey provides occasion for a hostelry motif and, consequently, the introduction of diverse episodes, meetings, and varied character portraits. The characters Gil Blas meets are not always honest or of good social standing. They often lack refinement, as does Gil Blas himself. He makes fun of himself for his own initial naïveté, yet he can also be vain and pretentious. Most important, he shows remarkable determination.

Lesage makes use of the grotesque (according to FURETIÈRE's definition, a mixture of the bizarre, the extravagant, and the ridiculous) in a similar manner as SCARRON or even MARIVAUX. And yet Gil Blas reflects something deeper. The novel is Freudian before its time and influences Marivaux, for example, through its exploration of different zones of consciousness and motivation.

The tale is told through a series of ironic, sometimes touching, episodes describing the people whom Gil Blas meets, both exemplary and ridiculous, that are unified by the narrator's voice. Some of the characters are unforgettable. The novel is highly entertaining and moralistic in the sense that Lesage uses the story to depict the dangers of vice, but it is not a work of social criticism. Lesage comments on human nature, not social systems.

FURTHER READING
France, Anatole. *The Latin Genius.* Translated by Wilfrid S. Jackson. London: John Lane and the Bodley Head; New York: Dodd, Mead, 1924.
Longhurst, Jennifer. "Lesage and the Spanish Tradition: *Gil Blas* as a Picaresque Novel." *Studies in Eighteenth-Century French Literature Presented to Robert Niklaus.* Edited by J. H. Fox, M. H. Waddicor, and D. A. Watts. Exeter, England: Exeter University Press, 1975, 123–137.

ADVENTURES OF JEROME BARDINI (AVENTURES DE JERÔME BARDINI)

JEAN GIRAUDOUX (1930)   Like Giraudoux's other works, *The Adventures of Jerome Bardini* is an engaging story that also reflects the uncertain times in which it was written. Perhaps Giraudoux's most modern novel, it tells the story of Jerome Bardini's journey of self-discovery.

Tired of the monotony of everyday life, Jerome decides to run away from Paris, work, his wife, and children to move to New York, where he can live the unencumbered existence of a foreigner, free from others and from responsibility. Jerome quickly discovers that his destiny is to be otherwise. One day in a park he meets Stephanie and they begin an affair. Stephanie, however, realizes that Jerome is incapable of remaining in a relationship and decides it is better to leave him before he can leave her.

Destiny then places a lost child in Jerome's path. Jerome becomes attached to "The Kid," only to find himself alone once more when The Kid's family is found. Fate has an ironic sense of humor. Jerome, who sought only to free himself from human entanglements, first falls in love with a woman and then with a child, realizing, in the end, that human beings are meant to be together. He ultimately returns to Paris to assume his responsibilities.

FURTHER READING

Body, Jacques. *Jean Giraudoux: The Legend and the Secret.* Translated by James Norwood. Rutherford, N.J.: Fairleigh Dickinson University Press; London; Cranbury, N.J.: Associated University Presses, 1991.

LeMaître, Georges Edouard. *Jean Giraudoux: The Writer and his Work.* New York: Ungar, 1971.

Le Sage, Laurent. *Jean Giraudoux, Surrealism and the German Romantic Ideal.* Urbana: University of Illinois Press, 1952.

ADVENTURES OF TELEMACHUS (LES AVENTURES DE TÉLÉMAQUE, FILS D'ULYSSE) FRANÇOIS DE SALIGNAC DE LA MOTHE FÉNELON (1699)

Supposedly the fourth book of Homer's *Odyssey,* Fénelon's work asserts from the start its debt to classical antiquity. In this work of pedagogical fiction, Ulysses' son Telemachus sets out in search of his father under the guidance of Mentor, who is, in fact, the disguised goddess Athena. This adventure story reflects the influence of classical antiquity on 17th-century French literature. It also bears the mark of the travel literature so popular among readers after the period of European exploration.

The real purpose of the journey is to teach Telemachus about ethics and politics. Telemachus's experiences transform and mature him. Like the duc de Bourgogne, the heir to the French throne for whom the tale is written, Telemachus is a future ruler. The *Adventures,* then, may be characterized as a mirror for princes inspired by both the virtues of classical antiquity and the Christian tradition. Like Dante's Virgil, in the *Inferno,* Mentor represents virtue and reason, toward which he guides his disciple, just as Fénelon was the moral guide for the duc de Bourgogne. Unfortunately, Fénelon's efforts never came to fruition; his pupil died before he could take the throne.

Mentor warns Telemachus against seeking pleasure, luxury, and war. For these reasons and because it echoes the arguments in Fénelon's critical *Letter to Louis XIV,* the work is considered a critique of Louis XIV's reign. It is also a work of utopian politics. There are two utopian governments within *Telemachus,* Salente and La Bétique. La Bétique recalls a golden age. In Salente, under Mentor's influence, King Idoménée rejects all luxury and forms a policy based on a return to the land and the simplicity and virtue of rustic life. Basing his work on a strict social hierarchy of seven classes and slaves, Fénelon essentially puts forth the traditional notion of monarchy with a strong aristocracy as the best form of government.

Immediately popular, *The Adventures of Telemachus* was one of the most read books of French literature until World War I. Along with La Fontaine's *Fables,* this text has long been a staple of the French student's literary diet.

FURTHER READING

Chydenius, Johan. *Humanism in Seventeenth-Century Spirituality.* Helsinki: Societas Scientiarum Fennica, 1989.

Janet, Paul. *Fénelon, His Life and Works.* Port Washington, N.Y.: Kennikat Press, 1970.

Rothkrug, Lionel. *Opposition to Louis XIV: The Political and Social Origins of the French Enlightenment.* Princeton, N.J.: Princeton University Press, 1965.

AGAINST THE GRAIN (À REBOURS) JORIS-KARL HUYSMANS (1884)

Last in the line of a noble family, des Esseintes, the main character of this novel vainly seeks fulfillment in vice and pleasure until he realizes the futility of this endeavor and becomes a recluse away from vulgar society. In the country, he creates a world of his own. His house becomes the perfect expression of his aesthetic taste, a refined decadence that rejects all banality. Des Esseintes covers his walls with exquisite cloth. His furniture consists of period pieces. The library is full of the writings of Latin decadents, mystics of all ages, and the poetry of Charles Baudelaire, Paul Verlaine, and Stéphane Mallarmé.

A sensual being, des Esseintes seeks to satisfy his senses through things created by humans, not by nature. In fact, he rejects nature. Nor is he particularly interested in art, which he sees as too realist (see REALISM). Des Esseintes prefers to create his own strange works of art that appeal directly to the senses, but they, too, tend to be perversions of nature. Des Esseintes explores literature, perfumes, flowers, gemstones (with which he decorates his tortoise's shell), Gustave Moreau's paintings, eroticism, and the illusion of travel. He plays symphonies on a mouth organ and creates other "symphonies" of odors and perfumes by crossbreeding flowers. He keeps a cricket in a cage suspended from the ceiling. Some critics have compared des Esseintes's collecting of physical and intellectual sensations to the collecting of knowledge in GUSTAVE FLAUBERT's BOUVARD AND PÉCUCHET.

Unfortunately, des Esseintes's attempt to create a refined aesthetic existence lead to excess and, ultimately, nervous collapse. Overcome by terrible nightmares, he suffers a crisis of nerves. The doctors are barely able to save him from madness, the effect of the artificial world des Esseintes has created for himself and that nearly destroys him.

The only solution is an agonizing return to society and the company of others. Faith in God is another possible solution but one that characters in Huysmans's subsequent novels will pursue, not des Esseintes, who is unable to make what becomes, in Huysmans's mind, the ultimate spiritual journey. Huysmans's contemporary Jules Barbey d'Aurevilly once said of Against the Grain, "After a book like this one, the author is left no choice but the mouth of a pistol or the feet of the cross." Huysmans chose the cross.

In this work, Huysmans breaks away from the NATURALISM of his earlier works, arguing that naturalism is a dead end as it depicts only the man of instinct and ignores the soul. Huysmans's systematic representation of the decadent style (see DECADENTISM) thus departs from his previous ZOLA-inspired naturalist works while retaining the Naturalists' accumulation of detail. It is Huysmans's most significant work.

One year before the publication of Against the Grain, PAUL BOURGET used decadence in reference to Charles Baudelaire in his Essays on Contemporary Psychology. The term decadence is derived from the Latin decadere, meaning "to fall from." Associated with a loss of values and moral decline, in literature deca-

dence represents a rejection of realism and naturalism in favor of SYMBOLISM. With this novel Huysmans introduces a new literary school whose adherents number among them AUGUSTE VILLIERS DE L'ISLE D'ADAM and the poet Stéphane Mallarmé. A year after the novel appeared, Mallarmé wrote a poem "Prose for des Esseintes." In fact, the character of des Esseintes became a cult figure.

Against the Grain also had an impact on later SURREALISM. Against conformity, decadent works often reveal a fascination with the grotesque and fantastic that is also reminiscent of some romantic works (see ROMANTICISM).

Huysmans's decadence marks a return to Flaubertian realism. Similar to some of Flaubert's characters, des Esseintes tries to eliminate the distinction between text and reality, to make them one. Imagination and illusion become reality as the character manipulates his experience. Des Esseintes represents an escape from materialism, bourgeois values, MODERNISM, and POSITIVISM, the hallmarks of 19th-century European civilization.

FURTHER READING

Banks, Brian. The Image of Huysmans. New York: AMS Press, 1990.

Gilman, Richard. Decadence: The Strange Life of an Epithet. New York: Farrar, Straus and Giroux, 1979.

Nalbantian, Suzanne. Seeds of Decadence in the Late Nineteenth-Century Novel. New York: St. Martin's Press, 1983.

Praz, Mario. The Romantic Agony. Translated by Angus Davidson. New York: Oxford University Press, 1970.

ALAIN-FOURNIER (Henri-Alban Fournier) (1886–1914)

From the beginning, Alain-Fournier lived a life full of dreams and fantasies that would come to bear on his one great novel, The WANDERER. If his childhood was somewhat melancholy, Alain-Fournier compensated for this by dreaming of a lost paradise. Fournier interpreted even life's little events as signs of some larger purpose.

In 1903, when Fournier entered secondary school in Paris, he became friends with Jacques Rivière, with whom he later corresponded almost daily. The two friends were different in character. Rivière was analytical and interested in ideas, whereas Fournier seemed to fear that ideas might tarnish the power of imagination. Despite the difference in character, this friendship dominated Fournier's life. In fact, Rivière married Fournier's sister.

In secondary school, Fournier's teachers introduced him to symbolist literature (see SYMBOLISM). In 1906, he discovered the works of Paul Claudel. These two influences confirmed his belief in the merging of word and thought, of the totality of art.

Another important event occurred the year before when Fournier briefly met a young woman who, although he never saw her again, became the focus of Fournier's dreams. After failing the university entrance exam, Fournier completed his military service and then took a position as secretary to the banker and financier Claude Casimir Perier. He began to publish a few articles and stories. Fournier's encounter with the works of André GIDE conflicted with the ideas he had derived from Claudel's Catholicism. In 1909, experiencing a religious crisis, Fournier traveled to Lourdes. When World War I began, he entered the army only to be one of the first soldiers to fall on the battlefield. In 1913, the *Nouvelle Revue Française* published Fournier's one famous novel, *The Wanderer,* a delicate work that clearly bears the influence of symbolism. Fournier brought together a sense of the real and the magical, as he sought to express a spiritual ideal.

FURTHER READING

Arkell, David. *Alain-Fournier: A Brief Life (1886–1914).* Manchester, New York: Carcanet, 1986.
Ford, Edward. *Alain-Fournier and Le grand Meaulnes (The Wanderer).* Lewiston, N.Y.: Edwin Mellen Press, 1999.
Gurney, Stephen. *Alain-Fournier.* Boston: Twayne, 1987.

ALGERIA TRILOGY: THE BIG HOUSE (LA GRANDE MAISON) (1952); FIRE (L'INCENDIE) (1954); TUNISIAN LOOM (LE MÉTIER À TISSER) (1957) MOHAMMED DIB

The Big House (1952), which won the Feneon Prize, is the first in this trilogy that tells the story of a young man named Omar. It begins with his experience of the misery of the urban working poor living in squalid conditions on the eve of World War II. The reader begins to understand the plight of the Arab population under colonial power and the reasons for their subsequent revolt, which are presented in a manner that recalls the works of the American writers John Steinbeck and John Dos Passos.

In volume two, *Fire,* Omar moves briefly to the countryside, where he discovers that the fellahins, or rural peasants, are as poor as urban workers. There he witnesses the outbreak of a fire that will soon spread across Algeria, a fire that "will keep on burning, slowly, blindly, until its bloody flames embrace the whole countryside with their sinister glow." Led by Hamid Sarady, a militant communist come from the city, the local populace rises up against injustice and oppression. In their struggle they rediscover a sense of meaning and heroism. The novel goes on to describe realistically the subsequent suppression of this movement and the harsh reality of war. In volume three, *Tunisian Loom,* Omar returns to the city, where he becomes an apprentice to a carpet weaver. The "fire" has now spread to the cities.

In this novel of apprenticeship, Omar matures into adulthood in the midst of trauma. He witnesses the rise of political consciousness while simultaneously experiencing the first pangs of desire for Zhor, a young woman who represents freedom. The themes of love and politics are thus intertwined.

In 1959, pursued by colonial authorities, Dib left Algeria for France. These first three novels came to serve as a national literary monument and mark the birth of modern Algerian literature. While Dib's realism draws from Western literary traditions, these works also draw from Algerian traditions in legends, songs, and poems.

FURTHER READING

Ahmad, Fawzia. *A Study of Land and Milieu in the Works of Algerian-Born Writers Albert Camus, Moulous Feraoun, and Mohammed Dib.* Lewiston, N.Y.: Edwin Mellen Press, 2004.
Joyaux, Georges J., Albert Memmi, and Jules Roy. "Driss Chraïbi, Mohammed Dib, Kateb Yacine and Indigenous North African Literature," *Yale French Studies* 24, Midnight Novelists (1959), 30–40.

ANTOINE BLOYÉ PAUL NIZAN (1933)

This sharp critique of bourgeois society opens with the

burial of Antoine Bloyé. The principal character of the novel, Antoine, is a railroad worker modeled on Nizan's father, who makes his way out of his original social class. In a manner that recalls 19th-century Realist novels (see REALISM), particularly the works of ÉMILE ZOLA, Nizan equates the railroad with the rise of the modern capitalist industrial system. "Antoine," he writes, "was caught like an insect in this quivering web of railway lines."

One day, Antoine confronts "nothingness," a concept associated with the German philosopher Martin Heidegger. (Nizan held a Ph.D. in philosophy from the Sorbonne). As he walks down the street, Antoine realizes the inevitability of his own death as well as the world's indifference to it and, as Nizan writes, "It takes a great deal of determination and creation to escape from nothingness." Antoine may have the determination and ambition to rise up out of the working class, but he lacks this deeper force, unlike his son Pierre, who, in CONSPIRACY, finds meaning in political struggle against social injustice. Because Antoine succeeds in attaining a position in management, he winds up in charge of the men who had once been his equals. This is what destroys him in the end, as Antoine discovers that he has cut himself off from his roots. In one poignant moment, Antoine looks down on Pierre after his birth and "thinks of his own death that will come and he contemplates his son who is nothing yet, who will betray him, who will perhaps detest him, or who will die."

Antoine Bloyé announces themes central to Nizan's oeuvre, in particular, betrayal and social mobility (which Nizan views as a form of betrayal). Moreover, he is critical of those who are concerned only with their career and success and, as a result, never engage in self-reflection.

FURTHER READING

McCarthy, Patrick. "Sartre, Nizan, and the Dilemmas of Political Commitment," *Yale French Studies,* no. 68, *Sartre after Sartre* (1985): 191–205.

Redfern, W. D. *Paul Nizan: Committed Literature in a Conspiratorial World.* Princeton, N.J.: Princeton University Press, 1972.

Schalk, David L. "Professors as Watchdogs: Paul Nizan's Theory of the Intellectual and Politics," *Journal of the History of Ideas* 34, no. 1 (January–March 1973): 79–96.

Scriven, Michael. *Paul Nizan: Communist Novelist.* New York: St. Martin's Press, 1988.

Stoekl, Allan. "Nizan, Drieu, and the Question of Death," *Representations,* no. 21 (Winter 1988): 117–145.

Suleiman, Susan Rubin. "The Structure of Confrontation: Nizan, Barrès, Malraux," *MLN* 95, no. 4, French Issue (May 1980): 938–967.

Wasson, Richard. "'The True Possession of Time': Paul Nizan, Marxism and Modernism," *Boundary* no. 2 (Winter 1977): 395–410.

ARAGON, LOUIS (1897–1982)

Louis Aragon was a poet and novelist whose collective works make sense only in the context of his life and the historical, cultural, and political framework in which he wrote. Because he was an illegitimate child, Aragon's mother passed him off as her brother. His father, prefect of police, could not have officially recognized his son without compromising his career. In fact, his father invented the name Aragon. The circumstances of his birth and upbringing may explain Aragon's continued exploration of the question of identity. It certainly led to his rejection of the bourgeois world of "appearances." Much of his writing reflects Aragon's interest in the "lying truth" of literature and the possibility of determining oneself through the writing process.

As a child, Aragon was an avid reader, fascinated from early on with language. He began writing in 1908, at the age of 11, first dictating stories to his aunts. He was drawn to the works of JULES VERNE, STENDHAL, MAURICE BARRÈS, and Henry Bataille, to the Russian novel, and, under the influence of an uncle, to SYMBOLISM, fauvism, cubism, and the Russian ballet.

In 1915, Aragon began to study medicine and met ANDRÉ BRETON, who was also a medical student. The two liked the same literature and became friends. At this point, Breton had already published some poems. He introduced Aragon into literary and artistic circles. Unfortunately, World War I interrupted their studies and Aragon only rejoined Breton in 1919. Together with Philippe Soupault they established a literary review entitled *Literature.* By 1920 Aragon was publishing his first poems and articles reflecting his interest in the question of modernity.

Like Breton, Aragon was associated with the DADA movement and SURREALISM, and he made an important contribution to the latter. Aragon's surrealist world, as it appears in *Anicet* and PARIS PEASANT, for example, is magical, vibrant, and sad all at once. Aragon's originality lies in his exploration of the marvelous in the quotidian, where imagination and rationalism intersect. Breton described him as a "skillful detector of the strange in all its forms." Throughout his life, Aragon remained interested in the relationship between reality and subjectivity. The influence of the symbolists is apparent in his lyrical style. Furthermore, during a 1922 trip to Berlin, Aragon was introduced to hypnotism, which generally fascinated the surrealists and is reflected in his *Wave of Dreams* (1924), Aragon's answer to Breton's *Surrealist Manifesto.*

In 1922, Aragon gave up his medical studies, against his family's wishes. He saw himself as part of a generation compelled to rebel against the prewar intellectuals who had sacrificed the young to protect a corrupt social order. Like Breton and others, Aragon subsequently turned to the political left.

Aragon's novel *Anicet,* published in 1921, is both a detective story and a work of apprenticeship. After participating in Dada "manifestations," Aragon wrote a parody of FÉNELON'S ADVENTURES OF TELEMACHUS (1922), and from 1923 to 1927 he worked on his *Defense of the Infinite,* a novel of novels that consisted of some 1,500 pages of literary collage reflecting, among other things, the anguish of expressing love in words. Aragon burned most of this work in Spain in 1927; only certain fragments were published during his lifetime. Aragon once wrote, "I envy those who can blend eroticism with expression." As in *Paris Peasant, Defense of the Infinite* illustrates the incompatibility of eroticism and its expression. In these works Aragon also considered the process of writing itself.

Aragon broke from the surrealists in 1927 when he joined the Communist Party, and in 1928 he met ELSA TRIOLET. From that point on Aragon was increasingly drawn to SOCIALIST REALISM. Aragon's *Treatise on Style* (1928) indicates that he was seeking a new direction. In the *Treatise,* Aragon considers the realm of individual freedom, arguing that the only criterion for defining inspiration is the discovery of new means of expression.

Aragon's writing subsequently became increasingly militant, especially in the 1930s. He wrote his one manifesto, *For a Socialist Realism,* in 1935, outlining principles to which he adhered in his series of novels *The Real World,* the first of which is *The Bells of Basel,* a critique of THIRD REPUBLIC France (1870–1940). Aragon's Balzacian (see BALZAC) RESIDENTIAL QUARTER, the second in the *Real World* series, focusing on the antagonism between two brothers, earned him the Renaudot Prize.

With Triolet, ANDRÉ MALRAUX, and ANDRÉ GIDE, Aragon traveled to the Soviet Union. The publication of his poem "Red Front" in 1932, however, brought on legal problems as well as Aragon's rupture with Breton. He was later drawn into political action in the Spanish civil war. In 1936–37, Aragon organized a group of antifascist intellectuals in defense of Spanish culture. During World War II, he organized a resistance group, directing a clandestine publication called *French Letters.* Aragon was considered the great poet of the Resistance, and his poems were passed underground during the Occupation years. After the Liberation of France in 1945, Aragon presided over the National Committee of Writers until the onset of the cold war. Because of his political stance, Aragon was deprived of his civil rights for 10 years.

Aragon believed that "all novels must appeal to a belief in the world as it is, even if it is to oppose it." Journalist, combatant, and participant in the intellectual Resistance against occupied France, Aragon wrote highly political work as he continually sought to show how the individual is caught in the historical process.

The revelation of Soviet leader Joseph Stalin's crimes in the 1950s had a tremendous impact on his work. Yet despite this and the political tensions of the cold war, Aragon remained faithful to the communist cause. Although he stopped working on *The* COMMUNISTS, Aragon refused to reject the link he saw between communism and literature, redefining socialist realism by promoting a combination of communism and literature as the means to express feeling. Aragon subsequently produced three important works, his *Unfinished Novel; Holy Week,* a novel about the painter Théodore Géricault; and a poem, *Fou d' Elsa.* In this period, Aragon's writing is freer than ever before as he reflects upon the conflict between reality and utopian dreams. With André Maurois, Aragon wrote *The Parallel History of the United States and the Soviet Union, 1917–1960* (1962). His famous poem, *Elsa* set in 15th-century Spain, recounts the fall of Grenada and looks toward Elsa, the woman of the future, as a source of hope and renewal. Love becomes the basis for reality.

The Soviet-led Warsaw Pact invasion of Czechoslovakia in 1968 brought on the final collapse of Aragon's idealist dreams. His last works focus on the relationship between art and history. As he alternates between prose and verse, in a manner reminiscent of the surrealists, Aragon's final novels explore the theme of the mirror as he examines the relationship between subject and object and, again, the question of identity.

To trace Aragon's life in his works is a rewarding endeavor. In the development of his imagination, his exploration of the self and the theme of love, and his political engagement, one sees the overlapping of the writer, his ideas, and politics in a fascinating and complex use of language.

FURTHER READING

Adereth, Maxwell. *Elsa Triolet and Louis Aragon: An Introduction to Their Interwoven Lives and Works.* Lewiston, N.Y.: E. Mellen Press, 1994.

Brosman, Catherine Savage. *Malraux, Sartre and Aragon as Political Novelists.* Gainesville: University of Florida Press, 1964.

Caute, David. *Communism and the French Intellectuals, 1914–1960.* New York: Macmillan, 1964.

Duruzoi, Gerard. *History of the Surrealist Movement.* Translated by Alison Anderson. Chicago: University of Chicago Press, 2002.

Kimyongur, Angela. *Socialist Realism in Louis Aragon's Le Monde Reel Series.* Hull, England: University of Hull Press, 1995.

ARGENS, JEAN-BAPTISTE DE BOYER, MARQUIS D' (1703–1771)

Son of an official to the parliament of Aix-en Provence, Jean-Baptiste de Boyer followed in his father's footsteps by studying law. He later undertook a brief military career that ended after sustaining an injury from a fall from his horse. Boyer wrote on a variety of subjects, among them his-

tory, philosophy, and religion. He was a prolific writer, too, producing numerous philosophical and moral essays and about 10 novels. His works may generally be categorized as presenting the ideas of ENLIGHTENMENT philosophers to a general audience. Invited by Frederick II to Berlin, Boyer became director of *Belles Lettres* at the Prussian Academy.

The marquis d'Argens's fictional works include his *Jewish Letters, Cabalist Letters,* and *Chinese Letters.* However, he is most famous as the author of one of the most popular LIBERTINE novels of the 18th century, *THÉRÈSE PHILOSOPHE.* D'Argens was inspired by a scandal in 1731, in which a priest was accused of seducing and impregnating a young woman. In this novel, the main character, Thérèse, describes her lessons in eroticism, first by a couple of penitents, then by the libertine Madame de Bois-Laurier. At the end of the novel she allies herself with a count who brings her to his château and allows her to enjoy the pleasures of the flesh without fear of pregnancy.

Thérèse articulates one of the principles of libertine philosophy, the notion that passion and desire are natural. According to her, they are gifts from God. D'Argens's work is particularly notable for his promotion of the very modern notion that sex, for men and women equally, is for pleasure, not necessarily for procreation. He thus liberates Thérèse from the limits of the domestic sphere in which a woman's only roles are those of wife and mother.

FURTHER READING

Bush, Newell Richard. *The Marquis d'Argens and His Philosophical Correspondence; A Critical Study of d'Argens' Lettres Juives, Lettres Cabalistiques, Lettres Chinoises.* New York: Thesis Columbia University, 1953.

AROUND THE WORLD IN EIGHTY DAYS (CINQ SEMAINES EN BALLON)

JULES VERNE (1873)   One of Jules Verne's best-loved works, this novel recounts the adventures of an English gentleman, Phileas Fogg, who makes a bet with his friends that he can circle the globe in 80 days. Fogg sets off with his French servant, Jean Passepartout, (which means "John passes everywhere"). Suspected of having robbed a bank, they are followed by a policeman, Inspector Fix.

The novel was inspired by an article that appeared in 1870 arguing that it would be possible to circumnavigate the globe in 80 days thanks to the construction of the Suez Canal. Verne uses this article as his starting point, as always blending adventure with science. The novel reflects the power of European civilization to dominate the globe. Like a fairy tale, the marvelous and the modern combine to entertain the reader, yet something serious and philosophical lurks beneath the surface.

In India, Fogg saves the life of Aude, a young widow who, according to Indian tradition, should have been placed on her husband's funeral pyre to be cremated with him. In China, the group encounters even more adventures. Phileas is now accompanied by Aude, and Fix remains hot on their trail. Unfortunately, since they are constantly on the move, Fix cannot arrest Fog, as the warrant never arrives on time. Finally, they arrive in America, where Fogg thwarts an Indian attack on a transcontinental train. Once they arrive at the East Coast, violent storms prevent the departure of any ships. Fogg finally manages to charter a boat. When it runs out of fuel, they are forced to sacrifice the ship's masts. Finally, Fogg and his friends arrive in England only to be arrested. Proven innocent, Fogg is released but he fears he has lost his bet. In fact, because of the time lag, he has gained 24 hours and succeeded in his task. Overcome with joy, Fogg asks Aude to marry him.

In *Around the World in Eighty Days,* Verne continues to explore the concepts of time and space, as in his JOURNEY TO THE CENTER OF THE EARTH. Fogg's journey is possible only because of the 19th-century revolution in transportation along with its effect on the perception of geographical space. Moreover, one of Verne's objectives is to teach the reader about the geography and character of the countries Fogg and his friends visit, responding to the reading public's fascination with travel literature, scientific discoveries, geography, and history. Verne's interest in scientific advances is reflected in the precision of his language. The travel literature genre also allows Verne to engage in social criticism through the comments of Passepartout.

Around the World in Eighty Days is more than an engaging adventure story. Verne uses his fertile imagination to draw the reader into a novel that is as much about developments in science and technology as it is about exciting escapades. Verne makes use of every possible form of transportation to bring his travelers to the end of their journey, from elephants and sleighs to trains. Like those of the great explorers of the 16th century, Fogg's journey is also linked to the process of European colonization, another recurring theme in Verne's writing.

Time is also an important subject in Verne's novels. Not only does the journey take place within the time frame of 80 days, but the regions through which Fogg travels allow for the characters to travel "back in time" as they cross through less-developed regions. The journey both begins and ends in England, Europe's most extensive empire during the 19th century. Verne explores both its expanse and its limits, for example, in India in the "sacrifice" of the wife after the death of her husband. The various regions through which Fogg travels exist at different stages of development, socially, economically, and technologically, thus marking the transition from old to new worlds. While the modern-day reader might have a different view, Verne's approach reflects 19th-century Europe's fascination with humankind's power to conquer Earth's natural obstacles. Since scientific and technical progress are not spread equally around the globe, Fogg's journey sometimes carries him into the past, again manifesting Verne's interest in the relationship of humankind to time and space.

FURTHER READING

Born, Franz. *Jules Verne, the Man Who Invented the Future.* Translated by Juliana Biro. Englewood Cliffs, N.J.: Prentice Hall, 1964.

Butcher, William. *Verne's Journey to the Center of the Self: Space and Time in the "voyages Extraordinaires."* New York: St. Martin's Press; London: Macmillan, 1990.

Costello, Peter. *Jules Verne: The Inventor of Science Fiction.* London: Hodder and Stoughton, 1978.

Evans, I. O. *Jules Verne and His Work.* Mattituck, N.Y.: Aeonian Press, 1976.

Freedman, Russell. *Jules Verne, Portrait of a Prophet.* New York: Holiday House, 1965.

Lottman, Herbert R. *Jules Verne: An Exploratory Biography.* New York: St. Martin's Press, 1996.

ARTAMÈNE, OR THE GREAT CYRUS (ARTAMÈNE, OU LE GRAND CYRUS)
MADELEINE DE SCUDÉRY (1649–1653)   On the surface, this highly popular 10-volume serial novel recounts important events and personages from Persian antiquity as Artamène overcomes a series of military and emotional obstacles to join his true love, Mandane. Nominally drawn from Persian history, the novel in fact recounts the military and romantic adventures of the Frondeurs. (The Fronde was a 17th-century aristocratic rebellion against the crown or, more particularly, the policies of the first minister, Cardinal Mazarin.) The main character, Artamène, represents the famous Frondeur the Grand Condé; Mandane is Madame de Longueville. Lydiane is Françoise d'Aubigné, wife of burlesque writer PAUL SCARRON.

Madeleine de Scudéry's depiction of exotic lands and cultures held great appeal for her audience. Even more attractive was the fact that it is a roman à clef, revealing the world of the *précieuses* (see PRECIOSITY) to the reader. Intercalated secondary stories are dispersed throughout the text. One tells of De Scudéry's platonic relationship with Paul Pélisson whereby her life becomes the model for love and fidelity in the manner of the *précieuses*. The novel paints an idealized portrait of *précieuse* society and manners. Its subtle psychological analysis makes it, along with MADAME DE LAFAYETTE's *PRINCESS OF CLÈVES,* a precursor to the French psychological novel.

FURTHER READING
Aronson, Nicole. *Mademoiselle de Scudéry.* Translated by Stuart R. Aronson. Boston: Twayne, 1978.
Davis, Joanne. *Mademoiselle de Scudéry and the Looking Glass.* New York: P. Lang, 1993.
Harth, Erica. *Cartesian Women: Versions and Subversions of Discourse in the Old Regime.* Ithaca, N.Y.: Cornell University Press, 1992.
McDougall, Dorothy. *Mademoiselle de Scudéry, Her Romantic Life and Death.* New York: B. Blom, 1972.

ASTREA (L'ASTRÉE) HONORÉ D'URFÉ (1607–1627)   This first great serial novel, more than 5,000 pages long, had a tremendous impact on 17th-century French literature and society. Its aristocratic audience waited impatiently for each new volume to appear. Readers acted out the plots, and various episodes were reproduced in the innumerable beautiful tapestries decorating the walls of aristocratic homes. The first and second parts were published in 1610, the third in 1619, the fourth part edited, and the fifth added in 1627 by d'Urfé's secretary, Balthazar Bruno. Another ending was been attributed to GOMBERVILLE.

The pastoral novel par excellence, *Astrea* is set in d'Urfé's native region of Forez in southeastern France. The novel depicts a mythical golden age in the fifth century. This fantastic background is what drove contemporary writers such as PAUL SCARRON, ANTOINE FURETIÈRE, and others to the BURLESQUE and to incorporate realist elements into their works.

The opening scene places the main characters, Céladon and Astrée, nominally a shepherd and shepherdess, on the banks of the Lignon River. Their speech and manners, however, are those of courtiers, not simple rustics. Calédon has been banished by his mistress, Astrée, who suspects that he has been unfaithful. Their situation is further complicated because their families hate each other and have forbidden marriage between the two lovers. This Shakespearean element is reinforced by many episodes of disguise and transvestism typical of Renaissance literature.

Desperate, Calédon throws himself into the river but is saved by water nymphs. Later, he resists Princess Galatea's offer of love, still hoping that Astrée will one day allow him to return. Eventually she does, in the last volume. The numerous and lengthy digressions from the main story line are typical of early modern fiction, the pastoral novel in particular. Most often the narrative turns back to a sophisticated discussion of love made famous by the *précieuses* (see PRECIOSITY). Recurring digressions refer to the "Fountain of Love's Truth." This magic fountain has been cast under a spell by a disappointed lover so that it no longer reflects one's true love in its clear water. Supposedly, the spell can be undone only by the sacrificial death of two ideal lovers. Fortunately, this never proves necessary.

Secondary story lines depict the love and adventures of Diane and Sylvandre, Phillis and Lycidas, and Hylas and the nymph Galathée. These intercalated stories and the additional inclusion of poems, songs, and letters give the novel its narrative complexity. D'Urfé's frequent inclusion of letters marks the work as a prototype of the EPISTOLARY NOVEL, so popular in the following century.

Astrea reflects a new interest in the analysis of love and emotion under the influence of Italian and Spanish sentimental literature, frequently in the pastoral form. If one considers the novel's historical context, the fascination with a mythical golden age for lovers is perhaps not surprising. The Edict of Nantes, ending the French wars of religion, had only been signed in 1598 and the French were ready for the restoration of peace and order in society.

Astrea has been characterized as baroque for its elaborate relationships, symmetry, and narrative complexity; synthesizing elements from medieval ROMANCES, the sentimental novel (see SENTIMENTALISM), and Italian and Spanish pastorals. *Astrea* depicts an idealized world in which lovers must overcome numerous obstacles that prevent them from consummating their relationship. In the medieval romance, that consummation would have been principally physical. In *Astrea*, two kinds of love are promoted simultaneously. The first is a Neoplatonic spiritual love. Some of d'Urfé's characters seem to speak with the voice of the philosopher Descartes in his promotion of reason over passion. The other love is strictly erotic. It is perhaps this combination that contemporary readers found so compelling.

FURTHER READING

Hembree, James M. *Subjectivity and the Signs of Love: Discourse, Desire, and the Emergence of Modernity in Honoré d'Urfé's L'Astrée.* New York: P. Lang, 1997.

Hinds, Leonard. *Narrative Transformations from L'Astrée to Le Berger Extravagant.* West Lafayette, Ind.: Purdue University Press, 2002.

Horowitz, Louise K. *Honoré d'Urfé.* Boston: Twayne, 1984.

Jehenson, Myriam Yvonne. *The Golden World of the Pastoral: A Comparative Study of Sidney's New Arcadia and d'Urfé's L'Astrée.* Ravenna, Italy: Longo, 1981.

McMahon, Mary Catharine, Sister. *Aesthetics and Art in the Astrée of Honoré d'Urfé.* New York: AMS Press, 1969.

Urfé, Honoré d'. *L'Astrée.* Translated with an introductory essay by Steven Randall. Binghamton, N.Y.: Medieval and Renaissance Texts and Studies, 1995.

ATALA, OR THE LOVE OF TWO SAVAGES IN THE DESERT (ATALA OU LES AMOURS DE DEUX SAUVAGES DANS LE DÉSERT) FRANÇOIS-RENÉ CHATEAUBRIAND (1801)

Inspired by his voyage to America in 1791 and by the French massacre of the Natchez in Louisiana in 1727, Chateaubriand wrote *Atala, or the Love of two Savages in the Desert,* depicting the morals and values of "savages" in the New World. Like RENÉ, *Atala* is an episode in the *GENIUS OF CHRISTIANITY,* suggesting the beauty and poetry of the Christian religion, but published separately. At the same time, Chateaubriand's love of nature and his evocation of passion and feeling in this work mark it as a great romantic novel (see ROMANTICISM).

According to the account, an elderly Indian named Chactas tells his story to a young Frenchman, René, who has come to America to escape an unhappy life. As a young man, Chactas is taken prisoner and condemned to death. Atala, a Christian, falls in love with him and helps him to escape.

Together they journey through the wilds of America, eventually arriving at the refuge of a missionary, Father Aubry. Chactas is ready to convert to Christianity in order to marry Atala. Unfortunately, on her deathbed, Atala's mother extorted a promise from her daughter that Atala would remain a virgin and devote her life to God. All through their travels Atala has been tormented by the memory of her vow. Desperate, she poisons herself. There is a painful death scene as Chactas and Father Aubry witness Atala's last moments and the two men bury her in great sadness. The burial scene is the subject of a hauntingly romantic painting by Anne-Louis Girodet-Trioson.

Through the character of Father Aubry, Chateaubriand depicts the beauty of Christianity when it is not distorted by human will (as exemplified through Atala's mother). His powerful evocations of nature, passion, and tragic love mark this text as supremely romantic. At the same time the theme of the noble savage gives it the flavor of an 18th-century work. Both *Atala* and *René* are moralistic and sentimental works in which Chateaubriand contrasts savage and civilized societies. In the end, he believes that Christianity will improve upon the virtue of humans in a state of nature.

FURTHER READING

Bouvier, Luke. "How not to Speak of Incest: Atala and the Secrets of Speech," *Nineteenth-Century French Studies* 30, nos. 3 and 4 (2002): 228–242.

Call, Michael J. *Back to the Garden: Chateaubriand, Senancour and Constant.* Saratoga, Calif.: Anma Libri, 1988.

Maurois, André. *Chateaubriand: Poet, Statesman, Lover.* Translated by Vera Fraser. New York: Greenwood Press, 1969.

Smethurst, Colin. *Chateaubriand, Atala, and René.* London: Grant and Cutler, 1995.

ATLANTIDA (L'ATLANTIDE) PIERRE BENOIT (1918)

As was often the case with Benoit, he chose an exotic setting for his novel, this time the desert. Antinéa, descended from Atlantis, draws travelers into her palace. Once they have succumbed to her charms, she murders her guests, making a collection of their mummies.

When two French officers arrive in this strange land, one of them, Saint-Avit, falls hopelessly in love with Antinéa, whereas his companion, Morhange, remains strangely unmoved. Disappointed, Antinéa persuades Saint-Avit to murder Morhange, after which he manages to escape from her clutches. In the end, however, incapable of overcoming his passion, Saint-Avit returns to Antinéa and certain death.

Atlantida won the grand prize of the Académie Française. Fantasy novels were a popular genre at the time and Benoit was particularly successful in writing them. As simple adventure novels one reads for pleasure, they stand out in contrast to contemporary symbolist (see SYMBOLISM) and naturalist (see NATURALISM) novels. *Atlantida* was adapted to film in 1921.

AUDOUX, MARGUERITE (1863–1937)

Audoux is the pseudonym for Marguerite Don Quichotte. Hers was a hard life. Shortly after her mother's death from tuberculosis, Marguerite and her sister, Madeleine, were abandoned by their alcoholic father. Marguerite would later raise the child abandoned in turn by her sister.

The two girls were initially taken in by an aunt and then sent to a provincial orphanage where they were raised by nuns. Audoux was subsequently sent to work on a farm, where she was inspired by her reading of FÉNELON's *ADVENTURES OF TELEMACHUS.* Desiring another kind of life, Audoux left for Paris at the age of 18. She earned her living as a seamstress and she wrote, despite a debilitating eye condition.

With little money, Audoux worked hard to support herself and her niece. In 1895 she set up her own atelier and took her mother's family name, Audoux, in place of the absurd Don Quichotte, the name given to her father, also an abandoned child, by a town employee. As of 1904, Audoux was participating in the meetings of a small group of artists and writers, the Carnetin Group, that included Valéry Larbaud, Francis Jourdain, Léon-Paul Fargue, and CHARLES-LOUIS PHILIPPE. When the latter died, Audoux contributed to the edition of the *Nouvelle Revue Française* (New French review) dedicated to Philippe's memory.

Audoux's friends from the Carnetin Group encouraged her to publish *Marie-Claire,* Audoux's fictionalized memoirs describing the misery and poverty of her childhood. Her captivatingly simple and natural style earned the praise of ANDRÉ GIDE. Audoux's most successful work, *Marie-Claire,* was published in 1910 with a preface by JEAN GIRAUDOUX. It won the Femina Prize in 1910. ALAIN-FOURNIER was so charmed by the work that he dedicated an article to it in the *New French Review* that same year.

Audoux continued to write novels such as *The Fiancée* (1910), *Marie-Claire's Atelier* (1920), *From the City to the Mill* (1926), and *Gentle Light* (posthumous, 1937) as well as articles. None of her later works was as successful as *Marie-Claire.* Audoux is considered to be one of the first populist or proletarian writers of the 20th century.

AURÉLIA GÉRARD DE NERVAL (POSTHUMOUS 1855)

In this, Nerval's last work, hope and peace are ultimately found in the mystical vision of Aurelia. The backdrop for the work is Nerval's fascination with both the Orient and Germany. In the first part, Nerval depicts a series of dreams through which a metamorphosis occurs to reveal a mysterious, unnerving other world of spirits. The narrator's despair grows until, at its height, he hears a voice crying out in the night. The narrator recognizes that it comes from Aurelia.

In the second part, the epigraph "Eurydice! Euri-duce!" recalls Orpheus's descent into hell. Dark visions and a mood of despair reign in this work as Eurydice/Aurelia is lost once more, just as she was in the myth. The narrator then sets off on a new path, this time to Paris. At the Dubois hospital, he meets his double, whom the narrator calls Saturnin. Ultimately, he finds peace in his soul through a mystical interpretation of these painful and confusing experiences.

Nerval wrote *Aurélia* in a period of madness and despair leading up to his suicide in January 1855. It was the author's last attempt to express his creativity. After *Aurélia*, he no longer felt capable of writing. The central theme of the eternal feminine is recurring in Nerval's works. Despite the note of despair, however, there is in this case the hope of redemption. *Aurelia* thus reflects Nerval's personal mythology.

Nerval's astonishing blend of dreams and reality reflects the romantic fascination with dream states and the inner, subjective experience (see ROMANTICISM). This particular quality also led to Nerval's influence on the surrealist movement (see SURREALISM).

FURTHER READING

Beauchamp, William. *The Style of Nerval's "Aurélia."* The Hague: Mouton, 1976.

Gilbert, Claire. *Nerval's Double: A Structural Study.* University, Miss.: Romance Monographs, 1979.

Jones, Robert Emmet. *Gérard de Nerval.* New York: Twayne, 1974.

Knapp, Bettina Liebowitz. *Gérard de Nerval, the Mystic's Dilemma.* Tuscaloosa: University of Alabama Press, 1980.

MacLennan, George. *Lucid Interval: Subjective Writing and Madness in History.* Rutherford, N.J.: Fairleigh Dickinson University Press, 1992.

Miller, David. *There and Here: A Meditation on Gérard de Nerval.* Frome, Somerset, England: Bran's Head Books, 1982.

Prendergast, Christopher. *The Order of Mimesis: Balzac, Stendhal, Nerval, Flaubert.* Cambridge: Cambridge University Press, 1986.

Strauss, Jonathan. *Subjects of Terror: Nerval, Hegel and the Modern Self.* Stanford, Calif.: Stanford University Press, 1998.

AURÉLIEN LOUIS ARAGON (1946) This masterpiece from Aragon's mature period explores the difficulties between a couple, Aurélien and Bérénice.

The novel opens in 1922, while the epilogue takes the characters to the tragic events of May 1940, with the Nazi occupation of France.

With the exception of one article by the playwright Paul Claudel, the novel was not well received, as it did not fit with the general postwar mood. Only later was *Aurélien* recognized by critics as an important novel. It is the story of a young soldier, Aurélien, broken by his experience in World War I, and Bérénice, a young provincial woman completely in love with Aurélien. However, Bérénice cannot accept her lover's idleness and skepticism, nor the wild life he leads in Paris in the 1920s. She thus leaves him.

At the end of the novel, the lovers find each other again in the year 1940. Aurélien has become a reactionary with fascist leanings, while Bérénice's political views are far more humanitarian. She dies in his arms, hit by an errant bullet as they are driving in a car.

Part of Aragon's *Real World* cycle of novels, *Aurélien* reflects Aragon's political views, as do so many of his works. The love story between Aurélien and Bérénice symbolizes France, divided in 1940 into two camps. Such a theme was difficult for readers to accept in 1946, just one year after the Liberation. A number of critics have noted that the sociohistorical perspective of the novel recalls BALZAC's HUMAN COMEDY.

FURTHER READING

Adereth, Maxwell. *Elsa Triolet and Louis Aragon: An Introduction to Their Interwoven Lives and Works.* Lewiston, N.Y.: E. Mellen Press, 1994.

Brosman, Catherine Savage. *Malraux, Sartre and Aragon as Political Novelists.* Gainesville: University of Florida Press, 1964.

Caute, David. *Communism and the French Intellectuals, 1914–1960.* New York: Macmillan, 1964.

Kimyongur, Angela. *Socialist Realism in Louis Aragon's Le Monde Réel Series.* Hull, England: University of Hull Press, 1995.

AYMÉ, MARCEL (1902–1967) Aymé was one of six children whose mother died when he was two years old. Consequently, Aymé went to live with his grandparents in the Jura region. Because of his grandfather's virulent anticlerical views, Aymé's grandmother was not able to have her grandson baptized until 1908, a scene the author recalls in his novel *The*

Green Mare (1933). When his grandmother died in 1910, Aymé had to move once more, this time to live with an uncle.

Aymé's childhood was marred not only by the loss of close family members but also by a serious illness from which he recovered in time to go to French-Rhineland Germany to complete his military service. In 1923, he moved to Paris, where he had no fixed employment for some time. Aymé worked at different times in a bank, as an extra in films, in an insurance company, and, finally, as a journalist.

Aymé lived in Montmartre, and his intimate knowledge of this Parisian neighborhood provided much rich material for his subsequent works. In 1925, he fell ill again, and during a long period of convalescence he began working on a novel. *Brûlebois* (1926), a novel depicting the working class Aymé knew so well, was only moderately successful. Aymé's second novel, *Round Trip* (1927), similarly portrays the street life and cafés of working-class Parisian neighborhoods. Then in 1929, *Hollow Field,* a novel drawing on Aymé's recollections of life in the provinces, won the prestigious Renaudot Prize. From that point on, Aymé lived by his pen, producing more or less a book a year until the end of his life.

The Green Mare was a particularly successful novel that was later adapted to film. Set in the fictitious village of Claquebue, the plot focuses on the rivalry between the Hadouin and Maloret families. The social and financial rise of the Hadouins is due to the birth of a green mare who observes the villagers' love lives and disputes from her stable. The feud between the two families also allows Aymé to reflect on political, religious, and property conflicts among the villagers.

In 1934, Aymé published a series of tales in which the reader rediscovers the author's taste for the marvelous, as well as his remarkable ability to blend the everyday with the fantastic. These and other works manifest Aymé's humor and sensitivity, as well as his reflections on the human condition, sometimes through allegorical animal figures. Elements of the fantastic reappear in the short story *Passe-Muraille* (1943), in which an ordinary office worker can walk through walls. In another work a young woman with the power to be in more than one place at a time re-creates herself thousands of times over to experience numerous erotic encounters. These Kafkaesque stories, however marvelous, nevertheless end in tragedy.

All his life, Aymé remained distant from politics as well as contemporary literary movements. In fact, it was never entirely clear what his stance was even in the most troubled of times politically. After the Liberation in 1945, Aymé was one of the writers who, to no avail, came out in defense of Robert Brasillach. After World War II, Aymé began writing for the theater, although he continued to produce novels and short stories, all of which offer his uniquely humorous critique of society and the foibles of humanity. A successful and well-known author, Aymé is not always considered a great writer, perhaps unfairly, given his singular capacity to describe real people, whether from the country or the city or somewhere in between.

FURTHER READING

Brodin, Dorothy R. *The Comic World of Marcel Aymé*. Paris: Nouvelles Éditions Debresse, 1964.
———. *Marcel Aymé*. New York: Columbia University Press, 1968.

AZIYADÉ Pierre Loti (1879)   Inspired by Loti's stay in Constantinople (Istanbul), this novel tells the story of an English naval officer named Loti who falls in love with Aziyadé, a young Circassian woman whose haunting green eyes he spies from a distance through the screen of a harem. The two are able to meet through the efforts of Loti's friends, a Macedonian named Samuel and Achmet, a Turk. Theirs is a passionate, if impossible, love. Eventually Loti is called back to England. At first he considers staying in order to remain near Aziyadé but, in the end, decides he must leave. Aziyadé withers away from sadness. When Loti hears of her death, he signs up again for service in Turkey and subsequently dies in battle.

Loti's first novel, *Aziyadé* received little or no attention; however it does present major themes that resurface in the author's other works: beautiful faraway lands where civilization has "stopped," the Westerner's fascination with a simple people, coupled with a sense of alienness in a place where he is "but a stranger without shelter."

Rich in description, the novel is partly epistolary, a device that allows for the two cultures to confront as civilization (Europe) intrudes on freedom (Turkey). In contrast to contemporary literary trends, Loti does not attempt to create a realist novel (see REALISM). Its appeal lies in its fantastic and exotic elements. At the same time, Loti hints at the novel's historical context by making reference to the Balkan crisis concluded by the Treaty of San Stefano (1878).

FURTHER READING

Barthes, Roland. "Pierre Loti: Aziyadé." In *New Critical Essays.* Berkeley: University of California Press, 1990.

Blanch, Lesley. *Pierre Loti: Portrait of an Escapist.* London: Collins, 1983.

———. *Pierre Loti: The Legendary Romantic.* San Diego: Harcourt Brace Jovanovich, 1983.

Hartman, Elwood. *Three Nineteenth-Century French Worters/Artists and the Maghreb: The Literary and Artistic Depictions of North Africa by Théophile Gautier, Eugène Fromentin and Pierre Loti.* Tübingen, Germany: Narr, 1994.

Hughes, Edward J. *Writing Marginality in Modern French Literature: from Loti to Genet.* Cambridge, New York: Cambridge University Press, 2001.

Lerner, Michael. *Pierre Loti's Dramatic Works.* Lewiston, Me.: E. Mellen Press, 1998.

Szyliowicz, Irene. *Pierre Loti and the Oriental Woman.* New York: St. Martin's Press, 1988.

B

BAGPIPERS, THE (LES MAÎTRES SON-NEURS) GEORGE SAND (1853)

One of Sand's well-loved pastoral novels, or *romans champêtres, The Bagpipers* is set in 1828 at a *veillée,* a peasant gathering in the evening for storytelling. An old villager, Depardieu, tells the story of his youth in the 1770s. As a young man, Depardieu was called Tiennet and he had two friends, his pretty cousin Brulette and Joset.

A dreamer, Joset is taken for a village idiot who, unfortunately, cannot sing as his friends do. Brulette and Tiennet suspect there is a hidden reason for Joset's inability to join them. They eventually discover that Joset, in fact, secretly makes enchanting music on a flute he has made from a reed.

Joset's musical career flourishes when he joins Huriel's father, a master bagpiper, as his apprentice. After a year and a half, however, Joset falls ill and believes that only Brulette may cure him. The reader suspects that Joset has always harbored a deep love for her. Brulette appears with Tiennet. There they encounter Thérence, who is caring for Joset. She is the mysterious young woman who caught Tiennet's eye years before when the youths were preparing for their communion.

One day, Brulette accepts a bouquet from Huriel as a sign of love, inciting Joset's jealousy. Meanwhile, Huriel's sister, Thérence, accepts a bouquet from Tiennet, while Joset realizes that art is all that matters to him. In defining himself through music, however, Joset concurrently defines himself as other. His sole passion is music but this marginalizes Joset.

Condemned to solitude, Joset turns increasingly inward, and dies alone in sad contrast to the two happy couples.

The last in Sand's series of *romans champêtres, The Bagpipers* seems to signal a departure from Sand's firm belief in the restorative power of peasant morals and values, in contrast to bourgeois, urban, market values. Sand's novels hearken back to HONORÉ D'URFÉ'S ASTREA in their depiction of a utopia of love. In this instance, however, there is a hint that Sand may be losing faith in the regenerative power of rural life. The novel's conclusion appears to represent Sand's own conflict, torn between art and life, a tension she was able to reconcile in INDIANA and CONSUELO.

FURTHER READING

Crecelius, Kathryn J. *Family Romances: George Sand's Early Novels.* Bloomington: Indiana University Press, 1987.

Glasgow, Janis, ed. *George Sand: Collected Essays.* Troy, N.Y.: Whitston, 1985.

Hofstadter, Dan. *The Love Affair as a Work of Art.* New York: Farrar, Straus & Giroux, 1996.

Naginski, Isabelle Hoog. *George Sand: Writing for her Life.* New Brunswick, N.J.: Rutgers University Press, 1991.

Peebles, Catherine. *The Psyche of Feminism: Sand, Colette, Sarraute.* West Lafayette, Ind.: Purdue University Press, 2003.

Powell, David A. *George Sand.* Boston: Twayne, 1990.

Schor, Naomi. *George Sand and Idealism.* New York: Columbia University Press, 1993.

Vitaglione, Daniel. *George Eliot and George Sand.* New York: Peter Lang, 1993.

BALCONY IN THE FOREST, A (UN BALCON EN FORÊT) JULIEN GRACQ (1958) Grange, an officer candidate in World War II, is charged with guarding a fort in the woods. There he meets and falls in love with a young woman named Mona, and their passion is heightened by the surrounding presence of nature, a frequent theme in Gracq's works. In a silent, snowy world lost in the depth of the forest, the war seems far away and forgotten. Recurring themes such as expectation and the significance of a given historical context are present. At the same time, the story is both inside and outside of history.

One day the couple's peaceful existence is disrupted by a rumor that the army is approaching. Then the curtain of silence falls once more, this time with a sense of anguish and foreboding typical of Gracq. Gracq's ability to create a strange and autonomous world parallel to our own reflects the influence of the surrealist movement on his writing (see SURREALISM). In a manner that recalls the works of ANDRÉ GIDE and LOUIS ARAGON, Gracq seeks to go beyond reality in order to attain some transcendent or metaphysical truth. Michel Mitrani adapted the novel to film in 1978.

BALZAC, HONORÉ DE (1799–1850) The image Balzac has left us is that of a vibrant bon vivant dressed in a white cashmere housecoat, working late into the night, fueled by endless cups of coffee made from unroasted beans. One of the most prolific writers of the 19th century, Balzac wrote more than 90 novels, 30 tales, five plays, and many review articles and works of literary criticism, but his life was also marked by financial difficulties, for he liked luxuries and was never careful about spending or investing in doomed business ventures.

Balzac's mother came from a Parisian bourgeois family, but his father was from the southern region of the Tarn. He arrived in the capital on foot but went on to lead a successful career in government administration. Balzac's mother always favored his brother, who may have been illegitimate, and sent Balzac away to boarding school. In fact, Balzac never went home once to his family between 1807 and 1813. He later described his experience at school in his novel *Louis Lambert*.

In 1814, Balzac left for Paris, where his father wished for him to pursue a career in law; he even went as far as to intern with a notary but decided on a literary career at the age of 20. At first Balzac wrote a quantity of mediocre works, such as *Cromwell*, under a pseudonym. In a letter to his sister Laure written in 1822, Balzac referred to these works as "veritable literary rubbish." He always refused to have them published under his own name. Nonetheless, Balzac's experience as a legal apprentice and his early unsuccessful attempts as a writer are reflected in a number of his novels.

The first novel signed under Balzac's name is *The Chouans, or Brittany in 1799*, published in 1829. It was followed by *The Physiology of Marriage*. The highly successful *Chouans* is a romantic and dramatic story of love and war that bears the influence of Sir Walter Scott, whom Balzac admired greatly. The publication of this novel opened up a period of tremendous literary productivity that, nevertheless, posed no obstacle to Balzac's active social life, extensive travels, amorous adventures, attempts at politics, and ruinous financial escapades. Moreover, the positive reception of his subsequent works opened up to him the doors to the most famous Parisian salons, such as that of Madame Récamier. There he met contemporary writers such as VICTOR HUGO, ALFRED DE VIGNY, ALEXANDRE DUMAS, and the romantic painter Eugène Delacroix (see ROMANTICISM). As of 1830, Balzac's novels followed one another in rapid succession.

Balzac often drew on his own experiences as well as his rich fantasy life for his novels. One might even argue that in his case, life resembles art. Women played a significant role in his life. The first, a woman 22 years older named Madame de Berny, whom he met in 1810, initiated him into society. Until her death in 1836, Berny played the roles of mother, lover, and friend to the aspiring writer, serving as an important influence on his development. At one point Balzac fell in love with the marquise de Castries, who selfishly toyed with his feelings. The author, however, took his revenge in his novel *The Duchess of Langeais*.

At the beginning of 1830, Balzac published his "scenes from private life" consisting of six separate novellas. Together they form the first part of *The HUMAN COMEDY* (1829–1847). With these works, Balzac became a distinguished writer with an increasingly broad readership, particularly among women. He also became the target of censors. The publication of *The Magic Skin* (1831), Balzac's most imaginative and original work, determined his fame. Drunk with success, Balzac turned into a dandy who spared no expense on his horses, servants in livery, a private box at the opera, and walking canes with carved silver handles.

The 1830s also witnessed Balzac's political conversion from liberal to a conservative defender of throne and altar. In his introduction to the *Human Comedy,* Balzac, for example, depicted the principles on which his work was based, saying, "Man is neither good nor bad; he is born with instincts and capabilities; society far from depraving him as Rousseau asserts, improves him, makes him better; but self interest also develops his evil tendencies. Christianity, above all Catholicism, being . . . a complete system for the repression of the depraved tendencies of man, is the most powerful element of the social order." "Religion and Monarchy," Balzac went on to say, "[are] two necessities."

A number of other novels date from roughly the same period, such as *The Vicar of Tours, Colonel Chabert, Ferragus, The Girl with the Golden Eyes, The Country Doctor,* and *Eugénie Grandet.* These are diverse works that evoke the many and varied layers of French society, ranging from the aristocrats and petit bourgeois of Paris to inhabitants of the provinces. In them, Balzac began to develop social themes that he continued to explore in subsequent works.

In 1832, Balzac received an anonymous letter from an admiring female reader. He later discovered that it came from the hand of Eveline Hanska, a Polish countess. She was perhaps the most important woman in Balzac's life, and after years of correspondence, he was finally able to marry her in 1850. This epistolary relationship, however, by no means prevented Balzac from entering into other romantic liaisons, including one with the countess Guidoboni-Visconti.

Despite time and energy invested in his love life and society, Balzac continued to write, producing *Seraphita* and *Father Goriot* in 1835. In the latter, he introduced his system of characters that reappear from one novel to the next. In 1836 Balzac published *Lily of the Valley,* whose character Madame de Mortsauf was based on Balzac's great friend Madame de Berny, who died that same year.

At roughly the same time, Balzac founded a review, The *Paris Chronicle,* at great personal expense. As his financial situation became increasingly complicated, Balzac was even forced into hiding to escape arrest. The beginning of 1838 found him in Sardinia, where he hoped to exploit the famous silver mines of classical antiquity. Meanwhile, *César Birotteau, The Old Maid,* and the beginning portions of *Lost Illusions* and *Scenes from a Courtesan's Life* all appeared.

By 1839, Balzac was engaged in trying to defend a notary whom he had encountered in his work as a journalist and who was accused of murder. Unfortunately, Balzac was unable to save Peytel from execution. He also tried once more to establish a journal, the Parisian Review, that he planned to edit himself. Only three issues ever came out. In this ill-fated review, however, Balzac published two famous articles, the first a scathing critique of Sainte-Beuve's *Port-Royal* and the other in praise of Stendhal's Charterhouse of Parma.

Balzac's sad financial state obliged him to give up his villa, Les Jardies, but by the end of 1841 he was negotiating with editors over his plan for the *Human Comedy* and writing the preface to the first volume, in which he outlined his vast literary scheme. In this 17-volume set of 91 novels Balzac depicted in detail French society during the Bourbon Restoration and under the July Monarchy (1814–48) and succeeded in revealing the social and psychological tensions that derived from the conflict between revolutionary individualism (see French Revolution) and the remnants of the Old Regime social order.

In his fictional universe, Balzac introduced around 2,500 characters, many of whom reappear from one novel to the next. Certain character types are manifest in Balzac's work. Like Stendhal's Julien Sorel from *The Red and the Black,* Eugène de Rastignac (who first appears in *Father Goriot*) and Lucien de Rudempré (*Lost Illusions*) represent the ambitious young man, one successful, the other less so. Upon his arrival in Paris, Rastignac begins his ascent up the social ladder partly by means of seduction. He even goes so far as to marry the daughter of his former mistress.

Rudempré, in contrast, is a poet who fails to adapt to society's cruel ways and who commits suicide at the age of 30, after having been falsely accused of murder. A recurring theme in these and other novels is ambition.

Balzac's female characters tend to differ according to age, yet regardless of their stage in life, they are always subject to the constraints of the civil code. At 30 a woman may be beautiful and seductive. Later she may be more maternal, willing to sacrifice herself for those whom she loves. Balzac thus portrays the stages in a woman's life through figures such as the young seductress (A THIRTY-YEAR OLD WOMAN) and the devoted mother (LILY OF THE VALLEY).

Balzac also created a number of unsettling characters, such as Vautrin the convict (*Father Goriot* and others), Corentin the policeman, and the dubious Maxime de Trailles. Yet these characters are perhaps the best able to reveal the forces at work in society. Finally, monomaniacal figures such as Félix Grandet (EUGÉNIE GRANDET) and Gobseck (*Gobseck*) reveal the destructive power of passion. Perhaps immodestly, Balzac compared his *Human Comedy* to Dante's *Divine Comedy*. Most important, however, Balzac explored the intersection of the real and the ideal in the novel form while unveiling the theatrical nature of the world.

In 1841 Madame Hanska's husband died. Nonetheless, two years passed before Balzac joined her in St. Petersburg. By the end of his stay, Balzac had determined to marry her but this meant struggling to earn an income sufficient to support his longtime admirer. In 1845, Balzac joined Hanska in Dresden whence they traveled to Italy, Paris, Holland, and Belgium. The situation was complicated, however, by threats of blackmail from Balzac's servant/mistress, Louise Breugnot. The year 1846 was also difficult as Madame Hanska gave birth to a stillborn child whom they named Victor-Honoré. That same year, however, Balzac finally acquired a house in Paris that he deemed worthy of his future bride. With his usual profligacy, he set out to furnish it in a manner that led him, once more, into financial straits.

Both *COUSIN BETTE* and *COUSIN PONS* were published in 1846–47. They were to be Balzac's last great works,

for at this point the master of fiction was worn out and ill. Nonetheless, he traveled once more to Ukraine, where Madame Hanska's family tried to prevent their marriage. She, too, seems to have had some doubts, perhaps because of Balzac's financial difficulties.

The revolutionary year of 1848 was marked by personal failure for Balzac, who was once more turned down for election to the Académie Française. Only Lamartine and VICTOR HUGO spoke on his behalf. Disappointment led to disappointment until, finally in 1850, Balzac married Hanska in Ukraine. The couple and their children set off for Paris, arriving on May 21 at the home Balzac had taken such care to prepare for them. Strangely, no one answered the bell for the caretaker had gone mad and was hidden in a dark corner of the unlit house.

Already in a weakened state, Balzac had to take to his bed. By August 18 he was in the last throes of death when Hugo came to see him. On August 21, 1850, Balzac was buried in the Père Lachaise cemetery, the place from which his character Rastignac had cried out his challenge to the city of Paris, "to the two of us now!" According to legend, Balzac's last words were to cry out for the doctor Bianchon, a character he had created in the *Human Comedy*.

In many ways, Balzac's life resembles that of his favorite characters. Despite all the energy spent on quixotic schemes, love affairs, and social life, he was driven by ambition that led him to work like a demon, tirelessly editing and reediting his manuscripts deep into the night. Balzac's remarkable gift for observation is evident in his wonderfully rich descriptions whether they be of a Parisian social gathering, a provincial town, clothing, furnishings, or one of his extraordinary characters.

Karl Marx's collaborator, Friedrich Engels, argued in 1888 that Balzac's true sympathies lay with the nobility. Yet Balzac was also a great satirist who could paint the death of the old social order with perspicuity. His works reflect the great 19th-century literary struggle between IDEALISM and REALISM. Some critics compare his work with the English writer Charles Dickens. Along with GUSTAVE FLAUBERT (1821–1880) and ÉMILE ZOLA (1840–1902), Balzac was one of the founders of French realism.

FURTHER READING

Allen, James Smith. *Popular French Romanticism: Authors, Readers and Books in the Nineteenth Century.* Syracuse, N.Y.: Syracuse University Press, 1981.

Canfield, Arthur Graves. *The Reappearing Characters in Balzac's Comédie Humaine.* Westport, Conn.: Greenwood Press, 1977.

Carrère, Jean. *Degeneration in the Great French Masters.* Translated by Joseph McCabe. Freeport, N.Y.: Books for Libraries Press, 1967.

Gerson, Noel Bertram. *The Prodigal Genius: The Life and Times of Honoré de Balzac.* Garden City, N.Y.: Doubleday, 1972.

Marceau, Félicien. *Balzac and His World.* Translated by Derek Coltman. Westport, Conn.: Greenwood Press, 1976.

Maurois, André. *Prometheus: The Life of Balzac.* New York: Harper and Row, 1966.

Pritchett, V. S. *Balzac.* New York: Harmony Books, 1983.

Robb, Graham. *Balzac: A Life.* New York: Norton, 1994.

Smith, Edward C., III. "Honoré de Balzac and the 'Genius' of Walter Scott: Debt and Denial," *Comparative Literature Studies* 36, no. 3 (1999): 209–225.

BAPHOMET PIERRE KLOSSOWSKI (1965)

Baphomet is a historical novel in the sense that it draws from King Philip IV (the Fair)'s suppression of the Knights Templar in 1307. Baphomet refers to the name of the idol that the Templars supposedly worshiped. At the heart of the novel lies an important theological question. While waiting for the Day of Judgment, what happens to the soul if it is separated form the body? Klossowski describes them as breaths. The Grand Master of the Temple argues that souls retain their identity, while Ogier, a page, says that they can move from one identity to another. Ogier is executed for sowing discord. He subsequently reappears as Baphomet. Perhaps surprisingly, Teresa of Avila, Nietzsche, and Octave, a character from Klossowski's trilogy, *The LAWS OF HOSPITALITY,* also make an appearance in this novel. In 1994, Klossowski drew from this work to write a play, *Immortal Adolescent.* The combination of fiction and theology as well as the question of evil are recurring themes in many of Klossowski's works.

FURTHER READING

Hill, Leslie. *Bataille, Klossowski, Blanchot: Writing at the Limit.* Oxford, New York: Oxford University Press, 2001.

Gallop, Jane. *Intersections: A Reading of Sade with Bataille, Blanchot and Klossowski.* Lincoln: University of Nebraska Press, 1981.

BARBUSSE, HENRI (1873–1935)

Barbusse grew up in Paris, where his father was a playwright. He thus naturally fell into literary circles, publishing his first poems in 1895. Barbusse was a precocious child, beginning work as a journalist just out of secondary school. Catulle Mendès, his father-in-law, introduced Barbusse to the works of the symbolists (see SYMBOLISM), an influence on the budding writer, who published his first novel, *The Supplicants,* in 1903. His second novel, *Hell,* published in 1908, shocked the public because of its explicit love scenes and its pessimistic, antireligious tone.

In 1914, at the age of 41, Barbusse joined the army and was distinguished for his service during World War I. His most famous work by far, *UNDER FIRE* (1916) offers a realistic description of the soldier's experience in the trenches. At first, this work, too, offended the public because of its honesty. Along with DORGELÈS' *WOODEN CROSSES, Under Fire* one of the most powerful combat novels of the war. With the subtitle "Journal of a Squad," its central theme is fidelity among men as it depicts the horror of life in the trenches through a series of brutal and moving images. This remarkable work won the Goncourt Prize in 1917. That same year, Barbusse founded the Republican Association of Former Soldiers (L'Association Républicaine de Anciens Combattants). Barbusse's experience in the trenches not only inspired this singular work, it also led him to join the pacifist movement.

The war also inspired Barbusse's novel *Clarté,* in which an ordinary French soldier returns from the battlefield certain that war is the product of bourgeois society and that revolution is necessary to save humanity from its suffering. In 1918, Barbusse founded *Clarté,* a pacifist journal, to promote fraternity among peoples and nations. Not surprisingly, like many other intellectuals of the interwar period, Barbusse subsequently joined the Communist Party in 1923. He traveled several times to the Soviet Union, supported Stalin, and even wrote a biography of the Soviet leader, *Stalin,* published in 1935.

Barbusse's novel *Chains* (1925) reflects the author's leftist politics as it traces the notion of fraternity through human history, from prehistoric times to 1914. The central theme of this work is, not surprisingly, the need for social reform. Despite his political stance, Barbusse came under attack from other members of the Communist Party after the publication of *The Judases of Jesus* (1927), and for articles subsequently published in his journal *Monde* (*World*), in which he tried to bring together communist intellectuals and other writers.

Barbusse also participated in the Association of Revolutionary Writers and Artists, founded in 1932. Their journal, *Commune* (1933–39), was directed by Barbusse, ANDRÉ GIDE, and ROMAIN ROLLAND. Inspired by NATURALISM, Barbusse was an heir to ÉMILE ZOLA, sharing with his predecessor, whom he greatly admired, a similar sense of aesthetics and social justice. Barbusse is remembered today as a convinced pacifist. He died in 1935 on his way to Moscow, and his funeral in Paris was attended by an enormous crowd of veterans and leftists.

FURTHER READING

Field, Frank. *Three French Writers and the Great War.* Cambridge: Cambridge University Press, 1975.

Green, M. J. *Fiction in the Historical Present: French Writers in the Thirties.* Hanover, N.H.: University Press of New England, 1986.

Klein, Holger. ed., *The First World War in Fiction.* London: Macmillan, 1976.

BARRÈS, MAURICE (1862–1923)

A writer and politician, Barrès was born into a bourgeois family. Two events in particular marked his life and subsequent viewpoints, an unhappy experience in boarding school and the defeat of the French by the Prussians in 1870.

In secondary school, Barrès read the works of poets who would later influence his style, most notably THÉOPHILE GAUTIER and Charles Baudelaire. He brought their works with him to Paris in 1883 when he moved into the bohemian Latin Quarter, ostensibly to study law although he was far more interested in literature.

In Paris he began to meet other writers such as VICTOR HUGO, who impressed Barrès immensely, and Hippolyte Taine, an important influence on Barrès's later works. It was the height of the naturalist period (see NATURALISM), and Barrès initially joined their circle where he was first received by ALPHONSE DAUDET. He later met with the group of writers associated with ÉMILE ZOLA. Nevertheless, he always remained somewhat apart, perhaps manifesting the sign of what would later develop into his central theme, the cult of the self. In this atmosphere of competing literary movements, Barrès tasted and explored all that the literary world had to offer.

As a writer, Barrès left his mark in a confluence of action, art, and thought that has come to be called *Barrésisme* and that influenced other writers such as PIERRE DRIEU LA ROCHELLE, ANDRÉ MALRAUX, LOUIS ARAGON, and HENRI DE MONTHERLANT. The central idea in Barrès's works is the cult of the self.

Borrowing from the language of mysticism, Barrès sought the means to discover and develop the self, recalling Stendhal's notion of egoism as affirmation of oneself vis-à-vis the world. He spoke of the self as "the child I create each day." While a principal source for Barrès's cult of the self is Stendhal, he also drew on Lord Byron, Goethe, Benjamin Disraeli, CHATEAUBRIAND, Alphonse de Lamartine, and Napoleon. He was, in effect, a romantic, and as was the case with the romantics, Barrès's cult of the self held an equal potential for rebellion (see ROMANTICISM). Seeking new sources of inspiration, he traveled to Italy, Spain, Greece, and the Orient, until political scandal and instability at the turn of the century compelled him to reconsider French society in a new way.

Barrès wrote with passionate egoism in rich, elaborate language and violent imagery. Drawing on the legacy of Stendhal, he sought both an exalted state of emotion and an intellectual analysis of feeling, drawing the conclusion that it is necessary to channel emotions into a positive force that allows one to create or re-create the self. Barrès firmly believed that each individual must seek his or her own particular truth, their *raison d'être,* and rejected anyone who did not share the same ideal.

In 1884, Barrès established a literary revue, *Traces of Ink (Taches d'encre),* at the ripe age of 22. He also produced a trilogy: *Under the Eye of the Barbarians* (1888), *A Free Man* (1889), and *Bérénice's Garden,* (1891). In these novels Barrès focuses on three factors: intelligence, sensibility, and will. Furthermore, he contrasts two distinct forces, intelligence and emotion. *Bérénice,* for example, represents the part of the self that is distinct from intelligence, the part that communes with nature and spirit. Barrès argues that "it is instinct, far superior to analysis, that makes the future, that dominates over the unexplored parts of my being."

One side of Barrès's family came from the province of Lorraine, the other from the Auvergne. His exploration of the former led Barrès to seek unity with others on the basis of a shared culture that supersedes the individual in a manner that recalls once again the romantic movement. He was thus able to draw the cult of the self into the sphere of nationalism, whereby the self is defined on a larger scale.

This shift in Barrès's thinking led him to participate actively in public life. Barrès's political career began in 1889 when he was elected deputy to the city of Nancy. By 1906, at the age of 44, he was elected deputy of Paris and received into the Académie Française. Barrès was a staunch Catholic and nationalist, and his politics were troubling for many of his contemporaries in the period following the World War I.

Perhaps ironically, Barrès was influenced by German intellectual and literary trends. He believed that tradition and national unity should serve as the basis for social and moral progress. These ideas are articulated most clearly in his trilogy, *The Novel of National Unity,* which comprises *The* UPROOTED (1897), *Call to the Soldier* (1900), and *Their Faces* (1902). In all these works there is an underlying tension between Barrès's aesthetic sense and his nationalism. In a subsequent series of novels, *Bastions of the East* (1905), *Colette Baudouche* (1909) and *Genius of the Rhine* (1920), Barrès's obsession with Germany is evident, as well as his fascination with the notion of harmony between beauty and spirit.

Barrès's greatest novel is arguably SACRED HILL, published posthumously. In this rich and complex journal of Barrès's soul, the author expressed his ideas on literature and politics. Barrès had a profound impact on an entire generation prior to World War I. After the war, however, the reading public lost interest in his works. Dismissive of his patriotism, readers preferred

the writings of ANDRÉ GIDE, MARCEL PROUST, and ANDRÉ BRETON.

In the end, it is difficult to classify Barrès. What appear at first glance to be contradictions in his thinking in fact unify his works. Ultimately, he sought to combine intelligence and intense emotion, whether in terms of the individual or the nation.

FURTHER READING

Curtis, Michael. *Three against the Third Republic: Sorel, Barrès, and Maurras.* 1959. Westport, Conn.: Greenwood Press, 1976.

Doty, Charles Stewart. *From Cultural Rebellion to Counterrevolution: The Politics of Maurice Barrès.* Athens: Ohio University Press, 1976.

Field, Trevor. *Maurice Barrès: A Selective Critical Biography (1848–1979).* London: Grant and Cutler, 1982.

Guérard, Albert Léon. *Five Masters of French Romance: Anatole France, Pierre Loti, Paul Bourget, Maurice Barrès, Romain Rolland.* New York: Scribners, 1916.

BATAILLE, GEORGES (1897–1962)   A novelist and essayist, Georges Bataille was born in the Auvergne, where he had had an unhappy childhood. His blind and syphilitic father died in 1915 and his own health was fragile. Moreover, like others of his generation, Bataille suffered from the trauma of war-torn Europe. After secondary school, Bataille entered seminary. Not long afterward, however, he decided to train to be an archivist. Between 1918 and 1922 Bataille studied at France's prestigious École des Chartes, after which he accepted a post at the national library. After one more stint at a Benedictine monastery on the Isle of Wight, Bataille abandoned his faith.

Bataille had a remarkably active intellectual life from the very beginning of his career. In 1929 he began directing the review *Documents* and contributing to *Critique Sociale.* Always intellectually curious, in 1931–32 he studied Hegel with Alexandre Kojève. By 1935 he was active with ANDRÉ BRETON, Paul Élouard, PIERRE KLOSSOWSKI, and others in forming the group Counter-Attack, whose members were inspired to revolution by a combination of SADE, Fourier, and Nietzsche. One year later he participated in the creation of the "College of Sociology," whose purpose was to examine society and the sacred. Finally, Bataille also established the journal *Acéphale*. As for his writing, Bataille often published under a pseudonym. *Madame Edwarda* (1941), for example, was published under the name Pierre Angélique. In 1943, Bataille left Paris and moved to Vézelay for health reasons. He subsequently worked as a librarian in Carpentras and Orléans. In 1946 he established yet another review, *Critique*.

Although he was not always appreciated in his lifetime, Bataille's work ultimately significantly influenced both French and international intellectual circles. He wrote on a broad array of subjects from mysticism to the economy. Central to his philosophy are the concepts of the Impossible and the Inner Experience, which he envisioned as a journey to the limits of the possible. For Bataille, the subjective experience culminates in a burst of Dionysian excess that brings forth both suffering and fulfillment. In this thinking, Bataille is thus close to Nietzsche, for whom thought is simultaneously affirmation and negation of the world. Bataille is equally close to the experience of mystics who plunge into an ultimate union with the absolute. For Bataille, however, there is no divine absolute. Rather one must go to the limits through laughter, excess, expense, enjoyment, eroticism, the unknown, death, transgression, negation, or anguish. Such are the objects of Bataille's focus.

Bataille, moreover, works from the Hegelian concept of negativity. For the 19th-century German philosopher Georg Hegel, negativity is the basis for a dialectic that moves toward a world of spirit. In contrast, Bataille came to consider the dialectic in terms of an awareness of death as the foundation of all useful action. Consequently, Bataille juxtaposed the Possible and the Impossible, Knowledge and the Absence of Knowledge, Good and Evil, the two essential aspects of human nature. Bataille's extremism is again reminiscent of Nietzsche, particularly in his later works.

This vision informs Bataille's novel *Blue of Noon*, written in 1934 but not published until 1957. In this roman à clef, the character of Lazare, a militant leftist, is inspired by Simone Weil. Troppmann represents the monstrous, or the Impossible. In this highly symbolic novel, Bataille writes with rage and fury, in contrast to the contemporary NOUVEAU ROMAN's focus on technique. Central to Bataille's thinking is the notion of death as necessarily beyond our comprehension and yet opening up for us the way to freedom. The themes of eroticism, transgression, and death present in *Blue of Noon* mark all of Bataille's works.

FURTHER READING
Boldt-Irons, Leslie Anne, ed. *On Bataille: Critical Essays.* Albany: State University of New York, 1995.

Botting, Fred, and Scott Wilson, eds. *Bataille: A Critical Reader.* Oxford, Malden, Mass.: Blackwell, 1998.

Connor, Peter Tracey. *Georges Bataille and the Mysticism of Sin.* Baltimore: Johns Hopkins University Press, 2000.

Dean, Carolyn J. *The Self and Its Pleasures: Bataille, Lacan, and the History of the Decentered Subject.* Ithaca, N.Y.: Cornell University Press, 1992.

Gemerchak, Christopher M. *The Sunday of the Negative: Reading Bataille, Reading Hegel.* Albany: State University of New York, 2003.

Irwin, Alexander. *Saints of the Impossible: Bataille, Weil, and the Politics of the Sacred.* Minneapolis: University of Minnesota Press, 2002.

Jay, Martin. *The Limits of Limit-Experience: Bataille and Foucault.* Berkeley: University of California, Center for German and European Studies, 1993.

Libertston, Joseph. *Proximity, Levinas, Blanchot, Bataille and Communication.* The Hague, Boston: M. Nijhoff, 1982.

Rella, Franco. *The Myth of the Other: Lacan. Deleuze, Foucault, Bataille.* Translated by Nelson Moe. Washington, D.C.: Maisonneuve Press, 1994.

Surya, Michel. *Georges Bataille: An Intellectual Biography.* Translated by Krzysztof Fijalkowski and Michael Richardson. London, New York: Verso, 2002.

BAZIN, HERVÉ (1911–1996)

This author's actual name was Jean-Pierre Hervé-Bazin, as he added Bazin to his name upon his marriage to Marie Bazin, sister of the French academician René Bazin. The publisher Bernard Grasset gave him the name we know today, Hervé Bazin, when he published his most famous work, VIPER IN HAND in 1948. The previous year, Bazin received the Apollinaire Prize for his collection of poetry entitled *Day*.

Bazin was raised by his grandmother while his parents were in China. Not a particularly talented student, he practiced a number of professions before turning to journalism, writing for *Paris Echo* (*L'Echo de Paris*) and *L'Information*. He gained notoriety as a writer with the publication of *Viper in Hand,* an autobiographical novel drawing on his experience as an adolescent in a broken family. The novel attained international renown and was translated into some 40 languages. Bazin's contemporary, COLETTE, called the novel scandalous. He went on to write other novels that include *Head against the Wall,* 1949; *Death of a Pony,* 1950; *The Owl's Cry,* 1972; *Le Matrimoine,* 1967; and *Madame X,* 1975.

Viper in Hand evokes the author's unhappy childhood while offering a critique of provincial bourgeois society that, in the end, leads the main character to violence and rebellion. The publication of the novel followed a difficult period in Bazin's life related to a break with his family, an unstable professional life, depression, divorce, and remarriage. *Head Against the Wall* follows in a similar vein with its tone of vengeful irony. In this work Bazin recounts a period of time spent in a hospital after a car accident. It is followed by *Death of a Pony,* a novel that continues the story begun in *Viper in Hand.*

Bazin subsequently became increasingly concerned with political and social problems, preoccupations reflected in his novels *Rise up and Walk,* 1952; *Whom I Dare to Love,* 1956; and *In the Name of the Son,* 1960. Bazin painted a particularly sensitive portrait of the underprivileged in *The Blessed of Desolation* (1970), the story of a volcanic explosion on an island, after which Tristan da Cunha tries to organize assistance for the island's suffering population.

The theme of family is central to Bazin's works, a reflection of the troubled relationship he had with his own. Bazin received the Grand Prize for Literature in Monaco in 1957 and was accepted into the Académie Goncourt. He continued writing until the end of his life.

FURTHER READING
Brosman, Catherine Savage. *French Novelists Since 1960.* Detroit: Gale Research, 1989.

BEAUTIFUL TENEBROUS (*UN BEAU TÉNÉBREUX*) JULIEN GRACQ (1945)   In the fall of 1940, Gracq wrote the prologue to this, his second novel while in a prisoner of war camp. Liberated in 1941 for health reasons, Gracq returned to France, where he completed *Beautiful Tenebrous* in 1942. It was not published until 1945.

The first two-thirds of the novel come from the character Gérard's journal. In the last part, an anonymous narrator takes over the story. The setting is a hotel by the sea in Brittany where a group of people have come to spend their summer vacation. Inspired by Goethe's *Elective Affinities,* Gracq's characters reveal their equally complicated and intertwined relationships. There is Gérard, the university student, the beautiful Christel, Jacques, Henri, and Irene. Each character, in the end, comes to embody the truth of him- or herself.

The "beautiful tenebrous" is Allan, the very embodiment of temptation. Allan has entered into a suicide pact with Doloris. Gracq's abundance of reflections and images creates a sense of unsettling discontinuity that a number of critics have remarked on. Moreover, there are several intertextual references. For example, the title comes from a poem by Gérard Nerval and the double suicide is inspired by a poem by Alfred de Vigny. Finally, the very subject of the novel refers to the surrealist discussion on suicide (see SURREALISM).

BEAUVOIR, SIMONE DE (1908–1986)   An existentialist philosopher and writer, Simone de Beauvoir was one of the most significant authors of the 20th century and the founder of modern FEMINISM. Born in Paris, Simone de Beauvoir rejected the conservative, Catholic, bourgeois values of her family at a young age. She was a brilliant student who received a degree from the Sorbonne in 1929. At the age of 21, Beauvoir was the youngest student ever to pass a degree in philosophy. She took second place. JEAN-PAUL SARTRE took first place, on his second attempt.

Beauvoir met Sartre at the Sorbonne, and they became lifelong companions, although she had affairs with other men and women. All her life Beauvoir wanted to write great literature, and she succeeded in combining philosophy and literature in her subsequent writings. An existentialist philosopher in her own right (see EXISTENTIALISM), Beauvoir shared with Sartre a commitment to writing, politics, and philosophy.

Beauvoir's first essays, *Pyrrhus and Cineas* (1944) and *For a Moral Ambiguity* (1947), correspond to philosophical ideas expressed by Sartre in *Being and Noth-*

ingness (1943). In 1943 Beauvoir gave up teaching to devote herself entirely to writing and published her first novel, *She Came to Stay.* Drawing on Beauvoir's experience with Sartre and with one of her students, the novel depicts the psychosexual tension among three people. The novel was well received, as was *The MANDARINS* (1954), a novel that won the Goncourt Prize.

From the 1950s through the 1970s, Beauvoir played an increasingly important role in French intellectual life, particularly in the expression of her belief in the individual's absolute right to freedom. As of 1958, she concentrated on writing her memoirs, in which she analyzes her intellectual and personal development over the years. At the same time, she continued to write in a variety of genres on topics pertinent to her times.

The Blood of Others (1944) focuses on the theme of social responsibility compelled by historical circumstances and reflects Beauvoir's Marxist leanings. The novel is set in France during the Occupation, telling the story of Jean Blomart, a Resistance leader who struggles with his fate after inadvertently causing the death of his colleagues and the woman he loved. One of the most important existential novels of the Resistance, *The Blood of Others* raises ethical questions as it explores the moral dilemma rising from the tension between responsibility toward oneself, those one loves, and humanity overall. Like *All Men Are Mortal* (1946), this novel reflects Beauvoir's philosophical stance in a manner that echoes her *Ethics of Ambiguity* and her ideas on human freedom and existentialist transcendence. The theme of the relationship between the individual and the movement of history is a recurring one in Beavoir's works.

The central theme to *All Men Are Mortal* is human mortality and our desire for immortality. In this novel, an actress believes that a mysterious man will carry her immortal soul onward after she dies. Obsessed with this idea, she is unable to experience life fully in the present. She is thus the antithesis of Beauvoir's existential philosophy. The novel was not well received despite its focus on a fundamental question of the human condition.

The Mandarins explores the role of leftist intellectuals in postwar society and their personal and political anguish as they struggle with the revelations about Stalinist Russia. Should they denounce the labor camps and risk failing to promote revolution? The problems of World War II society surface repeatedly in Beauvoir's works as she considers the question: whom must society sacrifice for the survival of the collective?

In 1947, Beauvoir spent five months in the United States. There she met the writer Nelson Algren, with whom she had an affair for several years. Their relationship is explored in *The Mandarins.* The following year she published *America from Day to Day,* condemning Americans for their racism. During this period, Beauvoir also began to consider the question of women.

Beauvoir is perhaps best known for *The Second Sex* (1949), a 1,000-page treatise on the female condition that lays the foundation for modern feminism. Considered scandalous at the time of its publication, the first volume traces gender relations and the subjugation of women throughout history. The second volume depicts women's experience from childhood to old age. This work examines the female condition along the lines of existentialist philosophy.

Beauvoir argued that, throughout history, men have compelled women to be "the other"; that is to say, men have assumed the human standard to be male. In deconstructing the myth of the feminine, Beauvoir examined the Western conception of women's roles, as girl, wife, mother, lesbian, and prostitute. Her fundamental argument is that "One is not born but becomes a woman."

Some critics have argued that Beauvoir, nonetheless, continued to hold up manhood as the ideal type. In fact, her work is important in that Beauvoir made the notions of womanhood and femininity contingent rather than objective concepts. Beauvoir was thus one of the first thinkers to argue that social norms play a role in the definition of the self. Twenty years after its publication, Beauvoir regretted not having drawn a more radical conclusion to this work. It scandalized the public, nonetheless, and came to have a real impact on the feminist movement only in the 1970s.

In her multivolume memoirs, Beauvoir attempted a direct, honest, and sincere reflection on her life and times. The first volume, *Memoirs of a Dutiful Daughter* (1958), traces her life from childhood, through her years as a student, her first attempts at writing, and

Sartre's captivity in Germany. Subsequent volumes, *Prime of Life* (1960), *The Force of Circumstance* (1963), *A Gentle Death* (1964), and *All Said and Done* (1972), together depict the passage from an age of apprenticeship into a mature sense of self.

Sartre's death in 1980 inspired Beauvoir's moving *Adieux: A Farewell to Sartre* as well as her *Conversations with Sartre*. Beauvoir's style is clear and concise, reflecting her work as a journalist. It is also frequently didactic, with an emphasis on psychological analysis. Beauvoir's collective works significantly influenced the development of modern French literature and thought. She sought to make of her own life a work of art and to show how intellectuals write to reveal a truth that may change the world. Upon her death in 1986, Beauvoir was buried alongside Sartre in Paris's Montparnasse cemetary.

FURTHER READING

Appignanesi, Lisa. *Simone de Beauvoir.* Harmondsworth, England: Penguin, 1988.

Arp, Kristana. *The Bonds of Freedom.* Chicago: Open Court Publishing, 2001.

Bair, Dierdre. *Simone de Beauvoir: A Biography.* New York: Summit Books, 1990.

Bauer, Nancy. *Simone de Beavoir, Philosophy and Feminism.* New York: Columbia University Press, 2001.

Evans, Mary. *Simone de Beauvoir: A Feminist Mandarin.* London: Tavistock, 1985.

Fallaize, Elizabeth. *The Novels of Simone de Beauvoir.* London: Routledge, 1988.

Keefe, T. *Simone de Beauvoir. A Study of her Writings.* Totowa, N.J.: Barnes and Noble, 1984.

Moi, Toril. *Feminist Theory and Simone de Beauvoir.* Oxford: Blackwell, 1990.

———. *Simone de Beauvoir.* Oxford: Blackwell, 1994.

BECKETT, SAMUEL (1906–1989)   Beckett
is one of those rare writers who abandoned his mother tongue to construct his life's work in another language. Ironically, in his world of fiction the individual discovers himself only through his *inability* to communicate with others, destroying himself in order to know himself and to realize that he is nothing.

Born into a bourgeois Irish Protestant family, Beckett was a brilliant student who earned his bachelor of arts in French and Italian from Trinity College Dublin

in 1927. In 1928 he began his studies at the École Normale Supérieure in Paris, where he studied René Descartes and Marcel PROUST. He met and became friends with James Joyce, a profound influence on Beckett's work, won a prize for poetry in 1930, and wrote a serious essay on Proust published in London in 1931.

As of 1931, Beckett wandered between London and Paris. The years 1933–36 were particularly difficult both morally and financially. Still, Beckett continued to be productive, publishing *More Pricks than Kicks* in 1934 and beginning work on *Murphy* (1938). In 1936–37 he traveled to Germany, after which he returned to settle in Paris.

During World War II, Beckett joined the Resistance and was forced to flee with his wife into the countryside to escape the Gestapo. During the day he worked on a farm; at night he wrote his last novel in English, *Watt* (1942). After the war, Beckett took up writing in French, producing his famous trilogy: *Molloy* (1951), *Malone Dies* (1951), and *The Unnameable* (1953).

Beckett is probably best known for his drama. His most famous play is *Waiting for Godot* (1952), translated into some 18 languages. Yet he was a prolific writer in a wide variety of genres and media, including radio, television, and film, in addition to his important translations of Eugenio Montale, René Crevel, Paul Éluard, ANDRÉ BRETON, and Arthur Rimbaud into English. In 1964 he wrote the screenplay for *Film,* in which Buster Keaton played the principal role. He received the Nobel Prize in Literature in 1969. Despite his fame, Beckett remains a mysterious and solitary figure, due in part to his style and the underlying philosophy of his works. Whether in novels or plays, the central theme of Beckett's writings is the fundamental problem of communication. For Beckett, the individual exists in isolation from others even when not alone.

In *Murphy* (1938), the principal character seeks to separate himself from others whose presence disturbs Murphy's awareness of his own existence. At the same time, the fact that others *are* present confirms his identity for the simple reason that others hear him. A similar notion pervades Beckett's dialogues, in which each character speaks essentially in monologue. There is no real communication between them. In *MOLLOY* (1951), the question of language reasserts itself as speech again confirms Molloy's existence. Beckett carries this pessimistic concept even further in *The UNNAMEABLE,* a novel in which speech creates only the illusion of existence.

Beckett was, at best, suspicious of women, yet he understood that love between a man and a woman perpetuates the species and thus contributes to humanity's continued if meaningless existence. The only solution to this problem of the human condition is to turn in on oneself in search of solitude. In all of his works, the impossibility of understanding the other is the dominant theme. One speaks to have the sense of living, to pass time; the presence of the other is necessary to prove the existence of the speaker. There is no distinction between past and future in this life of endless repetition. "Time has stopped," says Vladimir in *Waiting for Godot,* as the individual is constrained to live solely in the present. The tragedy of the human condition is to be caught between the need for and the meaninglessness of speech.

Beckett's early works bear the seeds of themes particularly present in his writing after 1946. Realistic passages describe neighborhoods in London and Dublin, for example, but the principal depiction of space in Beckett's work is one of imagination. His characters tend to turn inward both morally and physically. They are melancholy creatures who apprehend the world by means of compulsive questioning. Each action and movement is subject to interrogation. At the center of Beckett's fictional world is the self, seized by the agony of existence.

Beckett continually explores the role of language and its deceptive nature. Rather than revealing truth, language creates illusion that leads to despair at its realization. According to Gilles Deleuze, it is this notion that made television, with its capacity to transcend words, so attractive to Beckett, who remained, nonetheless, attentive to his own use of words and their musicality. One last pervasive element in Beckett's works is laughter, a laughter of despair at the tragedy of life and the human condition. Recurring themes are time, waiting, the quotidian, solitude, alienation, wandering, noncommunication, decay, and death.

Beckett's work is principally defined by his use of language. His characters have no psychological depth but are mere shadows. Most of all they are voices out of the silence that surrounds them. Not surprisingly, an existentialism reveals itself in Beckett's language. Word, speech, and the body are one. Moreover, each character exists outside of history and time, just as Beckett's French exists on its own, outside other contemporary literature. Beckett's writing symbolizes the uprootedness of modern life. His greatness as a writer lies in his ability to speak as any man. As he once wrote in *The Unnameable,* "I speak but I have nothing to say, nothing but the words of others."

FURTHER READING

Bair, Dierdre. *Samuel Beckett: A Biography.* New York: Summit Books, 1990.
Cronin, Anthony. *Samuel Beckett: The Last Modernist.* New York: Harper Collins, 1997.
Dukes, Gerry. *Samuel Beckett.* London: Penguin, 2001.
Gordon, Lois. *The World of Samuel Beckett, 1906–1946.* New Haven: Yale University Press, 1996.
McCarthy, Patrick A. *Critical Essays on Samuel Beckett.* Boston: G. K. Hall, 1986.
Pattie, David. *The Complete Critical Guide to Samuel Beckett.* London; New York: Routledge, 2000.
Rathjen, Friedhelm, ed. *In Principle, Beckett Is Joyce.* Edinburgh: Split Pea Press, 1994.

BEDROOM PHILOSOPHERS, THE (*LA PHILOSOPHIEDANSLEBOUDOIR*) DONATIEN-ALPHONSE-FRANÇOIS, MARQUIS DE SADE (1795)

In this libertine tale, the misogynist sodomite Dolmancé and his accomplices give lessons in deviancy to a young woman named Eugénie in the boudoir (bedroom) of Madame de Sainte-Ange. Together they convince Eugénie to reject all traditional values concerning motherhood, vaginal sex, and the importance of family. They urge her to join them in challenging nature herself, a consistent theme in Sade's works. When her mother arrives to pick up Eugénie, she is gang raped and sodomized. The novel ends in ultimate cruel torture. Injected with venereal disease, Madame de Mistival's vagina is sewn closed with red thread, symbolizing the destruction of motherhood and, by extension, all bourgeois values.

"Yet another effort, Frenchmen, if you want to live in a republic," a pamphlet included in *Bedroom Philosophers* makes its connection to revolutionary politics explicit. The problem, in Sade's view, is that despite its avowed purpose of creating a republic of virtue, the revolutionary government cannot destroy evil, an intrinsic element in human nature. Society must recognize the consequences of human passion that may be negative. In this way, *Bedroom Philosophers* emphasizes the most important theme in Sade's novels. Sade's extension of ENLIGHTENMENT materialism differs from DIDEROT, for example, in its rejection of progress. Sade thus deviates significantly from ideas central to 18th-century thought.

FURTHER READING

Barthes, Roland. *Sade, Fourier, Loyola.* Translated by Richard Miller. New York: Farrar, Straus and Giroux, 1976.

Du Plessix Gray, Francine. *At Home with the Marquis de Sade.* New York: Simon and Schuster, 1998.

Fabre, Jean. "Sade et le roman noir." In *Le Marquis de Sade. Paris: Armand Colin, 1968.*

Heine, Maurice. "Le Marquis de Sade et le roman noir." In *Le Marquis de Sade,* edited by Gilbert Lély. Paris: Gallimard, 1950.

Kehrès, Jean-Marc. "Libertine Anatomies: Figures of Monstrosity in Sade's *Justine, ou les malheurs de la vertu,*" *Eighteenth-Century Life* 21, no. 2 (1997): 100–113.

Schaffer, Neil. *The Marquis de Sade: A Life.* New York: Knopf, 1999.

Weber, Caroline. "The Sexist Sublime in Sade and Lyotard," *Philosophy and Literature* 26, no. 2 (2002) 397–404.

BEL-AMI GUY DE MAUPASSANT (1885)   *Bel-Ami,* Maupassant's second novel (after *A Life,* 1883), moves away from depictions of peasant life prevalent in his earlier works to contemporary Paris. It is the portrait of an amoral man in an amoral world in which ideals and morals are an illusion. Only the cynic can win at society's game by recognizing that success lies in appearance.

A young man from the provinces, Georges Duroy arrives in Paris nearly penniless but burning with ambition. The son of Norman tavern keepers, within three years Duroy has become the self-styled baron Du Roy de Cantel, "Bel-Ami" to his intimates, chief editor of *La Vie française,* and the husband of its director's daughter.

The story of Duroy's meteoric rise in society is a tale of seduction. Women promote Bel-Ami's career,

socially and professionally. DuRoy's first lover is Clotilde de Marelle, whom he periodically abandons when fortune dictates change. She remains closest to him, however, their bond somehow surviving the vicissitudes of Duroy's itinerant love affairs. She is his *"gentille maîtresse"* (kind mistress).

Bel-Ami first leaves Clotilde for the wife of his friend Georges Forestier. Georges and he had served in the army together in North Africa. In fact, Georges gave Duroy his first chance by introducing him to the world of journalism. After Georges's death, Bel-Ami takes over his position at the newspaper and his wife, Madeleine, without whose assistance he would never have managed to produce his first article.

To secure his future, Bel-Ami then seduces Madame Walter, the wife of the newspaper's director. Meanwhile, he arranges for Madeleine to be caught with her lover, an important government minister, and subsequently divorces her, but not before he has assured himself half of her estate. Once M. Walter has made a fortune speculating on the stock market over the Moroccan question, Bel-Ami now free, drops Madame Walter to seduce Suzanne, her daughter. Suzanne willingly runs away with Bel-Ami. The novel ends with their grand marriage ceremony. Upon leaving the church, Bel-Ami and Clotilde exchange a wordless glance ensuring that they will once again resume their love affair.

Bel-Ami's rise in society is thus dependent on women. Each is different in character and personality, yet their primary function is to serve as a tool for Bel-Ami's success. Madeleine Forestier is a talented journalist by nature who will do anything to satisfy her passion for political intrigue. Madame Walter is awkward but sincere. She suffers the most, as she witnesses her own daughter's marriage to the only man she had ever loved, the only one who had ever stirred her passion.

As for Bel-Ami, he desires women not just for what they can do for him but also to satisfy his own needs. Maupassant seems incapable of depicting women as anything other than objects of desire or as seductresses, hence certain critics' argument that Maupassant's view of women is essentially negative.

Maupassant's depiction of Parisian journalists and politicians was realistic enough that readers sought to identify recognizable people in the novel's characters. Certainly Maupassant's own experiences made his portrayal more believable. *Bel-Ami* is reminiscent of HONORÉ DE BALZAC's *LOST ILLUSIONS* except that Bel-Ami triumphs rather than being defeated in a cutthroat world. *Bel-Ami* also recalls ÉMILE ZOLA's MONEY in its satirical treatment of the press. Most important, Maupassant's portrayal of human nature as grasping for money, power, and pleasure is bleak. The novel was a great success but also scandalous. Some readers were disturbed either by the degree of pessimism or by his unkind portrait of Parisian journalism, to which Maupassant responded, "I simply wanted to tell the story of an adventurer similar to the ones we bump elbows with every day in Paris and whom one meets in every existing profession."

FURTHER READING

Haig, Stirling. "The Mirror of Artifice: Maupassant's *Bel-Ami*." In his *The Madame Bovary Blues: The Pursuit of Illusion in Nineteenth-Century French Fiction.* Baton Rouge: Louisiana State University Press, 1987, pp. 152–162.

Ignotus, Paul. *The Paradox of Maupassant.* New York: Funk and Wagnalls, 1968.

Jackson, Stanlye. *Guy de Maupassant.* Folcroft, Pa.: Folcroft Library Editions, 1974.

Lerner, Michael. *Maupassant.* London: Allen and Unwin, 1975.

Sherard, Robert Harborough. *The Life, Work, and Evil Fate of Guy de Maupassant (gentilhomme de letters).* Folcroft, Pa.: Folcroft Library Editions, 1976.

Steegmuller, Francis. *Maupassant: A Lion in the Path.* Freeport, N.Y.: Books for Libraries Press, 1972.

Sullivan, Edward D. *Maupassant: The Short Stories.* Great Neck, N.Y.: Barron's Educational Series, 1962.

BELLY OF PARIS, THE (LE VENTRE DE PARIS) ÉMILE ZOLA (1873)   This third novel in Zola's ROUGON-MACQUART series, a "Natural and Social History of a Second Empire Family," focuses on Les Halles, the central marketplace in Paris. The story is centered on Florent, an idealist who is mistakenly arrested and subsequently escapes prison. Seven years later he finds his half-brother (who inherited their uncle's fortune) in Paris, married to Lisa Macquart. Together the couple owns a successful delicatessen in Les Halles. Under an assumed name, Florent becomes a market inspector and gets to know the merchants,

learning about their dreams and woes, their jealousies and disagreements. In the evening, unbeknown to them, Florent participates in a secret society that is plotting against the government. When Lisa denounces him, Florent is sent away once more.

Zola conceived *The Belly of Paris* as a companion novel to *VENUS OF THE COUNTING HOUSE*. Both novels explore the world of the bourgeoisie, the pillar of the Second Empire, driven by greed, ambition, and an appetite for wealth. Zola was equally fascinated by Les Halles, its architecture, activity, and superabundance of goods. The market is itself an omnipresent character, like the train in *La Bête Humaine,* or the still in *L'ASSOMMOIR.* The market is the belly of Paris, its stomach, compelling the reader to consider its symbolic meaning. Zola's incomparable descriptions of food excite desire. At first glance the body of Paris is active and healthy, but beneath the surface is disease. True to his naturalist project (see NATURALISM), Zola explores the relationship among the individual, heredity, and the environment.

Many of the characters in the novel represent the working poor who find order in the rhythm of their daily lives, although the time may come when they will awaken. Like Silvère from the first volume of the Rougon-Macquart series, Florent seeks a society based on love and justice, in stark contrast to the traitorous Lisa, who, with a streak of cruelty lurking beneath the honest merchant's face, reveals the truth of petit bourgeois mentality.

FURTHER READING

Armstrong, Marie-Sophie. *Hugo's 'egouts' and Le Ventre de Paris, French Review* 69, no. 3. (February, 1996): 394–408.

Lathers, Marie. *Bodies of Art. French Literary Realism and the Artist's Model.* Lincoln: University of Nebraska Press, 2001.

BEN JELLOUN, TAHAR (1944–)   Ben Jelloun is a Moroccan writer who moved to Paris in 1971 and began working as a journalist for *Le Monde*. He studied philosophy at the University of Rabat, Morocco and wrote his first poem, "Dawn of the Flagstones," after the brutal suppression of demonstrations in Casablanca in 1965. His poetry bears the influence of Paul Verlaine and Arthur Rimbaud.

Equally at home in Arabic and French, Ben Jelloun chose to write in the latter. He earned his doctorate in social psychology. *The Greatest of Solitudes* (1977), an essay drawn from his thesis, is a reflection on the profound emotional and sexual solitude experienced by North African immigrant workers in France. His research also provided material for *Solitary Confinement,* a poem/novel in which the author takes up again the theme of despair among foreign workers. Over and over in his writings, Ben Jelloun gives voice to the victims of social injustice. Dominant themes are exile, injustice, and oppression, the identity of women, eroticism, and racism. What makes Ben Jelloun's works particularly appealing to readers is his unusual blend of Maghrebine traditions with very modern writing. He consistently evokes a sense of existential solitude in a rich, poetic voice. Ben Jelloun's fictional works consist of a blend of genres and cultural influences that range from traditional Arabic thought to Friedrich Nietzsche and Jorge Luis Borges.

In his first autobiographical novel, *Harrouda* (1973), Ben Jelloun describes his childhood in Fez and Tangiers. Fez symbolizes the ancient Islamic world while Tangiers represents a blend of Islamic and Western traditions. This work is both a novel and a poem evoking the mystical prostitute of a Moroccan city. *Harrouda* thus evokes a traditional character from Moroccan folklore while recalling the figure of the witch/prostitute reminiscent of the Celestina of Spanish literature.

In *Moha* (1978) and *Public Writer* (1983), Ben Jelloun abandons the first-person narrative to offer a critique of traditional society through the words of an idiot, in the tradition of Dostoyevsky, and a writer. At the same time, Ben Jelloun does not ignore the problem of Moroccan independence, rather, he evokes the humiliation central to much North African and Maghrebine literature of the 20th century. The victims of this humiliation extend beyond the realm of colonial politics to encompass, in their own way, women and children.

In *The SAND CHILD* (1985) and *The SACRED NIGHT* (1987), Ben Jelloun introduces the theme of women in Islamic society. He gained notoriety as a writer when these two novels together won the Goncourt Prize. In these works, Ben Jelloun discovered his own

voice. Written in the form of a traditional oral tale, these poetic novels recall the Islamic oral tradition in a manner reminiscent of *A Thousand and One Nights.* Together they offer a fairly sharp critique of Moroccan society, a theme central to Ben Jelloun's earlier works as well. In these two novels, Ben Jelloun tackles head-on the problem of women in Islamic society and their lack of personal freedom. At the same time, the influence of the Argentinian writer Jorge Luis Borges, whom Ben Jelloun admired greatly, is evident. Ben Jelloun further explores the relationship between France and North Africa in *With Downcast Eyes* (1991), *State of Absence* (1992), and *Corruption* (1994), as well as in a collection of short stories, *First Love Is Always the Last* (1995). Time and again, Ben Jelloun subtly and poetically calls for women's emancipation, sensitive as he is to all forms of injustice and oppression. In this sense, Ben Jelloun's fiction echoes his writing on the immigrant worker experience.

The father figure is frequently central in North African literature as is evident in the writings of Ben Jelloun, DRISS CHRAÏBI, and Mohammed Choukri, since he represents power in the social, economic, and political order. Ben Jelloun's later works seem to reevaluate the figure of the patriarch and he appears in a less harsh light than in *The Sand Child* and *The Sacred Night.* In *Silent Day in Tangiers,* for example, Ben Jelloun sensitively evokes an old man's reflections as he approaches death, isolated and ill. In *With Downcast Eyes,* a young girl idealizes her father who has gone to work in France.

Ben Jelloun is one of the "second generation" of francophone North African writers. Born after World War II, these writers, like KATEB YACINE, concentrate less on immediate concerns over decolonization and tend to be more innovative in their approach to fiction. At the same time, they are willing to abandon a linear narrative for a more synchronic vision of time. These writers tend to focus, too, on the broader issues of identity and alienation.

Ben Jelloun began by writing poetry and his gifts as a poet continue to shape his writing. Moreover, he is conversant with and engaged in postmodern, poststructuralist debates in literature (see POSTMODERNISM; POSTSTRUCTURALISM). This is precisely the quality that seems to attract his Western audience. There is an inherent tension in Ben Jelloun's works between traditionalism and modernity as he explores the bonds that unite the universe.

FURTHER READING

Cazenave, Odile. "Gender, Age, and Narrative Transformations in Tahar Ben Jelloun," *French Review* 64, no. 3 (February 1991): 437–450.

Fayad, Marie. "Borges in Tahar Ben Jelloun's *L'Enfant du sable:* Beyond Intertextuality," *French Review* 67, no. 2 (December 1993): 291–299.

Marrouchi, Mustapha. "Breaking Up/Down/Out of the Boundaries: Tahar Ben Jelloun," *Research in African Literatures* 21, no. 4 (Winter 1990): 71–83.

Zahiri, Mohammed, and Rachid Ameziane-Hassani. "The Father Figure in Tahar Ben Jelloun: *La Nuit Sacrée, Jour de Silence à Tanger,* and *Les Yeux baissés,*" *Callaloo,* 15, no. 4 (Autumn 1992): 1105–1109.

BENOIT, PIERRE (1886–1962)

Like many budding authors, in 1908 Pierre Benoit went to Paris. There he studied literature and met other writers such as ROLAND DORGELÈS. When he finished his studies, Benoit took a position working for the undersecretary of state for fine arts. He later became librarian for the Ministry of Education, dividing his time between working and writing. In 1914, Benoit published his first collection of poems, dedicated to MAURICE BARRÈS, then another in 1920. Benoit is best known, however, as a novelist.

Koenigsmark (1918), Benoit's first novel, was a great success. It was followed by *ATLANTIDA*, which received the grand prize for the novel from the Académie Française. For the next 40 years, Benoit wrote roughly one novel per year, all popular escapist fantasies. Rich in imagination, Benoit meticulously described exotic settings, often drawing from his own experience as he traveled widely and met a number of important historical figures. These journeys provided much material for the exotic flavor of his novels. He also described his experiences in a series of published articles.

In 1929 Benoit was elected president of the Society of Gens de Lettres, an important literary society, and to the Académie Française in 1931. He voluntarily withdrew from the Académie in 1959, in support of the writer Paul Morand whose candidacy was opposed due to his collaboration with the Vichy government.

Benoit's adopted homeland was the French province of Quercy. Life in *"La France profonde,"* too, with its rural setting, inspired his novels. Benoit was a popular writer and many of his works were subsequently adapted to radio, theater, television, and film. His last novel, *Dead Loves* (1961), is dedicated to the memory of his wife.

Benoit's novels share a few unusual characteristics. For example, each has 227 pages and the heroine's name always begins with the letter *A*. Moreover, the general plotline is similar from one novel to the next. Often inspired by the belle epoque, or the interwar years, Benoit argued that a novelist's duty is to reflect his own time. He was such a master of mystery and suspense that the rather obvious devices he used often go by unnoticed as the reader is captivated by the unexpected and "Rocambolesque" events of the plot in a manner that recalls the work of ALEXIS PONSON DE TERRAIL.

BERGERAC, SAVIEN CYRANO DE (1619–1655)

The name Cyrano de Bergerac immediately calls to mind Edmond Rostand's 1897 play based loosely on Cyrano's life. The real Cyrano was, in fact, a famous swordsman who belonged to a company of Gascon musketeers. After being wounded twice, the second time at the siege of Arras in 1640 by a sword to the neck, Cyrano de Bergerac gave up his military career and turned to literature and philosophy.

Cyrano's mentor was the great mathematician and philosopher Pierre Gassendi. Gassendi was a libertine, an Epicurean, and an empiricist. The influence of Gassendi's thought on Cyrano is particularly evident in his posthumously published works THE STATES AND EMPIRES OF THE MOON (1657) AND SUN (1662), published together under the title *The Other World.* These two works recount Cyrano's fantastic voyages into space, first to the moon and then to the sun. His imaginative encounters with people beyond Earth allow Cyrano to comment satirically on contemporary politics and society.

Cyrano de Bergerac also wrote two plays, *La Mort d'Agrippine* (1654), condemned for blasphemy, and *Le*

Pédant joué (1654), which drew on his unhappy experience as a young student. He died in Paris in 1655 when a wooden plank fell on his head. While he was known as both a duelist and as a writer, his reputation as an author was established after his death through the publication of *The States and Empires of the Moon and Sun.* Not fully appreciated during his own lifetime, Cyrano's stories influenced later works such as Jonathan Swift's *Gulliver's Travels* and Voltaire's MICROMÉGAS.

FURTHER READING

De Jean, Joan. *Libertine Strategies: Freedom and the Novel in Seventeenth-Century France.* Columbus: Ohio State University Press, 1981.

Harth, Erica. *Cyrano de Bergerac and the Polemics of Modernity.* New York: Columbia University Press, 1970.

Lanius, Edward. *Cyrano de Bergerac and the Universe of the Imagination.* Geneva: Droz, 1967.

BERNANOS, GEORGES (1888–1948) Bernanos's father was a staunch monarchist whose influence remained with his son throughout his life. In 1906, while studying law and literature in Paris, Bernanos joined a group of students connected with the conservative political movement L'Action Française. This was the beginning of his active commitment to political issues. However, his nationalism went beyond the abstract concept of the fatherland to encompass the suffering people for whom he felt great sympathy and responsibility. These sentiments are apparent in his writings. Bernanos's early works often reveal his nostalgia for a France of the past, for a Christian monarchy. His novels such as UNDER SATAN'S SUN (1926) and *Diary of a Country Priest* were successful with the public, the latter earning its author recognition from the Académie Française. A number of his works were adapted to film.

Having volunteered to fight, Bernanos spent World War I in the trenches. As was true for many of his contemporaries, this experience left a lasting imprint on Bernanos. He was particularly disillusioned by propaganda that falsified the real conditions in which soldiers lived and fought. The principal figures in Bernanos's writings often reflect the author's wartime experience, as is manifest in the recurring theme of combat.

In 1917, Bernanos married Jehanne Talbert d'Arc, a descendant of one of Joan of Arc's brothers, with whom he had six children. To support his family, Bernanos worked as an insurance inspector, writing his first novel in railway cars and train station cafés as he made his rounds. He gave up this position in 1926 to devote himself to writing, and his first novel, *Under Satan's Sun,* was published that same year. It reflects the disillusionment of Bernanos's generation following the war. The metaphysical aspect of the novel is revealed in the character of the Devil. Bernanos's Catholicism differs from that of FRANÇOIS MAURIAC, for example, in the sense that in Bernanos's novels, the devil takes on form. For Bernanos, Satan is a real force at work in the world and the soul is the battleground between evil and grace. This fundamental conflict is at the heart of this and other works by Bernanos.

Stark contrasts mark Bernanos's writing. On one hand, he depicts humanity's great sins, its egoism, injustice, and alienation of the weak. On the other, he promotes the fight for grace and sanctification. Salvation, however, may not be easy to attain. Bernanos's struggling Christians are often confronted with temptation, suffering, and moments of profound despair. In *Under Satan's Sun,* Abbé Donissan tries to save Mouchette and his battle with the Devil is fraught with torment. *Diary of a Country Priest* depicts the silent suffering, physically and spiritually, of a young provincial priest who cannot pray. It is a sober, moving work in which the character of the priest, marginalized in modern, consumer society, lives between good and evil.

In the 1930s, Bernanos began to turn away from the traditional right, particularly in light of the rise of fascism. In *The Great Fear of Right-Thinkers* (1931), for example, Bernanos offers a critique of the reign of materialism and the moral abnegation of French society through the lonely prophet Édouard Drumont.

In 1935, Bernanos published a detective novel, *A Crime,* and in 1936, *Diary of a Country Priest.* Then, in 1937, he published *The New History of Mouchette,* in which a young girl rebels against an unjust world, is deceived, and finally commits suicide. The tone of the novel corresponds to sentiments raised by the violent civil war in Spain. Almost no writer who lived through the troubled times that marked the first half of the 20th century was capable of remaining silent in the face of war and its consequences, and Bernanos was no different. As a politically engaged humanist, in *Grand Cemeteries Under the Moon* (1938) Bernanos denounced the violence of the Spanish civil war. He frequently spoke of his "fraternal solidarity with the universal church of combatants, living and dead," and condemned society's injustice and moral degradation.

Profoundly disturbed by the rise of National Socialism in Germany, Bernanos left Europe in 1938. He went first to Paraguay and later Brazil, where he published a number of articles supporting General Charles de Gaulle and the French Resistance. He also published MONSIEUR OUINE in 1943, a novel in which a village, consumed by boredom, represents modern society. Monsieur Ouine is the unwitting force of evil that causes the village to disintegrate.

In 1945, at the invitation of De Gaulle, Bernanos returned to France but refused all offers for a public position. Bernanos's pessimistic view of postwar society appears in two posthumous publications, *What to Do with Liberty* (1953) and *French People, If Only You Knew* (1961). During the winter of 1947–1948, Bernanos worked on the screenplay of *Dialogue of the Carmelites,* a work that evokes many of the themes dear to Bernanos: fear, anguish, death, and, ultimately, the communion of saints. Bernanos died in 1948 in the American Hospital in Neuilly.

FURTHER READING

Balthasar, Hans Urs von. *Bernanos: An Ecclesial Existence.* San Francisco: Ignatius Press, 1996.
Blumenthal, Gerda. *The Poetic Imagination of Georges Bernanos.* Baltimore: Johns Hopkins University Press, 1965.

BERNARDIN DE SAINT-PIERRE, JACQUES-HENRI (1737–1814)

A lively imagination and the influence of ROUSSEAU made Bernardin de Saint-Pierre an idealist in praise of nature. He is most famous for his pastoral novel, PAUL AND VIRGINIA, a work marking Bernardin de Saint-Pierre as a precursor to ROMANTICISM.

Trained as an engineer, Bernardin de Saint-Pierre traveled widely from France to Germany, Holland, Russia, Poland, Austria, and Malta, frequently in search of employment. In 1767 he left for a post on the Isle de France (present-day Mauritius), an experience that gave him the material for his writing. Bernardin de Saint-Pierre's experience living in a French colony overseas led him to castigate its administrative hierarchy and the horrors of slavery.

Upon his return to Europe in 1770, Bernardin de Saint-Pierre found himself out of work yet again. This is when he turned to writing. At the same time, he also attended Mademoiselle de Lespinasse's salon of the Encyclopédistes (see ENCYCLOPEDIA), where he met other literary figures such as DIDEROT.

Bernardin de Saint-Pierre's first work, *Voyage to the Isle de France* (1773), was not particularly well received. In contrast, his *Studies of Nature* (1785–87) was so popular that he even received marriage proposals. This success removed the financial obstacles over which he had struggled for so long. The third edition of *Studies of Nature* included the celebrated novel *Paul and Virginia.*

In 1792, Bernardin de Saint-Pierre was appointed head of the Royal Gardens. As an avid supporter of Napoleon, he received a pension and the medal of the Legion of Honor in 1806. Bernardin de Saint-Pierre was accepted into Académie Française in 1803.

Romantic and imaginative, Bernardin de Saint-Pierre lived in a world of his own dreams. Frustrated by the discrepancy between his vision of the world as it should be and reality, he promoted the idea of a natural society based on virtue, far from the corrupting influence of civilization, echoing similar arguments made by Rousseau.

FURTHER READING

France, Anatole. *The Latin Genius.* Edited by Wilfrid S. Jackson. London: John Lane the Bodley Head; New York: Dodd, Mead and Co., 1924.

BESSETTE, GÉRARD (1920–2005)

A Québecois writer, Bessette studied classics in secondary school and earned a doctorate in literature in Montreal. He traveled in Europe and Mexico, after which he began a career as a university professor, teaching in several Canadian and U.S. institutions. He began his parallel literary career publishing poetry. He contributed to a number of literary reviews and to Radio-

Canada. Along with his poetry, Bessette produced a series of novels all of which bear the mark of Freudian psychoanalysis. Equally evident is the influence of James Joyce and William Faulkner in these works that challenge social values in contemporary society.

In *The Semester* (1979), Bessette tells the story of a professor of French-Canadian literature named Omer Marin. Employed at Princess University in Narcotown, Professor Marin closely resembles the author. In the last semester of his teaching career, Marin teaches a course focused on the analysis of a Québecois novel, *Serge Between the Dead,* written by Gilbert La Rocque. Marin's approach draws entirely, even obsessively, from Freud's psychoanalytic method.

The lines between the character of Marin and Bessette are blurred to such an extent that the novel refers to Bessette's oeuvre as Marin's, only slightly disguised. Bessette thus plays with the notions of identity and authorship. In the novel, Bessette applies Freud's analysis to his own writing, viewing its stream of consciousness as the work of his subconscious mind. Moreover, the theme of the Oedipus complex, applied to the individual and to Québec as a whole, is pronounced.

As Marin analyzes La Rocque's novel for his students, he treats it as a dream that, with Freud's tools, he can deconstruct in such as way as to reveal the inner workings of the author's mind. If his students resist his conclusions, Marin turns his Freudian analysis against them with accusations of repression and an "unresolved oedipus complex." The student who responds most enthusiastically to Marin's lectures and who proceeds to expand on his analysis is Sandra Karolanski, with whom Marin subsequently has an affair, literally stimulated by her psychosexual analysis. Finally, not satisfied with limiting his analysis to literature, Marin applies the same method to everyday life and to his own motivations.

Another undercurrent in the novel plays with Marin's character as emblematic of Odysseus. Fearful of old age and death, Marin attempts to leave behind "children of the mind," the one means open to him of achieving immortality since he has not been successful in procreation. "Omer said to himself, his hand married his pen." The complex structure of the novel is built upon three levels that consist of La Rocque's novel, Marin's commentary, and Marin's novel (the one we read). Implicit in the work is a critique of the system of higher education.

The central character of *Not for Every Eye* (1960) is an enigmatic and miserly figure who accepts employment with a bookseller in a small provincial town. He rents a room from a woman separated from her husband. As a Roman Catholic, she cannot obtain a divorce. The two have a sordid affair. Meanwhile, the protagonist is fairly satisfied with his job until his boss directs him to sell certain books banned by the church, for a high price, to particular clients. It is not entirely clear why the protagonist chooses instead to sell a copy of an *Essay on Morals* to a young high school student at a local Catholic school.

The bookseller is distraught and desires to get rid of both his untrustworthy employee as well as the compromising books. The protagonist takes advantage of his employer's discomfiture to sell the books for his own profit, earning enough to set himself up in Montreal, where, for several months, he has no need of employment. Distracted by the pleasures of life in the city, the protagonist gives up writing in his journal and so the narrative ends.

Bessette frequently challenges taboo subjects while evoking the narrowness of conformist provincial society dominated by a Catholic hierarchy. He is particularly sharp in his depiction of individuals who profit from a warped, hypocritical value system. Finally, Bessette is fundamentally concerned with the relationship between the individual and his or her means of expression, that is to say, language itself. At the heart of his writing, then, is an epistemological question, how do we know what we know?

FURTHER READING

Jameson, Frederic. "Reveries Narcotowniennes," *Yale French Studies,* no. 65. *The Language of Difference: Writing in Quebec(ois)* (1983): 499–500.

Perron, Paul, and Brian Massumi. "On Language and Writing in Gerard Bessette's Fiction," *Yale French Studies,* no. 65. The Language of Difference: Writing in Quebec(ois) (1983): 227–245.

Seliwoniuk, Jadwiga. "Gerard Bessette and His Dream of 'Genarration,'" *Yale French Studies,* no. 65. The Language of Difference: Writing in Quebec(ois) (1983): 246–255.

BETI, MONGO (1932–2001)

Mongo Beti is the pen name of Alexandre Biyidi, a writer born in Cameroon whose first novel, *Cruel City* was published in 1954 when the author, then publishing under the name Eza Boto, was only 22 years old. Beti received his higher education in France, where he remained, returning to Cameroon only for brief periods. Beti was thus a writer in an exile of his own choosing. Nonetheless, the burning issues of his native Africa are central to Beti's work.

Beti's early works are marked by a biting challenge to the colonial system drawn from the author's own experience, particularly his early education by missionaries. As much as he is critical of the French colonial system, he is also opposed to the regime of Ahmadou Ahidjo in independent Cameroon, against which he published a sharp attack in the form of a pamphlet that was condemned by the French in 1972. A politically engaged writer, in 1978 Beti established a new review entitled *Black People, African People.*

There are two distinct periods in Beti's writing career. His first novels, *Cruel City, Poor Christ of Bomba* (1956), *Mission Accomplished* (1957), and *King Lazarus* (1958), all focus on the colonial period. Subsequent novels such as *Remember Ruben* (1974), *Perpetua and the Habit of Unhappiness* (1974), and *Lament for an African Pol* (1979) all deal with questions facing postcolonial Africa. Together these works bring to life the African experience from the 1930s to the 1970s.

Mission Accomplished is the story of Jean-Marie Medza, who has failed the oral exam for the baccalaureate and returned to his village. Medza suffers from a sense of his own inadequacy. Misjudged by the people around him, he responds by behaving inappropriately. Ultimately, he is incapable even of love. The structure of the novel subtly recalls the oral tradition.

Always outspoken against injustice and oppression, in *Perpetua* Beti focuses on the subjugation of African women. There is no freedom in a corrupt, postcolonial system run by drunken men and a harsh military regime. Least free of all are women. Perpetua is, like other women, a victim. Against her will she is forced into a marriage by her mother. Her husband, an ambitious government official, is cruel. Beaten even when she is pregnant, Perpetua suffers added humiliation when her husband takes a second wife. As he continually fails his exams for promotion, Perpetua's husband forces her to sleep with one of his superiors. When Perpetua falls hopelessly in love with a young athlete, her husband, for all intents and purposes, imprisons her. There she dies at the age of 20, malnourished, pregnant, and ultimately alone.

After 1974, Beti's novels such as *The Two Mothers of Guillaume Ismaël Dzwetama* (1984), *The Revenge of Ismaël Dzwetama* (1984), and *The Story of a Madman* (1994) focus on the corruption and disorder in African society after independence and, as such, recall the works of contemporary writers such as AHMADOU KOUROUMA and SEMBÈNE OUSMANE.

Beti consistently resists cultural assimilation, yet there is some irony in his stance given the fact he chooses to live in France. He is critical of NEGRITUDE and, in particular, the works of CAMARA LAYE. In the end, Beti opposes much that is associated with traditional African life.

FURTHER READING

Arnold, Stephen H. *Critical Perspectives on Mongo Beti.* Boulder, Colo.: Lynne Rienner, 1998.

Dramé, Kandioura. *The Novel as Transformation of Myth: A Study of the Novels of Mongo Beti and Ngugi wa Thiong'o.* Syracuse, N.Y.: Maxwell School of Citizenship and Public Affairs, Syracuse University, 1990.

John, Elerius Edet. *Creative Responses of Mongo Beti and Ferdinand Oyono to Historical Realities.* Lagos, Nigeria: Paico, 1986.

Priebe, Richard K. "Critical Perspectives on Mongo Beti," *African Studies Review* 42, no. 3 (December 1999): 196–198.

BITTER VICTORY (LE SANG NOIR) LOUIS GUILLOUX (1935)

Bitter Victory tells the sad story of a fascinating character, Cripure, a provincial philosophy teacher who is as hateful, dirty, and grotesque as he is generous, thoughtful, and intelligent. The character of Cripure is based on a high school teacher named Georges Palante whom Guilloux liked very much and who ended his own life just as Cripure does. The name Cripure is ironically derived from Immanuel Kant's *Critique of Pure Reason.* Cripure's gift is to disclose the painful reality of human existence. Cripure unveils social hypocrisy and the stifling constraints of provincial bourgeois society. He also raises philosophical questions in his struggle to understand the meaning of life.

Cripure seeks solace in writing a historical novel but is unsure of himself. The novel is to be called *Chrestomathie of Despair*. However, at one point, Cripure considers changing the title to *Bouclo and Pécuporte* or *Boucri and Pécupure,* obviously playing on his own name but also making an intertextual reference to GUSTAVE FLAUBERT'S *BOUVARD AND PÉCUCHET*. Guilloux thus seems to mock Cripure's search for truth. Some critics have compared Cripure to Don Quixote in his futile battle against social injustice. The novel also recalls the works of Guilloux's friend ALBERT CAMUS in its evocation of the individual's relationship to the world and the impossibility of happiness, a metaphysical tragedy that leads Cripure to suicide.

A number of critics have discussed the similarities between Guillou and JEAN-PAUL SARTRE, whose novel *NAUSEA* was published three years after *Bitter Victory*. Like Sartre's character Roquentin, Cripure is isolated from society. A frustrated intellectual, he feels as if he is suffocating in the narrow life of the small provincial town in which he lives. He is tormented by Monsieur Nabucet, a stereotypical bourgeois. When his frustrations prove to be too overwhelming he seeks refuge in a café, again like Roquentin. Because of his enormous size, he is physically unappealing, and this only augments his sense of suffering from the world's hostility. As a result, he often suffers from dizziness that resembles Roquentin's nausea. In each case, the ailment is a result of the character's unease at contact with the world.

Set in a provincial town, the novel is really about the problem of war, though it takes place far from the trenches. The black blood of the French title represents the stifling of human beings by the injustice of society. The theme of asphyxiation is common to other novels of the inter-war period. ROGER MARTIN DU GARD's Antoine Thibault, for example, observes his own death by poison gas.

Critics generally consider *Bitter Victory* to be Guilloux's greatest work. It was a tremendous success. In fact, ANDRÉ GIDE considered it one of the great novels of the 20th century. All Guilloux's works reflect his concern for political and social injustice. He writes in the tradition of populist writers with a sense of the farcical that recalls the writing of ANDRÉ MALRAUX.

FURTHER READING
Brombert, Victor. *The Intellectual Hero.* Chicago: University of Chicago Press, Phoenix Books, 1964.

Green, Francis J. "Louis Guilloux's Le Sang Noir: A Prefiguration of Sartre's La Nausée," *French Review* 43, no. 2 (December 1969): 205–214.

Green, Mary Jean Matthews. *Louis Guilloux, An Artisan of Language.* York, S.C.: French Literature Publications, 1980.

Peyre, Henri. *The Contemporary French Novel.* New York: Oxford University Press, 1955.

Redfern, W. D. *Louis-Guilloux: Ear-Witness.* Amsterdam, Atlanta: Rodopi, 1998.

BLAIS, MARIE-CLAIRE (1939–)

Born in Quebec, Blais published her first novel, *Mad Shadows,* in 1959. It was followed by *Tête Blanche* (1960) and *The Day is Dark* (1962) as well as a collection of poems. These early works evoke the difficulty and cruelty in relationships between adults and children in a style that blends fairy tale with poetry.

With the support of American literary critic Edmund Wilson, Blais received a Guggenheim fellowship. As of 1963, she spent several years in Boston and on Cape Cod. There she wrote *A SEASON IN THE LIFE OF EMMANUEL* (1965), which won the Médicis Prize in 1966. Blais's works were particularly well received in France, in fact better than in Canada, as her vision of the unhappiness and misery that pervade Quebecois society is often unsettling to Canadian readers.

Blais's writings have been translated into some 15 languages. In 1976, Blais won the Belgian-Canadian Prize for her oeuvre, and in 1993 she was elected to the Royal Academy of Belgium. *Journey of a Writer* (1993) recounts her experience in New England. She later divided her time between Quebec and Key West, Florida.

A Season in the Life of Emmanuel tells the tragic story of a family seen in part from the perspective of an infant. Under the vigilant eye of Grandmother Antoinette, members of the family live and die. Among them are the mystical Heloise, Pomme "the seventh," and Jean the Thin, the poet who adds his voice to the narrative. Through their multiple perspectives, the themes of suffering, redemption, and tragedy emerge with dark humor. In this novel, Blais skillfully subverts the traditional rural novel genre associated with writers such as LOUIS HÉMON.

Blais's trilogy that includes *The Manuscripts of Pauline Archange* (1968), *To Live! To Live!* (1969), and *Dürer's Angel* (1970) together offer a critique of a society incapable of understanding the young and their spirit of rebellion. These autobiographical works reflect Blais's use of writing as the means of defining herself and her life. *St. Lawrence Blues* (1973) explores the richness of the French dialect in Quebec, while *A Literary Affair* (1992) and *Sacred Voyagers* (1992) examine the temptation of evil.

Nights in the Underground (1978), *Deaf to the City* (1979), and *Anna's Visions* (1982) make up another cycle of novels more experimental in nature. Characters and sensations merge into one as the reader passes from one state of consciousness to another. *Deaf to the City* was inspired by a painting of the Norwegian symbolist Edvard Munch. An underlying theme in all these works is solitude and the individual's fundamental isolation. In *These Festive Nights* (1995) a group of young intellectuals and artists comment on contemporary society. Blais has also produced poetry and plays.

The manner in which Blais evokes the violence and unhappiness hidden in the depths of the Quebecois family recalls the writings of William Faulkner. Children are denied childhood and laughter. In consequence, they burn inwardly with rebellion. While Blais raises problems pervasive in contemporary society, she provides no answers. Yet the bleakness of her vision is tempered somewhat by her dark humor. Nonetheless, the underlying message that life is full of solitude that ends only in death dominates her works. Perhaps the most unhappy of all are those who survive to struggle in their loneliness.

FURTHER READING

Green, Mary Jean Matthews. *Marie-Claire Blais.* New York: Twayne, London: Prentice Hall International, 1995.
Stratford, Philip. *Marie-Claire Blais.* Toronto: Coles, 1974.

***BLANCHE OR FORGETTING* (BLANCHE OU L'OUBLI)** LOUIS ARAGON (1967) Set in 1965, this novel plays with the power of words. It is the supposed autobiography of the narrator, a linguist named Geoffroy Gaiffer who recalls his love for Blanche, a woman whom he loved passionately in the 1920s. Using the technique of internal monologue, Aragon has Geoffroy attempt to recapture the image of the woman whom he abandoned years before. Frustrated by the impossibility of language to express truly one's experience, Geoffroy suffers from a sense of his own impotency. He thus differs from MARCEL PROUST, who affirmed the power of words to actualize experience. Obsessed with GUSTAVE FLAUBERT's *SENTIMENTAL EDUCATION*, Geoffroy recalls the parting of Madame Arnoux and Frédéric in that novel as he ends, "I hid my face in my hands in order to see nothing but oblivion, the hot cinders of forgetfulness." Again recalling Madame Arnoux, Blanche offers a lock of her now white hair.

Parallel to Geoffroy's autobiography is Marie Noire's novel about the love between Geoffroy and Blanche. Her use of words is different from that of Geoffroy as she tries to re-create the truth about the past. Marie Noire is memory itself. As the novel progresses, words change along with the characters such that, when Blanche reappears, she is unrecognizable. The division of the novel into these two parts allows Aragon to explore the writing process by deliberately unveiling the creation of fictional characters. In this exploration of the novel itself, Aragon unveils the process of writing fiction. Moreover, the intertextual references to Flaubert add yet another dimension to the complex relationship between reality and fiction. Like many of Aragon's works, this novel blends reality and imagination, leaving the reader in a state of uncertainty.

The relationship between art and life in Aragon's career as a writer is very close. In terms of style, he draws on contemporary techniques in fiction associated with the New Novel (see *NOUVEAU ROMAN*) at the same time as he hearkens back to his earlier Surrealist period (see SURREALISM). Dedicated to "the unhappy crowd," the novel does not entirely abandon Aragon's political commitment as it recalls Karl Marx's call for the novelist to re-create the world.

FURTHER READING

Adereth, Maxwell. *Elsa Triolet and Louis Aragon: An Introduction to Their Interwoven Lives and Works.* Lewiston, N.Y.: E. Mellen Press, 1994.

Brosman, Catherine Savage. *Malraux, Sartre and Aragon as Political Novelists.* Gainesville: University of Florida Press, 1964.

Caute, David. *Communism and the French Intellectuals, 1914–1960.* New York: Macmillan, 1964.

Duruzoi, Gerard. *History of the Surrealist Movement.* Translated by Alison Anderson. Chicago: University of Chicago Press, 2002.

Kimyongur, Angela. *Socialist Realism in Louis Aragon's Le Monde Réel Series.* Hull, England: University of Hull Press, 1995.

BLANCHOT, MAURICE (1907–2003)

Blanchot once described literature as "not only a real experience, but a fundamental experience that calls everything into question, even itself, even the dialectic . . . art is infinite protest." Throughout his career as essayist, literary theorist, and novelist, Blanchot continuously sought to define and explain "the space of literature." His position in the history of French literature is ambiguous, for his writing is difficult and complex. Moreover, Blanchot never adhered to a contemporary literary movement, school of thought, or political party. He was never a surrealist or existentialist (see SURREALISM; EXISTENTIALISM). In fact, he was often silent. Little known among the general reading public, Blanchot was most appreciated by a narrow intellectual elite that included thinkers such as Gilles Deleuze, Jacques Lacan, GEORGES BATAILLE, and Michel Foucault among others. Today, Blanchot is principally recognized for his literary theory.

From a staunch Catholic family, Blanchot was first introduced to French literature by his father, who was a teacher. Around 1923, Blanchot left home to study philosophy and German at the University of Strasbourg. Then in 1929, he went to Paris intending to study medicine but was drawn instead into the world of journalism.

As a young man, Blanchot was associated with the political Right, although he refused to collaborate with the VICHY REGIME during World War II. The trauma of those years (Blanchot narrowly escaped execution against the wall of his own home in 1944) led him to withdraw increasingly from public life. For more than 10 years, he lived in self-imposed, internal exile in the south of France. During these years, he concentrated on literature and his own writing.

Blanchot's first novel, THOMAS THE OBSCURE (1941), is an unsettling work in which the characters appear to be strangely detached from the world. The novel also reveals a central theme to Blanchot's works, the powerlessness of language. It was followed by *Aminabad* (1942), a bizarre, Kafkaesque novel centered on a house whose inhabitants are governed by the law of an inaccessible top floor. In *Death Sentence* (1948), set during the Munich crisis when Hitler was threatening to invade Czechoslovakia and the opening of World War II, the principal character, like Thomas, experiments with love only; J. dies and Nathalie is (literally) petrified. The predominant theme of this work is absence.

The theme of the impossibility of communication reappears in *Most High* (1948), a novel in which a nurse kills Henri Sorge (whose name may signify a Heideggerian state of anguish) because he never reveals himself in conversation. The problem of communication is yet again the focus of *Infinite Conversation* (1969). The unending conversation to which Blanchot refers is one in which he himself engaged throughout his life, a ceaseless dialogue with philosophy, literature, and mythology, past and present.

Blanchot's subsequent writings tended to be shorter and denser although they treat the same core themes as his earlier works. Over time, Blanchot's fiction was increasingly denuded of all characteristics associated with traditional narrative forms. His works are frequently marked by a sense of anguish. Characters are but shadows through whom the reader dimly perceives another world. The reader must, in fact, abandon all normal conventions when approaching the text, particularly given that, for Blanchot, writing/literature is an experience that does not exist. There is no subject, no action, no meaning. Blanchot, instead, sought to offer a neutral space of experimentation through which it is possible so discern the singularity of the human experience. Unlike the surrealists, for example, Blanchot did not believe that art or literature could change the world. He did, however, believe it could be subversive. At the same time, Blanchot evoked a Hegelian sense of a universal, unifying spirit.

FURTHER READING

Foucault, Michel. *Maurice Blanchot, The Thought from the Outside.* Translated by Brian Massumi. New York: Zone Books, 1987.

Gregg, John. *Maurice Blanchot and the Literature of Transgression.* Princeton, N.J.: Princeton University Press, 1994.

Hill, Leslie. *Bataille, Klossowski, Blanchot: Writing at the Limit.* Oxford, New York: Oxford University Press, 2001.

Holland, Michael, ed. *The Blanchot Reader.* Oxford, Cambridge, Mass.: Blackwell, 1995.

Iyer, Lars. *Blanchot's Vigilance: Literature, Phenomenology, and the Ethical.* New York: Palgrave Macmillan, 2005.

Shaviro, Steven. *Passion and Excess: Blanchot, Bataille, and Literary Theory.* Tallahassee: Florida State University Press, 1990.

Smock, Ann. *What Is There to Say?* Lincoln: University of Nebraska Press, 2003.

BLOY, LÉON (1846–1917)

Bloy once stated, "I write only for God." An ardent Roman Catholic, Bloy was also interested in social reform. Unfortunately, he often expressed his concerns in a violent and vituperative tone that alienated his contemporaries. He is most famous for his semiautobiographic novels such as *The Hopeless One* (1886) and *The WOMAN WHO WAS POOR* (1897).

Bloy was born into a large family in Perigueux, where his father served as a government functionary. At first, Bloy studied drawing and architecture in Paris. However, his meeting with Jules Barbey d'Aurevilly in 1867 marked an important turning point in his life. It was then that Bloy underwent his conversionary experience and chose a literary career.

In 1873, Bloy tried a variety of jobs to support himself with an attempt to launch his writing career but the beginning was difficult, recalling BALZAC's early experiences. His religious intransigence made it increasingly challenging to find a publisher. Finally, Bloy began to write for a small journal called the *Black Cat*. These were important years for Bloy in other ways as well. In this period he met Anne-Marie Roulé, both his parents died, and Bloy attempted monastic life. In 1882, Anne-Marie was locked up as insane, a personal catastrophe

for both of them. Nonetheless, Bloy published his first two books in 1884, but the violence of his attacks against society caused a scandal.

Bloy tried, unsuccessfully, to start his own journal. He also began writing *The Hopeless One*. The autobiographical genre suited Bloy, leading him to think about writing a second novel, but he was desperately in need of money. Like Balzac's character Lucien de Rubempré (*LOST ILLUSIONS*), Bloy turned to journalism.

In 1890 he married Jeanne Molbech, the daughter of a Danish poet. In 1891, angry over the way JORIS-KARL HUYSMANS caricatured him in *Down There,* Bloy left with his wife for an extended stay in Denmark. By 1894 he had returned to writing novels, but this was a personally painful year during which two of his children died. He used this experience in another autobiographical novel, *The Woman Who Was Poor.* In 1900 Bloy returned to France. He died in 1917, profoundly marked by the traumatic experience of World War I.

Like his contemporary PAUL BOURGET, Bloy was a Catholic writer. Religion is the unifying factor in his writings, all of which reflect Bloy's search for the absolute. For Bloy, everything is symbolic. Fundamentally a mystic, Bloy focused on human anguish. Like many of his contemporaries, Bloy also rebelled against bourgeois life and values, often with violence. "The bourgeois is an idolater enslaved by the visible." Bloy inspired early 20th-century French Catholics and influenced the works of GEORGES BERNANOS, Franz Kafka, Nikolai Berdyaev, and Thomas Merton.

FURTHER READING

Brady, Sister Mary Rosalie. *Thought and Style in the Works of Léon Bloy.* New York: AMS Press, 1969, c.1946.

Polimeni, Emmanuela. *Léon Bloy: The Pauper Prophet, 1846–1917.* New York: Philosophical Library, 1951.

BLUE OF NOON (LE BLEU DU CIEL)

GEORGES BATAILLE (1935) As with all of Bataille's works, violence, death, and eroticism mark this novel, yet lying beneath the surface is a quest for the sacred and the infinite. The protagonist, Troppmann (whose Franco-German name means "too much man" undertakes a nihilistic journey of sexual perversion, drunkenness, ecstasy, and excess against the backdrop of a general strike in Spain and the rise of National Socialism in Germany. War is looming as Troppmann first separates from his libertine, drunken wife, Dorothea (Dirty), and then takes up with Lazare, a militant communist in France. Like Dorothea (who once defecated in her clothes), Troppmann lives an utterly depraved life. One evening he stabs his neighbor at dinner with a fork. He then goes on to say that he once almost had sex with a corpse.

Troppmann is suicidal, manic, full of self-loathing, and violent. He is the epitome of Bataille's notion of the Impossible. As he listens to Lazare and her father talking about one's responsibility to care for the downtrodden, Troppmann concludes that communists are no better than Christians. At one point Lazare takes control of a prison rather than a weapons depot as expected. Troppmann admires this senseless act. If Lazare represents political engagement, Troppmann represents nihilism. The final haunting images from the novel involve Troppmann and Dorothea having passionate sex in a graveyard in Germany with marching Hitler Youth in the background.

In this and other works by Bataille, eroticism and desire have the power to transform reality. Love, poetry, and death flow into the same experience of excess that so fascinates the author. Moreover, like MAURICE BLANCHOT, Bataille seeks to push the limits of writing as much as those of human experience.

FURTHER READING

Boldt-Irons, Leslie Anne, ed. *On Bataille: Critical Essays*. Albany: State University of New York, 1995.

Botting, Fred, and Scott Wilson, eds. *Bataille: A Critical Reader*. Oxford, Malden, Mass.: Blackwell, 1998.

Connor, Peter Tracey. *Georges Bataille and the Mysticism of Sin*. Baltimore: Johns Hopkins University Press, 2000.

Dean, Carolyn J. *The Self and Its Pleasures: Bataille, Lacan, and the History of the Decentered Subject*. Ithaca, N.Y.: Cornell University Press, 1992.

Gemerchak, Christopher M. *The Sunday of the Negative: Reading Bataille, Reading Hegel*. Albany: State University of New York, 2003.

Jay, Martin. *The Limits of Limit-Experience: Bataille and Foucault*. Berkeley: University of California, Center for German and European Studies, 1993.

Rella, Franco. *The Myth of the Other: Lacan. Deleuze, Foucault, Bataille*. Translated by Nelson Moe. Washington, D.C.: Maisonneuve Press, 1994.

BOOK FOUR (QUART LIVRE DE PANTAGRUEL) FRANÇOIS RABELAIS (1552) The full version of the *Quart Livre de Pantagruel* (*The Fourth Book of Pantagruel*) appeared in 1552, not long before Rabelais's death. Similar to the proceeding volumes in this epic tale of Gargantua and Pantagruel, this work is difficult to interpret. With each subsequent volume in the series, Rabelais increases the anecdotal material interspersed throughout the narrative. While the characters' journey continues, Rabelais makes an effort to make their travels more believable by introducing geographical elements from contemporary works. The concept of *Pantagruélisme*, first introduced in BOOK THREE, is expanded on here as the journey focuses on the search for *dive bouteille*. Rabelais continues to present the reader with a number of amusing scenes that disguise deeper meaning. With the islands of Ennasin and Cheli, Rabelais appears to be commenting on contemporary fashions. His attack on the legal world is renewed as well.

During a storm at sea, each character reacts differently to the life-threatening situation, allowing Rabelais to develop further themes he introduced in earlier works, such as the question of free will. Panurge's character has taken on an unfortunate turn for the worse. He continually invokes the Virgin Mary and the saints, praying for a miracle. He is once again chastised by the wise Pantagruel for his fear of death and his misguided notions of religion. In the subsequent chapters on the Macraeons, Rabelais expands on the questions of death and the immortal soul, showing the influence of his benefactor, Guillaume du Bellay.

The text's unity is derived from Rabelais's attack on contemporary politics, religion, materialism, and idealism. In the section on Quaresmeprenant, Rabelais attacks religious extremism, whether Catholic or Protestant. Some critics have argued that Quaresmeprenant represents Holy Roman emperor Charles V, who came under attack in earlier works as well. The Island of Chaneph focuses on the problem of hypocrisy as seen in the Abbaye de Thélème in *Gargantua*. Rabelais takes on a more serious tone in Pantagruel's dinner with his servants, interpreted as representing the last supper. While his meaning is often obscure or illusive, these themes carry through. The text is marked by thematic rather than narrative unity, although the use of the journey gives some overall structure to the text.

FURTHER READING

Bakhtin, Mikhail. *Rabelais and his World.* Translated by Hélène Iswolsky. Cambridge, Mass.: MIT Press, 1968.

Cave, Terrence. *The Cornucopian Text: Problems of Writing in the French Renaissance.* Oxford: Clarendon Press, 1979.

Febvre, Lucien. *The Problem of Unbelief in the Sixteenth Century: The Religion of Rabelais.* Translated by Beatrice Gottlieb. Cambridge, Mass.: Harvard University Press, 1982.

Screech, Michael. *Rabelais.* Ithaca, N.Y.: Cornell University Press, 1979.

BOOK OF THE CITY OF LADIES, THE (LE LIVRE DE LA CITÉ DES DAMES) CHRISTINE DE PIZAN (1405)

Christine de Pizan is one of the earliest female authors to write in defense of women. The text is an allegory based on an architectural metaphor. With the assistance of three august ladies—Reason, Justice, and Rectitude—Christine undertakes the construction of the City of Ladies. "On the flat and fertile plain" of the "field of Letters," Christine "takes up the trowel of her pen."

Influenced in part by Italian humanism, Christine seeks to redefine nobility as rooted in virtue rather than bloodlines. This utopian capital will open its gates only to women of virtue. The city will serve as a legitimization of women: their intellect, virtue, and their contribution to society. Here women will be protected from misogynist attacks. In a companion text, *The Book of Three Virtues,* Christine provides a handbook leading the way into the city of female virtue. This text is a treatise on the moral education of women of all stations, thus sharing a similar purpose as her mirror for princes, *The Book of the Body Politic.*

In *The Book of the City of Ladies,* Christine engages in the work of an intellectual or literary historian, redefining the canon of classical texts as she formulates an argument against the misogynist tradition in Western literature. Her unspoken adversary is JEUN DE MEUN, whose ROMANCE OF THE ROSE is an example of literature condemning the nature of women. Christine de Pizan's reaction to the image of women as morally, intellectually, and physically weak makes her one of the principal participants in the Quarrel of the *Romance of the Rose.*

This work is of particular interest to feminist scholars today for its handling of themes such as self-knowledge, authority (especially female authority), justice, and virtue. In *The Book of the City of Ladies,* legendary female figures are reassessed in a positive light. Dido is remembered for the construction of another city, Carthage, rather than for her love of Aeneas. Semiramis, too, is honored for her role as a city builder, not for her incestuous relationship with her son. The opening of the text subtly reminds the reader of the obstacles motherhood and domestic responsibilities may pose to a woman's intellectual pursuits. In shocking ways this text reexamines the role of women in literary history. Moreover, its author openly assumes a position of literary authority herself.

FURTHER READING

Altmann, Barbara K., and Deborah L. McGrady, eds. *Christine de Pizan: A Casebook.* New York: Routledge, 2003.

McLeod, Enid. *The Order of the Rose: The Life and Ideas of Christine de Pizan.* Totowa, N.J.: Rowman and Littlefield, 1976.

Quilligan, Maureen. *The Allegory of Female Authority: Christine de Pizan's Cité des dames.* Ithaca, N.Y.: Cornell University Press, 1991.

Willard, Charity Cannon. *Christine de Pizan: Her Life and Works.* New York: Persea Books, 1984.

BOOK THREE (TIERS LIVRE DES FAITS ET DITS HÉROÏQUES DU NOBLE PANTAGRUEL) FRANÇOIS RABELAIS (1546)

The *Tiers Livre des faits et dits héroïques du noble Pantagruel (The Third Book of the Heroic Acts and Words of the Noble Pantagruel)* appeared 12 years after *Gargantua* and was placed almost immediately on the Catholic Church's Index of Banned Books. On the surface a continuation of Pantagruel's story, this volume focuses on Panurge's search for a wife. This quest serves as the basis for more comedic adventures; however, Panurge's character has changed since the reader first met him. He has become more serious, more reflective.

While the book appears to retain the loose structure of Rabelais's earlier works, the text can be divided into three principal parts that give it overall coherence. The first part is Panurge's famous praise of debts. The central section is the marriage quest, and the third is the *"pantagruélion."*

Panurge is a complex character. While he is extremely erudite, thus displaying Rabelais's own tremendous erudition, his intellect is sterile. His endless talk may impede both action in daily life and, ultimately, knowledge of God. Rabelais points to the ambiguity of the human condition. We must act and yet we constantly fall victim to our own ignorance.

In his praise of debt, Panurge offers a clever argument that debt is a necessary part of life that, in fact, encourages Christian virtues such as faith, hope, and charity. This view is countered by the wise Pantagruel, who seems to have his hands on life's ropes, whereas Panurge, despite his ability to rationalize, does not. Still, readers continue to like Panurge, as they did from the first, for his exuberant language and comic nature.

As is always the case with Rabelais's humorous stories, Panurge's search for a wife is a platform for the exploration of deeper questions about the human condition. Some scholars view it as a negative contribution to the literary debate on women, the *querelle des femmes.* Panurge approaches a variety of characters to ask advice on the question of marriage, again allowing Rabelais to explore several facets of a single issue through different voices. Trouillogon gives an altogether negative view of marriage. The doctor Rondibilis takes a physiological perspective, arguing that marriage offers a proper channel for lust. Hippothadée speaks with the voice of the Evangelists, quoting from St. Paul's letter to the Corinthians. When Panurge expresses his fear of being a cuckold, Hippothadée recommends that he put his trust in God, for his own sake and for that of his wife. Panurge receives advice of a less rational nature from witches, mutes, jesters, soothsayers, and others. Again, comedy disguises serious themes that include an examination of human reason, knowledge, and superstition. In the end, Rabelais seems to suggest that we must learn to trust in forces beyond human nature. At the same time, only knowledge leads to truth. The usual mixture of comedy, erudition, and verbal acrobatics makes this one of Rabelais's best works. At the same time and for the same reasons, its meaning is not always accessible to the reader.

FURTHER READING

Bakhtin, Mikhail. *Rabelais and his World.* Translated by Hélène Iswolsky. Cambridge, Mass.: MIT Press, 1968.

Cave, Terrence. *The Cornucopian Text: Problems of Writing in the French Renaissance.* Oxford: Clarendon Press, 1979.

Febvre, Lucien. *The Problem of Unbelief in the Sixteenth Century: The Religion of Rabelais.* Translated by Beatrice Gottlieb. Cambridge, Mass.: Harvard University Press, 1982.

Screech, Michael. *Rabelais.* Ithaca, N.Y.: Cornell University Press, 1979.

BOSCO, HENRI (1888–1976) Bosco's great love for the richness and beauty of Provençal life is reflected in his works, the central themes of which find their source in his solitary childhood in the Avignon countryside.

A talented musician, botanist, and lover of language and literature, Bosco had a fine classical education that led him to describe Homer, Hesiod, Virgil, Plato, Dante, Petrarch, and the troubadours as "the poets of my life." Bosco completed an advanced degree in Italian at the University of Florence. Throughout his life, Bosco held dear the natural connection that exists both historically and spiritually between Provence and Italy.

During World War I, Bosco fought in the Dardanelles. When the war was over, he spent the next 10 years teaching comparative literature in Naples. At the same time, he contributed to a Provençal literary journal called *The Fire,* and thus began to attract the attention of readers. His first two novels were *Pierre Lampédouze* (1924) and *Irene* (1928), both "pastiches," as is the case with much of Bosco's writing.

Bosco lived and taught in many places. From 1931 to 1935 he worked in Rabat, Morocco where he founded the Alliance Française of Morocco and directed a local literary review. His writing earned him a significant number of prestigious prizes that includes the Renaudot Prize in 1945, the Louis Barthou Prize in 1947, the Ambassador's Prize in 1949, the National Grand Prize for Arts and Letters in 1953, the Grand Prize for Young People's Literature in 1959, the Grand Prize for Mediterranean Literature in 1965, and, in 1968, the Grand Prize for Literature from the Académie Française.

His most famous piece of children's literature, *Culotte the Donkey* (1937), made such a lasting impression that readers sometimes forget that Bosco was more than an author of children's literature. ANDRÉ GIDE described *Culotte* as "an exquisite, strange and miraculous book." Bosco said himself that his writing does not fit into a particular genre. "I write narrative. Narrative is necessary for me to indirectly attain poetry," having "a poetic temperament that cannot be realized in verse." With his lyrical and musical prose, Bosco captured the spirit of the earth, its shadows and its light.

Most of Bosco's novels are set in Provence, although he denied being a regional writer. "I am a human writer," he said. "My characters only appear to be from Provence. They are most of all universal and human . . . neither good nor bad, but alone." Some part of Bosco's characters compels them to search for some sacred mystery in silence and nature, thus reflecting Bosco's mysticism. In *Théotime,* for example, Geneviève arrives at a Provençal farm, where she discovers that she is capable of mystical communication with nature. Meanwhile, Pascal, her cousin, keeps a journal in which he writes, "the more I am alone, the more I attain the invisible." The two characters share Bosco's understanding of the mystical, even supernatural, connection between mankind and the world.

Inspired by nature, Bosco believed that a primitive magic exists between humankind and the earth. Nature leads us toward some ultimate spiritual union. In this respect, Bosco was a romantic (see ROMANTICISM). Bosco is buried in the Luberon, the land that he so loved.

FURTHER READING
Sussex, R. T. *Henri Bosco, Poet-novelist.* Christchurch, New Zealand: University of Canterbury Press, 1966.

BOURBON RESTORATION   The Treaty of
Fontainebleau, signed on April 11, 1814, exiled Napoleon Bonaparte to the island of Elba off the coast of Italy, and marked the beginning of the reign of Louis XVIII, the brother of Louis XVI. Louis XVIII subsequently signed a charter guaranteeing the French constitution. His reign therefore cannot be considered a return to the OLD REGIME despite the return of a Bourbon monarch to the throne. A representative government remained in place although dominated by a wealthy elite. Many Frenchmen and women, however, remained loyal to Napoleon, who returned to power for the famed Hundred Days after escaping from Elba in March 1815. One finds numerous references to the Bourbon Restoration in 19th-century French literature, such as STENDHAL's *The Red and the Black.*

BOURGEOIS NOVEL (ROMAN BOURGEOIS) ANTOINE FURETIÈRE (1666)   The *Bourgeois Novel,* whose title may refer to Scarron's *Roman Comique,* is the story of two middle-class girls, Javotte and Lucrèce, in the market for love and marriage. The *Bourgeois Novel* offers a satirical description in meticulous detail of middle-class Parisian life. It pokes fun at the language and style of the *précieuses* (see PRECIOSITY) as well as Furetière's contemporary, CHARLES SOREL, whose name can be found in anagram form in the character of Charrosselles.

As a realist novel, the *Roman Bourgeois* offers a stark contrast to the heroic and pastoral novels so popular at the time. It is in this manner that Furetière, along with PAUL SCARRON and CHARLES SOREL, was innovative in challenging contemporary literary norms even if, in the case of Furetière, the narrative tends to be rather dull. Conversations are recounted as having taken place in the past, distancing one from the events described in a way that is unnatural to the modern reader. Still, Furetière's writing is innovative in its realistic portrayal of daily life and through the insertion of the narrator's voice into the story. While this device was not particularly well received at the time, it had a later influence on other works exploring the role of narrative such as DIDEROT's *Jack the Fatalist.*

BOURGET, PAUL (1852–1935)   This poet, novelist, and literary critic, the son of an esteemed mathematician, was born in Amiens. After secondary school, Bourget moved to Paris, where he continued his studies in literature. He died in Paris in 1935.

Bourget's first published works were poetry, emphasizing the self-exploration of the human heart. This theme plays into Bourget's later psychological novels. A versatile thinker, Bourget turned from poetry to writing *Essays on Contemporary Psychology* (1883). This sensational work reveals Bourget's moralist tendencies as well. From psychology, Bourget turned to novels.

He also wrote criticism for a number of prominent French literary journals.

The publication of *The Disciple* in 1899 marked Bourget's transition in a new direction. Like other writers he remained concerned with the problems of contemporary society. He turned away from positivist, naturalistic trends, however, to focus on the state of the soul or conscience. From this point on, Bourget's novels were all marked by a combination of religion, morality, and psychology.

For a long time, critics considered Bourget to be the psychological novelist par excellence. In fact, a lack of intellectual rigor may mark him more as a moralist than a psychologist. He wrote in a sometimes heavy, oratorical style. Bourget's later works reflect a conservative promotion of royalist and Catholic interests, not unlike the writings of LÉON BLOY.

Bourget's works also reveal the fin de siècle malaise that may be linked to parallel movements in European intellectual life. Some thinkers considered the positivist belief in science to be insufficient as a means to interpret the human condition. The reaction against positivism is connected to a revolt against bourgeois materialism, such as we find, for example, in the works of BALZAC.

FURTHER READING

Baumer, Franklin L. *Modern European Thought: Continuity and Change in Ideas, 1600–1950.* New York: Macmillan, 1977.

Carter, John Hannibal. *A Study of Social Problems in the Novels of Paul Bourget with Reference to those of Balzac's Comédie Humaine.* Urbana, Ill.: PhD Thesis, 1944.

Singer, Armand E. *Paul Bourget,* Boston: Twayne, 1976.

BOUVARD AND PÉCUCHET (BOUVARD ET PÉCUCHET) GUSTAVE FLAUBERT (1881)

Flaubert's last, unfinished novel, *Bouvard and Pécuchet* (1881), reflects Flaubert's bitterness in the last years of his life despite the admiration he received from naturalist writers (see NATURALISM) such as GUY DE MAUPASSANT and from his friend GEORGE SAND.

The two principal characters, Bouvard and Pécuchet, engage in ambitious encyclopedic research into agronomy, archaeology, medicine, and literature, among other disciplines, but meet only with failure. Some critics view Flaubert's work as an attack on science. It is more likely that Flaubert meant to attack a lack of method.

Failure then, as in *MADAME BOVARY* and *SENTIMENTAL EDUCATION,* is a major theme of this novel. In the end, Bouvard and Pécuchet return to their original profession as copyists. Their (or rather Flaubert's) *Dictionary of Received Ideas* is added as an appendix to the novel. Bouvard and Pécuchet's disappointing efforts reflect another recurring theme in Flaubert's works revealing the banality and meaninglessness of ordinary life.

FURTHER READING

Brombert, Victor. *The Novels of Flaubert.* Princeton, N.J.: Prineton University Press, 1973.

Culler, Jonathan. *Flaubert and the Uses of Uncertainty.* Ithaca, N.Y.: Cornell University Press, 1974.

Orr, Mary. *Flaubert Writing the Masculine.* Oxford: Oxford University Press, 2000.

Porter, Laurence M., ed. *Critical Essays on Gustave Flaubert.* Boston: G. K. Hall and Co., 1986.

BRASILLACH, ROBERT (1909–1945)

Brasillach was born in the southern French city of Perpignan but his early childhood passed in Morocco, where Brasillach's father was stationed in the colonial army. When their father died in combat in 1914, Brasillach and his sister returned with their mother to Perpignan, their childhood marked by the violence and sacrifice of war. Nonetheless, Brasillach was a successful student, first in the provinces and then in Paris, where he discovered the joys of literature and theater. At the age of 21, Brasillach published a biography of Virgil (1931) and, in 1938, a celebrated biography of the 17th-century French writer Pierre Corneille. Over the course of his career, Brasillach wrote in a variety of genres, producing novels, journalism, *A History of Film, A History of the War in Spain,* an *Anthology of Greek Poetry,* and two plays.

Like GEORGES BERNANOS, Brasillach was drawn to the right-wing political group L'Action Française, sharing with its members the promotion of nationalism and pacifism, a disdain for parliamentary democracy, and a respect for Germany as a rising power. He was only 23 years old when Charles Maurras appointed Brasillach director of the group's literary reviews, a position he held from 1932 to 1939. Brasillach quickly revealed his talent as a writer as he produced a number of judicious reviews on contemporary authors such as Charles Péguy, MARCEL PROUST, MAURICE BARRÈS, JEAN GIRAUDOUX, Jean Anouilh, CÉLINE, BERNANOS, HENRI DE MONTHERLANT, FRANÇOIS MAURIAC, and COLETTE, among others.

During the interwar period, Brasillach produced a series of novels that includes *Child of the Night* (1934), *The Bird-Seller* (1936), and *Like Old Times,* the story of a lost paradise (1937) and *Seven Colors,* a declaration of the end of youth framed by the contemporary conflict between fascists and communists (1939). As of 1934, Brasillach also began to write political journalism, expressing his views on the Spanish civil war and his opposition to communism, thus participating in the public debate among intellectuals interested in the political future of Europe. *The Siege of Alcazar* (1939) focuses on the civil war in Spain. A decisive moment in Brasillach's life was his witnessing of the 1938 Nazi party Nuremburg rally (described in *Seven Colors*). Furthermore, Brasillach wrote anti-Semitic articles for the journal *I Am Everywhere* (*Je suis partout*).

During World War II, Brasillach worked as a collaborationist journalist. He was taken prisoner in 1940 and freed in 1941, the year he published *Before the War (Notre avant-guerre),* his political and intellectual confession. He then took his place once again as chief editor for *I Am Everywhere.* Brasillach supported Marshal Pétain and the French collaboration while contributing to other right-wing journals such as *National Revolution* and *Paris Chronicle.* In addition, Brasillach wrote a novel, *The Conqueror,* 1943, and *Six Hours to Waste* (1953), a collection of literary portraits, all during the Occupation.

Among fascist intellectuals, Brasillach was both unusual and courageous. Firm in his convictions, Brasillach refused to go into hiding after the Liberation, instead turning himself in to the police when he learned that his mother and brother-in-law had been arrested. Brasillach was condemned to death for giving information to the enemy in a trial that lasted only five hours. He was executed on February 6, 1945, despite a petition signed by François Mauriac, Jean Anouilh, PAUL CLAUDEL, ALBERT CAMUS, and Jean-Louis Barrault. In prison

he wrote a collection of poems, an essay on André Chénier, and his *Letter to a Soldier of the 60th Class.*

Those who defended Brasillach did so on the basis of his enormous literary talent. In the context and mood of 1945, however, he could not be allowed to live, in order to protect literature and the nation. Brasillach faced the firing squad with dignity. As SIMONE DE BEAUVOIR wrote, "we wanted the death of the editor of *I am Everywhere,* not of this man who was dying so well."

FURTHER READING

Beauvoir, Simone de. "Eye for an Eye." Translated by Mary McCarthy, *Politics* (July–August 1947).

Kaplan, Alice Yaeger. *The Collaborator: The Trial and Execution of Robert Brasillach.* Chicago: Chicago University Press, 2000.

Tame, Peter D. *The Ideological Hero in the Novels of Robert Brasillach, Roger Vailland, and André Malraux.* New York: Peter Lang, 1998.

Tucker, William R. *The Fascist Ego: A Political Biography of Robert Brasillach.* Berkeley: University of California Press, 1975.

BREAK OF DAY (*LA NAISSANCE DU JOUR*) COLETTE (1928)

After a childhood in the Burgundian countryside and later the turbulence of Paris, the narrator leaves for Saint-Tropez in search of peace and tranquility. In her fifties, she has left Paris to escape the torments of love and to aspire to the wisdom of Sido, her mother. However, Vial, a young decorator, attracts her. Furthermore, Hélène Clément, a young artist, is also in love with the narrator, becoming jealous to the point where a crisis is likely to ensue. The narrator hesitates between desire and reticence, finally choosing the wisdom of her mother. "Little loves of summer die here at the same time as the shadow that circles my lamp."

A highly autobiographical novel, *Break of Day* reflects recurring themes in Colette's work, such as the joy and pain of sensual awakening, the trials of love, jealousy, wisdom, and maturity.

FURTHER READING

Flieger, Jerry Aline. *Colette and the Fantom Subject of Autobiography.* Ithaca, N.Y.: Cornell University Press, 1992.

Kristeva, Julia. *Colette.* Translated by Jane Marie Todd. New York: Columbia University Press, 2004.

Francis, Claude, and Fernande Gontier. South Royalton, Vt.: Steerforth Press, 1999.
Stewart, Joan Hinde. *Colette*. New York: Twayne, 1996.

BRETON, ANDRÉ (1896–1966)

A medical student when World War I broke out, Breton served in the army as a neuropsychiatrist. When the war was over, together with Philippe Soupault and LOUIS ARAGON (whom Breton had met while in medical school), Breton established a literary journal in 1919, ironically entitled *Literature*. The journal's simple title belies the rebelliousness that lay behind the burgeoning literary and cultural movement known as SURREALISM. An early influence on Breton was the work of the symbolists (see SYMBOLISM). In fact, the term *surrealism* comes from the poet Guillaume Apollinaire.

In the early 1920s, Breton broke away from the DADA movement to articulate his new program in the first *Surrealist Manifesto,* published in 1924. Breton rejected the traditional pillars of Western literature and culture. A radical, his goal was to situate a new form of literature and life outside the bounds of bourgeois conventions. As stated in the manifesto, the surrealist project was "to discover the unexploited riches of psychic life." In the course of his career, Breton collaborated on several surrealist journals: *Literature* (1919–24), *The Surrealist Revolution* (1924–29), *Surrealism in the Service of the Revolution* (1930–33), and *Minotaur* (1933–39).

Opposed to both NATURALISM and REALISM, Breton turned instead to psychoanalysis as the means to penetrate the subconscious. Through the act of automatic writing, he sought to break into new states of consciousness beyond the limits of reason to reveal hidden depths of the human spirit. Adopting the concept from the poet Rimbaud, Breton asserted that the imagination could "change life." He was interested in dreams, hypnosis, free association, and coincidence. According to Breton, passionate love is another source of liberation and creativity and his encounters with women inspired some of Breton's greatest surrealist works. Through the ecstasy of love, the woman introduces the writer to yet another new form of consciousness, thereby also giving access to the surreal.

Breton's particular style of writing developed out of automatism, as is evident in *Magnetic Fields,* written in collaboration with Philippe Soupault. Other masterpieces of automatic writing include *Soluble Fish* (1924), Breton's most magical work, and *Immaculate Conception* (1930), cowritten with Paul Éluard. Another important segment of Breton's writing is dedicated to theory. He not only produced three surrealist manifestos (1924, 1929, and 1942), but also *The Political Position of Surrealism* (1935) and *Surrealism between the Two Wars* (1942).

In terms of defining a literary movement, the first manifesto is the most innovative and the most significant. In it Breton rejects all realism in favor of a literature that blends dreams with reality through "pure psychic automatism," a process of writing that allows for free expression of the subconscious. The second and third manifestos retain the same principles in art but are politically oriented and divisive, leading to the exclusion of some members of the group.

Breton's greatest works by far are *NADJA* (1928), *Communicating Vases* (1932), and *MAD LOVE* (1937). Consistent with the surrealist approach, these works combine narrative with images, including photographs and drawings which are intended to replace description. *Nadja* and *Mad Love* were inspired by love affairs, as was *Arcane 17* (1945), a novel that expresses the surrealist notion of a couple. The latter work also reflects Breton's interest in the occult, as the title, taken from tarot card, suggests.

Communicating Vases is a work of philosophy in which Breton analyzes his adherence to communism as he seeks a world in which action is "the sister of dreams." The first part of the work consists of a Freudian analysis of dreams. The second is a surrealist analysis of the meaning of coincidental or chance events. The last part expresses Breton's belief that freedom and the true expression of desire are possible only in a society liberated through a Marxist revolution. Breton thus links Marxism and surrealism. Like many contemporary artists and intellectuals, Breton joined the Communist Party in 1927, although he turned his back on the Soviet Union after the Moscow show trials of 1935.

In 1940, concerned over the government of VICHY FRANCE, Breton left for the United States. When he returned after the war, he was increasingly obsessed with occultism and alchemy, and with trying to keep the surrealist movement alive. His *Anthology of Black Humor* (censored in 1940 for its iconoclasm and not published until 1950) serves as a synthesis of surrealism and 20th-century culture in general.

Recalling certain aspects of the 19th-century romantic movement (see ROMANTICISM), Breton's "pure psychic automatism" was intended to reconcile the dream world and reality. Breton's life and art merged into one, just as the surrealist movement demanded that it should. He was a larger-than-life figure, authoritarian, but also full of passion, energy, and a desire to live and to struggle. This is what made Breton such an important figure in the interwar period, when most people had lost faith in society and its values. Breton spearheaded a powerfully innovative and romantic movement of the young that spread throughout the world and changed our vision of life and art.

FURTHER READING

Balakian, Anna, and Rudolf E. Kuenzli. eds., *André Breton Today*. New York: W. Locker and Owens, 1989.

Carrouges, Michel. *André Breton and the Basic Concepts of Surrealism*. Translated by Maura Prendergast. Tuscaloosa: University of Alabama Press, 1974.

Caws, Mary Ann. *André Breton*. [Undated ed.] New York: Twayne; London: Prentice Hall International, 1996.

———. *Surrealism and the Literary Imagination: A Study of Breton and Bacheard*. The Hague: Mouton, 1966.

Polizzotti, Mark. *Revolution of the Mind: The Life of André Breton*. New York: Da Capo Press, 1997.

BRIDGE BEYOND, THE *(PLUIE ET VENT SUR TÉLUMÉE MIRACLE)* SIMONE SCHWARZ-BART (1972)

In remarkably rich and beautiful language, in this novel Schwarz-Bart portrays strong women who reveal essential truths through their life experiences. The author was inspired to write this work by a woman she knew growing up in Guadeloupe. Yet this is not the story of just one woman, it honors all Caribbean women.

Schwarz-Bart recounts the lives of four generations of women from the Lougandour family, each of whom learns to survive life's hardships with dignity and grace. Minèrve, Toussine or Reine Sans Nom, Victoire, and Télumée serve as yet another manifestation of Schwarz-Bart's homage to black women. Strong, resilient, dignified, and beautiful, each woman seeks to define herself even as her identity changes over the course of her life. Their lives may end in solitude but never in despair.

Older generations introduce the younger into the successive stages of a woman's life with humor and wisdom. The water, wind, and land are recurring images connected to a woman at various points in her life. Toussine, for example, is described as "a piece of the world, an entire country, a wreath of negresse, a boat, a sail, the wind." When Man Cia sees Télumée she says of the girl, "You will be on earth like a cathedral."

Water has multiple symbolic meanings as purifier, as life itself, as peace. Woman is a boat that travels through the river of life that is both rough and smooth. Woman is fruit, birds, and trees, signifying fruition. The natural world, central to this text, may sometimes threaten humankind but in the end it provides. The island nourishes and nurtures, just as woman does. Deeply sensual and erotic, woman's body is ever present.

The novel's characters have depth and dimension partly because of Schwarz-Bart's rich, textured language full of rhythm and sound that simultaneously reflects oral culture and female identity. Written in French, her writing is imbued with Creole expressions that reveal the spirit and culture of the Caribbean. At the same time, Schwarz-Bart offers a realistic view of life as a cycle of good and bad, joy and suffering, while revealing, at the same time, the historical problems faced by poor blacks in the Caribbean even after slavery is abolished.

The legacy of racism and colonialism is readily apparent. Télumée, for example, goes to work in the Desaragne household, only to have the "master" of the house attempt to rape her. This is not the only ignominy Télumée is obliged to endure but the white family cannot destroy her; Télumée is too sure of her own identity.

Man Cia and Reine Sans Nom try to explain to her the master-slave relationship in a fable that mimics Caribbean oral traditions in which animals serve as allegorical figures representing human blacks and whites, making it easier to confront subjects too difficult to tackle head-on. These women are capable of facing the harsh realities of life yet their vision is not bleak. There is a certain degree of resignation in their outlook but not passivity. They are strong, certainly stronger than the men, who have been broken by poverty, drink, and despair. This is a story of the resistance and survival that defines the women whom Schwarz-Bart admires and celebrates. Schwarz-Bart once described this work as "a kind of memory that I wanted to restore."

FURTHER READING

McKinney, Kitzie. "Memory, Voice and Metaphor in the Works of Simone Schwarz-Bart." In Mary Jean Green, Karen Gould, Micheline Rice-Maximien, Keith Walker, and Jack Yeager, eds. *Postcolonial Subjects: Francophone Women Writers.* Minneapolis: Minneapolis University Press, 1996.

Ormerod, Beverley. *An Introduction to the French Caribbean Novel.* London: Heinemann, 1985.

Wallace, Karen Smyley. "The Female and the Self in Schwarz-Bart's *Pluie et vent sur Télumée miracle,*" *French Review* 59, no. 3 (February 1986): 428–436.

Wilson, Elizabeth Betty. "History and Memory in *Un Plat de porc aux bananes vertes* and *Pluie et vent sur Télumée miracle,*" *Callaloo* 15, no. 1, The Literature of Guadeloupe and Martinique (Winter 1992): 179–189.

BRUNO, G. (PSEUDONYM FOR AUGUSTINE TUILLERIE) (1838–1912)

G. Bruno, or Augustine Tuillerie, was the wife of Alfred Tuillerie, a well-known philosopher and friend of the French sociologist Émile Durckheim. She chose her pseudonym in honor of the heretical Italian philosopher Giordano Bruno, burned at the stake in Rome by the Inquisition in 1600.

Bruno was a fairly prolific writer. In addition to the well-known TOUR DE FRANCE, she wrote a novel *Francinet.* Generations of schoolchildren were brought up on *Tour de France,* subtitled "Duty and the Fatherland." This successful novel was republished into the beginning of the 20th century and served as a text for elementary schoolchildren.

BUBU OF MONTPARNASSE (BUBU DE MONTPARNASSE) CHARLES-LOUIS PHILIPPE (1901)

In this novel, Pierre Hardy, young and idealistic, tries to help Berthe Méténier break away from her pimp, "small but strong" Maurice Bélu, or Bubu. Alternating chapters move back and forth from Pierre to Bubu, with Berthe caught in between. In the end, Pierre fails. Berthe remains under Bubu's control. Generous of spirit, Pierre is baffled by the forces of money and violence. Strangely, perhaps, Pierre treats Bubu with sympathy for "He became a pimp because he was living in a society where there are powerful men who control jobs and who want women and so there must be pimps who provide them." One might argue that Berthe represents resignation and acceptance of the social order while Bubu stands for revolt.

The theme of the prostitute recalls its treatment by HONORÉ DE BALZAC in *Scenes of a Courtesan's Life,* in VICTOR HUGO's *Marion Delorme,* DUMAS FILS's CAMELIA, JORIS-KARL HUYSMAN's *Marthe,* and ÉMILE ZOLA's NANA. Philippe similarly draws on the naturalist tradition (see NATURALISM) in his sometimes crude depiction of the prostitute's life. Berthe reveals society's corruption, its emphasis on power and money, and its indifference to the abuse of innocent victims. Berthe, however, resembles characters from the works of the Russian novelist Fyodor Dostoyevsky more than contemporary French naturalists. Pierre is moved by love and pity to try and save Berthe, but the Christian virtues of poverty, charity, and suffering are powerless against power and strength. Philippe speaks with the voice of the people in a style that reflects the simplicity and poverty of the social class on whom he focuses his attention. Philippe's novel stands in contrast to contemporary literary movements such as DECADENTISM, SYMBOLISM, and NATURALISM (although he draws, in part, from the latter). His detailed examination of those forced to live in the depths of society bear the influence of socialism and anarchism. At the same time, there is evidence of Philippe's interest in Nietzschean philosophy.

BURLESQUE

Frequently associated with the baroque movement in the arts and literature, burlesque novels appeared in France in the early 17th century in opposition to the linguistic excesses of the *précieuse* (see PRECIOSITY) heroic novel. Influenced by the literature of classical antiquity, medieval fables, RABELAIS, and the Spanish picaresque novel, particularly *Don Quixote,* the burlesque's bourgeois realism stands in contrast to the idealism of the *précieuses.* Usually narrated in the first person, burlesque novels depict the contradictions in human nature and the triviality of daily life. In contrast to the idealized hero of the *précieuse* novel, the burlesque offers instead an antihero. Often using creative language in the tradition of Rabelais, the burlesque switches back and forth between comedy and realism, making use of parody, satire, farce, and the grotesque to weave an imaginative tale. Some of the most important burlesque works are CHARLES SOREL's *The Comical History of Francion* and *The Extravagant Shepherd,* PAUL SCARRON's COMICAL ROMANCE, and CYRANO DE BERGERAC's STATES AND EMPIRES OF THE MOON AND SUN. The burlesque novels of the 17th century influenced VOLTAIRE, the romantics, and some modern authors.

BUTOR, MICHEL (1926–)

A writer and professor of literature with an international reputation, Michel Butor grew up in Paris, beginning his studies at the Sorbonne in 1945, first in literature and then in philosophy. He met ANDRÉ BRETON in 1946, whose surrealist movement seems to have made an impression on Butor's subsequent works (see SURREALISM). Butor's two passions are writing and traveling. After completing his studies, he left France for Egypt. He has since been invited to speak at universities around the world.

Butor first acquired literary fame through his novels PASSING TIME, published in 1956, and *Modification,* which won the Renaudot Prize in 1957. Although he is associated with the NOUVEAU ROMAN, Butor's writing exists in a class by itself.

Since 1960, Butor has experimented with new ways of writing, inspired by his travels and his boundless curiosity, as is evident in novels such as *Mobile* (1962) and *Boomerang* (1978). Butor has also written a number of essays in which he has likewise made a significant contribution to literary and cultural studies, particularly through his fictional conversations with contemporary literary critic and theorist Béatrice Didier, 17th-century poet Charles Perrault, and the German composer Ludwig van Beethoven.

Nonlinear in structure, Butor's works bear little resemblance to the traditional novel, as he prefers to play with time and space in innovative and sometimes surprising ways. In *Passing Time,* for example, he takes the reader through a labyrinthine city in a narrative that rejects chronological order. *Modification,* written in the second person plural, addresses the reader directly. Ostensibly a journey from Paris to Rome, in fact the movement of the novel is again nonlinear, with multiple twists and turns that superimpose a mental geography onto the physical.

In compete intellectual freedom, Butor explores writing with indirect quotations, discontinued and broken narrative, variations on a single theme, recurring images, and the reversal of signifier/signified. As such, Butor has made a significant impact on the development of contemporary literature. By playing with typesetting, collage, and any and every means that comes to mind, Butor has produced a varied oeuvre that seeks to encompass the diversity of modern life. As a result, it is fascinating for the reader to trace the metamorphoses in Butor's works over time.

Despite his rejection of linearity and continuity, Butor's works nevertheless retain a certain overall coherence. His writings can be divided into groups of five novels that each shares a similar structure. Some of his published novels are complete, others are works in progress. Still others are just beginning. His is an ever-expanding project that builds on connections linking one work to another. As a "new novelist," Butor shares with NATHALIE SARRAUTE and ALAIN ROBBE-GRILLET the desire to break down the novel's traditional form and structure.

FURTHER READING
Faulkenburg, Marilyn Thomas. *Church, City and Labyrinth in Brontë, Dickens, Hardy, and Butor.* New York: P. Lang, 1993.

Grant, Marian A. *Michel Butor, L'Emploi du Temps.* London: Edward Arnold, 1973.

Lydon, Mary. *Perpetuum Mobile: A Study of the Novels and Aesthetics of Michel Butor.* Edmonton: University of Alberta Press, 1980.

McWilliams, Dean. *The Narratives of Michel Butor: The Writer as Janus.* Athens: Ohio University Press, 1978.

Spencer, M. C. *Michel Butor.* New York: Twayne, 1974.

Waelti-Walters, Jennifer R. *Michel Butor: A Study of His View of the World and a Panorama of His Work.* Victoria, B.C.: Sono Nis Press, 1977.

C

CAMILLE (LA DAME AUX CAMÉLIAS)

ALEXANDRE DUMAS FILS (1848) *Camille* is the title of both a novel (1848) and a play (1852), both of which were remarkably successful. Bridging two eras, Camille represents elements of both ROMANTICISM and REALISM.

According to the story, a young man of good family, Armand Duval, falls in love with a courtesan, Marguerite Gautier. The pure and passionate love they share causes Marguerite to withdraw from her world, peopled with characters among whom she knows Armand could never belong. The lovers escape to a small house in the country where they enjoy an idyllic life together until Armand's father secretly approaches Marguerite.

The old man realizes that Armand and Marguerite are truly in love with each other, but he points out to her that their affair is an obstacle to Armand's future. Moreover, Armand's younger sister cannot marry the man she loves because of his scandalous behavior. Marguerite agrees to sacrifice her own happiness for Armand and leaves. Armand, however, knows nothing of this noble gesture. He believes that Marguerite was bored and threw him over to find a wealthier lover.

Later, Armand meets Marguerite again in Paris, where she has become the mistress of the comte de Varville. Overcome with anger, Armand throws a considerable sum of money at her that he has just won gambling, saying that now they are even.

Marguerite is wounded to the core. Not only has Armand humiliated her by this gesture but he flaunts his new mistress. Marguerite, always delicate of health, succumbs to tuberculosis, the 19th-century disease of love. Her faithful servant Nanette reveals to Armand his error and he arrives at Marguerite's deathbed at her last breath. The novel serves as the basis for Giuseppe Verdi's opera *La Traviata,* performed for the first time in Venice in 1853.

FURTHER READING

Maurois, André. *Three Musketeers: A Study of the Dumas Family.* Translated by Gerard Hopkins, London: Cape, 1957.

Saunders, Edith Alice. *The Prodigal Father, Dumas Père et fils and the Lady of the Camellias.* London, New York: Longmans Green, 1951.

Schwarz, Henry Stanley. *Alexandre Dumas, fils, Dramatist.* New York: B. Blom, 1871.

CAMUS, ALBERT (1913–1960)

An existentialist writer, philosopher, and journalist (see EXISTENTIALISM), Albert Camus was born into a poor family in Algiers. His father was an agricultural laborer who died in 1914 during World War I, leaving his wife and Camus in difficult circumstances, "halfway between misery and sunshine." Yet Camus drew from this experience in positive ways, saying, "Poverty was never a misfortune for me: it was radiant with light. Even my revolts were brilliant with sunshine. They were almost always . . . revolts for everyone, so that every life might be lifted into that light." Camus's writings are replete with the images of sun and sea that dominated his youth. His mother, for whom Camus felt great tenderness, spoke little and was nearly illiterate. She may be the source for the theme of silence one frequently notes in Camus's works.

As a student, Camus studied philosophy and wanted to become a teacher, but in 1930 he contracted tuberculosis and was unable to sit for his exams. Camus's encounter with illness made him sharply aware of his own mortality. Another significant influence on Camus's early years was his teacher Jean Grenier, who introduced him to the philosophy of Friedrich Nietzsche. Together these experiences helped to shape Camus's understanding of humanity's place in the world.

In 1934 Camus married Simone Hié; this first marriage lasted only two years. At the time, Camus was working at various jobs, trying to pay for his studies. He briefly joined the Communist Party and was assigned to work on party relations with Arab nationalists. He also lived out his passion for the theater, establishing his Labor Theater in 1935. Years later in *The Future of Tragedy* (1955), Camus argued that modern society needs tragedy as much as ancient Greece needed Sophocles or the 17th century Corneille.

In 1936, Camus earned a degree having concentrated on Christian metaphysics and Neoplatonism. He left his wife and went to travel in Central Europe. Upon his return to Algeria Camus collaborated with three friends on a play about a 1934 insurrection in Asturias during the Spanish civil war.

A militant antifascist, peace activist, and supporter of Republican Spain, Camus was actively engaged in contemporary political and social problems. He left the Communist Party in 1937, for example, when the party refused to support Algerian independence. In his life and in his writings, Camus sought to serve witness to all that he experienced as a child growing up in poverty and through which he learned "the true sense of life."

By 1937 Camus had begun work as a journalist for the *Alger Républicain* newspaper in which he promoted Arab emancipation. The year 1937 also witnessed the publication of Camus's first work, *L'Envers et l'endroit* (The Wrong Side and the Right Side), that brings together in one volume five texts that are part short story and part essay. In them, Camus combines moments drawn from everyday life, personal experiences as a child, and those encountered in recent travels, along with philosophical reflection. In other words, Camus explores the moral significance of the things he has seen and heard. The title hints at the relationship between death and life, a common theme in Camus's writing. In the last story, for example, a woman constructs her own tomb and then dies.

Camus saw beauty in the world but also despair. In his mind, the two are allied. "There is but one freedom," Camus wrote, "to put oneself right with death. After that, everything is possible." Death may be ever-present but there is also light, sunshine, and beauty. Happiness is possible. Ultimately, the recognition of death leads to the conditions for rebellion. "There is no love for life," he wrote, "without despair for life."

For Camus, rebellion is a creative act as "art challenges the real, but does not escape from it." For Camus, beauty offers the means of transcendence; art offers a substitute universe. The artist is a rebel because he or she refuses to accept the world as it is. The dialectic in Camus's thought is derived from his belief that human consciousness both explores the negativity of the world and realizes its potential, leading to a new synthesis.

For Camus, this act of rebellion was situated in writing. He once wrote, "If you want to be a philosopher, write novels." In *Intelligence and the Scaffold* (1943) Camus defined the novel as something that offers to humankind our destiny. Yet journalism, too, provided an outlet for Camus's intellectual and creative energy.

In 1940, Camus moved to Paris and began working for *Paris Soir* (Paris Evening). The following year he married Francine Faure. He also wrote his "cycle of the absurd" that includes: *The STRANGER* (1942), *The Myth of Sisyphus* (an essay; 1942), *The Misunderstanding* (a play; 1944), and *Caligula* (a play; 1944). These works earned Camus recognition as a major voice for the concerns of his generation. The fundamental question he addresses in them is, How is one to live life so that there is meaning?

In 1935, Camus began working on *A Happy Death* (not published until 1971). This work laid the foundation for *The Stranger*. By his name and the peaceful manner with which he greets death, the principal character in *A Happy Death* prefigures the character of Mersault in *The Stranger*. A central theme in many of his works is the question of silence, into which characters such as Mersault seem to have fallen. It becomes necessary to speak, however, when silence no longer accords with the world.

In *The Myth of Sisyphus* (1942), Camus explains his concept of the absurd in relation to death. Since there is only this world and none other, the only happiness one can find is in one's connection to the physical environment, thus the emphasis in *The Stranger,* for example, on Mersault's relationship to the sun and sea.

Camus explores different sorts of individuals who have attained the life of conscious understanding of the absurd, such as the seducer, the actor, the adventurer, and, above all, the Greek hero Sisyphus, condemned for eternity to push a boulder up a mountain only to have it fall again to the bottom. Death and silence force man to confront the absurdity of his condition, and it is only by consciously recognizing the absurd that he can overcome it. The search for a personal ethic is thus derived from a sense of one's own humanity and the need to struggle to give meaning to one's existence.

During World War II, Camus participated in the Resistance, publishing articles in *Combat,* an underground newspaper established in 1943. Camus's play *The Misunderstanding* opened that same year and *Caligula* in 1945. Like modern man, Caligula understood that God is dead and the world unlivable. Despite this starkly pessimistic vision, in *Letters to a German Friend* (1944) Camus foresaw the defeat of the Nazis and was able to express his concern for human rights and liberty, as well as his belief in the necessity of preserving moral values in political life.

In his first two works published after the war, *The PLAGUE* (1947) and *The Rebel* (1951), Camus articulated his notion of existentialism, in contrast to that of JEAN-PAUL SARTRE and others with whom he differed, in part, over the notion of political "engagement." Published at a time when Camus was particularly distressed by politics, *The Plague* evokes the danger of fascism, recognizable by its mass graves, crematoria, and the trains that deliver their victims. Unlike Sartre and other contemporary writers, Camus clearly defined the enemy. For the principal character, Rieux, the plague could

always return. There is no guarantee against it, no historical process leading inevitably to a brighter future, no obvious Marxist solution to the world's problems. Camus's personal rebellion is based on a deep-seated faith in human nature even as he rejects the experience of history.

Camus was criticized by his contemporaries for having a metaphysical vision of rebellion rather than promoting a material or political revolution. In fact, in *The Rebel,* a philosophical essay, Camus declares the modern notion of a material revolution to be a failure. All rebels, he argued, from the MARQUIS DE SADE to the poet Arthur Rimbaud to the German philosopher Friedrich Nietzsche, all reveal nostalgia for order. Political rebellions have been an even greater failure as their leaders have tended to transform themselves into tyrants. Camus finds this to be as true for the leaders of the Reign of Terror during the FRENCH REVOLUTION as it was for Hitler and Stalin. Such men have denied God and authority to become Gods themselves. In contrast, Camus offers the possibility of a revolt whereby we become ourselves in solidarity with others.

Published in the midst of the cold war, *The Rebel* was one of the first literary works to critique Stalinism and Nazism on the same grounds. Because he denied a Marxist interpretation of history, Camus was attacked by leftist intellectuals such as Sartre and ANDRÉ BRETON. Camus's break with Sartre dates from 1952. If Sartre can be characterized as being filled with the horror of life, Camus was equally filled with love. He may have had his moments of despair but Camus never abandoned his faith in human values.

Camus was subsequently torn apart, personally and intellectually, by the Algerian war. In *The FALL* (1956), Camus's fundamental humanism turns to pessimism as he considers the moral decay of humanity in the postwar world. This novel evokes a powerful sense of solitude. In 1957, Camus also published a collection of short stories entitled *Exile and the Kingdom;* he also continued to write for the theater, successfully adapting Dostoyevsky's *The Possessed,* to the stage in 1959.

Camus won the Nobel Prize in Literature in 1957 for an oeuvre that "brings to light the problems of our day." An ardent supporter of liberty and human rights, Camus was once described by Sartre as "the admirable conjunction of a man, an action, an oeuvre." Certain critics such as Roland Barthes have characterized Camus's writing as classical in the sense that his novels are well structured and written in a sober style (see CLASSICISM). At the same time, there is both humor and irony in Camus's writing, a dark humor that recalls the works of ALFRED JARRY. His plays are as important as his novels and explore similar themes. Together, Camus's works hold a significant place in the history of modern literature for their exploration of both the misery and the grandeur of the human condition. Camus was working on yet another novel, *The First Man* (posthumous 1994), when he died, unexpectedly and prematurely, in a car accident in 1960. He was 47 years old.

FURTHER READING

Aronson, Ronald. *Camus and Sartre: The Story of a Friendship and the Quarrel That Ended It.* Chicago: University of Chicago Press, 2004.

Brée, Germaine. *Camus.* New Brunswick, N.J.: Rutgers University Press, 1972.

Brosman, Catharine Savage. *Albert Camus.* Detroit: Gale Group, 2001.

Burnier, Michel-Antoine. *Choice of Action: The French Existentialists on the Political Front Line.* Translated by Bernard Murchland. New York: Random House, 1968.

Cruickshank, John. *Albert Camus and the Literature of Revolt.* New York: Oxford University Press, 1960.

Jackson, Tommie Lee. *The Existential Fiction of Ayi Kwei Armah, Albert Camus, and Jean-Paul Sartre.* Lanham, Md.: University Press of America, 1997.

Mairowitz, David Zane, and Alain Korkos, edited by Richard Appignanesi. *Introducing Camus.* New York: Totem Books, 1998.

Poster, Mark. *Existential Marxism in Postwar France.* Princeton, N.J.: Princeton University Press, 1975.

Sartre, Jean-Paul. "Reply to Albert Camus." Translated by Benita Eisler in *Situations.* New York: Braziller, 1965.

Sprintzen, David A., and Adrian van den Hoven, eds. and trans. *Sartre and Camus: A Historic Confrontation.* Amherst, N.Y.: Humanity Books, 2004.

CANDIDE VOLTAIRE (1759)

The great ENLIGHTENMENT philosopher VOLTAIRE was a mature man when he wrote *Candide* from his country estate, Ferney, outside Geneva. At this point in his life he had experienced personal disillusionment. The Prussian ruler Frederick II had not lived up to Voltaire's expectations as an enlightened despot, the Seven Years' War, a terrible earthquake in Lisbon (1755), and the conflict over the ENCYCLOPEDIA together created a sense of pessimism that reveals itself through Voltaire's ironic style.

Candide is the story of a young, naive, illegitimate son of a minor nobleman in the German lands. From the beginning, Candide responds enthusiastically to the optimistic theories of his tutor, Dr. Pangloss, whose mantra is that "all is for the best in the best of all possible worlds." At the opening of the novel, Candide is growing up happily in Westphalia at the château of baron Thunder-ten-Tronck. Unfortunately, Candide is driven out when the baron discovers his love for (and escapades with) the baron's daughter, Cunégonde.

Thus begins a series of horrific adventures of war, injustice, cruelty, slavery, and intolerance that challenge Pangloss's optimistic teachings. Candide is forcibly conscripted into the Bulgar army. He finally escapes to Holland, where he encounters injustice and hypocrisy, recurring themes for Voltaire. Candide also finds Pangloss, who is suffering from syphilis. From Pangloss he learns that the château of Thunder-ten-Tronck was attacked by the Bulgar army. Cunégonde was raped and disemboweled. The soldiers also killed the baron and his wife and son.

Fortunately for Candide and Pangloss, they encounter a kind Anabaptist merchant named Jacques who takes them under his wing. The three head off on the merchant's ship for Portugal but the ship sinks in a storm. Jacques dies. Somehow, Candide and Pangloss make it to shore when a terrible earthquake strikes Lisbon. They try to help the victims but are arrested by the Inquisition. Pangloss is hanged, Candide flogged.

An old woman suddenly appears, taking Candide away to an isolated house to care for him. There he meets again the splendid Cunégonde. She was indeed raped and disemboweled, but "one does not always die from these two accidents." Cunégonde is now mistress of both Don Issachar, a Jewish banker, and the Grand Inquisitor of Lisbon. Threatened by her rivals, Candide kills them both and escapes with Cunégonde and the old woman by boat to America.

As they travel, the old woman tells the sad story of her life. Born to a pope and a princess, she began life with every advantage but suffered cruelly thereafter. The old woman then invites the others to tell their equally miserable tales. Slowly, Candide begins to comprehend the existence of evil. Once they arrive at Buenos Aires, Candide and Cunégonde are separated. The old woman has advised Cunégonde to accept the attentions lavished on her by the governor. Candide must continue his flight from the long arm of the Inquisition.

Candide and his valet, Cacambo, head off to find refuge with the Jesuits in Paraguay. There they discover Cunégonde's brother, who has also miraculously escaped death at the hands of the Bulgars, only to be killed by Candide when the young baron refuses to let Candide marry his sister. After the murder, Candide and Cacambo are forced to flee once again and are almost eaten by cannibals. Starving, they travel toward Cayenne. The two come across an old boat and, floating aimlessly down a river, discover the utopian paradise of Eldorado. Here all really *is* "the best in the best of all possible worlds." There is delicious food, peaceful and happy inhabitants, a kind ruler, religious tolerance. Yet even Eldorado cannot squelch Candide's desire to rejoin Cunégonde. The hapless travelers leave, loaded down with gifts. They have 100 sheep carrying food and a fortune in jewels and gold. Unfortunately, along their journey Candide's sheep die one by one. By the time they arrive in Surinam, only two remain. Candide sends Cacambo to Buenos Aires to purchase Cunégonde's freedom. They arrange to meet in Venice.

Of course Candide is tricked out of his last two sheep. He then heads for Bordeaux with a persecuted intellectual named Martin. Martin speaks to Candide about good, evil, and human nature. In contrast to Pangloss, Martin believes that evil dominates over good. As if to illustrate his point, the two witness a brutal battle between a Spanish and a Dutch ship.

From Bordeaux, Candide goes to Paris but, echoing themes found in the works of Rousseau, is quickly disillusioned after being tricked by thieves disguised as a priest, an aristocrat, and a false Cunégonde. Candide is unjustly arrested but bribes a police officer to release him. From there he travels toward England with Martin. They witness the public execution of an admiral who is guilty of not having killed enough men.

Deterred by this experience, Candide decides it is time to go to Venice. At first he finds neither Cacambo nor Cunégonde. Instead he stumbles across Paquette, a former servant of the baron Thunder-ten-Tronckh, who is living with a monk named Giroflée. After they too have exchanged tales of misfortune, Candide decides to visit lord Pococurante, who is reputed never to suffer unhappiness. Candide is impressed but Martin suggests that the great lord may not be as happy as he seems.

During carnival, Candide dines with six deposed monarchs. There he finds Cacambo, who has been enslaved. Candide learns that Cunégonde is waiting for him near Constantinople. On the galleys, Candide recognizes Pangloss and the young baron, who, once again, escaped death. Candide purchases their freedom as well as Cunégonde's although she is now very ugly.

Candide is horrified when he recovers Cunégonde who is horribly disfigured. Still, he marries her. He gets rid of the young baron, who continues to resist their marriage, by sending him back to the galleys. With his last few diamonds, Candide purchases a small farm where, together with Cunégonde, Paquette, brother Giroflée, Pangloss, and Martin, he turns to work as a source of solace from unhappiness. Hence the famous line, we must "cultivate our garden."

Voltaire's novel addresses the problem of human suffering. Why is there so much evil in the world? At the ripe age of 64, Voltaire realized that what he saw in the world around him was in stark contrast to contemporary trends in philosophy, the German philosopher Gottfried Leibniz in particular. In fact, Pangloss's mantra is a distortion of Leibnizian philosophy. Candide, too, is an optimist.

On a symbolic level the search for Cunégonde becomes a search for happiness. Eldorado is the Enlightenment utopia, a state governed by reason. There is no suffering, crime, or war. The simplicity of Eldorado's religion fits with Voltaire's deism. In this ideal community there is a respect for science and education as the means to ensure happiness. The foundations of this society are equality and fraternity. In this masterpiece of a genre he created, the philosophical tale (*conte philosophique*), Voltaire illustrates the problems of injustice, cruelty, and simple fate, which impede human happiness. The solution to need, idleness, and vice is work.

In considering the problem of evil, Voltaire suggests that one must consider the particular source of human unhappiness, be it war, intolerance, inequality, privilege, superstition, ignorance, or oppression, all of which are Enlightenment themes. Voltaire examines evil not in a metaphysical sense but in the context of human society. His litany of incredible and absurd suffering is intended to bring readers up short so that they will come to recognize evil in the real world. The rhetorical device he uses so effectively to do so is irony, saying one thing but meaning another. Moreover, this approach was particularly suited to the conditions of OLD REGIME censorship.

Some critics have characterized the novel as rococo because of its light, frivolous, and playful style, in sharp contrast to the miserable events recounted. Yet the juxtaposition is deliberate in order to lead the reader to the conclusion that the world *should* be different from what it is. Voltaire's message is effectively conveyed by the philosophical tale. This genre is neither fiction nor philosophy, rather a mixture of both. In consequence, there is no need to be realistic, a quality much debated in 18th-century fiction.

Voltaire draws on the tradition of the picaresque novel in these works whose characters tend to be allegorical figures. Candide represents optimism; Cunégonde, the search for love; Pangloss, the futility of metaphysics; Cacambo, friendship and loyalty; and Martin, pessimism. Each character represents an abstract idea. Other philosophical tales written by Voltaire are ZADIG, MICROMÉGAS, and THE WORLD AS IT IS. In each tale a central philosophical theme runs through a series of episodic adventures. Moreover, Voltaire is able simultaneously to poke fun at the contemporary novel form. Some critics have compared *Candide* to DIDEROT'S *JACK THE FATALIST* (1773).

This novel, published anonymously in 1759, is one of numerous clandestine works of the Old Regime. Of all of Voltaire's writings, it is also the one with which readers today are the most familiar. *Candide* reflects central themes of Enlightenment thought, and Voltaire was one of its greatest voices.

FURTHER READING

Bonneville, Douglas A. *Voltaire and the Form of the Novel.* Oxford: Voltaire Foundation, 1976.

Bottiglia, William F. *Voltaire's "Candide": Analysis of a Classic.* Geneva: Institut et Musée Voltaire, 1964.

Cutler, Maxine G., ed. *Voltaire, the Enlightenment, and the Comic Mode: Essays in Honor of Jean Sareil.* New York: P. Lang, 1990.

Sherman, Carol. *Reading Voltaire's Contes: A Semiotics of Philosophical Narration.* Chapel Hill, N.C.: Department of Romance Languages: Distributed by University of North Carolina Press, 1985.

Wade, Ira O. *Voltaire and "Candide."* Princeton, N.J.: Princeton University Press, 1959.

CAPTAIN FRACASSE THÉOPHILE GAUTIER **(1863)** Gautier was a writer at ease with evoking the past, as is evident from this novel set in the age of Louis XIII. The novel opens in an abandoned château in Gascony during the first half of the 17th-century, where the last of the Sigognac family lives in misery, his only companions an old valet, a nag, and a cat. Suddenly a troupe of itinerant actors disturbs his lazy solitude by asking for a night's lodging. They form a bizarre group. There is Blazius, the drunken pedant; Tyran, the good-natured giant; Matamore; Léandre; and Scapin. The men are accompanied by four women: Séraphina, Isabelle, Zerbine, and Dame Léonarde. This good-humored troupe's language reflects the style of the period as Gautier skillfully imitates the verbal intricacy of the *précieuses* (see PRECIOSITY). Enchanted, the young baron de Sigognac decides to link his fate to the troupe of actors. Together they set off for Paris, where baron de Sigognac hopes his fortune may improve. When Matamore dies, Sigognac takes his place in the troupe under the name Captain Fracasse. He also falls in love with Isabelle. As they travel along, the group encounters a series of adventures affording Gautier the opportunity to echo an earlier picaresque tradition through pleasant descriptions of the countryside with its villages, inns, taverns, various dives, and theaters.

Sigognac's fate takes a turn for the worse when the troupe meets the duke de Vallombreuse, an arrogant aristocrat who takes a liking to Isabelle. When she rejects the duke's overtures, Vallombreuse kidnaps her and takes her to his château. Sigognac and the other actors besiege the château to rescue Isabelle. Sigognac seriously wounds Vallombreuse in a duel. Vallombreuse's father appears to take his son away, whom he believes to be dead. When the old man sees Isabelle, he recognizes in her his only daughter, who had been abducted. Meanwhile, Sigognac also believes that he has killed the duke and decides to return to his château so as not to embroil his friends in further trouble.

Fortunately, Vallombreuse is not dead. He is healed of his wound along with his passion for Isabelle. Vallombreuse and Sigognac reconcile. Sigognac subsequently marries Isabelle. The novel continues with further adventures.

Inspired by PAUL SCARRON's COMIC ROMANCE, Gautier's manifests his great gift for description in bringing to life the period of Louis XIII.

FURTHER READING

Richardson, Joanna. *Théophile Gautier, His Life and Times.* London: M. Reinhardt, 1958.

Smith, Albert Brewster. *Ideal and Reality in the Fictional Narratives of Théophile Gautier.* Gainesville: University of Florida Press, 1969.

Snell, Robert. *Théophile Gautier, A Romantic Critic of the Visual Arts.* Oxford: Clarendon Press; New York: Oxford University Press, 1982.

Tennant, P. E. *Théophile Gautier.* London: Athlone Press, 1975.

CARDINAL, MARIE (1929–2001)

Born in Algeria, Marie Cardinal studied philosophy in Paris. From 1953 to 1960 she taught at the universities of Salonika (Greece), Lisbon (Portugal), and Montreal (Canada). In 1961 she began work as an editor, working for two major French publishing houses, Gallimard and Grasset.

As a writer she produced some of the most important works of contemporary French feminist literature (see FEMINISM), sharing with HÉLÈNE CIXOUS, for example, an emphasis on the relationship between the word and the body, or writing the body. She was interested in the writing process as a means of self-identification. Cardinal's most famous work, *The WORDS TO SAY IT,* won the Prix Lettré in 1976. It has been translated into at least 18 languages and is thus known throughout the world.

Influenced by Freudian psychoanalytical theory, Cardinal makes frequent use of repetitions in her works, as she tries to re-create experience through the writing process. For Cardinal, as for Freud, madness exists already in infancy if not in utero. Recurring themes are disorder, death, the absence of the father, a woman's relationship to her mother, a mother's guilt, a woman's identity as a writer, and writing as a means of giving birth to oneself.

In all of her works there is a complex relationship among the protagonist/narrator/writer. While they are not exactly one and the same, the lines are blurred. As Cardinal once said, "I need to be the woman in each of my novels." Cardinal thus chose a genre midway between the novel and autobiography as the means to liberate and transform woman as literary subject.

Cardinal's belief that the writing process transforms the writer is evident in works such as *The Words to Say It* and *In Other Words.* According to Freud, children will repeatedly re-create painful experiences through play to be able to substitute a passive role in those events for an active one. For Cardinal, a similar empowerment occurs through repetition in writing. As a result, many of her works exist as variations on a theme. The metaphor she uses is from embroidery. She refers to a stitch that is sewn (repeated) over several times. Moreover, Cardinal makes a deliberate link between one novel and the next. "In each of my manuscripts I repeat a passage from an earlier manuscript, in order to make a chain, to show that I am writing one single book that will be made up of all my books."

Cardinal develops her themes of order and disorder particularly in *The Words to Say It* and *Great Disorders.* A related theme is entropy, a force of disorder that affects human relations and ultimately leads toward death. It is not possible to avoid death but one can take measures against the negative effects of entropy. At the same time, it must be recognized and accepted as part of oneself. If one attempts to suppress the force of disorder, the "Thing" as she refers to it in *The Words to Say It,* whatever that may be for a given individual, the result is madness.

The experience of family life is central to her writings. The two dominant themes in relation to the family are the absence of the father and the symbiotic relationship that exists between mother and daughter, an important theme in feminist literature generally. The absent father is juxtaposed with the omnipresent mother. Moreover, the mother-daughter relationship is paralleled by the author's relationship to her *motherland*, Algeria. Cardinal refers to Algeria as her "true mother," a land that is nourishing. Moreover, a mother's agony finds its parallel in the suffering of Algeria in civil war, destroyed as a woman is by patriarchal, colonial society.

If the mother-daughter relationship is a powerful one, it also engenders guilt. The mother always feels guilt vis-à-vis her children. "I did not want to lower my eyes, I did not obey, I disobeyed! I am guilty of having disobeyed people, their rules, their laws, their culture, their morality, that which they call the 'eternal feminine,' and the astronomical price for this disobedience are the lives of my two children. . . . I did not stay in my place. . . . I created a disaster." Furthermore, the woman who leaves her place in hearth and home for a male profession like writing is even more culpable. Yet Cardinal shows how a woman may work her way to a feminist point of view. Women come to share power equally with men by appropriating language for themselves. Woman gives birth to literature and to herself through writing.

FURTHER READING
Durham, Carolyn A. "Feminism and Formalism: Dialectical Structures in Marie Cardinal's *Une Vie pour Deux*," *Tulsa Studies in Women's Literature* 4.1 (Spring 1985): 83–99.

———. "Patterns of Influence: Simone de Beauvoir and Marie Cardinal," *French Review* 60, no. 3 (February 1987): 341–348.

Stephens, Sonya, ed. *A History of Women's Writing in France.* Cambridge: Cambridge University Press, 2000.

CARMEN PROSPER MÉRIMÉE (1845)
After traveling through Spain in 1830, Mérimée published his "Letters from Spain," a blend of travel notes and fiction recounting bullfights, execution, sorcery, and the story of a bandit named José Maria. These letters become the foundation for *Carmen*. The initial narrator has come to Spain on an archaeological expedition. There he encounters a bandit, José Navarro, and a savagely beautiful femme fatale, a Gypsy girl named Carmen.

José is a fairly serious, disciplined young soldier until he is bewitched by the beautiful Carmen. Under her influence, José becomes first a deserter, then a bandit, and, finally, a murderer. In a perverse act of love, José ends by murdering the woman who has possessed his soul, an act that leads inevitably to his own death. The narrator has received permission to visit José, at that point a convicted murderer, prior to his execution. It is a story of tragic love, of passion powerful enough to lead a man astray.

While on duty, José is ordered to bring Carmen to prison but he allows her to escape and then follows her. At first Carmen returns his love but quickly tires of him and his jealousy. When her husband returns from prison, José murders him saying that he, José, is Carmen's true husband.

José tries to convince Carmen to run away to America, where they could live an honest life, but she will have none of it. Carmen wants her freedom. Moreover, she has now fallen in love with a picador named Lucas. In an argument, Carmen casts the ring José has given her to the ground and he kills her in a fit of passion.

Carmen reflects a renewed interest in sorcery in the 19th century. The beguiling Gypsy even warns José that she only brings unhappiness to those who love her. Unfortunately a victim of destiny, José is a man who can love only one woman, to the point of his own destruction.

The exotic setting and powerful portrayal of love and death reflect themes prevalent in romantic literature. Yet Mérimée departs from romantic lyricism in favor of a sober, concise style that recalls the works of his friend STENDHAL. An interest in the fantastic, the odd, and the cruel, while typical of the dark side of romanticism, drew some criticism. A strange epilogue follows in which Mérimée discourses on the language and culture of the Gypsies, giving the reader the sense of an unsettling distance between the author and his subject. In fact, critics accused Mérimée of unnatural coldness, which is in stark contrast to the themes of tragic love, murder, and death.

FURTHER READING
Bowman, Frank. *Prosper Mérimée: Heroism, Pessimism, and Irony.* Berkeley: University of California Press, 1962.

Gould, Evlyn. *The Fate of Carmen*. Baltimore: Johns Hopkins University Press, 1996.

Raitt, A. W. *Prosper Mérimée*. New York: Scribner, 1970.

CASTLE OF ARGOL, THE (*AU CHÂTEAU D'ARGOL*) Julien Gracq (1938)

In this first novel, Gracq reveals his power over words. A fantastic and dark tale, *The Castle of Argol* is reminiscent of the works of Edgar Allan Poe, whom Gracq admired greatly. This novel also raises aesthetic and moral issues. It was first rejected by Gallimard and then accepted by José Corti, a publisher close to the surrealist movement (see SURREALISM).

The story takes place in Brittany at a castle in the middle of a forest, near the sea. Albert, the owner, is a wealthy intellectual, very different in character from his friend Herminien, whom he invites for a visit. When Herminien arrives, he has a beautiful young woman named Heide with him, whose name, by chance is engraved on an ancient tombstone in the cemetery. Gracq frequently introduces mysterious and prophetic signs into his works. In this case, the signs of foreboding increase until one day, Albert sees Herminien, armed, entering the forest with Heide.

Albert is suspicious when he sees Herminien depart with Heide. At dark, he goes off in search of them as a storm is approaching, only to find Heide, bound, naked, and bleeding, the victim of rape. Herminien, meanwhile, has disappeared. Gracq frequently makes use of the theme of enclosure that evokes a feeling of suffocation. Moreover, the use of the snake metaphor to describe Herminien presages the violence and death he will bring to the castle. One of Gracq's gifts as a writer is his astonishing ability to create a sense of foreboding.

Albert brings Heide back to the castle. Once she is healed, Heide goes off in search of Herminien, eventually finding him in a mysterious place where he is suffering from a fall off a horse. Herminien, in turn, goes back to the castle to recover from his wounds. Relations among the three become increasingly tense. Albert also rapes Heide. Herminien takes Albert through a secret passage that leads to Heide's room. Heide poisons herself. In revenge, Albert murders Herminien.

The relationship between the two men is complicated, each man serving as both the double and the opposite of the other, ultimately necessitating, perhaps, the destruction of one or both. Despite her many qualities, Heide is reduced to a sexual object as she passes from one man to the other. The chapter entitled "The Swim" falls at the center of the novel and serves as a sort of climax. As the three swim away from the shore one day, they momentarily attain equality until Heide is nearly engulfed by the waves. Albert and Herminien save her and all three swim to safety, but a spell has been broken and the chapter ends in Gracq's inimitable silence.

In this novel, Gracq reveals his debt to the German philosopher Hegel. The antithesis in the work is situated in the juxtaposition of Albert and Herminien, light and dark, the spiritual and the material, contemplation and action. Moreover, in the "Notice to the reader," Gracq refers to the German composer Richard Wagner, stating that *The Castle of Argol* is a "demonic version" of *Parsifal*. The novel thus blends surrealism with the Gothic novel and ROMANTICISM. André Breton praised this violent and highly abstract novel.

FURTHER READING
Dobbs, Annie-Claude, and Kathleen Flosi-Good. "The Problematics of Space in Julien Gracq: Fiction and Narration in a Chapter of Au Chateau d'Argol," *Yale French Studies,* no. 57, Locus: Space, Landscape, Décor in Modern French Fiction (1976): 86–108.

Rodina, Herta. "Sign and Design: Julien Gracq's Au Chateau d'Argol," *French Review* 64, no. 4 (March 1991): 659–666.

CASTLE OF THE CARPATHIANS, THE (*LE CHÂTEAU DES CARPATHES*) Jules Verne (1892)

Set in Transylvania near a village called Werst, this mysterious story takes place in and around an abandoned castle that generates strange rumors and legends. One day, smoke appears to be coming from the castle keep. Full of fear, a young forester, Nick Deck, and doctor Patak go to investigate. Bizarre events ensue. A little later, Count Franz de Telek arrives in Werst. He has been traveling in an attempt to forget his sorrow over the death of his fiancée, the singer name Stilla. One day Stilla appears to him and leads him into a trap whereby he is locked up in the castle. There he discovers Rodolphe de Gortz's dark secret. Rodolphe was the last of the lords to have lived in the castle. The police arrive and free the count but the rumors continue.

The novel's wide range of characters broadly represents the three orders associated with OLD REGIME society; the clergy, the nobility, and the third estate. Consequently, nearly every reader could identify with one or another of the personalities that make up this story.

Like Verne's other works, *Castle of the Carpathians* makes use of recent discoveries in science and technology and thus reflects the enormous change in these fields that took place over the course of the 19th century. While this novel reflects traditional themes associated with gothic novels, the ending, in which superstitious fears of the supernatural are at least partly put to rest by scientific explanations, fits with Verne's other works. POSITIVISM battles against legend and superstition. The reader, like the villagers, is taken in at first by the mysterious events that take place in and around the castle. The dialectic between scientific progress and myth that Verne depicts represents two very different worlds and ways of thinking. The novel comes to rest somewhere in between the two as, in the end, Verne denies that science can provide all the answers to humanity's questions. Verne reveals in this novel the power of his imagination and his ability to draw the reader into a fascinating tale full of drama and suspense. At the same time, he reflects seriously on the nature of civilization.

FURTHER READING

Born, Franz. *Jules Verne, the Man who Invented the Future.* Translated by Juliana Biro. Englewood Cliffs, N.J.: Prentice Hall, 1964.

Butcher, William. *Verne's Journey to the Center of the Self: Space and Time in the "voyages Extraordinaires."* New York: St. Martin's Press; London: Macmillan, 1990.

Costello, Peter. *Jules Verne: The Inventor of Science Fiction.* London: Hodder and Stoughton, 1978.

Evans, I. O. *Jules Verne and His Work.* Mattituck, N.Y.: Aeonian Press, 1976.

Freedman, Russell. *Jules Verne, Portrait of a Prophet.* New York: Holiday House, 1965.

Lottman, Herbert R. *Jules Verne: An Exploratory Biography.* New York: St. Martin's Press, 1996.

CÉLINE, LOUIS-FERDINAND (LOUIS FERDINAND DESTOUCHES) (1894–1961)

Céline grew up in a modest household in Paris. After engaging in a series of apprenticeships, he joined the army in 1914 and was seriously wounded in the first few months of World War I, during a voluntary mission. After his recovery, Céline was sent to work in the French consulate in London. From there he went to Africa, returning to France when he fell ill from malaria. After the war, he completed his medical degree in Rennes and married the daughter of a professor of medicine. Céline's doctoral thesis on Philippe Semmelweis's work on disease prevention, a veritable literary work itself, was completed in 1924.

Céline's real name was Destouches. He took up the pen name Céline in order not to prejudice his medical career. He took a position with the League of Nations in the department of epidemiology and was sent to Geneva from 1924 to 1927 and on mission to America and Central Europe. He eventually divorced his wife to pursue a long affair with an American dancer, Elizabeth Craig, who introduced him to the notion of artistic creation derived from "internal necessity."

When Céline's position in Geneva was not renewed, he returned to Paris and wrote his most famous novel, JOURNEY TO THE END OF THE NIGHT, which won the Renaudot Prize in 1933. It was followed later by DEATH ON THE INSTALLMENT PLAN. An even more despairing work than, *Journey, Death on the Installment Plan* blurs the boundaries between fiction and reality.

Disappointed that Céline was clearly abandoning his role as a fellow traveler, leftist critics who had praised *Journey* were critical of the latter work. Angry at this rejection, at professional difficulties, and especially at losing a position at the medical clinic in Clichy to a Lithuanian Jew, Céline began writing vitriolic antisemitic and anticommunist works. Drawing from the German philosopher Friedrich Nietzsche's *Genealogy of Morals,* Céline pushed Nietzsche's argument even further, to blame the Judeo-Christian tradition and socialism for the triumph of a democracy of the weak. Ironically, Céline's obscenely vitriolic tracts are not without some lyrical passages. These were republished separately in 1959 under the title *Ballet with No Music, No One, Nothing.*

Céline's real difficulties began with the publication of these anti-Semitic works. *Guignol's Band* (1944) marks his return to literature at the very moment its author was obliged to flee France as a collaborationist. He passed through Germany to Denmark where he was, nonetheless, imprisoned. Condemned in France for treason, Céline did not return until his amnesty in 1951. Upon his return, Céline was blacklisted by contemporary writers such as LOUIS ARAGON, JEAN-PAUL SARTRE, and the National Committee of Writers.

Céline subsequently struggled to regain the recognition he felt his due as a writer and very nearly succeeded with *From One Chateau to Another* (1957) and *North* (1960). He died in 1961 while finishing *Rigodon* (posthumous, 1969), the third volume in a series of imaginary adventures in the Third Reich.

Céline's novels are clearly autobiographical to a considerable degree. For example, the narrator of a number of his works is named Ferdinand, Céline's second given name. The surnames Destouches and Céline are present. Finally, the contemporary historical setting is clear. The difference between the events Céline describes and his own life has to do with degree. The events in his novel tend to be darker and more exaggerated. His characters are pushed to their limit.

Céline attained notoriety in particular for *Journey to the End of the Night,* a novel that transformed contemporary literature by its freedom and crude style. According to the author, the vocabulary he uses is antibourgeois. In fact, it is the language of the street. His syntax and style are complex, overflowing with neologisms, crude language, obscenities, as well as the language of medicine and philosophy. Céline often makes use of repetitions and redundancies, juxtapositions, interjections, and exclamations. Normal punctuation gives way to question marks. The result is a fragmented narrative that mimics the emotion carried by the spoken word. Céline's powerful and innovative use of language is used to depict life as an object of derision, to the absurdity of which man may never be able to adapt. Céline's works represent the most radical and corrosive form of the absurdism that marked early 20th-century literature. A visionary, physically disabled during the war, scandalized by the interwar period, Céline expressed the weak side of EXISTENTIAL-ISM. His characters are threatened from within and from without, "man naked, stripped of everything, even faith in himself," as Céline put it.

Despite his racism and his generally right-wing political views, Céline's innovative approach to the novel has guaranteed him a place in literary history. Nonetheless, the reaction of French readers to the mention of Céline's name even today remains largely negative. In their minds, it is impossible to separate the man from his works. By and large, Céline is remembered for his stance during the war.

FURTHER READING

Bouchard, Norma. *Céline, Gadda, Beckett: Experimental Writings of the 1930s.* Gainesville: University of Florida Press, 2000.

Buckley, William K., ed. *Critical Essays on Louis Ferdinand Céline.* Boston: G. K. Hall, 1989.

Green, M. J. *Fiction in the Historical Present: French Writers and the Thirties.* Hanover, N.H.: University Press of New England, 1986.

Hewitt, Nicholas. *The Life of Céline: A Critical Biography.* Oxford, Malden, Mass.: Blackwell, 1999.

Klein, Holger, ed. *The First World War in Fiction.* London: Macmillan, 1976.

Knapp, Bettina Liebowitz. *Céline, Man of Hate.* Tuscaloosa: University of Alabama Press, 1974.

Luce, Stanford, ed. and trans. *Céline and His Critics: Scandals and Paradox.* Saratoga, Calif.: Anma Libri, 1986.

McCarthy, Patrick. *Céline.* New York: Penguin Books, 1977.

Solomon, Philip H. *Understanding Céline.* Colombia: University of South Carolina Press, 1992.

Vitoux, Frédéric. *Céline: A Biography.* Translated by Jesse Browner. New York: Paragon House, 1992.

Wohl, Robert. *The Generation of 1914.* Cambridge, Mass.: Harvard University Press, 1979.

CHAMINADOUR MARCEL JOUHANDEAU (VOL. I, 1934; VOL. II, 1936; VOL. III, 1941)

Chaminadour contains themes found in other works by Jouhandeau, such as *Pincegrain* (1924) and *PRUDENCE HAUTECHAUME* (1927). The first two volumes of *Chaminadour* draw on Jouhandeau's experience as a child, while the third is set in adulthood.

Published in intervals, *Chaminadour* is Jouhandeau's depiction of provincial life in his native city of Guéret. His experience growing up in the provinces as well as his mother's almost daily missives provides much of the material for these works that bring to life the many and varied characters that people any small town. Jouhandeau evokes the pettiness of petit bourgeois merchants and their families, yet his depiction is not wholly pessimistic, as Jouhandeau reveals his sensitivity to the COMÉDIE HUMAINE. An admirer of Jouhandeau, ANDRÉ GIDE praised his clear and concise style as much as his perceptive exploration of the question of good and evil.

CHANSONS DE GESTE

The *chansons de geste* were medieval epic poems written in verse paragraphs (*laisses*) of varying length. In old French, *geste* meant heroic deeds. *Chanter de geste* was to sing an epic song. The SONG OF ROLAND, recounting the life and death of Charlemagne's valiant knight Roland, is a superb example of the *chanson de geste*.

The *chansons de geste* were performed in public by *jongleurs,* wandering minstrels whose performances, accompanied by music, entertained the public at fairs, marriages, or dinners held in the lord's castle. They reflect the predominantly male values of feudal society with its combination of chivalric and Christian themes.

These heroic stories recount the events of a community: a people, a nation, or a kinship group. They consequently lay the foundation for the concept of the nation in French literature. They are associated with the period of the Crusades. The *chansons de geste* differ from the medieval ROMANCES, which emphasize the individual's emotions and search for identity within the community over national or religious zeal.

FURTHER READING

Daniel, Norman. *Heroes and Saracens: An Interpretation of the Chansons de Geste.* Edinburgh: Edinburgh University Press, 1984.

Hindley, A. *The Old French Epic: An Introduction: Texts—Commentaries—Notes/* by Alan Hindley and Brian J. Levy. Louvain, Belgium: Peeters, 1983.

Kay, Sarah. *The Chansons de Geste in the Age of Romance: Political Fictions.* Oxford: Clarendon Press, New York: Oxford University Press, 1995.

Keller, Hans-Erich, ed. *Romance Epic: Essyas on a Medieval Literary Genre* Kalamazoo: Medieval Institute Publications, Western Michigan University, 1987.

Kellogg, Judith. *Medieval Artistry and Exchange: Economic Institutions, Society, and Literary Form in Old French Narrative.* New York: P. Lang, 1989.

CHARRIÈRE, ISABELLE DE (ISABELLA AGNETA VAN TUYLL VAN SEROORSKERKEN) (1740–1805)

"Belle van Zuylen," as she was called, was born in Holland but her culture was eminently French. Encouraged by her parents, she received a remarkable education for a woman of her time and displayed from an early age a talent and taste for writing. At the age of 20 she published anonymously a novel, *The Nobleman,* in which she spoke out against the biases of her class. While she is most famous for her EPISTOLARY NOVELS, de Charrière also wrote pamphlets, drama, and opera. She was politically engaged particularly during the French Revolution. Initially a supporter of the Revolution, de Charrière later turned against Jacobin excesses.

After a series of suitors, de Charrière eventually chose to marry Charles-Emmanuel de Charrière, formerly a tutor to her brother, and moved with him to his modest family estate in Switzerland. There she wrote her two great epistolary works, LETTERS OF MISTRESS HENLEY, and *Letters from Switzerland* (i.e., *Letters from Neuchatel; LETTERS WRITTEN FROM LAUSANNE; and Caliste, or Continuation of Letters Written from Lausanne*). In these works Charrière is primarily interested in observing the intimate. She engages in social criticism through her sometimes satirical observations of domestic and conjugal life. At the heart of all her works is an exploration of human freedom. Her characters are frequently confronted with the necessity of choosing between actions but the choice is never obvious. Characters may avoid making a decision, sometimes with unhappy consequences. Because she writes from a feminist perspective, it is usually the female character who suffers from male indecision, particularly in an age that denied women autonomy either within or outside of marriage. The problem of marriage is central to her works, as it was to her life. *Letters from Mistress Henley,* in particular, is considered to be at least partly autobiographical. The themes of freedom and suffering she shared with her lover, BENJAMIN CONSTANT, with whom she had an affair from 1787 to 1796. His novel *ADOLPHE* was influenced by de Charrière. Ironically, de

Charrière also had an influence on CORINNE, a novel written by GERMAINE DE STAËL, Constant's subsequent lover.

In contrast to most sentimental novels, de Charrière's heroines are appealing but not perfect. The literary critic SAINTE-BEUVE considered Marianne of *Mistress Henley* one of the most touching female characters in French literature. He spoke highly, too, of de Charrière's style, saying that she wrote with a light touch and simple tone. Her contemporaries evidently agreed. *Mistress Henley* and *Letters from Switzerland* were immediately popular. She is frequently compared to Jane Austen for both her style and her emphasis on the significance of small events in daily life. De Charrière, too, interweaves the domestic, the emotional, and the economic in her depiction of 18th-century society and, in particular, its effect on women, challenging Rousseau's model of domestic virtue in *The New Heloise*.

FURTHER READING

Beebee, Thomas O. *Epistolary Fiction in Europe, 1500–1850.* Cambridge: Cambridge University Press, 1999.

Bérenguier, N. "From Clarens to Hollowpark. Isabelle de Charrière's Quiet Revolution," *Studies in Eighteenth-Century Culture* 21 (1991): 219–243.

Hinde Stewart, Joan. "The Novelists and Their Fictions." In *French Women and the Age of Enlightenment.* Edited by Samia I. Spencer. Bloomington: Indiana University Press, 1984, 197–211.

———. *Gynographs: French Novels by Women of the Late Eighteenth Century.* Lincoln: University of Nebraska Press, 1993.

Jackson, Susan K. "Publishing Without Perishing: Isabelle de Charrière, a.k.a. *la mouche du coche.*" In *Going Public: Women and Publishing in Early Modern France.* Edited by Elizabeth C. Goldsmith and Dena Goodman. Ithaca, N.Y.: Cornell University Press, 1995.

CHARTERHOUSE OF PARMA, THE (LA CHARTREUSE DE PARME) STENDHAL (1839)

The Charterhouse of Parma opens with the arrival of French troops in Milan in 1796. Robert, a French officer billeted with a Milanese family, introduces the reader to the del Dongo household which includes the reactionary, pro-Austrian marquis del Dongo, his wife the marquise, and her sister, Gina, the widow of a French officer. Fabrice, the marquise's son, is born a year later and the implication is that he is the love child of the marquise and Robert.

Given his parentage, it is perhaps not surprising, then, that Fabrice grows up dreaming of Napoleon's glory. In 1815, when Napoleon returns to power for the Hundred Days, Fabrice runs off to join him with his aunt's blessing. Spirited and romantic (see ROMANTICISM), Fabrice finally arrives at Waterloo on the afternoon of the great battle, but the French army is already retreating. The description of Waterloo is considered one of the most famous passages in the novel. Sadly, Fabrice does not entirely understand what takes place around him and is obliged to depend on the advice of others less naive than he.

Upon his return to Italy, Fabrice must retire to Parma with his aunt, as he is now suspect to Milanese authorities. Meanwhile, Gina has married the duke of Sanseverina through the patronage of her lover, count Mosca, the prime minister of the court at Parma. She occupies a brilliant position at court and uses her influence to promote Fabrice's career.

Once Fabrice is living in Parma, his aunt's romantic love for him is revealed. Fabrice, however, is tormented by the thought that something may be lacking in his heart, making him incapable of passionate love, and so he avoids his aunt's overtures although he admires her sincerely. What follows is a period of "crystallization," for Mosca and Gina, and Gina and Fabrice, reflecting Stendhal's theory on love.

The politics of court life in this petty absolutist monarchy are complex. A true Machiavellian, Gina maneuvers superbly until Fabrice's antics lead him into trouble. As the result of an insignificant love affair, Fabrice kills his rival in a duel and is imprisoned in the infamous tower of Farnese by Mosca's political rivals. There Fabrice discovers passion, falling desperately in love with Clelia, the prison director's daughter. The two had met once before when their situations were nearly reversed. Clelia hesitatingly responds to the handsome prisoner, and the two devise a series of ingenious ways to communicate with each other from a distance. Fabrice finally discovers his qualities of energy and heart when he meets Clelia. Through the mediation of a woman and love, themes in Stendhal's works overall, Fabrice's internal conflicts are resolved.

Meanwhile, Gina plans Fabrice's escape. He is at first unwilling to leave the prison, where he can at least remain near Clelia. Finally, Clelia convinces him that he must flee, as he is increasingly in danger of being poisoned by his enemies. In the course of his escape, Clelia's father is given a strong dose of opium. Clelia vows to the Virgin that if her father survives she will never see Fabrice again. She consequently obeys her father's wishes and marries the marquis Crescenzi. For his part, Fabrice enters the church, a military career no longer being possible.

In the interim, the old prince of Parma has died, in fact secretly poisoned by a radical poet, Ferrante Palla, on the instructions of Gina, who seeks revenge for Fabrice's imprisonment. The prince is succeeded by Ranice-Ernest V and Mosca successfully suppresses a revolt.

When Fabrice returns to Parma he falls into danger yet again. Only Gina's successful manipulation of the prince spares him. She then leaves Parma with Mosca, whom she marries. Fabrice rises quickly in his ecclesiastical career and establishes renown as a preacher. Eventually, he succeeds in meeting Clelia again and the two initiate a secret and passionate affair in which each of the lovers finally tastes of happiness until the demise of their child leads quickly to Clelia's death. Fabrice retires to a monastery (the Charterhouse of Parma) and dies shortly thereafter, as does Gina. Only Mosca survives.

The starting point of the novel is a true story from Renaissance Italy when Alexander Farnese became pope through the patronage of his aunt's lover. Stendhal then places the story in the 19th century, enriching it with his own recollections of the Napoleonic Wars and the details of contemporary history.

In this masterpiece of fiction, Stendhal's gift as a writer is at its height. The author's own passion for the glory of Napoleon, adventure, love, and love of Italy are all revealed in the character of Fabrice. Beyond Stendhal's signature clarity of style, the writing attains the quality of a romantic poem while, at the same time, offering a series of philosophical and moral reflections. Stendhal reveals, too, his deftness at psychological analysis, reminding the reader of his admiration for LACLOS.

The novel received little attention at the time of publication but is recognized today as one of the most significant novels of the 19th century, as important to the first half of the century as FLAUBERT's SENTIMENTAL EDUCATION is to the second. It is a story that blends love, ambition, and politics, themes present in Stendhal's other novels, particularly The RED AND THE BLACK. Stendhal's contemporary HONORÉ DE BALZAC praised the work as "the novel Machiavelli would have written had he lived in the 19th century."

FURTHER READING

Alter, Robert in collaboration with Carol Cosman. *A Lion for Love: A Critical Biography of Stendhal.* New York: Basic Books, 1979.

Auerbach, Erich. *Mimesis: The Representation of Reality in Western Literature.* Translated by Willard R. Trask. Princeton, N.J.: Princeton University Press, 1953.

Fineshriber, William. *H. Stendhal the Romantic Rationalist.* Philadelphia: R. West, 1977.

Girard, René. *Deceit, Desire and the Novel: Self and Other in Literary Structure.* Translated by Yvonne Freccero. Baltimore, London: Johns Hopkins University Press, 1976.

Green, Frederick Charles. *Stendhal.* New York: Russell and Russell, 1970.

Hemmings, F. W. J. *Stendhal, A Study of His Novels.* Oxford: Clarendon Press, 1964.

Keates, Jonathan. *Stendhal.* New York: Carroll and Graf, 1997.

May, Gita. *Stendhal and the Age of Napoleon.* New York: Columbia University Press, 1977.

CHATEAUBRIAND, FRANÇOIS-RENÉ, VICOMTE DE (1768–1848)

Born in Saint-Malo to an old noble family whose fortune was in decline, Chateaubriand developed into one of the leading writers of the French romantic movement in literature (see ROMANTICISM). Chateaubriand was educated in Rennes and then spent two idyllic years at the family château of Comborg with his sister, Lucile, an important influence in his life. She was the first to inspire Chateaubriand to write, after long walks in the countryside during which he waxed poetic. Nervous and sensitive, Lucile probably committed suicide in 1804. Her death was a painful loss to her brother.

Chateaubriand briefly considered a naval career, then the priesthood but, in the end, rejected both, choosing instead to become a writer. Chateaubriand also witnessed important historical events, including the beginning of the French Revolution. In 1791, he escaped the dangers of revolutionary France by traveling to America, where he spent five months. While his itinerary is not entirely certain, his travels did include Niagara and Florida (home of the Natchez). Chateaubriand was particularly struck by his discovery of Native Americans, an experience that profoundly influenced his writings. As he once wrote, "In these savage regions, the soul is pleased to sink itself into an ocean of forests . . . and so to find itself alone before God."

Short of money, Chateaubriand was obliged to return to France where he joined the army of émigré aristocrats and was wounded. He subsequently fled to London. These were difficult years. In 1798–99, his mother and another sister died. His financial and personal situations were precarious. These experiences, along with émigré life in general, contributed to his conversion to devout Roman Catholicism. In a review of GERMAINE DE STAËL's *On Literature,* he wrote "I believe, with Pascal, that only the Christian religion can explain the human condition." This view permeates Chateaubriand's subsequent writings.

By 1800, Chateaubriand decided to return to France, where he published some of his greatest works, such as the GENIUS OF CHRISTIANITY (1802), of which ATALA and RENÉ formed a part. These works were extraordinarily well received by the public, *Atala* in particular.

A man of versatility, Chateaubriand then undertook a diplomatic career in 1803, traveled to the Orient (which provided further inspiration for his writing), became a supporter of the Bourbon Restoration, and finally, a minister of France. The most important woman in Chateaubriand's life was inarguably Juliette Récamier. Every afternoon he presided with her over a salon held in the Parisian convent of the Abbaye-aux-Bois, where she had retired due to financial constraints. In 1848, the great romantic died in the presence of Madame Récamier, who cut off a lock of his hair and placed a bouquet of Verbena on his breast. He was buried according to his wishes in his birthplace, the epitaph reading "a great French writer desired to rest here in order to hear nothing but the sea and the wind."

Along with ROUSSEAU, Chateaubriand also made a major contribution to the genre of autobiography with his *Memoirs from Beyond the Grave.* In this work Chateaubriand struggles to understand himself and the world in which he lives. Moreover, there are autobiographical elements in a number of his novels. Critics frequently point to the parallels between Chateaubriand and his character, René.

Chateaubriand's life and work bridged two centuries, and this resulted in the overlapping of literary genres one finds in his works. His interests ranged from scientific to literary. He wrote in the tone of both 18th-century Rousseauesque sensibility and 19th-century romantic passion. Witnessing the fall of the Old Regime may have induced Chateaubriand to turn to romanticism, with its emphasis on the individual's unease and uncertainty in modern life. René certainly suffers from melancholy and this metaphysical uncertainty.

Disillusionment led Chateaubriand and other romantic writers to become fascinated with an idealized or mythical past. Chateaubriand's fascination with nature and the power of feeling and imagination also mark him as a romantic. Similarly, the recurring theme of the exotic journey in his works reflects elements of romantic thought while offering Chateaubriand the opportunity to comment on contemporary French society and values.

FURTHER READING

Bouvier, Luke. "How Not to Speak of Incest: Atala and the Secrets of Speech," *Nineteenth-Century French Studies* 30, nos. 3 and 4 (2002): 228–242.

Call, Michael J. *Back to the Garden: Chateaubriand, Senancour and Constant.* Saratoga, Calif.: Anma Libri, 1988.

Maurois, André. *Chateaubriand: Poet, Statesman, Lover.* Translated by Vera Fraser. New York: Greenwood Press, 1969.

Smethurst, Colin. *Chateaubriand, Atala, and René.* London: Grant and Cutler, 1995.

CHÂTEAUBRIANT, ALPHONSE DE BRÉDENBEC DE (1877–1951)

Châteaubriant grew up in Brittany under the influence of his grandfather, a painter, and his father, a musician. His first novel, *Monsieur des Lourdines* (1911), which depicts the countryside of his youth, won the Goncourt Prize.

Nonetheless, its author remained in relative obscurity until the publication of *La Brière* (1923), an epic novel that brought to life the provincial culture of Nantes and earned the grand prize of the Académie Française. These two novels evoke the peasant's mystical attachment to the land, presaging certain themes that would appear in Châteaubriant's later works. A loner, Châteaubriant's one friend in the world of literature was ROMAIN ROLLAND.

Châteaubriant was mobilized in 1914 for World War I. Like so many others, his four years at the front marked him for life. His experience during the war left him with a desire to return to the origins of human society, a golden age untainted by the rationalism that had, in his mind, so evidently failed to lead to progress.

As of 1915, Châteaubriant was increasingly drawn to mysticism as he sought God outside of institutionalized religion. With *The Lord's Response* (1932), a mystical work that speaks out against materialism and modern egoism, Châteaubriant's writing moved in a new direction both politically and spiritually as he dreamed of a renewed medieval era that would emerge out of Germany's National Socialism.

When he returned to France from his travels in Germany, Châteaubriant wrote *La Gerbe des forces* (not translated, 1937), depicting a new religion capable of replacing individualism and intellectualism with a primitive communion with the earth. During World War II, Châteaubriant founded *La Gerbe*, a major right-wing newspaper that defended the German occupation of France. After the war, he was condemned to death in absentia as he had taken refuge in an Austrian monastery where he remained until his death in 1951, writing his last essays, *Writings from the Other Shore* (1950) and *Letter to a Dying Christian* (1951). Châteaubriant's collection of texts, *Posthumous Trial of a Visionary*, was published posthumously in 1987, provoking a debate on the possible rehabilitation of its author.

FURTHER READING

Chadwick, Kay. *Alphonse de Châteaubriant: Catholic Collaborator.* Oxford, New York: P. Lang, 2002.

CHAWAF, CHANTAL (1948–)

Chantal Chawaf married a Syrian and moved with him to Syria, where she had two children. Upon her return to France she began her career as a writer. She has traveled widely. Her writings portray the many and varied experiences of women, from the threat of male violence to motherhood, tasting the joys of domestic life, fighting illness, seeking a lover, or witnessing the death of one's father. In essence, Chawaf explores every aspect of a woman's life. As she explains in *The Body and the Word* (1992), Chawaf's FEMINISM is marked by a deliberate attempt to break with male language in order to develop an entirely new vocabulary, like that of the myth or fairy tale, in an effusive writing that exudes the intimate. Her overflowing accumulation of words pours out in a stream.

The trauma of her birth is a recurring theme in Chawaf's writings as is evident in her first novel, *Mother Love/Mother Earth,* published in 1974. In September, 1948, doctors pulled the infant Chawaf from her mother's body after her parents' car was shelled by the Germans during the war. Two major themes in her writing are the relationship between mother and daughter and sensual love from a woman's perspective.

After combing through the archives in Boulogne, Chawaf wrote *The Black Overcoat* (1998), exploring the violence that killed her parents and so many others. Obsessed with the idea that her life began in blood, the blood of her mother and the blood of war, Chawaf was able to overcome a sense of her own madness only by seeking to understand her relationship to other victims. In the end, she chose life and to speak out, through her writing, against war.

Chawaf's style is representative of the *écriture féminine* of French feminist literature (see FEMINISM) as she seeks to write *from* the body. Her belief that the body can speak through writing reflects her innovative understanding of the relationship between the body and the word.

FURTHER READING

Benstock, Shari. "From the Editor's Perspective: Women's Literary History: To Be Continued," *Tulsa Studies in Women's Literature* 5, no. 2 (Autumn 1986): 165–183.
Davidow, Ellen-Messer. "The Philosophical Bases of Feminist Literary Criticisms," *New Literary History* 19, no. 1, Feminist Directions (Autumn 1987): 65–103.
Gilbert, Sandra M., and Susan Gubar. "Sexual Linguistics: Gender, Language, Sexuality," *New Literary History* 16,

no. 3, On Writing Histories of Literature (Spring 1985): 515–543.

Jardine, Alice A., and Anne M. Menke. "Exploding the Issue: "French" "Women" "Writers" and "The Canon"?" *Yale French Studies,* no. 75, The Politics of Tradition: Placing Women in French Literature (1988): 229–258.

Kraemer, Don. "Abstracting the Bodies of/in Academic Discourse," *Rhetoric Review* 10, no. 1 (Autumn 1991): 52–69.

CHÉRI COLETTE (1920)

Chéri, or darling, refers to Fred Peloux, the son of one of Léa de Lonval's companions. An aging courtesan, Léa built her entire life on the foundation of her beauty and her quest for sensual pleasure.

Chéri, young and adored, has grown up in the atmosphere of indolent luxury that surrounds women like Léa, with whom he has an affair until his mother marries him off to a rich young woman named Edmée. Not until Chéri leaves on his honeymoon does Léa realize the depth of her passion, a love that, at her age, is sure to be the last. Chéri returns, however, and the two come together again and declare their love for the first time. Then, one morning, Léa suddenly tells Chéri to leave, giving in with bitterness to her conscience and her age.

With a plot centering on an older mistress, a wealthy young wife, and a handsome young man, this novel appears on the surface to be a light work depicting the libertine ways of the belle epoque. In fact, Colette wrote a tragedy. In her own words *Chéri* is one of her most bitter works. It certainly has great psychological depth and thus marks an important stage in Colette's development as a novelist.

Despite the novel's title, Léa is in fact the principal character, a woman accustomed to pleasure who discovers true passion only when it is too late. Recognizing her age, Léa renounces the love that has awakened within her. As a result, she is forced to mourn her love and her past life at the same time.

Novels traditionally depict female characters as capricious, unaware, and passive. In this novel, Colette reverses the stereotype. Chéri is the passive character. Léa's assertiveness combined with autobiographical elements made the novel shocking for contemporary readers. Its exploration of the themes of love and passion at every stage of life is a hallmark of Colette's works.

FURTHER READING

Olken, I. T. "Aspects of Imagery in Colette: Color and Light," *PMLA* 77, no. 1 (March 1962): 140–148.

CHRAÏBI, DRISS (1926–)

One of the most important North African writers of the 20th century, Chraïbi was born in Morocco. He attended secondary school in Casablanca and left for France in 1945, where he completed his studies in chemical engineering in 1950. For a time, Chraïbi studied psychology and then traveled in Europe before becoming a producer for France Culture radio in 1959. He also began to develop an interest in literature and theater and taught North African literature at the University of Laval-Quebec in Canada before returning permanently to France in 1971.

Chraïbi's first novel, *Simple Past,* published in 1954, marks the author as one of a generation of North African writers who rebelled against the patriarchal traditions of Islamic society. This novel led to such an outcry in a period of heightened nationalism that Chraïbi publicly repudiated his own work, an action he later regretted. *Simple Past* focuses on the family and social values of traditional Moroccan society. In this and subsequent works, Chraïbi engaged in a sharp critique of both North African and European society. *The Butts* (1955) evokes the misery of North African immigrant workers in France. *The Donkey* (1955) speaks out against the failure of decolonization and the despair to which it has led. In *Death to Canada* (1975) Chraïbi turned his sharp eye on Western society. *Flutes of Death* (1981) marks a shift in Chraïbi's works as he begins to explore North African Berber culture. *Mother Spring* (1982) and *Birth at Dawn* (1986), the first two volumes of a trilogy, depict the introduction of Islam into the Maghreb and the Christian-Arab encounter in Spain. While Chraïbi never abandons his critical stance, these later works are less harsh. Chraïbi's early novels are full of tension. "We are nervous writers," he once said.

FURTHER READING

Joyaux, Georges J., Albert Memmi, and Jules Roy, "Driss Chraïbi, Mohammed Dib, Kateb Yacine and Indigenous North African Literature," *Yale French Studies,* no. 24, Midnight Novelists (1959): 30–40.

Yetiv, Isaac. "Iconoclasts in Maghrebian Literature," *French Review* 50, no. 6 (May 1977): 858–864.

CINQ-MARS ALFRED DE VIGNY (1826)

Bored by the monotony of military life, Alfred de Vigny turned to literature, joining the romantic movement (see ROMANTICISM). In 1826 he published his only novel, *Cinq-Mars*, a historical romance set during the reign of France's king Louis XIII. Vigny focuses the drama on the conflict between the king's first minister, Cardinal Richelieu, and the nobility. Criticized by SAINTE-BEUVE for historical inaccuracy, Vigny responded in "Reflections on the Truth in Art" (1829), in which he argued that art should reveal "the truth of observation on human nature and not on the authenticity of fact."

This tragic novel tells the story of the marquis de Cinq-Mars, an ambitious young man seeking to play a role in court politics. He bears all the marks of high birth, generosity and nobility mixed with dreams of grandeur. It is possible that Vigny saw parallels between the reign of Louis XIII and his own time with the defeat of the nobility by 19th-century egalitarianism.

Opposed to the powerful Richelieu's absolutist policies, Cinq-Mars joins a conspiracy against him, counting on the king's support. The conspirators enter into a secret agreement with Spain. Meanwhile, Richelieu is informed of the plot by Father Joseph, leading to Cinq-Mars' imprisonment and eventual execution. Richelieu triumphs. Marie de Gonzague, his love for whom had inspired Cinq-Mars's ambitious dreams, only realizes that she returns Cinq-Mars's affection when it is too late. She accepts to marry the king of Poland as pragmatism wins out over emotion. The novel explores all the sordid aspects of court factionalism and politics, reminiscent of MADAME DE LAFAYETTE's *PRINCESS OF CLÈVES*.

Cinq-Mars bears the influence of gothic novels, such as Anne Radcliffe's well-liked stories, the historical novels of Sir Walter Scott, all popular among contemporaries, and of the romantic movement overall. Vigny reveals the tension between two parallel worlds, one of politics and the other of dreams—in other words, the romantic's world. With its blend of history and fiction, *Cinq-Mars* was well received by the public.

FURTHER READING

Kelly, Linda. *The Young Romantics: Victor Hugo, Sainte-Beuve, Vigny, Dumas, Musset, and George Sand and Their Friendships, Feuds and Loves in the French Romantic Revolution.* New York: Random House, 1976.

Shwimer, Elaine K. *The Novels of Alfred de Vigny: A Study of their Form and Composition.* New York: Garland Publishers, 1991.

CIXOUS, HÉLÈNE (1937–)

Cixous is one of the most important figures in contemporary French feminist writing (see FEMINISM). Like CHANTAL CHAWAF, Cixous is interested in the relationship between a woman's body and the word. In other words, she, too, believes that the body speaks through writing. Her own relationship with the word is passionate, conflicted, and ultimately, carnal.

Cixous was born in Oran, Algeria, where her childhood was marked by war and the death of her father in 1948. Moreover, she was raised in a German-Jewish household and her mother tongue is German, which sometimes results in an unusual and ambiguous use of syntax. Cixous also plays with words as she questions the concept of identity, as mother and as woman, through an exploration of her social, cultural, and religious roots.

Cixous went to France in 1955 to study English literature and wrote her doctoral dissertation on James Joyce. She began teaching at the university level. In 1968, along with a group of scholars, she created the University of Vincennes, where she was subsequently appointed chair of English literature. In 1969, she established a literary journal, *Poetics*, with two other women scholars. She has traveled widely, notably to the United States and Canada, where she has also taught. A prolific writer, Cixous has produced some 20 novels, plays, and works of literary criticism.

Like Julia Kristeva, Roland Barthes, Jacques Derrida, and Luce Irigaray, Cixous is interested in the relationship between sexuality and writing. Her own writing celebrates the female body. According to Cixous, once a woman has escaped the confines of male writing and male thought, she can begin to appreciate her sense of self through her own image and that of other women. In offering such an approach to women's literature, Cixous creates a new mythology whose characters depict the birth and rebirth of woman, in desire and in pain. A woman's appropriation of herself takes place through the creation of a new language of the body, heart, memory, and subconscious. "Woman must write herself."

Furthermore, through her writing, Cixous engages in a psychoanalytical exploration of the feminine. Reading and writing are, for her, the means to grapple with the enigma of male/female relations. She has been criticized for her psychoanalytical style, influenced by Jacques Lacan, and marked by a superabundance of images. Nonetheless, Cixous has been instrumental in establishing a new form of literature that lies somewhere between myth and novel.

In her essay *Exit* (1975), Cixous argues that Western civilization is based on a set of hierarchical values that juxtapose order and chaos, self and other, light and dark, good and evil, and, ultimately male and female, a way of thinking that must be broken down. Part of a group of poststructuralist, theoretical feminists (see POST STRUCTURALISM), Cixous further outlined her theory of women's writing in *The Laugh of the Medusa* (1975), in which she argues that the Western tradition in literature has always given primacy to the phallus. Arguing against Freudian sexual theories about women, Cixous (along with Luce Irigaray) has argued that for women to write, they must first locate the source of their sexual pleasure. Moreover, Cixous thinks that women have a distinct advantage. The nature of women's bodies sets them closer to the symbolic. Both men and women, she argues, need to understand the relationship between sexuality and writing. The problem for women thus far has been that they have been speaking and writing from the male perspective.

Through its inherently deconstructive nature, women's writing (*écriture féminine*) will develop a new system of expression that will lead to union and a return to the mother's body by speech/writing in "white ink" (breast milk). *Écriture féminine* is not based on representational language. It is a stream of words, flowing in connection to the rhythm of the body, ultimately wiping out the dichotomy of self/other. She praises COLETTE and MARGUERITE DURAS for having produced truly feminine writing.

FURTHER READING

Cixous, Hélène, and Catherine Clément. *The Newly Born Woman.* Translated by Betsy Wing. Minneapolis: University of Minnesota Press, 1986.

Conley, Verena Andermatt. *Hélène Cixous: Writing the Feminine.* Lincoln: University of Nebraska Press, 1991.

Marks, Elaine. "Review Essay: Women and Literature in France," *Signs* 3 (1978): 832–842.

Marks, Elaine, and Isabelle de Courticron, eds. *New French Feminisms: An Anthology.* Amherst: University of Massachusetts Press, 1980.

Sellers, Susan, ed. *Writing Differences: Readings From the Seminar of Hélène Cixous.* New York: St. Martin's Press, 1988.

Shiach, Morag. *Hélène Cixous: A Politics of Writing.* London: Routledge, 1994.

Showalter, Elaine, ed. *The New Feminist Criticism: Essays on Women, Literature and Theory.* New York: Pantheon, 1985.

CLASSICISM (C. 1660–1685)

Classicism refers to a period in French literature coinciding with reign of Louis XIV, particularly the years 1660–1685. This literary and cultural movement is thus consistent with the period of royal absolutism when art, architecture, and literature were put in service of the king's glory. From 1687 to 1694 the literary world was rocked by a debate between the so-called Ancients and Moderns. Nicolas Boileau, the theoretician of classicism and defender of the Ancients, opposed Charles Perreault and the Moderns.

Following in the footsteps of the philosopher René Descartes, classicism established literary and linguistic rules in the name of reason and inspired by the culture and values of classical antiquity, especially the classical emphasis on balance and harmony. Drawing on Aristotle's *Poetics*, classicism tends to classify works according to an established hierarchical order. Tragedy, for example, is considered superior to Comedy.

Classicism also unites literature and morality, following Horace's dictum that one should blend the pleasant with the useful. Classicism promoted literature that was to please the reader with its eloquence and good style, giving the reader the impression of direct contact with the writer. Not surprisingly, the epistolary tradition comes close to meeting these standards. One of the greatest works of the period is GUILLERGAUE's *PORTUGUESE LETTERS*.

Classicism's respect for language and its proper use also draws on the tradition of classical antiquity. Classicism seeks to promote the dignity and grandeur of the French language using classical Latin texts as a model. Under the tutelage of the Académie Française, established in 1635, adherents to classicism aspired to a purity and clarity of language they associated with the great Latin writers. With this goal in mind, the Académie Française produced an official French grammar, dictionary, and works on poetics and rhetoric. The classicists took a derisive view of technical terms associated with professional vocabularies and colloquial language. In this respect, they were elitist. DIDEROT and d'Alembert's ENCYCLOPEDIA thus reflects a reaction against this hierarchical approach to knowledge. ANTOINE FURETIÈRE's dictionary of 1690 likewise competed with the Académie's official work by allowing for a more comprehensive view of the French language.

The term classicism was coined in the 18th century as writers and scholars looked back on earlier literary movements. Classicism then falls between the baroque and ROMANTICISM. Classicism seeks to explore the universal in the physical world and in human nature. The romantics' focus on the particular and the unique is, in part, a reaction against the universalism of classicism. Slightly tongue-in-cheek, STENDHAL argued that romanticism refers to writers who wish to please the public of their own time while classicism regards writers who wish to please their great-grandfathers.

The nature of classicism is somewhat contradictory as it blends conservatism with innovation. We tend to think of classicism as rigid and constraining in its insistence on certain academic rules (unity of time, place, and action in theater or believability and good taste in novels). However, in attempting to approximate the sublime and the natural, classicism is also an expressive and elegant style in literature.

CLAUDINE AT SCHOOL (*CLAUDINE À L'ÉCOLE]*) COLETTE (1900)

First in the Claudine series, this novel was initially published under the name *Willy,* the nickname of Colette's first husband, Henry Gauthier-Villars. It was not until a court decision of 1955 that Colette was officially recognized as coauthor, whereas she in fact created the unforgettable character of Claudine.

Claudine is a young woman living in an isolated French country village. She has no mother and her father is constantly distracted by his work. He may be affectionate but he is also eccentric. Claudine finds refuge in her garden and with her cat yet she fervently desires someone with whom to share her life. "I feel my spirit is sore because I, who do not like to dance, would like to dance with someone whom I adore with all my heart because I would want that someone to relax with, to whom I could tell everything that I now confide only to Fanchette [the cat] or to my pillow (not even my diary) because I miss this person like mad; I am humiliated, and I would not give myself up to anyone but the one I would love and know completely—dreams that will never come true."

The entire novel thus reflects this tension between desire and disappointment. Claudine's everyday life is centered on her experiences at school, she where she is often judged as impertinent or even cruel. Claudine first seeks love and affection from a young teacher, Aimée Lanthenay, and then, when rejected, consoles herself by mistreating Aimée's sister Luce, who seems to enjoy it. Aimée chooses instead to giver herself to the headmistress, Mademoiselle Sergent, in a lesbian relationship that becomes increasingly open and obsessive, to the point where the students are sometimes left entirely on their own.

Such relationships are further complicated by a male teacher's attraction to Aimée, and the school superintendent, who is drawn to any young flesh, Claudine in particular. All the while, lessons continue in French composition, arithmetic, drawing, sewing, and music and preparations for the final exam are underway.

Claudine at School is the story of a young woman's awakening to sensuality, eroticism, and cruelty. One has the sense that Claudine's future will be rich and unusual like Claudine herself. Attractive and yet inspiring unease in the reader, Claudine is one of Colette's most powerful and eminently seductive characters.

FURTHER READING
Ladenson, Elizabeth. "Colette for Export Only," *Yale French Studies,* no. 90. Same Sex/Different Text? Gay and Lesbian Writing in French (1996): 25–46.

Rogers, Juliette M. "The 'Counter-Public Sphere': Colette's Gendered Collective, *MLN* 3, no. 4, French Issue (September 1996): 734–746.

CLAUDINE IN PARIS (*CLAUDINE À PARIS*) COLETTE (1901)

Second in Colette's Claudine series, *Claudine in Paris* was, like CLAUDINE AT SCHOOL, published under Colette's husband's name, Willy. Not until 1955 was Colette officially recognized as coauthor, despite the fact that the character of Claudine was her own creation.

At the opening of the novel, Claudine and her father leave their home for Paris. Uprooted and cut off from her garden and life in the countryside, Claudine begins to wither away. Life in Paris becomes more interesting only once she meets her effeminate cousin, Marcel, with whom she gets along well. Marcel confides to her his love for an older boy, while extracting from Claudine similar confessions. But Claudine's tales of love for another schoolgirl are only fiction, concocted to satisfy Marcel's obsessive curiosity and voyeurism. Claudine's chance meeting with Luce, the school friend who was supposedly the object of her desire, leaves her disillusioned and depressed as Luce is being "kept" by an older man.

Life is transformed, however, when Claudine meets Marcel's father and falls hopelessly in love with him. Little by little he begins to return her love, despite Marcel's fits of jealousy, and asks Claudine's father for her hand in marriage.

Like most of Colette's works, *Claudine in Paris* has a strong autobiographical tone. Moreover, the novel evokes Parisian society and the world of theater in the first decade of the 20th century, with its libertinism and sexual ambiguity, hallmarks of Colette's writing. The novel also explores the nature of adolescence and the sensual awakening that accompanies this stage of life in particular, likewise a common theme in Colette's works. The novel offers a powerful blend of desire and feeling, flesh and spirit.

FURTHER READING

Ladenson, Elizabeth. "Colette for Export Only," *Yale French Studies,* no. 90. Same Sex/Different Text? Gay and Lesbian Writing in French (1996): 25–46.

Rogers, Juliette M. "The 'Counter-Public Sphere': Colette's Gendered Collective, *MLN* 3, no. 4, French Issue (September 1996): 734–746.

CLAUDINE'S HOME (*LA MAISON DE CLAUDINE*) COLETTE (1922)

Claudine's Home consists of 30 chapters, each one focused on a particular memory, place, person, or feeling. Together they bring to life Colette's vision of the world while evoking her experience growing up in the French countryside. There are animals, often present in Colette's works, and Sido, her wise mother, even Bel-Gazou, Colette's daughter. The rhythm of the writing alternates between the lyrical and the lively.

The title of this work is somewhat misleading as *Claudine's Home* does not form part of the Claudine cycle, Colette's first series of novels (see CLAUDINE AT SCHOOL, and CLAUDINE IN PARIS). When *Claudine's Home* was published, Colette was already a mature writer who had developed her own style to perfection, as she depicts a simple vision of the world enmeshed in family relations and the details of everyday life. Colette's publishers insisted that the title refer to Claudine, Colette's unforgettable and highly popular character.

FURTHER READING

Ladenson, Elizabeth. "Colette for Export Only," *Yale French Studies,* no. 90. Same Sex/Different Text? Gay and Lesbian Writing in French (1996): 25–46.
Rogers, Juliette M. "The 'Counter-Public Sphere': Colette's Gendered Collective, *MLN* 3, no. 4, French Issue (September 1996): 734–746.

CLEANED OUT (*LES ARMOIRES VIDES*) ANNIE ERNAUX (1974)

Cleaned Out is the story of Denise Lesur, a young woman studying literature at the university who has an illegal abortion and struggles with her sense of alienation. She is from a family of very modest background. Her parents run a small grocery and café in Normandy. Her happy childhood is disturbed when her parents send her to a more exclusive school where Denise discovers that she does not fit in. She tries to compensate by adopting the language and values of the middle-class girls with whom she studies. Denise's sense of identity is further shaken at the university where she meets Marc, a law student from a good family, with whom she has an affair. When she discovers that she is pregnant, Marc is unsympathetic. Denise becomes angry and frustrated at the realization that she is caught between two worlds. She has abandoned the culture of her parents and yet is ultimately excluded from the middle class because of her origins. She reflects on literature as she undergoes the abortion, recognizing that literature has no words to describe her experience. There is "not a single passage to describe what I am feeling now, to help me through my difficult moments." As a woman from the lower classes, she is one of the voiceless.

In this autobiographical novel, Ernaux introduces all the themes that she continues to explore in her subsequent works: a woman's struggle for sexual freedom, the problem of social mobility, the role of literature in society, and the way in which language and education promote social injustice. In her exploration of female social and personal identity, Ernaux's novel reflects fundamental themes of feminist literature (see FEMINISM).

FURTHER READING

McIlvanney, Siobhán. *Annie Ernaux: The Return to Origins.* Liverpool, England: Liverpool University Press, 2001.

Thomas, Lyn. *Annie Ernaux: An Introduction to the Writer and Her Audience.* Oxford, New York: Berg, 1999.

CLELIA (CLÉLIE) MADELEINE DE SCUDÉRY (1645–1660)

Like *ARTAMÈNE OR THE GREAT CYRUS*, this 10-volume serial novel is only nominally set in Roman antiquity. A masterpiece of salon literature, Clelia in fact paints an idealized portrait of *précieuse* society. Its most famous feature is the "Map of the Land of Tenderness" (*Carte du Tendre*). This map of love drawn from a woman's perspective and creating a space in which she has control, explains to the lover what he should and should not do. If he passes through "Pretty Verse" and "Sincerity," he will arrive at "Tenderness-on-Esteem." However, should he travel through "Negligence," he will only end up in "Obliteration." The map is the equivalent of a 17th-century board game. Extraordinarily successful, it immediately spawned a number of imitations.

Modern readers may find it odd that the plot is less important than the description of its action but this reflects the *précieuse* fascination with language. The interest in language arose at a time when the French language was not yet fixed by the Académie Française. The movement away from action toward description also reflects new developments in prose, largely promoted by women authors such as CATHERINE DESJARDINS and MADAME DE LAFAYETTE. The sophisticated language and elaborate word games promoted by the *précieuses* came under attack from a variety of critics, such as the French playwright Molière in his *Précieuses ridicules* (1659), for its affectedness. Nonetheless, conversations in the narrative appear exactly as they might have taken place in Madeleine de Scudéry's salon, where the principle subjects of discussion were love, marriage, and literature.

FURTHER READING

Aronson, Nicole. *Mademoiselle de Scudéry.* Translated by Stuart R. Aronson. Boston: Twayne, 1978.

Davis, Joanne. *Mademoiselle de Scudéry and the Looking Glass.* New York: P. Lang, 1993.

Harth, Erica. *Cartesian Women: Versions and Subversions of Discourse in the Old Regime.* Ithaca, N.Y.: Cornell University Press, 1992.

McDougall, Dorothy. *Mademoiselle de Scudéry, Her Romantic Life and Death.* New York: B. Blom, 1972.

CLIGÉS CHRÉTIEN DE TROYES (1176)

This tale, often called the "anti-Tristan" ROMANCE, tells of the love between Fenice and Cligés. Her love for Cligés is so pure that Fenice has a servant secretly give her husband a magic potion on their wedding day so that he will enjoy her favors only in his dreams. Fenice thus remains a virgin and faithful to her true love. At the same time, Fenice states explicitly that she does not wish to relive with Cligés a painful love affair like that of the mythic Tristan and Iseut. After a series of adventures, typically for Chrétien in the form of single combat, Cligés and Fenice are reunited through a ruse by which she fakes her death. The tale is set at Arthur's court but also draws on Greco-Byzantine legends and reflects contemporary politics. *Cligés* manifests, too, Chrétien's remarkable ability to portray his characters' psychological and emotional states.

FURTHER READING

Frappier, Jean. *Chrétien de Troyes: The Man and His Work,* Translated by Robert J. Cormier. Athens: Ohio University Press, 1982.

Lacy, Norris. *The Craft of Chrétien de Troyes: An Essay on Narrative Art.* Leiden, Netherlands: Brill, 1980.

Leupin, Alexandre. *Le Graal et la Littérature.* Lausanne, Switzerland: L'Age d'Homme, 1982.

Troyes, Chrétien de. *Arthurian Romances.* Translated by William W. Kibler. London: Penguin, 1991.

COCTEAU, JEAN (1889–1963)

Known principally as a cinematographer, Jean Cocteau also expressed his creativity in a variety of forms including novels. Cocteau was born into a wealthy bourgeois family in Paris. His happy childhood was marred by the sudden, unexplained suicide of his father. Nonetheless, he began to develop his poetic skills at a young age, beginning to write poetry as of 1906. His poems were first presented to the public at the Salle Femina on the Champs-Élysées in 1908. From 1909 to 1911, he ran a short-lived literary journal, *Shéhérazade,* with Maurice Rostand.

Cocteau participated in artistic and literary circles with figures such as the painter Picasso, composer Igor Stravinsky, ANDRÉ GIDE, and COLETTE. After 1910, when he met MARCEL PROUST, Sergey Diaghilev, and the Ballet Russe, Cocteau began moving in avant-garde circles in 1911. Long interested in drawing and design, he designed two successful posters for the ballet *Specter of the Rose* and wrote the plot summary for *The Blue God* in which Vaslav Nijinksy danced the principal role.

Inspired by Gide, Cocteau traveled to North Africa. Upon his return to France, he was stunned by Stravinsky's *Rite of Spring.* Cocteau became friends with the composer and, in this innovative and artistic milieu, produced a mixed work *Potomak,* comprised of prose, poems, and drawings. For Cocteau, poetry rises out of a union of the conscious and the unconscious.

In 1913, Cocteau met the famous pilot Roland Garros, who inspired what was to become a prominent theme in Cocteau's works, that of the angel. He subsequently founded and directed yet another short-lived review, *Word,* with the illustrator Paul Iribe. At this point, Cocteau also discovered the works of the German philosopher Friedrich Nietzsche, whom he greatly admired and who remained a significant influence on Cocteau throughout his life.

During World War I, Cocteau served with the Red Cross on the Belgian front. His wartime experience inspired *Thomas the Imposter,* a novel that introduces the theme of death into Cocteau's works. Upon his return to Paris, Cocteau again frequented literary and artistic circles, associating with composer Erik Satie, poets Max Jacob, Guillaume Apollinaire, and Blaise Cendrars, among others. With Picasso and Satie he prepared the ballet *Parade* in Rome for which Cocteau wrote the book and Satie the music. In Paris, too, Cocteau continued to work with the Ballet Russe. A performance in 1917 met with resistance from the public cause for what Apollinaire would describe as its SURREALISM.

Cocteau then moved beyond the ballet to musical circles, becoming the spokesperson for a group of young musicians, the group of six, which included Georges Auric, Louis Durey, Arthur Honneger, Darious Milhaud, Francis Poulenc, and Germaine Tailleferre. Ever blending diverse art forms, Cocteau began to experiment with theatrical poetry in an approach that shares principles with cubist painting.

In 1919, Cocteau met his companion RAYMOND RADIGUET. Together the two authors wrote and traveled. Under Radiguet's influence, Cocteau turned away from the avant-garde as his subsequent works on aesthetics indicate (*The Professional Secret* and *Vocabulary,* 1922). At the same time, he continued to write poetry and for the theater. Radiguet's death in 1923 came as a tremendous blow, driving Cocteau first to opium and then a return to Catholicism. Nonetheless, he remained productive, writing, acting, and playing the role of Mercutio in his adaptation of *Romeo and Juliette.*

From 1924 to 1929, Cocteau spent long periods at the seaside, where he brought together his works of criticism in *Call to Order.* At Christmas in 1926, he met the young writer Jean Desbordes. Cocteau's support for Desbordes's novel *I Adore* as well as his own *White Book,* in which he explicitly addresses the question of homosexuality, particularly shocked French Roman Catholics. Cocteau's *Letter to Jacques Maritain* marks Cocteau's break with Catholicism.

By 1929, Cocteau was again treated for opium abuse. He wrote an essay on the advantages and disadvantages of drug use in *Opium,* followed by a novel, *The HOLY TERRORS,* about the ill-fated consequences of holding onto an imaginary paradise.

In 1932, the year in which his first film, *The Blood of a Poet,* was released, Cocteau began an affair with Princess Nathalie Paley, the niece of Russian czar Alexander III. Cocteau once articulated his views on bisexuality: "A normal man, from the point of view of sexuality, ought to be capable of making love with anyone or anything. Vice begins with the choice."

From 1930 onward, Cocteau's work in theater and film became increasingly important. In 1947 he met the painter Édouard Dermif, whom he accepted as his adoptive son and heir and, in 1950, Francine Weisweiller, who became his mistress. The three traveled widely together. Their experiences inspired Cocteau's subsequent writing. After World War II, Cocteau's career as a filmmaker took off. He was chosen to be president of the Cannes Film Festival in 1955 and was elected to the Académie Française.

Cocteau's principal novels are *Thomas the Impossible* and *The Holy Terrors.* He found inspiration in a wide range of literature from Sophocles to Stendhal to legends of the Holy Grail. He characterized his own work as poetry, whether referring to a novel or a film.

Cocteau's written works are supplemented by a significant body of artistic work that includes murals, paintings, tapestries, and stained-glass window designs. He gathered together a broad array of themes and ideas in his last great work, *Requiem.* Cocteau died following a heart attack in 1963.

Contemporaries criticized Cocteau's work for being too diverse, yet this is its most remarkable quality, along with his uncanny ability to evoke the dark part of ourselves where a mystical light shines nevertheless.

FURTHER READING

Brown, Frederick. *An Impersonation of Angels: A Biography of Jean Cocteau.* Harlow, England: Longmans, 1969.

Tsakiridou, Cornelia A., ed. *Reviewing Orpheus: Essays on the Cinema and Art of Jean Cocteau.* Lewisburg, Pa.: Bucknell University Press, 1997.

COLETTE (GABRIELLE-SIDONIE COLETTE) (1873–1954)

Colette grew up in the French countryside in a household where her father encouraged her to read while her mother, Sido, shared with Colette her love of nature. Colette's first husband, in turn, encouraged her to write. Colette subsequently developed her own unique voice, explicitly sensual and erotic, distinct from contemporary trends in literature.

As Colette grew, she dreamed of love and escape from village life. It came to her suddenly in the form of Henri Gauthier-Villars, or Willy, as he was called. Willy had an illegitimate child by a married woman who died in 1891. The child, Jacques, was sent to live with the Colette family. Colette, already anxious for life to begin, was attracted to Willy, an ambitious Parisian. They married in 1893, and Willy introduced Colette to the bohemian life of Paris. The following year, Colette made the painful discovery that Willy had a mistress. To her own detriment, Colette accepted the situation. Depressed, she decided to join him in his own game. Colette, Willy, and Georgie Raoul-Duval left for the music festival in Beyreuth, Germany, in 1901 as a ménage-à-trois. Colette had become, in her own words, Willy's slave, an experience she evokes in the Claudine series. In 1906 Colette began an affair with Mathilde de Morny, or Missie, who helped her to finally disengage from Willy. Willy profited as long as possible from Colette's success and finally left, with another woman, in 1906. The couple divorced in 1910.

Colette made famous the village of her birth by evoking a lost paradise of childhood. The four novels that make up the Claudine series are *CLAUDINE AT SCHOOL, CLAUDINE IN PARIS, Claudine Married* (1902), and *Claudine and Annie* (1903). The last novel appeared during the period when Colette had separated from Willy. The first three novels in the Claudine cycle were signed with the name of this man who sought notoriety, although Colette was the true author.

When Colette divorced Willy she began working as a mime in a music hall, where her experience with the motley crowd she found there inspired subsequent novels. Colette later turned to journalism. She was a nonconformist and a feminist before her time who discovered herself in the process of writing, along with her freedom and her genius.

Having inherited her mother's love of nature, Colette had a singular ability for depicting the beauty of the landscape, be it Burgundy or Provence, with a rich vocabulary that arouses the senses in passages of pure poetry. Above all, Colette was able to resurrect the links between nature and childhood, the marvel of discovery and joy that a child finds in nature. She was equally capable of evoking the connection between a love affair and the season in which it was born, or died. In sum, all her life Colette remained extraordinarily sensitive to what one feels in relation to one's environment.

Despite her nostalgic evocations, Colette's childhood was not always easy. Her mother married twice. With the first husband, Jules Robineau-Duclos, she had a son and a daughter, Achille and Juliette, to whom Sido was passionately attached. With her second husband, Jules Colette, a former military officer who lost a leg in 1859, she had two more children, Gabrielle-Sidonie (Colette) and Léo.

When Colette's sister, Juliette, married in 1885 she demanded her inheritance. This necessitated the family's moving from their home in Saint-Sauveur to Châtillon-Coligny, where Achille was living. The move was extremely painful for Colette and her brother Léo, who never quite recovered from it. Their sister hanged herself after receiving communion in 1908.

In *My Mother's House,* Colette carefully works through her memories of childhood, particularly in relation to her mother, who was to remain an important character in Colette's subsequent writings. Colette once wrote, "If a child could tell the story of his childhood while going through it, the tale would perhaps consist only of intimate dramas and deceptions but he does not write until adulthood. Nonetheless he believes he has kept intact the memories of childhood. I am skeptical of my own." Still, she believed that all our sentiments are rooted in childhood and in a complex mixture of memory and imagination.

In *Sido* (1930), Colette recalls her childhood as a time of freedom, desire, and discovery. Central to the narrative is her mother, who reigns over the garden where she shares with Colette her bond with nature. Moreover, Colette seeks to understand the nature of her mother, whose relationship to life and to her husband seems to embody the concept of love. Colette evokes the power of her mother's scent, making Sido the epitome of femininity, the essence of womanhood.

Colette's language and her exploration of herself in relation to her mother explain her interest to contemporary feminist writers.

Colette began her career in journalism in 1910, writing for *Le Matin.* As of 1911 she was producing a story a week in a column called "The Tales of a Thousand and One Mornings," or, as of 1913, "Colette's Journal." She married one of the newspaper's editors, Henry de Jouvenal, in 1912. Shortly thereafter she gave birth to a daughter, Colette, nicknamed Bel-Gazou. A baroness as of her marriage, Colette began to write of her experience in the music hall, the central themes of which are love and grief. Henry was handsome, seductive, and like Willy, unfaithful. Theirs was a turbulent relationship.

The difficulties of World War I, her husband's seductive nature, and his success as a diplomat all contributed to the breakup of Colette's second marriage. As she and Henry grew increasingly apart, Colette undertook the "sentimental education" of his son, Bertrand, from an earlier marriage. By 1925 the couple had divorced and Colette broke with Bertrand as well.

The twenties were the years of Colette's glory. Famous for her novels and her writings on war and society such as *Long Hours* (1917), *Children in the Ruins* (1917), *In the Crowd* (1918), and *The Lighted Room* (1918), Colette was made a cavalier of the Legion of Honor in 1928. Other honors include election to the Belgian Royal Academy of French Language and Literature, presidency of the Académie Goncourt, and the Grand Medal of the City of Paris.

In 1926 Colette took up acting again in adaptations of *Chéri* and *The Vagabond.* She also wrote theater critiques, scenarios, and dialogues. In 1932, she even briefly opened a cosmetics boutique. She traveled widely, in North Africa, Spain, Germany, Austria, Romania, and New York.

The outbreak of World War II as well as health problems that eventually reduced her to life in a wheelchair put an end to her journeys. In 1935, however, she happily married Maurice Gondeket. A Jew, Gondeket was imprisoned during the winter of 1941–42. It is likely that Colette's fame earned his release. Gondeket subsequently hid in the unoccupied Free Zone until 1944. Through all of this, Colette continued to be astoundingly prolific, producing *The End of Chéri* (1926), *Break of Day* (1928), *The Other Woman* (1929), *The Cat* (1933), *Duo* (1934), *Bella Vista* (1937), *Toutounier* (1939), *Hotel Room* (1940), *Julie de Carneilhan* (1941), *Képi* (1943), and *Gigi* (1944).

At the same time, Colette also wrote essays in the tradition of Montaigne—a mixture of memories, reflections, anecdotes, and short stories in *These Pleasures* (1932), *The Pure and the Impure* (1941), *Looking Backwards* (1941), *Nudity* (1943), *Paris from my Window* and *Three . . . Six . . . Nine* (1944), *Beautiful Seasons* (1945), *Evening Star* (1946), *Intermittent Journal* (1949), *Blue Lantern* (1949), and *Familiar Territory* (1949). In Colette's words, these were "neither memoirs nor a journal. My reader must resign himself: a lamp for day or night, blue between two red curtains tightly stuck to the window like a butterfly that falls asleep on a summer morning, my beacon does not light up things of a size to astonish."

The many aspects of love were Colette's preferred themes: one's first sensual experience, jealousy, homosexuality, disenchantment, a broken heart, and satisfaction. Colette was one of the first women writers to explore themes of love, sensuality, and sexuality with complete freedom. She has thus been recognized by contemporary French feminist writers as laying the foundation for women's writing (see FEMINISM). Her open eroticism is astounding and powerful, particularly as it is combined with her sensitivity to the details of emotion and sensation. If Colette was able to write in this way, it is because she plumbed the depths of her own sensual experience and suffering. Colette knew fame, fortune, and beauty. She had many lovers. As she grew older, her vision continually expanded to absorb the changes in life and the new pleasures they afforded.

Colette once explained that writing was not a calling; rather for her it was a necessity, to earn her living and to gain her independence. In the process of writing, she also gained a sense of herself as a woman and as a writer. She was sympathetic to all forms of passion, offering no lessons in morality, no set of values, simply an acceptance of nature and life as it is and a commitment to authenticity. In any case, she was unforgettable. In the playwright Jean Anouilh's words, "You are not at all a decent woman Madame Colette. You are proud shamelessness, wise pleasure, insolent freedom, the type of girl who is the ruin of the most sacred institutions and of families."

FURTHER READING

Best, Victoria. *Critical Subjectivities: Identity and Narrative in the Work of Colette and Marguerite Duras.* Oxford, New York: Peter Lang, 2000.

Corbin, Laurie. *The Mother Image: Self-Representation and the Mother-Daughter Relation in Colette, Simone de Beauvoir, and Marguerite Duras.* New York: Peter Lang, 1996.

Dormann, Geneviève. *Colette: A Passion for Life.* Translated by David Macey and Jane Brenton. New York: Abbeville Press, 1985.

Eisinger, Erica Mendelson, and Mari War McCarty. *Colette: The Woman, the Writer.* University Park: Pennsylvania State University Press, 1981.

Flieger, Jerry Aline. *Colette and the Fantom Subject of Autobiography.* Ithaca, N.Y.: Cornell University Press, 1992.

Francis, Claude, and Fernande Gontier. *A Charmed World: Colette, Her Life and Times.* New York: St. Martin's Press, 1993.

Goudeket, Maurice. *Close to Colette; An Intimate Portrait of a Woman of Genius.* Westport, Conn.: Greenwood Press, 1972; 1957.

Huffer, Lynn. *Another Colette: The Question of Gendered Writing.* Ann Arbor: University of Michigan Press, 1992.

Kristeva, Julia. *Colette.* New York: Columbia University Press, 2004.

Ladimer, Bethany. *Colette, Beauvoir, and Duras: Age and Women Writers.* Gainesville: University Press of Florida, 1999.

Lottman, Herbert. *Colette: A Life.* Boston: Little, Brown, 1991.

Marks, Elaine. *Colette.* Westport, Conn.: Greenwood Press, 1981; 1960.

Mitchell, Yvonne. *Colette: A Taste for Life.* New York: Harcourt Brace Jovanovich, 1977; 1975.

Peebles, Catherine. *The Psyche of Feminism: Sand, Colette, Sarraute.* West Lafayette, Ind.: Purdue University Press, 2003.

Sarde, Michèle. *Colette: Free and Fettered.* Translated by Richard Miller. New York: Morrow: 1980.

Stewart, Joan Hinde. *Colette.* Boston: Twayne, 1983.

Thurman, Judith. *Secrets of the Flesh: A Life of Colette.* New York: Knopf, 1999.

COMICAL ROMANCE, THE PAUL SCARRON (1651–1657)

The *Comical Romance* is Paul Scarron's most famous work. This parody recounts the adventures of a group of itinerant actors, their lives and loves, as they travel from village to village in provincial France. Scarron does not hesitate to parody the manners and morals of the *"menu peuple"* or common people. Numerous secondary BURLESQUE and gallant stories, drawing on the Spanish picaresque tradition, are interspersed throughout the main narrative.

Actors with names such as Destiny and Star meet up with a wide variety of characters: a hack writer named Ragotin, grooms and innkeepers, and a ridiculous provincial buffoon who tries to ape sophisticated Parisian wit. Scarron's style, and the burlesque in general, is full of contrasts, notably between comedy and realism.

The 19th-century novelist THÉOPHILE GAUTIER drew from Scarron's *Comical Romance* for his *CAPTAIN FRACASSE* (1863). Gautier aptly praised Scarron's style as "an excellent prose, full of frankness and allure, of irresistible gaiety . . . while tending toward the comedic, there is still a certain tender grace and poetry in his descriptions of love." Certainly, Scarron's contemporaries would have agreed with this assessment.

FURTHER READING
Armas, Frederick A. de. *Paul Scarron.* New York: Twayne, 1972.
Phelps, Naomi Forsythe. *The Queen's Invalid; A Biography of Paul Scarron.* Baltimore: Johns Hopkins University Press, 1951.

COMMUNISTS, THE LOUIS ARAGON (1949)

In this vast panorama of six volumes, Aragon traces the history of France in a particularly dramatic period that Aragon described as "convulsive and apocalyptic." The work begins with the Nazi-Soviet pact of 1939 and ends with the French defeat by Nazi Germany in 1940. Aragon celebrates the heroism of the Communist Party in France, in his opinion, the only force capable of defending liberty and the nation during the German Occupation. This work serves as a historical document in its realistic depiction of the different forces at play in French society during this turbulent period.

With a remarkable attention to detail, Aragon evokes heroes and traitors, exemplary resistance fighters and hesitant and timorous intellectuals Joseph Gigois appears at first glance to be a secondary character, whereas he conveys the essential message of this work

about the beauty of hope and will. The love between Cécile Wisner and Jean de Moncey expresses Aragon's famous idea that "woman is the future of man."

The multiple layers of the novel's construction reflect Aragon's past adherence to SURREALISM and its continued influence on his vision of the world. In fact, there is no sharp division between Aragon's surrealist period and the *Real World* cycle of novels, in which *The Communists* holds an important place. Aragon continued to use the collage technique associated with surrealism, including, for example, portions of historical documents incorporated into the narrative while retaining a poetic sensibility.

A convinced communist, Aragon experienced a crisis of conscience following Stalin's death in 1955, leading him to rewrite this novel in 1966. The later version reflects shifts in Aragon's ideology and style and includes a sharp critique of Stalinism. Some critics have noted Aragon's ability to blend fiction and reality in a way that leads to some ultimate truth.

FURTHER READING
Adereth, Maxwell. *Elsa Triolet and Louis Aragon: An Introduction to Their Interwoven Lives and Works.* Lewiston, N.Y.: E. Mellen Press, 1994.
Brosman, Catherine Savage. *Malraux, Sartre and Aragon as Political Novelists.* Gainesville: University of Florida Press, 1964.
Caute, David. *Communism and the French Intellectuals, 1914–1960.* New York: Macmillan, 1964.
Duruzoi, Gerard. *History of the Surrealist Movement.* Translated by Alison Anderson. Chicago: University of Chicago Press, 2002.
Kimyongur, Angela. *Socialist Realism in Louis Aragon's Le Monde Réel Series.* Hull, England: University of Hull Press, 1995.

CONDÉ, MARYSE (1937–)

Novelist, playwright, and essayist, Maryse Condé was born in Guadeloupe. She left for Paris in 1953, where she studied at the Sorbonne. In 1961, Condé married an actor from Guinea. She then taught for 12 years in Ghana. Forced to leave Africa for dissident activities, Condé returned to Paris, where she subsequently worked as a journalist.

Condé's first novel, *Heremakhonon,* was published in 1976 and appeared again in a revised edition under the title *Waiting for Happiness* in 1988 although it was not particularly well received. *Children of Ségu* (1984), in contrast, was an instant success. This novel consists of two volumes that tell the story of the royal family of Mali from the 18th to the middle of the 19th century. In this work, Condé blends history and fiction. The city of Ségou in Mali, is central to this narrative tracing the history of Africa through the experience of one kingdom. At the end of the 18th century, Ségu is a powerful warrior kingdom. However, over the course of time, it falls into decline, victim of internal divisions, the imposition of Islamic law, the slave trade, and later the introduction of Christianity and French culture. At the same time, Condé traces the parallel decline of a once powerful family, the Traore. Despite the violence and suffering that marks the African experience, Condé offers a sense of optimism, particularly in the image of women who bear within themselves both hope and life itself.

Condé has written some 10 novels and has become one of the most internationally renowned francophone writers of the 20th century. Other novels include *Season in Rihata* (1981), *Tree of Life* (1987), and *Colony of the New World* (1993). During her writing career, Condé has developed her own particular style. At the heart of all her works is the question of identity as is evident in *I, Tituba, Black Witch of Salem* (1986) and *The Last of the African Kings* (1992). Her characters are usually of Caribbean or African-American origin. The Caribbean world is the setting for CROSSING THE MANGROVE (1989) and *Windward Heights* (1995). The themes of exile and alienation are also central to Condé's works. Mother/child relationships are often traumatic, broken by absence and death. The search for one's mother is thus symbolic of exile.

Condé divides her time between New York and Guadeloupe. In speaking of her own life experience Condé sees wandering and self-imposed exile as a source of renewal. In consequence, she has come to define herself outside the constraints of race, nation, language, or class, all limitations that Condé fundamentally rejects. She argues strongly against an obsession with the past. Thus, in contrast to a number of other francophone writers of her generation, Condé is disillusioned by the myth of "mother Africa." Consequently, her writing stands in opposition to works associated with NEGRITUDE.

FURTHER READING

Alexander, Simone A. James. *Mother Imagery in the Novels of Afro-Caribbean Women*. Columbia: University of Missouri Press, 2001.

Krüs, Patricia. *Claiming Masculinity as Her Own: Cultural Identity and Caribbean Women's Writing*. Leiden, Netherlands: Universiteit Leiden, 2001.

Suk, Jeannie. *Postcolonial Paradoxes in French Caribbean Writing: Césaire, Glissant, Condé*. Oxford: Clarendon, 2001.

CONFESSIONS OF A CHILD OF THE CENTURY, THE (*LA CONFESSION D'UN ENFANT DU SIÈCLE*) ALFRED DE MUSSET (1836)

In the opening section of this autobiographical novel, Musset describes the "malady of the century," a disease he suffers along with his entire generation. Following the glory of the French Revolution and the Napoleonic Empire, Musset's generation felt deceived, overcome by a sense of purposelessness. Octave, the principal character of the novel, symbolizes this generation.

The novel is divided into five parts. In the first part, nineteen-year-old Octave is in despair, having discovered that his mistress has betrayed him. Desgenais, Octave's cynical friend, tries to tempt him into a life of pleasure, suggesting that Octave give up on his illusions of love. At first, Octave is unable to follow Desgenais's advice. He waits at night outside his lover's window, obsessed and sad, and he drinks. When he discovers that his former mistress has also betrayed her subsequent lover, Octave finally gives in to cynicism and depravity, only to discover that a life of pleasure is not satisfying.

When his father dies, Octave leaves Paris and returns to the country to live the quiet and simple life of his father. For a time he is indeed tranquil, until meeting a young widow, Brigitte Pierson. At first, she tries to keep distance between them, realizing that Octave has feelings for her. Ultimately, passion dominates reason and the couple declare their love for each other. For a while they are happy but Octave becomes increasingly and unreasonably jealous and suspicious. It is as if he cannot separate Brigitte from the women he has known in the past. His behavior gradually breaks down their relationship, leading to painful scenes between them. At last they decide to leave for Paris.

In the final part of the novel the appearance of Brigitte's childhood friend, Henri Smith, leads to the couple's separation. Henri is clearly in love with Brigitte and this incites Octave's already jealous nature. At one point he poises a knife above Brigitte as she lies sleeping. Octave later discovers a letter in which Brigitte refuses Henri, although she loves him, out of a sense of loyalty to Octave. Finally, he lets her go, saying that at least only one of the three then will suffer.

Musset was 26 when he published his *Confessions,* just three years after meeting and parting with his former lover, GEORGE SAND. *Confessions* tells the story of their affair from Musset's point of view and reflects his willingness to share a burden of responsibility for the death of their love. After Musset's death, Sand also wrote of their affair in *Her and Him.* (Musset's brother then responded with *Him and Her.*) Influenced by the confessions of St. Augustine, CHATEAUBRIAND'S *RENÉ,* and BENJAMIN CONSTANT'S *ADOLPHE,* Musset's novel reveals the author's complicated character, one that is simultaneously pathetic, sarcastic, and yet seductive as he performs the autopsy of his affair with Sand. It is a story of obsession, jealousy, and sexual possession, themes that inspired Diane Kuys's 1999 film, *Enfants du siècle (Children of the Century).*

In a broader context, Musset explores "the death of feeling" experienced by his generation. Musset's suffering compels him to speak out, but there is no sense of hope; rather, his vision of the future is marked by the self-annihilation that he, in fact, experienced.

FURTHER READING

Hofstadter, Dan. *The Love Affair as a Work of Art.* New York: Farrar, Straus and Giroux, 1996.

Levin, Susan M. *The Romantic Art of Confession.* Columbia, S.C.: Camden House, 1998.

Majewski, Henry. *Paradigm and Parody: Images of Creativity in French Romanticism.* Charlottesville: University Press of Virginia, 1989.

Sedgwick, Henry Dwight. *Alfred de Musset, 1810–1857.* Port Washington, N.Y.: Kennikat Press, 1973.

CONFESSIONS OF COUNT ***, THE (LES CONFESSIONS DE COMTE DE ***) CHARLES PINOT DUCLOS (1741)

One of the most popular LIBERTINE NOVELS published in France between 1741 and 1760, *The Confessions of Count **** went through more than 25 editions before the end of the century. The story unfolds as an older relative, narrating in the first person, offers the moral lesson of his own experience to a younger relative caught up in the turbulence of worldly social life. The first part of the novel consists of a series of amorous episodes in the young count's life. In the second part, the count falls in love with a good woman who eventually draws him away from his dissolute life.

There are parallels in the novel to CRÉBILLON'S WAYWARD HEAD AND HEART. In fact, MONTESQUIEU wrongly attributed *The Confessions* to Crébillon. Both novels are set during the regency that followed the death of Louis XIV. Both begin with a young man's entry into society and his apprenticeship in the ways of love and libertinism under the tutelage of an older woman. Finally, the main character retreats from the world to seek happiness in a more stable life.

If Duclos and Crébillon deal with many of the same themes, their writing style differs. While Crébillon carefully explores the psychology of the individual, Duclos seems to march ahead, offering a series of intrigues with no real connection between them. The first part of the novel lacks the sense of development found in Crébillon. At the same time, one could argue that his many love affairs accentuates the count's conclusion that mondaine pleasure is, in the end, a deception. Lovers take up with another and leave each other for little reason. Human relations count for nothing. Even sexual relations are not really erotic encounters. In this way Duclos reveals himself to be a moralist. His sociological approach to the count's adventures unmasks the hypocrisy of social life among the nobility, the financial and judicial families, and the bourgeoisie.

The second part of the novel, with the story of Madame de Selve, differs from the first as the count begins to reflect on himself and his way of life. His transformation takes place in three stages. He sees his friend Senecé destroyed by passion for an immoral woman. He then meets an innocent young woman named Julie, whom he decides to help solely for the sake of doing good, arriving at a Rousseauian conclusion that "there must exist in the heart a particular sense that is superior to all others" (see ROUSSEAU). Finally, he meets Madame de Selve, with whom he eventually discovers true pleasure "with his wife who is his friend."

Duclos ends the novel with the successful domination of reason over passion. Unlike NERCIAT, he was unable to promote pure hedonism. Rather Duclos seems to argue for social reform. For Duclos, redemption may ultimately be found in bourgeois values and in the intimacy of daily life.

FURTHER READING

Free, L. R. *Virtue, Happiness and Duclos' "Histoire de Madame de Luz."* The Hague: Martinus Nijhoff, 1974.

Meister, Paul. *Charles Duclos, 1704–1772.* Geneva, Switzerland: Droz, 1956.

Silverblatt, Bette Gross. *Maxims in the Novels of Duclos.* The Hague: Martinus Nijhoff, 1972.

Thompsett, E. "Love and Libertinism in the Novels of Duclos," *SVEC,* 137, 1975.

CONFIANT, RAPHAEL (1951–)

Born in Martinique, Confiant writes novels that celebrate Creole language and literature as in *Bitake-A* (1985), *Mamzelle Dragonfly* (1987), and his very successful *The Negro and the Admiral* (1988), set in Fort-de-France in the 1940s. He also produced *Eau-de-café* (1991), *Alley of Sighs* (1994), *Gouverneur des dés* (1995), and *La Vierge du Grand Retour* (1996); these works have not been translated into English. Confiant has also written an autobiographical work entitled *Ravines du devant-jour* (1993) and several works on Creole language and literature.

Confiant's novels are full of humor as they evoke daily life in Martinique among all levels of society. A number of his works spill over with characters too numerous to identify as in *Alley of Sighs,* which focuses on a particular meeting place in Fort-de-France during an uprising in 1959.

Confiant blends Creole with invented words and vocabulary drawn from old Norman and Breton dialects. Creative and imaginative, his manner of expression recalls the writing of RABELAIS in its humor and CÉLINE in its use of popular language.

Confiant sees Creole as the foundation for cultural identity in Martinique. It is the product of the intersection of several cultures, European, African, and indigenous. Hence, an underlying theme in his works is difference, something that marks not only society in general but the family as well. Like MARYSE CONDÉ, for Confiant slavery is a point of origin for the cultural hybridization that marks the Antilles. Because he argues for a distinct Creole identity, Confiant rejects defining the people of Martinique as African and is thus opposed to the concept of NEGRITUDE.

A non-Western aesthetic marks Confiant's writings. There is no one dominant narrative voice; rather, many voices join in collective expression. Moreover, his approach to time is nonlinear as overlapping narratives, not always in agreement with one another, recount the same event.

CONQUERORS, THE (LES CONQUÉRANTS) ANDRÉ MALRAUX (1928)

This novel tells the story of a general strike and insurrection in Canton, China, in 1925. The novel is full of heroic characters who are almost allegorical figures; Malraux received criticism for this. Renski, for example, is a Dilettante while Rebecci is a Terrorist. Cheng-Dai is a Moderate. Garine, the character who most reflects Malraux's concern with oppression and human dignity, is the determined and forceful Conqueror.

Malraux's style is almost cinematographic, thereby heightening the dramatic feeling of the novel. Rather than one principal character, a group of characters with varied points of view offer a polyphonic commentary on both historical and philosophical questions. Heavily symbolic, Malraux evokes powerful images to explore the human condition.

This novel marked a turning point in Malraux's career as a writer. It is the first of three novels focusing on social and political questions in the Far East, following Malraux's return to Europe in 1926 from Saigon. *The Conquerors* also offers the first evidence of Malraux's own political engagement. Influenced by Marxism, Malraux promotes revolutionary political action. However, the heroes of this novel are less concerned with the human material or economic condition than with human dignity. At the center of Malraux's exploration of human values is the notion of fraternity, another recurring theme in his works. Whether one considers the culture and civilization of the West or of the East, life is absurd and one must define one's own existence in the face of the world's indifference.

FURTHER READING

Van den Abbeele, Georges. "L'Asie fantome: or Malraux's Inhuman Condition," *MLN* 115, no. 4, French Issue (September 2000): 649–661.

CONSPIRACY, THE (LA CONSPIRATION)

PAUL NIZAN (1938)   In this novel drawn from his experience as a youth, Nizan returns to the question of alienation and isolation, also a theme in his earlier work, *Aden Arabia,* in which Nizan spoke out against the colonial system. With its polyphonic, fragmented narrative, *Conspiracy* offers different points of view that fit together like the pieces of a puzzle to reveal a whole. An important and recurring theme is betrayal.

In this novel, four young men—Rosenthal, Laforgue, Pluvinage, and Bloyé, the son of Antoine Bloyé in Nizan's novel of the same name—start an avant-garde review entitled *Civil War.* Led by Rosenthal, they then decide to start a real revolution, going so far as to secure the emergency plans for the city. They are enthralled with the idea of political action, but, in the end, there is no revolution. Rosenthal commits suicide and Pluvinage joins the police, while Laforgue and Bloyé, still optimistic, continue their militant activism.

Along with ANTOINE BLOYÉ and THE TROJAN HORSE, *Conspiracy* reflects themes that mark all the works of Nizan, as a convinced communist. Nizan's principal concern is with the reality of what takes place in his society and the suffering of the common man in an unjust world.

FURTHER READING

Redfern, W. D. *Paul Nizan: Committed Literature in a Conspiratorial World.* Princeton, N.J.: Princeton University Press, 1972.

Schalk, David L. "Professors as Watchdogs: Paul Nizan's Theory of the Intellectual and Politics," *Journal of the History of Ideas* 34, no. 1 (January–March 1973): 79–96.

Scriven, Michael. *Paul Nizan: Communist Novelist.* New York: St. Martin's Press, 1988.

Suleiman, Susan Rubin. "The Structure of Confrontation: Nizan, Barrès, Malraux," *MLN* 95, no. 4, French Issue (May 1980): 938–967.

Wasson, Richard. "'The True Possession of Time:' Paul Nizan, Marxism and Modernism," *Boundary* 5, no. 2 (Winter 1977): 395–410.

CONSTANT, BENJAMIN (1767–1830)

Benjamin Constant was born in Lausanne, Switzerland, to a French Protestant family that had emigrated in the 17th century. Constant's mother died early, leaving her son in the care of his father, a captain in a Swiss regiment, who turned his education over to a series of tutors, some better than others.

As a child, Constant was precocious. He read avidly but was nervous, impressionable, and unbalanced, despite his extensive learning. Constant retained certain adolescent characteristics into adulthood, in his weakness of character, emotionalism, and tendency toward the melodramatic. Throughout his life Constant carried on a series of love affairs, often with older women of strong yet maternal character. Two important women in his life were also writers, GERMAINE DE STAËL and ISABELLE DE CHARRIÈRE. Along with his weakness for women, Constant had an equal inclination for gambling that caused him difficulty.

In 1798, Constant became a French citizen. After joining the opposition to the Napoleonic Empire in 1802, Constant returned to Switzerland, where he participated in the group led by Germaine de Staël, with whom he had begun an affair in 1794. In the beginning he did not make a favorable impression on the woman who was to play such a tremendous role in his adult life. In the end, however, the couple carried on a turbulent relationship for 17 years. In later years, like his character Adolphe, Constant's only desire was to escape.

In 1815, Constant made a political about-face, deciding to support Napoleon. His efforts were rewarded when Napoleon named Constant a counselor of state during the Hundred Days of Napoleon's return to power in 1815. Constant began to establish a reputation as a politician. In 1824, he became a deputy of Paris in the National Assembly and a leading voice of opposition to the Bourbon Restoration. Constant was an immensely popular political figure, revealed in the public demonstrations of mourning after his death. His contemporaries clearly recognized Constant as a politician. However, he is principally remembered today as the author of an autobiographical novel, *ADOLPHE,* written in 1806 but not published until 1816, in London. Constant never considered it an important work. Neither did the reading public, show overwhelming interest in the novel until the end of the 19th century.

In 1808, Constant secretly married Charlotte von Hardenberg, only informing Madame de Staël two years later. His marriage to Charlotte did not hinder him from other emotional attachments. In 1814 he met and fell passionately in love with Juliette Récamier (CHATEAUBRIAND's longtime companion). She never returned Constant's affection. Throughout his life Constant struggled between a pressing physical need for women and his desire for independence. Similar to Constant's experience with Madame de Staël, Adolphe wishes for independence but is caught in a love affair that no longer affords him pleasure. He wishes to break with his lover, Ellénore, but fears hurting her despite increasing alienation.

An important theme in Constant's life and works is individual liberty, a concept much influenced by the French Revolution. For Constant, the question of liberty was always an ambiguous one. Both he and Adolphe had weak characters. The theme of liberty is also reflected in his other writings, particularly his diaries (*Journeaux intimes*) and in the story of his childhood (*Le Cahier rouge*).

Not unlike CHATEAUBRIAND, Constant bridges the 18th and 19th centuries and their literary worlds of classicism and ROMANTICISM. The anxiety and sense of solitude Adolphe experiences are romantic, while the tone and style of Constant's writing are classical.

FURTHER READING

Call, Michael J. *Back to the Garden: Chateaubriand, Senancour, and Constant.* Saratoga, Calif.: Anma Libri, 1988.

Cruickshank, John. *Benjamin Constant.* New York: Twayne, 1974.

Fontana, Biancamaria. *Benjamin Constant and the Post-revolutionary Mind.* New Haven, Conn.: Yale University Press, 1991.

Heck, Francis S. *Spiritual Isolation in French Literature from Benjamin Constant and Senancour.* Madrid: Dos Continentes, 1971.

Wood, Dennis. *Benjamin Constant: A Biography.* London, New York: Routledge, 1993.

CONSUELO GEORGE SAND (1842) Consuelo is the story of a young Spanish musician who arrives in Venice with her mother. At the age of 10, Consuelo is singing in the streets when Porpora, a real-life Italian composer (1686–1776), discovers her and undertakes to give Consuelo more formal musical training. The theme of music, central to the novel, reflects Sand's frequent concern with the relationship between art and life. Other novels focus on theater (*Castle of the Deserts*), the pictorial arts (*Mosaic Masters*), and dance (*Albine Fiori*).

With Porpora's aid, Consuelo is hired by the Venice Opera. Now 18 years old, she falls in love with another young singer, Anzoletto, who betrays her. Other singers are jealous of her success. Porpora then decides to send Consuelo to Bohemia with money and his recommendation. There Consuelo becomes a singing teacher for the Rudolstadt family.

Sand introduces 18th-century intellectual and mystical movements through the mother of this family, Wanda, who is descended from King Georges Podiebrad, a follower of secret traditions associated with the religious reformers Jan Hus and Jean Ziska. Wanda leads a religious and nationalistic secret society of illuminists called the Invisible Ones. In fact, when Consuelo joins the Rudolstadt family, her employer thinks that she is the reincarnation of one of his ancestors.

In the Rudolstadt household, Consuelo meets Wanda's son, count Albert, who also loves music. Their encounter ultimately leads to a union whereby Consuelo becomes the countess of Rudolstadt. The power of love to overcome social barriers is a frequent theme in Sand's works, perhaps reflecting the experience of her own parents. Sand's father was an aristocrat, her mother the child of a fowler. The discrepancy in her parents' backgrounds may explain, in part, Sand's political engagement in favor of worker and peasant rights. The second part of the novel in particular, "The Countess of Rudolstadt," bears the mark of the Catholic priest Félicité de Lamennais's humanitarian mysticism and the philosopher Pierre Leroux's socialism, two important influences on Sand's thought.

During a trip to Berlin, Consuelo, now countess, comes to understand the strain between the ENLIGHTENMENT rationalism of Frederic II and VOLTAIRE and spiritually oriented thinkers represented by the Invisible Ones. Sand thus depicts certain trends associated with 18th century thought, such as Freemasonry. The novel is marked by an atmosphere of occultism, popular in the 18th century. Sand makes allusions, for example, to the gothic novels of writers like Anne Radcliffe. At the same time, she reveals the fundamental tension between Enlightenment thought and ROMANTICISM, of which she is a proponent. In an approach that echoes ROUSSEAU, Sand argues that happiness and love are the source for moral regeneration.

Under Wanda's guidance, Consuelo is initiated into the secret society. In a surprising turn of the plot, Albert falls ill and is believed to be dead. Consuelo subsequently falls for an Italian named Liverani, for whom she feels exactly the same emotions as Albert once aroused in her. Not understanding how this is possible, Consuelo is torn by inner conflict only to discover that Albert and Liverani are, in fact, the same man. Meanwhile, Consuelo rises quickly in the secret society for she is blessed with "the capacity to combine love and virtue, happiness and duty."

In sum, and in accord with one of Sand's principal themes, Consuelo begins life as a woman oppressed by an unjust world yet manages to overcome all obstacles to join Albert in a life of shared love and fulfillment. In the end, happiness, passion, and love vanquish all obstacles as in a number of Sand's other successful novels such as INDIANA and FRANÇOIS THE WAIF.

FURTHER READING

Crecelius, Kathryn J. *Family Romances: George Sand's Early Novels.* Bloomington: Indiana University Press, 1987.

Glasgow, Janis, ed. *George Sand: Collected Essays.* Troy, N.Y.: Whitston Publishing Company, 1985.

Hofstadter, Dan. *The Love Affair as a Work of Art.* New York: Farrar, Straus and Giroux, 1996.

Naginski, Isabelle Hoog. *George Sand: Writing for her Life.* New Brunswick, N.J.: Rutgers University Press, 1991.

Peebles, Catherine. *The Psyche of Feminism: Sand, Colette, Sarraute.* West Lafayette, Ind.: Purdue University Press, 2003.

Powell, David A. *George Sand.* Boston: Twayne, 1990.

Schor, Naomi. *George Sand and Idealism.* New York: Columbia University Press, 1993.

Walton, Whitney. "Writing the 1848 Revolution: Politics, Gender and Feminism in the Works of French Women of Letters," *French Historical Studies* 18, no 4 (Autumn 1994): 1001–1024.

CONTEMPORARY HISTORY (*HISTOIRE CONTEMPORAINE*), 4 VOLS. ANATOLE FRANCE

This series of four novels tells the story of the academic Monsieur Bergeret who offers his reflections on people and society. In the first volume, *Elm Avenue* (1897), Monsieur Bergeret works as a professor in a provincial university. A skeptic, he observes and comments on the world around him, especially the elite, composed of the archbishop, the two priests Lantaigne and Guitrel, the prefect, the archivist, and a retired general. When he needs to relax, Monsieur Bergeret withdraws to Paillot's bookstore.

Volume two, *The Straw Mannequin* (1898), refers to the figure Madame Bergeret uses for sewing clothes. When she betrays Monsieur Bergeret with one of his own disciples, Monsieur Bergeret, renouncing women forever, leaves her to go live with Monsieur Goubin, to whom he expresses his bitter ruminations on conjugal life. *The Amethyst Ring* (1899) refers to a bishop's ring. In this volume, Lantaigne and Guitrel compete with each other for promotion. In the end, the Machiavellian Guitrel wins out.

When the Dreyfus affair in which a Jewish officer is falsely tried and convicted of treason in 1894 breaks out, Monsieur Bergeret openly supports the officer accused of treason but is alone in his position and thus subject to criticism from society. Bergeret seeks peace in his work and in the company of his dog, Riguet. At his point, Monsieur Bergeret is offered a position at the Sorbonne in Paris. This is where the reader finds him in the last volume, *Monsieur Bergeret in Paris* (1901). Still supporting Dreyfus, Bergeret again comes under attack. Ultimately, his philosophical nature allows Monsieur Bergeret a watchful and ironic perspective on the world that finally affords him some peace.

FURTHER READING

Durant, Will. *Anatole France: The Man and His Work.* Girard, Kansas: Haldeman-Julius, 1925.

Guérard, Albert Léon. *Five Masters of French Romance: Anatole France, Pierre Loti, Paul Bourget, Maurice Barrès, Romain Rolland.* New York: Scribner, 1916.

Jefferson, Alfred Carter. *Anatole France: The Politics of Skepticism.* New Brunswick, N.J.: Rutgers University Press, 1965.

May, James Lewis. *Anatole France: The Man and His Work: An Essay in Critical Biography.* Port Washington, N.Y.: Kennikat Press, 1970.

Tylden-Wright, David. *Anatole France.* New York: Walker, 1967.

CORINNE, OR ITALY (*CORINNE, OU L'ITALIE*) Germaine de Staël (1807)

Like Madame de Staël's earlier novel *Delphine, Corinne* reflects the author's own life and experience as a cosmopolitan intellectual torn between desires of the heart and the mind. The romantic feminism that finds its fullest expression in the works of George Sand finds its roots in Staël's writing that bridges Enlightenment thought with Romanticism. For Staël, women represent true individuality of the heart. Women are victims of society and male weakness, perhaps because of their passionate nature.

In *Corinne,* two young people meet in Rome. Lord Oswald Nelvil is English, in poor health, and suffering because his father died before they could reconcile. Corinne, a well-known Italian poet, has escaped from her family to Rome, where she seeks to live an independent life. As they fall in love, the two explore Italy, its art, literature, philosophy, and life. Oswald wants to marry Corinne, but, upon his return to England, he marries the woman his father had chosen for him. Corinne is devastated and, half-mad, dies of a broken heart.

Exiled from France, Staël traveled in Germany in 1804–05, a journey that led her to pay homage to those countries in *On Germany* and *Corinne.* Like the writings of a number of other prominent European intellectuals with whom she was associated, many of them romantics, Staël's novel fits into the broader context of her aesthetic vision. Oswald, consequently, represents utilitarian (moral, political, or social) art, whereas Corinne is a poetess, an individual whose subjective meditation on beauty is reflective of romanticism as well as Staël's particular view of the role literature plays in society.

In *The Influence of Literature upon Society,* Staël rejects the notion that modern literature should be judged by the standards of antiquity (classicism). Drawing on Montesquieu, Staël believed instead that literature should reflect the political, social, and cultural institutions of the nation that gave it birth. Moreover, Staël draws a distinction between the literatures of northern and southern Europe. By arguing that there is no objective definition of beauty, Staël suggests that the value of art lies in its capacity to reflect culture. As a romantic, she also believes that literature should express feeling. *Corinne,* thus, serves as the practical manifestation of Staël's theoretical work.

Moreover, Staël uses the story of Corinne to explore the relationship between gender and culture. Just as Italy was overrun by foreign armies, so a woman of genius is forced to submit to the patriarchal order, in politics and in personal life. Corinne (read Staël) is celebrated as a great poet in Italy, whereas she would have been rejected in revolutionary France. The overlapping themes of family, politics, and patriarchy are the foundation for this work.

In fact, it turns out that Corinne's and Oswald's families are connected. Corinne is the product of an Anglo-Italian marriage. Oswald's father had known her in England but rejected Corinne as a potential wife for his son because of her artistic nature. Instead he chose her half-sister Lucile, who is far more "English." Torn between passion and duty, the Italian and the English, Corinne understands why Oswald chooses her sister. Sadly, the result is the annihilation of female genius by the patriarchal order.

Staël makes clear the problem for an independent woman. Corinne must die, not because she is a victim of her passion as much as because she has been marginalized by the social order. Readers have traditionally viewed *Corinne* as an autobiographical novel reflecting on the notion that a woman of genius has no place in the world.

FURTHER READING

Christopher-Herold, J. *Mistress to an Age: A Life of Mme de Staël.* New York: Bobbs-Merrill, 1958.

Gutwirth, Madelyn. *Madame de Staël, Novelist: The Emergence of the Artist as a Woman.* Urbana: University of Illinois Press, 1978.

Hess, Carla. *The Other Enlightenment: How French Women Became Modern.* Oxford, Princeton, N.J.: Princeton University Press, 2001.

Hogsett, Charlotte. *The Literary Existence of Germaine de Staël.* Carbondale: Southern Illinois University Press, 1987.

Smith, Bonnie G. "History and Genius: The Narcotic, Erotic, and Baroque Life of Germaine de Staël," *French Historical Studies* 19, no. 4 (Autumn 1996): 1059–1081.

Trouille, Mary Seidman. *Sexual Politics in the Enlightenment.* Albany: State University of New York Press, 1997.

COUNT D'ORGEL'S BALL (*LA BAL DU COMTE D'ORGEL*) RAYMOND RADIGUET (1924)

In this novel, Mahaut, the count d'Orgel, is married to a beautiful young woman named Anne. Together they befriend an idle young man named François de Seryeuse. François and Anne fall for each other but Anne does not wish to betray her husband and so asks Madame de Seryeuse to call her son away. François's mother lets her son know of Anne's request, but, instead of respecting her wishes, he comes to a masked ball held by the count. Worn out emotionally, Anne faints and tries to confess her love for François to her husband, but he will not listen as he is more concerned with keeping up appearances. He pays no attention to Anne's torment. In fact, he chooses the costume that François wears to the ball.

The story is modeled on the 17th-century novel by MADAME DE LAFAYETTE, *The Princess of Clèves*, in which a virtuous young woman confesses to her husband that she loves another man. Taking this dramatic step seems the only way to preserve her honor, fearing as she does that she will give in to her passion. For the characters of Anne and Mahaut, Radiguet also drew from two of his friends, Edith and Étienne de Baeumont. The novel contains other unusual or eccentric characters such as the exiled Russian prince Naroumof, Hortense d'Austerlitz, Mirza the Persian, and his wealthy and seductive American niece, Hester Wayne.

Radiguet's subtle psychological analysis recalls the writing of MARCEL PROUST and lays the foundation for the future *NOUVEAU ROMAN*, as an omniscient narrator offers varied interpretations of the characters' reactions and emotions. The character thus becomes an object of literary discourse.

FURTHER READING

Crosland, Margaret. *Raymond Radiguet: A Biographical Study with Selections from his Work.* London: Owen, 1976.

McNab, James P. *Raymond Radiguet.* Boston: Twayne, 1984.

COUNTERFEITERS, THE (*LES FAUX MONNAYEURS*) ANDRÉ GIDE (1926)

Bernard Profitendieu discovers a love letter written to his mother revealing that he is not, in fact, the son of the old judge Profitendieu. Strangely liberated by this news, Bernard leaves a note explaining his departure from his parents' home. From that point on a series of overlapping adventures take place involving Bernard and his two friends, Olivier and Vincent, sons of the magistrate Molinier, who is a colleague of judge Profitendieu.

The two boys' uncle, Édouard, plays a central role in the novel. Bernard is anxious to meet this novelist, who is particularly close to Oscar despite the ambiguous nature of their relationship. By chance, Bernard finds Édouard's baggage claim ticket at the train station and steals his suitcase. Inside he finds Édouard's journal, which reveals that Édouard is writing a novel called *The Counterfeiters*. Bernard also finds a desperate letter from Édouard's former lover, Laura, who is pregnant by Vincent and living in penury away from her husband. The appearance and reappearance of the baggage claim ticket is an example of Gide's *"mise en abyme"* technique, whereby he reproduces themes and patterns on more than one level in the text in order to explore the question of fate.

The novel Édouard is writing becomes the subject of *Gide's* novel when Édouard meets Madame Sophroniska, who questions him closely on the subject. This reflection on the novel takes place as the broader narrative continues. Madame Sophroniska is a psychiatrist who is treating Boris, the young man whom Édouard is searching for, as he is the grandson of Édouard's friend the old pianist La Pérouse. Boris returns with Édouard to the school where his grandfather is teaching. There, to gain acceptance into a group of rough boys, Boris agrees to pretend to commit suicide in his grandfather's class, but the gun is loaded and Boris needlessly dies. These boys are the counterfeiters of the novel's title. Bernard, in the end, returns to his father's house. He had been working as Édouard's secretary until the latter gives up on his novel.

The Counterfeiters is a novel about adolescence. Like Gide's other works, such as *LAFCADIO'S ADVENTURES,* it consists of a series of overlapping, interconnected subplots. On one level, is Olivier's and Bernard's discovery of love, Olivier for his uncle, and Bernard for Édouard's former lover, Laura (pregnant and abandoned by Vincent) and then her sister, Sarah. Vincent ends up mad and in misery after murdering his subsequent lover, Lilian. On another level, *The Counterfeiters* is a novel of apprenticeship, as Olivier and Bernard acquire experience in the world through the two older men who are both writers, Édouard and Olivier's mentor, the repellant Passevant. Finally, there is the darker subplot involving the counterfeiters Georges and Strouvilhou, who drive Boris to his death. The fact that Édouard is writing a novel called *The Counterfeiters* compels the reader to ask just who the real counterfeiters are, the two boys or the two writers?

Gide said that this novel offers a synthesis of his life and thought. Certain autobiographical elements are present, as in Édouard's homosexuality. There are also recurring themes found in Gide's oeuvre, such as a philosophical reflection on adolescence as a force of life.

The Counterfeiters also must be examined within the context of a generation of writers who experimented with new narrative forms, laying the foundation for the NOUVEAU ROMAN. The concept of the novel within a novel allows Gide to theorize on the nature of this genre and to test his own innovative ideas. As Édouard writes his novel within a novel of the same name, he also reveals that his greatest failing is his inability to grasp reality. *The Counterfeiters* reflects a general loss of faith in the capacity of literature to depict reality. In *NAUSEA*, for example, SARTRE's principal character states that one must choose either "to live or to tell" (*vivre ou raconter*). SAMUEL BECKETT's characters, too, struggle with simultaneous failure and necessity of language. Hence the modern novel, for Gide and for others, increasingly focused on the act of writing itself and on the relationship between language and life.

FURTHER READING

Bettinson, Christopher D. *Gide: A Study*. London: Heinemann; Totowa, N.J.: Rowman and Littlefield, 1977.

O'Brien, Justin. *Portrait of André Gide: A Critical Biography*. New York: Octagon Books, 1977; 1953.

O'Keefe, Charles. *Void and Voice: Questioning Narrative Conventions in André Gide's Major First-Person Narratives*. Chapel Hill: Department of Romance Languages, University of North Carolina, 1996.

Salz, Lily. "André Gide and the Problem of Engagement," *French Review* 30, no. 2 (December 1956): 131–137.

Sheridan, Alan. *André Gide: A Life in the Present*. Cambridge, Mass.: Harvard University Press, 1999.

Stoltzfus, Ben. "André Gide and the Voices of Rebellion," *Contemporary Literature* 19, no. 1 (Winter 1978): 80–98.

Walker, David, ed. *André Gide*. London, New York: Longman, 1996.

COUNT OF MONTE CRISTO, THE (LE COMTE DE MONTE CRISTO) ALEXANDRE DUMAS (1848)

This serial novel first published in the *Journal des Débats* is arguably Dumas's most famous work, competing successfully with EUGÈNE SUE's *MYSTERIES OF PARIS*. When this extraordinary adventure story was published, Dumas was principally known by his contemporaries as an innovator in the theater, the first to introduce romantic drama to the French stage (see ROMANTICISM). With *The Count of Monte Cristo*, Dumas's great gift as a dramatist is turned to fiction.

The Count of Monte Cristo is a dramatic story of revenge inspired by an anecdote from the *Memoirs of the Police Archives* in Paris published in 1838 by Jacques Peuchet. According to one police file, a young shoemaker from Nîmes was engaged to a wealthy orphan in 1807. Four jealous friends caused him to be falsely imprisoned as a spy. He was not released until 1814. While incarcerated, an Italian priest told him of a lost treasure. Upon his release, the young man made use of the treasure and various disguises to wreak vengeance on those who had betrayed him, just as Dumas's count would do.

In the prologue to the novel, Dumas himself and a friend, Albert de Morcerf, meet a stranger in 1838 in Rome during carnival. Dumas recognizes the count of Monte Cristo as the mysterious man who welcomed him and Napoleon on the island of Monte Cristo, previously thought to be deserted. There is, in fact, a small island east of Elba named Montecristo that Dumas once saw from a distance.

In Rome, the count is an extravagant and generous host to the two young men. Moreover, he saves Albert, who has been kidnapped by bandits. In return, Albert offers to introduce the count to Parisian society. This allows the count to carry out his plans for revenge against those who had betrayed him as a young man.

The novel is divided into three basic parts, each centered on a separate city. The sections have their own internal narrative unity, but only together do they complete the story of the count's life. The first portion begins in Marseille, the city where Edmond Dantès lived with his aging father. On the eve of his marriage to the lovely Mercedes, Edmond is betrayed by his friends and condemned to life as a state prisoner in the terrible Château d'If for unwittingly passing on a compromising letter revealing the exiled Napoleon's plans to return to France. While he is gone, Edmond's beloved father dies in penury, waiting for his son's return.

In prison, Edmond meets a fellow prisoner with whom he converses, at first, through a wall. The Abbé Faria tells Edmond of a fabulous treasure buried on the island of Monte Cristo. Sadly, it is only the abbé's death that allows Edmond his spectacular escape. Edmond replaces his friend's corpse and is thrown from the walls of the château. With his knife he rips open the bag and swims to safety. This first part of the novel ends with Morrel's just recompense for fidelity, for the count rewards virtue with the same vigor that he punishes deceit.

The second part of the novel begins in Rome 10 years later. Having found Faria's treasure, Edmond has refashioned himself into the count of Monte Cristo. Manipulating the two young men, the count finds his entrée back into Paris. He stops first in Marseille, to weave the first threads of his elaborate tapestry of revenge. One by one those who were traitors to friendship and love are meted out their just reward.

In Paris, the count finds his betrayers. After his arrest, Mercedes had married Edmond's rival Fernand Mondego, who has become the comte de Morcerf, Albert's father. Danglars, his accomplice, has been transformed into a baron and a wealthy banker. The third of his betrayers, Villefort, is now procurer to the king, a high royal office. When the count of Monte Cristo arrives in Paris, he brings with him Haydée (whom the count rescued), the daughter of a Pasha who was cruelly destroyed by Fernand. One by one, the count brings each traitor to his downfall, exacting

a kind of divine retribution that indicates the influence of Dante's *Divine Comedy* on Dumas's novel.

The Count of Monte Cristo is a dramatic story of mythic proportions inspiring innumerable editions, translations, and adaptations to theater and film even today. The novel also poses serious questions about evil and justice. If God does not act, does man have the right to punish others by retaliation? If one is Christian, must one always turn the other cheek? The count of Monte Cristo is beyond good and evil; he is a force of destiny. He recalls the biblical figure of Joseph in Egypt, and the theme of revenge was popular among readers.

Like Dumas's other novels, *The Count of Monte Cristo* is a theatrical romantic novel, offering the count as a Byronic figure who abandons Paris in the end, to return to a mythical Orient with his lovely Haydée. Finally, the count of Monte Cristo is the epitome of the romantic hero, ultimately destined to solitude.

At the same time, Dumas turns a critical eye to social values of the period even as he unravels the threads of one of the great mystery novels of all time. The count's experience allows Dumas to reflect on the injustices of the judicial system. The count, in meting out justice to members of the new elite, embodies values that stand in stark contrast to those of the BOURBON RESTORATION. One might argue, too, that Edmond is inspired by the Napoleonic myth. The FRENCH REVOLUTION made possible the entry of new men and women into the elite. How else could a woman like Mercedes have become a countess? The self-made count of Monte Cristo seems to represent the fluidity in postrevolutionary society that engenders both new possibilities and a sense of instability. He lives, moreover, every man's dream-come-true by transforming himself from pauper into prince.

FURTHER READING
Hemming, F. W. J. *Alexandre Dumas: The King of Romance.* New York: Scribner, 1979.
Ross, Michael. *Alexandre Dumas.* Newton Abbot, England; North Pomfret, Vt.: David and Charles, 1981.
Stowe, Richard. *Dumas.* Boston: Twayne, 1976.

COURTLY LOVE (C. 12TH CENTURY) Courtly love idealized passionate love between a knight and his lady. Although it arose at the same time as the cult of

the Virgin Mary in the Roman Catholic tradition, courtly love contained fewer religious elements than the contemporaneous code of chivalry. At the same time, courtly love drew on the values of the chivalric code. Courtly love exalted women. The knight was to fight and to overcome obstacles to win his lady's favor. Ideally, his allegiance to her, like his allegiance to his lord, was for life. Courtly love frequently involved adulterous relationships, thus reversing social reality whereby aristocratic marriages were arranged by two families. With courtly love, the union was by choice. Just as the knight was a vassal to his lord, he was also a vassal to his lady. This also reversed the social order. In reality, a woman was dominated by her husband.

Courtly love was praised in song and poetry by professional poets, the troubadours. Courtly love was defined in the medieval ROMANCES, and its focus on the love relationship between two individuals contributed to the gradual secularization of culture in the Middle Ages. It is reflected in an altered form in *précieuse* novels of the 17th century (see PRECIOSITY).

COUSIN BETTE (LA COUSINE BETTE)

HONORÉ DE BALZAC (1846) Like many of Balzac's novels, this literary masterpiece is at least partly autobiographical, drawn from the author's own love affairs. The novel focuses on a bourgeois family in Paris, the Hulots, whose status in society is derived from the successful careers under Napoleon of two brothers, one of whom is Hector Hulot. As he grows older, Hector becomes increasingly obsessed with sex, becoming "the prodigal father." Lisbeth Fischer, or Cousin Bette, is a vengeful, resentful, and manipulative old maid determined to wreak havoc on her family since she had once been in love with Hector but he married her cousin Adeline instead.

Modeled on Balzac's great love and, later, wife, Madame Hanska, Adeline's character is somewhat ambiguous. She is all goodness, natural nobility, loyal, guided always by a sense of Christian charity, consequently, anathema to feminist critics. She is destroyed, in the end, by these very qualities. To save her husband she offers herself for money to an earlier would-be seducer, but he is no longer interested. Humiliated, Adeline gains nothing but a disfiguring nervous tick and moral collapse.

Hector is not Bette's only failed love. She later becomes protector of a Polish artist, Wenceslas Steinbock. Bette desires revenge when he abandons her guidance for love of Hector's daughter Hortense, to whom he offers his sculpture of Samson destroying a lion, the embodiment of male strength. The sculpture may also represent Bette's strength denied, leaving her dispossessed.

Bette decides to play on Hulot's sexual obsessions and almost succeeds in ruining the family. She uses the courtesan Valerie Marneffe as her weapon for revenge. Valerie seduces Hector. When the financial repercussions of his lifestyle become too burdensome, Hector disappears, leaving his wife to worry and wonder what has become of him.

Balzac plays on the parable of the prodigal son. Forgiven three times by his loving wife, Hector, "the prodigal father," finally drives Adeline to her death by offering, within her hearing, to make a kitchen maid his wife. Another biblical theme, the golden calf, is articulated by Crevel, to whom Adeline offers herself in despair, saying that France has "returned to biblical times." The golden calf of 19th-century bourgeois Parisians is money.

Beneath the surface of the novel runs the myth of Napoleon. Hulot's early years are associated with the myth of meritocracy under Napoleon I. His decline into sexual and moral degeneracy corresponds to a general social decline that begins with the fall of the Napoleonic Empire.

The richness of Balzac's dialogue between a range of archetypal characters that includes a buffoon, a hag, and a virtuous mother is almost theatrical, hence Balzac's popularity with his readers. Like the marquise de Merteuil in LACLOS's *DANGEROUS LIAISONS*, Crevel and Valerie Marneffe in the end die punished for their sins. Adeline dies for or because of her virtue. Bette dies of pneumonia. Only Hector goes on to have an affair with a cook whose apprentice he later marries. Good and evil have no absolute meaning, it seems.

Cousin Bette is the companion novel to Balzac's *COUSIN PONS*. This novel, together with *Cousin Pons*, was one of the last great works the writer produced before his death in 1850. In each he echoes the Balzacian theme of materialism in 19th-century bourgeois society and its threat to the stability of the family as the fundamental unit of civil society.

The underlying question to *Cousin Bette* seems to focus on the tension between two basic human drives, eros and thanatos, love and death. Balzac's subtle evocation of 19th-century bourgeois life points to the problems inherent in modern urban society, much as Freud did later in *Civilization and Its Discontents.*

FURTHER READING

Allen, James Smith. *Popular French Romanticism: Authors, Readers and Books in the Nineteenth Century.* Syracuse, N.Y.: Syracuse University Press, 1981.

Carrère, Jean. *Degeneration in the Great French Masters.* Translated by Joseph McCabe. Freeport, N.Y.: Books for Libraries Press, 1967.

Jameson, Fredric. "*La Cousine Bette* and Allegorical Realism," *PMLA* 86, no. 2 (March 1971): 241–254.

Kanes, Martin, ed. *Critical Essays on Balzac.* Boston: G. K. Hall, 1990.

Smith, Edward C. III. "Honoré de Balzac and the 'Genius' of Walter Scott: Debt and Denial," *Comparative Literature Studies* 36, no. 3 (1999): 209–225.

COUSIN PONS Honoré de Balzac (1847)

Cousin Pons is the companion novel to Balzac's *Cousin Bette.* Sylvain Pons, like Bette, is a "poor relation," the title given to the two novels together. Sylvain, a gentle, bachelor musician whose great and equally kind friend is a German musician named Wilhelm Schmucke, is harassed to death by wealthier family members jealous of his one treasure, an art collection.

In *Cousin Bette,* a woman is the aggressor. In contrast, Sylvain, a male relative, is the victim. Balzac often thought in terms of pairs, whether juxtaposed, as in these two novels, or complimentary. Balzac wrote *Cousin Pons* to compete with the enormously popular serial novels of Eugène Sue. This novel, together with *Cousin Bette,* was among the last great works the writer produced before his death in 1850. In each he echoes the Balzacian theme of materialism in 19th-century bourgeois society and the threat it poses to the stability of the family as the fundamental unit of civil society.

FURTHER READING

Allen, James Smith. *Popular French Romanticism: Authors, Readers and Books in the Nineteenth Century.* Syracuse, N.Y.: Syracuse University Press, 1981.

Carrère, Jean. *Degeneration in the Great French Masters.* Translated by Joseph McCabe. Freeport, N.Y.: Books for Libraries Press, 1967.

Kanes, Martin, ed. *Critical Essays on Balzac.* Boston: G. K. Hall, 1990.

Smith, Edward C. III. "Honoré de Balzac and the 'Genius' of Walter Scott: Debt and Denial," *Comparative Literature Studies* 36, no. 3 (1999): 209–225.

CRÉBILLON FILS (CLAUDE-PROSPER JOLYOT DE) (1707–1777)

Crébillon *fils* (the younger) studied in Paris at the famous Jesuit college, Louis-le-Grand. Crébillon's father had also been a writer, tragic poet, and dramatist of some skill whose talent was comparable to that of Voltaire. It may have been difficult for the son to grow up in his father's footsteps. Contemporaries did not always compare them favorably. In 1732 he published his first novel, *Letters of the Marquise of M*** to the Count of R***.* Unfortunately it received only a lukewarm response from readers.

At the time, Crébillon was an active participant in dissolute Parisian social life involving actors, singers, and writers. Around 1733 they formed several riotous societies where they met together to dine and drink. Crébillon's first success as an author came in 1734 with the anonymous publication of a supposedly Japanese story, *Tanzaï and Néardané,* attacking the papal bull "Unigenitus," which had condemned the Jansenists. For this work, Crébillon was briefly imprisoned.

In 1736 the first part of his LIBERTINE novel, *The Wayward Head and Heart,* appeared. Subject to censorship, the second and third parts were published in the Netherlands in 1738. In 1742 he published his even more scandalous *Sopha,* for which he was banished by the government for a time from Paris. His writing career continued despite his exile. In 1754 Crébillon published a translation of Eliza Haywood's *Unfortunate Foundlings,* a popular English novel and, a few months later, *Ah! What a Story* and *The Night and the Moment.*

Crébillon was able to return to Paris in 1759 because Madame de Pompadour, mistress to Louis XV and a great patroness of the arts, secured him, somewhat ironically, a position as royal censor for literature. Even as he fulfilled his responsibilities as censor, Crébillon continued to write, but there was not much response to his *Chance by the Fireplace* (1763), *Letters of the Duchess of *** to the Duke of **** (1768), or the *Athenian Letters* (1771). His reputation as a writer was in decline. The libertine novel of the first half of the 18th century could no longer compete in the period of Rousseau's *The NEW HELOISE*.

Crébillon died in 1777. He left mixed opinions among his contemporaries. Some considered him a mysogynist, others a charming philosopher. Typical of the libertine novelist, Crébillon described a corrupt and immoral world of aristocrats whose main purpose is the pursuit of amorous relationships. The operative words are "to take," "to possess," and "to leave." He wrote with a clear and witty style that shows his ability to manipulate language subtly as well as a clear understanding of human nature. In his preface to *The Wayward Head and Heart,* Crébillon breaks with the tradition whereby the author asserts the authenticity of the story on which the novel is based. In this he echoes Rousseau's introduction to *The NEW HELOISE*. Like the BURLESQUE writers, Crébillon sought to describe human nature as it really is, in a manner both useful and amusing.

FURTHER READING
Conroy, P.-V., Jr. *Crébillon fils: Techniques of the Novel.* Oxford: Voltaire Foundation, 1972.

CRENNE, HÉLISENNE DE (MARGUERITE BRIET) (C. 1515–1560)

Now considered one of the most important early French women writers, Hélisenne de Crenne produced a number of semi-autobiographical works arguing in favor of virtue and defending women's writing. Born in Abbeville, Hélisenne was married about 1530 to Philippe Fournel, Seigneur de Crenne. The marriage was apparently not a happy one and the couple separated about 1539, at which point Hélisenne moved to Paris.

The TORMENTS OF LOVE (1538), describing an unhappy love affair, is Hélisenne de Crenne's most famous and most popular work. This novel draws on the tradition of the medieval ROMANCE. At least seven editions were published in the 16th century. Some scholars consider this to be France's first psychological novel, written more than a century before Madame de Lafayette's *PRINCESSE DE CLÈVES* (1678). In addition to *The Torments of Love,* Hélisenne wrote a semiautobiographical epistolary novel, *Personal and Invective Letters* (1539), in which she argued in favor of women's literary activity. She also wrote *Madame Hélisenne's Dream* (1540), an allegorical fable, and translated parts of Virgil's *Aeneid.*

Comparable to CHRISTINE DE PIZAN, Hélisenne wrote with a strong authorial voice, often in the first person. She writes convincingly of a woman's experience as a wife and as an author, and her message had great appeal to the female audience of the 16th century. Her style is erudite, perhaps too much so for some contemporary readers. A product of her intellectual and cultural environment, French Renaissance humanism, her works bear the influence of the Latin classics and Boccaccio.

FURTHER READING
Crenne, Hélisenne [Marguerite Briet]. *The Torments of Love.* Edited and translated by Lisa Neal. Minneapolis: University of Minnesota Press, 1996.
Nash, Jerry C. "Constructing Hélisenne de Crenne: Reception and Identity." In *Por le soie amisté: essays in honor of Norris J. Lacy.* Edited by Keith Busby and Catherine M. Jones. (Faux Titre; no. 183), Amsterdam, Atlanta: Rodophi, 2000.
Randall, Catherine. "Positioning Herself: A Renaissance-Reformation Diptych." In *Attending to Early Modern Women.* Edited by Susan D. Amussen and Adele Seeff. Newark: University of Delaware Press; London; Cranberry, N.J.: Associated University Presses, 1998.
Wood, Diane S. *Hélisenne de Crenne: At the Crossroads of Renaissance Humanism and Feminism.* Madison, N.J.: Fairleigh Dickinson University Press; London; Cranberry, N.J.: Associated University Presses, 2000.

CRIME OF SYLVESTER BONNARD, THE (LE CRIME DE SYLVESTRE BONNARD) ANATOLE FRANCE (1881)

In part one, "The Log," through an unexpected act of generosity, Sylvester Bonnard acquires a manuscript that has long been the object of his desire. In the second part, "Jeanne Alexandre," Sylvester battles against the hypocrisy of society when he steals Jeanne, a poor orphan, away from her nasty guardian so she can marry one of his students.

Like other characters created by France, Monsieur Bergeret, for example, Sylvester Bonnard resembles the author in his love of books. A humanist drawn to the ideas and values of classical antiquity, Sylvester Bonnard's only crime is in challenging the social order. This is the source of the novel's humor, through which France gently calls into question accepted social values and conventions. France also plays with a light hand on the self-centeredness that makes us blind to reality. Sylvester Bonnard, for example, may be able to interpret texts, but he has little understanding of real life. Slowly, Sylvester relinquishes the narrow vision of an old bachelor to live a more concrete life that unites body and spirit. Reflecting France's own values, Sylvester Bonnard reveals the importance that France attached to tolerance and kindness.

FURTHER READING

Durant, Will. *Anatole France: The Man and his Work.* Girard, Kansas: Haldeman-Julius, 1925.

Guérard, Albert Léon. *Five Masters of French Romance: Anatole France, Pierre Loti, Paul Bourget, Maurice Barrès, Romain Rolland.* New York: Scribner, 1916.

Jefferson, Alfred Carter. *Anatole France: The Politics of Skepticism.* New Brunswick, N.J.: Rutgers University Press, 1965.

May, James Lewis. *Anatole France: The Man and His Work. An Essay in Critical Biography.* Port Washington, N.Y.: Kennikat Press, 1970.

Tylden-Wright, David. *Anatole France.* New York: Walker, 1967.

CRIMES OF LOVE (ALINE ET VAL-COUR) DONATIEN-ALPHONSE-FRANÇOIS, MARQUIS DE SADE (1793)

This collection of short gothic tales is the gentlest of Sade's works. Closer to the traditional *roman noir* (gothic novel) of the 18th century, violence and murder take place in an isolated castle, but there are no explicitly erotic and cruel scenes. Consequently, this is the first book published under the author's full name. Like Sade's other works, *Crimes of Love* expands on themes prevalent among ENLIGHTENMENT philosophers: materialism, the authority of nature, and the relationship between reason and passion. In Sade's case, however, such themes are pushed to the extreme.

FURTHER READING

Barthes, Roland. *Sade, Fourier, Loyola.* Translated by Richard Miller. New York: Farrar, Straus and Giroux, 1976.

Du Plessix Gray, Francine. *At Home with the Marquis de Sade.* New York: Simon and Schuster, 1998.

Fabre, Jean. "Sade et le roman noir." In *Le Marquis de Sade.* Paris: Armand Colin, 1968.

Heine, Maurice. "Le Marquis de Sade et le roman noir." In *Le Marquis de Sade.* Edited by Gilbert Lély. Paris: Gallimard, 1950.

Schaffer, Neil. *The Marquis de Sade: A Life.* New York: Knopf, 1999.

Weber, Caroline. "The Sexist Sublime in Sade and Lyotard," *Philosophy and Literature* 26, no. 2 (2002): 397–404.

CROSSING THE MANGROVE (TRAVER-SÉE DE LA MANGROVE) MARYSE CONDÉ (1989)

The setting of this novel is the author's native Guadeloupe. It consists of a series of episodes with multiple narrators, all of whom come from the village of Rivière du Sel. The villagers have come together for the funeral of Francis Sancher, who only lived with them for one year. The secret crime that haunts the novel and the curse that leads to Sancher's death represents slavery.

One of the most enigmatic figures to speak is Xantippe, yet he best expresses Condé's literary vision. Xantippe's story is, in part, a creation myth. With rich imagery and sensual language, Condé evokes the origins of this land. The notion of origin or identity is central to this and other works by Condé. Moreover, it is a particularly significant theme in relation to Caribbean culture, born out of forced migration and slavery. Rather than viewing Africa as the Caribbean people's point of origin, Condé places it in slavery itself.

While there is some reference to Africa in the narrative, Condé's rejection of NEGRITUDE leads her to focus on the Caribbean land and its people's connection to it. While the narrative at times resembles a folktale, its tone is not one of nostalgia for the past. Condé evokes the sometimes troubling consequences of modernization that entail, among other things, assimilation into French culture. "I saw schools open and, not believing my ears, I heard children chanting 'our ancestors the Gauls.' . . . " Yet despite the Caribbean people's tragic beginning and subsequent suffering, Condé offers a pantheistic vision of the world in which hope endures, particularly in women's narratives.

FURTHER READING

Alexander, Simone A. James. *Mother Imagery in the Novels of Afro-Caribbean Women.* Columbia: University of Missouri Press, 2001.

Krüs, Patricia. *Claiming Masculinity as Her Own: Cultural Identity and Caribbean Women's Writing.* Leiden, Netherlands: Universiteit Leiden, 2001.

Suk, Jeannie. *Postcolonial Paradoxes in French Caribbean Writing: Césaire, Glissant, Condé.* Oxford: Clarendon, 2001.

CURTIS, JEAN-LOUIS (1917–1995)

An English teacher in Bayonne and then Paris, Curtis spent long periods in England and in the Mediterranean, on journeys that inspired novels such as *Tea Under the Cypruses* (1969).

Curtis's third novel, *Forests of the Night* (1947), won the Goncourt Prize. In subsequent novels, some more successful than others, Curtis ignored the dominant trends in the literature of the period, the NOUVEAU ROMAN with its emphasis on the psychological, preferring instead to focus on a depiction of contemporary society.

Young Men (1946) is situated in the period before and during World War II, the first volume in a series of three novels that includes *Forests of the Night,* depicting a small town on the line of demarcation during the German Occupation. The last novel of the three, *Just Causes* (1954), describes the period just after the Liberation.

In *The Forties* (1966), the principal characters of *Young Men* reappear, older and with their own children, to deal with the problems of postwar consumer society, the subject of other novels by Curtis such as *The Young Couple* (1967) and *The Pensive Reed* (1971).

In yet another trilogy that includes *Hidden Horizon* (1978), *Halfway Down the Road* (1980), and *The Beating of my Heart* (1981), the heroes of May 1968 gradually return to the more conservative values of their parents, precisely the values they had once so vehemently rejected. Curtis continued to draw from the contemporary sociopolitical context in his novel *Wild Swan* (1962), about a character named Gilles Ferrus, who grew up during the Algerian War.

Curtis wrote novels in a variety of genres. A number of his works may be characterized as novels of apprenticeship, while others are science fiction (*A Neon Saint,* 1956) or detective stories (*The Temple of Love,* 1990). Curtis also published essays on literature, parodies, and translations from English.

D

DABIT, EUGÈNE (1898–1963) Dabit was born in the Somme region but he grew up in the neighborhood of Montmartre in Paris; his knowledge and love of that city inspired many of his novels.

When he finished school, Dabit became an apprentice, first to a locksmith and then to an ironworker. Attracted to art, he began painting in 1912, and when World War I began (1914) he was hired to run an elevator. By 1916, he was out of work and left for the front. Inspired by his reading in the trenches, of the works of CHARLES-LOUIS PHILIPPE, Dabit became interested in writing.

In 1919 he returned to Paris, where his parents, formerly a delivery man and a concierge, had opened a small hotel, the Hôtel du Nord. At this point Dabit was still dreaming of becoming an artist. He went to art school and even sold a few paintings before turning entirely to writing.

Dabit first worked on his memories from the war. The writers ROGER MARTIN DU GARD and Léopold Chauveau both encouraged Dabit to continue. In 1928 he married a young artist named Beatrice Appia, and, in 1931, his novel HÔTEL DU NORD won the Populist Prize.

The very title makes it evident that Dabit's novels were partly autobiographical. In *Hôtel du Nord,* Dabit depicts the occupants of a small hotel run by a couple named Lecouvreur. The hotel is destined to be demolished, symbolizing the precarious existence of poor Parisians. The adaptation of *Hôtel du Nord* to film by Marcel Carné in 1938 became one of the classics of French cinema. *Petit Louis* (1939) is a novel of apprenticeship, likewise focusing on working-class Paris, in which Louis grows up peacefully, only to have his vision of the world turned upside down by the war. Between the trenches and brothels, Louis discovers just how ugly the world can be.

Dabit's literary and intellectual life was particularly vibrant after 1930. He associated with writers such as ANDRÉ MALRAUX, HENRI BARBUSSE, and ROMAIN ROLLAND, among others. Dabit also signed the Manifesto of the Proletarian School of writers and was a member of the Association of Revolutionary Writers and Artists. Although a convinced leftist, Dabit chose not to join a political party.

From 1932 to 1936 Dabit contributed to a number of literary reviews and newspapers, and in 1932 he published *Villa Oasis or the False Bourgeois*. In this novel, Irma and Julien come from the working class but aspire to a bourgeois lifestyle. In *Faubourgs of Paris* (1933) Dabit describes the city he knew so well and revealed his dismay at the way in which modern urban life makes the world a sad and ugly place; "I am no longer attached to my old neighborhood. I get lost like a provincial. My city has changed. It has become more menacing, inhuman, artificial, almost monstrous." In *A Recent Death* (1934) Dabit depicts the reactions of his family members to the death of Alfred Singer with simplicity and candor, revealing their loss of values and humanity. This novel is thus similar in theme to *Fau-*

bourgs of Paris in its focus on the problems associated with modern urban life.

In that same year, Dabit also published *The Island,* a collection of three short stories inspired by his experience on Majorca, his refuge from the turbulence of Paris, where he lived each year from May until September. Inspired by paintings he saw in the Prado museum in Madrid, Dabit also wrote an essay on Spanish painting.

The Green Zone (1935) again focuses on the difficulties of life in Paris that drive the main character to ultimately escape to the suburbs. In *Way of Life* (1935), Dabit offers a series of depressing portraits of working-class life with its prostitution, despair, and suicide.

In 1936 Dabit traveled with a group of writers that included ANDRÉ GIDE to the Soviet Union, where he died, probably of typhus. He is buried in the Père Lachaise cemetery in Paris. Gide's *Return from the USSR* is dedicated to Dabit.

Most of Dabit's works focus on the lives of the poor in working-class neighborhoods of Paris. He was attached to these people and described their problems and difficulties with gentleness and artistry. As a result, Dabit was frequently characterized by his contemporaries as a populist writer, something to which he objected. Dabit simply sought to portray the troubled times through which he lived: "I can only be sensitive to the tragedy of our destiny." His writing reflects a tension between pessimism and joy.

DADA Dada, born in a bar in Zurich, Switzerland, in 1916, entailed a derisive and provocative statement on art. Romanian poet Tristan Tzara chose the name for this early 20th-century literary and cultural movement deliberately for its obvious lack of meaning. In 1918 Tzara published his Dada Manifesto, saying "there is a great, negative, destructive work to accomplish." Through this movement, he and his collaborators sought to destroy the illusions of humanist art.

Dada quickly became an international movement, spreading to New York, Cologne, Berlin, Amsterdam, Barcelona, and Paris, where Tzara arrived in 1920. The most vibrant years of Dadaism were from 1920 to 1922, when it shared with SURREALISM a combination of ironic humor and radical skepticism. The movement

died out in 1922, after a conference in which ANDRÉ BRETON and others sought to define modernism while castigating Dadaism. Early French writers associated with Dada include the poet Paul Éluard, LOUIS ARAGON, Philippe Soupault, and Breton, along with other writers associated with the *Nouvelle revue française* (New French Review).

Dada constitutes a reaction against Western civilization and the set of social values that Dadaists and others viewed as having led to the outbreak of violence and destruction in World War I. Dada emerged at a point in history when a sense of demoralization seemed the only natural response to the disaster of war. In some sense, then, Dada was a radicalization of despair. The Dadaists created scandals with exhibitions and performances that manifested their goal of freeing themselves entirely from the past. Anarchist, nihilist, and iconoclastic, Dada reemerged in the 1960s in painting and "happenings."

Dadaists promoted non-sense as a challenge to established principles in art and society. They did so by blending literature, art, poetry, photography, sound, and action. In art, for example, Dadaists made use of unusual materials such as wire and matches, language and slogans. They sought through art to destroy, not to create, and thus gave birth to their own myth of being subversive, even terrorist. In some ways, Dada marks the birth of truly modern art.

DADIÉ, BERNARD (1916–) Born in the Ivory Coast, Dadié completed his studies at the École Normale Supérieure William Ponty Dakar, in Senegal, earning a degree in government administration in 1935. The next year he began work at the Institut Fondamental d'Afrique Noir, a center for research on Africa. In 1947, he returned to the Ivory Coast, where he took an active stance against the colonial system and engaged in work for the Social Democratic Party. He was subsequently arrested and spent 16 months in prison. In 1960 Dadié traveled to the United States and to Italy, experiences that furnished much of the material for his subsequent novels. After independence, Dadié was appointed minister of culture.

Beyond his political career, Dadié retained a lifelong interest in literature. One of the most prolific writers of francophone Africa, Dadié has produced a series of autobiographical novels that includes *Climbié* (1956), *African in Paris* (1959), *One Way: Bernard Dadié Observes America* (1964), and *The City Where No One Dies* (1968).

In *Climbié,* Dadié draws from his own life experience to tell the story of a gifted student who makes his way from a village to the prestigious William Ponty School. Climbié gradually develops a political consciousness that ultimately leads him to rebel against the colonial system. As a result, he is prevented from holding a position in government administration that his studies had prepared him for.

Just before the war, Climbié participates in a general strike in Dakar. Arrested and imprisoned by colonial authorities, he learns that the colonial social hierarchy exists even in prison, where French prisoners receive preferred treatment over African detainees. Despite this experience, Climbié still has hope for a brighter future of peace and brotherhood. This novel recalls CAMARA LAYE's *BLACK CHILD* in its evocation of the tension felt by Africans torn between two very different cultures.

Dadié has also written short stories, collections of African tales, and a number of plays. Dadié's works tend to target both colonial power and certain aspects of postcolonial society, while bringing to life traditional African culture in a manner reminiscent of TAHAR BEN JELLOUN. In 1965, Dadié won the Grand Prix Littéraire de l'Afrique Noir. All of his works reflect his interest in traditional African culture and his political militancy.

DAMNED, THE (*LÀ-BAS*) JORIS-KARL HUYSMANS (1891)

In this novel banned by railway booksellers, Huysman's character Durtal picks up where Des Esseintes of *AGAINST THE GRAIN* left off. He, too, rejects the society of other men. He also rejects des Esseintes's pure aestheticism, but not his desire for sensual experience. Like des Esseintes, Durtal explores all possibilities leading him to adultery with the hysterical wife of a Catholic writer and, ultimately, to black magic with an excommunicated priest. Satanism might have destroyed him if Durtal had not kept in contact with a small group of intellectuals. Ultimately, Durtal realizes that there is a limit to evil, but not to beauty and love.

Huysmans retains some elements of his earlier NATURALISM in terms of an accumulation of detailed observation. Yet this novel at the same time serves as a denunciation of naturalism. Both Huysmans's and Durtal's fascination with the Middle Ages has a romantic quality and something more. The accumulation of detail associated with naturalism turns into a deciphering of symbols and signs ultimately leading to a new spiritual journey that Huysmans recounts in *En Route, Cathedral,* and *The Oblate.* Ultimately, one must consider Huysmans's works as a unified whole, perhaps more so than almost any other writer.

FURTHER READING

Banks, Brian. *The Image of Huysmans.* New York: AMS Press, 1990.

Gilman, Richard. *Decadence: The Strange Life of an Epithet.* New York: Farrar, Straus and Giroux, 1979.

Nalbantian, Suzanne. *Seeds of Decadence in the Late Nineteenth-Century Novel.* New York: St. Martin's Press, 1983.

Praz, Mario. *The Romantic Agony.* Translated by Angus Davidson. New York: Oxford University Press, 1970.

DANGEROUS LIAISONS (*LES LIAISONS DANGÉREUSES*) PIERRE-AMBROISE CHODERLOS DE LACLOS (1782)

The two principal characters in this LIBERTINE, EPISTOLARY NOVEL, the Count de Valmont and the Marquise de Merteuil, former lovers, are unforgettable. Equally cynical and intelligent, together they manipulate the more naive characters of the novel. At the opening, Valmont has decided to seduce the virtuous but comely Présidente de Tourvel while the Marquise is bent on revenge against the Count de Gercourt, who is supposed to marry a young innocent named Cécile de Volanges. Cécile's charm is purely physical. Her lack of intelligence makes her a perfect prey to Valmont and Merteuil.

Merteuil demands that Valmont give up his pursuit of the Présidente de Tourvel in order to seduce Cécile. They succeed in their plans. Tourvel falls madly in love with Valmont, to the point of her destruction, and Cécile is both impregnated by Valmont and engages in another affair with a young gentleman without fortune, the chevalier Danceny. In the course of their machinations, Merteuil realizes that Valmont has developed real feelings for Tourvel. This is disturbing to the Marquise, who demands that he abandon his lover. When Valmont does so, Tourvel dies of a broken heart. Only then does Valmont realize that, for the first and only time, he was himself in love.

Valmont and the Marquise declare war on each other and military metaphors abound (Laclos was a military man). To seduce is to conquer. In the end, Valmont allows Danceny to kill him in a duel but not before he has published his correspondence with the Marquise, revealing their machinations in all their infamy. The Marquise ends her days disfigured by disease and in debt, rejected by society. Cécile enters a convent.

In his preface, Laclos writes "It seems to me . . . that one does a service to moral principles to reveal the means by which those with bad morals corrupt those with good." In the end, Valmont and the Marquise de Merteuil are punished, but there remains some ambiguity in Laclos's stance nonetheless. Scholars continue to debate his position on the question of evil.

The novel created an uproar. What was particularly shocking to his contemporaries was Laclos's depiction of a combination of intelligence and a will to destroy others that challenged the foundation of the social order. *Dangerous Liaisons* depicts an aristocracy in pursuit of pleasure whose world would be destroyed seven years later by the French Revolution. The origin of the nobility's power is found in the military tradition of the Middle Ages. No longer able to assert their status through military combat, they choose conquest by seduction, a game of social power. Between Valmont and the Marquise, letters become weapons that, once published, destroy the authors themselves. They never actualize the erotic and sexual nature of their relationship except through their epistolary duel.

The epistolary novel was already well established when Laclos wrote *Dangerous Liaisons*. The genre arguably began with GUILLERAGUE's PORTUGUESE LETTERS. MONTESQUIEU and ROUSSEAU perfected the art, but the genre reached its height with Laclos, master of the novel in the form of letters. His orchestration of multiple voices allows for a multifaceted view of separate events. The novel was an instant success, perhaps because it was so shocking. Fifty editions were published between 1782 and 1815. It was condemned as

late as 1832. The novel was rediscovered in the twentieth century by authors such as ANDRÉ GIDE, MARCEL PROUST, ANDRÉ MALRAUX, François Mauriac, and MICHEL BUTOR. It has also benefited from a renewed interest in 18th-century and feminist studies.

In their manners and style, the two heroes follow in the tradition of 18th-century libertine and erotic literature (there are intertextual references to CRÉBILLON FILS, for example), but for them, seduction is more than a diversion. Valmont and the Marquise believe that reason may dominate over feeling, a common theme in 18th-century literature and philosophy. Laclos's stance, however, is ambiguous. Whether the characters represent reason (Valmont, Merteuil) or emotion (the Présidente de Tourvel), in the end, neither value system can protect them from destruction.

The themes of language and writing are central to the text. Salon discourse is transformed into a battle in which each participant tries to destroy others through wit and reason. The act of seduction is so closely linked to the act of writing that writing and reading replace the act of making love. This is clearest in the episode in which Valmont writes to Tourvel using a courtesan's naked buttocks as a writing table.

Language is the means of manipulation. It is also the means of self-creation. In her famous letter on autodidacticism, Merteuil makes a direct assertion of her identity: "I can say that I am my own creation." She also reveals something of the double-edged sword all women encountered as she privately takes pleasure in being seduced but is, at the same time, required to show resistance. A woman's private and public self are not the same. Echoing Rousseau, Laclos makes a strong argument about the importance of a woman's reputation in a world of false appearances. Equally central to the text is the question of identity. What is striking about Valmont in the course of the novel is his change of identity. At the start a libertine, he eventually finds his heart, but this does not prevent his ultimate destruction.

Dangerous Liaisons is arguably the greatest masterpiece of 18th-century epistolary fiction. While Laclos offers his critique of 18th-century aristocratic society in the language of libertinism, he also draws on the tradition of 17th-century baroque spirituality in all its sensuality, offering a literary parallel to Bernini's moving sculpture of the *Ecstasy of Saint Theresa*.

FURTHER READING

Altman, Janet G. *Epistolarity: Approaches to a Form.* Columbus: Ohio State University Press, 1982.

Becker-Theye, Betty. *The Seducer as Mythic Figure in Richardson, Laclos and Kierkegaard.* New York: Garland, 1988.

Brinsmead, Anne-Marie. *Strategies of Resistance in Les Liaisons Dangereuses: Heroines in Search of "Author- ity."* Lewiston, N.Y.: E. Mellen Press, 1989.

Brooks, Peter. *The Novel of Worldliness.* Princeton, N.J.: Princeton University Press, 1969.

Conroy, Peter V. *Intimate, Intrusive and Triumphant: Readers in Les Liaisons Dangereuses.* Amsterdam, Philadelphia: J. Benjamins, 1987.

Diaconoff, Suellen. *Eros and Power in Les Liaisons Dangereuses.* Geneva: Droz, 1979.

Free, Lloyd R., ed. *Laclos: Critical Approaches to Les Liaisons Dangereuses.* Madrid: José Porrúa Turanzas, D.L., 1978.

Rosbottom, Ronald C. *Choderlos de Laclos.* Boston: Twayne, 1978.

Roulston, Christine. *Virtue, Gender and the Authentic Self in Eighteenth-Century Fiction: Richardson, Rousseau, and Laclos.* Gainesville: University of Florida Press, 1998.

Sol, Antoinette Marie. *Textual Promiscuities: Eighteenth-Century Critical Rewriting.* Lewisburg, Pa.: Bucknell University Press, 2002.

Thelander, Dorothy R. *Laclos and the Epistolary Novel.* Geneva: Droz, 1963.

DARK CHILD (*L'ENFANT NOIR*) Camara Laye (1953)

In this autobiographical novel, Laye tells the story of his childhood in Guinea, growing up with his father, a successful goldsmith, and his mother, whose presence in many ways dominates the author's reflections on the past. The rhythm of life is governed by natural cycles of labor, harvests, and traditional cultural practices and rites. Laye sensitively evokes the poetry and mystery of Africa in this nostalgic work.

The novel traces the author's life from 1933 to 1948 as he describes the solidarity of the African community and the inner tension experienced by Laye as he began to develop as an individual. Laye started his studies in the village Islamic school but later left for a French school in Conakry. From the beginning, the themes of exile and separation that mark all Laye's works are present.

The tension Laye feels is derived from opposing pressures. The male figures in the novel, Laye's father, a well-respected self-made man, and his uncle, an accountant in a French firm, encourage Laye to forge his own way in life. His mother, in contrast, represents the solidity of family life and tradition. Strong female figures are important in this matrilineal society, and Daman, Laye's mother, is particularly well regarded in the community because of her magical powers. She is the author's mother but she is also mother Africa herself, a woman who can communicate with animals, particularly the crocodile, her family totem. The community respects Daman because she uses her gifts for their collective benefit.

Laye once explained that his motivation in writing this work was to preserve his culture and "this love that unites us so closely with one another, that makes of our tribes, our families . . . compact groups . . . so much in accord, so peaceful, so inter-connected."

Laye originally wanted to call this novel *Child of Guinea* but his French editor changed it to *Dark Child*. It was one of the first African novels to receive international attention, winning the Charles Veillon Prize in 1954. Laye's first novel, *Dark Child* does not address questions of colonialism or independence central to other contemporary African novelists such as Ahmadou Kourouma, René Maran, and Mohammed Dib.

FURTHER READING

Bernard, Paul R. "The Writings of Camara Laye," *French Review* 56, no. 6 (May 1983): 936–937.

Burness, Donald. "The Radiance of Camara Laye," *Journal of Black Studies* 2, no. 4 (June 1981): 499–501.

Hale, Thomas A. "From Written Literature to the Oral Tradition and Back: Camara Laye, Babou Condé, and *Le Maître de la parole:* Kouma, Lafolo and Kouma," *French Review* 55, no. 6, Literature and Civilization of Black Francophone Africa (May 1982): 790–797.

King, Adele. *Rereading Camara Laye.* Lincoln: University of Nebraska Press, 2002.

———. *The Writings of Camara Laye.* London: Heinemann, 1980.

Lee, Sonia. *Camara Laye.* Boston: Twayne, 1984.

DAUDET, ALPHONSE (1840–1897)

Daudet was born in Nîmes, where his father owned a silk manufactory, but the family was forced to move to Lyon when the business failed. A sensitive child, Daudet did not at first appreciate the rainy weather of Lyon nor the humiliating experience of poverty. There was some compensation, however, in boating and playing hooky from school. When his family's financial situation worsened, Daudet was obliged to leave school in search of work. He went first to Alès but, apparently lonely and unhappy, took the road to Paris to join his brother at the age of 17. There he decided to embark on a literary career.

Daudet at first led a precarious Bohemian life, recalling the experience of BALZAC's character Lucien in LOST ILLUSIONS, but by 1858 he had published a collection of poetry called Les Amoureuses (The Lovers) and was writing for Parisian journals. Although Daudet was interested in writing for the theater, as this was more lucrative, he was not terribly successful. Daudet continued to struggle until a writer friend (Ernest Lépine) helped him secure a position as a secretary, affording him financial stability. Together they collaborated on several plays until Daudet's health problems required a journey to his native south of France. Daudet also traveled to Corsica and Algeria, all of which provided material for his writing.

Daudet's experience in the Midi (southern France) led to his famous LETTERS FROM MY MILL, while his travels in Algeria influenced his popular novel TARTARIN DE TARASCON. Daudet is also known for his Monday Tales and an autobiographical novel, The Little Thing, among other works. In fact, Daudet was a fairly prolific writer, producing some 17 novels, some of which were adapted for the theater.

Daudet is principally remembered and still treasured by French readers as a Provençal writer who captured the mood and character of southern French culture. He was friends with FLAUBERT, ZOLA, the brothers GONCOURT, and de MAUPASSANT, and his writing echoes elements of the naturalist school, but he remained essentially independent. Daudet asserted, too, that "he liked to leave some things unsaid." He is considered a precursor to Zola in his exploration of ordinary people's lives. Like many 19th-century writers, Daudet was interested in pointing to the lies and illusions that seem to be at the foundation of contemporary society. In theme and subject matter he is also frequently compared to Charles Dickens.

Daudet was a talented writer capable of diverse genres. Letters from My Mill has a strong element of the poetic, Tartarin de Tarascon the burlesque, and Jack, REALISM. Most of all, Daudet's work is rich in imagination and fantasy. His writing has a childlike appeal that continues to attract readers today. Daudet was particularly gifted in bringing to life a rustic world through his rich language peppered with provincial expressions.

FURTHER READING

Dobie, Vera G. Alphonse Daudet. Folcroft, Pa.: Folcroft Library Editions, 1974.

Roche, Alphonse. Alphonse Daudet. Boston: Twayne, 1976.

Sachs, Murray. The Career of Alphonse Daudet. A Critical Study. Cambridge, Mass.: Harvard University Press, 1965.

DAUMAL, RENÉ (1908–1944)

At the age of 15 or 16, Daumal began adventuring into the realm of the unknown, exploring the limits of consciousness and experience. Through alcohol, drugs, tobacco, noctambulism, and even partial asphyxiation, Daumal and his friends, the "phreres simplistes" (simple brothers), sought to explore the degree to which one may have or gain control over one's consciousness. With these companions, Daumal also shared a taste for poetry, particularly that of Arthur Rimbaud and GÉRARD DE NERVAL. For Daumal, poetry is more than literature; it is a fundamental approach to life, an attitude he referred to as "experimental metaphysics."

In 1925, Daumal began preparing for entrance into the prestigious École Normale Supérieure in Paris; however, he failed the entrance exam and began studying philosophy at the Sorbonne instead. Daumal's reading taste was eclectic and included works on occultism, theosophy, and mysticism. Even as he studied, Daumal experimented with opium and began writing.

Along with a group of young writers, in 1928 Daumal established a short-lived journal, Le grand Jeu (The big game). Only three editions were published. Influenced by the surrealist movement (see SURREALISM), Daumal and his collaborators shared with the surrealists a revolutionary spirit that called into question traditional social and aesthetic values. Daumal, in particular, sought in both life and art a sense of purity and authenticity. Nonetheless, when ANDRÉ BRETON asked

Daumal to join the surrealists in 1929, Daumal refused with disdain.

Daumal was, unfortunately, frustrated in his attempts to reconcile dialectical materialism associated with Marxist thought (see MARXISM) and spirituality. Discouraged and suffering from poor health, Daumal eventually found solace in the teachings of philosopher Alexander Salzmann. Daumal subsequently turned to Oriental philosophy. He began studying Sanskrit and attained such a level of competence that he wrote *Sanskrit: Grammar, Poetry, Theater* (published by his brother in 1985). Daumal's fascination with Hinduism lasted throughout his life and was an important influence on his writing and in the development of his own brand of mysticism.

Daumal once wrote: "Everything that we adore is a cadaver, except God. . . . This is why I say: my body is dead, my voice is dead; all of science is a cadaver. . . ." Drawing from Eastern philosophy, Daumal sought mastery over his body, his instincts, and his intellect. This was in stark contrast to the excesses of his youth, something Daumal reflected on in *A Night of Serious Drinking* (1939). Again in contrast to his past experiences, Daumal cried out against all forms of illusion or artificial paradise that might be induced by drugs and alcohol.

Daumal has sometimes been accused of being a nihilist. However, his desire to create rather than to destroy is more than evident in his unfinished novel *MOUNT ANALOGUE* (posthumous 1952). In this final work, the reader finds the culmination of Daumal's development as a writer and thinker, reflected in the novel's blend of surrealist elements, metaphysics, and Hindu philosophy. Written when Daumal was already suffering from tuberculosis, this allegorical tale recounts the struggle undertaken by a group of mountaineers to attain the summit of a secret mountain. Suffering increasingly from illness, Daumal died in 1944 at the age of 36.

FURTHER READING

Daumal, René. *The Powers of the Word: Selected Essays and Notes, 1927–1943.* Edited and translated by Mark Polizotti. San Francisco: City Lights Books, 1991.

———. *Rasa, of Knowledge of the Self: Essays on Indian Aesthetics and Selected Sanskrit Studies.* Translated by Louise Lande Levi. New York: New Directions, 1982.

Rosenblatt, Kathleen Ferrick. *René Daumal: The Life and Work of a Mystic Guide.* Albany: State University of New York Press, 1999.

DEATH ON THE INSTALLMENT PLAN (MORT À CRÉDIT) LOUIS FERDINAND CÉLINE (1936)

This novel recounts the troubled childhood and adolescence of Ferdinand Bardamu, the principal character in Céline's previous novel, *JOURNEY TO THE END OF THE NIGHT*. The only child of petty merchants, Ferdinand, like the author, grows up in Paris and tries his hand at various apprenticeships before going off to war in 1914.

In a series of anecdotes, the first part of the novel reflects the pathos of Ferdinand's life, crushed as he is by his parents and his environment. Ferdinand's story denies the possibility of liberation through class struggle, hence the novel's rejection by leftist critics who had earlier praised *Journey*. Céline shows how the family itself is responsible for one's dissatisfaction with life. Ferdinand is intimidated daily by his parents, and his rebellion is purely personal, never political, leading, in the end, only to silence.

Tragicomic and full of local color, *Death on the Installment Plan* reflects Céline's innovative and powerful use of language as well as his ability to reveal the tension and turbulence of the inter-war period. Moreover, it is a narrative of rage and violence against his childhood. Ferdinand, the narrator, feels no pity for his parents, whose only concern is material survival. The only positive character is the narrator's grandmother. However, her influence is insufficient to prevent Ferdinand from becoming like his father. One day, overcome with rage, Ferdinand nearly murders his father. The second part of the novel recounts Ferdinand's subsequent experience in England as secretary to Courtial des Pereires, the vicious director of a scientific review who ends up committing suicide.

The novel contains strong autobiographical elements. The narrator shares Céline's first name and, like all of Céline's novels, is written in the first person. In this and other works, Céline offers his view of the human condition as weak and hopeless. Céline reveals the tragedy of modernity by evoking the atomization of individuals in contemporary life. His style is, as always, innovative, nonconformist, antibourgeois, and antiestablishment. Moreover, Céline uses the coarse language of the street while overturning all the rules of syntax to give the reader the impression of violent emotion.

FURTHER READING

Bouchard, Norma. *Céline, Gadda, Beckett: Experimental Writings of the 1930s.* Gainesville: University of Florida Press, 2000.

Buckley, William K., ed. *Critical Essays on Louis Ferdinand Céline.* Boston: G. K. Hall, 1989.

Green, M. J. *Fiction in the Historical Present: French Writers and the Thirties.* Hanover, N.H.: University Press of New England, 1986.

Hewitt, Nicholas. *The Life of Céline: A Critical Biography.* Oxford, Malden, Mass.: Blackwell, 1999.

Knapp, Bettina Liebowitz. *Céline, Man of Hate.* Tuscaloosa University: University of Alabama Press, 1974.

Luce, Stanford, ed. and trans. *Céline and his Critics: Scandals and Paradox.* Saratoga, Calif.: Anma Libri, 1986.

McCarthy, Patrick. *Céline.* New York: Penguin Books, 1977.

Solomon, Philip H. *Understanding Céline.* Colombia: University of South Carolina Press, 1992.

Vitoux, Frédéric. *Céline: A Biography.* Translated by Jesse Browner. New York: Paragon House, 1992.

Wohl, Robert. *The Generation of 1914.* Cambridge, Mass.: Harvard University Press, 1979.

DEBACLE, THE   See *The* DOWNFALL.

DECADENTISM

The term *decadentism* was first used by historians in the 1830s to refer to the end of the Roman Empire and to the late Roman poets. More important, from the Latin *cadere,* meaning "to fall," decadentism refers to a 19th-century literary movement contemporary with SYMBOLISM and opposed to NATURALISM. It is associated with writers such as Jules Laforgue, JORIS-KARL HUYSMANS, PAUL BOURGET, Rémy de Gourmont, and Octave Moreau.

Paul Bourget discussed the decadent aesthetic in his *Essays on Contemporary Psychology* (1883), in reference to Charles Baudelaire, whose poetry, with its emphasis on the beauty of that which is lethal, is an important influence on the development of decadentism, along with the pessimistic philosophy of Arthur Schopenhauer.

The first genuine decadent novel is Joris-Karl Huysmans's *AGAINST THE GRAIN* (1884), in which the principal character's fascination with the artificial, the rare, and the odd, Huysmans's subtle blending of mysticism and sensuality, and an interest in the occult all reflect principal themes of decadentism. Decadent writers were, on the whole, antibourgeois, nonconformist, and interested in modernity only in its artificiality.

DELPHINE GERMAINE DE STAËL (1802)

In this EPISTOLARY NOVEL written in the tradition of JEAN-JACQUES ROUSSEAU'S *JULIE, OR THE NEW HELOISE,* Delphine, a young widow, is in love with Léonce, who loves her in return. Unfortunately, social constraints bar their union over and over again. In the first instance, Delphine compromises herself to protect the honor of a female friend. Léonce is naturally jealous. Unaware of Delphine's true intentions, he is tricked by Sophie de Vernon into marrying her daughter, Mathilde. When Sophie dies, Léonce discovers the truth, rekindling his love for Delphine. Yet because he does not believe in divorce, he cannot leave Mathilde. Overcome with sadness, Delphine enters a convent.

When the FRENCH REVOLUTION abolishes the monasteries, Delphine is released from her vows. Léonce finds her again and it seems that happiness is finally possible until Léonce, again inspired by a sense of duty, joins the civil war only to be executed as an aristocrat. Delphine poisons herself.

Léonce describes Delphine saying, "You love liberty the way you love poetry or religion or anything capable of ennobling and exalting humanity: and the ideas one believes to be alien to women are perfectly reconciled in your kind nature." Unfortunately, the tragedy lies in Delphine's refusal to hide her true nature from society, thus making her vulnerable.

Staël deftly blends personal sentiments and analysis of the human heart and soul with reflections on contemporary society and politics. In this early feminist work, Staël explores the theme of a female desire for liberty in a society whose laws and expectations are oppressive to women, laying the foundation for GEORGE SAND's feminist ROMANTICISM. Staël, in fact, bridges the ENLIGHTENMENT and the romantic movement. Like her lover, BENJAMIN CONSTANT, Staël was interested in the concepts of liberty and individualism and the inevitable tension between the individual and society.

FURTHER READING

Christopher-Herold, J. *Mistress to an Age: A Life of Mme de Staël*. New York: Bobbs-Merrill, 1958.

Gutwirth, Madelyn. *Madame de Staël, Novelist: The Emergence of the Artist as a Woman*. Urbana: University of Illinois Press, 1978.

Hess, Carla. *The Other Enlightenment: How French Women Became Modern*. Princeton, N.J., Oxford: Princeton University Press, 2001.

Hogsett, Charlotte. *The Literary Existence of Germaine de Staël*. Carbondale: Southern Illinois University Press, 1987.

Smith, Bonnie G. "History and Genius: The Narcotic, Erotic, and Baroque Life of Germaine de Staël," *French Historical Studies* 19, no. 4 (Autumn 1996): 1,059–1,081.

Trouille, Mary Seidman. *Sexual Politics in the Enlightenment*. Albany: State University of New Work Press, 1997.

DESJARDINS, CATHERINE (MADAME DE VILLEDIEU) (1640–1683)

Catherine Desjardins was a prolific writer. In the course of her literary career she produced more than 14 novels, fictional memoirs, poetry, and plays. One startling piece is an erotic sonnet *Jouissance* (*Enjoyment*), written in her youth. For such a work to be written and published by a young unmarried woman was surprising at the time. She was perhaps inspired by her great passion for a nobleman named Antoine Villedieu. Desjardins never married the man with whom she carried on a lengthy and tumultuous affair, but after his death she signed her works "Madame de Villedieu." She eventually married Claude-Nicolas de Chaste in 1677.

As a novelist, Desjardins is known for historical fiction. She theorized, too, on the genre she chose to write in, taking a remarkably modern approach to the relationship between fiction and history. She argues that her novels, like the DISORDERS OF LOVE, are simply another kind of history. Desjardins was interested in the motivations that lie behind historical action. She takes an essentially psychological approach to the effects of private history on public history, arguing that human emotion (love in particular) is the driving force behind political intrigue. She is comparable, in this respect, to MADAME DE LAFAYETTE. Desjardins also gives prominent attention to the role of women. Not surprisingly, she was criticized by contemporary writers such as Pierre Bayle and Boileau for distorting the truth.

FURTHER READING

Beasley, Faith Evelyn. *Revising Memory: Women's Fiction and Memoirs in Seventeenth-Century France*. New Brunswick, N.J.: Rutgers University Press, 1990.

Goldsmith, Elizabeth C. *Publishing Women's Life Stories in France, 1647–1720: From Voice to Print*. Women and Gender in the Modern World. Aldershot, England: Ashgate, 2001.

Lalande, Roxanne Decker, ed. *A Labor of Love: Critical Reflections on the Writings of Marie-Catherine Desjardins (Mme de Villedieu)*. Madison, N.J.: Fairleigh Dickinson University Press; London: Associated University Presses, 2000.

Morrissette, Bruce. *The Life and Works of Marie-Catherine Desjardins (Mme de Villedieu): 1632–1683*. Washington University Studies. New Series. Language and Literature, no. 17. Saint Louis: Washington University Press, 1947.

DEVIL IN THE FLESH, THE (LE DIABLE AU CORPS) RAYMOND RADIGUET (1923)

Set in 1918, this novel features an adolescent narrator named François who tells the story of how he met Marthe, a bit older than he and engaged to a soldier at the front. The novel was written when Radiguet was between the ages of 16 and 18. It was published in the year of his premature death at 20. The novel is partly autobiographical, as Radiguet did have an affair with an older woman named Alice when he was only 14, but, as Radiguet wrote, "They wanted to read in my book a confession. What a mistake."

The story begins when François is 16 years old. The upheaval of wartime and the freedom he is allowed by his parents permit François a good deal of independence. When he meets Marthe, they begin an affair. Marthe marries her fiancé, Jacques, nonetheless, when he is home on leave. Once he is gone and she has her own apartment, she and François have even greater freedom and François ends up practically living with Marthe. Trouble comes when Marthe discovers she is pregnant. Overwhelmed, François abandons her and Marthe dies not long after giving birth to her child, calling out for François.

The novel's power lies in Radiguet's description of François, whose experience is that of a man although he is, in reality, still only a child. The narrator opens the novel with the words "It is but a child that I must lead through an adventure that even a man of experience would find difficult." In French, the word *adventure* has an ambiguous meaning. Moreover, the expression "to have the devil in one's flesh," used to refer to naughty children, took on an erotic meaning after the publication of Radiguet's novel. It is a novel of "initiation," a love story, a psychological novel, and a tragedy all at once. Written in a simple, sober style, the novel ends on a moralist note, despite its scandalous content. Contemporary readers were disturbed that the novel did not show the respect due to soldiers when, in fact, it is war that created the conditions for the affair between François and Marthe.

FURTHER READING
Crosland, Margaret. *Raymond Radiguet: A Biographical Study with Selections from his Work.* London: Owen, 1976.
McNab, James P. *Raymond Radiguet.* Boston: Twayne, 1984.

DEVIL'S POOL, THE (LA MARE AU DIABLE) GEORGE SAND (1846)

In this work from her series of pastoral novels, or *romans champêtres,* Sand depicts the simple, poetic, laborious life that she finds in her native province of Berry. *Devil's Pool* tells the story of Germain, a widowed peasant with three children, who agrees to marry a wealthy widow. He sets off on a visit to his betrothed with his children and a young woman named Marie who is going into domestic service. Along the way, the travelers get lost and have to spend the night outdoors under the stars, near the Devil's Pool. There they timidly speak of love and marriage. Despite certain difficulties, Germain follows his heart and upon his return, marries Marie rather than the wealthy widow.

The novel reflects Sand's belief, in contrast to her contemporary, GUSTAVE FLAUBERT, that literature should be idealist (see IDEALISM). That is the avowed purpose of her art. Sand paints a world in which hard work and simple virtues serve as the foundation for moral regeneration. In contrast to HONORÉ DE BALZAC's *The Peasants,* written at roughly the same time, Sand prefers to depict country life not in terms of class struggle but as the means for social salvation. Echoing themes found in the works of JEAN-JACQUES ROUSSEAU, Sand shows

that the peasantry has retained values long abandoned by the bourgeoisie and urban life. Inspired, in part, by Virgil's *Georgics,* Sand argues that collective labor in the midst of nature will save humankind. Marriage, too, overcomes class conflict to symbolize fundamental human unity. Sand thus opposes the values of love and labor to those of the modern market economy and society, to promote the salutary role of love in human existence.

FURTHER READING
Crecelius, Kathryn J. *Family Romances: George Sand's Early Novels.* Bloomington: Indiana University Press, 1987.
Glasgow, Janis, ed. *George Sand: Collected Essays.* Troy, N.Y.: Whitston, 1985.
Hofstadter, Dan. *The Love Affair as a Work of Art.* New York: Farrar, Straus and Giroux, 1996.
Naginski, Isabelle Hoog. *George Sand: Writing for her Life.* New Brunswick, N.J.: Rutgers University Press, 1991.
Peebles, Catherine. *The Psyche of Feminism: Sand, Colette, Sarraute.* West Lafayette, Ind.: Purdue University Press, 2003.
Powell, David A. *George Sand.* Boston: Twayne, 1990.
Schor, Naomi. *George Sand and Idealism.* New York: Columbia University Press, 1993.
Vitaglione, Daniel. *George Eliot and George Sand.* New York: Peter Lang, 1993.

DEVIL UPON TWO STICKS, THE (LE DIABLE BOITEUX) ALAIN RENÉ LESAGE (1707)

Lesage's interest in literature first manifested itself in translations of Spanish works, and the influence of that literary tradition on his own writing is marked. *The Devil upon Two Sticks* reflects Spanish influence and yet the style (the only thing that matters in the words of ANATOLE FRANCE) is unmistakably French.

This very popular novel borrows its setting from Velez de Guevara's *Diablo cojuelo,* in which a demon, Asmodée, lifts the roofs of Madrid to reveal to Cléo, a student, the private lives of its inhabitants. Such a device in the hands of Lesage becomes a satire of Parisian mores. The novel contains 16 chapters of lively anecdotes interspersed with two longer sentimental stories. Its realistic depiction of human nature made the novel an instant success, so much so that legend tells us two noblemen drew swords over the last available copy.

FURTHER READING

France, Anatole. *The Latin Genius.* Translated by Wilfrid S. Jackson. London: John Lane and the Bodley Head; New York: Dodd, Mead, 1924.

Longhurst, Jennifer. "Lesage and the Spanish Tradition: *Gil Blas* as a Picaresque Novel," *Studies in Eighteenth-Century French Literature Presented to Robert Niklaus.* Edited by J. H. Fox, M. H. Waddicor, and D. A. Watts. Exeter, England: Exeter University Press, 1975, 123–137.

DIARY OF A COUNTRY PRIEST, THE (*JOURNAL D'UN CURÉ DE CAMPAGNE*)

GEORGES BERNANOS (1936)   Written as the private journal of a young provincial priest, the very structure of this novel suggests that the writer, as such, and the priest share a sacerdotal quality. The unnamed priest is naive, timid, weak, and in poor health when he arrives in a country village to take up his post. Despite his good intentions, the villagers greet all his plans with a hostility he cannot comprehend. Moreover, there are serious problems in the family that inhabits the local château. Chantal, the count's daughter, is rebellious, as her father is having an affair with the governess while her mother is overcome with grief and anger since the death of their son. Evil is present in the village of Ambricourt, in the mud, the night, in death, and in hatred. In the midst of all these difficulties, the priest's only solace is in conversations with an older priest and the local doctor. In the end, however, the priest, capable of great and gentle love for the souls in his care, triumphs over evil and offers redemption.

Diary of a Country Priest is the most popular and the most moving of Bernanos's novels. There is no fascinating intrigue or complicated plot; it is simply the journal of a country priest whose efforts to improve the spiritual life of his parishioners often end in failure. Keeping a journal serves as catharsis. It is a personal confession that allows the priest to take stock of his own conscience. In the end, it becomes a necessary means of self-examination and self-expression. The priest describes events and his thoughts with meticulous care. Above all, it is a journal about the state of a soul, a powerful first-person narrative that draws the reader into the priest's suffering conscience.

The culminating passage in the novel involves a conversation between the priest and the countess. The priest has come to the château to try and effect reconciliation between Chantal and her mother. In a moment of epiphany, the countess attains a state of grace and thanks the priest for the peace she has finally found through him. That very night, she dies in her sleep. What follows is the priest's agonizing death from stomach cancer, a death that symbolizes the priest's extraordinary Christlike character.

The novel also explores the meaning of poverty and misery, in the life of the priest and in the lives of his parishioners, as poverty is an essential element in the Christian faith. Bernanos's message recalls the works of LÉON BLOY, whose writings he discovered during the painful years of World War I. The character of the priest recalls another of Bernanos's characters, the abbé Donissan in UNDER SATAN'S SUN. Both are ultimately pure beings who suffer from tragic solitude in a modern world devoid of spirituality.

FURTHER READING

Balthasar, Hans Urs von. *Bernanos: An Ecclesial Existence.* San Francisco: Ignatius Press, 1996.

Blumenthal, Gerda. *The Poetic Imagination of Georges Bernanos.* Baltimore, Md.: Johns Hopkins University Press, 1965.

DIB, MOHAMMED (1920–2003)

Born into a family of modest means in Algeria, Dib engaged in a variety of professions before turning to journalism and teaching. In 1950–51, he worked as a journalist for *Alger républicain,* the communist daily newspaper of colonial Algeria. The militantism of this newspaper influenced Dib's first novels. Dib was a member of a group of Algerian writers that included ALBERT CAMUS. Along with Camus and KATEB YACINE, Dib came to be recognized as one of the most important contemporary Algerian writers. His first novel, *The Big House* (1952), which won the Feneon Prize, was the first of a trilogy that includes *FIRE* (1954) and *Tunisian Loom* (1957). These three novels together are entitled *ALGERIA.*

This trilogy depicts life in colonial Algeria and the gradual rise of political consciousness among its people. Highly realist, the novel tells the story of Omar, who first experiences urban misery, then the first peasant uprisings in the countryside, and, finally, the birth of an industrial proletariat. All three novels reflect Dib's interest in the power of language. *Algerian Sum-*

mer (1959) depicts the world and vision of the Algerian bourgeoisie during the war of liberation. Dib was driven out of Algeria in 1959 for supporting the Algerian independence movement, and he left for France.

Dib's first novels draw from realist and naturalist traditions in fiction (SEE REALISM and NATURALISM). In *Who Remembers the Sea* (1962), however, Dib abandons realism for an apocalyptic vision that recalls Picasso's painting *Guernica* in its violent and sensual imagery that continues to inform subsequent novels such as *On the Savage Banks* (1964), *Dance of the King* (1968), and *God in Barbarity* (1970). In his later works, Dib's style becomes increasingly mystical and abstract.

Dance of the King, God in Barbarity, and *The Hunter* evoke the richness of life in independent Algeria through the different types of speech associated with certain kinds of characters. Arfia and Rodwan are former resistance fighters who realize that their personal memories are no longer significant. At the same time, there is a power in their recollection of brushes with death that others cannot entirely comprehend. Then there is Kamel Waëd, who is compelled by the prevailing order to direct the army to intervene against a group of intellectuals who have gone into the countryside to help the poorest of peasants. Dib gives the impression of the power of any given discourse to influence and even override the individual's conscience and consciousness. Dib further explores the power of language in *Habel,* the story of an Algerian exiled in Paris who has a vision of the angel of death who instructs Habel to "give each thing a precise name." It is a story of love and madness as Habel gives himself over entirely to his obsession and to a woman named Lily.

A second trilogy that includes *Orsol Terrace* (1985), *Eve's Slumber* (1989), and *Marble Snow* (1990) evokes once more a very different literary landscape from Dib's earlier works. Focusing on the psychological and affective relationships between people, these novels are both tender and cruel. At the same time, they reflect a sense of wisdom about life derived from experience. Dib reveals his fascination, too, with the relationship between mother and child. *If God Wills It* (1998) depicts massacres in an Algerian village and reflects Dib's profound sense of the writer's responsibility to society.

An underlying theme in many of Dib's works is the anxiety produced by modernization. Occasionally this anxiety gives way to madness. Dib has also produced tales for children and a number of articles that reflect his engagement in political issues.

FURTHER READING
Ahmad, Fawzia. *A Study of Land and Milieu in the Works of Algerian-Born Writers Albert Camus, Moulous Feraoun, and Mohammed Dib.* Lewiston, N.Y.: E. Mellen Press, 2004.
Joyaux, Georges J., Albert Memmi, and Jules Roy. "Driss Chraïbi, Mohammed Dib, Kateb Yacine and Indigenous North African Literature," *Yale French Studies,* no. 24, Midnight Novelists (1959): 30–40.

DIDEROT, DENIS (1713–1784)

Born in Langres to a petit bourgeois family, Diderot rose to become one of the greatest philosophers of the French ENLIGHTENMENT. He wrote on philosophy, art, and natural history and produced novels and plays. His most significant work is arguably the ENCYCLOPEDIA, the great collaborative project of the Enlightenment philosophers intended to eradicate ignorance and superstition by offering a compendium of all human knowledge.

Diderot was first educated by the Jesuits in Langres and later studied theology at the Sorbonne, in Paris. In 1726 he received a master of Arts degree from the University of Paris. There he lived by tutoring and by his pen, translating and publishing philosophical works, the first of which was an annotated and edited edition of Shaftesbury's *Essay on Merit and Virtue* (1745). Shaftesbury's thinking remained an important influence on Diderot's later works. In Paris that he first met two important figures in his life, Antoinette Champion, a seamstress whom he secretly married in 1743, and JEAN-JACQUES ROUSSEAU.

Diderot's marriage collapsed after a few years but two other women were central to his life in later years, Madeleine de Puisieux, for whom he wrote INDISCRETE JEWELS, and, Sophie Volland. The correspondence between Diderot and Volland provides a rich source for understanding the development of Diderot's thought. Known for his radical ideas, Diderot was even imprisoned. His books were often censored, confiscated, or published after his death. His startling and scandalous novel *The Nun,* for example, was written in 1760 but not published until 1796. This novel of a young woman forced to take her vows is an apology for individual liberty, one of the most important themes in Diderot's works and to the project of the Enlightenment.

The permission to begin work on what was initially to be a translation of English scholar Ephraim Chambers *Cyclopedia* was accorded in 1746, the same year that Diderot produced his *Philosophical Thoughts,* a work that was almost immediately condemned by the parliament of Paris. Diderot was described to the lieutenant of police in Paris as "a very dangerous man who speaks scornfully of the holy mysteries of our religion." For 26 years Diderot worked as principal editor of the *Encyclopedia.* He collaborated with the mathematician Jean Le Rond d'Alembert on this work that was, in the end, much more than a translation of Chamber's work. With 17 volumes of text and 11 volumes of illustrations, this was no easy task. The *Encyclopedia* was also threatening to both church and state as its more than 60,000 articles challenged existing social and political institutions and beliefs. Diderot was imprisoned for his supposedly dangerous ideas; the *Encyclopedia* was condemned by the pope and subjected to the censor's harsh treatment. Nonetheless, it was an enormous success that, according to some scholars, lay the foundation for the French Revolution by creating a new political vocabulary.

The circle of Enlightenment philosophers, such as Rousseau, David Hume, Claude Adrien Hélvetius, abbé Guillaume Thomas Raynal, novelist Lawrence Stern, and Jean-François Marmontel, constituted Diderot's network of friends. Rousseau had his great moment of illumination that led to his *Discourse on the Origin of Inequality* on his way to visit Diderot in the prison of Vincennes. Although there are strong parallels in their thinking, Diderot broke with Rousseau in 1757. The origin of their dispute is a line from Diderot's play *The Bastard:* "Only the mean man is alone," which Rousseau took as a reference to himself.

Some of the great enlightened despots of the 18th century were also among his contacts. Along with d'Alembert, Diderot was elected to Frederick the Great's Academy of Berlin in 1751. Catherine II of Russia was an even greater patroness of Diderot. In 1765 she purchased Diderot's library to save him from financial ruin. From 1773 to 1774 he visited her in St. Petersburg, where together they held lengthy conversations on a variety of social and political issues.

On his return from Russia, Diderot oversaw the French edition of Catherine II and Marshall Betskoi's *Plans and Statutes for different Establishments ordered by Empress Catherine II,* edited his own *Observations* on Catherine II's constitutional project (the *Nakaz*), published his *Memoirs for Catherine II* and his *Plan for a University for the Government of Russia.* The topic of education was important for Catherine in her attempts to refashion Russian society along Western lines. It was equally important to the Enlightenment philosophers as the means to eradicate ignorance and refashion Western society on rational lines.

The years 1757 and 1758 were fertile for Diderot as a dramatist. He wrote several plays, *The Bastard or Trials of Virtue, Conversations with Dorval,* and *Family Man* as, well as theoretical works that include a *Discourse on Dramatic Poetry,* and the famous *Letter to d'Alembert* in 1758. Along with the aforementioned line from *The Bastard,* this public letter led to the final breach with Rousseau, who disagreed on the question of theater as a pedagogical tool to promote social virtue.

From theater Diderot turned to art criticism. He wrote his first *Salon* in 1759 for Grimm's *Literary Correspondence.* He then wrote eight others between 1759 and 1781. In this period, Diderot also produced his greatest novel, *The Nun.* Between 1762 and 1764 he wrote a first draft of *Rameau's Nephew,* reedited in 1773. Interestingly, this work was not published in French until 1821–23, from Goethe's translation into German of 1805. Diderot continued to write prolifically. In 1769 he wrote *D'Alembert's Dream.* The *Supplement to Bougainville's Voyage* dates from 1772. This work, along with the *History of the Two Indies,* on which he collaborated with the Abbé Raynal, indicts the systems of colonialism and slavery and calls into question the foundations of Western civilization.

Whether he wrote fiction or nonfiction, Diderot continually emphasized the importance of individual liberty and the necessity of grounding society on a notion of natural virtue, all the while acknowledging the tensions that necessarily exist between these two ideas. His goal as a writer and philosopher was to bring everything out into the open and to reveal the truth, whatever that may be, about society, institutions, and human nature. The 19th-century literary critic SAINTE-BEUVE described Diderot as "the first great writer who belongs to modern democratic society."

FURTHER READING

Burbank, P. N. Diderot: A Critical Biography. New York: Knopf, 1992.

Diderot, Denis. La Religieuse. Edited by Roland Desné. Paris: Garnier-Flammarion, 1968.

Loy, Robert J. Diderot's Determined Fatalist: A Critical Appreciation of Jacque le Fataliste. New York: Crown Press, Columbia University, 1950.

MacPhail, Eric. "Diderot and the Plot of History," New Literary History 30, no. 2 (1999): 439–452.

Wilson, Arthur. Diderot. New York: Oxford University Press, 1972.

DISCIPLE, THE PAUL BOURGET (1889) The

Disciple is the story of a student who decides to apply practically the naturalistic literary theories he has learned to his own life. Focusing on the theme of morality versus science, The Disciple marks a turning point in Bourget's career as a writer. From this point on, Bourget's novels increasingly combine morality, religion, and sociology. Long considered a master of the psychological novel, Bourget's approach reflects the fin de siècle malaise shared by a generation of young thinkers who turned against positivist and naturalistic trends in science and literature (see POSITIVISM and NATURALISM).

From 1850 to the end of the 19th century, these two movements dominated the literary world. Bourget, however, participated in a counter movement that rejected materialism in search of spiritual regeneration. Bourget thus shares the interests of other writers such as ANDRÉ GIDE, MARCEL PROUST, PAUL VALÉRY, and ROMAIN ROLLAND. MAURICE BARRÈS called this new generation of thinkers Les Déracinés (the uprooted).

Beyond challenging intellectual developments associated with Darwin, Freud, and Nietzsche, recent events such as the French defeat at the hands of the Prussians and the crushing of the Paris Commune in 1871 contributed to the general sense of disorientation that led some writers to turn inward. Bourget's Disciple reflects this exploration of the psychological

as an antidote to science. After the publication of The Disciple, Bourget's novels became increasingly royalist and Catholic in tone, recalling the works of his contemporary LÉON BLOY.

FURTHER READING

Baumer, Franklin L. Modern European Thought: Continuity and Change in Ideas, 1600–1950. New York: Macmillan, 1977.

Carter, John Hannibal. A Study of Social Problems in the Novels of Paul Bourget with Reference to those of Balzac's Comédie Humaine. Urbana, Ill., Ph.D. Thesis. 1944.

Singer, Armand E. Paul Bourget. Boston: Twayne, 1976.

DISORDERS OF LOVE, THE (LES DÉS-ORDRES DE L'AMOUR) CATHERINE DESJARDINS, MADAME DE VILLEDIEU (1675) In this work

of historical fiction, Catherine Desjardins tells three stories drawn from the recent past to examine the cause of "disorder" in France in the late 1500s, a period marked by civil and religious war. She looks at the rise of the Catholic League, Marshal de Bellegarde's betrayal of France, and the death of Givry d'Anglure, one of Henry IV's most trusted advisers. In each instance, she traces the origins of political events to their source. For Desjardins this is always love. As she states directly, "the diverse intrigues that comprise this story prove convincingly that love is the force behind all other human passions. If one were to examine the secret motives behind the revolutions within monarchies, one would discover inevitably that this passion is the culprit or at least the accomplice of them all."

In placing passion above reason, Desjardins moves away from the traditional Christian stance on the human condition, at least in its ideal state. Distancing herself from the Cartesian view that reason can govern emotion, Desjardins contributes to a refashioning of the literary discourse on love so prominent in 17th-century fiction. Echoing the language and view of the précieuses (see PRECIOSITY), HONORÉ D'URFÉ presented a utopian vision of love in a mythical golden age. As writers such as Desjardins and MADAME DE LAFAYETTE began to take a more psychological approach to their analysis of human emotion, they lead us in new directions reinforced by libertine novelists such as JEAN-BAPTISTE DE BOYER, MARQUIS D'ARGENS.

FURTHER READING

Beasley, Faith Evelyn. *Revising Memory: Women's Fiction and Memoirs in Seventeenth-Century France.* New Brunswick, N.J.: Rutgers University Press, 1990.

Goldsmith, Elizabeth C. *Publishing Women's Life Stories in France, 1647–1720: From Voice to Print. Women and Gender in the Modern World.* Aldershot, England: Ashgate, 2001.

Lalande, Roxanne Decker, ed. *A Labor of Love: Critical Reflections on the Writings of Marie-Catherine Desjardins (Mme de Villedieu).* Madison, N.J.: Fairleigh Dickinson University Press; London: Associated University Presses, 2000.

Morrissette, Bruce. *The Life and Works of Marie-Catherine Desjardins (Mme de Villedieu): 1632–1683* Washington University Studies. New Series. Language and Literature, no. 17. Saint Louis: Washington University Press, 1947.

DJEBAR, ASSIA (1936–)

Assia Djebar was born in Algeria. Her father was a teacher who, contrary to tradition, chose to have his daughter educated in a French school. A passionate reader and brilliant student, in 1955 Djebar went on to study at the prestigious École Normale Supérieure in Paris. Along with her husband, Djebar participated in the Algerian war of liberation, and their experiences furnished much of the material for her subsequent works. The theme of women's emancipation runs throughout Djebar's writings and is associated with the liberation of Algeria from French colonial rule. For Djebar the two problems are inextricably linked. Djebar's early works include *Mischief* (1957), *Impatient Ones* (1958), and *Children of the New World* (1962). One of her greatest works, *Naïve Larks* (1967), is an exploration of a North African woman's discovery of her own body.

As of 1980, Djebar's writings turned more markedly feminist in their exploration of the tension between traditional Arab women, enclosed and veiled, and contemporary women seeking emancipation despite the resistance of a good portion of society. This theme is central, for example, to *Algerian Women in their Apartment* (1980), in which Djebar skillfully blends her own personal experience with a historical perspective. In *Fantasia, An Algerian Cavalcade* (1986) she traces the conquest of Algeria from 1830 to the war of independence in 1962. A SISTER TO SCHEHERAZADE (1987) reflects on female solidarity. In *So Vast the Prison* (1995), Djebar recalls her mother and grandmother, while *Algerian White* (1996) and *Oran, a Dead Language* (1997) examine the problems of contemporary Algeria.

Along with other works of fiction, Djebar has also produced a film focusing on the difficulties of love for a couple that result from the fundamental differences between men and women. Perhaps North Africa's most famous woman writer, Djebar skillfully reveals women's voices and expressions, the problem of cultural identity, national and personal independence, and colonialism and patriarchy.

FURTHER READING

Donadey, Anne. *Recasting Postcolonialism: Women Writing Between Worlds.* Portsmouth, N.H.: Heinemann, 2001.

Elia, Nada. *Trances, Dances and Vociferations: Agency and Resistance in Africana Women's Narratives.* New York: Garland, 2001.

Erickson, John. "Women's Space and Enabling Dialogue in Assia Djebar's *L'Amour, la fantasie.*" In *Post-Colonial Subjects: Francophone Women Writers,* edited by Mary Green et al. Minneapolis: University of Minnesota Press, 1996.

Merini, Rafika. *Two Major Francophone Women Writers, Assia Djebar and Leila Sebbar: A Thematic Study of their Works.* New York, P. Lang, 1999.

DOCTOR FAUSTROLL (GESTES ET OPINIONS DU DOCTEUR FAUSTROLL, PATAPHYSICIEN) ALFRED JARRY (1911)

In this fantastic novel, the hussar René-Isidore Panmuphle, finds Doctor Faustroll (whose name is obviously derived from a combination of Faust and troll), in his cellar, flooded with wine and spirits of various sorts, preparing to embark on a journey by boat along with characters he has taken from books and with a monkey as cabin boy.

This odd collection of characters leaves Paris, traveling from sea to sea, stopping in different ports. When they come across a monster sailor, Faustroll kills everyone except for their host. The monkey's ghost is then sent to purchase canvas and to get a painting machine working that will re-create different worlds. Doctor Faustroll subsequently acts as if he is dying and enters into correspondence with Lord Kelvin, a physicist to whom he imparts the secret of "Pataphysics," and attempts to calculate the surface of God.

This is a complicated and, at times, perplexing work. "Pataphysics" is "the science of imaginary solutions" that Jarry's character Ubu invented in another work. It is a science of particulars that reflects late 19th-century symbolist thought (see SYMBOLISM). Moreover, each of Faustroll's ports of call recalls the work of a different writer or artist, Stéphane Mallarmé, LÉON BLOY, and Paul Gaugin among them. The Rabelaisian undercurrent to the novel is strong (see RABELAIS). However, there are also references to the Bible, Homer, and science in general, as Jarry creates a fantastic world that exists outside of reality. Not surprisingly, *Doctor Faustroll* was an inspiration to later surrealists (see SURREALISM).

FURTHER READING

Beaumont, Keith. *Alfred Jarry: A Critical and Biographical Study.* St. Martin's Press, 1984.

Fell, Jill. *Alfred Jarry, an Imaginary Revolt.* Madison, N.J.: Farleigh Dickinson University Press, 2005.

LaBelle, Maurice Marc. *Alfred Jarry, Nihilism, and the Theater of the Absurd.* New York: New York University Press, 1980.

Lennon, Nigey. *Alfred Jarry: The Man with the Axe.* Los Angeles: Panjandrum Books, 1984.

Murphy, Patrice. "Rabelais and Jarry," *French Review* 51, no. 1 (October 1977): 29–36.

Shattuck, Roger. *The Banquet Years: The Arts in France, 1885–1918: Alfred Jarry, Henri Rousseau, Erik Satie, Guillaume Apollinaire.* New York: Harcourt Brace, 1958.

DOCTOR PASCAL (*LE DOCTEUR PASCAL*) ÉMILE ZOLA (1893)

The last novel in Zola's ROUGON-MACQUART "natural and social history of a Second Empire family," *Doctor Pascal* finally breaks the hold of biological determinism on the descendants of Adelaïde Fouque. The theme of heredity and the environment's impact on the individual is at the heart of Zola's naturalist project in literature (see NATURALISM).

Doctor Pascal, a Rougon, is a biologist who earns his living as a doctor while pursuing his study of heredity, thus allowing him to examine his own family from a supposedly objective standpoint. He is a learned man who believes in social and moral progress. He is drawn to POSITIVISM and yet senses that there is something more to life than what science reveals to us.

Like Zola's own encounter and love affair with Jeanne Rozerot, Doctor Pascal's life changes when he falls in love with his niece, Clotilde, the daughter of Pascal's brother, Aristide Saccard (*MONEY*). In a moment of spiritual crisis, Clotilde tries to destroy her uncle's records of the family. She wants to erase the taint that finds its origins in Aunt Dide's madness. Pascal catches Clotilde and explains his purpose, ultimately convincing her to abandon her faith in favor of science. The novel thus reflects tensions in 19th-century French society that pitted older religious traditions against modern science and the notion of progress. In the end, Pascal, the scientist, is a conciliator.

Clotilde becomes Pascal's mistress. Once in love, however, Pascal begins to question his own faith in science. To put an end to gossip, and because of his poverty, Pascal forces Clotilde to leave, not realizing that she is pregnant with their child. Clotilde becomes a symbol of hope for the future of humanity as the novel ends with the image of a mother nursing her child.

In this last volume, the hereditary weakness with which the series began is ultimately defeated. The novel and the series end on a positive note. There is something beyond the question of biological determinism. In contrast to the series's opening, fertility is no longer a curse. Rather it offers the possibility of redemption.

FURTHER READING

Butor, Michael, and Michael Saklad. "Zola's Blue Flame," *Yale French Studies*, no. 42, Zola (1969): 9–25.

DOMINIQUE EUGÈNE FROMENTIN (1863)

Eugène Fromentin's only novel, *Dominique*, is an autobiographical work recounting the author's unfulfilled passion for a childhood friend. Fromentin published the novel when he was 43 years old, 15 years after the death of the woman he loved.

Dominique, the main character, describes his passion for Madeleine and their mutual renouncement. He writes as a settled, reasonably happy family man and mayor of his village. The work is thus a Bildungsroman or novel of apprenticeship, written in retrospect. The protagonist, Dominique, realizes that knowledge of oneself comes from one's own sensations, memories, habits, and emotions, not from outside of oneself. In fact, it is experience and self-reflection that create one's identity. *Dominique* is consequently also a psychological novel.

Fromentin, a successful artist, wrote the way he painted, perhaps with even greater sensitivity. While there is no complex or dramatic plot, the novel evokes the poetry of feeling and memory. Fromentin wrote with a discrete style and a delicacy of expression that is almost chaste. The harmonious nostalgia for emotions and seasons he invoked resembles a painting of a familiar landscape.

Dominique was published in 1862 in the renowned literary journal the *Revue des deux mondes*. Dominique de Bray is an orphan, raised in the country by an aunt and a young teacher. By nature a sensitive young man, he is also guided by instinct. As an adolescent he is a dreamer. At secondary school, he loves only poetry and his one great friend, Olivier.

Olivier's cousin, Madeleine, disturbs him profoundly when they meet, but she is two years older. Madeleine marries Alfred de Nièvres. However, she and Dominique remain friends. Nonetheless, Dominique feels sharply his unrequited love. He wishes to remain near Madeleine, in order to at least reveal his soul to her even if he cannot reveal his love. Not surprisingly, his passion becomes too painful to bear in silence. Madeleine, generous of heart, is sensitive to Dominique's pain and wishes to cure him but soon realizes that she loves him in return. As a result, she decides she must distance herself from him forever.

Meanwhile, Dominique has failed in his literary career. He ultimately returns to his property in the country, where he leads a peaceful life as a country gentleman, mayor, husband, and father.

Fromentin successfully portrays the renouncement of a young man's love when he realizes that he cannot have what he desires most. Moreover, Fromentin treats the honorable yet painful decision made by Dominique and Madeleine with great delicacy of feeling. As Fromentin draws from his own experience as a youth, the tone is confessional. In the end, Dominique is at peace with himself, the most one can hope for when confronted with the impossible.

Like many romantic novels, (see ROMANTICISM) a significant theme is the abandonment of an unrequited passion. Fromentin's descriptions of nature, particularly the melancholy aspects of autumn, are similarly romantic. At the same time, the author leads the reader in a new direction. Turning away from romantic passion, Fromentin offers instead a sort of melancholy wisdom on social and moral constraints.

FURTHER READING
Evans, Arthur R. *The Literary Art of Eugène Fromentin: A Study in Style and Motif.* Baltimore: Johns Hopkins University Press, 1964.

Hartman, Elwood. *Three Nineteenth-Century French Writer/Artists and the Maghreb: The Literary and Artistic Depictions of North Africa by Théophile Gautier, Eugène Fromentin and Pierre Loti.* Tübingen, Germany: Narr, 1994.

Mickel, Emanuel J. *Eugène Fromentin.* Boston: Twayne, 1981.

Wright, Barbara. *Eugène Fromentin: A Life in Art and Letters.* Bern, New York: Peter Lang, 2000.

DORA BRUDER PATRICK MODIANO (1997)

Arguably Modiano's greatest work, *Dora Bruder* evokes a Paris in which memory and reality overlap and become indistinguishable. Modiano once said, "Like all those people who have neither a native land nor roots, I am obsessed with my prehistory and my prehistory is the troubled and shameful period of the Occupation: I have always had the feeling, for obscure reasons related to my family, that I was born out of this nightmare. The dim light of this period is for me like the Gironde was for Mauriac or Normandy for La Varende; that is where I come from."

In this novel, the author is in search of a 15-year-old girl whose name he comes across by chance in an old newspaper. Dora Bruder disappeared on December 31, 1945, when she was deported to German concentration camp. Born in 1926 to a family of immigrants from eastern Europe, Dora lived with her family in a series of hotel rooms in the working-class neighborhoods of north Paris.

Modiano weaves back and forth between Dora's life and his own. Although he did not experience the war, his parents did. Modiano's father was an Italian Jew who lived in occupied Paris with his Belgian wife. The figure of Modiano's father haunts a number of his works as the author grapples with the question of whether his father was a collaborationist.

Critics have often characterized Modiano's works as "autofiction" because of their ambiguity and obscurity. To what degree is *Dora Bruder* autobiographical? To what degree is it history? It is in part the work of a historian, as Modiano reaches into Dora's past. The significance of an ordinary girl takes on new meaning as she comes to represent the shocking collective experience of French Jews during the war. Moreover, Modiano breaks a taboo that has only recently been challenged in a serious way: the truth of French collaboration in the deportation of Jews.

Modiano searched the French archives for evidence of Dora's fate, evidence that is included in this collage-like text that builds on a few, slim historical facts. The end of the novel recounts Dora's initial imprisonment, her transfer to the Drancy transit camp, and, finally, her deportation to Auschwitz. The novel includes an intertextual reference of JEAN GENET's *Miracle of the Rose,* a novel written from the same Tourelles prison where Dora is temporarily held.

Modiano's work is marked by the anguish of forgetting that makes it difficult to untangle the autobiographical elements in the novel from the author's quest for Dora, a rebellious girl who is in some ways Modiano's double. Moreover, Modiano's search for Dora appears to be connected to Modiano's struggle to understand his father and to come to terms with his own Jewish identity. He even imagines a moment when his father might have seen Dora, as if he wishes to link his own destiny with that of the lost girl. In the end, however, he concludes, "I believe that she will remain anonymous forever, she and all the other shadows arrested on that night." Modiano thus raises certain ethical questions as he explores the relationship between fiction and reality, literature and history.

The novel is marked by a sense of tragedy as Modiano attempts to revive the memory of someone who disappeared from history without a trace. Dora represents the pain and suffering of the entire Jewish community. For Modiano, the Occupation is a concentrated microcosm of the human condition with all its vitality and horror.

FURTHER READING

Avni, Ora. "Patrick Modiano: A French Jew?" *Yale French Studies,* no. 85, Discourses of Jewish Identity in Twentieth-Century France (1994): 227–247.

Bridges, Victoria. "Patrick Modiano: Quartier Perdu," *Yale French Studies.* Special Issue: After the Age of Suspicion: The French Novel Today (1988): 259–263.

Guyot-Bender, Martine, and William Vander Wolk, eds. *Paradigms of Memory. The Occupation and Other Histories in the Novels of Patrick Modiano.* New York: Peter Lang, 1998.

Kawakami, Akane. *A Self-Conscious Art: Patrick Modiano's Postmodern Fictions.* Liverpool, England: Liverpool University Press, 2000.

Mitchell, Constantina. *Shaping the Novel: Textual Interplay in the Fiction on Malraux, Hébert, and Modiano.* Providence: Berghahn Books, 1996.

Morris, Alan. "Patrick Modiano." In Michael Tilby, ed. *Beyond the Nouveau Roman. Essays on the Contemporary French Novel.* Providence: Berg, 1990, 177–200.

Morris, Alan. *Patrick Modiano.* Oxford, Washington, D.C.: Berg, 1996.

Nettelbeck, Colin. "Novelists and Their Engagement with History: Some Contemporary French Cases," *Australian Journal of French Studies* 35 (1998): 245–248.

Sherman, Timothy H. "Translating Memory: Patrick Modiano in the Postmodern Context," *Studies in Twentieth Century Literature* 16, no. 2 (Summer 1992): 289–303.

Vander Wolk, William. *Rewriting the Past. Memory, History and Narration in the Novels of Patrick Modiano.* Amsterdam, Atlanta: Faux-Titre No. 129, Rodopi, 1997.

DORGELÈS, ROLAND (1885–1973) Dorgelès

is the pseudonym for Roland Lécavalé, who was born in Amiens and studied at the École des Beaux-Arts in Paris, where he frequented bohemian circles of artists and writers. He began his own career as a journalist and then joined the infantry in World War I. The horrors of life in the trenches inspired Dorgelès's most famous novel, WOODEN CROSSES, which won the Femina Prize in 1919. In this novel, Dorgelès depicts the French soldier's everyday experience. "To tell of your long misery, I also wanted to laugh, to laugh your laugh."

Wooden Crosses was followed by *The Beautiful Woman's Cabaret* (1919) and *The Raising of the Dead* (1923), a novel that casts a bitter eye on the period following World War I. A similar spirit marks the disillusioned characters in *Saint-Magloire* and *If It Were True?* (1934), a science fiction novel asserting the unperfectability of humanity. Dorgelès's pessimistic conclusions concerning the human condition likewise color *Everything Is* for Sale (1956) and Down with Money (1965), novels whose very titles express the mood of the author and his times.

Dorgelès also experimented with travel novels in Caravan Without Camels (1928), On the Mandarin Road (1925), Under the White Cap (1942), and Tropical Route (1944). Far more successful were his nostalgic works evoking the bohemian life of Montmartre: Montmartre My Country (1928), The Château of Fog (1932), When I Was in Montmartre (1936), Bohemian Bouquet (1948), Unaltered Portraits (1952), Good Times on the Hill (1963), and The Marquis of Poverty (1971).

During World War II, Dorgelès served as a correspondent. His novel Identity Card (1945) explores the problems of occupied France. In 1945 Dorgelès was elected president of the Goncourt Academy, of which he had been a member since 1929. He died in Paris in 1973.

FURTHER READING

Field, Frank. Three French Writers and the Great War. Cambridge: Cambridge University Press, 1975.
Klein, Holger, ed. The First World War in Fiction. London: Macmillan, 1976.
Wohl, Robert. The Generation of 1914. Cambridge, Mass.: Harvard University Press, 1979.

DOWNFALL, THE (LA DÉBÂCLE) ÉMILE ZOLA (1892)   Nineteenth in Zola's 20-novel ROUGON-MACQUART series, a "Natural and Social History of a Second Empire Family," The Downfall recounts the defeat of Napoleon III's army at Sedan during the Franco-Prussian War (1870–71). In accordance with his naturalist doctrine (see NATURALISM), Zola depicts the reality of war through the experience of foot soldiers, among whom the reader finds Jean Macquart, the central character in Zola's novel EARTH, along with Maurice Levasseur, a student who participates in the bloody defeat of the Paris Commune.

With his naturalist colleagues, Zola had previously explored the experience of war in his Médan Evenings, preparing the way for World War I writers such as HENRI BARBUSSE and ROLAND DORGELÈS. Zola was not interested in the cause of war but in its demystification, seeking to reveal the responsibility of various social groups for violent conflict. Reflecting intellectual and scientific trends associated with Darwin and Freud, Zola makes a statement about war in general, as a law of nature connected to humanity's death instinct, an unavoidable part of the historical process. War proves the absurdity of human existence. At the same time, Zola also reinforced general public opinion over the Franco-Prussian War, according to which France was defeated by incompetent leaders and a corrupt regime. Ultimately, the novel evokes Zola's fundamental commitment to the notion of the individual placing the needs of the collective before his own.

FURTHER READING

Tintner, Adeline R. "A Bibliographical and Biographical Note: Henry James's Markings in Zola's La Debacle," Henry James Review 17, no. 2 (Spring 1996): 204–207.

DRIEU LA ROCHELLE, PIERRE (1893–1945)   Drieu La Rochelle was born in Paris and studied at the prestigious École Libre des Sciences Politiques. He failed his qualifying exam and was consequently unable to pursue a diplomatic career. Drieu grew up reading MAURICE BARRÈS, Rudyard Kipling, and Friedrich Nietzsche with great interest. When World War I broke out, Drieu left enthusiastically for the front. Wounded and subsequently hospitalized, he wrote a collection of poems, Interrogation (1917), praising the mystical fraternity that exists among soldiers.

After the war, Drieu experimented with varied artistic and political movements of the period, from communism to SURREALISM to fascism. He also began his career as a writer, producing The Back of the Canteen (1920), Civil Status (1921), Measure of France (1922), some short stories, and, in 1925, A Man Buried in Women, a novel about the deception of time and love dedicated to LOUIS ARAGON. At the end of the 1920s, Drieu was also writing numerous articles as he became increasingly active politically. The dominant theme in Drieu's writing is his denunciation of social decadence. Drieu was merciless in his attacks on bourgeois society and values.

Drieu's father died in 1934; his mother had died in 1925. In Dreaming Bourgeoisie he recalls his parents. According to the plot, Camille le Pesnel marries Agnès Ligneul around the year 1890. Because he does not love her, he keeps his former mistress as well. Agnés, nonetheless, feels bound to her husband and remains faithful to him despite the advantageous proposition she receives when they are facing difficult times. The novel then shifts the narrator's voice to Geneviève, Agnès's daughter, whose brother, Yves, has died a hero's death at the front.

In his well-known *Comedy of Charleroi* (1934), Drieu traces the experience of a soldier in World War I. The work consists of six short stories. In *Comedy,* a former soldier visits the battlefield of Charleroi with the mother of a fallen comrade and is disgusted by her, as she represents all that is wrong with society. Drieu had, in fact, participated in that battle.

Will o' the Wisp (1931) represents the period in Drieu's life between his experiments with surrealism and his move toward fascism. It also reflects the author's pessimistic view of society in the interwar period. The principal character, Alain, miserable with his lover and himself, commits suicide. Then, in *Diary of a Fragile Man* (1934), in the course of, again, six short stories, Drieu evokes, among other things, the experience of a couple whose love is undermined by jealousy. GILLES (1939), Drieu's partly autobiographical novel, offers an explanation as to why a young man could be drawn to the political right in uncertain times.

In addition, Drieu wrote about 40 essays and some 600 articles. Drieu's political views were passionate and complex. By 1934, he had shifted distinctly to the right. Fascinated by the theatricality of fascism, he came to believe that the movement would be capable of regenerating Europe. Yet in 1944 he published *Straw Dogs,* depicting his disillusionment with fascism. In the winter of that same year, Drieu attempted suicide for the first time. He subsequently wrote *The Memoirs of Dirk Raspe,* published posthumously in 1966. Drieu also wrote for the theater, notably *Cold Water* (1931), *The Man in Charge* and *Charlotte Corday* (1944).

Drieu evoked the deception and disillusionment of an entire generation, particularly among those who had experienced life in the trenches of World War I. As he gradually embraced fascism, Drieu showed a tendency toward a mystical vision of Europe and his own nation. After 1940, he collaborated with the German occupiers until he realized the horror of Hitler's regime. However, he later came to the conclusion that communism would inevitably triumph. Protected by friends such as ANDRÉ MALRAUX, at the Liberation Drieu committed suicide on the day he learned of the warrant for his arrest.

FURTHER READING

Cadwallader, Barrie. *Crisis of the European Mind: A Study of André Malraux and Drieu La Rochelle.* Cardiff: University of Wales Press, 1981.

Green, M. J. *Fiction in the Historical Present: French Writers and the Thirties.* Hanover, N.H.: University Press of New England, 1986.

Kaplan, Alice Y. *Reproductions of Banality: Fascism, Literature, and French Intellectual Life.* Minneapolis: University of Minnesota Press, 1986.

Klein, Holger, ed. *The First World War in Fiction.* London: Macmillan, 1976.

Leal, Robert Barry. *Drieu La Rochelle.* Boston: Twayne, 1982.

Reck, Rima Drell. *Drieu La Rochelle and the Picture Gallery Novel: French Modernism in the Interwar Years.* Baton Rouge: Louisiana State University Press, 1990.

Soucy, R. *A Fascist Intellectual: Drieu La Rochelle.* Berkeley, Los Angeles, London: University of California Press, 1979.

Zelden, Theodore. *France 1848–1945,* Vol. 5, "Anxiety and Hypocrisy." Oxford: Oxford University Press, 1979.

DUCLOS, CHARLES PINOT (1704–1772)

Duclos once stated: "I was a real libertine because of my temperament and I did not really begin to concentrate on literature until satiated with libertinism, sort of like those women who offer to God what the Devil no longer wants." Grammarian, moralist, historian, and novelist, Charles Duclos was a talented conversationalist and writer, if at times difficult of character and sharp with words.

Duclos was born in Brittany to a wealthy commercial family. In 1721 he left for Paris to study law but spent more time in libertine pursuits. Concerned, his mother called him home. When he returned to Paris in 1726 he was drawn more to literature than to his previous pastimes. This time the Parisian cafés he visited were frequented by atheists and materialists.

Duclos was a witty man. His conversational ability was so great that he was accepted into the Académie des Inscriptions et Belles-Lettres before having published a single work. Not surprisingly, Duclos was welcome in literary and philosophical circles. Madame de Pompadour and Louis XV were his benefactors, assuring him the position of historiographer of France in 1750. Duclos also served as mayor of his native town of Dinan. Although his relationship with the *Encyclopédists* was sometimes strained (see ENCYCLOPEDIA), in later years he corresponded with VOLTAIRE and MONTESQUIEU. A member of the London and Berlin Academies, Duclos was accepted into the Académie Française in 1746, to which he was appointed perpetual secretary in 1762.

Over the course of his lifetime, Duclos produced a wide variety of works. His two famous LIBERTINE NOVELS were *The HISTORY OF MADAME DE LUZ* and *The CONFESSIONS OF THE COUNT OF ****. Like his contemporary CRÉBILLON FILS, Duclos theorized on the novel, arguing that its purpose is to give an illusion of truth. STENDHAL admired Duclos for his ideas and his style of writing, saying that "one draws from [Duclos] the juice of man's knowledge."

FURTHER READING

Free, L. R. *Virtue, Happiness and Duclos' "Histoire de Madame de Luz."* The Hague: Martinus Nijhoff, 1974.
Meister, Paul. *Charles Duclos, 1704–1772.* Geneva: Droz, 1956.
Silverblatt, Bette Gross. *Maxims in the Novels of Duclos.* The Hague: Nijhoff, 1972.
Thompsett, E. "Love and Libertinism in the Novels of Duclos," *SVEC* 137 (1975).

DUJARDIN, ÉDOUARD (1861–1949)

Born near Blois to a Norman family, Dujardin attended secondary school in Rouen and Paris. He later studied music at the conservatory in Paris along with Claude Debussy, but Dujardin was already showing the interest in literature that would govern his future career.

Dujardin played an important role in the symbolist movement as a writer, editor and theoretician (see SYMBOLISM). Influenced by the poet Stéphane Mallarmé, composer Richard Wagner, and philosopher Arthur Schopenhauer, Dujardin founded *La Revue Wagnérienne* in 1885. He directed *La Revue indépendante* from 1886 to 1888. Both of these journals were important to the symbolist movement.

Dujardin is principally known today as the writer of the first novel to use the interior monologue or stream of consciousness. His novel *WE'LL TO THE WOODS NO MORE* influenced diverse writers such as James Joyce, Virginia Woolf, ANDRÉ GIDE, SAMUEL BECKETT, and NATHALIE SARROUTE, among others.

FURTHER READING

Genova, Pamela Antonia. *Symbolist Journals: A Culture of Correspondence.* Aldershot, England; Burlington, Vt.: Ashgate, 2002.
McKilligan, Kathleen M. *Édouard Dujardin, Les Lauriers sont coupés and the Interior Monologue.* Hull, England: University of Hull, 1977.

DUMAS, ALEXANDRE (1802–1870)

When Dumas's father, a famous Napoleonic general who had fallen on hard times, died, his family was left in difficult straits. Alexandre was obliged to take a position as clerk in a notary's office. He was only 15 years old. At the age of 21, he abandoned this uninspiring career to make his fortune in Paris. There he applied his energies to literature, ultimately with remarkable success. By 1825 Dumas was collaborating with librettist Adolphe de Leuven on vaudeville works that, in the end, were not performed. Despite this inauspicious beginning, Dumas's career as a writer soared. In his time, Dumas was known as both playwright and novelist. Today we remember him principally for his novels.

Dumas's life was adventurous, like the novels he wrote, full of duels, love affairs, travel, and the company of artists and writers. His liaison with a seamstress, Catherine Labay, produced a son in 1824, ALEXANDRE DUMAS FILS (in English, Junior).

Dumas had a varied career. For a time, he worked as librarian to the duc d'Orléans but resigned this post for political reasons. A convinced republican, Dumas participated in the revolutions of 1830 and 1848. He ran for office twice but was never elected. In 1860, inspired by the Italian independence movement, Dumas joined General Giuseppe Garibaldi's army in Italy, where he spent four years before returning to Paris.

A born adventurer, Dumas loved travel but he was also sometimes obliged to do so for political reasons or to escape his debts, despite the fortune he made writing. Dumas produced 91 plays, some 100 novels, numerous articles, and even a cookbook. He is particularly famous today for his historical romances like *The Three Musketeers* trilogy and *Queen Margot*. He has often been criticized for a sloppy style but his abundant imagination, lively dialogues, intrigues, sympathetic heroes, and terrible villains make his novels a pleasure to read.

At the outset, Dumas intended to write for the theater. He first acquired fame and fortune with his *Henry III and His Court* (1829). This historical drama, performed at the Comédie Française theater, marked Dumas as a leader of romantic theater (see ROMANTICISM). While no one reads anymore his early novels such as *Captain Paul* (1838), *The Adventures of John Davis* (1840), or *Georges* (1843), Dumas's later historical fiction remains popular. Moreover, it is difficult to articulate the tremendous impression Dumas's works made on contemporary readers. His writing for the theater had a significant impact on his historical fiction; all of Dumas's novels are, in their own way, powerfully theatrical.

A British performance of Shakespeare's *Hamlet* marked a turning point in Dumas's life. From then on he was fascinated and inspired by history's exceptional men and events, in which he found an endless reservoir of material. The Scottish novelist Sir Walter Scott, whose works were nearly as compelling in France as in his native Britain, was also a significant influence on Dumas.

Dumas once wrote, "What is history? A nail on which I hang my novels." In 1838, he met Auguste Maquet, a young history teacher, with whom he collaborated for many years. Eventually Maquet took Dumas to court saying that he should be recognized as coauthor of the novels they had worked on together, in order to receive royalties. Maquet lost. All of Dumas's most famous historical works were produced in the 1840s: the d'Artagnan trilogy, the Valois romances that include *Queen Margot*, and *The Count of Monte Cristo*, arguably Dumas's most popular novel. He was so successful that in 1845 the journalist Eugène Mirecourt accused Dumas of running a "fiction factory," arguing that it is impossible for one man to produce so prolifically. Dumas took him to court and won.

In 1847, Dumas built his own theater, the Théâtre Historique, at enormous expense. There he put on adaptations of his novels such as *Queen Margot* and *The Three Musketeers,* as well as original works for the stage such as *The Demoiselles of Saint-Cyr* (1843). Audiences were enthusiastic but still Dumas could not pay his debts. In the same year he constructed his theater, Dumas also completed his luxurious residence, the Château of Monte Cristo in Marly-le Roi. The result of his extravagance was financial disaster.

Dumas left for Belgium in 1851, where he worked on his memoirs, published after his return to France in 1853, along with more novels. Back in France, Dumas founded a newspaper, *The Musketeer,* and a literary weekly, *The Monte Cristo,* but his financial situation remained precarious. When he encountered opposition from Napoleon III, Dumas headed off on new escapades, joining Garibaldi's revolution. He spent four years in Naples, where he irritated the Neapolitans, who considered Dumas an opportunist.

Once again Dumas returned to Paris, where new journalistic endeavors failed, inspiring him to journey to Russia in 1858. The results of this voyage were two more travelogues, *Adventures in the Caucasus* (1859) and *Travels in Russia* (1865). Dumas had already published memoirs of his travels in Switzerland, Southern France, and Italy among others. Dumas's travel journals also made popular reading among his contemporaries.

Dumas once said that in the course of his life he earned 18 million gold francs. But he spent as fabulously as he earned. At the end of his life he was broke but happy and had to be taken in by his son and daughter. In his last years Dumas said of death, "I will tell her a story and she will be kind to me."

Dumas wrote more than 300 volumes. He was not the best writer from a strictly literary standpoint but that is perhaps not the best standard by which to judge an author who was, first and foremost, a creator of myths that live on today. Dumas's unforgettable characters continue to inspire readers and movie producers. Of all the romantic writers, along with BALZAC and HUGO, Dumas is the most read today. As his biographer, André Maurois, wrote, "Dumas was a hero out of Dumas. . . . He turned his own life into the finest of his novels."

FURTHER READING

Bell, David F. *Real Time: Accelerating Narrative from Balzac to Zola.* Urbana: University of Illinois Press, 2004.

Hemming, F. W. J. *Alexandre Dumas. The King of Romance.* New York: Scribner, 1979.

Maurois, André. *Three Musketeers. A Study of the Dumas Family.* Translated by Gerard Hopkins. London: Cape, 1957.

Ross, Michael. *Alexandre Dumas.* Newton Abbot, Devon, England; North Pomfret, Vt.: David and Charles, 1981.

Schopp, Claude. *Alexandre Dumas: Genius of Life.* New York: Franklin and Watts, 1988.

Stowe, Richard. *Dumas.* Boston: Twayne, 1976.

DUMAS, ALEXANDRE, *FILS* (1824–1895)

One imagines that it might be difficult to follow in the footsteps of a father as legendary as ALEXANDRE DUMAS *père,* creator of unforgettable adventure stories like *The* THREE MUSKETEERS, *The* COUNT OF MONTE CRISTO, and QUEEN MARGOT. Alexandre Dumas *fils* (in English, Junior), the natural son of Alexandre Dumas and a seamstress named Catherine Labay, seems not to have suffered. Not surprisingly, there are a number of interesting parallels in the lives of the two Dumas.

As a child, Dumas *fils* studied at boarding school in Paris until the age of 17. He earned a number of first prizes on finishing secondary school; in this respect he was unlike his father, who never put much effort into his schoolwork. Upon completion of his studies, Dumas went to live with his father for six months until he decided, in 1842, to set off on his own.

Dumas was so successful in sowing his wild oats that by 1845 he had accumulated more than 50,000 francs in debt, an enormous sum by any reckoning. Dumas must have inherited something of his father's character as well as a talent for writing.

He once said, "not knowing how to do anything, I turned to literature." In 1845 he published a volume of poetry, *Sin of Youth.* Appropriately named, this work received little attention. After a voyage to Spain with his father, Dumas published his first novel, *The Adventures of Four Women* (1846). Disappointed with this first attempt at novel writing, Dumas realized that his real gift lay in the observation of daily life. CAMILLE (*La Dame aux camélias*), his first experiment in this new direction, was an enormous success. The character of

Marguerite Gautier is modeled on Marie Duplessis, Dumas's mistress, whom he met in 1844. Dumas was only 24 when his reputation as a writer was assured.

Over the next three years, Dumas produced a dozen novels, enough to improve his financial situation. Then he turned to his great love, the theater, again falling in his father's footsteps. *Camille* was adapted to the stage. Dumas was even more successful in writing for the theater than he had been as a novelist, although he did publish one more novel, *The Clemenceau Affair* (1866).

Dumas wrote mostly REALIST plays such as *A Question of Money* (1857), *Natural Son* (1858), and *Prodigal Father* (1859). In 1860, Dumas suffered an illness due to overwork. He did not pick up his pen again until 1864.

Dumas's approach to theater was like that of DIDEROT. Theater must have a moral, didactic purpose such as we see in *Madame Aubray's Ideas* (1867). Dumas's later plays were similar in purpose and sometimes scandalous in their depiction of Parisian mores and society. Dumas was elected to the Académie Française in 1874.

FURTHER READING

Maurois, André. *Three Musketeers: A Study of the Dumas Family.* Translated by Gerard Hopkins. London: Cape, 1957.

Saunders, Edith Alice. *The Prodigal Father, Dumas père et fils and the Lady of the Camellias.* London, New York: Longmans Green, 1951.

Schwarz, Henry Stanley. *Alexandre Dumas, fils, Dramatist.* New York: B. Blom, 1871.

DURAS, MARGUERITE (1914–1996)

Duras is the pen name of Marguerite Donnadieu, taken from the name of a town in southwest France where the author's father was born. A talented writer who ultimately attained international fame, Duras was born in the French colony of Indochina. Her childhood was difficult. Of modest background, Duras's parents were tempted by the dream of success in the colonies, but this was not to be. Duras's father died when she was only four years old, leaving her mother, a teacher, with three children to raise in extreme financial difficulty. After working for many years, she bought a piece of land, thinking that she would finally have security, only to discover that she had been swindled. The land she purchased flooded six months of the year and was thus impossible to cultivate.

At boarding school in Saigon, Duras discovered her own sensuality and the power of desire when she met "the lover" described in her novel of the same name, a rich, young Chinese man with whom she shared her first experience in love and social transgression. The difficulties of a childhood spent with her struggling mother, an older brother caught up in drugs, and a younger brother who was slightly retarded and whom she loved dearly left a lasting mark on Duras that is reflected in her writing.

In 1932, Duras went to study law, mathematics, and political science in Paris. Adjustment to life in France was not easy. She met and married Robert Antelme, giving birth to a stillborn child in 1942. That same year, Duras met the actor Dionys Mascolo. For a time, the three worked together. Duras and Antelme then divorced in 1947, the year Duras gave birth to her son Jean Mascolo.

As of 1943, Duras and Antelme were active in the Resistance movement, and in 1944 Antelme was arrested and deported to Dachau concentration camp, the year that Duras joined the Communist Party (only to be expelled from it in 1950). Antelme was liberated in 1945 and published his reflections on his experience in *The Human Species* in 1947. This was also the subject of Duras's work *Douleur* (Pain, 1985).

Duras began writing during World War II. Her first novel, *The Shameless,* was published in 1943. It was followed by *Tranquil Life* in 1944, a work that recalls the novels of FRANÇOIS MAURIAC in its evocation of the simple joys of provincial life. The writer RAYMOND QUENEAU was responsible for introducing the work to the editors at Gallimard.

Inspired by American writers of "the lost generation," Duras wrote her first autobiographical work, SEA WALL, in 1950, in which she offered a sympathetic portrait of those oppressed by the colonial system. It was her first great success and was later adapted to film. In this novel, Duras also described her family and her experience as a child. It is the first work in which she introduces the figure of her mother, who reappears in

her famous novel LOVER, 30 years later. She is courageous, stubborn, loved, hated, and respected all at once. Duras's exploration of her relationship with her mother has attracted the attention of modern feminist writers (see FEMINISM).

As a militant communist, Duras gathered together a group of leftist artists and intellectuals in her Paris apartment. She also wrote prolifically. In her next four novels, *Sailor from Gibraltar* (1952), *Little Horses of Tarquina* (1953), *Entire Days in the Trees* (1954), and *The Square* (1955), Duras began to experiment with a new narrative style. She gained notoriety with the publication of MODERATO CANTABILE in 1958. Duras is especially well known for the highly successful film *Hiroshima, mon amour,* directed by Alain Resnais and released in 1960, based on Duras's novel of the same name and for which she also wrote the screenplay. In that same year, Duras published *The English Lover.*

At this point in her career, Duras was writing on the margins of the NOUVEAU ROMAN movement as the formal elements in her novels cede place to detail, motif, silence, and hesitation. Her writing is marked by the weight of the *unsaid.* However, Duras ultimately stood apart from the NOUVEAU ROMAN group, convinced that their approach would only lead, in the end, to sterility. Her writing turned in yet another direction with *The RAVISHING OF LOL V. STEIN,* the first in a series of increasingly enigmatic novels that includes *The Vice-Consul* (1965), *India Song* (1973), *Lover* (1971), *The Woman of the Ganges* (1973), and *Venice in the Calcutta Desert* (1976). Duras continued to draw from her own experiences in these novels, although she insisted, "The story of our life, of my life, does not exist." In fact, it is difficult to distinguish between autobiography and fiction in her works.

Duras was active in the student protest movement of 1968, the events of which renewed her revolutionary dreams, reflected in such publications as *Destroy, She Said* (1969), a work that addresses the tension between desire and social conventions. Duras subsequently turned increasingly to film, producing *Destroy, She Said* (1969), *The Yellow Sun* (1970), *Nathalie Granger* (1973), *India Song* (1975), and *The Truck* (1977).

In *Woman to Woman,* Duras engages in a dialogue with Xavière Gauthier. In this feminist work she explores the female condition. Contemporary feminist writers have recognized Duras's contribution to women's writing (*écriture féminine*) in her exploration of a woman's social and sexual identity.

From 1970 to 1980, Duras continued to write for film. Furthermore, in *Les Lieux de Marguerite Duras* (1977), Duras engages in a dialogue with screenwriter Michele Porte about her life. In her later years, Duras suffered from poor health. Nonetheless, the presence of her last companion, Yann Andréa, marks her writing after 1980. In *Summer 80,* Duras and Andréa watch a child on the beach, while *Yann Andréa Steiner* (1992) describes their life together. In 1983, Andréa himself wrote *M.D.,* about Duras's near-death experience in a detoxification program.

Once recovered, Duras published her extremely successful autobiographical novel *Lover* (1984), about her childhood in Indochina. *Lover* won the Goncourt Prize. Disturbed by Jean-Jacques Annaud's adaptation of that novel to film, Duras wrote *The Lover from Northern China* (1991), reworking the same story in a different way. Finally, in *To Write,* one of her last works, Duras explained what writing meant to her. Independent and original, Duras became almost a cult figure, inspiring both admiration and hatred.

The principal themes in Duras's novels are love and desire, pain and destruction. Each of her characters is haunted by a secret, obsessive, and enigmatic suffering that builds up to a cry of despair, often to the point of madness. The suffering that Duras describes is born out of desire. Occasionally, she hints at the possibility of liberation through love, yet the individual remains, at heart, bound and burdened by social constraints.

Duras's novels are frequently built around a single event, a crisis without resolution. At the same time, Duras explores the relations between characters who inevitably fall back into their own solitude. Beneath the surface runs the current of passion and desire, the expression of which is always somewhat hesitant, reflecting the tension that exists between silence and speech. Desire is never exhausted, nor is it ever entirely fulfilled. Duras's world is one of the unfinished, the incomplete, the unsatisfied. Her powerful use of language unveils the tension that underlies our existence. Her characters are marginalized and strange, living in

a world apart. Moreover, there is a musicality to her language, written in a style that gives precedence to dialogue over pure narrative. Duras perhaps found her fullest creative expression in writing for film. Her writing is sober, rhythmic, unadorned, and yet powerful in its emotional intensity.

FURTHER READING

Adler, Laure. *Marguerite Duras: A Life.* Translated by Anne-Marie Glasheen. Chicago: University of Chicago Press, 2000.

Ames, Sanford Scribner, ed. *Remains to Be Seen: Essays on Marguerite Duras.* New York: Peter Lang, 1988.

Best, Victoria. *Critical Subjectivities: Identity and Narration in the Work of Colette and Marguerite Duras.* Oxford, New York: Peter Lang, 2000.

Cohen, Susan. *Women and Discourse in the Fiction of Marguerite Duras: Love, Legends, Language.* Amherst: University of Massachusetts Press, 1993.

Corbin, Laurie. *The Mother Mirror: Self-Representation and the Mother-Daughter Relation in Colette, Simone de Beauvoir, and Marguerite Duras.* New York: Peter Lang,. 1996.

Knapp, Bettina, ed. *Critical Essays on Marguerite Duras.* New York: G. K. Hall; London: Prentice Hall International, 1998.

Murphy, Carol J. *Alienation and Absence in the Novels of Marguerite Duras.* Lexington, Ky.: French Forum, 1982.

Ramsay, Raylene L. *The French New Autobiographies: Sarraute, Duras, and Robbe-Grillet.* Gainesville: University of Florida Press, 1996.

Selous, Trista. *The Other Woman: Feminism and Femininity in the Work of Marguerite Duras.* New Haven, Conn.: Yale University Press, 1988.

Vircondelet, Alain. *Duras: A Biography.* Translated by Thomas Buckley. Normal, Ill.: Dalkey Archive Press, 1994.

D'URFÉ, HONORÉ (1548–1625) A soldier and a writer, Honoré d'Urfé' had a fascinating life story. In 1584 he joined the Order of the Knights of Malta and later fought for the Catholic League in the French wars of religion. In 1600 d'Urfé married his beautiful sister-in-law, Diane de Châteaumorand, after her marriage to his brother Anne Comte d'Urfé had been annulled. Neither marriage was happy. In 1615 d'Urfé separated from his wife and spent most of his time at the court of Savoy, where he held the position of chamberlain. In 1616 he took up arms again, first

for the duke and then in 1625 for Louis XIII against the Spanish. He died that same year from injuries sustained in battle when he fell from his horse.

During his years in Savoy, d'Urfé came up with the plot of his famous novel, ASTREA, set in his native region of Forez in southeastern France. This enormously successful work runs over 5,000 pages and is divided into five parts. The fourth part was edited and the fifth added by his secretary, Balthazar Bruno. Another sequel is attributed to GOMBERVILLE. Astrea is the first great serial novel in the history of French literature. Addressed to an aristocratic audience, it was immensely popular. As readers waited for subsequent volumes to be published, they sometimes acted out the characters' parts.

With many lengthy digressions, the principal plot tells the story of Celadon and Astrée, nominally a shepherd and shepherdess. Astrea is thus the preeminent pastoral novel. Set in a mythical golden age, the characters carry on an elaborate discourse on love. These supposedly rustic characters have the manners and speech of aristocrats and courtiers. This is precisely what contemporary writers such as ANTOINE FURETIÈRE and PAUL SCARRON reacted against by introducing realist elements into their works. The main plot of Astrea may be partly autobiographical, drawing on the story of Anne and Honoré d'Urfé's separate marriages to the same woman. Some episodes may also draw from the life of Henry IV, a renowned lover.

D'Urfé wrote other works as well, such as moral letters and poetry, but it is Astrea that marks his place in the annals of French literary history. The novel has been characterized as baroque for its elaborate relationships, symmetry, and narrative complexity. The narrative structure incorporates poetry, prose, and songs interspersed throughout the principal and secondary plots. Astrea had an immediate impact on the précieuses (see PRECIOSITY) and later on Rousseau.

FURTHER READING

Hembree, James M. Subjectivity and the Signs of Love: Discourse, Desire, and the Emergence of Modernity in Honoré d'Urfé's L'Astrée. New York: Peter Lang, 1997.
Hinds, Leonard. Narrative Transformations From L'Astrée to Le Berger Extravagant. West Lafayette, Ind.: Purdue University Press, 2002.
Horowitz, Louise K. Honoré d'Urfé. Boston: Twayne, 1984.
———. Honoré d'Urfé. Boston: Twayne, 1984.
Jehenson, Myriam Yvonne. The Golden World of the Pastoral: A Comparative Study of Sidney's New Arcadia and d'Urfé's L'Astrée. Ravenna, Italy: Longo, 1981.
McMahon, Mary Catharine, Sister. Aesthetics and Art in the Astrée of Honoré d'Urfé. New York: AMS Press, 1969.
Urfé, Honoré d'. L'Astrée. Translated by with an introductory essay by Steven Randall. Binghamton, N.Y.: Medieval and Renaissance Texts and Studies, 1995.

E

EACH MAN IN HIS NIGHT (CHAQUE HOMME DANS SA NUIT) Julien Green (1960)

The principal character of this novel, arguably Green's greatest work, is Wilfred, a salesman in a clothing store in the United States. Wilfred's financial situation improves considerably when he receives an inheritance after the death of an uncle who, like his nephew, was a marginalized Roman Catholic living among Protestants.

A devout and sincere Catholic, Wilfred also has a disturbing capacity to seduce women. Wilfred senses something diabolical at the core of his being. When he seduces Phoebe, the wife of his cousin James Knight, Wilfred turns to confession in search of solace. To merit the grace he is accorded, Wilfred decides he must settle up past accounts and goes off in search of his friend Max, with whom he had a troubled relationship. In the course of their meeting, Max kills Wilfred. As he is dying, Max asks Wilfred for forgiveness, to which Wilfred responds, "Yes."

The Christian symbolism in this dramatic scene is apparent, and yet at Wilfred's funeral, a disturbing conversation takes place in which Wilfred's conformist mother and cousins discuss the meaning of his last words. Recurring themes in Green's work are the conflict between body and spirit and the presence of evil in the human heart. A convert from Protestantism to Roman Catholicism, Green struggled throughout his life to come to terms with his own faith.

FURTHER READING

Burne, Glenn S. *Julian Green*. New York: Twayne, 1972.
Cooke, Gerard. *Hallucination and Death as Motifs in the Novels of Julien Green*. Washington, D.C.: Catholic University of America Press, 1960.
Dunaway, John M. *The Metamorphoses of the Self: The Mystic, the Sensualist, and the Artist in the Works of Julien Green*. Lexington: University Press of Kentucky, 1978.
Green, Julien. *The Apprentice Writer*. New York: M. Boyars, 1993.
Kostis, Nicholas. *The Exorcism of Sex and Death in Julien Green's Novels*. The Hague, Paris: Mouton, 1973.
Newbury, Anthony H. *Julien Green: Religion and Sexuality*. Amsterdam: Rodopi; Atlantic Highlands, N.J.: Humanities Press, 1986.
O'Dwyer, Michael. *Julien Green: A Critical Study*. Dublin, Ireland; Portland Ore.: Four Courts Press, 1997.
Wildgen, Kathryn Eberle. *Julien Green: The Great Themes*. Birmingham, Ala.: Summa, 1993.
Ziegler, Robert. "From Writing to Scripture: The Character as Text in Julien Green's Le Voyageur sur la terre," *French Review* 63, no. 5 (April 1990): 819–826.

EARTH (LA TERRE) Émile Zola (1887)

At the opening of this powerful novel, the old peasant Fouan can no longer take care of his fields. As much as he resists the idea, Fouan is obliged to divide his property among his children: "Jesus-Christ," a poacher so called for his appearance, Fanny who is married to a wealthy farmer named Delhomme, and Buteau. The division of property is acrimonious. Sometime later, another conflict over property arises that pits Buteau and his wife, Lise, against Françoise, Fouan's granddaughter, who marries an outsider, Jean Macquart (see *The* DOWNFALL).

Tensions in the family arise when Lise slices Françoise open with a scythe, killing her and her unborn child as well. When Buteau and Lise realize that old Fouan has witnessed their crime, they brutally murder him in turn. Jean decides to rejoin the army. He reappears in *The Downfall* and in the last novel in the ROUGON-MACQUART series, *DOCTOR PASCAL*.

This 15th novel in the Rougon-Macquart series resembles *L'ASSOMMOIR* and *GERMINAL* in its focus on laboring classes rather than the bourgeoisie. Critics challenged Zola's brutal depiction of peasant life. Breaking away from the myth of pure, simple country life associated with writers such as JEAN-JACQUES ROUSSEAU, GEORGE SAND, and Jules Michelet, Zola's portrait is far from idyllic. Zola challenged beliefs and values long associated with peasant culture, reflecting his belief that the writer must scientifically observe and document the world as he encounters it (see NATURALISM). Zola desired always to tell the truth.

The setting of the novel is the Beauce, the region where Zola's mother was born. Drawing on his own experience, he brings to life the poverty and endless labor of the peasants' life. He reveals the brutal aspects of peasant character: the harshness, superstition, and fundamental conservatism. To make the novel as realistic as possible, Zola consulted Jules Guesde, a socialist, to learn about the deleterious effects of inheritance laws, the threat of imported grain, and the peasants' resistance to modern agricultural methods. Jesus-Christ speaks as a socialist and recalls the revolutionary events of 1848 that led to the overthrow of King Louis Philippe. Hippolyte Taine's argument concerning the impact of heredity, the environment, and circumstance is another important influence on this work and Zola's writing overall.

Zola once wrote that he wanted "to write the living poem of the Earth but in human terms." In this he was successful. Zola manifests a profound sensitivity to the human condition, to agricultural cycles and human cycles marked by timeless occasions of birth, marriage, and death. The earth itself is an overwhelming presence in the novel, the way the train is in *LA BÊTE HUMAINE* or the still in *L'ASSOMMOIR*. Certainly the relationship of characters to the earth is central to the novel. While the concept of property is important to the novel, it does not reflect Zola's fundamental purpose. Each character may be defined by his or her relationship to the land in such a way that humanity, weak and humbled, confronts the immense power of the earth, fertile and nourishing, yet also the cause of human suffering.

FURTHER READING

Bell, David. *Real Time: Accelerating Narrative from Balzac to Zola.* Urbana: University of Illinois Press, 2004.

Berg, William J., and Laurey K. Martin. *Émile Zola Revisited.* New York: Twayne; Toronto: Maxwell Macmillan Canada; New York: Maxwell Macmillan International: 1992.

Bloom, Harold, ed. *Émile Zola.* Philadelphia: Chelsea House. 2004.

Bowlby, Rachel. *Just Looking: Consumer Culture in Dreiser, Gissing and Zola.* New York: Methuen, 1985.

Brown, Frederick. *Zola: A Life.* Baltimore: Johns Hopkins University Press, 1996.

Chessid, Ilona. *Thresholds of Desire: Authority and Transgression in the Rougon-Macquart.* New York: P. Lang, 1993.

Gallois, William. *Zola: The History of Capitalism.* Oxford, New York: P. Lang, 2000.

Lethbridge, Robert, and Terry Keefe, eds. *Zola and the Craft of Fiction.* Leicester, England; New York: Leicester University Press, 1990.

Lukács, Georg. *Studies in European Realism.* Translated by Edith Bone. New York: Grosset and Dunlop, 1964.

Petrey, Sandy. *Realism and Revolution: Balzac, Stendhal, Zola and the Performance of History.* Ithaca, N.Y.: Cornell University Press, 1988.

ECHENOZ, JEAN (1947–)

Influenced by the rhythm of jazz music, Echenoz evokes sound in words. A versatile writer, Echenoz is able to parody the adventure stories of Conrad in *The Unhappy Team,* write a detective story in *Lake,* as well as structure a novel based on a piece of jazz music in *Cherokee* (also inspired by *The Maltese Falcon*), all with equal skill. Playing with sound, color, and language, Echenoz reveals his creativity and imagination in fantastic electronic flies (*Lake*) and the stunning description of an earthquake in Marseilles (*We Three*).

Echenoz is a very private person, and not much is known about his life. He has occasionally written articles for the French Communist Party paper, *L'Humanité*. He also worked for a number of years as a therapist. After studying sociology in Paris, Echenoz turned to writing, winning the Médicis Prize for *Cherokee* in 1983. Like many contemporary intellectuals, Echenoz was disillusioned by the failure of the political left, as is reflected in his subject matter, particularly in his evocation of modern urban life. Moreover, in his attention to contemporary language and his subtle rejection of society's fascination with media and image, Echenoz reveals his connection to philosophers such as Guy Debord (*Society of the Spectacle*) and Jean Baudrillard (*Simulacra and Simulation*), who have explored the relationship between image and reality in the postmodern world (see POST-MODERNISM).

In *The Greenwich Meridian* (1979), Echenoz experiments with abstract constructions inherited from the *NOUVEAU ROMAN*. This style, however, hampered his creative expression. Subsequent novels reflect a shift in his writing that has become increasingly spontaneous and vibrant as, for example, when he creates his own inimitable world of wasters and detectives roaming the streets of Paris and its suburbs.

Echenoz is capable of a subtle evocation of history and modern life through his description of ordinary objects that suddenly take on a new and strange appearance under the author's ironic gaze. Much of his humor comes from the way in which Echenoz plays with the methods of other writers such as Joseph Conrad and John Le Carré. At the same time, Echenoz brings to his works sonority and a rhythm whose flow evokes the very sense of modern life.

Echenoz participates in a movement that began in the 1980s that aims at bringing literature into closer contact with mass culture and art. He thus draws from popular fiction including comic strips, detective stories, and science fiction, to create his narrative form in novels that are humorous, entertaining, and full of adventure. At the same time, he is able to evoke the incoherence of modern life.

FURTHER READING

Bertens, H. *The Idea of the Postmodern: A History*. London: Routledge, 1995.

Tilby, M., ed. *Beyond the Nouveau Roman: Essays on the Contemporary French Novel*. Oxford: Berg, 1990.

ELEMENTARY PARTICLES, THE (*LES PARTICULES ÉLÉMENTAIRES*) MICHEL HOULLEBECQ (1998)

This powerful and bleak look at contemporary life was translated into 25 languages and won the November Prize in 1998, although the debate among judges was bitter. The principal character, Michel Djerzinski, is, like the author, abandoned by his parents. This leaves him cold and distant from others. He becomes a scientist who experiments on animal cloning.

The only person Michel is at all close to is his half-brother Bruno. The two men are completely different. Bruno is obsessed with sex, and through him the reader sees the degree to which our culture, too, is permeated with sex, eroticism, and "dreams of eternal youth." Bruno is driven by desire to the point of madness. Michel, in contrast, remains detached from the world, completely absorbed in his research. Michel believes that if he succeeds in his experiments, he will be able, through cloning, to separate sex from reproduction, thereby bringing peace to humanity. Certain autobiographical elements are present in this novel that coldly examines social disorder and dysfunction.

Houllebecq seems to suggest that human begins are being surpassed by the very civilization that they have created. Advances in the sciences, in particular, have created the conditions for biological mutations that may replace humanity, as it is now, with something new. Social values, materialism in particular, have likewise contributed to humanity's downfall. Materialism has led to the birth of a culture of desire and excessive individualism. The solution will be a new society that values the collective rather than the individual. Cloning will free humanity from the necessity of sexual reproduction. In consequence, the family and lineage will no longer be important.

In this novel, Houllebecq imaginatively combines molecular biology with quantum physics, drawing on Danish physicist Niels Bohr's theory of complementar-ity. This becomes the theme of the narrative as Houlle-becq juxtaposes Michel (representing objectivity) with Bruno (subjectivity). Together they reveal the spiritual crisis of modern society in which human relations have become distorted and love is impossible. At the same time, the two brothers also represent the nonseparabil-ity of quantum theory in "a society composed of indi-viduals who feel isolated, separated from one another, meeting in a neutral space . . . we are ourselves com-posed of elementary particles, unstable aggregates, in permanent movement."

ÉMILE JEAN-JACQUES ROUSSEAU (1762)

In *Émile,* composed of five books, Rousseau relates the story of raising his ideal pupil, Émile, from infancy to adult-hood, thus tracing the different stages of human development. From the very beginning of Émile's life, Rousseau lays out his plans for a wholesome and natural upbringing. With this combined pedagogical treatise and novel, Rousseau introduced a new era in progressive education. In 1788, the novelist GERMAINE DE STAËL wrote that Rousseau "succeeded in restoring happiness to childhood."

Rousseau has Émile breastfed by his mother (not the general practice among aristocratic women in the 18th century). Nor is Émile swaddled as other infants are, but allowed freedom of movement. He is gradu-ally accustomed to cold and hardship, not so that he suffers, but to attain a level of autonomy necessary for life's later challenges. One of the greatest lessons Émile must learn is self-control. He must have command over his body and his emotions. Freedom comes from self-sufficiency.

Rousseau's pedagogical theories reflect philosophi-cal trends that originate in the epistemology of the late 17th century. Influenced by John Locke's theory of the tabula rasa (the notion that the human mind at birth is a blank slate), as many Enlightenment thinkers were, Rousseau follows sensationist theories. According to this empirical approach, human beings acquire knowl-edge through their senses and experience. Rousseau puts these theories into practice in designing Émile's education.

Rousseau believed that sensations come before ideas. In fact, according to Rousseau, a child is not born with reason. Hence, for many years, Émile's edu-cation focuses on experience rather than books. Émile learns through good examples from his tutor and through hands-on experience. In line with his general philosophical agenda, Rousseau's plan is to educate Émile to be both "Natural Man," as well as a morally and intellectually independent and productive mem-ber of society. For this reason, Émile must not be afraid of hard work or manual labor. He must learn a trade or skill (carpentry, for example).

The last book introduces Émile to Sophie, his future spouse. Book five serves as a romantic novel within the pedagogical treatise. Rousseau and Émile set out as "knights errant" on a quest that leads to the discovery of Sophie, courtship, separation, and finally reunion and marriage. In this last book Rousseau outlines the best education for the woman who will make an ideal wife and mother. Beyond the search for Émile's spouse, the two knights errant are on a quest for an ideal past when man and woman were not yet corrupted by society. Through Sophie, Rousseau hearkens back to a "golden age" of humans in the state of nature where intuition (female) is superior to reason (male).

Émile's education nurtures the innate virtue that is within everyone. He is honest, loyal, sensitive, and compassionate. Sophie is his perfect mate. Brought up by loving parents in a wholesome environment, far from the temptations of society, Sophie dreams of finding a husband like Telemachus from the novel by FRANÇOIS DE SALIGNAC DE LA MOTHE FÉNELON. Sophie will make Émile attentive to her needs but she will not be a coquette. Nor will she be overly educated. Émile will have the great joy of teaching her what she does not know. In return, her natural compassion and nur-turing spirit will meet his needs. She will be a doc-ile and loving wife. While Rousseau's vision of female education may not meet the criteria of 21st-century society, it met with great response in the 18th century. A careful reading of his text reveals the complementar-ity inherent in Rousseau's notion of the ideal conjugal relationship.

By emphasizing feeling (physical or emotional), Rousseau implicitly argues that emotions are part of human nature and thus bestowed by God. Rousseau's deist approach to religion brought him into conflict with the state and the church. His clearest articulation of "natural religion" is found in the "Profession of Faith of a Savoyard Vicar," in *Émile.* The expression of respect for the conscience of the individual, beyond the dictates of institutional religion, brought accusations of unorthodox religious views. *Émile* was consequently banned in Roman Catholic France and Calvinist Switzerland. Rousseau's argument in favor of "moral autonomy" influenced the German Enlightenment philosopher Immanuel Kant's thinking. Furthermore, the value Rousseau attached to emotion or intuition fed into ROMANTICISM.

Critics in political and ecclesiastical circles disapproved of *Émile's* intellectual and spiritual education, but the general public responded enthusiastically. As popular as Rousseau's *JULIE, OR THE NEW HÉLOÏSE, Émile* inspired many Europeans to raise their children *à la Jean-Jacques. Émile* was famous throughout Europe and had a direct influence on pedagogical theory for many years. Women desired to follow the example of the virtuous Sophie, much as they desired to imitate Julie. Rousseau offered a space in which a woman's "nature" might reach its fullest potential, albeit within a domestic sphere. Through it, Rousseau contributed to changing the concept of childhood, as a distinct period in human development.

In his *Confessions,* Rousseau urged readers to consider his works as a whole. His political theory as well as his fiction offer solutions to 18th-century social problems by proposing a plan to reform the individual (*Julie, or the New Héloïse* and *Émile*) together with society (*The Social Contract*).

FURTHER READING

Cassirer, Ernst. *The Question of Jean-Jacques Rousseau.* Edited and translated by Peter Gay. Bloomington: Indiana University Press, 1963.

Daniels, Charlotte. *Subverting the Family Romance: Women Writers, Kinship Structures and the Early French Novel.* Lewisburg, Penn.: Bucknell University Press; London: Associated University Presses, 2000.

Kelly, Christopher. "Taking Readers as They Are: Rousseau's Turn From Discourses to Novels," *Eighteenth-Century Studies* 33, no. 1 (1999): 85–101.

Morgenstern, Mira. *Rousseau and the Politics of Ambiguity: Self, Culture and Society.* University Park: Pennsylvania State University Press, 1996.

Riley, Patrick, ed. *The Cambridge Companion to Rousseau.* Cambridge: Cambridge University Press, 2001.

Steinbrügge, Lieselotte. *The Moral Sex: Woman's Nature in the French Enlightenment.* Translated by Pamela E. Selwyn. New York: Oxford University Press, 1995.

Wolff, Larry. "Then I Imagine a Child: The Idea of Childhood and the Philosophy of Memory in the Enlightenment," *Eighteenth-Century Studies* 31, no. 4 (1998): 377–401.

ENCYCLOPEDIA (ENCYCLOPÉDIE) (1751–1772)

The *Encyclopedia,* or *Rational Dictionary of the Sciences, Arts, and the Crafts,* was edited by the philosopher, playwright, and novelist DENIS DIDEROT and mathematician Jean d'Alembert and constitutes the greatest collaborative project of the French ENLIGHTENMENT. This collected work consists of 17 volumes of text and 11 volumes of engravings. Originally conceived of as a translation of Scottish globemaker Ephraim Chamber's *Cyclopedia,* the project quickly took on larger proportions as its authors attempted to put together a compendium of all human knowledge that epitomizes the spirit of the Enlightenment.

The authors of the more than 60,000 articles shared a belief that greater human knowledge would lead to greater human happiness. For the *encyclopédists,* the arts and trades, too, offered a model for progress. To them, knowledge makes economic, social, and political progress possible. The overall purpose of the work was to teach people how to think critically and objectively about everything, including such controversial topics as religion, legal justice, and social and political institutions. In consequence, the *Encyclopedia* and its editors met with resistance. Diderot was imprisoned. The French government temporarily banned the work, and the pope placed it on the Index of Banned Books.

While it is unwise to draw a direct line from the Enlightenment philosophers or the *Encyclopedia* to the French Revolution, it is clear that new ideas began to penetrate society. The *Encyclopedia* was a major vehicle for the spread of Enlightenment ideas.

FURTHER READING

Chartier, Roger. *The Cultural Origins of the French Revolution.* Translated by Lydia G. Cochrane. Durham, N.C.: Duke University Press, 1991.

Darnton, Robert. *The Business of Enlightenment: A Publishing History of the Encyclopédie, 1775–1800.* Cambridge, Mass.: Belknap Press, 1979.

Gay, Peter. *The Age of Enlightenment.* New York: Time, Inc., 1966.

Mornet, Daniel. *Les Origines intellectuelles de la Révolution française, 1715–1787.* Paris: A. Colin, 1967.

ENLIGHTENMENT (LE SIÈCLE DES LUMIÈRES) (1688–1815)

The Enlightenment represented emancipation from ignorance and superstition by reason—the power of light (*lumière*) over darkness. Consequently, this period is often called the Age of Reason. Enlightenment thinkers questioned traditional authorities, civil and religious. They asked fundamental questions about life, God, human nature, good and evil. Enlightenment thought emphasized the importance of human dignity and basic rights such as freedom of expression and freedom of religion. One of the best examples of Enlightenment literature is François Arouet de Voltaire's CANDIDE (1758). Voltaire turns a critical eye toward almost every aspect of 18th-century socioeconomic and intellectual life with a great deal of satirical humor. The sharply ironic refrain of Voltaire's character Pangloss, "the best of all possible worlds," forces the reader to question perceived truths about the human condition.

In the course of the 17th-century Scientific Revolution, progress had meant intellectual progress. For the most part, 17th-century thinkers did not bring science into direct conflict with religion, although that was sometimes how their work was perceived. By the 18th century, some thinkers were beginning to question whether religious truth could ever be known with any certainty. Innovative as they were, Enlightenment philosophers formed an unusual group in both their nonreligious and their philosophical views and reading habits. Their views on religion, for example, were not representative of society as a whole. DENIS DIDEROT's novel THE NUN is a battle cry against aristocratic families and the church that together forced unwilling "prisoners" into convents rife with sexual and moral abuse. Diderot exaggerated the problems of conventual life to make a point against organized institutional religion and what he considered barbaric social practices that undermined individual freedom and dignity. Still, 18th-century French society remained profoundly Christian, even as the reading public's taste expanded to include new genres, particularly the novel. Much as readers were frequently titillated by libertine novels like DANGEROUS LIAISONS, those same readers were shocked by CHODERLOS DE LACLOS's direct challenge to accepted moral and ethical behavior. Even more scandalous were the pornographic novels of the libertine MARQUIS DE SADE, who pushed the aims of Enlightenment thought to their most extreme conclusions.

Influenced by the English philosopher John Locke, Enlightenment thinkers by and large believed that through the application of reason, human beings could create better societies and better people. For some, the arts and trades offered a model for progress. An increase in human knowledge was the best way to achieve progress. Hence, an emphasis on education was also a significant aspect of Enlightenment thought. Enlightenment thought is fundamentally optimistic in its faith in rationalism as a means to move society forward. The point to all of their works was to apply a rational, critical approach to determine the laws governing the natural world and society. Enlightenment philosophers engaged in a common undertaking to influence society. The ENCYCLOPEDIA: *the Rational Dictionary of the Sciences, Arts, and Crafts* (completed in 1772) was perhaps their greatest project. One of its contributors, JEAN-JACQUES ROUSSEAU, wrote works that bridge the Age of Reason and ROMANTICISM. Initially banned by the French government for its attack on the social and political order, the *Encyclopedia,* edited by Diderot and mathematician Jean d'Alembert, professed to offer a compendium of all human knowledge. It praised science and the arts while questioning religion and authority. It criticized intolerance, injustice, and social institutions. Its authors believed that greater human knowledge would lead to greater human happiness.

Since knowledge meant progress, many Enlightenment thinkers focused on the importance of education as a means of reform as well as social control. Nonetheless, the leaders of this intellectual movement remained largely suspicious of the common people's ignorance and superstition. Enlightenment thinkers took a utilitarian approach to education, frequently arguing that education should be geared to socioeconomic standing. Thus, old and new ways of thinking continued to coexist. Even as 18th-century thinkers developed a new appreciation for the lower classes and a broader definition of citizen, theirs remained a society based on inequality and privilege that began to break down only with the FRENCH REVOLUTION. The onset of romanticism and a return to conservative politics on the European continent following the defeat of Napoleon in 1815 turned literature in a new direction, away from reason and toward passion as a source of truth about the human condition.

FURTHER READING

Berlin, Isaiah. *The Age of Enlightenment.* New York: Houghton Mifflin, 1956.

Darnton, Robert. *The Business of Enlightenment.* Cambridge, Mass.: Harvard University Press, 1979.

Gay, Peter. *The Age of Enlightenment.* New York: Time, Inc., 1966.

Roche, Daniel. *France in the Enlightenment.* Translated by Arthur Goldhammer. Cambridge, Mass.: Harvard University Press, 1998.

Rusher, William, and Ken Masugi. *The Ambiguous Legacy of the Enlightenment.* Lanham, Md.: University Press of America; Claremont: Claremont Institute, 1995.

EN ROUTE JORIS-KARL HUYSMANS (1895) A companion novel to *The Damned, En Route* continues the story of Durtal's spiritual journey, which is, in fact, Huysmans' own story of conversion to Roman Catholicism. When he discovers that mysticism, occultism, and black magic are as unsatisfying as reclusive aestheticism (see AGAINST THE GRAIN), Durtal returns to society. One day, contemplating the painter Matthias Grünewald's *Crucifixion* (a late 15th-century painting in Colmar, Germany), Durtal is taken by the beauty of sacred art and begins to recognize its profound meaning. Thus begins his journey to salvation and monastic life. The end of Huysmans's tale of conversion is told in *The Cathedral* and *The Oblate.* Together they reveal the unity of Huysmans's oeuvre.

FURTHER READING

Banks, Brian. *The Image of Huysmans.* New York: AMS Press, 1990.

Gilman, Richard. *Decadence: The Strange Life of an Epithet.* New York: Farrar, Straus and Giroux, 1979.

Nalbantian, Suzanne. *Seeds of Decadence in the Late Nineteenth-Century Novel.* New York: St. Martin's Press, 1983.

EPISTOLARY NOVEL The great age of the epistolary novel was the 18th century, which witnessed the rise of the novel as a popular genre often associated with women. Although this form of fiction fell out of fashion at the beginning of the 19th century, the epistolary novel contributed to the great novel form of the 19th century not only for its sentimentality but also for its social commentary. More than 150 epistolary novels appeared between 1750 and 1778 alone.

Epistolary novels are associated, too, with the rise of realism in fictional literature that began in the 17th century. They sometimes give the appearance of autobiography, as in GIL BLAS, MANON LESCAUT, *The* WAYWARD HEAD AND HEART, or *The* LIFE OF MARIANNE. A standard presentation for the epistolary novel is often a manuscript supposedly discovered by the editor who is really the author. The editor then professes to publish the letters because they serve as a moral lesson. The letters may be monophonic (written by one fictional writer), as in the case of *The* PORTUGUESE LETTERS, or multiphonic (by more than one fictional writer) as in DANGEROUS LIAISONS.

Although there are earlier examples of the epistolary novel, such as *The Portuguese Letters* and *The* PERSIAN LETTERS, the genre really took off in 1732 with CRÉBILLON's *Letters of the Marquise de M***.* The high point is ROUSSEAU's *The* NEW HELOISE. Preeminence is also given to LACLOS's *DANGEROUS LIAISONS.* By the 19th century, writers showed disdain for this form of fiction. VICTOR HUGO called them "conversations of deaf-mutes."

A number of 18th-century epistolary novels were written by men: ROUSSEAU, MONTESQUIEU, LACLOS, for example. Yet as women began to read and increasingly to write fiction, their first choice was often the novel in the form of letters. Letter writing was an activity that allowed women a public voice when they could not hold an official public position. The letter is by nature a means of determining one's identity, of self-expression. It is also necessarily subjective.

Love is a common theme in 18th-century fiction and it remains so with the epistolary novel. When such novels are written by women, marriage becomes a central topic. Because women were denied, for the most part, an existence independent from a male protector, the choice of a husband was important. The heroine of such novels is of a type, young, beautiful, virtuous. However, there is rarely a precise description of her physical appearance. In contrast to the LIBERTINE novel, where the male figure is central to the narrative, in the epistolary novel he is frequently observed from the female perspective. Male characters are often depicted as weak, indecisive creatures unworthy of a woman's constancy. To the 18th-century mind, the epistolary novel was suited to women because of its focus on the intimate, the domestic, the female sphere. In terms of themes and subject matter, the epistolary novel is closely tied to the SENTIMENTAL NOVEL.

EREC AND ENIDE (EREC ET ENIDE)
CHRÉTIEN DE TROYES (12TH CENTURY)   The principal theme of *Erec and Enide* is the struggle between love and valor. To save his reputation as a knight, Erec sets off on a course of adventure with his beloved wife, Enide, through which he is able to prove, in the end, both his prowess and his love. In the prologue, Chrétien states that he will not be like the *jongleurs* that "mangle" stories; rather he will give structure to this tale. At the same time, he experiments with "interlacing" by breaking up the linear development of the main plot with other lines of action. HÉLISENNE DE CRENNE's *The TORMENTS OF LOVE*, for example, draws from the tradition of the medieval ROMANCE, of which *Erec and Enide* is an illustration.

FURTHER READING
Frappier, Jean. *Chrétien de Troyes: The Man and His Work.* Translated by Robert J. Cormier. Athens: Ohio University Press, 1982.
Lacy, Norris. *The Craft of Chrétien de Troyes: An Essay on Narrative Art.* Leiden, Netherlands: Brill, 1980.
Troyes, Chrétien de. *Arthurian Romances.* Translated by William W. Kibler. London: Penguin, 1991.

ERL-KING, THE (LE ROI DES AULNES)
MICHEL TOURNIER (1971)   Twice in his life, Abel Tiffauges is spared punishment for his actions through chance alone. Before World War II, the burly Tiffauges is a mechanic working in Paris. When, in 1940, he is taken prisoner of war in Kaltenborn, where he is surrounded by young Germans, Tiffauges is suddenly overcome by a powerful image of Germany as a land of symbols, legends, and magical signs.

Tiffauges subsequently encounters a young Jewish boy, Ephraim, while discovering, at the same time, the horrors of Auschwitz. One day, Tiffauges carries Ephraim safely out of Kaltenborn on his shoulders, fulfilling his self-proclaimed prophecy, "My triumphal end will be, if God wills it, to walk across the earth with a star, more radiant and golden than that of the three kings, on my neck." Thanks to Ephraim, Tiffauges is redeemed while discovering the sacred meaning of, literally, bearing something. If Tiffauge's death in the peat bogs brings back the myth of the erl-king, his journey across the swamps with the child on his shoulders also recalls the legend of Saint Christopher. The novel ends on a surprisingly light note given its sobering subject matter.

Lengthy and complex, the novel's structure is built on the concept of duality and opposition. Two symmetrical currents run through the work. The first part takes place in France, the second in Germany. Slowly, in the first half of the novel, Tiffauges comes to comprehend the signs that ultimately reveal his destiny. Upon meeting the child Ephraim, Tiffauges experiences a reversal of values and meaning through the notion of carrying, metaphorically signifying the essence of Christianity.

Tiffauges's ambiguity lies in his dual identity as an ogre (Tournier draws from Goethe's poem "Der Erlkönig"), traditionally an abductor of children, and a savior who literally and figuratively carries the child out of danger. As is frequently the case in Tournier's works, the author introduces and reinterprets traditional myths. In the end, the novel's sense of ambiguity remains, nonetheless, unresolved, as a secret remains forever undisclosed.

Disturbing, confusing, and engaging all at once, *The Erl-King* won the Goncourt Prize. The novel bears a similar structure to Tournier's *FRIDAY* (1967) in its foundation in myth and legend, its nostalgia, and its evocation of instinctual sexuality. Like *Friday,* this work is equally humorous, sober, and lyrical. In a *New York Times* book review on September 3, 1972, Janet Flanner called *The Erl-King* "the most important novel to appear in France since PROUST."

FURTHER READING

Anderson, Christopher. *Michel Tournier's Children: Myth, Intertext, Initiation.* New York: P. Lang, 1998.

Cloonan, William J. *Michel Tournier.* Boston: Twayne, 1985.

Davis, Colin. *Michel Tournier, Philosophy and Fiction.* Oxford: Clarendon Press; New York: Oxford University Press, 1988.

Edwards, Rachel. *Myth and the Fiction of Michel Tournier and Patrick Grainville.* Lewiston, N.Y.: E. Mellen Press, 1999.

Petit, Susan. *Michel Tournier's Metaphysical Fictions.* Amsterdam, Philadelphia: J. Benjamins, 1991.

Platten, David. *Michel Tournier and the Metaphor of Fiction.* New York: St. Martin's Press, 1999.

Worton, Michael, ed. *Michel Tournier.* London, New York: Longman, 1995.

ERNAUX, ANNIE (1940–) Born in Normandy to a family of modest background, Ernaux trained to be a schoolteacher. She lives in Paris and has written nine autobiographical works: *CLEANED OUT* (1974), *They say Nothing* (1977), *A FROZEN WOMAN* (1981), *A MAN'S PLACE* (1983), *A WOMAN'S STORY* (1987), *SIMPLE PASSION* (1991), *Exteriors* (1993), *I Remain in Darkness* (1997), and *Shame* (1997). She first gained notoriety when *A Man's Place* won the Renaudot Prize.

As a writer, Ernaux is interested in the social sciences and in the way that literature relates to society and politics. She is an *engagé* writer, to use the Sartrean term (see JEAN-PAUL SARTRE), concerned with social injustice, sexuality, and the female condition. *Cleaned Out,* for example, is the story of a young woman who has an illegal abortion. Ernaux wrote the novel in the mid-1970s, at a time when a vociferous debate on abortion and contraception was raging in France. True to her principles, Ernaux wrote the novel in witness to contemporary events.

She writes about social class and the female condition in a straightforward, even clinical manner that is always fundamentally physical. Certain themes reap-pear in all her works as she tells the story of her life many times over from different perspectives.

Ultimately, the act of writing is an act of self-transformation. Ernaux is concerned with the voices that literature has traditionally silenced, women and the working class in particular. Consequently, she seeks to fill a particular gap. As a feminist writer, the problem of the female condition is important to Ernaux (see FEMINISM). One of the most important influences on her writing are the works of SIMONE DE BEAUVOIR, the founder of modern French feminism. She shares with Beauvoir a focus on women's particular experiences. Ernaux's female characters struggle with their identity as daughters, wives, and mothers, as they strive to assert their right to live their own lives as they choose.

A central theme in all her works is social mobility. Here Ernaux also draws from her own experience. Her parents, originally of peasant origin, owned a small grocery and café in a working-class neighborhood of a provincial town. Her mother in particular desired more for her daughter. Ernaux was subsequently sent to a more exclusive school than she might otherwise have attended. Ultimately, she rose above her parents' station to enter the middle class as well as the world of Parisian intellectuals. Yet the question of social identity has been difficult for her to grapple with. Ernaux's characters exist as insiders and outsiders, caught between two worlds or, as she puts it, seated between two chairs, a position that is none too comfortable. Ernaux uses terms drawn from the French sociologist Pierre Bourdieu as she explores power relations, referring to the dominant and the dominated (the middle class and working class, respectively). Hence she implicitly makes a political statement that questions the validity of middle-class values as the one legitimate standard for society. The basic problem for her characters is that they lose their sense of identity even as social mobility opens their lives up to new possibilities.

For Ernaux, social mobility in France is inextricably linked to education. While education serves as the means for social mobility, at the same time the educational system reinforces social injustice as it promotes a language that reflects and reaffirms social status. Finally, as Ernaux is fundamentally interested in identity, it is not surprising that she focuses on relationships within the family, particularly the relationship between mother and daughter. All her novels offer an intimate exploration of the author's own life.

FURTHER READING

McIlvanney, Siobhán. *Annie Ernaux: The Return to Origins.* Liverpool, England: Liverpool University Press, 2001.

Thomas, Lyn. *Annie Ernaux: An Introduction to the Writer and Her Audience.* Oxford, New York: Berg, 1999.

ERNST, MAX (1891–1976)   One of the many young men who returned from the front after World War I completely disillusioned by the failure of traditional values, Max Ernst turned to anarchy and the irrational. Principally known as a surrealist artist (see SURREALISM), Ernst also produced a surrealist or irrational novel, *Kindness Week.*

Prior to World War I, Ernst lived in the German city of Cologne, where he attended university classes in art, history, and philosophy. There he met members of the avant-garde Blue Rider group of artists, discovered the art of the mentally ill, read German romantic literature (see ROMANTICISM), and decided to become a painter.

After the war, Ernst formed a DADA group in Cologne in 1919 along with German artists Hans Arp and Johannes Baargeld. In 1922 he left for Paris, where he collaborated with the surrealists ANDRÉ BRETON and LOUIS ARAGON, and the poet Paul Éluard on their review *Literature.*

Ernst developed a technique called "frottage," the painter's equivalent to Breton's "automatic writing," whereby he rubbed various objects through paper. Ernst also worked on set design for the Ballet Russe and made sculptures. In 1941 he left France for the United States, where he edited a journal *VVV* from 1942 to 1944 with Breton and artist Marcel Duchamp. He also worked on "dripping" paintings frequently associated with Jackson Pollock. Ernst lived for a time in Arizona with the American painter Dorothea Tanning. He returned to France in 1953. Ernst was rejected by the surrealists when he won the Biennale Grand Prize for painting in Venice in 1954.

FURTHER READING

Hopkins, David. "Hermetic and Philosophical Themes in Max Ernst's 'Vox Angelica' and Related Works," *Burlington Magazine* 134, no. 1076 (November 1992): 716–723.

Hubert, Renée Riese. "Max Ernst: The Displacement of the Visual and the Verbal," *New Literary History* 15, no. 3, Image/Imago/Imagination (Spring 1984): 575–606.

———. "The Fabulous Fiction of Two Surrealist Artists: Giorgio de Chirico and Max Ernst," *New Literary History* 4, no. 1 (Autumn 1972): 151–166.

Spies, Werner. *Max Ernst Collages: The Invention of the Surrealist Universe.* Translated by John William Gabriel. New York: Abrams, 1991.

ETCHERELLI, CLAIRE (1934–)   Born in Bordeaux, the daughter of a longshoreman, Etcherelli worked for two years on a factory assembly line, an experience that inspired her novel *Élise,* a work that won the Femina Prize in 1967 and was adapted to film by Michel Drach.

In *A Traveling Tree* (1978), Etcherelli evokes daily life in the context of dramatic political events such as the war in Algeria and the Soviet-led invasion of Czechoslovakia in 1968. The theme of politics is particularly pronounced in this novel as Etcherelli tells the story of a woman living on the margins of society who joins in the student rebellion in France of 1968. She participates in the riots, having returned to Paris on the day that the Warsaw Pact tanks entered Prague. The narrative then breaks as hope gives way, in this case, to disillusionment. Etcherelli's style is simple and lyrical as she writes in witness to the misery of working-class life with its poverty and social marginalization with an authority derived from her own experience.

Etcherelli is often characterized as a proletarian writer, but this classification is not entirely fair. Etcherelli explores the misery of the human condition certainly, but she does so with warmth and, ultimately, with a cry of hope for the possibility of a better life. At the same time, her heroines are unable to separate their own personal tragedy from that of the collective.

Élise, for example, is the story of a young Frenchwoman from the provinces who comes to Paris in the 1950s to work in an automobile factory and falls in love with an immigrant worker. Through the prism of their love Etcherelli reflects on the war in Algeria and its social consequences. Élise's vision of the world changes dramatically as she is exposed to racial tensions and the exploitation of workers in the context of socioeconomic change after World War II. Had she stayed in the provinces, Élise would have lived out her life within the confines of traditional domesticity. Instead, she experiences political awakening. Hers is the story of a young woman's liberation from her family and, eventually, from her Algerian lover, to make her own way in the world. Etcherelli wrote *Élise* at the height of the situationist movement, led by philosopher Guy Debord, and her novel reinforces his theme of alienation outlined in *Society of the Spectacle*. Etcherelli evokes the alienation of working-class women, in particular, much as SIMONE DE BEAUVOIR did for women of the bourgeoisie.

Etcherelli's works form part of the postwar renaissance of women's literature in which female writers such as MARIE CARDINAL, ANNIE ERNAUX, HÉLÈNE CIXOUS, CHANTAL CHAWAF, and others redefine the traditional understanding of gender relations. Through this feminist literature women writers also seek to define and redefine themselves (see FEMINISM).

EUGÉNIE GRANDET HONORÉ DE BALZAC

(1833) In this novel of provincial French life, Félix Grandet, a wealthy miser, tyrannizes his household, which includes his wife, his daughter Eugénie, and a servant named Nanon. In November 1819, the family plans a celebration of Eugénie's 23rd birthday. Two families, the Cruchots and the Grassins, both of whom wish to marry a son to Eugénie, are invited, along with a surprise guest, the elegant and charming cousin Charles, who has come from Paris. Balzac thus sets the reader up from the beginning to consider the contrast between these two worlds, Paris and the provinces.

Eugénie falls hopelessly in love with Charles, who, little by little, begins to return her affections. Unfortunately, his visit is marred by tragedy when a letter arrives announcing the death of Charles's debt-ridden father by suicide. Félix Grandet coldly refuses to help his nephew. Eugénie, moved by her cousin's suffering, offers him all the gold her father has given her so he can try to make his fortune in the Indies. In return, Charles offers her a gift of portraits of his parents. The two lovers kiss and promise to marry. Charles heads off to make his fortune, leaving a void as Eugénie returns

to the routine of her daily life. When Félix discovers Eugénie's gift to Charles he is overcome with anger and locks his daughter away in her room. Saddened by this turn of events, Eugénie's mother weakens and dies.

Félix is obliged to make up with his daughter as she is the sole inheritor of her mother's wealth, but their life remains dreary. Eventually Félix dies too, still admiring his coins. Silent for all this time, Charles finally writes to Eugénie telling her that he as made an advantageous marriage. Eugénie then resigns herself to marrying Cruchot but only if he agrees that the marriage will not be consummated and (faithful to her lover to the end) to pay off her uncle's (Charles's father) debts. Upon the death of her husband, Eugénie returns to her family home to lead a sad and lonely life, in the end economizing like her father, only the difference is that she gives to charity.

Certain of Balzac's recurring themes are evident in this novel. More than one character in the HUMAN COMEDY reveals the destructive effects of maniacal obsession, such as Grandet's love for money. The conflict between reason and passion is revealed as intrinsic to human nature. Eugénie's hopeless and faithful love reminds the reader of Adeline in COUSIN BETTE. Both characters portray an idealized concept of female virtue that, in the end, is piteous. Finally, Balzac believed that the family, not the individual, should be the true social unit, and his vivid portrayal of a degenerate society in which this basic value has been lost reflects this.

FURTHER READING
Allen, James Smith. *Popular French Romanticism: Authors, Readers and Books in the Nineteenth Century.* Syracuse, N.Y.: Syracuse University Press, 1981.

Carrère, Jean. *Degeneration in the Great French Masters.* Translated by Joseph McCabe. Freeport, N.Y.: Books for Libraries Press, 1967.

Kanes, Martin, ed. *Critical Essays on Balzac.* Boston: G. K. Hall, 1990.

Smith, Edward C. III. "Honoré de Balzac and the 'Genius' of Walter Scott: Debt and Denial," *Comparative Literature Studies.* 36, no. 3 (1999): 209–225.

EXISTENTIALISM
A philosophical and literary movement, existentialism developed in the pes-

simistic period that followed World War II as the horrors of that experience seemed to offer irrefutable proof of the absurdity of life. In a world without God or moral values, human liberty takes on new significance. Fulfillment is possible only through the recognition of one's freedom to act and in acceptance of the fundamental irrationality of life.

The term *existentialism* was first coined by JEAN-PAUL SARTRE to define his own work. It was not used to encompass broader schools of thought until the late 1950s. The clearest articulation of his approach is found in *Being and Nothingness* (1943).

Existentialism is associated with an emphasis on the isolation of the individual in a hostile world. Moreover, the individual's actions take on meaning only in the context of the self. As ALBERT CAMUS wrote in *The STRANGER*, "You will never be happy if you continue to search for what happiness consists of." It is the exercise of one's freewill through freedom of choice that is determinant. Existentialists acknowledged that the consequences of one's decisions may be negative; what is important is to carry though with that decision unhesitatingly. Generally associated with leftist politics and the notion of political engagement, existentialism had an impact on the development of the NOUVEAU ROMAN and the theater of the absurd. Existentialist literature is most often associated with the works of Sartre, Camus, and SIMONE DE BEAUVOIR, among others.

FURTHER READING

Burnier, Michel-Antoine. *Choice of Action: The French Existentialists on the Political Front Line.* Translated by Bernard Murchland. New York: Random House, 1968.

Poster, Mark. *Existential Marxism in Postwar France.* Princeton, N.J.: Princeton University Press, 1975.

F

FALL, THE (LA CHUTE) ALBERT CAMUS
(1956) One of Camus's most successful novels, *The Fall* is divided into six parts, the first of which begins when Jean-Baptiste Clamence offers to serve as interpreter to a patron in a dubious bar in Amsterdam called the Mexico City, introducing himself as a "penitent judge." Clamence accompanies the other man through the Jewish quarter, where he evokes all of the horrors of the German occupation of World War II. He speaks of Holland as a country of merchants and dreamers. Clamence then leaves his acquaintance before a bridge as he has vowed never to cross a bridge again at night. The two men arrange to meet again the next day.

On the second day, Clamence speaks of his past life, explaining that at one time he had been a brilliant lawyer living happily in Paris. He had been a defender of noble causes. He had a good opinion of himself. In fact, Clamence viewed himself as superior to most men. Then, one autumn evening he heard a strange sound on a bridge in Paris. He went home feeling disturbed and when he looked in the mirror it seemed as if his smile had doubled.

Clamence continues his story on the third day. Clamence thought he heard a laughing voice pursue him. Doubt began to wind its way slowly into his life, revealing to him the ridiculous falseness of his moral superiority and smug self-satisfaction. From then on, Clamence's life began to change as he became a penitent judge. The laugh he heard on the bridge had revealed to him his vanity. Clamence's crisis of conscience only

augmented when he angrily found fault with a driver. Clamence realized that his relationships with women had also been based on vanity. As he continued his intense self-examination, Clamence suddenly recalled that a few years earlier he had seen a woman throw herself into the Seine one evening and he did nothing to save her.

The story continues on the fourth day as the two men visit a nearby island. Clamence explains that having recognized his own duplicitous nature he decided to seek out love and friendship but only met with the peremptory judgment of other men. He then began to think that life is nothing but a comedy and humanity itself deceitful. He became derisive, going so far as to try and make himself repulsive to others.

Later that day on the boat bringing the two men back to Amsterdam, Clamence speaks of the beauty of Greece before returning once more to his confession. He explains how he had sought love in vain. Then he turned to debauchery. He became increasingly unhappy until he finally admitted his guilt and the guilt of all men, reflecting that Christ had offered an example through his death on the cross.

On the fifth day, Clamence is ill with a fever and his companion visits him in his room. He tells of how he stole water from a dying man when he was a prisoner of war. In his cupboard a Van Eyck painting is hidden. The police are looking for it. Clamence hopes that one day he will be arrested. Finally, he reveals his notion of the penitent judge. Clamence "confesses" to other men the sins that they might have committed. He turns to the mirror so that he and his companion may also accuse themselves. Once one becomes a penitent, it is possible to judge and thus set oneself free. Despite his fever, Clamence wants to get up and see the falling snow. Then he returns to bed. Each time Clamence approaches a stranger he hopes it will be a policeman. But the stranger he met in the bar is a lawyer from Paris, like him.

In this novel, Camus mocks the values he had praised in *The Rebel. The Fall* thus marks a turning point in his career by pessimistically evoking the theme of solitude while underemphasizing the notion of solidarity. Moreover, Camus's writing style is more vibrant and theatrical. The denunciation of complacent self-satisfaction reflects the moral struggle of Camus and other intellectuals in the postwar period. Clamence is familiar with eloquent language but recognizes that it is nothing but a lie. John the Baptist, Clamence's namesake, announced the coming of a savior, but for Clamence there is no messiah. In the modern world, all is silent with the exception of those who judge. Camus's message appears to be directed at those intellectuals who judge others but never themselves. A great success, *The Fall* remains one of the most read French novels today.

FURTHER READING

Brée, Germaine. *Camus.* New Brunswick, N.J.: Rutgers University Press, 1972.

Brosman, Catharine Savage. *Albert Camus.* Detroit: Gale Group, 2001.

Mairowitz, David Zane, and Alain Korkos. *Introducing Camus.* Edited by Richard Appignanesi. New York: Totem Books, 1998.

Poster, Mark. *Existential Marxism in Postwar France.* Princeton, N.J.: Princeton University Press, 1975.

FASCISM

Disillusionment with 19th-century liberalism tilled the ground for the rise of fascism in the 1920s and 1930s. The rise of fascism was a sign that LIBERALISM was collapsing. Industrialization had created a mass, faceless society. Moreover, traditional humanist values had been shaken to the core by the trauma of World War I. Many members of fascist movements in Europe were young, postwar youth who wished to re-create the camaraderie of the trenches. As the German writer Thomas Mann put it in 1919, "fascism is a disease of the times."

Although fascism spread throughout Europe in the interwar period, it was particularly strong in Germany and Italy. As a political movement, fascism fed on fears of the spread of communism, as well as economic instability. Fascists expressed hostility to liberal values and institutions. Hence fascism involved a rejection of democracy, something that German dictator Adolf Hitler described as "the systematic cultivation of human failure," while promoting militarism and imperialism. War, according to the Italian fascist leader Benito Mussolini, for example, would give people "the stamp of honor if they are willing to rise up and meet it." In France, the fascist movement originated in antirepublicanism of the 19th century but is particularly associated with the collaborationist Vichy regime (see VICHY FRANCE).

A number of writers from the early 20th century deal with the rise of fascism in the interwar period. While writers such as DRIEU LA ROCHELLE and PAUL NIZAN evoke the attraction of fascism at a time when Europe was experiencing a crisis in values, others offer a critique of this menacing trend, among them JULES ROMAINS, ANDRÉ MALRAUX, and FRANÇOIS MAURIAC.

FATHER GORIOT (LE PÈRE GORIOT)

HONORÉ DE BALZAC (1835)   One of Balzac's masterpieces, *Father Goriot* introduces Balzac's system of reappearing characters in the collection of novels that his HUMAN COMEDY comprises. Astonishingly, Balzac feverishly produced the novel in the course of three days and three nights. One of his most famous characters, Eugène de Rastignac, is the protagonist. Drawing on Shakespeare's *King Lear, Father Goriot* was first published in 1834 in the *Revue de Paris* and offers that pessimistic view of bourgeois society that is another recurring theme in Balzac's works.

The novel is set in 1819. The provincial Rastignac arrives in the capital and reveals his great ambition to conquer Paris. The novel thus opens with one of Balzac's principal themes, the relationship of Paris to the provinces.

Rastignac encounters Father Goriot in the Parisian boarding house where they both live. Goriot is an enigmatic figure who leads a strange nocturnal existence. At 69, he is the oldest resident of the boarding house whose other inhabitants offer a wide array of characters that reflects Balzac's versatility as a writer, including the famous criminal Vautrin.

Goriot, one of Balzac's great monomaniacal characters, arrived in 1813 after retiring from business. At first, his income allowed Goriot to live in the pension's best apartment. Gradually, however, his wealth diminishes and the old man is obliged to move into increasingly modest lodgings. Finally, he ends up in the attic. The other residents treat him as a scapegoat and suspect that he has squandered his wealth on women.

Rastignac is from a noble family whose wealth has also been depleted. Thanks to a recommendation from his aunt, he is invited to balls held by Madame de Beauséant, one of the most influential hostesses in Paris. One evening he falls for the countess Anastasie de Restaud, who turns out to be one of old Goriot's daughters. The next day Rastignac visits her home, but his clumsy behavior offends her and he is sent rudely away.

Rastignac then returns to the home of Madame de Beauséant, where he meets the duchess of Langeais. His behavior is still not up to Parisian standards but at least he learns about Goriot's past. Goriot was a merchant who made his fortune before the FRENCH REVOLUTION and then devoted his wealth to his two daughters, Anastasie and Delphine. After giving them a fine education and a dowry, he married Anastasie to the count de Restaud and Delphine to a wealthy banker, Nucingen.

Goriot's children have since abused his generosity and now scorn him. Moreover, he is nearly dispossessed. The story he hears brings tears to Rastignac's eyes. Madame de Beauséant makes use of the story to give Rastignac advice; he should make his way in society through women. She suggests that he begin by approaching Delphine.

Upon his return to the pension, Rastignac decides that he will help Goriot. Vautrin (who, like Rastignac, appears in several novels) recognizes Rastignac's ambition and tries to convince him to seduce a fellow resi-dent in the house named Victorine Taillefer and then kill her brother so that she might inherit the family's enormous wealth. A percentage of her inheritance would naturally go to Vautrin. Rastignac refuses. He prefers to follow Madame de Beauséant's advice.

Rastignac recounts his subsequent meeting with Delphine to her father and the two become strangely complicitous. Rastignac indeed becomes Delphine's lover and thereby learns of her financial problems. Her marriage is a failure. Her husband has taken over their fortune and she has nothing. She even asks Rastignac to play roulette for her and, when he wins, announces that he has saved her.

Goriot is in despair when he learns of his daughter's misfortune. Rastignac, meanwhile, begins to realize just how much money one needs to succeed in Parisian society. Vautrin turns out to be a convict who escaped from prison. He arranges for a friend to murder Victorine's brother, throwing the residents of the pension into chaos.

With the last of his savings, Goriot once more tries to help his daughters but to no avail. His situation declines both economically and personally. Goriot falls ill and dies, essentially of a broken heart, without leaving behind enough money for a proper funeral. His daughters do not even visit him on his deathbed and yet Goriot forgives them, acknowledging his own responsibility. Rastignac is obliged to pay for the old man's burial. Accompanied by his friend Christophe, a medical student called in to care for Goriot, Rastignac sees Father Goriot to his final resting place, the cemetery of Père Lachaise. From the heights of the cemetery, Rastignac looks down on Paris and challenges the city with his famous line: "Now, for the two of us."

Rastignac reappears in LOST ILLUSIONS and a number of other novels that form part of the *Human Comedy*, allowing the reader to witness his transformation from a poor, idealistic, provincial youth to a successful, ambitious minister of France. Rastignac's determination to conquer Paris is a sort of vengeance that reveals Balzac's subtle appreciation of the truth about human nature in all its ambiguity.

FURTHER READING

Kanes, Martin, ed., *Critical Essays on Balzac*. Boston: G. K. Hall, 1990.

FELICIA André-Robert, Andréa de Nerci-at (1775)   Not nearly as scandalous as Nerciat's later pornographic works, *Felicia,* his first novel, is also his most delightful. It is a typical recitation of the libertine's "education," but unlike the first-person narratives of Crébillon fils and Duclos, Felicia does not recount her adventures to warn readers away from a life of pleasure, rather to encourage them. It is her way of life that brings happiness. Nerciat seems to write for his own pleasure as well, and this fits with his philosophy of life.

Drawing on the picaresque tradition and adventure novels, Nerciat offers a veritable cornucopia of characters and circumstances far different from the narrow aristocratic world described by Crébillon. Moreover, Nerciat's setting is provincial rather than Parisian. Intercalated stories allow Neciat to introduce new characters constantly. Characters do not have psychological depth but are appealing in their manner and vivacity.

Comic and burlesque elements are evident from the beginning. Felicia, for example, is born on a battlefield. Independent and frivolous, she is an avid reader of Boyer's *Thérèse Philosophe.* She is one of the few female characters in 18th-century literature who is not simply the passive object of male pleasure. Her promotion of the idea that sensation alone guarantees the reality of one's existence parallels trends in Enlightenment thought.

Condemned by authorities and adored by readers, *Felicia* went through 22 editions between 1775 and 1800. In Stendhal's words on reading Nerciat, "I become absolutely crazy; the possession of a real mistress, previously the object of all my wishes, could not have plunged me into such a torrent of sensuality."

FURTHER READING

Ivker, B. "The Parameters of a Period-piece Pornographer, Andréa de Nerciat," *SVEC* 98 (1972).

Wilkins, K. "Andréa de Nerciat and the Libertine Tradition in Eighteenth-Century France," *SVEC* 256, (1988).

FEMINISM

One might argue that French feminism, that is to say the struggle for recognition of a woman's just role in society, began with the French Revolution. As a literary movement, however, it is largely associated with the articulation of new ideas about women's writing that emerged in the 1970s.

Simone de Beauvoir's *The Second Sex* (1949) is perhaps *the* foundational text of the modern feminist movement. Although it was subject to harsh criticism when first published, with the burgeoning of the feminist movement in the 1970s (given impetus by events of the 1960s) *The Second Sex* inspired renewed and positive interest among a number of women who began to theorize on the definition of women's writing (*écriture féminine*).

These women posited "writing" in contrast to traditionally male-dominated "literature." Rather than viewing women's artistic production within the confines of a male paradigm, feminist writers sought to define a particularly female domain. A number of publishers began to produce series of women's collections. Writers such as Catherine Clément, Julia Kristeva, and Xavière Gauthier began to explore new, feminist-oriented interpretations of psychoanalysis in relation to women's creativity and artistic production.

De Beauvoir, who declared herself a feminist only in the 1970s, created the term *féminitude,* analogous to Negritude, or the notion of being defined as other in relation to a (white) male standard. Meanwhile, writers such as Hélène Cixous and Monique Wittig began to reexamine the relationship of word and body. A number of works of feminist fiction are thus autobiographical in nature, the novels of Cixous, Beauvoir, and Marguerite Duras among them.

Drawing on one's own experience is perhaps only natural in a movement intended to reconstruct and reevaluate female identity in a manner the defies the myth of the "eternal feminine." Feminist writers seek to restore women to themselves on both a theoretical and a practical level. Thus, feminist literature appears in a variety of genres: essays, novels, poetry, and drama, as women writers sought to redefine woman as an autonomous *subject.* Common themes are female sexuality, motherhood, relationships, illness, and work.

The term *French feminism* was actually coined by American scholars despite the fact that it refers to an intellectual and literary movement situated in France. A particularly important text is Hélène Cixous's *The Laugh of the Medusa* (1976). According to Cixous, female sexuality transcends the phallocentric thought of male. She shares her focus on female sexuality with Annie Leclerc (*Woman's Word* [1974] and *Coming Into Writing* [1977]) and Luce Irigaray (*This Sex Which Is Not One* [1977]), among others. A number of newly established women's journals focused on similar questions. In the mid-1970s certain highly regarded intellectual journals produced special "women's issues." Of particular note is the 1975 *L'Arc,* devoted to Simone de Beauvoir. With *Newly Born Woman* (1976), Clément and Cixous introduced a new series called Feminine Future.

FURTHER READING

Cixous, Hélène, and Catherine Clément. *The Newly Born Woman.* Translated by Betsy Wing. Minneapolis: University of Minnesota Press, 1986.

Conley, Verena Adermatt. *Hélène Cixous.* Lincoln: University of Nebraska Press, 1984.

Marks, Elaine. "Review Essay: Women and Literature in France," *Signs* 3 (1978): 832–842.

Marks, Elaine, and Isabelle de Courtivron, eds. *New French Feminisms: An Anthology.* Amherst: University of Massachusetts Press, 1980.

FÉNELON, FRANÇOIS DE SALIGNAC DE LA MOTHE (1651–1715)

Theologian and writer, pedagogue and politician, Fénelon had a diverse career. His role in political and theological disputes makes him one of the major figures of the reign of Louis XIV.

Born in Périgord of an old noble family, Fénelon studied at the University of Cahors and later at the seminary of Saint-Sulpice. He entered the priesthood in 1675. Through his connections at court, he was appointed tutor to the duc de Bourgogne in 1689, presumed heir to the throne. In his role as pedagogue, Fénelon wrote several important works. The first, *The Treatise on the Education of Girls* (1689), served as the theoretical foundation for the curriculum at Saint-Cyr, a school for noble girls established by Louis XIV and his morganatic wife, Madame de Maintenon, in 1686. For the education of the duc de Bourgogne, Fénelon produced three other fictional texts, his *Fables* and *The Adventures of Telemachus* (1699) and *The Dialogues of the Dead* (1700), a series of conversations between important figures from the past following a classical philosophical model that emphasizes the relationship between virtue and politics.

Despite his prominence at court, Fénelon suffered disgrace for his role in the theological dispute over quietism and was forced into exile to his bishopric in Cambrai in 1697. Further problems emerged with the appearance of *The* ADVENTURES OF TELEMACHUS in 1699, which Louis XIV interpreted as an attack on his reign. Fénelon was elected to the Académie Française in 1693. He also participated in the literary debate the Quarrel of the Ancients and the Moderns through his posthumous letter to the Academy (1714).

From the perspective of literary history, Fénelon's most important work is *The Adventures of Telemachus.* Put forth as the fourth book of Homer's *Odyssey,* Ulysses's son Telemachus goes off in search of his father. In the tradition of Dante and Virgil, he is guided by Mentor, in reality, the goddess Athena. Through his travels, Telemachus learns about ethics, politics, mythology, and, most important, the principles inspired by classical antiquity and the Catholic Reformation that mark all of Fénelon's writings: simplicity, moderation, and virtue. Laying the foundation for ROUSSEAU, Fénelon was ahead of his time in advocating an approach to education that was to be both agreeable to the child and useful.

Fénelon is sometimes considered a precursor to the ENLIGHTENMENT, although he was in fact a defender of absolutism. Nearly all his works manifest his views on the problems in contemporary French society. He frequently promoted the virtues of simple, rustic life as opposed to the decadence of the court. At the same time, he defended the notion of a strictly ordered society. His understanding of the social hierarchy was one in which all social groups would function on the basis of traditional values. Those values found their purest form in that brew of the purity of morals associated with countryside over city, and in the legacy of classical antiquity combined with piety and notions of Christian virtue. He believed that the provincial nobility, unspoiled by the decadence of court life, inherently possess this combination of virtues and could, therefore, lead society into a future of domestic prosperity and peace.

FURTHER READING

Chydenius, Johan. *Humanism in Seventeenth-Century Spirituality*. Helsinki: Societas Scientiarum Fennica, 1989.

Janet, Paul. *Fénelon, His Life and Works*. Port Washington, N.Y.: Kennikat Press, 1970.

Rothkrug, Lionel. *Opposition to Louis XIV: The Political and Social Origins of the French Enlightenment*. Princeton, N.J.: Princeton University Press, 1965.

FERAOUN, MOULOUD (1913–1962)

Born into a family of poor peasants, Feraoun was one of a generation of young Algerian writers educated in French schools. He became a teacher and was assassinated in 1962 at the very end of the Algerian war of independence. Feraoun believed in the possibility of maintaining a relationship between the French and Arab communities, particularly in the battle against poverty, itself a source of much of the violence in society. A great friend of ALBERT CAMUS, Feraoun expressed his admiration in "Letter of an Algerian Muslim to Albert Camus."

Feraoun wrote a number of novels, the first of which was *Poor Man's Son* (1950), an autobiographical work that won the grand prize for literature of the city of Alger. This novel essentially tells the story of the author's own upbringing. The son of poor peasants, he was destined to become a shepherd until access to education enabled his escape from poverty. Set in a mountain village where the misery and harshness of life are overwhelming, men and women struggle to eke out a meager existence from the arid land. The style is sober and biting yet reflects Feraoun's love of the Algerian people. His best-loved novel, *Poor Man's Son,* contributed to bringing Algerian literature to the attention of a broader reading public.

Feraoun also wrote *Earth and Blood* (1953), *The Paths That Rise* (1957), his *Journal* (1962), and *Letters to His Friends* (posthumous, 1969). In this work he was also one of the first writers to explore the difficulties of mixed couples as the story focuses on an Algerian man married to a French woman with whom he returns to his native land. Together Feraoun's writings reveal the inner tension experienced by Algerians who are were also attached to French language and culture. A true humanist, Feraoun sought to express and promote the dignity of all men, including the most miserable and poorest.

FLAUBERT, GUSTAVE (1821–1880)

Flaubert was born in Rouen, where his father was a surgeon. As a result, one of the amusements Flaubert shared with his sister Caroline was to visit the hospital morgue. Despite this somewhat morbid pastime, Flaubert's childhood was a peaceful one. Flaubert's parents favored his older brother, and so Gustave was often left to his own devices.

Each summer the Flaubert family went to the sea. There, in 1836, the future author met Maurice Schlesinger, director of the *Gazette and Musical Review of Paris*. More important, Flaubert met Schlesinger's wife, Élisa. Hopelessly in love, each day he would pick up her red-and-black coat from the beach. This proved to be one of his most formative experiences, as it inspired a lasting passion that left its mark on his works *Memoirs of a Madman* (1838), *November* (1842), and SENTIMENTAL EDUCATION (1869).

A precocious writer, Flaubert published his first works while still in high school. In 1841 he began his law studies in Paris, to his father's approval and his own dismay. Flaubert failed his second-year exam in 1843, the year he met his great friend the future writer and photographer Maxime du Camp and began working on *Sentimental Education*.

Flaubert's friendship with Du Camp was an important one although their views on life differed significantly. Disagreeing with du Camp, who was anxious to make his way in the world, Flaubert once wrote, "To be known is not my principal goal. I envisage something better: to please myself, and this is more difficult." Nonetheless, the two friends traveled together from 1849 to 1851 in France, Egypt, Turkey, and Greece. These experiences furnished Flaubert with material for his later novels SALAMMBÔ (1862) and *The Temptation of Saint Anthony* (three versions).

Flaubert suffered his first attack resulting from a neurological disorder that resembles epilepsy in 1844. "I felt myself all of a sudden carried away by a torrent of flames," he described it. Flaubert subsequently gave up his law studies and returned to his family in Croisset, near Rouen. With occasional journeys to Paris and some more extensive travels in the Orient, Flaubert lived in Croisset, largely shut off from the world, where he labored over his manuscripts.

The first version of *Sentimental Education* was completed in 1845, and that same year Flaubert traveled to Italy with his sister and her husband. He was particularly struck by a Bruegel painting that inspired his *Temptation of Saint Anthony*. The following year was a difficult one as Flaubert lost both his father and his sister, who died in childbirth. Flaubert took in his mother and niece, for whom he would care into adulthood. These losses augmented his pessimistic view of the world. Flaubert also witnessed the revolution of 1848, an experience that further disillusioned him along with others of his generation.

Back in Paris for a time, Flaubert met Louise Collet in 1844, a beautiful blue-stocking poet he first encountered in a sculptor's studio and who was to become his mistress. They carried on a stormy relationship for roughly 10 years. Flaubert continued to spend time with du Camp, and during a walking tour the two decided to write a work together inspired by their strolls along fields and beaches. Du Camp was to write the even chapters and Flaubert the odd. They later abandoned this idea. In the meantime, Flaubert was hard at work on *Temptation,* a draft of which he read aloud to du Camp and another friend, Louis Bouilhet, both of whom declared it unpublishable: "You need to throw this in the fire and never talk about it again."

After a period abroad, Flaubert returned to France determined, nonetheless, to devote himself to literature, and he began working on the scandalous (at the time) MADAME BOVARY. For 56 painful months Flaubert struggled over his manuscript, finally published in 1857. Flaubert was tried in court for his "attack on good morals and religion," but he was exonerated. However, the publicity over the case, which coincided with the poet Charles Baudelaire's similar trial for *Flowers of Evil,* only served to increase the public's interest in the novel. Flaubert became famous.

Marked by his experience, Flaubert turned away from contemporary society and manners to the past, beginning work on *Salammbô,* a romance set at the end of the First Punic War, in 1857. Published in 1862, it was a great success. The year 1863 saw Flaubert back in Paris

once more, where he began to correspond with GEORGE SAND. She was to become a great friend. By 1869, Flaubert had completed his second version of *The Temptation of Saint Anthony* (finally published in 1874).

Sentimental Education, eventually published in 1869, was not well received. Only a few writers, such as ÉMILE ZOLA and Sand, came out in support of this work. Disappointed over the reception, Flaubert suffered from further health problems, his mother's death, and financial constraints. Moreover, his last version of *Temptation* was poorly received. But he persevered, working on his ultimately unfinished novel, BOUVARD AND PÉCUCHET (1881), a work that reflects Flaubert's bitterness in the last years of his life despite the admiration he received from naturalist writers (see NATURALISM) such as GUY DE MAUPASSANT and again, Sand.

In 1875, Flaubert's niece's husband went bankrupt and the author did everything in his power to save them from utter ruin, to the point of sacrificing his own financial stability. Unfortunately, he met with little gratitude and found himself in an awkward situation. Sand even offered to purchase Flaubert's home for him. Flaubert declined and Sand died six months later. Meanwhile, he continued to work on *Bouvard and Pecuchet,* in which he depicts the inability to acquire knowledge on the part of the principal characters that manifests itself in supreme mediocrity.

It was George Sand who asked Flaubert to write something not marked by a sense of desolation. Flaubert's response was the *Three Tales* (1877) that include "A SIMPLE HEART," "The Legend of Saint Julian Hospitaler," and "Hérodias." One of Flaubert's most popular works, "A Simple Heart" tells the story of one woman's life of virtue. Unfortunately, Sand died when Flaubert was still at work on these stories. He said that he wanted to bring his readers to tears with the *Tales,* but it was he who wept bitterly at Sand's funeral.

As Flaubert's continued to experience financial difficulties, Prime Minister Jules Ferry obtained a post for him as a curator as well as a pension. In 1880 Flaubert died, worn out and anxious. Zola, EDMOND DE GONCOURT, ALPHONSE DAUDET, and De Maupassant, among others, attended his funeral.

A perfectionist, Flaubert struggled over his texts for years, producing, for example, three separate versions of *Sentimental Education* before finally publishing it in 1869. Although the Goncourt brothers had praised certain passages from *November,* Flaubert waited another 13 years before publishing that work. In all his writings, it was particularly important to Flaubert that his presence as author be absolutely absent from the text: "Every work [of literature] is blameworthy if the author allows himself to be revealed."

Flaubert also carried out meticulous research before putting pen to paper. After an astounding amount of research in preparation for writing the story of Salammbô, he then struggled six years seeking to perfect his style. Flaubert's aesthetic sensibility was strong and his goal of creating beauty is reflected in his incessant, unending editing of his manuscripts. His mastery of language is particularly evident in his careful construction of each phrase and in his precise use of vocabulary. Flaubert would sometimes check for repetitions of words through 30 or 40 lines. He was particularly attentive to moments of transition between description and narration or dialogue. Finally, he has been particularly noted for his use of represented discourse (*style indirect libre*), a technique that allows the author to comment discreetly on the characters without interfering in the narrative.

Flaubert's work bridges ROMANTICISM and REALISM. Perhaps he inherited from his father the scientific method of analysis that he applied in his own search for the truth that lies beneath appearances. In fact, some contemporaries criticized Flaubert for his apparent detachment and objectivity, accusing him of being insensitive to moral and other issues.

Some of Flaubert's works, such as *Salammbô,* reflect clearly romantic themes such as fantasy, exoticism, and death. Moreover, the underlying current of disillusionment may also be interpreted as romantic. Flaubert's writing is marked by the author's love of beauty as well as a sense of desolation, despair, and even nihilism that results from his disillusionment with and horror of bourgeois society and its values. On some fundamental level, Flaubert was a critic of humanity and the society in which "we are all in a desert; no one understands anybody."

There is a profound connection between Flaubert's writing and the romantic movement as a whole. As a young man, he was a great admirer of VICTOR HUGO, one of the fathers of French romantic literature. Describing his own experience as a youth, Flaubert once wrote, "I have no idea of what other students dreamed. Ours, however, were superbly extravagant, the last reaches of Romanticism that has spread even to us and that, compromised by a provincial milieu, made our heads boil. One was not merely troubadour, rebel and Oriental, one was above all an artist . . . one exhausted one's eyes reading in the dormitory, one carried a dagger in the pocket like Antony. One student . . . shot himself in the head, another hung himself with his tie. We probably didn't deserve much praise. But what hatred of all platitudes! What impulses of grandeur! How we admired Victor Hugo." On a fundamental level, Flaubert's characters experience a painful abundance of sensations and emotions that cannot be sustained. Like characters created by SAINT-BEUVE, STENDHAL, and GAUTIER, Flaubert's romantic heroes and heroines are disillusioned with the world and the desires of their own hearts. Flaubert embraced the romantic ideal and, better than most, was able to express the melancholy it led to.

Flaubert was also a naturalist and realist, particularly in his depictions of provincial and Parisian life as marked by marriage, love, and money. Flaubert considered humanity and the world as made for art rather than art as something made for mankind. While a number of critics have compared Flaubert to Balzac, Flaubert surpassed the author of the *HUMAN COMEDY* in his capacity to transpose sensation into true feeling.

Flaubert worked like a Benedictine, dedicating his life to literature the way a monk would devote his life to God. He was a perfectionist to the point of tormenting himself. In Zola's words Flaubert's genius lay in his combination of "ardent poetry and cold observation." Flaubert built on both Balzac and Stendhal's concept of the novel. In a manner similar to the naturalist approach (see NATURALISM), Flaubert argued that "literature will become more and more like science; it will *expose*." Flaubert's observations reflect a remarkable objectivity, yet his own emotions and fertile imagination still permeate his work. It is his gift for irony, perhaps, that made it possible for him to take a detached stance from the world he paints so meticulously. Structuralist and poststructuralist criticism (see STRUCTURALISM and POST-STRUCTURALISM) has deemphasized Flaubert's realism, arguing instead that Flaubert refrains from drawing conclusions about his observations. He is thus not a realist but an "indeterminist." Recent scholarship also confirms Flaubert's place in the development of the modern novel, particularly in his use of "represented discourse."

FURTHER READING

Brombert, Victor. *The Novels of Flaubert*. Princeton, N.J.: Princeton University Press, 1973.

Chambers, Ross. "An Invitation to Love: Simplicity of Heart and Textual Duplicity in 'Un Coeur simple'" in *Story and Situation: Narrative Seduction and the Power of Fiction*. Minneapolis: University of Minnesota Press, 1984.

Constable, E. L. "Critical Departures: *Salammbô*'s Orientalism," *MLN* 111, no. 4 (1996): 625–646.

Culler, Jonathan. *Flaubert and the Uses of Uncertainty*. Ithaca, N.Y.: Cornell University Press, 1974.

LaCapra, Dominick. *'Madame Bovary' on Trial*. Ithaca, N.Y.: Cornell University Press, 1982.

Orr, Mary. *Flaubert Writing the Masculine*. Oxford: Oxford University Press, 2000.

Porter, Laurence M., ed. *Critical Essays on Gustave Flaubert*. Boston: G. K. Hall, 1986.

FLEURIOT, ZÉNAÏDE (1829–1890)

Zénaïde Fleuriot was born in Brittany, and her identity as a Bretonne was important to her. Over the course of her career, Fleuriot wrote 83 novels for young people. Her works are out of date for young readers today but at the time they were very popular. Fleuriot wrote in a clear and natural style, emphasizing the real. Her works are thus a sign of the literary period in which she lived and wrote. Her REALISM only increased the popularity of her novels, which reflect important religious and political events of her day. Fleuriot's novels include *A Mother's Heart* (1863), *Caline* (1881), *The Hothead Clan* (1887), and *Sun Beam* (1891). A number of her works were published in the *Bibliothèque Rose* series (children's editions) and in the *Bibliothèque Bleue* (inexpensive volumes noted for their blue covers).

FORMALISM

Associated first with Russian formalism, the "new critics" of the 1920s rejected the notion of interpreting literature within its historical context. Formalists are equally opposed to making links between a text and the author's biography. Instead, formalists view the text as existing in its own right. As the term suggests, formalism emphasizes internal form over content.

The term *formalism* first came into use in the 1940s in reference to a close reading of the text that is viewed as a composite of literary devices. The "achieved content" of a work is what gives a piece of literature its meaning. Neither the author's original intention nor the reader's understanding is important. A text inherently possesses organic unity and a unique structure that gives it meaning. A work of literature or art, according to the formalist, is thus entirely self-contained.

Formalist readings focus on the use of images, motifs, and linguistics, as each separate element of the text, as in a living organism, contributes to its meaning. The emphasis is on aesthetic elements and literary devices. At the same time, formalists seek to reveal universal truths even while concentrating on elements that are unique to a given work. Formalists also often focus on tension, irony, and ambiguity.

In France, formalism is particularly associated with the theories of the Swiss linguist Ferdinand de Saussure. It is essentially a reaction against a traditional approach that views art and literature as connected to life. Formalism exists, too, as a reaction against the sociological approach to writing associated with NATURALISM and REALISM.

FOUNDLING, THE (SANS FAMILLE) HECTOR MALOT (1878)

Malot's most famous work, *The Foundling*, tells the story of an orphan boy's adventures and misadventures until he finds his parents once again. Unlike Malot's other novels, *The Foundling* is still popular with children today. It is also an example of a kind of children's literature particularly popular in the 19th century.

In these stories, a child hero essentially in search of self learns about life, society, human nature, and morality. Good and evil are clearly distinguished. Other examples of the genre include ALPHONSE DAUDET's *Little Thing*, JULES VALLÈS's *Child*, and Jules Renard's *Carrot Top*.

Rémi, an abandoned child, is taken in by Vitalis, a traveling showman. With a monkey and three trained dogs, they travel about France on a series of picaresque adventures. When death separates them, Rémi goes to live with Lise and her peasant family. Finally, he sets off to travel again with Mattia the Italian. He has a dramatic experience in a coal mine and meets numerous strange and dangerous people until he finds his real parents.

The travel theme allows the reader to learn about different parts of the country in a manner that echoes GEORGE BRUNO's TOUR DE FRANCE. At the same time, Malot manages to create a world in which Rémi lives out his adventures yet is protected by surrogate parents. The presence of alternative authority figures teaches children to think in different ways about justice, authority, security, and happiness. Moreover, these parental figures have different characters. Through these role models the child is also allowed to consider various possibilities in relation to his own personality and desires.

This classic of children's literature is rich in drama and even violence, yet tempered by humanitarian gestures. A mixture of melodrama and fairy tale, *The Foundling* is also marked by a gently moralizing tone. Rémi's experiences allow Malot to reveal his own sensitivity to social reality and his ability to transmit that awareness to his readers. The specific context of the 19th-century tension between bourgeoisie and proletariat is apparent. In contrast to Jules Vallès's work, there is no rebellion against family and society but, rather, a fatalistic acceptance. In the end, Malot promotes the bourgeois values of family and work. Dreams of a stable family life are reinforced by the author's focus on a lost child whose journey allows the author to move from the level of fantasy to reality.

FRANCE, ANATOLE (1844–1924) The son of a Parisian bookseller, Anatole France first worked as a proofreader and later took a position as librarian for the French Senate. An extremely versatile writer, France wrote in a wide variety of genres that includes poems, essays, literary criticism, novels, short stories, plays, and an opera. However, he is principally remembered as a novelist.

A well-known writer during the Third Republic, France spoke out against the arrest of Alfred Dreyfus, a Jewish officer falsely accused and convicted of treason in 1894, and anticlericalism. As a pacifist, France was opposed to French participation in World War I. He was elected as a member of the Académie Française in 1896. He won the Nobel Prize in literature in 1921.

The most astonishing aspect of France's work is its variety. He published his first book, *Alfred de Vigny,* in 1868. This was followed by a series of poems that appeared in 1873, dedicated to the poet Charles-Marie Leconte de Lisle. In 1876 he published *The Bride of Corinth,* a drama in verse followed by short poems, that was performed at the Odéon in 1902 and the Opéra Comique in 1922.

In 1877, France married Marie-Valérie Guérin de Sauville, with whom he had a daughter. The couple divorced in 1893. In 1879, he produced two short stories published together, "Jocasta" and "The Skinny Cat." France finally gained real notoriety in 1881 with the publication of *The CRIME OF SYLVESTER BONNARD.* In this highly successful novel, the principal character engages in an intellectual quest for wisdom.

In *Jean Servien* (1882), France evokes his passion for the actress Élise Devoyod. This work was followed by *My Friend's Book* (1885), *Balthasar* (1889), and *Thaïs* (1890), "the story of a sinner who became a saint and a saint that sinned." The latter was so extraordinarily successful that Jules Massenet set the story to music. *Thaïs* was performed at the Paris Opéra in 1894. Writing prolifically, France produced a *Tales from a Mother-of-Pearl Casket* in 1892 and *Queen Pédanque* (1893). He also continued to write articles of literary criticism, published later in five volumes under the title *Literary Life.* The first volume appeared in 1888.

The Red Lily (1894) was inspired by France's passion for Madame Arman de Caillavet, with whom he began an affair in 1888. It was adapted to the stage in 1899. *Epicurus' Garden* (1894) draws on the philosophy of the ancient thinker. In 1895, France produced yet another collection of tales, *The Well of Sainte-Claire,* and in the following year was elected to the Académie Française. France also wrote the preface to MARCEL PROUST's first book, *Pleasures and Days,* and in 1897, the first volume of France's very popular series, *Contemporary History,* that includes the novels *Elm Avenue, The Wicker Mannequin, The Amethyst Ring,* and *Monsieur Bergeret in Paris.*

In these four novels, France offers a critique of French society at the time of the Dreyfus affair, contemporaneous with ÉMILE ZOLA's *"J'accuse"* (1898). France also signed the petition of intellectuals calling for a new trial of Dreyfus, at the request of Proust.

The character of Monsieur Bergeret in *Contemporary History* bears a resemblance to his creator. Other novels by France are also of an autobiographical nature, such as *My Friend's Book* (1885) and *Little Pierre* (1918). The latter novels reflect a nostalgia for childhood that marks their place in the history of children's literature, an emerging genre at the turn of the century. France also wrote historical novels such as *The GODS WILL HAVE BLOOD,* his greatest work, about the period of the Reign of Terror during the FRENCH REVOLUTION.

France's other political writings include *Social Opinions* (1902), the preface to *A Lay Campaign* (1905), and *Toward Better Times* (1909). His involvement in contemporary social and political debates did nothing to impede his literary production. *Small Happiness* was published in 1898; *Pierre Nozière* in 1899; *Crainquebille* in 1902; *Comic History* in 1903; a mediocre work of history, *The Life of Jeanne d'Arc,* in 1908, the same year as *PENGUIN ISLAND,* a scarcely veiled critique of French society. France also wrote *The Tales of Jacques Tournebroche* (1908), *The Latin Genius* (1913), *Revolt of the Angels* (1914), *On the Glorious Path—What the Dead Say* (1916), and *Life in Bloom* (1922). France's last works are touched with sadness brought on by the war, inspiring him to look back to his childhood in an attempt to recapture a sense of peace.

In his later years France was less involved in political debates. Nonetheless, throughout his life as a writer, he promoted tolerance and freedom as fundamental human values. A number of his characters confront religious or political fanaticism. Through their voices, France expresses the bitterness and skepticism that contemporary events inspired in the minds of many writers. Moreover, France equally exposed the pettiness of provincial officials and Parisian intellectuals with his own particular brand of irony. His tone of disenchantment is particularly noted in the character of Monsieur Bergeret.

France lived most of his life in Paris, where he was active in literary circles. In fact, in *REMEMBRANCE OF THINGS PAST* Proust partially based his character of Bergotte on Anatole France. Profoundly disturbed by the war, France withdrew from public debates in 1914. A gently rational skepticism marks the thought of this man to whom contemporaries referred as "the good master." France wrote with a style marked by subtle nuances of language and a tone of gentle irony, yet he has been criticized for creating characters that appear more as the incarnation of ideas than as living beings.

FURTHER READING

Jefferson, Alfred Carter. *Anatole France: The Politics of Skepticism.* New Brunswick, N.J.: Rutgers University Press, 1965.

May, James Lewis. *Anatole France: The Man and His Work. An Essay in Critical Biography.* Port Washington, N.Y.: Kennikat Press, 1970.

Tylden-Wright, David. *Anatole France.* New York: Walker, 1967.

FRANÇOIS THE WAIF (FRANÇOIS LE CHAMPI) GEORGE SAND (1848)

First published in 1848 as a serial novel in the *Journal des débats, François the Waif* was published as a single volume in 1849. Part of a series of pastoral novels (*romans champêtres*) that includes *PETITE FADETTE* and *The DEVIL'S POOL, François the Waif* opens with a young abandoned boy, poor and hungry, who encounters the saintly Madeleine Blanchet, the wife of a miller.

François has been taken in by an old woman, Zabelle, who needs money and who hopes that when the boy has grown he will work for her. Moved by their plight, Madeleine undertakes to help Zabelle and François, despite her watchful mother-in-law and a suspicious, avaricious husband, Cadet. Madeleine's life is further complicated by Blanchet's mistress, La Sévère, who is tyrannical and manipulative, out only for her own gain.

Jealous of Blanchet's respect for Madeleine, La Sévère convinces her lover that the relationship between Madeleine and François (now a young man) is not as innocent as it appears. Although this is not the case, Madeleine is compelled by Blanchet to drive François from the house. Both are heartbroken.

François finds employment elsewhere and proves his worth but cannot forget Madeleine, whom he loves like a mother. After the miller's death, François returns, only to find Madeleine near death, her affairs in terrible order due to the machinations of La Sévère. François returns the mill to working order and defeats La Sévère. In the end, François and Madeleine marry, much as Sand's parents had done even though they, too, were of different social classes.

Some critics have suggested that the novel is partly autobiographical. In 1847 Sand was experiencing the first stages of a growing affection for a younger man, Victor Borie, some of whose traits François shares. Madeleine, with her strong maternal instinct, even as a lover, represents George Sand. Moreover, Sand's humanitarian outlook can be found in her defense of a child that society has marginalized, despite his nobility of spirit and mind. Drawn to socialist principles, along with a group of local socialists, Sand in fact came to the assistance of an abandoned girl, petite Fanchette, in 1843.

Written in a charming, delicate style that evokes all the beauty of Sand's native province of Berry, *François the Waif* paints an idealized vision of rural life with its potential for moral purity, as yet untainted by modern, urban life. The principal theme running through Sand's pastoral novels centers on the power of love to overcome social prejudice and injustice, thus marking them as romantic fiction (see ROMANTICISM).

FURTHER READING

Crecelius, Kathryn J. *Family Romances: George Sand's Early Novels.* Bloomington: Indiana University Press, 1987.

Glasgow, Janis, ed. *George Sand: Collected Essays.* Troy, N.Y.: Whitston, 1985.

Hofstadter, Dan. *The Love Affair as a Work of Art.* New York: Farrar, Straus and Giroux, 1996.

Naginski, Isabelle Hoog. *George Sand: Writing for her Life.* New Brunswick, N.J.: Rutgers University Press, 1991.

Peebles, Catherine. *The Psyche of Feminism: Sand, Colette, Sarraute.* West Lafayette, Ind.: Purdue University Press, 2003.

Powell, David A. *George Sand.* Boston: Twayne, 1990.

Schor, Naomi. *George Sand and Idealism.* New York: Columbia University Press, 1993.

Walton, Whitney. "Writing the 1848 Revolution: Politics, Gender and Feminism in the Works of French Women of Letters," *French Historical Studies* 18, no. 4 (Autumn 1994): 1,001–1,024.

Vitaglione, Daniel. *George Eliot and George Sand.* New York: Peter Lang, 1993.

FRANCOPHONE

The term *francophone* refers to a body of literature written in French but not necessarily in France. The underlying question is, does a shared linguistic community mean a shared cultural community? Some francophone writers such as the first president of Senegal Leopold Senghor argued yes, going so far as to suggest a new term, *"francité,"* or, roughly speaking, "Frenchness." Is there one francophone literature? Or many? To refer to literature in French in the singular or the plural has different and often politically charged meanings.

Francophone literature is generally characterized as inhabiting two distinct zones. The first consists of regions such as parts of Switzerland, Belgium, and Canada, where French is the mother tongue. The second is comprised principally of areas in Africa and the Caribbean where French was introduced by colonizers.

In the course of the 20th century, the debate over francophone literature focused on the possibility of reconciling the notion of a shared linguistic culture with one's own distinct cultural identity. This can be problematic, particularly in Quebec and Africa, where questions of assimilation and/or provincialism are central to literature. Francophone literature is thus extremely varied from one part of the world to another. This diversity is what enriches the body of literature written in French as a whole, particularly as francophone writers have often articulated and promoted their distinct cultural heritage. This is not to say that francophone literature has always met with the warmest reception in France, although that has changed in recent years.

The recognition of autonomous francophone literatures outside of France is relatively recent as the debate has, for some time, focused on whether these should be considered regional literatures, peripheral, or overseas. Any such characterization naturally assumes primacy of France itself and bears the legacy of imperialism.

The rise of francophone literature is first associated with the NEGRITUDE movement and Senghor's anthology of literature, published in 1948 with a preface by JEAN-PAUL SARTRE. The movement then continued in the 1950s with the works of such writers as CAMARA

LAYE and MONGO BETI, among others, who received support from leftist intellectuals in France.

After independence, in the 1960s a second generation of African writers not only grappled with decolonization but also sought to explore and express the spirit of Africa, often producing works imbued with expressions from native languages such as the writings of AHMADOU KOUROUMA. In both Africa and Quebec, these writers produced a new set of "classics" that made their way into the respective school systems.

Most frequently, the goal of francophone literatures has been to express a separate cultural identity, often the product of cultural contact in an imperialist context, as something rich, distinct, and legitimate in its own right. In French Canada, the production and dissemination of literature written in French is sometimes considered act of resistance. In the Antilles, writers such as SIMONE SCHWARTZ-BART, RAPHAEL CONFIANT, and Patrick Chemoiseau have sought to reconcile their people with the past while unveiling the richness of Caribbean culture.

In Africa, the celebration of francophone literary expression in the Negritude movement gave way to dissatisfaction and disillusionment. In North Africa, francophone literature of the first generation of Maghreb liberation writers, such as KATEB YACINE and MOHAMMED DIB, lays the foundation for postliberation writers whose works explore the complexity of Franco-Arab cultural contact. Literature thus becomes the means of questioning Arab culture as much as French colonization.

FRENCH REVOLUTION

FRENCH REVOLUTION   The French Revolution is often associated with the storming of the Bastille, a royal prison in Paris that symbolized monarchical abuse of power in the popular mind, on July 14, 1789. Of course, the overthrow of this prison is only one of many events associated with the downfall of OLD REGIME society and the subsequent rise of a republican government in which sovereignty came to reside in a representative assembly rather than in the person of the king. The causes of the revolution lay in urgent financial crises and in the fact that political and social realities were no longer aligned as the boundaries between social classes blurred in the second half of the 18th century. Principles of ENLIGHTENMENT thought,

such as liberty and equality, contributed to a climate in which it was possible for French men and women to consider alternate forms of government.

The French Revolution lasted 10 years, ending with Napoleon's rise to power in 1799. Four distinct periods make up the revolutionary decade. The National Constituent Assembly (1789–91), which produced France's first written constitution, the Legislative Assembly (1791–92), the National Convention (1792–93), and the Directory (1795–99). Despite the reversals and violence associated with the Reign of Terror, during which King Louis XVI, his wife Marie Antoinette, and thousands of aristocrats and opponents of the regime were guillotined, the French Revolution is noted for signifying the first time in history that a Western country completely rejected the notion of monarchical government.

Old Regime society was one based on privilege and inequality. One of the first things the revolutionaries did was to assert that "men are born free and equal in rights." During this 10-year period, France redefined itself as a nation and developed the defining feature of the modern Western world, representative government.

Eighteenth-century writers such as JEAN-JACQUES ROUSSEAU, DENIS DIDEROT, VOLTAIRE, and MONTESQUIEU together contributed to laying the foundation for the French Revolution with their trenchant critique of Old Regime society. Nineteenth-century novelists frequently struggled with the legacy of the Revolution. STENDHAL's *The Red and the Black* illustrates the way in which the Revolution paved the way for upward mobility, while BENJAMIN CONSTANT's concept of individual liberty is derived from principles associated with the 18th century. Still other 19th-century writers struggled with unfortunate aspects of the Revolution. In *The Gods Will Have Blood*, ANATOLE FRANCE evokes the tragedy of the Reign of Terror. ALFRED DE MUSSET offers an example of the romantic's disillusionment with postrevolutionary society in his *Confessions of a Child of the Century*.

FRIDAY (VENDREDI OU LES LIMBES DU PACIFIQUE) MICHEL TOURNIER (1967)

When Robinson Crusoe lands on a lonely island he is in despair until he decides to reorganize the world in which he finds himself by establishing laws and a penal code. The appearance of Friday, a young native, makes Robinson's civilizing mission possible, until a violent, unanticipated explosion of gunpowder shatters Robinson's convictions. Under Friday's tutelage, however, Robinson eventually breaks free from the shackles of civilization to celebrate nature, laughter, play, and the sun. Thus Robinson returns to an age of innocence. When circumstances make it possible to return to society, Friday chooses to leave the island as he has never experienced civilization. Robinson remains on the island to continue his happy life as natural man in a natural environment. Robinson's subsequent solitude, a recurring theme in this author's works, allows Tournier to explore Western philosophical traditions as Robinson reflects on his situation.

Typical of Tournier's works, *Friday* draws on a legend reinterpreted along the lines of the author's particular philosophical train of thought. In writing this work, Tournier draws on a tradition that includes works by the English authors Daniel Defoe, Robert Louis Stevenson, and JULES VERNE. *Friday* also reflects Tournier's shared interests with his former fellow student, the structural anthropologist Claude Lévi-Strauss.

Tournier rewrote *Friday* in a children's version in 1977. This highly successful novel is one of Tournier's most famous works, reflecting his interest in the relationship between literature and philosophy.

FURTHER READING

Anderson, Christopher. *Michel Tournier's Children: Myth, Intertext, Initiation.* New York: P. Lang, 1998.

Cloonan, William J. *Michel Tournier.* Boston: Twayne, 1985.

Davis, Colin. *Michel Tournier, Philosophy and Fiction.* Oxford: Clarendon Press; New York: Oxford University Press, 1988.

Edwards, Rachel. *Myth and the Fiction of Michel Tournier and Patrick Grainville.* Lewiston, N.Y.: E. Mellen Press, 1999.

Petit, Susan. *Michel Tournier's Metaphysical Fictions.* Amsterdam, Philadelphia: J. Benjamins, 1991.

Platten, David. *Michel Tournier and the Metaphor of Fiction.* New York: St. Martin's Press, 1999.

Worton, Michael, ed. *Michel Tournier.* London, New York: Longman, 1995.

FROMENTIN, EUGÈNE (1820–1876) Born

in La Rochelle, at age 19 Fromentin left for Paris, where he began his career not as a novelist but as a painter.

Fromentin traveled extensively in North Africa, making three long journeys between 1846 and 1853. He was taken by the light, the colors, and the desert. The beauty of North Africa became his inspiration for painting works that were admired by the naturalists (see NATURALISM) for their precise drawing and use of color. In fact, Fromentin achieved some renown as an Orientalist.

Fromentin's career as a writer was varied. Troubled by the Franco-Prussian War (1870–71) and the fall of the Paris Commune, Fromentin, once peace was declared, left for Belgium and Holland to visit museums. This journey resulted in *Past Masters* (*les Maîtres d'antrefors*), similar to two earlier works of art criticism, *Artistic Visits* (1852) and *Simple Pilgrimages* (1856).

From his travels in North Africa, Fromentin also produced a number of travel journals, his first attempts at literature. *A Summer in the Sahara* (1857) and *A Year in the Sahel* (1858) were quite popular. GEORGE SAND, the historian Jules Michelet, and SAINTE-BEUVE all praised them. Although Fromentin was a successful professional artist, his paintings were not as original as his sensitive writing, much appreciated by GUSTAVE FLAUBERT and the GONCOURT brothers.

Fromentin's only novel, *DOMINIQUE,* is an autobiographical work recounting his unfulfilled passion for a childhood friend who married and died at the age of 27. It is a bildungsroman that recalls CONSTANT's reflections on his own character in *ADOLPHE. Dominique* reflects an important stage in 19th-century Sensibility. Turning away from romantic passion, (see ROMANTICISM) Fromentin offers instead a sort of melancholy wisdom on social and moral constraints.

FURTHER READING

Evans, Arthur R. *The Literary Art of Eugène Fromentin: A Study in Style and Motif.* Baltimore: Johns Hopkins University Press, 1964.

Hartman, Elwood. *Three Nineteenth-Century French Writer/ Artists and the Maghreb: The Literary and Artistic Depictions of North Africa by Théophile Gautier, Eugène Fromentin and Pierre Loti.* Tübingen, Germany: Narr, 1994.

Mickel, Emanuel J. *Eugène Fromentin.* Boston: Twayne, 1981.

Wright, Barbara. *Eugene Fromentin: A Life in Art and Letters.* Bern, New York: Peter Lang, 2000.

FROTH ON THE DAY DREAM (L'ÉCUME DES JOURS) BORIS VIAN (1947)

Praised by ALAIN ROBBE-GRILLET, this novel is on the surface a traditional, tragic love story. Beautiful and sad, according to RAYMOND QUENEAU *Froth* is "the most poignant contemporary love story."

Colin, young and rich, is in love with Chloe, whom he marries. They seem destined for happiness. Colin's friend Chick is a disciple of the philosopher Jean-Sol Partre (read JEAN-PAUL SARTRE) and loves Alice. They too seem suited to each other. But shortly after their wedding Chloe falls ill and, despite all the efforts of Professor Mangemanche, dies.

This is the story of individuals subsumed and destroyed by mysterious and implacable forces beyond their control. Colin, ruined by his loss, remains alone. Alice murders Partre, whom she believes has made Chick irremediably unhappy. Chick also dies. The novel closes on the death of a mouse caught in a cat's mouth that leaves behind 11 blind orphans. In this work Vian creates an absurd vision of the world that oscillates between poetry and anguish, reflecting the profound sadness of life.

This novel reveals the untrustworthy nature of language, teaching the reader to be suspicious of words while simultaneously suggesting that playing with words and their meaning can be a means of transforming reality. In this work Vian takes cliché expressions literally, modifies words, and makes puns while also revealing the musicality of language. Although Vian's most famous work, this novel did not receive much attention when it was published, catching the public's eye only after Vian's death in 1959.

FURTHER READING
Jones, Christopher M. *Boris Vian Transatlantic: Sources, Myths and Dreams.* New York: P. Lang, 1998.

FROZEN WOMAN, A (LA FEMME GELÉE) ANNIE ERNAUX (1981)

A Frozen Woman explores a woman's transition from childhood to adulthood. In this autobiographical novel, the narrator recalls growing up in her parents' home. They ran a small grocery and café in a provincial town. The narrator's mother was ambitious for her daughter to move up in society and so sent her to a more exclusive school than she might otherwise have attended. The narrator relates her experience as an adolescent and the sexual awakening that accompanies that period. She becomes a teacher and marries a solidly middle-class man and has a family, only to discover that the concerns of domestic life have turned her into a frozen woman. In this novel, Ernaux continues her exploration of themes found in all her works, the consequences of social mobility, identity, and the female condition, drawing from her own life experience.

FURTHER READING
McIlvanney, Siobhán. *Annie Ernaux: The Return to Origins.* Liverpool, England: Liverpool University Press, 2001.
Thomas, Lyn. *Annie Ernaux: An Introduction to the Writer and Her Audience.* Oxford, New York: Berg, 1999.

FRUITS OF THE EARTH (LES NOURRITURES TERRESTRES) ANDRÉ GIDE (1897)

Not a novel per se, this long prose poem is central to an understanding of Gide's philosophy of life and his aesthetic vision that are prevalent in subsequent works of fiction such as LAFCADIO'S ADVENTURES, The IMMORALIST, STRAIGHT IS THE GATE, and TWO SYMPHONIES. *Fruits of the Earth* promotes an aesthetic vision built on the concept of the individual's sensuality and sexuality freed from all social and moral constraints.

A first-person narration addressed to Nathaniel, *Fruits of the Earth* is equally directed to the reader. The narrator proposes that, after reading the text, Nathaniel throw it away and begin to live his own life. The narrator then goes on to recount his travels, particularly in Italy and North Africa, where he tasted the "fruits of the earth," both sensual and sexual. The underlying theme of homosexuality runs as a current throughout this work as the narrator carefully recounts his journey of self-discovery that leads to an ultimate freeing of the senses. In 1935, Gide took up the same themes again in *New Fruits,* proving his adherence to an aesthetic developed early in his career. *Fruits of the Earth* thus announces the principal literary and moral themes of Gide's oeuvre. At its publication, however, this work received little attention. For the first 10 years only 500 copies were sold. Later, *Fruits of the Earth* inspired generations of young people in their rebellion against conventional morality and bourgeois values, best articulated in Ménalque's line from *The Immoralist,* "Families, I hate you." Equally important to an understanding of Gide's works is the assertion of his homosexuality.

FURTHER READING

Bettinson, Christopher D. *Gide: A Study.* London: Heinemann; Totowa, N.J.: Rowman and Littlefield, 1977.

O'Brien, Justin. *Portrait of André Gide: A Critical Biography.* New York: Octagon Books, 1977; 1953.

O'Keefe, Charles. *Void and Voice: Questioning Narrative Conventions in André Gide's Major First-Person Narratives.* Chapel Hill: Department of Romance Languages, University of North Carolina Press, 1996.

Sheridan, Alan. *André Gide: A Life in the Present.* Cambridge, Mass.: Harvard University Press, 1999.

Stoltzfus, Ben. "André Gide and the Voices of Rebellion," *Contemporary Literature* 19, no. 1 (Winter 1978): 80–98.

Walker, David, ed. *André Gide.* London, New York: Longman, 1996.

FURETIÈRE, ANTOINE (1619–1688) Born

in Paris to a bourgeois family, Furetière first studied law. As a man of letters, friend of La Fontaine, and well-respected by contemporary playwrights Racine and Molière, Furetière was elected to the Académie Française in 1652.

Furetière wrote a variety of works, including the satire and BURLESQUE for which he is renowned. In 1655 he published a selection of poetry, in 1658 a *New Allegory or the History of Recent Troubles in the Realm of Eloquence,* satirizing PRECIOSITY, and from 1648 to 1653, the *Aeneid Travesty.* Today he is most famous for his *Universal Dictionary,* published posthumously in Holland in 1690. Written at the same time as the Académie Française's official dictionary, Furetière was accused of plagiarism and thrown out of the Académie. With its preface by the philosopher Pierre Bayle, Furetière's dictionary is the richest encyclopedic dictionary of the 17th century, broader than that of the Académie, which includes only literary language. Furetière's provides technical terms, old expressions, idioms, and proverbs. It is so complete that the Jesuits of Trévoux republished it in the 18th century to compete with DIDEROT's ENCYCLOPEDIA.

Furetière's most famous literary work is his BOURGEOIS NOVEL (1666). Similar in theme and spirit to Molière's *Bourgeois Gentleman,* this work offers a pessimistic account of middle-class life. Divided into two parts, the second contains an attack on the style of Furetière's contemporary, CHARLES SOREL. Despite this critique, Furetière joins company with Sorel, CYRANO DE BERGERAC, and PAUL SCARRON in their departure from the pastoral and heroic novels of the period.

G

GALZY, JEANNE (1883–1977) Born to a traditional Protestant family in the southern French city of Montpellier, Galzy began her writing career as a poet. Her poetry and novels were largely unnoticed until the publication of *A Woman Among the Boys* (1917), *The Reclining* (1923), and *The SURPRISE OF LIVING* (1969). Galzy also published a number of historical and biographical works that include *The Intimate Life of André Chenier,* as well as biographies of GEORGE SAND and Saint Theresa of Avila. In all, she wrote 12 novels. Galzy's writings frequently speak out against the fate of women forced to accept life within the confines of bourgeois society.

Galzy studied at the École Normale Supérieure at Sèvres. She had barely begun her teaching career when she fell seriously ill and was hospitalized, an experience that inspired her novel *The Reclining*. She was a prolific writer and member of the Femina Prize jury. Her most famous work, *The SURPRISE OF LIVING* (1969), is an important contribution to the history of lesbian and feminist literature (see FEMINISM).

FURTHER READING

Garreta, Anne F., and Josyane Savigneau. "Same Sex/Different Text? Gay and Lesbian Writing in French," *Yale French Studies,* no. 90 (1996): 214–234.

GARGANTUA FRANÇOIS RABELAIS (1534) *La Vie très horrifique du grand Gargantua* (which means "The Very Horrific Life of the Great Gargantua"), Pantagruel's father, continues with themes and topics first introduced in *Pantagruel,* but Panurge's comic role in the first book is played in the second by the character of Brother Jean des Entommeures.

The structure of this work has greater unity than *Pantagruel:* however, the same themes of education, religion, and warfare continue to serve as the basis for Rabelais's enquiry into human nature and ethics. The study of behavior was typical of Renaissance thought and bears the influence of the Christian humanist Desiderius Erasmus. An especially burning issue for Rabelais and his contemporaries was religion in a period of religious war. As in his other works, Rabelais uses a mixture of comedy and satire to promote reform. Rabelais's evangelical, humanist, utopian spirit is revealed in the organization of the Abbaye de Thélème. In Greek, "thelema" means will, thus reflecting the question of free will so central to contemporary religious debates. In this antimonastery, the residents are *not* bound by vows to remain there for life. Hypocrites and lawyers are excluded, two species of characters whom Rabelais repeatedly attacks. Traditional doctrinal and liturgical elements of Catholicism, such as the veneration of the saints and the Virgin Mary, are deemphasized. Each resident has his own private chapel, again reflecting trends in evangelical religion condemned by Rome. Rabelais's stance on religious questions echoes that of MARGUERITE DE NAVARRE. As in the *HEPTAMERON,* Rabelais, too, shows his concern with the active rather than the contemplative life.

Humanist themes are also apparent in Rabelais's presentation of education and warfare. The episode of the "picrochiline" war is a vehicle for Rabelais's critique of wars of aggression, a theme found again later in the works of FÉNELON. Moreover, this episode allows Rabelais to comment on the nature of kingship. The prince should have a Renaissance education, encompassing all the disciplines noted above. Only a man of broad culture can govern rightly. Rabelais's king is one of divine right. The religious element of secular rule is thus not ignored, but it does not sanction the prince's abuse of customary rights and privileges. Rabelais's explication of divine right monarchy parallels early modern texts on political theory such as Jean Bodin's *Six Books of the Republic*. The king must protect the subjects of his realm. In consequence, there may be just wars, but Rabelais suggests that wars of aggression are not so. The book concludes with the Enigma, a multilayered poem, the solution to which is provided by Brother Jean. This text within a text continues to serve as a subject of debate by scholars. Like *Pantagruel,* this rich humanist text reveals Rabelais's extraordinary mastery of language.

FURTHER READING

Bakhtin, Mikhail. *Rabelais and His World.* Translated by Hélène Iswolsky. Cambridge, Mass.: MIT Press, 1968.

Cave, Terrence. *The Cornucopian Text: Problems of Writing in the French Renaissance.* Oxford: Clarendon Press, 1979.

Febvre, Lucien. *The Problem of Unbelief in the Sixteenth Century: The Religion of Rabelais.* Translated by Beatrice Gottlieb. Cambridge, Mass.: Harvard University Press, 1982.

Screech, Michael. *Rabelais.* Ithaca, N.Y.: Cornell University Press, 1979.

GARGANTUA AND PANTAGRUEL   See
separate entries on *Gargantua, Pantagruel, Book Three,* and *Book Four.*

GASPARD OF THE MOUNTAINS (GASPARD DES MONTAGNES)   HENRI POURRAT (1922–1931)   Pourrat's most famous work, *Gaspard of the Mountain* consists of four volumes written between 1918 and 1931. *The Chateau with Seven Doors or, Gaspard's Children* (1922), *The Beautiful Shepherdess's Auberge or, When Gaspard Returned to War* (1925), *The Pavilion of Love or, Gaspard and the Bourgeois of Ambert* (1930), and *The Tower of the East or, When Gaspard Ends the Story* (1931), published together in 1960 under the title *The Gallantries, Farce and Adventure of Gaspard of the Mountains.* The story takes place over the course of 28 *veillées,* gatherings of peasants, that provide a framework for the novel and an excuse for the numerous descriptions of customs, beliefs, and stories told during the evening. Gaspard's innate virtue recalls JEAN-JACQUES ROUSSEAU's idealistic view of country life. This work celebrates friendship, family, farm, and village. Some critics, however, criticized the novel's lack of depth and realism.

The central story focuses on Anne-Marie, the daughter of Jean-Pierre Grange, who is forced to leave his estate at Chenerailles for several days. The consequences of his departure are horrifying. A stranger arrives. When Anne-Marie accidentally cuts off the fingers on one of his hands, he swears to take revenge. When Anne-Marie's father arranges for her to marry a solid bourgeois gentleman, her husband turns out to be none other than the man she had injured. Anne-Marie is raped and abandoned, and her only defense against her husband's attacks is Gaspard. Aside from the central story of Gaspard and Anne-Marie, numerous digressions are allowed by the nature of the *veillée* that introduce bandits, village idiots, corrupt priests, and even werewolves. *Gaspard* won the Académie Française's grand prize for the novel.

GAUTIER, THÉOPHILE   (1811–1872)
Remembered now as an eccentric and romantic figure with yellow gloves, long hair, and his famous red waistcoat, Théophile Gautier was born in Tarbes. Encouraged in his literary endeavors by his father, Gautier later went to secondary school in Paris, where he met a number of the major literary and cultural figures of his era, such as Gérard de Nerval, HONORÉ DE BALZAC, and VICTOR HUGO, whom Gautier admired all his life. He first attempted painting but later turned to writing as a career. Gautier wrote abundantly in a variety of genres: travel journals, novels, articles, and poetry. Gautier's travel accounts draw on his own experiences along with purely imaginative journeys across time as in the *The Romance of a Mummy* (1858).

He is principally remembered today for his novels, especially CAPTAIN FRACASSE.

At the beginning of his career Gautier was linked to the romantic movement (see ROMANTICISM). Gautier's public defense of Hugo's HERNANI clearly places him among the romantics. Moreover, Gautier's early poetry is written under a romantic influence, as is manifest in the themes of time and death, and in evocative landscapes.

Gautier's association with the romantics changed with the publication of his novel MADEMOISELLE DE MAUPIN in 1835. The famous preface to that work is now considered to be Gautier's declaration of the doctrine of art for art's sake. "There is nothing that is truly beautiful other than that which serves no purpose; all that is useful is ugly." Gautier believed that art has nothing to do with morality or politics; it must exist in its own right. He searched for beauty, which alone is, in his mind, superior and eternal.

With his belief in the supernatural, Gautier sought something beyond reality that he might evoke through the power of his imagination. Consequently, he argued that of all literary forms, poetry offers a primacy of sensation that links it to sculpture and painting, two other privileged art forms. Gautier's interest in form itself was particularly influential on the poet Charles Baudelaire, who dedicated his *Flowers of Evil* to Gautier.

With the exception of *Captain Fracasse*, Gautier is no longer read. Nonetheless, he wrote at the crossroads of 19th-century literary currents, playing an important role in the development of aesthetic theory. His aesthetic vision of art for art's sake, with its disdain for morality, sentimentality, or progress, contributed to the development of a new art form. Gautier was admired by contemporaries such as Baudelaire and GUSTAVE FLAUBERT, among others, for his sense of the artist's dignity, his love of beauty and form, and his voluptuous language and, ultimately, for making a "religion of art."

FURTHER READING

Snell, Robert. *Théophile Gautier, A Romantic Critic of the Visual Arts.* Oxford: Clarendon Press; New York: Oxford University Press, 1982.

Tennant, P. E. *Théophile Gautier.* London: Athlone Press, 1975.

GEMINI (*LES MÉTÉORES*) MICHEL TOURNIER (1974)

Not surprisingly, this is the story of twin brothers so alike and so intimately connected that they appear to be almost one. Beneath the surface lies the theme of incestuous homosexual love. Unfortunately, the perfect union between Jean and Paul is broken when Jean decides that he must explore the world on his own. Desperate, Paul pursues his brother until, in an accident in a Berlin tunnel, Paul loses an arm and a leg.

According to the fable Paul relates, every human being is a twin devoured by his sibling in the womb. Humankind's subsequent torment is solitude. The irony is that our salvation also lies in solitude, in the internal search for what we have lost, our double. The character of Alexander searches for his lost self in homosexual love, parallel to Paul's quest for Jean. The novel thus echoes Plato's theory of reminiscence and the notion that to know oneself is to recall lost knowledge. In this picaresque, sometimes grotesque adventure, Tournier leaves little open to the interpretation of the reader as he engages in his own internal analysis of the text in a manner that to some critics appears almost presumptuous.

FURTHER READING

Anderson, Christopher. *Michel Tournier's Children: Myth, Intertext, Initiation.* New York: P. Lang, 1998.

Cloonan, William J. *Michel Tournier.* Boston: Twayne, 1985.

Davis, Colin. *Michel Tournier, Philosophy and Fiction.* Oxford: Clarendon Press; New York: Oxford University Press, 1988.

Edwards, Rachel. *Myth and the Fiction of Michel Tournier and Patrick Grainville.* Lewiston, N.Y.: E. Mellen Press, 1999.

Petit, Susan. *Michel Tournier's Metaphysical Fictions.* Amsterdam, Philadelphia: J. Benjamins, 1991.

Platten, David. *Michel Tournier and the Metaphor of Fiction.* New York: St. Martin's Press, 1999.

Worton, Michael, ed. *Michel Tournier.* London, New York: Longman, 1995.

GENET, JEAN (1910–1986)

Born in Paris, Jean Genet was abandoned by his mother, a seamstress and maid, and was raised as a ward of the state. At one point he was sent to live with a foster family in the countryside. Then, after being accused of stealing, Genet was sent to a particularly harsh reformatory. To escape, at the age of 19 he joined the military. Thus began a life of wandering, begging, stealing, prostitution, and regular periods of incarceration.

Genet composed his first poem, "Man Condemned to Death," and his first novel, OUR LADY OF THE FLOWERS, from a prison cell. *Our Lady* (1944), *Querelle of Brest* (1947), and *Miracle of the Rose* (1946) all celebrate an underworld peopled with homosexuals and thieves. These novels also reflect Genet's fascination with imprisonment and death. In 1948, Genet was convicted of burglary for the tenth time, which meant automatic life imprisonment. JEAN-PAUL SARTRE, ANDRÉ GIDE, and JEAN COCTEAU, all admirers of Genet's works, intervened on his behalf and Genet was pardoned. Sartre even wrote a biography of Genet, *Saint-Genet: Actor and Martyr.*

In the 1940s, Genet began writing for the theater, producing *The Maids* (1947), *Deathwatch* (1947), *The Balcony* (1957), *The Blacks* (1959), and *Screens* (1961). He also wrote his memoirs, *The Thief's Journal* (1949). Genet was also actively engaged in politics as a militant supporter of the Palestinian cause, the Black Panther movement, as well as the rights of prisoners and immigrant workers.

Genet's relationship with the United States was tense. Although he was active in the Black Panther movement and lectured at a number of American universities, he was not welcome to U.S. authorities. He was asked to leave the country in 1968 and was refused a visa in 1973. His film *Love Song* was censored, as were his writings. In the mid-1940s, Doubleday expressed an interest in publishing Genet's works in English, until the publisher actually read them.

Whether as dramatist, poet, or novelist, Genet wrote all his works on the margins of society about an underworld of thieves and homosexuals. With a violent and provocative eroticism, Genet celebrates crime, betrayal, prostitution, and homosexuality, all of which are intertwined in the world he creates. He also writes poetically about the beauty of the male body and the pleasures of masturbation in minutely detailed descriptions that overflow with sensuality and a richness of language that stuns the reader.

Some critics have been surprised that Genet never engaged directly in the struggle for homosexual rights. He seemed instead to desire to preserve the marginalized nature of homosexual life, a society within a society that functions on the basis of its own values. He often and disturbingly equates homosexuality with betrayal. In *Funeral Rights,* for example, he describes the death of one of his lovers, Jean Decarnin, a resistance fighter shot down in 1944 at the age of 20. Strangely, Genet praises the collaborator who betrayed Jean. He even goes so far as to praise the Nazis, who were Jean's enemies, saying, "It is natural for piracy, the ultra-mad banditry of Hitler's adventure, to arouse hatred in decent people, but deep admiration and sympathy in me." Then he imagines that Jean's soul lives in the matchbox in his pocket. Only slowly does the reader come to understand that Genet's expression is one of profound grief that he is incapable of expressing in ordinary language. Instead he dreams of cannibalism, of consuming, literally, his dead lover's body.

Genet makes absolutely no concession to conventional morality. He rather turns morality on its head in his revolt against bourgeois Christian values. The central theme to all of his works is theft, "more beautiful than prostitution." Theft is, by its very nature, an assault on the foundation of bourgeois society, private property. Genet makes ironic use of Christian vocabulary in the construction of his particular and peculiar system of ethics, for example, thieves are saints and angels. Of equal significance are the police. In *Querelle of Brest,* the symbiotic relationship between the thief and the policeman is explicit. Mario the detective and Querelle the criminal are lovers even though Mario is trying to solve the crimes that Querelle has committed.

In another reversal of Christian values, Genet argues that it is better to rob the poor than the rich. Better still is to steal from a friend. Theft is the means of purification and liberation. Genet's aim seems to be to assert himself through his acts to prove that he is not simply acted upon. When one steals, "one feels alive."

Genet writes disturbingly of betrayal as something to be proud of. In the world he describes, there is no mythical code of loyalty among thieves. In fact, all of Genet's works are marked by a rejection of the dominant culture and its values. Genet exists as an individual whose fate is of his own choosing. "Only I am responsible for the being in which others have sought to imprison me." It is his sense of living on the margins, perhaps, that leads to his distinction between sexual pleasure and sexual intimacy. It is with harsh pleasure that Genet asserts, "I bugger the world." Yet those who have understood Genet's works to be nothing more than pornography have missed the point. Genet did more than explore society's underworld. His emphasis on destruction and death has a far deeper meaning. It is all of our destruction that concerns him.

Genet once said that he "did not write books in order to liberate homosexuals." "Literature," he said, "doesn't begin by positing the problem of homosexuality or Marxism or whatever. It begins by constructing a sentence. . . . I wrote my books for a completely different reason: for the *taste* of words." What is perhaps most important is that Genet's writing is profoundly and movingly sensual.

Over the years, Genet made several suicide attempts, finally succeeding in 1986 in a Parisian hotel. He supposedly suffered from an accidental fall: however, he is generally believed to have ended his own life.

FURTHER READING

Bersani, Leo. "The Gay Outlaw," *Diacritics* 24, no. 2/3, Critical Crossings (Summer–Autumn 1994): 4–18.

Botsford, Keith. "Jean Genet," *Yale French Studies,* no. 8, What's Novel in the Novel (1951): 82–92.

Brooks, Peter, and Joseph Halpern. *Genet, A Collection of Critical Essays.* Englewood Cliffs, N.J.: Prentice Hall, 1979.

Gaitet, Pascale. *Queens and Revolutionaries: New Readings of Jean Genet.* Newark: University of Delaware Press; London: Associated University Press, 2003.

Jones, David Houston. *The Body Abject: Self and Text in Jean Genet and Samuel Beckett.* Oxford, New York: P. Lang, 2000.

McMahon, Joseph H. *The Imagination of Jean Genet.* New Haven, Conn.; London: Yale University Press, 1963.

Plunka, Gene A. *The Rites of Passage of Jean Genet: The Art and Aesthetics of Risk-Taking.* Rutherford, N.J.: Fairleigh Dickinson University Press; London: Associated University Presses, 1992.

Sartre, Jean-Paul. *Saint Genet, Actor and Martyr.* Translated by Bernard Frechtman. New York: Pantheon, 1983.

Stewart, Harry E. *Jean Genet: A Biography of Deceit, 1910–1951.* New York: P. Lang, 1989.

White, Edmund. *Genet: A Biography.* New York: Knopf, 1993.

Winkler, Josef. *Flowers for Jean Genet.* Translated by Michael Roloff. Riverside, Calif.: Ariadne Press, 1997.

Yaeger, Henry J. "The Uncompromising Morality of Jean Genet," *French Review* 39, no. 2 (November 1965): 214–219.

GENEVOIX, MAURICE (1890–1980)

From life as a student at the École Normale Supérieure in Paris where he was preparing to become a teacher, Genevoix suddenly found himself in the trenches of World War I. Seriously wounded in 1915, the next year he was back at the front, fighting at Verdun, the longest battle of the war. After the war, Genevoix devoted himself to literature. His early works recount the difficulties he and his comrades encountered in the trenches. His description of their daily confrontation with death is straightforward rather than dramatic and is thus comparable to the combat novels of LOUIS-FERDINAND CÉLINE, HENRI BARBUSSE, and ROLAND DORGELÈS. Genevoix's memoirs of the war are expressed in five volumes, *Under Verdun* (1916), *War Nights* (1917), *On the Threshold of Guitounes* (1918), *Mud* (1921), and *Savings* (1923). Later, in his essay *Facing Death,* Genevoix recalls his encounter with death with supreme stoicism.

This first body of works, drawn from Genevoix's experience in the war, was followed by a series of novels inspired by life in his native countryside, the Loire valley. These are the works for which he is principally remembered and which mark Genevoix as a regional writer. Some critics have argued that Genevoix's regional novels are the logical outcome of his combat literature; the experience of war made it necessary for him to seek renewal in the countryside.

Enchanted by nature, Genevoix had a passion for the earth, water, trees, and animals of the Loire. He depicts the territory of his birth and the people who inhabit it with delicate sensitivity. RABOLIOT, the most famous of his works, received the Goncourt Prize in 1925. In this novel, Genevoix depicts the merciless struggle between Raboliot, a poacher, and Bourrel, a gendarme. Driven to desperation, in the end Raboliot murders Bourrel. *Raboliot* was followed by *The Last*

Hunt (1938), a remarkable description of a hunt from the perspective of the prey; *Eva Charlebois* (1944); *Framboise and Bellehumeur* (1942); *Adventure Is in Us* (1952); *Fatou Cissé* (1954); *Agnes, the Loire and the Boys* (1962); *Behind the Hills* (1964); *The Lost Forest* (1967); and *Lorelei* (1978).

As an amateur naturalist, the third body of works Genevoix produced focuses on the beasts that animate nature: *Tender Bestiary* (1969), *Enchanted Bestiary* (1969), and *Bestiary without Forgetting* (1971). Beneath the surface of these works lie the two themes of the joy of life and the acceptance of death.

Genevoix has frequently been characterized either as a combat novelist or as a regional writer. In his works recounting life in the Loire, he draws inspiration from GUY DE MAUPASSANT, on whose works Genevoix had written his master's thesis and whose tradition he follows in careful attention to detail. Genevoix's writing can best be described as romantic realism (see ROMANTICISM and REALISM). Unlike the harsher realist novels of HONORÉ DE BALZAC or ÉMILE ZOLA, Genevoix's novels contain a poetic lyricism. There is constant dialogue between the writer and nature and life itself. The heroes of his novels are usually simple people who are close to nature, as the author was himself. The appeal of Genevoix's regional novels lies in the fact that the author seems to recapture the traditional relationship between humans and nature of an earlier and simpler time.

Genevoix was elected to the Académie Française in 1946 and served as secretary to that body from 1958 to 1973. In 1970, he received the Grand Prix National for his collected works.

FURTHER READING

Gerson, Stephane. "Une France Locale: The Local Past in Recent French Scholarship," *French Historical Studies* 26, no. 3. (Summer 2003): 539–559.

Ó Dúill, Micheál. *Three Twentieth-Century Novelists of Rural Life: Friedrich Griese, Pádhraic Óg Ó Conaire, and Maurice Genevoix.* Frankfurt-am-Main, Germany; New York: P. Lang, 1992.

GENIUS OF CHRISTIANITY, THE (LE GÉNIE DU CHRISTIANISME) FRANÇOIS-RENÉ CHATEAUBRIAND (1802)

Chateaubriand's great work, *The Genius of Christianity,* was fortuitously published on April 14, 1802, just four days before Napoleon and Pope Pius VII signed the Concordat restoring relations between the French state and the Roman Catholic Church. As a consequence, this work and the Concordat were inextricably linked in the public's mind, and that contributed to the success of *Genius.*

Chateaubriand was inspired to write *Genius* after the deaths of his mother and a sister in 1798. At the same time, he attempted to atone for his *Essay on Revolutions (1797),* in which he stated that Christianity is no more than a historical fact.

In *Genius,* Chateaubriand wrote an apology for Christianity by exploring its history, architecture, monuments, and influence on the arts. He attempted to prove that Christianity is the religion that is "the most poetic, the most human, the most favorable to liberty, arts, and letters." The work consists of four main parts: dogma and doctrine, the poetics of Christianity, arts and literature, and liturgy and practice. His fundamental argument is that Christianity promotes both social order and liberty.

While Chateaubriand wrote *Genius* principally in praise of the Christian religion, it also contains political and moral commentaries. According to the 19th-century critic SAINTE-BEUVE, it is not a great book. Romantic (see ROMANTICISM) historians such as François Guizot and Jules Michelet disapproved of Chateaubriand's anecdotal approach to religious history. Nonetheless, it played a role in a popular movement of spiritual renewal with 19th- and 20th-century readers alike drawn to its religious sentimentalism. In France, generations of schoolchildren read parts of *Genius* well into the 20th century.

Genius marks a moment in time as well as revealing Chateaubriand's religious sentiments. It reflects a conservative, religious aspect of romanticism as seen, for example, in Chateaubriand's evocation of the feelings invoked by Christian cemeteries. The work does not consist of a unified whole; rather, it is a collection of diverse fragments written in a variety of genres that appealed to its readers. One can pick up and put down the book at will, unconstrained by a narrative line.

Genius also served as an inspiration to the movement of Gothic revival. Its nationalistic tone in praise of French Gothic architecture parallels Goethe's and

Friedrich Schlegel's arguments on the German Gothic style. Together they echo Edmund Burke's fascination with the sublime that so marked 19th-century romantic thought. Chateaubriand had a significant impact on VICTOR HUGO, who turned the cathedral into a powerful character itself in *The HUNCHBACK OF NOTRE DAME*.

FURTHER READING

Call, Michael J. *Back to the Garden: Chateaubriand, Senancour and Constant*. Saratoga, Calif.: Anma Libri, 1988.

Maurois, André. *Chateaubriand: Poet, Statesman, Lover*. Translated by Vera Fraser. New York: Greenwood Press, 1969.

Smethurst, Colin. *Chateaubriand, Atala, and René*. London: Grant and Cutler, 1995.

GENLIS, STÉPHANIE-FÉLICITÉ DU CREST, COMTESSE DE (1746–1830)

A prolific writer over the course of her long career, Madame de Genlis produced more than 140 volumes. Today she is remembered by scholars for her role in developing 18th-century pedagogical theater (*théâtre d'éducation*) and as an early female novelist. Genlis is also remembered for her memoirs. While not particularly original in style, they depict life at the court of Louis XVI in a lengthy series of lively anecdotes.

In the 19th century, Madame de Genlis's writings received mixed reviews. CHATEAUBRIAND, the poet Alphonse de Lamartine, and VICTOR HUGO all praised her to some degree. She annoyed STENDHAL. Nonetheless, that writer recommended Madame de Genlis's works to his sister Pauline in 1803. While BALZAC was also critical, GEORGE SAND appreciated Madame de Genlis as "a good lady and one that has been too much forgotten, and who had real talent. . . . I owe my first socialist and democratic instincts to her." The reading public also appreciated Genlis's writings, which were republished into the 19th century and beyond.

Although born in the provinces, Madame de Genlis was living in Paris by the age of 10. Her father faced financial ruin and at age 13, Genlis and her mother were under the protection of the financier Lancelot de La Popelinière. In 1763, Genlis married Charles Alexis Bruslart, comte de Genlis, later marquis de Sillery. A talented musician and a cultivated woman who read widely, she was successful in society. She later became mistress to the duc de Chartres, the future King Louis-Philippe, and governess to his children. Louis-Philippe remembered her as a hard teacher; "she raised my sister and me with ferocity."

Genlis began writing by composing pedagogical plays for private theatricals (*théâtre de société*). In fact, her first publications were *Theater for Young People* and *Théâtre d'éducation*. These first literary attempts were welcomed enthusiastically, not only in France but across Europe.

In 1782, Genlis published her lengthy epistolary novel *ADÈLE AND THÉODORE*. While the novel was generally a success, it also incited some negative comments. Due to its support for religion, this work caused Genlis's break with the ENLIGHTENMENT philosophers. Early in her career, Madame de Genlis had associated with philosophers such as Jean le Rond d'Alembert (editor with DIDEROT of the *ENCYCLOPEDIA*), Melchior Grimm, Jean-François Marmontel, and Jean-François de La Harpe. Genlis initiated a personal war against the philosophers, whom she blamed for inciting the people to revolution "to destroy temples, religion, and to massacre kings." In consequence, Genlis spoke out strongly against the *Encyclopedia*.

Nonetheless, Genlis was not entirely opposed to the FRENCH REVOLUTION. She even welcomed revolutionaries into her salon. She was later disillusioned by the course of revolutionary politics (her husband was executed, for example). Genlis went into exile in 1791 and lived abroad for nine sometimes painful and difficult years.

In 1800, Genlis returned to France, where Napoleon offered her a pension and appointed her an inspector of primary schools. The republication of the *Encyclopedia* made Genlis feel that religion was once again menaced. She subsequently produced a series of works attempting to renew traditional moral principles.

Genlis died in 1830, having seen her former pupil accede to the throne of a restored monarchy and having lived herself through a total of 11 political regimes. Over the course of her long and productive career she produced a variety of works that include pedagogical texts, plays, tales, novels, and short stories. Her overriding purpose, regardless of the genre in which she wrote, was to promote morality in an agreeable and acceptable manner. In this she was influenced by 17th-century literary styles for, as she said, "clarity, naturalness, purity, and elegance are the indispensable marks of good style."

FURTHER READING

Schroder, Anne L. "Going Public Against the Academy in 1784: Madame de Genlis Speaks out on Gender Bias," *Eighteenth Century Studies* 32, no. 3, Constructions of Femininity (Spring 1999): 376–382.

Wyndham, Violet. *Madame de Genlis, a Biography.* New York: Roy Publishers, 1960.

GEORGICS, THE (LES GÉORGIQUES) CLAUDE SIMON (1981)

This novel consists of three interwoven stories, that of L.S.M., a general in Napoleon's army, a volunteer in the Spanish civil war, and a soldier in World War II. Simon offers a dramatic depiction not only of three distinct historical periods but also of their shared elements. Death, disillusionment with politics, failure, and defeat combine against the individual confronted with the tide of history.

The structure of the first part of the novel, focusing on L.S.M., is, like much of Simon's works, deliberately complex, collagelike, and disorganized. Simon even switches back and forth from italics to regular typescript. Moreover, his story remains somehow incomplete. In the second part, which takes place during World War II, the narrative is on somewhat firmer ground. The soldier, a descendent of L.M.S., gives the reader a sense of the moving experience of every military hero. Throughout the novel there are also recollections of the civil war in Spain with its bloody street battles.

Beneath the surface flows the cycle of the seasons reminding the reader that nature and history are united as forces that exist and repeat themselves beyond the power of humanity, individual or collective. The last part of the novel recounts the general's end, abandoned and betrayed, signifying universal decline. Simon subtly evokes the chaotic nature of history. History, an unending cyclical force, overwhelms the individual, hence Simon's choice to present three different men at three different times, whose experience is fundamentally the same. Moreover, like a painter, Simon seeks to capture the beauty in suffering.

FURTHER READING

Britton, Celia. *Claude Simon: Writing the Visible.* Cambridge: Cambridge University Press, 1987.

———, ed. *Claude Simon.* London, New York: Longman, 1993.

Duncan, Alistair B. *Claude Simon: Adventure in Words.* Manchester, England; Manchester University Press, 2003.

———. *Claude Simon, New Directions: Collected Papers.* Edinburgh: Scottish Academic Press, 1985.

Evans, Michael. *Claude Simon and the Transgressions of Modern Art.* New York: St. Martin's Press, 1988.

Gould, Karen. *Claude Simon's Mythic Muse.* Columbia, S.C.: French Literature Publications, 1979.

GERMINAL ÉMILE ZOLA (1885)

The 13th volume in Zola's ROUGON-MACQUART series, *Germinal* remains one of his most famous and compelling works. After *L'Assommoir*, it is the second novel in which Zola focuses his attention on the lives of workers, in this case, miners. Zola's stated purpose was to write a political novel describing a miners' strike during the SECOND EMPIRE, and the central theme of *Germinal* is the struggle between labor and capital, one of the most pressing issues for 19th-century European society. In the novel the reader finds Zola's dream of "one fraternal people making of the world a unique city of peace, truth and justice." While *Germinal* is not the first novel in French to explore the lives of workers, it is certainly one of the most powerful to do so.

The story takes place in the north of France, in Montsou, a name invented by Zola but derived from Montceau-les-Mines, a mining town that experienced bloody strikes and anarchist movements similar to those related in the book. In French, Montsou also signifies "mountain under the earth." When Zola began working on the novel in 1884, he drew from an actual event. True to his naturalist doctrine (see NATURALISM), Zola visited the area where miners had recently carried out a long strike in order to document accurately what took place, studying the miners' working conditions, rituals, mores, habits, and diseases. He descended into mines and interviewed workers, taking hundreds of pages of notes in preparation for writing.

There are several layers to the novel. Beyond the struggle between labor and capital, important themes include love, sex, and jealousy. More important, the murderous impulse that marks the Rougon-Macquart family raises its bloody head in this novel as well, as Zola continued to explore the role of heredity in determining character.

In this story, Étienne Lantier, Gervaise Macquart's son (see *L'Assommoir*), is both generous and intelligent, but circumstances force him to leave his post as a railroad machinist in Paris after an altercation with his boss. Finding himself out of work in the midst of an industrial crisis that has touched the north of France, Étienne sets off in search of employment. He arrives in Monstou to work in the mines, where he discovers the intolerable conditions to which the workers have become completely resigned. Through the Maheu family, with whom he lives and works, Étienne witnesses the miners' acquiescence to their miserable existence, and he contacts a socialist leader in Lille. He begins to read radical literature, spreading the gospel of revolution among his compatriots. When the mine owners decide to reduce workers' salaries, Étienne leads them in a strike and it seems he has convinced them to share in his dream of a more just society. Meanwhile, Étienne has also fallen in love with Catherine, who is the mistress of a brutal worker named Chaval.

Unfortunately for the workers, the mining company refuses to negotiate. Although Étienne has established an insurance fund, the strike begins before the workers have accumulated enough cash to protect themselves. As the situation worsens, the desperate miners begin to break machinery, sabotage the mines, and attack the bourgeois management. Soldiers are called in to restore order. When troops confront the miners, the conflict ends in blood.

At one point, the starving workers approach Hennebeau, a mine administrator, demanding bread. After a month and a half of suffering, the workers end the strike, convinced that it is impossible for them to fight injustice. It has all been for nothing. Then on the day the miners return to work, the anarchist Souvarine floods the mines, trapping the workers below ground. Maheu is killed, as is his daughter Catherine, who dies in Étienne's arms before help arrives. Étienne is saved and returns to Paris in the spring, a season that promises new life, while the miners continue their miserable lives. In spite of his family history of alcoholism,

violence, and murder, Étienne has the potential to be a hero. Moreover, despite the tragedy it recounts, the novel ends on a note of hope in the possibility that future worker rebellions may ultimately force change onto society after a slow "germination that will burst the earth, fertilized by the blood of martyrs."

Germinal is primarily a political novel in which the Maheu family represents the workers' struggle against capital. In taking the side of the exploited, Zola meticulously reveals the suffering and despair that drive the miners to attack one another even violently. Nonetheless, the workers' courage in the face of misery stands in sharp contrast to the capitalists' paternalism and greed. Skillfully using animal metaphors and harsh juxtapositions, Zola portrays the stark opposition between the bourgeoisie's life of ease and the labor of beasts that consigns the miners to a living hell. Zola seems to fear the fierce tensions that plague society and that threaten to explode at any moment. Placing his hope in the development of class consciousness, Zola promotes the role of trade unions and legal means ultimately to effect change. Zola's powerful cry for justice resonated with many of his contemporaries. When Zola died, a group of miners attended his funeral shouting "Germinal!"

FURTHER READING

Grant, Elliott Mansfield. *Zola's Germinal, A Critical and Historical Study.* Leicester, England: Leicester University Press, 1962.
Walker, Philip D. *Germinal and Zola's Philosophical and Religious Thought.* Amsterdam. Philadelphia: J. Benjamins, 1984.

GERMINIE LACERTEUX EDMOND AND JULES ALFRED HUOT DE GONCOURT (1865)

Arguably the finest novel written by the GONCOURT brothers, *Germinie Lacerteux* tells the sad adventures of a servant girl. The novel begins with Germinie telling a story from her childhood to her old mistress. The novel ends with a view of Germinie's inconspicuous tomb in the corner of a cemetery. The authors are clearly sympathetic to Germinie's sad plight, all the while minutely detailing her gradual degradation until death. Written in an innovative style, the novel strives to depict social reality and is thus representative of the REALIST movement in 19th-century literature. The authors produce a remarkable depiction of lower-class life. At the same time, the Goncourts begin to take literature in a new direction. Many critics consider the preface to *Germinie Lacerteux* to be the NATURALIST manifesto. The preface defines the novel as "the great, serious, impassioned and living form of literary study and of social enquiry." The Goncourt brothers masterfully blend art and science in this story that draws from a real-life case.

The novel is based on the life experience of Rose Malingre, a devoted servant to the Goncourt family for over 25 years, who, they later discovered, lived a double life. In the novel, Germinie is a poor girl from the country who falls into ruin in Paris. Determined to survive, she enters domestic service to a pious old noble spinster, Mademoiselle de Varandeuil, and, under her influence, becomes devout. Unfortunately, Germinie falls in love with a neighbor's son, Jupillon, who is unworthy of her affection. Jupillon drags Germinie further and further into ruin, to the point of prostitution and abject misery. At one point, Germinie discovers that she is pregnant after having been raped and subsequently gives birth to a stillborn child. The novel is rife with lies, drunkenness, and theft, strangely coupled with illusions of love. Torn between faith and passion, Germinie suffers terribly before dying of tuberculosis. The Goncourts' style is rich and evocative as they explore, in ZOLA's words, "the cadaver of the human heart."

FURTHER READING

Billy, André. *The Goncourt Brothers.* New York: Horizon Press, 1960.

Goncourt, E. *The Goncourt Journals, 1851–1870.* New York: Greenwood Press, 1968.

Grant, Richard B. *The Goncourt Brothers.* New York: Twayne, 1972.

GIDE, ANDRÉ (1859–1951)

Gide was the only son of a wealthy and austere Protestant family. After his father died, Gide was raised almost exclusively by women. Gide's schooling was anything but regular and literature was, at first, a refuge from the world. Highly strung, anxious, and sickly, Gide often suffered from doubt and uncertainty as a young man. At school he turned in on himself, so much so that some of his teachers thought he was not very bright.

Throughout his life, Gide was caught between conflicting desires for liberty and conformity, sensuality and austerity.

Gide's development as a writer reflects his struggle to find his own way independently of the conflicting elements that marked his childhood. Two elements in particular mark Gide's writing, his religious upbringing and CLASSICISM. With the exception of his early experimentation with symbolism, Gide's works may be classified as classical in structure and style. He knew literature well, both classical and contemporary, and what is most striking in his own writing is a combination of classicism and modernity. Gide translated Shakespeare into French and was particularly drawn to the works of Russian author Fyodor Dostoyevsky, French essayist Michel Montaigne, and Czech writer Franz Kafka.

When Gide began his writing career, it was under the influence of the symbolist movement (see SYMBOLISM). However, as of 1895, Gide broke away from the symbolists and quickly developed his own ironic style. He also began to express the themes that permeate his works from that point on, an emphasis on the sensual in particular. He frequently focused on the problem of happiness.

The austere Protestantism of Gide's childhood appears in *TWO SYMPHONIES* and *STRAIT IS THE GATE*, while the theme of homosexuality is present in *FRUITS OF THE EARTH*, *The IMMORALIST*, and *The COUNTERFEITERS*. Gide is also well known for his autobiographical works, *If It Die*, in particular. The tension in Gide's works and thoughts is principally derived from the combination of moral rigor and a strong desire for freedom. At times, homosexuality appears to be a means to attain liberty; at others, it is a source of unease. When Gide does call traditional morality into question, he does so by celebrating homosexuality and by calling for a sexual liberation that will exalt the senses and the body. Not surprisingly, this aspect of Gide's writing was considered scandalous by some of his contemporaries. For the same reasons, Gide played an important role in breaking down certain taboo subjects.

From 1893 to 1895, Gide traveled in North Africa, a journey that had a tremendous impact on his life, because this is when he discovered his homosexuality. Upon his return to France, however, Gide nonetheless married his cousin Madeleine, whom he had loved since adolescence. The love Gide felt for his wife was purely spiritual and their marriage was never consummated. Gide wrote his first novel, *The Notebooks of André Walter* (1890), for his wife; the work reflects a strange combination of dreams and inhibitions. It is the story of a young man who wears himself out because his rich inner life of the mind and imagination make decisions impossible and his life ends in failure. This novel was not successful.

Amyntas (1904) draws on Gide's experience in North Africa, thus making it part of a literary tradition that includes the works of GUSTAVE FLAUBERT, EEUGÈNE FROMENTIN, and PIERRE LOTI. It also contributes to opening a dialogue in literature about homosexuality. What is remarkable in Gide's oeuvre is his unrelenting pursuit of truth, about himself, about homosexuality, and about sexuality in general. Moreover, in a broader context he explores the relationship of language to sense experience. His is a language of desire.

Gide began writing *Corydon* in 1907. Although it was published earlier in a private edition, *Corydon* appeared in a commercial edition only in 1925. At this point Gide had discovered Sigmund Freud, who, to his amazement, echoed Gide's own views on sexuality and homosexuality. In fact, Gide hoped that Freud might write the preface to *Corydon*. This was not to be the case. *Corydon*, nonetheless, remains a significant work in the tradition of homosexual literature, particularly in its focus on sexual repression. Moreover, Gide's approach anticipates more recent theories in feminist literature about writing the body (see FEMINISM).

Gide's participation in the founding of the *New French Review (Nouvelle Revue française)* in 1909 was an important step in his professional life as it gave Gide the opportunity to promote contemporary writers. He encouraged the DADA movement, carried on an open discussion with the novelist ROGER MARTIN DU GARD, and convinced PAUL VALÉRY to return to writing.

Each of Gide's own works appears to be the exploration of temptations that the author himself experienced. *Fruits of the Earth,* in particular, reveals the many possibilities for sensual enjoyment if one is open to them. It is the story of a young man who explores all of his sensual desires while rejecting social and cultural constraints. For Gide, true freedom exists only in the moment for one who is in a constant state of rebirth in a manner that recalls certain elements of existentialist philosophy (see EXISTENTIALISM). Many readers responded enthusiastically to this view of the world. Despite the recurring theme of freedom, Gide recognized that there are constraints. One may even be tortured by one's desires.

The Immoralist reveals the danger of losing one's sense of self due to outside influences. Religious fervor poses similar risks, as is evident in the story of Alissa and Jerome in *Straight Is the Gate*. In this novel, Gide draws from his experience with his wife, Madeleine, while *The Return of the Prodigal Son* is a reflection on hedonism. In these works Gide shows that he has already developed into a mature writer, although at the time he was not widely known to the general public.

Gide's first literary success was LAFCADIO'S ADVENTURES, a novel he called a *"sotie,"* a term that comes from medieval comic plays. *Lafcadio's Adventures* fits into the adventure novel genre in a manner that recalls ALAIN FOURNIER's *The LAST DOMAIN*. It also reveals the danger of allowing oneself an excess of personal freedom. Lafcadio reflects Gide's concept of the *"acte gratuit,"* the notion that one may act, for no particular reason or purpose, for pure pleasure. The gratuitous act may refer to a murder without motivation, committed, as in Lofcadio's case, on impulse, much like the murder on the beach in ALBERT CAMUS's *The STRANGER*. The concept originates in the works of the American writer Edgar Allan Poe. To be oneself, free from society and from one's own past, is the central theme, hearkening back to *Fruits of the Earth*.

A major turning point occurred in Gide's life in 1917 when he met and fell in love with the man who would become his lover, Marc Allégret, an encounter Gide's wife quickly became aware of. The result was an internal conflict reflected later in *Two Symphonies*, a novel in which a pastor provokes the suicide of a young blind girl. *The Counterfeiters,* in contrast, allows for the possibility of determining one's fate as an individual. This novel seems to signify the moment when Gide finally found peace with himself.

Gide's stature as a writer and thinker was on the rise following World War I; and his influence on the generation of intellectuals that formed between 1920 and 1935 was enormous. This is not to say that Gide had no critics. Some of his works were considered scandalous. *The Counterfeiters,* however, was another terrific success.

In 1925, Gide traveled to the Congo and Chad, an experience that led him to denounce the abusive nature of the colonial system, publishing *Travels in the Congo* in 1927 and *Return from Chad* in 1928. His contact with the colonial system led Gide to question the conditions necessary for personal freedom. Like many other intellectuals in the 1930s, Gide was drawn to communism as the solution to problems of social injustice. In the end, he was unable to accept the constraints of SOCIALIST REALISM. However, along with ANDRÉ MALRAUX, LOUIS ARAGON, and others, Gide was active in the antifascist movement.

Gide had been invited to the Soviet Union with LOUIS GUILLOUX, EUGÈNE DABIT, as well as other writers. His hopes were dashed when he saw the reality of Stalinist society with its poverty, corruption, lack of freedom of expression, and the cult of Stalin. When he returned to France, Gide decided to bear witness to what he had seen. He was one of the first leftist intellectuals to denounce the Stalinist system in his famous *Return From the USSR* (1936), a subject treated by SIMONE DE BEAUVOIR in *The MANDARINS.* The publication of Gide's testimony had a significant impact on intellectual debates of the period and met with hostility on the part of many leftists who did not want to accept Gide's depiction of Soviet society. To many of his compatriots, Gide appeared to be a traitor to the Russian Revolution.

After the outbreak of World War II, Gide hesitated before breaking with the *New French Review,* then run by DRIEU LA ROCHELLE. He eventually left for Africa and did not return to France until 1945. Gide's oeuvre, whose themes were first articulated in *Fruits of the Earth,* his role as a founder of the *New French Review,* and his denunciation of fascism, colonialism, and Stalinism together earned him the Nobel Prize in Literature in 1947.

Certain characteristics such as a break from naturalist and realist novels (see NATURALISM and REALISM)

mark the works of Gide as he participated in 20th-century literary movements that challenged traditional concepts of the novel. Along with MARCEL PROUST, Gide laid the foundation for the NOUVEAU ROMAN with its self-referential and innovative approach. In fact, the only one of his works that he called a novel is *The Immoralist.*

Gide had a tendency to play with the relationship between the reader and the text. In *Paludes,* for example, a parody of symbolist views on the relationship between art and life, a writer espouses aesthetic views in opposition to the novel and yet he is writing one himself. In *The Counterfeiters,* Gide breaks up the chronology and plays with the notion of a novel in the process of being written. All through the work Édouard struggles to write a novel of the same name. When *he* abandons the idea, Gide's novel ends.

Gide made use of an unsettling technique, *"la mise en abyme,"* or a repetitious frame story to reinforce the sense of external laws that govern one's fate. Certain objects appear and reappear in the course of Gide's novels. In the case of Michel in *The Immoralist,* it is his wife's scissors. For Édouard in *The Counterfeiters,* it is his baggage claim ticket. This technique brings the process of writing to the surface by emphasizing the ambiguous relationship among author, text, and reader.

Another principal theme in Gide's works is *disponibilité* (openness) to potential experiences, free from social or moral constraints. An ethical question is thus at the heart of Gide's approach, in which a first-person narrator may follow an ethical decision to its logical and sometimes destructive conclusion. Michel sacrifices his wife in *The Immoralist,* Alyssa sacrifices her own and Jerome's happiness, and Gertrude becomes the victim of the pastor's manipulation of religion in *Two Symphonies.* Ironically, in the fullest sense of the word, Gide's method of first-person narrative heightens the sense of objectivity as the narrator, often unconsciously, reveals the truth of himself.

Gide produced a series of remarkable literary characters that pursue their own particular path to the very end. They also reflect general truths about the human condition. Gide observes the human character with the eye of a naturalist, in the end showing the world that, no matter how hard one tries to create an independent existence, it is impossible to escape one's own environment and one's own character. In *Strait Is the Gate,* for example, Alissa refuses Jerome in her struggle to control her own sensual nature and is, ultimately, unsuccessful. While Gide's determinist view of personality may be derived in part from his Protestant upbringing, it also reflects his emphasis on the importance of determining one's authentic self.

A number of critics have noted that Gide not only explores the human psyche but also offers the possibility of striving for an ideal, despite his recognition of one's very real limitations. From childhood on, Gide sought to cultivate his own difference, as is apparent in his journal. He engaged in an examination of conscience and ultimately found the means to justify himself vis-à-vis his mother, his wife, and society in general. Gide's personal struggle also needs to be understood in the context of his time as the problems of modern life run beneath the surface of his works.

FURTHER READING

Bettinson, Christopher D. *Gide: A Study.* London: Heinemann; Totowa N.J.: Rowman and Littlefield, 1977.

O'Brien, Justin. *Portrait of André Gide: A Critical Biography.* New York: Octagon Books, 1977; 1953.

O'Keefe, Charles. *Void and Voice: Questioning Narrative Conventions in André Gide's Major First-Person Narratives.* Chapel Hill: Department of Romance Languages, University of North Carolina Press, 1996.

Parnell, Charles, "André Gide and His Symphonie Pastorale," *Yale French Studies,* no. 7. André Gide, 1869–1951 (1951): 60–71.

Salz, Lily. "André Gide and the Problem of Engagement," *French Review* 30, no. 2 (December 1956): 131–137.

Sheridan, Alan. *André Gide: A Life in the Present.* Cambridge, Mass.: Harvard University Press, 1999.

Stoltzfus, Ben. "André Gide and the Voices of Rebellion," *Contemporary Literature* 19, no. 1 (Winter 1978): 80–98.

Walker, David, ed. *André Gide.* London, New York: Longman, 1996.

GIGI Colette (1943)   Like many of Colette's novels, *Gigi* is the story of an adolescent's introduction to love, her sensual awakening. Gilberte (Gigi) lives a quiet life, raised by her mother, "Mamita," and her grandmother, Madame Alvarez, in a modest apartment in Paris. As Gigi's family is somewhat unusual in social standing, manners are important, particularly to Great Aunt Alicia, who long ago had her time of glory in society and is especially concerned with introducing her niece to the ways of the world.

The rhythm of daily life is broken only by occasional visits from Gaston Lachaille, the son of one of Madame Alvarez's former lovers. Handsome and privileged, Gaston seems to find sanctuary in the simplicity and warm welcome he finds in Madame Alvarez's home. Over time, it becomes apparent that "Tonton" (uncle) Gaston has come to appreciate Gigi's entrance into womanhood.

Gigi is naive, innocent, and unsure. Despite certain vicissitudes, however, Gigi ends up marrying Gaston, declaring, "I would rather be unhappy with you than live without you." Themes in the novel, common to Colette's works overall, are the awakening of love and sensuality, the pleasures of everyday life, adolescence, and innocence.

FURTHER READING

Best, Victoria. *Critical Subjectivities: Identity and Narrative in the Work of Colette and Marguerite Duras.* Oxford, New York: Peter Lang, 2000.

Corbin, Laurie. *The Mother Image: Self-Representation and the Mother-Daughter Relation in Colette, Simone de Beauvoir, and Marguerite Duras.* New York: Peter Lang, 1996.

Dormann, Geneviève. *Colette: A Passion for Life.* Translated by David Macey and Jane Brenton. New York: Abbeville Press, 1985.

Eisinger, Erica Mendelson, and Mari War McCarty. *Colette: The Woman, the Writer.* University Park: Pennsylvania State University Press, 1981.

Flieger, Jerry Aline. *Colette and the Fantom Subject of Autobiography.* Ithaca, N.Y.: Cornell University Press, 1992.

Francis, Claude, and Fernande Gontier. *A Charmed World: Colette, Her Life and Times.* New York: St. Martin's Press, 1993.

Goudeket, Maurice. *Close to Colette: An Intimate Portrait of a Woman of Genius.* Westport, Conn.: Greenwood Press, 1972; 1957.

Huffer, Lynn. *Another Colette: The Question of Gendered Writing.* Ann Arbor: University of Michigan Press, 1992.

Kristeva, Julia. *Colette.* New York: Columbia University Press, 2004.

Ladimer, Bethany. *Colette, Beauvoir, and Duras: Age and Women Writers.* Gainesville: University Press of Florida, 1999.

Lottman, Herbert. *Colette: A Life.* Boston: Little, Brown, 1991.

Marks, Elaine. *Colette.* Westport, Conn.: Greenwood Press, 1981; 1960.

Mitchell, Yvonne. *Colette: A Taste for Life.* New York: Harcourt Brace Jovanovich, 1977; 1975.

Peebles, Catherine. *The Psyche of Feminism: Sand, Colette, Sarraute.* West Lafayette, Ind.: Purdue University Press, 2003.

Sarde, Michèle. *Colette: Free and Fettered.* Translated by Richard Miller. New York: Morrow, 1980.

Stewart, Joan Hinde. *Colette.* Boston: Twayne, 1983.

Thurman, Judith. *Secrets of the Flesh: A Life of Colette.* New York: Knopf, 1999.

GILLES PIERRE DRIEU LA ROCHELLE (1939)

Divided into three parts, this novel traces the life of Gilles Gambier. Raised in a bourgeois family whose values the author rejects, in the first part of the novel Gilles goes off to World War I, where he proves to be equally capable of both courage and cowardice. On leave in Paris, Gilles decides that he needs to find a wife. While visiting the family of a slain comrade, Gilles meets Myriam, the daughter of a financier. Although he loves her, he principally marries her for her money. Later, thanks to the wife of the minister of defense, Gilles is offered a position in the Ministry of Foreign Affairs.

The second part of the novel focuses on Gille's varied attempts to forge a career. Ultimately disillusioned, he returns to the front hoping for death, but he survives and, after the war, becomes involved with an avant-garde group that is an offshoot of ANDRÉ BRETON's surrealists (see SURREALISM). However, Gilles begins to think that the surrealists are no better than right-wing political movements. He turns to journalism but abandons that too, when his pregnant mistress, Pauline, is struck with cancer.

In the third part of the novel, Gilles takes up the sword once again as a militant nationalist and goes off to seek death in Spain. Like ANDRÉ MALRAUX's *MAN'S HOPE,* the ending of this novel is situated in the Spanish civil war. Gilles dies before a successful Republican attack and thus ends his days uncertain over the future of fascism. The only certainty is the author's pessimism.

Gilles reflects major political and social movements of the period. Some critics have even argued that the pregnant Pauline's cancer refers to the crushing of a fascist demonstration in 1934. To save her from uterine cancer, the doctor must kill the child. Pauline dies nonetheless, just as France is dying. Drieu thus offers an implicit critique of a bourgeois capitalist system that leads only to sterility and death.

Drieu's most famous novel, *Gilles* is partly autobiographical. Drieu convincingly shows how, in the uncertainty of the interwar period, a young man might be drawn to the political right. Drieu was bitterly opposed to what he considered bourgeois decadence, a recurring theme in his works. Like his other novels, *Gilles* reflects the crisis in values that marked the period between the two world wars. Unlike Malraux and LOUIS ARAGON, who turned to leftist politics, Drieu became increasingly pessimistic and isolated. Nonetheless, this work accurately documents its historical context, revealing one side of the rift among intellectuals in this period. Like LOUIS-FERDINAND CÉLINE and ROBERT BRASILLACH, Drieu accepted fascism as a possible solution to social problems. Only at the end of his life did Drieu recognize his error. He committed suicide in 1945.

FURTHER READING
Cadwallader, Barrie. *Crisis of the European Mind: A Study of André Malraux and Drieu La Rochelle.* Cardiff: University of Wales Press, 1981.

Green, M. J. *Fiction in the Historical Present: French Writers and the Thirties.* Hanover, N.H.: University Press of New England, 1986.

Kaplan, Alice Y. *Reproductions of Banality: Fascism, Literature, and French Intellectual Life.* Minneapolis: University of Minnesota Press, 1986.

Klein, Holger, ed. *The First World War in Fiction.* London: Macmillan, 1976.

Leal, Robert Barry. *Drieu La Rochelle.* Boston: Twayne, 1982.

Reck, Rima Drell. *Drieu La Rochelle and the Picture Gallery Novel: French Modernism in the Interwar Years.* Baton Rouge: Louisiana State University Press, 1990.

Soucy, R. *A Fascist Intellectual: Drieu La Rochelle.* Berkeley, Los Angeles, London: University of California Press, 1979.

Zelden, Theodore. *France 1848–1945,* Vol. 5, "Anxiety and Hypocrisy." Oxford: Oxford University Press, 1979.

GIONO, JEAN (1895–1970)   Giono once said of himself, "I believe that I have had something all my life for which I thank the gods. That is a great capacity to be happy. I am happy with nothing, with a pen, a pipe, with I don't know what, a leaf from a tree, a butterfly, the sun, it doesn't matter what, even the rain."

Giono was considered by ANDRÉ MALRAUX to be one of the greatest novelists of the time, and Giono's love for life and his native Provence is the quality that most marks his works. With the exception of his time spent in the trenches of World War I and a few trips to Italy, Scotland, and the balearic islands in the Atlantic, Giono spent his life in or near the city of his birth, Manosque.

Giono was sent to the front in 1916 and survived the horrific battle of Verdun, where many of his comrades were killed. This experience turned him into a vocal pacifist in the 1930s. In 1920, Giono married Élise Maurin, a young teacher in his native town of Manosque. The couple had two daughters. During the interwar period, Giono wrote poems, stories, and an unfinished novel, *Angelica,* set in the Middle Ages. He became friends with Lucien Jacques, a poet and painter who encouraged Giono to pursue his vocation as a writer. Giono's first completed novel, *The Birth of Odysseus,* was rejected by publishers. *Hill* (1928), however, was a great success and was awarded the American Brentano Prize. When the bank he was working in closed, Giono decided to devote himself entirely to writing.

At this point he purchased a house outside of Manosque, where he spent most of the rest of his life. There he wrote RENEWAL, a novel that won the English Northcliffe Prize. With his wartime experience far enough in the past to be dealt with, Giono also wrote *The Last Flock,* in which he juxtaposed the experience of trench warfare with the hope of renewal through the traditions of peasant life. In 1932 he published *John the Blue,* evoking his childhood in Provence and, in 1934, one his most beautiful novels, *Song of the World,* the first of his works to be set in the mountains.

Giono's works are first and foremost a pleasure to read but this quality does not deny them depth. He is a writer whose image in the minds of readers and critics has evolved over time. Giono is now recognized as one

of the great French novelists of the 20th century, his works published in a Pléiade edition of eight volumes. His principal focus is the relationship of humankind to nature, a connection that is complicated, ever changing, and contradictory; it is always fundamental. For a long time Giono was considered to be a rural novelist for his celebration of peasant life. Again, though, even in his earliest works there is a profundity that merits fuller consideration as Giono evokes equally the joy and fear that mark the human condition. Common themes unite, for example, *Hill* (1928), the story of a group of men who save their village from the ravages of nature, and *Renewal,* in which the principal character saves his once deserted village while overcoming his own savage instincts. In *That My Joy Last* (1935), the inhabitants of a plateau struggle against boredom until the unexpected arrival of a stranger named Bob renews their hope in life, in the end, unfortunately, only to fail. In *Mountain Battles* (1937) villagers again fight together against natural disaster. One has the sense of Giono's appreciation for the power of nature, and our humility in the face of it. These novels do not create a utupian vision of the world. Nonetheless, Giono's evocation of our relationship to nature at times reaches a state of euphoria. There is power in his depiction of sensations that leaves the reader with the impression of inebriation with life itself.

Two Knights of the Storm marks a shift in Giono's fiction writing. The novel, written between 1938 and 1943, was first published in a collaborationist journal. It was only published as a separate volume in 1965. Considered a chronicle, *Two Knights* introduces a narrative style that recalls village oral tales in tone and structure. Another shift in Giono's writing is related to his personal experience, notably his arrest and imprisonment in 1939 for pacifism. Giono's pacifist views are evident in his *Salute to Melville* (1940). Originally intended as a biographical essay on the author of *Moby-Dick,* Giono transformed this work into a novel as well.

During World War II he was declared a deserter and was arrested twice, once in 1939 and again in 1944. On the first occasion he was freed with the support of ANDRÉ GIDE. The second time Giono was imprisoned on suspicion of collaboration, although there were no real grounds for his arrest. Although *Two Knights* had been published in a collaborationist journal, Giono was actively engaged in support of Jews and other victims of persecution under VICHY FRANCE.

These difficult times seem to have invigorated Giono's writing. In 1945, he created the memorable Angelo, the principal character in his Hussar cycle of novels. *Hussar on the Roof* (1951) brought Giono back into the public eye. Different in tone from his earlier works, *Hussar on the Roof* introduces a young aristocrat, the illegitimate son of an Italian duchess who takes refuge in France after killing an Austrian spy. He encounters an epidemic of cholera in Provence and survives by reason of his bravery and kindness, and with the help of a young woman named Pauline. The series begins in the 19th century with Angelo's story and ends in the 20th with his grandson (also named Angelo).

While working on *Hussar*, Giono continued to write chronicles full of impossibly passionate crimes and excesses of all kinds. All are recounted in the first person. The most famous of these "oral" chronicles is *A King Without Pleasure* (1947), in which a policeman charged with capturing a murderer commits suicide when he realizes that he has the same violent tendencies as the suspected criminal.

In Giono's most modern novel, *Strong Souls* (1949), the author breaks away from the traditional narrative form to present two parallel accounts of a series of events. While both are believable, they contradict each other and the reader is left to choose between the two. *Noé* (1947) is yet another innovative work in which Giono tells a series of unconnected stories.

In 1952 Giono published *The Polish Mill*, evoking one family's problems among themselves and with the outside world. In the last years of his life, Giono pursued a variety of literary projects that included historical fiction as well as the adaptation of a number of his earlier works to the stage. He also continued to write short stories and novels in which the natural world serves as a device to reveal the truth of the human condition.

FURTHER READING

Ford, Edward. *Jean Giono's Hidden Reality.* Lewiston, Me.: E. Mellen Press, 2004.

Goodrich, Norma Lorre. *Giono: Master of Fictional Modes.* Princeton, N.J.: Princeton University Press, 1973.

Lawrence, Derek W. "The Transitional Works of Jean Giono," *French Review,* Special Issue. no. 1 (Winter 1970): 126–134.

Redfern, W. D. *The Private World of Jean Giono.* Oxford: Blackwell and Mott, 1967.

Smith, Maxwell A. "Giono's Cycle of Hussar Novels," *French Review* 35, no. 3 (January 1962): 287–294.

GIRAUDOUX, JEAN (1882–1944)

GIRAUDOUX, JEAN (1882–1944) Although Giraudoux is principally remembered today as a playwright, he was also one of a number of contemporary writers who changed the form of the novel in the interwar period. The diverse nature of his writings includes literary criticism, essays, novels, plays, and screenplays. He established his reputation as one of the great French playwrights of the 20th century, laying the foundation for the likes of SAMUEL BECKETT and Eugène Ionesco.

Giraudoux grew up in the provinces in a family of modest means. A brilliant student, he went to Paris in 1900 on a scholarship, where his secondary-school teacher introduced him to German culture. This turned into a passionate interest that Giraudoux continued to pursue at the École Normale Supérieure and during a stay in Germany in 1905 that lasted several months. From there, Giraudoux went to Harvard in 1906, returning to Paris the following year, where he began working for a literary review before launching a diplomatic career in 1910. He published his first novel, *The Provincials,* in 1909.

Wounded in World War I, Giraudoux became a convinced pacifist after the war. He chose to pursue a diplomatic career in Paris and abroad while continuing to write. He produced a series of novels that include *Simon the Pathetic* (1918), a collection of three short novels focusing on a single character, *Elpénor* (1920), *Suzanne and the Pacific* (1921), MY FRIEND FROM LIMOUSIN, and *Bella* (1926). In 1928, Giroudoux met the actor Louis Jouvet and began writing for the theater, adapting *My Friend* to the stage as *Siegfried* in 1928. The two collaborated together over the next 10 years, producing the 12 plays that brought Giraudoux fame.

Giraudoux was appointed commissioner of information in 1939, the year that he published *Full Power,* an essay discussing contemporary political problems.

In 1940 he retired from public life but continued to write. As World War II progressed, Giraudoux's works became increasingly dark, *Sodom and Gomorrah* (1943) and *Without Power* (posthumous 1945) in particular.

Giraudoux's works need to be understood within the context of the interwar period. His experience in World War I led him to denounce the absurdity of war. Moreover, his career as a diplomat allowed him the opportunity to consider from up close the problems European society confronted between 1918 and 1938. *Adorable Clio* (1920) evokes the fraternity among soldiers in the Great War. By and large, Giroudoux's writings are marked by the conflict between France and Germany, as we see in *My Friend from Limousin*, the story of a young French writer wounded in World War I who suffers from amnesia. He is treated by a German nurse and becomes a great philosopher during the Weimar Republic, Germany's democratic government in the interwar period. The novel reflects Giraudoux's conviction that the tension between France and Germany was one of the most pressing problems of his day. This novel won the Balzac Prize and was Giraudoux's first great success. *The Trojan War Will Not Take Place* illustrates the impossibility of avoiding war in certain circumstances, while *Electra* begins with a family conflict that expands to encompass war itself. In *Sodom and Gomorrah*, Giraudoux announces the coming of the end of the world, and in *Full Power* he specifically censures the politics responsible for war.

The heaviness of the war theme in Giraudoux's writings is counterbalanced by his appreciation of provincial society. A perhaps surprising aspect of Giraudoux's writing is his tendency to escape into the supernatural, the marvelous, and the mythical. His style has often been characterized as *précieux* (see PRECIOSITY) and is replete with word games, allegories, parody, and antitheses. Giraudoux particularly liked to parody myths and legends with burlesque humor. *Elpénor*, for example, is a retelling of Homer's *Odyssey*. The underlying theme to this and other works is self-discovery and return, as in *The ADVENTURES OF JEROME BARDINI*.

Giraudoux's novels are unusual in their lack of emphasis on characters or plot. Plot structures may be nearly absent as in *Simon the Pathetic* or simply a parody as *Suzanne and the Pacific* mimics *Robinson Crusoe*. Giraudoux's characters seem more like shadows or symbols than real people. Characters such as we find in *Elpénor* and *Suzanne and the Pacific*, for example, recall the theatrical works of Luigi Pirandello. They are aware of themselves as literary characters moving from one book to another. At the same time, these characters are powerfully independent. It is as if their mythical nature necessitates their meeting other legendary characters, as Suzanne, for example, meets Robinson Crusoe. What are most striking about Giraudoux's works are his remarkable style and his quality of imagination as he sought to create a world apart, unencumbered by everyday life, a mythical world.

As a mature writer, two principal, overlapping themes emerge in his works: Europe's disarray in the interwar period and love. *Bella* depicts a conflict between two families involved in politics, each with a separate idea of what Europe should be. Their ideological conflict is the setting for a love story. On the surface, *Églantine* (1927) tells the story of a young woman drawn to two older men. Beneath the surface run deeper currents concerned with the fate of Europe, youth and old age, among others. From this point on in Giraudoux's career, the love between a man and a woman comes to represent the future of society.

Readers and theatergoers alike tend either to be enchanted with Giraudoux or to dislike his style. Regardless, Giraudoux's oeuvre reflects the mind of a lucid thinker, full of humor and yet increasingly disturbed by events of the 20th century that seemed to prophesy an unhappy destiny for humankind.

FURTHER READING

Body, Jacques. *Jean Giraudoux: The Legend and the Secret.* Translated by James Norwood. Rutherford, N.J.: Fairleigh Dickinson University Press; London; Cranbury, N.J.: Associated University Presses, 1991.

Korzeniowska, Victoria. *The Heroine as Social Redeemer in the Plays of Jean Giraudoux.* Oxford, New York: P. Lang, 2001.

LeMaître, Georges Edouard. *Jean Giraudoux: The Writer and his Work.* New York: Ungar, 1971.

Le Sage, Laurent. *Jean Giraudoux, Surrealism and the German Romantic Ideal.* Urbana: University of Illinois Press, 1952.

GIRL WITH THE GOLDEN EYES, THE (LA FILLE AUX YEUX D'OR) HON-ORÉ DE BALZAC (1834)

Dedicated to the French romantic painter Eugène Delacroix, this novel forms the last part of a triology usually titled *The Thirteen* that includes *Ferragus* and *The Duchess of Langeais*. *The Girl with the Golden Eyes* begins with a depressing portrait of Paris. "Thus the exorbitant movement of the proletariat, the corrupting influence of the interests which consume the two middle classes, the cruelties of the artist's thought, and the excessive pleasure which is sought for incessantly by the great, explain the normal ugliness of the Parisian physiognomy." Parisians are driven by a desire for wealth and pleasure, implicitly raising the problem of materialism in 19th-century thought. Recurring themes throughout the work are moral degeneracy and its accompanying metaphorical ill health.

It is the story of Henri de Morsay, illegitimate child of Lord Dudley and the marquise de Vordac, neither of whom has shown much interest in their son. Henri is educated by a learned priest who guides the talented, athletic, and handsome young man in the ways of the world. His friend is Paul de Manerville. Separately, they encounter the fascinating and seductive "girl with the golden eyes," a "woman of fire." In the course of a stroll, the as yet unknown beauty wordlessly expresses interest in Henri, who discovers that she is Spanish and well guarded by her chaperone. Rising to the challenge, Henri decides to seduce her.

The lovers arrange to meet secretly. Their first encounter in a rundown house is strange and passionate. Balzac makes suitable reference to the gothic novels of Anne Radcliffe. In fact, there are a number of intertextual references in the novel, to ROUSSEAU, Choderlos de LACLOS, and the 19th century German writer Johann Wolfgang von Goethe, all of which contribute to the tone of mystery and underlying evil. A decrepit old woman resembling the wicked witch of fairy tales portentously presides over the meeting. She turns out to the girl's Georgian mother who has sold her daughter for material gain, to whom we do not know. Paquita, as the stranger is called, mysteriously explains that she and Henri have but 12 days to love each other. Henri is overcome by passion, despite his initial blasé attitude, driven by Paquita's exoticism and wild sensuality. "She was an Oriental poem."

Unsure but seduced nonetheless, Henri returns to Paquita again. Paquita is the lover a man can only imagine but she is dangerous and unstable. She asks Henri to run away with her. Evoking the romantic's fascination with the exotic, Balzac writes "Asia is the only country where love can unfold his wings." However, Henri suspects Paquita and plans revenge for her treachery. On the night he plans to murder her, Henri witnesses Paquita's violent and bloody death throes, stabbed by the marquise, Paquita's mistress, who turns out to be Henri's half sister, yet another illegitimate child of Lord Dudley.

Reminiscent of Delacroix's erotic and violent painting *The Death of Sardanapalus*, *The Girl With the Golden Eyes* is itself a romantic work (see ROMANTICISM) in its fascination with exoticism, erotic sensuality, violence, and mystery. At the same time, Balzac's critique of 19th-century materialism marks this novel's place in contemporary intellectual movements.

FURTHER READING
Allen, James Smith. *Popular French Romanticism: Authors, Readers and Books in the Nineteenth Century.* Syracuse, N.Y.: Syracuse University Press, 1981.
Bresnick, Adam. "The Paradox of *Bildung:* Balzac's *Illusions Perdues,*" *MLN* 113, no. 4 (1998): 823–850.
Carrère, Jean. *Degeneration in the Great French Masters.* Translated by Joseph McCabe. Freeport, N.Y.: Books for Libraries Press, 1967.
Kanes, Martin, ed. *Critical Essays on Balzac.* Boston: G. K. Hall, 1990.
Smith, Edward C. III. "Honoré de Balzac and the 'Genius' of Walter Scott: Debt and Denial," *Comparative Literature Studies* 36, no. 3 (1999): 209–225.

GODBOUT, JACQUES (1933–)

A man of many talents, Godbout has been a novelist, poet, painter, journalist, and filmmaker all at once. Godbout attended the university of Montreal, where he wrote his master's thesis on the French poet Arthur Rimbaud. From 1954 to 1957 he taught in Ethiopia. Upon his return to Canada Godbout began work as a director for the National Film Board of Canada. He was also active in establishing the review *Liberty* and in founding the

Secular Movement for French Language. Finally, Godbout was instrumental in forming the union of Quebecois writers, to which he was elected president in 1977.

Godbout began his literary career in the 1950s with the publication of several collections of poetry; however, he is best known for his novels. For Godbout the novel is a sort of poem. One of the principal contemporary Quebecois writers, his early novels include *Aquarium* (1962), *Knife on the Table* (1965), and *Hail Galarneau* (1967).

Galarneau, whose story Godbout picks up again in *Galarneau's Times* (1993), is a dreamer and poet, slightly confused by life, who runs a snack bar out of an old bus. He has been betrayed by his wife and by a society that has pushed him to its margins. Ironically, Galarneau decides to rebuild his life by closing himself up in his house. A naive and solitary character, Galarneau tells his story in a first-person narrative drawn from his journal.

Godbout writes with a remarkable freedom of structure and style. His novels tend to be short, composed of a series of scenes that recall cinematographic techniques. His manner of expression is at once violent, tender, and full of irony. In *D'Amour P.Q.* (1972), for example, the novelist Thomas D'Amour is turned into a character by the secretary who types his manuscripts.

Godbout is frequently inspired by contemporary politics and social issues. Ecological and political questions inform *Dragon Island* (1976) and *The Heads at Papineau* (1981). Moreover, Godbout also raises questions concerning nationalism and modernity.

An American Story (1986) recounts the experience of Gregory Francoeur, who leaves Quebec for a series of misadventures in California. This novel reflects one of the dominant themes in Godbout's writing, the question of national identity, and reveals the sense of disillusionment among Quebecois intellectuals after the failed referendum on independence in 1980. Francoeur is a nationalist intellectual who leaves Quebec for a sabbatical in California. He is also in search of happiness. Francoeur's personal life is closely linked to political questions. By going to California, he is able to escape, for a brief period, his marriage and life in Quebec. Moreover, with distance, Francoeur can reflect on the problem of Quebecois cultural identity. He is unable to restrain himself from political activism, however, even in the United States. He participates in a clandestine organization that helps foreign leftists immigrate illegally to the United States and is arrested. Once released, he returns to Canada.

Godbout writes in a simple and original style. Beneath the surface, however, one has the sense of a language and culture in danger as his works explore the problem of francophone cultural identity in North America. Godbout has won a number of literary prizes in Canada, Belgium, and France.

GOD'S BITS OF WOOD (LES BOUTS DE BOIS DE DIEU) OUSMANE SEMBÈNE (1960)

This powerful novel recounting a strike among railway workers in Dakar, Senegal, is drawn from the author's own experience. It is written in rich, poetic language that evokes events that took place from 1947 to 1948 on the Dakar-Niger railroad as strikers sought equal pay for African workers and subsidies for all children of polygamous fathers.

In the novel, the workers and their families struggle to sustain themselves during the long strike. For Sembène, a militant Marxist, this is a story of class conflict. It is also a story about the injustice of the colonial system. Women, who play an important role in the novel, are desperate to feed their families. One of them, Ramatoulaye, is arrested when she slaughters a ram. She and others receive harsh treatment from the police. The women communicate to the authorities in broken French. The French, however, do not know a word of Wolof, the native language. The ram that is slaughtered is called Vendredi (Friday), the Muslim day of worship. Sembène sees little in religion that can help the people. It is as impotent as the castrated ram slaughtered by a group of women.

Women are even more alienated than men in this society, and yet they play an active role in the struggle for change. When the women march to Thiès, the third city on the Dakar-Niger line, they are symbolically led by a blind woman, who under normal conditions would have been marginalized in society because of her disability. Other female characters likewise challenge traditional ways of thinking. Penda, a prostitute, becomes a leader in the strike. Ad'jibid'ji wants to become a train driver. Polygamy represents traditional African cultural practices that the French fail to respect. Sembène makes it clear that the old ways are not compatible with the new.

One of Sembène's characters in his novel *Black Docker* echoes the author saying "You wish to become a writer? You will never be a good one until you defend a cause. You see, a writer should go in front, to see things as they really are." In *God's Bits of Wood,* Sembène has found a cause. Sembène wrote this novel between 1957 and 1959 to educate the masses and make them politically conscious. As the character Tiémoko says, "This strike is like a school." The people must rely on themselves to change the system, because existing social, economic, and political institutions are all unjust. The strike is long and arduous, and yet these people are heroic in their determined battle that ultimately ends in triumph. While Sembène's account is generally historically accurate, in reality the workers' grievances were not redressed until five years later.

FURTHER READING

Aire, Victor O. "Didactic Realism in Ousmane Sembène's *Les Bouts de bois de Dieu," Canadian Journal of African Studies* 11, no. 2 (1977): 283–294.

Gadjigo, Samba, et al., eds. *Ousmane Sembène: Dialogues with Critics and Writers.* Amherst: University of Massachusetts Press, 1993.

Murphy, David. *Sembène: Imagining Alternatives in Film and Fiction.* Oxford: J. Curry; Trenton, N.J.: Africa World Press, 2001.

Smith, Craig. "The Stereography of Class, Race, and Nation in *God's Bits of Wood," Research in African Literatures* 24, no. 1 (1993): 51–56.

Tsabedze, Clara. *African Independence from Francophone and Anglophone Voices: A Comparative Study of the Post-Independence Novels by Ngugi and Sembène.* New York: P. Lang, 1994.

GODS WILL HAVE BLOOD, THE (LES DIEUX ONT SOIF) ANATOLE FRANCE (1912)

A historical novel, *The Gods Will Have Blood* is composed of a series of conversations and digressions of all kinds situated in the period of the Reign of Terror during the FRENCH REVOLUTION. It is thus similar in subject to *NINETY-THREE* by VICTOR HUGO. At first glance, the principal character is Citizen Brotteux des Ilettes, a former banker during the OLD REGIME who, during the Terror, leads a miserable life making marionettes in his attic while philosophizing about life.

The real hero of the story, however, is the young painter Évariste Gamelin, a student of the revolutionary artist Jacques-Louis David, a true historical personage. Évariste is an austere and fanatical revolutionary who becomes a member of the revolutionary tribunal. He also falls passionately in love with Élodie Blaise. Divided between austerity and desire, Évariste develops as a character in the midst of the Revolution and its varied consequences. Around him are his mother, a woman of the people; his sister, who flees France with an aristocrat; an elegant intriguer; a priest; and a monk.

The author carried out meticulous research to depict accurately the real historical events that serve as the context for the narrative. He kept a detailed journal of the revolution as it progressed day by day. He evokes the uprising of royalists in the Vendée region, the assassination of the radical journalist Marat, foreign war, and Robespierre's Reign of Terror, to which the title refers.

Évariste, convinced like Robespierre that virtue and terror are necessary to save the republic, embraces his destiny as a number of principal characters die by the guillotine. From his seat on the tribunal, Évariste is merciless to the victims of the Revolution. At the same time, he is capable of a pure and tender love for his mistress. In the end, Évariste dies side by side with Robespierre. When the day comes for his execution, the cart carrying Évariste to his death passes beneath Élodie's window. A woman's hand emerges to drop a red carnation at Évariste's feet. His eyes fill with tears as he contemplates her sweet gesture of farewell, turning his gaze to the guillotine's bloody blade. In the end the gods will always have blood.

After the Thermidorian counterrevolution that ended the Reign of Terror, a period of reaction, luxury, and corruption began under the Directory. Élodie finds a new lover and life goes on. The novel reflects France's fundamental ideas about life, society, and the human condition, some of which he had already expressed in *PENGUIN ISLAND.* France shows how, even in the midst of the most dramatic political events, individuals may only perceive dimly the significance of what takes place around them. In the figure of Évariste, France warns of the cruelty of which men are capable, especially when they believe they possess an absolute truth. Finally, in the character of Élodie, France expresses his belief that it is the duty of the living to let go of the dead and to go on. Élodie is as sincerely tender with her new lover as she was with the former.

Some critics have argued that France's characters tend to lack life and exist more as the expression of an idea than as a living being. Nonetheless, *The Gods Will Have Blood* has remained a compelling work as France successfully evokes the atmosphere of this period in French history.

FURTHER READING

Jefferson, Alfred Carter. *Anatole France: The Politics of Skepticism.* New Brunswick, N.J.: Rutgers University Press, 1965.

May, James Lewis. *Anatole France: The Man and His Work. An Essay in Critical Biography.* Port Washington, N.Y.: Kennikat Press, 1970.

Tylden-Wright, David. *Anatole France.* New York: Walker, 1967.

GOMBERVILLE, MARIN LE ROY DE (1600–1674)

This Parisian-born writer produced a variety of works in several genres. He wrote poetry, history, and two novels. An active member of the Académie Française, to which he was admitted in 1634, Gomberville worked on the plan for its official dictionary of the French language along with FURETIÈRE, who was subsequently cast out for supposed plagiarism when he produced his own dictionary.

Of Gomberville's two novels, the first, *Cythérée* (1622), is a pastoral. Its interest at the time lay in the fact the shepherds and shepherdesses who fill its pages were real people recognizable to contemporary readers.

The five-volume novel POLEXANDRE is Gomberville's most ambitious work. In it he turns away from the pastoral setting to trace the adventures of Polyxandre as he travels to the Canary Islands, the Antilles, and Mexico in search of the island of Princess Alcidiane. Influenced by the travel accounts so popular among 17th-century readers, the novel is full of history and geography, including the history of Mexico as it was known at the time. He also wrote a conclusion to HONORÉ D'URFÉ's unfinished novel *L'ASTRÉE,* usually called Gomberville's sequel.

FURTHER READING

Wadsworth, Philip, A. *The Novels of Gomberville: A critical Study of Polexandre and Cythérée.* New Haven, Conn.: Yale University Press; London: Oxford University Press, 1942.

GONCOURT, EDMOND (1822–1896) and JULES DE (1830–1870)

Edmond-Louis-Antoine Huot and Jules-Alfred Huot de Goncourt were two brothers who collaborated on a variety of literary endeavors. Two dandies who manifested a broad interest in literature and culture, they were larger-than-life figures on the 19th-century French literary stage who left a mark on their age and beyond. The Goncourts were closely associated with other great literary figures of their day including GUSTAVE FLAUBERT, ÉMILE ZOLA, THÉOPHILE GAUTIER, GUY DE MAUPASSANT, and JORIS-KARL HUYSMANS, among others. ALPHONSE DAUDET was the executor of Edmond Goncourt's will.

Edmond and Jules had very different personalities. Edmond was taciturn, Jules enthusiastic. Their characters came to bear on the way they approached their work, and the combination was effective. Each brought to their collective work his particular sensibility. Edmond carefully planned each work while Jules was more concerned with style. They collaborated on or jointly conceived their greatest works.

The brothers are remembered best today for their literary *Journal,* a collaborative effort that Edmond continued to produce on his own after his brother's death. The *Journal,* nine volumes published between 1885 and 1896, consists of the Goncourts' commentary on contemporary literary, artistic, and social life. As "contemporary historians" the Goncourts describe cultural and social events and discuss questions of taste and aesthetics. Moreover, they are theoreticians of REALISM.

The vision of Edmond and Jules was to paint life as they saw it by exploring all social categories, from the aristocracy to the laboring classes, in their works. They were modern writers in the sense that they deliberately examined every aspect of contemporary society, in all its complexity. Critics often refer to their approach as scientific or medical. The Goncourt brothers thus wrote novels that mark the transition from realism to NATURALISM. The coauthors present GERMI-NIE LACERTEUX, for example, as a "true novel" in that it offers sharp observations on contemporary social and moral ills. At the same time, the brothers moved beyond realism in their clinical approach to the examination of human passions. While the Goncourt brothers have made clinical observations about society, they never did so at the expense of style, for they wrote in a rich, voluptuous, and sensual language. Abandoning traditional syntax, the brothers sought to develop an original vocabulary. They called this the artist's writing (*l'écriture artiste*). Critics have argued that this style is somewhat contrived; it was certainly not popular for long. Yet the Goncourts' writing reflects exciting and innovative movements in literature during the 19th century. Throughout their careers, the Goncourt brothers adhered to a realist vision of the novel along with contemporaries such as Zola, STENDHAL, HONORÉ DE BALZAC, and FLAUBERT.

The brothers wrote prolifically. In addition to their *Journal* (considered by some critics to be their masterpiece), the Goncourts produced a series of novels, not all of which they wrote together, such as *In 18 . . .* (1851), *Men of Letters* (1860), *Sister Philomène* (1861), *Renée Mauperin* (1864), *Germinie Lacerteux* (1865), *Manette Salomon* (1867), *Charles Demailly* (1868), and MADAME GERVAISAIS (1869). *Germinie Lacerteux* is arguably the best among them. They also wrote history, some unsuccessful dramas, and works of art criticism. The Goncourts were particularly interested in Japanese art.

Before his death, Edmond bequeathed part of his fortune to establish a literary society composed of 10 members, to award a prize annually for the best imaginative prose work. This is the distinguished Prix Goncourt that continues to be awarded today.

FURTHER READING

Billy, André. *The Goncourt Brothers*. New York: Horizon Press, 1960.

Goncourt, E. *The Goncourt Journals, 1851–1870*. New York: Greenwood Press, 1968.

Grant, Richard B. *The Goncourt Brothers*. New York: Twayne, 1972.

GRACQ, JULIEN (1910–) Julien Gracq, whose real name was Louis Poirer, had a peaceful childhood walking along the Loire River and reading Edgar Allan Poe, JULES VERNE, and STENDHAL, one of his most beloved authors. Gracq was a brilliant student. He graduated with a degree in history and geography from the prestigious École Normale Supérieure in Paris and began a double career as a professor and writer, producing a remarkable oeuvre that marks his place in the history of modern French literature. His principal novels include *The CASTLE OF ARGOL* (1938), *BEAUTIFUL TENEBROUS* (1945), *The OPPOSING SHORE* (1951), and *A BALCONY IN THE FOREST* (1958), all of which have a pronounced poetic quality and bear the influence of the surrealist movement (see SURREALISM). This is particularly noticeable in his collagelike series of images that together inspire self-reflection.

In 1931 Gracq traveled to Venice then Brittany, both of which became settings for future novels. In his first novel, *The Castle of Argol,* Gracq acknowledges in the preface his debt to the 19th-century German philosopher Hegel and to surrealism. Gracq had read NADJA in 1930 and was an admirer of ANDRÉ BRETON. Breton, who rejected the traditional novel form, praised this work that shares certain characteristics with surrealist novels. It also bears the influence of Hegelian thought in the confrontation between nature and spirit.

The plotline of Gracq's novels tends to be less important than the atmosphere in which enigmatic characters, who seem as if they have no real identity, are open to whatever comes their way. The only one of Gracq's novels that has a clearly defined plot, *The Castle of Argol,* also appears to draw from Goethe's *Elective Affinities.* Set in Brittany, it is a story of union and separation as two friends, Albert and Herminien, fall in love with the same young woman, Heide. The novel ends in tragedy as Heide commits suicide and Albert murders Herminien. In a manner typical of Gracq's later works, nature seems to prophesy their sad end.

Mobilized during World War II, Gracq was imprisoned in a German prisoner of war camp in 1940 and was subsequently repatriated for health reasons. *A Balcony in the Forest* reflects in part Gracq's experience during the war. This work, too, bears all the qualities of mystery and poetry peculiar to Gracq's writings as he evokes a secret world of signs and symbols that may lead one toward the truth, if only one is able to recognize those signs.

In 1947 Gracq published a collection of prose poems entitled *Grand Liberty,* then he moved to Paris to teach history and geography at a secondary school where he remained until his retirement in 1970. Gracq gained real notoriety in 1951 when he won and then refused to accept the prestigious Goncourt Prize for *The Opposing Shore* because he felt such honors bring attention to the writer rather than to the work. He wished to remain detached from the literary scene, a position he had outlined in a 1950 pamphlet, "Literature of the Stomach." In that essay, Gracq reveals his concern that the creative spirit of literature had been crushed by the weight of commercialism, journalism, and the lure of literary prizes.

The Opposing Shore is the most ambiguous of Gracq's novels. With no historical or geographical setting, the novel simply paints a verbal picture of seascapes as a tumbledown Venetian-like city is slowly eaten away by an ocean that oddly seems to represent freedom. Gracq evokes a similar feeling in his fourth novel, *A Balcony in the Forest,* only in that work the forest predominates. In all his works, Gracq shows a concern for spatial order. In fact, each work is situated within a prescribed space: a building, a balcony, a room, a road. Gracq's novels thus examine the relationship between representational and textual space in an ambiguous manner. Gracq's interest in geography marks his writing. By far the most important element in his novels is his description of landscape, more so than story line or the exploration of thought and feeling. The natural environment in which his novels are set is omnipresent, a character in its own right, full of magical and strangely sensual secrets. Yet with his remarkable blend of narrative and pure poetry, Gracq creates a sense of mystery that leaves the reader with a feeling of uncertainty as to whether it is a world of menace or promise.

Just as Gracq draws on his training in geography, so his interest in history marks his novels, though he abandons chronology even as he attempts to evoke history. According to Gracq, history became important to literature only in the 19th century, when writers began to situate their works within their own time and context. In the end, as a consequence of his surrealist approach to fiction, Gracq rejects the notion of cause and effect, preferring instead an irrational world of dreams. As a surrealist, Gracq attempts to make each scene in his novels appear as a painting, thus linking narrative to visual imagery.

In *Peninsula,* a collection of short stories published in 1970, Gracq no longer makes any pretense of creating a plot. Other works include a study of ANDRÉ BRETON (1948), a collection of essays (*Preferences,* 1961), two volumes of criticism (*Lettrines,* 1967, and 1974), *In Reading, in Writing* (1980), and a series of autobiographical works, *The Form of a City* (1985), *Around the Seven Hills* (1988), and *Notebooks of a Long Journey* (1992).

Gracq's own study of Breton, published in 1948, reflects his debt to the surrealist movement. Written at the time when Breton had returned to France after the war and was trying to relaunch the movement, Gracq's study analyzes Breton's works as a reader, not as a member of the movement. Gracq is not, in other words, writing a history of the surrealist movement. He is principally interested in Breton's writing style and in his view of the relationship between literature and life. Gracq finds the origins of the surrealist movement in German ROMANTICISM, although he, like others, also recognizes the influence of French writers such as ALFRED JARRY and the poet comte de Lautréamont on the birth of the movement.

Lettrine is the term used by printers for the letter placed at the opening of a chapter or paragraph. In these works of literary criticism, Gracq offers a series of varied writing fragments that include reflections on literature, particularly the works of CHODERLOS DE LACLOS, FRANÇOIS-RENÉ CHATEAUBRIAND, VICTOR HUGO, STENDHAL, HONORÉ DE BALZAC, GUSTAVE FLAUBERT, and MARCEL PROUST, mixed with travel descriptions, reminiscences, and portraits of family and friends. Like the *lettrine,* each piece could serve as the opening to a potential work of literature. The two volumes of *Lettrines* reflect Gracq's connection to the surrealist movement. Although the works do not include images, the *Lettrines* are a collage nonetheless, recalling the works of Breton and LOUIS ARAGON.

Gracq's *In Reading, in Writing* (1981), a collection of texts written in the 1970s, brought the author to the attention of a broader reading public. This work offers his visions of the connection between reading and writing, which he sees as a continuous process. It also includes reflections on the relationship between literature and the visual arts, on literary history, and on his own oeuvre. *In Reading, in Writing* is a more unified work than the *Lettrines*.

Gracq evokes an otherworldly sense of time and space, marginal domains full of magical possibilities. His writing is poetic, lyrical, sensual, and rich in imagery. Moreover, Gracq is particularly sensitive to the rhythm and sound of words and phrases, writing in a dynamic and highly musical style. Rejecting traditional REALISM, Gracq instead depicts aspects of everyday life that take on a strange appearance when they come in contact with a mysterious other world.

In all his works, Gracq appears to be principally concerned with the senses. Gracq's characters often seem to be expecting a message that reveals itself only to one who has abandoned him- or herself entirely to nature. It is difficult to classify and even to describe Gracq's unique poetic world.

FURTHER READING

Dobbs, Annie-Claude, and Kathleen Flosi-Good. "The Problematics of Space in Julien Gracq: Fiction and Narration in a Chapter of Au Chateau d'Argol," *Yale French Studies,* no. 57, Locus: Space, Landscape, Décor in Modern French Fiction (1976): 86–108.

Rodina, Herta. "Sign and Design: Julien Gracq's Au Chateau d'Argol," *French Review* 64, no. 4 (March 1991): 659–666.

GRAFFIGNY, FRANÇOISE DE (FRANÇOISE D'ISSEMBOURG D'HAPPONCOURT) (1695–1758)

Françoise de Graffigny was neither beautiful nor rich nor particularly happy in her life, but she had a gift for writing and produced one of the great works of EPISTOLARY fiction of the 18th century, LETTERS OF A PERUVIAN PRINCESS.

Born to a recently ennobled family (1660), Françoise married François Huguet de Graffigny in 1712. It was not a happy marriage and the three children she bore all died young. Her husband was brutal and

jealous. They separated in 1723 and Graffigny's husband died two years later. Widowed at 30, within a few years she lost both of her parents. Alone and with few resources, Graffigny attached herself to the court of Lorraine. There she fell in love with a young officer, Léopold Desmarets, the one great love of her life. Their liaison, not without its difficulties, lasted until 1743.

Political circumstances forced Graffigny to leave Lorraine for Paris in 1738. On her way she spent time with VOLTAIRE and his mistress, the scholar Madame du Châtelet. In Paris, her initial benefactress was the duchesse de Richelieu. When she died in 1740, Graffigny faced serious financial difficulties and was forced to retire to a convent, but by 1742 she had moved into a home she rented with two friends, near the Luxembourg palace in Paris.

Graffigny's participation in Parisian intellectual and cultural life may have compensated for her financial problems. She met with artists and writers, among whom were DUCLOS, CRÉBILLON, MARIVAUX, ROUSSEAU, the mathematician JEAN LE ROND D'ALEMBERT, and DIDEROT. Together they ate and drank and discussed liberty and literature. With this group Graffigny shared her first attempts as a writer.

Graffigny's greatest success as an author was *Letters of a Peruvian Princess*. Instantly popular, between 1747 and 1835 this work went through 77 editions and translations, not including continuations by other authors. Expertly crafted, this epistolary novel elegantly combines exoticism, social criticism, feminism, and sentimentalism.

From the novel, Graffigny turned to drama. Her first play, *Cénie* (1750), was fairly successful on the Parisian stage. Even Rousseau, who condemned the theater and denigrated women writers, praised *Cénie*. Graffigny's next attempt, *Aristide's Daughter,* was a failure. The play was produced in April 1758. Disappointed and physically weak, Graffigny died in December of the same year.

FURTHER READING

Altman, J. G. "Making Room for Peru. Graffigny's Novel Reconsidered." In *Dilemmes du roman. Essays in Honor of G. May.* Edited by C. Lafarge. Saratoga, Calif.: Anma Libri, 1989, 33–46, and "Graffigny's Epistemology and the Emergence of Third-World Ideology." In *Writing the*

Female Voice. Edited by E. C. Goldsmith. Boston: Northwestern University Press, 1989, 172–202.

Landy-Houillon, I. *Lettres portugueses, Lettres d'une Péruvienne et autres romans d'amour par letters*. Paris: Garnier-Flammarion, 1983.

Showalter, E. "The Beginnings of Mme de Graffigny' Literary Career." In *Essays on the Age of Enlightenment in Honor of I.O. Wade*. Edited by J. Macary. Geneva: Droz, 1977, 293–304, and "Madame de Graffigny and her Salon," *Studies in Eighteenth-Century Culture* 6 (1977): 377–391.

GRAINVILLE, PATRICK (1947–)

After completing his studies at the Sorbonne in Paris, Grainville became a professor of literature. Each of his novels evokes a nostalgia for adolescence and a Dionysian celebration of love. Rejecting the banality of everyday life, Grainville's characters exist instead in a dream world, such as Tokor, who is obsessed with a lost people in *The Flamboyant* (1976), or Martel, who seeks to revive Scandinavian mythology in *The Last Viking* (1980).

The Flamboyant is one of Grainville's most successful novels, winning the Goncourt Prize in 1976. It centers on an unusual friendship between William Irrigal and the insane and cruel African king Tokor Yaki Yumalta. The two set off across Africa in search of the Diorles, a lost sacred people. They travel through a fantastic landscape shaped as much by their own dreams and secret desires as anything else. Meanwhile, an insurrection in the capital threatens King Tokor's state.

Lush forests evoke primordial forces, typical of Grainville's works, which frequently focus on a search for passion and eroticism connected to nature. Grainville writes with energy and a sense of the poetic. Critics have often characterized his writing as baroque.

In subsequent novels, Grainville explores lost love (*Red-haired Diana*, 1978), the world of animals (*Shadow of the Beast*, 1981), a secret labyrinth (*Black Fortresses*, 1982), the South (*The Cave of Heaven*, 1984), Egypt (*Paradise of Storms*, 1986), America (*The Painter's Studio*, 1988, and *Anger*, 1992), the mystery of initiation (*Orgy; Snow*, 1990 and *Angels and Falcons*, 1994), and Sri-Lanka (*The Link*, 1996).

Grainville's world is one of innocence and primitive splendor. Grainville's entertaining works distance themselves from contemporary avant-garde movements in literature.

FURTHER READING

Edwards, Rachel. *Myth and the Fiction of Michel Tournier and Patrick Grainville*. Lewiston, N.Y.: E. Mellen Press, 1999.

GREEN, JULIEN (1900–1998)

Born in Paris to American parents, Green enjoyed a happy childhood in a large and pious family full of love. Green's parents were originally from the American South. The seventh child, Green grew up spoiled by his five older sisters and his mother. A tender and loving atmosphere reigned in this close-knit family.

Green was extremely attached to his mother, who raised him to read the Bible and whose puritan tendencies compelled her to try and protect him from the dangers of sin and sex. In high school, Green often felt isolated and different from other students, in part the result of growing up in an English-speaking household. Not only did his mother speak little French, but she also raised her children on romantic myths of the American South. Despite his solitary nature, Green was not unhappy. His first experience with pain came with the death of his mother in 1914. A number of Green's later works are marked by a sense of having been abandoned. He subsequently suffered through a series of spiritual crises linked to homosexuality, sin, and the question of evil, a recurring theme in Green's works. The title of one of his novels, *EACH MAN IN HIS NIGHT*, seems to sum up Green's concerns.

In 1916, Green left his mother's faith and converted to Roman Catholicism, shortly after his father. At first he intended to enter the Benedictine order of monks. Instead, he joined the American Field Service in 1917, where he served as an ambulance driver on the Italian front of World War I. Forced to confront death time and again, Green was horrified by his experience in the war. Upon his return home, Green encountered death yet again when his sister Retta died at the age of 22, the victim of a pulmonary disease contracted while serving as a nurse during the war.

After the war, Green left for America to pursue his studies at the University of Virginia, graduating in 1922. Solitary as always, and sometimes ostentatiously pious, Green also discovered his homosexuality when he fell in love with a fellow student, whom he called Mark. Throughout his life he was caught in a conflict between his own sensual nature and a spiritual quest. During this period Green also reconnected with his American family, whose property would become the setting for some of Green's subsequent works. Green's first publication, *The Psychiatrist's Apprentice,* was published in English in the university's literary review.

Upon his return to France in 1922, Green briefly considered a career as a painter before deciding to devote himself to a literary career. In 1924, he published his first major work, a *Pamphlet Against the Catholics in France,* in which he reproached French Catholics for their indifference to both the threat of damnation and the mystery of religion. Although it received little attention from the reading public, *Pamphlet* provided its author with entrance into Parisian literary circles.

That same year, Green also discovered happiness in love when he met his lifelong companion, Robert de Saint-Jean. Success soon followed. GEORGES BERNANOS praised Green's first novel, *Mount Cinère* (1926), saying "Courage, Green. Your work is good." Nonetheless, the first period in Green's career as a writer is marked by a somber tone and with the triumph of violence and cruelty.

Green published *Voyager on Earth* in 1926. In this series of short stories, he explores the boundary between reason and madness. Characters in the stories are preyed upon by their own violence and passion as they abandon themselves to excesses of all sorts. The monotony of life drives them to madness. Frightening hallucinations and murderous dreams presage their tragic fates. Only the approach of death seems to offer them a certain calm. The sense of the beyond is a reflection of Green's Catholicism. Mystical and poetic, *Voyager* straddles the line between realism and the subjective experience.

Critics often characterized Green's writing as neo-realist (see REALISM). Pessimism and despair reign in ADRIENNE MESURAT (1927). In his novels, love and hate both inevitably lead toward disaster. There is an overpowering sense of the unavoidable abyss against which human beings are powerless. Green's characters are almost primitive in that their desires, fears, anger, and cries of anguish are disordered, leading willy-nilly to madness and murder. At this time, Green was still living with his family in Paris, where he remained until 1932, stifled by their close proximity. "Adrienne Mesurat was me," he wrote, "surrounded by prohibitions that drove me crazy." Even after his father's death in 1927, Green lived with his sister until her death in 1979.

The publication of LEVIATHAN (1929), however, marked a new period in Green's career as he withdrew from religion to enjoy the pleasures of the flesh. *The Other Sleep* (1931), whose title recalls the works of the 17th-century theologian Blaise Pascal, explores the appeal of homosexuality.

Together these novels reflect Green's pessimistic visions of the human condition, a vision that condemns us to solitude in the face of madness and death. At the same time, elements of REALISM reflect his admiration for HONORÉ DE BALZAC, from whom Green draws his interest in human psychology. Green's bitter tone resurfaces in *The Strays* (1932). In fact, Green's oeuvre reflects a lifelong spiritual struggle in which he vacillates between despair and calm.

Green traveled to the United States in 1933–34, where he renewed his family ties and began to conceive *Faraway Country,* a work he would complete only in 1987. From 1934 to 1940, Green set off in a new direction that reflects his interest in Eastern spirituality, expressed in *The Visionary* (1934), *Midnight* (1936), and *Varouna* (1940). While his pessimism is still evident in these works, it is tempered by his evocation of another mystical reality where one may find deliverance. Green's venture into mysticism, however, constitutes but one stage in his ongoing spiritual journey.

During World War II, Green fled to the United States, where he taught, participated in conferences, translated the poet Charles Péguy, and published his memoirs in English. *Memoirs of Happy Days* received the Harper Prize. As an American citizen, Green was drafted and sent to work in the Office of War Information.

Another spiritual crisis, beginning in 1939, influenced a third series of novels that reflect the tension between carnal desire and religious faith. The character of Joseph Day in MOÏRA (1950) becomes a killer out of religious fanaticism. This novel also returns to the theme of homosexuality, first introduced in *The Other Sleep.*

Upon his return to France in 1945, Green wrote a number of works that continued to reflect his renewed faith. In *Each Man in His Night*, arguably Green's greatest novel, love and faith are reconciled. These later works reflect the tension between faith and uncertainty. Yet they also reveal an attempt to reconcile faith and literature. The underlying pessimism in Green's thought is qualified by his belief that suffering ultimately leads to salvation.

In the 1950s Green also tried his hand at writing for theater, producing three plays, *South* (1953), *Shadow* (1954), and *The Enemy* (1958), at which point he turned to autobiography. His *Journal* (four volumes) traces his own spiritual journey and expresses a nostalgia for the lost innocence of childhood. "God speaks gently to children," he says, "and often without words. Creation offers the child all the vocabulary he needs in the leaves, clouds, running water or a patch of light. It is the secret language not taught in books that children know so well." In these volumes, Green explores his struggle to attain a balance in life between body and spirit, the material and the spiritual.

In his later years, Green continued to be productive in a variety of genres that includes essays, biography, and autobiography. He was elected to the Académie Française in 1971. Asserting his identity as an American, in 1996 Green stated that he no longer considered himself a part of the Académie. A tormented man and a powerful writer, Green reveals a fundamental dualism in his works. As the epigraph of *Moïra* states, "Purity is only found in heaven or in hell."

FURTHER READING

Burne, Glenn S. *Julian Green*. New York: Twayne, 1972.

Cooke, Gerard, Mother. *Hallucination and Death as Motifs in the Novels of Julien Green*. Washington, D.C.: Catholic University of Merica Press, 1960.

Dunaway, John M. *The Metamorphoses of the Self: The Mystic, the Sensualist, and the Artist in the Works of Julien Green*. Lexington: University Press of Kentucky, 1978.

Green, Julien. *The Apprentice Writer*. New York: M. Boyars, 1993.

Kostis, Nicholas. *The Exorcism of Sex and Death in Julien Green's Novels*. The Hague, Paris: Mouton, 1973.

Newbury, Anthony H. *Julien Green: Religion and Sexuality*. Amsterdam: Rodopi; Atlantic Highlands, N.J.: Humanities Press, 1986.

O'Dwyer, Michael. *Julien Green: A Critical Study*. Dublin; Portland Ore.: Four Courts Press, 1997.

Wildgen, Kathryn Eberle. *Julien Green: The Great Themes*. Birmingham, Ala.: Summa, 1993.

Ziegler, Robert. "From Writing to Scripture: The Character as Text in Julien Green's Le Voyageur sur la terre," *French Review* 63, no. 5 (April 1990): 819–826.

GUIBERT, HERVÉ (1955–1991)

The central and most important theme in Guibert's works is the body, particularly the relationship of his body to AIDS, the disease to which he succumbed in 1991 at the age of 36. Guibert explores through his disease the connection between subject and object in a manner that recalls postmodern feminist writing (see POSTMODERNISM and FEMINISM). More important, he also made a significant contribution in bringing the subjects of homosexuality and AIDS into the open.

Guibert began writing as a critic, principally for *Le Monde*, one of France's most prestigious newspapers. Guibert was also a photographer fascinated by the power of images. He produced several works on photography and spoke of "an infiltration of the photo into the text," or image, verbal or otherwise, as a means to unleash the text, a notion that pervades a number of his works.

Guibert created a scandal by openly depicting his life as a homosexual in *Voyage with Two Children* (1982), *Arthur's Whims* (1983), *The Dogs* (1982), *Wounded Man* (1983, film adaptation by Patrice Chéreau), *Crazy about Vincent* (1989), and *The Blind* (1985). His discussion of homosexuality in these works runs the gamut from innocent to crude. Described as pretentious, narcissistic, provocative, and stubborn, Guibert was not afraid to reveal everything about himself and his life, to the point of having himself filmed in the hospital as he lay dying. *Modesty and Shame* was shown on French television a month after Guibert's death. His writings reveal sadomasochistic tendencies, in sex and in life. Guibert violently rejected the values of his family and wanted to hurt them, particularly his wife, Christine. A number of his works are centered on his family, such as *Suzanne and Louise* (1980), *My Parents* (1986), and *The Gangsters* (1988). In contrast to the animosity he felt toward his family, Guibert was extremely attached to his lovers.

Guibert's first novel introducing the subject of AIDS is *Crazy about Vincent* (1989), in which the narrator discusses his lover, Vincent, a bisexual drug addict who begins to show signs of having AIDS. While Guibert reflects on this first contact with the disease, he also celebrates their sexual relationship. The narrator meets Vincent in 1982, and their relationship lasts until Vincent's death from a drug overdose in 1988. The narrator, writing as if in a diary, is both curious and afraid. He has nightmares that are a combination of sexual fantasy and fear. At the same time, he is fascinated by Vincent's body. Guibert alters the traditional diary form as he tells the story backward, from death to the birth of love.

Guibert discovered that he had AIDS in 1988. From that point on, the theme of AIDS and its ravaging effects on his body became central to his works, particularly in his AIDS trilogy, *To the Friend Who Did Not Save My Life* (1990), *Compassionate Protocol* (1991), and *Cytomégalovirus* (posthumous, 1992). At the same time, Guibert continued to write works of pure fiction such as *My Valet and Me* (1991), *Man in the Red Hat* (posthumous, 1992), and *Paradise* (posthumous, 1992).

Vacillating between depression and acceptance, Guibert wrote his AIDS trilogy in an attempt to "go to the limit of unveiling the self." In doing so, he created what some critics consider to be a new genre, that of the "false novel" or "autofiction," lying somewhere between fiction and reality. Guibert's style moves from first-person to third-person narrative and back again, yet he remains the principal character in his works, speaking openly of things one normally keeps secret. Always fascinated with the body, whether in words or in image, with AIDS Guibert's attention shifts to the body in decay.

In the AIDS cycle Guibert seeks at times to escape illness, at others to reconcile himself to his body, and, ultimately, to find refuge in writing. *Cytomégalovirus* is the journal of his experience in the hospital as he slowly lost his vision. His inability to read or write is central to this work for Guibert *must* write. Writing and life have become one. The day after his 36th birthday, Guibert tried to commit suicide. He died 11 days later from complications following that attempt.

As a gay writer, Guibert participated in a group who sought to bring the early debate on AIDS out of a purely scientific and moral discourse into the field of literature. *Compassionate Protocol,* for example, evokes the feeling shared by many AIDS patients of having a body haunted by ghosts from the past, including the past of one's own body. Guibert blurs the line between subject and object or, in this case, subject and disease, in a manner that recalls feminist theorist Julia Kristeva's treatment of motherhood. *To the Friend Who Did Not Save My Life* describes the early stages of Guibert's struggle with AIDS, as well as the last phase of the life of his friend and mentor, Michel Foucault.

Combined with Guibert's work in photography, the concept of writing the body, associated with contemporary feminist literature, takes on new meaning. Guibert offers a glimpse of the experience and treatment of AIDS in France, as well as the powerful relationship between pain and desire.

FURTHER READING

Apter, E. "Fantom Images: Hervé Guibert and the Writing of 'sida' in France." In T. F. Murphy and S. Poirier, eds. *Writing AIDS: Gay Literature, Language, and Analysis.* New York: Columbia University Press, 1993.

Orban, Clara. "Writing, Time and AIDS in the Works of Hervé Guibert," *Literature and Medicine* 18, no. 1 (1999): 132–150.

Sarkonak, Ralph Williams. *Angelic Echoes: Hervé Guibert and Company.* Toronto, Buffalo: University of Toronto Press, 2000.

Schehr, Lawrence R. "Thanatopsis: Writing and Witnessing in the Age of AIDS." Review Essay. *Modern Fiction Studies* 48, no. 3 (2002): 746–750.

Stambolian, G., and E. Marks, eds. *Homosexualities and French Literature.* Ithaca, N.Y., London: Cornell University Press, 1979.

GUILLERAGUES, GABRIEL JOSEPH DE LAVERGNE, VICOMTE DE (1628–1685)

Guilleragues was both a diplomat and a writer. As Ordinary Secretary of the Chamber and Cabinet of His Majesty, Guilleragues drafted letters for Louis XIV. In 1679 he was sent as French ambassador to Constantinople (present-day Istanbul), where he died. Guilleragues's greatest literary work is his *Letters of a Portuguese Nun* (1669).

Published anonymously in 1669, the *Letters of a Portuguese Nun* was immediately attributed to Guilleragues. This immensely popular work inaugurated the genre of the EPISTOLARY NOVEL that was to become so popular in the 18th century. In a series of five monophonic letters structurally comparable to the five acts of a tragedy, Mariane, abandoned by her dashing French lover, writes from her provincial convent of her lost love. The style is simple and direct in its appeal, hence deemed "realist" by contemporary readers.

In a manner characteristic of the genre, the author presents himself as the editor of a collection of genuine letters. Contemporary readers viewed the letters as realistic, due less to the author's device than to the passion evoked by the letters themselves. Like GOMBERVILLE and MADELEINE DE SCUDÉRY, Guilleragues turned away from the bucolic pastoral setting of HONORÉ D'URFÉ. His concentrated story line, so different from the encyclopedic digressions of L'ASTRÉE, proved to be more popular with the reading public. In the 18th century, the monophonic epistolary novel reappears with MADAME DE GRAFFIGNY's LETTERS OF A PERUVIAN PRINCESS (1747). However, the greatest works in this genre are polyphonic: MONTESQUIEU's PERSIAN LETTERS (1721), ROUSSEAU's JULIE, OR THE NEW HELOISE (1761), and CHODERLOS DE LACLOS's DANGEROUS LIAISONS (1782).

The moving depiction of a woman seduced and abandoned made this work an immediate literary success. Published by a Parisian house that specialized in popular "mondaine" literature, the *Letters of a Portuguese Nun* went through 20 editions in the 17th century. The initial publication of the *Letters* was followed by a series of anonymous "responses" supposedly written by Mariane's lover. These, too, contributed to the work's commercial success. Even the title of the book took on a meaning of its own. The famous letter writer Madame de Sévigné used the term *"faire une portuguese"* to refer to a tender and passionate letter like the ones found in the novel.

Contemporary debates on the work were lively. Even at the time there were arguments over the letters' authenticity, although some critics argued that it does not matter who the author is as long as the sentiments expressed are real. CATHERINE DESJARDINS made a similar argument in defense of her own works. Other critics condemned the reading public for its scurrilous interest in a nun's amatory transgressions.

Despite the general attribution of the work to Guilleragues, modern scholars have debated the gender of the author or have taken a psychological approach in analyzing the letters. Anna Klobucka suggests that one needs to take into account the national identity of the text itself. If the letters are genuine, then the work is Portuguese; if they are fictional, then it is French. From the romantic period of the 19th century to the feminist postmodern of the 20th, this text has been significant in defining the concept of Portuguese national identity.

FURTHER READING

Klobucka, Anna. *The Portuguese Nun: Formation of a National Myth.* Lewisburg, Pa.: Bucknell University Press, 2000.

GUILLOUX, LOUIS (1899–1980)

Guilloux was born into a family of modest means. His father, a cobbler and militant socialist, introduced Guilloux at a young age to leftist politics. All of Guilloux's writings bear this influence, particularly in their concern for the fate of the poor and suffering. A gifted student, Guilloux was inspired to pursue a literary career by his reading of JEAN-JACQUES ROUSSEAU, JULES VALLÈS, and ROMAIN ROLLAND. From 1916 to 1918 he taught high school in his native Brittany.

Guilloux moved from the provinces to Paris in 1918, where he earned his living by teaching and in journalism. His literary career began with the publication of his first novel, *House of the People* (1927), a work that evokes his childhood and his father's militancy. In the next decade, Guilloux produced his three most important novels: *Confidential File* (1930), *Angelina* (1934), and BITTER VICTORY (1935).

During the interwar period, Guilloux was as active in leftist politics as his father had been. He returned to Brittany in 1930. Although he was sympathetic to their program, he never joined the Communist Party. Guilloux was secretary to the international Congress of Writers for the Defense of Culture in 1935. He supported the Spanish Republicans against Franco and, in 1936, traveled to the Soviet Union along with a group of writers that included ANDRÉ GIDE. Upon their return, Guilloux was offered a position as editor of the literary section of a leftist newspaper. When he refused to denounce Gide's *Return from the USSR,* however, Guilloux was forced to resign. Moreover, the disillusionment that he, like Gide, experienced on his trip to the Soviet Union led him to break completely with the Communist Party in the following year.

Guilloux received the Populist Prize in 1942 for *Bread of Dreams* and the Renaudot Prize in 1949 for *The Game of Patience.* He received the Grand Prize from the Académie Française for the totality of his works in 1973. A well-known writer, after World War II, he worked on adapting the works of the Polish-born English novelist Joseph Conrad and ROGER MARTIN DU GARD to television.

During the war Guilloux remained in Brittany, working to establish cooperation between communist and noncommunist resistance fighters. He also undertook a mission for the U.N. High Commission on Refugees investigating conditions in camps for displaced persons in Germany, Italy, and Greece. After the Liberation in 1945, he served as an interpreter to the U.S. Army, an experience that inspired *O.K. Joe* (1976).

While working for radio and television, Guilloux continued to write novels after the war, producing *Absent from Paris* (1952), *Parpagnacco or the Conspiracy* (1954), and *Lost Battles* (1960), a novel in which he takes up again the question of social injustice. *Confrontation* (1967) is in the form of a police investigation but is principally the story of a man in search of his past.

Guilloux is often associated with the writer EUGÈNE DABIT, due to their shared interest in the life of the poor and humble. Such is the focus of *House of the People* and *Angelina.* In *Confidential File* and *Bitter Victory,* Guilloux describes the atmosphere of provincial French towns during the war. *Bitter Victory* is particularly powerful in its evocation of the base character of the provincial elite. At the same time, the novel movingly depicts the character of Cripure, a touching philosophy teacher suffocated by the narrowness of provincial life. *Bitter Victory,* Guilloux's masterpiece, best encapsulates the author's vision of the world. Critics have often compared Cripure to a modern-day Don Quixote who battles against the world's injustices.

Above all, Guilloux is sympathetic in his treatment of characters forced to confront the sometimes ridiculous nature of their destiny. More than anything, this sincere and spontaneous compassion marks Guilloux's works. He strives to give voice to the voiceless in society as, for example, in the interior monologue of a lonely man in a small village who has been abandoned by his wife (*Lost Coco,* 1978). Guilloux also wrote a series of autobiographical works (*Notebooks, 1921–1944* and *1944–1974*), as well as translating a number of works from English into French.

Guilloux's literary voice is linked to his politics. He brings to life the pain of everyday life that results from the way human beings treat one another, whether by greed, indifference, or ignorance. Guilloux thus serves as the prophet of the victims of an unjust society. He speaks of their hopes, their struggles, their lost battles, not to explain them but simply as witness to them. Guilloux's great friend ALBERT CAMUS once said, "I like and admire the work of Guilloux, who neither flatters nor scorns the people of whom he speaks and who restores to them the one greatness that can never be torn from them, that of truth."

FURTHER READING

Brombert, Victor. *The Intellectual Hero.* Chicago: University of Chicago Press, Phoenix Books, 1964.

Green, Francis J. "Louis Guilloux's Le Sang Noir: A Prefiguration of Sartre's La Nausée," *French Review* vol. 43, no. 2 (December 1969): 205–214.

Green, Mary Jean Matthews. *Louis Guilloux: An Artisan of Language.* York, S.C.: French Literature Publications, 1980.

Peyre, Henri. *The Contemporary French Novel.* New York: Oxford University Press, 1955.

Redfern, W. D. *Louis-Guilloux: Ear-Witness.* Amsterdam, Atlanta: Rodopi, 1998.

H

HÉBERT, ANNE (1916–2000) Born in Quebec, Hébert grew up among artists and writers. Because of poor health, she received a private education. Moreover, her father was a poet and literary critic who had a strong impact on his daughter's intellectual development. During her adolescence, another important influence was her cousin, Saint-Denys Garneau. Through them, Hébert began to frequent literary circles. In 1953 she started work as a scriptwriter for the Canadian National Film Bureau. She then received a fellowship from the Canadian Royal Society and moved to Paris. From that point on, Hébert lived mainly in France but made frequent trips to Quebec, and her writings reflect an ongoing connection to the land of her birth.

At the beginning of her literary career, Hébert published a series of short stories in which she introduced a profound sense of the tragic that marks all her works. She skillfully evokes the effect of the passions and fate on the individual's destiny in *Silent Rooms* (1958) and subsequent works. Hébert's poetry, too, is often marked by a strong feeling of anguish. The theme of solitude dominates much of her writing.

In *KAMOURASKA* (1970), arguably Hébert's most powerful work, past and present overlap. On one level, the narrative takes place while a woman watches over her dying husband in the course of the night. On another, it is the story of that woman's life, Elisabeth Aulnières, who recalls her passionate love for Dr. Nelson and its terrible consequences. In the stillness of the sickroom, an atmosphere of suspicion reigns. Elisabeth is weighted down by guilt that seems not to have diminished over time.

As in so many of her works, Hébert's novels manifest a combination of the real and the mythical. *Children of the Black Sabbath* (1975) is a story of incest and witchcraft set in a Quebecois convent, while *IN THE SHADOW OF THE WIND* (1982) recounts the strange disappearance of two girls from a fishing village along the Saint Lawrence River. This novel consists of several different perspectives on the tragic event that shakes this small English-speaking village. *Burden of Dreams* (1991) explores the disquieting behavior of a group of adolescents suffering from some evil secret and thus echoes Hébert's earlier work *The Torrent* (1950).

FURTHER READING

Gould, Karen. "Absence and Meaning in Anne Hébert's *Les Fous de Bassan*," *French Review* 59, no. 6, Special Issue on Quebec (May 1986): 921–930.

Green, Mary Jean. "Dismantling the Colonizing Text: Anne Hébert's *Kamouraska* and Assia Djebar's *L'Amour, la fantasia*," *French Review* 66, no. 6 (May 1993): 959–966.

Green, Mary Jean. "The Witch and the Princess: The Feminine Fantastic in the Fiction of Anne Hébert," *American Review of Canadian Studies* 15, no. 2 (Summer 1985): 137–146.

Knight, Kelton W. *Anne Hébert: In Search of the First Garden.* New York: P. Lang, 1998.

Pallister, Janis L. *The Art and Genius of Anne Hébert: Essays on her Works: Night and the Day Are One.* Madison, N.J.: Fairleigh Dickinson University Press, 2001.

Paterson, Janet M. "Anne Hébert and the Discourse of the Unreal," *Yale French Studies*, no. 65, The Language of Difference: Writing in Quebec(ois) (1983): 172–186.

Russell, Delbert. *Anne Hébert*. Boston: Twayne, 1983.

HÉMON, LOUIS (1880–1913)

Born in France, Hémon left his homeland at the age of 23 to travel after the death of his wife. He spent eight years wandering in England before settling in Canada. There he lived first in Quebec, then in Montreal, before moving to the forest where he lived and worked with a family of lumberjacks. Hémon shared their life, reflecting on their culture and values in his novel *MARIA CHAPDELAINE* (posthumous 1914). First published as a serial novel, this work evokes the experience of French settlers in Canada. The novel did not attract the attention it deserved until 1924, at which point Hémon suddenly acquired fame. He was run over by a train in 1913. A number of his other novels were also published posthumously, including *Voilà, Beauty* (1923), *Colin-Maillard* (1924), *Fighting Malone, Pugilist* (1926), and *Monsieur Ripois and the Nemesis* (1950). Hémon's writing had been described as clear and uncomplicated yet rich in details about everyday life. He has since been recognized for his important contribution to Canadian francophone literature.

HEPTAMERON, THE MARGUERITE DE NAVARRE (1558)

Marguerite de Navarre was the sister of France's king Francis I and the queen of Navarre. Although she died in 1549, the collection of 72 stories called *The Heptameron*, published in 1558, is attributed to her and her court circle, despite some 19th-century scholars who argued that it was really the work of her contemporary BONAVENTURE DES PÉRIERS. Marguerite may not have penned all the stories herself and there is no definitive text. Seventeen different manuscripts have survived.

The Heptameron is modeled on Boccaccio's collection of tales, the *Decameron* (1353), an important work of the Italian Renaissance. The first French translation of Boccaccio appeared in 1414. A new translation was commissioned by Marguerite de Navarre in 1545. The 15th and 16th centuries saw the rise of the short story as an important literary genre generally.

The setting for the telling of these tales is a monastery, where a group of travelers have taken refuge from severe flooding and other difficulties. To entertain themselves they undertake to tell each other stories over the course of eight days in an attempt to re-create the original *Decameron*—or 100 stories. The participants, five men and five women, are meant to tell true stories. In fact, the symbolic or metaphorical meaning of the stories is what counts. As the characters discuss the various tales, their conversations allow for digressions into other areas. In consequence, the problem of truth and language is a recurring one in the text.

The contemporary sociopolitical context is important for understanding this work, which reveals the social and spiritual problems of its day. This was a period of cultural change across Europe. A centralized monarchy was in the process of constructing an identity for France as a nation-state, culturally and politically rivaling Italy, Spain, and England. It was a period in which the traditional aristocracy faced the challenge of rising commercial, legal, and bureaucratic classes. Society also experienced a flourishing and sometimes acrimonious debate on the nature of women, the *querelle des femmes*. Finally, cultural change included the effects of theological and ideological shifts that accompanied the Reformation. The Reformation emphasized the importance of the individual's conscience and personal relationship with God, in opposition to traditional ecclesiastical authority. One of the main themes of this text focuses on religion. Other themes include gender roles and the relationships between the individual and society and fiction and reality.

Like her contemporary HÉLISENNE DE CRENNE, Marguerite de Navarre leads literature toward a modern world in which the individual's subjective experience is perceived as being shaped by social and cultural institutions. Their emphasis on gender issues is likewise innovative. Marguerite de Navarre points out how social, economic, and political considerations may determine a woman's fate in ways detrimental to her personal happiness. At the same time, the text ends by praising marriage as an institution that should ideally create a space in which the individual may safely experience the fulfillment of desire. Like de Crenne, too,

Marguerite de Navarre lays the foundation for the later development of the SENTIMENTAL NOVEL.

FURTHER READING

Armstrong, Nancy. "Literature as Women's History: A Necessary Transgression of Genres," *Genre* 19 (1986): 347–369.

Freccero, Carla. "Rewriting the Rhetoric of Desire in Marguerite de Navarre's *Heptameron*." In *Contending Kingdoms: Historical, Psychological, and Feminist Approaches to the Literature of Sixteenth-Century England and France*. Edited by Marie-Rose Logan and Peter Rudnytsky. Detroit: Wayne State University Press, 1989.

Tetet, Marcel. *Marguerite de Navarre's "Heptameron": Themes, Language and Structure*. Durham, N.C.: Duke University Press, 1973.

HERNANI VICTOR HUGO **(1830)** Although *Hernani* is a drama, not a novel (principally performed today as an opera by Verdi), it is a significant work in the rise of ROMANTICISM in 19th-century France and thus has a bearing on developments in fiction. Hugo made his first theoretical statement on the romantic movement in his *Preface to Cromwell* (1827). Even before its first performance at the Comédie Française on February 25, 1830, *Hernani*, Hugo's theory made manifest, was subject to censorship and attacked by critics. *Hernani* launched a veritable literary war (the Battle of *Hernani*), pitting the young avant-garde "moderns" led by THÉOPHILE GAUTIER and including DUMAS, BALZAC, and the poet Gerard de Nerval, against an older generation of writers who staunchly defended classical principles (see CLASSICISM) in drama and fiction, and a conservative bourgeois public.

Set in 16th-century Spain, the plot is replete with passion and pathos. Doña Sol has three suitors: Hernani, an outlaw whose love she returns; Don Carlos, the king of Spain; and her uncle, an old duke named Don Ruy Gomez. The first act outlines the rivalry among the three men. Despite their enmity, Don Ruy Gomez adheres to the Castilian code of honor and does not turn Hernani over to the king, even when he has discovered the young couple's love for each other. In return, Hernani fatefully promises to forfeit his life to Don Ruy Gomez at the sounding of a horn. The two men conspire against Don Carlos, who has abducted

Doña Sol. Also chivalrous, Don Carlos pardons them once he has acceded to the throne of the empire. Jealous, nonetheless, Don Ruy Gomez desires revenge and sounds the horn on the eve of Hernani and Doña Sol's wedding. The couple takes poison and dies in each other's arms. Don Ruy Gomez subsequently commits suicide as well.

Hernani reflects characteristics of Romantic drama in its historical setting, its expression of passion, and its mixture of comedy and tragedy, the grotesque and the sublime. Such juxtapositions are typical of Hugo's writing. Moreover, Hernani is a particularly romantic hero, a solitary man with a strong sense of honor. Fate inevitably leads him to a tragic death, a result in part of the perfect yet impossible love he shares with Doña Sol.

FURTHER READING

Brombert, Victor. *Victor Hugo and the Visionary Novel*. Cambridge, Mass.: Harvard University Press, 1984.

Evans, David O. *Social Romanticism in France: 1830–1848*. New York: Octagon, 1969.

Maurois, André. *Victor Hugo and His World*. Translated by Oliver Bernard. New York: Viking, 1966.

Peyre, Henri. *Victor Hugo: Philosophy and Poetry*. Translated by Roda P. Roberts. University: University of Alabama Press, 1980.

Richardson, Joanna. *Victor Hugo*. London: Weidenfeld and Nicolson, 1976.

HISTORY OF MADAME DE LUZ (HISTOIRE DE MADAME DE LUZ) CHARLES PINOT DUCLOS **(1740)** This LIBERTINE novel opens with the statement: "It seems a woman's virtue is a stranger to this world, against which everything conspires." Not surprisingly, the novel recounts the sad series of misadventures that one by one erode the main character's virtue.

Madame de Luz marries her husband out of duty, not inclination. Nonetheless virtuous and angelic, she remains faithful to him and resists her passionate desire for her cousin, Saint-Géran. The downward spiral begins when Madame de Luz is compelled to give in to the sexual desire of a corrupt official to save her husband, who has been accused of conspiracy. Tormented by her conscience, she distances herself from her cousin and devotes herself to her duties as spouse. Unfortunately, fortune turns against her yet again when she is abused by a gentleman in the countryside where she has taken refuge from society. She turns to her confessor for help but, overcome with desire, he drugs and rapes her. Finally, as a widow, Madame de Luz could have married her true love but, unable to overcome her despair, she dies, followed shortly thereafter by Saint-Géran.

Duclos was a libertine, a man who loved nothing more than good food, wine, and women, yet the conclusion to his novel recalls the PRINCESSE DE CLÈVES's retreat. When confronted with an impossible love, only a rejection of passion can guarantee tranquility for the heart and soul. At the same time, Duclos's representation of virtue unrewarded, in contrast to prevalent themes in the SENTIMENTAL NOVEL, presages characters such as VOLTAIRE's Mlle De Saint-Yves and Cosi-Sancta, or even SADE's Justine. The theme of suffering despite virtue raises interesting moral questions in all these works. Madame de Luz and Saint-Géran are the two innocent characters in this novel, yet they are the ones who are punished. Where, then is justice? Where is God?

FURTHER READING

Free, L. R. *Virtue, Happiness and Duclos' "Histoire de Madame de Luz."* The Hague, Netherlands: Martinus Nijhoff, 1974.

Meister, Paul. *Charles Duclos, 1704–1772.* Geneva: Droz, 1956.

Silverblatt, Bette Gross. *Maxims in the Novels of Duclos.* The Hague, Netherlands: Nijhoff, 1972.

Thompsett, E. "Love and Libertinism in the Novels of Duclos," *SVEC 137,* 1975.

HOLY TERRORS, THE (LES ENFANTS TERRIBLES) JEAN COCTEAU (1929)

In this novel, with its fairy tale-like tone and sense of the mythological and the fantastic in a manner that recalls ANDRÉ GIDE, Cocteau offers emancipation to the generation that grew up in the interwar period.

The novel opens with a snowball fight among boys on a school ground. Paul seeks the one he loves and admires, Dargelos, in order to take his part but is struck by a snowball that has a rock hidden inside it. At the moment he falls, Paul is fixated on the boy whom he adores and whom he never meets again. Paul's great friend, Gérard, as taken with Paul as Paul is with Dargelos, gently takes his friend home, where he spends several weeks recuperating from a weakness in the chest.

Elisabeth, Paul's sister, is a sort of mythical goddess who cares for her brother and their invalid mother, who dies shortly thereafter, leaving the children alone in the fantasy life they share in their bedroom, the place in which Paul and Elisabeth play out their most extravagant dreams in games of the subconscious. They adore each other as much as they tear each other apart. Their strange existence on the margins of reality attracts Gérard, who joins their life, slowly transferring his love from Paul to Elisabeth. When Elisabeth decides to begin a career as a model, she meets Agatha, who becomes the fourth person in their strange collective.

The shared room becomes a magic chamber in which love grows. Paul eventually falls in love with Agatha, who strongly resembles Dargelos, although he does not realize it at first. Even when Elisabeth decides to marry, the magic is not broken, as her husband Michael dies the night of their wedding in a car accident, as if a fairy has intervened to protect the four from any outside intruder. It seems as if nothing can touch the couple at the center of the group, the brother and sister.

Together they all move into Michael's house, inherited by Elisabeth. Paul eventually realizes his love for Agatha. Both he and Agatha confide their love for each other separately to Elisabeth who, overcome with jealousy, begins to work her subtle machinations in the dark of night to preserve Paul untouched. She persuades Gérard that Agatha loves him, persuades Agatha to marry Gérard because Paul does not love her, and convinces Paul that Agatha loves Gérard. Gérard and Agatha indeed marry, driving Paul to take the poison he was mysteriously sent by Dargelos, becoming Dargelos's victim once again in the closed space of a room that finds its parallel in the snowball and the poison. As he is dying, Paul learns of his sister's betrayal and of Agatha's love but it is too late. Elisabeth takes a revolver and shoots herself at the very moment her brother dies.

Death is recurring theme in Cocteau's works. In this novel, the intensity of their imaginary life makes death a necessity to protect the fusion of brother and sister into one. The language of the subconscious permeates this work, depicting a world marked by the contradictory elements of childlike innocence and morbid eroticism, purity, and perversity. The novel was adapted to film in 1950.

FURTHER READING
Brown, Frederick. *An Impersonation of Angels: A Biography of Jean Cocteau.* Harlow: Longmans, 1969.
Tsakiridou, Cornelia A., ed. *Reviewing Orpheus: Essays on the Cinema and Art of Jean Cocteau.* Lewisburg, Pa.: Bucknell University Press, 1997.

HOPE (L'ESPOIR) ANDRÉ MALRAUX (1937)

Like Malraux's earlier works set in the Far East, *The* CONQUERORS (1928), *The* ROYAL WAY (1930), and MAN'S FATE (1933), *Hope* depicts men in the conditions of revolution, in this case the revolution that gives way to the Spanish civil war, in which Malraux participated. The principal themes are fraternity, the tension between action and ideology, heroism, despair and, finally, hope.

The first part, "Lyrical Illusion," evokes the sense of fraternity and hope that drove the Spanish people to rise up against their miserable conditions. Sentimental in tone, this portion of the novel evokes the notion of liberty. In order to realize the conditions of liberty, however, it is necessary to organize and *act,* as change does not arise from sentiment. The theme of action leads into the section "Organise the Apocalypse."

To prepare for a confrontation with general Francisco Franco's army, members of the Communist Party play an important role in this phase of the civil war. They alone are capable of the organization necessary to defeat Franco. In "Being and Doing," the anarchists and communists share a passion for justice. However, the anarchists represent the disorder that cannot be allowed if the Republicans are to succeed. Manuel, a communist and a doer, takes command, illustrating Malraux's fundamental belief that action and art are the two means available to give meaning to our lives. The anarchist Hernandez, in contrast, shares with Manuel a

belief in fraternity but does not know how to act. He is shot by the Falangists.

For Manuel, fraternity means action. In the last part of the novel, Manuel focuses on an ideological war. The hope of the republicans rests on a desire to give meaning to the lives of the suffering Spanish people. In contrast to Hemingway's depiction of the Spanish civil war, Malraux focuses on the collective rather than the individual. The very notion of fraternity, so fundamental to Malraux's thinking, is the antidote to humiliation and degradation. What is important is that which binds people together in flesh and blood. The hope of the novel's title is, indeed, man's hope.

In this as in other works, Malraux examines humanity at the moment we confront a powerful force such as History or War or Death. In this context, hope becomes an ethical value, as we attempt to overcome our destiny. In the end, Malraux approaches the Spanish civil war with an optimism derived from his view of human nature absent in the works of GEORGES BERNANOS and PIERRE DRIEU LA ROCHELLE, who also wrote on this subject.

FURTHER READING
Rowland, Michael L., and Sonja G. Stary. "Mask and Vision in Malraux's L'Espoir," *French Review,* Special Issue. no. 6, Studies on the French Novel (Spring 1974): 189–196.
Stolzfus, Ben. "Hemingway, Malraux and Spain: For Whom the Bell Tolls and L'espoir," *Comparative Literature Studies* 36, no. 3 (1999): 179–194.

HÔTEL DU NORD EUGÈNE DABIT (1929)

This novel describes the lives of the occupants of a small hotel on the canal Saint-Martin in Paris, run by a couple named Lecouvreur. The inhabitants of the Hôtel du Nord are, like the other residents of the neighborhood, poor, uprooted, and fundamentally sad. Dabit depicts the monotony of their daily lives, filled with work and suffering. The death by drowning of an unknown young woman seems to represent the bitterness of these lives. Only a strange hope glimmers in the character of an old bourgeois gentleman who seeks, at the end of his life, the liberty that only a life of poverty can offer.

The novel has strong autobiographical elements as Dabit draws on the experience of his parents, a former deliveryman and a concierge, who opened their own small hotel in Paris. The novel was immediately successful. Its adaptation to film by Marcel Carné is one of the classics of French cinema. *Hôtel du Nord* won the Populist Prize for its depiction of working-class life, a common theme in Dabit's works.

HOULLEBECQ, MICHEL (1958–   )

Michel Houllebecq was abandoned by his parents. At the age of six, he went to live with his grandmother, a communist whose name he later adopted. As a student, Houllebecq distinguished himself from early on for his remarkable analytical abilities. Other students nicknamed him Einstein.

In 1975, Houllebecq began the study of agronomic engineering, earning a diploma in 1978. In 1980 he married a classmate's older sister. Their son was born in 1981, but the couple divorced soon after. Houllebecq subsequently suffered from depression and was hospitalized several times.

Houllebecq launched his literary career at the age of 20 with the publication of his poetry but began to attain notoriety with his biography of H. P. Lovecraft, published in 1991. In 1994, he published his first novel, *Extension of the Domain of Struggle.* Translated into several languages, this work brought Houllebecq to the attention of a broader reading public. In 1998 he won the national grand prize for literature for talented young writers.

Houllebecq produced *Interventions,* a series of critical essays, along with his second novel, ELEMENTARY PARTICLES, which won the Prix Novembre in 1998. Houllebecq subsequently moved to Ireland, where he lived for several years in County Cork. He later moved onto Spain. Always a contentious figure, Houllebecq was taken to court in 2002 after being accused of making racist statement against Muslims in his third novel, *Platform.* This novel begins with the line "Father died last year," instantly recalling the opening of ALBERT CAMUS's novel *The* STRANGER.

Readers tend either to love or to hate Houllebecq's work. Some consider him a prophet. Others praise him for telling the bitter truth about human existence in the modern world. For still others, he is a mediocre writer who uses crude language to portray sex and desire or who treats intellectuals with condescension. Nonetheless, his works are best-sellers.

Houllebecq is noted for his critique of Americanization and globalization. He is particularly adept at pointing out society's weaknesses. At times one has the sense that he enjoys rubbing salt in the wound as he suggests the impossibility of true communication between human beings in the postmodern world (see POSTMODERNISM). Houllebecq once wrote, "The value of a human being is measured today by his economic efficiency and his erotic potential." This seems to sum up Houllebecq's vision of the world.

HUGO, VICTOR (1802–1885)

A politically engaged writer, poet, novelist, dramatist, critic, journalist, and historian, Victor Hugo was a giant of 19th-century French literature. He was a leader of the romantic movement in France (see ROMANTICISM), as well as a staunch republican.

Born in the provincial city Besançon, Hugo had a difficult childhood. His father was a general who moved with some frequency from one garrison to another, and his parents separated.

Hugo chose a literary career early. In 1816 he wrote, "I want to be CHATEAUBRIAND or nothing." He surpassed his goal. With his brothers and as early as 1819, Hugo established a literary journal, the *Literary Guardian,* which lasted until 1821.

The next year was important both personally and professionally. In 1822 Hugo married Adèle Foucher, a childhood friend. At roughly the same time, he also published his first collection of poetry and wrote his first novel, *Bug-Jargal* (1820, 1826), the story of a slave rebellion in Santo Domingo. In 1823 another novel appeared, *Han d'Islande,* in 1824 more poetry, and in 1827 a failed play, *Cromwell.* Hugo's first expression of romantic theory is the *Preface to Cromwell* (1827). In this text he articulated the difference between romantic theater and classical tragedy, a genre he called artificial. Modern romantic drama, he argued, is closer to life in its mixture of the sublime and the grotesque, a juxtaposition that readers often associate with Hugo's own writing.

In these early years Hugo and his wife had their first three children; the author also lost his father and was nominated to the prestigious Legion of Honor. He also continued to write, publishing *Orientals* in 1829, a collection of poetry that appealed to his contemporaries' romantic sensibilities, particularly their taste for the exotic. That same year Hugo published another novel, *The Last Day of a Condemned Man,* in which he made a humanitarian appeal for the end of the death penalty.

Meanwhile, the Hugo apartment became a central meeting place for a circle of romantics referred to as the *Cénacle.* But the young couple's comfortable domestic situation was disturbed when SAINTE-BEUVE seduced Hugo's wife. Later, in 1833, Hugo found some comfort when he met and fell in love with the actress Juliet Drouet. She remained Hugo's mistress until her death in 1883.

The performance of HERNANI at the Comédie Française in 1830 was a fabulous success, bringing Hugo certain fame and assuring victory for the younger generation of romantics in their struggle against the old guard. In 1830, Hugo's fourth child, Adèle, was born. Although his private life was complicated by both joys and sorrows, Hugo continued to work tirelessly.

The July Revolution of 1830 had a tremendous impact on Hugo and his generation of romantic writers. Social action became increasingly important from this moment on and is reflected in their works. Hugo said, "Romanticism, so often badly defined, is all in all, and this is its real definition, nothing more than Liberalism in literature. . . . Freedom in art, freedom in society; that is the double goal." Hugo's great respect for the people as a collective is apparent in many of his works.

The years 1830 to 1843 were particularly productive for Hugo. His first great novel evoking life in medieval Paris, *The* HUNCHBACK OF NOTRE DAME, was published in 1830. Moreover, he produced four collections of poetry that demonstrate his maturation as a poet. Despite some failures in writing for theater, *Ruy Blas* (1838) turned out to be another dramatic masterpiece. Finally, after three failed tries, in 1841 Hugo was elected to the Académie Française. A journey along the Rhine in 1840 led to a remarkable travel journal, *The Rhine* (1842). At the same time, Hugo developed the idea for another historical drama, *The Burgraves,* which failed miserably in 1843, leading him to give up on the theater.

In 1843 Hugo's eldest daughter drowned on her honeymoon. In July of that year, Hugo was returning with Juliette from a holiday in the Pyrenees when he read of Léopoldine's death in a newspaper. Hugo was heartbroken. Nonetheless, between 1843 and 1851, Hugo continued to write poetry and the beginning of what would later become his powerful novel *Les* MISÉRABLES, but he was unable to complete anything and published no works during this period.

Suffering from the loss of his daughter, Hugo turned his attention to political life and spoke out increasingly on behalf of various humanitarian causes. After the Revolution of 1848, Hugo was elected to the French National Assembly. However, his opposition to Louis-Napoleon Bonaparte's coup d'état in 1851 drove Hugo into exile. Having failed to incite a revolt, he took a night train from Paris to Brussels dressed as a worker. At this point a convinced republican, Hugo continued to denounce the French government from abroad and his fame grew. Ironically, nearly 20 years in exile assured his reputation.

Ultimately settling on the English Channel island of Guernsey, Hugo wrote standing in the "lookout" of his house. He was at the height of his brilliance as a writer. Rising at 6:00 A.M. every day, Hugo worked in a small room with windows looking out across the sea to the coast of France, surrounded by his wife and children and with Juliette installed nearby. From Guernsey, he produced a number of works, among them a collection of poems entitled *Punishments* (1853), in which he spoke out against the tyrannical regime of the "Little Napoleon." When Louis-Napoleon, now Emperor Napoleon III, offered him amnesty in 1859, Hugo refused, further solidifying his reputation as a symbol of the republic. Hugo's status as an exile only added to his prestige both in France and abroad.

Contemplations, a masterful collection of poems focusing on spiritual, metaphysical, and philosophical questions, was published in Paris and Brussels in 1856. In the preface to this series of 158 poems, Hugo announced his examination of "human existence as it leaves the enigma of the cradle and ends with the enigma of the coffin." His exploration of his own pain and suffering makes him an everyman. As he wrote, "When I speak of me, I speak of you."

Hugo's wife died in 1858. Despite his loss, he continued to be productive finishing one of his greatest novels, *Les Misérables* (1862), during this period. In 1864, he published "William Shakespeare," a long essay in which he articulated his theory of genius. In addition to more poetry, Hugo also wrote two additional novels, TOILERS OF THE SEA (1866) and *The MAN WHO LAUGHS* (1869).

Hugo returned to Paris in triumph in 1870, where he was elected to the National Assembly. There he continued his struggle against injustice, speaking out in favor of amnesty for participants in the PARIS COMMUNE and going so far as to resign publicly during one session. Disillusioned by politics, he returned to Guernsey for nearly a year but was then elected as senator of Paris in 1876.

Most of the works that appeared between 1870 and 1885 were begun while Hugo was in exile. These works in various genres include *The Terrible Year* (1872), NINETY-THREE (1874), *Acts and Words* (1875–76), the last series of *The Legend of the Centuries* (1877–83), and *The Art of Being a Grandfather* (1877), poems inspired by Hugo's two grandchildren, Georges and Jeanne. Hugo also produced *Story of a Crime* (1877), written against Napoleon III, *The Pope* (1878), *Supreme Pity* (1879), *Religions and Religion* (1880), *The Mule* (1880), and *The Four Winds of the Spirit* (1881). Upon his death, Hugo also left behind a number of manuscripts that were published posthumously, including *The End of Satan* (1886), *Things Seen* (1887–1900), *God* (1891), *France and Belgium* (1892), *Fatal Years* (1898), and *Postscript to my Life* (1901).

Hugo's later years were marked by some difficult moments, including the death of two of his children and a kind of senile eroticism that strained his relationship with Juliette. Still, he was showered with honors. In 1880 there was a public celebration on the 50th anniversary of *Hernani* and in 1892 an official celebration in Paris of Hugo's 90th birthday.

This powerful voice of poetry and politics died in 1885, two years after the death of his longtime companion, Juliette Drouet. Following his funeral, an enormous crowd accompanied Hugo's body from the Arc de Triomphe on the Champs-Élysées to its resting place in the Pantheon. His fame continued to grow after his death.

Hugo was a lyrical writer whose style reveals a remarkably creative use of metaphor. He believed that the poet has a visionary and prophetic role to play in society as a spiritual guide to progress. As a result, the themes of social injustice and human suffering appear in many of his works. There is even the possibility of overcoming oppression. Though Quasimodo lies down to die with the corpse of his beloved Esmerelda after her execution in the public square (in *The Hunchback of Notre Dame*), Jean Valjean in *Les Misérables,* succeeds in overcoming all obstacles.

Hugo's writing, as varied as it is, shares certain characteristics, first and foremost, a tendency to contrasts, and his almost Manichean struggle between good and evil manifests itself in a variety of forms. Hugo frequently presented a battle between two hostile camps. Yet conflict may evolve into unity, as in the character of Jean Valjean.

A legendary figure who created monuments of 19th-century fiction, Hugo remains one of the most read novelists in the history of French literature. At the time, his legendary status was due in part to his exile but also to the position he ultimately attained as a symbol of the French THIRD REPUBLIC. Moreover, Hugo was and still is noted for his prolificacy, diversity, eloquence, compassion, and poetic expression. Finally, he was principally concerned with the question of evil that takes the form of social injustice. That concern marks his place in literary history as a visionary who sought to reconcile his understanding of life's purpose with the reality of human history. As a poet Hugo influenced Charles Baudelaire, Arthur Rimbaud, Stéphane Mallarmé, and the surrealists (see SURREALISM).

FURTHER READING

Brombert, Victor. *Victor Hugo and the Visionary Novel.* Cambridge, Mass.: Harvard University Press, 1984.

Evans, David O. *Social Romanticism in France: 1830–1848.* New York: Octagon, 1969.

Halsall, A. W. *Victor Hugo and the Romantic Drama.* Toronto, Buffalo, N.Y.: University of Toronto Press, 1998.

Houston, John Porter. *Victor Hugo.* Boston: Twayne, 1988.

Hudson, William Henry. *Victor Hugo and His Poetry.* London: Harrap, 1918.

Ireson, J. C. *Victor Hugo*. Oxford, New York: Clarendon Press, 1997.

Maurois, André. *Victor Hugo and His World*. Translated by Oliver Bernard. New York: Viking, 1966.

Peyre, Henri. *Victor Hugo: Philosophy and Poetry*. Translated by Roda P. Roberts. Tuscaloosa: University of Alabama Press, 1980.

Porter, Laurence M. *Victor Hugo*. New York: Twayne, 1999.

Raser, Timothy Bell. *The Simplest of Signs: Victor Hugo and the Language of Images in France*. Newark: University of Delaware Press, 2004.

Richardson, Joanna. *Victor Hugo*. London: Weidenfeld and Nicolson, 1976.

Robb, Graham. *Victor Hugo*. New York: W. W. Norton, 1997.

Stevens, Philip. *Victor Hugo in Jersey*. Shopwyke Hall, Chichester, England: Phillimore, 1985.

VanderWolk, William. *Victor Hugo in Exile: From Historical Representations to Utopian Vistas*. Lewisburg, PA: Bucknell University Press, 2006.

HUMAN COMEDY, THE (*LA COMÉDIE HUMAINE*) HONORÉ DE BALZAC (1829–1847)

This series of 91 novels in 17 volumes, a veritable parallel literary universe, constitutes Balzac's greatest achievement as a writer. It is comparable to Walter Scott's *Waverly* novels depicting Scottish life (Scott was an influence on Balzac), but greater in scope. Balzac said that, in creating the *Human Comedy,* he wanted to "compete with the civil state." *The Human Comedy* is divided into three parts. The first, "Studies in Nineteenth-Century Mores," consists of 6 further divisions: Scenes from Private Life, Provincial Life, Political Life, Military Life, and Country Life. The second part is devoted to "Philosophical Studies" and the last to "Analytical Studies."

Like STENDHAL, Balzac was a subtle observer of 19th-century French society, able to explore contemporary history with a subtle, psychological approach. Balzac focused on the dynamics of social forces at work in French society, revealing the tensions resulting from the conflict between revolutionary individualism and the remnants of OLD REGIME society in all its rigidity. Perhaps immodestly, Balzac compared his *Human Comedy* to Dante's *Divine Comedy*.

In his introduction to the 1842 edition, Balzac defends his right to call these collected novels the *Human Comedy:* "Chance makes the world's greatest novelist: to be fecund one need only study it. French society should be the historian; I should only be the secretary. In drawing the inventory of vices and virtues, in assembling the principal deeds of passion, in depicting characters, in choosing principal social events, in creating types through a union of several homogeneous characters, perhaps I can write the history forgotten by so many historians, that of mores."

Balzac indeed succeeds in weaving a rich and varied tapestry of Parisian and provincial life in France from the Restoration to the July Monarchy (1814–48). This collection of novels includes literary masterpieces such as *FATHER GORIOT, LOST ILLUSIONS,* and *EUGÉNIE GRANDET.* The series employs the device of reappearing characters. One figure may play a minor role in one novel yet is central to another. Of the more than 2,000 characters, about 500 appear in more than one work. Balzac's seemingly inexhaustible production of novels reveals his attempt to compete with the enormously popular serial novelist EUGÈNE SUE. Balzac's parallel world is peopled with an array of characters and qualities from heroes to criminals, the self-interested and the generous, cold manipulators and sensitive souls. In effect, he portrays the range of human life as we know it.

In his introduction to the series, Balzac also wrote that his idea for the *Human Comedy* came out of a comparison of humanity and "animality." Here, he manifests the influence of contemporary trends in science and mysticism. Balzac believed that society resembles nature; thus social and class distinctions (merchant, poet, nobleman, or priest, for example) are like "social species." Drawing on an epistemological tradition that focuses on the effects of environment on human development, Balzac chooses to focus on people and their material culture to produce this history of manners. Disagreeing with ROUSSEAU that society corrupts, he believed civilization can improve humankind, particularly through the Roman Catholic religion. In the end, his conclusions are fairly conservative. Yet with such a range of characters, there is also a certain ambiguity in Balzac's approach. Readers may find something morally disturbing in the fact that Balzac's hero is the ambitious Rastignac, or that the criminal Vautrin resurfaces continually, apparently challenging the victory of good over evil.

FURTHER READING

Allen, James Smith. *Popular French Romanticism: Authors, Readers and Books in the Nineteenth Century.* Syracuse, N.Y.: Syracuse University Press, 1981.

Bresnick, Adam. "The Paradox of *Bildung*: Balzac's *Illusions Perdues*," *MLN* 113, no. 4 (1998): 823–850.

Carrère, Jean. *Degeneration in the Great French Masters.* Translated by Joseph McCabe. Freeport, N.Y.: Books for Libraries Press, 1967.

Kanes, Martin, ed. *Critical Essays on Balzac.* Boston: G. K. Hall, 1990.

Smith, Edward C. III. "Honoré de Balzac and the 'Genius' of Walter Scott: Debt and Denial," *Comparative Literature Studies* 36, no. 3 (1999): 209–225.

HUNCHBACK OF NOTRE DAME, THE (NOTRE-DAME DE PARIS) VICTOR HUGO (1831)

Hugo once thought of calling this novel "What there is in a bottle of ink." Writing under extreme financial pressure with a family to support, he finished *The Hunchback of Notre Dame* with the last drop of ink from a bottle purchased expressly for the purpose of writing the novel. According to the author, he was inspired to write it after finding the Greek word *ananke* (fate) in a dark recess of the cathedral. In the novel, it is Frollo who engraves the word in stone.

Tormented by desire, dean of the cathedral of Notre-Dame Claude Frollo falls violently in love with a beautiful Gypsy girl named Esmerelda, who, accompanied by her faithful goat, Djali, earns her living by dancing and telling fortunes. Esmerelda is proud and silent but also, as she later reveals, sensitive to the plight of others. She lives among the teeming hoards of false beggars, thieves, and assorted riffraff that make up the "court of miracles." Overcome by his passion for her, Frollo instructs his protégé, the cathedral's deformed bell-ringer, Quasimodo, to kidnap Esmerelda. Out of pity, Frollo had raised the monstrous Quasimodo and now governs him with a harsh hand.

Captain Phoebus Châteaupers saves Esmerelda from the attempted kidnapping and she subsequently falls in love with him. Unfortunately, Pheobus is a callous man who looks upon Esmerelda as only yet another amo-rous adventure. Meanwhile, Quasimodo has been sent to the pillory for the attempted crime. Moved by pity at his plight, Esmerelda brings him something to drink thus stirring the Quasimodo's undying love for her.

Unwittingly, Esmerelda arranges to meet Phoebus and is on the point of giving herself to him when Frollo suddenly appears and stabs Phoebus. Then, because Esmerelda has again refused his advances, Frollo arranges for her to be accused of Phoebus's murder.

Esmerelda is brought before the cathedral to be hanged but Quasimodo rescues her, taking the Gyspsy girl into the church where she can claim sanctuary. In his descriptions of the bell tower, Hugo skillfully evokes a literary chiaroscuro that reveals the cathedral's mysteries. Quasimodo has brought Esmerelda into his lair where they are surrounded by hideous gargoyles. When a group of beggars and criminals, Esmerelda's friends from the court of miracles, attack the cathedral, Quasimodo misunderstands their attempt to rescue the girl and drives them back, hurling stones down onto them but to no avail in the end. Driven on by his dark passion, in the chaos, Frollo attempts to seduce Esmerelda. When he is rebuffed once more he then turns her over to a half-crazed beggar woman who abhors Gypsies since they once stole her beloved daughter. The woman in turn gives Esmerelda over to the authorities, realizing too late that Esmerelda is in fact her lost child. Esmerelda is brought to court again and hanged. Once Quasimodo discovers the role his master played in Esmerelda's downfall, in one of Hugo's most powerful and famous passages, he hurls Frollo from the top of the cathedral and goes to die in the paupers' grave, clinging to Esmerelda's lifeless body.

Hugo's novel both reflects and inspired contemporary interest in the Middle Ages, a period that fascinated many romantics as is evident in architect Eugène Viollet-le-Duc's subsequent efforts to restore the cathedral to its original state. In fact, the real hero of the novel is the cathedral, with its gargoyles, columns, stained-glass windows, sculptures, and dark recesses. It is, as Hugo eloquently described, a book in stone. The cathedral plays a central role in the novel, taking on a personality and power of its own as monstrous passions reveal themselves within its sacred space.

In this tale set in 15th-century Paris, Hugo created unforgettable characters, although some critics have described them as flat. Lacking in subtlety, each character represents a type. Frollo is the evil traitor; Phoebus the frivolous and uncaring young lover. Even the beautiful Esmerelda is an equally conventional character, yet she remains strangely touching.

This romantic novel offers a tragic depiction of human destiny and impossible love, in particular the horror of being unloved. Hugo's language is overflowing and rich. The epitome of the gothic romantic novel, *The Hunchback of Notre Dame* was an immediate success and remains so today with numerous adaptations. Not historically accurate, Hugo's gripping descriptions of medieval Paris, particularly its street life, have nonetheless become the stuff of legend that reflects the author's tremendous creative power. The plot may be exaggerated but Hugo's evocation of medieval Paris is powerful and lyrical. His depictions of its mysterious streets and their inhabitants also reflect his enduring interest in the lives of the poor, the suffering, and the outcast. The novel thus finds a parallel in contemporary political movements in defense of the poor and disadvantaged in which Hugo participated. His contemporary, EUGÈNE SUE, praised this novel that explores the question of fate, a theme central to this and other works by Hugo. In *The Hunchback of Notre Dame* as he did later in LES MISÉRABLES, Hugo manages to give body and soul to visions, to give life to symbols, and to give a sense of historical reality to the products of his own vibrant imagination.

FURTHER READING

Brombert, Victor. *Victor Hugo and the Visionary Novel.* Cambridge, Mass.: Harvard University Press, 1984.

Evans, David O. *Social Romanticism in France: 1830–1848.* New York: Octagon, 1969.

Maurois, André. *Victor Hugo and His World.* Translated by Oliver Bernard. New York: Viking, 1966.

HUSSAR ON THE ROOF, THE (*LE HUSSARD SUR LE TOIT*) JEAN GIONO (1951)

With the publication of *Hussar on the Roof,* one of Giono's masterpieces, the author regained his status as a writer after having been falsely accused of collaboration during World War II. The setting, as with many of Giono's novels, is his native Provence during an outbreak of cholera. Death is everywhere.

Angelo Pardi, an officer, is the illegitimate son of an Italian duchess seeking refuge in France. Traveling on horseback, he is shocked to come upon what appears to be a completely deserted village where he discovers endless corpses contorted unto horrifying positions, attacked by rats and dogs. The heat is stifling and Angelo suffers from exhaustion, thirst, and confusion.

He moves on to yet another village only to discover the same horror. Angelo finally comes across another living person, a doctor who has come, too late, to aid the victims of cholera. He teaches Angelo how to try to revive the dying, but they are unsuccessful. When the doctor falls ill, Angelo comforts *"le petit français"* (the little Frenchman) in his last agonizing hours only to find himself alone again, although he has overcome his earlier fear.

Angelo finally arrives in Manosque, where he hopes to find his foster brother. Upon his arrival, however, disaster strikes yet again and Angelo is almost lynched when he is mistaken for a poisoner. To escape, he spends several days hiding on rooftops, accompanied by a cat. There he has time to reflect on life. For food, he makes forays into people's apartments, in one of which he encounters the lovely Pauline de Théus. She offers him hot, sweet tea, which seems like a miracle after his days on the roof.

When he descends, Angelo meets a slightly comical if saintly nun who has remained in her convent despite the epidemic, in order to wash the dead. Angelo helps her. Meanwhile, more and more of the townspeople are escaping into the countryside, where they set up a huge camp. Giuseppe, Angelo's foster brother, is one of the men in charge. Disturbed because the families of the sick are banished from the camp, Angelo sets off again only to come across Pauline once more.

The two young people travel on together but are picked up and quarantined. Escape is necessary yet again. One night they stay with an old doctor who philosophizes about the nature of cholera. When Pauline falls ill, Angelo cares for her and manages to save her life. He brings her safely to her elderly husband and then sets off for Italy. Despite their attraction for each other, throughout their adventures the couple remain chaste. Ultimately, in a sequel, they come together. The final novel of the series, narrated by the grandson of Angelo and Pauline, recounts her death.

Hussar on the Roof, abounds with sadness, scent, light, and feeling. It is clear, and in keeping with Giono's pacifist views, that cholera represents war. Inspired by STENDHAL's *CHARTERHOUSE OF PARMA,* Angelo bears a certain resemblance to Fabrice del Dongo in the latter novel. In Angelo, Giono explores the theme of the solitary hero as he reveals the conflicting and contradictory tendencies in human nature.

FURTHER READING

Ford, Edward. *Jean Giono's Hidden Reality.* Lewiston, Me.: E. Mellen Press, 2004.

Goodrich, Norma Lorre. *Giono: Master of Fictional Modes.* Princeton, N.J.: Princeton University Press, 1973.

Lawrence, Derek W. "The Transitional Works of Jean Giono," *French Review,* Special Issue, No. 1 (Winter 1970): 126–134.

Redfern, W. D. *The Private World of Jean Giono.* Oxford: Blackwell and Mott, 1967.

Smith, Maxwell A. "Giono's Cycle of Hussar Novels," *French Review* 35, no. 3 (January 1962): 287–294.

HUYSMANS, JORIS-KARL (1848–1907)

Huysmans's Dutch father moved to Paris where he met and married a Frenchwoman. After his father's death, when Huysmans was eight years old, his childhood was difficult. He once described it as "a humiliating and broken life." When he finished school, Huysmans entered government service as a functionary in the Ministry of the Interior until his retirement in 1898. Born Georges Charles Marie, Huysmans took the Dutch form of his name at the time of his first publication. His Dutch name was reserved, however, for his persona as author. Huysmans's colleagues knew him as Georges.

The element of continuity within change that marks Huysmans' oeuvre is remarkable. His writing passed from one identifiable stage to another while retaining an overall sense of unity and sincerity. Various influences worked upon Huysmans' growth as a writer. He was first a follower of the poet Charles Baudelaire, publishing a collection of prose poems in 1874. He then turned to REALISM and NATURALISM in a style reminiscent of the GONCOURT brothers.

Marthe (1876), a novel on prostitution, was published one year prior to Edmond de Goncourt's *Élisa.* The VATARD SISTERS reveals the misery of working-class life through the lives of two women. *Down Stream* and *Living Together* depict the trivial and solitary lives of André and Jean Folantin, two men ultimately tormented by failure. In certain ways, these two characters resemble Huysmans himself. Although he was a successful writer, Huysmans lived a somewhat lonely, misogynist existence. Nonetheless, his novel *Becalmed (En Rade)* focuses on married life. Huysmans's pessimism bears the influence of the German philosopher Arthur Schopenhauer.

The first shift in Huysmans's career is the result of his connection with ÉMILE ZOLA. In 1880 Huysmans contributed a short story, "Rucksack," to Zola's *Médan Evenings,* the "manifesto" of the naturalists. Huysmans was fascinated with modern art, and his style is influenced by the impressionist movement in painting. In fact, his impressionist writing style left its mark on late 19th-century fiction. In addition, Huysmans wrote several monographs on Parisian neighborhoods. Together these works offer a remarkable picture of Parisian life in the 1880s.

By the mid-1880s however, Huysmans had moved in an entirely new direction, beyond naturalism and impressionism, abandoning these earlier styles for DECADENCE. *AGAINST THE GRAIN* marks yet another decisive shift in Huysmans's development as a writer. This novel not only signifies Huysmans' entrance into this new genre but serves as the decadents' bible.

It is the story of Des Esseintes, the last of a noble family who chooses to live in a refined, solitary retreat where he satisfies his desire for pleasure in rather unusual ways like keeping a cricket in a cage. Des Esseintes retires to a life of refined aestheticism that is a perversion of nature, as he attempts to create an artificial world to replace the natural. Huysmans's character becomes the epitome of the fin de siècle decadent.

Against the Grain is an important novel in the history of French literature as it marks a decisive break from naturalism. It is also a significant turning point in Huysmans's life. His contemporary Jules Barbey d'Aurevilly once said of *Against the Grain,* "After a book like this one, the author is left no choice but the mouth of a pistol or the feet of the cross."

D'Aurevilly's remark is particularly apt as the next significant shift in Huysmans's progress as a writer is closely linked to his conversion to Roman Catholicism. Two companion novels, *The* DAMNED and EN ROUTE, depict the character Durtal's conversion based on Huysmans' own experience. *The Damned* begins with Durtal's exploration of the occult, magic, and satanism that the reader first saw with des Esseintes. By the end of the novel, Roman Catholicism appears as a possible solution to Durtal's search for spiritual fulfillment. His final conversion takes place in *En Route*.

Huysmans's conversion was sincere and, in a sense, not surprising. He first fell in love with the beautiful stained-glass windows of Chartres cathedral and the monks' illuminated manuscripts. Huysmans's love of art led him to religion. With his newfound spirituality, he turned to medieval art, architecture, and Gregorian chant. *The Cathedral* contemplates the symbolism of Gothic architecture in the cathedral of Chartres. As his fascination with religious symbolism grew, so did Huysmans's spiritual development. He made a number of spiritual retreats to monasteries. In 1898 Huysmans was received as an oblate by the Benedictines. In 1901, he returned to Paris, where he wrote *The Oblate* and *The Crowds of Lourdes* in response to Zola's work. Huysmans's final works are mystical, prayerful writings.

Taken as a whole, Huysmans's writings are profoundly honest, autobiographical works that allow the reader to witness every step in the author's intellectual and spiritual development. Like a number of his characters (Folantin and des Esseintes, for example), Huysmans was disdainful of a world peopled with, as he called them, idiots. His early novels thus depict characters leading useless, absurd lives.

Despite the marked shifts in style, there is an underlying unity to Huysmans's works. Characteristic traits are precise description, sincerity, and an impressionist influence. Huysmans's originality lies in his ability to make writing visual; his writing is as painting. Even if he was not as popular as Zola or MAUPASSANT, Huysmans left a lasting mark on French literary history.

FURTHER READING

Banks, Brian. *The Image of Huysmans.* New York: AMS Press, 1990.

Gilman, Richard. *Decadence: The Strange Life of an Epithet.* New York: Farrar, Straus and Giroux, 1979.

Nalbantian, Suzanne. *Seeds of Decadence in the Late Nineteenth-Century Novel.* New York: St. Martin's Press, 1983.

Praz, Mario. *The Romantic Agony.* Translated by Angus Davidson. New York: Oxford University Press, 1970.

I

ICELAND FISHERMAN, AN (PÊCHEUR D'ISLANDE) PIERRE LOTI (1886)

Yann, a tall sailor, and a young woman named Gaud meet at a ball where they dance together all evening. Gaud falls hopelessly in love with Yann and waits impatiently for him to return from Iceland, where he is fishing for cod. Unfortunately, when he returns, Yann ignores Gaud, who sadly begins to think about death.

During the next fishing season, Gaud's father dies and she loses all her money gambling. Obliged to go live with an old woman Moan, Gaud cares for Sylvestre, Yann's friend, who subsequently dies in China during his military service. One day Yann returns and, out of the blue, asks Gaud to marry him. She accepts. After six blissful days Yann leaves again for the sea. He never returns. The novel ends with Gaud walking to the edge of a cliff overlooking the sea, where, advancing slowly, she calls, "I'm coming, Yann."

Despite the novel's tragic end, it was popular with contemporary readers, who appreciated Loti's powerful evocation of life dominated by the sea. Beyond the love story of Yann and Gaud, the character of Sylvestre is a powerful reminder of a young man's courage in the face of death.

FURTHER READING

Blanch, Lesley. *Pierre Loti: Portrait of an Escapist.* London: Collins, 1983.
———. *Pierre Loti: The Legendary Romantic.* San Diego: Harcourt Brace Jovanovich, 1983.
Hartman, Elwood. *Three Nineteenth-Century French Worters/Artists and the Maghreb: The Literary and Artistic Depictions of North Africa by Théophile Gautier, Eugène Fromentin and Pierre Loti.* Tübingen, Germany: Narr, 1994.
Hughes, Edward J. *Writing Marginality in Modern French Literature: from Loti to Genet.* Cambridge, New York: Cambridge University Press, 2001.
Lerner, Michael. *Pierre Loti's Dramatic Works.* Lewiston, Me.: E. Mellen Press, 1998.

IDEALISM

Idealism is essentially a philosophical approach to literature whereby art becomes a means to transcend reality. Associated in 19th-century poetry with the works of Charles Baudelaire and the symbolists (see SYMBOLISM), idealism is also found in novels such as those written by GEORGE SAND in which love is presented as a source of personal, moral, and political regeneration. The term *idealism* is sometimes used pejoratively to refer to literature that deliberately ignores the unpleasant aspects of life.

IMMORALIST, THE (L'IMMORALISTE) ANDRÉ GIDE (1902)

In this novel Michel, the principal character, calls together his closest friends to confess the story of his life and explains, anticipating its conclusion, that "to know how to free oneself is nothing; the difficult thing is to know to be free."

Michel's story begins with the four friends' last meeting on the occasion of Michel's marriage to Marceline, not out of love but rather a sense of obligation after the death of his father. After their marriage, Michael and Marceline set off for Tunisia, but when they arrive, Michel falls seriously ill with tuberculosis and he coughs blood. At first he tries to hide his illness, not wishing to show any sign of weakness.

Michel thinks he has little hope of recovery but Marceline refuses to give up. Under her care, Michel slowly begins to recover. One day, to distract him, Marceline brings home an Arab child named Bachir. Full of admiration for the child's abundant health, Michel subsequently puts all his energy into healing, embracing anything that seems to do him good. He also becomes increasingly absorbed with his own body. He goes to the public park where he finds the children who play there attractive and entertaining. However, Michel wishes to go there alone or with Bachir, not with his attentive wife. As he watches, Michel's senses begin to awaken, causing an "exaltation of his senses and flesh."

Unfortunately, the approach of winter forces Michel indoors. Moktir, one of the children who often visits the couple, steals a pair of scissors, thinking that Michel has not seen. Michel says nothing but from that moment on, Moktir becomes his favorite. With spring comes Michel's complete recovery. Realizing that he has been neglecting Marceline, Michel vows to love her more.

The couple decides to leave Biskra. On their last night, unable to sleep, Michel goes onto the terrace but the calm disturbs him and he is overcome with the tragedy of life. Before returning to bed he opens a Bible haphazardly to the Gospel of John: "Now you gird your loins and go where you want to go; but when you are old, you will stretch out your hands."

From North Africa, Michel and Marceline travel to Italy, where Michel realizes that his experience has changed him. He sees too that his education, upbringing, and habits have stifled him. He emerges from the sea and sun feeling "not quite robust but capable of being so, harmonious, sensual, almost handsome."

To signify his sense of physical renewal, Michel decides to shave his beard and yet he is unsure. "It seemed to me that one could see my naked thought." Fearing that Marceline will somehow impede the transformation he is undergoing Michel tries to hide it. He even begins to take pleasure in his dissimulation. One day, however, he barely escapes being run over by the coach Marceline is traveling in to meet him. The near miss brings the couple closer together than they have ever been. In Sorrento, Michel receives a letter from a friend announcing that there is a position open at the prestigious Collège de France in Paris. The couple returns to France and moves for the summer into the country house Michel inherited from his mother.

When they arrive in Normandy, Marceline announces that she is pregnant. Michel prepares his lectures for the fall and, with the help of Charles, plans improvements for his land, even sending away two farmers who had left certain fields uncultivated. At the beginning of the school year, Michel and Marceline return to Paris where they live in some luxury. Michel, however, is unhappy. Only Ménalque seems to understand Michel's philosophy. Michel's encounter with his old friend provokes a certain philosophical examination of life and the choices one makes, as Ménalque lives an independent existence, unencumbered and free. The contrast between Ménalque's existential and ontological isolation and Michel's own situation causes Michel to reflect on his responsibility toward others.

Upon his return, Michel learns that in his absence, Marceline has had a miscarriage. Once she has apparently recovered, they travel again. Michel imagines that perhaps he will love Marceline again as he did in Sorrento. As they journey, however, Marceline's health deteriorates. She, too, coughs blood as Michel had done on their first journey. She is weak and she knows that Michel has no tolerance for weakness.

Michel pushes her on. He wants to return to North Africa. In the evenings he abandons her to wander through the streets. As she continues to weaken, Michel drives them on mercilessly, compelled by his own obsessive impulse. In Algeria, Marceline is near death. Yet she suffers alone in their room as Michel goes out into the night with Moktir, only to return for Marceline's last sigh.

Michel's story ends there. He is at a loss. The days run by and now he counts only on the friends he has called to his side saying "Take me away from here; I cannot do it myself."

The Immoralist needs to be understood within the context of Gide's reading of German philosopher Friedrich Nietzsche and psychoanalyst Sigmund Freud. Written a year after the publication of Freud's *Interpretation of Dreams* and Nietzsche's *The Will to Power*, the character of Michel can be characterized as both Nietzschean and Freudian, a being who seeks to live by and for his own pleasure. He thus serves as an example of Gide's concept of the *"acte gratuit,"* or gratuitous act. A principal theme in Gide's works is that of *disponibilité* (openness) to potential experiences, free from social or moral constraints. An ethical question is thus at the heart of Gide's approach, in which a first-person narrator may follow an ethical decision to its logical and sometimes destructive conclusion. Ultimately, he promotes the idea of living in freedom. Although there are autobiographical elements to the novel, the narrator nonetheless creates a sense of distance from Gide's life through the character of Ménalque, who also serves as the catalyst for Michel's coming to self-awareness.

FURTHER READING

Bettinson, Christopher D. *Gide: A Study.* London: Heinemann; Totowa, N.J.: Rowman and Littlefield, 1977.

Sheridan, Alan. *André Gide: A Life in the Present.* Cambridge, Mass.: Harvard University Press, 1999.

Stoltzfus, Ben. "André Gide and the Voice of Rebellion," *Contemporary Literature* 19, no. 1 (Winter 1978): 80–98.

Walker, David, ed. *André Gide.* London, New York: Longman, 1996.

INDIANA GEORGE SAND (1832)

Like George Sand herself, the principal character of this novel set on the island La Réunion, Madame Delmare, or Indiana, is unhappily married. She wants true love to deliver her from her misery. Her first attempt at salvation through an affair is with Raymon, the former lover of Madame Delmare's creole servant, Noun. Raymon may love Indiana but he is an egotist, seeking first and foremost to satisfy his own desires. Noun naturally never forgives Raymon for his betrayal, and seeks revenge. One day, Noun's desire for vengeance leads her to seduce Raymon in Madame Delmare's own room. When Indiana discovers their betrayal, she is pained by what appears to be the inevitability of male desire leading to infidelity. Noun drowns herself.

Madame Delmare's next lover is Ralph, who has always loved her. With Ralph, Indiana finally finds the true love she has been seeking for so long. Echoing VILLIERS DE L'ISLE D'ADAM, like any true romantic passion (see ROMANTICISM), it appears that the love between Indiana and Ralph may only fulfill itself in death. Romantic novels frequently focus on a yearning for the unattainable, a love that transcends everyday experience. In what is intended to be their final kiss on the edge of a torrential flow of water, they are miraculously saved by what appears to be divine intervention. Sand thus allows her lovers to live out their lives in peace and happiness, reflecting her principal belief in love as the source of moral regeneration.

FURTHER READING

Booker, John T. "Indiana and Madame Bovary: Intertextual Echoes," *Nineteenth Century French Studies* 31, nos. 3 and 4, (Spring-Summer 2003): 226–236.

Vest, James M. "Fluid Nomenclature, Imagery and Themes in George Sand's 'Indiana,'" *South Atlantic Review* 46, no. 2 (May 1981): 43–54.

INDISCRETE JEWELS, THE (LES BIJOUX INDISCRETS) DENIS DIDEROT (1748)

In this LIBERTINE novel, the ENLIGHTENMENT philosopher DENIS DIDEROT tells the story of a bored sultan who uses a magic ring to make women's genitals talk. Diderot wrote this work for his mistress at the time, Madeleine de Puisieux, who was also a writer.

Like CRÉBILLON FILS's novel *The Sofa*, in which a man turns into a couch in order to watch women, Diderot's tale is likewise one of oriental voyeurism. A number of 18th-century libertine novels were partly inspired by Antoine Galland's translation of *Arabian Nights* and reflect a general interest among readers in exotic lands as a consequence of European exploration that began in the late 15th century.

Although later in his life Diderot regretted having written this novel, it does serve as another expression of his general philosophical ideas. Like *JACK THE FATALIST, Indiscrete Jewels* emphasizes the importance of those unexpected and varied experiences that make human beings feel alive. Drawing from English philosopher John Locke, Diderot expands on sensationist theory to argue that boredom can be relieved only by changing experience. At the same time, Diderot uses a series of short narratives and commentaries in this libertine novel to peel back layers of hypocrisy and ignorance in order to reveal the truth of human relations, a major theme in his works.

FURTHER READING
Burbank, P. N. *Diderot: A Critical Biography.* New York: Knopf, 1992.
Loy, Robert J. *Diderot's Determined Fatalist: A Critical Appreciation of Jacque le Fataliste.* New York: Crown Press, Columbia University, 1950.
MacPhail, Eric. "Diderot and the Plot of History," *New Literary History* 30, no. 2 (1999): 439–452.
Wilson, Arthur. *Diderot.* New York: Oxford University Press, 1972.

INQUISITORY, THE (*L'INQUISITOIRE*)
ROBERT PINGET (1962) A former servant of the Château de Broy, nearly deaf, answers questions throughout almost the entire novel, although the reader never fully comprehends his motivations. The steward of the château has disappeared, soon to be followed by another servant. These events lie at the origin of the investigation. The château is located in one of Pinget's fictional provinces, Agapa.

The old servant in question left the château almost a year before. He recounts his work experience, explaining to the questioner about the region, the château, his employers' habits (Monsieur Louis and Monsieur Jean), as well as those of their friends and acquaintances. Does he tell all this out of a desire to fulfill his duty? Because he is guarding a secret? All we know is that the old servant is worn out. The novel ends with the words, "I am tired."

There are things that the servant forgets, consciously or not, and contradictions appear in his story. For example, not until the end of the novel does the old man recall that an amateur astronomer (Monsieur Pierre) lives in the castle keep. He thus had three masters. The novel concludes with the servant exhausted and the mystery unsolved.

Pinget said that he began writing *The Inquisitory* with nothing to say, simply a need to express himself. While there are certain traditional elements to this novel, there are parodies as well. At the center of the novel is a marriage banquet that in its detail recalls the writing of GUSTAVE FLAUBERT or ÉMILE ZOLA. As a NOUVEAU ROMAN, the work reflects Pinget's interest in the word, speech, and language. The old servant's words reveal the inaccessibility of truth. The old servant refuses or is unable to respond directly to the questions asked. It is possible that he witnessed some sort of criminal activity but we can never be sure, because there are too many inconsistencies in his answers. In the end, the reader is left confused by this, nevertheless, compelling work.

FURTHER READING
Henkels, Robert M. *Robert Pinget: the Novel as Quest.* Tuscaloosa: University of Alabama Press, 1979.
Reid, Martin. "Robert Pinget," *Yale French Studies,* Special Issue: After the Age of Suspicion: The French Novel Today (1988): 97–100.
Rosmarin, Léonard. *Robert Pinget.* New York: Twayne Publishers; London: Prentice Hall, 1995.

IN SEARCH OF LOST TIME   See REMEMBRANCE OF THINGS PAST.

INSIDE (*DEDANS*) HÉLÈNE CIXOUS (1969) As the title implies, in this novel a female narrator explores an inner, private space that exists in opposition to an external space. Inside is quiet intimacy, the personal. Outside is the humming of the many, as opposed to the few.

Inside is naturally connected to the family and, in this case, is related to the Jewish tradition of understanding the family as a line of fathers that extends from the past into the future. The narrator explores her memories as they relate to the different members of her family, united by love, tenderness, and circumstance. Cixous has said that the novel also serves as a metaphor for Algeria from the 1940s through the 1960s.

Cixous's exploration of an inner world is influenced by Irish novelist James Joyce, the subject of her doctoral dissertation. Her writing is difficult, complex and sometimes obscure. Nonetheless, the underlying message is clear. One must grasp the secret life of the inside.

The novel reflects a style and set of core beliefs associated with women's writing (*écriture féminine,* see FEMINISM). *Inside* received the Médicis Prize.

FURTHER READING
Cixous, Hélène, and Catherine Clément. *The Newly Born Woman.* Translated by Betsy Wing. Minneapolis: University of Minnesota Press, 1986.

Conley, Verena Andermatt. *Hélène Cixous: Writing the Feminine*. Lincoln: University of Nebraska Press, 1991.

Marks, Elaine. "Review Essay: Women and Literature in France," *Signs* 3 (1978): 832–842.

Marks, Elaine, and Isabelle de Courticron, eds. *New French Feminisms: An Anthology*. Amherst: University of Massachusetts Press, 1980.

Sellers, Susan, ed. *Writing Differences: Readings From the Seminar of Hélène Cixous*. New York: St. Martin's Press, 1988.

Shiach, Morag. *Hélène Cixous: A Politics of Writing*. London: Routledge, 1994.

Showalter, Elaine, ed. *The New Feminist Criticism: Essays on Women, Literature and Theory*. New York: Pantheon, 1985.

IN THE SHADOW OF THE WIND (LES FOUS DE BASSAN) ANNE HÉBERT (1982)

On the night of August 31, 1936, Olivia and Nora disappear from a small, English-speaking fishing village on the banks of Canada's Saint Lawrence River. The cries of the seabirds evoked by the novel's French title echoes the villagers' torment over this loss. Yet perhaps the village itself has contributed to the crime with its stifling atmosphere and narrow vision.

Six different voices narrate the story, each from his or her own perspective. Some recount the event at the moment of its occurrence; others do so many years later. Typical of Hébert's novels, the story is one of stifling, violent passion and desire.

Olivia and Nora are both on the edge of womanhood, each slowly awakening to her body and desire. In consequence, they represent both innocence and sinfulness. Fifty years later the murderer confesses his crime in a letter to a friend. Steven Brown's narrative reveals his fascination with and fear of the young women's budding sexuality. The murderer is mesmerized by the two young women. Yet he expresses no regret or remorse over their rape and murder. His own family life had been harsh and Steven had left Griffin Creek for five years before returning to commit his heinous crime.

In this powerful and austere work, male characters appear as menacing. Female characters are full of life

and spirit. The motivations for the rape and murder thus raise deeper questions about women's sexuality and the way in which it can be threatening to men. In fact, the narrative echoes passages from Genesis, indicting woman for tempting man. An element of Roman Catholic Jansenist thought with its emphasis on original sin is present in this work as well as in Hébert's *KAMOURASKA*. For Hébert, man is evil, and perhaps also mad.

Nicolas Jones, the pastor who opens the novel with his recollections of 1936, the year not only of the murder but also of his wife, Irene's, suicide due to their unhappy marriage, is likewise unbalanced. Jones fills his home with portraits of male ancestors who visually represent the continuity of male power and authority but, beneath it all, there is a sense of doubt and uncertainty. The two spinsters, Pat and Pam, who have never subjected themselves to male power, respond to the pastor's message by putting up female faces and names to challenge the male portraits. Male versus female power is thus a dominant theme in this novel. In the end, the attempt to suppress and silence the female body is unsuccessful. Olivia's lyrical poem rises up out of the sea. *In the Shadow of the Wind* won the Femina Prize.

FURTHER READING

Gould, Karen. "Absence and Meaning in Anne Hébert's *Les Fous de Bassan*," *French Review* 59, no. 6, Special Issue on Quebec (May 1986): 921–930.

Green, Mary Jean. "The Witch and the Princess: The Feminine Fantastic in the Fiction of Anne Hébert," *American Review of Canadian Studies* 15, no. 2 (Summer 1985): 137–146.

Knight, Kelton W. *Anne Hébert: In Search of the First Garden.* New York: P. Lang, 1998.

Pallister, Janis L. *The Art and Genius of Anne Hébert: Essays on her Works: Night and the Day Are One.* Madison, N.J.: Fairleigh Dickinson University Press, 2001.

Paterson, Janet M. "Anne Hébert and the Discourse of the Unreal," *Yale French Studies,* 65, The Language of Difference: Writing in Quebec(ois) (1983): 172–186.

Russell, Delbert. *Anne Hébert.* Boston: Twayne, 1983.

J

JACK THE FATALIST AND HIS MASTER (JACQUES LE FATALISTE) Denis Diderot (1778)

With *Jack the Fatalist,* Diderot introduces a new kind of realism in fiction. Drawing from the philosophical ideas of the 17th century English philosopher John Locke, Diderot recognized that nature itself is varied. He argued that literature should reflect this multiplicity. The ultimate purpose of this novel is to challenge the notion of free will.

Jack is a brave, intelligent, and generous valet. In contrast, his master is idle, difficult, and entirely dependent on Jack. Together they journey to what is at first an unknown destination, conversing all the way on a variety of topics. Influenced by Lawrence Stern's *Tristram Shandy* and the picaresque tradition, in this novel Jack and his master undergo a series of misadventures for which the master is responsible. Because of him Jack finds himself attacked by brigands and is imprisoned.

Diderot engagingly addresses the reader directly in the novel. The mixture of narrators and breaks in the linear structure of the narrative make it a strikingly innovative and modern novel that examines the question of philosophical determinism. At the same time, Jack's determinism is linked to Diderot's vision of humankind's destiny and liberty. Echoing the principle theme of *The NUN,* he asserts that "a sequestered human being falls into regret, languishment, insanity or despair." The solution to the problem of human fulfillment, if not human happiness, is to lead a life of virtue in the company of others. For this Jack is rewarded, making him a just counterpoint to the principal character in RAMEAU'S NEPHEW. As they travel from one inn to another, Jack and his master discuss important philosophical questions: As individuals, are we free to act or do we follow a prescribed destiny? What is virtue? What is vice? And as always with Diderot, how does one deal with the problem of language and meaning?

Diderot continues along the path he established in earlier works of challenging ethical and moral norms. Each episode within the narrative poses a moral question that cannot be answered by relying on normal social standards of behavior and conduct. The most obvious example is the innkeeper's story about Madame de la Pommeraye, who, to take revenge on a former lover, tricks him into marrying a prostitute. Against all odds, the marriage is a happy one. Diderot has once again convincingly challenged OLD REGIME social order.

FURTHER READING

Burbank, P. N. Diderot: *A Critical Biography.* New York: Knopf, 1992.

Loy, Robert J. *Diderot's Determined Fatalist: A Critical Appreciation of Jacque le Fataliste.* New York: Crown Press, Columbia University, 1950.

MacPhail, Eric. "Diderot and the Plot of History," *New Literary History* 30, no. 2 (1999): 439–452.

Wilson, Arthur. *Diderot.* New York: Oxford University Press, 1972.

JACK THE REBEL (JACQOU LE CRO-QUANT) EUGÈNE LE ROY (1898)

The most significant work of the Perigordian writer Eugène Le Roy, *Jack the Rebel* depicts peasant life in Perigord region in Southwestern France at the end of the 19th century through the eyes of its protagonist, the laborer Jack. This realist novel (see REALISM) is a brutal, pessimistic portrait of rural life. At the same time, Le Roy manifests his empathy for the peasants' humble existence, hard work, and anger against their former lords. LeRoy is known today as a popular regional novelist capable of evoking the rich flavor of the Perigord region with sensitivity and sympathy for its people.

JACQUES VINGTRAS TRILOGY: CHILD (L'ENFANT) (1879); BACHELOR (LE BACHELIER) (1881); THE INSURREC-TIONIST (L'INSURGÉ) JULES VALLÈS (1886)

This autobiographical trilogy written by one of 19th-century France's most renowned revolutionaries, traces the life of Jacques Vingtras from childhood to adulthood, ending on the barricades of the PARIS COMMUNE in 1871.

In the first volume, *Child,* the narrator, who represents Vallès, recounts an unhappy childhood in the provinces where he is raised by narrow-minded, authoritarian parents. Starved for affection and understanding, Jacques leaves the constraints of petit-bourgeois life for Paris.

Vallès produced the first volume in a four-month period, living in exile after having been condemned to death in absentia for his participation in the insurrection of the Paris Commune. It first appeared in a journal in 1879 under a pseudonym and was finally published as a separate volume in 1881. The dedication, with its sharp invective against two bulwarks of social stability, the family and the school, caused a scandal.

In the second volume, *Bachelor,* Jacques Vingtras arrives in Paris at the age of 17. With no job and no money, he takes up work here and there to make ends meet, but there seems to be no escape from misery, and he joins others who are also the victims of social injustice.

The second volume was also written during the author's period in exile. It first appeared in installments under the title "Memoirs of a Rebel" in the journal *The French Revolution, The People* having refused to publish it after the scandal caused by the first volume. Like *Child, The Bachelor* also denounces the French system of education for producing only "victims of books." It also recounts the hero's initiation into political activism. In fact, *The Bachelor* may be read as an introduction to the literary and political history of 19th-century France. Frustrated by the moral and political crisis resulting from the failure of the 1848 Revolution, the novel closes with the hero's cry against himself, "Coward!"

The last volume of the Jacques Vingtras trilogy, *The Insurrectionist,* tells of the hero's open rebellion against bourgeois society of the Second Empire. Jacques joins the insurrection of the Paris Commune in 1871 only just to escape with his life at the end of the "Bloody Week" in May, during which the Thiers government violently suppressed the Communards. Dedicated to the fallen heroes of the Commune, *The Insurrectionist* speaks to all victims of social injustice. Despite the Commune's defeat, the possibility of hope remains with the dawn of a new era of workers' consciousness.

Stylistically, the novel offers a literary collage that includes passionate articles Vallès wrote during the period of the Commune and published in *The Cry of the People.* The novel is a remarkable mixture of history and fiction, allegory and REALISM. Some critics have argued that Vallès's trilogy even constitutes a return to NATURALISM. Because of the sensitivity of the subject matter—the history of the Commune's violent suppression—*Jacques Vingtras* was excluded for a long time from literary collections. It is now recognized for its realism in depicting a particular period in the history of France and as a literary catharsis for both author and reader.

FURTHER READING

Bouvier, Luke. *Writing, Voice, and the Proper: Jules Vallès and the Politics of Orality.* Amsterdam, Atlanta: Rodolpi, 1998.

Langford, Rachael. *Jules Vallès and the Narration of History: Contesting the French Third Republic in the Jacques Vingtras Trilogy.* Bern, New York: P. Lang, 1999.

Long, Robin McArthur. *Self, Language and the Social in the Writings of Jules Vallès (1832–1885): The Jacques Vingtras Trilogy.* Lewiston, N.Y.: E. Mellen Press, 2004.

JARRY, ALFRED (1873–1907)

A brilliant student, in 1888 Jarry moved with his mother from the Breton countryside to Rennes, where, in high school, he met the now famous physics teacher Monsieur Hébert, about whom his students wrote poems and plays in which "Father Heb" is given the role of the king of Poland. In 1891, Jarry left for Paris, where he began to frequent literary circles.

Having failed the entrance exam for the prestigious École Normale Supérieure, Jarry chose a career in literature instead. By 1893 he was publishing regularly in various literary reviews, particularly the well-known *Mercure de France*. This journal published Jarry's first substantive work, *Minutes of Sand: Memorial,* a mixture of prose and verse influenced by both SYMBOLISM and DECADENTISM. This collection includes "Guignol," in which Father Heb has been transformed into Jarry's legendary character, Father Ubu.

Discharged from military service for health reasons, in 1896 Jarry published *King Ubu*. This play caused a scandal, not so much for its content as for its style. A number of critics simply took it as a farce, as Jarry's "ubuesque" writing rejects all the traditional rules of dramatic writing. It is theater of the absurd. In an article entitled "On the Uselessness of Theater to Theater," Jarry had already articulated his approach, called "pataphysics," a method by which he sought to challenge both reason and language.

Jarry's revolutionary approach to drama had an impact on his writing of fiction and the way he lived his life. He rejected traditional social norms as much as conventional forms of literature. He thus chose to live on the margins of society, solitary and poor, as if he were the extravagant King Ubu himself. He also continued to write prolifically and to participate in puppet theater. A number of articles published in *The White Review* brought Jarry to the attention of a broader reading public in 1900–1903. Unfortunately, poverty and alcoholism caused his health to disintegrate to the point where by 1906, then seriously ill, Jarry was experiencing mystical visions that he describes in *The Tassel*.

Jarry had a remarkable talent to play with words and etymology in the practice of "pataphysics," engendering a plurality of language that recalls the writing of Irish novelist James Joyce. Critics have sometimes accused Jarry of being overly intellectual, describing his writing as *"précieux"* (see PRECIOSITY) and SYMBOLIST. Jarry owes his reputation principally to the character of Ubu. Other novels include *Days and Nights,* (1897), *Love Visits* (1898), SUPERMALE (1902), and DOCTOR FAUSTROLL (posthumous, 1911).

FURTHER READING

Beaumont, Keith. *Alfred Jarry: A Critical and Biographical Study*. St. Martin's Press, 1984.

Fell, Jill. *Alfred Jarry: An Imaginary Revolt*. Madison, N.J.: Farleigh Dickinson University Press, 2005.

LaBelle, Maurice Marc. *Alfred Jarry, Nihilism, and the Theater of the Absurd*. New York: New York University Press, 1980.

Lennon, Nigey. *Alfred Jarry: The Man with the Axe*. Los Angeles: Panjandrum Books, 1984.

Murphy, Patrice. "Rabelais and Jarry," *French Review* 51, no. 1 (October 1977): 29–36.

Shattuck, Roger. *The Banquet Years: The Arts in France, 1885–1918: Alfred Jarry, Henri Rousseau, Erik Satie, Guillaume Apollinaire*. New York: Harcourt Brace, 1958.

JEALOUSY (LA JALOUSIE) ALAIN ROBBE-GRILLET (1957)

Set somewhere in Africa, a group of characters develop under the watchful eyes of the narrator, a jealous husband who is, at one and the same time, both present and not present. The novel is replete with methodical descriptions of surroundings and gestures. Sequences of events are repeated with slight modification, giving the impression of a schizophrenic state of mind. There are three characters, yet only two of them are "named." A. is the narrator's wife. She and her unnamed husband represent the colonial worldview, yet they are uncertain about the future. Franck, A.'s presumed lover, and Christine, in contrast, offer a more modern perspective on the colonial world as they seem to be more aware of the problems associated with that era.

The plot contains little action, in fact, nothing much happens at all. The reader has simply the narrator's perception of reality that he continually reformulates. Robbe-Grillet's customarily long and minute descriptions inform the narrator's internal monologue. In this and other works, Robbe-Grillet emphasizes the subjectivity of his characters. The jealous husband, for example, reacts to the world only in light of his obsession.

For the writer, the objective description of a subjective experience is the only reality.

Jealousy and Robbe-Grillet's earlier novel, *Erasers* (1953), introduce the NOUVEAU ROMAN. In these earlier works, Robbe-Grillet's writings still retain certain elements of the traditional novel even as he experiments with a new approach to writing fiction. Subsequently, the world of objects increasingly takes precedence over the world of the mind, thus challenging the humanism associated with the traditional novel. Robbe-Grillet's emphasis on objects in relation to reality recalls GEORGES PEREC's equally materialist vision in THINGS.

Jealousy was initially a commercial failure, yet not long after, it was translated into some 30 languages, as it continued to provoke debate among literary theorists. Over time, the novel gradually attracted the attention of a broader reading public.

FURTHER READING

Angelini, Eileen M. *Strategies of "Writing the Self" in the French Modern Novel: C'est moi, je Crois.* Lewiston, N.Y.: E. Mellen Press, 2001.

Carrabino, Victor. *The Phenomenological Novel of Alain Robbe-Grillet.* Parma: C.E.M., 1974.

Fletcher, John. *Alain Robbe-Grillet.* London, New York: Methuen, 1983.

Harger-Grinling, Virginia, and Tony Chadwick. *Robbe-Grillet and the Fantastic: A Collection of Essays.* Wesport, Conn.: Greenwood Press, 1994.

Leki, Ilona. *Alain Robbe-Grillet.* Boston: Twayne, 1983.

Morrissette, Bruce. *Intertextual Assemblage in Robbe-Grillet from Topology to the Golden Triangle.* Fredericton, New Brunswick: York Press, 1979.

Ramsay, Raylene L. *The French New Autobiographies: Sarraute, Duras, and Robbe-Grillet.* Gainesville: University Press of Florida, 1996.

Smith, Roch Charles. *Understanding Alain Robbe-Grillet.* Columbia: University of South Carolina Press, 2000.

Stoltzfus, Ben. *Alain Robbe-Grillet and the New French Novel.* Carbondale: Southern Illinois University Press, 1964.

JEAN-CHRISTOPHE ROMAIN ROLLAND (1904–1912)

A monumental work in 10 volumes, *Jean-Christophe* was first published in 17 parts in the *Cahiers de la Quinzaine,* edited by the poet and essayist Charles Péguy, a journal to which Rolland also contributed a number of other works. The novel tells the story of Jean-Christophe Krafft, born in a peaceful village in the German Rhineland.

From a musical family, Jean-Christophe is likewise a musician. His experience as a child and his discovery of music, his apprenticeship as an adolescent, his first loves and subsequent introduction to pain and injustice serve as the material for the first three books: *Dawn, Morning,* and *Adolescence.*

In the fourth book, *Rebellion,* Rolland uses the character of Jean-Christophe to attack social values that stand in sharp contrast to the inherent nobility of the novel's hero. Jean-Christophe suffers under the constraints of narrow provincial society. He dreams of a wider world, of going to France. When he is involved in a fight between peasants and soldiers, he kills an officer and is forced to flee. Jean-Christophe thus does go to Paris, the setting for the next three books: *Marketplace, Antoinette,* and *At Home,* united under the title *Jean-Christophe in Paris.*

Jean-Christophe encounters numerous difficulties as he attempts to establish himself in the world of artists and intellectuals. In *Friends,* he meets Olivier Jeannin, with whom he shares a similar vision and aspirations. The two young men decide to live together. The friendship between Jean-Christophe, who is ethnically German, and Olivier, who is French, represents Rolland's belief in fraternity and understanding between nations and peoples, a recurring theme in his works. Their arrangement lasts until Olivier's marriage. The union is not a happy one and several years later Olivier and his wife go their separate ways.

Friends, The Burning Bush, and *The New Day* share the general title *The Journey's End.* In the course of these volumes, Olivier dies in a riot. Jean-Christophe, who has also participated, flees once more, this time to Switzerland, in despair. A painful affair with Anna Braun almost drives him to suicide, but he finally attains peace in the solitude of the Swiss mountains. There he regains both a sense of balance and inspiration, having heard the voice of God from the burning bush. In the end, Jean-Christophe eventually finds love with a young woman he knew from his youth.

Rolland's profound love for and knowledge of music runs like a hidden current through this novel. Jean-Christophe is a young man full of emotion and spirit who goes through a spiritual/intellectual crisis during which he is, for a time, drawn to skepticism. Ultimately, he finds spiritual fulfillment, even moments of ecstasy, through music and nature in a pantheistic and ultimately romantic vision of the world (see ROMANTICISM), as Jean-Christophe perceives the "divine Essence" that unites all things. As his life continues, Jean-Christophe suffers from the tension between his inner joy and creative spirit and his disillusionment with society. Nonetheless, in the end, nothing can dim his inner light, nor challenge his sense that creativity comes from God.

The novel ends with Rolland's plea for pacifism. In the preface to the last volume, the author speaks from one generation to the next: "I wrote the tragedy of a generation that will disappear. I did not try to dissimulate either their voices or their virtues, their heavy sadness or chaotic pride, their heroic efforts or their dejection . . . men of today, young men, trample over us and go forward. Be greater and happier than we." In these volumes, Rolland tries to impart his vision of the world while depicting the atmosphere among European intellectuals at the turn of the 20th century, sometimes with a tone of accusation, sometimes with lyricism. He offers a veritable catalogue of ideas, movements, and ideologies that are, in part, what make this work so complex.

FURTHER READING

Aronson, Alex. *Romain Rolland: The Story of a Conscience.* Bombay, India: Padma, 1946.

Beckwith, William Hunter. *The Formation of the Esthetic of Romain Rolland.* New York: New York University Press, 1936.

Starr, William Thomas. *Romain Rolland and a World at War.* New York: AMS Press, 1971.

———. *Romain Rolland. One Against All. A Biography.* The Hague, Paris: Mouton, 1971.

JOUHANDEAU, MARCEL (1888–1979)

Marcel Jouhandeau grew up in a provincial town where his father and mother ran a butcher shop. He was raised primarily by the women in his family; his grandmother Blanchet, who ran a bakery in a nearby street, was particularly important in his upbringing in an atmosphere of Catholicism and mystical spirituality. Jouhandeau was to be concerned with religious questions all his life.

As a child, Jouhandeau first came under the influence of a young woman who introduced him to devotional literature, particularly the works of 17th century the Spanish Mystic St. John of the Cross. Later, as an adolescent, an older woman, Madame Alban took on the role of spiritual guide. She encouraged Jouhandeau to enter a religious order. Jouhandeau certainly wished to escape from the confines of a narrow provincial life, although he was at the same time endlessly fascinated by the characters he encountered in his native Guéret.

Instead of entering religious life, Jouhandeau left for Paris in 1908, where he studied at the Sorbonne. He began writing in 1909, keeping a detailed journal in which he recorded his reflections, descriptions of people he met, poems, and stories. He once referred to himself as a "notary of life." Having discovered his homosexuality, Jouhandeau broke free from his pious upbringing and began to celebrate in writing his appreciation of the male body. Nonetheless, Jouhandeau felt guilty before God and decided he must struggle against his inclinations. He was never entirely successful; yet in a moment of spiritual crisis, Jouhandeau burned his manuscripts in 1912, the year he took up a teaching career. Jouhandeau taught at Saint-Jean de Passy from 1913 to 1949.

By 1914, Jouhandeau was writing again and published his first stories, *Pincengrain,* in 1924. His *"Comédie Humaine"* explores the unforgettable characters that inhabit a provincial town, such as Clodomir the murderer, PRUDENCE HAUTECHAUME with her clothing store, and Madame Bodeau, with her brothel. This work caused a scandal in Guéret, as all of the characters were recognizable to its residents. This would be the case with Jouhandeau's subsequent works as well. Jouhandeau said that he never really left Guéret. Certainly his mother's almost daily letters continued to furnish him with material even as he lived his rather complicated life in Paris. As a teacher, Jouhandeau diligently fulfilled his duties yet he also lived a double life in which he pursued sexual adventures on the side. During World War I, he served as secretary to an officer and lived a quiet life, fulfilling his duties and studying Greek. He also began work on *The Intimate*

Life of Monsieur Godeau, in which he evokes his painful discovery of his own homosexuality.

Saddened by the death of an old school friend, Léon Laveine, Jouhandeau wrote a letter of condolence to his rich and beautiful widow, whom he later referred to as the duchess. After the war, Jouhandeau returned to his post as a schoolteacher and, in 1919, published the first part of *Théophile's Youth* in the prestigious *Nouvelle Revue Française* (New French Review). Jouhandeau was thus introduced into the circle of writers associated with that journal, ANDRÉ GIDE and ROGER MARTIN DU GARD among them. Moreover, Laveine's widow welcomed him into her social gatherings. He continued to write and publish prolifically until the end of his life.

In 1928, Jouhandeau met Elisabeth Toulemon, a former dancer, whom he referred to as Élise in his later works. She gathered a circle of writers and artists in her home that included artist and writer Max Jacob and JEAN COCTEAU. The couple eventually decided to marry. Élise knew about Jouhandeau's secret life but seems to have hoped that conjugal life would put an end to his sexual adventures. Their wedding took place in 1929.

For the first few years they were happy enough, until Jouhandeau began to regret his loss of freedom. Divorce was impossible so Jouhandeau continued his escapades and the couple bumbled along as couples do. Jouhandeau drew on their experience for *Monsieur Godineau Married* (1933), MARITAL CHRONICLES (1938), *Scenes from Conjugal Life* (1938), and *The Imposter* (1950). He also wrote *Élise, the Architect* (1951), *The Incredible Day* (1951), *Jaundice* (1956), *Eternal Trial* (1959), *Domestic Menagerie* (1948), and *New Bestiary* (1953), among other novels. Moreover, a number of Jouhandeau's works focus on the character of Élise's mother, such as *The Farm Gone Mad* (1950), *Galande* (1953), and *Madame Apremont* (1954).

Jouhandeau and his wife eventually took in a young girl named Céline as an adopted daughter. When, as an adolescent, she had a child whom she named Marc, they raised him as a sort of foster grandchild. Concerns over Céline and then Marc held the couple together until Élise's death in 1971.

By far the greatest source for Jouhandeau was the collection of journals he kept throughout his life. He published the journal of his life as a teacher in 1957,

as well as 28 volumes of his *Journaliers* between 1961 and 1983.

Torn throughout his life between religion and desire, Jouhandeau explored homosexuality in *On Baseness* (1939), *Chronicle of a Passion* (1944), *Don Juan's Notebooks* (1947), *Elegy of Sensuality* (1951), as well as in his diaries. His varied and contradictory beliefs and experience later led him to explore moral questions in his *Algebra of Moral Values* (1935), *Elements of Ethics* (1955), and *Reflections on Aging and Death* (1956). In the end, Jouhandeau proved to be a moralist in a manner that recalls the writings of André Gide.

JOURNEYMAN JOINER OR COMPANION OF THE TOUR DE FRANCE, THE (LE COMPANION DU TOUR DE FRANCE) GEORGE SAND (1840)

In this novel, Sand reveals her adherence to socialist thought. Pierre Huguenin, a carpenter, belongs to a workers' organization typical of certain 19th-century socialist circles. Chance takes him to work near a noble family. The father of this family, the count de Villepreux, is skeptical, cynical, and depressed but hides his true feelings. One of his daughters, Josephine, is a heartless seductress who torments one of Pierre's friends with her capricious demands. The other daughter, Yseut, is as in love with Pierre as he is with her. Romantic heroes both, each of them seeks an emotional and philosophical ideal (see ROMANTICISM). Unfortunately, the discrepancy in their social status is an obstacle to their love. In the end, Pierre chooses duty to his comrades over love.

Set in 1823, the novel reflects problems resulting from modernization and industrialization. *The Journeyman Joiner* marks a shift in Sand's thinking. In her pastoral novels such as INDIANA, FRANÇOIS THE WAIF, and *The DEVIL'S POOL,* love conquers all obstacles, and reflects Sand's belief that love is the source of both personal and social regeneration. In *The Journeyman Joiner,* Sand is inspired by the socialist, humanitarian principles of her friend Pierre Leroux. The characters of Pierre and his comrades voice Sand's concern with social inequality and injustice and her desire to promote human dignity. This sentimental love story, a trademark of Sand's fiction, is thus placed within a broader context.

Unlike her contemporaries HONORÉ DE BALZAC and ÉMILE ZOLA, however, Sand does not adhere to the principles of REALISM, even as she grapples with contemporary social reality. Sand's IDEALISM lies beneath the surface, echoing themes found in ROUSSEAU. Yseut, in fact, reads Rousseau. Moreover, Pierre is a hero worthy of Jean-Jacques, intelligent and noble in spirit if not in birth. Together Yseut and Pierre are forced to confront the injustice of social institutions that would bar their union.

Sand expresses concern for the man of the people who, despite two revolutions (1789 and 1830), continues to suffer. She thus shares a similar social conscience to her contemporary VICTOR HUGO. With this novel, Sand lays the groundwork for later works focusing on working-class conditions such as *Mr. Antoine's Sin* (1845) and *Black Town* (1860). Most bourgeois readers were not receptive to Sand's promotion of proletarian interests. For them, *The Journeyman Joiner* was a scandalous novel.

FURTHER READING

Crecelius, Kathryn J. *Family Romances: George Sand's Early Novels.* Bloomington: Indiana University Press, 1987.

Glasgow, Janis, ed. *George Sand: Collected Essays.* Troy, N.Y.: Whitston, 1985.

Hofstadter, Dan. *The Love Affair as a Work of Art.* New York: Farrar, Straus and Giroux, 1996.

Naginski, Isabelle Hoog. *George Sand: Writing for her Life.* New Brunswick, N.J.: Rutgers University Press, 1991.

Peebles, Catherine. *The Psyche of Feminism: Sand, Colette, Sarraute.* West Lafayette, Ind.: Purdue University Press, 2003.

Powell, David A. *George Sand.* Boston: Twayne, 1990.

Schor, Naomi. *George Sand and Idealism.* New York: Columbia University Press, 1993.

Vitaglione, Daniel. *George Eliot and George Sand.* New York: Peter Lang, 1993.

Walton, Whitney. "Writing the 1848 Revolution: Politics, Gender and Feminism in the Works of French Women of Letters," *French Historical Studies* 18, no. 4 (Autumn 1994): 1,001–1,024.

JOURNEY TO THE CENTER OF THE EARTH (*VOYAGE AU CENTRE DE LA TERRE*) JULES VERNE (1864)

In this fantastic tale, one of Verne's most popular, Professor Lidenbrock, a German geologist, discovers a 16th-century manuscript written by the Icelandic alchemist Arne Saknüssen, who professed to have discovered the route to the center of the earth. Lidenbrock decides to follow Saknüssen's trail, taking with him his nephew, Axel, and Hans, an Icelandic guide. There could not be two more different personalities than the phlegmatic Hans and the passionate Lidenbrock, and that reveal Verne's ability to portray varied characters.

The explorers enter the earth through the Sneffels crater. The course of their journey is fraught with difficulties; Axel is lost and Professor Lidenbrock fears that they will die of thirst. It is also full of wonders. Together they cross a subterranean sea miraculously illuminated by a strange electrical phenomenon. On the banks they see giant prehistoric plant life and witness a battle between dinosaurs. They experience a wild storm and a shipwreck, discover a fossilized man and a living creature neither man nor monkey. They also discover traces of Arne Saknüssen's earlier passage as in a rusty, engraved dagger. Disaster ensues when, in order to break through an impasse, the explorers use dynamite. When they are thrown out of the Stromboli crater by the power of the blast, their adventure ends.

Journey to the Center of the Earth reflects Verne's fascination with geology and the volcanic activity at the heart of the earth's origins. The reader is aware of Verne's belief in a mysterious life force as he attempts to trace the history of the earth in a transdisciplinary approach that blends myth and science with faith in technological progress, recurring themes in Verne's works. Verne's writing is marked by a deep knowledge of contemporary science and technology. In addition to his novels, Verne wrote an *Illustrated Geography of France and Its Colonies* (1868). Verne's fiction manifests a concern with precise, accurate details.

The concepts of space and time are likewise central to Verne's writings. Verne was fascinated with the relationship between humans and society, space and time. In this journey 120 kilometers beneath the earth's surface, Verne's characters discover a completely different world. As they travel deeper and deeper, they go back in time to prehistoric periods. In consequence, there is a direct relationship between the distance traveled (space) and history (time).

To describe the geological layers leading to the earth's core, Verne relies on contemporary science, much of it theoretical rather than proven as, at that point, geologists had explored only approximately 15 kilometers beneath the earth's surface. Verne's novel has an expressly didactic purpose, to teach geology and geography. The earth serves Verne's purpose as an inexhaustible source of inspiration. The journey reflects, too, the themes of conquest and domination that mark Europe's experience in the 19th century, a period of tremendous change in society, science, and technology. This is the century of the agricultural and scientific revolutions, innovations in transportation, urbanization, medicine, education, and philosophy, the century of Charles Darwin and French philosopher Auguste Comte. Verne's novel not only reflects this varied context but also popularizes recent discoveries for a reading public equally interested in discoveries in fields as diverse as geology, paleontology, mineralogy, aeronautics, and astronomy. Verne subtly interweaves rationalism with fantasy, expressing the view that progress in science will improve the world.

FURTHER READING

Born, Franz. *Jules Verne, the Man Who Invented the Future.* Translated by Juliana Biro. Englewood Cliffs, N.J.: Prentice Hall, 1964.

Butcher, William. *Verne's Journey to the Center of the Self: Space and Time in the "Voyages Extraordinaires."* New York: St. Martin's Press; London: Macmillan, 1990.

Costello, Peter. *Jules Verne: The Inventor of Science Fiction.* London: Hodder and Stoughton, 1978.

Evans, I. O. *Jules Verne and His Work.* Mattituck, N.Y.: Aeonian Press, 1976.

Freedman, Russell. *Jules Verne, Portrait of a Prophet.* New York: Holiday House, 1965.

Lottman, Herbert R. *Jules Verne: An Exploratory Biography.* New York: St. Martin's Press, 1996.

JOURNEY TO THE END OF THE NIGHT (VOYAGE AU BOUT DE LA NUIT) LOUIS FERDINAND CÉLINE (1932)
This novel, begun in 1929 and published in 1932, won the Renaudot Prize. Céline described it as his "one truly mean novel," "Man naked, stripped of everything, even faith in himself." With it, Céline broke away from the subjective approach prevalent in many contemporary novels and returned to REALISM. *Journey to the End of the Night* is also considered one of the first "absurd" novels, an influence on the existentialists (see EXISTENTIALISM).

According to the plot, Ferdinand Bardamu, a medical student wounded in 1914, is traumatized after discovering the horrors of war. As he recovers in Paris, Ferdinand begins to understand that war benefits those who do *not* participate in it. The disdain that leads officers to use their troops as canon fodder reigns everywhere. In an attempt to escape the ravages of war, Ferdinand leaves for Africa, only to discover that the tentacles of war reach everywhere. Ferdinand is disgusted by the colonial system and begins to see the world as divided by class and race, each exploiting or exploited by another. Ill almost to the point of death, Ferdinand sets off for America.

Ferdinand's journey consists of endless nightmares in which he encounters a world of shame, crime, death and violence. Ferdinand's nihilist view of life reflects the crisis in values of the interwar period. Like others of his generation, Céline's experience in the Great War shaped his view of society and the human condition. While some intellectuals turned to the left, others, like Céline, turned to the right. What unites them is the horror of a war that called into question all moral and social values and that led, in turn, to another war of monstrous proportions.

Journey to the End of the Night is an important work in the history of the autobiographical novel. Moreover, Céline's innovative use of language ensures this novel's place in the history of literature as it transformed contemporary literature by its freedom and crude style. The novel is full of the violent and obscene language of the street mixed with medical and philosophical terms. The images of blood, defecation, and vomit in the first part of the novel recall the combat literature of MAURICE BARRÈS and ROMAND DORGELÈS. Céline's powerful and creative use of language depicts life as an object of derision, to the absurdity of which humans may never be able to adapt.

FURTHER READING

Bouchard, Norma. *Céline, Gadda, Beckett: Experimental Writings of the 1930s.* Gainesville: University of Florida Press, 2000.

Buckley, William K., ed. *Critical Essays on Louis Ferdinand Céline*. Boston: G. K. Hall, 1989.

Green, M. J. *Fiction in the Historical Present: French Writers and the Thirties*. Hanover, N.H.: University Press of New England, 1986.

Hewitt, Nicholas. *The Life of Céline: A Critical Biography*. Oxford, Malden, Mass.: Blackwell, 1999.

Klein, Holger, ed. *The First World War in Fiction*. London: Macmillan, 1976.

Knapp, Bettina Liebowitz. *Céline, Man of Hate*. University Tuscaloosa: University of Alabama Press, 1974.

Luce, Stanford, ed. and trans. *Céline and His Critics: Scandals and Paradox*. Saratoga, Calif.: Anma Libri, 1986.

McCarthy, Patrick. *Céline*. New York: Penguin Books, 1977.

Solomon, Philip H. *Understanding Céline*. Colombia: University of South Carolina Press, 1992.

Vitoux, Frédéric. *Céline: A Biography*. Translated by Jesse Browner. New York: Paragon House, 1992.

Wohl, Robert. *The Generation of 1914*. Cambridge, Mass.: Harvard University Press, 1979.

JULIE, OR THE NEW HELOÏSE (LA NOUVELLE HELOISE) JEAN-JACQUES ROUSSEAU (1761)

This tremendously popular EPISTOLARY NOVEL (72 printings were published between 1761 and 1800) describes the passionate love affair of Julie d'Etange and her tutor, Saint-Preux. In the title, *Julie, or The New Héloïse*, every French reader immediately recognized JEAN-JACQUES ROUSSEAU's reference to the 12th-century lovers Abelard and Héloïse. Like Julie, Héloïse was Abelard's pupil. Angered by Abelard's treatment of Héloïse, her uncle sent his servants in the night to castrate Abelard. These two illustrious intellectuals, Abelard and Heloise, ended their days in monastic communities. As their letters bear witness, the link between them survived even the horrors of shame and mutilation. The epistolary novel was a popular genre in the 18th-century. Although Rousseau implicitly suggests in the preface that these letters are fictional, the form lends credence to the truth behind the story of two ill-fated lovers.

Julie is divided into two parts. The first describes how Julie and Saint-Preux fall in love but are forced to part, thwarted by constraints due to the difference in their social status. When a friend and benefactor,

the English nobleman Edward Bomston, tries to argue in favor of their marriage, Julie's father is irate, prohibiting Julie from ever seeing Saint-Preux again. Saint-Preux is inconsolable and near suicide when Edward offers them refuge on his estate. Out of duty to her father, Julie refuses. In the second part, Julie agrees to marry her father's friend Wolmar. Together they create a utopian community in the idyllic countryside where Saint-Preux eventually joins them. Here virtue and duty reign. However, the harmony of this refuge from society's corruption lies only on the surface. As she is dying, Julie confesses that she has never overcome her love for Saint-Preux.

The character of Julie proved inspirational to many 18th-century women. She is the "unheroic heroine" who has experienced passionate love and yet overcomes her desire in the name of duty. Julie's maternal and nurturing role holds the utopian community of Clarens together on an emotional level. Wolmar is the rational theoretician and leader, the community's head; Julie is its heart. Through the character of Julie, Rousseau validates a woman's role within the family and in society. Moreover, despite her undying love for Saint-Preux, Julie is a faithful and dutiful wife. Notwithstanding its tragic end, the character of Julie legitimizes a woman's intuitive and compassionate nature.

If Wolmar is daunting in his control over himself and the other members of the community, Saint-Preux inspires sympathy through his sentimental and passionate attachment to Julie. His character might be described as weak, but his emotions are strong. The reader is touched that two lovers, so evidently made for each other, are not allowed to join in matrimony. Nonetheless, only death parts them.

In the first part of the novel Rousseau gives us a taste of the lyricism that seems to restore life to the stultified neoclassical style of 17th- and early 18th-century French literature. His eulogies in praise of nature presage the romantic movement (see ROMANTICISM), as his image of Saint-Preux, kissing the stones touched by Julie's feet, foreshadows Goethe's epitome of the romantic hero Werther.

The novel abounds with passion, but there is also moral didacticism, particularly in the second part. *Julie, or the New Heloise* is thus representative of the 18th-century sentimental epistolary novel, reminiscent of NEOCLASSICISM in its call to place virtue and duty above passion, and a precursor of romanticism.

Rousseau makes a significant contribution to the Western literary tradition with *Julie, or the New Heloise* as he combines political philosophy with the novel. He tells us that the family must serve as the moral and ethical basis of society. From the beginning there is a struggle between passion and virtue, love and duty. Rousseau's approach to these juxtapositions is ambiguous. There is a value to emotion as much as reason, the byword of the ENLIGHTENMENT; yet, in the end, only by overcoming passion are the moral values necessary to the individual's happiness and the good of society established. In this respect, Rousseau reminds us of the values of classical antiquity.

In his *Discourse on the Origin of Inequality* (1755), Rousseau put forth his basic argument that we are born good but are corrupted by society's bad institutions. Wolmar and Julie attempt to create a world safe from the vice of civilized society at Clarens. In this way, Julie is connected to Rousseau's great pedagogical novel, *ÉMILE*. Both works are intended to outline Rousseau's project to reform the individual, thus making the virtuous person who will inhabit the virtuous society of *The Social Contract*.

FURTHER READING

Cassirer, Ernst. *The Question of Jean-Jacques Rousseau*. Edited, and translated by Peter Gay. Bloomington: Indiana University Press, 1963.

Daniels, Charlotte. *Subverting the Family Romance: Women Writers, Kinship Structures and the Early French Novel*. Lewisburg, Penn.: Bucknell University Press; London: Associated University Presses, 2000.

Kelly, Christopher. "Taking Readers as They Are: Rousseau's Turn From Discourses to Novels," *Eighteenth-Century Studies* 33, no. 1 (1999): 85–101.

Morgenstern, Mira. *Rousseau and the Politics of Ambiguity: Self, Culture and Society*. University Park, PA: Pennsylvania State University Press, 1996.

Riley, Patrick, ed. *The Cambridge Companion to Rousseau*. New York; Cambridge: Cambridge University Press, 2001.

Steinbrügge, Lieselotte. *The Moral Sex: Woman's Nature in the French Enlightenment*. Translated by Pamela E. Selwyn. New York: Oxford University Press, 1995.

Wolff, Larry. "Then I Imagine a Child: The Idea of Childhood and the Philosophy of Memory in the Enlightenment," *Eighteenth-Century Studies* 31, no. 4 (1998): 377–401.

JULIETTE DONATIEN-ALPHONSE-FRANÇOIS, MARQUIS DE SADE (1797)

In contrast to Sade's innocent and virtuous Justine (see JUSTINE), her sister Juliette is a true libertine (see LIBERTINISM). The story of her life consists of endless scenes of infanticide, cannibalism, murder, and lesbianism. Juliette was first corrupted by the mother superior of her convent, who then threw her out when Juliette's family lost their fortune. Juliette sees no alternative but prostitution.

Her first two lovers are powerful men, one of whom roasts virgins for his dinner. Juliette also has a female lover, Clairwil. In a parody of contemporary secret societies, Juliette and her accomplices in the Society of the Friends of Crime engage in theft, rape, and murder. These actions lead not to their ruin, however, but to wealth and happiness. The contrast between Justine's virtue unrewarded and Juliette's experience is a shocking statement on Sade's part. Not only do Juliette and her collaborators engage in deviant behavior, so too do important historical personages such as Catherine II of Russia and Pope Pius VI.

Echoing themes in Sade's other works, *Juliette* promotes the ENLIGHTENMENT concept of individual freedom in the extreme. The materialism of contemporary Enlightenment thinkers like DIDEROT is also pushed to the furthest possible limit. Hedonism becomes Sade's moral law as a result of people's fundamental isolation from one another. In this astonishing work, Sade also serves as a precursor to Sigmund Freud in his exploration of humankind's hidden drives.

FURTHER READING

Barthes, Roland. *Sade, Fourier, Loyola*. Translated by Richard Miller. New York: Farrar, Straus and Giroux, 1976.

Du Plessix Gray, Francine. *At Home with the Marquis de Sade*. New York: Simon and Schuster, 1998.

Fabre, Jean. "Sade et le roman noir." In *Le Marquis de Sade*. Paris: Armand Colin, 1968.

Heine, Maurice. "Le Marquis de Sade et le roman noir." In *Le Marquis de Sade*. Edited by Gilbert Lély. Paris: Gallimard, 1950.

Kehrès, Jean-Marc. "Libertine Anatomies: Figures of Monstrosity in Sade's *Justine, ou les malheurs de la vertu*," *Eighteenth-Century Life* 21, no. 2 (1997): 100–113.

Schaffer, Neil. *The Marquis de Sade: A Life*. New York: Knopf, 1999.

Weber, Caroline. "The Sexist Sublime in Sade and Lyotard," *Philosophy and Literature* 26, no. 2 (2002): 397–404.

JULY MONARCHY   Pressure on the Bourbon monarchy rose in 1827 due to economic crisis and as Liberals who supported Republican ideals (see LIBERALISM) increased their hold on power in elections held that year. In response, in 1829 Charles X brought a reactionary, prince Jules de Polignac, into his government. Opposition to his reign was further fueled by romantics (see ROMANTICISM) such as VICTOR HUGO. Hugo, in fact, called romanticism "liberalism in literature."

Charles X's attempt to carry out a coup d'état on July 26, 1830, by dissolving the Chamber of Deputies and disenfranchising a majority of voters, led to riots, demonstrations, and, ultimately, revolution. He was forced to abdicate on August 2, leaving the throne to his grandson, whom liberals rejected in favor of Louis-Philippe.

The Revolution of 1830 was thus a victory for French liberals. The subsequent regime is known as the July Monarchy, as well as the "bourgeois monarchy," for its promotion of the wealthy middle class that benefited from industrialization. The regime nonetheless met with opposition from workers who called for universal manhood suffrage. They were suppressed by government troops, and censorship restrictions were put in place as well as restrictions on the right to form organizations.

The two 19th-century writers who most successfully evoked the period of the July Monarchy are HONORÉ DE BALZAC in his series of novels *The HUMAN COMEDY* and GUSTAVE FLAUBERT in *SENTIMENTAL EDUCATION*.

JUSTINE, OR THE MISFORTUNES OF VIRTUE (JUSTINE, OU LES MALHEURS DE LA VERTU) DONATIEN-ALPHONSE-FRANÇOIS, MARQUIS DE SADE **(1791)** *Justine, or the Misfortunes of Virtue* is an expanded version of an earlier text Sade wrote in 1787. It is continued in the even more shocking *The New Justine* (1797). The theme is the pleasure of evil. Drawing on ENLIGHTENMENT thought, Sade argues that nature, the supreme authority, justifies cruelty. "Men will never understand that there is no sort of taste, however bizarre or criminal, that does not derive from the organization that we have received from nature."

Justine is a poor but beautiful and virtuous orphan cast out on her own at the age of 12. She is as blond and innocent as her sister Juliette is dark and vicious. In contrast to centuries-long moral traditions, however, Juliette is rewarded with wealth and happiness while Justine suffers endlessly.

In this first-person narrative, the trusting Justine recounts episode after episode in which she is abused by cold libertines seeking their own pleasure (see LIBERTINISM). Through rape, blood, torture, and tears, her tormentors remain unmoved. At the same time, there is tremendous irony in Sade's subtle play of language. Justine's abusers describe shockingly erotic scenes in the most polite and formal language possible. Justine is only warned of the danger of her situation when her opponents (or supposed protector's) language changes from the formal to the informal. Informality and increasing vulgarity signal coming brutality.

The libertines Justine meets have physical abnormalities that contribute to their ferocious sexual drive. Military and animal metaphors abound in the descriptions of orgies. Moreover, there is a juxtaposition of the profane and sacred through metaphors for sexual organs: military and animal for male organs, religious for female. Despite all the tortures that she undergoes, Justine retains her unshakable faith in virtue.

There are certain parallels between Justine and the popular 18th-century *roman noir* or Gothic novel. The typical Gothic novel, however, attempts to convey the exceptional nature of the heroine and her sufferings. This is decidedly not the case with Justine. Her tormentors repeatedly remind her that she is always replaceable. Sade's cold rationalism and systematic cruelty challenge the notion that virtue is rewarded.

During the Enlightenment, the writers of the ENCYCLOPEDIA sought to produce a compendium of all human knowledge. Sade expands the practice in Justine to include knowledge of the dark side of human nature. M. de Corville chides Justine for not wanting to tell all the wretched details of her experience, saying that such knowledge reveals the truth of the human heart. In the end, Justine's sister Juliette converts to a life of virtue and the two sisters intend to live together but Justine is struck by lightening. The fate of Justine, lifeless and mutilated, is not a just one, in contrast to the disfigurement undergone by LACLOS'S Marquise de Merteuil IN *DANGEROUS LIAISONS.*

Sade draws, too, on a literary tradition running from Madame de LAFAYETTE to Madame de TENCIN that explores pain and suffering. In contrast to their works, the cold rationalism of Sade's libertines is extraordinary. Torrents of blood, tears, and semen flow in fortresses that serve a practical, not a symbolic purpose. The libertine seeks only to pursue his or her own pleasure undisturbed by the outside world. Sade's libertines exhibit a remarkable sense of detachment, never guilt or remorse.

FURTHER READING

Barthes, Roland. *Sade, Fourier, Loyola.* Translated by Richard Miller. New York: Farrar, Straus and Giroux, 1976.

Du Plessix Gray, Francine. *At Home with the Marquis de Sade.* New York: Simon and Schuster, 1998.

Kehrès, Jean-Marc. "Libertine Anatomies: Figures of Monstrosity in Sade's *Justine, ou les malheurs de la vertu," Eighteenth-Century Life* 21, no. 2 (1997): 100–113.

Schaffer, Neil. *The Marquis de Sade: A Life.* New York: Knopf, 1999.

Weber, Caroline. "The Sexist Sublime in Sade and Lyotard," *Philosophy and Literature* 26, no. 2 (2002): 397–404.

KAMOURASKA Anne Hébert (1970)

KAMOURASKA Anne Hébert (1970)   The narrative of this novel takes place during a single night, as Elisabeth Aulnières watches over her dying husband, Jerome Rolland, whom she married 18 years before and whom she bore eight children. As she waits in the quiet, death-filled room, her mind wanders over her past life. Jerome is Elisabeth's second husband. Twenty years earlier she was married to Antoine Tassy, seigneur of Kamouraska, a debauched brute. At the time, driven by unhappiness, Elisabeth turns to Doctor Georges Nelson, with whom she has an affair. When she becomes pregnant by her lover, Elisabeth reconciles with her husband for appearances' sake.

Eventually, Elisabeth and Georges decide to murder Antoine. They arrange for Aurilie Caron to seduce and then poison him. But their plan fails. Georges then undertakes the 200-mile journey to Kamouraska and kills Antoine himself. Afterward, he leaves Elisabeth, who is suspected of her husband's murder but acquitted of all charges in a trial. Elisabeth then escapes into a dull, conventional life by marrying Jerome. During the night of waiting, her past returns in a hallucinatory stream. Hébert's abrupt and brusque style of writing only adds to the sense of unreality.

Some scholars have seen a relation to colonialism in this novel. In 1840, Elizabeth La Corriveau was tried for the murder of her husband by the queen's court and hung in an iron cage. Her death thus became associated in the popular mind with the British conquest of Quebec. Hébert's character hearkens back to this episode in Canadian history passed down in oral tradition. Mostly, the tragic tale reflects Hébert's startling ability to evoke the unforeseen consequences of passion and fate on individual destiny.

FURTHER READING

Green, Mary Jean. "Dismantling the Colonizing Text: Anne Hébert's *Kamouraska* and Assia Djebar's *L'Amour, la fantasia*," *French Review* 66, no. 6 (May 1993): 959–966.

———. "The Witch and the Princess: The Feminine Fantastic in the Fiction of Anne Hébert," *American Review of Canadian Studies* 15, no. 2 (Summer 1985): 137–146.

Knight, Kelton W. *Anne Hébert: In Search of the First Garden.* New York: P. Lang, 1998.

Pallister, Janis L. *The Art and Genius of Anne Hébert: Essays on Her Works: Night and the Day Are One.* Madison, N.J.: Fairleigh Dickinson University Press, 2001.

Paterson, Janet M. "Anne Hébert and the Discourse of the Unreal," *Yale French Studies,* no. 65, The Language of Difference: Writing in Quebec(ois) (1983): 172–186.

Russell, Delbert. *Anne Hébert.* Boston: Twayne, 1983.

KINDNESS WEEK (UNE SEMAINE DE BONTÉ) Max Ernst (1934)

KINDNESS WEEK (UNE SEMAINE DE BONTÉ) Max Ernst (1934)   Also a film directed by Jean Desvilles, *Kindness Week* is a surrealist novel (see SURREALISM) composed of 182 collages divided into segments, each focusing on a different day of the week. Ernst was particularly noted for his collages. As he once put it, "When one brings two distant realities together on an apparently antipathetic plane (that which in simple language is called 'collage'), an exchange of energy transpires, provoked by this very meeting."

Most of Ernst's writings appeared in surrealist literary reviews. As is the case with *Kindness Week,* he combines the visual and the verbal in a collage form that we have come to associate with the surrealist movement. Other examples are found in the works of ANDRÉ BRETON and LOUIS ARAGON. The reader is also an observer as he or she contemplates the juxtaposition of text and image. Moreover, with an approach that both constructs and deconstructs our normal understanding of the world, Ernst's work possesses a new and obscure language that forces the reader to *read* differently.

FURTHER READING
Hopkins, David. "Hermetic and Philosophical Themes in Max Ernst's 'Vox Angelica' and Related Works," *Burlington Magazine* 134, no. 1076 (November 1992): 716–723.

Hubert, Renée Riese. "Max Ernst: The Displacement of the Visual and the Verbal," *New Literary History* 15, no. 3, Image/Imago/Imagination (Spring 1984): 575–606.

———. "The Fabulous Fiction of Two Surrealist Artists: Giogio de Chirico and Max Ernst," *New Literary History* 4, no. 1 (Autumn 1972): 151–166.

Spies, Werner. *Max Ernst Collages: The Invention of the Surrealist Universe.* Translated by John William Gabriel. New York: Abrams, 1991.

KING LAZARUS (LE ROI MIRACULÉ)
MONGO BETI (1958)   Set in 1948, this novel depicts a world that seems to be falling apart in the years following World War II but the Essazam tribe can focus on nothing but the fact that their king, Essomba Mendouga, has converted to Christianity after being miraculously cured of an illness that represents the collapse of their society. He had been the strongest voice and symbol of tradition, and now his conversion threatens the tribe, whose elders have become but a shadow of their former selves. Theirs is a last-gasp effort to save a dying civilization.

The two central figures, Father Le Guen, the missionary priest, and Essomba Mendouga, the tribal chief with 100 wives, stand in stark contrast each other and yet together represent the identity of colonial Africa. Looking back at a long history in which this tribe lived and struggled, free from any outside influence, Beti condemns the Western subversion of traditional African society. This is the fourth novel in a series by Beti focusing on the problem of colonialism that includes *Cruel City* (1954), *Poor Christ of Bomba* (1956), and *Mission Accomplished* (1957). These early works evoke the confusion that derives from the movement away from traditional African culture associated with colonialism. Echoing RENÉ MARAN's *BATOUALA,* Beti explores the problem of cultural conflict that ultimately leads to the demise of African civilization. At the same time, Beti criticizes aspects of African culture as well, particularly its patriarchal system and the oppression of women.

FURTHER READING
Arnold, Stephen H. *Critical Perspectives on Mongo Beti.* Boulder, Colo.: Lynne Rienner, 1998.

Dramé, Kandioura. *The Novel as Transformation of Myth: A Study of the Novels of Mongo Beti and Ngugi wa Thiong'o.* Syracuse, N.Y.: Maxwell School of Citizenship and Public Affairs, Syracuse University, 1990.

John, Elerius Edet. *Creative Responses of Mongo Beti and Ferdinand Oyono to Historical Realities.* Lagos, Nigeria: Paico, 1986.

Priebe, Richard K. "Critical Perspectives on Mongo Beti," *African Studies Review* 42, no. 3 (December 1999): 196–198.

KISS OF THE LEPER, THE (LE BAISER AU LÉPREUX) FRANÇOIS MAURIAC (1922)
Jean Péloueyre is rich but unattractive. Under the influence of their priest, his family marries him off to Noémie, but the marriage is a failure. Noémie tries to be submissive but is only filled with disgust for her husband, and Jean sadly realizes that for her, his touch is like the leper's kiss. When Noémie is tempted by her passion for a young doctor, she tries to turn back to her husband but finds she can no longer tolerate him. Jean then leaves for Paris, where he cares for a victim of tuberculosis, catches the illness, and dies.

Having read German philosopher Friedrich Nietzsche, Jean comes to the conclusion that he is a slave, not a master. He is in a sense a martyr. By his contact with the tubercular patient, Jean ensures his own death and Noémie's liberation. Mauriac characteristically evokes the landscape around Bordeaux that he loved, a landscape that gives comfort to the dying Jean.

In the end, Noémie abandons all hope of love to care for her father-in-law after Jean's death. Perhaps Jean's sacrifice has inspired Noémie in her widowhood. Or perhaps she only plays the part of a saintly widow, revealing Mauriac's concern over religious hypocrisy. The blend of sensuality and mysticism in this work is typical of Mauriac, as is his critique of bourgeois society. Moreover, the theme of human isolation is a recurring one in Mauriac's novels.

FURTHER READING

Bessent, Edna. "Solitude in the Novels of François Mauriac," *French Review* 8, no. 2 (December 1934): 129–134.

Garaudy, Roger. *Literature of the Graveyard: Jean-Paul Sartre, François Mauriac, André Malraux, Arthur Koestler.* Translated by Joseph M. Bernstein. New York: International Publishers, 1948.

Penn, Dorothy. "Three French Writers of Contemporary Catholic Realism: The Inner Consciousness Studied by Georges Bernanos, Henri Ghéon, and François Mauriac," *French Review* 12, no. 2 (December 1938): 128–137.

Speaight, Robert. *François Mauriac: A Study of the Writer and the Man.* London: Chatto and Windus, 1976.

KLOSSOWSKI, PIERRE (1905–2001)

Born in Paris to a family of Polish origin, Klossowski grew up in a highly artistic environment. His father was an art historian and painter, his mother a student of the painter Pierre Bonnard, while his brother was the well-known painter Balthus. Klossowski, too, was also at first interested in drawing.

As of 1914, Klossowski traveled with his parents to Germany, Switzerland, and Italy. He was intellectually drawn both to the traditions of classical antiquity and to German philosophy. This combination came to influence all of Klossowski's subsequent works.

In 1923, Klossowski returned to Paris, where he associated with the Austrian poet Rainer Maria Rilke and ANDRÉ GIDE among others, and discovered the writings of the marquis de SADE as well as psychoanalysis. Still fascinated with German philosophy, Klossowski began reading the works of Friedrich Nietzsche and Søren Kierkegaard. Klossowski also collaborated on a translation of the German Romantic poet Friedrich Hölderlin. In 1934, Klossowski became friends with GEORGES BATAILLE, with whom

he participated in the "College of Sociology" and the journal *Acéphale*.

Equally significant was the next stage in Klossowski's development, an intense exploration of religion in the years 1939–43, and one might just as easily classify him a theologian as a novelist. Klossowski studied theology and entered the Dominican order as a novitiate. He subsequently converted to Lutheranism before returning once more to Catholicism. Klossowski's religious passage provided the material for *Deferred Vocation* (*Vocation suspendue*), published in 1950. In this work of autobiographical fiction, Jerome, a seminarian and the principal character of the novel, vacillates between two very different strains of Catholicism, devotion and inquisition. In the end, a conspiracy leads to his being defrocked. In this work, Klossowski reflects on the nature of religious calling as well as on the concept of grace.

Klossowski's most significant work is his trilogy published in 1965 under the title *The LAWS OF HOSPITALITY*, which includes *Roberte ce soir* (1954), *The Revocation of the Edict of Nantes* (1959), and *Souffleur* (1960). Fascinated with the writings of de SADE and under the influence of Bataille, Klossowski began to write a series of works in which he explored the notion of evil. Together these works reflect on the relationship between body and soul, and on salvation. A number of his ideas find their roots in the writings of the Roman orator Tertullus and in St. Augustine. Despite the fact that discussions between characters may border on the heretical, theological questions are at the heart of this trilogy as much as Klossowski's other works. The style and some of the themes draw from the writings of Sade, especially *Philosophy in the Bedroom,* as Klossowski blends digressions, descriptions, and fragments of diaries in a manner that is essentially baroque. On a deeper level, Klossowski seems to define literature as a verbal substitution for both carnal and spiritual reality.

The BAPHOMET, Klossowski's last significant work of fiction, draws in part from Nietzsche's conception of time and history. Klossowski also produced a series of essays that include *Diana at Her Bath* (1956), *A Deadly Desire* (1963), *Nietzsche and the Vicious Circle* (1969), *Living Money* (1970), and *Resemblance* (1985). *Diana* at Her Bath draws from the classical myth in which the hunter Acteon, who has seen Diana bathing, is transformed into a stag that is then devoured by his own herd. In Klossowski's mind, however, this myth becomes the means to explore the centrality of metamorphosis in Western thought. Toward the end of his career, Klossowski returned to the visual arts to focus almost exclusively on drawing.

FURTHER READING

Gallop, Jane. *Intersections: A Reading of Sade with Bataille, Blanchot and Klossowski.* Lincoln: University of Nebraska Press, 1981.

Hill, Leslie. *Bataille, Klossowski, Blanchot: Writing at the Limit.* Oxford, New York: Oxford University Press, 2001.

KNIGHT OF THE CART (LANCELOT) CHRÉTIEN DE TROYES (12TH CENTURY)

The Knight of the Cart is the first tale to come down to us depicting the adulterous and passionate love between Lancelot and Guinevere. In the prologue, Chrétien reveals that this ROMANCE was inspired by countess Marie de Champagne and her court. It reflects the COURTLY LOVE ideal that flourished under her patronage as the lovers explore their feelings in a highly stylized language. Scholars continue to debate whether courtly love is a reflection of social practice or an idealization. Chrétien's Lancelot makes a religion of courtly love, even genuflecting as he leaves Guinevere's bed.

Lancelot differs from Chrétien's other romances, which seem to promote courtly love *within* marriage. There is also some evidence of ironic humor that calls into question Lancelot's character, evident in the scene where he duels somewhat ridiculously behind his back in order to keep his eyes on Guinevere.

This romance and *The KNIGHT WITH THE LION (YVAIN)* were probably written at the same time, as there are intertextual references between the two stories. The underlying theme of Lancelot's struggle to save and be united with Guinevere as her lover is based on *contrapasso,* whereby the punishment must fit the crime. Because Lancelot hesitates at the beginning of the tale to accept a ride in a cart, signifying criminality and shame, he must later make up for this transgression by showing willingness to fulfill his lady's commands instantly. Along with *The STORY OF THE GRAIL (PERCEVAL),*

this romance was left unfinished by Chrétien and was completed by an otherwise unknown clerc named Godefroy de Lagny. HÉLISENNE DE CRENNE's *The TORMENTS OF LOVE* draws, for example, from the tradition of the medieval romance such as we find in the works of Chrétien de Troyes.

FURTHER READING

Frappier, Jean. *Chrétien de Troyes: The Man and His Work.* Translated by Robert J. Cormier. Athens: Ohio University Press, 1982.

Lacy, Norris. *The Craft of Chrétien de Troyes: An Essay on Narrative Art.* Leiden, Netherlands: Brill, 1980.

Troyes, Chrétien de. *Arthurian Romances.* Translated by William W. Kibler. London: Penguin, 1991.

KNIGHT WITH THE LION (YVAIN) CHRÉTIEN DE TROYES (12TH CENTURY)

Some scholars consider *The Knight with the Lion* to be Chrétien's most perfect ROMANCE. Like *EREC AND ENIDE,* the story depicts the struggle between love and valor. Yet whereas Erec takes his bride with him on his quest, Yvain abandons his love to prove his valor in the tournaments, failing to return to her at the promised time. Accompanied by a lion whom he saved from a fire-breathing dragon, Yvain must struggle to redefine himself by becoming the ultimate defender of ladies in need. This romance in particular manifests the elements of magic and fantasy opposed by "realists" such as JEAN RENART.

FURTHER READING

Frappier, Jean. *Chrétien de Troyes: The Man and His Work,* Translated by Robert J. Cormier. Athens: Ohio University Press, 1982.

Lacy, Norris. *The Craft of Chrétien de Troyes: An Essay on Narrative Art.* Leiden, Netherlands: Brill, 1980.

Leupin, Alexandre. *Le Graal et la Littérature.* Lausanne, Switzerland: L'Age d'Homme, 1982.

Troyes, Chrétien de. *Arthurian Romances.* Translated by William W. Kibler. London: Penguin, 1991.

KOUROUMA, AHMADOU (1927–2003)

Born in the Ivory Coast, Kourouma was sent at the age of seven to live with a maternal uncle, according to tradition. He was later sent to high school in the Sudan but was expelled for political activities. At that point, he was forcibly conscripted into the French colonial army and fought in Indochina. When he had completed his military service, Kourouma continued his studies in Paris and Lyon, ultimately becoming a lawyer. He returned to the Ivory Coast to practice law until he was exiled for political reasons. Arrested, imprisoned, and released, Kourouma subsequently spent time in Algeria, Cameroon, and Togo.

Kourouma's greatest novel, SUNS OF INDEPENDENCE, was first published in Montreal in 1968 then in Paris in 1970. A highly significant work in the history of the African novel, *Suns of Independence* offers a moving critique of both pre- and postcolonial African society. Through the character of Fama, a disinherited prince, and his wife, Salimata, Kourouma unveils the political, economic, and social turmoil associated with the rise of an independent fictional *"République des Ébenes."* The break with the past has led to the fall of the traditional elite and the parallel rise of a new, corrupt, political order that leads Fama to despair. Twenty years later, Kourouma produced a second novel, *Monnew,* an equally powerful work that evokes the colonial period.

Kourouma is highly critical of contemporary African politics and society, revealing the hypocrisy of government leaders who speak about progress and development yet whose actions reflect a backward, at times superstitious mentality. Kourouma seems particularly concerned with the lack of moral and spiritual values of this new society that marks so clearly the death of old Africa. At the same time, Kourouma evokes the old ways of thinking about the intimate connection between humans and nature, spirits and gods, in rich, beautiful language. One of the most striking elements in Kourouma's writing is his blending of French with native Malinke idioms and expressions.

Kourouma makes clear that history has resulted in a sharp divide between two worlds and two cultures. Nonetheless, he does not hearken back to the past. Kourouma is equally balanced in his evocation of traditional African society, whose hierarchy was neither more nor less rational than that which existed in the early years of independence.

FURTHER READING

Schikora, Rosemary G. "Narrative Voice in Kourouma's *Les Soleils des Independences,"* *French Review* 55, no. 6, Literature and Civilization of Black Francophone Africa (May 1982): 811–817.

Sellin, Eric. *"Les Soleils des Independences."* Review Article, *French Review* 44, no. 3 (February 1971): 641–642.

L

LA BÊTE HUMAINE ÉMILE ZOLA (1890)

First published in serial form in the winter of 1889–90 (see ROMAN FEUILLETON), this novel is the 17th in Zola's ROUGON-MACQUART series. *La Bête Humaine* tells the story of Jacques Lantier, the son of Gervaise Macquart (see *L'ASSOMMOIR*) and brother of Claude (*The BELLY OF PARIS, MASTERPIECE*), Étienne (*GERMINAL*), and *NANA*.

Jacques is a train mechanic who witnesses a murder. He suspects Roubaud, the assistant station master in Le Havre, and his wife, Séverine. Séverine subsequently seduces Jacques, who is fascinated by her. The very fact that she has committed a violent crime appeals to him, as Jacques is himself tormented by murderous fantasies, a family trait that is a central theme to Zola's collected works. In accordance with naturalist principles (see NATURALISM), Zola traces the effect of heredity and environment on the individual. Some critics were shocked by the novel's violence, while others, such as ANATOLE FRANCE, praised it. Characters in the novel reflect humanity's basest instincts: sexual deviancy, child abuse, murder, and corruption.

In a moment of crisis, Séverine describes to Jacques the murder that she and Roubaud committed. Jacques, overcome, kills Séverine. Rather than feeling remorse, Séverine's murder is a catharsis for him; Jacques finally experiences a sense of calm. Reflecting on the murder, he thinks to himself, "Did it all go back so far, to the evil which women had perpetrated upon his sex, to the sense of grievance accumulated from male to male ever since that betrayal in the depths of some cave?"

The first murder in the novel is based on a real case that occurred in 1860 when a judge was murdered in the first-class carriage of a train. Other murders in the novel are likewise based on fact. Zola was particularly impressed by the case of English serial murderer Jack the Ripper (1888), whose murderous character can be compared to Jacques Lantier. Anticipating Freud in *Totem and Taboo* (1913), moreover, Zola links sexual desire with the death impulse that lies at the heart of human society. Jacques is marked by a hereditary impulse to murder. He wants to conquer woman and to destroy her.

At the time, atavism was a subject of debate among criminologists. Zola, too, manifests a fascination with the notion that our behavior may have primitive origins as he explores the conflict between atavistic instinct and reason. Victim of some internal, uncontrollable drive, "A person kills only from an impulse that springs from his blood and sinews, from the vestiges of ancient struggles, from the need to live and the joy of being strong."

At the end of the novel, Jacques is caught with his assistant's wife. On a speeding locomotive, Jacques and this man are locked in a struggle to the death. As the two fall beneath the train, gripping each other to the violent end, the train hurtles forward, driverless, full of drunken, singing solders leaving for the front, a blind beast plunging forward toward catastrophe.

The train is an overwhelming presence in the novel, much as Les Halles, the central marketplace in Paris, is in *The Belly of Paris,* the still in *L'Assommoir,* the mine in *Germinal,* or the stock exchange in MONEY. The first passenger train service in France began in 1837. Society greeted the introduction of this new technology with both admiration and trepidation. While the rise of the railroad reflects technological progress, as "the human beast," it also represents regression.

The train is both witness and agent to events, active and passive, anthropomorphized. The locomotive is female. The railroad is linked to industrialization and serves as a theme in a number of contemporary works, literary and otherwise. Zola's descriptions parallel Monet's painting of Paris's Saint-Lazare railroad station and JORIS-KARL HUYSMANS's depictions of Montparnasse.

FURTHER READING

Bell, David. *Real Time: Accelerating Narrative from Balzac to Zola.* Urbana: University of Illinois Press, 2004.

Berg, William J., and Laurey K. Martin. *Émile Zola Revisited.* New York: Twayne; Toronto: Maxwell Macmillan Canada; New York: Maxwell Macmillan International, 1992.

Bloom, Harold, ed. *Émile Zola.* Philadelphia: Chelsea House, 2004.

Bowlby, Rachel. *Just Looking: Consumer Culture in Dreiser, Gissing and Zola.* New York: Methuen, 1985.

Brown, Frederick. *Zola: A Life.* Baltimore: Johns Hopkins University Press, 1996.

Chessid, Ilona. *Thresholds of Desire: Authority and Transgression in the Rougon-Macquart.* New York: P. Lang, 1993.

Gallois, William. *Zola: The History of Capitalism.* Oxford, New York: P. Lang, 2000.

Lethbridge, Robert, and Terry Keefe, eds. *Zola and the Craft of Fiction.* Leicester, England; New York: Leicester University Press, 1990.

Lukács, Georg. *Studies in European Realism.* Translated by Edith Bone. New York: Grosset and Dunlop, 1964.

Petrey, Sandy. *Realism and Revolution: Balzac, Stendhal, Zola and the Performance of History.* Ithaca, N.Y.: Cornell University Press, 1988.

LA CALPRENÈDE, GAULTIER DE COSTE, SEIGNEUR DE (1609?–1663)

The playwright and novelist La Calprenède was born in the Dordogne region of France and studied in Toulouse. From there he went to Paris, where he entered a guards' regiment and in 1650 he became gentleman-in-ordinary to the royal household. In 1663, La Calprenède died rather ignominiously from a fall from his horse.

La Calprenède wrote long, heroic romances, the most famous of which are *Cassandra* (10 volumes, 1642–45) and *Cleopatra* (12 volumes, 1647–58). La Calprenède's lengthy and complex works of morality and sentiment contributed to the establishment of the genre of historical romance. Fairly inaccessible to the modern reader, they were popular into the 18th century. His historical settings drew from earlier periods such as the fall of the Macedonian and Roman Empires and the foundation of the French monarchy. Despite the setting, many of the novels' characters were recognizable as people the author knew from Parisian salons. This element of realism was also appealing to his audience.

La Calprenède wrote a number of other works as well, such as *Faramond* (1661) and *The Tales or Diversions of Princess Alcidiane* (1661). He also wrote plays, none of which was as successful as his novels. The best of his drama is *The Count of Essex,* performed in 1638, from which the great playwright Corneille drew his tragedy of the same name.

FURTHER READING

Hill, Herbert. *La Calprenède's Romances and the Restoration Drama.* Reno: University of Nevada Press, 1910–1911.

Pitou, Spire. *Calprenède's Faramond: A Study of the Sources, Structure, and Reputation of the Novel.* Baltimore: Johns Hopkins University Press; London: H. Milford, Oxford University Press, 1938.

LACLOS, PIERRE-AMBROISE CHODERLOS DE (1741–1803)

Choderlos de Laclos was born to a recently ennobled family of bourgeois origin. He chose a military career but suffered initially from class prejudice as the military hierarchy was traditionally the domain of the old nobility of the sword. On the side, Laclos wrote a variety of works: letters, poems, literary criticism, libertine stories, an essay in praise of Marshall Vauban that got him into trouble with the military establishment, and essays on the condition of women. But his greatest work is the EPISTOLARY NOVEL *DANGEROUS LIAISONS,* in which he reached the height of that genre so popular in the 18th century. This novel depicts the dissolute morals of the aristocracy.

Laclos was engaged politically during the French Revolution. He first supported revolutionary leader Philippe-Égalité and later the radical Jacobins, who at one point imprisoned him. Laclos very nearly fell under the blade of the guillotine but survived. A great admirer of Napoleon Bonaparte, Laclos resumed his military career at the age of 59 and died of dysentery in the siege of Taranto, Italy.

Laclos seduced and later married Marie-Soûlange Duperré. In contrast to the cynical depiction of upper-class marriages found in *Dangerous Liaisons,* correspondence reveals that he was an affectionate and attentive husband. He may even be described as a feminist. Inspired by JEAN-JACQUES ROUSSEAU's *Discourse on the Origins of Inequality,* Laclos argued that society had enslaved women.

As an author, Laclos needs to be considered in both his literary and historical contexts. His active participation in the turbulent years of revolution and under Napoleon marked his opinions as they are revealed in his writings. While the majority of his works are not generally remarkable, he did produce one of the greatest masterpieces of the 18th-century literary tradition. In *Dangerous Liaisions,* Laclos manifests his critical view of OLD REGIME society and its morals or lack thereof. In its complexity and subtle weaving of the characters' voices, he created a work that may arguably be designated as the epitome of the epistolary novel genre.

FURTHER READING

Altman, Janet G. *Epistolarity: Approaches to a Form.* Columbus: Ohio State University Press, 1982.

Becker-Theye, Betty. *The Seducer as MythicFigure in Richardson, Laclos and Kierkegaard.* New York: Garland, 1988.

Brooks, Peter. *The Novel of Worldliness.* Princeton, N.J.: Princeton University Press, 1969.

Rosbottom, Ronald C. *Choderlos de Laclos.* Boston: Twayne Publishers, 1978.

Roulston, Christine. *Virtue, Gender and the Authentic Self in Eighteenth-Century Fiction: Richardson, Rousseau, and Laclos.* Gainesville: University of Florida Press, 1998.

Sol, Antoinette Marie. *Textual Promiscuities: Eighteenth-Century Critical Rewriting.* Lewisburg, Pa.: Bucknell University Press, 2002.

Thelander, Dorothy R. *Laclos and the Epistolary Novel.* Geneva: Droz, 1963.

LADIES' PARADISE, THE (AU BONHEUR DES DAMES) ÉMILE ZOLA (1883)

Octave Mouret is blessed with a good head for business. From his first wife's small Parisian boutique he develops an enormously successful department store, The Ladies' Paradise. His purpose is to arouse desire, his "sole passion was the conquest of Woman. He wanted her to be queen in his shop; he had built this temple for her in order to hold her at his mercy. His tactics were to intoxicate her with amorous attentions, to trade on her desires."

The context for the novel is contemporary urban planning. Under Napoleon III, Baron Haussmann (Baron Hartmann in the novel) undertook a series of redevelopment projects in the 1850s aimed at modernizing the city of Paris. In the novel, Mouret takes advantage of new modes of transportation and expanding markets associated with the Industrial Revolution generally and its impact on the Parisian economy.

Mouret manifests the stereotypical capitalist's view of workers as expendable and exploitable until he falls in love with one of his own employees, the modest and virtuous Denise, a protofeminist who defends workers and women from a threatening patriarchal order. She is the one woman in this novel who refuses to become a commodity. Hinting again at socioeconomic change initiated by the Industrial Revolution, the store is compared to a machine. "Denise felt that she was watching a machine working at high pressure; its dynamism seeming to reach to the display windows themselves." She ultimately persuades Mouret that improving working conditions will not lower profits. At the end of the novel, after overcoming numerous obstacles, the couple marries.

True to his naturalist program (see NATURALISM), in this 11th volume in the ROUGON-MACQUART series, Zola was motivated by his desire to explore and reveal all aspects of Second Empire society. He focuses here on the great 19th-century Parisian department stores. The Ladies Paradise is modeled on Le Bon Marché, the first Parisian department store and, until the 20th century, the largest in the world. Zola was interested in their structure, organization, and connection to the banking industry. He was fascinated by the rise of modern advertising, iron-and-glass architecture, and their power to change

Parisian commerce. Moreover, the department store is depicted as a public space for women that defines the bourgeois image of female propriety and taste.

The Ladies Paradise offers a picture of the socioeconomic transition associated with the rise of 19th-century bourgeois consumer society. At the same time, it is a story in which love triumphs while, perhaps surprisingly, simultaneously promoting the dominant economic system. Even as Zola depicts with genuine admiration the rise of these enormous business ventures, he simultaneously depicts the fall of small, family-run boutiques, incapable of competing with enterprises like The Ladies Paradise, which employ scores of workers and can buy in bulk. In the end, Mouret's hard heart is softened by a woman who serves as a balance between idealism and pragmatism. Zola wanted his novel to be "a poem of modern activity," "to express the century." In a period marked by pessimism, Zola offered a romantic if material solution to life's struggles.

FURTHER READING

Felski, Rita. *The Gender of Modernity.* Cambridge, Mass.: Harvard University Press, 1995.

Thompson, Hannah, ed. *New Approaches to Zola. Selected Papers from the 2002 Cambridge Centenary Colloquium.* London: Émile Zola Society, 2003.

LAFAYETTE, MARIE-MADELEINE PIOCHE DE LA VERGNE, MADAME DE
(1634–1693) This famous woman author is noted for having written the first modern psychological novel, *The PRINCESS OF CLÈVES* (1678). Born in Paris to a family of minor nobility, Madame de Lafayette had a distinguished career. When her father died in 1649, her mother remarried the uncle of the celebrated letter writer Madame de Sévigné. As a result of this connection, the two women became friends. In 1651 Madame de Lafayette was named *demoiselle d'honneur* to queen of France, Anne of Austria. Her situation at court put her in a position to marry, in 1655, a man 20 years her elder, Count François de Lafayette, who was from a noble family of significantly higher status than her own. By 1670, Madame de Lafayette was spending much less time at court, although her experience there provided much of the material for her writing. In Paris

she held a salon frequented by men and women of culture such as her great friend the essayist François La Rochefoucauld. Although she wrote short stories and novels, she did not put her name to them, as she felt it inappropriate for a woman of her rank. She even denied having written *The Princess of Clèves,* although she participated in the literary debate it spawned. Toward the end of her life she played a diplomatic role to the court of Savoy. Her historical novels, *The Princess of Montpensier* and *The Princess of Clèves,* by far her most renowned work, share themes central to Madame de Lafayette's thought: appearance versus reality, the relationships between love and pain and love and marriage, the role of women in society, the conflict between public and private life particularly for women, political factions, and, most important, the problem of virtue.

FURTHER READING

Danahy, Michael. *Feminization of the Novel.* Gainesville: University of Florida Press, 1991.

DeJean Joan. *Libertine Strategies: Freedom and the Novel in Seventeenth-Century France.* Columbus: Ohio State University Press, 1981.

Green, Anne. *Privileged Anonymity: The Writings of Madame de Lafayette.* Oxford: Legenda, 1996.

Haig, Sterling. *Madame de Lafayette.* New York: Twayne, 1970.

Kaps, Helen Karen. *Moral Perspective in La Princesse de Clèves.* Eugene: University of Oregon Press, 1968.

Kuizena, Donna. *Narrative Strategies in The Princesse de Clèves.* Lexington, Ky.: French Forum, 1976.

Paulson, Michael G. *Facets of a Princess: Multiple Readings of Madame de la Fayette's "La Princesse de Cleves."* New York: P. Lang, 1998.

Redhead, Ruth Willard. *Themes and Images in the Fictional Works of Madame de Lafayette.* New York: P. Lang, 1990.

Tiefenbrun, Susan W. *A Structural Analysis of The Princesse de Clèves.* The Hague: Mouton, 1976.

LAFCADIO'S ADVENTURES (LES CAVES DU VATICAN) ANDRÉ GIDE (1914) A complicated adventure story, *Lafcadio's Adventures* is one of Gide's best-known works, famous in large part for its principal character. Lafcadio represents Gide's concept of *l'acte gratuit,* or "the gratuitous act."

With its deliberately disjointed narrative, *Lafcadio's Adventures* contains overlapping intrigues. The first involves the conflict between ultra-Catholic Julius and his brother-in-law Anthime, an atheist and freethinker. For a time the two exchange viewpoints, only to return to their original convictions at novel's end. The second plotline involves Protos and his band of crooks, while the last involves Lafcadio's adventures.

After the sudden and unexpected conversion of Anthime, Julius is instructed by his dying father, the old count Juste Agénor de Baraglioul, to search for a young Romanian named Lafcadio Wluiki. As a result, Lafcadio discovers that he is the illegitimate son of the count. Lafcadio has a last, moving conversation with his father. When the old man dies, Lafcadio inherits part of his fortune. On that very day, chance has it that Lafcadio has the opportunity to save Julius's eldest daughter, Genevieve.

In the third part of the novel, the setting is the southern city of Pau, in Gascony, where a band of criminals is at work. They spread the rumor that the pope has been abducted and is being held either in the cellar of the Vatican or in the château of Saint-Ange, while a double has taken his place. One member of the band is Protos, a former school friend of Lafcadio and a bad influence. Meanwhile, another of Julius's brothers-in-law, Amédée Fleurissoire, heads off to Rome to save the pope as if on a modern-day crusade. While Carola tries to protect him, Protos watches carefully, concerned that even Amédée might realize that it is all a hoax. One day, on a train between Rome and Naples, Lafcadio murders Amédée.

Lafcadio lives out Gide's concept of the "free act." Just as he was able to act heroically to save Genevieve in Paris, he is equally capable of murder. Protos sees Lafcadio throw Amédée's body off the train and so tries to convince him that his only choice now is to join the band of criminals. Horrified, Lafcadio refuses.

Amédée's death is not without unforeseen consequences. Carola, who believes that Protos is guilty of the crime, denounces him to the police. In return, Protos kills her and is then imprisoned for *two* murders. Lafcadio meanwhile suffers from remorse, suddenly aware of his victim's humanity. Moreover, he feels guilty that Protos is imprisoned, in part, for his own crime. Lafcadio is further torn by Genevieve's offer of love.

There is obviously nothing realistic about this novel. The author himself even called it a "sotie," rather than a novel. It is pure entertainment, a parody of a detective novel. Despite its complicated plot full of fantastic twists and turns, the novel rests on a solid philosophical base as Gide explores the concept of the *acte gratuit*. A common theme in Gide's works is the potential for the individual to lead an independent life, open to all possible choices, like the character of Ménalque in *The* IMMORALIST. This theme is a reflection of Gide's own approach to life, clearly outlined in his more confessional works such as *If It Die*. Lafcadio's completely gratuitous act is to throw Amédée Fleurissoire from a train. It represents the arbitrary nature of the choices one makes in life as much as it demonstrates the author's rich imagination. The theory of the gratuitous act is derived principally from the works of Friedrich Nietzsche and Fyodor Dostoyevsky and constitutes a defiance of God and the world's supposed moral order. Because of this and the novel's dark humor, *Lafcadio's Adventures* was of great interest to the surrealists (see SURREALISM). It was equally scandalous to Roman Catholics. Gide's examination of freedom and its consequences in this novel is a continuation of themes found in *STRAIT IS THE GATE* and *The Immoralist*. Moreover, his fractured narrative reflects Gide's rejection of the traditional novel form as well as his taste for parody.

FURTHER READING

Bettinson, Christopher D. *Gide: A Study.* London: Heinemann; Totowa, N.J.: Rowman and Littlefield, 1977.

O'Brien, Justin. *Portrait of André Gide: A Critical Biography.* New York: Octagon Books, 1977; 1953.

O'Keefe, Charles. *Void and Voice: Questioning Narrative Conventions in André Gide's Major First-Person Narratives.* Chapel Hill: Dept. of Romance Languages, University of North Carolina Press, 1996.

Salz, Lily. "André Gide and the Problem of Engagement," *French Review* 30, no. 2 (December 1956): 131–137.

Sheridan, Alan. *André Gide: A Life in the Present.* Cambridge, Mass.: Harvard University Press, 1999.

Stoltzfus, Ben. "André Gide and the Voices of Rebellion," *Contemporary Literature* 19, no. 1 (Winter 1978): 80–98.

Walker, David, ed. *André Gide.* London, New York: Longman, 1996.

LAINÉ, PASCAL (1942–)

A brilliant student, Lainé earned a degree in philosophy and began his teaching career first in high school, then at the university level. His first novel, *B Like Barrabas,* published in 1967, was followed by *Irrevolution* (1971). That novel won the Médicis Prize, while *Web of Lace* won the Goncourt Prize in 1974.

One of Lainé's gifts is his ability to point out the problem of inequality between the sexes and different social classes through a series of minute observations. *Web of Lace,* for example, is the story of Pomme, a simple and shy shampoo girl in a beauty salon who falls in love with a university student too caught up in himself to recognize her qualities.

Beyond the concept of social injustice, several other distinct strains run through Lainé's writings. One theme focuses on the pain caused by an absent or neglectful father as in *Land of Shadows* (1982) and *Water of the Mirror* (1979). In contrast, *Tender Cousins* (1979) and *Jeanne's Pleasure* (1984) recall the LIBERTINE novels of the 18th century. Lainé's works are not of equal literary quality.

LAKE (LE LAC) JEAN ECHENOZ (1989)

The principal character of this novel, Chopin, is a solitary entomologist and private detective. The intrigue begins when he meets Suzy, who is funny and a bit crazy. Suzy's husband, an embassy secretary, disappeared without a trace six years before. One surprise follows another as the reader slowly begins to notice signs of the missing man.

The novel has a tightly knit plot written in a style that recalls comic strips. It is humorous and ironic in its evocation of modern society. Echenoz grasps the culture, spirit, and atmosphere of contemporary urban life, symbolized by his dialogues that defy all rules of punctuation and the use of ellipses to reflect the rhythm of life. Echoenoz's creative use of language, moreover, recalls the style of RAYMOND QUENEAU. The *Lake* is a highly entertaining detective story that reflects a movement in fiction in the 1980s away from the sterile theoretical approach of the NOUVEAU ROMAN.

FURTHER READING

Bertens, H. *The Idea of the Postmodern: A History.* London: Routledge, 1995.

Tilby, M., ed. *Beyond the Nouveau Roman: Essays on the Contemporary French Novel.* Oxford: Berg, 1990.

L'ASSOMMOIR (ÉMILE ZOLA) (1877)

In this seventh volume of the ROUGON-MACQUART series on the "Natural and Social History of a Second Empire Family," Gervaise Macquart, a laundress, moves to Paris from the provinces with her lover, Auguste Lantier, and their two sons, Claude and Étienne (see GERMINAL). Lantier, a hatter, is lazy and unfaithful and ultimately abandons Gervaise and their children to run off with Adèle.

Struggling to survive, Gervaise meets Coupeau, a roofer, at old Colombe's cabaret under the sign of a bludgeon (*l'assommoir,* in reference to the nearby slaughterhouse). Like *l'assommoir,* the still serves as an equally ominous sign foreshadowing Gervaise's downfall. The two decide to set up house together and it seems at first that the couple may find happiness in marriage despite the difficulties of a worker's life. With hard work and saving they manage to prosper; they even have a daughter, Nana (see Zola's novel of the same name).

But fate intervenes when Coupeau falls from a roof and breaks his leg. Unable and unwilling to return to work, he depletes their savings. Moreover, Coupeau begins to sink slowly into a drunken stupor. For a time, Gervaise struggles bravely and opens her own laundry. No matter how hard she works, though, she is unable to repay to Goujet the loan that allowed her to start her own business. At one point Lantier reappears and becomes friends with Gervaise and Coupeau, then he tries to seduce his former lover.

When Coupeau turns violent, a bad situation takes a turn for the worse. Gervaise loses her laundry and turns to prostitution. She too begins to drink. Coupeau ends his days in a hospital, dying from a fit of delirium tremens witnessed by Gervaise, whose demise soon follows. The orphaned Nana becomes a florist and a kept woman.

Earlier novels in the Rougon-Macquart series described the bourgeoisie. In this novel, Zola turned to the moral and physical degradation of the working class. True to his naturalist doctrine (see NATURALISM), Zola sought to bring to life social classes hitherto neglected in literature. Like FLAUBERT, Zola used the technique of *style indirect libre* (represented discourse) to comment on the world of Parisian workers. *L'Assommoir* allowed Zola to explore further the degradation of society and the corresponding moral decay of its members. The workers of Paris are victims of their conditions marked by misery, alcoholism, and brutality.

L'Assommoir was first published as a serial novel. In the 1877 complete edition Zola added a preface asserting "this is a work of truth, the first novel of the common people." Clearly this was an exaggeration. A number of novels had already focused on the common people such as EUGÈNE SUE's *The MYSTERIES OF PARIS,* VICTOR HUGO's *LES MISÉRABLES,* and the GONCOURT BROTHERS' *GERMINIE LACERTEUX.* Nonetheless, *L'Assommoir* was innovative. In it, Zola recounts the degeneracy of a woman distinguished only by her dream of finding security in a protective nest. Although Gervaise begins as a woman of high character, by the end of the novel she has become no more than a caricature of herself. Like others of her kind, she disappears into anonymity and death. Moreover, Zola again uses represented discourse to reinforce the sense of Gervaise's anonymous voice, particularly at the point of death. Zola anticipates the writing of CÉLINE; street language and the language of food and digestion permeate this novel that emphasizes the plight of the urban working poor with graphic descriptions of bodily functions that further challenged the conservative bourgeois order.

Critics have often noted the discrepancy between Zola's naturalist theory (literature as science) and practice, whereby the author's imagination necessarily comes into play. Moreover, contemporary critics also disapproved of the naturalist program because of the pessimism that marks these works. Criticized from the right and from the left, the novel caused a scandal that ultimately contributed to Zola's success. HUYSMANS, BOURGET, and the symbolist poet Stephane Mallarmé, however, praised it.

Like ALPHONSE DAUDET, GUSTAVE FLAUBERT, the GONCOURT BROTHERS, and GUY DE MAUPASSANT, Zola depicts a woman brought down by moral and physical suffering. At first glance, it thus appears that he has taken up the negative image prevalent among the bourgeoisie of the worker as inclined to dissipation. Moreover, Zola's incorporation of street language contributes to the rough depiction of the urban poor. However, Zola's workers are victims, and some have dreams of improving their lives, like Gervaise at one point. But failure is unavoidable in an unjust society. In the end, despair leads to hope in Zola's later work GERMINAL, hope that a workers' revolution may ultimately overcome social injustice and lead to a new society.

FURTHER READING
Baguley, David. "Event and Structure: The Plot of Zola's *L'Assommoir,*" *PMLA* 90, no. 5 (October, 1975): 823–833.

Donaldson-Evans, Mary. *Medical Examinations: Dissecting the Doctor in French Narrative Prose, 1857–1894.* Lincoln: University of Nebraska Press, 2000.

Furst, Lillian. *L'Assommoir: A Working Woman's Life.* Masterwork Studies Series. Boston: Twayne, 1990.

Gallois, William. *Zola: The History of Capitalism.* Oxford, New York: P. Lang, 2000.

Lukács, Georg. *Studies in European Realism.* Translated by Edith Bone. New York: Grosset and Dunlop, 1964.

LAWS OF HOSPITALITY, THE (LES LOIS DE L'HOSPITALITÉ) PIERRE KLOSSOWSKI (1965)

The Laws of Hospitality brings together three of Klossowski's earlier novels: *Roberte ce soir* (1953), *The Revocation of the Edict of Nantes* (1959), and *Souffleur* (1960). Klossowski skillfully blends meditation, dialogue, and eroticism to explore, in part, recurring themes in many of his works such as the problem of communication. Particularly influential on Klossowski's thinking are the 17th-century writer Blaise Pascal's *Pensées* as well as the writings of the marquis de SADE.

In *Roberte ce soir,* Klossowski pushes the laws of hospitality to an extreme. In front of her husband, Roberte offers her body to all the guests who come into their home, perhaps even the nephew who is living with them. If the soul alone is important, then it does not matter what one does with the body. Moreover, eroticism becomes a path to knowledge. Roberte is surprised by her own experiences and desires. In the preface to this work, Klossowski explained that Roberte signifies his entire oeuvre.

The Revocation of the Edict of Nantes is composed of interlaced excerpts from Octave's and Roberte's private diaries. Octave collects paintings by a fictitious artist named Tonnerre, who is inspired by the works of two 19th-century French painters, Gustave Courbet and Théodore Chassériau. Meanwhile, Roberte has become a radical deputy and a member of the commission on censorship, through which she discovers the world of sexual perversion, which she decides matter-of-factly to pursue more fully in her search for freedom. Octave continues to observe her escapades until his death, perhaps even after. The subject matter of Tonnere's paintings is an effective counterpoint to Roberte's excesses. The mood of mysticism and eroticism in this work inspired a film by Pierre Zucca in 1979.

In the last volume of the trilogy, *Souffleur,* similar situations between Octave and Roberte are carried even further. Both more comical and more complex than Klossowski's earlier works, this volume continues to blend fiction and reality. As in Gothic novels, the world is recognizable and apparently real, yet one is never really sure. All three volumes focus on the same principal characters, Octave, an older theology professor, and Roberte, his young wife. Klossowski's writing is marked by an unusual mixture of diary entries and theological debates interwoven with erotic scenes. Ultimately, Klossowski seeks to convey the incommunicability of language, a recurring theme in his writing.

FURTHER READING

Gallop, Jane. *Intersections: A Reading of Sade with Bataille, Blanchot and Klossowski.* Lincoln: University of Nebraska Press, 1981.

Hill, Leslie. *Bataille, Klossowski, Blanchot: Writing at the Limit.* Oxford, New York: Oxford University Press, 2001.

LAY   The first definition of a lay is a lyrical composition expressing the joy or pain of a character who experiences an adventure not recounted in the lay. A later definition is broader and encompasses specific rules applied to a short narrative in verse such as we see in the medieval LAYS OF MARIE DE FRANCE. The term was subsequently used in reference to a narrative recounting a marvelous or fantastic adventure through which the hero or heroine attains access to a different reality often associated with a fairy's love for a mortal or some other supernatural encounter.

A number of lays draw from the Celtic tradition and belong to a genre of courtly literature related to the CHANSONS DE GESTE and ROMANCES that inspired a number of 16th-century writers such as HÉLISENNE DE CRENNE. Most medieval vernacular literature was intended to be sung or recited aloud, accompanied by music. The lays, however, constitute a more literary stage in the transition from oral to written culture.

LAYE, CAMARA (1928–1980)   Born in Guinea, Laye spent his childhood between Kouroussa, the provincial town where his father worked as a goldsmith, and his mother's village. As a child, Laye first went to an Islamic school in his native village before attending a technical school in Conakry, the capital. Having received a scholarship, like many other talented students of his generation, Laye left for Paris, where he continued his studies while working in an auto factory.

Laye's first novel, DARK CHILD (1953), re-creates the author's childhood. In it he recalls his father, a well-respected self-made man who remained connected with his ancestors through a small, black serpent. Even more important is the figure of his mother, who was reputed to possess magical powers against evil. Laye depicts with sensitivity and affection the solidarity of the rural community he grew up in, bringing to life his personal memories of the rhythm of agricultural life in a manner that recalls the works of Marcel Pagnol and MAURICE GENEVOIX. *Dark Child* was popular with many readers but it troubled some contemporary African intellectuals who felt that the writer's principal obligation should be to participate in the struggle against colonialism.

In 1954, Laye published *The Radiance of the King,* influenced by Czech writer Franz Kafka, whom Laye admired greatly. He once described Kafka as "Europe's greatest writer and my greatest influence. When critics find my novels difficult it is because they don't know Kafka." This novel tells the story of Clarence, a white man who has been rejected by his peers and sets off in search of the king. It is a novel of apprenticeship as Clarence unwittingly goes through the rites of initiation associated with traditional African culture, thus reversing the problem of racial alienation in African society. Some scholars have interpreted Laye's decision to have a white man complete the rite as symbolizing unity among African and European peoples.

Once Guinea attained independence in 1958, Laye accepted a position in the Ministry of Information. Unfortunately, his strained relations with the dictatorial regime of Sekou Touré necessitated Laye's departure for Senegal in 1963, where he continued to work as a writer in exile. *Dream of Africa* appeared in 1966. In this work, Laye recounts his return to his native land. When Laye was informed that the title *Dramouss* had been translated into English as *Dream of Africa,* he responded, "Ah, Dramouss in Africa is a genie of prayer to Mohammed and the Archangel Gabriel." The novel's critique of colonial and postcolonial Guinea reflects Laye's personal disillusionment with independence that led him into exile.

The Guardian of the Word (1978) resurrects one of the great epics of the African tradition. In this work Laye adapts the legend of Sundiata, a 13th-century leader who was exiled and later returned to his native land to defeat its conquerors and build his own empire. In 1963, Laye approached a "griot," or traditional storyteller, named Babou Condé and taped him telling his version of this legend that parallels Laye's own life experience of dealing with questions of personal, collective, and cultural identity. Some critics have said that this is not really a novel, just a transcription. Others value the preservation of an oral source. Still others see in Laye's adaptation clear elements of the author's own style as he brings together oral and written traditions much like AHMADOU KOUROUMA.

Laye's works have not always been received with equal warmth by African readers. While *Dark Child* was a success, subsequent works were not as popular. To understand why this was the case, one must consider the political and social context of the period in which he was writing. Recent scholarship tends to offer a more balanced assessment of Laye's contribution to francophone African literature. Laye was deeply attached to the traditions of his native land yet he was forcibly distanced from them. At the same time, his experience in Europe has marked his writing as much as exile. Underlying themes in all Laye's works are alienation and personal freedom. Together Laye's works reflect the author's own journey to self-understanding as he explores the notion of identity.

FURTHER READING

Bernard, Paul R. "The Writings of Camara Laye, *French Review* 56, no. 6 (May 1983): 936–937.

Burness, Donald. "The Radiance of Camara Laye," *Journal of Black Studies* 2, no. 4 (June 1981): 499–501.

Hale, Thomas A. "From Written Literature to the Oral Tradition and Back: Camara Laye, Babou Condé, and *Le Maître de la parole:* Kouma, Lafolo and Kouma," *French Review* 55, no. 6, Literature and Civilization of Black Francophone Africa (May 1982): 790–797.

King, Adele. *Rereading Camara Laye.* Lincoln: University of Nebraska Press, 2002.

———. *The Writings of Camara Laye.* London: Heinemann, 1980.

Lee, Sonia. *Camara Laye.* Boston: Twayne, 1984.

LAYS OF MARIE DE FRANCE, THE (12TH CENTURY)

The Lays of Marie de France consist of a prologue and 12 poems dating from the second half of the 12th century. Although some scholars have questioned her authenticity, the author was undoubtedly a Frenchwoman, probably living in England at the time she wrote the poems. In the prologue, Marie de France dedicates the lays to Henry II, king of England. They were most likely circulated at the English court in the 1170s.

Written in the vernacular, the *Lays* belong to a genre of courtly literature related to the CHANSONS DE GESTE and ROMANCES born in the rich culture of southern France, in Provence and Languedoc. Most medieval vernacular literature was intended to be sung or recited aloud, accompanied by music. Marie de France's *Lays,* written in octosyllabic rhyming couplets, represent a more literary stage in the transition from oral to written culture.

The *Lays* were popular in the Middle Ages and were translated into several languages including Norse, Middle English, and Middle High German. They are stories of love and passion whose female protagonists include beautiful young women married unhappily to older men, devoted wives, brave young maidens (one of whom is pregnant outside of wedlock), and adulteresses. Marie de France is generally sympathetic to the plight of women. Although some of her lovers are punished, it is for their wickedness, not for adultery.

Only in the 12th century did marriage became a sacrament, as wealthy families sought contractual agreements in the interest of property and lineage. Aristocratic marriages were not by choice, and a woman, in particular, had no say in the selection of her husband. Ironically, in this same period, courtly love reversed social reality by placing the woman in a position of dominance. The feudalization of love mirrored the male relationship between a lord and his vassal, redefining gender roles outside of marriage. In the tradition of Andreas Capellanus's *The Art of Courtly Love* (1186), outlining the dynamics of courtly love and its connection to the code of chivalry, the *Lays* of Marie de France set a foundation for love and passion as central themes of Western literature while revealing the qualities and virtues of aristocratic court culture in the Middle Ages. HÉLISENNE DE CRENNE's *The DISORDERS OF LOVE,* for example, draws from the tradition of medieval romances such as we find in the *Lays* of Marie de France.

FURTHER READING

Burgess, G. S. *Marie de France, Text and Context.* Manchester, England: Manchester University Press, 1987.

Kinoshita, Sharon. "Two for the Price of One: Courtly Love and Serial Polygamy in the *Lais* of Marie de France," *Arthuriana* 8, no. 2 (1998): 33–55.

McCracken, Peggy. *The Romance of Adultery: Queenship and Sexual Transgression in Old French Literature.* Philadelphia: University of Pennsylvania Press, 1998.

Muir, Lynette R. *Literature and Society in Medieval France. The Mirror and the Image 1100–1500.* London: Macmillan, 1985.

Rothschild, Judith Rice. *Narrative Techniques in the Lais of Marie de France: Themes and Variations.* Vol 1. North Carolina Studies in the Romance Languages and Literatures 39. Edited by Juan Battista Avalle-Arce. Chapel Hill: University of North Carolina Department of Romance Languages, 1974.

Spearing, A. C. "Love and Power in the Twelfth Century, with Special Reference to Chrétien de Troyes and Marie de France." In *The Olde Daunce: Love, Friendship, Sex, and Marriage in the Medieval World.* Edited by Robert R. Edwards and Stephen Spector. Albany: SUNY Press, 1991.

Stevens, Sonya, ed. *A History of Women's Writing in France.* London, New York: Cambridge University Press, 2000.

LEBLANC, MAURICE (1864–1941)   Leblanc's
father, a merchant in Rouen, wanted his son to pursue a business career. Instead, Leblanc headed for Paris, where he first studied law before turning to literature. Leblanc began by writing for a number of newspapers, including *Gil Blas* and *Le Figaro,* while participating in naturalist and symbolist circles (see NATURALISM and SYMBOLISM) frequented by figures such as GUY DE MAUPASSANT and the Belgian poet Maurice Maeterlinck, whose mistress was Leblanc's sister Georgette.

Leblanc's early works such as *A Woman* (1893), *Work of Death* (1896), *Armelle and Claude* (1897), *Here are the Wings* (1898), and *Enthusiasm* (1901), drawing on his experience as a youth growing up in Normandy, recall the psychological approach of PAUL BOURGET. Leblanc also wrote a number of short stories that bear the influence of Maupassant, GUSTAVE FLAUBERT, and LÉON BLOY. Leblanc's play, *Pity* (1904), was accepted by the Free Theater in Paris (Théâtre Libre).

Leblanc had already shown a talent for psychological analysis in *A Woman,* and he received encouragement to continue writing from figures such as ALPHONSE DAUDET and Bloy. Unfortunately, with the decline of the psychological novel, interest in Leblanc's writings waned until 1905, when he was engaged by the publisher Pierre Lafitte to write a detective novel. Leblanc is most famous for his series of novels featuring the unforgettable character Arsène Lupin.

Leblanc's first detective novel, *The Arrest of Arsène Lupin,* gave birth to an extraordinary adventurer. Immediately successful with the reading public, it was followed by nine other novels published together under the title *Arsène Lupin, Gentleman Thief.* The character of Arsène Lupin took over Leblanc's career. The author once said, "He follows me everywhere. He is not my shadow; I am his." Arsène Lupin is like a Robin Hood of modern times, infinitely appealing in his sense of justice and gallantry.

Leblanc went on to write *Arsène Lupin Against Sherlock Holmes* (1908), *The Hollow Needle* (1909), *813* (1910), *The Crystal Stopper* (1912), *Arsène Lupin's Secrets* (1913), *Burst of Shells* (1915), *The Golden Triangle* (1917), *The Isle of Thirty Coffins* (1919), *Tiger's Teeth* (1920), *The Clock Strikes Eight* (1923), *The Countess of Cagliostro* (1924), *The Girl with the Green Eyes* (1927), *Barnett and Cie* (1928), *Mysterious Dueling* (1928), *La Barre Leaves* (1930), *Woman with Two Smiles* (1932),

Victory of the Worldly Brigade (1934), and *Cagliostro's Revenge* (1935).

Arsène's first escapades resemble those of Sherlock Holmes, as the reader is surprised at the end by a brilliant and surprising solution to the mystery. Leblanc quickly began to develop increasingly complicated plots as Arsène gives up theft for more serious adventures in search of lost treasure or solutions to mysteries drawn from French history. The first novels were published in serial form, so the narrative is punctuated by dramatic twists and turns to the plot. In *The Hollow Needle,* for example, the secret hideout of the French kings becomes Arsène's refuge. In *The Crystal Stopper* and *813,* Arsène turns to politics and diplomacy. With the outbreak of World War II in 1939, Leblanc's novels took on a markedly nationalist tone as Arsène, too, confronts the invading Germans.

The popularity of Leblanc's series was due in part to Leblanc's style and his interesting plots. Above all, the mocking, almost superhuman character of Arsène Lupin draws the reader in. Arsène Lupin is full of charm, clever, even spiritual. For many readers, he seemed to encapsulate the French spirit. A number of Leblanc's works were also adapted to stage, screen, and television. The overwhelming popularity of the character of Arsène Lupin caused a number of Leblanc's other works to be overlooked.

LÉLIA GEORGE SAND (1833; 1839)

First published in 1833, *Lélia* was completely reworked by Sand for publication again in 1839. One of Sand's early novels, *Lélia* is a highly psychological gothic work that recounts the story of Lélia d'Almovar who, at the opening of the novel, is frustrated by inaction and self-examination.

A young poet, Sténio, is in love with her. Lélia cares for him but having been hurt in an earlier love affair, she fears submitting to him. She also has a close friend and confidant, Trenmor, of whom Sténio is jealous. Trenmor has become a sort of spiritual director for Lélia, and an atmosphere of religiosity permeates their story.

Meanwhile, Magnus the hermit is the only one who has not entirely succumbed to Lélia's charm. He considers her a dangerous seductress. Torn among these

three men, Lélia decides to enter religious life. Soon she becomes abbess, bringing true Christian spirit to the life of the convent. Unfortunately, Sténio is unable to overcome his love for Lélia. He comes to the convent and asks for one conversation with her. Realizing the truth of Lélia's feelings for him, and that she will now always remain unattainable, Sténio kills himself.

When Magnus discovers Sténio's body, he is even more convinced that Lélia is dangerous. He convinces the outside world of Lélia's demoniacal nature and, as a result, Lélia is imprisoned for the rest of her life. When Lélia dies, Trenmor buries her at the edge of the lake, across from Sténio's tomb.

Written during the first period of Sand's literary career, this romantic novel (see ROMANTICISM) depicts an ideal and impossible love. In the first version, Lélia is killed by Magnus, whereas the second reflects Sand's more pacifist ideas. Successful both in France and abroad, *Lélia* focuses on Sand's theme of love.

FURTHER READING
Crecelius, Kathryn J. *Family Romances: George Sand's Early Novels.* Bloomington: Indiana University Press, 1987.
Cornell, Kenneth. "George Sand, Emotion and Idea," *Yale French Studies,* no. 13 Romanticism Revisited (1954): 93–97.
Sivert, Eileen Boyd. "Lélia and Feminism," *Yale French Studies,* no. 62, Feminist Readings: French Texts/American Contexts (1981): 45–66.

LEROUX, GASTON (1868–1927)

Lawyer, journalist, and novelist, Leroux gained notoriety as a writer of detective novels featuring Rouletabille, a resourceful and sympathetic amateur detective. A second series of popular novels features Chéri-Bibi.

Born in Paris, Leroux first worked as a lawyer before turning to journalism, then fiction. He began covering trials for a daily newspaper in 1894. Later he wrote "exclusives" on topics as varied as an expedition to the North Pole and the rescue of Russian sailors after the battle of Chemulpo in the Russo-Japanese War of 1904. In fact, the troubled climate of prerevolutionary Russia is the background for several of Leroux's novels.

In 1903, Leroux wrote his first serial novel, *The Double Life of Théophraste Longuet.* This is the fantastic story of a dull, ordinary worker who discovers that he is the reincarnation of the bandit Cartouche. He subsequently sets off in search of treasure. However, Leroux's literary career truly began with the publication of *The Mystery of the Yellow Room* in 1907. The plot involves a stereotypical murder mystery that takes place in a sealed room from which no one appears to have entered or departed. The mystery is solved by a clever 18-year-old journalist, Rouletabille, who then becomes the central figure in a series of novels. In each instance, Rouletabille is highly rational in his approach to solving the crimes he encounters. As our senses may deceive us, he seems to say, only logic and reason can lead us to the answer. At the same time, Leroux's writing is anything but dry.

The Mystery of the Yellow Room was successful enough for Leroux to devote himself entirely to literature. He left Paris for Nice, where he produced nine volumes of *The Extraordinary Adventures of Joseph Rouletabille* between 1907 and 1922. *The Woman in Black's Perfume* (1908) tells the story of Rouletabille's background. *Rouletabille in Russia* (1913) is set in Moscow during the period of nihilist political assassinations, while *The Black Castle* and *Rouletabille's Strange Marriage* (1914) are typical adventure stories. In the latter novel, Rouletabille travels to the war-torn Balkans to rescue his fiancée from a bandit.

Leroux also tried his hand at popular novels in the style of EUGÈNE SUE's *The MYSTERIES OF PARIS*, producing *The Mysterious King* (1908–09), *A Man in the Night* (1910), *Queen of the Sabbath* (1910–11), *The Infernal Column* (1926), *The Mohicans of Babel* (1926), and the *Chéri-Bibi* series (five volumes, 1913–25), which focus on the adventures of a young man sentenced to the galleys for a murder he did not commit.

Leroux's best novels include *The Man Who Saw the Devil* (1908) and *The Haunted Chair* (1910), which takes place in the Académie Française, where three scholars suddenly die after giving their inaugural speech. In an ironic twist, at the end of the novel the illiterate Gaspard Lalouette is elected to the haunted chair. In Leroux's masterpiece, *The Phantom of the Opera* (1910), Erik, imprisoned in the body of a monster, falls in love with an opera singer and takes her to his mysterious kingdom.

Leroux wrote some forty novels, a number of which are marked by a slightly ironic and patriotic tone that reflects the time in which they were written. Leroux's style is flamboyant, his dialogues peppered with slang. Moreover, he had a gift for narrative and suspense. Leroux's sense of the mysterious was noted by later surrealists (see SURREALISM). An extraordinarily popular writer, Leroux was the last of the great serial novelists.

LE ROY, EUGÈNE (1836–1907)

Le Roy was born in the Dordogne. His identity as a writer is closely linked to his native region of Périgord. LeRoy served in Africa and Italy, beginning a career as a government functionary in 1860. While he wrote several scholarly works on the history of Périgord, today he is principally known as a regional novelist. LeRoy first established his reputation with the publication of *Frau's Mill* in 1895. His most significant work, *Jack the Rebel*, appeared in 1898.

Le Roy's later works are less well known. They include *Nicette and Milou* (1901), *Stony Landscape* (*Le Pays des pierres,* 1906), and *The People of Aubéroxque* (1907). All of Le Roy's writings offer the hearty flavor of his native Périgord and sensitivity toward its people.

LESAGE, ALAIN-RENÉ (1668–1747)

Very little is known of Lesage's character but he seems to have been possessed of an independent spirit. Unlike many contemporary writers, Lesage neither benefited from royal patronage nor that of the Parisian literary salons. Some scholars have argued that Lesage's fiction stands somewhat apart from the general development of the French novel, occupying instead a place in the broader development of European literature. Its influence is particularly strong on certain English novels.

Lesage came from a modest bourgeois family. His father was a lawyer, notary, and registrar of the royal court. Lesage received his early education from the Jesuits. His parents died when he was young and Lesage's uncle and guardian squandered his inheritance. Consequently, Lesage was poor when he left for Paris in 1690 to study law and philosophy.

In 1694, Lesage married the beautiful, virtuous, and penniless Marie Elizabeth Huyard. He was by all accounts a decent, honest husband and father. Lesage's career as a novelist and playwright began when the abbé Lyonne suggested that he introduce Spanish golden age literature to France. Thus Lesage turned to literature as a means to support his family. He began with translations of Fernando de Rojas and Félix Lope de Vega. His first literary success came with a comedy, *Crispin, Rival of His Master,* in 1707. In the same year, Lesage published his popular romance, *The DEVIL UPON TWO STICKS.* Several editions were published in 1707, and the novel continued to be reprinted with some frequency until 1725, when Lesage made changes that gave the novel its present form.

The first two parts of Lesage's second novel, *The ADVENTURES OF GIL BLAS DE SANTILLANE,* appeared in 1715. Lesage worked on this novel for many years. The third part was published in 1724 and the fourth in 1735. It is a story of upward mobility, tracing the adventures of Gil Blas from unwilling thief to aristocrat.

In addition to these two novels, Lesage wrote prolifically for street theater, producing more than a hundred pieces. His best theatrical work, *Turcaret* (1709), is a comedy satirizing the world of finance. The play was popular in Parisian salons. Nonetheless, until 1740 Lesage and his family led a somewhat precarious existence. Estranged from his two sons who had become actors, Lesage and his wife went to live with the third, a canon at the Cathedral of Boulogne. Lesage died there peacefully in 1747.

FURTHER READING

France, Anatole. *The Latin Genius.* Translated by Wilfrid S. Jackson. London: John Lane and the Bodley Head; New York: Dodd, Mead, 1924.

Longhurst, Jennifer. "Lesage and the Spanish Tradition: *Gil Blas* as a Picaresque Novel," *Studies in Eighteenth-Century French Literature Presented to Robert Niklaus.* Edited by J. H. Fox, M. H. Waddicor, and D. A. Watts. Exeter, England: Exeter University Press, 1975, 123–137.

LES MISÉRABLES VICTOR HUGO (1862)

The central figure in *Les Misérables* is Jean Valjean, a victim of society sentenced to the galleys for having stolen bread to feed his starving family. Twenty years later, Jean Valjean is released, but the brutal experience of the galleys has turned him into a social pariah. All that is left in him is hate. Only the saintly bishop of Digne,

Monseigneur Myriel, the incarnation of Christian virtue, deigns to help Jean, who returns the bishop's kindness by stealing his most precious possessions, some silver candleholders.

Arrested by the police, Jean faces a return to the galleys until Monseigneur Myriel exculpates him. This profoundly humanitarian gesture signals the beginning of Jean Valjean's transformation. Until this moment he has experienced only the iron hand of an inflexible law and cruelty. Monseigneur Myriel offers him kindness and mercy. Filled with remorse and the first stirring of his own humanity, Jean begins the long and arduous process of self-rehabilitation.

The reader finds him next living in the Pas-de Calais under the name Monsieur Madeleine. Now a wealthy industrialist respected for his virtue and generosity, Monsieur Madeleine is even elected mayor of the town and receives the medal of the Legion of Honor. Among his numerous charitable acts, Monsieur Madeleine rescues Cosette, the illegitimate daughter of one of his employees, Fantine. Fantine had been seduced by a student who subsequently abandoned her. Fantine leaves Cosette in the care of an innkeeper, Thénardier, who mistreats and abuses her.

Unfortunately, Monsieur Madeleine's generous act draws the attention of Javert, a policeman. Javert suspects Monsieur Madeleine's identity and decides to set a trap for him. Monsieur Madeleine hears that an unfortunate soul has been arrested for theft and is accused of being Jean Valjean. He subsequently suffers a crisis of conscience, the famous "tempest in a human skull," as he realizes that he must reveal his identity to the court to save the other man who has been falsely accused.

Fortunately, Monsieur Madeleine is able to escape along with Cosette, whom he rescues from the Thénardiers (her mother has died). Together they seek refuge in a convent in Paris, Le Petit Picpus, where Jean Valjean takes up a position as gardener and Cosette receives an education. Meanwhile, Javert continues to search for his prey.

Hugo then introduces Marius, a young law student, son of a colonel in the Napoleonic army who disappeared in the Battle of Waterloo. Hugo at one point digresses to describe in detail that historical military engagement. Once Jean Valjean and Cosette are living openly in Paris, Marius falls in love with the young woman, whom he encounters in the Luxembourg Gardens. Naive and passionate, Marius and his compatriots, among whom is the legendary Parisian street urchin Gavroche (Thénardier's abandoned son), fight on the barricades in the Revolution of 1832. Most of the young heroes die except for Marius. Despite his anxiety that he might lose Cosette, Jean Valjean rescues Marius in a famous scene, dragging him with superhuman effort through the sewers of Paris. Meanwhile he has also saved Javert's life. Javert, humiliated by his enemy's kindness and shaken by seeing his principles destroyed, throws himself into the Seine.

Marius and Cosette plan to marry. Unaware of what he owes him, Marius learns of Jean Valjean's true identity and insists that Jean gradually distance himself from Cosette. Heartbroken, Jean leaves his adopted daughter. Once the truth is revealed, Marius and Cosette return to Jean, who, on his deathbed, receives them with love and dies like a saint.

Les Misérables is an enormous tome of five parts and 10 volumes, written partly in reaction to EUGÈNE SUE's popular serial novel, *The MYSTERIES OF PARIS*. Hugo adopts some of the devices of the serial novelist to keep the reader's attention. Jean Valjean, for example, hides himself in a deceased nun's casket to leave the convent. Not all of the adventures are believable.

Hugo began working on the novel in 1845, but political events interrupted him for the next 12 years. The novel was finished only in 1862. It is marked by Hugo's turn to republicanism and his political exile. In both his political life and his writing, Hugo adhered unwaveringly to humanitarian principles and political views that have a tremendous impact on the novel. He makes a strong statement against a repressive judicial system, reflecting his sympathy for the misery of the lower classes. In fact, the poor people of Paris are collectively a major character in the novel. Hugo's stated purpose is to condemn "the degradation of man in the proletariat, the fall of woman because of hunger, the atrophy of the child by the night." In this epic of good and evil, however, Hugo offers no plan for social reform. The work simply expresses the author's moral conscience. In his struggle against fate, Jean Valjean becomes a Christ-like figure who expiates the sins of humanity. In *Les Misérables,* the theme of mercy and its redemptive or regenerative quality predominates. To a great extent, the novel reflects Hugo's own character. Still, the influence of GEORGE SAND and the works of the utopian socialists is also apparent.

In the course of this complex, interwoven plot, Hugo runs the gamut from indignant to satirical to declamatory; he is powerful and generous. Hugo's sensitive depiction of life in a convent, his juxtapositions of the beautiful and the ugly (typical of his writing), and the parallel between historical events and the development of particular characters all reveal the author's versatility. *Les Misérables* had a profound influence on later developments in the French novel.

FURTHER READING

Brombert, Victor. *Victor Hugo and the Visionary Novel.* Cambridge, Mass.: Harvard University Press, 1984.

Evans, David O. *Social Romanticism in France: 1830–1848.* New York: Octagon, 1969.

Hudson, William Henry. *Victor Hugo and His Poetry.* London: Harrap, 1918.

Maurois, André. *Victor Hugo and His World.* Translated by Oliver Bernard. New York: Viking, 1966.

Peyre, Henri. *Victor Hugo: Philosophy and Poetry.* Translated by Roda P. Roberts. Tuscaloosa: University of Alabama Press, 1980.

Richardson, Joanna. *Victor Hugo.* London: Weidenfeld and Nicolson, 1976.

LETTERS FROM MY MILL (*LETTRES DE MON MOULIN*) ALPHONSE DAUDET (1869)

This collection of letters written in the form of a first-person narrative established Daudet's reputation as a writer and set the tone for later novels situated in Provence that are among his best. Daudet never lost touch with his southern French roots, describing the people and landscape of that region with great sympathy.

In the preface to *Letters,* the narrator states that he has purchased a mill in Provence where he can pursue his dreams in peace, away from the dirt and bustle of Paris. There was, in fact, a real mill abandoned for some 20 years not far from Daudet's home, inhabited by rabbits and an owl. There Daudet wrote, at least in his imagination, most of the *Letters.*

Published first in the press, together these tales reveal the Provençal character with a mixture of emotion, malice, and humor. Daudet's charming and simple style, which is both natural and conversational, demonstrates his sensitivity to the details of ordinary people's lives. His picturesque characters, such as the provincial poet, shepherd, and gourmand priest, bring to life the character of Provence. In Daudet's own words, "It is my favorite book . . . because it brings back the most beautiful hours of my youth." The *Letters* continues to be a favorite among his readers as well; it remains today the best known of Daudet's works.

FURTHER READING

Dobie, Vera G. *Alphonse Daudet*. Folcroft, Pa.: Folcroft
   Library Editions, 1974.
Roche, Alphonse. *Alphonse Daudet*. Boston: Twayne, 1976.
Sachs, Murray. *The Career of Alphonse Daudet. A Critical
   Study*. Cambridge, Mass.: Harvard University Press, 1965.

LETTERS OF A PERUVIAN PRINCESS (LETTRES D'UNE PÉRUVIENNE) Fran-

çoise de Graffigny (1747)   In this finely crafted EPISTOLARY NOVEL, Graffigny elegantly combines exoticism with social criticism, feminism with sentimentalism. Zilia, a Peruvian princess, tells her story in a series of 38 letters to her lost love, Aza. Immediately popular, by the end of the 18th century the novel had gone through 42 editions and continued to be published into the 19th century. The second edition, of 1752, added three letters to the initial text.

The Spanish ship that carries Zilia off on the day intended for her wedding to Aza is taken by the French. The captain, Déterville, brings her to France. Déterville and his sister Céline introduce Zilia to Western civilization that she, then, comments on and criticizes in her letters to Aza. Déterville, of course, falls hopelessly in love with Zilia. Despite the fact that Aza is now in Spain, has converted to Christianity, and married a Christian woman, Zilia remains faithful to her first vow and refuses Déterville. At the same time, she wishes to retain his friendship.

Graffigny's novel simultaneously draws on two models. As a SENTIMENTAL NOVEL focusing on the theme of an abandoned woman, *Letters of a Peruvian Princess*

follows in the pattern set by GUILLERAGUE's *Letters of a Portuguese Nun*. As a novel of social criticism, it draws on the tradition of the foreigner's observations on European life mastered by MONTESQUIEU in *The Persian Letters*.

The theme of exoticism was popular in the 18th century and was often linked to the notion of the noble savage. CHATEAUBRIAND carries this idea into the 19th century in *Atala* and *René*. Zilia is, nonetheless, unique. She is a "savage," impressed by European technology and yet critical of social mores. She is also the victim of a brutal system of colonization. Some scholars have argued that she is one of the first politically conscious heroines of the Third World. While she remains in France for the rest of her life, Zilia never really *becomes* French. Nor is she ever entirely persuaded that Western values are superior to those of her own culture.

Graffigny's novel is innovative in that it does not offer a traditional conclusion. Zilia does not languish and die of a broken heart, nor does she enter a convent, nor does she marry; she remains independent. Such an ending was disturbing to Graffigny's contemporaries. Her independence results from a small property and income that Déterville has assured for her, implying, as Virginia Woolf does more than a century later, that a woman's independence, intellectual and otherwise, necessitates money and a room of one's own.

Graffigny's work is also innovative in directly confronting the problem of language and communication, more so even than Montesquieu, or Voltaire in *The Huron*. Zilia is at first incapable of understanding or communicating in French. She tells her story by knotting cords, the method of writing in her land. As she gradually learns to speak French, she raises questions about language and meaning, object and sign, about the limits of verbal communication. When she visits the opera, Zilia feels that music and gesture may approximate more closely natural communication between human beings.

As Zilia's knowledge of French grows, so does her realization that language does not always reveal the truth; sometimes it disguises it. Zilia notices this particularly with women, as she remarks on the discrepancy between the words women use and their real thoughts and feelings. In the end, she arrives at a similar conclusion to ROUSSEAU. There are obvious parallels between Zilia's comments and the Parisian letters in *The New Héloïse.* Society has lost any sense of authenticity. Appearance has superseded reality; hence Zilia's ambivalent view of the French. They are not mean people but they are frivolous and superficial.

Graffigny thus precedes Rousseau in criticizing society's moral decadence. Presaging, too, DIDEROT in *The Nun,* Zilia is stunned, for example, at the practice of sending younger children into monasteries to keep the family property intact, as Déterville's mother at one point considers for Céline. She is critical, too, of a social order that permits the rich to live luxuriously while the poor suffer. Some scholars have even suggested that Graffigny's argument is a precursor to socialism.

Given her concern with social injustice, it is not surprising that Graffigny comments on the question of women in society, in Zilia's words: "What strange people who, at the same time, shower women with respect and scorn them." Letter 34, added to the second edition, expands on the feminist theme by addressing the problem of women's education. Graffigny argues in favor of an education that would form women as responsible beings, worthy of respect in a society that would no longer subjugate them.

FURTHER READING

Altman, J. G. "Making Room for Peru. Graffigny's Novel Reconsidered." In *Dilemmes du roman. Essays in Honor of G. May.* Edited by C. Lafarge. Saratoga, Calif.: Anma Libri, 1989, 33–46, and "Graffigny's Epistemology and the Emergence of Third-World Ideology." In *Writing the Female Voice.* Edited by E. C. Goldsmith. Boston: Northwestern University Press, 1989, 172–202.

Showalter, E. "The Beginnings of Mme de Graffigny's Literary Career." In *Essays on the Age of Enlightenment in Honor of I.O. Wade.* Edited by J. Macary. Geneva: Droz, 1977, 293–304, and "Madame de Graffigny and Her Salon," *Studies in Eighteenth-Century Culture* 6 (1977): 377–391.

LETTERS OF MISTRESS FANNY BUT-LERD, THE (*LETTRES DE MISTRISS FANNI BUTLERD*) MARIE-JEANNE RICCOBO-NI (1757)   In this highly popular EPISTOLARY NOVEL, Fanny writes a series of 116 mostly short letters to her lover, Charles Alfred, count of Erford. The novel

is monophonic; there are no letters from Charles to Fanny, but it is clear from the context that he has written back to her. Like the majority of sentimental epistolary novels of the 18th century (see SENTIMENTAL NOVEL), Fanny Butlerd is the story of an, in this case, ill-fated love affair. Clearly the relationship is more important to Fanny than to Charles, who abandons her to marry someone else. Fanny is honest with herself, recognizing that she has sacrificed herself completely to a man unworthy of devotion. In the end she is angry and contemptuous of his behavior. When she finally breaks contact with him, she does so in a clear and dignified manner. The tragedy lies in the fact that Fanny has wasted her love on someone who never really existed except in her own mind. The notion that love is a product of the imagination makes Riccoboni's novel a precursor to PROUST.

The theme of male duplicity runs through Riccoboni's works. In *The History of the Marquis du Cressy* a man abandons his lover to marry a wealthy widow. He subsequently seduces his lover again, driving his wife to suicide. Still, Riccoboni's depiction of gender relations is not without subtlety. If men are insensitive and cruel it is because society has made them so. Morally weak, they take advantage of an economic, legal, and social system that subjugates women. Riccoboni may consequently be described as a social realist.

The novel bears the influence of contemporary English writer Samuel Richardson in tone and setting despite the marked differences in character. Moreover, as in Richardson's works, such as *Pamela,* the interior drama undergone by Fanny is more important than exterior events. The use of one voice reflects the heroine's solitude and is thus comparable in theme and structure to GUILLERAGUE's LETTERS OF A PORTUGUESE NUN and GRAFFIGNY's LETTERS OF A PERUVIAN PRINCESS. Few other characters are invoked. The novel focuses fully on Fanny's emotions.

Riccoboni once wrote, "Buffon speaks of love as a man. The physical is good, he says, the moral is nothing. A woman would have thought the opposite." Fanny gives herself to her lover conscious of all that she risks in society and she does so willingly to make him happy. There is not the somber and violent passion of PRÉVOST; Fanny resembles more Julie's deliberate approach to Saint-Preux in ROUSSEAU's *The New Héloïse.*

Riccoboni addresses class issues along with gender. Her political protest is against a feudal order of exploitation. At the same time, there is ambiguity. Men even treat women of their own class badly. Riccoboni reveals a pessimistic concept of love based on what she considers the profound incompatibility between the sexes. On the positive side, she also seems to seek a moral contract under which men and women would both be held to the same ethical standard.

FURTHER READING

Cook, Elizabeth Heckendorn. *Epistolary Bodies: Gender and Genre in the Eighteenth-Century Republic of Letters.* Stanford, Calif.: Stanford University Press, 1996.

Sol, Antoinette-Marie. *Textual Promiscuities: Eighteenth Century Critical Rewriting.* Lewsiburg, Pa.: Bucknell University Press, 2002.

Stewart, Joan Hinde. *The Novels of Madame Riccoboni.* Chapel Hill: University of North Carolina Press, 1976.

LETTERS OF MISTRESS HENLEY, THE (LETTRES DE MISTRISS HENLEY PUBLIÉES PAR SON AMIE) ISABELLE DE CHARRIÈRE (1784)

This EPISTOLARY NOVEL is Isabelle de Charrière's response to Samuel de Constant's "antifeminist" novel *Sentimental Husband,* in which the main character is tormented by his insensitive and unkind wife. The story line of Charrière's work is essentially the same as CONSTANT's. A young woman marries an older man already established in his routine. She has nothing to contribute to their life together. She must simply adjust. The wife in Constant's novel is portrayed as mean-spirited. In contrast, Charrière's depiction of the woman's plight is far more sensitive.

The question at the heart of the novel is the problem of reconciling reason and emotion, a question that was central to 18th-century thought. In both works the husband makes reason the foundation for a happy household. In *Mistress Henley,* Marianne, a spontaneous and passionate woman, is tormented by her husband's excessive rationality. The problem with Marianne's marriage is incompatibility. Contemporaries suspected that Mistress Henley was, in fact, Isabelle de Charrière. While the novel is not entirely autobiographical, Charrière's correspondence indicates certain parallels between her experience as a wife and that of Marianne. Although the novel was published anonymously, it became a fashion to guess who the models for her characters were.

The novel was well received in Holland and Switzerland, and became famous in France after the publication of a pirated edition in 1785 that included *Sentimental Husband, Mistress Henley,* and an anonymous *Justification of Mr. Henley.* Charrière publicly disclaimed this publication, the *Justification* in particular, in the *Journal de Paris* in 1786.

The setting of *Mistress Henley* is England. In a series of six letters to a female friend, Marianne describes her unhappy marriage. There is no tragedy in the novel but there is despair. The man's first marriage had been a happy one and he has a daughter from this "first bed." Marianne is young, spontaneous, and spirited. Her small attempts to contribute to the household always lead to failure and increasing alienation. Charrière essentially asks if women must always be held responsible for happiness in a marriage. Do men not also bear some accountability?

The story ends sadly. Unhappy as she is, Marianne will not go so far as to commit suicide as she is expecting a child, but tells her friend "in a year or two, I will either be reasonable and happy or I will be no more." The underlying problem is that a wife must conform to her husband's expectations. The only way for Marianne to become "happy and reasonable" is through a process of self-annihilation. The marginalization of women in society is a fundamental theme in Charrière's novels.

Mistress Henley, written in response to Constant's novel, also raises the question of female authorship. Marianne requests that the friend to whom she writes ensure that her letters be published. Through the main character, then, Charrière asserts a woman's right to write, to participate in a public sphere. Moreover, at the same time that she challenges Constant, Charrière also subtly but surely throws down the gauntlet to ROUSSEAU as well. Hollowpark, an apt name for the Henley estate, is a counterpoint to the utopian community of Clarens in *The New Héloïse.* It is as if Marianne follows Rousseau's advice in choosing a husband not out of passion but because he is reasonable. The consequences for Marianne are no better than they are for

Rousseau's Julie. *Mistress Henley* challenges the norms of 18th-century aristocratic society by considering the problem of female dependence. It is also in many ways a modern drama in its depiction of marriage as based more often on misunderstanding, miscommunication, and incompatibility than overt tragedy.

FURTHER READING

Beebee, Thomas O. *Epistolary Fiction in Europe, 1500–1850.* Cambridge: Cambridge University Press, 1999.

Bérenguier, N. "From Clarens to Hollowpark. Isabelle de Charrière's Quiet Revolution," *Studies in Eighteenth-Century Culture* 21 (1991): 219–243.

Hinde Stewart, Joan. "The Novelists and Their Fictions." In *French Women and the Age of Enlightenment.* Edited by Samia I. Spencer. Bloomington: Indiana University Press, 1984, 197–211.

———. *Gynographs: French Novels by Women of the Late Eighteenth Century.* Lincoln: University of Nebraska Press, 1993.

Jackson, Susan K. "Publishing Without Perishing: Isabelle de Charrière, a.k.a. *la mouche du coche.*" In *Going Public: Women and Publishing in Early Modern France.* Edited by Elizabeth C. Goldsmith and Dena Goodman. Ithaca, N.Y.: Cornell University Press, 1995.

LETTERS WRITTEN FROM LAUSANNE (LETTRES ÉCRITES DE LAUSANNE AND CALISTE OU SUITE DES LETTRES ÉCRITES DE LAUSANNE) ISABELLE DE CHARRIÈRE (1785, 1787)

This EPISTOLARY NOVEL is written in two parts. The first depicts a mother who writes to her cousin about her daughter's marriage prospects. Cecile is an attractive girl, not perfect but lively and engaging. Although she is of good birth, she has no fortune. This severely limits her potential suitors. The novel is open-ended. The reader never finds out whether Cécile marries. According to the literary critic SAINTE-BEUVE, "that is the true end, the only right ending. To have gone further would have been to spoil [the novel]." Despite its general popularity, the citizens of Neuchâtel, Switzerland, near Charrière's home, did not receive the novel well due to its depiction of provincial Swiss life.

The second part, often considered as a novel apart, is the story of Caliste, a former actress. She once performed in the play *The Beautiful Penitent,* and this becomes the story of her life. Caliste was raised as a courtesan by her mother and later educated by an older man to whom she was mistress. The narrator is a man of good birth who once loved her but was too weak to challenge social norms and his father's prohibitions to marry Caliste. Later he made a respectable marriage, as did she, or at least one based on stability. Still, Caliste always regretted the loss of William and she died after a miscarriage but also from a broken heart. Her death leaves William in despair.

Cécile and Caliste resemble each other in their inability to determine their own destiny, and this trait manifests Charrière's pessimistic view of the female condition. The recurring themes in this and other novels by Charrière concern the powerlessness of women in the marriage market and the social constraints that lead to female marginalization. Charrière explores the question of human freedom and, in particular, the suffering of women due to male indecision. In this way the novel influenced both BENJAMIN CONSTANT and GERMAINE DE STAËL. In his passivity and lethargy, and his regret for his own mistakes, William also presages the ROMANTIC hero. There are parallels, too, with ROUSSEAU's NEW HÉLOÏSE. When Julie dies, however, she goes to God. For Caliste, there is no promise of paradise. Caliste's death argues against a philosophy that asserts human happiness or pleasure as seen, for example, in the LIBERTINE novel.

FURTHER READING

Beebee, Thomas O. *Epistolary Fiction in Europe, 1500–1850.* Cambridge: Cambridge University Press, 1999.

Hinde Stewart, Joan. "The Novelists and Their Fictions." In *French Women and the Age of Enlightenment.* Edited by Samia I. Spencer. Bloomington: Indiana University Press, 1984, 197–211.

———. *Gynographs: French Novels by Women of the Late Eighteenth Century.* Lincoln: University of Nebraska Press, 1993.

Jackson, Susan K. "Publishing Without Perishing: Isabelle de Charrière, a.k.a. *la mouche du coche.*" In *Going Public: Women and Publishing in Early Modern France.* Edited by Elizabeth C. Goldsmith and Dena Goodman. Ithaca, N.Y.: Cornell University Press, 1995.

LIBERALISM

Liberalism is the philosophy that emerged in response to industrialization and modernization in the 19th century. It thus reflects the efforts of the middle class to attain political rights corresponding to their economic rights. In France, liberalism is often associated with the JULY MONARCHY.

Liberalism carries over elements of ENLIGHTENMENT thought, particularly in its faith in science, rationalism, and progress. As a philosophy, liberalism is organized around 18th-century thoughts on freedom. Liberty and equality are the two principal terms associated with the FRENCH REVOLUTION of 1789. Drawing on this legacy, 19th-century liberalism focused on basic personal freedoms. Liberty means a new form of government in which the people are sovereign. Hence liberalism, with its corresponding emphasis on individualism, became possible only through the political conditions established by the French Revolution. However, liberals never espoused a true democracy. They promoted middle-class economic and political interests instead. STENDHAL offers a particularly clear depiction of the clash between liberalism and the forces of reaction in his novel The RED AND THE BLACK.

LIBERTINISM   In the 17th-century, libertinism primarily signified an intellectual openness or a willingness to challenge traditional views, especially in terms of religious dogma. Epicurian and materialist, 17th-century libertines believed that the physical world is organized around certain laws that can be determined through the use of reason. The independence of spirit associated with 17th-century libertinism can be found in the works of such authors as TRISTAN L'HERMITE and SAVIEN CYRANO DE BERGERAC.

If 17th-century libertinism is associated principally with impiety, in the 18th-century the freethinking spirit is linked even more closely to immorality in a world of aristocrats whose main purpose is to seek pleasure. By the 18th century, then, libertinism is associated with debauchery.

Authors such as SADE, CRÉBILLON FILS, LACLOS, RESTIF DE LA BRETONNE, and NERCIAT used eroticism to promote a philosophy of militant rationalism. The primacy of nature and the notion of humans as animals leads to a necessary emphasis on the pursuit of physical pleasure. Nonconformist in morality, religion, and politics, the 18th-century libertine novel is a philosophical reaction to the idealism of the previous century. Libertine novels are philosophical novels that promote materialism and rationalism. As a result, they may also signify an unwillingness to submit to authority that manifests itself in a challenge to the social order.

Libertinism is not synonymous with eroticism or pornography, although libertine novels may contain elements of both, since their morality is based on the expression of natural instincts rather than on their suppression. If they were judged on this idea alone, one could argue that nearly every 18th-century novel is libertine. The historian Robert Darnton's studies of 18th-century reading habits examine requests to publishers for combinations of books that are, at first glance, surprising. A reader might order philosophical works, histories, works critical of absolutism, along with libertine and pornographic novels, all of which share the quality of challenging the social order in some way.

There are two principal sorts of libertine novel. The first is the "roman galant," such as the works of Crébillon, DUCLOS, DIDEROT, or Laclos. The second is the cynical novel in which the "heros" are adventurers, prostitutes, actresses, in other words, not characters drawn from the aristocratic milieu of other libertine novels. There are numerous intertextual references between libertine novels marking the parameters of discourse.

Each individual is called upon to obey his or her own nature. The human condition, then, is defined by needs and desires, no longer by theology. Human beings cannot subsequently be blamed for their vices. Libertine novels are marked by an abandonment of metaphysics for a world, this world, in which each creature exists for its own sake and for the sake of immediate pleasure of the senses and mind. Such an approach may be carried to extremes in the case of Laclos (cruel manipulation) or Sade (violence).

Since the libertine novel gives primacy to feeling love remains a major theme, but it no longer contains the sentimental, hyperbolic exaggerations, adventures, and disguises so prevalent in the works of D'URFÉ, LA CALPRENÈDE, or MADELEINE DE SCUDÉRY. Instead of depicting how human beings should be, it aspires to show are the really are. The authors, challenged by censorship, frequently wrote prefaces to explain how their works are in fact useful by showing the dangers of living by vice.

The libertine novel displays a didactic realism. It is not a genre that promotes women. The aristocratic characters that people these novels live in a world of dissimulation, even more marked among women than men. These are tales of conquest that allow the male hero a new sort of glory through the conquest of a lover. Military metaphors abound, as in the language of Laclos's count de Valmont. The search for pleasure, or perhaps simply distraction, veils a fear of the meaninglessness of one's life characteristic of the aristocracy at the end of the OLD REGIME.

LIFE, A USER'S MANUAL (*LA VIE MODE D'EMPLOI*) GEORGES PEREC (1978)   This remarkable, encyclopedic reconstruction of modern life won the prestigious Médicis Prize in 1978. In one sense, the purpose of the novel is to draw up an inventory of reality through the interweaving of multiple stories. The last section of the novel is meant to give a scientific character to the work. Some 700 pages long, the novel recounts in minute detail life in a Parisian apartment building. This is what gives the novel its structure. Simultaneously, Perec follows a pattern from the game of chess called "the knight's tower," in which the knight stops once on each square of the board. Hence, the structure of the novel is also mathematical in form. The apartment building consists of 10 squares, is 10 stories high, and is 10 apartments wide. For each square there is one chapter. The 42 parts to each chapter also draws from a mathematical algorithmic principle.

The novel, not surprisingly, has a feeling of the bizarre. The principal character, Bartlebooth, is a blend of Herman Melville's character Bartleby, whose refrain was "I would prefer not to do it," and Barnabooth, a character created by the writer Valéry Larbaud, full of desire to act, to live, to create, and to travel. Bartlebooth spends 20 years painting 500 seascapes at different places throughout the world, then another 20 years putting them back together as puzzles after having treated them with a solvent that renders them blank. At his death, Bartlebooth holds a *w*-shaped piece of the puzzle while the piece he needs is an *x*.

The image of the puzzle is central to the text. Perec deliberately plays with the relationship between image and word, turning language into something material.

Thus language becomes an object, signified by the *w* and the *x*. W also refers to the character of Winkler, who drove Bartlebooth into the obsessive game that leads to his death, Winkler's revenge, for reasons the reader never understands. The significance of the letter *w* carries over into other works, as in the imaginary land of *w* associated with the Nazis in Perec's autobiography. *X* may represent the mathematical unknown that Bartlebooth has not taken into account, or it can be transformed into the Nazi swastika. If only he could have transformed the *x* into a *w*. Bartlebooth's elaborate system breaks down when he encounters a space he cannot fill.

The epigraph of the novel, "Look with all your eyes, look," is taken from Jules Verne and represents the novel's purpose, as Perec attempts to evoke the richness and complexity of the world. There is a tension between a desire to say everything and, at the same time, to leave the enumeration and classification of things, a recurring theme in Perec's work, open-ended. The novel reflects trends present in the works of other OuLiPo writers. In fact, the novel is dedicated to the leader of that movement, RAYMOND QUENEAU. For the OuLiPo writers, formal constraint is a fundamental principle of creativity. The novel is replete with an endless profusion of lists that overwhelm the reader with a waterfall of images, as in the lists of ports, ships, and material objects that Bartlebooth draws up in the course of his travels. In the lists of images that abound throughout the text, objects are illuminated or obscured by the movement of the sun as Perec plays with light and shadow, both literally and figuratively. "I seek at the same time the eternal and the ephemeral" is the epigraph of one chapter.

FURTHER READING

Andrews, Chris. "Puzzles and Lists: Georges Perec's *Un homme qui dort*," *MLN* 111, no. 4 (1996): 775–796.

Bellos, David. *Georges Perec: A Life in Words.* Boston: Godine, 1993.

Motte, Warren F. Jr. "Georges Perec on the Grid," *French Review* 57, no. 6 (May 1984): 820–832.

———, ed. *Oulipo: A Primer of Potential Literature.* Lincoln: University of Nebraska Press, 1986.

Schwartz, Paul. *Georges Perec, Traces of His Passage.* Birmingham, Ala.: Summa Publications, 1988.

LIFE OF MARIANNE, THE (*LA VIE DE MARIANNE*) PIERRE CARLET DE MARIVAUX (1731–1742)

The Life of Marianne bears certain resemblances to Marivaux's other unfinished novel, *The* UPSTART PEASANT. Both works are pseudomemoirs written in the first person that tell a story of upward mobility. These "memoirs," written later in life, recount the experiences of an orphan turned countess. A notice (*avertissement*) at the beginning of the novel announces that the manuscript, found in the cupboard of a country house, was written by a woman named Mariannne to a female friend.

Marianne recounts her suffering at the hands of an unfaithful lover. Valville falls in love with Marianne but, because of her uncertain social background, his family opposes their marriage. When he meets Mademoiselle de Varthon, of whom his family does approve, he marries her instead. Poor Marianne can do nothing. Her situation reveals the plight of women in 18th-century society, abandoned for social and economic reasons, as do characters of MARIE-JEANNE RICCOBONI. Marianne is in some ways an ideal 18th-century woman as she is essentially passive and submissive to her destiny. At the same time, Marivaux challenges standard views of a woman's role by allowing Marianne to assert herself through writing. Marianne's recollections of being 15, a vivacious, sensitive young woman who discovers the world and love, are interspersed with her more mature philosophical reflections.

What is remarkable in Marivaux's narrative is that there is more than one Marianne. The older, wiser narrator is the same and yet not the same as the younger, naive, character. In contrast to Jacob in Marivaux's *The Upstart Peasant,* Marianne undergoes a metamorphosis. Literary theorist Béatrice Didier has remarked on the process of self-creation within the narrative framework through the interaction between the author/narrator/character who manipulates the past, present, and future to create the story of a life.

In some ways, this is a traditional narrative drawing on the picaresque tradition. Marivaux's innovation lies in his profound psychological analysis that leads into the development of his own style, called "marivaudage." This distinctive style was sometimes criticized by contemporaries as pretentious. Its affectation recalls the 17th-century *précieuses* (see PRECIOSITY).

FURTHER READING

Haac, Oscar A. *Marivaux.* New York: Twayne, 1974.
Jamieson, Ruth. *Marivaux: A Study in Sensibility.* New York: Octagon Books, 1969.
Marshall, David. *The Surprising Effects of Sympathy: Marivaux, Diderot, Rousseau, and Mary Shelley.* Chicago: University of Chicago Press, 1988.
Rosbottom, Ronald. *Marivaux's Novels: Theme and Function in Early Eighteenth-Century Narrative.* Madison, N.J.: Fairleigh Dickinson University Press, 1974.

LIFE ON EPSILON (*LA VIE SUR EPSILON*) CLAUDE OLLIER (1972)

This is the story of four astronauts, O., Perros, Quilby, and Rossen, who land on the planet Epsilon. Their spaceship is in need of repair and all communication has been cut off. Epsilon is the fifth planet that O. explores, it is divided into five parts, and it is the fifth book in Ollier's cycle of novels.

Life on Epsilon begins as O. decides to join his colleagues who have gone off to explore the planet when strange things begin to occur. Before finding each of his friends, O. is overcome either by cloudlike blades that send him into his past, luminous veils that reveal to him an agonizing future, or waves that cause him to lose consciousness. As a result, O. begins to lose his grasp on reality, a frequent theme in Ollier's works. Meanwhile, O.'s companions have returned to the ship and restored communication. As he returns, O. is overwhelmed yet again with uncertainty about his experiences on Epsilon. Perhaps they have all been an illusion.

As in Ollier's earlier novel, MISE EN SCÈNE, on which this science fiction version is based, the author continues to explore the nature of reality. At the same time, he makes use of the science fiction genre to play with the question of writing itself. Ollier thus uses older literary models to test the limits of the imaginary, not unlike other NOUVEAU ROMAN writers such as ALAIN ROBBE-GRILLET and MICHEL BUTOR.

FURTHER READING

Lindsay, Cecile. *Reflexivity and Revolution in the New Novel: Claude Ollier's Fictional Cycle.* Columbus: Ohio University Press, 1990.

LILY OF THE VALLEY (*LE LYS DE LA VALLÉE*) HONORÉ DE BALZAC (1835)

Lily of the Valley was inspired by Balzac's reading of SAINT-BEUVE'S novel *The SENSUAL MAN* (*Volupté*), which he criticized as badly written, weak, and puritanical. Balzac decided then to create a heroine, Henriette, who would prove to be a virtuous woman by her own taste and inclination. The novel reveals Balzac's fascination with the human social species articulated in his introduction to the HUMAN COMEDY. *Lily of the Valley* also offers the reader one of Balzac's archetypal characters. Madame de Mortsauf is a devoted mother willing to sacrifice her self interest for the sake of her children. As Balzac put it, "The unknown struggle which goes on in a valley of the Indre between Madame de Mortsauf and her passion is perhaps as great as the most famous of battles. On one the glory of the victor is at stake, in the other it is heaven." In this novel, Balzac again manifests his sensitivity in exploring the many and varied aspects of human nature, in particular the tension between reason and passion as revealed through the dynamics of social and familial life.

FURTHER READING

Allen, James Smith. *Popular French Romanticism: Authors, Readers and Books in the Nineteenth Century.* Syracuse, N.Y.: Syracuse University Press, 1981.

Carrère, Jean. *Degeneration in the Great French Masters.* Translated by Joseph McCabe. Freeport, N.Y.: Books for Libraries Press, 1967.

Kanes, Martin, ed. *Critical Essays on Balzac.* Boston: G. K. Hall, 1990.

Smith, Edward C. III. "Honoré de Balzac and the 'Genius' of Walter Scott: Debt and Denial," *Comparative Literature Studies* 36, no. 3 (1999): 209–225.

LITTLE PRINCE, THE (*LE PETIT PRINCE*) ANTOINE DE SAINT-EXUPÉRY (1943)

This extraordinary work blends a wondrous tale with reflections on friendship and love. Written for children, the novel is, in reality, for anyone, young or old, who bears within her- or himself vulnerability and a propensity for solitude. Saint-Exupéry's experience as an aviator is reflected in this story of a pilot who breaks down in the Sahara Desert, where, far from civilization, he encounters a strange and compelling little boy, astonishingly at ease in this deserted place.

"Please . . . draw me a sheep." With these simple words the friendship between the Little Prince and the pilot begins. Unfortunately none of the sheep that the narrator draws satisfies the Little Prince, until, finally, he draws a box with holes in it saying that the sheep is inside. The Little Prince has other concerns as well that are not immediately apparent to the pilot. By asking questions, though, he gradually comes to learn the Prince's story.

The Little Prince comes from a tiny planet where, each day, he has to pull out the baobab roots that threaten to overrun things as well as to clean out the planet's three volcanoes. One day he finds a beautiful flower, a rose that he comes to love. She is vain and demanding, causing the Little Prince to suffer so much that he eventually takes advantage of some migrating birds to escape from her. Exacting as she is, the rose's attitude is, in reality, a defense against her frailty and vulnerability.

As in VOLTAIRE'S *MICROMÉGAS*, the Little Prince travels from one planet to another where he encounters an array of perplexing characters—a vain man, a king, a businessman who thinks he owns the stars because he counts them, a drinker who drinks to forget that he drinks, and a geographer. The Little Prince concludes that adults are strange and not very serious.

After wandering on earth for some time, the Prince finds himself in a rose garden and is shocked to discover that his flower is not unique, despite all her protestations to the contrary. Then he meets a fox and all becomes clear. In a moving scene that holds the key to the entire work, the fox asks the Prince to tame him. "So far, for me you are just a little boy like a hundred thousand other little boys. I do not need you. You don't need me either. For you I am a fox like a hundred thousand other foxes. But if you will tame me, we will need one another. For me you will be unique in all the world. I will be unique for you." "I am beginning to understand," says the Little Prince. "There was a flower. . . . I think she tamed me." The fox reveals to the Prince the essence of life, love, and friendship, saying "One only sees clearly with the heart. The essential is invisible." Overcome with a desire to return to his planet, the Little Prince allows himself to be bitten by a poisonous snake and disappears in the night after doing his best to comfort the pilot who has become attached to him.

Saint-Exupéry exhibits a remarkable and moving sensitivity to the psychology of a child. In a compelling tone of naive trust, Saint-Exupéry shows how poetry, love, tolerance, and respect for others are the true riches in life. The novel is dedicated to Saint-Exupéry's friend Léon Werth, "when he was a child."

FURTHER READING

Cate, Curtis. *Antoine de Saint-Exupéry: His Life and Times.* New York: Paragon House, 1990.

Master, Brian. *A Student's Guide to Saint-Exupéry.* London: Heinemann Educational, 1972.

Mooney, Philip. *Belonging Always: Reflections on Uniqueness.* Chicago: Loyola University Press, 1987.

LORRIS, GUILLAUME DE (MID-12TH CENTURY)

We know almost nothing of Guillaume de Lorris except that he is the author of the first part of *The Romance of the Rose,* continued some 40 years later by JEAN DE MEUN. In this allegorical dream vision, the narrator, who is also the lover, finds himself in the garden of Diversion, where he discovers his love, the rose. Initially received by Fair Welcome, he is thwarted in his pursuit of the rose by Shame, Fear, Refusal, and Slander. The unfinished poem ends with the frustrated lover shut out of the castle of Jealousy.

Typical of medieval ROMANCES, the poem is written in 4,000 lines of octosyllabic rhyming couplets. It offers an intriguing mixture of two genres, the courtly lyric and the courtly romance. This overlapping of forms finds its parallel in the blurring of lines between the lover and the narrator, fiction and reality, and the rose (the flower) and Rose (the lady). HÉLISENNE DE CRENNE's *The TORMENTS OF LOVE,* for example, draws from the medieval tradition of romances such as we see in the works of Guillaume Lorris.

FURTHER READING

Arden, Heather. *The Romance of the Rose.* Boston: Twayne, 1987.

Luria, Maxwell. *A Reader's Guide to the Roman de la Rose.* Hamden, Conn.: Archon, 1982.

LOST ILLUSIONS (LES ILLUSIONS PERDUES) HONORÉ DE BALZAC (1837–1843)

Lost Illusions has been characterized as a reverse bildungsroman. The novel tells the story of Lucien de Rudempré's transformation from a naive, provincial poet to an ambitious Parisian journalist. In contrast to the traditional bildungsroman, however, this is not about Lucien's moral development but, rather, his disillusionment. The novel is divided into three parts: "Two Poets, 1837," "A Distinguished Provincial in Paris, 1839," and "Eve and David, 1843." Together they form the eighth volume of Balzac's HUMAN COMEDY. Set in 1821–22, the novel looks back on the JULY MONARCHY.

The underlying themes of the novel relate to political, social, and economic power in 19th-century French society. Lucien's career as poet/novelist turned journalist allows Balzac to comment on contemporary intellectual life and the way in which literature has been tarnished by materialism. A number of Balzac's works may be characterized as antimaterialist. Although Balzac wrote *Lost Illusions* when ROMANTICISM was already beginning to fade, the novel describes the rise of that 19th-century literary and cultural movement.

Lucien's career begins in the provincial city of Angoulême. His disillusionment with a society incapable of recognizing his genius augments with his move to Paris. Balzac thus turns again to his common theme juxtaposing the mores and manners of Parisians and provincials. Lucien is one of Balzac's monomaniacal figures. If Goriot (in *FATHER GORIOT*) was obsessed with his daughters, Lucien's single passion is to become a poet and to be recognized as such. Lucien runs away to Paris with his older lover, Anaïs de Bargeton, who promptly abandons him when Lucien does not appear as promising a venture in Paris as he had been in the provinces. Lucien can find a publisher neither for his novel nor his volume of poetry. Despite the moral warnings of his romantic circle of idealist friends, sharing equally their poverty and intellectual life, Lucien is seduced by the glitter of the journalist's life and the seductive beauty of a young actress. The close relationship between literature and politics is revealed when Lucien turns to journalism. Despite his initial success, in the end Lucien is attacked by liberals and royalists alike. He returns to Angoulême.

David Séchard, Lucien's devoted friend and brother-in-law, serves as a counterpoint to Lucien's ambition. David, who remains in Angoulême, is never tempted by

Lucien's illusory goals. David toils tirelessly to support his family and, from a distance, Lucien, by his publishing business and his attempts to invent a cheaper method for manufacturing paper. He is exploited both by the capitalist system he does not entirely understand and is ultimately brought down unintentionally by Lucien. David's and Lucien's experiences allows Balzac to comment acidly on economic issues related to book production in the 19th century, the corruption of the literary world, as well as contemporary social values, his stated purpose in the *Human Comedy*.

When Lucien returns to Angoulême, he unwittingly contributes to David's arrest for debt. Overcome with anguish, Lucien leaves a note stating that he intends to commit suicide. As he awaits the night, Lucien encounters the Spanish Jesuit Carlos Herrera, who convinces him that self-interest and ruthless ambition are what should guide him in life. Balzac's novel *Scenes from a Courtesan's Life* describes Lucien's return to Paris, where he is initially successful in entering aristocratic circles, much like STENDHAL's Julien Sorel of *The Red and the Black*. Eventually, however, Lucien likewise fails, finally committing suicide in prison. In this novel, Carlos Herrera turns out to be Jacques Collin, alias Vautrin, the criminal figure in *Father Goriot* who tries to manipulate Rastignac. Ultimately, he becomes head of the Paris police.

Balzac wrote *Lost Illusions* as a serial novel to compete with popular works like EUGÈNE SUE's *MYSTERIES OF PARIS*. Just as this novel reveals changes in book production and literary life, so does Balzac's novel indicate the author's practical need to write novels appealing to a less sophisticated but broader readership. Remarkably, Balzac's novels lose very little in the process. In *Lost Illusions,* Balzac attempts to "give expression to ideas through images." For him, the novelist is the true poet.

FURTHER READING

Allen, James Smith. *Popular French Romanticism: Authors, Readers and Books in the Nineteenth Century*. Syracuse, N.Y.: Syracuse University Press, 1981.

Bresnick, Adam. "The Paradox of *Bildung*: Balzac's *Illusions Perdues*," *MLN* 113, no. 4 (1998): 823–850.

Carrère, Jean. *Degeneration in the Great French Masters*. Translated by Joseph McCabe. Freeport, N.Y.: Books for Libraries Press, 1967.

Kanes, Martin, ed. *Critical Essays on Balzac*. Boston: G. K. Hall, 1990.

Smith, Edward C. III. "Honoré de Balzac and the 'Genius' of Walter Scott: Debt and Denial," *Comparative Literature Studies* 36, no. 3 (1999): 209–225.

LOTI, PIERRE (1850–1923)

Pierre Loti is the pseudonym of Louis Marie Julien Viaud, born in Rochefort-sur-Mer into a modest family of three children. His elder sister was 19 years older than Pierre. They were close, nonetheless, sharing a love of music and painting. From early childhood on, Pierre was fascinated by the sea. Moreover, his brother Gustave's stories of his experience as a sailor inspired Pierre to follow in his footsteps.

Pierre's happy childhood was interrupted by the death of Gustave, buried at sea in 1865. Moreover, his father was accused of theft and spent some days in prison. Although he was later acquitted, Pierre's father was required to pay back the sum supposedly stolen and lost his job, leaving the family in difficult straits.

Pierre entered the naval academy in 1867 and served for more than 42 years, traveling around the world. The journal he kept from 1866 until 1918 provided most of the material for his writing. During a tour in 1872, Pierre sent his sister three articles based on his journal entries about Easter Island. She had the articles published in the journal *L'Illustration*. Friends later suggested turning his entries from a passage through Constantinople in 1876–77 into a novel. His subsequent story of an English officer's love affair with a green-eyed beauty became *AZIYADÉ*.

Aziyadé did not receive much notice. His second work, *Loti's Marriage* (1872), "by the author of *Aziyadé*," was much more successful. This novel draws on Loti's experience in Tahiti and provides the source of his pseudonym. *Loti* means "flower" in the Tahitian language. His third novel, *Romance of a Spahi* (1881), was signed Pierre Loti. As a naval officer, Loti did not have the right to publish works under his own name without permission from a superior.

A spate of novels followed, some set in Brittany such as *My Brother Yves* (1883), his highly successful *ICELAND FISHERMAN* (1886), and *Sailor* (1892). *Ramantcho* is set in Basque country; *MADAME CHRYSANTHÈME*, the inspiration for Puccini's opera *Madame Butterfly,* (1887) and *The Third Youth of Madame Prune* (1895) are set in Japan while *Fantom of the Orient* (1887) and *The Disenchanted* (1906) are both set in Turkey.

Loti's travels clearly fueled his literary imagination, and the reading public responded enthusiastically to his mixture of adventure and exoticism, particularly as he wrote during a period in which the naturalists (see NATURALISM) dominated the literary scene. Loti's novels manifest a melancholy nostalgia for beautiful yet fundamentally inaccessible other worlds of ancient yet crumbling civilizations symbolized, for example, by the last full bloom of the chrysanthemum just before it withers and dies. Loti is drawn to what he sees as the primitive, human spirit of the Orient untainted by the progress of civilization. At the same time, he evokes his own sense of exile. Always appreciative of the exotic beauty of faraway lands and people, Loti realizes that he will always remain something of a stranger. Although he was not particularly oriented toward political life, Loti did speak out in favor of the Turks, in their conflict with the Greeks and Armenians, and, during World War I, the Germans.

Because of the strong links between Loti's personal journal and his novels, the line between fiction and reality is blurred. Descriptions of theatrical and puppet performances make explicit Loti's interest in and recognition of the question of mimesis. His works appear as a collage consisting of real letters, documents, and personal accounts superimposed on the product of fantasy and imagination. Moreover, by the nature of his sources, the relationship between author and narrator is also ambiguous.

Readers also enjoyed Loti's travel journals and short stories, but his five dramatic works were not nearly as successful. A popular writer, Loti was elected to the Académie Française in 1891. In his acceptance speech, he made a point of attacking the naturalists.

FURTHER READING

Barthes, Roland. "Pierre Loti: Aziyadé." In *New Critical Essays.* Berkeley: University of California Press, 1990.

Blanch, Lesley. *Pierre Loti: Portrait of an Escapist.* London: Collins, 1983.

———. *Pierre Loti: The Legendary Romantic.* San Diego: Harcourt Brace Jovanovich, 1983.

Hartman, Elwood. *Three Nineteenth-Century French Writers/ Artists and the Maghreb: The Literary and Artistic Depictions of North Africa by Théophile Gautier, Eugène Fromentin and Pierre Loti.* Tübingen, Germany: Narr, 1994.

Hughes, Edward J. *Writing Marginality in Modern French Literature: From Loti to Genet.* Cambridge, New York: Cambridge University Press, 2001.

Lerner, Michael. *Pierre Loti's Dramatic Works.* Lewiston, Me.: E. Mellen Press, 1998.

Szyliowicz, Irene. *Pierre Loti and the Oriental Woman.* New York: St. Martin's Press, 1988.

LOUIS LAMBERT HONORÉ DE BALZAC (1832–1835)

The partly autobiographical novel *Louis Lambert* describes Balzac's experience in secondary school (collège) and his subsequent philosophical development. Like *Seraphita,* it also reflects Balzac's fascination with metaphysics and mysticism in the 1830s. Like Balzac, Lambert is influenced by Swedish philosopher and mystic Emanuel Swedenborg (1688–1772). In this novel, Balzac argues in favor of Christianity as the only real religion since the beginning of the world.

According to the story, Balzac the narrator and Lambert are fellow students in Paris, both fascinated by philosophy. Lambert goes so far as to write his own treatise on metaphysics, synthesizing Swedenborg's theories with materialist views and the Austrian physician Anton Mesmer's (1734–1815) work on hypnosis. Unfortunately, one of Lambert's teachers destroys his work and Lambert has to leave the school. Lambert goes to Paris to continue his philosophical studies but is disillusioned. He appears in LOST ILLUSIONS as part of the circle of romantic idealists with whom Lucien de Rudempré associates until seduced away from literature by journalism.

In *Louis Lambert,* disenchantment with Paris leads Lambert to return to his original Swedenborgian mysticism. Lambert decides to live in the country with an uncle. There he falls in love with a beautiful Jewish woman, Pauline de Villenois, but he is already losing his mind. His passion for Pauline pushes Lambert over the edge. The night before his wedding Lambert goes insane, entering into a trance that lasts until his death three years later. Pauline nurses him until the end. The romantic (see ROMANTICISM) elements of mysticism, passion, and madness are immediately evident in this and other works produced by Balzac in the 1830s.

FURTHER READING
Allen, James Smith. *Popular French Romanticism: Authors, Readers and Books in the Nineteenth Century.* Syracuse, N.Y.: Syracuse University Press, 1981.
Bresnick, Adam. "The Paradox of *Bildung:* Balzac's *Illusions Perdues,*" *MLN* 113, no. 4 (1998): 823–850.
Carrère, Jean. *Degeneration in the Great French Masters.* Translated by Joseph McCabe. Freeport, N.Y.: Books for Libraries Press, 1967.
Kanes, Martin, ed. *Critical Essays on Balzac.* Boston: G. K. Hall, 1990.
Smith, Edward C. III. "Honoré de Balzac and the 'Genius' of Walter Scott: Debt and Denial," *Comparative Literature Studies* 36, no. 3 (1999): 209–225.

LOUISE DE LA VALLIÈRE   See VICOMTE DE BRAGELONNE

LOVER, THE (*L'AMANT*) MARGUERITE DURAS (1984)   This autobiographical work is Duras's most powerful novel about the birth of passion and over-whelming desire. The Lover is already a man, rich, and Chinese. The girl is white, 15 years old, and a student in a boarding school in Saigon, South Vietnam. They are two beings as different from each other as two people could be. Everything separates them—age, sex, culture—yet they come together with a burning and desperate passion. He loves her beyond reason. She tears herself up, and him, vacillating between desire and rebellion, silence and humiliation. In the end, he cannot escape tradition and culture, and so he marries the Chinese woman his father has chosen for him. She returns to France to become a great writer. Neither one forgets. Passion has marked them for life.

This is the eternal story of impossible, first love and the birth of passion. The Lover is entirely captivated but cannot escape the constraints of his own culture, a recurring theme in Duras's works. The girl may not be truly in love but is certainly a prisoner to her passion as much as her obsession with the idea of the great book she will one day write.

The novel develops around a series of images. There is colonial Saigon, with its incessant rumors, preju-dices, narrowness, and long, muddy river. There are images, too, of Duras's mother, distant from herself and others, her elder brother who is always watch-ing, and her dearly loved younger brother. Duras's "snapshots" make for the fragmented structure of the novel. It also makes the reader somewhat of a voyeur, somewhat like the figure of Duras's brother. With its intensely poetic, rhythmic, and musical language, the novel gives the reader the impression of slow breath-ing. It was an instant success, partly due to its confes-sional tone. *Lover* received the Goncourt Prize in 1984, bringing Duras international fame as a writer. Trans-lated into 40 languages, it was also adapted to film by Jean-Jacques Annaud in 1992. Disturbed by his inter-pretation, Duras wrote *The Lover from Northern China* (1991), reworking the same story in a different way.

FURTHER READING
McNeece, Lucy Stone. "The Reader in the Field of Rye: Mar-guerite Duras' L'Amour," *Modern Language Studies* 22, no. 1 (Winter 1992): 3–16.
Morgan, Janice. "Fiction and Autobiography/Language and Silence: L'Amant de Duras," *French Review* 63, no. 2 (December 1989): 271–279.

LUCIEN LEUWEN STENDHAL (1833–1836), PUBLISHED 1894   The theme of a young man's struggle in life runs through most of Stendhal's novels. In this unfinished novel, the principal character Luc-ien, the son of a wealthy Parisian banker, is blessed. His father and mother care for him; he is wealthy. In fact, he has everything to make him happy from the outset of life, unlike Stendhal's character Julien Sorel, who must make his own way. However, Lucien is not content. He feels he must earn good fortune through his own merit.

As a young second lieutenant, Lucien is sent to the garrison in Nancy, at the beginning of the JULY MON-ARCHY. The local aristocracy believes he is a republican and he surprises them with his social ambitions. Luc-ien is soon admitted into the best salons of this provin-cial town, where he falls in love with a young widow, Madame de Chasteller. When he hears a rumor that she is pregnant by a rival, Lucien leaves Nancy in despair.

Back in Paris, Lucien's father helps him get a post in the Ministry of the Interior, where Lucien enters the world of money and power. He does brilliantly but is scornful of the society in which he finds himself. When his father dies suddenly, Lucien pays off his debts and leaves Paris for a diplomatic post abroad. According to Stendhal's notes, Lucien was eventually to reconcile with Madame Chasteller upon discovering that she had, in fact, never betrayed him.

Another writer, Madame Jules Gaulthier, suggested the plot of the novel to Stendhal. Its structure and themes are reminiscent of HONORÉ DE BALZAC's COMÉDIE HUMAINE, especially since Lucien Leuwen was originally intended to have three parts, the first depicting provincial life, the second life in Paris, and the third life in cosmopolitan Europe.

It is possible that Stendhal never finished the novel since he could never have published such a sharp critique of society while occupying a government post himself. Lucien's character seems closest of all Stendhal's heroes to that of the author. Lucien is a romantic hero (see ROMANTICISM), typical of Stendhal in the sense that social constraints frustrate his natural energy and passion. Nonetheless, Lucien remains faithful to his republican ideals.

In its portrayal of 19th-century society and its values, Lucien Leuwen echoes themes found in Stendhal's masterpiece, The RED AND THE BLACK. Some critics have praised the novel as an astute political work raising serious questions about the exercise of power. Others see in it an accurate representation of both the fall of the aristocracy and the rise of a cynical bourgeoisie, especially after 1830.

FURTHER READING

Alter, Robert, in collaboration with Carol Cosman. *A Lion for Love: A Critical Biography of Stendhal.* New York: Basic Books, 1979.

Auerbach, Erich. *Mimesis: The Representation of Reality in Western Literature.* Translated by Willard R. Trask. Princeton, N.J.: Princeton University Press, 1953.

Fineshriber, William. *H. Stendhal the Romantic Rationalist.* Philadelphia: R. West, 1977.

Girard, René. *Deceit, Desire and the Novel: Self and Other in Literary Structure.* Translated by Yvonne Freccero. Baltimore, London: Johns Hopkins University Press, 1976.

Green, Frederick Charles. *Stendhal.* New York: Russell and Russell, 1970.

Hemmings, F. W. J. *Stendhal: A Study of His Novels.* Oxford: Clarendon Press, 1964.

Keates, Jonathan. *Stendhal.* New York: Carroll and Graf, 1997.

May, Gita. *Stendhal and the Age of Napoleon.* New York: Columbia University Press, 1977.

LYRICISM   Lyricism is a term first and foremost associated with poetry, but its characteristics have manifested themselves in the novel as well. Originally, lyricism referred to ancient compositions that were chanted or sung to the accompaniment of music. Subsequently, lyricism applied only to poetry that recalled the rhythm or character of the odes of classical antiquity. In the modern era, lyricism came to denote poetry *or* fiction that expresses the grandeur and nobility of intense emotions.

In the 17th century lyricism was most evident in the works of the *précieuses* (see PRECIOSITY), who encountered opposition from the proponents of CLASSICISM. While classicism tended to dominate the literature of the 18th century, certain writers such as JEAN-JACQUES ROUSSEAU produced works marked by a lyrical tone that lay the foundation for the subsequent movements of SENTIMENTALISM and ROMANTICISM. After romanticism, the legacy of lyricism continued to manifest itself in the poetry of writers such as Guillaume Apollinaire, Paul Verlaine, and Arthur Rimbaud, whose influence extended into other realms of fiction.

MADAME BOVARY GUSTAVE FLAUBERT (1857)

Living a reclusive life at home in Croisset, Flaubert worked five long years on this very popular novel that provoked a scandal. Madame Bovary has become an iconic figure whose sufferings, even if she brings them on herself, may nonetheless arouse the reader's sympathies.

Although Flaubert began working on *Madame Bovary* in 1851, the idea for the novel was conceived in 1849 when friends criticized his reading of *The Temptation of Saint Anthony,* suggesting that Flaubert might have more success if he undertook a more concrete subject. The novel first appeared in serial form (see ROMAN FEUILLETON) in *La Revue de Paris,* a journal founded by Flaubert's friend Maxime Du Camp. Authorities disapproved of the novel's liberalism. In fact, Flaubert was taken to court for immorality, as was *La Revue.* Fortunately, Flaubert was acquitted. When the novel was published as a volume by Michel Lévy in 1857, its success was assured. The court proceedings had made the novel and Flaubert famous. Critics approved of the work, particularly CHARLES AUGUSTINE SAINTE-BEUVE and Charles Baudelaire. Flaubert, however, was disturbed by the trial experience and turned to the past for his next novel, *SALAMMBÔ.*

Despite the accusations against Flaubert, one could argue that *Madame Bovary* is, in its own way, a novel of morality. It is the story of Emma Bovary, a young woman dissatisfied with her life and, consequently, the victim of her own unrealizable and unrealistic dreams. Emma suffers from the mediocrity of provincial life.

Critics have frequently commented that Flaubert's characters are believable "types," so much so that they have entered the vernacular. Flaubert draws on his life experience and, more important, his own feelings, in particular his passion for an older, married woman whom he met in 1836, Élisa Schlésinger, and his relationship with Louise Colet, a bluestocking poet whom he met in 1844 and with whom he had a stormy relationship for a decade. Perhaps this is why Flaubert says "Madame Bovary is me." Later he wrote, "When I wrote the scene of Madame Bovary's poisoning, I had the taste of arsenic in my mouth. . . . My imaginary characters affect me, pursue me, or rather it is me who is in them." Flaubert's identification with his characters gives power to his writing.

The novel opens with Charles Bovary, a young student in a provincial secondary school who becomes a country doctor. Dominated by his mother, Charles is married off to an older widow who loves him passionately but who rules him with an iron hand. After her death, Charles meets Emma while treating her father, a wealthy farmer, for an illness.

Emma received a convent education where, in the company of provincial society girls, she read romantic novels. Emma consequently desires the passion and romance she has read about in books. Her marriage to Charles brings her only disillusionment. She finds village life suffocating. At one point, Emma does try to make her marriage work by promoting her husband's career. She encourages him to experiment on a young patient with a clubfoot; the experiment leads to disastrous results when the young man's leg must be amputated.

An invitation to a ball held by the marquis de Vaubyessard, where Emma dances with a viscount, brings all her wild dreams back to the surface, and she can no longer tolerate her miserable existence. Depression and a nervous illness inspire Charles to move with his wife, to whom he is utterly devoted, to a larger town, Yonville-l'Abbaye. Emma is pregnant.

In Yonville, the Bovarys meet several characters crucial to the novel, among them Homais, the progressive and anticlerical pharmacist, and Léon Depuis, a handsome young man serving as clerk to the notary. Léon falls in love with Emma, who enjoys his company but does not at first respond to his overtures in the way he would like. After Emma's baby is born, Emma and Léon incite comment from the neighbors when he is seen accompanying her home. Finally, though, bored himself with life in Yonville and frustrated by a love he sees is hopeless, Léon leaves for Paris.

Léon's departure leaves an unexpected void in Emma's life until, shortly thereafter, she is seduced by Rodolphe Boulanger, an elegant country gentleman. Emma unfortunately precipitates the end of their relationship by showing up unexpectedly at his home several times and by generally throwing all caution to the wind. Moreover, she is insistent that they run away together. After putting her off several times, Rodolphe finally agrees to leave with Emma at a given time, but on the eve of their departure he abandons her. Suffering from this terrible blow, Emma again falls ill, believing that she will die of sadness. Charles tends her devotedly for weeks.

When Emma recovers from her illness, Charles suggests that, to give her pleasure, they attend the opera in Rouen. There Emma again meets Léon. Charles foolheartedly suggests that Emma remain in Rouen for a few days on her own. So begins the long-awaited and torrid affair between Emma and Léon. Emma finds an excuse to return weekly to Rouen. Happy in her new love, Emma luxuriantly gives in to all of her desires, going into debt to a merchant, L'Heureux, who finally

threatens her with humiliating legal repercussions. Léon, already disenchanted with Emma's extravagant demands, refuses to help. Frantic, Emma tries to prostitute herself to Rodolphe only to be humiliatingly rejected. Finally, in the last stage of desperation, Emma coerces the pharmacist's assistant to give her arsenic, with which she poisons herself. At her burial, Charles cries out, "It is fate's fault."

This pessimistic line is the moral of Flaubert's cheerless story, which serves as an indictment of commonplace bourgeois values. Emma's downfall is caused by the opposition of dreams to reality. Ethically unsettling, the novel condemns neither marriage nor adultery and consequently had a profound influence on the realists (see REALISM). It is possible that Flaubert's ambiguous depiction of marriage also influenced GEORGE SAND, with whom he corresponded for 13 years.

The applicability of the American author Henry James's statement, "art and morality are two perfectly different things," pertains to Flaubert, whose ambition was to strive for "pure art." One of Flaubert's great gifts was his ability to create characters who are simultaneously recognizable types and individuals. Flaubert is innovative in his use of *"style indirect libre"* (represented discourse), which creates an unsettling problem of perspective since the reader is uncertain whether the narrator or the character is speaking. This device marks Flaubert's contribution to the rise of the modern novel.

FURTHER READING

Brombert, Victor. *The Novels of Flaubert*. Princeton, N.J.: Princeton University Press, 1973.

Culler, Jonathan. *Flaubert and the Uses of Uncertainty*. Ithaca, N.Y.: Cornell University Press, 1974.

LaCapra, Dominick. *'Madame Bovary' on Trial*. Ithaca, N.Y.: Cornell University Press, 1982.

Orr, Mary. *Flaubert Writing the Masculine*. Oxford: Oxford University Press, 2000.

Porter, Laurence M., ed. *Critical Essays on Gustave Flaubert*. Boston: G. K. Hall, 1986.

MADAME CHRYSANTHEMUM (*MADAME CHRYSANTHÈME*) PIERRE LOTI (1887) Drawing on Loti's personal journal, *Madame Chrysanthème* tells the story of a young naval officer's love affair with

a gentle Japanese maiden he meets in Nagasaki. The story becomes the inspiration for Giacomo Puccini's opera *Madama Butterfly*. Like Loti's other works, *Madame Chrysanthème* manifests a melancholy nostalgia for beautiful yet fundamentally inaccessible other worlds of ancient civilizations symbolized, for example, by the last full bloom of the chrysanthemum just before it withers and dies. Loti is drawn to what he sees as the primitive, human spirit of the Orient, untainted by the progress of civilization. At the same time, he evokes his own sense of exile. Always appreciative of the exotic beauty of faraway lands and people, Loti realizes that he will always remain something of a stranger.

FURTHER READING

Blanch, Lesley. *Pierre Loti: Portrait of an Escapist.* London: Collins, 1983.
———. *Pierre Loti: the Legendary Romantic.* San Diego: Harcourt Brace Jovanovich, 1983.
Hartman, Elwood. *Three Nineteenth-Century French Writers/ Artists and the Maghreb: The Literary and Artistic Depictions of North Africa by Théophile Gautier, Eugène Fromentin and Pierre Loti.* Tübingen, Germany: Narr, 1994.
Hughes, Edward J. *Writing Marginality in Modern French Literature: from Loti to Genet.* Cambridge, New York: Cambridge University Press, 2001.
Lerner, Michael. *Pierre Loti's Dramatic Works.* Lewiston, Me.: E. Mellen Press, 1998.
Szyliowicz, Irene. *Pierre Loti and the Oriental Woman.* New York: St. Martin's Press, 1988.

MADAME GERVAISAIS EDMOND HUOT DE GONCOURT (1869)

The setting of this novel by Edmond and Jules de Goncourt is Rome in three guises: the antique, the baroque, and the contemporary Italian City, and was written under the influence of the scholar abbé J. Gaume's *The Three Romes. Journal of a Voyage in Italy,* three volumes (1856). The Goncourt brothers spent five weeks in Rome that same year. (Their notes were published posthumously in 1896 as *Notes on Italy.*) The brothers returned again to Italy once they had decided to set a novel in Rome.

The model for the principal character, Madame Gervaisais, is the Goncourt brothers' aunt, Nephtalie Lebas de Courmont. Nephtalie had two sons, one of whom was sickly and died at the age of 10. After her eldest child's death, Nephtalie moved to Rome with her second son and mixed in elite social circles until her spiritual "conversion" in approximately 1842. Nephtalie died of tuberculosis in 1844 as she was preparing to meet the pope. All these elements, life in Rome, a sickly child, conversion, and death connected to a meeting with the pope, make their way into the novel.

Madame Gervaisais also resembles the authors themselves, particularly in her rediscovery of a taste for painting. One possible reading of the novel thus entails an ontological analysis of the various elements that make up Madame Gervaisais's very being. Beyond her traits drawn from Nephtalie or the Goncourts themselves, Madame Gervaisais is also a creature of the brothers' imaginations. She is nearly a caricature of a mystic as she reads Saint François de Sales's works of devotion and mortifies herself. In fact, their depiction caused Sainte-Beuve to accuse the Goncourts of having no real understanding of Roman Catholic piety. Madame Gervaisais is a baroque beauty who slowly destroys herself. The evocation of the baroque, however, is only of passing interest to the Goncourts.

The novel demonstrates the Goncourt brothers' descriptive powers. Although he criticized them for misunderstanding Catholic mysticism, Sainte-Beuve also remarked in his notes, "The goal is description. Madame Gervaisais' feelings are only an accident, the means for an invasion of painting in literature."

FURTHER READING

Billy, André. *The Goncourt Brothers.* New York: Horizon Press, 1960.
Goncourt, E. *The Goncourt Journals, 1851–1870.* New York: Greenwood Press, 1968.
Grant, Richard B. *The Goncourt Brothers.* New York: Twayne, 1972.

MADEMOISELLE DE CLERMONT FÉLICITÉ DE GENLIS (1802)

Madame de Genlis's *Mademoiselle de Clermont* is a revival of the 17th-century historical novel and recalls MADAME DE LAFAYETTE's *Princesse de Montpensier*. The basic plot is drawn from a story Genlis once heard from a relative who had been a close friend of the novel's heroine. Genlis heard the story about 1772 but did not decide to write the novel until 1802. *Mademoiselle de Clermont* was an immediate success and was republished numerous times until 1880.

According to the anecdote, Louise Marie Anne de Bourbon-Condé (who went under the name Mademoiselle de Clermont) fell deeply in love with Louis de Melin, prince d'Épinay. Although the prince was of high birth, he could not pretend to the hand of a princess of the blood. According to legend, Mademoiselle de Clermont and Melun married secretly. Unfortunately, shortly thereafter he died from a hunting accident. Genlis thus borrowed the framework for her novel from history in this story of pure and tragic love, chivalry, and idealism. At the same time, she offers a contrast to the SENTIMENTAL NOVEL often associated with ROUSSEAU's New Heloïse.

In a manner that recalls Madame de Lafayette's PRIN-CESS OF CLÈVES, the story takes place at court, allowing Genlis to comment on the lies, spying, and constraints of etiquette associated with court life. Court society is like a theater where appearances are what counts, regardless of an individual's true feelings. The theme of appearance versus reality is a common one in the French literary tradition and is most often associated with the works of Rousseau.

Mademoiselle de Clermont and her lover encounter numerous obstacles to their happiness that surpass the problem of birth. Political interests nearly prevent their union as Mademoiselle de Clermont's brother wishes to marry his sister to a foreign ruler. In the conflict between duty and passion, the lovers must also struggle against social constraints. At court, every word and gesture is the subject of scrutiny. Even after their clandestine marriage, Mademoiselle de Clermont is required to attend the king, externally unperturbed by the fact that her husband is dying. In fact, she is unable to attend him on his deathbed. The duties of a princess come before those of a wife.

Genlis's style recalls the CLASSICISM of the period she depicts. The portraits of her principal characters are suitably vague, while their expressions of love are dignified, even obscure. The profound love between Mademoiselle de Clermont and Melun develops in stages. It is not love at first sight. Consequently, Genlis's heroes differ from those of contemporary female novelists such as Madame Riccoboni or Madame de Cottin. This charming novel was much admired by contemporary readers and marks a transition from the classic historical novel into the romantic (see ROMANTICISM).

FURTHER READING

Harmand, Jean. A Keeper of Royal Secrets; Being the Private and Political Life of Madame de Genlis. London: E. Nash, 1913.
Schroder, Anne L. "Going Public Against the Academy in 1784: Madame de Genlis Speaks out on Gender Bias," Eighteenth Century Studies 32, no. 3, Constructions of Femininity (Spring 1999): 376–382.
Wyndham, Violet. Madame de Genlis: A Biography. New York: Roy, 1960.

MADEMOISELLE DE MAUPIN THÉOPHILE GAUTIER (1835)

In the famous preface to this novel, Gautier declared the doctrine of art for art's sake by rejecting any intrusion of criticism or morality into artistic creation. Gautier thus marked his final break with the romantic movement (see ROMANTICISM).

This EPISTOLARY NOVEL depicts the life of a singer at the end of the 17th century. Madeleine de Maupin is alone in the world, fairly wealthy, energetic, and romantic. Her romantic idealism leads her to disguise herself as a man to learn from experience how men's views on life differ from those of women. Her first revelations of the male perspective are discomfiting. However, quickly enough Madeleine begins to enjoy her new life of gallantry that leads to a series of surprising adventures. The sister of a friend falls madly in love with her and she is forced into a duel because she refuses to marry another young woman. Ultimately, she winds up in a château, still pursued by a female admirer, Rosanette, along with Albert, a sentimental young man who suspects that Madeleine may not be exactly as she appears. Finally, still trying to console Rosanette, Madeleine gives in to Albert.

The novel is rich in digressions as well as description, drawing on both the 17th-century tradition in fiction and on 18th-century libertine novels (see LIBERTINISM). Gautier breaks from tradition with his irreverent disdain for morality, at the same time as he manifests his aesthetic refinement.

FURTHER READING

Barsoum, Marlène. Théophile Gautier's Mademoiselle de Maupin: Toward a Definition of 'Androgynous Discourse.' New York: P. Lang, 2001.

Richardson, Joanna. *Théophile Gautier, His Life and Times.* London: M. Reinhardt, 1958.

Smith, Albert Brewster. *Ideal and Reality in the Fictional Narratives of Théophile Gautier.* Gainesville: University of Florida Press, 1969.

Snell, Robert. *Théophile Gautier: A Romantic Critic of the Visual Arts.* Oxford: Clarendon Press; New York: Oxford University Press, 1982.

Tennant, P. E. *Théophile Gautier.* London: Athlone Press, 1975.

MAD LOVE (*L'AMOUR FOU*) ANDRÉ BRETON (1937)

This novel articulates the surrealist conception of a couple (see SURREALISM), as Breton evokes the "mad love" he feels for his wife, Jacqueline. The love he experiences is the epitome of the surrealist manner of life of which love and its "convulsive" beauty are its greatest expressions.

This novel that is not quite a novel reflects Breton's belief in the significance of chance and coincidence. In chapter four, for example, Breton analyzes "Sunflower," a poem he wrote in 1932. It is a product of the "automatic writing" process, by which the writer attains free expression of his subconscious mind, unconstrained by reason. The places in Paris the poem depicts are those through which he later strolls with Jacqueline on the first night they spend together. Other signs also appear to give meaning to Breton's experience. A friend points out a poster bearing the name Reverdy, the poet to whom Breton dedicated "Sunflower."

Coincidence, in Breton's mind, signifies necessity and confirms the overlapping of the real and the imaginary. The surrealist's attention to the strange makes mad love possible. This work inspired a generation of artists and intellectuals who sought to attain the mythic heights of the mad love evoked by Breton.

FURTHER READING
Balakian, Anna, and Rudolf E. Kuenzli, eds. *André Breton Today.* New York: W. Locker and Owens, 1989.

Carrouges, Michel. *André Breton and the Basic Concepts of Surrealism.* Translated Maura Prendergast. Tuscaloosa: University of Alabama Press, 1974.

Caws, Mary Ann. *André Breton.* New York: Twayne, n.d.; London: Prentice Hall International, 1996.

———. *Surrealism and the Literary Imagination: A Study of Breton and Bacheard.* The Hague: Mouton, 1966.

Polizzotti, Mark. *Revolution of the Mind: The Life of André Breton.* New York: Da Capo Press, 1997.

MAGIC SKIN, THE (*LA PEAU DE CHAGRIN*) HONORÉ DE BALZAC (1831)

Magic Skin reflects influences at work during Balzac's early years as a writer, particularly the works of the German writer E. T. A. Hoffmann (1776–1822). Moreover, when Balzac's mother miraculously recovered from an illness, he began to read the works of thinkers such as Jacob Boehme (1688–1772), Emanuel Swedenborg (1688–1772), and Anton Mesmer (1734–1815), all of which had an impact on *Magic Skin*. While this novel is perhaps not Balzac's most refined work, it is certainly unique. It is divided into three parts: "The Talisman," "Woman with no Heart," and "Agony."

Set in 1830, the novel opens when young Raphaël du Valentin has just gambled his last coin and lost. Hopeless, he decides to commit suicide but must wait for dark before throwing himself into the Seine. As he wanders along, he enters an antique store in which he confides his sorrow to an enigmatic shopkeeper who offers him a magic skin that can grant the owner's wishes. As a warning, the shopkeeper tells Raphaël that with each wish, the skin shrinks, leading inexorably toward death. "If you possess me you will possess everything, yet you will belong to me."

At this point, the young man's friends turn up looking for him. Together they set off for an evening of pleasure. In the course of an evening marked by excess, Raphaël agrees to tell the story of his life and explain his desire to commit suicide. His litany of family problems, financial problems, and problems in love are what have driven him to despair.

Raphaël lives in poverty in Paris while trying to write (much like Lucien in LOST ILLUSIONS, and Balzac himself) when a friend leads him into a life of debauchery. As his situation worsens, Raphakl begins to make wishes on the skin, first for money. This is when the real trouble starts. By the third part of the novel, Raphaël is still making wishes with no consideration for the consequences. Upon the rediscovery of a lost love, he decides to marry and drops the skin into a well in an attempt to avoid the Faustian destiny he chose and cannot escape. To save him, Raphaël's lover,

Pauline, *wishes* to commit suicide. When Raphaël stops her, it is he who dies.

Magic Skin is a romantic work (see ROMANTICISM), not only for its tragic end but for the Faustian deal that leads inevitably to it. The tension in Raphaël's life between reason and passion that is likewise romantic is also a recurring theme in Balzac's works overall.

FURTHER READING

Allen, James Smith. *Popular French Romanticism: Authors, Readers and Books in the Nineteenth Century.* Syracuse, N.Y.: Syracuse University Press, 1981.

Carrère, Jean. *Degeneration in the Great French Masters.* Translated by Joseph McCabe. Freeport, N.Y.: Books for Libraries Press, 1967.

Kanes, Martin, ed. *Critical Essays on Balzac.* Boston: G. K. Hall, 1990.

Smith, Edward C. III. "Honoré de Balzac and the 'Genius' of Walter Scott: Debt and Denial," *Comparative Literature Studies* 36, no. 3 (1999): 209–225.

MAILLET, ANTONINE (1929–)

A French-Canadian novelist and playwright born in New Brunswick, in many of her works Maillet focuses on the lost culture of the Acadians of Nova Scotia. Her most famous novel, *PÉLAGIE* (1979), won the Goncourt Prize. A true storyteller, Maillet creates marvelous characters and fantastic tales like the story of Pélagie, who, with a cart full of her belongings and children, sets off with her friends from the U.S. state of Georgia. For 10 years they travel north, back to their homeland, joined along the way by other exiled Acadians. Maillet's use of language is playful, creative, and original as she revives the Acadian dialect of the 18th century. Her knowledge of RABELAIS, on whom she wrote her doctoral dissertation, is readily apparent.

Maillet began her literary career with the publication of a play consisting of a series of monologues by a clever old house cleaner. With its rich language it was an instant success. Maillet continued to write novels as well as other works for the theater. Her most significant works have contributed to the reclamation of the lost Acadian culture that lingers on in an oral tradition that Maillet makes every attempt to preserve. She has become a legendary figure in Acadia, although some contemporary writers have accused her of an overly nostalgic vision of the past.

In *On the Eighth Day* (1986) and *L'Oursiade* (not translated, 1990), Maillet turns away from Acadian characters while continuing to favor fantastic legends and tales. *The Confessions of Jeanne de Valois* (1992) is a more serious work. In this novel, an elderly nun recounts her life in a Quebecois convent while reflecting on recent history.

FURTHER READING

Dinwoodie, C. "Where is Acadia?" *British Journal for Canadian Studies* 1 (1986): 15–29.

Fitzpatrick, Marjorie A. "Antonine Maillet: The Search for a Narrative Voice," *Journal of Popular Culture* 15, no. 3 (Winter 1981): 4–13.

Smith, Donald. *Voices of Deliverance: Interviews with Quebec and Canadian Writers.* Toronto: Anansi, 1986.

MALONE DIES (MALONE MEURT) SAMUEL BECKETT (1951)

In this novel a senile and wretched old man tries to write the story of a man and woman. He begins by inventing the character of Sapo but then interrupts the narrative to offer an apparently irrelevant list of his possessions. The immobile old man cannot move from his bed and so draws his possessions forward with the aid of a stick. The image is one of ultimate degradation and decrepitude. As the old man continues his story, new characters come into his head: Louis (more than one), Malone, and, Macmann. Then Malone slowly falls apart, in body and mind, as his story reaches its delirious and sordid end.

This second volume of Beckett's trilogy that also includes *MOLLOY* and *The UNNAMEABLE* evokes the sense of a mysterious abyss from which issues a strange and uncertain voice. Malone's voice speaks but it is incoherent and disjointed. No outside event or influence breaks the illusion of reality that Malone lives. He seems to exist only internally. His voice is the direct expression of the self, offering an unending and uncontrolled stream of words that do nothing to redeem him. Eminently modern and pessimistic, Beckett's novel challenges a dominant concept in Western philosophy since Descartes, the notion that thought, expressed through language, affirms one's existence.

FURTHER READING

Bair, Dierdre. *Samuel Beckett: A Biography*. New York: Summit Books, 1990.

Cronin, Anthony. *Samuel Beckett: The Last Modernist*. New York: Harper Collins, 1997.

Dukes, Gerry. *Samuel Beckett*. London: Penguin, 2001.

Gordon, Lois. *The World of Samuel Beckett, 1906–1946*. New Haven, Conn.: Yale University Press, 1996.

McCarthy, Patrick A. *Critical Essays on Samuel Beckett*. Boston: G. K. Hall, 1986.

Pattie, David. *The Complete Critical Guide to Samuel Beckett*. London, New York: Routledge, 2000.

Rathjen, Friedhelm, ed. *In Principle, Beckett Is Joyce*. Edinburgh: Split Pea Press, 1994.

MALOT, HECTOR (1830–1907)

Hector Malot moved from Rouen to Paris to work in a notary's office and study law while embarking at the same time on a literary career. Although he ultimately became a well-respected literary critic, Malot was most famous for his idealist novels.

Malot's successful first novel, *Lovers* (1859), was followed by *Spouses* (1865) and *Children* (1866). Together this trilogy is entitled *Victims of Love*. A prolific writer, between 1859 and 1896 Malot published an astonishing 70-novels, some of which consist of several volumes. Among them are *The World's Inn* (4 volumes, 1875–76), *Marriage Battles* (3 volumes, 1877), *Doctor Claude* (2 volumes, 1879), *Rowdy Bohemia* (3 volumes, 1880), *Romain Kalbris* (1869), and *A Second Empire Marriage* (1873). Malot's most famous work, which is still read today, is The FOUNDLING (1878). This story of an orphan's adventures was followed by *Family life* in 1893. In 1896, Malot published his *Novel of My Novels*, a literary autobiography.

Malot's novels may generally be characterized as naturalist (see NATURALISM). Because of their didactic, moralizing tone, they are mostly forgotten today with the exception of *The Foundling*, which remains a classic of children's literature.

MALRAUX, ANDRÉ (1901–1976)

While Malraux ultimately became one of the more remarkable literary figures of the 20th century as an adventurer, novelist, and humanist, his beginnings were surprisingly inauspicious. After his parents separated in 1905, Mal-raux went with his mother to live in the Parisian suburbs, where his grandmother had a small grocery store. His escape from the troubles of daily life was in literature. At the age of 17, Malraux quit school and left for Paris, where he spent a great deal of time in libraries, museums, and theaters. He also took courses at the Guimet Museum and the École du Louvre, where he took up the study of Sanskrit.

An admirer of Max Jacob, Pierre Reverdy, and Blaise Cendrars, Malraux participated in avant-garde artistic and literary circles in the period following World War I and published his first article, "On the Origins of Cubist Poetry," in 1920. At the astonishingly young age of 19, Malraux became the literary editor of Sagittarius Publishing while contributing to various avant-garde journals and associating with the likes of JEAN COCTEAU, PIERRE DRIEU LA ROCHELLE, RAYMOND RADIGUET, the writer André Suarès, and artists Pablo Picasso, and Georges Bracque. His first longer work, a fantastic tale entitled *Paper Moons*, was published in 1921.

Malraux went on to write a series of shorter pieces he called *"farfelu,"* eccentric works that reflect his sense that the world is indifferent to human aspirations. In these writings, Malraux reveals the crisis of disillusionment in traditional Western values that marked the interwar period. In 1922 he published "Pneumatic Rabbits in a French Garden," inspired by the work of contemporary avant-garde painters.

At the age of 20 Malraux married Clara Goldschmidt, a young woman of Franco-German origin. Meanwhile, his articles attracted the attention of ANDRÉ GIDE. Shortly thereafter, Malraux began contributing to the famous *Nouvelle Revue française* (New French Review). Always passionate about art, Malraux also traveled across Europe visiting museums and studying expressionist art and film.

In 1923, a series of poor investments led Malraux to leave for Cambodia with Clara and a childhood friend. Malraux was also particularly enamored of Khmer art. Together they undertook an archaeological expedition through the jungle along the ancient royal road. Unfortunately, they took several Khmer statues from a temple at Banteaï-Srey. Upon their return to the Cambodian capital of Phnom Penh, they were arrested for pillaging ruins. At first condemned to three years in prison, Malraux was released after a group of French artists and intellectuals signed a petition on his behalf. Disturbed by his encounter with the French colonial administration, a year later Malraux returned to the Vietnamese city of Saigon, where he established an anticolonial journal, *Indochina Enchained,* with the lawyer Paul Monin. In the end he was disappointed with his first attempts at militancy and returned to Paris. His brief experience as a journalist, however, had a significant impact on his development as a militant political activist and writer.

On his journey home, Malraux worked on revisions of his essay, *The Temptation of the West* (1926), structured as a series of letters exchanged between two men, one from France and one from China, in which each offers his impression of the other's culture. With remarkable perspicacity, Malraux wrote, "the world is invading Europe," arguing that the Europeans' traditional perspective on the world was no longer adequate. Upon his return to France, Malraux published three novels set in the Far East, *The CONQUERORS* (1928), *ROYAL WAY* (1930), and *MAN'S FATE* (1933). By age of 30, Malraux was a famous writer, in no small part due to the publication of these timely works reflecting themes that he had already introduced in *The Temptation of the West.*

Influenced by Marxism, Malraux argued for the necessity of revolutionary political action. His heroes, however, are less concerned with our material condition than with oppression and the denial of human dignity. At the heart of his works is the promotion of human values. Influenced, too, by the German philosopher Friedrich Nietzsche and Russian writer Fyodor Dostoyevsky, Malraux likewise engaged in a deliberate search for the meaning of life. *Man's Fate* evokes two episodes in the Chinese revolution of 1925–27. It also reflects an important recurring theme in Malraux's works, that of fraternity. Rather than focusing on a single character, this novel offers a collective of men who willingly sacrifice their lives for a cause. Malraux's approach to fundamental ontological questions presages the works of existentialist writers such as ALBERT CAMUS, JEAN-PAUL SARTRE, and SIMONE DE BEAUVOIR (see EXISTENTIALISM).

During the interwar period, Malraux established two publishing houses before taking a position at Gal-

limard publishers as artistic director in 1929 and as an author in 1933. His position as artistic director offered him the opportunity to do some of the things he loved most, to travel around the world in search of works of art as he organized various exhibitions. In 1934, for example, he flew over the deserts of Yemen in search of ancient ruins.

Like many contemporary intellectuals, as of 1933 Malraux was increasingly concerned with the rise of fascism in Europe. At first he turned towards the Communist Party and was the only noncommunist invited to Moscow to attend the first Congress of Soviet Writers, where he spoke out in favor of creative freedom and against the constraints of SOCIALIST REALISM.

As of 1935, Malraux entered a new period in which he focused on the struggle against fascism. He did more than write about it, however. Malraux participated in the Spanish civil war, fighting with a group of international volunteers against General Francisco Franco. Malraux drew from this experience for his novel *MAN'S HOPE.*

Disillusioned by Franco's victory as well as the signing of the Nazi-Soviet Pact of 1939, Malraux turned away from communism, and in 1940 he volunteered to fight in a tank division during World War II. Wounded and captured, he later escaped into the unoccupied Free Zone of France. While in captivity, Malraux worked on two novels that he never completed. Their very titles powerfully evoke the times in which they were written: *The Reign of Evil* and *The Demon of the Absolute.* Malraux also worked on *Struggle with the Angel,* the first volume of which was published in Lausanne, Switzerland, in 1943 with the title *The Walnut Trees of Altenburg.* In this as in other works, Malraux probes the meaning of life as well as concepts like civilization and culture. There are horrifying scenes such as an unforgettable gas attack on Russian soldiers. Such events evoke the presence of evil in the modern world.

Malraux joined the Resistance in 1944 and was once again arrested, then released when the Germans withdrew from Toulouse, the city where he had been imprisoned. He continued in the Resistance movement in the region of Alsace-Lorraine, despite his grief over the death of Josette Clotis, his lover with whom he had two children. (These two sons died in an automobile accident in 1961). In 1948, Malraux married his sister-in-law, Marie-Madeleine Lioux, similarly a widow with children.

In 1945, Malraux met General Charles de Gaulle, an encounter that inaugurated an entirely new phase in the author's life. He subsequently served as minister of information in de Gaulle's provisional government from 1945–46. Malraux then withdrew from politics for a time and turned to reflections on art. At this point, he had determined that humanity had two ways of giving meaning to life, action and art. Furthermore, for Malraux, art gives us the possibility of meaning in the face of death. In this period he produced some of his greatest works on art, such as *Voices of Silence* (1951), *Saturn: An Essay on Goya* (1950), *Museum without Walls* (3 volumes, 1952, 1954, and 1955), as well as volume one of *The Metamorphosis of the Gods* (1957).

When de Gaulle returned to power in 1958, Malraux accepted a position as minister of cultural affairs, which he held from 1959 to 1969. In that role he initiated a project for the restoration of monuments in Paris as well as a system of *maisons de culture* (cultural centers) all over France. Throughout his life Malraux was concerned with the relationship between art and life. His aesthetic vision rested on the notion that art represents something that exists beyond this world. Since art is the negation of time and space, an expression of the spirit, so art defies death and allows one to transcend one's own mortality and to surpass an ordinary vision of reality and truth.

In 1969 Malraux gave up on politics to focus on history, fate, and death, subjects that had always preoccupied him. He described humans as "the only animal that knows he will die." Thus death is a central issue in his works. It is death, ironically, that defines life. Yet how is one to give meaning to both? The only solution, according to Malraux, is to act, either in the sphere of politics or in art, both of which offer the means to define oneself. One must, in Malraux's words, establish an "anti-destiny" in the face of the tragedy of history and the inevitability of death. Malraux had published his own "Anti-Memoirs" in 1967.

Malraux rejected the traditional narrative form. His writing tends to be disjointed and cinematographic as he moves from one scene to another. In each instance the perspective is that of one character. No omniscient narrator is present. Nonetheless, critics have sometimes commented that Malraux's characters, driven by inner obsessions, become almost allegorical figures that are too abstract to be real.

At the heart of Malraux's thinking is an idea that becomes the driving force in one's life. Malraux's heroes tend either to confront history, to create art, or to manifest the power of fraternity. He once wrote, "I seek that crucial region of the soul where evil confronts fraternity," as is evident in *Man's Fate* and *Hope*. Moreover, Malraux lived his own life according to the principles articulated in his writing. If he essentially argued that one must say no to history, he did so by engaging in political struggles against fascism and colonialism, bearing witness to the fact that one does have the possibility of transforming history and one's own fate through action and art. These underlying concepts make of Malraux's oeuvre a unified and consistent whole that unites politics with metaphysics as art and life blend into one.

FURTHER READING

Bevan, David. *André Malraux: Towards the Expression of Transcendence.* Kingston, Ontario: McGill-Queen's University Press, 1986.

Cadwallader, Barrie. *Crisis of the European Mind: A Study of André Malraux and Drieu La Rochelle.* Cardiff: University of Wales Press, 1981.

Cate, Curtis. *André Malraux: A Biography.* New York: Fromm International, 1997.

Dorenlot, Françoise, and Micheline Tison-Braum, eds. *André Malraux: Metamorphosis and Imagination.* New York: New York Library Forum, 1979.

Greshoff, C. J. *An Introduction to the Novels of André Malraux.* Cape Town, South Africa: A. A. Balkema, 1975.

Kline, T. Jefferson. *André Malraux and the Metamorphosis of Death.* New York: Columbia University Press, 1973.

Lebovics, Herman. *Mona Lisa's Escort: André Malraux and the Reinvention of French Culture.* Ithaca, N.Y.: Cornell University Press, 1999.

Lyotard, Jean François. *Signed, Malraux.* Translated by Robert Harvey. Minneapolis: University of Minnesota Press, 1999.

———. *Soundproof Room: Malraux's Anti-aesthetics.* Translated by Robert Harvey. Stanford, Calif.: Stanford University Press, 2001.

Madsen, Axel. *Malraux: A Biography.* New York: Morrow, 1976.

Righter, William. *The Rhetorical Hero: An Essay on the Aesthetics of André Malraux.* London: Routledge and Kegan Paul, 1964.

Shaanan, Avraham. *Writers in War and Resistance.* Sherbrook, Quebec, Canada: Éditions Naaman, 1986.

Tame, Peter D. *The Ideological Hero in the Novels of Robert Brasillach, Roger Vailland and André Malraux.* New York: Peter Lang, 1998.

Todd, Olivier. *Malraux: A Life.* New York: Knopf, 2004.

MAMMERI, MOULOUD (1917–1989)

Mammeri was born in Algeria of Berber descent, and his mother tongue was Kabyl. The author learned French, the language in which he wrote, at school. Mobilized during World War II, Mammeri fought in Italy, France, and Germany before returning to Algeria in 1947.

Mammeri began writing in 1940 but his first novel, *Forgotten Hill,* was not published until 1952. This work, the first in a trilogy recounting the many and varied stages of Algerian history, evokes the inner tension of a group of adolescents in a Kabyl village torn between the disparate forces of ancient Berber traditions reinforced by Islam and modernization and colonialism. *Sleep of the Just* (1955) brings to life the rise of Algerian national consciousness and the ineluctable movement toward independence among a people increasingly disillusioned by the colonial experience. In *Opium and the Stick* (1965) Mammeri indicates the necessity for each Algerian to participate in the war of independence.

Throughout his life, Mammeri both promoted and celebrated Berber language and culture, publishing translations of Berber poems, tales, and a grammar. These efforts were viewed with suspicion by Algerian officials, who pressed for Algerian Arab-Islamic identity. Both novelist and anthropologist, after independence in 1962, Mammeri directed a research center at the University of Algiers, where he also held the chair in Berber. His work on the ancient literature of Kabyl was suppressed twice by the authorities between 1974 and 1980. Mammeri's writings ultimately led to a struggle in the Algerian university system for freedom of expression. His novel *The Crossing* (1982) and a series of short stories reflect the author's bitterness at his treatment. Not until 1992, three years after his death, did an international conference award Mammeri's works the recognition they deserve.

FURTHER READING

Vulor, Ena C. *Colonial and Anti-Colonial Discourses: Albert Camus and Algeria, and Intertextual Dialogue with Mouloud Mammeri, Mouloud Feraoun, and Mohammed Dib.* Lanham, Md.: University Press of America, 2000.

MANDARINS, THE (LES MANDARINS)

SIMONE DE BEAUVOIR (1954)   One of Beauvoir's most thoughtful and successful novels, *The Mandarins* won the Goncourt Prize. Beauvoir draws from her own experience as a writer to depict the moral and political preoccupations of leftist intellectuals in the period following World War II. In 1945, Beauvoir, JEAN-PAUL SARTRE, Maurice Merleau-Ponty, Raymon Aron, and others established a leftist journal, *Les Temps modernes* (Modern Times). This became the inspiration for *The Mandarins* and its theme of the intellectual's commitment to politics.

The central characters are Dubreuilh, his wife, Anne, and his friend Henri. The dynamics of their relationship are complicated. Anne and Henri, for example, have entirely different views on life. Anne believes in absolutes and is haunted by the idea of death. Henri is dedicated to political action and life. While he shares with Dubreuilh a commitment to leftist politics, the two men also differ from each other. For Henri, the questions of literature and aesthetics are meaningless so long as there is injustice in the world. With an unrealistic optimism, Dubreuilh believes that political action and art can work together toward the same end. Anne gradually grows more distant from her husband and has an affair with an American writer. In the end, unable to reconcile herself to circumstances, she plans to commit suicide. Despite certain ruptures in their friendship, Henri and Dubreuilh decide to join forces once again although there is an underlying sense of futility to their actions at the end of the novel.

Readers recognized Beauvoir, Sartre, and ALBERT CAMUS in the three central characters. The novel explores the difficult relationship between leftist writers and the Communist Party after World War II, as well as what Beauvoir perceived to be the gradual capitulation of intellectuals. Simone de Beauvoir shows how intellectuals, particularly the existentialists (see EXISTENTIALISM), became like the Chinese mandarins, respected yet impotent, while revealing at the same time the problem for the leftists of defining a militant aesthetic. Beauvoir's style is simple and sober as she engages in a sincere exploration of her experience in certain intellectual circles. The novel can thus be said to lead into her memoirs.

FURTHER READING

Appignanesi, Lisa. *Simone de Beauvoir*. Harmondsworth, England: Penguin, 1988.

Arp, Kristana. *The Bonds of Freedom*. Chicago: Open Court, 2001.

Bair, Dierdre. *Simone de Beauvoir: A Biography*. New York: Summit Books, 1990.

Bauer, Nancy. *Simone de Beauvoir, Philosophy and Feminism*. New York: Columbia University Press, 2001.

Evans, Mary. *Simone de Beauvoir: A Feminist Mandarin*. London: Tavistock, 1985.

Fallaize, Elizabeth. *The Novels of Simone de Beauvoir*. London: Routledge, 1988.

Keefe, T. *Simone de Beauvoir. A Study of her Writings*. Totowa, N.J.: Barnes and Noble, 1984.

Moi, Toril. *Feminist Theory and Simone de Beauvoir*. Oxford: Blackwell, 1990.

———. *Simone de Beauvoir*. Oxford: Blackwell, 1994.

MAN IN THE IRON MASK   See VICOMTE DE BRAGELONNE.

MANON LESCAUT ABBÉ ANTOINE-FRANÇOIS PRÉVOST D'ÉXILES (1731)   *Manon Lescaut* is the final book of a larger novel by Prévost, *The Memoirs and Adventures of a Man of Quality*. In *Manon*, Prévost's most famous work, the Man of Quality is the narrator, who meets the chevalier des Grieux twice. Hence the narrative's division into two distinct yet connected parts.

At the opening of the novel, the narrator arrives in the town of Pacy-sur-Eure. In front of a cabaret are two carts filled with a group of prostitutes who are being exiled to America. One of the women is Manon Lescaut. The narrator is intrigued by her beauty. Curious to know more, he is directed by a guard to a young man overcome with grief. The chevalier des Grieux has followed the convoy of prostitutes from Paris. Out of violent passion for Manon, he will continue to follow her to America. Unfortunately he has used all his money either trying to free her or paying the guards for the right to speak with his lover. Now he is penniless. The sympathetic Man of Quality gives des Grieux money and arranges with the guards to let the two lovers speak together as they continue their ill-fated journey.

Two years later, the Man of Quality passes through Calais on his way to London and recognizes des Grieux. The two men are pleased to see each other. Des Grieux thanks his benefactor warmly again, explaining that he has just returned from America. That evening they meet at the narrator's hotel where des Grieux tells his story.

Des Grieux was young and from a good family, pursuing his studies in theology, when he met Manon one day as he was traveling. She was being sent by her parents against her will to a convent. Like a bolt of lightening, des Grieux is struck by her beauty, and the couple almost immediately decide to run off together despite the warnings of des Grieux's most loyal and wise friend, Tiberge, another theology student.

As des Grieux abandons principles, family, and his studies, the two lovers run away to Saint-Denis, where for three weeks they live a life of passion in perfect harmony. Slowly des Grieux begins to feel remorse and thinks that he will ask his father's permission to marry Manon. Manon thinks otherwise and dissuades him, saying that some country relatives can help them out of their financial difficulties. Naive, des Grieux acquiesces. In reality, Manon has secretly taken a wealthy lover.

At this moment, des Grieux's father's servants arrive and carry him home. Des Grieux cannot believe that Manon would betray him. He is in despair. To prevent him from returning to Paris, des Grieux's father locks him in his room. Slowly des Grieux recovers and decides to return to his studies, in which he is extraordinarily successful. One day, after a brilliant recitation at the Sorbonne, Manon reappears and all of des Grieux's resolutions disappear. Des Grieux abandons the seminary and the couple runs off yet again.

Over and over, des Grieux is forced by circumstances to recognize Manon's infidelity and her need for luxury and pleasure. When the house in which they have been living in Chaillot burns down, all their money is lost. Manon's wayward brother suggests that des Grieux prostitute Manon. Incensed but desperate, des Grieux turns to the life of a gambler and trickster in order to support his lover. With the means to give Manon the comforts she desires, all goes well until fortune turns against them yet again. The couple is robbed by their servants. As always, Manon's solution is to seek a wealthy lover. When the couple tries to trick the latest, he has them thrown in prison. Des Grieux eventually escapes and frees Manon as well but their troubles do not end. The next man who presents himself to Manon is the son of the last lover. When he too is tricked by the couple, they are arrested once more. This time des Grieux's father ensures Manon's exile before getting his son out of prison.

Des Grieux is unable to control his passion for Manon and, as we know, follows her to America, where they decide to marry. Unfortunately, the governor's son is also in love with Manon. Des Grieux wounds him in a duel and the lovers run off to the wilds, where Manon dies. Des Grieux, lies down on her grave and waits for death himself but is found by the indefatigable Tiberge, who brings him back to France. There he discovers that his father has died of grief in the interim. At this point, des Grieux meets again the Man of Quality, and the story ends.

This first-person narrative by Prévost offers a metaphysical examination of the possibility of reconciling love and morality. The conclusion is ambiguous. Novelist and philosopher, Prévost raises the very modern question of subjective reality. Des Grieux is subject to passions and emotions beyond his control. "Persons of noble character can be stirred in a thousand different ways; it seems as if they have more than five senses and that they receive ideas and sensations that go beyond the ordinary limits of nature." Prévost deals with one of the fundamental questions of ENLIGHTENMENT thought concerning the relationship between reason and passion, a question that inevitably leads into ROMANTICISM. The moral lesson is, on the surface, a traditional condemnation of the passions. The ambiguity arises from the suggestion that amorous passion may be the central experience of one's life, something derived from nature itself, and yet Prévost is unable to overcome his pessimism about the possibility of happiness.

FURTHER READING
Frail, Robert J. *Realism in Samuel Richardson and the Abbé Prévost.* Lewiston, N.Y.: E. Mellen, 2005.
Kory, Odlile A. *Subjectivity and Sensitivity in the Novels of the Abbé Prévost.* Paris, Brussels; Montreal: Didier, 1972.
Lazzaro-Weis, Carol M. *Confused Epiphanies: L'abbé Prévost and the Romance Tradition.* New York: P. Lang, 1991.
Segal, Naomi. *Unintended Reader: Feminism and Manon Lescaut.* Cambridge, New York: Cambridge University Press, 1986.
Smernoff, Richard. *L'abbé Prévost.* Boston: Twayne, 1985.

MAN'S FATE (LA CONDITION HUMAINE)

ANDRÉ MALRAUX (1933)   *Man's Fate* reflects themes that Malraux had already introduced in an essay *The Temptation of the West* (1927). This novel is one of three focusing on the Far East; the others are *The CONQUERORS* (1928) and *The ROYAL WAY* (1930). Malraux's fascination with Asia stems from his experience of living in Indochina, where he was active in the anticolonial movement.

The narrative is interwoven with Malraux's reflections on politics, love, fate, human dignity, art, and philosophy. Moreover, Malraux's cinematographic style in *Man's Fate* as a sequence of images of a group of characters with varied points of view provides a polyphonic and varied perspective on events in the novel.

Man's Fate depicts an uprising that took place in Shanghai in 1927 during the Chinese Revolution. A group of communists led by Kyo rises up against the government. Initially successful, the insurgents are subsequently unsure what strategy to pursue in relation to Chiang Kai-shek, the leader of the Republic of China, whose army marched on the city ensuring the revolution's success. When Chiang establishes a new government and demands that the communists disarm, they refuse. Kyo then meets with the central committee of the Communist Party to discuss the matter, only to discover that they are opposed to any outright confrontation with the Kuomintang, Chiang Kai-shek's political party.

Kyo, half-Japanese, half-European, lives for the revolution, which gives meaning to his life. Tchen is a terrorist seeking blood. In contrast, Hemmelrich is tortured by his inability to act, and the final struggle offers him liberation. Ferral, the capitalist, is driven solely by his desire for power. Tchen dies in a second failed attempt at Chiang Kai-shek's life, while Kyo and his friend Katow are taken prisoner, brutally tortured, and killed. Following his death, Kyo's mistress, May, decides to take up the struggle in his place.

The revolution allows each character to define him- or herself and reflects Malraux's belief that political action is one of the two ways in which we can challenge the absurdity of our own existence, the other being artistic creation. This is how we create our "antidestiny." In contrast to the pessimistic view of PIERRE DRIEU LA ROCHELLE, Malraux believes that by engaging history, we can triumph over fate.

The title of the novel in French is "The Human Condition," which asserts the philosophical nature of Malraux's inquiry. Characters attempt to make sense of their lives in terms of history, while a sense of fraternity spares them the anguish of a truly existential crisis. An admirer of German philosopher Friedrich Nietzsche, Malraux sought to determine how one might redefine oneself if God is indeed dead, asking "what does one do with man's soul if there is neither God nor Christ?" In the end, suffering leads to redemption as in Kyo's case, whereby "it is easy to die when one does not die alone."

FURTHER READING

Constable, Liz. "Economies of Lethal Emotions in La Condition humaine," *MLN* 115, no. 4, French Issue (September 2000): 573–599.

Hiddleston, J. A. *Malraux—La Condition humaine.* London: Edward Arnold, 1973.

Kastely, James L. "Revolution and Isolation in La Condition humaine," *Twentieth Century Literature* 35, no. 4 (Winter 1989): 458–479.

Roudiez, Leon S. "La Condition humaine: An Awareness of Other," *Twentieth Century Literature* 24, no. 3, André Malraux Issue (Autumn 1978): 303–313.

MAN'S PLACE (LA PLACE) ANNIE ERNAUX (1983)

The title of this novel in French is *La Place,* a word with multiple meanings. It can be a public square (and Ernaux indeed considers the question of public space), a place in the basic sense of the word, or one's position or status in society. In this novel, Ernaux once again focuses on the question of social mobility and social identity as the narrator tells the story of her father's life and its implications for her own.

The daughter returns home for her father's funeral and is forced to confront the difference between her present position, well-ensconced in the middle class, and her origins. Ernaux thus considers the relationship of the individual to larger sociopolitical power structures. Through the narrator, Ernaux explores the process and consequences of socialization in a powerful and intimate work set within the context of social and cultural change in postwar World War II France.

In school, the narrator's father had read *The* TOUR OF FRANCE, a novel intended to reinforce traditional values. He thus grew up with a strong sense of community centered on village life and then lived through the turmoil of World Wars I and II. Ultimately he rose up from his peasant origins to own his own shop, through hard work and as a result of general socioeconomic change. Still, he remained unsure of his own identity. He rejected his past along with the dialect spoken by his parents, yet was uncertain of his new place in society. Ernaux's novel is almost an ethnological or anthropological study as she explores class, power, and social relations through the prism of a father and a daughter.

FURTHER READING

McIlvanney, Siobhán. *Annie Ernaux: The Return to Origins.* Liverpool, England: Liverpool University Press, 2001.

Thomas, Lyn. *Annie Ernaux: An Introduction to the Writer and Her Audience.* Oxford, New York: Berg, 1999.

MAN WHO LAUGHS, THE (L'HOMME QUI RIT) VICTOR HUGO (1869)

Gwynplaine was disfigured in childhood by a roving band of criminals who kidnap children for public street performances. As a result, he has a permanent grin on his face, hence "the man who laughs." His friend Déa is blind. Eventually a kind vagabond named Ursus welcomes him into a troupe that performs an allegorical drama called "Chaos Vanquished" in which the spiritual triumphs over the material.

The audience enjoys the show and Gwynplaine becomes quite well known. One day he is recognized as the baron Clancharlie, who had been abducted as a child from his family (not the only kidnapping in Hugo's works). Gwynplaine subsequently returns to his rightful place in society. He enters the House of Lords, where he defends the poor. In one particularly moving speech, Gwynplaine weeps openly but the audience breaks into laughter when they see the man who laughs cry. Angry and disillusioned, Gwynplaine runs away to find Déa and Ursus, but when he finds them Déa is dying. Feeling hopeless, Gwynplaine commits suicide.

The theme of laughter is central to the novel. In contrast to the laughter of the crowds before which he performs, Gwynplaine's laughter is false. It is the laughter of self-mutilated humanity. *The Man Who Laughs* echoes a number of themes found in Hugo's other works such as *The HUNCHBACK OF NOTRE DAME* and *NINETY-THREE*. Most of Hugo's novels engage in social criticism that reflects the influence of utopian socialists such as Claude Saint-Simon and Charles Fourier. In this and other novels Hugo draws a contrast between the purity of nature and the corruption of society that is similar to arguments made by JEAN-JACQUES ROUSSEAU. Like many of his contemporaries, ÉMILE ZOLA in particular, Hugo contemplates the human condition.

FURTHER READING

Brombert, Victor. *Victor Hugo and the Visionary Novel.* Cambridge, Mass.: Harvard University Press, 1984.

Evans, David O. *Social Romanticism in France: 1830–1848.* New York: Octagon, 1969.

Hudson, William Henry. *Victor Hugo and His Poetry.* London: Harrap, 1918.

Maurois, André. *Victor Hugo and His World.* Translated by Oliver Bernard. New York: Viking, 1966.

Peyre, Henri. *Victor Hugo: Philosophy and Poetry.* Translated by Roda P. Roberts. Tuscaloosa: University of Alabama Press, 1980.

MAN WHO SLEEPS, THE (L'HOMME QUI DORT) GEORGES PEREC (1967)   The principal character of this novel is addressed as "you" in a style reminiscent of MICHEL BUTOR's novel *MODIFICATION*. The protagonist of Perec's work is a 25-year-old

student living in a tiny room in Paris who becomes alienated from the world around him. He does not take his exam in sociology or respond when friends knock at his door. He has become apathetic.

The origin of his apathy came "one day in May when it was too hot, a text too hard to follow, a bowl of Nescafé suddenly bitter . . . [and] something broke." Perec makes a number of literary allusions to other writers who, as he saw it, created the literary space for *A Man Who Sleeps,* such as Herman Melville, Franz Kafka, MARCEL PROUST, Dante, and James Joyce. The novel's title is taken from Proust's REMEMBRANCE OF THINGS PAST and the epigraph from Kafka. The latter explains to the protagonist what he must do: "You don't need to leave the house. Stay at the table and listen. Don't even listen, simply wait. Don't even wait, stay absolutely silent and alone. The world will come and offer itself to you so that you can unmask it. It cannot do otherwise. Enraptured, it will writhe before you." The novel thus treads a line between passivity and self-abnegation, and its conclusion is open-ended. The protagonist waits for a train at the Place de Clichy. He has returned to the world, but what will happen next?

FURTHER READING

Andrews, Chris. "Puzzles and Lists: Georges Perec's *Un homme qui dort,*" *MLN 111, no. 4* (1996): 775–796.

Bellos, David. *Georges Perec: A Life in Words.* Boston: Godine, 1993.

Motte, Warren F. Jr. "Georges Perec on the Grid," *French Review* 57, no. 6 (May 1984): 820–832.

Motte, Warren, ed. *Oulipo: A Primer of Potential Literature.* Lincoln: University of Nebraska Press, 1986.

Schwartz, Paul. *Georges Perec, Traces of His Passage.* Birmingham, Ala.: Summa, 1988.

Richardson, Joanna. *Victor Hugo.* London: Weidenfeld and Nicolson, 1976.

MARAN, RENÉ (1887–1960)   Maran was born in Martinique, where his father served as a clerk in the French administration although his parents were originally from French Guiana. In 1894, Maran's father was stationed in Gabon and his parents decided that their son should attend a boarding school in Bordeaux rather than accompany them to Africa. Maran published his first collection of poems, most of which

he wrote while still a student, in 1909. After secondary school, Maran accepted a minor post in the French colonial administration in Congo. His experience there furnished him with the material for his most significant novel, *Batouala* (1921).

In this work, Maran describes daily life and traditions in a Congolese village. It was perhaps the first time in literature that a novel focused on the African people and their culture in a positive light, laying the foundation for the subsequent rise of NEGRITUDE as a movement in 20th-century African fiction. The whites, who represent the French colonial presence in Africa, appear as a pathetic group of corrupt drunkards, merciless in their treatment of indigenous peoples. In his preface, moreover, Maran powerfully denounces the colonial system.

At the same time, the novel is far more than a polemical tract against European colonialism. Maran brings to life the richness of African culture in a vividly poetic voice. Much to the author's surprise *Batouala* won the Goncourt Prize. It also created such a scandal that Maran was obliged to resign from his position in colonial administration. Maran also wrote several remarkably poetic works on animals in the African bush that include *The Book of the Bush* (1934) and *M'Bala the Elephant* (1943).

FURTHER READING

Cameron, Keith. *René Maran*. Boston: Twayne, 1985.
Cook, Mercer. "René Maran," *French Review* 17, no. 3 (January 1944): 157–159.
Fabre, Michel. "René Maran. The New Negro and Negritude," *Phylon* (1960–   ) 36, no. 3 (1975): 340–351.
Ojo-Ade, Femi. *René Maran, the Black Frenchman; A Bio-Critical Study*. Washington, D.C.: Three Continents Press, 1984.

MARIA CHAPDELAINE LOUIS HÉMON (1914)

A simple yet powerful work, *Maria Chapdelaine* was first published as a serial novel in 1914. Republished in 1921, it was an instant success. For 18 months Hémon lived and worked with a family of lumberjacks in the Canadian forest. Samuel and Laura, the couple for whom he labored, had four sons and a daughter, Maria.

Three men seek Maria's hand: Eutrope Gagnon, a peasant; Lorenzo Surprenant, who leaves Canada for the United States, and François Paradis, sometimes a lumberjack, sometimes a worker, full of life and adventure. One day while gathering blueberries, Maria and François fall in love. Although François must leave, he promises to return to Maria for Christmas when they will marry.

When Christmas comes, François indeed sets out to rejoin Maria but is caught in a terrible storm and dies. Since, as Hémon put it, "peasants never die of a broken heart," Maria goes on, driven by her profound attachment to the land and her people. Nonetheless, part of Maria dies along with François. When Eutrope returns from the forest for the spring sowing, Maria agrees to marry him out of a sense of duty.

It is the priest who convinces Maria of her place in the great chain of life. Although he is not entirely sympathetic, he persuades Maria of her duty: "To make yourself upset for no reason and to discourage the whole household makes no sense and God does not like it . . . a girl like you, pleasant to look at and in good health, courageous and a good housekeeper is made for helping one's old parents first and then for marrying and establishing a Christian family." Maria, obedient and submissive, believes that God has spoken to her through the priest.

Most of the characters in the novel are real people who later recognized themselves in Hémon's work. Hémon portrays the French-Canadian peasant's strength of character with sympathy born out of a shared experience. These are people who live in solitude, and Hémon describes with touching simplicity their hard lives, Maria's sacrifice, and the family's intimate connection to the land. Central themes are labor, love, and death.

MARIE DE FRANCE (12TH CENTURY)

One of two medieval French women writers, Marie de France was the first woman of her time to have successfully written in the vernacular. We have very little biographical information on Marie de France, but her writings (The LAYS and her *Fables*) reveal something of her identity. Marie de France probably lived in England in the last quarter of the 12th century with connections to the court of King Henry II and his queen, Eleanor of Aquitaine. In the epilogue of her version of

Aesop's *Fables* (the earliest extant collection of fables in the Western tradition), Marie asserts her authorial voice in a way similar to her 15th-century successor, CHRISTINE DE PIZAN, stating "My name is Marie and I come from France (Marie ai num, si sui de France)."

It is clear from her writings that Marie de France was well educated and from a good family. She may have been educated in a convent; she was perhaps an abbess. Clearly, she was familiar with the interests and values of aristocratic society. Marie de France's stories were well known and translated into several other languages including Norse, Middle English, and Middle High German. Her *Lays* (a term referring to short stories written in verse; see LAY) set a foundation for love and passion as central themes of Western literature while revealing the qualities and virtues of aristocratic court culture in the Middle Ages.

FURTHER READING

Burgess, G. S. *Marie de France, Text and Context.* Manchester, England: Manchester University Press, 1987.

Kinoshita, Sharon. "Two for the Price of One: Courtly Love and Serial Polygamy in the *Lais* of Marie de France," *Arthuriana* 8, no. 2 (1998): 33–55.

McCracken, Peggy. *The Romance of Adultery: Queenship and Sexual Transgression in Old French Literature.* Philadelphia: University of Pennsylvania Press, 1998.

Muir, Lynette R. *Literature and Society in Medieval France. The Mirror and the Image 1100–1500.* London: Macmillan, 1985.

Rothschild, Judith Rice. *Narrative Techniques in the Lais of Marie de France: Themes and Variations.* Volume 1. North Carolina Studies in the Romance Languages and Literatures, 39th ed., ed. Juan Battista Avalle-Arce. Chapel Hill: University of North Carolina Department of Romance Languages, 1974.

Spearing, A. C. "Love and Power in the Twelfth Century, with Special Reference to Chrétien de Troyes and Marie de France." In *The Olde Daunce: Love, Friendship, Sex, and Marriage in the Medieval World.* Edited by Robert R. Edwards and Stephen Spector. Albany: SUNY University Press, 1991.

Stevens, Sonya, ed. *A History of Women's Writing in France.* London, New York: Cambridge University Press, 2000.

MARITAL CHRONICLES (*CHRONIQUES MARITALES*) MARCEL JOUHANDEAU (1938)

In this semiautobiographical work, Jouhandeau reflects on the contradictory impulses that drive us to marry. The novel is divided into three parts, the first of which describes one's simultaneous attachment for and disgust with the home in which one was raised. The second part depicts Jouhandeau's life with Élise, his wife, who is both enchanting and tormenting. The love between them is passionate and also ambiguous, partly because of Jouhandeau's bi-sexual orientation. The third part focuses on questions of religion and mysticism. Jouhandeau's great gift, recalling the works of ANDRÉ GIDE, is to unveil the secrets of the human heart as well as the conflict between good and evil.

MARIVAUX, PIERRE CARLET DE (1688–1763)

Playwright and novelist, Pierre Carlet de Marivaux was born in Paris. Like many other novelists of the period, he was initially trained in law. As a young man Marivaux chose instead a career as a writer. In the 1720s he founded *The French Spectator,* modeled on the famous English journal. He participated in Parisian literary salons and, in 1742, was elected to the Académie Française, where he later took the side of the Moderns in the renowned literary quarrel between those who argued in favor of a classical model (see CLASSICISM) and those who proposed a more innovative approach to assessing the quality of literature. At the time, Marivaux was famous for his comedies in which love always triumphs, such as *The Surprise of Love* (1722), *The Game of Love and Chance* (1730), and *The Legacy* (1736).

Marivaux's gift to posterity is a particular style of writing known as "marivaudage." This unique style was sometimes criticized by contemporaries as pretentious. Its affectation recalls the 17th-century *précieuses* (see PRECIOSITY). Marivaux deliberately developed his particular writing style, stating, "If there is in France a generation of men who have greater finesse of spirit than ever before, then there needs to be new words and signs to express the new ideas of this generation."

Marivaux is also known for his two unfinished novels, *The LIFE OF MARIANNE* (1731–41) and *The UPSTART PEASANT* (1734–35), in which he aptly depicts middle-class life. Marivaux is a sharp observer of society, painting a clear picture of differences in language and class, as well as the abuses of a hierarchical society.

Marivaux's heroes tend to be noble in character but not in birth. His characters' generosity and sincerity mark Marivaux as a humanist whose writing promotes an optimistic sensitivity to human suffering rendered lightly through comic scenes.

Marivaux's subtle, rather modern technique of writing exploits the possibilities of first-person narrative, so common to 18th-century fiction, by juxtaposing the motivations, actions, and reactions of the main character with those of the narrator. Both these novels emphasize self-fashioning as a theme through Marivaux's subtle exploration of feeling and sentiment.

Both novels are about upward social mobility. The novels complement each other through the distinction between *Marianne's* emphasis on female sensibility and *Upstart's* focus on masculine sensuality. Consequently, the two together reveal the gendered contrasts typical of 18th-century literature, a topic of increasing interest to modern scholars.

FURTHER READING

Haac, Oscar A. *Marivaux*. New York: Twayne, 1974.

Jamieson, Ruth. *Marivaux: A Study in Sensibility*. New York: Octagon Books, 1969.

Marshall, David. *The Surprising Effects of Sympathy: Marivaux, Diderot, Rousseau, and Mary Shelley*. Chicago: University of Chicago Press, 1988.

Rosbottom, Ronald. *Marivaux's Novels: Theme and Function in Early Eighteenth-Century Narrative*. Madison, N.J.: Farleigh Dickinson University Press, 1974.

MARTHE Joris-Karl Huysmans (1876) Huysmans's first novel, *Marthe* tells the story of a flamboyant redheaded Parisian prostitute at the end of the Second Empire. The novel falls in Huysmans's naturalist stage (see NATURALISM). Like his other early realist works (see REALISM), *Marthe* offers a pessimistic and despairing look at a sad, mediocre world.

Marthe was first published in Brussels, Belgium, and was immediately forbidden by French censors because the subject matter was considered scandalous. Huysmans argued, however, that he had intended to write an antierotic, artistic, moral novel, not a work of pornography. The novel appeared one year before EDMOND DE GONCOURT's novel about a prostitute, *Élisa*. In fact, Huysmans wrote to Goncourt, "I have the most sincere and strong admiration for your talent; accept then this novel as witness to my profound respect for the author of *Germinie Lacerteux* and so many other marvelous works." Huysmans sought Goncourt's support in fending off the charge that *Marthe* is a pornographic novel.

FURTHER READING

Banks, Brian. *The Image of Huysmans*. New York: AMS Press, 1990.

Gilman, Richard. *Decadence: The Strange Life of an Epithet*. New York: Farrar, Straus and Giroux, 1979.

Nalbantian, Suzanne. *Seeds of Decadence in the Late Nineteenth-Century Novel*. New York: St. Martin's Press, 1983.

Praz, Mario. *The Romantic Agony*. Translated by Angus Davidson. New York: Oxford University Press, 1970.

MARTIN DU GARD, ROGER (1881–1958)

Roger Martin du Gard was an extraordinarily popular novelist born outside Paris to a bourgeois family of some means. In 1890, Martin du Gard's grandmother died. This first encounter with death left a lasting impression on him. Martin du Gard once said that for him, literature became a means to cheat death. His interest in literature developed early. When he was nine years old, he met an older boy on his summer vacation who wrote tragedies in verse in a notebook he carried with him. This inspired Martin du Gard, who began writing as well.

Raised as a Roman Catholic, Martin du Gard studied at parochial schools. One priest introduced him to the works of the Russian novelist Leo Tolstoy, a writer who was to remain a lasting influence throughout Martin du Gard's life. At the same time, Martin du Gard discovered ÉMILE ZOLA, whose works also made a deep impression on him. Martin du Gard wrote in the 19th-century tradition of NATURALISM associated with Tolstoy as well as such French novelists as the GONCOURT brothers and Zola. Martin du Gard's highly structured novels reflect his interest in the relationship of the individual to his or her historical context. Just as the naturalists sought to comment on contemporary society with an objective eye, so Martin du Gard evoked the experience of World War I in *The Thibaults* and the Dreyfus affair in *Jean Barois*. Moreover, Martin du Gard took up other pressing themes such as the tension between the material and the spiritual, homosexuality, incest, and contemporary political problems.

From 1902 to 1903, Martin du Gard fulfilled his military service. Although he had no taste for army life, this was an important period in his development as he met a number of intellectuals of diverse backgrounds with whom he engaged in passionate discussions on the merits and weaknesses of naturalism and who encouraged him to pursue a literary career. These discussions led him to conceive of a new approach to fiction that would focus on dialogue. For a time, he considered a career in medicine, and a number of his works contain admirable doctors as central figures. Instead, Martin du Gard studied at the Sorbonne and at the Écoles des Chartes, France's prestigious school for training archivists. His preparation there gave him an appreciation for historical research, as is evident in his subsequent novels.

After completing his studies, Martin du Gard married Hélène Foucault, a devout Catholic. Their marriage was not a particularly happy one, as the author's later journals reveal. From 1906 to 1908, he worked on *Life of a Saint,* the story of a country priest named Luc Hardel. Martin du Gard's ambitious plan was to develop fully a character in relation to his historical context. Unfortunately, he never felt that he was fully able to grasp the nature and character of a country priest. In fact, he suffered serious doubts about his vocation as a writer.

The theme of the individual's ability to fool himself recurs in his novels. As the character of Antoine Thibault wrote to his nephew, "one has to fumble about for a long time before knowing *who* one is." In this period of self-doubt, Martin du Gard paused for a moment to study psychotherapy before publishing his first novel, *To Become!* in 1909, which explores the disillusionment of his generation. This first novel introduces the themes and style that mark Martin du Gard's later works. Stylistically, the emphasis is on dialogue, as he sought above all to avoid the intervention of the author's voice into the narrative. In some respects, Martin du Gard's novels thus recall the style and method of James Joyce, the Irish novelist.

For the next three years, Martin du Gard worked on his second novel, *Jean Barois* (1913), the story of an intellectual torn between religion and science. Over time, Barois abandons his faith to join a circle of progressive intellectuals who establish a journal that speaks out, among other things, about the Dreyfus affair in which a Jewish officer was falsely accused and convicted of treason in 1894. One day Barois has an accident and is shocked to realize that his first impulse is to pray. Only at the point of death does he thus return to Roman Catholicism. Jean Barois's character reflects the inner conflict of an entire generation. Barois's moral crisis also paves the way for the existentialist search for authenticity (see EXISTENTIALISM). ALBERT CAMUS wrote the preface to the Pléiade edition of Martin du Gard's works.

Jean Barois attracted the attention of the prestigious *Nouvelle Revue française* (New French Review); from that point on Martin du Gard participated in the literary circle associated with that journal. He formed a particularly close friendship with ANDRÉ GIDE that lasted until the latter's death in 1951. Martin du Gard later praised Gide's contribution to modern French literature in *Recollections of André Gide* (1951). Martin du Gard's associates seem to have admired his generosity and upstanding character as well as the high value that he placed on friendship. He developed close working relationships with other writers as well, including MARCEL JOUHANDEAU and EUGÈNE DABIT.

In 1920, Martin du Gard began work on his most ambitious project, an eight-volume cycle of novels entitled *The THIBAULTS* (1922–40), which focuses on the relationship between two brothers very different in character yet fundamentally linked by blood. During the first decade of this work, Martin du Gard passed through a series of personal crises. First his daughter, whom he loved dearly, married his old friend Marcel Coppet. Their union inspired Martin du Gard to write a short story on the theme of incest between a brother and a sister. Then in 1931 Martin du Gard and his wife were in a serious automobile accident that necessitated a fairly long convalescence.

Upon his recovery, Martin du Gard wrote a psychological drama, *Taciturn Man,* performed at the Comédie des Champs Élysées in 1913. It is the story of a man who painfully becomes aware of his homosexuality. Incapable of acting on his feelings, he chooses instead to commit suicide. The following year, Martin du Gard tried his hand at yet another genre, publishing a series of sketches on village life in a work entitled *Postman.* At this point, Martin du Gard returned again to *The Thibaults,* for which he envisioned a new ending. He also worked on the screenplay for a film version of Zola's *La Bête Humaine,* which was never produced.

The three volumes of *Summer, 1914* appeared together in 1936, recounting events of the last two months before the outbreak of World War I as Martin du Gard successfully evokes this tense period in history, fraught with both ideological and political conflicts. In 1937, he received the Nobel Prize "for the force and artistic truth of his cycle *The Thibaults,* in which he depicted human conflicts and important aspects of contemporary life."

The next year, Martin du Gard wrote the *Epilogue* to the Thibaults cycle; it was published in 1940. During World War II, Martin du Gard worked on yet another lengthy novel, *Lieutenant-Colonel Maumont* (published posthumously in 1983), in which he explored, through a soldier's eyes, the experience of the war, Nazism, the Resistance, and Liberation. Recurring themes in this work are death, the meaning of life, sexuality, religion, pacifism, tolerance, and the dangers of fanaticism.

Martin du Gard holds an important place in the history of contemporary French literature. As an idealist, moralist, and humanist, he carefully considered the most pressing social, religious, and political questions of his day as he sought new values to replace those of bourgeois society and Roman Catholicism. Whether religious or political, Martin du Gard was skeptical of all fanaticism. More than the heir to naturalism, he also made a significant contribution to the development of the modern novel. In Camus's words, "he was perhaps the only one [of his generation] to proclaim the literature of today and to bequeath it the problems that would both crush it and offer it some hope . . . his oeuvre is also one of doubt, of reason deceived yet persevering, of ignorance recognized." Martin du Gard was one of the first writers of his generation to realize that if we no longer have God, then we have no choice but to join with others. In this sense his fundamental thinking recalls the works of André Malraux.

FURTHER READING

Barbert, Gene J. "Roger Martin du Gard: Recent Criticism," *French Review* 41, no. 1 (October 1967): 60–69.

Boak, Denis. *Roger Martin du Gard.* Oxford: Clarendon Press, 1963.

Gibson, Robert. *Roger Martin du Gard.* New York: Hillary House, 1961.

Jouejati, R. *The Quest for Total Peace: The Political Thought of Roger Martin du Gard.* London, Totowa, N.J.: F. Cass, 1977.

O'Nan, Martha. *Roger Martin duGard Centennial, 1881–1981.* Brockport, N.Y.: Department of Foreign Languages, State University of New York College, 1981.

Ru, Yi-Ling, *The Family Novel: Toward a Generic Definition.* New York: P. Lang, 1992.

Savage, Catharine H. *Roger Martin du Gard.* New York: Twayne, 1968.

Schalk, David L. *Roger Martin du Gard: The Novelist and History.* Ithaca, N.Y.: Cornell University Press, 1967.

Taylor, Michael John. *Martin du Gard-Jean Barois.* London: Edward Arnold, 1974.

Hall, Thomas White. "A Note on the So-Called Change in Technique in Les Thibault of Roger Martin du Gard," *French Review* 27, no. 2 (December 1953): 108–113.

MARTYRS, THE François-René Chateaubriand (1809)

On the surface, *The Martyrs* is a romantic (see ROMANTICISM) story of two lovers, Eudore and Velléda. As an apology for Christianity, *The Martyrs* echoes CHATEAUBRIAND's *The Genius of Christianity.* A Christian soldier in the Roman army, Eudore is transformed from religious indifference to zealous martyrdom in a Roman stadium. Chateaubriand thus explores the struggle between Christianity and paganism, a theme that surfaces more than once in his writings.

The love story recalls *Atala.* Once Velléda has succumbed to her passion for Eudore, she commits suicide out of regret. Like Atala, she had vowed to remain celibate. Once again, Chateaubriand movingly depicts two lovers reaching out for each other across a cultural and religious divide.

In contrast to some of the critiques of *Genius,* contemporary historians were impressed by Chateaubriand's brilliant depiction of antiquity. At the same time, Chateaubriand commented on recent political events in a way that was recognizable to contemporary readers. Moreover, Chateaubriand's conservative and sentimental religiosity, exoticism, and depiction of tragic love made contemporary readers appreciate the novel for its overwhelmingly romantic character.

FURTHER READING

Bouvier, Luke. "How Not to Speak of Incest: Atala and the Secrets of Speech," *Nineteenth-Century French Studies* 30, nos. 3 and 4 (2002): 228–242.

Call, Michael J. *Back to the Garden: Chateaubriand, Senancour and Constant.* Saratoga, Calif.: Anma Libri, 1988.

Maurois, André. *Chateaubriand: Poet, Statesman, Lover.* Translated by Vera Fraser. New York: Greenwood Press, 1969.

Smethurst, Colin. *Chateaubriand, Atala, and René.* London: Grant and Cutler, 1995.

MARXISM

Karl Marx and Friedrich Engels developed the theory we know as Marxism in response to social dislocation associated with modernization and industrialization. Marx was particularly concerned with the exploitation of the worker in a modern economy based on mechanized production that deprives workers of the possibility for creativity, spontaneity, and sensuality. In the 19th century, LIBERALISM, the philosophy of the middle class, was one side of the coin, while Marxism was the other.

Marxist theory rests on a materialist conception of history. Marx believed that the historical process has, since time immemorial, rested on class conflict and is leading inevitably toward a worldwide anticapitalist revolution. Marxist theory focuses on conflict and alienation in modern economic, social, and political life, redefining the Hegelian dialectic in order to develop a theory of dialectical materialism. The rise of leftist politics in the second half of the 19th century and into the 20th is reflected in literary movements such as REALISM and NATURALISM in the 19th century and SOCIALIST REALISM, SURREALISM, and EXISTENTIALISM in the 20th century. Marxism served as an ideological foundation for a number of leftist writers such as LOUIS ARAGON, ELSA TRIOLET, JEAN-PAUL SARTRE, ANDRÉ BRETON, and PAUL NIZAN.

MASTERPIECE, THE (L'ŒUVRE) ÉMILE ZOLA (1886)

In *The Masterpiece*, the 14th novel in his ROUGON-MACQUART series, Zola depicts the mood of Parisian artists' studios. In fact, he counted a number of contemporary artists among his friends. Zola knew Paul Cézanne from childhood, had been a staunch defender of Édouard Manet, and wrote numerous articles on art and aesthetics. In this novel Zola describes the struggles of a generation of young artists to introduce a new way of viewing art. In the process, he explores their lives, financial difficulties, friendships, and rivalries.

As the story of the Rougon-Macquart family continues, Claude Lantier, Gervaise's son by her alcoholic lover (see *L'ASSOMMOIR*), is obsessed with the idea of creating a masterpiece, but his hereditary weakness prevents him from accomplishing his dream. Increasingly absorbed by his art and distant from his wife, Claude hangs himself before an unfinished canvas. The Rougon-Macquart "Natural and Social History of a Second Empire Family" manifests Zola's naturalist approach to literature (see NATURALISM) by drawing on recent developments in the sciences, particularly the role of heredity in determining character.

Some contemporary artists are recognizable in the novel such as Andrea Solari, Antoine Guillemet, Camille Pissaro, and Manet. A number of critics have characterized Claude as a composite of Cézanne and Manet. In fact, disturbed by the portrayal of Claude, Cézanne broke with Zola after the novel was published. Zola's descriptions of art are rich and varied, echoing similar passages in the work of GUY DE MAUPASSANT.

The Freudian theme of the death instinct is present in this novel as it is in the Rougon-Macquart series overall. The question of artistic creation blends with that of sexuality, again, themes that lie at the heart of much of Zola's writing.

FURTHER READING

Bell, David. *Real Time: Accelerating Narrative from Balzac to Zola.* Urbana: University of Illinois Press, 2004.

Berg, William J., and Laurey K. Martin. *Émile Zola Revisited.* New York: Twayne; Toronto: Maxwell Macmillan Canada; New York: Maxwell Macmillan International, 1992.

Bloom, Harold, ed. *Émile Zola.* Philadelphia: Chelsea House, 2004.

Bowlby, Rachel. *Just Looking: Consumer Culture in Dreiser, Gissing and Zola.* New York: Methuen, 1985.

Brown, Frederick. *Zola: A Life*. Baltimore, Md.: Johns Hopkins University Press, 1996.

Chessid, Ilona. *Thresholds of Desire: Authority and Transgression in the Rougon-Macquart*. New York: P. Lang, 1993.

Gallois, William. *Zola: The History of Capitalism*. Oxford, New York: P. Lang, 2000.

Lethbridge, Robert, and Terry Keefe, eds. *Zola and the Craft of Fiction*. Leicester, England; New York: Leicester University Press, 1990.

Lukács, Georg. *Studies in European Realism*. Translated by Edith Bone. New York: Grosset and Dunlop, 1964.

Petrey, Sandy. *Realism and Revolution: Balzac, Stendhal, Zola and the Performance of History*. Ithaca, N.Y.: Cornell University Press, 1988.

MAUPASSANT, GUY DE (1850–1893)

EDMOND DE GONCOURT once described Guy de Maupassant as a true man of letters. Despite Maupassant's tragic end, he was a remarkably prolific writer and a fitting disciple of his mentor, GUSTAVE FLAUBERT.

Maupassant was born in Normandy. His father's family had originally come from Lorraine but his mother was of true Norman blood. Maupassant and his brother, Hervé, were raised by their mother (née Laure le Poittevin) after their parents' separation. Laure had a passion for literature. In fact, her brother Albert was a poet. She was also a childhood friend of Flaubert, whom Maupassant first met as a child.

Not surprisingly, Laure encouraged her son in his literary pursuits. She directed Maupassant's early education herself, encouraging him, for example, to read Shakespeare. Other than her supervision of his studies, she left him a great deal of freedom and Maupassant took advantage of this to wander the countryside happily. As a boy, Maupassant was strong and healthy. He spent many hours walking the fields and cliffs by the sea or going off in fishing boats, laying by a store of material from which he would later draw for his short stories of provincial peasant life. During these outings he also met the painters Jean-Baptiste Camille Corot and Claude Monet. The strong visual imagery present in Maupassant's works may bear witness to the influence of contemporary painters on his art.

At the age of 13, Maupassant's mother sent him to a parochial boarding school where he was miserable. Isolated from other students, he also developed a distaste for religion that lasted his entire life. Maupassant's only joy was writing poetry that infuriated his teachers. Forced to leave the school, Maupassant finished his studies at a boarding school in Rouen. Maupassant was 20 years old when the Franco-Prussian War broke out in 1870. He enlisted, later depicting his experience in his famous *Boule de Suif,* published in 1880 in ÉMILE ZOLA's *Médan Evenings.*

Like many young men, Maupassant longed for Paris. When the war ended, he took a position in the Naval Ministry; he later moved to the Ministry of Education. Always an astute observer, Maupassant drew on his experience as a government bureaucrat for his stories. He also threw himself enthusiastically into the pleasures of Paris and especially, on weekends, boating on the Seine with a group of friends.

The aspiring writer concentrated more on his writing career than he did on his official post. From 1873 to 1880, Maupassant struggled under the tutelage of Flaubert, who left a lasting imprint on his style and vision of an artist. He even did research for Flaubert's *BOUVARD AND PÉCUCHET.* Flaubert instilled in Maupassant the realist aesthetic (see REALISM), exhorting his pupil to observe the world closely and depict what he saw in precise detail. Flaubert also introduced Maupassant to ALPHONSE DAUDET, JORIS-KARL HUYSMANS, Zola, and the Russian writer Ivan Turgenev.

Maupassant first began his literary career writing various articles on literature, society, and politics for Parisian journals while he principally thought of himself as a poet. His first book, *Des vers,* published in 1880, is a collection of naturalist verse (see NATURALISM). Maupassant also tried his hand at drama, writing a series of plays for private performance. None was successful but Maupassant's engagement in theater may have left a mark on his writing in terms of his attention to the visual.

The publication of *Boule de Suif* launched the young author's career, inspiring Maupassant to leave his government post to concentrate on writing. He quickly developed into a popular writer. Parisian salons clamored for him, but Maupassant guarded his privacy, partly out of disdain and partly as a result of Flaubert's influence. Maupassant firmly believed that an artist's reputation should rest on the quality of his work alone.

He did not, however, live an entirely isolated existence. He had a series of brief love affairs but apparently never knew love as more than a physical experience. Having no lasting attachments may have colored his view of women, whom he often depicted negatively.

Once established as a professional writer, Maupassant was remarkably prolific. Each year between 1880 and 1890 he produced three to five volumes of short stories and novels in addition to various articles and reviews. His most important novels are BEL-AMI and PIERRE AND JEAN. Maupassant's fame earned him a solid fortune, allowing him to build a house in Normandy where he could work in solitude and hunt. He also traveled widely in France, Europe, and North Africa.

The first signs of the onset of mental illness appeared after 1885, although it is possible that earlier periods of discouragement and depression may be related. Maupassant suffered from syphilis, and mental illness ran in his family. His brother died insane at the age of 33. Despite continued productivity, Maupassant became increasingly obsessed with the monotony of human existence and with death. Moreover, he began to suffer from hallucinations. At first he was able to translate these experiences into fantastic stories. By 1889, however, his physical and mental states were in serious decline.

Maupassant's doctors sent him to the Alps and to the Côte d'Azur to rest but, by 1891 it was clear that he would not recover. He attempted and failed to slit his own throat in 1892. He was subsequently sent to an asylum where he died 18 months later, completely insane.

One of the finest writers of the naturalist school, Maupassant is also the great master of the French short story: sensual, impressionistic, and realist all at the same time. As a disciple of Flaubert, he concentrated on the development of a pure and precise style. His works often reflect on the temporality of human happiness and misery. For Maupassant there is no hope, no afterlife, only a pessimistic vision of the human condition that deepened as his illness progressed.

FURTHER READING

Haig, Stirling. "The Mirror of Artifice: Maupassant's *Bel-Ami*." In his *The Madame Bovary Blues: The Pursuit of Illusion in Nineteenth-Century French Fiction*. Baton Rouge: Louisiana State University Press, 1987, 152–162.

Ignotus, Paul. *The Paradox of Maupassant*. New York: Funk and Wagnalls, 1968.

Jackson, Stanlye. *Guy de Maupassant*. Folcroft, Pa.: Folcroft Library Editions, 1974.

Lerner, Michael. *Maupassant*. London: Allen and Unwin, 1975.

Sherard, Robert Harborough. *The Life, Work, and Evil Fate of Guy de Maupassant (gentilhomme de lettres)*. Folcroft, Pa.: Folcroft Library Editions, 1976.

Steegmuller, Francis. *Maupassant: A Lion in the Path*. Freeport, N.Y.: Books for Libraries Press, 1972.

Sullivan, Edward D. *Maupassant: The Short Stories*. Great Neck, N.Y.: Barron's Educational Series, 1962.

MAURIAC, FRANÇOIS (1885–1970)

Born in Bordeaux, Mauriac was raised by his mother, after the death of his father, in a large bourgeois Roman Catholic household. Even as an adolescent, Mauriac recognized his imprisonment by social rank, religion, and provincial life. These became the central elements in his novels, all of which are autobiographical in reflecting Mauriac's own struggle between faith and desire. Above all, Mauriac sought to depict with moral clarity the world he knew. Neither communist nor socialist, Mauriac was nonetheless capable of testifying against his own middle class when guilty of injustice. He consistently spoke out against excessive materialism and religious hypocrisy.

Like ROGER MARTIN DU GARD, Mauriac studied briefly at the École des Chartes, France's prestigious school for training archivists, before quitting to become a writer. He published his first collection of poems, *Joined Hands*, in 1909. This work drew praise from MAURICE BARRÈS, who thus contributed to Mauriac's success. Mauriac published three other collections of poems, *Farewell to Adolescence* (1911), *Storms* (1925), and *The Blood of Atys* (1940), all of which, like his works of fiction, reveal the tension between sin and sensuality. Similar themes mark his three successful plays, *Asmodée* (performed in 1937), *The Unloved* (1945), and *Fire on the Earth* (1950).

After the publication of these poems, Mauriac began to frequent literary circles in Paris where he associated with figures such as MARCEL PROUST and ANDRÉ GIDE.

In 1913, he married Jeanne Lafon. After the outbreak of World War I, Mauriac volunteered as an ambulance driver. By this time, he had established himself as one of the great writers of his generation.

Mauriac gained notoriety as a writer with the publication of KISS FOR THE LEPER (1922), although the novel was subject to criticism from Roman Catholic readers. Like *Kiss for the Leper*, *Génitrix* (1923), *Desert of Love* (1926), THÉRÈSE DESQUEYROUX (1927), and VIPERS' NEST (1932) all draw on his knowledge of the Bordelaise region. Mauriac later explored other genres, producing essays such as *The Life of Jean Racine* and *God and Mamon*. He was elected to the Académie Française in 1933.

Mauriac once wrote, "No drama can begin to live in my spirit that is not set in places where I have lived." In the pine forests, beaches, and vineyards surrounding his native city, Mauriac thus explored the world of family, one's own conscience, and, frequently, the relationship between the two. Mauriac sought to describe bourgeois society and the inner life of those who inhabit it. The countryside around Bordeaux is an overwhelming presence in Mauriac's works, creating an atmosphere that promotes the sensual passion of his characters.

A recurring image symbolizing the conflict within a family is the vipers' nest, as individuals suffer from a sense of isolation, misunderstanding, jealousy, and hatred. The family becomes a suffocating force upon which Mauriac casts a critical eye, frequently focusing on the presence of evil and his works reflect his Catholic faith. In his view, "no matter how miserable a man is, he can begin the apprenticeship to holiness." Recurring themes are temptation, suffering, redemption, and mercy. Mauriac seems to argue that even the worst passions are simply misguided efforts to gain love, the object of which should be God. In other words, we do not realize that what we are actually seeking is divine love.

Mauriac once said, "I am a Catholic who writes novels." The tone of his works differs significantly from other Catholic writers such as PAUL BOURGET and GEORGES BERNANOS. Catholic readers themselves were often skeptical of Mauriac's works, which all reflect in some way on the question of evil. In other words,

Mauriac's novels are not always uplifting. The weightiness of the subject matter, however, is countered by his immense gift of language.

Two distinct periods define his novels written before 1940. *Thérèse Desqueyroux*, Mauriac's most famous work, is typical of the first in its evocation of the presence of evil, as a woman stifled by her marriage attempts to poison her husband. The novel is sharply critical of bourgeois society. Despite its ominous title, *Vipers' Nest* is representative of the second period, in which one perceives a glimmer of hope. The narrator, an old man approaching death, castigates his beneficiaries for their selfishness, yet he attains a sense of peace at the end of his life. In *The End of the Night* (1935), a sequel to *Thérèse Desqueyroux*, Mauriac similarly introduces the possibility of spiritual redemption. Finally, *The Frontennac Mystery* (1933) evokes harmony within the family.

Mauriac repeatedly depicted characters that are separated from God, who wish to do good yet cannot. At the same time, the sensuality in his writing evokes the tension between body and spirit. When Catholics criticized Mauriac it was often for his all too credible and, they feared, perhaps tantalizing depiction of sin. For Mauriac, however, such a clear description of human weakness and temptation was necessary to prove that an absence of morality only leads to emptiness, which is the absence of God. Characters such as Thérèse, Louis, and Jean anguish over the fact that no one seems to love them for themselves, while Mauriac appears to argue that sexual relationships cannot ultimately satisfy our need for companionship. In Mauriac's own words, only Christ can vanquish solitude.

Disillusioned by World War II, Mauriac participated in the Resistance by publishing an underground newspaper during the German occupation. He was later a supporter of General Charles de Gaulle. In 1945, Mauriac tried unsuccessfully to intervene on behalf of BRASILLACH, who had been accused of collaboration. Although Mauriac was criticized from the Left and the Right for his political views, he continued to maintain an independent stance. He was also an outspoken critic of colonialism. He received the Nobel Prize in 1952 for "his penetrating analysis of the soul in the novel form."

After the war, the public's taste in literature shifted toward EXISTENTIALISM and the literature of the absurd. Although Mauriac continued to write novels, contemporary trends were not to his taste. He thus began to move in a new direction, openly defending Christian and humanist values while writers such as JEAN-PAUL SARTRE and ALAIN ROBBE-GRILLET were introducing an entirely new perspective on literature and the world. When he took up his pen in the name of politics, Mauriac did so out of a sense of moral duty. Sympathetic to the poor and the oppressed, he sought to promote tolerance and harmony among differing factions. His fundamental concern for truth and justice was a driving force throughout Mauriac's life. Until his death, he wrote a weekly column, first for *Express* and then for the *Literary Figaro,* in which he commented on the major issues of his day, including the war in Algeria, the return of de Gaulle to power, and the church. His memoirs, published in 1959, manifest the care with which he examined his own conscience as much as the problems of the outside world. In his later years, Mauriac wrote another successful novel, *Formerly Adolescent* (1969), inspired by the revolutionary events of 1968.

Mauriac also wrote a number of essays on religion, which reveal his struggle to live a Christian life in difficult times. His preoccupation with ethical and moral questions spilled over into his views on politics, especially in his critique of fascism and totalitarianism. Mauriac offered his reflections on life and the world in his *Journal* (4 volumes, 1934–51), and in his famous *Bloc-Notes* (1958), a collection of his articles published between 1952 and 1961. Independent and courageous, Mauriac never hesitated to take a stand that reflects his faith as a guiding force in his life.

FURTHER READING

Bessent, Edna. "Solitude in the Novels of François Mauriac," *French Review* 8, no. 2 (December 1934): 129–134.

Garaudy, Roger. *Literature of the Graveyard: Jean-Paul Sartre, François Mauriac, André Malraux, Arthur Koestler.* Translated by Joseph M. Bernstein. New York: International Publishers, 1948.

Penn, Dorothy. "Three French Writers of Contemporary Catholic Realism: The Inner Consciousness Studied by Georges Bernanos, Henri Ghion, and François Mauriac," *French Review* 12, no. 2 (December 1938): 128–137.

Speaight, Robert. *François Mauriac: A Study of the Writer and the Man.* London: Chatto and Windus, 1976.

MEMOIRS OF HADRIAN, THE (LES MÉMOIRES D'HADRIEN) MARGUERITE YOURCENAR (1951)

The Memoirs of Hadrian takes the form of a fictional letter written by the Roman emperor Hadrian to his son, Marcus Aurelius. Hadrian begins by describing his illness, only to progress into a broader and deeper reflection on life. A humanist and philosopher, Hadrian looks back on his experience as a head of state, administrator, military leader, and builder of cities. He explains that he has undertaken to write this letter "in order to define myself, to judge myself, perhaps, at least to know myself better before I die." The narrative thus takes the form of self-analysis. "I try to look back over my life to find in it a plan, but this artificial plan is nothing but an illusion of memory . . . too many roads lead nowhere, too many equations do not add up."

Hadrian recalls a time shortly after being named emperor when an overly zealous supporter murdered his enemies and his fear that, from then on, he would be viewed as a tyrant. Yet, Hadrian feels that he has successfully manipulated public opinion in his own favor. During his reign, Hadrian reveals that he has sought to discern then disseminate universal truths in various architectural and civic projects. His purpose was to promote the grandeur and values of Roman civilization, of which he sees himself, in part, as author.

The most traumatic event in Hadrian's past is clearly the suicide of Antinous, the young Greek man whom Hadrian loved. Only at the end of his life is Hadrian truly capable of accepting Antinous's death. Hadrian had once even considered suicide, asking a doctor to mark the place of his heart so that, in the event that he is not chosen emperor, his dagger will find its target quickly and surely. The challenge for Hadrian is to assimilate the fact that others might see life from a different perspective. This includes Antinous and the Jews who reject the Roman gods.

A watershed in Yourcenar's career as a writer, this very successful work brought the author fame for her ability to combine historical accuracy with fictional appeal.

FURTHER READING

Farrell, C. Frederick. *Marguerite Yourcenar in Counterpoint.* Lanham, Md.: University Press of America, 1983.

Horn, Pierre L. *Marguerite Yourcenar.* Boston: Twayne, 1985.

Howard, Joan E. *From Violence to Vision: Sacrifice in the Works of Marguerite Yourcenar.* Carbondale: Southern Illinois University Press, 1992.

Sarnecki, Judith Holland, and Ingeborg Majer O'Sickey, eds. *Subversive Subjects: Reading Marguerite Yourcenar.* Madison, N.J.: Fairleigh Dickinson University Press, 2004.

Savigneau, Josyane. *Marguerite Yourcenar: Inventing a Life.* Translated by Joan E. Howard. Chicago: University of Chicago Press, 1993.

Shurr, Georgia Hooks. *Marguerite Yourcenar: A Reader's Guide.* Lanham, Md.: University Press of America, 1987.

MEMOIRS OF THE COUNT OF COMMINGE, THE (*LES MÉMOIRES DU COMTE DU COMMINGE*) CLAUDINE-ALEXANDRINE GUÉRIN, MADAME DE TENCIN (1735)

Published anonymously in The Hague, this work of pseudomemoirs by Madame de TENCIN was successful with readers into the 19th century. The philosopher Jean-François de la Harpe described *Comminge* as equal to *The PRINCESS OF CLÈVES* (1678). An edition of 1804 combined the novels of Tencin, Marie-Madeleine de Lafayette and Marie-Louise de Fontaines in one volume.

The memoir novel was an important literary genre in the 18th century, its format lending authenticity to the story. Its emphasis on morality in a realistic setting arose in response to the exaggerated historical romance of the 17th century. Some of the most popular pseudomemoirs were PRÉVOST's *MANON LESCAUT* (1731), MARIVAUX's *The LIFE OF MARIANNE* (1731–42) and CRÉBILLON's, *The WAYWARD HEAD AND HEART* (1736). Most of these novels were written by male authors, women writers tending toward the EPISTOLARY NOVEL. Madame de Tencin's choice to write a memoir novel in a male voice is implicitly critical of a male-dominated social order.

Like Prévost's character of des Grieux, the hero recounts the story of his lost love. As a young man, Comminge fell in love at first sight with the beautiful Adelaïde de Lussan. With a Shakespearean twist that recalls the obstacles faced by the lovers in HONORÉ D'URFÉ's *ASTREA,* the pair's fathers are bitter enemies. Separated by their families, Adelaïde allows herself to be married off to secure Comminge's release, as he has been locked away on a family estate. Comminge enters a monastery.

Once she is widowed, Adelaïde goes in search of Comminge. To be near him, she disguises herself as a monk and joins the community. Always mourning his lost love, Comminge never realizes that she has been before his very eyes until the moment of her death. He writes his memoirs after her death, again recalling des Grieux. Interestingly, Prévost criticized the last scene of Tencin's novel for its lack of respect for religion. Neither character repents for having entered religious life on false grounds.

In an elegant and flowing style, the novel reflects the recurring themes of thwarted love as well as the tension between love and duty. At the same time, Madame de Tencin subverts the meaning of literary conventions typical of the 18th-century novel by challenging the legitimacy of social oppression like other contemporary women writers such as ISABELLE DE CHARRIÈRE.

FURTHER READING

Jones, S. "Madame de Tencin: An Eighteenth-century Woman Novelist." In *Woman and Society in Eighteenth-Century France.* Edited by E. Jacobs, W. H. Barber, et al. London: Athlone Press, 1979.

Stewart, Philip, *Imitation and Illusion in the Memoir-Novel, 1700–1750: The Art of Make-Believe.* New Haven, Conn.: Yale University Press, 1969.

MEN OF GOOD WILL (*LES HOMMES DE BONNE VOLONTÉ*) JULES ROMAINS (1932–1946)

This monumental, 27-volume novel covers the vast panorama of political, economic, and social life of France from 1908 to 1933. It focuses on the story of Jallez and Jerphanion, whose personal destinies blend with Romains's concept of unanimism, a philosophy that emphasizes the spirit of the collective over the individual in modern life. One a poet and the other a statesman, the two met as students and in their interests represent the intellectual world of their time.

Friendship naturally plays an important role in the novel as the means by which an individual is able to experience both the personal and the collective in relation to each other. Beneath the surface runs a moral current, a message of "goodwill." Whether in reflections on history or contemporary political life, good will among men is what offers hope for the future of humanity. This massive work reflects at one and the same time both ideal and real worlds.

Each volume explores a new world, whether academic, political, ideological, or scientific. Ultimately, Romains' global vision of the world reveals itself gradually, as the reader discovers the numerous and varied microcosms that make up life. Moreover, the novel reflects contemporary historical problems such as mounting social tension in the first decades of the 20th century, the trauma of World War I, the rise of fascism, and new cultural and intellectual movements such as SURREALISM. His principal concern is war. In its panoramic vision, the novel recalls the works of HONORÉ DE BALZAC, ÉMILE ZOLA, and the writer Georges Duhamel. In this complex work, Romains attempts to reconcile humanity struggling with the fragmentation of society associated with modernity.

The numerous volumes of Men of Good Will did not meet with equally positive reception. Romains envisioned a contemporary COMÉDIE HUMAINE, but some critics doubted that he was equal to the task. The first two volumes were well received, subsequent volumes less so. Still, Romains built up a solid readership that assured future sales.

FURTHER READING
Boak, Denis. Jules Romains. New York: Twayne, 1974.
Walter, Felix. "Unanimism and the Novels of Jules Romains," PMLA 51, no. 3 (September 1936): 863–871.

MÉRIMÉE, PROSPER (1803–1870) Prosper Mérimée's parents were both painters who, when the time came, discouraged their son from following in their chosen career path. Mérimée consequently entered government administration. From 1834 to 1860 he served as an inspector of historical monuments, a position that took him all over France and Mediterranean Europe and provided much of the material for his fiction.

The publication of Clara Gazul's Theater (1815) launched Mérimée's literary career. This work is ostensibly a translation by "Joseph L'Estrange" of the writings of a Spanish actress. Although a popular work, it was not a great financial success. The attention it drew, however, meant that Mérimée was in great demand in some of the more illustrious Parisian salons, such as that of Madame Récamier. Mérimée's reputation was clearly established with Mateo Falcone (1829), Venus of Ille (1837), Colomba (1840), and CARMEN (1845), highly successfully adapted to opera by Georges Bizet in 1873. A predecessor of GUY DE MAUPASSANT, Mérimée was also a master of the short story. Moreover, his fiction is representative of certain themes associated with ROMANTICISM.

Politically conservative, Mérimée was elected a senator during the SECOND EMPIRE. When the daughter of Mérimée's friend, the Spanish countess de Montijo, became the empress Eugénie, Mérimée began to frequent the court. He died several days after the fall of the Second Empire in 1870.

Most of Mérimée's works are situated in unusual places full of local color in a manner typical of romanticism. Yet Mérimée differs from many romantics in that he does not idealize these exotic locales. Moreover, he departs from romantic lyricism in favor of a sober, concise style that recalls the works of his friend STENDHAL. An interest in the fantastic, the odd, even the cruel, while typical of the dark side of romanticism, drew some criticism. Mérimée was accused of coldly depicting cruelty and violence in a manner unsettling to the reader, as in Carmen.

FURTHER READING
Bowman, Frank. Prosper Mérimée: Heroism, Pessimism, and Irony. Berkeley: University of California Press, 1962.
Gould, Evlyn. The Fate of Carmen. Baltimore, Md.: Johns Hopkins University Press, 1996.
Raitt, A. W. Prosper Mérimée. New York: Scribner, 1970.

MEUN, JEAN DE (D. 1305) Few details of Jean de Meun's life have passed down to us. He is renowned for his continuation of GUILLAUME DE LORRIS'S ROMANCE OF THE ROSE. Evidently connected with the intellectual milieu of the University of Paris, Jean de Meun's Romance reflects the manner of disputation associated with medieval scholasticism. This controversial poem was immediately popular and remained so well into the Renaissance. He is also known for his

translations of the fifth-century philosopher Boethius and the *Letters of Abelard and Heloise.* HÉLISENNE DE CRENNE's *The DISORDERS OF LOVE,* for example, draws from the tradition of the medieval romance much as we see in the works of Jean de Meun.

FURTHER READING

Arden, Heather. *The Romance of the Rose.* Boston: Twayne, 1987.

Luria, Maxwell. *A Reader's Guide to the Roman de la Rose.* Hamden, Conn.: Archon, 1982.

MICROMÉGAS VOLTAIRE (1752)   In this fantasy of science fiction that recalls CYRANO DE BERGERAC's *The STATES AND EMPIRES OF THE MOON AND SUN* (1657, 1662), Micromégas travels through the universe. The narrator meets him on one of the planets orbiting the star Sirius. As the genius Micromégas is 120,000 feet tall, the theme of this tale is the gigantesque, evoked by Voltaire with a sense of humor similar to that of RABELAIS.

Micromégas is an intelligent, cultivated man, not quite 250 years old, who studied at the Jesuit college on his planet. Because of his great intelligence he was able to figure out 50 of Euclid's propositions, 18 more than the Jansenist Blaise Pascal. Unfortunately, the leader of Micromégas's country becomes suspicious of him when Micromégas publishes a suspect book. He is accused of heresy and forced to defend himself. The court case lasts 120 years. In the end, the leader has Micromégas's book condemned by a group of lawyers who have never read it. Micromégas is banished from court for 800 years. Contemporary readers clearly saw the implicit references to OLD REGIME society, even to Voltaire's own experience.

Once in exile, Micromégas travels from planet to planet. Each place that he visits, such as Saturn and Earth, provides the opportunity for Voltaire to make a satirical remark on contemporary society. For example, he ridicules the astronomer William Derham (1657–1735). The story is about proportions; whether they are always scientifically accurate is not the point. Voltaire's ultimate purpose is revealed in Micromégas's remark, "I have traveled . . . but I have seen none who have not more desires than real wants, and more wants than they can satisfy."

On earth, Micromégas is introduced to the philosophy of Aristotle, Descartes, Malebranche, Leibniz, and Locke by that planet's inhabitants, who are microscopic in comparison to Micromégas yet full of conceit. In return, Micromégas offers them a book of philosophy that will explain everything. When they bring the book to the Academy of Sciences in Paris and open it, the pages are blank. Using the device of examining society through a foreigner's eyes, reminiscent of MONTESQUIEU's *PERSIAN LETTERS,* Voltaire offers his usual critique of society with great wit and humor.

FURTHER READING

Bonneville, Douglas A. *Voltaire and the Form of the Novel.* Oxford: Voltaire Foundation, 1976.

Cutler, Maxine G., ed. *Voltaire, the Enlightenment, and the Comic Mode: Essays in Honor of Jean Sareil.* New York: P. Lang, 1990.

Sherman, Carol. *Reading Voltaire's Contes: A Semiotics of Philosophical Narration.* Chapel Hill: University of North Carolina Department of Romance Languages, Distributed by University of North Carolina Press, 1985.

MISE EN SCÈNE CLAUDE OLLIER (1958)   The reader knows little about the protagonist of this novel, De Lassalle, other than that he is an engineer who has come to North Africa to find the road leading to a mine. The opening of the novel finds him in his hotel room, uneasy with his unfamiliar surroundings, full of noises and shadows that he finds difficult to identify. De Lassalle strains to construct a reassuring sense of reality, and this struggle is central to the novel as well as to Ollier's oeuvre, marking its place in the tradition of the *NOUVEAU ROMAN* (New Novel).

There are three interrelated crimes in the novel. The first, legendary crime took place years before. The second takes place in the novel's present time, while the third is only imagined, hence, Lassalle's confusion over reality and meaning. His attempt to map out a lost route and to uncover the significance of a mythical crime take on symbolic meaning. In the end, De Lassale succeeds in his task—objectively—but he is *subjectively* uncertain, ultimately incapable of mastering reality.

The novel is set in an outlying area where the French colonial presence is not strong. The arrival of the engineer is troubling to the local tribe because he is searching for a road to the mine and because he is interested in a murder. This means that more Europeans will soon come. The *"mise en scène"* or stage setting of the novel is the collective reaction of the local populace to these events. Ba Iken, who serves as guide and interpreter to Lassalle, introduces the engineer to the life of the local people. His language, a mixture of French and Arabic, represents the uneasy union between colonizer and colonized and reflects Ollier's fascination with the individual and language. Ichou, a young man who wishes to travel to the West, intervenes between Lassalle and Ba Iken, revealing the latter's deceptions. In the end, tribal consensus wins out; no one reveals the truth about the murder of De Lassale's predecessor to colonial authorities.

Like the NOUVEAU ROMAN writers MICHEL BUTOR and ALAIN ROBBE-GRILLET, Ollier creates a novel that is ostensibly of a work of detective fiction that serves the larger purpose of exploring the nature of reality. De Lassalle is searching for meaning. He seeks to attain an objective vision of the world, only to discover that reality is full of incomprehensible elements. The reader is left with a strange feeling that seems to echo De Lassalle's experience in the novel. This strangeness is a predominant characteristic in Ollier's other works as well. Moreover, violence is present but hidden from the eye, creating the sense of horror that Ollier found so fascinating.

FURTHER READING

Lindsay, Cecile. *Reflexivity and Revolution in the New Novel: Claude Ollier's Fictional Cycle.* Columbus: Ohio University Press, 1990.

MODERATO CANTABILE MARGUERITE DURAS
(1958) Anne Desbarèdes is a rich and idle young woman bored with life, until one day she witnesses the aftermath of a strange and tragic event. A man kills a woman in a nearby café and then passionately embraces her dead body. Chauvin, a former employee of Anne's husband, sees the murder. The shared experience brings these two together in a way that nothing else could have. They are of two different worlds.

The relationship between Anne and Chauvin grows stronger and stronger, obsessed as they both are with the memory of the "lovers of death." Anne gradually allows the gentle yet mysteriously violent passion that develops between them to draw her away from her conventional life until one evening she arrives late and drunk to a party in her home. Two days later she meets Chauvin for the last time, and their parting words strangely echo the opening of the novel as Chauvin says "I wish you were dead." Anne responds, "I already am."

In this novel, Duras reveals her innovative approach, abandoning all pretense of psychological analysis. The writing is stripped of detailed description or character portraits, while revealing the themes that lie at the heart of the author's works, love and death. *Moderato Cantabile* remains one of Duras's most successful novels.

In Duras's works, an isolated and strange event frequently brings together individuals who would otherwise have remained unconnected. Brought together by death and desire, they ultimately fall back into their own personal solitude, leaving the reader with the lingering sense of something unfinished.

Another frequent theme in Duras's works is a woman's struggle against the constraints of society. She has thus earned the recognition of other contemporary feminist writers (see FEMINISM). In this novel, Anne slowly abandons her conformist identity for freedom and self-knowledge. *Moderato Cantabile* also marks Duras's brief affiliation with the NOUVEAU ROMAN group.

FURTHER READING

Bassoff, Bruce. "Death and Desire in Marguerite Duras's Moderato Cantabile," *MLN* 94, no. 4, French Issue: Perspectives in Mimesis (May 1979): 720–730.

Bishop, Lloyd. "Classical Structure and Style in Moderato Cantabile," *French Review,* Special Issue No. 6 Studies on the French Novel (Spring 1974): 219–234.

Champagne, Roland A. "An Incantation of the Sirens: The Structure of Moderato Cantabile," *French Review* 48, no. 6 (May 1975): 981–989.

Coward, David. *Marguerite Duras, Moderato Cantabile.* London: Grant and Cutler, 1981.

Hirsch, Marianne. "Gender, Reading and Desire in Moderato Cantabile," *Twentieth Century Literature* 28, no. 1 (Spring 1982): 69–85.

Moskos, George. "Women and Fictions in Marguerite Duras's Moderato Cantabile," *Contemporary Literature* 25, no. 1 (Spring 1984): 28–52.

Welcher, Jeanne K. "Resolution in Marguerite Duras' Moderato Cantabile," *Twentieth Century Literature* 29, no. 3 (Autumn 1983): 370–378.

MODERNISM

MODERNISM In literature and art, modernism emerged in the early 20th century and is associated with writers such as Virginia Woolf, James Joyce, and MARCEL PROUST. In general, modernism reflects the legacy of ENLIGHTENMENT thought with its emphasis on reason and rationalism, the capacity for an individual to act as an autonomous being, as well as faith in science and progress.

In fiction, modernism emphasizes the subjective as in, for example, stream-of-consciousness writing. In consequence, there is a turn away from an omniscient third-person narrator in modernist fiction. Modernist literature is often marked by overlapping genres, fragmentation, pastiche, nonlinear depictions of time, a conscious exploration of the creative act, and a rejection of the traditional distinction between high and low culture. Modernism reflects a belief that art may create meaning and thus serve as a unifying force in life and society. Many critics consider the last stage of modernism to be STRUCTURALISM.

MODIANO, PATRICK (1945–)

MODIANO, PATRICK (1945–) The urban setting for Modiano's novels is evident from titles such as *Place de l'Étoile* (1968), *Ring Road* (1972), and *The Street of Obscure Shops* (1978). Moreover, the influence of ÉMILE ZOLA and the poet Charles Baudelaire is apparent in these novels, which reveal an enigmatic world peopled with characters uncertain of themselves. Finally, Modiano frequently evokes the period of the German occupation of Paris during World War II.

Although Modiano was too young to have experienced the Occupation, he imagines what it must have been like, exploring the existential uncertainty that marked this troubled period in history. Minute details give Modiano's novels their sense of REALISM, as he creates a world in which characters seem to play a role doled out by chance. Modiano's novels, with their blend of the tragic and the quotidian, thus unsettle the reader.

Modiano's novels are haunted by the presence of his mother, Luisa Colpeyn, a Belgian actress who went to Paris in 1940, and his father, Albert, an Italian Jew whose activities during the war are marked by a troubling obscurity. Modiano once described his upbringing as typical of "all the people who have neither a homeland nor roots." Principally concerned with memory, Modiano's works are, each in its own way, a quest for identity.

Modiano studied only a year at the Sorbonne before becoming a writer. In his early works, he evokes an imaginary world of collaborationists and Jewish heroes. In *Place de l'Étoile,* for example, the character of Raphaël Schlémilovitch meets LOUIS-FERDINAND CÉLINE and Sigmund Freud. The Place de l'Étoile refers to an intersection of several major boulevards in Paris as well as to the yellow stars Jews were forced to wear over their hearts during the Occupation.

In *Night Round,* likewise set in Paris during the Occupation, a double agent goes back and forth between the Gestapo and the Resistance. He is not, however, motivated by political cause or patriotic ideal, and the reader is uncertain as to what drives Swing Troubadour-Lamballe to deliver up the Resistance fighters to the Gestapo, only to martyr himself in the end. The reader follows the steps of this lost young man through an imagined Paris. Although Modiano draws on a specific historical context, he creates a setting that lies outside of time and space, even as it is recognizable. Finally, the figure of Modiano's father dominates *Ring Road* as Modiano seeks to understand what his father did during the war. In this novel, he creates an almost hallucinogenic world in which to place his father's activities, as in *Place de l'Étoile.*

The period of the Occupation that so fascinates Modiano exists in the partly imagined history of his family. By far the most autobiographical of Modiano's novels is *Family Record Book (Livret de famille),* published in 1977, in which Modiano attempts to retrace his parents' steps during the war. The point of origin for this novel is the day the narrator (read Modiano) enters his daughter's date of birth in the family's official record book and realizes that certain information about his parents is missing, such as their dates of birth and their real names. Modiano's attitude toward his own childhood as "an accident of the Occupation" lends a tone to his writing reminiscent of writers in exile.

Not surprisingly, Modiano's novels tend to introduce a character, somewhat like the author, in search of a ghost from the past. Guy Rolland in *Street of Obscure Shops,* a novel that won the Goncourt Prize, for example, suffers from amnesia and struggles to recover his memory. The narrator of *Dog of Spring* (1993) is obsessed with the photographer Francis Jansen and, in DORA BRUDER (1997), arguably Modiano's greatest work, the author himself is in search of a young Jewish woman who disappeared in the war.

Honeymoon (1990) is the story of a young woman who commits suicide in a hotel room in Milan. As Jean takes the train back to Paris, he reads the notice of her death in the newspaper and realizes that he once knew the dead woman. He subsequently seeks to reconstruct the image of Ingrid Teyrsen. The novel follows the form of detective fiction as Jean conjures up the links between himself and Ingrid, as when they each took a taxi or walked the same street. Jean's search for Ingrid is in fact a search for himself. A similar blurring of identity is noticeable in *Dora Bruder. Memory Lane* (1981), *Such Brave Boys* (1982), and *Blond Doll* (1983) seek to depict the myth of a happier time. *Flowers of Ruin* (1990) and *A Circus Passes* (1992) all similarly evoke a lost past. The search for a mythical past is frustrated in novels such as *Sad Villa* (1975), *Sunday in August* (1986), *Cloakroom of Childhood* (1989), and *Further from Forgotten* (1996), all of which evoke a sense of failure. Modiano also wrote a play, *Polka* (1974), and worked with the filmmaker Louis Malle on the dialogues for the film *Lacombe Lucien* (1974).

There is some ambiguity in the criticism on Modiano's fiction. Some critics view him as a writer who has broken with tradition and yet his works are not considered avant-garde. Others view his novels as traps in which the reader is lost in the relationship of the author to text and text to context, as Modiano abandons the traditional narrative form. The underlying theme in Modiano's first three novels is the issue of being both French and Jewish. Some of his principal concerns are the question of identity, both personal and collective, as well as the lost voices of the past.

Modiano's works are nourished by the uncertainties of his past and his own identity, the quest for which marks a number of his novels. Moreover, touched by the death of his brother in 1957, Modiano also evokes a powerful sense of absence in many of his works. Obsessed with the period just prior to his birth and the evil associated with it, Modiano evokes a sense of guilt and strangeness. His novels are both of this world and outside of it. In 1984, Modiano received the Pierre de Monaco Foundation Prize for his oeuvre.

FURTHER READING

Avni, Ora. "Patrick Modiano: A French Jew?" *Yale French Studies,* no. 85, Discourses of Jewish Identity in Twentieth-Century France (1994): 227–247.

Bridges, Victoria. "Patrick Modiano: Quartier Perdu," *Yale French Studies,* Special Issue: After the Age of Suspicion, The French Novel Today (1988): 259–263.

Guyot-Bender, Martine, and William Vander Wolk, eds. *Paradigms of Memory: The Occupation and Other Histories in the Novels of Patrick Modiano.* New York: Peter Lang, 1998.

Kawakami, Akane. *A Self-Conscious Art: Patrick Modiano's Postmodern Fictions.* Liverpool, England: Liverpool University Press, 2000.

Mitchell, Constantina. *Shaping the Novel: Textual Interplay in the Fiction on Malraux, Hébert, and Modiano.* Providence, R.I.: Berghahn Books, 1996.

Morris, Alan. "Patrick Modiano." In Michael Tilby, ed. *Beyond the Nouveau Roman. Essays on the Contemporary French Novel.* Providence, R.I.: Berg, 1990, 177–200.

Morris, Alan. *Patrick Modiano.* Oxford, Washington, D.C.: Berg, 1996.

Nettelbeck, Colin. "Novelists and Their Engagement with History: Some Contemporary French Cases," *Australian Journal of French Studies* 35 (1998): 245–248.

Sherman, Timothy H. "Translating Memory: Patrick Modiano in the Postmodern Context," *Studies in Twentieth Century Literature* 16, no. 2 (Summer 1992): 289–303.

Vander Wolk, William. *Rewriting the Past. Memory, History and Narration in the Novels of Patrick Modiano.* Amsterdam, Atlanta: Faux-Titre No. 129, Rodopi, 1997.

MODIFICATION MICHEL BUTOR (1957) In this novel, Léon Delmont presents the reader with a minute description of his thought process as he travels by train from Paris to Rome. Lost in time and space for the period of this journey, Léon contemplates his intention to bring his mistress, Cécile, who is in Rome, back to Paris with him. The longer he thinks about this, the more he is convinced that Cécile's charm will be lost if she is no longer in Rome. Instead, Léon considers the possibility of bringing his wife, Henriette, from Paris to Rome. As this internal monologue continues, Cécile and Henriette merge into one. Like Léon, Cécile and Henriette exist outside of time and space. In the end, Léon simply appears as inept and incapable of bringing order into his life.

Modification belongs with *PASSING TIME, Milanese Passage,* and *Degrees,* to the first period in Butor's works. It is written in the second-person plural, addressing the reader directly in a manner that breaks down the usual notion of a novel's character. Like other theorists and practitioners of the *NOUVEAU ROMAN,* such as ALAIN ROBBE-GRILLET, Butor challenges the traditional structure of the novel.

FURTHER READING

Faulkenburg, Marilyn Thomas. *Church, City and Labyrinth in Brontë, Dickens, Hardy, and Butor.* New York: P. Lang, 1993.

Lydon, Mary. *Perpetuum Mobile: A Study of the Novels and Aesthetics of Michel Butor.* Edmonton, Canada: University of Alberta Press, 1980.

McWilliams, Dean. *The Narratives of Michel Butor: The Writer as Janus.* Athens: Ohio University Press, 1978.

Spencer, M. C. *Michel Butor.* New York: Twayne, 1974.

Waelti-Walters, Jennifer R. *Michel Butor: A Study of his View of the World and a Panorama of His Work.* Victoria, B.C.: Sono Nis Press, 1977.

MOÏRA JULIEN GREEN (1950)

Joseph Day, a timid and austere Protestant, suffers from the mocking of other students at the university. His life is further complicated when Simon commits suicide out of frustrated love for him. As for Joseph, he tries his best to ignore his own passionate nature.

One day Joseph is again troubled when his landlady tells him that he is sleeping in the beautiful Moïra's former bed. From that moment on, Joseph is haunted by unwanted and obsessive images. Meanwhile, Joseph's fellow students decide it is time for Joseph to lose his virginity. They send Moïra to seduce him. Mad with despair and regret, he murders her the following morning and buries her body in the garden. When his friend Bruce Praileau tries to convince Joseph to flee, he refuses, renouncing both his freedom and his passion in the same moment.

Like *ADRIENNE MESURAT, Moïra* depicts the problem of good and evil, as well as the question of dualism, recurring themes in Green's works. Recalling the novels of GEORGES BERNANOS and FRANÇOIS MAURIAC, Green reveals his profound pessimism over the human condition.

FURTHER READING

Cooke, Gerard Mother. *Hallucination and Death as Motifs in the Novels of Julien Green.* Washington, D.C.: Catholic University of America Press, 1960.

Dunaway, John M. *The Metamorphoses of the Self: The Mystic, the Sensualist, and the Artist in the Works of Julien Green.* Lexington: University Press of Kentucky, 1978.

Kostis, Nicholas. *The Exorcism of Sex and Death in Julien Green's Novels.* The Hague, Paris: Mouton, 1973.

Newbury, Anthony H. *Julien Green: Religion and Sexuality.* Amsterdam: Rodopi; Atlantic Highlands, N.J.: Humanities Press, 1986.

MOLLOY SAMUEL BECKETT (1951)

In this novel, Molloy, a decrepit specimen of humanity, has received a strange command to write down his memories. Unfortunately, he is incapable of recalling the past with any accuracy. Molloy can call to mind only recent events, and in no particular order. Often his memories make no sense. Some he may have invented. Molloy's internal voice also tells him to take his bicycle and visit his mother. He wanders along in confusion and gets lost in a forest, limping and then crawling. He finally collapses after murdering a coal merchant.

The novel then shifts to Moran, who has in turn received a mysterious order to look for Molloy. His search quickly degrades into the same aimlessness that Molloy experienced. Any distinction between the two characters is ambiguous. Moran begins to fall apart. Like Molloy he limps and then suddenly grows old. Moran's son abandons him and he loses all his possessions, ending up as a vagabond. As the novel progresses and individual characters deteriorate so does the structure and language of the novel. Moreover, the reality it depicts is no longer certain, leaving the reader profoundly unsettled.

Beckett's first novel, *Murphy* (1938), was written in English, the author's native tongue. With *Molloy,* the first novel in a trilogy that includes *MALONE DIES* and

The UNNAMEABLE, the author turns to French. In each novel the characters are less distinct individuals than simply voices, as is common in Beckett's writing. This approach announces motifs that reappear in his theatrical works, such as the well-known *Waiting for Godot.*

Disjointed as it is, *Molloy* retains a vague sense of narrative that diminishes with Beckett's subsequent novels. In these works, Beckett's fundamental pessimism about the human condition recalls JEAN-PAUL SARTRE'S *NAUSEA.*

FURTHER READING
Bair, Dierdre. *Samuel Beckett: A Biography.* New York: Summit Books, 1990.
Cronin, Anthony. *Samuel Beckett: The Last Modernist.* New York: Harper Collins, 1997.
Dukes, Gerry. *Samuel Beckett.* London: Penguin, 2001.
Gordon, Lois. *The World of Samuel Beckett, 1906–1946.* New Haven, Conn.: Yale University Press, 1996.
McCarthy, Patrick A. *Critical Essays on Samuel Beckett.* Boston: G. K. Hall, 1986.
Pattie, David. *The Complete Critical Guide to Samuel Beckett.* London, New York: Routledge, 2000.
Rathjen, Friedhelm, ed. *In Principle, Beckett Is Joyce.* Edinburgh: Split Pea Press, 1994.

MONEY (L'ARGENT) ÉMILE ZOLA (1891)
The 18th novel in Zola's ROUGON-MACQUART series, a "Natural and Social History of a Second Empire Family," *Money* examines the financial world of 19th-century Paris. It tells the story of the financier Aristide Saccard, who comes to Paris to gain his fortune. He is full of energy and will, qualities that Zola admires, as we see in the character of Octave Mouret (*The LADIES' PARADISE*). Saccard is a modern man who grasps the movement of capital. Creating his own bank, he dominates the stock exchange and struggles against his rival, Gundermann, a Jewish banker. Saccard is supported in his struggle by Caroline Hamelin's love for him. According to some critics, Caroline is central to the novel as a symbol of hope and joy. When his bank fails and he is once again ruined financially, Saccard flees to the Netherlands to engage in new financial ventures.

Echoing *VENUS OF THE COUNTING HOUSE* and *The Ladies' Paradise,* the theme of money and its role in Second Empire France is, not surprisingly, the central theme of this novel. Zola explores the golden age of banks and the stock exchange, analyzing the mechanisms of finance, investment, and speculation. He exposes the powerful allure of money. Despite his condemnation of capitalism and the corrosive force of money, Zola shows respect for Saccard, who remains undaunted in spite of his failures. Saccard is energetic and creative, a life force. Characters like him reflect Zola's fundamental respect for those who struggle against the death instinct. They are the victorious ones and bear some similarities to characters in BALZAC's novels, a profound influence on Zola's development as a writer.

FURTHER READING
Grant, Richard B. "The Jewish Question in Zola's L'Argent," *PMLA* 70, no. 5 (December 1955): 955–967.
Wasserman, Renata R. "Financial Fictions: Emile Zola's L'argent, Frank Norris' The Pit, and Alfredo de Taunay's O encilhamento," *Comparative Literature Studies* 38, no. 3 (2001): 193–214.

MONSIEUR OUINE GEORGES BERNANOS (1946)
The mysterious murder of a servant unleashes a wave of passion and hatred in the somnolent village of Fenouille, symbolic of the sin and unhappiness of the modern world. Each character seems to possess an evil secret that consumes and destroys him. Monsieur Arsène, the mayor, is feeble and repulsive, despite his obsession with cleanliness. The Chatelaine de Néréis, Jambe-de-Laine, is debauched and perhaps the mistress of the mayor. Monsieur Ouine, a retired professor and nihilist, doubts all meaning, a view he passes on to his pupil Steeny.

Mystifying, hateful links bind these people together. Each character explores the deepest, darkest secret about him- or herself and others, as if a poison has worked its way into the community. The enigmatic nature of personal relations is a sign of evil. While Monsieur Ouine is not himself evil incarnate, he is the essence of passivity and nihilism, the dangers of which spread to others. When the servant is murdered, the atmosphere of tension and destruction swells, threatening to overcome the village, revealing itself in madness, suspicion, and suicide. In a strangely sacrificial rite of purification, the villagers lynch Jambe-de-Laine.

The pervasive sense of evil that marks this novel is typical of Bernanos's works. For him, the existence of evil is a product of modern life deprived of divine illumination. It is a mysterious and enigmatic evil that emerges from a world in chaos. The consequences of the unresolved murder carry this novel beyond the limits of detective fiction to explore fundamental metaphysical questions about the human condition.

FURTHER READING

Balthasar, Hans Urs von. *Bernanos: An Ecclesial Existence.* San Francisco: Ignatius Press, 1996.

Blumenthal, Gerda. *The Poetic Imagination of Georges Bernanos.* Baltimore, Md.: Johns Hopkins University Press, 1965.

MONTESQUIEU, CHARLES-LOUIS DE SECONDAT, BARON DE LA BRÈDE ET DE (1689–1755)

Moralist, political theorist, and philosopher, Montesquieu also wrote one of the most important EPISTOLARY NOVELS of the 18th century, *The PERSIAN LETTERS.* Born in Bordeaux to a Parliamentary family, Montesquieu, like MARIVAUX, first studied law before turning to writing. In 1708 he left for Paris, although he never forgot his Bordelaise roots. He was a member of the Parliament of Bordeaux and helped found the Bordeaux Academy of Sciences.

The Persian Letters were published anonymously in Amsterdam in 1721. It is possible that Montesquieu did not want to attract attention to himself, given his position as a magistrate. The novel was immediately successful, securing Montesquieu increased participation in Parisian literary salons. From this point on, Montesquieu spent more time in Paris, although he continued to manage his family's provincial estates. With his literary reputation on the rise, Montesquieu was accepted into the Académie Française in 1728. According to legend, the prime minister, Cardinal Fleury, opposed his acceptance into the Académie on the basis of letter 24 in *The Persian Letters,* in which both Louis XV and the pope are likened to magicians. Particularly controversial under the OLD REGIME was his attack on despotism.

For the next two years, from 1728 to 1731, like the two principal characters in his novel, Usbek and Rica,

Montesquieu traveled extensively throughout Europe studying geography, climate, diplomacy, economy, and culture. This period of research gave him the foundation for his most famous political treatise, *On the Spirit of Laws,* published anonymously in Geneva in 1748. One of the most important works of political theory to come out of the French ENLIGHTENMENT, *On the Spirit of Laws* caused a great stir as well as serious opposition on religious and political grounds. Montesquieu responded to the attacks in 1750 with his *Defense of the Spirit of Laws,* a brilliant explication of his political thought. Nonetheless, by 1751 this work had been placed on the Roman Catholic Church's Index of Banned Books and condemned by the Sorbonne. This did not diminish its success among readers. By 1750, 22 editions had been published.

In *On the Spirit of Laws,* Montesquieu argued that laws are neither universal nor absolute. They depend on the particularities of climate, culture, and systems of government. *The Persian Letters,* an epistolary novel presenting the impressions of two Persians traveling in France, serves as an effective literary counterpoint to the political theory Montesquieu expresses in the *Spirit of Laws.*

FURTHER READING

Conroy, Peter V. *Montesquieu Revisited.* New York: Twayne; Toronto: Maxwell Macmillan Canada; New York: Maxwell Macmillan International, 1992.

Cook, Elizabeth Hackendorn. *Epistolary Bodies: Gender and Genre in the Eighteenth Century Republic of Letters.* Stanford, Calif.: Stanford University Press, 1996.

Dargan, Edwin Preston. *The Aesthetic Doctrine of Montesquieu: Its Application in His Writings.* New York: B. Franklin, 1968.

Goodman, Dena. *Criticism in Action: Enlightenment Experiments in Political Writing.* Ithaca, N.Y.: Cornell University Press, 1989.

Gunny, Ahmad. "Montesquieu's View of Islam in the *Lettres persanes,*" *Studies on Voltaire and the Eighteenth Century* 174. Oxford: Voltaire Foundation, 1978.

Kra, Pauline. "Montesquieu and Women." In Samia I. Spencer, ed. *French Women and the Age of Enlightenment.* Bloomington: Indiana University Press, 1984.

Pucci, Suzanne. "Orientalism and Representation of Exteriority in Montesquieu's *Lettres persanes,*" *The Eighteenth Century: Theory and Interpretation* 23 (Fall 1985): 263–279.

Shackleton, Robert. *Essays on Montesquieu and on the Enlightenment.* Oxford: Voltaire Foundation and the Taylor Institute, 1988.

Schaub, Diana. *Erotic Liberalism: Women and Revolution in Montesquieu's Persian Letters.* Lanham, Md.: Rowman & Littlefield, 1995.

MONTHERLANT, HENRI DE (1896–1972)

Novelist, playwright, and essayist, Henri de Monetherlant was born in Paris to an aristocratic, Catholic family. He was an only child. Financial difficulties necessitated his family's move into his maternal grandparents' home where two uncles were already living. They were to become the inspiration for Montherlant's novel *The Bachelors* (1933).

From a young age, Montherlant was drawn to the literature of classical antiquity. Throughout his life he continued to read and reread Plutarch's *Lives* and the works of Seneca, and to reflect on the philosophy of the Stoics. The influence of these thinkers is apparent in his later writings.

By the age of 12, Montherlant had decided to become a writer. As a student, he developed a close relationship with another male student, much to the consternation of the school's administration. Montherlant was subsequently forced to leave the school. He once said, "this creature is the only one I loved in my entire life." Unlike ANDRÉ GIDE, for a long time Montherlant was not able to express his view of homosexuality openly, although this adolescent experience with love later inspired the play *The City in Which the Prince Is a Child* (1951) and the novel *The Boys* (1973).

Montherlant's father died in 1914. As his mother was also dying, she requested that her son delay before volunteering to fight in World War I. Consequently, Montherlant did not leave for the front until 1915. Seriously wounded in 1918, he finished his military service as an interpreter for the U.S. Army.

Montherlant's literary career began with the publication of *Morning Rises* in 1920, although the work was rejected by 11 different publishers before finally being accepted. When his grandmother died, Montherlant sold her house and left for several years to wander across Spain, North Africa, and Italy, where he sought to recapture the sense of fraternity he had experienced with other soldiers at the front. His travels inspired *At the Fountains of Desire* (1927), *The Little Child of Castille* (1929), and *A Lone Traveler Is a Devil* (1945). In 1930 he began work on *Desert Rose,* not published until 1968, a work in which he offered his reflections on colonialism in North Africa. However, Montherlant hesitated to publish opinions that might be considered unpatriotic.

In this novel, Lieutenant Auligny, a young officer stationed in Morocco, begins to question France's colonial policy and ultimately asks to be relieved of his command because he is unwilling to participate in military operations against local inhabitants. He then leaves for Fez, Morocco where, ironically, he is killed by a group of Arabs when he refuses to take up arms against them, becoming the victim of his own honesty and charity.

Montherlant returned to France in 1932, only to be disgusted by what he perceived as society's weakness and degradation. He shared with BARRÈS a sense of decadence and egoism, a cult of the self reminiscent of STENDHAL and, more distantly, CHATEAUBRIAND. A number of his works reflect nostalgia for childhood and a celebration of the body as Montherlant sought to evoke a virile masculinity that found its counterpoint in misogynism. In *The Dream* (1922) and *Funeral Chant for the Dead at Verdun* (1924), for example, Montherlant juxtaposed masculine heroism to feminine feeling. His love for athletics and bullfighting inspired *The Olympics* (1924) and *The Bestiary* (1926), a novel in which Alban Bricoule must fight a dangerous bull to earn the favors of Soledad. Strangely, once he has killed the bull, Alban rejects Soledad. The bullfight turns out to have been an important rite of passage through which Alban discovers his own identity. Montherlant's description of the bullfight blends the mystical with the erotic.

After 1932, Montherlant's reflections on politics and heroism led him to the conclusion that a German victory might be a fitting outcome to Europe's crisis. There is an ambiguity in Montherlant's works derived from a combination of Christian charity and a Nietzschean disdain for the weak. In 1934, he published *The Bachelors,* a novel about old noblemen incapable of adapting to modern life. That novel won the grand prize of the Académie Française. On an entirely different note, *Useless Service* (1935) evokes the conflict between the spirit and the intellect. Montherlant's writings reveal contradictory tendencies of sacrifice and abandon, austerity and sensuality. Above all, Montherlant was opposed to the mediocrity and decadence of contemporary society, a frustration that sometimes led him to try and escape into the past.

In 1924, Montherlant broke his engagement with one woman and in 1934 with another. This experience provided some of the material for a cycle of novels entitled UNMARRIED GIRLS, which includes *Unmarried Girls* (1936), *Pity for Women* (1936), *The Demon of Good* (1937), and the successful *Lepers* (1939). Despite the rather unlikable character of Pierre, in these novels Montherlant posed serious questions about relations between men and women, love and marriage, in a manner that appealed to a broad audience.

In 1938, in the turbulent period leading up to the outbreak of World War II, Montherlant spoke out against the Munich agreement between Germany, Great Britain, France and Italy, producing a series of articles against war mongering that were published together in a volume entitled *Fall Equinox*. In 1940, Montherlant left again for the front, this time as a war correspondent but quickly returned to Paris. He then moved to the south where he remained until 1941 and wrote *Summer Solstice* (1941). A commission to write a play drew him back to Paris. *The Dead Queen* (1942) was an enormous success. The only other work Montherlant wrote during the war was *No One's Son* (1943).

After the Liberation, Montherlant was perplexed to discover that he was under investigation for collaboration during the war. However, *Texts Under the Occupation* proved these suspicions wrong. Nonetheless, Montherlant suffered from the experience. After 1940, he by and large devoted himself to theater, often turning to religious or historical subjects. His most successful plays were *The Dead Queen, The Master of Santiago* (1947), and *The City Whose Prince Is a Child* (1951).

Montherlant was elected to the Académie Française in 1960. In 1963 he wrote yet another novel, *Chaos and the Night,* in which he considered the question of approaching death. He completed *The Boys* in 1969 and another novel, *My Master Is an Assassin* in 1971,

in which he examined the absence of pity among men. Certain critics have commented that these novels, including *Desert Rose,* almost come too late, in the sense that Montherlant was for various reasons unwilling to broach certain themes until later in his life. In *The Boys,* Montherlant finally revealed the secret of his love for another boy when they were in school. In this work, Montherlant blends the spiritual and the sensual in a story that allows love to vanquish in the end. It is a work full of mystery and grace. *Desert Rose,* as we have seen, is critical of France's colonial policy. One has the sense that Montherlant wished to end his life with a clean slate. Having lost the use of one eye, Montherlant committed suicide in 1972, a gesture in which he demonstrated his unwillingness to live in what he considered to be a weakened and undignified state.

Montherlant's knowledge of classical culture and Christian spirituality mark his oeuvre in which one finds a fundamental tension between stoicism and a love of pleasure. A recurring theme is the notion that the world is chaos followed by night. While this is indeed the title of one novel, it is the atmosphere that permeates others. Montherlant was in the end a disillusioned moralist whose pessimism marks his works. He is principally remembered today for his plays.

FURTHER READING

Becker, Lucille Frackman. *Henry de Montherlant: A Critical Biography.* Carbondale: Southern Illinois University Press, 1970.

Gerrard, Charlotte Frankel. *Montherlant and Suicide.* Madrid: J. Porrúa Turanzas, 1977.

Johnson, Robert Brown. *Henry de Montherlant.* New York: Twayne, 1968.

MOUNT ANALOGUE: A NOVEL OF SYMBOLICALLY AUTHENTIC NON-EUCLIDEAN ADVENTURES IN MOUNTAIN CLIMBING (*LE MONT ANALOGUE*)

RENÉ DAUMAL (1952) This unfinished novel reflects the complex philosophy Daumal developed over his lifetime. One finds in it hints of his brush with SURREALISM as well as his interest in Hinduism and Eastern philosophy more generally.

A novel of initiation, *Mount Analogue* is the story of a group of adventures who set off to climb a secret mountain located on a distant island. The group is led by Professor Sogol, whose name is an anagram of the Greek *logos* or reason. Before the climbers even begin their ascent, they must abandon all conventional notions of reality and experience. Only by embracing humility and the truth of their own weakness can they succeed. All those driven by curiosity or greed fail.

The group originally consisted of 12, until four decided not to participate, at least not at first. The four later undertake a parallel ascent but they do so for the wrong reasons and so are destroyed in a storm.

The mountaineers' progress is slow. They move in stages from one refuge to another. In each instance, however, they must prepare the refuge for others who may follow. Their journey, literally and figuratively, is one undertaken in company and in a spirit of collaboration.

Daumal died before finishing his manuscript, but he left behind notes that allow us to understand the novel's purpose, as well as its future development. "You climb. You see. You descend, you can't see anymore; but you have seen. . . . When you cannot see anymore, you can at least still know."

The novel is highly symbolic. The mountain seems to represent the possibility of rising above the limits of ordinary human existence to attain a metaphysical sense of absolute union. Furthermore, the only way to ascend the mountain is by analogy. In Daumal's mind, there is a fundamental relationship between the visible and the invisible. Herein lies the law of the universe.

In Daumal's vision mystical thought is superior to rational thought. For example, two members of the expedition are brothers; one is round and the other rectangular. Together they symbolize the original form of the world uniting the sphere and the four-sided figure into one. Daumal's cosmogony is even more apparent in the story of the hollow men and the bitter rose (*les homes creux el la rose amère*). According to this legend, hollow men are ordinary bad men and the rose is wisdom. Two twins seek to conquer the rose. Mo, the first, falls to the hollow men. Ho, the second, succeeds and become a complete man, Ho-Mo. Whether in the legend of the hollow men and the rose or because each member of the expedition bears a different trait of the original, complete man, Daumal's ideal is to unite all aspects of humanity.

FURTHER READING
Daumal, René. *The Powers of the Word: Selected Essays and Notes, 1927–1943.* Edited and translated by Mark Polizotti. San Francisco: City Lights Books, 1991.
Daumal, *Rasa, of Knowledge of the Self: Essays on Indian Aesthetics and Selected Sanskrit Studies.* Translated by Louise Lande Levi. New York: New Directions, 1982.
Rosenblatt, Kathleen Ferrick. *René Daumal: The Life and Work of a Mystic Guide.* Albany: State University of New York Press, 1999.

MUSSET, ALFRED DE (1810–1857)

Alfred de Musset is one of the most fascinating personalities of the 19th-century literary scene. He left his mark on posterity as much by his public and literarily publicized love affair with GEORGE SAND as for his poetry, drama, and an autobiographical novel, *CONFESSIONS OF A CHILD OF THE CENTURY*.

Musset was born in Paris into a family of some means and he grew up in a cultured environment. A brilliant student, he was a young man of diverse talents. For a time, his choice of career was uncertain. He studied law, then medicine; he was also a talented draftsman and musician. Only after his father's death did Musset finally decide to become a writer. A high-school friend, VICTOR HUGO's brother-in-law, introduced Musset to the great writer's literary circle, the *cénacle*, and Musset became an ardent admirer of Hugo. Musset was more a man of the world than a man of letters, although his writing captivated ALFRED DE VIGNY and SAINTE-BEUVE.

A precocious writer, Musset published his first collection of poetry, *Tales of Spain and Italy*, at age 19, shocking an audience who did not expect Musset's tone of irony from a supposed disciple of Hugo. A first love affair turned out to be a painful disappointment, convincing Musset to view women as duplicitous. Musset later said that this affair had spoiled him for love. His later works all reflect closely his emotional and psychological state at the time of writing.

Musset's first play, *Venetian Night,* was a failure, closing after one performance. All his later dramatic works were intended to be read rather than performed. The most famous of these, *Lorenzaccio,* was well received in 1834. It is Musset's dramatic masterpiece.

In 1833, he the writer met GEORGE SAND and it seemed at first that she might be the woman who could cure him of his inability to love. Beautiful, intelligent, and bold, Sand inspired Musset and they entered into a tumultuous love affair that lasted for eight months, then continued on and off until 1847. In 1833 they traveled together to Italy, where Musset fell seriously ill. During his convalescence, Sand fell in love with Musset's young doctor, Pagello, when there were already tensions between the two lovers/writers. This caused the first rupture in their relationship. Although they later attempted to resume their affair, it was never successful. Their relationship nonetheless plays a significant role in both authors' works. *Lorenzaccio* draws on the Italian experience while revealing at the same time Musset's skeptical view of life and politics.

Critics have often characterized Musset as a man with an adolescent mind and a number of his principal characters are on the verge of entering adulthood, not full of vigor and determination but doubtful and wounded before their life has even begun. Both *Lorenzaccio* and *Confessions* are examples. In *Confessions* (1836), the main character, Octave, like Lorenzo, represents both Musset himself and his entire generation of young men disappointed in their political aspirations, skeptical of the possibility of action, and dubious about women, love, and religion. Despair over lost innocence and moral idealism lead to debauchery, the only apparent alternative to boredom and frustration.

After 1838, Musset seemed to lose inspiration. He suffered from a heart condition, too much drinking, and life of general depravity. Musset was elected to the Académie Française in 1853, the same year that he was appointed librarian to the Ministry of Education, but he no longer wrote. He died four years later, his demise largely ignored. Musset's most creative period was during his youth and ended by 30. A debauched dandy, Musset was never able to choose art over pleasure, yet was well aware of the serious nature of this conflict. The best of his works, then, in any genre, are confessional, always revealing a man torn between dissolution and the possibility of salvation through art.

FURTHER READING

Hofstadter, Dan. *The Love Affair as a Work of Art.* New York: Farrar, Straus and Giroux, 1996.

Levin, Susan M. *The Romantic Art of Confession.* Columbia, S.C.: Camden House, 1998.

Majewski, Henry. *Paradigm and Parody: Images of Creativity in French Romanticism.* Charlottesville: University Press of Virginia, 1989.

Sedgwick, Henry Dwight. *Alfred de Musset, 1810–1857.* Port Washington, N.Y.: Kennikat Press, 1973.

MY FRIEND FROM LIMOUSIN (SIEGFRIED ET LE LIMOUSIN) JEAN GIRAUDOUX (1922)

At the opening of this novel World War I has ended and Jean discovers among the articles of a German journalist whole pages signed S.V.K. that were, in fact, written by his friend Jacques Forestier, a French writer who disappeared in 1915. With the help of a German friend, Jean discovers that Siegfried von Kleist (S.V.K.) is in reality Jacques.

Suffering from amnesia, Jacques had been found on the battlefield and was subsequently treated by a German nurse. After the war, he became one of the great thinkers of the Weimar Republic, Germany's democratic government in the interwar period, a moral guide completely unaware of his true identity. Jean brings Siegfried/Jacques to his native province of Limousin in an attempt to stir his memory.

Giraudoux grew up in the Limousin, a countryside that remained dear to him. This novel forms part of a trilogy that includes *Bella* (1926) and *Églantine* (1927). Together they reflect Giraudoux's concern for European society in the interwar period, particularly in terms of Franco-German relations. Giraudoux's career as a diplomat made him especially aware of contemporary political problems.

While the novel reflects the historical context of Europe between the two wars, it also stands apart. Critics have often commented on Giraudoux's *précieux* style (see PRECIOSITY) that may make this novel heavy going for readers today. At the time of its publication, however, *Siegfried and the Limousin* was a remarkable success. It was adapted to the stage in 1928 under the title *Siegfried*.

FURTHER READING

Body, Jacques. *Jean Giraudoux: The Legend and the Secret.* Translated by James Norwood. Rutherford, N.J.: Fairleigh Dickinson University Press; London, Cranbury, N.J.: Associated University Presses, 1991.

Korzeniowska, Victoria. *The Heroine as Social Redeemer in the Plays of Jean Giraudoux.* Oxford, New York: P. Lang, 2001.

LeMaître, Georges Edouard. *Jean Giraudoux: The Writer and his Work.* New York: Ungar, 1971.

Le Sage, Laurent. *Jean Giraudoux, Surrealism and the German Romantic Ideal.* Urbana: University of Illinois Press, 1952.

MYSTERIES OF PARIS, THE (*LES MYS-TÈRES DE PARIS*) EUGÈNE SUE (1842–1843)

One of the first serial novels published in France, *The Mysteries of Paris* appeared in the Parisian *Journal des débats* in 1842–43. A masterpiece of the genre, *The Mysteries* was an instant success. The novels tells the story of Rodolphe, a German nobleman who tries to expiate his past sins by turning into a modern-day knight errant. Disguised as a worker, he plumbs the depths of the Parisian underworld to protect the innocent and right wrong. There he meets Fleur-de-Marie, an unhappy young woman forced into prostitution by the shrewish Chouette, who has raised her. Rodolphe becomes Fleur-de-Marie's protector, saving her more than once from her enemies. Eventually, Rodolphe discovers that Fleur-de-Marie is in fact his daughter. Returning with her to Germany, Rodolphe restores Fleur-de-Marie to her rightful place in society. Unfortunately, she is haunted by her past. Refusing to marry the man she loves, Fleur-de-Marie enters a convent. Rodolphe dies on the very day that his daughter takes the veil. She follows him to the grave shortly thereafter.

The novel offers a broad cast of characters, from the malevolent Chouette to the honest worker Morel. Novels by authors such as RESTIF DE LA BRETONNE and HONORÉ DE BALZAC had already exposed the underside of Parisian life. Sue's contemporary GEORGE SAND promoted humanitarian socialist principles in her novels. Sue was the first, however, to bring together so many disparate elements into a novel about society. His realistic descriptions did much to promote a critique of contemporary social institutions, echoing the socialist platform in the period leading up to the Revolution of 1848. He thus laid the foundation for VICTOR HUGO's masterpiece *LES MISÉRABLES.*

The Mysteries was so popular that readers of all social classes lined up for the latest installment. Sue made a fortune even as he made a political statement, seeking to convince his readers that the suffering classes are victims rather than criminals. While it may have been entertained by a string of murders, kidnappings, and other gruesome crimes, drawing on the traditions of the English gothic novel, the reading public imbibed at the same time Sue's message about social justice. Leading into REALISM, Sue shows how suffering may not be the result of vice. Inhumane social conditions also contribute.

FURTHER READING

Palmer Chevasco, Berry. *Mysterymania: The Reception of Eugène Sue in Britain 1838–1860.* Oxford, New York: P. Lang. 2003.

MYSTERIOUS ISLAND, THE (*L'ÎLE MYS-TÉRIEUSE*) JULES VERNE (1874)

Similar to *TWENTY THOUSAND LEAGUES UNDER THE SEA, Mysterious Island* is an adventure story based on the experience of a small group of castaways. There are five characters: captain Cyrus Smith, an engineer; Gédéon Spilett, a journalist; a black named Nab; Pencroff, a sailor; and Harbert, a child, all of whom escape from the American Civil War by balloon. Over the ocean, their engine is disabled and they must abandon all heavy objects, including gold, to survive. The castaways are thus cut off literally and figuratively from the world they once knew.

They wind up on a deserted island with no resources. They name it Lincoln, after the American president. Unprepared for the fate that has befallen them, they are fortunate in the presence of Cyrus, who seems to produce miracles. Cyrus makes fire from lentils, determines the topography of the island, makes bows and arrows, metal and chemicals. He builds a shelter in a cave and begins to domesticate animals. In fact, under Cyrus's guidance the five castaways relive the process of human history.

All the while, there is the sense that some mysterious power seems to be watching over them. Assistance appears out of nowhere; the engineer is magically rescued. Finally, there is a message telling them where to find Ayrton, a former convict from another Verne novel. When they are saved from a pirate attack by a mysterious explosion, it turns out that Captain Nero (of *Twenty Thousand Leagues Under the Sea*) is responsible. The five men meet the famous navigator in time to witness his death. Fortunately, he warns them about a volcanic explosion that will take place on the island. It is through Nemo that the castaways escape from the island and return to civilization.

Influenced by Daniel Defoe's *Robinson Crusoe,* Verne depicts the efforts of these five to form a new community. Yet Verne's characters differ from Defoe's. If Robinson Crusoe was an 18th-century philosopher, Verne's castaways represent knowledge and a 19th-century view of civilization based on science and humankind's ability to conquer nature. A number of themes recur in Verne's works. As in *AROUND THE WORLD IN EIGHTY DAYS, Mysterious Island* also reflects Verne's interest in European colonization and the underlying idea that Europe can impose its standards and values on the rest of the world. The castaways/colonists must survive not just for survival's sake but to perpetuate a tradition. They will "turn the island into a little America! . . . build cities there and establish railroads, install the telegraph, and one great day the island will be transformed." Verne's "colonists" also reflect an idealist vision that bears the marks of both POSITIVISM and political theorist Claude-Henri Saint-Simon's utopian socialism. These men live together in society and are thus capable of progress in a way that one is not is not when in isolation. Verne thus depicts an ideal world where differences of race or class disappear before the collective. In the end, the needs of the individual can be met only within the context of the community.

Verne's fascination with geology is likewise apparent in this novel through its detailed description of the geological structure of the island. The island's volcanic origin is important for the outcome of the story, but it relates to themes also found in *JOURNEY TO THE CENTER OF THE EARTH,* in which the fire at the earth's core and the earth's volcanic origins represent life.

Verne continues in his tradition of blending science and fantasy. This novel forms part of a series called "The Extraordinary Voyages." Verne asserted that his purpose in writing these adventure stories was "to depict Earth, and not only the Earth, but the universe." His writings reveal the revolutionary nature of technological change in the 19th century that resulted in an altered understanding of society, time, and space. Despite his faith in the power of science and technology to improve the world, Verne also shows that science cannot explain certain things. Through his exploration of our relationship to the environment, Verne also raises existential, metaphysical, and philosophical questions.

FURTHER READING

Born, Franz. *Jules Verne, the Man Who Invented the Future.* Translated by Juliana Biro. Englewood Cliffs, N.J.: Prentice Hall, 1964.

Butcher, William. *Verne's Journey to the Center of the Self: Space and Time in the "Voyages Extraordinaires."* New York: St. Martin's Press; London: Macmillan, 1990.

Costello, Peter. *Jules Verne: The Inventor of Science Fiction.* London: Hodder and Stoughton, 1978.

Evans, I. O. *Jules Verne and His Work.* Mattituck, N.Y.: Aeonian Press, 1976.

Freedman, Russell. *Jules Verne, Portrait of a Prophet.* New York: Holiday House, 1965.

Lottman, Herbert R. *Jules Verne: An Exploratory Biography.* New York: St. Martin's Press, 1996.

NADJA A**NDRÉ** B**RETON** **(1928)**   Nadja is a mysterious and fascinating young woman Breton meets by chance who embodies the spirit of SURREALISM. She is a real person, a "wandering soul" in the streets of Paris to whom Breton is first drawn because of her bizarre makeup. For a brief moment, Nadja enters Breton's life and he sees the world through her eyes, those of a mad woman who ends up in an asylum.

Their encounters take place between October 4 and 12, 1926, after which Nadja disappears. The epilogue, written in praise of a love and beauty that is "not dynamic or static but convulsive," was written in 1927. Breton felt that he was better able to define himself after knowing Nadja. He reedited the novel in 1963.

Nadja is the phantom at the heart of the book that reveals the presence of another dimension, the subconscious world of everyday life. She reminds Breton and the reader of a metaphysical abyss full of dreams, fears, uncertainties, and death. This deepest part of the self rises to the surface in this extraordinary work. Nadja is more than a character in a novel: She is a necessity; she is destiny.

The novel takes place on two levels, that of the real world and that of the mind. In the prologue, Breton poses the question, "Who am I?" In response, the narrative serves as an autobiographical evocation of the psychic relationship between the imaginary and the real. Interspersed throughout the novel are photographs and drawings by Nadja, all of which lend the story authenticity. Breton's most romantic work, *Nadja* is also a supreme example of surrealist literature, with its seamless blending of the world of dreams and reality.

FURTHER READING
Balakian, Anna, and Rudolf E. Kuenzli, eds. *André Breton Today.* New York: W. Locker and Owens, 1989.
Carrouges, Michel. *André Breton and the Basic Concepts of Surrealism.* Translated by Maura Prendergast. Tuscaloosa: University of Alabama Press, 1974.
Caws, Mary Ann. *André Breton.* New York: Twayne, n.d.; London: Prentice Hall International, 1996.
———. *Surrealism and the Literary Imagination: A Study of Breton and Bacheard.* The Hague: Mouton, 1966.
Polizzotti, Mark. *Revolution of the Mind: The Life of André Breton.* New York: Da Capo Press, 1997.

NANA É**MILE** Z**OLA** **(1880)**   Nana is a strikingly modern novel. Its central theme of desire is centered on the courtesan Nana's remarkable body, capable of inspiring desire in men and women alike. It is a fascinating and dangerous body, "a golden beast," a force of its own whose very odor overtakes reason and the senses. Zola's contemporary the painter Édouard Manet was so impressed with Zola's character that he gave the title *Nana* to his painting of the courtesan Henriette Hauser. In his portrait Hauser appears as an enticingly plump young woman whose glance reaches out coyly to the observer. Nana, however, is more. She is the very embodiment of Venus. In the end, though, the malady that disfigures and destroys her serves as an allegory for a diseased society.

The novel is divided into two symmetrical parts. The first describes Nana's rise and fall as an actress, the second her meteoric rise and ultimate demise as a courtesan. In this ninth volume in the ROUGON-MACQUART series, Zola continues the exploration of debauchery he began in *L'ASSOMMOIR*. In fact, Nana Coupeau is the daughter of that novel's principal character, Gervaise. In his notes for the novel, Zola described Nana's character as "good natured above all else . . . never does harm for harm's sake and feels sorry for people. . . . At first very slovenly, vulgar; then plays the lady and watches herself closely . . . simply by means of her sex and her strong female odor, she destroy[s] everything she approaches . . . turning society sour just as women [menstruating] turn milk sour."

One winter, Nana runs away from her parents' miserable life only to become a prostitute. She is eventually hired by the Variety Theater. Although she can neither sing nor dance, Nana is taken on for her strikingly beautiful, even mesmerizing body. When she appeared on stage, nearly naked but for her long golden hair, "every man was under her spell. A wave of lust was flowing from her as from a bitch in heat, and it had spread further and further until it filled the whole house."

Nana quickly becomes one of the most sought-after women of the SECOND EMPIRE. Thus despite her squalid beginnings, Nana winds up in a sumptuous mansion where her bedroom becomes a place of worship. In her unending drive for pleasure, she thoughtlessly destroys the men who desire her, ruining their fortunes and families, driving them to suicide. Once he is ruined for good, the charming Vandeuvres locks himself in the stable with his horses and sets it on fire. "You could hear [the horses] lashing out, throwing themselves against the doors, and screaming just like human beings." Even the empress's chamberlain, Muffat, is not spared Nana's voracious appetite. Long repressed by his catholic upbringing, Muffat is completely overcome when he encounters Nana. "She was the Golden Beast, as blind as brute force, whose very odor corrupted the world. Muffat gazed in fascination, like a man possessed, so intently that when he shut his eyes to see no more, the Beast reappeared in the darkness, larger, more awe-inspiring, more suggestive in

its power. Henceforth it would remain before his eyes, in his very flesh, forever." He ends up playing a dog and bear on Nana's bedroom carpet taking pleasure in his humiliation. Over and over, Zola refers to beasts, instinct, the notion of Nana devouring everything before her in a frenzy of sensual greed. The imagery is overpowering. Zola's skillful use of language provokes an almost physical sensation in the reader who begins to grasp the voracious appetite of Nana and her bewitching power over men who see and desire nothing more than her sex.

Zola's notes indicate that despite her basic goodness, Nana "ends up regarding man as a material to exploit, becoming a force of nature, a ferment of destruction," until her death at the age of 19. Her once legendary body horribly disfigured by smallpox, Nana ends her days at the outbreak of the Franco-Prussian War (1870) as a crowd in the street cries, "To Berlin, to Berlin."

This "poem of male desires," as Zola referred to it, was not the first scandalous and yet alluring novel about a prostitute. Earlier examples include PRÉVOST D'ÉXILES's *MANON LESCAUT,* DUMAS FILS's *CAMILLE,* EUGÈNE SUE's popular *MYSTERIES OF PARIS,* the GONCOURTS' *Elisa,* and HUYSMANS's *MARTHE* among others. What makes Nana different, however, is Zola's shift away from the stereotypical depiction of the prostitute as seductive yet principally an object of sympathy. Nana is dangerous because she is able to cross boundaries between different social classes. Vigorous, healthy, good-humored, and energetic, Nana is far from an object of pity; she becomes the means whereby Zola continues his systematic critique of SECOND EMPIRE society. Moreover, Zola seeks to destroy the romantic myth of the courtesan by exposing the world of prostitution and the men who maintain it by weakness or vice in a study that can legitimately be called sociological.

Adhering to his naturalist program (See NATURALISM), in this work Zola continues to study the effects of heredity on the Rougon-Macquart family. For 10 years, Zola gathered information for the novel, observing theater life and race track events, following public scandals and police raids, and interviewing men who frequented courtesans. Published at the same time as his *Experimental Novel,* Zola attempted to show that, to a degree, imagination is irrelevant in naturalist literature. Rather the novelist must observe and document as if he were carrying out a scientific experiment. His aim was to situate a character in a given environment and then note what happens. This approach to literature drew criticism from some Zola's contemporaries, who argued that the novelist cannot simply observe the movements of his characters; he must inevitably participate in plot and character development.

Critics found Zola's views and subject matter shocking. Yet he was not alone. Dumas fils said that France's defeat was due to prostitution, while the writer Paul de Saint-Victor was even more precise: "Who can say how much energy was destroyed, strength enervated and spirit debilitated by that laxity of morals. Who can measure the degree to which it contributed to our fearful misfortunes?" With the notable exception of Zola's friend GUSTAVE FLAUBERT, few critics praised his work. Nonetheless, the novel's subject matter was titillating to contemporary readers. *Nana* was first published as a serial novel (see ROMAN FEUILLETON) in 1879. When it was published in book form in 1880, 55,000 copies were sold on the first day.

FURTHER READING

Brooks, Peter. "Storied Bodies or Nana at Last Unveiled," *Critical Inquiry* 16, no. 1 (Autumn 1989): 1–32.

Chitrus, Bernice. *Reflecting on Nana*. London, New York: Routledge, 1991.

Donaldson-Evans, Mary. "Pricking the Male Ego: Pins and Needles in Flaubert, Maupassant, and Zola," *Nineteenth Century French Studies* 30, nos. 3 and 4 (Spring-Summer 2002): 255–266.

NATURALISM (1865–1890)

The term *naturalism* was first used by Jules Antoine Castagnary in an art critique of 1863, in contrast to REALISM. This literary movement, spearheaded by ÉMILE ZOLA, competes with science to represent nature. Like a doctor or scientist, the writer carefully observes the world, examining the human as a physical and chemical machine interacting with the environment. Zola picked up the term in 1865, arguing, "the Naturalists take up a study of nature at its very sources, replacing metaphysical man with physiological man, no longer separating him from the environment that determines him."

Drawing on the realist movement, naturalism was first inaugurated with the publication of the GONCOURT brothers' novel *GERMINIE LACERTEUX* in 1865. In their preface, the coauthors provided a definition of this new literary movement. In contrast to popular serial novels, the Goncourts offered what they hoped would be a "true novel" that studies all social classes, the lower class in particular, drawing on recent developments in medicine and physiology. Zola greatly admired the Goncourts' work, launching his own brand of naturalism that also draws on medical studies, particularly those of the physiologist Claude Bernard (1813–78), in his ROUGON-MACQUART series.

In 1865–66, Zola produced a series of articles articulating his work in developing this new literary form adapted to the modern era. Through a series of efforts that include literary articles, a defense of painters such as Édouard Manet, the publication of *THÉRÈSE RAQUIN*, and, in particular, the scandal caused by the publication of *L'ASSOMOIR*, Zola drew together at his home in Médan a group of young writers such as JORIS-KARL HUYSMANS and GUY DE MAUPASSANT. These naturalists acknowledged their debt to GUSTAVE FLAUBERT, whose *MADAME BOVARY* was especially influential on their work, along with the writings of the Goncourts, HONORÉ DE BALZAC, and STENDHAL. The naturalists existed both inside and outside of France; the height of their movement was 1880–94. They were gradually torn apart by dissension within the group and by challenges from other new literary movements such as the BOURGET-influenced psychological novel, SYMBOLISM, and the decadents.

NAUSEA (*LA NAUSÉE*) JEAN-PAUL SARTRE (1938)

This novel reflects Sartre's notion, fully articulated in *Being and Nothingness* (1943), that consciousness has physicality. In this work, nausea is the manifestation of consciousness. "A discrete and insurmountable nausea perpetually reveals my body to my consciousness."

Antoine Roquentin, a solitary, idle bachelor of 35, lives in the fictional city of Bouville, a port that resembles Le Havre, where Sartre was living and teaching at the time. After quitting his job in Indochina, Roquentin, tired of travel and what he had thought would be adventures, begins work on a biography of an 18th-century aristocrat, the marquis de Rollebon, while keeping a journal, the text on which the novel is based. The journal opens with an undated entry in which Roquentin notes that his perception of objects has changed, inspiring him with a feeling of disgust and strangeness. Roquentin begins to wonder if he is going mad.

As the journal continues, Roquentin tries to analyze his experience, to discover the origin of the alteration in his perspective. He considers how he first noticed the change in ordinary objects like a pipe, a fork, or a door handle, even in the people he habitually encounters such as the man he frequently sees at the library while doing his research on Rollebon.

To escape the torment of these strange and unexpected sensations, Roquentin takes refuge in a noisy café where life appears to be going on as normal. Although the café Mably gives him a tentative sense of security, Roquentin still feels alone. Occasionally he sleeps with Françoise but he does not love her and cannot talk to her. Roquentin begins to realize that he can never return to a past in which he did not feel estranged from the objective world. He has become imprisoned in his solitude so much so that it surprises him to see other men in conversation. One day he has become immobilized to the point that it is impossible for him to pick up a stray piece of paper lying in the street. It is as if Roquentin has entirely lost his will. All that he feels is the nausea that has extended to his very hands.

At first Roquentin worked on the biography of Rollebon because it gave him satisfaction. He even had sympathy for this figure from the past. Gradually, however, Roquentin's sense of well-being gives way to disillusionment with the tenuous nature of his results. Moreover, over time he begins to feel nauseated even when he is in the café. To overcome it, he plays his favorite blues song, "Some of These Days." For a time the nausea dissipates as Roquentin loses himself in the music.

He then leaves the café to walk in the streets, where he suddenly experiences envy for a woman he encounters as she seems to be suffering from some real trouble, whereas his own torment is ephemeral. At the library

he discovers that his acquaintance, the self-taught man, is systematically reading books in alphabetical order. The idleness of a Sunday afternoon when the people of Bouville go out in the streets to enjoy themselves only augments Roquentin's sense of solitude. For a moment he almost wishes to seek adventure as he had in the past, but this sensation, too, quickly fades.

One day Roquentin receives a letter from Anny, an actress whom he once loved and whom he often recalls, who wants to meet him in Paris. Their relationship had always been complicated and Roquentin hesitates, afraid that he will not be able to meet Anny's expectations. He visits the local museum where is his struck unpleasantly by a series of portraits of smug, bourgeois "bastards" exposed on the walls. His work on Rollebon has become meaningless, and he wonders what will become of his life now that he has nothing to occupy himself with. He lunches with his friend from the library who only bores him with humanitarian, socialist platitudes. Roquentin finds satisfaction nowhere. The violence of his nausea becomes so powerful that he abruptly leaves his friend. He realizes that the existence of things outside himself has become too much; the objective world only reveals his own inner weakness.

Roquentin decides to leave Bouville and go to Paris to see Anny, who has also changed. She explains to him that she no longer believes in the "perfect moments" that she had formerly tried to orchestrate. She no longer even feels capable of passion. When they part, Roquentin has the feeling that Anny has no desire to see him again. As his sense of psychological torment increases, Roquentin begins to have visions in which the city is peopled with monstrous beings.

In certain respects, Roquentin resembles ALBERT CAMUS's character Meursault in *THE STRANGER*. Each of these characters exists solely in the sense that they are passive recipients of experience. Life happens to them. Not until the end of the novel, in the public garden, does Roquentin have a clear sense of the unreality of conventional things, beliefs, and values. Not long after, he thinks again about his biography of Rollebon, indicating that, perhaps through the creative act, his life will attain a sense of purpose. The novel thus reflects Sartre's existentialist philosophy (see EXISTENTIALISM) and the notion that one is defined solely by one's existence and actions. Through the choices that we make, we determine our own reality through constant questioning.

FURTHER READING

Brée, Germaine. *Camus and Sartre: Crisis and Commitment.* London: Calder and Boyars, 1974.

Glynn, Simon, ed. *Sartre: An Investigation of Some Major Themes.* Aldershot, England: Avebury; Brookfield, Vt.: Gower, 1987.

Howells, Christina. *Sartre: The Necessity of Freedom.* Cambridge, New York: Cambridge University Press, 1988.

Jackson, Tommie Lee. *The Existential Fictin of Ayi Kwei Arma, Albert Camus and Jean-Paul Sartre.* Lanham, Md.: University Press of America, 1997.

Kern, Edith. *Existential Thought and Fictional Technique: Kierkegaard, Sartre, Beckett.* New Haven, Conn.: Yale University Press, 1970.

McBride, William L. *Existentialist Literature and Aesthetics.* New York: Garland, 1997.

Thody, Philip Malcolm Waller. New York: St. Martin's Press, 1992.

Wilcocks, Robert. *Critical Essays on Jean-Paul Sartre.* Boston: G. K. Hall, 1988.

NAVARRE, MARGUERITE DE (1492–1549)

Marguerite de Navarre was the sister of France's king Francis I, the queen of Navarre, and grandmother of Henry of Navarre, the future Henry IV. Her court at Béarn was a center of cultural and literary patronage in Renaissance France. Sympathetic to the rise of Protestantism, Marguerite de Navarre patronized other reform-minded writers such as BONAVENTURE DES PÉRIERS and FRANÇOIS RABELAIS, who dedicated his BOOK THREE to her.

Marguerite de Navarre's most famous work, the HEPTAMERON, is modeled after the 14th century italian author Giovanni Boccaccio's *Decameron.* Like her contemporary HÉLISENNE DE CRENNE, Marguerite manifests the influence of Boccaccio on French letters as well as a new sensibility to gender issues the great Italian writer did not share. Marguerite also wrote Neo-Platonist religious poetry, *The Mirror of the Sinful Soul* (1531) and *Prisons* (1547). In contrast to these works focusing on a renunciation of the world, the *Heptameron* is about how to live in the real world. Along with Hélisenne de

Crenne, Marguerite de Navarre leads French literature in a new direction toward the development of the SENTIMENTAL NOVEL. Writing in a period of religious and political change, her work emphasizes the significance of subjective experience. With a surprisingly modern approach, Marguerite de Navarre shows how the subjective experience is shaped by social institutions. Marguerite is particularly interested in the role of women in society and the ways in which aristocratic women in particular are subject to outside political and social forces. Marguerite de Navarre is, thus, one of the principal participants in the debate on the nature of women, the *Querelle des femmes.* The *Heptameron* is one of the classics of French literature, assuring Marguerite de Navarre's dominant position in the literary world of 16th-century France.

FURTHER READING

Armstrong, Nancy. "Literature as Women's History: A Necessary Transgression of Genres," *Genre* 19 (1986): 347–369.

Freccero, Carla. "Rewriting the Rhetoric of Desire in Marguerite de Navarre's *Heptameron.*" In *Contending Kingdoms: Historical, Psychological, and Feminist Approaches to the Literature of Sixteenth-Century England and France.* Edited by Marie-Rose Logan and Peter Rudnytsky. Detroit, Mich.: Wayne State University Press, 1989.

Tetet, Marcel. *Marguerite de Navarre's "Heptameron": Themes, Language and Structure.* Durham, N.C.: Duke University Press, 1973.

NEDJMA KATEB YACINE (1956)

Myths and history permeate this work in which Yacine ponders the question of national and cultural identity. The cyclical structure of the novel reflects an Arab sense of time in which past and future are closely connected. Nedjma is a beautiful, enigmatic woman, the daughter of a Frenchwoman and an Algerian who is loved to the point of obsession by four men, Rachid, Lakhdar, Mourad, and Mustapha. Nedjma haunts their dreams.

Rachid is engaged in parallel quests to discover his own identity, that of the Algerian people, his father's murderer, and Nedjma's origins. When Rachid learns that Nedjma has unwittingly married her half-brother, he kidnaps her and takes her to Nahdor, a mythical place in the mountains. When Rachid takes Nedjma away from her husband and her home, he displaces her, removing Nedjma from the present in order to resituate her in an idealized past, to give her a new life in this mythical place where men live in harmony with nature. When Nedjma emerges naked from the bath, she is like nature, a symbol of fruition. For Rachid as for the others, she is associated on a fundamental level with the idea of Algeria, and so they desire her.

Yacine had a cousin named Nedjma whom he loved but who was married to someone else. The Nedjma of the novel is a sort of ideal woman, mother, sister, lover, and, most important, an allegorical representation of Algeria. Yacine once said, "Nedjma is the soul of Algeria, torn apart since its origin and ravaged by too many exclusive passions." Yacine's exploration of Algerian national identity is closely linked to his critique of the French colonial system. Yacine is equally critical of his compatriots who collaborate with the French in their own interests.

With its cyclical or circular sense of time, this prose poem has been characterized as representative of the NOUVEAU ROMAN approach associated with writers such as ALAIN ROBBE-GRILLET, MICHEL BUTOR, and NATHALIE SARRAUTE. Yacine structures his novel in concentric narrative circles. It begins and ends with the phrase, "I do not have an identity card."

The novel consists of six parts and 12 short chapters. Its outside structure is deceptive, however, as the narrative is serpentine. Themes rise to the surface, recede, then reappear. Various scenes are repeated from different narrative perspectives, like a literary statue in the round that one approaches successively from different sides. Rachid, Lakhdar, Mourad, and Mustapha each offer their own distinct perspective.

None of these men ultimately possesses Nedjma. She eludes them. The reader, moreover, only comes to know her through the four men, never directly as a character in her own right. Still, there is something larger than life about her, as Yacine draws from myths and legends to tell his story. Her lovers struggle over Nedjma, just as real men compete for Algeria. Each of the four men is willing to undergo almost anything, including prison, pain, and humiliation, to attain the Nedjma of their dreams. Recurring images are of prison and the knife.

FURTHER READING

Aresu, Bernard. *Counterhegemonic Discourse from the Maghreb: The Poetics of Kateb's Fiction.* Tübingen, Germany: G. Narr, 1993.

Joyaux, Georges J., Albert Memmi and Jules Roy. "Driss Chraïbi, Mohammed Dib, Kateb Yacine, and Indigenous North African Literature," *Yale French Studies,* no. 24, Midnight Novelists (1959): 30–40.

Salhi, Kamal. *The Politics and Aesthetics of Kateb Yacine: From Francophone Literature to Popular Theater in Algeria and Outside.* Lewiston, N.Y.: E. Mellen Press, 1999.

Tcheho, Isaac Celestin. *The Novel and Identity in Algeria: A Study of the Works of Mohammed Dib, Mouloud Feraoun, and Kateb Yacine, 1950–1966.* Cameroon: Master's Thesis University of Yaoundé s.n., 1980.

NEGRITUDE (NÉGRITUDE)

RENÉ MARAN, who wrote the novel *Batouala* in 1921, is generally considered to be a precursor of Negritude. The actual term Negritude was coined by the Martinican poet Aimé Césaire in 1935. The concept of Negritude is equally associated with Senegalise poet and statesman Leopold Sédar Senghor.

Negritude asserts the values and aesthetics of francophone Africa and promotes African consciousness of its own distinct cultural identity. In the 1920s, Negritude came to be associated with Pan-Africanism. Negritude writers affirm the strength of African civilization, making it a source of pride despite an oppressive colonial system.

Césaire defined Negritude as "the simple recognition of the fact that one is black, and acceptance of this fact, of our black destiny, of our history and our culture." For Senghor, Negritude is a concept that transcends divisions such as Arab or black. "Negritude is a fact, a culture," he wrote. In Senghor's view, moreover, the strength of African culture is drawn from its proximity to nature and to one's ancestors. JEAN-PAUL SARTRE said that Negritude is "the negation of the negation of black man."

In the second half of the 20th century, a second generation of francophone writers from Africa and the Caribbean began to challenge the concept of Negritude in an attempt to define francophone literature in new ways, particularly in the period following independence. RAPHAEL CONFIANT, for example, deemphasizes African roots to focus on Caribbean culture as a unique expression of varied cultural and historical influences.

NERCIAT, ANDRÉ-ROBERT, ANDRÉA DE (1739–1800)

Military man, cosmopolitan adventurer, novelist, and intellectual, Nerciat was born in Dijon, where his father, a lawyer, served in the parliament of Bourgogne. However, Nerciat's family is originally from Naples. Nerciat is principally remembered today for his LIBERTINE NOVEL, *FELICIA OR MY ESCAPADES*.

Nerciat had an extremely varied career. In 1775 he entered the king's guard as a lieutenant colonel. An avid traveler, he crossed Europe in the military and as a diplomat. He was also a member of several learned societies. In 1783 Nerciat married Angélique Condamin de Chaussan. When the French Revolution struck just six years later, Nerciat was forced to emigrate. He first entered the Prussian army and by 1798 was serving as chamberlain to Queen Caroline of Naples. As her envoy to the pope, Nerciat was arrested for treason and imprisoned by the French. He died of consequences related to his detention in 1800.

Nerciat is the last 18th-century writer of light, indecent, erotic novels associated with the likes of CRÉBILLON FILS. His creativity is apparent in his invention of a new vocabulary of pleasure. Despite its prohibition by censors, *Felicia,* a popular novel, was republished numerous times.

Nerciat produced other libertine and even pornographic works. His eroticism reflects his philosophy of life whereby sexual satisfaction is essential to human happiness. His characters do not think of the afterlife but seek pleasure in the present. His is a materialist morality of pleasure. Yet, Nerciat's eroticism is different from that of SADE because it lacks cruelty. Nerciat also challenges the taboos of bourgeois society. Equality among classes rests on the search for pleasure in which each individual engages.

FURTHER READING

Ivker, B. "The Parameters of a Period-piece Pornographer, Andréa de Nerciat," *SVEC* 98 (1972).

Wilkins, K. "Andréa de Nerciat and the Libertine Tradition in Eighteenth-Century France," *SVEC* 256 (1988).

NERVAL, GÉRARD DE (GÉRARD LABRUNIE) (1808–1855)

Nerval is the pseudonym for Gérard Labrunie, one of the most fascinating romantic writers of the 19th century (see ROMANTICISM). Nerval's father was a surgeon in Napoleon's army. His mother, the daughter of a merchant, died in 1810 in Prussian Silesia, where she had followed her husband on a military campaign. After his mother's death, Nerval was raised by an uncle in the countryside. He was a dreamy and sensitive child, drawn to his uncle's books. One result was a fascination with esoteric doctrines that lasted throughout his life.

When his father returned to France in 1814, Nerval moved with him to Paris, where he attended high school, becoming friends with another future writer, THÉOPHILE GAUTIER. A precocious writer, Nerval published his first poems at age 18, and at 20 he gained renown for his translation of Goethe's *Faust* (1828). Nerval also met the great romantic writer VICTOR HUGO. Like Hugo and other liberal intellectuals of the period, Nerval was a republican, participating in student demonstrations, for which he was briefly imprisoned in 1832. To please his father, Nerval began to study medicine although literature was his true calling. But when he received an inheritance from his grandfather, Nerval abandoned his studies and traveled to Italy in 1834.

Upon his return to France, Nerval became one of the more flamboyant participants in the bohemian life of Paris. He fell in love with the actress Jenny Colon, one of several female figures who reappear in his fiction. She was the inspiration for Nerval's character AURELIA. Over time, the memory of this woman took on mythic proportions in Nerval's mind and she is present, in some form, in most of his greatest works.

Interested in theater, Nerval used his inheritance to establish a short-lived review, *Le Monde dramatique.* Its failure led to Nerval's financial ruin. He subsequently earned his living by writing for a variety of contemporary journals. He collaborated with ALEXANDER DUMAS PÈRE on a number of plays, notably *The Alchemist* and *Leo Burckhart.*

In 1838, Jenny Colon married a musician, a decision that was, not surprisingly, painful for Nerval. That same year Nerval traveled to Germany with Dumas

père. It was a significant journey in Nerval's development as a writer. This was the country of Faust and the
country where his mother died; these and other reasons contributed to Nerval's fascination with German
culture. In 1839 he was in Vienna, where he met the
pianists Franz Liszt and Marie Pleyel, with whom he
fell in love. She and Sophie Davies (who is transformed
into the fictional character of Adrienne) joined Colon
as the mystical and mythical female figures who came
to dominate Nerval's imagination.

Nerval's life changed dramatically in 1841 when
he experienced his first mental crisis and was hospitalized for several months. From this point on, all of
Nerval's writings were affected by his encounter with
madness that is reflected in a blurring of dreams and
reality. The superimposition of these two realities gives
Nerval's work its particular, fascinating character. His
world is one of signs and symbols revealed in a night
of dreams.

In 1842, several months after Jenny Colon's death,
Nerval left France for an extended voyage to Greece,
Egypt, Syria, and Constantinople, an experience he
recounted in his *Journey to the Orient* (published in final
form in 1851). He continued to travel in Belgium, Holland, England, and Germany while working as a journalist and producing various dramas and librettos. But
as of 1851, Nerval experienced more frequent bouts of
madness that required hospitalization. Between these
periods of confinement, he traveled, often spending
time in his native province of Valois.

Nerval's last and greatest works, *Daughters of Fire* (a
series of novellas that includes SYLVIE, 1854), *Chimeras*
(a collection of sonnets, 1854), and AURELIA (posthumous, 1855), together reflect Nerval's powerful personal mythology. Especially pronounced is his sense of
the eternal feminine.

Desperate to understand himself and torn between
a world of dreams and reality, Nerval sought a way to
communicate with a world of spirits. He felt a connection to all the sufferings of humanity as he himself
suffered from metaphysical angst, mystical anguish,
and apocalyptic visions. In *Pandora*, for example, the
eternal feminine becomes a demon, reflecting Nerval's tortured state of mind. And yet there is also a
hint of redemption in his last writings, found in the

images of the Virgin Mary, Isis, Jenny/Aurelia, and
Eurydice.

Nerval's works reflect the romantics' fascination
with the internal, subjective experience. Moreover, in
his rich writing, the Christian notion of redemption
combines with ancient myths as the author seeks the
means to purify the soul.

In the last tragic year of his life Nerval was home-
less, sometimes sleeping outside, sometimes spending
the night with friends. He was unable to write and frequently in despair. On January 26, 1855, he committed suicide by hanging himself from a railing in Paris.

FURTHER READING

Beauchamp, William. *The Style of Nerval's "Aurélia."* The
    Hague: Mouton, 1976.
Gilbert, Claire. *Nerval's Double: A Structural Study.* Jackson:
    University of Mississippi: Romance Monographs, 1979.
Jones, Robert Emmet. *Gérard de Nerval.* New York: Twayne,
    1974.
Knapp, Bettina Liebowitz. *Gérard de Nerval, the Mystic's
    Dilemma.* Tuscaloosa: University of Alabama Press, 1980.
MacLennan, George. *Lucid Interval: Subjective Writing and
    Madness in History.* Rutherford, N.J.: Fairleigh Dickinson
    University Press, 1992.
Miller, David. *There and Here: A Meditation on Gérard de
    Nerval.* Frome, Somerset, England: Bran's Head Books,
    1982.
Prendergast, Christopher. *The Order of Mimesis: Balzac, Stend-
    hal, Nerval, Flaubert.* Cambridge, England: Cambridge
    University Press, 1986.
Strauss, Jonathan. *Subjects of Terror: Nerval, Hegel and the
    Modern Self.* Stanford, Calif.: Stanford University Press,
    1998.

NIGHT (LA NUIT) ELIE WIESEL (1958)   This
powerful autobiographical novel opens in 1941.
Eliezer Wiesel's father is a well-respected member of
the Jewish community in Sighet, a small town in Transylvania (Romania), if somewhat distant from his own
family members. His son, Elie, is serious, drawn to the
mystical tradition in Judaism. Moché the Beadle, Elie's
former teacher, returns to Sighet and warns the Jews
of the impending German threat, but no one believes
him. They think he is mad. Even when the Germans
arrive many Jews are unwilling to confront the situation. Moché tells Elie, "Man questions God and God

answers. But we don't understand His answers. We can't understand them." In these lines Moché reveals to the reader the crisis of faith that is at the heart of this work.

In 1944, German troops entered the town. The Jews are first enclosed in ghettos, then deported to concentration camps. The cattle cars in which they travel are crowded; conditions are horrible. One woman goes mad, prophetically screaming "Fire! I can see a Fire . . . It is a furnace." Some of the men tie her up and gag her since she cannot keep quiet.

Once they arrive in the concentration camp of Birkenau, Elie indeed smells burning flesh. He and his father are separated from his mother and sisters. The image of fire returns when Elie witnesses babies thrown into the flames. Miraculously, Elie and his father manage to stay together. Their heads are shaved, they have showers, and receive prison uniforms. Elie's arm is tattooed with a number. From now on he will be identified as A-7713. Soon thereafter, Elie and his father are moved to another camp where they are beaten, whipped, malnourished, and worn down by labor.

The question of faith looms large. "Never shall I forget that night," Elie recalls, "the first night in camp, which has turned my life into one long night, seven times cursed and seven times sealed. . . . Never shall I forget those flames which consumed my faith forever." Where is God when a boy is hanged, struggling against the rope that slowly suffocates him? For Elie, God is hanging on the gallows.

Elie witnesses a boy who kills his own father for a piece of bread, reflecting the tremendous toll that concentration camp life takes on the human spirit. One reaches the point where the only thing that counts is survival. Morality shrivels up and dies in the human body subject to unspeakable horror.

Somehow, Elie and his father survive. Then, as the Soviet army approaches the camp, the prisoners are forced to march to Buchenwald, Germany. All are near death. Elie's father weakens and eventually dies. The Germans are determined to exterminate the remaining Jews but the arrival of American tanks on April 11, 1945, puts a halt to the plan. Elie is rescued but in a mirror he sees not a living boy but a corpse.

This first volume of a trilogy, *Night* is a masterpiece. It also offers a painful portrait of Eliezer Wiesel's horrific experience as a young boy. It has since become one of the classics of Holocaust literature, offering a window onto the horror of the Jewish experience through the eyes of a 12-year old. The narrator's simple depiction of daily life in the concentration camps raises profound philosophical questions about life, the human spirit, and God, as Elie slowly acquires wisdom in equal proportion to his pain. His experience is brutal and shocking, perhaps even more so because the story is that of a child. As he recounts the death of family and friends, he wonders, as does the reader, how it is possible to live on after such an experience. Moreover, he tells not only the story of his family but the story of the entire Jewish people. The burden of survival is heavy; it is also a recurring theme in Wiesel's works. Wiesel once described his difficulty in writing *Night*: "I felt incapable and perhaps unworthy of fulfilling my task as survivor and messenger. I had things to say, but not the words to say them."

The two other volumes in the *Night* trilogy are *Dawn* and *The Accident.* They are less overtly autobiographical than the first. *Dawn* tells the story of a Jewish terrorist in Palestine who suffers through the night before he is to execute a captured British soldier. As he waits for dawn, Elisha confronts the ghosts of his past. In *The Accident,* the narrator whose name is also Eliezer and who is a holocaust survivor, has tried to commit suicide by jumping in front of a taxi in New York City. He survives and even decides to live by "learning to lie well." All three volumes conclude as the narrator recognizes himself in a reflection.

FURTHER READING

Fine, Ellen S. *Legacy of Night, the Literary Universe of Elie Wiesel.* Albany: State University of New York Press, 1982.

Mass, Wendy, ed. *Reading on Night.* San Diego, Calif.: Greenhaven Press, 2000.

Stern, Ellen Norman. *Elie Wiesel, Witness for Life.* New York: Ktav Publishing House, 1982.

Wiesel, Elie. *Night: With Related Readings.* St. Paul, Minn.: EMC/Paradigm, 2003.

NIGHT FLIGHT (VOL DE NUIT) ANTOINE DE SAINT-EXUPÉRY (1931) This novel, whose pref-

ace was written by ANDRÉ GIDE, evokes the heroic era of early commercial aviation. It is the story of the director of an air mail company, Rivière, and his team of pilots. Rivière, who wants above all to succeed and to prove that the plane is a superior means of transportation to the train, makes his pilots undertake dangerous night flights to deliver mail.

One of the pilots, Fabien, headed for Buenos Aires, disappears in a storm, sacrificed for the success of Rivière's enterprise. Rivière tells his pilots they should never fear death, to give their all to their mission, in sum, to act "as if there is something that surpasses, in value, human life." His pilots indeed live by this creed. The prompt delivery of the mail becomes a sacred act. Rivière is harshly critical of weakness and failure and does not care in the least whether he appears to be just or unjust. At the same time, Rivière stands among his men, not above them. When Fabien's wife arrives seeking news of her husband, Rivière realizes that love and duty are two equally necessary and irreconcilable ideals.

Partly autobiographical, Saint-Exupéry's work brings to life the pilot's sense of honor, self-sacrifice, and willingness to abandon all that is dear to him for a larger purpose. Two types of men appear in this novel. Rivière represents the sort of man who is capable of forging the will of others. Rigid and intransigent in his pursuit of ideals, Rivière represents the qualities that, for Saint-Exupéry, are virtues. Fabien, the complement to Rivière, is a pilot who understands the notion of self-sacrifice and who dies carrying out his duty, facing death in the skies with strength and composure. Fabien and the other pilots follow orders and take risks because of their chosen profession. They submit to duty voluntarily because that is what they believe in. Duty involves both courage and self-sacrifice. This ethic that places the collective above the individual marks all of Saint-Exupéry's works. Moreover, the pilots' recognition of the constraints of duty makes them aware of their own greatness.

Like HENRI DE MONTHERLANT and ANDRÉ MALRAUX, Saint-Exupéry is both a humanist and an idealist in his reflections on man's place in history, his moments of greatness and of frailty. An adventure story, *Night Flight* was a popular novel and won the prestigious Femina Prize.

FURTHER READING

Cate, Curtis. *Antoine de Saint-Exupéry: His Life and Times.* New York: Paragon House, 1990.

Master, Brian. *A Student's Guide to Saint-Exupéry.* London: Heinemann Educational, 1972.

Mooney, Philip. *Belonging Always: Reflections on Uniqueness.* Chicago: Loyola University Press, 1987.

NIMIER, ROGER (1925–1962)

One of Nimier's characters in his novel *The Blue Hussar* said, "I belong to that happy generation that was twenty years old when the civilized world ended." The same could be said for Nimier himself. Nimier wrote in a bitter tone born of the experience of World War II and a disappointed dream of heroism. His sense of gloom only grew in the course of demobilization, postwar purges, and the beginning of the cold war. Nimier considered himself to be the heir of STENDHAL and CÉLINE, and his depiction of war recalls the experiences of both Fabrice del Dongo (CHARTERHOUSE OF PARMA) and Ferdinand Bardamu (JOURNEY TO THE END OF THE NIGHT). Because of Nimier's novel *The Blue Hussar* (1950), as well as JEAN GIONO'S HUSSAR ON THE ROOF, a group of writers who shared their views came to be known as the Hussars.

In contrast to the political engagement of writers such as ALBERT CAMUS and JEAN-PAUL SARTRE, in the 1950s Nimier manifested instead a haughty disdain and a tendency toward right-wing politics, going so far as to rehabilitate collaborationist writers like LOUIS FERDINAND CÉLINE and PAUL MORAND. Nimier sought to renew values associated with a Stendhal-like egoism, the search for pleasure, aristocratic elegance, and irony. He also preferred to write in a more classical style than the forms introduced by the NOUVEAU ROMAN. An admirer of JEAN GIRAUDOUX and JEAN COCTEAU, Nimier nonetheless quickly developed his own writing style.

Nimier is the pseudonym of Roger de la Perrière, who was born in Paris, where his father was an inventor and engineer and his mother a retired violinist. Nimier worked his way through school, ultimately earning a degree in philosophy from the Sorbonne. During World War II, he volunteered and was wounded. His first novel, *Unknown Woman,* was published only posthumously in 1968; however, *Swords* (1948), *Perfidy,* and *The Blue Hussar* in particular were all very successful.

In his novel *Sad Children* (1939), a group of young men play the game of love and ambition. The character of Le Barsac tries to prevent the marriage of his son Raoul to Tessa, a young secretary, despite the fact that Le Barsac is already married to Odette. Le Barsac's 15-year-old son Olivier then decides it would be amusing to push Odette into an affair with a lawyer. The consequences are that Olivier ends up in a desperate state and Odette dies. Then war breaks out. When Olivier returns in 1947, he briefly becomes Tessa's lover, and when their relationship ends, he decides to become a writer.

Olivier finds success as a writer but not in love. Although he loves Dominique, he marries her friend Catherine instead. Catherine is charming and aristocratic. Nonetheless, after his marriage Olivier finds that he is living only on the margins of high society. Filled with a sense of his own solitude, he plays the social game with no real satisfaction. Three days after his wedding and, more important, after the death of Dominique, Olivier drives his sports car at 130 kilometers per hour into a construction site and dies, strangely foreshadowing Nimier's own death in 1962. There are, however, no real grounds for the suspicion that Nimier's automobile accident was a suicide. As the writer Marcel Aymé pointed out, Nimier had a passenger in the car whom he barely knew.

Sad Children is marked by a melancholy and cynical tone, particularly in its evocation of society's decadence and degradation in the period leading up to the war. Finally, there is Nimier's fascination with death and his disturbing assertion that it is better to die a violent death at a young age than to linger on in life. Written in a sober style, this novel is about failure and the loss of hope.

The Blue Hussar evokes the experience of an entire generation as it describes the experience of a Hussar squad at the end of World War II through a series of monologues. The principal characters are Saint-Anne, a young volunteer, and Sanders, an old Resistance fighter. Set in 1945–46, the Hussar squad is sent as an occupying force to Germany. Sanders, simultaneously passionate about life and disillusioned, dreams like a true romantic of dying in this last campaign (see ROMANTICISM). Sanders shares a mistress with Saint-Anne, a young German woman named Rita. When Rita kills Saint-Anne, Sanders finds himself alone once again. When he finally returns to France, Sanders again recognizes the importance of friendship and justice, fundamental values of which he had lost sight during the war.

Nimier also served as the director of the series *Livre de Poche Classique,* inexpensive editions of classical novels introduced by famous contemporary writers. Nimier was likewise a successful journalist and columnist, a literary consultant to Gallimard, and a screenwriter, collaborating with Louis Malle on the screenplay for *Elevator to the Scaffold* (1957), the first of the New Wave films.

FURTHER READING

Hewitt, Nicolas. *Literature and the Right in Postwar France: the Story of the "Hussars."* Oxford, Washington, D.C.: Berg, 1996.

NINETY-THREE (*QUATRE-VINGT TREIZE*) VICTOR HUGO (1874)

In this novel, set in Brittany during the year of the Reign of Terror during the French Revolution, Hugo again focuses on the theme of the suffering people. Michelle Fléchard is a widow with three children who is protected by a republican battalion though she remains loyal to the monarchy. In a parallel plotline, the conservative marquis de Lantenac struggles against Cimourdain, a representative of the people. In the course of a subsequent battle, Fléchard's three children are taken hostage by the Vendéens (inhabitants of the region) who are under attack in a fortress. As they are about to die in a fire, Lantenac manages to save them.

Lantenac subsequently faces death as a traitor to the Revolution. His nephew Gauvain, a staunch republican, nevertheless cannot accept that Lantenac will be guillotined and helps him to escape, taking his place in prison. Inflexible to the end, Cimourdain has Gauvain executed despite their friendship and then commits suicide.

In 1870, Hugo returned to Paris after nearly 20 years in exile. Despite his own strong republican views, Hugo was still able to turn a critical eye on the French Revolution. In this novel he chooses 1793, as a point of examination. Hugo argues essentially that the Revolution of 1789 quickly became reactionary, and he draws parallels to the 1871 PARIS COMMUNE. Hugo subtly raises important questions about the nature of the Terror through the personal struggle between his characters. Like the German romantic writer Georg Büchner, Hugo depicts history as flowing with a force of its own, unimpeded by human morality. Hugo is gifted in portraying individuals forced into pacts with evil for their own survival and against their own higher principles, as always skillfully revealing the struggles, contradictions, and juxtapositions inherent in the human condition.

FURTHER READING

Brombert, Victor. *Victor Hugo and the Visionary Novel.* Cambridge, Mass.: Harvard University Press, 1984.

Evans, David O. *Social Romanticism in France: 1830–1848.* New York: Octagon, 1969.

Hudson, William Henry. *Victor Hugo and His Poetry.* London: Harrap, 1918.

Maurois, André. *Victor Hugo and His World.* Translated by Oliver Bernard. New York: Viking, 1966.

Peyre, Henri. *Victor Hugo: Philosophy and Poetry.* Translated by Roda P. Roberts. Tuscaloosa: University of Alabama Press, 1980.

Richardson, Joanna. *Victor Hugo.* London: Weidenfeld and Nicolson, 1976.

NIZAN, PAUL (1905–1940)

JEAN-PAUL SARTRE once described Nizan by saying, "His eyes were Marxist, and his ears, and his head." The son of a railway worker, Nizan nonetheless had an elite education. He studied the classics and philosophy yet did not choose an academic career. In all his writings, Nizan reminded writers and intellectuals of their obligation to be politically engaged. He situated all his characters squarely in their socioeconomic context. This is not surprising, given his Marxist orientation. Moreover, Nizan was a true realist (see REALISM) who did not hesitate to offer a brutal description of life, even of his own youth. Nizan's university years were marked by a profound uneasiness that led him to question contemporary politics and society. These years are the background for *Conspiracy,* a novel focusing on a group of Parisian students making their first foray into love and politics. This novel earned Nizan a certain notoriety.

In 1926 Nizan sought to escape the stifling atmosphere of bourgeois society and the closed world of Parisian intellectual life. He thus left for Aden, Yemen, in 1926, where he was equally disillusioned by the French colonial system, an experience that inspired *Aden Arabia* (1931). Most critics see his experience in Yemen as the determining factor in Nizan's embrace of communism and political activism.

Upon his return to France, Nizan joined the Communist Party. He received a degree in philosophy from the Sorbonne at the same time as Sartre, with whom he also attended high school, and SIMONE DE BEAUVOIR. Nizan taught philosophy in Bourg-en-Bresse from 1931 to 1932 but was fired for his political activism. Invited to the International Congress of Soviet Writers in 1934, Nizan actually edited *The Trojan Horse* while in the Soviet republic of Tajikistan. He then devoted himself completely to the party through his journalism. At the same time, Nizan published his own translations from Democritus, Epicurus, and Lucretius in *The Materialists of Antiquity.*

One of his famous pamphlets, *Watchdogs* (1932), contains a virulent attack on bourgeois university circles as Nizan criticized abstract philosophy that screens young people from reality. Nizan directed his attack against the academic philosophers of the THIRD REPUBLIC, promoters of idealist philosophy who failed to take into consideration the truth of the human condition with all of its illness, misery, poverty, and war. "We are living," he wrote, "in a time when philosophers abstain. They are living in a scandalous state of separation; there is a scandalous distance between what philosophy declares and what happens to men."

Obviously written from a Marxist perspective, Nizan's pamphlet accuses contemporary philosophers of perpetuating bourgeois society and values. It ends by calling on a new generation of young philosophers to struggle against the "watchdogs" and to place philosophy at the service of the proletariat. ANDRÉ GIDE called the tract "a sign of the times," although he was critical of its repetitive style. *Watchdogs* is in essence a critique of the ivory tower, as Nizan sought to convince intellectuals that philosophy is an act, not just a reflection. The problem with the university system, as he saw it, was that professors had taken over the role of the clergy in the OLD REGIME, as the men who persuade others to accept the social order when, in Marx's terms, the point is to change it. The notion of betrayal, a recurring theme in Nizan's works, is also evident in Nizan's attack on intellectuals.

Nizan went on to write novels such as ANTOINE BLOYÉ (1933) and THE TROJAN HORSE (1935). His CONSPIRACY won the Interallié Prize in 1938. Between 1935 and 1939 he published a series of articles on international politics addressing in particular the Spanish civil war and events leading up to the outbreak of World War II. In 1939, he quit the Communist Party because of the Nazi-Soviet pact. Nizan's colleagues in the party accused him of betrayal when he abandoned their common cause. Sartre, however, later came to Nizan's defense when he wrote the preface to a 1960 edition of *Aden Arabia*. Nizan's decision to leave the party must have been a difficult one, as he saw party membership as the one real option for an intellectual.

Nizan's oeuvre stands as a coherent, unified, and consistent whole. His principal motivation was political engagement, yet he skillfully blended fiction and action in the interest of revolution. Nizan spoke out repeatedly against inauthenticity, colonialism, and capitalism. At heart a secular humanist, Nizan once said, "The two most revolting objects in earth are a church and a prison." In all his works Nizan proclaimed his faith in the power of revolutionary ideas to transform society. He was to become one of the most widely read writers by leftist students in the 1960s, respected for both his revolutionary stance and his principles in abandoning the Communist Party. Along with the writings of JULES VALLÈS, Nizan's novels are almost unique as politically engaged works of real literary quality. Mobilized in 1939, Nizan died during the battle of Dunkirk in 1940 at the age of 35.

FURTHER READING

McCarthy, Patrick. "Sartre, Nizan, and the Dilemmas of Political Commitment," *Yale French Studies,* no. 68, Sartre after Sartre (1985): 191–205.
Redfern, W. D. *Paul Nizan: Committed Literature in a Conspiratorial World*. Princeton, N.J.: Princeton University Press, 1972.
Schalk, David L. "Professors as Watchdogs: Paul Nizan's Theory of the Intellectual and Politics," *Journal of the History of Ideas* 34, no. 1 (January–March 1973): 79–96.
Scriven, Michael. *Paul Nizan: Communist Novelist.* New York: St. Martin's Press, 1988.
Stoekl, Allan. "Nizan, Drieu, and the Question of Death, "*Representations,* no. 21 (Winter 1988): 117–145.
Suleiman, Susan Rubin. "The Structure of Confrontation: Nizan, Barrès, Malraux," *MLN* 95, no. 4, French Issue (May 1980): 938–967.
Wasson, Richard. "'The True Possession of Time:' Paul Nizan, Marxism and Modernism," *Boundary* 5, no. 2 (Winter 1977): 395–410.

NOUVEAU ROMAN (NEW NOVEL)

The *nouveau roman* was developed by a generation of writers who emerged after World War II opposed to the traditional novel form. Prime examples of the new novel are found in the works of ALAIN ROBBE-GRILLET, MICHEL BUTOR, CLAUDE SIMON, NATHALIE SARRAUTE, ROBERT PINGET, and CLAUDE OLLIER. Initially an intense movement, the group dissolved in the 1970s as participating writers increasingly went their own way. Some even returned to more traditional narrative forms. The *nouveau roman* novels are principally associated with the Éditions de Minuit publishing house.

Nouveau roman novelists rejected the notion of literature existing in service to ideology. As they were not politically oriented, their works then differ from politically engaged writers like ALBERT CAMUS and JEAN-PAUL SARTRE. Characters in the *nouveau roman* lack a sense of unity or cohesion. Instead, *nouveau roman* novels tend to emphasize the anonymity of the individual in modern, consumer society. Moreover, they are far from the humanist tradition in their deemphasis of the individual.

In the *nouveau roman* there are no stories in the traditional sense. Rather, authors play with and subvert chronology and deliberately confuse narrative voices. According to *nouveau roman* writers, traditional narrative cannot truly apprehend reality. Consequently, an ontological questioning of reality marks these works. Sarraute, for example, explicitly rejected the idea that literature conforms to our sense of reality. Authors were concerned with the *process* of creating a novel; literature is thus no longer the product of inspiration.

Nouveau roman writers developed instead a science of literature. In 1960, Butor spoke at the Sorbonne on "the novel as research." Robbe-Grillet argued that composition is more important than content. The novel contains nothing and expresses only itself, nothing else. Moreover, it is constantly in the process of reinventing its own rules. In these works stories often become puzzles.

Having rejected traditional concepts of character and narrative in their *"anti-romans,"* all that was left to the *nouveau roman* writers was the process of writing itself. In their laboratory for writing, these authors frequently played with word games, metonymy, and metaphor. The result is often disconcerting to the reader, who recognizes in their works the influence of MARCEL PROUST, the Irish writer James Joyce, and the American author William Faulkner. These novels also often focus on minute descriptions of objects and places.

NUN, THE (*LA RELIGIEUSE*) DENIS DIDEROT (1796)

Written in 1760 but not published until 1796, *The Nun* is arguably Diderot's most famous novel. In Diderot's own words, "I do not think that anyone has ever written such a terrifying satire of convents." It is the story of Suzanne, a young woman forced into monastic life by her parents. Her attempt to leave the convent through legal proceedings fails. In consequence, Suzanne is tormented and abused by her fellow nuns. When she finally moves to another convent, she is corrupted by her lesbian mother superior. Not surprisingly, *The Nun* was deemed a scandalous novel at the time of its publication, although this may have added to its popularity.

Suzanne's life is based on the true story of Marguerite Delamarre, whose attempt to abandon religious life likewise failed. Diderot and several literary friends wished to entice their friend, the marquis de Croismare, who had taken an interest in the real Suzanne's story, back to Paris from his country estate. Pretending to be Delamarre seeking assistance, Diderot wrote to the marquis through an intermediary, and the marquis responded. This series of letters is attached to the novel as a "post-preface" that deliberately blurs the lines between fiction and reality. When the marquis offers Marguerite a position in his household, Diderot is forced to kill off his character.

The novel fits clearly into Diderot's larger philosophical agenda. Man is a social creature according to Diderot. It is unnatural for human beings to live in isolation as one does in a convent. The novel is not necessarily an attack on religion, despite Diderot's atheism. Suzanne prays genuinely for comfort and guidance. It is rather an attack on religious and social institutions that victimize women for the sake of property and deny them individual liberty. If man is a social animal, then a denial of human nature and its basic needs, including sexual needs, necessarily leads to illness and perversion. The portraits of Suzanne's three mother superiors together illustrate the process of dehumanization that takes place when human beings are obliged to deny their nature. Madame de Moni is a visionary, Sister Sainte-Christine a sadist, and the Abbess of Arpajon a lesbian. As with his other works, such as INDISCRETE JEWELS, Diderot's purpose is to reveal a truth otherwise shrouded in hypocrisy or ignorance. A surprisingly modern novel, the engaging story draws the reader into Suzanne's anguish.

The novel bears the influence of English writer Samuel Richardson, whose works Diderot admired greatly. He even wrote an elegy in praise of Richardson in the year of that author's death. *The Nun* echoes some of the themes in *Pamela* in its first-person narrative and its pathos. In writing *The Nun*, Diderot wished to imitate Richardson in producing a work of fiction that is believable, moving, and morally useful.

The Nun also bears witness to Diderot's interest in the visual arts. Suzanne frequently paints portraits as she describes scenes from her life as if they were on an artist's canvas. The novel also reflects Diderot's interest in moral theater. The liveliness of the dialogues described by Suzanne is confirmed by the novel's successful adaptation to film.

By combining elements of the memoir novel and the EPISTOLARY NOVEL, Diderot evokes the feeling of a personal journal similar to PRÉVOST's *MANON LESCAUT*, MARIVAUX's *LIFE OF MARIANNE*, or CRÉBILLON FILS's *WAY-*

WARD HEAD AND HEART. Diderot's powerful depiction of the development of consciousness through a series of formative experiences is similar to the 19th-century experiential novel. In fact, ZOLA saw Diderot as the precursor to this later genre.

FURTHER READING

Burbank, P. N. *Diderot: A Critical Biography.* New York: Knopf, 1992.

Diderot, Denis. *La Religieuse.* Edited by Roland Desné. Paris: Garnier-Flammarion, 1968.

Loy, Robert J. *Diderot's Determined Fatalist: A Critical Appreciation of Jacque le Fataliste.* New York: Crown Press, Columbia University, 1950.

MacPhail, Eric. "Diderot and the Plot of History," *New Literary History* 30, no. 2 (1999): 439–452.

Wilson, Arthur. *Diderot.* New York: Oxford University Press, 1972.

O

OBERMANN Étienne Pivert de Senancour
(1804) In this EPISTOLARY NOVEL, the narrator, a
young man named Obermann, meditates on nature
while confessing the state of his soul. Obermann writes
a series of letters to his oldest and dearest friend at
the end of his youth, recalling the experiences of his
life thus far. Like a knight errant, he wanders through
life seeking fulfillment, but each obstacle only leaves
him increasingly dissatisfied with life. The underlying
theme of the conflict between imagination or the world
as one desires it to be and reality lies at the heart of
this novel, just as it had in Senancour's earlier work
Aldomen or Happiness in Obscurity (1795). But whereas
Aldomen ultimately found a sense of purpose in the
simple pleasures of conjugal life in the countryside,
Obermann only feels a sense of impotence as he realizes that his dreams are all unattainable.

The plot has little action, reflecting Obermann's
sense that "the real life of man is within." At the age
of 20, already dissatisfied with life's prospects, Obermann leaves his family and runs away to Switzerland.
Alone and disappointed, he takes to writing as solace.
Obermann's experiences closely resemble those of the
Senancour, who also fled from his family to Switzerland. Consequently, most critics regard the novel as
autobiographical.

The novel opens with Obermann deciding to leave
his family in Lyon. He feels that life may be opening
up for him as he searches for a place to live. Echoing the experience of JEAN-JACQUES ROUSSEAU, Ober-

mann chooses Switzerland, traveling like Rousseau's
character Saint-Preux through the countryside, where
nature's beauty seems to offer the possibility of resolv-
ing the tension between the individual and society.

One day while climbing in the mountains, Obermann sheds the trappings of society as he sheds his
clothes, feeling for a moment that he is free. He finds
comfort in nature's order and harmony, a divine order
that he now understands he must seek to replicate in
life. It is a moment of clarity in which he perceives the
relationship among humans, nature, and God in the
pantheistic terms so prevalent in romantic thought (see
ROMANTICISM). When Obermann descends from the
mountain he feels spiritually prepared to fulfill his role
in life.

Shortly thereafter, Obermann is obliged to travel
to Paris to take care of his financial affairs. His return
to the city with its dirt, disease, and injustice is disturbing. As a result, Obermann isolates himself from
others. Like CHATEAUBRIAND's René, Obermann suffers
from the romantic disease. He is maladjusted, incapable of living in society, and very aware of his own
limitations. He tries returning to Fontainebleau, where
he has happy memories from his youth, but even there
he finds no solace. He needs the raw beauty of the
mountains.

Unfortunately, Obermann's financial affairs have
not turned out well. He loses his fortune and returns
to Lyon, where he hopes to reconnect with his dear
friend, the "vous" to whom he addresses the letters. At

this point there is a gap in the letters when, presumably, there is no need for the friends to correspond since they are living in the same city.

A few years later, the letters resume. Obermann is again meditating on nature, but he has come to the conclusion that solitude in nature is not sufficient for one's fulfillment. He needs to love others. His friend has abandoned their once shared values for success in the world. As he struggles both with disappointment in friendship and with his changing perception of the relationship between man and nature, Obermann suspects that society ruins the individual, distorting his taste and desire, diverting him from simple truths. Some critics have argued that Obermann's turn away from nature reflects Senancour's apparent hostility to Christianity. Nature represents a divine order that has failed humanity.

The other great disappointment for Obermann is in love. He meets again the woman he once loved and lost. She is unhappily married. Again, Obermann suffers regret for what might have been. Finally, disillusioned with love, friendship and nature, Obermann returns to the mountains to write. Literature may offer some comfort by giving him a purpose, even if it is an artificial one. He no longer has faith in the natural or the divine order. One must live as best one can.

Obermann bears the influence of both BERNARDIN DE SAINT-PIERRE and Jean-Jacques Rousseau, but Senancour takes their idyllic descriptions of nature and love in a new direction. There are lyrical depictions of alpine landscapes worthy of his mentors, but Obermann's melancholy meditations on nature reflect an underlying dissatisfaction with life and with himself. At the same time, there is a strange ambiguity in Senancour's novel. Obermann is somehow still capable of imagining a better sort of human existence, for himself and for others. Society has caused human beings to suffer, not human nature itself.

For Senancour, Obermann's frustration was real. When he wrote this novel, the author was living in exile, his marriage failed, his family fortune lost, all at a time in life when a young man should be establishing himself. Like his character, Senancour felt that his youth and its potential had passed. Obermann explores precisely these years (from the age of 20 to

29), recounting his efforts to find the ideal environment for a life of personal fulfillment. By the time *Obermann* was republished in 1833, Senancour was 63 and no longer suffered from the malaise of youth. He had largely forgotten this earlier work when the literary critic SAINTE-BEUVE's preface to the 1833 edition finally brought Senancour's work to the public's attention. It has subsequently come to hold its place in the literary history of France as one of the first romantic novels. Obermann's strain of the romantic disease leads the reader in the direction of EXISTENTIALISM. Senancour describes a metaphysical malaise that inevitably develops as we becomes conscious of ourselves. The resulting turn inward is both incurable and irreversible.

FURTHER READING
Brooks, Van Wyck. *The Malady of the Ideal: Obermannn, Maurice de Guérin and Amiel.* Folcroft, Pa.: Folcroft Library Editions, 1973.

Call, Michael J. *Back to the Garden: Chateaubriand, Senancour, and Constant.* Saratoga, Calif.: Anma Libri, 1988.

Heck, Francis S. *Spiritual Isolation in French Literature from Benjamin Constant and Senancour.* Madrid: Dos Continentes, 1971.

OHNET, GEORGES (1848–1918)

Born in Paris during a year of revolution, Georges Ohnet began his literary career writing political journalism. From there he turned to drama. His novels, however, brought him fame. Ohnet wrote a succession of serial novels (ROMAN FEUILLETON) under the general title "Battles of Life." These popular novels first appeared in journals such as *Le Figaro, L'Illustration,* and the *Revue des deux mondes.* Ohnet later published them separately. His most successful novels were *Serge Panine* and *The Forge Master,* perhaps his only novels remembered today.

A great admirer of GEORGE SAND, Ohnet was, not surprisingly, opposed to REALISM. Critics have often focused on Ohnet's imitative, commonplace style. Nonetheless, he wrote popular novels of moral idealism that are well structured and logical, and they reveal the author's sense of the dramatic. *The Forge Master,* adapted to the stage in 1883, was a great success; its performance at the Gymnase theater ran for a year. A number of his works were successfully adapted to stage or screen. Ohnet is sometimes called the PAUL

BOURGET of the poor. The principal focus of his fictional works is the basic contrast between nobility of birth and nobility of spirit. Although they are now mostly read by scholars, Ohnet's works represent the tremendously successful 19th-century serial novels, so much so that ALBERT CAMUS studied them out of an interest in popular novels.

OLD REGIME

The *ancien régime* (Old Regime) is a term designating the social and political system that existed in France prior to the FRENCH REVOLUTION of 1789. Under the monarchy a hierarchically ordered society fixed one's position by birth. Under the king were three estates, or orders: clergy, nobility, and the third estate consisting of common people. In this patriarchal society, the monarchy represented itself as the metaphorical father figure of society. Moreover, the patriarchal system was mirrored in each individual family and served as the basis of social order. The Roman Catholic Church and the crown converged to secure the stability of French society. The French Revolution brought an end to Old Regime society by establishing a new form of government in which sovereignty resided in the nation through representative government. A number of 18th-century writers, such as DENIS DIDEROT, MONTESQUIEU, VOLTAIRE, and CHODERLOS DE LACLOS, who made abundantly clear the meaninglessness of aristocratic life in *DANGEROUS LIAISONS*, paved the way for the Revolution through their trenchant criticism of Old Regime society. In the 19th century, BALZAC in particular skillfully evoked the tensions derived from the conflict between the remnants of Old Regime society and the emerging modern world in his *HUMAN COMEDY*.

OLLIER, CLAUDE (1922–)

Ollier was born in Paris, studied law, and during World War II was deported as a laborer to Germany. In 1950, he left France for Africa to work as a government functionary. There he wrote his first novel, *MISE EN SCÈNE*. Ollier called this "an Arab story." This novel won the Médicis Prize and brought him to the attention of the reading public. In 1955 Ollier decided to devote himself entirely to literature. His first writings consisted

of short narratives, some of which were published as *Navettes (Shuttle Service)* in 1967.

Mise en Scène was followed by a cycle of eight novels, the first of which were *Child's Game* and *Keeping Order* (1961), evoking colonial life at the end of the 1950s. The principal theme of *Keeping Order* is blindness. A man uncovers the criminal actions of racist police in a North African village. If he speaks out, he will be killed and so is, in a sense, awaiting death, separated from the outside world by the window of his apartment. The blindness to which Ollier refers is the blindness of the colonial system, of the corrupt police, and of the witness who hesitates over which course to take.

These two novels were followed by *Indian Summer* (1963) and *Nolan's Fall* (1967). In the second half of the series, Ollier transposed themes found in *Mise en Scène* into science fiction in *LIFE ON EPSILON* (1972). He then did the same with *Keeping Order,* which in its new form became *Enigma* (1974). Ollier wrote science fiction partly in hommage to JULES VERNE, whom he acknowledged to be an influence on his writing. The year 1974 also witnessed the publication of *Our, or Twenty Years After*. The last volume of the cycle, *Fuzzy Sets,* appeared in 1975. In it, the hero returns to his point of origin. Thereafter, Ollier's writing became largely autobiographical, drawing on his experience both in and outside of France.

Ollier shared with ALAIN ROBBE-GRILLET the invention of "total objectivity" in literature. For Ollier, the terms *objective* and *subjective* had no real meaning, rather "literature is a selection and combination of grammatical forms, not an extension of psychology." His writings are thus marked by a depersonalization of the subject that recalls the NOUVEAU ROMAN (new novel) style. In his discussions of literature, Ollier emphasized the role of the reader and the relationship between the reader and the text as much as that of the author and the text. He went so far as to say that the relationship of author to text is secondary, not to the reader but to earlier texts. In other words, Ollier saw literature as a long chain in which each new piece is derived in some degree from what preceded it.

Ollier also thought that all important books and films deal in some way with terror. "The primordial relationship between man and these works is one of terror, terror born of the juxtaposition of two worlds." This prevailing sense of opposing worlds results in a sense of oscillation in Ollier's novels between contradictory ideas.

Ollier once wrote, "My characters do not symbolize anything. They wear themselves out reflecting on the world around them, that is to say, on the fictional world, that is to say on literature. If there is anything that 'prowls' in my books, it is undoubtedly the sense of uselessness that results from this fatigue!" *Nolan's Fall* is, for example, above all a rereading of the three preceding novels. Its themes are those of these three books, plus its own reading. "The reality of a book," he argued, "is the totality of its TEXT."

FURTHER READING

Lindsay, Cecile. *Reflexivity and Revolution in the New Novel: Claude Ollier's Fictional Cycle.* Columbus: Ohio University Press, 1990.

ONE HUNDRED TWENTY DAYS OF SODOM (LES 120 JOURNÉES DE SODOM) DONATIEN-ALPHONSE-FRANÇOIS, MARQUIS DE SADE (1785)

The novel *120 Days of Sodom* has been described in a recent biography as Sade's most important work. Sade wrote the manuscript when he was imprisoned on the King's order in the Bastille. The manuscript was written on small pieces of paper glued together and rolled into a tube that could easily be hidden. When Sade believed the manuscript to have been lost in a fire resulting from the storming of the Bastille in 1789, he supposedly cried "tears of blood." In fact, the manuscript had been rescued by another prisoner. Having made its way to Germany, the manuscript was rediscovered and first published in 1904. A French edition appeared in 1929.

This novel is marked by an extraordinary combination of LIBERTINISM blended with philosophical discourse. Four wealthy, powerful men tucked away in a fortress carry on an orgy for several months. Sade takes aim here at 18th-century social hierarchy by making them a duke, a bishop, a magistrate, and a financier. They are accompanied by their wives and a collection of male and female victims to their sexual experiments. The story is augmented by the erotic tales of four women, echoing the narrative structure of the Italian writer Giovanni Boccaccio's *Decameron*. In this work, Sade continues his

deviant version of the ENLIGHTENMENT project to make a compendium cataloguing all forms of knowledge.

FURTHER READING

Barthes, Roland. *Sade, Fourier, Loyola.* Translated by Richard Miller. New York: Farrar, Straus and Giroux, 1976.
Du Plessix Gray, Francine. *At Home with the Marquis de Sade.* New York: Simon and Schuster, 1998.
Fabre, Jean. "Sade et le roman noir." In *Le Marquis de Sade.* Paris: Armand Colin, 1968.
Heine, Maurice. "Le Marquis de Sade et le roman noir." In *Le Marquis de Sade.* Edited by Gilbert Lély. Paris: Gallimard, 1950.
Schaffer, Neil. *The Marquis de Sade: A Life.* New York: Knopf, 1999.
Weber, Caroline. "The Sexist Sublime in Sade and Lyotard," *Philosophy and Literature* 26, no. 2 (2002): 397–404.

OPPOSING SHORE, THE (LE RIVAGE DES SYRTES) JULIEN GRACQ (1951)

As are all of Gracq's novels, *The Opposing Shore* is full of mystery and multiple layers of symbolism. For 300 years, the states of Orsenna and Farghestan have been living in suspended hostility. One day, Aldo, a young aristocrat from Orsenna, feels compelled to investigate the enemy shore with which he is strangely fascinated, and he takes off in his boat. As a result of his actions, war breaks out and Orsenna is destroyed, all because Aldo tempted fate.

To Aldo, Orsenna represents tradition, order, and the past, while Farghestan symbolizes the irrational and the future. As a result it is at once attractive and menacing. Aldo is heroic in his personal courage to try and escape the past, only his attempt, unfortunately, leads to tragedy for his people.

This work reflects Gracq's association with the surrealist movement (see SURREALISM). Gracq called the novel an "awakened dream." Gracq's recurring theme of expectation and foreboding is particularly pronounced. Some critics have questioned Gracq's fascination with death and an apocalyptic vision.

Probably Gracq's best-known work, *The Opposing Shore* won the Goncourt Prize in 1951. Gracq, refused to accept the prize, however, in accordance with principles articulated in *Literature of the Stomach,* an essay in which he rejected the contemporary literary scene, its commercial quality in particular.

OUR LADY OF THE FLOWERS (NOTRE-DAME DES FLEURS) Jean Genet (1944)

SIMONE DE BEAUVOIR described how "For several months we have heard about an unknown poet that Cocteau discovered in prison and whom he thinks is the greatest writer of our time." That writer was Jean Genet, who wrote his first novel, *Our Lady of the Flowers,* in prison. JEAN COCTEAU, arranged for the novel's publication in 300 expensively bound copies. Genet's writing impressed both de Beauvoir and JEAN-PAUL SARTRE, who in 1952 published a psychological biography of Genet, *Saint Genet.* The positive reception of this work among some of the greatest intellectuals and writers of the day, along with Cocteau's success in convincing a judge to give Genet a light sentence because of the author's creative genius ("one does not imprison a Rimbaud"), earned Genet fame.

The principal characters of the novel, the drag queen Divine, the pimp Darling Daintyfoot, a young thief named Our Lady of the Flowers, and Seck Gorgui, are apparently born out of Genet's imagination. There is nonetheless a certain ambiguity. Genet may argue that these characters are purely fictional but statements such as "I first met Divine in Fresnes prison . . ." and ". . . Darling's real name is supposed to be Paul Garcia" call the relationship between fiction and reality into question.

The novel consists of three overlapping narratives. The first is the "confession" of Genet as he awaits his trial in prison. The second is a reflection on the life and death of Divine beginning with a depiction of Divine's funeral as she is carried to her grave by a group of transvestites. In this plot line, Our Lady of the Flowers confesses to murder and draws Darling away from Divine. In depicting Divine, Genet borrowed from his experience as a male prostitute in the streets of Montmartre. In fact, Genet once showed a photograph to a friend saying, "This is a picture of me when I was Divine." The third narrative tells the story of Divine's childhood. Here Genet again draws from his own experience. Moreover, Divine's real name, Louis Culafroy, is that of a boy Genet knew growing up in a village east of Paris. The narratives weave in and out of one another as Divine and Genet share the same sexual fantasies. "For a period of two days," he says, "between my four bare walls, I experienced with him and through him

every possibility of an existence that . . . got so mixed up it became more real than the real one."

The atmosphere of the marvelous is strong in this masturbation fantasy that is superimposed on writing that again recalls the genre of confession. The words are those of a criminal writing in prison. It is unclear how long he will remain incarcerated, so he creates a fantasy world that is sexually stimulating. The narrator masturbates while imagining the characters of Divine and her lovers.

Genet wrote while in prison and often suffering from hunger. Yet he produced an astonishing work of sexual fantasy in a mystical language that challenged contemporary bourgeois sensibilities. Like all of Genet's novels, *Our Lady of the Flowers* is at least partly autobiographical. At the heart of Genet's writing is the question of sexual identity. Death, perversion, transvestitism, sodomy, masturbation, and prostitution are all recurring themes in Genet's works, which depict gay culture in Montmartre between the two world wars. Like FLAUBERT, Genet explores the social mores of a particular segment of French society, in this case that of a marginalized group. In certain respects, Genet's writing equally recalls the works of the GONCOURT brothers or ÉMILE ZOLA, who, in their own historical context, likewise sought to give voice to the outcast.

Genet's writing style is cinematographic as he moves seamlessly from one scene into another in a montage style. The prison life Genet evokes is shockingly poetic. Crime makes Genet worthy of beauty, of the men he desires. "Now I am exhausted with inventing circumstances in which he loves me more and more. I am worn out with the invented trips, thefts, rapes, burglaries, imprisonments and treachery in which we were involved." Genet reflects voluptuously on murder, the murderer as a God. Genet also offers a celebration of the male body and all of its bodily functions. Even a fart becomes a thing of poetry, a "pearl." Genet's dense and voluptuous prose hearkens back to the writing of MARCEL PROUST, whom Genet greatly admired. Reading a copy of Proust's *Guermantes' Way* that he surreptitiously acquired in prison inspired Genet to begin writing. Although Genet's exploration of gay culture is in some ways almost sociological, he felt no need to create a sense of reality. Again, like Proust, Genet drew from everyday life yet his writing his highly philosophical, emphasizing reflection over the events depicted.

FURTHER READING

Brooks, Peter, and Joseph Halpern. *Genet, A Collection of Critical Essays.* Englewood Cliffs, N.J.: Prentice-Hall, 1979.

Lucey, Michael. "Genet's Notre-Dame-des-Fleurs: Fantasy and Sexual Identity," *Yale French Studies,* no. 91, Genet: In the Language of the Enemy (1997): 80–102.

Sartre, Jean-Paul. *Saint Genet, Actor and Martyr.* Translated by Bernard Frechtman. New York: Pantheon, 1983.

White, Edmund. *Genet: A Biography.* New York: Knopf, 1993.

P

PANTAGRUEL FRANÇOIS RABELAIS (1532) *Les Horribles et Épouvantables Faits et Prouesses du très rennomé Pantagruel, Roi des Dipsodes, fils du Grand Gargantua (The Horrible and Terrible Acts of the Well-Known Pantagruel, King of the Dipsodes, Son of the Great Gargantua),* was first published under the pseudonym Alcofribas Nasier, an anagram of Rabelais's full name. Although some of his contemporaries did not think this work sufficiently serious for a humanist of Rabelais's stature, it made its author an instant success. This work, condemned by the Sorbonne University as were Rabelais's other books, draws on earlier literary traditions such as the *roman chevaleresque* and the *roman d'aventure* to tell the story of Pantagruel's birth, childhood, and education. In Paris, Gargantua meets Panurge, one of the principal characters of the series. Together Pantagruel and Panurge set off on a series of adventures.

This first section allows Rabelais to contrast the medieval scholastic tradition of rote learning to a new pedagogical approach promoting mental and physical exercise, a Renaissance education, calling for students to be trained in a variety of disciplines including language, classical thought, music, the natural sciences, medicine, and arts. Gargantua's famous letter to his son lays out a plan for Pantagruel's education by satirically treating medieval scholasticism and the general intellectual rigidity of the Sorbonne. This discussion contrasting old and new forms of education blends into a philosophical exploration of humankind's rai-son d'être, themes that are expanded in Rabelais's later works.

The book is loosely structured, highly comical, and lively in action and speech. Rabelais's interspersed anecdotes and comic parody of sacred texts mark the centrality of Rabelais's works in the history of laughter. His verbal proliferation, word games, and imaginative vocabulary reflect elements of Renaissance thought, in particular, the influence of the humanist Desiderius Erasmus. The same excess found in Rabelais's use of language is paralleled in his comic images of eating, drinking, and bodily functions. Rabelais's imaginative exploration of language stands in sharp contrast to the rigidity of academic and legal discourses. Blended humor and seriousness break down for a moment the traditional duality in Western thought between body and soul.

FURTHER READING

Bakhtin, Mikhail. *Rabelais and His World.* Translated by Hélène Iswolsky. Cambridge, Mass.: MIT Press, 1968.

Cave, Terrence. *The Cornucopian Text: Problems of Writing in the French Renaissance.* Oxford: Clarendon Press, 1979.

Febvre, Lucien. *The Problem of Unbelief in the Sixteenth Century: The Religion of Rabelais.* Translated by Beatrice Gottlieb. Cambridge, Mass.: Harvard University Press, 1982.

Screech, Michael. *Rabelais.* Ithaca, N.Y.: Cornell University Press, 1979.

PARIS COMMUNE

PARIS COMMUNE The context of the Paris Commune is the Franco-Prussian War (1870–71), in which the French were defeated by Prussia and Napoleon III sent into exile in England. In February 1871, France witnessed the election of a monarchist-dominated National Assembly. The leader of the provisional government was Adolphe Thiers. Many Parisians were resentful of the presence of the occupying Prussian army and the wealthy French who had abandoned the city. When French troops seized weapons in the neighborhood of Montmartre in March 1871, a crowd formed and two generals were executed, leading to the siege of Paris by French government troops. The Paris Commune tried to defend the city while initiating liberal social and economic reforms. Smaller uprisings against the conservative government also took place in some provincial cities. In May government troops led an assault on the capital, defeating the Paris Commune. Some 25,000 Parisian died in this bloody civil war. VICTOR HUGO and JULES VALLÈS both actively supported the Commune, and Vallès was condemned in absentia for his participation. Vallès's character JACQUES VINGTRAS evokes the author's own experience as he fights on the barricades in 1871.

PARIS PEASANT (LE PAYSAN DE PARIS)

LOUIS ARAGON (1926) Though often considered a novel, *Paris Peasant* is difficult to classify by genre. Written in Aragon's surrealist period (see SURREALISM), this work recalls ANDRÉ BRETON's *Last Steps*. It is the story of a man who endlessly rediscovers his city with a fresh eye that allows him to appreciate life, the city, and their relationship to each other. One of the most famous passages in the text and the one most often remembered describes the long-since demolished opera. Equally significant is the "Preface to a modern mythology" or "Peasant's Dream."

With this work, Aragon made a significant contribution to the surrealist movement with his free-flowing train of thoughts and dreams. Aragon's oft-noted attention to detail is evident. At the same time, this work serves as more than a Parisian's guide to his city. Aragon blends passages from newspaper articles, advertisements, announcements, signs, and inscriptions in a collage technique often associated with surrealism. He deftly displays the power of his imagination and his appreciation for the wonders of daily life. As an athe-ist, Aragon found meaning in the quotidian and thus explored shops and views, the passage by the opera, brothels and cafés in a poetic style that affirms life. This work successfully unites reality with the imagination, senses, and spirit. *Paris Peasant* is a sort of intellectual adventure that brings together language and thought in a surprising and engaging manner. The text also explores the relationships among love, eroticism, and language.

FURTHER READING

Adereth, Maxwell. *Elsa Triolet and Louis Aragon: An Introduction to Their Interwoven Lives and Works.* Lewiston, N.Y.: E. Mellen Press, 1994.

Brosman, Catherine Savage. *Malraux, Sartre and Aragon as Political Novelists.* Gainesville: University of Florida Press, 1964.

Caute, David. *Communism and the French Intellectuals, 1914–1960.* New York: Macmillan, 1964.

Duruzoi, Gerard. *History of the Surrealist Movement.* Translated by Alison Anderson. Chicago: University of Chicago Press, 2002.

Kimyongur, Angela. *Socialist Realism in Louis Aragon's Le Monde Réel Series.* Hull, England: University of Hull Press, 1995.

PASSING TIME (L'EMPLOI DU TEMPS)

MICHEL BUTOR (1956) In this innovative novel, Jacques Revel, a young Frenchman, is living in England for professional reasons. Cold and foggy, the town of Bleston is in some way Jacques's enemy. He decides to keep a journal of his period in "exile." The process of writing is, for him, a process of self-discovery.

At one point, Jacques is wandering like the legendary Athenian Theseus, lost in a labyrinth of city streets. He encounters two sisters who show him the way, each one, in turn, loved and lost. The city is a monster, like the Minotaur Theseus defeated in that labyrinth of old, mysteriously responsible for the attempted murder of Jacques's friend George Burton. In a novel within the novel, *The Murder of George Burton,* the evil secrets of the city are revealed.

For both Burton and Jacques, the need to write represents a struggle, again like that of Theseus, to find one's way. Unfortunately, the project fails. In the end, Jacques is unable to decipher the world.

Butor's second novel, *Passing Time,* reflects the author's ideas about the writing process through which one explores the world and discovers new modes of expression. Writing is the search for truth and for oneself. *Passing Time* received the Féneon Prize in 1956.

FURTHER READING

Faulkenburg, Marilyn Thomas. *Church, City and Labyrinth in Brontë, Dickens, Hardy, and Butor.* New York: P. Lang, 1993.

Grant, Marian A. *Michel Butor, L'Emploi du Temps.* London: Edward Arnold, 1973.

Lydon, Mary. *Perpetuum Mobile: A Study of the Novels and Aesthetics of Michel Butor.* Edmonton, Canada: University of Alberta Press, 1980.

McWilliams, Dean. *The Narratives of Michel Butor: The Writer as Janus.* Athens: Ohio University Press, 1978.

Spencer, M. C. *Michel Butor.* New York: Twayne, 1974.

Waelti-Walters, Jennifer R. *Michel Butor: A Study of His View of the World and a Panorama of His Work.* Victoria, B.C.: Sono Nis Press, 1977.

PASTORAL NOVEL

PASTORAL NOVEL   Popular in the 17th century, the pastoral novel is characterized first and foremost by its bucolic setting, far from civilization, in which idealized shepherds and shepherdesses engage in a discourse analyzing love. The pastoral novel draws from 16th-century Spanish and Italian works of a similar nature.

The pastoral novel is frequently linked to the baroque. During the reign of Louis XIV, pastoral elements could be found in court festivals, balls, and dances that, together, contributed to the rise of the opera as a dramatic and musical medium.

The narrative is often complicated by a series of lovers who must overcome both internal and external obstacles to consummate their relationship. Lovers in disguise frequently mistake each other. Pastoral novels are marked by the combination of a Neoplatonic ideal of a spiritual love with eroticism. The preeminent French pastoral novel is HONORÉ D'URFÉ'S ASTREA. Through its subtle analysis of human sentiments, particularly love, the pastoral leads to the rise of the psychological novel.

PASTORAL SYMPHONY (*LA SYMPHONIE PASTORALE*) ANDRÉ GIDE (1919)

PASTORAL SYMPHONY (*LA SYMPHONIE PASTORALE*) ANDRÉ GIDE (1919)   In this lyrical work, Gide recounts the story of a Protestant pastor who encounters a poor, blind orphan whom he decides to raise with his family. Gertrude is vermin-ridden and filthy when she arrives in the pastor's home. On top of being blind, Gertrude has never learned to speak. Despite his wife's resistance, the pastor decides to help the child out of Christian charity. The consequences of his gesture are tragic.

As Gertrude begins to open up, the pastor is struck by the beauty of her words and her soul. He is as unaware of his growing love for her as he is of the pain this attachment causes his wife. The pastor is caught unawares yet again when his son Jacques declares his love for Gertrude and his desire to marry her. The pastor responds with what he thinks is the voice of a spiritual mentor when, in fact, it is the voice of a jealous man who realizes that his own son is his rival. Jacques obeys his father's wishes and leaves on a trip to the mountains.

Meanwhile, a doctor believes that he can operate on Gertrude's eyes and give her sight. At this point, Gertrude has gone to live in the home of a virtuous woman whom she helps in teaching and raising a few other blind girls. The operation on Gertrude is successful, but when she returns to the pastor's home, her eyes are opened both literally and figuratively. Gertrude realizes that she has always loved Jacques, not the pastor as she had once believed. Moreover, she sees the pain on his wife's face caused by her own presence, so Gertrude ends her life. Jacques, who reveals to his father that both he and Gertrude have converted to Roman Catholicism, enters a religious order of monks.

The pastor is devastated and yet the outcome of the story is of his own making. He believed that he lived according to the gospel that calls for us to love one another. This becomes the means by which he can justify his love for Gertrude. The pastor reveals the very human weakness that allows us to reason away what we desire. While the pastor deliberately refuses to consider the words of Saint Paul (on sin), he concentrates on Jesus' words of love. Jacques is the opposite, emphasizing instead Saint Paul's words on duties. Thus the father and son confront each other on both theological and personal grounds.

Pastoral Symphony appears to be written in striking contrast to both *LAFCADIO'S ADVENTURES* (published five years before) and *The Counterfeiters,* written about five years after. Gide once explained that he felt compelled to write this book that fits in with a number of his earlier works, such as *The Immoralist, Strait Is the Gate,* as well as *Lafcadio's Adventures.* In each instance, Gide explores the concept of the *"acte gratuit,"* or gratuitous act, one committed on impulse solely to satisfy one's desire. A recurring theme in this and other works is the tension between the desire to live an independent life and one's responsibility toward others.

It is also possible that Gide's own spiritual crisis, as he wrestled with his Protestant upbringing, led him to write this story of the blind girl that had been so long in his head. Moreover, in 1917 Gide fell in love with a young man who seems to parallel the character of Gertrude in *Pastoral Symphony.*

FURTHER READING

Bettinson, Christopher D. *Gide: A Study.* London: Heinemann; Totowa, N.J.: Rowman and Littlefield, 1977.

O'Brien, Justin. *Portrait of André Gide: A Critical Biography.* New York: Octagon Books, 1977; 1953.

O'Keefe, Charles. *Void and Voice: Questioning Narrative Conventions in André Gide's Major First-Person Narratives.* Chapel Hill: Dept. of Romance Languages, University of North Carolina, 1996.

Parnell, Charles, "André Gide and His *Symphonie Pastorale,*" *Yale French Studies,* no. 7, André Gide, 1869–1951 (1951): 60–71.

Salz, Lily. "André Gide and the Problem of Engagement," *French Review* 30, no. 2 (December 1956): 131–137.

Sheridan, Alan. *André Gide: A Life in the Present.* Cambridge, Mass.: Harvard University Press, 1999.

Stoltzfus, Ben. "André Gide and the Voices of Rebellion," *Contemporary Literature* 19, no. 1 (Winter 1978): 80–98.

Walker, David, ed. *André Gide.* London, New York: Longman, 1996.

PAUL AND VIRGINIA (PAUL ET VIRGINIE) Jacques-Henri Bernardin de Saint-Pierre (1788)

In this sentimental pastoral novel, narrated by an old man who supposedly knew the characters involved, two European children, Paul and Virginia, are raised by their mothers on the Isle de France (Mauritius). Madame de la Tour, a widowed noblewoman, and Margaret, a woman abandoned by her lover, live quietly in the countryside with their two slaves, Domingo and Mary. Paul and Virginia's mutual love and tenderness grow day by day in this tranquil world surrounded by maternal love.

When Virginia becomes a young woman, her mother is persuaded to send her to France to complete her education in the household of a wealthy aunt. Class issues come into play even in this remote spot. Virginia is from a noble family; Paul is not.

Paul is desolate when Virginia leaves but, despite his fears, she remains true to him. She is unmoved by Parisian society and its ways, so different from the life of innocence and virtue she has always known. Tragedy ensues upon Virginia's return to the island. At the entrance to the harbor, Virginia's ship is destroyed by a storm. Out of modesty, Virginia refuses to undress to allow a sailor to bring her ashore. Before Paul's eyes, Virginia dies.

Bernardin de Saint-Pierre clearly drew from his experience living on the Isle de France, but what he describes is not the colonial system he knew but, rather, some earlier period of his imagination that approximates Rousseau's state of nature. Bernardin's promotion of virtue and nature, in opposition to the corruption of the civilized world, mark him as Rousseau's collaborator and a precursor to Romanticism. This very popular novel was praised by Chateaubriand in *The Genius of Christianity.* The poet Alphonse de Lamartine, Balzac, and Flaubert all acknowledged a debt to Bernardin de Saint-Pierre.

FURTHER READING

France, Anatole. *The Latin Genius.* Edited by Wilfrid S. Jackson. London: John Lane the Bodley Head; New York: Dodd, Mead, 1924.

PÉLAGIE Antonine Maillet (1979)

This epic tale brings to life a forgotten moment in Canadian history. In 1755 British troops deported the French-speaking population of Acadia in Nova Scotia into exile along the eastern coast of North America. One generation later the exiles return, led by Pélagie-la-Charrette, the leader of the Acadian diaspora, a sort of female Moses who leads her people on a 10-year journey back to the land of their birth. With a miserable wooden cart that gives her the name "la charrette," packed full of her belongings and children, Pélagie sets off northward from the state of Georgia accompanied by a group of friends. Along the way they pick up other displaced Acadians who have heard of their quest. Together they experience a series of fantastic adventures and misadventures until finally they reach their promised land. But their former home has been occupied by the British and the fertile land of La Grand' Pré destroyed. Pélagie dies after seeing the fertile plain once more. Her people must continue north without her. The continued existence of the Acadians as a distinct people will now depend solely on culture and tradition. The female values embodied by Pélagie stand in stark contrast to patriarchal British power.

The narrative consists of three levels. The first takes place in the 1770s when the Acadians return to their homeland. The second, set in the 1880s, features Pélagie's descendant, Pélagie-la-Gribouille. The last, set in 1979 at the time of the novel's writing, carries on the oral tradition of the Acadian people. The narrative is marked by characteristics of oral culture that include popular sayings and proverbs, refrains and repetitions. Moreover, Maillet revives the Acadian dialect, vocabulary, and expressions of the 18th century. *Pélagie* won the prestigious Goncourt Prize in 1979.

FURTHER READING

Dinwoodie, C. "Where Is Acadia?" *British Journal for Canadian Studies* 1 (1986): 15–29.

Fitzpatrick, Marjorie A. "Antonine Maillet: The Search for a Narrative Voice," *Journal of Popular Culture* 15, no. 3 (Winter 1981): 4–13.

Smith, Donald. *Voices of Deliverance: Interviews with Quebec and Canadian Writers.* Toronto: Anansi, 1986.

PENGUIN ISLAND (*L'ÎLE DES PEN-GOUINS*) ANATOLE FRANCE (1908) In this philosophical tale that recalls the works of VOLTAIRE, France satirizes Western civilization. Drawing inspiration from Breton myths, France gives a fantastic origin to French society in the transformation of a flock of penguins into humans by Saint Maël.

The work is composed of eight books that relate French history in an ironic tone. For example, Draco and the Draconites are recognizable as the Bourbon rulers of France, while Lyrot and Colomban represent Dreyfus, the Jewish officer falsely accused and convicted of treason in 1894, and ÉMILE ZOLA. It is a wondrous tale and yet strangely realistic at the same time, as France exposes the irresponsibility of the THIRD REPUBLIC, ready to throw itself into the second world war. The last and most visionary book, entitled "Future Times: History without End," gives free expression to France's pessimism as he envisions the fall of capitalist society and depicts the absurdity of history with no memory of its past errors, destined to repeat the same mistakes over and over again.

France reveals his adherence to the general values of the political left. At the same time, in contrast to most leftist intellectuals, he is skeptical of great historical movements that promise a golden future. Rather, his values are drawn from the philosophy of the ancient Greek philosopher Epicurus, much as we see in his *Epicurus' Garden* (1894). *Penguin Island* also bears the traces of ENLIGHTENMENT thought in its rejection of all dogma and ideological certainty. Beneath the surface runs the current of France's inimitable and ironic humor.

FURTHER READING

Durant, Will. *Anatole France: The Man and his Work.* Girard, Kans.: Haldeman-Julius, 1925.

Jefferson, Alfred Carter. *Anatole France: The Politics of Skepticism.* New Brunswick, N.J.: Rutgers University Press, 1965.

May, James Lewis. *Anatole France: The Man and His Work. An Essay in Critical Biography.* Port Washington, N.Y.: Kennikat Press, 1970.

Tylden-Wright, David. *Anatole France.* New York: Walker, 1967.

PEREC, GEORGES (1936–1982) Perec was born into a family of Polish-Jewish immigrants. After World War II, during which his father died at the front in 1940 and his mother in Auschwitz, Perec was raised in Paris by an aunt and uncle. He began by studying history and sociology and, between 1954 and 1962, wrote several novels that were not published. As of 1961 Perec decided to devote himself entirely to literature and was subsequently recognized for his virtuosity of technique. His novel *THINGS, A STORY OF THE SIXTIES* (1965) earned the Renaudot Prize. *LIFE, A USER'S*

MANUAL (1975) received the prestigious Médicis Prize. Perec showed an interest not only in fiction but also in theater, music, and film, adapting A MAN WHO SLEEPS (1967) to film in 1975. A number of Perec's works were published posthumously.

Perec's novels tend to tell not one story but several simultaneously, all of equal importance. The reader is almost overwhelmed by Perec's ability to play games with language, an interest he shared with RAYMOND QUENEAU. Perec participated in Queneau's "Workroom of Potential Literature," or OuLiPo. Perec is likewise associated with the NOUVEAU ROMAN (new novel) movement, but he was more than a "new novelist." Some critics have interpreted his writing word "games" as a means to disclose the ambiguous relationship between the individual and the world that is also reflected in Perec's attention to material reality.

Perec's innovative approach to writing lies at the heart of his works. In A Void (1969), for example, he made use of the "lipogram," a literary device that requires the writer to avoid using a particular letter of the alphabet. In this novel, it is the letter e. The absence of that letter in this astonishing work naturally changes its whole tenor, as it does not allow for feminine endings, for example. This is a detective novel whose subject is the disappearance of the letter e. The encyclopedia is missing the E volume, and hospital bed number five (signifying e in the alphabet) is missing from a ward with 26 beds. The reader encounters such diverse elements as a large family suffering from a "maldiction," Albanian spies, the rewriting of famous poems, and numerous literary allusions. The novel was initially criticized as nothing more than literary "acrobatics." In his postscript, however, Perec indicated that his concern was with writing itself.

Perec's techniques, of course, place constraints on the writer. At the same time, one could argue that they also liberate the author from the necessity of imparting a message. For Perec techniques such as the lipogram led him to "the zero degree of constraint, at which point all becomes possible once more."

The development of Perec's approach can be traced to Things, which is, at first glance, a traditional novel telling a story about life in the 1960s. Here Perec enu-merates the objects envied by Jerome and Sylvie. His technique of proliferation was later perfected in Life, A User's Manual, whose attention to detail recalls the REALISM of Flaubert. Moreover, Perec ascribes political significance to objects, as his descriptions of people obsessed with having things serves as a critique of modern consumer society. Things ends with a quotation from Communist theorist Karl Marx.

Les Revenentes (not translated, 1972) is also marked by excess as is evident, for example, in its carefully depicted orgy scene. Freedom, excess, and constraint are subjects of debate among the orgy's participants. The novel shows the influence of Roland Barthes's Sade, Fourier, Loyola and the poststructuralist movement in general (see POSTSTRUCTURALISM). The orgy is part of a plan by a group of characters to steal jewelry from the bishop of Exeter's guests as, in the confusion, no one will notice what they are doing. Certain scenes recall De Sade's 120 DAYS OF SODOM.

Life, A User's Manual is perhaps Perec's greatest work. The novel derives its structure from an apartment building. A series of stories emerge around the figure of Bartlebooth, who spent 20 years working on 500 paintings that are puzzles. Bartlebooth then spends the next 20 years putting the puzzles together, only to die in the end when an unforeseen w forbids their conclusion. A number of secondary elements also appear in the novel, such as the word killer and the seller of trinkets. In essence, Bartlebooth represents Perec's approach to writing and his belief in the impossibility of naming the totality of things.

Together, Perec's works explore the question of existence/nonexistence, as characters are torn between a sense of detachment and a desire to act. The clearest example of this tension is found in the character of Bartlebooth, a blend of the American-writer Herman Melville's character Bartleby, whose refrain was "I would prefer not to do it," and Barnabooth, a character created by the French novelist Valery Larbaud, full of desire to act, to live, to create, and to travel. Bartlebooth represents the tension between plenitude and emptiness.

Another attempt at ordering things appears in Think/Catalog (1985). Perec then returns to the puzzle in 53 Days (1989), an attempt to rewrite STENDHAL'S

The CHARTERHOUSE OF PARMA, just as *Things* was in certain respects a reprise of FLAUBERT's SENTIMENTAL EDUCATION. Perec turned to autobiography in *W, or the Remembrance of Childhood* (1975), only to say that because of his parents' deaths, "I have no memories of childhood."

Perec's autobiographical works are particularly marked by the theme of absence. He may have said that he had no childhood memories but, parts of his early childhood are revealed in his writings. In *W*, he wrote, "Until about my twelfth year, my history only takes up a few lines: I lost my father when I was four, my mother when I was six; I spent the war in various boarding schools in Villard-de-Lans. In 1945 my father's sister and her husband adopted me." *W* is a complex work in which two stories weave in and out of each other in alternating chapters. The underlying theme of absence appears, too, in *A Sleeping Man* and *I am Born* (1990).

In 1978, after winning the Médicis Prize, Perec defined his quest as the desire to explore every possible way of writing, in every genre. One example of his experimental approach is the mathematical base for the structure of his texts and the use of the grid, as in a crossword puzzle: "The construction of the grid is a fastidious task, minute, compulsive, a sort of arithmetic based on letters. . . . it is a system of primary constraints where the letter is omnipresent but the language is absent."

Perec's work has been described as sociological fiction, Oulipian exercise, autobiography, and hyperrealism. In his own view, other literature simply created the space for his construction of literary puzzles. Perec died at 45 of lung cancer.

FURTHER READING

Andrews, Chris. "Puzzles and Lists: Georges Perec's *Un Homme qui dort,*" *MLN*, 111, no. 4 (1996): 775–796.
Bellos, David. *Georges Perec: A Life in Words.* Boston: Godine, 1993.
Motte, Warren F., Jr. "Georges Perec on the Grid," *French Review* 57, no. 6 (May 1984): 820–832.
———, ed. *Oulipo: A Primer of Potential Literature.* Lincoln: University of Nebraska Press, 1986.
Schwartz, Paul. *Georges Perec, Traces of his Passage.* Birmingham, Ala.: Summa, 1988.

PERGAUD, LOUIS (1882–1915)

Like his father, Pergaud was a country schoolteacher, close to children and to nature in the Jura region where he grew up. After his marriage, Pergaud left teaching and moved to Paris in 1907. He returned to teaching in 1909 after a brief stint working for the water company. Pergaud began his writing career as a poet but acquired fame with *From Goupil to Margot,* a collection of country tales that won the Goncourt Prize in 1910; *The Button War* (1912); and *The Novel of Miraut, Hunting Dog* (1913), a work that reflects Pergaud's feeling for animals.

The eight short stories that make up *From Goupil to Margot* are drawn from Pergaud's childhood experiences in provincial France. They reveal the tension between human and beast that marks rural life. Pergaud has frequently been noted for his remarkable gift of observation, his love for the natural sciences, and his sensitivity to animal psychology.

Over the next four years, Pergaud produced his greatest works. *The Revenge of the Crow* was published in 1911, and in 1912 his masterpiece, *The Button War.* In this novel, Pergaud tells the story of a group of children between the ages of 10 and 14 who are divided into two opposing factions. In the course of their battles, the losers are humiliatingly shorn of their buttons, only to be punished once more when they return home to their parents. Despite the enmity between them, the children form a united front before the adults as they protect each other from "authority." Courage, a spirit of adventure, and notions of honor and friendship blend in this novel with cruelty and humiliation in a persuasive depiction of the psychology of children. The novel was adapted to film by Yves Robert in 1962.

In 1914 Pergaud published the darker *Story of Miraut.* In this work a peasant couple acquires Miraut, a hunting dog, who becomes a bone of contention between the husband, an avid hunter who loves the solitude of the forest, and his wife, who desires a more comfortable, material life. Meanwhile, Miraut commits one misdeed after another. Eventually, the couple decides to separate. After they have gone, Miraut returns again and again to his former home. Beaten down, Miraut comes to realize that he has been abandoned and cries out in hunger and sadness at the cruelty of the human beings who have neglected him. In this touching novel, Pergaud offers a realistic depiction of rural life and values.

Mobilized during World War I, Pergaud died in 1915. His body was never recovered. Just before leaving for the front, he submitted a collection of poems, *The Rustics,* to his publisher. They appeared posthumously in 1921. Pergaud also left behind an unfinished novel, *Lebrac, Lumberjack,* that continues the story of one of the characters from *The Button War.* His *Life of Animals* (1923), *Mélanges* (1938), as well as *Correspondence* (1955) were all published after the author's death.

PÉRIERS, BONAVENTURE DES (C. 1510–1544)

Bonaventure des Périers has left a slightly tarnished reputation to posterity. Born to a noble family in Burgundy, he was first a tutor to several noble families. In 1536 he became secretary to Marguerite de NAVARRE, his patron. Some 19th-century scholars have suggested that the *HEPTAMERON* was his work. Like Marguerite de Navarre, Bonaventure des Périers was a humanist who shared her sympathy for the Protestant Reformation.

While he also wrote some fairly mediocre poetry, Bonaventure des Périers is best known for his *Cymbalum Mundi,* a series of four dialogues written in the style of the Roman satirist Lucian and his *NOVEL PASTIMES AND MERRY TALES. Cymbalum Mundi* was banned by the Sorbonne university for its anti-Christian views. The work was so scandalous that Marguerite de Navarre was obliged to disavow it, although she continued to protect its author until 1544. Under sharp attack for his heretical ideas, Bonaventure des Périers moved to Lyon, a city more tolerant of liberal ideas than Paris. There he lived in poverty until 1544, when he committed suicide by falling on his sword.

Bonaventure des Périers's series of stories, *Novel Pastimes and Merry Tales,* was published posthumously in Lyon. These short stories written in a simple, direct style give evidence of Bonaventure des Périer's skill as a narrator. This work marks his place as a significant contributor to 16th-century humanist prose.

FURTHER READING

Gauna, Max. *Upwellings: First Expressions of Unbelief in the Printed Literature of the French Renaissance.* Rutherford, N.J.: Fairleigh Dickinson University Press; London, Cranberry, N.J.: Associated University Presses, 1992.

Krailsheimer, A. J. *Three Sixteenth-Century Conteurs.* London: Oxford University Press, 1966.

PERSIAN LETTERS, THE (LES LETTRES PERSANES) MONTESQUIEU, CHARLES-LOUIS DE SECONDAT, BARON DE (1721)

In this EPISTOLARY NOVEL, two imaginary Persians travel to France. In their letters home they comment on Parisian morals and society. The novel is extraordinarily modern in its promotion of cultural relativity, an approach that contributed to the rise of sociology as a discipline. The epistolary novel dates from the 17th-century with GUILLERAGUE's *LETTERS OF A PORTUGUESE NUN.* In *The Persian Letters,* Montesquieu creates a masterpiece of the genre, expressing an abundance of ideas in an interlocking series of 161 polyphonic letters. This work reinspired the 18th-century vogue in epistolary fiction of which ROUSSEAU's *The NEW HÉLOÏSE* and LACLOS's *DANGEROUS LIAISONS* are particularly notable examples.

The novel covers the last few years of the reign of Louis XIV and the regency. Despite their professed Eastern values, Usbek and Rica offer an essentially Western rationalist critique of European social institutions, making this one of the great texts of the French ENLIGHTENMENT. Like the *ENCYCLOPEDIA* and other projects of this period, *The Persian Letters* is marked by a critical spirit and an emphasis on liberty, humanity, rationalism, and secularism. Because of its Enlightenment themes, the novel was published anonymously in Holland, a standard procedure at the time for books challenging the French censors.

According to the story, two Persian lords, Usbek and Rica, leave for France in 1711 on a journey that lasts for eight years. Usbek is attached to his native land yet is forced to escape for political reasons. He is enlightened and honest, qualities that have earned him enemies at a corrupt court. He is sorry to leave his five wives. In contrast, Rica is younger and therefore more desirous of adventure. Sharply observant and humorous, he is ready to attend the Parisian salons with their witty company and beautiful women.

Some scholars argue that the novel consists of three basic parts. The first and third concentrate on Persia.

In the first, Usbek and Rica set off on their travels. The third focuses on the disorder in Usbek's harem. The middle portion offers the travelers' reactions to French life and society with interspersed commentary on Persia, other parts of Europe, and Russia. Other scholars argue that there is no unified structure to the text although a series of letters occasionally deals with a particular topic. The argument against a unified structure is based on the notion that Montesquieu's novel can be compared to the contemporary rococo movement in the arts.

Having crossed Persia, Turkey, and Italy, Usbek and Rica arrive in Paris in 1712. From France, they correspond with 25 of their compatriots in Persia. Their exchange allows Usbek and Rica to keep up with what takes place at home and offers the possibility of drawing contrasts and comparisons between East and West. The two Persians are interested in everything: politics, behavior, and culture, the role of women, economic life, and religion. They comment on what they observe. At one point in their travels, they go in separate directions, and this leads to correspondence between them as well, allowing for a clearer picture of the differences in their characters.

Questions of women and marriage are central to the text. The French are viewed as licentious and frivolous, similar to their depiction in GRAFFIGNY'S LETTERS OF A PERUVIAN PRINCESS. Montesquieu also points to problems in the harem system. At times Persian customs are depicted as horrifying, on other occasions as worthy of emulation. The last 15 letters dealing with the crisis in Usbek's harem end with the suicide of his once favorite wife, Roxane, after she has declared her hatred for Usbek and her right to personal freedom. Contemporary readers were fascinated by the harem story with its combination of exoticism and eroticism.

The final crisis in the harem also provides Montesquieu with the opportunity to return to another important theme, despotism. Implicit in this discussion is a criticism of Louis XIVs' reign and the subsequent regency. The disorder in the harem is in contrast to the ideal of family life in the passages on the Troglodytes, who live together on the basis of mutual generosity and understanding. Here Montesquieu offers his argument against the view of human nature as naturally aggressive associated with the English political theorist Thomas Hobbes. Whether he discusses sexual relations or other topics, Montesquieu makes use of the differences between Persian and French culture to comment on all aspects of society.

Usbek and Rica's comments on Parisian society furnish a critical picture of 18th-century upper-class life. Montesquieu borrows from the moralist Jean de La Bruyère the technique of producing characters who are both individuals and representative of specific social groups. In utilizing this technique, he is particularly effective in depicting the nobility. Through Usbek, Montesquieu ridicules the vanity of nobles and promotes the 18th-century idea of meritocracy. For this and other reasons, many readers have considered *The Persian Letters* as a precursor to his *Spirit of Laws.*

FURTHER READING

Conroy, Peter V. *Montesquieu Revisited.* New York: Twayne; Toronto: Maxwell Macmillan Canada; New York: Maxwell Macmillan International, 1992.

Cook, Elizabeth Hackendorn. *Epistolary Bodies: Gender and Genre in the Eighteenth Century Republic of Letters.* Stanford, Calif.: Stanford University Press, 1996.

Dargan, Edwin Preston. *The Aesthetic Doctrine of Montesquieu: Its Application in his Writings.* New York: B. Franklin, 1968.

Goodman, Dena. *Criticism in Action: Enlightenment Experiments in Political Writing.* Ithaca, N.Y.: Cornell University Press, 1989.

Gunny, Ahmad. "Montesquieu's View of Islam in the *Lettres persanes,*" *Studies on Voltaire and the Eighteenth Century* 174. Oxford: Voltaire Foundation, 1978.

Kra, Pauline. "Montesquieu and Women." In Samia I. Spencer, ed. *French Women and the Age of Enlightenment.* Bloomington: Indiana University Press, 1984.

Pucci, Suzanne. "Orientalism and Representation of Exteriority in Montesquieu's *Lettres persanes,*" the *Eighteenth Century: Theory and Interpretation* 23 (Fall 1985): 263–279.

Shackleton, Robert. *Essays on Montesquieu and on the Enlightenment.* Oxford: Voltaire Foundation and the Taylor Institute, 1988.

Schaub, Diana. *Erotic Liberalism: Women and Revolution in Montesquieu's Persian Letters.* Lanham, Md.: Rowman & Littlefield, 1995.

PETITE FADETTE George Sand (1849)

One of Sand's *romans champêtres,* or pastoral novels, *Petite Fadette* opens with twin brothers living in Sand's native province of Berry. When he grows up, Landry falls in love with Petite Fadette, whom everyone supposes to be a witch since her grandmother had passed on to Fadette certain secrets. Sylvinet suspects that they are in love and tells his father, who eventually, if reluctantly, agrees to their marriage.

Disappointed with the outcome of the Revolution of 1848, Sand left Paris and returned to her family estate of Nohant, where she wrote, among other works, *Petite Fadette,* celebrating the simple, hard, yet noble life of the countryside, which stands in contrast to modern urban bourgeois values. Written at the same time as HONORÉ DE BALZAC's *The Peasants,* Sand's novel is marked by a discernible difference. Sand is an idealist, not a realist (see IDEALISM; REALISM). Echoing JEAN-JACQUES ROUSSEAU, she depicts country life as a source of universal moral regeneration through love and labor. Some critics accused Sand of exaggerating her positive view of rural life. Nonetheless, *Petite Fadette* reflects the guiding principles that lie at the heart of all Sand's works.

FURTHER READING

Crecelius, Kathryn J. *Family Romances: George Sand's Early Novels.* Bloomington: Indiana University Press, 1987.

Glasgow, Janis, ed. *George Sand: Collected Essays.* Troy, N.Y.: Whitston, 1985.

Hofstadter, Dan. *The Love Affair as a Work of Art.* New York: Farrar, Straus and Giroux, 1996.

Naginski, Isabelle Hoog. *George Sand: Writing for Her Life.* New Brunswick, N.J.: Rutgers University Press, 1991.

Peebles, Catherine. *The Psyche of Feminism: Sand, Colette, Sarraute.* West Lafayette, Ind.: Purdue University Press, 2003.

Powell, David A. *George Sand.* Boston: Twayne, 1990.

Schor, Naomi. *George Sand and Idealism.* New York: Columbia University Press, 1993.

Walton, Whitney. "Writing the 1848 Revolution: Politics, Gender and Feminism in the Works of French Women of Letters," *French Historical Studies* 18, no. 4 (Autumn 1994): 1001–1024.

Vitaglione, Daniel. *George Eliot and George Sand.* New York: Peter Lang, 1993.

PHILIPPE, CHARLES-LOUIS (1874–1909)

Of modest background, Philippe's father was a craftsman and his mother a domestic servant. Throughout his life Philippe was plagued with poor health, small stature, and a scar on his face that he later hid with a beard. At the age of 12, Philippe was sent to boarding school. After secondary school, he failed the entrance exam to the local polytechnic university. Interested in literature, Philippe read symbolist poetry (see SYMBOLISM) and entered into correspondence with the poet Stéphane Mallarmé. He also met ANDRÉ GIDE and a group of writers who established a socialist literary review, *The Enclosure.*

Philippe decided to seek work in the capital and in 1886 found employment with the city of Paris, where he remained until his death, earning a modest salary as a low-level administrator while pursuing his writing career. Philippe published his *Four Stories of Poor Love* in 1897, a work that bears the mark of symbolist influence. In 1898 he published *Good Madeleine and Poor Marie* and, in 1900, a short version of *Mother and Child.* The complete work did not appear until after Philippe's death, published under the stewardship of Gide. It is the fictionalized story of Philippe's life from birth until age 20 and is dedicated to his mother. "You will pick up your glasses to read these words," he wrote. "You will spell out word by word saying it's a big book full of words. Well, Mama, each of these words is for you." The book, in fact, helped Philippe's mother to accept his career as a writer as it proved he could earn a living by his pen.

Philippe's parents dreamed that their son would rise in society, but that was not the author's vision. Perhaps because of his origins, in his writing Philippe chose to describe the world of the humble and poor. His writing thus differs from the contemporary literary movements of DECADENTISM and NATURALISM, both of which, he felt, modify or alter reality in the interest of artistic effect. At the same time, Philippe drew from naturalism, despite his critique. Most important, he sought to describe accurately the realities of rural life. Moreover, he convincingly made use of popular speech. Influenced by the Russian writer Leo Tolstoy, Philippe was one of the first populist writers in France.

Philippe's encounter with a prostitute furnished the material for his most famous work, *BUBU OF MONTPAR-*

NASSE (1901). To write this novel, Philippe explored the world of Parisian whores. He was particularly interested in the economic and social origins of prostitution. This novel clearly marks Philippe's style and content as closer to contemporary Russian novelists than the French Naturalists.

As of 1885, Philippe was associated with anarchist circles. Although he did not engage in violent activities himself, his vision contains traces of anarchist theory. A number of his works reflect the author's fascination with power in a manner that recalls works of the german philosopher Friedrich Nietzsche. In *Father Partridge,* which nearly won the Goncourt Prize in 1903, a blacksmith named Partridge, too ill to work, is accompanied in his tragic journey toward suicide by a young man named Jacques Bousset, who quits his job when there is a strike and drags his feeble friend to Paris. Partridge, too weak and ill to sustain life in the city with all its force and energy, dies.

In *Croquignole* (1906), an office worker believes he has become rich after receiving a small inheritance. Yet he ends up by making his friend Claude miserable by destroying the life of Angèle, a wise seamstress. Here is yet another triangular relationship that recalls *Bubu of Montparnasse.* Once again, Philippe introduces the theme of a man with power who dominates the weak. In the end, however, Croquignole informs his colleagues that he is not sure that "one has to live" after all. Croquignole enjoys his inheritance as long as he can. When it is gone, he cannot bear the thought of returning to his old life, where "He arrived at work in the morning. First he took out of his drawer: pen, pencil, don't forget the eraser, and he spread out three rulers all at once. After that he had nothing left to do but sit. He sat. . . . " His colleagues are all apathetic, overcome by the weight of existence; Croquignole at least sought for a time to break free.

The death of his father in 1907 inspired Philippe to write *Charles Blanchard.* Left unfinished, the novel was not published until 1913. Philippe also produced a number of chronicles and tales in which, recalling *Bubu,* thieves and murderers (treated again with some sympathy) attack the social institutions of the rich.

Philippe died of meningitis at the age of 35. He left behind a body of work that gives voice to the suffering of the poor in an unjust society. As Philippe once wrote, "There are two sorts of men on earth: those who protest and those who don't." Philippe chose to protest.

PIERRE AND JEAN (PIERRE ET JEAN)
GUY DE MAUPASSANT (1888)   This novel opens with a family on a fishing trip, in the harbor outside of Le Havre. In the boat are Mr. Roland, an obtuse retired jeweler from Paris, his wife, and their two sons Pierre and Jean. Also present is a young widow, Madame de Rosémilly.

Upon their return, the Roland family discovers that an old family friend, Maréchal, has bequeathed his fortune to Jean. Pierre is jealous; he wonders why he did not share in the inheritance. Struggling with his feelings, Pierre decides to move forward with his career. He chooses an apartment to set up his medical practice, thinking that he can ask his brother to lend him the money for the first months' rent. Unwittingly, Madame Roland chooses the very same apartment for Jean's law office.

His frustration increasing, Pierre suddenly remembers a portrait of Maréchal that has disappeared from view. Pierre asks his mother what has happened to it. When she reluctantly produces the portrait, it is clear that Jean bears a strong resemblance to Maréchal. Without ever addressing the issue explicitly, Pierre lets Madame Roland know that he has discovered her secret. Pierre is tormented by the thought that the mother he revered once had a lover, and that she is just like other women. Maupassant's subtly negative view of women is revealed in Pierre's reflections on his mother. It is a theme the resurfaces in Maupassant's other works. Women are either objects of desire or seductresses.

Meanwhile, Jean announces that he and Madame de Rosémilly have decided to marry. No longer able to contain himself, Pierre argues with Jean, revealing the truth of Jean's birth within their mother's hearing. A painful scene ensues; Madame Roland is a broken woman. A few days later, Jean informs the family that a transatlantic ship is looking for a doctor. Pierre applies for the position, putting much needed distance between himself and his family. Only at the last moment, as the ship departs, does Pierre gesture to his mother in a way that begins to relieve her suffering.

Flaubert's influence on Maupassant's NATURALISM in this novel is evident, particularly in the precise descriptions of Le Havre. Moreover, Maupassant begins the novel with a preface in which he declares his vision of art and of the writer's freedom of expression.

FURTHER READING

Ignotus, Paul. *The Paradox of Maupassant.* New York: Funk and Wagnalls, 1968.

Jackson, Stanlye. *Guy de Maupassant.* Folcroft, Pa.: Folcroft Library Editions, 1974.

Lerner, Michael. *Maupassant.* London: Allen and Unwin, 1975.

Steegmuller, Francis. *Maupassant: A Lion in the Path.* Freeport, N.Y.: Books for Libraries Press, 1972.

Sherard, Robert Harborough. *The Life, Work, and Evil Fate of Guy de Maupassant (gentilhomme de lettres).* Folcroft, Pa.: Folcroft Library Editions, 1976.

Sullivan, Edward D. *Maupassant: The Short Stories.* Great Neck, N.Y.: Barron's Educational Series, 1962.

PINGET, ROBERT (1919–1997)

Pinget was born in Switzerland. Although he studied law, his real interests were poetry, music, and painting. Thus in 1946 he gave up his legal career and moved to Paris, where be began to study painting at the Beaux Arts school. There he became a follower of the abstract painter Georges Bracque. In 1950, he gave up painting in favor of literature.

Pinget is associated with the NOUVEAU ROMAN (new novel). He participated in important conferences on the New Novel in Cerisy in 1971 and in New York City in 1982. His novel *The* INQUISITORY won the Critics Prize in 1962, while *Someone* was awarded the Femina Prize in 1965. Pinget also won the National Grand Prize for Literature (*Grand Prix National des Lettres*) in 1987.

Although influenced by SAMUEL BECKETT, Pinget does not carry the sense of negation and the absurd as far as his mentor. The two writers were friends and translated each other's works. Each novel Pinget wrote has its own "inquisitory" that leads toward the solution of an enigma. In the end, however, words themselves are more important than what is said or done. Crit-

ics have argued that Pinget has in essence written just one book several times over, each time perfecting to a greater degree his particular and often indiscernible quest. The critic Jean-Claude Lieber described Pinget's writing as "a gigantic construction site where the last word remains to be written."

Pinget's style is marked by brief dialogue; words are essential in order to grasp something that ceaselessly disappears. "What misery," Pinget writes, "to have undertaken to write that." Only what he means by "that" is never entirely clear. And so Pinget sets out to write "it" again, differently. There is little action in his stories, just situations.

Pinget's first publication was a collection of short stories, *Between Fantoine and Agapa,* that introduces the imaginary geographical space for almost all of his subsequent novels. His first novel, *Mahu, or the Material,* appeared in 1952 and offers a series of surrealist situations (see SURREALISM). This work is particularly noted for the character of Mahu. Pinget created a number of celebrated characters peculiarly his own such as Mahu, Baga, Mortin, and M. Songe, for whom he is remembered. Recurring themes are the quest and forgetting. It is possible to forget what one has said, as well as what one has written. An underlying question, too, focuses on identity. Do the characters know their own identity?

In the 1950s, Pinget began his association with the Éditions de Minuit publishing house and was considered for a time as representative of the NOUVEAU ROMAN movement. But he rejected all theorizing about the writing process. His goal was to create a narrative voice that was anonymous and neutral. Pinget's later works have the tone of detective fiction. Recurring themes are the presence of evil, boredom, anguish, and uncertainty.

An example of a mystery never revealed in its entirety and typical of Pinget's works is found in *Clope's Dossier* (1961). As in Pinget's other works, there is little action. Clope appears to be the central character but the reader does not learn much about him. We know he shot a goose and that he has been falsely accused of murdering his mother and must prove his innocence. But Pinget focuses his attention equally on other characters such as Philippard and Mortin, Verveine, Toupin, Pommard the judge, and a young mother named Simone who is constantly occupied with changing and dressing her son, Guillaume. In the end, we know nothing about what has happened to Clope's case. As a NOUVEAU ROMAN writer, Pinget seeks to evoke a multiplicity of experiences that together constitute reality.

Pinget wrote about the writing process as "opening the faucet of the subconscious," thus recalling the "automatic writing" of the surrealists. Pinget's novels explore the process of writing and the role of the writer in today's world, a world that in his view has rejected God. The influence of German philosopher Friedrich Nietzsche is evident. Pinget's principal concern, then, is "the way of saying things." His writing style has an oral quality. Moreover, the use of the first person gives a sense of proximity to the subconscious. The boundaries between doing, saying, and writing are all blurred. As the narrator of *Someone* says, "I write like that, the way one speaks, the way one sweats." Writing and saying are one. "The ear," he said, "makes tyrannical demands. . . . I am not interested in what is said or meant, but in the way it is said."

FURTHER READING

Henkels, Robert M. *Robert Pinget: The Novel as Quest.* Tuscaloosa: University of Alabama Press, 1979.

Reid, Martin. "Robert Pinget," *Yale French Studies,* Special Issue: After the Age of Suspicion: The French Novel Today (1988): 97–100.

Rosmarin, Léonard. *Robert Pinget.* New York: Twayne, London: Prentice Hall, 1995.

PIZAN, CHRISTINE DE (C. 1364–1431)

Christine de Pizan was one of France's first professional female writers. Another was arguably the 12th-century author MARIE DE FRANCE. Christine de Pizan was born in Venice around 1364 but moved to Paris with her family in 1369, where her father had accepted an appointment at the court of Charles V. She received a remarkably sophisticated education for a woman of her time, encouraged first by her father and then by her husband, Étienne du Castel, whom she married in 1380. The marriage was happy but short-lived. Étienne died in 1389.

Widowed at 25 with a family to support, Christine took up her pen, from which flowed a wide range of works: poetry, biography, politics, books of chivalry, religion, and philosophy. She is best known today for *The BOOK OF THE CITY OF LADIES,* in which she engages in the work of a literary historian, redefining the canon of classical texts as she formulates an argument against the misogynist tradition in Western literature. Christine is one of the principal figures in the Quarrel of the ROMANCE OF THE ROSE, debating the nature of women.

Some of her other works include moving lyric poetry in which she grieves over the loss of her husband, *The Path of Long Study, The Book of Fortune's Change,* an allegory of her widowhood after which Christine becomes a man, and *The Book of the Body Politic.* In the latter work of political theory, the metaphor of the body bears the direct influence of the English political theorist John of Salisbury's *Policraticus* and the works of Aristotle. This mirror for princes outlines the ideal education for the moral development of the prince, defining the ruler's responsibilities and the structure of society as it continues in the tradition of synthesizing classical and Christian thought. *The Book of the Body Politic* thus reflects the legacy of medieval scholasticism, the explication of texts through traditional glosses. To cite ancient philosophers such as Plutarch, Aristotle, or Seneca, for example, was to provide validity for one's argument, especially for a woman writer, as Christine points out.

Despite the patronage of powerful figures at the French court, Christine was in certain respects a writer in exile. Her threefold "alienness" stemmed from her position as a foreigner, a professional, and a woman. These three elements contributed to her sense of self. Like Marie de France, in all of her writings Christine asserts a strong authorial voice, "I, Christine." She identifies herself as an individual, a woman, a writer, even visually through her manuscript illuminations, produced in an all-female studio.

Frequently recurring themes in her work include dreams, the intervention of nature, allegorical figures, autobiographical elements, and, most often, discussion of the moral and intellectual capacity of women. With the rise of women's studies in recent years, Christine de Pizan has become an object of increased interest to literary historians.

FURTHER READING

Altmann, Barbara K., and Deborah L. McGrady, eds. *Christine de Pizan: A Casebook*. New York: Routledge, 2003.

McLeod, Enid. *The Order of the Rose: The Life and Ideas of Christine de Pizan*. Totowa, N.J.: Rowman and Littlefield, 1976.

Quilligan, Maureen. *The Allegory of Female Authority: Christine de Pizan's Cité des dames*. Ithaca, N.Y.: Cornell University Press, 1991.

Willard, Charity Cannon. *Christine de Pizan: Her Life and Works*. New York: Persea Books, 1984.

PLAGUE, THE (LA PESTE) ALBERT CAMUS (1947)

A powerful work, *The Plague* expresses Camus's profound faith in man. The novel opens a new cycle in Camus's works, focusing on the unlikely connection between rebellion and solidarity among men. Camus began writing in 1941, although the novel was not published until 1947, when he was further troubled by events that marked the character of the postwar world, such as the assimilation of Eastern Europe into the Soviet empire as well as French colonial policy.

In the novel an epidemic of the plague breaks out in Oran, Algeria. The novel opens with the lines, "The unusual events described in this chronicle occurred in 194- in Oran. Everyone agreed that, considering their somewhat extraordinary character, they were out of place there. For its ordinariness is what strikes one first about the town of Oran …" The novel is structured like a tragedy in five acts.

The disease of the title represents evil, whether of natural, human, or historical origin. As the plague may always return, so it is everyone's concern. It is the great equalizer because no one can escape its deadly grasp regardless of position or class. Highly moralistic, the novel speaks out movingly against violence. Moreover, in the background of this chronicle of a collective experience of death is the sea and freedom. As the novel portrays, humankind cannot live in conditions that deny freedom.

The first part opens with Dr. Rieux finding a dead rat on his staircase. Later that day he accompanies his wife to the train station. She is suffering from poor health and is leaving to recover in the countryside. A few days later, a newspaper reports the death of 6,000 rats. Anxiety in the town rises. Monsieur Michel, the concierge of Rieux's building, becomes mysteriously ill and despite all his good efforts, the doctor is unable to save him.

In the second "act," people's behavior begins to change as the city becomes increasingly isolated from the outside world. Rambert, a Parisian journalist, tries desperately to return to his lover in France, further emphasizing the underlying theme of separation. Cottard, who had earlier tried to commit suicide, is strangely satisfied with the general suffering. Grand, a minor bureaucrat, concentrates on the novel he wishes to write, rewriting the first sentence over and over. Father Paneloux expresses himself in a fiery sermon calling on the city's inhabitants to recognize their just punishment. Tarrou carefully chronicles daily events in the course of the epidemic while organizing sanitary squads.

Tarrou believes the plague is both universal and inescapable, yet he struggles on, saying "We must keep endless watch on ourselves lest in a careless moment we breathe in somebody's face and fasten the infection on him." Tarrou decides to become "a saint without God." Later, he too succumbs to the disease. Doctor Rieux brings him into his own home to nurse Tarrou through his last agonizing days.

As the crisis mounts, the death rate rises precipitously. It is hardly possible to bury all the bodies in common graves. There are protests and looting yet in the end most inhabitants seem resigned to their fate. There are no more illusions. People simply wait.

The fourth part covers the period from September to December (the plague broke out in April). Rambert finally finds a way out of the city but decides to stay and join in the struggle with Rieux and Tarrou. The protracted death of the official Othon's son provokes reflection on the suffering of the innocent. The priest, Paneloux, retreats into his faith, clutching his crucifix at the moment of death, having refused to call Rieux for help. Father Paneloux's death represents the ultimate failure of dogmatic and rigid Christian theology. In contrast, Rieux and Tarrou, though their humanitarian efforts, offer the possibility of a secular moral life based on a profound sense of human dignity. Tarrou and Rieux manage to sneak out of the city for a rejuvenating swim in the sea. By Christmas, the rats have returned and Grand survives the plague thanks to a new serum.

In the final act, the plague finally recedes, leaving behind its last victims. Tarrou dies, bequeathing his notebooks to Rieux. Cottard goes mad and is arrested. Rieux learns of his wife's death. The city finally opens its gates on a beautiful day in February and its inhabitants celebrate even as they recognize "the absurdity of their existence and the precariousness of the human condition." The hitherto unnamed narrator reveals himself to be Doctor Rieux, who asserts that the plague may someday return.

An epidemic of typhus in Algeria in 1941–42 inspired Camus's novel, as did the horrifying experience of World War II. In 1942, he wrote, "I want to express by means of the plague, the suffocation that we have suffered and the atmosphere of menace and exile that we have experienced." At one point he considered calling the novel *The Exiles*, reflecting his belief that human destiny is marked by the fear of suffering and death, imprisonment, exile, and separation. The underlying theme of separation is pervasive and seems to encompass the experience Camus and others underwent during the war. At the time, Camus was separated from his wife (who was born in Oran) and his native land.

A number of critics have pointed out the absence of women in the text or that those women who are present are but shadows. Rieux's mother, for example, is silent, much like Camus's own mother. In 1946 Camus wrote in his journal, "*Plague*: it is a world without women and therefore stifling [*irrespirable*]." The absence of women underscores the theme of separation. Love is evoked through their absence.

The Plague is essentially a philosophical exploration of the question of evil inspired by difficult times. Camus writes of "the brown plague," recognizable by the trains that bear its victims to their death, its mass graves, and crematoria. Moreover, he makes this evil everyone's problem and everyone's responsibility. Non-Marxist in orientation, the hero of the novel, Rieux, rejects class conflict in favor of a struggle that will unite all humanity. The novel thus marks an important stage in Camus's intellectual development in its affirmation of the human potential to live with one another in solidarity, not as strangers (see *The STRANGER*).

For Camus, one of the great problems of modern society is its belief in logic and ideologies that deny the human spirit. He thus focuses on lucidity and courage as the two essential human qualities. One may abandon oneself to defeat and see in punishment the hand of God, or else one can find dignity and freedom in rebellion and solidarity. Later, in *The FALL*, Camus mocks his own humanism.

An allegory for France under the German Occupation, Camus's depiction of evil differs from that of his contemporary, JEAN-PAUL SARTRE in *The FLIES*. For Sartre, the purpose was to oppose the injustice of a particular regime. He criticized Camus for confusing communism and Nazism. For Camus, the plague served as a metaphor for a more abstract and metaphysical concept of evil.

FURTHER READING

Aronson, Ronald. *Camus and Sartre: The Story of a Friendship and the Quarrel That Ended It.* Chicago: University of Chicago Press, 2004.

Brosman, Catharine Savage. *Albert Camus.* Detroit: Gale Group, 2001.

Cruickshank, John. *Albert Camus and the Literature of Revolt.* New York: Oxford University Press, 1960.

Mairowitz, David Zane, and Alain Korkos. Edited by Richard Appignanesi. *Introducing Camus.* New York: Totem Books, 1998.

PLANETARIUM, THE (*LA PLANÉTARIUM*) NATHALIE SARRAUTE (1959) The characters in this novel reveal a unifying theme in Sarraute's works. Each more or less anonymous character is but one part of a constellation, subject to forces of attraction and repulsion beyond their control and even their awareness. Each character exists as a form and image made by others, thus raising the ontological problem of existence within inexistence.

The plot of the novel, framed by the story of a family, is without real significance. Alain Guimier, newly married and poor, tries to convince his aunt to turn over a large apartment to him so that he can gain the approval of his in-laws. Alain has also written a thesis and wishes to launch a literary career, so he seeks guidance from an established writer, Germain Lemaire.

This thinly developed plot is the backdrop for an exploration not of the objective world, but of the subjective representation of it. A corresponding sense of anguish marks the work because for each character some apparently insignificant detail renders life unbearable because it erodes the sense of reality. A confluence of multiple, subjective visions of the world is expressed in broken dialogues that reveal the degree to which each character is isolated from the others.

The novel reflects themes Sarraute first introduced in *Tropismes* (1939). Influenced by the Russian writer Fedor Dostoyevsky, MARCEL PROUST, James Joyce, and Virginia Woolf, Sarraute seeks to reveal the unknown territory that exists on the margins of human consciousness. Considered one of the great examples of the NOUVEAU ROMAN, this work reflects Sarraute's interest in her own particular brand of psychological analysis, rather than in defining new forms of writing. Nonetheless, her skillful use of language and innovative approach to fiction set an example for other contemporary writers.

FURTHER READING

Barbour, Sarah. *Nathalie Sarraute and the Feminist Reader: Identities in Process.* Lewisburg, Pa.: Bucknell University Press; London: Associated University Presses, 1993.

Besser, Gretchen. *Nathalie Sarraute.* Boston: Twayne, 1979.

Jefferson, Ann. *Nathalie Sarraute, Fiction and Theory: Questions of Difference.* Cambridge, New York: Cambridge University Press, 2000.

Minogue, Valerie. *Nathalie Sarraute and the War of Words: A Study of Five Novels.* Edinburgh: Edinburgh University Press, 1981.

O'Beirne, Emer. *Reading Nathalie Sarraute: Dialogue and Difference.* Oxford, New York: Clarendon Press, 1999.

Ramsay, Raylene L. *The French New Autobiographies: Sarraute, Duras, and Robbe-Grillet.* Gainesville: University of Florida Press, 1996.

Temple, Ruth. *Nathalie Sarraute.* New York: Columbia University Press, 1968.

Watson-Williams, Helen. *The Novels of Nathalie Sarraute, Towards an Aesthetic.* Amsterdam: Rodopi, 1981.

POLEXANDRE MARIN LE ROY DE GOMBERVILLE (1629–1637)

In this lengthy novel (five volumes), Gomberville recounts the adventures of Polexandre as he travels in search of the island of princess Alcidiane. His journey takes him to the Canary Islands, the Antilles, and Mexico. Clearly influenced by contemporary travel accounts, Gomberville's narrative shows the interesting overlapping of history and geography so common to the early modern period. The text includes the entire history of Mexico as it was known at the time.

FURTHER READING

Wadsworth, Philip A. *The Novels of Gomberville, A Critical Study of Polexandre and Cythérée.* New Haven, Conn.: Yale University Press; London: Oxford University Press, 1942.

PONSON DU TERRAIL, PIERRE ALEXIS, VICOMTE DE (1829–1871)

Born in Montmaur, near the Alps, Ponson du Terrail went against his family's wishes that he become a naval officer and left for Paris where he fought in the mobile guard during the Revolution of 1848, attaining the rank of captain. His passion, however, was literature. After several false starts, Ponson du Terrail published his first significant work, *Les Coulisses du monde,* a novel on contemporary mores, in 1852. A series of novels in a wide array of genres followed: historical fiction, adventure, fantasy, pedagogy, and country tales. By far his most important work is *Parisian Dramas,* serial novels based on the adventures of the larger-than-life Rocambole, a romantic bandit (see ROMANTICISM), in revolt against society. The character was so successful that Ponson de Terrail continued Rocambole's adventures in 20 volumes that appeared in the Parisian press from 1859 to 1884.

Ponson du Terrail knew instinctively how to create an atmosphere of suspense. He created larger-than-life characters such as Rocambole, who became a favorite of contemporary caricaturists. Rocambole entered the annals of legend, his character even adapted to film. Immensely popular, Ponson du Terrail was an enormously prolific writer of popular serial novels, a genre that made its debut in the 1840s with such famous works as EUGÈNE SUE's *The MYSTERIES OF PARIS,* Frédéric Soulié's *The Devil's Memoirs,* and ALEXANDRE DUMAS's *The COUNT OF MONTE CRISTO,* among others.

Critics have frequently commented on Ponson du Terrail's overly simple style, grammatical errors, repetitions, and unbelievable plot twists. Yet this last quality is precisely what pleased his audience, avid for dramatic scenes and fantastic adventures; they did not even notice the incorrect grammar. Rather, his readers waited impatiently for the next installment of Rocambole's escapades.

One of the most famous serial writers of the 19th century, Ponson du Terrail was received into the Legion of Honor in 1866 at the same time as GUSTAVE FLAUBERT. When the Franco-Prussian war broke out in 1870, Ponson du Terrail left for Orléans, where he led a company of fighters. He then took refuge in Bordeaux, where he died of illness in 1871.

POSITIVISM Positivism is a 19th-century empirical philosophy that views sense perception as the only valid basis for human knowledge. In France, it is principally associated with Auguste Comte, who developed a philosophical system intended to supersede theology and metaphysics. Comte's system was built on a hierarchy of the sciences beginning with mathematics and culminating in sociology, a new discipline at the time. According to Comte, there are three stages in the development of each science: the theological, the metaphysical, and the positive or scientific. Positivism is reflected in the literary movements of NATURALISM and REALISM, as writers such as ÉMILE ZOLA and HONORÉ DE BALZAC sought to observe society from a rational, objective stance. The fascination with science that marks positivism is reflected as well in the novels of JULES VERNE.

POSTCOLONIALISM Postcolonialism is associated with Edward Said's *Orientalism* (1978) and *Culture and Imperialism* (1993), in which Said argues that Western literature depicting non-European societies has served as a means to maintain Western political and cultural dominance over others. Postcolonialism is an open-ended term referring to literature that explores the experience of former European colonies from the period of colonization to the present. The question of identity is central to these works. The theme of the center and periphery is equally significant, as indigenous writers grapple with the relationship between the two. One might assume that indigenous literatures share certain qualities because of the colonial experience. However, postcolonial discourse reveals both similarities and differences, and one might argue that difference is increasingly celebrated in these works.

Postcolonial discourse is also associated with POSTMODERNISM as the postmodern rejection of metanarratives is useful to postcolonial theorists, even as some of these writers accuse postmodernists of ethnocentrism. Postcolonial literature has, in fact enriched postmodern discourse. Some theorists have, for example, questioned the validity of describing the First and Second Worlds in terms of economic systems and the Third World solely in terms of the colonial experience, thus challenging a binary opposition such as one associates with structuralist theory (see STRUCTURALISM).

POSTFEMINISM Like POSTCOLONIALISM, postfeminism is both concerned with the question of identity and associated with POSTMODERNISM, although its relationship to the latter is, for some theorists, problematic. The term originated in the 1980s.

On one hand, FEMINISM may be viewed as seeking to allow women to participate equally with men in the project of ENLIGHTENMENT and in the related assertion of an autonomous, rational self. On the other hand, such a project may simply accept, if not reinforce, the traditional patriarchal order that makes man the standard and woman the other (see SIMONE DE BEAUVOIR). One might argue that the pluralism central to postmodern thought may create the conditions in which it is possible to celebrate difference, thereby rejecting the binary opposition male/female that places greater value on the male (see STRUCTURALISM).

Some postfeminist theorists argue in favor of completely reevaluating concepts of gender as can be seen, for example, in the writings of MONIQUE WITTIG. As theorist Jane Flax has argued, feminist theory, "like other forms of Post-modernism . . . should encourage us to tolerate and interpret ambivalence, ambiguity, and multiplicity as well as to expose the roots of our needs for imposing order and structure no matter how arbitrary and oppressive these needs may be." Like other forms of postmodernism, postfeminism challenges the notion of metanarratives that give meaning to the world and define our reality. Unfortunately, the problem of multiplicity lies in its potential to lean toward extreme relativism and to deny the political aims of feminist theory.

Like postcolonial theorists, some postfeminists argue that postfeminism offers an alternative view of reality that will enrich the broader postmodern discourse by introducing a perspective of the world as seen from the margins. As such, postfeminism may possess a transformative power to challenge the dualism of traditional Western thought. Moreover, the view of woman as a nomadic subject allows for the recognition and appreciation of differences between women and within woman.

POSTMODERNISM

In literature, philosophy, and the social sciences, the theory of postmodernism is the means of grappling with the postmodern condition of the late 20th and early 21st centuries. Characteristics of the postmodern world are globalization, later consumer capitalism, mass media, and postindustrial service-oriented economies. In literature postmodernism is associated with POSTSTRUCTURALISM. Postmodernist literature tends to deemphasize the individual in nonlinear narratives.

Postmodernism refers to a condition that arose after MODERNISM, but it is difficult to determine exactly when this transition took place. Modernism, or an expression of modernity, is associated with ENLIGHTENMENT rationalism, faith in the notion of an autonomous individual, science, and progress. With postmodernism, the notion of progress becomes obsolete.

The definition of Postmodernism was perhaps best articulated in France by the philosophers Jean-François Lyotard and Jean Baudrillard. Like poststructuralists, they rejected the concept of metanarratives that give meaning to reality. Following their lead, postmodernists celebrate disorder, disunity, and fragmentation, in contrast to modernism, which even in disorder seeks an underlying sense of unity. For postmodernists, there is no signifier/signified. Everything is a signifier, thus everything is relative. According to Baudrillard, in the postmodern world there are no originals, only copies or what he called "simulacra."

Postmodernism questions the traditional hierarchy of knowledge. It tends, moreover, to be political, as it also challenges power relations and certain core values of Western civilization such as the dominance of a white, male, European patriarchal order.

Early postmodernists such as Jacques Derrida and Michel Foucault focused on an analysis of discourse. Derrida in particular introduced the theory of deconstruction and the notion of defining discourse by what it is not rather than what it is. Postmodernism is associated with phenomenology and semiotics, the study of signs and symbols, their meaning, and their relationship to one another.

POSTSTRUCTURALISM

For poststructuralists, language is unstable, therefore there is no concrete truth to be found in literature. Poststructuralism accepts certain elements of STRUCTURALISM and Swiss linguist Ferdinand de Saussure's linguistic analysis but rejects the idea that one can determine meaning with any certainty.

Structuralism assumes that a truth exists in a metalanguage, be it linguistic, philosophical, or sociological. Structuralism thus rests on the conviction that the structure of language produces reality. For structuralists the understanding of reality is determined by language. The difference between structuralism and poststructuralism is the latter suggests there is no one relationship between signifier and signified.

Out of poststructuralism emerged deconstruction, whereby the reader focuses on what is *not* revealed in overarching structures. Rather than seeking coherence, deconstruction thus focuses on disunity. Deconstruction is principally associated with the theories of the philosopher Jacques Derrida, who argued that it is not possible to be objective about structures. Derrida developed the concept of deconstruction to reveal the ambiguities in the text. Poststructuralism denies the possibility of standing outside language. Rather, it focuses on the reader's engagement with the text. In Derrida's words, "there is no outside of the text."

Poststructuralism and deconstruction reexamine the concept of the self in relation to the binary oppositions central to structuralist thought. Derrida, for example, considers Western philosophy to be permeated with binary oppositional values, but he sees these, first, of all as permeable and, second, as a reflection of power relations. The goal of poststructuralists is to reexamine the relationship between binary pairs, for example, good/bad, masculine/feminine, and light/dark. Poststructuralism thus tends to be political in its concern over hierarchy and power relations. Poststructuralist works challenge the values and experience of Western civilization manifest in phenomena such as colonialism, racism, sexism, and homophobia. The primary critics of poststructuralism challenge the relativism in this approach to literature that denies truth. Poststructuralism is associated with POSTMODERNISM.

POURRAT, HENRI (1887–1959) One of the most famous regional authors, Pourrat never moved to Paris but remained in his native region of the Auvergne. The son of a grocer, Pourrat suffered from poor health to the point of being forced to abandon his studies in agronomy due to tuberculosis. From then on, he lived a sedentary life. A prolific writer, Pourrat was inspired by the rugged beauty of the Auvergne to explore the relationship between humans and nature and the power of both.

Pourrat's greatest work, GASPARD OF THE MOUNTAINS (1922–1931), published in four volumes, brought Pourrat fame. The series includes *The Chateau with Seven Doors or, Gaspard's Children* (1922), *The Beautiful Shepherdess's Auberge or, When Gaspard Returned to War* (1925), *The Pavilion of Love or, Gaspard and the Bourgeois of Ambert* (1930), and *The Tower of the East or, When Gaspard Ends the Story* (1931), and was published together in 1960 under the title *The Gallantries, Farce and Adventure of Gaspard of the Mountains*. In this work, Pourrat offers a rich depiction of rural life. The structure of the novel is built on the tradition of the *veillées,* evening gatherings where peasants come together to work and tell stories. In the course of 28 *veillées,* old Marie tells the tale of Gaspard and Anne-Marie. As a writer and ethnographer, Pourrat brings peasant life to literature in this popular novel.

Pourrat went on to publish *The Bad Boy* (1926), *Mountains and Marvels* (1934), and *Georges, or April Days* (1940). Other works that evoke life in the Auvergne are *Wild Gardens* (1923), *The Green Line* (1929), *To Touch the Earth* (1936), *November Veillée* (1927), *Orchard Gate* (1938), *The Man at the Spade*

(1939), *Christmas Wheat* (1942), and *Blessed Passion* (1946). In his description of peasants and peasant life, Pourrat recalls the writing of ALPHONSE DAUDET. Some critics have noted a tension between the voice of the writer and that of the people he describes.

Nonetheless, a profound sensitivity to oral culture marks all his works. Beginning in 1908 and over the next 50 years, Pourrat collected local tales that he transcribed with great poetic sensibility. His *Treasury of Tales* (1948–62) consists of 13 volumes of fables, legends, and oral traditions of the rural Auvergne that might otherwise have been lost to posterity. Pourrat described his collection of folklore as "the original mythology of the French," and his *Treasury* as "an attempt to understand something about the rural world that is in the process of disappearing, to grasp something that should not disappear." Pourrat once explained to a student about to interview some peasant women about folklore that he should never write down what they are saying in front of them or they will stop talking. Rather he advises the student simply to listen and to observe the "singing phrases that appear in these tales." Pourrat died in 1959 near the village where he was born.

PRECIOSITY Due to its elaborate and refined use of language, this 17th-century literary and cultural movement is often associated with the baroque. Born in the sophisticated culture of the *précieuse* salons, this movement promoted a Neoplatonic conception of love that emphasized the importance of women, best expressed in the novels of Madeleine de SCUDÉRY. Complex, sometimes hyperbolic language articulated distinctions and definitions in a range of human emotions, resulting in an idealization of manners based on gallantry (a manner of pleasing others).

Précieuse novels draw on the tradition of medieval COURTLY LOVE and ROMANCES in their idealization and respect for women, although the perfect union is spiritual rather than physical. The movement likewise bears the influence of HONORÉ D'URFÉ's *L'ASTRÉE.*

This protofeminist movement advocated divorce and free love rather than the subjection of women in marriage. Concerned with nobility of spirit rather than birth, the précieuses also challenged the strictly hierarchical structure of 17th-century society. They were often attacked by contemporaries for affectation, and the sharpest critique can be found in Molière's *Précieuses ridicules* (1659). Despite this negative assessment of preciosity, this literary and cultural movement's subtle analysis of love and language led to new movements in fiction, such as the psychological novel, an example of which is Madame de LAFAYETTE's PRINCESS OF CLÈVES.

PRÉVOST D'ÉXILES, ABBÉ ANTOINE-FRANÇOIS (1697–1763) Prévost is known today for his famous memoir novel, MANON LESCAUT. In the 18th century, however, Prévost was considered an important figure in ENLIGHTENMENT intellectual life and one of its greatest novelists.

Prévost lived an adventurous life. He entered the Jesuit novitiate twice, but his stay was interrupted each time by military engagements. In 1720 Prévost entered the Benedictine order, but the religious life did little, in the end, to protect him from scandal.

Prévost left France for Holland, where he published a satirical and libertine novel on the regency, *The Adventures of Pomponius (1724).* In 1728 he broke with his order and published the first two volumes of *Memoirs and Adventures of a Man of Quality.* At this point, Prévost attempted to live by his pen, devoting himself to literature and various escapades. Within 12 years he had produced his most important works, always in the midst of scandalous love affairs or financial crisis. Having traveled to England, Prévost was then forced to quit that country as well when he was suspected of wanting to marry his employer's daughter. His flight from England was followed by yet another period of turbulence and creativity, again in Holland. There he finished *Man of Quality,* inserting into it *The Story of the Chevalier des Grieux and Manon Lescaut,* and began his second great novel, *The English Philosopher or the Story of Mr. Cleveland* (1731). Prévost subsequently returned to the Benedictines in France and published a far more discreet novel, *The Dean of Coleraine* (1735). Unable to sustain a trouble-free life, Prévost was beset by more financial and personal problems from his ever imprudent behavior. As always Prévost's creativity did not suffer despite his difficulties. He went on to write two

historical biographies, *Marguerite d'Anjou* (1740) and *William the Conqueror* (1742), followed by three more short LIBERTINE NOVELS, *History of a Fair Greek* (1740), *Memoirs on the History of Malta* (1741), and *Memoirs of M. Montcal* (1741). Prévost then turned to translations and editing as a surer means of financial stability. With two exceptions, *Memoirs of an Honest Man* (1745) and *Moral World* (1760–64), Prévost gave up on fiction. He translated Cicero, and from the English, *The Voyages of Robert Lade.* This led him to continue working on travel literature, an immensely popular genre in the 18th century. From 1745 until 1759, at one volume per year, Prévost produced a *General History of Voyages.* This project precedes that of the ENCYCLOPEDIA but shares a similar purpose, to gather all knowledge of different continents and cultures. In this and other similar works written in this period we find the origins of anthropology as a discipline. Prévost also translated the English novelist Samuel Richardson's *Clarissa* and *Sir Charles Grandison,* along with lesser-known English novels. Richardson's works were extremely influential in the rise of the SENTIMENTAL NOVEL.

Prévost created a complex emotional world that reflects his frustrating search for liberty and an authentic interior life. His narrative structure is marked by complex intrigues, dramatic reversals, violence, and passionate desire, and may be linked to the baroque style in the arts. But Prévost's work also leads into ROMANTICISM. In all his works, Prévost emphasizes guilt and responsibility. Characters discover the paradoxical consequences of their own actions over which they have no real control. Prévost's characters find themselves the unwitting authors of their own unhappiness. Consequently, Prévost reveals the subjective nature of reality.

FURTHER READING
Frail, Robert J. *Realism in Samuel Richardson and the abbé Prévost.* Lewiston, N.Y.: E. Mellen, 2005.

France, Anatole. *The Latin Genius.* Translated by Wilfrid S. Jackson. London: John Lane the Bodley Head; New York: Dodd, Mead, 1924.

Kory, Odlile A. *Subjectivity and Sensitivity in the Novels of the abbé Prévost.* Paris, Brussels, Montreal: Didier, 1972.

Lazzaro-Weis, Carol M. *Confused Epiphanies: L' Abbé Prévost and the Romance Tradition.* New York: Peter Lang, 1991.

Segal, Naomi. *Unintended Reader: Feminism and Manon Les-caut.* Cambridge, New York: Cambridge University Press, 1986.

Smernoff, Richard. *L' abbé Prévost.* Boston: Twayne, 1985.

PRINCESS OF CLEVES, THE (LA PRIN-CESSE DE CLÈVES) MADAME DE LAFAY-ETTE (1678)

Nominally set at the court of Henry II, this historical novel was unusual at the time in that it focused on a period in history relatively close to the one in which it was written. Madame de Lafayette realistically describes life at court as a sort of fish bowl in which each participant's words and actions are closely scrutinized by everyone else. Beneath the surface of gallantry and luxury lies a society driven by ambition. Similar to CATHERINE DESJARDINS, for Madame de Lafayette, the moral and psychological truth of human interaction is more important than historical accuracy, although this was problematic to contemporary readers.

The story of the Princess of Cleves, or Mademoiselle de Chartres, as she starts out, is at first glance a familiar one. The plot is set in 1558 in the last years of Henry II's reign. The lovely and virtuous Mademoiselle de Chartres appears at court for the first time and stuns the elegant and gallant crowd with her remarkable beauty. The equally virtuous Prince of Cleves falls in love with her at first sight and is determined to make her his wife. They duly marry, although the princess respects but does not love her husband. She subsequently falls hopelessly for a dashing courtier, the duke of Nemours, who returns her affection with similar passion. The princess's mother warns her against the danger of giving in to a passion that is sure to stain her reputation and reduce her to the state of ordinary women and then dies, leaving her daughter to struggle on her own. Fearful that she may succumb to her weakness, the princess confesses to her husband that she loves another man and so wishes to retreat from society to protect her virtue and reputation. Despite her display of confidence in him, circumstances lead the prince to believe that his wife has betrayed him and he dies with a broken heart. Although she is free, the princess is tormented by the thought that, despite her innocence, she has caused the death of an hon-

orable man and the best of husbands. Although she maintained her reputation, the princess acknowledges the depth of her passion for a man who was not her husband and her mother's dying words have been imprinted on her heart. Moreover, she is sure that the duc's love for her could never last and fears the pain of one day discovering that he has left her for another. The princess thus refuses to marry her lover and retires completely from society only to die a few years later. Her pessimistic view that love can never triumph over the pettiness of human nature, jealousy, and infidelity was shared by some of her contemporaries in the last third of the 17th century.

The publication of *The Princess of Cleves* provoked a lively literary debate. The text bears elements of two other genres, the medieval ROMANCES and the novella of Italian origin. Contemporary critics argued that some of the more unbelievable episodes made *The Princess of Cleves* resemble these familiar genres. However, the nearly contemporary historical setting made the reader expect a realist novel.

Other writers contributed to a similar transformation in prose writing. Like Madame de Lafayette, Catherine Desjardins (Madame de Villedieu), and César Richard wrote shorter works in a more contemporary historical setting to comment on, if not critique, society. Because of its realistic setting, contemporary readers were disturbed when characters did not behave in ways that conformed to social norms, such as the princess's confession to her husband. The debate over "versimilitude" in prose was important in the 17th century. *The Princess of Cleves* was not believable to contemporary readers because of the heroine's actions. The text itself deliberately emphasizes the contrast between the heroine's behavior and that of the other women at court who also struggle, albeit in a different manner, with the problems of love and fidelity.

Some scholars have argued that the novel is a prototype for the 19th-century bildungsroman. The heroine's education is central to the novel and it takes place first under the tutelage of the princess's mother. After her mother's death, however, the princess must make her way alone, largely by means of self-analysis in terms of her feelings and behavior. This central aspect of the novel may draw from the tradition of the novella, such as MARGUERITE DE NAVARRE'S HEPTAMERON, in which a group of courtiers search for the truth about men and women, love and society. The difference here is that *The Princess of Cleves* comes to no universal conclusion. The princess's decision to retire from society can be applied only to herself.

The novel's emphasis on psychological analysis marks it as innovative. While MADELEINE DE SCUDÉRY also focused on the characters' self-analysis and on love, the analytical parts of her work were marginal to the narrative. In *The Princess of Cleves*, analysis is pivotal to the text. The action of the plot is less important than the character's internal debate and decision-making process.

FURTHER READING

Kaps, Helen Karen. *Moral Perspective in La Princesse de Clèves.* Eugene: University of Oregon Press, 1968.

Kuizena, Donna. *Narrative Strategies in The Princesse de Clèves.* Lexington, Ky.: French Forum, 1976.

Paulson, Michael G. *Facets of a Princess: Multiple Readings of Madame de Lafayette's "La Princesse de Clèves."* New York: P. Lang, 1998.

Tiefenbrun, Susan W. *A Structural Analysis of The Princesse de Clèves.* The Hague: Mouton, 1976.

PROUST, MARCEL (1871–1922)

Proust was born into a family of some means. His father, Adrien Proust, was a doctor, and his mother, Jeanne Weil, was from a wealthy Jewish family. Proust was consequently raised in a highly cultured environment, and his mother and grandmother introduced him to fine literature at a young age. He spent his summers in the countryside at an aunt's house and later by the sea in Normandy. These experiences provided landscapes for his later works. Legend has it that the fastidious, sickly, eccentric Proust retired from society to his cork-lined room in order to write. In fact, Proust continued to participate in the social and cultural life of Paris until his death.

From childhood on, he suffered from poor health due to asthma. Ultimately, complications related to asthma led to Proust's premature death. Not a particularly diligent student, after high school Proust completed a year of military service in Orléans. This experience inspired the episode at Doncières in his great novel REMEMBRANCE OF THINGS PAST. Proust received a degree in literature in 1892 and launched his career as a writer with a series of articles published in several literary journals. Because of his family's wealth, Proust lived a life of ease. At the same time, one has the sense of a growing self-awareness. Friends with other young men from privileged Parisian families, Proust was introduced into the sophisticated society of Parisian salons, where he met Robert de Montesquiou, a homosexual poet linked with symbolist writers (see SYMBOLISM) and the model for the baron de Charlus in Proust's novel. As of about 1892, Proust began to realize his own homosexual tendencies. His relationship with the composer Reynaldo Hahn was a source of real happiness in Proust's life.

A careful and thoughtful observer, Proust was increasingly convinced that literature and philosophy constitute the essence of life. His *Pleasures and Days,* whose preface was written by ANATOLE FRANCE, was published in 1896. It consists of a series of short stories on the vanity of worldly society that reflects the themes of illness and solitude. Between 1895 and 1899, Proust worked on what he hoped would be his first autobiographical novel, *Jean Santeuil,* but abandoned it, dissatisfied, in 1901. The manuscript was discovered 30 years after Proust's death in a hat box. In 1898, Proust openly supported Dreyfus, the Jewish officer falsely accused and convicted of treason in 1894, soliciting Anatole France's signature for a petition drawn up in the officer's behalf. Proust also attended ÉMILE ZOLA's trial after the publication of *J'accuse;* echoes of these momentous events in contemporary history find their way into *Remembrance.*

Proust's fascination with the world of art grew in the period 1899–1904, particularly after his discovery of English writer John Ruskin, thanks to Hahn's cousin, Marie Nordlinger-Riefenstahl. After abandoning *Jean Santeuil,* Proust turned to translations of Ruskin, and his study of the English scholar's work was crucial to the genesis and development of Proust's novel. By the end of 1899, he was already thinking of translating Ruskin's *The Amiens Bible.* After Ruskin's death, Proust made pilgrimages in his honor to Amiens and Venice. He later traveled to Holland. In the course of his journey between 1990 and 1902, Proust became increasingly convinced of his calling. In his published works on Ruskin, Proust outlined his notion of time regained, the cornerstone of *Remembrance.*

Devastated by his father's death in 1903 and that of his mother in 1905, Proust retired to a sanatorium before returning to Paris, where he settled on the Boulevard Haussmann. In 1907 Proust produced a series of articles, the most important of which was an extract from his future novel, "Impressions of the Road from an Automobile," that appeared in *Le Figaro.* In 1908 he wrote a series of short "pastiches" in which he examined the writings of BALZAC and SAINTE-BEUVE. The true beginning of *Remembrance* dates to that year, when Proust began writing fragments in a notebook given to him by a friend. His writing process was one of "montage," as he created characters and scenes that he was to connect only later. Proust viewed the structure of the novel as analogous to the architecture of a cathedral, again drawing on Ruskin.

The origin of *Remembrance of Things Past* lies in Proust's critique of the 19th-century writer and critic Sainte-Beuve, in particular, the latter's tendency to equate an author's biography with his work. For Proust, the important biography is that of the work itself, not that of its writer. *Against Sainte-Beuve* also contains the first version of the madeleine scene in which a pastry dipped into a cup of tea powerfully evokes a past memory, as taste and sensation together spark what Proust referred to as "involuntary memory." Involuntary memory reveals continuity between two experiences and, subsequently, one's own true essence. Ultimately, Proust deemphasized experience in favor of memory and perception. At first, Proust intended to write a work blending the essay and novel forms that would illustrate the relationship between art and everyday life. It was to conclude with a critique of Sainte-Beuve in the form of a conversation between Proust and his mother.

Proust offered his manuscript to the director of the *Mercure de France* in 1909. At that point, the novel had already surpassed the author's original plan and had begun to take on a life of its own. Both the *Mercure* and *Le Figaro* rejected Proust's manuscript. One reader simply could not see what it was about, especially after reading a lengthy account of tossing and turning in bed on a sleepless night. The novel appeared to lack purpose.

Despite the rejections, as of 1910 Proust was hard at work on his new project, centered on the character of Charles Swann. Four extracts were published in *Le Figaro* in 1912–13. But several publishing houses again refused his manuscript. Criticized by ANDRÉ GIDE, *Swann's Way* was finally published in 1913 by Bernard Grasset at the author's expense. An interview with the author published prior to the publication of *Swann's Way* explained the background of Proust's novel. At the time, Proust was living through the troubled period that was to inspire the "Albertine cycle."

In February 1913 Proust hired as his chauffeur Alfred Agostinelli, whom he had met several years before. Their tempestuous relationship dissolved when Agostinelli abruptly left and died shortly thereafter in a plane crash under the name Marcel Swann, the name he had chosen to use when he took his flying lessons. Proust was devastated by this loss. Agostinelli had left Paris with no warning, and Proust was subsequently unsuccessful in getting him to return. A number of literary critics have argued that Agostinelli was the model for Albertine in *Remembrance.* It has been argued that on more than one occasion Proust "translated" men in his life into the characters of women in his novel.

His health deteriorating, Proust continued to work through the next difficult years when financial problems necessitated a move from Boulevard Haussmann to a less expensive neighborhood. The second part of *Remembrance, Within a Budding Grove,* won the Goncourt Prize over ROLAND DORGELÈS's *WOODEN CROSSES* in 1919. Success inspired Proust to continue the project that was to occupy him and, in the end, wear him out, until his death in 1922 at the age of 51.

Often in poor health and weakened by his efforts, Proust finally completed the seven volumes that *Remembrance* comprises. *The Guermantes Way,* volume 1, appeared in 1920, *The Guermantes Way,* volume 2, and *Sodom and Gomorrah,* volume 1, in 1921. Shortly thereafter, Proust suffered an attack at a museum exhibition of Dutch paintings; he was looking again at Vermeer's *View from Delft.* It was the last exhibition he would see, and his experience inspired the death scene of the Bergotte character in his novel. He published

Sodom and Gomorrah, volume 2, in 1922 and then came down with pneumonia, to which he succumbed in that same year. Struggling to finish his novel even while deathly ill, Proust may be said to have sacrificed his life to his work. One day he announced to his housekeeper, Celeste, that he had finally written "the end." Proust's brother Robert, published *The Fugitive* (*Albertine disparue*) and *Time Regained* (*Temps retrouvé*) after his death.

The first correct edition of *Remembrance* was not published until 1954. *Remembrance* is not the work of sudden inspiration. It is rather a life's work whose genesis was long and complicated. It is, moreover, the history of both an era and of one man's consciousness in a subtle blending of fiction and reality. The identities of the narrator, Marcel, and Proust converge against the backdrop of the decline of the aristocracy and the rise of the bourgeoisie in the Belle Époque. Meanwhile, the characters of Vinteuil the musician, Elstir the painter, and Bergotte the writer offer a vision of a parallel reality in this human comedy that recalls on some level the works of Dante and HONORÉ DE BALZAC. Art emerges from life to reveal that literature *is* life.

All of Proust's works are marked by a deep interest in art and writing and convey the creative process at work. Proust rejected the notion that art is nothing more than aesthetics, rather, art allows one to rise above the mediocrity of daily existence to reveal "true life." A writer is thus more than a storyteller. By creating a distinctive style, the artist/writer restores the real, spiritual world. It is in the process of writing that the writer comes to understand and subsequently to reveal the essence of things. This did not prevent Proust from being a keen observer of the real world, and he was certainly able to depict the human comedy in a sometimes sharp and satirical tone.

Recurring themes are childhood, love, desire, jealousy, homosexuality, literature and art, time, and space. Moreover, Proust's famously long, sinuous phrases reflect his vision of the relationship between art and music. "It is impossible," he once wrote, "that a piece of music or a painting that moves us does not correspond to a spiritual reality." In the end, the reader is left wondering, has Proust written a novel or philosophy? Perhaps both.

Proust's works mark an important transition in the history of the novel. In the 1930s and 1940s, a period of SURREALISM and then political "engagement," not much attention was paid to Proust. In the second half of the 20th century, however, Proust's lifelong project of *Remembrance* was finally recognized as one of the greatest works of the 20th century and of all French literature. Proust inspired a new generation of writers that includes JEAN COCTEAU, JEAN GIRAUDOUX, and FRANÇOIS MAURIAC.

Most of Proust's work is written in the first person and emphasizes a subject through whom the reader is introduced to the world. Proust pioneers such modern themes in literature as the relativity of consciousness and the centrality of the subjective self, thereby laying a foundation for future writers such as those associated with the NOUVEAU ROMAN movement. Like Proust, they too sought to elaborate a theory of the novel from *within* the novel itself. NATHALIE SARRAUTE in particular found in Proust's concept of memory sensitivity what she referred to as tropisms.

FURTHER READING

Auerbach, Erich. *Mimesis.* Translated by Willard R. Trask. Princeton, N.J.: Princeton University Press, 1953.

Bersani, Leo. *Marcel Proust. The Fictions of Life and of Art.* Oxford: Oxford University Press, 1965.

Descombes, Vincent. *Proust: Philosophy of the Novel.* Translated by Catherine Chance Maskey. Palo Alto, Calif.: Stanford University Press, 1992.

Ellison, David R. *The Reading of Proust.* Baltimore: Johns Hopkins University Press, 1984.

Hayman, Ronald. *Proust: A Biography.* New York: Harper Collins, 1990.

Ladenson, Elisabeth. *Proust's Lesbianism.* Ithaca, N.Y.: Cornell University Press, 1999.

Landy, Joshua. "Proust, His Narrator, and the Importance of Distinction," *Poeticsa Today* 25, no. 1 (Spring 2004): 91–135.

Painter, George. *Proust's Narrative Techniques.* Geneva: Droz, 1965.

Shattuck, Roger. *Marcel Proust.* Princeton, N.J.: Princeton University Press, 1982.

Tadié, Jean-Yves, *Marcel Proust.* Translated by Evan Cameron. N.Y.: Viking, 2000.

White, Edmund. *Marcel Proust.* New York: Penguin, 1999.

PRUDENCE HAUTECHAUME Marcel Jouhandeau (1927) Set in the provincial town of Chaminadou—in fact Jouhandeau's native city of Guéret—*Prudence Hautechaume* is the story of a lonely, bored old woman who, at the end of a long day tending her shop, climbs to the attic from whence she spies on her neighbors. When Prudence commits a petty crime, the town takes its revenge by putting her in prison.

This is one of a series of novels in which Jouhandeau explores the truth of human nature as it is revealed through the prism of provincial life. As with *Pincegrain* (1924) and *Chaminadour*, *Prudence Hautechaume* caused some concern in Guéret as a number of the characters were recognizable to its residents. This work, along with Jouhandeau's other novels, received the praise of André Gide for its strength and beauty, as well as for its exploration of good and evil, a recurring theme in Gide's own works.

PSYCHOLOGICAL NOVEL Psychological novels explore the inner nature of a character or characters. The first psychological novel in the history of French literature is generally considered to be Madame de Lafayette's *Princess of Clèves* (1678). The psychological novel is often associated with the first half of the 19th century, however, and novels such as Constant's *Adolphe* and Stendhal's *The Red and the Black*. There is also a connection to Romanticism in these works, as the focus of the psychological novel is the individual's highly subjective experience. Early 19th-century psychological novels also bear the influence of Jean-Jacques Rousseau's *Julie*. Perhaps the best example of the psychological novel, nonetheless, came later with Proust's *Remembrance of Things Past*. Post-Freudian psychological novels often focus on the expression of the subconscious, sexuality, and repression.

QUEEN MARGOT (LA REINE MARGOT)

ALEXANDRE DUMAS (1845) Like Dumas's other historical romances, *Queen Margot* presents a compelling picture of love, hatred, intrigue, and murder. Set in 16th-century Renaissance France, the novel focuses on the character of Marguerite de Valois (Queen Margot), the daughter of Henry II and Catherine de' Medici. Its historical setting is the period of the French wars of religion. Charles IX, the present king, marries Marguerite to Henry of Navarre, her cousin and a Protestant, the future king Henry IV.

Political and religious tensions lead to the murderous Saint Bartholomew's Day Massacre in 1572, during which Margot supports her husband. Charles is poisoned. In the midst of powerfully dramatic events, Margot loses her lover, whose head she carries in her lap as her carriage takes her to its burial place. Like his other novels, Dumas is unsurpassed in his ability to draw on exceptional historical events to weave a tale that entrances his readers.

FURTHER READING

Bell, David F. *Real Time: Accelerating Narrative from Balzac to Zola.* Urbana: University of Illinois Press, 2004.

Hemming, F. W. J. *Alexandre Dumas: The King of Romance.* New York: Scribner, 1979.

Maurois, André. *Three Musketeers. A Study of the Dumas Family.* Translated by Gerard Hopkins. London: Cape, 1957.

Ross, Michael. *Alexandre Dumas.* Newton Abbot, Devon, England; North Pomfret, Vt.: David and Charles, 1981.

Schopp, Claude. *Alexandre Dumas: Genius of Life.* New York: Franklin and Watts, 1988.

Stowe, Richard. *Dumas.* Boston: Twayne, 1976.

QUENEAU, RAYMOND (1903–1974)

A poet and novelist, Queneau was born and raised in Le Havre. In 1920, he left his native city for Paris to study philosophy. An avid reader, Queneau possessed an encyclopedic knowledge that reflects a broad range of intellectual interests. By 1924 he had joined surrealist circles (see SURREALISM) with whom he remained connected until his break with ANDRÉ BRETON in 1929.

In 1932 Queneau traveled to Greece, where he began working on *WITCH GRASS* (1933), drawing from the 17th-century philosopher René Descartes's *Discourse on Method.* Queneau's purpose was the systematic reform and renewal of the French language in a style that combined mathematical rigor with humor and a spirit of innovation. Although the surrealists rejected the novel form per se, this work nonetheless reflects two questions central to surrealist thought and to Queneau's oeuvre: How is one to construct a novel? And what are the implications and possibilities of language? Queneau has been noted for his unusual ability to blend the rich texture of spoken French with precise, almost academic written language.

Queneau sought to imbue his writings with "linguistic realism" that reflects a desire for language to exist as a living thing, hence his interest in phonetic spelling. Moreover, Queneau conceived of novels as poems in which characters and situations "rhyme." *Gueule de Pierre* (not translated, 1934) centers on the astrological sign Pisces. It is the first in a series of novels that includes *Les Temps mêlés* (1941) and *Saint Glinglin* (1948). These novels reveal a theme that lies at the heart of all Queneau's works, the passage of time. As one character put it, "One never bathes one's feet twice in the same stream." For Queneau, time is circular or cyclical rather than linear. Moreover, the world as we experience it is illusory as is art. "People say that life is absurd. Nonetheless one lives. How do you reconcile yourself to that? How do you reconcile the absurd and life? By living absurdly, undoubtedly." Queneau's sense of humor tempers the underlying sense of tragedy in his works. Laughter becomes the answer to life's absurdity.

In 1937 he published his first collection of poems, *Chêne et Chien*, whose title in French reflects Queneau's interest in word games. In 1938, he joined Gallimard as an editor for whom he established and directed for 30 years the *Pléiade Encyclopedia*. The year 1938 is also when Queneau published *The Limon Children*, a novel in which the character of Chambernac sells his "Encyclopedia of Inexact Knowledge" to Raymond Queneau, who is writing a novel about a character named Chambernac.

Queneau was also a gifted storyteller who showed particular sensitivity in his depictions of female characters. At a time when many contemporary novelists were turning away from the evocation of emotions typical of popular literature, Queneau produced two powerful love stories, *Odile* (1937) and *A Hard Winter* (1939). *Odile* contains autobiographical elements that reflect, in part, on Queneau's break with Breton. Subtle autobiographical elements are evident in a number of Queneau's works. *A Hard Winter* is set during World War I in Le Havre.

Not all of Queneau's works, however, are autobiographical. *Pierrot My Friend* (1942) is the story of a whimsical character at a fun fair. *Skin of Dreams* (1944) is a cinematographic novel that explores the blurred boundaries between dream and reality, being and nonbeing. In 1947 Queneau published *Exercises in Style,* in which he retells the same insignificant anecdote in 99 different ways. In this work, Queneau demonstrates the creative power of language. He was supposedly inspired by a symphony that gave him the idea of *writing* variations on a theme. *Exercises in Style* was later adapted to the stage as a music hall show.

In 1947, Queneau published *We Always Treat Women too Well*, a parody of novels set during the Irish Revolution (1916–21). This work was followed by *The Intimate Journal of Sally Mara* (1950), in which a young Irishwoman keeps a journal in French in honor of her eccentric teacher.

After the war, Queneau undertook diverse activities that included writing songs and essays on painting and film. He also acted in small theatrical roles. In 1950 he published a series of essays on language in which he included a commentary on the absurdity of French orthography. Queneau himself often wrote phonetically, alternating between a humorous and an innovative approach with a highly literary style. His *Portable Cosmogony* (1950) brings together science and poetry in six songs written in verse, while in *Sunday of Life* (1952) the soldier Valentin Brû undertakes a Hegelian journey from innocence to self-knowledge. One of Queneau's greatest gifts, evident in this and other works, is his ability to merge the banality of everyday life with the fantastic. The real and the unreal are superimposed in works that depict various characters' search for wisdom.

Most of Queneau's characters are ordinary people—concierges, employees, and unemployed workers—whose heroism rises up from everyday life. The unexpected success of his novel ZAZIE IN THE METRO in (1959) brought Queneau to the attention of a broader reading public. In this famous work, Zazie is one of those ordinary characters who bring to life a fascinating world that lies, often unnoticed, right before our very eyes. In this work, Queneau confused language, the sexes, and provincial and urban culture.

In 1960, along with François le Lionnais and a few other friends, Queneau established OuLiPo, or the Workroom of Potential Literature. This group believed that writing is richer when constrained by arbitrary rules determined by the author, as if playing a game. Queneau's works reflect three important literary and philosophical movements of his time, surrealism, EXISTENTIALISM, and the *NOUVEAU ROMAN*. At the same time, his works stand apart.

Blue Flowers (1965) is arguably Queneau's master-piece. In this work, he recounts 700 years of medieval history. It is centered on the duc d'Ange, who dreams that he is Cidrolin who dreams in turn that he is the duc d'Ange. In this reflection on history, Queneau introduced dreams and psychoanalysis. The novel also reflects Queneau's interest in Eastern spirituality. His last novel, *Flight of Icarus* (1968), draws from the detective fiction genre to recount the story of a character from a novel stolen by a dishonest writer.

Queneau wrote 18 novels in addition to short stories, several volumes of poetry, translations of English and American literature, and hundreds of articles and book reviews. He has been called the "Rabelais of the twentieth century" and the "James Joyce of France." The concept of play is fundamental to an interpretation of his works. Play becomes the symptom of rebellion against the social order. He constantly toyed with language and its meaning. *The Limon Children,* for example, plays with the word for slime and lemon. The "glinglin" of *Saint Glinglin* signifies always and never. Zazie never enters the metro. The *"vol"* of *Le Vol d'Icare* (*The Flight of Icarus*) can mean both theft and flight.

There is a deliberate instability in Queneau's novels. He creates confusion, too, over names. Some characters have more than one name or do not know the names of other characters in the same novel. A name is thus not important to the essence of a person or object but arbitrary. In *Pierrot My Friend* Pierrot sets out on a trip to the south of France with two friends who are named but not identified. Only later does the reader discover, through their behavior, that Mésange and Pistolet are a chimpanzee and a wild boar. A number of Queneau's characters are orphans and therefore lack the history that allows for full identification. Finally, in *Sunday of Life,* Paul Bolucra's family name changes 50 times in the novel. The book opens with a disclaimer that alters the meaning of the one that often appears at the beginning of a film or television program: "As all of the characters in this novel are real, any resemblance to imaginary persons is accidental."

FURTHER READING

Bastin, Nina. *Queneau's Fictional Worlds.* Oxford, New York: P. Lang, 2002.

Guicharnaud, Jacques. *Raymond Queneau.* New York: Columbia University Press, 1965.

Hale, Jane Alison. *The Lyric Encyclopedia of Raymond Queneau.* Ann Arbor: University of Michigan Press, 1989.

Shorley, Christopher. *Queneau's Fiction: An Introductory Study.* Cambridge, New York: Cambridge University Press, 1985.

Stump, Jordan. *Naming and Unnaming: On Raymond Queneau.* Lincoln: University of Nebraska Press, 1998.

Thiher, Allen. *Raymond Queneau.* Boston: Twayne, 1985.

Velguth, Madeleine. *The Representation of Women in the Autobiographical Novels of Raymond Queneau.* New York: P. Lang, 1990.

R

RABELAIS, FRANÇOIS (1483–1553) François Rabelais, the prophet of laughter, is one of the great masters of French Renaissance prose. His epic work of several books recounting the adventures of the giants *Gargantua* and his son *Pantagruel* were written over a 20-year period. Together they ensure Rabelais' place in the annals of world literature.

A curious mixture of the grotesque, the bawdy, and the erudite mark all of Rabelais's works. A polymath, Rabelais was conversant in such diverse areas of knowledge as linguistics (he studied Greek, Hebrew, Arabic, and Latin), Latin and French literature, medicine, astronomy, botany, and mathematics. Rabelais is reputedly the first person to have performed a public dissection. Both a monk and a physician, Rabelais first entered a Franciscan monastery and later joined the Benedictines. He frequently satirized the monks and their way of life, although his thinking is profoundly influenced by the religious milieu in which he lived and worked.

Rabelais studied at the University of Montpellier, where he later taught, then traveled to Lyon, Paris, and Rome with the bishop du Bellay (an important influence on Rabelais' thought), finally ending up in Meudon, near Paris, until 1553, the year of his death. The full version of his fourth book was published in 1552. It raised a storm of protest among Protestants and Catholics alike.

Rabelais's epic of Gargantua and Pantagruel consists of at least four, books, GARGANTUA, PANTAGRUEL, BOOK THREE, and BOOK FOUR. In addition, most scholars agree that Rabelais wrote at least part of the posthumously published fifth book. In these works Rabelais proves himself a master of linguistic acrobatics, humor, satire, Renaissance humanist thought, theological disputes, and philosophical questions about the human condition. On the surface, these stories of the giants' adventures are comedies full of bodily functions and gross language, surprising to the modern reader. Beneath the surface lie many layers of interpretation. For this and other reasons, Rabelais's works are often difficult to understand. Serious treatment of contemporary political or religious questions is interspersed with comic anecdotes and obscene language.

In all his works, Rabelais promoted free speech and thought while challenging custom, authority, and their constraints. He was especially critical of the intellectual sterility of the Sorbonne and its scholastic method. Rabelais advocated a new approach to education and a reexamination of the basis for a life of faith in this world. While his books are loosely structured and overflowing with language and imagery, they are unified thematically.

The 16th century witnessed the rise of Protestantism and religious wars across Europe. This turbulent context is reflected in Rabelais's critique of religious extremism whether Protestant or Catholic. One of the great religious debates of the period focused on the issue of free will. Rabelais, influenced by the great humanist Erasmus, seems to argue in favor of free will (he was at least not in agreement with the Calvinist notion of predestination), while recognizing that human beings are victims of their own ignorance and superstition. Despite his own erudition, Rabelais's characters appear subliminally to challenge excessive faith in rationalism and objective knowledge as the basis for truth. One must also have faith in God. For Rabelais, extremist Protestants and Catholics alike lead people down the wrong path, either by denying free will or by placing excessive trust in relics and saints. In contrast, Rabelais argues that each individual must learn to live an active life in a space where reason and faith are not always clearly delineated yet are ever present.

Much has been said about the role of laughter in Rabelais's works. Drawing from classical texts, Renaissance writers viewed laughter as a particularly human gift. Humor could reveal something of the human condition because of its particularity and its universality. The medieval and early modern traditions in popular culture of carnival (*charivari*) and feasts of fools allowed ordinary people the opportunity to challenge power structures by depicting a "world turned upside down." It is in this context that we need to understand Rabelais's ease in combining serious philosophical inquiry with grotesque humor and elaborate descriptions of bodily functions.

Rabelais's works offer one of the best examples of the Renaissance concept of *copia,* a rich, abundant style of writing elaborated on by Erasmus in *On Abundance of Words and Ideas* (1512). Rabelais's versatility in exploring and exploiting language creates some of the wonder of his texts. His writings glorify the richness of eating and drinking, as well as language. This mixture of heterogeneous elements contributes to the difficulties readers and scholars alike have in coming to consensus on how the texts should be interpreted. Rabelais plays with language and perspective, exploring the facets of a given question from every side. The atmosphere of iconoclastic carnival that permeates his work influenced other Renaissance writers such as Bonaventure de Périers, Noël du Fail, and others who attempted to imitate Rabelais's style. His exploration of the human condition in a world of fantasy, comedy, and profundity marks his significance to French Renaissance humanism and the literary history of the West. While modern scholars continue to debate Rabelais's expression of Renaissance thought, writers of fiction such as Czech writer Milan Kundera acknowledge their debt to Rabelais's ability to break free from the constraints of literary traditions in order to articulate a new vision.

FURTHER READING

Bakhtin, Mikhail. *Rabelais and His World.* Translated by Hélène Iswolsky. Cambridge, Mass.: MIT Press, 1968.

Cave, Terrence. *The Cornucopian Text: Problems of Writing in the French Renaissance.* Oxford: Clarendon Press, 1979.

Febvre, Lucien. *The Problem of Unbelief in the Sixteenth Century: The Religion of Rabelais.* Translated by Beatrice Gottlieb. Cambridge, Mass.: Harvard University Press, 1982.

Screech, Michael. *Rabelais.* Ithaca, N.Y.: Cornell University Press, 1979.

RABOLIOT Maurice Genevoix (1925)

In this regional novel set in the Loire valley, Raboliot, a poacher, his dog Aïcha, his prey, and the land are all inextricably linked in a cycle of life. Raboliot's great enemy is the gendarme Bourrel, who represents an alien world of rules and laws. Raboliot's way of life is anathema to Bourrel, who hates the poacher. Ironically, Bourrel turns into the hunter and Raboliot the prey, to the point where Raboliot is forced to live in the forest like a beast, always on the run, cut off from his wife and children because of Bourrel's ceaseless pursuit. One day Raboliot receives permission to visit his family on the condition that afterward he leave the region permanently. When Bourrel comes upon them, Raboliot murders Bourrel in desperation.

The conflict between the two men is without mercy. Yet despite the theme of hatred and a violent end, the novel is marked by lyrical passages describing the countryside and its inhabitants in Genevoix's inimitable manner. *Raboliot* is his most famous novel, winning the Goncourt Prize in 1925. Genevoix writes in the classical tradition of the novel and of regional literature, treating his subjects with a sensitivity that recalls the works of George Sand.

FURTHER READING

Gerson, Stephane. "Une France Locale: The Local Past in Recent French Scholarship," *French Historical Studies* 26, no. 3. (Summer 2003): 539–559.

Ó Dúill, Micheál. *Three Twentieth-Century Novelists of Rural Life: Friedrich Griese, Pádhraic Óg Ó Conaire, and Maurice Genevoix.* Frankfurt am Main, Germany, New York: P. Lang, 1992.

RADIGUET, RAYMOND (1903–1923)

Precocious and talented, Radiguet began writing at age 15. The son of cartoonist Maurice Radiguet, Raymond was an excellent student but interested only in literature. A protégé of JEAN COCTEAU, he was also associated with avant-garde literary and artistic circles of Paris in the 1920s. Radiguet's first novel, DEVIL IN THE FLESH (1923), was considered scandalous for its depiction of an adulterous relationship between a young man and the wife of a soldier away at the front during World War I. His second novel, COUNT D'ORGEL'S BALL, inspired by MADAME DE LAFAYETTE'S PRINCESS OF CLEVES, also centers on an adulterous love affair in which a married woman, Anne d'Orgel, declares her love for François de Séryeuse to her husband, Mahout. The novel was published a year after Radiguet's premature death at the age of 20.

Both of Radiguet's novels shocked the contemporary reading public due to their subject matter. Both offer complex psychological analyses of love that recall the works of Madame de Lafayette and LACLOS. Radiguet, sought to imitate the moralist writings of the 17th and 18th centuries. His novels include maxims on life that serve as satirical commentary on contemporary society.

Radiguet was only 14 when he had an affair with a 24-year-old woman named Alice. That affair provided the essential material for his first novel. That same year he delivered some of his father's work to the publisher André Salmon, to whom Radiguet showed his own drawings, which were then published under the name Rajky. Radiguet subsequently found work as an editorial assistant for two weekly satirical journals. In 1918, Salmon introduced Radiguet to the poet Max Jacob, with whom the young man struck up a friendship that allowed him to frequent bohemian circles in Paris.

In 1919 Radiguet began associating with the early surrealists (see SURREALISM), occasionally contributing to their journal, *Literature.* That same year he also met Jean Cocteau, who further introduced Radiguet into literary society. Invited by Edith and Étienne de Beaumont to their evening gatherings, Radiguet mingled with their illustrious guests such as Cocteau, the composer Erik Satie, and the painter Pablo Picasso. The couple serves as the model for Mahaut and Anne d'Orgel in *Count d'Orgel's Ball.*

In his leisure time, Radiguet frequented the cafés of Montmartre, took drawing lessons, and met contemporary artists such as Amedeo Modigliani and Wassily Kandinsky. He also participated in the preparations for the first DADA activities in Paris, although he shortly thereafter criticized the movement. With Cocteau, Radiguet established an anti-Dada review. He also collaborated with Cocteau on the libretto for a comic opera, *Paul and Virginia,* for which Satie wrote the music and produced a musical, *The Wedding.*

In 1921 Radiguet met ANDRÉ MALRAUX, who like Cocteau admired the young writer's talents. He also met Beatrice Hastings, who had been Modigliani's model for the past two years. Theirs was a tempestuous relationship, due largely to Hastings's jealousy that Radiguet continued an affair with another woman despite his involvement with her.

In 1922 Radiguet entered into an agreement with the publisher Bernard Grasset, who offered him 1,500 francs monthly for *Devil in the Flesh* under the condition that he complete revisions of that novel and add an epilogue. Although Radiguet spent a good deal of time drinking, getting into debt, and associating with Cocteau's circle, he managed to complete the work and *Devil* was published in 1923. The novel was an instant commercial success due to Grasset's effective publicity campaign. Sales from *Devil* allowed Radiguet to move into more luxurious accommodations and to provide for his family.

Although former soldiers spoke out against the novel, *Devil* won the New World Prize. During a vacation spent with Cocteau and other friends, Radiguet completed *Count d'Orgel's Ball.* He had recently decided to put order in his life and give up his bohemian ways when he was struck by typhoid fever in December 1923. After his death, Cocteau undertook to edit the proofs of the novel. In 1952 Cocteau published an article "The Student Who Became My Teacher," in which he described Radiguet as a sort of talking plant. "In *Devil,* this plant recounts the mystery of its roots. In

Count d'Orgel's Ball this plant blooms—its perfume is the word."

FURTHER READING

Crosland, Margaret. *Raymond Radiguet: A Biographical Study with Selections from his Work.* London: Owen, 1976.

McNab, James P. *Raymond Radiguet.* Boston: Twayne, 1984.

RAMEAU'S NEPHEW (*LE NEVEU DE RAMEAU*) Denis Diderot (1762–1777)

Another of Diderot's posthumously published works (Diderot's original text was published only in 1891), *Rameau's Nephew* is a polythematic dialogue between "moi," the philosopher, and "lui," nephew of the famous composer Rameau. They first meet in a café at the Palais Royal in Paris and engage in a series of conversations on a wide variety of topics: the questions of genius, female education, immorality, the poor, flattery, and music, among others. Diderot's mastery of dialogue makes the novel innovative in form.

Rameau's nephew is an immoral, cynical, yet whimsical bohemian who has been cast out of his patrons' home because he has revealed their dissolute morals. Deliberately provocative, he denies friendship and virtue (both important to Diderot's conception of a moral society) and pokes fun at a worldly society that seeks out artists solely to make their dinner conversations more interesting. When Moi, the philosopher, challenges Rameau's Nephew on his cynical view of the world, suggesting that it is not possible to be happy if one leads an immoral life, Lui responds that it is society that has made him so. Lui goes so far as to condemn education as useless, instead praising the pursuit of a parasitic life as he recounts his experiences as a social buffoon.

Strikingly imaginative in form and language, *Rameau's Nephew,* like Diderot's other works of fiction, fits into his broader philosophical agenda. In this case, he returns to the notion of virtue as the basis for a happy society. Moreover, his emphasis on morality, virtue, education, and an unveiling of hypocrisy reflect elements of ENLIGHTENMENT thought more generally.

FURTHER READING

Burbank, P. N. *Diderot: A Critical Biography.* New York: Knopf, 1992.

MacPhail, Eric. "Diderot and the Plot of History," *New Literary History* 30, no. 2 (1999): 439–452.

Wilson, Arthur. *Diderot.* New York: Oxford University Press, 1972.

RAMUZ, CHARLES-FERDINAND (1878–1947)

Born in Switzerland, Ramuz earned a degree in literature at the University of Lausanne in 1900. Encouraged by his mother, Ramuz went to Paris, where he lived from 1900 to 1914, returning to Switzerland each year for vacations. He launched his career as a writer by publishing a collection of poetry in 1903 and then, in 1905, his first novel, *Aline,* which was nominated for but did not win the Goncourt Prize.

Throughout his many years in Paris, Ramuz retained a close connection to the region of his birth. *Jean-Luc* (1909), for example, is set in the Valais region of Switzerland. In *Aimé Pache, Vaudois Painter* (1911), and *The Life of Samuel Belet* (1913) Ramuz further developed his identity as a regional writer. In these two novels, the principal characters resemble the author in their discovery that their identity is closely linked to their provincial origins. Looking back on his years in Paris, in 1938 Ramuz wrote, "It is Paris itself that liberated me from Paris. It taught me its own language . . . [and] to make use of my own language." Ramuz marked the end of this first, fruitful period in his career with an essay, *Farewell to Many Characters* (1914).

During his years in Paris Ramuz sought to develop his poetic voice, one that would allow for a clear expression of his aesthetic vision. "My ideas come from my eyes," he said. "If I have teachers, they are painters." He found particular inspiration in the works of the painter Paul Cézanne and the composer Igor Stravinsky. For Ramuz, the artist or writer has a spiritual mission to promote a sense of unity between humankind and the natural world. In an essay, *Raison d'être* (1914), Ramuz further articulated his goals as a regional writer.

As Ramuz continued to develop his style, he gradually turned away from REALISM toward a deeper exploration of the relationship between the individual and the forces of destiny. Central themes of his later works are evil, as in *The Reign of the Evil One* (1915), war in *War in the Highlands* (1917), the end of the world in *Signs Among Us* (1919), miracles in *The Healing of Dis-*

ease (1917), and death in *Earth and Sky* (1921) and *The End of all Men* (1922). In these works, Ramuz's language changes in rhythm and syntax to approximate more closely spoken language. Such innovations did not always meet with the approval of readers expecting a more traditional narrative form.

The years following World War I were difficult for Ramuz, who felt isolated even in his native land. As of 1925, however, he began publishing with Bernard Grasset, which brought him back to the attention of the French reading public. Moreover, he earned the praise of contemporary writers such as Paul Claudel and Henri Barbusse. Ramuz also influenced other writers including Jean Giono, Henri Pourrat and Céline. The literary review *Cahiers de la quinzaine* devoted an entire issue to Ramuz in 1926. Ramuz's audience in Switzerland also began to expand. Between 1930 and 1932, he directed his own literary review, entitled *Today*.

The late 1920s and 1930s were the richest period in Ramuz's career as he produced Terror on the Mountain (1926), arguably his most powerful work, *Beauty on Earth* (1927), *Adam and Eve* (1932), *Farinet* (1932), *When the Mountain Fell* (1934), *A Boy from Savoy* (1936), and *If the Sun does not Return* (1937). In addition, Ramuz wrote essays on morals, aesthetics, and politics.

After winning the Romand Prize in 1930, Ramuz purchased a country house, La Muette. In 1936 he also won the Schiller Foundation's grand prize. In the last years of his life, Ramuz was touched by war and illness. He died in 1947, having published his last novel, *The Paper War* (1942), and two collections of short stories.

All of Ramuz's writings are firmly rooted in his native land, yet he managed to go beyond the limits of most regional novels to touch on the universal for all humankind. Opposed to bourgeois society and values, Ramuz promoted instead the peasant who lives by the rhythm and cycles of nature. That is not to say that humans' relationship with nature is easy. We confront the violence of nature, evil, and death, all of which menace the peasant community. If we foolishly attempt to challenge nature, we will only meet with a fall.

For Ramuz there is no sense to history. He was interested in neither communists nor fascists, nor in intellectual and literary trends. "Ours is a country too peaceful, one that has always remained distant from the great fevers that agitate Europe. We are a country not of arteries but of veins indolently carrying blood that is not fluid enough." Ramuz's distance from the major political questions of his day and contemporary intellectual movements, as well as his identity as a regional writer, have meant that he has often been underappreciated. However, certain innovative techniques such as his use of multiple narrative voices and perspective, along with his deemphasis of linear time, make him a precursor of certain characteristics associated with the nouveau roman.

RAVISHING OF LOL V. STEIN, THE (*LE RAVISSEMENT DE LOL V. STEIN*) Marguerite Duras (1964)

One night at a dance Lola Valérie Stein watches with horror as her fiancé, Michael, dances with another woman. Captivated, he follows her until dawn, abandoning Lol forever. Lol subsequently falls into a depression on the brink of madness. To save herself she marries and closes herself off from the world in an atmosphere of rigid order.

Back in the city where she was born, Lol runs into an old friend, Tatiana, and her lover, Jacques. Lol starts to spy on them, watching their amorous meetings from her hotel window. She eventually seduces Jacques and then, after spying on the couple one last time, falls asleep in a field of rye, finally liberated from her past.

In this work, Duras abandons the autobiography that defines many of her other works while keeping their central themes and style. Jacques is the narrator, yet the quality of his first-person narrative makes it apparent that it is neither Jacques nor an omniscient author who speaks, but an undefined observer. The theme of observer/observed is central to the work. As the novel progresses, a dialectical relationship develops between two similar acts of seduction. Lol, her fiancé, and Jacques are all equally fascinated by the power of seduction. Furthermore, it is only through an act of seduction that Lol can avoid falling into madness. Her sleep at the end of the novel is that of peaceful deliverance.

The novel may also be interpreted as a metaphor for the act of writing. The writer struggles against the constraints of language in an effort to reach that which exists *beyond* words. The notion of desire is connected to love and seduction, but also to language and the writing process. In *The Ravishing of Lol v. Stein,* Duras continues her exploration of a woman's emancipation, marking the author's contribution to feminist literature (see FEMINISM).

FURTHER READING

Andermatt, Verena. "Rodomontages of Le Ravissement de Lol v. Stein." *Yale French Studies* 57, Locus: Space, Landscape, Décor in Modern French Fiction (1979): 23–35.

Glassman, Deborah. "Fascinating Vision and Narrative Cure: Marguerite Duras's The Ravishing of Lol v. Stein," *Tulsa Studies in Women's Literature* 8, no. 1, Toward a Gendered Modernity (Spring 1989): 77–94.

REALISM   Literary theorist Erich Auerbach's seminal work of criticism, *Mimesis: The Representation of Reality in Western Literature* (1946), focuses on a gamut of writers that includes Homer, RABELAIS, MARGUERITE DE NAVARRE, CHARLES SOREL, ANTOINE FURETIÈRE, RESTIF DE LA BRETONNE, and DIDEROT. However, this literary and artistic movement is most often associated with the second half of the 19th century. Realism is opposed to idealism in its concentration on contemporary life and society. This movement had an impact on both literature and the visual arts. Gustave Courbet's painting *The Burial at Ornans* (1850–51) initiated the "realist battle" of painters and writers.

Champfleury (Jules Husson) first used the term *realism* in 1850. By 1857 he had brought together a series of articles defining this movement as one whereby the novelist should observe reality and describe the milieux he or she knows best. "The reproduction of nature by man will never be either a *reproduction* or an *imitation;* it will always be an *interpretation.*" The style is ideally neutral, even flat, but accessible to all readers.

In his preface to PIERRE AND JEAN, GUY DE MAUPASSANT suggested that the writer create a parallel reality that reflects the world. Consequently, realists drew their themes from everyday life, especially among the lower classes, hitherto ignored by most literary and artistic movements. Realism is also linked to contemporary political movements, especially the Revolution of 1848. Realists were primarily concerned with trends in modern life related to politics, economics, industry, and the rise of new social classes in the modern industrial age. Influenced by POSITIVISM, they were opposed to both ROMANTICISM and CLASSICISM.

GUSTAVE FLAUBERT's novel MADAME BOVARY is considered one of the first great realist works. Like the later naturalists, Flaubert sought documentation for his ideas. For example, the passage on Charles Bovary's disastrous treatment of the clubfoot reflects Flaubert's meticulous study of medical treatises. Flaubert thus sets the tone for "clinical observations" in literature. Characters in the modern realist novel tend represent a certain segment of social reality, such as Frédéric in SENTIMENTAL EDUCATION. One might argue that the realists' program was deepened by the naturalists, associated most frequently with their principal spokesman, ÉMILE ZOLA. The reading public sometimes found the realists' attention to sensation and banal or trivial circumstances disgraceful. The term *realist* eventually took on a pejorative meaning evoking the obscene, the vulgar, or the coarse.

RED AND THE BLACK, THE (LE ROUGE ET LE NOIR) STENDHAL (1831)   STENDHAL's novel *The Red and the Black,* famous for its trenchant criticism of 19th-century French society, bridges two centuries by laying a foundation for later writers such as MARCEL PROUST, ANDRÉ GIDE, ALBERT CAMUS, and the German philosopher Friedrich Nietzsche. Published in 1831, the novel did not receive much attention until the 20th century, when it earned its reputation as one of the great French novels of all time.

Stendhal usually referred to the novel as "Julien," the name of the principal character, who dominates the story. The plot was inspired by the real story of Antoine Berthet, a young man executed in 1828 after having shot his mistress in a local church.

The novel opens in the Jura region where Julien was born and raised. Julien is the third son of old Sorel, a peasant turned businessman who owns a sawmill. Unlike his brawny brothers, Julien has no interest in manual labor at the mill. He prefers books and dreams of glory. As a child, Julien once saw Napoleon's troops and this inspired a passionate admiration for the emperor. At first Julien wished to make his career in the army but chose the priesthood instead as a means of entrance into society.

With the support of the local priest, Julien is hired as tutor to the children of the mayor, M. de Rênal. Once installed in the Rênal household, Julien is overwhelmed by the beautiful and indulgent Madame de Rênal. Yet full of awkward pride, he refuses to accept a gift from her. Julien's innate pride attracts Madame de Rênal, who almost without realizing it, falls in love with him. Certain misunderstandings, moreover, fuel her passion.

When rumors begin to fly, Julien is obliged to leave town, and he subsequently sets off for the seminary in Besançon. Once there, he is unhappy as he has nothing in common with his coarse and unrefined peers. His only comfort is the abbé Pirard, who procures Julien a position in Paris as secretary to the marquis de la Môle. Julien's character and ambition assure his rise in Parisian high society. He is fascinated by Mathilde, the marquis's daughter, and eventually they become lovers. When Mathilde discovers that she is pregnant, she convinces her father to bestow property, a title, and a position in the hussars on Julien prior to their marriage. But just when Julien appears to be at the height of his fortune, a letter arrives from Madame de Rênal denouncing him for his past behavior. Angry, Julien returns to his hometown of Verrières and fires at his former mistress in the church.

Julien is subsequently arrested and condemned to death. Beyond attempted murder, Julien's crime is, in part, that of being a peasant who sought to rise above his station. In prison, he realizes he has always loved Madame de Rênal. He also finally understands the truth of himself and "never was this head so poetic as at the moment it was to fall."

Julien is buried in the countryside as he desired. Echoing the legendary gesture of Queen Marguerite de Navarre, Madame de Rênal carries Julien's head in her carriage as she follows the funeral procession. She dies three days later.

Julien embodies Stendhal's notion of "energy." Talented, manipulative, and yet susceptible, Julien is equally capable of success and weakness. He inspires esteem in others but lacks experience. His education nourished Julien's ambition but ultimately did not give him the means to satisfy it.

The FRENCH REVOLUTION of 1789, overthrowing the monarchy, made Julien's upward mobility possible. Julien's initial success is due, in part, to the breakdown of the OLD REGIME social order. A secret admirer of the great military leader Napoleon Bonaparte, Julien seeks to imitate his model's meteoric rise in society. The two principal routes of social mobility in the postrevolutionary period were through the army and the church. The red of the novel's title signifies the military and LIBERALISM associated with the early Napoleon, while the black refers to the church and conservatism.

The Red and the Black is partly the story of Julien's education in the social power of language. More than once he manages to transform himself through language, behavior, and dress, revealing another underlying theme: appearance versus reality. The falsity of appearance over meaningful reality (perhaps intellectual, perhaps emotional) is connected to dress, manners, ritual and ceremony, and language.

The novel is full of contrasting images. The clash between reform (liberalism) and reaction (conservatism) is mirrored in the themes of gender and class conflict. Even the female characters illustrates a juxtaposition of compliance and rebellion. The novel's two principal female characters are Julien's lovers. While Madame de Rênal embodies ROUSSEAU's ideal woman (Julien was a great admirer of Rousseau), Mathilde de la Môle, like Julien, rebels against her family's social position, only she is born an aristocrat. Mathilde is also a character with "energy." Proud and scornful of the society in which she finds herself, Mathilde courageously recognizes that she will eventually succumb to its demands.

Though the experience of Julien, Stendhal examines the issue of change in the 19th century: social, economic, and political. At one point in the story, Stendhal describes the novel as "a mirror carried along a road," yet the movement of the traveler results in a disjointed and broken image, revealing the uncertainty and anxiety that characterizes the modern era. The two great literary movements of the 19th century emphasizing the tension between the individual and society in this period of change are ROMANTICISM and REALISM. *The Red and the Black* reflects both.

Julien is a typical romantic hero whose story is one of self-discovery and self-definition. As he seeks to satisfy his ambitions, Julien suffers from an internal conflict between reason and passion that is one of the hallmarks of romanticism. Drawing on 18th-century thinkers who argued that knowledge is derived from the senses, Stendhal developed his own theories on the energetic and passionate individual's search for self-expression and fulfillment through the processing of emotional experiences. Through the character of Julien, the novel thus promotes this philosophy that is called Beylism (drawn from Stendhal's real name, Henri Beyle).

At the same time, Stendhal is considered one of the founders of realism. The novel depicts both a psychological and a social reality. The subtitle for *Le Rouge et le noir,* Chronicle of 1830, places this novel squarely in its historical context. The year 1830 was one of revolution. In July 1830 the reactionary monarch of the BOURBON RESTORATION, Charles X, attempted to dissolve the national assembly's Chamber of Deputies, limit the franchise, and increase censorship. Society's response was a series of demonstrations and revolts leading to the abdication of the king. The Revolution of 1830 was a victory for French liberals and the wealthy middle class, who benefited most from industrialization and modernization. Stendhal wrote that politics in a novel is "like a pistol shot in the middle of a concert." Yet politics and history (even when the author plays with chronology) are woven into the fabric of this text. Like Stendhal's other great novel, *The CHARTERHOUSE OF PARMA, The Red and the Black* brings to life the spirit of an age.

FURTHER READING
Auerbach, Erich. *Mimesis: The Representation of Reality in Western Literature.* Translated by Willard R. Trask. Princeton, N.J.: Princeton University Press, 1953.
Fineshriber, William H. *Stendhal the Romantic Rationalist.* Philadelphia: R. West, 1977.
Keates, Jonathan. *Stendhal.* New York: Carroll and Graf, 1997.
May, Gita. *Stendhal and the Age of Napoleon.* New York: Columbia University Press, 1977.

REDEMPTION CHANTAL CHAWAF (1989) The
principal character of this powerful novel, Charles de Roquemont, is obsessed with his brutal murder of a

former lover. He lives in Paris and spends his time alone, creating works of abstract art by cutting up the pages of a book with a razor, carefully gluing each word separately onto a piece of cardboard. One day he meets Olga in the Park Monceau. She is equally isolated by her writing and her desire for love. Olga senses Charles's madness yet is irresistibly drawn to him, even when their relationship becomes increasingly painful and disturbing.

The majority of Chawaf's works explore the meaning of what it is to be a woman. In *Redemption,* she moves beyond the world of feminine sensations and a writing of the body associated with the *écriture féminine* of feminist literature (see FEMINISM), to explore the writing of the psyche. In this novel, Chawaf enters the world of madness with a brutal and violent lyricism. She nonetheless retains her particular feminist style in the rhythm of her writing and her abundance of images that recall the works of HÉLÈNE CIXOUS and MARIE CARDINAL. The novel also contains descriptive passages of Canada and the stifling summer heat of the Park Monceau that are supremely poetic.

FURTHER READING
Benstock, Shari. "From the Editor's Perspective: Women's Literary History: To Be Continued," *Tulsa Studies in Women's Literature* 5, no. 2. (Autumn 1986): 165–183.
Davidow, Ellen-Messer. "The Philosophical Bases of Feminist Literary Criticisms," *New Literary History* 19, no. 1, Feminist Directions (Autumn 1987): 65–103.
Gilbert, Sandra M., and Susan Gubar. "Sexual Linguistics: Gender, Language, Sexuality," *New Literary History* 16, no. 3, On Writing Histories of Literature (Spring 1985): 515–543.
Jardine, Alice A., and Anne M. Menke. "Exploding the Issue: 'French' 'Women' 'Writers' and 'The Canon'?" *Yale French Studies,* no. 75, The Politics of Tradition: Placing Women in French Literature (1988): 229–258.
Kraemer, Don. "Abstracting the Bodies of/in Academic Discourse," *Rhetoric Review* 10, no. 1 (Autumn 1991): 52–69.

REMEMBRANCE OF THINGS PAST (IN SEARCH OF LOST TIME, À LA RECHERCHE DU TEMPS PERDU) MARCEL PROUST (1913–1927) From childhood on, all of Proust's life experience led inevitably toward *Remembrance of Things Past* (the title is also translated *In Search of Lost*

Time). Famous for its long, sinuous phrases, the novel reflects Proust's vision of art and music as life. Recurring themes are childhood, love, jealousy, homosexuality, literature, art, time, and place. *Remembrance* is both the last great novel of the 19th century and the first experimental novel of the 20th, laying the foundation for innovations in fiction that we now accept as commonplace.

The novel consists of seven volumes. *Swann's Way* (1913), *Within a Budding Grove* (1918), *The Guermantes Way* (1920–1921), *Sodom and Gomorrah* (1921–1922), *The Captive* (1923), *The Fugitive* (1925), and *Time Regained* (1927). At first, Proust envisioned only three volumes, but as time went on the novel grew of its own accord. Some critics have argued that the novel lacks a sense of unity. The author, however, compared his work to a cathedral of "rigorous construction." Digressions are a part of its subtle architecture.

With the exception of "Swann in Love," a section of *Swann's Way,* the novel is written in the first person, thus introducing into literature "I" that is the prism through which the reader encounters the world, philosophy, and an understanding of the relationship between art and life. On its most basic level, *Remembrance* is the story of one man's discovery of his calling as a writer. Only in the last volume, after a long and painful quest to discover a means of self-expression, does the narrator understand that it is in his own life that he can find the source of creativity and its voice. He ultimately finds salvation in the act of writing, experiencing a sense of deliverance and renewal in his discovery of "true life." The narrator's journey to self-understanding is not one of action, but of internal reflection.

In *Swann's Way,* the narrator recalls his childhood, the atmosphere that reigned in his family—including Françoise the servant with her peculiar ideas and ways, his grandmother's rules and principles—and all that made up the provincial world of fictional Combray. He seeks to recapture the source of joy that accompanies the sensations inspired by the taste of pastry dipped in a cup of tea. Ultimately, through the memory of this apparently insignificant act, a past life is reborn. Swann recalls, for example, the worldly Odette de Crécy who marries M. Swann, the neighbor at Combray who represents Parisian society.

Incorporated into this volume is the section "Swann in Love," the only portion of the novel written in the third person. It is the story of Swann's passion for Odette and the suffering that passion ultimately leads to. Swann had long been a part of high society. Through Odette, he is introduced to wealthy bourgeois circles. He begins to attend gatherings at the home of Monsieur and Madame Verdurin, with their pretensions of competing with the beau monde. In his descriptions of their salon, Proust offers comical and pointed depictions of the principal characters associated with up-and-coming members of the bourgeoise.

Swann falls madly in love with Odette and frequents the Verdurins in hopes of seeing her there. He is aware of the difference in their social status but, because of his passion, is incapable of restraining himself. Like the author, Swann has a strong aesthetic sensibility. He envisions Odette as a Botticelli-like beauty. However, after a brief period of rather uncertain happiness, Odette begins to withdraw and becomes increasingly indifferent to Swann's attentions.

Swann suffers in consequence as if he were experiencing a physical illness. One day, at a social gathering, he hears a bit of music he has always associated with Odette and realizes suddenly that the music does not signify his love for her, but rather he associates Odette with the music. Swann is overcome with sadness at the recollection of a happier time. Tortured by jealousy, he realizes too that their love is dying. He marries Odette nonetheless, scandalizing the narrator's parents, who disapprove of Swann's wife and their way of life. At this point the narrator takes up again his recollection of childhood in Combray.

In *Within a Budding Grove,* the narrator looks back on his sadness and disillusionment with Gilberte, who withdrew from him and whom he eventually forgets. He thinks back too on his fascination with the actress Berma (modeled on Sarah Bernhardt), on holidays spent with his grandmother by the sea in Normandy (at the fictional Balbec), and of the group of young girls he encounters there. He is particularly drawn to Albertine Simonet. While at Balbec, the narrator also meets Elstir, the painter, and his grandmother comes across an old friend at the hotel, Madame de Villeparisis, an aristocrat who is the aunt of the duc de Guermantes and a great aunt of Robert de Saint-Loup, with whom the narrator strikes up a friendship. This volume also introduces the duc de Guermantes's brother, Palamède, the baron de Charlus.

In *The Guermantes Way* we learn that the Guermantes family château is near Combray. The narrator's family also moves into an apartment in Paris that is next to the Guermantes' impressive home in the capital. As a result, the duchesse de Guermantes, Oriane, comes to dominate the narrator's thoughts, inspiring him with passion. The narrator also comes across the baron de Charlus again, who seeks to establish some as yet uncertain connection with him. The narrator aspires to enter aristocratic society and is eventually successful, thanks to the duchesse. He is also troubled in this volume by the death of his grandmother and the beginning of his relationship with Albertine.

The fourth volume, *Sodom and Gomorrah,* focuses on the narrator's experience in various milieux, the baron de Charlus's peculiar behavior, and aristocratic social circles, which the narrator depicts with a blend of irony and sympathy. The high point of this volume is a gathering at the home of the princesse de Guermantes. In his emotional life, the narrator is torn between Albertine with her strange habits (she represents Sodom) and the baron de Charlus (Gomorrah). The narrator, like Swann before him, is tormented by jealousy.

In *The Captive,* the narrator, despite his suffering, decides that Albertine should live with him. Unfortunately, this affords him only increasing unease. Even though Albertine has become his prisoner, she continues to evade him. Meanwhile, the narrator continues to frequent aristocratic society. He not only witnesses but assists in the downfall of the baron de Charlus. When he discovers the power of music to captivate the senses, he considers breaking off his relationship with Albertine, but, when he arrives home, Françoise informs him that Albertine is already gone.

In *The Fugitive,* formerly entitled "Albertine Disappeared," the narrator learns in a telegram that Albertine has died in a car accident and is overcome with his tragic loss, anguish, and jealousy that lingers on even after she is gone. The narrator again encounters Gilberte, whose mother, Odette, has since married the baron de Forcheville. The narrator subsequently travels to Venice, where he learns that his old friend Saint-Loup has married Gilberte. Once more, the narrator struggles to overcome his pain and suffering and to find a sense of inner peace.

In the last volume, *Time Regained,* the narrator returns to his childhood home at Combray. There he dreams of his past. This volume also includes a portrait of Parisian society during World War I. One day, the narrator spends a morning at the home of the princesse de Guermantes where, in a moment of epiphany, he realizes his vocation as a writer.

The origin of the work as a whole lies in an earlier literary project, Proust's plan for a critique of SAINTE-BEUVE—in particular that writer's equating of an author's biography with his oeuvre. For Proust, the one important biography is that of the author's work, not the author's life. Nonetheless, readers continue today to look for Proust in the narrator of *Remembrance.* Certainly the author drew openly from his own life experience, but only to create something that, as a work of art, transcends daily life. Herein lies Proust's philosophic and aesthetic vision. Life and literature, fiction and reality merge to create a new metaphysical reality.

The reader knows little about the narrator, who is only rarely referred to as Marcel. He is almost anonymous, yet through him the reader gains access to the world. On one level a chronicle of the belle époque, the novel is also something more. The narrator's development makes it a novel of apprenticeship as well, in the sense that he must learn to recognize the deceptive nature of society and love. Swann blazes the trail, but the narrator, in the end, surpasses his initial guide.

The entire plot is the story of one man becoming a writer, as Proust probes the depths of the narrator's consciousness, the object of the work. There are numerous characters with different personalities, but we see them all through the narrator's eyes. Gilberte, Saint-Loup, Charlus, the duchess of Guermantes, and Albertine are all perceived by the narrator as signs whose meaning he must discover. Charlus, for example, whom the narrator surprises with his male lover Jupien, signifies for the narrator homosexuality, which he sees as one point on a continuum of human sexual relations. Albertine's lesbian relations constitute the other end of the continuum.

The story of the writer's vocation is what ultimately gives a sense of unity to this immense work. The narrator first senses his calling at Combray, as he strolls along the Guermantes Way. Over time, worldly society and love emerge as obstacles to his vocation, whose deceptive nature he must recognize before he can satisfy his creative drive. Solitude and the profound depths of the self are the source of creativity, and they stand in opposition to society, which obscures the self. Proust's exploration of the obstacles to the language and life of the spirit—society and love—offer him the opportunity to engage in what is almost a psychological study of contemporary bourgeois and aristocratic society and manners. Moreover, love is a malady. Love is defined principally by absence, which gives birth to a painful desire for possession of the beloved that can never be realized. The impossibility of complete possession of the beloved—Odette for Swann, Gilberte or Albertine for the narrator, Rachel for Saint-Loup, and Morel for Charlus—engenders jealousy, the "shadow of love" that poisons the soul.

The famous episode of "involuntary memory," triggered by the taste of the madeleine pastry dipped in tea, resurrects the narrator's childhood experience and hints at an ideal world. Encounters and relationships with the novel's artists—Bergotte, Elstir, and Vinteuil—suggest the possibility of a transcendent world of creativity that exists beyond the self and society. Certain sensations inspire the narrator to write but, for a long time, he is unable to comprehend them. He even considers giving up his desire to become a writer, until the episode of involuntary memory that takes place at the end of the novel. At this point, the narrator finally understands the secret of involuntary memory as the foundation for creative expression. A sensation, in the present, recalls an old impression, and the combination transcends both to become something new, "something uncommon with both the past and the present that is much more essential than either one." The concept of involuntary memory makes its appearance in the works of CHATEAUBRIAND, NERVAL, and Baudelaire as well, but only Proust carries the idea to its logical conclusion. It is, moreover, the fundamental principle of his work.

In developing his theory, Proust draws on the philosophies of Arthur Schopenhauer and Friedrich Schelling, as art and music become the supreme activities of the spirit that give meaning to one's existence in the world. "It is impossible," he writes, "that a piece of music or a painting that moves us does not correspond to a spiritual reality." Thus the many passages devoted to the arts throughout the novel lay the foundation for the narrator's final apprehension of the truth. Art and literature constitute "our real life . . . reality as we have felt it to be."

The symmetry of the novel rests on the two poles of Combray, one at the beginning of the novel and the other at the end, which is also a beginning. In addition, there are the two "ways," two directions one could take for a walk and that represent two ways of life, the aristocratic and the bourgeois. These finally come together in *Time Regained*. At the end of the first volume, Marcel says that time cannot be regained; at the end of the last volume he says that it can. The novel's originality lies in part in its treatment of time. It is, furthermore, modern in its themes of homosexuality, the relativity of consciousness, and the centrality of the subjective self. Finally, *Remembrance* is also supremely modern in its elaboration of the theory of the novel within the novel.

FURTHER READING

Acunan, André. *The Proust Project.* New York: Farrar, Straus & Giroux, 2004.

Auerbach, Erich. *Mimesis.* Translated by Willard R. Trask. Princeton, N.J.: Princeton University Press, 1953.

Bersani, Leo. *Marcel Proust. The Fictions of Life and of Art.* Oxford: Oxford University Press, 1965.

Descombes, Vincent. *Proust: Philosophy of the Novel.* Translated by Catherine Chance Maskey. Palo Alto, Calif.: Stanford University Press, 1992.

Ellison, David R. *The Reading of Proust.* Baltimore: Johns Hopkins University Press, 1984.

Hayman, Ronald. *Proust: A Biography.* New York: Harper Collins, 1990.

Ladenson, Elisabeth. *Proust's Lesbianism.* Ithaca, N.Y.: Cornell University Press, 1999.

Landy, Joshua. "Proust, His Narrator, and the Importance of Distinction," *Poetics Today* 25, no. 1 (Spring 2004): 91–135.

Painter, George. *Proust's Narrative Techniques.* Geneva: Droz, 1965.

Shattuck, Roger. *Marcel Proust.* Princeton, N.J.: Princeton University Press, 1982.

Tadié. *Marcel Proust.* Translated by Evan Cameron. N.Y.:
  Penguin, 2000.
White, Edmund. *Marcel Proust.* New York: Penguin, 1999.

RENART, JEAN (C. 1180 TO 1250) Few
details of Jean Renart's life have passed down to us. He
was born near Senlis and had contact with the courts
of Flanders and Champagne. *The KITE* is addressed to
the count of Flanders and *The ROMAN DE LA ROSE OR
GUILLAUME DE DOLE* to Milon de Nanteuil, provost of the
cathedral chapter of Rheims. Not only does Jean Renart reveal his patronage connections to these important
personages, but he shows us something of daily aristocratic and bourgeois life. For this reason he has been
called one of the first realists.

In contrast to CHRÉTIEN DE TROYES's fantastic adventures, magic is absent from Jean Renart's stories and
they are situated in a believable and often identifiable
contemporary setting. His audience consisted of the
people surrounding those to whom he dedicated his
ROMANCES As he tells his stories, which are, as near
as we can tell today, his own, he makes reference to
a body of literature that he assumes his audience is
familiar with: the story of Tristan and Iseut, the lays
of MARIE DE FRANCE, the Arthurian legends of CHRÉ-
TIEN DE TROYES, and the works of Ovid, the Roman
poet, among others. Jean Renart asserts his authorial
voice, explaining his innovative inclusion of songs
into the text, stating that his tales may be both recited
and sung. The addition of intercalated songs into the
story has made Jean Renart of interest to modern literary critics. He asserts that they are included to make
his romances more interesting to his avowedly aristocratic audience. Jean Renart thus invented a new literary genre, the "lyric anthology," a form imitated by
subsequent medieval authors. HÉLISENNE DE CRENNE's
The TORMENTS OF LOVE, for example, draws from the
tradition of medieval romances such as we find in the
works of Jean Renart.

FURTHER READING
Beekman, Pauline. *Jean Renart and His Writings.* Paris: Droz,
  1935.
Durling, Nancy Vine. *Jean Renart and the Art of Romance:
  Essays on Guillaume de Dole.* Gainesville: University Press
  of Florida, 1997.

RENÉ FRANÇOIS-RENÉ DE CHATEAUBRIAND (1802)
René was first published as a part of Chateaubriand's
five-volume *GENIUS OF CHRISTIANITY,* in which he strives
to demonstrate that "Christianity has changed the
passions by changing the basis of vice and virtue."
Chateaubriand repeatedly juxtaposes earthly ills and
heavenly joys. Unhappiness in this life may lead to
sadness but there is always the possibility of future satisfaction.

The feeling of emptiness that is a consequence of
civilization leads inevitably to melancholy. Chateaubriand's romantic theory (see ROMANTICISM) on the
"vagueness of the passions" is best articulated in his
words "we are disillusioned before we have enjoyed."
He believed that the problem with contemporary society is derived from passions that have no object.

René is the epitome of the melancholy romantic
hero who may symbolically represent the demise of the
French aristocracy as a result of the FRENCH REVOLUTION
and the Napoleonic era. Moreover, Chateaubriand was
critical of the French Revolutionary government for
closing the monasteries, a haven for the kind of person
who is lost in modern society.

The reader knows from the introduction to *ATALA*
that René came to America to escape an unhappy life in
France. There he married an Indian woman but lives,
nonetheless, alone, away from society. He is troubled
by a deep-seated unhappiness revealed in the confession of his life, made to Chactas, a blind elderly chief
whom we meet in *Atala* as well, and the priest, Father
Souel. René clearly suffers from a "moral illness," diag-
nosed by the two older men as pride.

René begins his story with his childhood, in which the
reader detects parallels to Chateaubriand's own experience. René lives with an austere father and a loving sister. Haunted by thoughts of death, René seeks comfort
in sublime nature (another romantic theme) by climbing
Mt. Etna. Unfortunately, the experience does nothing to
resolve his existential crisis. René's one great comfort
is his sister, Amélie. Separated from her, René contemplates suicide. Always sensitive to her brother's moods,
Amélie realizes this and hurries to join him, making him
promise not to end his life. She then abruptly leaves.

Shortly thereafter, René receives a letter from Amélie saying that she is entering a convent. René tries

to stop her but does not succeed. She wishes him to accompany her to the altar. The situation is complicated by the tender feelings that René and Amélie share for each other. More than the natural love between a brother and sister, this is passionate love, most clearly on the part of Amélie. Some critics have argued, however, that René can be interpreted as a Cain-like figure, responsible in this case for his sister's incestuous love. Despairing, René leaves for America. Amélie dies caring for a sick nun. In a slightly difference context, the denial of the female is also a theme in *Atala* and *The* MARTYRS.

Chateaubriand acknowledges the influence of the 18th-century writer ROUSSEAU on his works, particularly in his approach to nature and feeling. Through his focus on these themes, Rousseau's works lead into romanticism. Chateaubriand is himself a romantic writer. At the same time, he attempts to create an antidote to the romantic "disease" by describing it in detail. René, the alienated and isolated hero who succumbs to his emotions, is much like the German writer Johann Wolfgang von Goethe's character Werther (*The Sorrows of Young Werther*).

The danger of tragic love is that it may isolate one from society. Chateaubriand, much like Goethe, rather than curing the disease of romanticism, created a fashion. He was as influential a writer in France as Goethe in Germany or Lord Byron in England. SENANCOUR's Obermann and CONSTANT's Adolphe bear the influence of René as well as the works of other great romantic writers such as ALFRED DE MUSSET, ALFRED DE VIGNY, VICTOR HUGO, and ALEXANDRE DUMAS (père). Chateaubriand's influence is particularly strong on STENDHAL's *The* RED AND THE BLACK.

FURTHER READING

Bouvier, Luke. "How Not to Speak of Incest: Atala and the Secrets of Speech," *Nineteenth-Century French Studies* 30, nos. 3 and 4 (2002): 228–242.

Call, Michael J. *Back to the Garden: Chateaubriand, Senancour and Constant.* Saratoga, Calif.: Anma Libri, 1988.

Maurois, André. *Chateaubriand: Poet, Statesman, Lover.* Translated by Vera Fraser. New York: Greenwood Press, 1969.

Smethurst, Colin. *Chateaubriand, Atala, and René.* London: Grant and Cutler, 1995.

RENEWAL (REGAIN) JEAN   GIONO (1930)

Renewal is the last in Giono's *Pan* trilogy that includes *Hill* and *One of the Baumugnes.* The theme of renewal refers to the regeneration of a Provençal village called Aubignane. At the opening of the novel, Aubignane has only three inhabitants: Panturle the poacher, Gaubert the blacksmith, and Mamèche, an old woman who lost her husband and child not long after her arrival in Aubignane. The other residents have left the village because the terrain is so arid. One would think the village completely abandoned if not for the sounds coming, from time to time, from Gaubert's forge.

One day, at his son's invitation, Gaubert also leaves. A bleak winter follows for Panturle and Mamèche. Mamèche then tells Panturle that he needs a wife if the village is ever to come to life again. Although he agrees in principle, it is difficult for Panturle to imagine. Living the life of a poacher has made him wild and uncivilized.

Mamèche then disappears at the same time as Gédémus the grinder is passing by with his assistant, a young woman named Arsule. As they cross an immense, barren, windy plateau near the village, they suddenly see a strange dark figure leaping in the grass. Unnerved, they head for Aubignane, where Panturle, now all alone, has been thinking about women. When he falls, Arsule is suddenly there to save him. She leaves the grinder for Panturle and quickly succeeds in taming him. Panturle, no longer a savage, begins to cultivate the land and, in the first year, produces the best wheat in the region. Drawn by his success, another family moves into the village. Arsule is expecting a child. Life in the village will go on because of Mamèche's sacrifice on the plateau. In this novel of rebirth, Giono anticipates contemporary environmental movements. The story was adapted to film by Marcel Pagnol in 1937.

FURTHER READING

Ford, Edward. *Jean Giono's Hidden Reality.* Lewiston, Me.: E. Mellen Press, 2004.

Goodrich, Norma Lorre. *Giono: Master of Fictional Modes.* Princeton, N.J.: Princeton University Press, 1973.

Lawrence, Derek W. "The Transitional Works of Jean Giono," *French Review,* Special Issue, no. 1 (Winter 1970): 126–134.

Redfern, W. D. *The Private World of Jean Giono.* Oxford: Blackwell and Mott, 1967.

Smith, Maxwell A. "Giono's Cycle of Hussar Novels," *French Review* 35, no. 3 (January 1962): 287–294.

RESIDENTIAL QUARTER (LES BEAUX QUARTIERS) LOUIS ARAGON (1936)

This second novel in Aragon's *Real World* cycle explores the tense relationship between two brothers, Armand and Edmond, who grew up in a provincial bourgeois household. Armand, the principal character, disappointed by the mediocrity of provincial life, goes to Paris before the World War I and discovers there the tense relationship between labor and capital. His brother, Edmond, a medical student, has an affair with Carlotta, the mistress of Quesnel, an older businessman who subsequently draws Edmond into his questionable dealings. In the end, Edmond is blackmailed by a policeman.

Meanwhile, Armand is living in misery. When he is hired to work in a factory where the workers are on strike, his apprenticeship in life continues as he discovers the harsh realities of the workers' existence. In the end he joins the strikers and their union.

Following his surrealist period (see SURREALISM), Aragon became increasingly militant as his devotion to the communist cause grew. Aragon's works are closely connected to his politics, as is evident in this novel focusing on the exploitation of workers and the corrupt nature of bourgeois capitalist society.

FURTHER READING

Adereth, Maxwell. *Elsa Triolet and Louis Aragon: An Introduction to Their Interwoven Lives and Works.* Lewiston, New York: E. Mellen Press, 1994.

Brosman, Catrherine Savage. *Malraux, Sartre and Aragon as Political Novelists.* Gainesville: University of Florida Press, 1964.

Caute, David. *Communism and the French Intellectuals, 1914–1960.* New York: Macmillan, 1964.

Duruzoi, Gerard. *History of the Surrealist Movement.* Translated by Alison Anderson. Chicago: University of Chicago Press, 2002.

Kimyongur, Angela. *Socialist Realism in Louis Aragon's Le Monde Réel Series.* Hull, England: University of Hull Press, 1995.

RESTIF DE LE BRETONNE, NICOLAS-EDMÉ (1734–1806)

The son of a wealthy peasant family, Nicolas Restif de la Bretonne did not begin his career as a writer. In 1750 he was apprenticed to a printer in Auxerre. Having become a journeyman in 1755, Restif de le Bretonne left for Paris, where he worked in the royal printing press of the Louvre and other printers' shops. This is where he also began to write.

In 1760 Restif returned to Auxerre to marry Agnés Lebègue. The couple lived separately for the most part and divorced in 1794. The early years together were hard ones for the family as Restif tried both to write and to print in order to make ends meet. Restif was still working as a printer when he wrote his first novel at the age of 33. His first success came in 1755 with the publication of *The Perverted Peasant,* which assured his reputation as an author. One of his best works, this novel went through 42 editions in England. In 1780 he fell in love with a young neighbor named Sara and began to write *The Perverted Peasant Woman,* which appeared in four volumes in 1784. From his relationship with Sara also comes *Sara, or the Last Adventure of a Forty-five-year-old Man* (1783).

Restif de la Bretonne was an astonishingly prolific writer of 203 volumes, many of which he printed himself. The material for his writing was drawn from his own experiences as a child in Auxerre, as a worker in Paris, and his libertine lifestyle. Much of his writing may be characterized as cynical and LIBERTINE. Both his life and his works are marked by sensuality. Despite his prolific production, his questionable character, scandalous works, and financial difficulties made him somewhat of a marginal character. By the end of his life he had sunk into an obsession with incest. He managed to live quietly during the revolutionary years in Paris, having built his own press in the rue de la Bûcherie. He died in poverty in 1806.

The ambiguity in his works arises from his position on vice. Restif de la Bretonne was driven by licentiousness but also concerned with morality. This marks him as different from SADE, who was simply fascinated by the question of evil. Restif's pornographic novel of 1798, *Anti-Justine,* echoes some of the principles found in Sade's works but differs in depicting eroticism without cruelty. As in NERCIAT's FELICIA, passion and pleasure are promoted as beneficial, and necessary parts of life.

Perhaps surprisingly, Restif de la Bretonne was also a great admirer of ROUSSEAU, similarly opposing the purity of rural life with the corruption of the city. Restif de la Bretonne was possibly the only 18th-century writer to come from the lower classes whose lives he depicted realistically and out of concern for social justice. His writings reflect his interest in prison and hospital reform, the problems of urban life and the working poor, along with the promotion of agriculture. He contributed to the development of the modern novel through his ability to observe society critically, making him comparable to BALZAC and ZOLA, whose realist novels so mark 19th-century fiction (see REALISM).

Toward the end of his life Restif de la Bretonne turned to autobiography with *The Life of My Father* and *M. Nicolas*. This genre allowed him to explore the evolution of an individual divided between a desire for moral purity and an irrepressible sexual drive. He appears to have attempted to rival Rousseau's *Confessions* as he unveiled his love life. Today Restif de la Bretonne is recognized for his place in the 18th-century tradition of the libertine novel, as well as for offering an interesting stage in the development of autobiography.

FURTHER READING

Coward, David. *The Philosophy of Restif de la Bretonne.* Oxford: Voltaire Foundation and the Taylor Institute, 1991.

Porter, Charles. *Restif's Novels or An Autobiography in Search of an Author.* New Haven, Conn.: Yale University Press, 1967.

Poster, Mark. *The Utopian Thought of Restif de la Bretonne.* New York: New York University Press, 1971.

RICCOBONI, MARIE-JEANNE (1714–1792)

Madame Riccoboni was a sentimental novelist (see SENTIMENTAL NOVEL) whose work was recognized during her lifetime, no small accomplishment for a woman of the 18th century, a period in which both women and the novel form were regarded with suspicion. The majority of her works are EPISTOLARY NOVELS written from the perspective of a woman and focusing on male/female relationships.

According to DIDEROT, Madame Riccoboni wrote "like an angel." Even Rousseau gave her a positive assessment. RESTIF DE LA BRETONNE, who was at least as suspicious of women writers as Rousseau, also praised her work. Her extraordinarily popular novels were published well into the 19th century and were recommended by subsequent authors such as the German writer Johann Wilhelm von Goethe, STENDHAL, and BALZAC.

Madame Riccoboni, née Laboras de Mézières, was born in Paris. In 1735 she married Antoine François Riccoboni, an actor and dramatist. Madame Riccoboni had attempted to act herself but was unsuccessful. As a novelist, however, she produced a number of popular novels such as *The LETTERS OF MISTRESS FANNY BUTLERD* (1757), *The History of the Marquis du Cressy* (1758), *Milady Juliette Catesby* (1759–60), and *Ernestine* (1765), considered by the philosopher Jean-François La Harpe to be her greatest work. She also produced three separate series of letters: *Adelaide de Dammartin* (1766), *Elizabeth Sophie de Vallière* (1772), and *Milord Rivers* (1776). Madame Riccoboni also wrote a novel based on the English novelist Henry Fielding's *Amelia,* as well as a conclusion to MARIVAUX's *LIFE OF MARIANNE*.

Madame Riccoboni started life with several counts against her. She was born out of wedlock to her father's mistress (he was later excommunicated for bigamy) and raised in a convent. Her relations with her mother were strained and Madame Riccoboni chose marriage to escape the tension of the family home. Unfortunately, the husband she chose was violent and unfaithful. The couple separated in 1755.

Following a literary discussion during which Marivaux's style was described as inimitable, Riccoboni decided to write a conclusion to *The LIFE OF MARIANNE* that reportedly surprised even Marivaux himself. It was published in 1761. This experience launched Riccoboni's literary career. Her first big success was *Fanny Butlerd,* an epistolary novel that may have been inspired by her own experience of abandonment by a lover who preferred to make an advantageous marriage. *Fanny Butlerd* was followed by the *Marquis du Cressy* (1758) and *Juliette Catesby* (1759).

Riccoboni may be described as an early feminist as her novels emphasize the themes of male infidelity, female vulnerability, and social hypocrisy. Riccoboni's correspondence with LACLOS, published in 1787, reveals her frustration with his character the Marquise de Merteuil, who manifested that masculine egoism that Riccoboni attacked in her novels. Riccoboni lost her royal pension with the fall of the monarchy and died in 1792.

FURTHER READING

Cook, Elizabeth Heckendorn. *Epistolary Bodies: Gender and Genre in the Eighteenth-Century Republic of Letters.* Palo Alto, Calif.: Stanford University Press, 1996.

Sol, Antoinette-Marie. *Textual Promiscuities: Eighteenth Century Critical Rewriting.* Lewsiburg, Pa.: Bucknell University Press, 2002.

Stewart, Joan Hinde. *The Novels of Madame Riccoboni.* Chapel Hill: University of North Carolina Press, 1976.

RINGUET, PHILIPPE (1895–1960)   Ringuet is the pen name of Philippe Panneton, a Quebecois writer who earned a degree in medicine in Montreal. One of the most important French Canadian writers of the first half of the 20th century, Ringuet practiced medicine intermittently from 1920 to 1940. He also traveled widely and had a broad range of intellectual interests. Along with Louis Francoeur, Ringuet produced a series of humorous pastiches of several contemporary French-Canadian writers.

Canada, its land and people, are central to Ringuet's works. His first novel, *Thirty Acres,* appeared in 1938 and earned the praise of critics who saw in it the height of the *"roman du terroir,"* or rural novel, in Canadian literature. This novel evokes the painful existence of a rural family that disintegrates as it confronts the forces of modernization upon entering the world of the urban working class. Ringuet also published a collection of short stories and tales in which one senses the power of destiny to crush the individual in a manner that recalls *Thirty Acres.*

Le Poids du jour (1949), in contrast, recounts Michel Garneau's rise in Montreal society. At the same time, the novel shares the theme of migration from the countryside to the city and the sense of loss that accompanies this transition from one mode of existence to another. Perhaps Ringuet's most powerful work, this novel offers a sympathetic portrayal of characters struggling against fate. The plot is set against a backdrop of 50 years of Canadian history, and its style stands in sharp contrast to the nostalgic tone of certain French-Canadian novels associated with writers such as LOUIS HÉMON.

After his mother's death, Michel discovers that he is the illegitimate son of this woman he so loved and his godfather, who has taken Michel under his wing in Montreal. Disappointed and disillusioned, Michel decides to focus his energy on attaining success. Ringuet makes use of Michel's experiences as he rises in society to offer a sharp critique of the crass materialism and philistinism of Montreal's high society. There is a marked contrast between Michel's generation and the next that tends toward greater intellectual depth and culture. Eventually Michel attains a sense of peace through his daughter with her broader, more humanitarian vision of the world. In all of his writings, Ringuet sought to create a sense of what it means to be North American. "We are not Europeans," he said. "We are and must endeavor to be Americans."

RIPENING SEED, THE (LE BLÉ EN HERBE)   COLETTE (1923)   Phil and Vinca grow up side by side. As they enter adulthood, Phil is the first to abandon the ways of childhood as he is drawn into his first love affair. With her woman's instinct, Vinca realizes that she needs Paul and so she follows him, spies on him, and waits for him. Paul, too, experiences some feelings of unease. Tormented by regret that is none too clear, he attempts suicide. Vinca offers herself to him to save Paul.

The underlying theme surfaces in a number of Colette's works, the notion that there is no age for passion. A girl of 15 is already a woman, sensitive and delicate. *The Ripening Seed* is written to celebrate the awakening of womanhood.

FURTHER READING

Dormann, Geneviève. *Colette: A Passion for Life.* Translated by David Macey and Jane Brenton. New York: Abbeville Press, 1985.

Eisinger, Erica Mendelson, and Mari War McCarty. *Colette: The Woman, the Writer.* University Park: Pennsylvania State University Press, 1981.

Huffer, Lynn. *Another Colette: The Question of Gendered Writing.* Ann Arbor: University of Michigan Press, 1992.

Kristeva, Julia. *Colette.* New York: Columbia University Press, 2004.

Lottman, Herbert. *Colette: A Life.* Boston: Little, Brown, 1991.

Marks, Elaine. *Colette.* Westport, Conn.: Greenwood Press, 1981; 1960.

Thurman, Judith. *Secrets of the Flesh: A Life of Colette.* New York: Knopf, 1999.

ROBBE-GRILLET, ALAIN (1922–)

It can be argued that Alain Robbe-Grillet transformed contemporary French literature. The publication of *Erasers* (1953) and *The Voyeur* (1955) met with resistance, though the latter won the Critics Prize. Nonetheless, Robbe-Grillet's new theory of the novel, articulated in *For a New Novel* (1963), had a tremendous impact on the way in which fiction came to be conceived and written.

Almost a legendary figure, Robbe-Grillet was the leader of the NOUVEAU ROMAN (new novel) school, a group of writers who rejected both neoconservatism and Sartrean political engagement (see JEAN-PAUL SARTRE) to explore new ways of writing fiction. The group includes such writers as MICHEL BUTOR, SAMUEL BECKETT, NATHALIE SARRAUTE, MARGUERITE DURAS, and CLAUDE OLLIER, among others.

Robbe-Grillet rejected the traditional novel form associated with writers such as HONORÉ DE BALZAC, arguing that REALISM, both natural and psychological, is simply not possible to attain in literature. Robbe-Grillet believed that the traditional Balzacian novel failed in its goal to describe reality precisely. Moreover, the traditional novel places humankind squarely at the center of things. With his "new realism," Robbe-Grillet showed how we share the world equally with the objects that surround us. Influenced by the philosopher Edmund Husserl, for whom objects exist outside any system of reference or thought, Robbe-Grillet's novels demand that we see the world as it really is, without coherence or any larger meaning. They thus emphasize objects within a materialist aesthetic vision. Hence Robbe-Grillet attempted to "treat objects with geometric precision," the same approach he would take in regard to his characters. In the 1960s and 1970s, Robbe-Grillet turned to film, in which the narrator's voice and the camera are conscious of their simultaneous proximity to and distance from the objective world.

Robbe-Grillet was raised in Brittany and Paris. He suffered deportation to Germany as a worker during World War II. After the war, Robbe-Grillet first worked as an agronomic engineer at the National Institute of Statistics. He began writing his first novel, *Regicide,* in 1948. Initially rejected, the novel was not published until 1978.

His second novel, *Erasers* (1953), draws from Sophocles' *Oedipus Rex.* In this work, inspector Wallas is ordered to investigate a murder that, in reality, has not yet taken place. Events make it such that he becomes the murderer he has been looking for. Moreover, the man he murders is his presumed father. Even time is symbolically affected as the hands on Wallas's watch stop at the hour of the murder. The plot thus both opens and closes at the same moment. As in many of Robbe-Grillet's works, there are minutely detailed descriptions that paradoxically produce a sense of uncertainty despite their precise nature. The relationship between Wallas's mind and the strange world he inhabits is somehow solidified by an object, the eraser that he compulsively purchases. The frequent references to the legend of Oedipus signify Wallas's failure.

The appearance of *The Voyeur* (1955) provoked a great deal of discussion among literary critics. It won the Critics Prize despite the fact that the jury was deeply divided. It is the story of a commercial traveler who fails to reveal to the reader the sexual crime he committed while on his rounds. The famed critics Maurice Blanchot and Roland Barthes both wrote articles in response to the publication of *Le Voyeur.* Blanchot focused on the sexual crime that provides the framework for the novel, whereas Barthes concentrated on Robbe-Grillet's descriptions and style.

JEALOUSY (1957) is a novel in which a husband describes the world around him with false objectivity as he is, in fact, interpreting all that he observes. In a number of subsequent works of literature and film, Robbe-Grillet made use of spy novels, comic strips, publicity, and erotic literature to write *The House of Assignation* (1965), *Project for a Revolution in New York*

(1970), *Topology of a Fantom City* (1976), *The Golden Triangle* (1978), and *Djinn* (1981), among others. These works are full of strange and mysterious organizations, diabolical doctors, drug traffickers, double agents, and naked young women who are kidnaped and suffer endless tortures. Yet Robbe-Grillet wrote these SADE-like stories with humor. The novels read like a series of visual images, and there is no attempt to make either the characters or the circumstances realistic. Robbe-Grillet's novels are highly cinematographic. He once said, "They have reproached me for being an engineer who writes, they have reproached me for being a writer who uses films as if I were painting." Whether in novels or in films, Robbe-Grillet engages in reconstructing spacio-temporal relations as he seeks to portray the illusion of reality.

Another shift in Robbe-Grillet's writing dates from 1976, when he undertook his "imaginary autobiography" for the Éditions de Minuit publishing house that sponsored another, similar work by the literary critic and theorist Roland Barthes at roughly the same time. Robbe-Grillet begins the work saying, "I have never spoken of anything but myself. Since it is internal, however, it is hardly apparent." What follows is a sort of autobiographical novel since Robbe-Grillet speaks through his double, Henri de Corinthe, a fantastic father/brother figure. This work was followed by *The Mirror* (1984), *Angélique* (1988), and *The Last Days of Corinthe* (1994). In his autobiographical works, Robbe-Grillet blends memories from childhood of family members with characters from literature such as Merlin or Madame Bovary, who become as real as his grandfather, for example.

FURTHER READING

Angelini, Eileen M. *Strategies of "Writing the Self" in the French Modern Novel: C'est moi, je Crois.* Lewiston, N.Y.: E. Mellen Press, 2001.

Harger-Grinling, Virginia, and Tony Chadwick. *Robbe-Grillet and the Fantastic: A Collection of Essays.* Wesport, Conn.: Greenwood Press, 1994.

Carrabino, Victor. *The Phenomenological Novel of Alain Robbe-Grillet.* Parma, Italy: C.E.M., 1974.

Fletcher, John. *Alain Robbe-Grillet.* London, New York: Methuen, 1983.

Leki, Ilona. *Alain Robbe-Grillet.* Boston: Twayne, 1983.

Morrissette, Bruce. *Intertextual Assemblage in Robbe-Grillet from Topology to the Golden Triangle.* Fredericton, N.B., Canada: York Press, 1979.

Ramsay, Raylene L. *The French New Autobiographies: Sarraute, Duras, and Robbe-Grillet.* Gainesville: University Press of Florida, 1996.

Smith, Roch Charles. *Understanding Alain Robbe-Grillet.* Columbia: University of South Carolina Press, 2000.

Stoltzfus, Ben. *Alain Robbe-Grillet and the New French Novel.* Carbondale: Southern Illinois University Press, 1964.

ROCHEFORT, CHRISTIANE (1917–1998)

Born in Paris, Rochefort had an extremely broad education. She studied art, medicine, and psychology, but her true passion was writing from a young age. Rochefort published a series of short stories before the success of her first novel, *Warrior's Rest* (1958), later adapted to film by Roger Vadim and starring Brigitte Bardot. *Warrior's Rest* was enormously successful, largely due to the openness with which it explores sexual themes while satirizing bourgeois society and values. *Children of Heaven* (1961), in contrast, offers a realistic portrayal of the daily life of Parisian children. Some critics have classified Rochefort as a populist writer because of this novel. The characterization, however, is not accurate. In this and all her works, Rochefort tended to focus on bourgeois society.

Rochefort's writings can be described as generally nonconformist, reflecting the political struggles of her day as well as the feminist movement (see FEMINISM). She was principally interested in and opposed to all forms of alienation. She thus sought to challenge social taboos as in *Springtime in the Parking Lot* (1969). Her steadfast promotion of freedom and happiness makes her works particularly accessible to the young. Aside from her novels which include *Cats Don't Care for Money* (1963), *A Rose for Morrison* (1966), *Archaos* (1972), *Still Happy That Summer Is Coming* (1975), *When You Go to See Women* (1982), *The Far Door* (1988, Médicis Prize), and *Conversations without Words* (1997), Rochefort also wrote essays and autobiography.

The title of *Cats Don't Care for Money* (*Stances à Sophie*) comes from a soldiers' song. In this novel, Céline suspects that she is making a mistake in marrying, not because of her husband's character but because of marriage itself. For her marriage signifies a kind of imprisonment that necessitates the renunciation of oneself. Nonetheless, she forges ahead, approaching marriage, ironically, as if entering religious life.

Céline tries to be a good wife to Philippe, who introduces her into solid bourgeois society as she has no money or connections of her own. Céline begins to rebel against social constraints and expectations when she realizes that Philippe does not really love her. Rather, he thinks of her as simply another possession, a charming creature meant to take care of him. He is not particularly interested in her as an individual with whom he has chosen to spend his life. Philippe's real interests are keeping up appearances, his new car, and launching a career in politics.

A Rose for Morrison (1966) seems to announce the revolutionary events that would occur two years after its publication. It was dedicated to the American folk singer Bob Dylan and refers to the Quaker who, in the presence of his wife and children, set himself on fire in front of the Pentagon to protest the Vietnam War. The novel took the public by surprise with its depiction of a flawed society run by politicians and technocrats whose hold on power is threatened by the energy of a younger generation that desires to live a fuller life. Rochefort's description is almost that of a police state that, through the educational system, conditions children from a young age to be obedient. The system suppresses desire and only the force of rebellious youth may eventually overcome a society that recalls the writings of the British writers George Orwell and Aldous Huxley.

In *Springtime in the Parking Lot,* Rochefort turns to the theme of homosexuality. Here a young man whose future is bleak leaves home after his father asks him to move away from the television screen—on which there is no picture. The set is broken, a powerful metaphor for the emptiness of their lives. Christophe is subsequently introduced into student circles with their vibrant political and philosophical debates. He meets a student of Chinese who argues about the weakness of both the communist and the capitalist systems and they become friends. Thomas lends Christophe his student ID so that he can try to pick up girls in the library.

Thomas soon becomes Christophe's protector. Meanwhile, both young men resist the homosexual love that develops between them until finally, Christophe shows Thomas the way to liberate his soul, his true nature, and his being. Both are taken by surprise at the force of their desire in body and in spirit.

Rochefort again reveals her idealization of youth in *Still Happy That Summer Is Coming.* In this novel, a group of high school students inspire one another to run away and pursue their dreams. Along the way they experience and question life and love. Recurring themes are homosexual love and rebellion against the adult world.

The title of *When You Go to See Women* comes from a line by the German philosopher Friedrich Nietzsche, "When you go to see women, don't forget your whisk." The novel then opens with the rewording of a passage from the poet Arthur Rimbaud's "Drunken Boat." The narrator, Bertrand, about whom the reader knows little, tells his story in the first person. It is an unsettling work, as Bertrand is a psychoanalyst with masochistic sexual leanings. His mistresses help him to realize his self-destructive desires, like the desire to be sodomized with a whisk. Some critics have interpreted Bertrand's masochism as a comment on contemporary society. Others read the novel as a critique of Freudian psychoanalytic theory.

The Far Door introduces another disturbing theme, incest. In this first-person narrative, a woman rebels against the painful circumstances in which she finds herself, refusing to become a victim. The novel shares with other works by Rochefort the theme of illicit relations, a reflection of the author's willingness to confront forbidden subjects. Moreover, in her works children often seduce adults, reflecting Rochefort's emphasis on the power of youth to challenge an enfeebled adult world.

Rochefort's novels reflect the utopianism of the 1960s. She wrote with humor in a style that sometimes recalls the tradition of RABELAIS. Her writings constitute an exercise in freedom and creativity while offering a critique of bourgeois, consumer society and its crass materialism. In *Children of Heaven,* for example, Rochefort attacks France's postwar natalist policy whereby the birth of each child brings the family a subsidy that allows for the purchase of a television set or a washing machine.

Rochefort emphasized the role of the subconscious in the writing process. "Writing is not thought. It is one hundred percent an act. Writing is located where thought is absent." Because Rochefort believed that our first impulse is to use the language of society, and because that language inherently constrains us, she sought to free herself from its limitations. Her writing can be characterized as feminist in its rejection of the traditional patriarchal order. Most important, Rochefort sought to escape a mode of thought determined by a dominant political and cultural system, often by playing with syntax and word formation.

FURTHER READING
Hutton, Margaret-Ann. *Countering Culture: The Novels of Christiane Rochefort.* Exeter, England: University of Exeter Press, 1999.
Paine, Pamela Fries. *Christiane Rochefort and the Dialogic: Voices of Tension and Intention.* New York: P. Lang, 2002.

ROLLAND, ROMAIN (1866–1944)
Trained as a historian, Rolland also had a passion for literature, music, and art. He studied at the prestigious École Normale Supérieure, earning a degree in history in 1889. He then left for Rome to work on his thesis, "The History of Opera in Europe Before Lulli and Scarlatti." While in Rome he also explored the Renaissance art of Italian masters such as Raphael and Michelangelo. These broad interests endured throughout his lifetime. In Italy, Rolland also began to develop his theory on the "musical novel."

Repelled by the decadence he saw in contemporary society, Rolland began a novel entitled *Savonarola* that was never completed but that highlights his interest in solitary characters who struggle against a debased world. He then turned to socialism and wrote *Wolves* (1898), inspired by the Dreyfus affair in which a Jewish officer was falsely accused and convicted of treason in 1894. He also developed an interest in the FRENCH REVOLUTION, which he treated in a series of plays. He became a regular contributor to his friend Charles Péguy's *Cahiers de la quinzaine* and began working too on a biography of Beethoven, published in 1903, in which he presents the great composer as a heroic figure.

Rolland's masterpiece, *Jean-Christophe*, a monumental work of 10 volumes published between 1904

and 1912, is divided into three parts, *Jean-Christophe, Jean-Christophe in Paris,* and *The Journey's End. Jean-Christophe* introduced into modern French literature the concept of the cyclical novel and set the standard for subsequent writers such as JULES ROMAIN, ROGER MARTIN DU GARD, and Georges Duhamel. Rolland had at first thought to model his hero on Beethoven. As he wrote, however, the novel began to take shape as a portrait of European society. Fearful for the future, Rolland used his novel to "plead for reconciliation among nations."

Above and beyond the 10 volumes of *Jean-Christophe,* Rolland also wrote biographies of the Renaissance artist Michelangelo (1905–06) and Russian writer Tolstoy (1911), as well as numerous articles on music. He particularly admired the works of Leo Tolstoy and, under his influence, developed his own brand of pantheism. In 1912, he left teaching to work on yet another novel, *Colas Breugnon,* the supposed journal of an artisan. Because of the war, the novel was not published until 1919.

Rolland spent the war years in Switzerland. He also continued to write, producing a series of articles published together under the title *Above the Fray* (1915), in which he once more called for peace among nations. Because of its pacifist message, the work was not well received, in France or abroad. "I am alone," he wrote. "These are the saddest days of my life. To the distress of my heart and mind are added personal sorrows." Although this work inspired vociferous debate, it also lost Rolland some of his friends. Nonetheless, he must have found some recompense in winning the Nobel Prize in Literature in 1916. At the same time, he kept a journal published in 1952 in which he developed ideas that were to appear in subsequent works.

In 1919 Rolland returned to Paris a politically engaged writer. There he attempted to start an international movement with his "Declaration of Independence of the Spirit." Although a thousand intellectuals from all over the world signed his declaration, his attempt to create a new movement was not successful. Rolland's pacifist views are also reflected in *Clérambeault, Story of a Free Conscience during the War* (1920).

Rolland shared antiwar sentiments with the writer HENRI BARBUSSE, although the two were not close. Rolland refused to contribute to Barbusse's journal, *Clarté,* just as he refused to contribute to communist journals, asserting that he was not a "party man." Rather, Rolland carefully guarded his position as an independent thinker. Troubled by events taking place in the USSR, Rolland rejected Stalin's dictatorship, saying that he "stood with the proletariat whenever it respects truth and humanity. Against the proletariat when it violates truth and humanity."

Rolland subsequently returned to Switzerland, where he began work on his next lengthy novel, *Enchanted Spirit* (1922–27), published in three volumes. During that period, Rolland developed an interest in Hinduism and theories of nonviolent resistance associated in particular with Mohandas Gandhi, the subject of a book he published in 1923. Under the influence of psychoanalyst Sigmund Freud, whom Rolland knew, he also wrote a work of self-analysis, *The Inner Journey,* covering the years 1926–42, in which he articulates his notion of the "oceanic feeling" described by Freud in *Civilization and Its Discontents.*

In 1934 he married a Russian citizen, Maria Koudacheva, whom he had met in 1929 and with whom he traveled to the USSR in 1935. Rolland had joined the Communist Party in 1930. During World War II he lived in Vézelay, home of the one of great romanesque cathedrals. In these last years of his life, Rolland turned to religion. Inspired by Friedrich Nietzsche and Tolstoy, idealism and rationalism, Rolland was a humanist with a passion for life and personal freedom. He sought to create a balance between his love of freedom and a sense of community that inspired him to embrace communism.

Rolland's fiction reflects his interest in history. Frequent backdrops for his writings are the Middle Ages, the Renaissance, and the French Revolution. He was particularly drawn to the conflict between the individual and society. Musical elements are strong as Rolland combines music criticism with reflections on the relationship of musical style to national character, indicating his affinity for the romantic (see ROMANTICISM). Rolland sought to create a musical novel by interweaving themes with one another as in a musical composition. Ultimately, the theme of fraternity indicates the way back to love and peace.

FURTHER READING

Aronson, Alex. *Romain Rolland: The Story of a Conscience.* Bombay, India: Padma Publications, 1946.

Beckwith, William Hunter. *The Formation of the Esthetic of Romain Rolland.* New York: New York University Press, 1936.

Starr, William Thomas. *Romain Rolland and a World at War.* New York: AMS Press, 1971.

———. *Romain Rolland: One Against All. A Biography.* The Hague, Paris: Mouton, 1971.

ROMAINS, JULES (1885–1972)

Louis Farigoule was born in the Auvergne but grew up in Paris, where he received a degree in philosophy from the École Normale Supéreieure in 1906. He taught from 1909 until 1914, when he chose a literary career instead. He adopted the pen name Jules Romains in 1902. Romains was associated with the literary group "de l'abbaye," whose interests extended from SYMBOLISM, to revolutionary socialism, to futurism. The underlying principle of all his works is a concept he called unanimism. Romains's first collection of poetry was published in 1908 under the title *Unanimist Life.* In 1910 Romains published his *Manual of Deification,* in which he articulated the metaphysics of unanism, or the notion of the collective spirit that unites beings and things.

Romains had a rich and varied career. A firm supporter of Franco-German relations, after World War I, he participated in PEN clubs as well as various diplomatic missions. At the beginning of the war, Romains, a pacifist, joined the army's ambulance service and was subsequently released from duty in 1915. In 1916, he expressed his antiwar sentiments in *Europe.* He is principally remembered as a playwright and for his serial novel, MEN OF GOOD WILL, a vast project based on Romains's vision of the modern world first articulated in *Unanimist Life.*

Probably best known for his drama, Romains is one of the most performed playwrights of the 1920s, along with Luigi Pirandello and George Bernard Shaw. Romains was also a careful observer of contemporary political and social life, as is evident in his essays such as *Today's Problems* (1931), *European Problems* (1933), and *The Couple France-Germany* (1935). Even as war loomed over Europe once more, Romains continued to advocate rapprochement.

Romains began writing his greatest work, *Men of Good Will,* in 1932. It consists of 27 volumes all structured around the concept of unanimism. The last volume was published in 1946. That same year, Romains was elected to the Académie Française. Unanimism, derived from "unanimous," is based on modern urban life and the sense of interconnectedness and communion that animates it. The writer is the interpreter of this collective spirit. Recurring themes are politics, the relationship of the individual to the historical process, and friendship. According to unanimist philosophy, the individual ought to renounce him- or herself, preferring to think and act as a part of a larger group. In poetry, unanimism emphasizes free verse, focusing on the crowd in the streets of modern urban centers.

By far his greatest work, *Men of Good Will* is Romains's clearest expression of unanimism. Rather than focusing on the individual, Romains turns to humanity itself in all its diversity. This polyphonic novel covers 25 years of French history (1908–33) and is encyclopedic in its treatment of every social class and political movement. There are approximately 600 characters overall and 40 main characters, yet Romains gives them distinct personalities. Romains makes use of comedy, tragedy, narrative, internal monologue, and dialogue to bring this work to life.

The novel is unified through the story of two intellectuals, Jerphanion and Jallez. Through them, Romains reflects on history, praising men of peace and good will in contrast to men of war. This novel recalls the work of ROMAIN ROLLAND, Romains's predecessor in producing a multivolume serial novel, JEAN-CHRISTOPHE. The underlying purpose of both works is to represent the hope and future of humanity through friendship.

Since the modern world has a tendency toward lethargy, according to Romains, the writer has an obligation try to awaken it, as he attempted in *The Boys in the Back Room* (1913), a novel in which a group of friends devises events intended to draw the inhabitants of a provincial city out of their sluggishness. Romains appears to have been somewhat skeptical of romantic love. Nonetheless, in *The Body's Rapture* (1922), he explores the idea of a sexual religion capable of reconciling the senses and the spirit.

During World War II, Romains left France for the United States and Mexico. Back in France after the Liberation, he continued to write novels and social commentary.

FURTHER READING
Boak, Denis. *Jules Romains.* New York: Twayne, 1974.
Walter, Felix. "Unanimism and the Novels of Jules Romains," *PMLA* 51, no. 3 (September 1936): 863–871.

ROMANCE Medieval romances were the poems and stories told by the TROUBADOURS, wandering poets and minstrels who entertained the public at fairs, marriages, and private castles. The romances are associated with the rise of courtly love.

As seen in the *CHANSONS DE GESTE,* there were strong links between religion and the culture of chivalry. Yet the romances also focus on the struggle of isolated individuals within the community. Often presenting obstacles to love, the romances shift attention away from the national and religious questions addressed in the epic poems, toward the individual's emotional struggle. In tournaments, knights vied with each other for a lady's favor while the troubadours sang praises of chivalrous love and the feats it inspires. Together they produced the great legends of medieval literary culture. Courtly love poems lay the foundation for love-centered explorations of the individual's emotions in French literature.

ROMANCE OF THE ROSE, THE GUILLAUME DE LORRIS AND JEAN DE MEUN (c. 1225–1270) This famous poem is written in two sections by two different authors, 40 years apart. The first part of 4,000 lines of octosyllabic rhyming couplets was composed by GUILLAUME DE LORRIS about 1225, roughly the same time that JEAN RENART wrote his ROMANCE of the same name. In this allegorical dream vision, the lover finds himself in the garden of Diversion where he falls in love with a rosebud. Initially received by Fair Welcome, the lover ultimately finds himself shut out of Jealousy's castle, and thus thwarted in his attempt to reach the rose. Jealousy is aided by allegorical characters representing Shame, Fear, Refusal, and Slander. Guillaume de Lorris's version of the *Romance of the Rose* is representative of the courtly romance genre.

The allegorical figures met by the lover in the garden direct the action of the plot. In Jean de Meun's continuation of the poem (17,500 lines), sometime in the 1260s, the style and form of the story change, despite the retention of the allegorical form.

Over 250 manuscripts of Jean de Meun's version of the *Romance of the Rose* exist, more than any other piece of vernacular literature from the Middle Ages with the exception of Dante's *Inferno*. Widely read and controversial from the start, the poem continued to be popular well into the Renaissance. CHRISTINE DE PIZAN responded to the poem's negative portrayal of women at the beginning of the 15th century, beginning what was arguably France's first literary debate, the Quarrel of the *Romance of the Rose*.

Jean de Meun is not alone in rewriting or adding to an existing text. The medieval literary tradition was based on translation and adaptation rather than innovation. However, Jean de Meun does so in a particularly assertive manner by poking fun at social conventions. In Guillaume de Lorris's version, the allegorical figures, positive (Fair Welcome) and negative (Slander), direct the action of the plot. With the exception of Jean de Meun's startling conclusion, in which the Lover, aided by Genius, Nature's confessor, and Venus, succeeds in deflowering the rose, Jean de Meun uses his narrative as a vehicle for diatribes on a vast array of subjects.

Often borrowing directly from writers of antiquity such as Ovid, Juvenal, and Boethius, Jean de Meun's narrative structure reflects the medieval scholastic tradition of disputation. The voices of his characters may often be interpreted in more than one way. Jean de Meun has been accused of being, among other things, a misogynist, but it is difficult to pin him down on any one viewpoint. He even excuses himself in advance to his potential critics, arguing that he is only retelling what others have said before him. Jean de Meun's use of irony allows him to challenge ecclesiastical and social values. Moving beyond the confines of the courtly romance, Jean de Meun's *Romance of the Rose* is a philosophical and epistemological work in addition to an allegorical romance. HÉLISENNE DE CRENNE's *The TORMENTS OF LOVE,* for example, draws from the tradition of the medieval romance of which *The Romance of the Rose* is a superlative example.

FURTHER READING

Arden, Heather. *The Romance of the Rose.* Boston: Twayne, 1987.
Luria, Maxwell. *A Reader's Guide to the Roman de la Rose.* Hamden, Conn.: Archon, 1982.

ROMANCE OF THE ROSE OR GUILLAUME DE DOLE, THE (JEAN RENART) (C. 1225)

Jean Renart's *Romance of the Rose* is usually referred to as *Guillaume de Dole* to avoid confusion with GUILLAUME DE LORRIS and JEAN DE MEUN's ROMANCE of the same name. *Guillaume de Dole* consists of 5,655 octosyllabic lines in rhyming couplets. Its theme of thwarted lovers who must struggle to be united or reunited is common to medieval romances.

The romance begins as the German emperor Conrad asks his minstrel, Jouglet, to entertain him with a story. Jouglet tells Conrad Jean Renart's *The Lay of the Shadow,* in which a knight pledges his love to a married lady. The lady refuses her lover's advances until she is moved when he desperately offers a ring to her reflection in water, casting it into a pool. Conrad asks the minstrel if such a beautiful and virtuous woman could exist in reality. Jouglet then describes a brave knight, Guillaume de Dole, and his sister Liénor. Jouglet's account of Liénor is so compelling that Conrad falls in love with her although he has never seen her. Conrad invites Guillaume to his court, eventually revealing his love for Guillaume's sister.

Conrad's plans are thwarted by his seneschal, who is jealous of Guillaume's potential challenge to his influence. The seneschal travels to Dole, where Liénor's mother unwittingly reveals to him that her daughter has a birthmark shaped like a rose on her thigh. The seneschal returns to court and speaks of the rose, implying that he knows Liénor intimately. Conrad and Guillaume are distraught. Meanwhile, Liénor, a strong female character, plans her revenge. She anonymously sends the seneschal some jewels as a token of love. The seneschal must wear them under his clothes if he wishes to enjoy the lady's favors. Liénor then appears at court, accusing the seneschal of having raped her and stolen her jewels. After a trial by ordeal, the seneschal and, in consequence, Liénor are proved innocent. The romance ends happily with the marriage of Conrad and Liénor.

The plot of the tale is fairly credible, marking the contrast between Jean Renart and CHRÉTIEN DE TROYES, whose idealized stories of Arthur's court are filled with magical elements. Moreover, Jean Renart does not place emphasis on the solitary knight who frequently engages in single combat. Contemporary literary critics have shown a renewed interest in Jean Renart's stories because of his realism. In *Guillaume de Dole* and his story *The Kite,* Jean Renart shows himself to be a careful observer of the daily life of aristocrats and ordinary people, painting charming pictures of children, food, and court life.

Guillaume de Dole is placed in the geographical space of the German empire. However, the romance is dedicated to Milon de Nanteuil, provost of the cathedral chapter of Rheims. Jean Renart fashions his story to meet his audience's interest by making reference to literature with which they would have been familiar. The tale thus reveals to today's reader a body of knowledge intrinsic to 13th-century aristocratic culture.

In his prologue, Jean Renart advertises the innovative crafting of his tale with a strong authorial voice. Incorporated into the romance are 46 songs. Together they provide a collection of contemporary songs from a variety of sources: courtly love songs, songs sung by women as they wove, pastorals, and dance songs. The author suggests that his story may be both read and sung. These multivocal layers of text are also of interest to modern critics. Jean Renart's creation of a new literary genre, the lyric anthology, influenced a number of later works.

FURTHER READING

Baldwin, John. *Aristocratic Life in Medieval France.* Baltimore: Johns Hopkins University Press, 2000.

Fox, John. *A Literary History of France: The Middle Ages.* London: Ernest Benn; New York: Barnes and Noble, 1974.

Zink, Michel. *Roman rose et rose rouge: Le Roman de la rose ou de Guillaume de Dole de Jean Renart.* Paris: Nizet, 1979.

ROMAN FEUILLETON (SERIAL NOVEL)

The origins of the serial novel lie in the 19th century with the rise of the press and mass production. In 1836 Émile de Girardin established a newspaper/journal, *La Presse,* in which he published the first serial novel. Girardin wanted both to increase the number of subscribers to his newspaper and to lower the subscription rate. His success starting a wave of serial novels in competing newspapers and led to a new sort of press, the novel journal.

Critics assailed this modern genre of "industrial literature." ALEXANDRE DUMAS took a journalist, Eugène Mirecourt, to court after being accused of running a "fiction factory." (Dumas won his case.) Opponents of the serial novel critized its aesthetic weakness, emphasis on emotion over style, theatrical effects, and melodrama. Not surprisingly, these novels were extremely popular with the reading public. EUGÈNE SUE's *MYSTERIES OF PARIS* is one of the best-known 19th-century serial novels but nearly all the major novelists of the period wrote in serial form at one time or another: Alexandre Dumas, PONSON DU TERRAIL, Xavier du Montepin, ZOLA, and BALZAC. The serial novel tradition was carried into the 20th century by MAURICE LEBLANC and GASTON LEROUX, for example. Most important, the rise of the serial novel is associated with developments in 19th-century society and the popular press.

ROMANTICISM (1780–1840)   Romanticism

was an intellectual and cultural movement that spanned both sides of the Atlantic and the entire European continent. Romanticism greatly affected aesthetic and artistic movements in poetry, fiction, music, and painting, reflecting the romantic emphasis on the individual and the irrational as a source of creativity and truth.

The ENLIGHTENMENT (1688–1815) emphasized reason and the notion that objective knowledge leads to progress. The romantic movement was in part a reaction against the rigidity of Enlightenment thought, raising questions about the use of reason and rationality. The romantics opposed restrictions on the individual (political, religious, or civil), and believed that such restrictions were ultimately derived from rationalism. The concurrent rise of industrial society, a consequence of the application of empirical knowledge to daily life, only increased the romantics' belief that the modern world created heightened conditions for the individual's alienation and isolation in the material world. Not surprisingly then, the movement also reflects changes in philosophy and history.

The emergence of nationalism in the post-Napoleonic era gave rise to a conservative romanticism that focused on a definition of nature and culture derived from the nation-state. STENDHAL's novel *The Red and the Black* depicts both the isolated romantic individual's struggle in society and the importance of nationalism to personal and cultural identity. Language was important to both romanticism and nationalism as the existence of different languages seemed to confirm the notion of an organic view of the world. Language is not the result of abstract reason or individual effort; it is the function of national or ethnic organisms. The FRENCH REVOLUTION revealed a belief that the state can be artificially constructed. The romantic notion of the nation was different. The nation is not the conscious joining of individuals but a natural union of people who share the same language, culture, and traditions.

The effects of industrialization and modernization on the European psyche caused some romantics to seek solace in an idealized past. Romantics were thus fascinated by traditional, rural peasant life since they believed that identity comes from what is unique and particular rather than from the general. They preferred custom and tradition to legislation and rejected the notion of absolute truths.

The romantics were critical of "modern" social change and so desired to look at the world in a new and different way. Their approach was largely antirational, but that did not mean rejecting science. For the romantics, nature was not a product but a process, an organism rather than a Newtonian machine. Nature was also a source of inspiration. Early romantics in particular sought an ideal union among humankind, nature, and God. Prominent themes in literature were love, nature, and beauty. CHATEAUBRIAND's novel *ATALA*, set among North America's "noble savages," is an example of the romantic's yearning for an unattainable and perfect unity with nature, God, and one's beloved.

On the whole, the romantics were introspective. They were also fascinated by the human potential for creative genius. As a result, they wanted to know what the self is like on the inside. The romantics might have talked about "practical reason," "fancy," "imagination," or simply "feeling," but they believed that the human mind possesses a special power that goes beyond the limits of passive understanding or knowledge acquired experientially (as described by Enlightenment thinkers such as John Locke and David Hume). Influenced by 18th-century sentimentalism (see SENTIMENTAL NOVEL) as seen in the works of JEAN-JACQUES ROUSSEAU such as *ÉMILE* or *JULIE,* the romantics believed that it is not reason that makes us human but emotions.

Art and literature were important because they represent the inner self. Music played a particularly significant role because it is unrestricted by physical form, place, and, in a sense, time. The world of art (including literature) was an ideal world as art is essentially a heavenly miracle; artistic genius could not be taught or learned. The romantic emphasis on the individual and human emotions (the inner self) became increasingly important and led into a fascination with the psychological. The manifestation of the dream became a popular topic on canvas and in literature. One need only call to mind the English artist Henry Fuseli's painting *The Nightmare.*

Romanticism brought extreme skepticism to the view of modernization and industrialization along with a mistrust of materialism. Later writers such as the existentialists (see EXISTENTIALISM) bring us back again to the importance of the irrational, which began with romanticism and as a reaction to rationalism associated with Enlightenment thought. With the romantics, subjectivity takes precedence over objectivity in the struggle between passion and reason.

FURTHER READING

Allen, James. *Popular French Romanticism.* Syracuse, N.Y.: Syracuse University Press, 1981.

Berlin, Isaiah. *The Roots of Romanticism.* Edited by Henry Hardy. Princeton, N.Y.: Princeton University Press, 1999.

Bishop, Lloyd. *The Romantic Hero and His Heirs in French Literature.* New York: P. Lang, 1984.

Bowman, Frank. *French Romanticism: Intertextual and Interdisciplinary Readings.* Baltimore: Johns Hopkins University Press, 1990.

Gautier, Théophile. *A History of Romanticism.* New York: Fertig, 1988.

Talbot, Émile. *Stendhal and Romantic Esthetics.* Lexington, Ky.: French Forum, 1985.

ROUGON-MACQUART SERIES ÉMILE ZOLA
(1871–1893) On the wall of his study Zola wrote "not a day without a line." The Rougon-Macquart series gives proof to his words. Over a 22-year period, Zola produced twenty novels tracing "The Natural and Social History of a Second Empire Family" (see SECOND EMPIRE).

In line with his naturalist doctrine (see NATURALISM), Zola wished "to replace the word doctor with the word novelist." Drawing on the physiologist Claude Bernard' *Introduction to Experimental Medicine* (1865), Zola sought to articulate the role of observation and experimentalism in literature. In particular, he was interested in the effect of heredity and the environment in determining human character and action.

The Rougon and the Macquart families are both descended from the wealthy and whimsical Adélaïde Fouque, or Aunt Dide, who ended her days in an asylum. The legitimate side of the family is descended from Aunt Dide and her husband, Pierre Rougon. With her lover, a wayward alcoholic named Antoine Macquart, she also had two children, Antoine and Ursule. Set in the period of the Second Empire, following Louis-Napoleon's coup d'etat in 1851, the Rougons represent the rising bourgeoisie. The Macquarts and the Mourets, a second illegitimate branch of the family, generally represent the working class, despite the success of Octave Mouret, the wealthy owner of a Parisian department store (*Ladies' Paradise*).

From the beginning, Zola turned a critical eye on venal republicans and naive idealists alike. In the first volume, none of these contemptible characters is willing to help the one idealist among them, Silvère, who has fallen in love with Miette, an orphan who dies on the barricades. Silvère is killed by a policeman and Aunt Dide goes crazy. Thus ends *The Fortune of the Rougons*, setting the stage for all subsequent events narrated in *VENUS OF THE COUNTING HOUSE*, 1872; *The Belly of Paris*, 1873; *Conquest of Plassans*, 1874; *Abbé Mouret's Sin*, 1875; *His Excellency Eugène Rougon*, 1876; *L'ASSOMMOIR*, 1877; *Page of Love*, 1878; *NANA*, 1880, *Piping Hot*, 1882; *The LADIES' PARADISE*, 1883; *Joy of Life*, 1884; *GERMINAL*, 1885; *The MASTERPIECE*, 1886; *EARTH*, 1887; *The Dream*, 1888; *LA BÊTE HUMAINE*, 1890; *MONEY*, 1891; *The DOWNFALL*, 1892; and *DOCTOR PASCAL*, 1893.

Recent criticism has explored the underlying movement throughout the Rougon-Macquart series from despair to redemption, reflecting changes in Zola's own life and view of the world. Certain characters from the first volume, like Sylvère the idealist, set the stage for others like Florent (*The Belly of Paris*) and Étienne (*Germinal*), just as Sylvère's love affair with Miette, a love that awakens sensuality but is frightening as well, introduces the theme of love and death prevalent in later novels (*Germinal, La Bête Humaine, Doctor Pascal*). Zola's repeated emphasis on the death instinct reflects contemporary developments in the field of psychoanalysis.

In these rich novels, like HONORÉ DE BALZAC's *COMÉDIE HUMAINE*, Zola not only details the experience of the Rougon Macquart families but also explores in great depth nearly every aspect of contemporary society: banking and the stock exchange, the marketplace, the church, politics, Parisian workers, prostitution, the bourgeoisie, department stores, the world of artists, peasants, the railroad, and the French defeat by Prussia in 1871. Together these novels offer an extraordinary history of 19th-century France.

FURTHER READING
Bell, David. *Models of Power: Politics and Economics in Zola's Rougon-Macquart*. Lincoln: University of Nebraska Press, 1988.

Chessid, Ilona. *Thresholds of Desire: Authority and Transgression in the Rougon-Macquart*. New York: P. Lang, 1993.

Frey, John Andrew. *The Aesthetics of the Rougon-Macquart*. Madrid: José Porrúa Turanzas, 1978.

Gallois, William. *Zola: The History of Capitalism*. Oxford, New York: P. Lang, 2000.

Haavik, Kristof H. *In Mortal Combat: The Conflict of Life and Death in Zola's Rougon-Macquart*. Birmingham, Ala.: Summa, 2000.

Warning, Rainer. "Zola's Rougon-Macquart: Compensatory Images of a 'Wild Ontology.'" MLN 113, no. 4, French Issue (September 1998): 705–733.

ROUSSEAU, JEAN-JACQUES (1712–1778)
In his *Confessions*, Rousseau wrote, "I am not made like any of those that I have seen; I dare to believe that I was not made like anyone in existence. If I am not worth more, at least I am different. If nature did well

or badly to break the mold after me, it is this that one cannot judge until having read me."

Few individuals have produced as wide a range of works as ENLIGHTENMENT thinker Jean-Jacques Rousseau, a playwright, composer, novelist, philosopher, political theorist, pedagogue, and psychologist. While his opera, *The Village Soothsayer* (1752), has long been forgotten, Rousseau's works are still widely read and debated among students and scholars of the 18th century.

Rousseau was born in Geneva, Switzerland, in 1712. Shortly after his birth his mother died, leaving him in the care of his father and a beloved aunt. While Rousseau had no formal education, he read enthusiastically as a child, first the novels left by his mother and then the works of the Greek writer Plutarch. The values of classical antiquity such as virtue, honor, duty, and citizenship were influential in Rousseau's thinking throughout his life. In *JULIE, OR THE NEW HÉLOÏSE* (1761), the principal characters, Julie and her husband, Wolmar, establish a utopian community at Clarens whose underlying principles are clearly derived from classical values. Each member of the community, including its leaders, must place duty before desire in the interest of the community at large. In theory, the Socratic equation of reason = virtue = happiness reigns at Clarens.

Rousseau was apprenticed to an engraver but ran away from his master and from Geneva when he was not yet 16 years old. He converted from Calvinism to Roman Catholicism under the protection of his benefactress and eventual lover, Madame de Warens. Rousseau's best articulation of his religious views is found in the "Profession of Faith of a Savoyard Vicar," included in *ÉMILE* (1762). For Rousseau moral development occurs as the result of self-exploration, not through the dictates of the church hierarchy, be it Protestant or Roman Catholic. Rousseau's argument that natural man is inherently good runs counter to the Christian concept of original sin. Hence, his ideas were rejected by the Protestant and Catholics churches alike. The censors' condemnation forced Rousseau to flee France although he eventually returned under an assumed name. He was officially permitted to return to France in 1770 provided that he not write anything against the government.

Rousseau's reputation as a philosopher began in Paris, where he first traveled in 1742. There he met a tavern servant, Thérèse LeVasseur, whom he eventually married in 1768. In his *Confessions,* Rousseau says that she bore him five children, all of whom he sent to an orphanage. While it is not clear that the story is true, it makes for one of the many apparent contradictions in his life and works. How is it that a man who abandoned his own children could later write one of the great theoretical works on education?

It was not until 1750, however, that the *Discourse on the Sciences and the Arts* guaranteed Rousseau's fame. In 1749, on his way to visit his friend Diderot (coeditor of the ENCYCLOPEDIA), who was imprisoned in the Château de Vincennes in 1749, Rousseau noticed an advertisement in the newspaper announcing an essay competition sponsored by the Academy of Dijon: "Has the restoration of the sciences and the arts helped to purify morals?" In his essay, Rousseau argues that progress in the sciences and arts has morally corrupted humanity. He criticizes European society's abandonment of human nature and its preference for appearance over reality, themes that reappear in all his works.

Rousseau published his *Discourse on the Origin of Inequality* in 1755. He begins this work with the romantic notion of the noble savage (SEE ROMANTICISM). According to Rousseau, the development of reason and the civilizing process have estranged human beings from their original nature. Foreshadowing Freud, Rousseau argues that natural man is inherently good; he is only later corrupted by society. Even social inequality is a result of the civilizing process. Rousseau's argument that human reason develops in the progression from natural to civilized man brought him into conflict with other Enlightenment thinkers who promoted human reason as the defining feature of humanity and the basis for social progress.

Rousseau's emphasis on man in the state of nature reflects a fascination with primitive peoples that he shared with his contemporaries. Following the period of European exploration and expansion in the 16th century, travel accounts and journals were tremendously popular among the reading public. While Rousseau never pretended to trace the development of human society with historical accuracy, the second *Discourse on the Origin of Inequality* offers groundbreaking analysis of human society, contributing to the formation of the social sciences as a discipline.

Rousseau's most famous example of political theory is *The Social Contract* (1762). Here he develops his concept of liberty in relation to duty, reflected in the general will. *Émile* serves as an effective counterpoint to *The Social Contract,* presenting Rousseau's plan to prepare his pupil to become a dutiful citizen and a virtuous man. In his *Confessions,* he argued that his works must be considered as a whole. His fundamental argument is that society corrupts human nature. "Man is born free; and everywhere he is in chains." Rousseau realized that his project of reform for the individual and society might reach a greater audience if he turned away from political theory to fiction, as we see in *Émile* and *Julie or The New Héloïse.*

Toward the end of his life, Rousseau turned to a completely different genre. In his last years, Rousseau wrote *The Confessions* (1770), *The Dialogues: Rousseau, Judge of Jean-Jacques* (1776), and *The Reveries of the Solitary Walker* (1776). These autobiographical works lay the foundation for modern concepts of psychology and the construction of the self.

The 18th century is known as the age of revolution and of reason. Eighteenth-century France contributed enormously to modern concepts of liberty and democracy. Rousseau participated in the intellectual world of the ENLIGHTENMENT philosophers. He contributed several articles to the ENCYCLOPEDIA. Yet by the end of his life, Rousseau was as isolated from his fellow philosophers as he was from the church.

At the heart of Rousseau's works is the question of human happiness. What is the good life? The philosophers of classical antiquity focused on this question too. Rousseau takes the reader in new directions, anticipating Marx and Freud as the conditions of the modern world placed increasing strain on the relationship between the individual and society. From the 18th century until today, scholars have argued over the tension in his work between the individual and the collective. Rousseau's novels emphasized the validity of both emotion and reason for the human condition. The return of lyricism in his passages in praise of love and nature laid the foundation for the sentimental

novel and romanticism. To date there is no common assessment of Rousseau. He is the father of SENTIMENTALISM, the precursor of ROMANTICISM, prophet of the FRENCH REVOLUTION, and foreshadower of totalitarianism, all in one.

FURTHER READING

Cassirer, Ernst. *The Question of Jean-Jacques Rousseau.* Edited and translated by Peter Gay. Bloomington Indiana University Press, 1963.

Daniels, Charlotte. *Subverting the Family Romance: Women Writers, Kinship Structures and the Early French Novel.* Lewisburg, PA: Bucknell University Press; London: Associated University Presses, 2000.

Kelly, Christopher. "Taking Readers as They Are: Rousseau's Turn from Discourses to Novels," *Eighteenth-Century Studies* 33, no. 1 (1999): 85–101.

Morgenstern, Mira. *Rousseau and the Politics of Ambiguity: Self, Culture and Society.* University Park Penn: Pennsylvania State University Press, 1996.

Riley, Patrick, ed. *The Cambridge Companion to Rousseau.* Cambridge, NY: Cambridge University Press, 2001.

Steinbrügge, Lieselotte. *The Moral Sex: Woman's Nature in the French Enlightenment.* Translated by Pamela E. Selwyn. New York: Oxford University Press, 1995.

Wolff, Larry. "Then I Imagine a Child: The Idea of Childhood and the Philosophy of Memory in the Enlightenment," *Eighteenth-Century Studies* 31, no. 4 (1998): 377–401.

ROUSSEL, RAYMOND (1877–1933)

Family wealth ensured a happy childhood for Roussel that the author looked back on throughout his life with fond memories. But growing up in ease did not protect him from difficult times later in life. As an adolescent, he studied music but decided at age 17 to devote himself to literature. Bent on discovering his genius, Roussel worked day and night for months on end, leading to exhaustion and a subsequent emotional crisis. The complete failure of his first novel, *The Understanding* (1897), came as such a shock that Roussel ended up in psychiatric care. Once recovered, he returned to his work and labored meticulously to develop his own style. Unfortunately for him, *The View* (1902) scarcely received any notice.

For the next five years, Roussel struggled to become a writer. He once said, "Sometimes I writhed on the ground in a crisis of rage, feeling that I could not succeed in giving myself the sensations of art to which I aspired." He finally found his literary voice in IMPRESSIONS OF AFRICA (1910). Once again, this novel received little attention from the reading public. Only the dramatist and poet Edmond Rostand declared that it could be adapted to the stage. Roussel had three separate versions performed in Paris, none of which was successful.

The subject of this work is the novel itself. Divided into two parts, the first 10 chapters offer a series of fantastic and incomprehensible scenes. In the second part, the narrator organizes the scenes into a plot. Certain elements seem to have been inspired by JULES VERNE. Characters experience a shipwreck and are captured by a black king. They subsequently enter a strange land where they encounter curious machines. The novel's originality lies in the way Roussel repeats diverse scenes in order to play with their meaning. Words do not lead to a sense of reality, but to other words. "I chose words," he said, "that are almost the same, for example, 'billard' and 'pillard.' Then I added words that are the same but have two different meanings, and I obtained two almost identical sentences. Once I found the two sentences, all I had to do was write a story that could begin with the first and end with the second."

Meanwhile, Roussel had begun work on a new novel, Locus Solus (1914). Set at Martial Canterel's magnificent villa at Montmorency, this novel opens up another world of strange and marvelous things. It is a parallel world in which the author again plays with words and images. A suitor (prétendant) gives rise to a soldier (reître en dents) with the aid of a young lady's multicolored teeth (dents). The young woman, first associated with the suitor, is then transformed into a machine. On the surface, Roussel appears to be telling a bizarre story, but the real adventure is one of words as he explores the possibility of creating a new reality out of language.

Sadly, this work met with no better reception than his earlier novels. It was likewise adapted to the stage but caused an uproar. Only the scandal it created brought Roussel fame. He determined that his problem derived from adapting novels to the stage and so

sought to write a play from the beginning, producing Star on Front in 1924. This work, too, was considered scandalous. Gradually, however, Roussel began to attract a small public. His last play, Dust of the Suns, was performed in 1926. Roussel's greatest work is, arguably, New Impressions of Africa (1932). It is also one of his last, although he subsequently articulated his views on the writing process in How I Wrote Certain of My Books (1935).

Unappreciated during his lifetime, Roussel's works are now recognized as marking an important moment in the history of modern fiction, particularly in their focus on the relationship between the writer and writing. Critics today view Roussel's works as some of the most striking examples of modern literature, however enigmatic they may be. Anticipating the focus of the NOUVEAU ROMAN, Roussel's poetry is marked by an obsession with objects—an image set in the base of a pen holder, a beach viewed from a distance, the label on a bottle of mineral water. Moreover, Impressions of Africa and Locus Solus each find their genesis in a word game, from which Roussel creates a richly imaginative world.

Roussel's works are less disconcerting to contemporary readers than they were at the time of their publication and are now viewed as precursors to both the NOUVEAU ROMAN and SURREALISM. ANDRÉ BRETON praised Roussel's vision and power of imagination, while ALAIN ROBBE-GRILLET and MICHEL BUTOR likewise expressed their admiration for his verbal skills.

FURTHER READING

Ashbery, John. Other Traditions. Cambridge, Mass.: Harvard University Press, 2000.

Ford, Mark. Raymond Roussel and the Republic of Dreams. Ithaca, N.Y.: Cornell University Press, 2001.

Foucault, Michel. Death and the Labyrinth: The World of Raymond Roussel. Translated by Charles Ruas. London, New York: Continuum, 2004.

Heppenstall, Rayner. Raymond Roussel: A Critical Study. Berkeley: University of California Press, 1967.

Roussel, Raymond. How I Wrote Certain of My Books. Translated by Trevor Winkfield. New York: SUN, 1977.

ROY, GABRIELLE (1909–1983)

This French-Canadian novelist first dreamed of becoming an actress before choosing a literary career. Throughout her life,

Roy sought to reach a broader international audience and she was largely successful in her endeavor. She remained isolated from Quebecois literary circles. Roy's first novel, *The TIN FLUTE* (1945), WAS AN INSTANT SUCCESS, WINNING THE PRESTIGIOUS FEMINA PRIZE IN 1947. It is a moving story written in the realist tradition (see REALISM), focusing on a family living in Montreal that suffers through the economic crisis of the 1930s and then the war. Roy's style is sober and yet familiar as she draws the reader into a closed world of urban misery.

In *Where Nests the Water Hen* (1950), Roy shifts the setting of her novel to depict the life of pioneers in northern Manitoba. This work includes lyrical descriptions of the countryside and yet Roy does not fail to portray the challenges that nature sometimes imposes. *Cashier* (1954) tells the story of an ordinary bank teller who ponders in his simple soul the deepest questions about human existence.

Roy's later work, *River without Rest* (1971), is unusual in that it consists of three short stories and a novel published together. Also set in the Canadian wilderness, it is the story of the Inuit and the challenge the arrival of white men and civilization imposes on local traditions. In this meeting of two different ways of looking at the world, Roy manifests her interest in the question of human destiny. In the end there is no one answer. Each man and woman must determine life's meaning for him- or herself. One's independent search for self-knowledge can result in tension as mankind also seeks to unite as one. In consequence, some of her characters seek to recapture a lost age of innocence.

One of the dominant themes in her work is the unity of humankind. Love between a man and a woman interests her less than brotherly love. In this, her thinking may reflect the Roman Catholic emphasis on the distinction between body and soul. Roy favors a pantheistic, transcendent union between man, nature, and God. Her philosophy rests on a sense of the cycles that make up life and death. Death gives meaning and value to each individual life.

Observation and imagination blend in works that reflect her love of the countryside. Over time, Roy's writing shifted from linear narrative. A number of her works comprise chapters that can be read independently and yet together constitute a unified whole.

Enchanted Summer (1973), for example, consists of a selection of memories from a summer spent at her house in the countryside outside of Quebec. In this and other works, Roy personifies nature, revealing the connection between man and his or her environment that, for Roy, has deep philosophical significance.

On the surface, this is a light, pastoral work in which Roy lovingly depicts the Quebecois region, its topography, flora, fauna, seasons, and the products of the land. Yet there is a deeper meaning. Recurring themes are the problems of industrial development, modernization, progress, solitude, hope, love, and despair. In each instance, Roy demonstrates her capacity to look at both the positive and the negative aspects of each of these prevailing themes.

Another central theme in many of her works is the journey. She frequently depicts immigrants or wanderers, and the desire for travel has both literal and metaphorical significance. Male characters tend to have greater freedom of movement, although women share equally in the desire for liberty. There is an inherent tension between the desire for the freedom of the open road and the security of domestic space. In the end, though, all roads lead to death.

FURTHER READING

Clemente, Linda M. *Gabrielle Roy: Creation and Memory.* Toronto: ECW Press, 1997.

Lewis, Paula Gilbert. "The Incessant Call of the Open Road: Gabrielle Roy's Incorrigible Nomads," *French Review* 53, no. 6, Numéro Spécial sur Le Québec (May 1980): 816–825.

Ricard, François. *Gabrielle Roy: A Life.* Translated by Patricia Claxton. Toronto: M & S, 1999.

Roy, Gabrielle. *The Fragile Lights of Earth: Articles and Memories, 1942–1970.* Translated by Alan Brown. Toronto: McClelland and Stewart, 1982.

ROYAL WAY, THE (LA VOIE ROYALE)

ANDRÉ MALRAUX (1930) This novel draws on Malraux's experience on an archaeological expedition in Cambodia. A young archaeologist named Claude Vannec and Perken, an adventurer, follow a path through the jungle leading to the great Khmer temples. As they travel, Claude and Perken discuss death and art, two themes of particular importance to Malraux.

Claude is searching for bas-reliefs on the ancient temples but, significantly, cannot break them free from the stone. The hammer fails him just as all the accouterments of civilization have weakened over time. The jungle thus takes on symbolic meaning, representing a metaphysical truth that lives on even when culture and civilization may die. Perken, in contrast, is trying to get enough money to buy arms for the tribe he has come to dominate.

Claude and Perken are captured by a Moi tribe where they find Grabot, a courageous and determined deserter who lived alone in the forest until the Moi blinded and enslaved him. When Claude and Perken find Grabot, he is naked and tied to a grindstone that he turns by crawling along the floor in a circle. When they ask him what has happened, Grabot answers "nothing." Despite his humiliating condition, Grabot has control of his life because he is thoroughly disdainful of death. Something in his vision inspires Perken, who says, "D'you see all those damn-fool insects making for that lamp, obeying the call of the light? The termites, too, obey the law of the anthill. . . . I will not obey." In the end, Perken dies of sceptic arthritis as he tries to avenge Grabot's death, even as he realizes that any attempt to do so is hopeless.

The Royal Way is a novel about failure and solitude. In this sense it is different from Malraux's other novels, in which he suggests the possibility of transcending fate. The work is heavily philosophical, and critics have accused Malraux of being too abstract. Others have noted the similarities between this novel and Joseph Conrad's *Heart of Darkness* in theme, plot, and character. As in other novels, Malraux explores human solitude in a world indifferent to our fate. "Death is there, don't you see, as the irrefutable proof of life's absurdity." Malraux was concerned with our place in the universe and our isolation in the face of death. The absurdity of life ultimately leads him to conclude that art may serve as our "anti-destiny."

FURTHER READING

Cordle, Thomas. "The Royal Way." *Yale French Studies,* no. 18, Passion and the Intellect, or: André Malraux (1957): 20–26.

Fallaize, Elizabeth. *Malraux, La Voie royale.* London: Grant and Cutler, 1982.

S

SACRED HILL, THE (LA COLLINE INSPIRÉE) MAURICE BARRÈS (1913)

In this novel, the three Baillard brothers, all of whom are priests, seek to evoke the mystical spirit of Lorraine on the sacred hill of Sion-Vaudémont. Together they establish the Institute of the Brothers of Our Lady on the Hill. The central figure is the eldest brother Léopold, whose fervor leads him to join with the prophet Vintras to form a new religious community. In consequence, a group composed in part of members of the church hierarchy forms against Léopold and his brothers. Even the general public views them as heretics who deserve to be excommunicated. One of the brothers, François, dies without receiving the sacraments. Having brought ruin to the group, Léopold finds himself alone and isolated.

One winter night while wandering through the snow, he is saved from eternal damnation through the efforts of a priest from Sion who sacrifices his own life to ensure Léopold's salvation. The words Léopold hears are "Troubled river, swallow yourself up in the ocean of the divine."

When this work was published in 1913, Barrès was already a famous writer and a member of the Académie Française. More lyrical than some of his other works, *The Sacred Hill* reflects Barrès's spirituality, his love for his native province, and his nationalism. Divided between CLASSICISM and ROMANTICISM, the novel influenced such writers as FRANÇOIS MAURIAC and GEORGES BERNANOS. Its message to modern readers is to warn against the dangers of unchecked idealism.

FURTHER READING

Curtis, Michael. *Three Against the Third Republic: Sorel, Barrès, and Maurras.* Westport, Conn.: Greenwood Press, 1976; 1959.

Doty, Charles Stewart. *From Cultural Rebellion to Counterrevolution: The Politics of Maurice Barrès.* Athens: Ohio University Press, 1976.

Field, Trevor. *Maurice Barrès: A Selective Critical Biography (1848–1979).* London: Grant and Cutler, 1982.

Guérard, Albert Léon. *Five Masters of French Romance: Anatole France, Pierre Loti, Paul Bourget, Maurice Barrès, Romain Rolland.* New York: Scribner, 1916.

SACRED NIGHT, THE (LA NUIT SACRÉE) TAHAR BEN JELLOUN (1987)

The Sacred Night takes up Ahmed/Zahra's story that began with *The SAND CHILD,* on the night of her father's death. As the title indicates, it is a sacred night, the 27th day of Ramadan when Muslims believe one's fate is determined. Just before he dies, Zahra's father, Hadj, frees her from her forced identity as a man (Ahmed), asking Zahra to forgive him for having denied her the right to live her life as a woman.

At one point, Hadj had not even given medicine to his wife and daughters, reserving it solely for himself. He later reveals "I had to stay alive in order to rebuild my life. What cowardice, what misery!" When he is about to die, Hadj confesses, "I saw in her arms a boy and not a girl. I was already possessed by madness. Never have I seen in you, your body, feminine features." In Arabic, Zahra means *flower;* metaphorically,

Zahra can now blossom into her true self. Hadj's dying words, however, do not make up for years of pain. Zahra says that "he will carry with him into his tomb the image of the monster he created." There is no sign of mourning from Zahra's sisters either, rather celebration of their father's death. The sisters play loud music as Zahra observes from a distance.

At night, Zahra sneaks into the cemetery where her father is buried and opens his grave, placing next to his body all evidence of her forced identity as a man, including a false photograph of her circumcision. She then takes the long bandage always wound tightly around her breasts and strangles her father's dead corpse with it. Ben Jelloun thus starkly reflects on male power over women in traditional Muslim society. That power is almost absolute. Zahra experiences a sort of death, even though she was not killed outright at birth. Rather she has been forced to remain silent about the very core of her identity. Her mother eventually goes insane because of the weight of her secret.

After her father's death, Zahra sets out to live a new life, and as she wanders from place to place, strange and dangerous things occur. The most significant event is her encounter with a blind mystic who introduces her to eroticism and mysticism and with whom she finds love. Zahra and the consul, as he is called, are inspired by the poetry of the Koran. With his hands, his "eyes at the ends of his fingers," the consul brings Zahra to life by awakening in her sensual awareness of her own body. "He sculpted me in a statue of flesh, desired and desiring."

Erotic love represents the ultimate, perfect union with God. However, the tradition of Sufi mysticism stands in direct contrast to the experience of men and women in everyday life. When Zahra is in prison, she imagines a beautiful light that comes from the heavens or from love. Through her love for the blind consul, Zahra learns that accepting darkness leads to light.

Zahra's understanding does not come immediately, however. In the course of her adventures she murders her uncle, is imprisoned, and, by her sisters, subjected to to female circumcision. The theme of vision is central to the text. Zahra even ties a bandage around her eyes so that she, too, is blind. When she is circumcised, the only reason the reader has a description of

the women who violate Zahra is because one of them tears off her blindfold. Men, too, are incapable of seeing a woman's body. Zahra's father is only the most extreme example. Other male characters, in their own way, are equally blind as they reduce a woman's body to its erotic parts. Only the blind man, who sees with his hands, perceives the true beauty of a woman's body. And only after many years does Zahra free herself from her past, liberated, finally, both physically and spiritually, to re-create for herself the consul's tranquility.

FURTHER READING

Cazenave, Odile. "Gender, Age, and Narrative Transformations in by Tahar Ben Jelloun," *French Review* 64, no. 3 (February 1991): 437–450.

Marrouchi, Mustapha. "Breaking Up/Down/Out of the Boundaries: Tahar Ben Jelloun," *Research in African Literatures* 21, no. 4 (Winter 1990): 71–83.

Zahiri, Mohammed, and Rachid Ameziane-Hassani. "The Father Figure in Tahar Ben Jelloun: *La Nuit Sacrée, Jour de Silence à Tanger,* and *Les Yeux baissés*," *Callaloo* 15, no. 4 (Autumn 1992): 1,105–1,109.

SADE, DONATIEN-ALPHONSE-FRAN-ÇOIS, MARQUIS DE (1740–1814)

Born in Paris, the infamous Marquis de Sade came from a prestigious noble family from Provence. Military man, writer, criminal, and revolutionary, this author brought ENLIGHTENMENT philosophy to its ultimate conclusion through pornographic novels of sexual cruelty.

Sade was initially educated in the country by his uncle, the abbé de Sade d'Ebreuil, but in 1750 he returned to Paris to continue his studies under the Jesuits. In 1755 he entered the military and participated in the Seven Years' War of 1754–1763 and that involved most major European powers. Under pressure from his family, Sade married Renée Pélagie Cordier de Launay de Montreuil in 1763. Five months after his marriage Sade was arrested for the first time. He would be arrested on many more occasions for violence, cruelty, torture, sodomy, and poisoning. The events of his life parallel those described in his novels. In 1772 Sade was charged with murder by the parliament of Provence and was executed in effigy. He had run away to Italy with his sister-in-law, whom he passed off as his wife. The death sentence was later revoked. Just as he was arrested on more than one occasion, so did he escape. In 1778, however, he was finally incarcerated by notorious *lettre de cachet* that denied the right of habeas corpus. By 1784 he had been transferred from the Château de Vincennes to the Bastille prison. He was moved yet again to another series of prisons after inciting the crowd outside the Bastille in 1789. Sade escaped the guillotine only by chance.

Sade was freed along with other victims of the *lettre de cachet* in 1794, at which point he began to participate in revolutionary politics. Nonetheless, he was rearrested in 1801 as the author of *JUSTINE* and *JULIETTE*. Sade's final place of internment was the hospital of Charenton, where, attended by his mistress Marie-Constance Quesnet, he directed plays attended by Parisian high society.

Sade's atheism is revealed in his *Dialogue between a Priest and a Dying Man,* not published until 1926. But he is known more for his sexual deviancy whose legacy is the term *sadism. Justine* was published in 1791, and *The New Justine* followed by *The History of Juliette Her Sister* in 1797. In the interim, Sade published his *Bedroom Philosophers* and *Aline and Valcour. THE 120 DAYS OF SODOM* was not published until the 20th century. Altogether Sade produced about 12 novels, most of them extremely long, 60 tales, and 20 plays. About one quarter of his manuscripts were destroyed under the Consulate and the Empire.

As a writer, Sade belongs to the revolutionary period in which he lived. He was in prison when the Revolution began (see FRENCH REVOLUTION). As a deviant aristocrat prone to immorality, Sade should have been everything the Revolution was against, yet he became its supporter. A number of his works were published only because of the new freedom of the press inaugurated by the Revolution. Perhaps the descriptions of violence and excess suited the spirit of contemporary events. In any case, his novels were a success.

Since the 1960s there has been renewed interest in Sade, who has been reexamined in the context of Enlightenment thought. He has been linked to the surrealist movement and, more recently, has undergone a controversial reading by feminist scholars (see SURREALISM, FEMINISM).

FURTHER READING

Barthes, Roland. *Sade, Fourier, Loyola.* Translated by Richard Miller. New York: Farrar, Straus and Giroux, 1976.

Du Plessix Gray, Francine. *At Home with the Marquis de Sade.* New York: Simon and Schuster, 1998.

Fabre, Jean. "Sade et le roman noir." In *Le Marquis de Sade.* Paris: Armand Colin, 1968.

Heine, Maurice. "Le Marquis de Sade et le roman noir." In *Le Marquis de Sade.* Edited by Gilbert Lély. Paris: Gallimard, 1950.

Kehrès, Jean-Marc. "Libertine Anatomies: Figures of Monstrosity in Sade's *Justine, ou les malheurs de la vertu,*" *Eighteenth-Century Life* 21, no. 2 (1997): 100–113.

Schaffer, Neil. *The Marquis de Sade: A Life.* New York: Knopf, 1999.

Weber, Caroline. "The Sexist Sublime in Sade and Lyotard," *Philosophy and Literature* 26, no. 2 (2002): 397–404.

SAINTE-BEUVE, CHARLES AUGUSTIN (1804–1869)

Nineteenth-century France's most famous literary critic and professor of literature, Sainte-Beuve also wrote a novel, *The SENSUAL MAN,* that clearly places his writing and thought within the romantic movement (see ROMANTICISM). Sainte-Beuve's lectures on literature provided much of the material for his written work.

Sainte-Beauve was born in Normandy, and his father died shortly after his birth. Deeply wounded by this loss, Sainte-Beuve's mother and aunt kept the father's memory alive, thus marking Sainte-Beuve's childhood. Until 1818 when he left for Paris to continue his secondary education, the piety of his family and the Roman Catholicism of his secondary school education were important influences on his development. In addition, when he was 16 years old, Sainte-Beuve read CHATEAUBRIAND's *RENÉ* and was overcome by the romantic hero of the novel. From then on, Catholicism and romanticism were interwoven in his works.

A gifted student, Sainte-Beuve showed an interest in psychology. His first inclination was to study medicine, and in 1823 he entered medical school, where he studied for four years. From early on, Sainte-Beuve manifested a sensibility to questions of the soul, strangely blended with a typical 19th-century faith in science. He was principally interested in the way the physical world shapes the moral world, as is apparent in his later works of criticism. Sainte-Beuve spoke of a "Science of the spirit."

The language of disease, so prevalent in Sainte-Beuve's writing, reflects his medical training. His studies also had an impact on his approach to literary analysis. Sainte-Beuve's later lectures on Chateaubriand, for example, declared the end of the *"mal de René,"* the *"mal du siècle,"* or the moral disease, associated with the romantics. While in medical school, Sainte-Beuve began to write for Parisian literary journals articles in favor of romanticism. He also met VICTOR HUGO and attended the writer's literary circle, the *cénacle.*

In 1829 and 1830 Sainte-Beuve published his first collections of poetry. Of no great quality, his early poems at least exhibit a youthful honesty along with a blend of tenderness and morbidity characteristic of romanticism. As a staunch supporter of romanticism, Sainte-Beuve sought its roots in the Renaissance, thus making this 19th-century literary and cultural movement part of a longer literary tradition.

Sainte-Beuve seemed to move ceaselessly from one influence to another, from romanticism to socialism to liberal Christianity. Another significant influence in his life was his mistress Adèle Foucher, the wife of Victor Hugo. During their affair he wrote *The Sensual Man,* a partly autobiographical confession of an idealized love affair drawing on his experience with Madame Hugo. Yet in 1836, Sainte-Beuve suffered from the end of his relationship with her and disappointment over the failure of a Catholic renewal. Needing time to recover, he went to Lausanne, Switzerland, where he began work on his history of Port-Royal and the Jansenist movement. In the end, however, he was never able to overcome his own religious skepticism.

Sainte-Beuve was elected to the Académie Française in 1843. In 1848, disturbed by the events associated with the revolution, he resigned his post at the Mazarin Library, going into voluntary exile to Belgium. There he worked on *Chateaubriand and His Literary Group during the Empire* (1860). Upon his return to France in 1849, Sainte-Beuve began to publish his famous *Causeries du lundi* (Monday chats) and, later, *Nouveaux Lundis* (New Mondays). Sainte-Beuve left his mark on the literary history of France principally as a literary critic. His other major works include *Literary Critiques*

and Portraits (6 volumes, 1832–39), *Portraits of Women* (1844), *Literary Portraits* (1844), and *Contemporary Portraits* (1846).

Sainte-Beuve had a true passion for literature. Although his own fiction was second rate, he was a monumental literary critic who attempted to place each writer in his or her own specific context, both personal and historical. He sought to reveal the artist's soul. Although he was a friend of the great writers of his day—Hugo (for a time), ALFRED DE MUSSET, and GEORGE SAND, among others—Sainte-Beuve could also be petty and mean. He was often jealous of contemporary writers, and his greatest works focus on literary figures of the past. He was also an important influence on future writers, including MARCEL PROUST.

Sainte-Beuve's particular combination of sensitivity and intuition lends itself to romanticism, particularly in his belief that the principal source of literary creation lies in the writer's subjectivity. At the same time, Sainte-Beuve was interested in placing literary movements in their historical, spiritual, and sociological contexts.

FURTHER READING
Call, Michael J. *Back to the Garden: Chateaubriand, Senancour and Constant.* Saratoga, Calif.: Anma Libri, 1988.
Chadbourne, Richard McClain. *Charles-Augustin Sainte-Beuve.* Boston: Twayne, 1977.
Proust, Marcel. *Against Sainte-Beuve and Other Essays.* London, New York: Penguin Books, 1988.

SAINT-EXUPÉRY, ANTOINE DE (1900–1944)
Born into an aristocratic family, Saint-Exupéry developed a passion for flying at a young age. He first served as a pilot in the army and then flew commercial flights. Saint-Exupéry's first novel, *Southern Mail* (1930), tells the story of the pilots who flew air mail service between the southern French city of Toulouse and North Africa. *Southern Mail* and NIGHT FLIGHT (1931) emphasize the values of courage and mutual assistance that bind pilots together. Recalling ANDRÉ MALRAUX's HOPE, Saint-Exupéry offers a sense of grandeur and, in his own particular fashion, an aerial vision of the world frequently expressed in intensely lyrical passages.

Alongside a feeling of grandeur, Saint-Exupéry reveals the fragility of the human condition. Moreover, his love of flying led him to consider the relationship between man and machine. Even in his reveries about the experience of flight, Saint-Exupéry expresses concern with the problems of mass society and its vulgar materialism, all of which are detrimental to humankind. In contrast, Saint-Exupéry sometimes chooses to celebrate childhood, those moments in which dreams and the spirit live fully.

After failing an entrance exam for the naval academy, Saint-Exupéry entered the army. Through a combination of determination and connections, he became a pilot. He left the army in 1923 as a reserve officer. An unhappy love affair and a brief stint in sales only filled him with a sense dread over the monotony of daily life. In compensation, Saint-Exupéry turned to the distractions of worldly society, flying, and literature.

In 1925 Saint-Exupéry published his first novel, *Aviator.* Its publisher, Gaston Gallimard, then offered him a contract for a second novel with a similar theme, although it took Saint-Exupéry some time to complete his next work, especially since he became a pilot for the air mail service between Toulouse and North Africa in the following year. This experience provided the material for his second novel. Prominent themes of *Southern Mail* (1929) are the pilot's meditative solitude in flight, the camaraderie that exists among pilots, and their sense of duty. Remarkably lyrical passages again depict the experience of flying.

The story is one of impossible love between Jacques Bernes, a pilot on the Toulouse-Dakar line, and Genevieve, a young woman whose life is in contrast to his highly regular and ordered one. The novel's rhythm and varied points of view give a cinematographic quality to Saint-Exupéry's writing and prepare the way for his next work, *Night Flight.* For this novel, Saint-Exupéry drew from his experience flying the line between Toulouse and South America, transatlantic flights he undertook as of 1929.

The principal character of *Night Flight,* Rivière, the director of operations, has a strong sense of discipline and responsibility for his pilots and the danger they face daily. The pilots reflect the human condition in all its glory and frailty. Flight is a metaphysical experience that allows for a moment of distance from the concerns of the world, allowing pilots the opportunity to live in the present in a way most men never experience. At the same time, their work provides a profound sense of accomplishment. The novel ends in tragedy as a pilot disappears in a storm over the Andes.

In 1931 Saint-Exupéry married and began working as a test pilot, then scriptwriter, lecturer, and correspondent in the Spanish civil war. Mobilized at the beginning of World War II, Saint-Exupéry later spent time in New York City, where he wrote *Combat Pilot* (1942), an autobiographical work in which he reflects on the war. This work contains some extraordinary moments of subtle analysis followed by poetic passages full of hope, a sense of sacrifice, and the power of the collective.

Saint-Exupéry's most famous work, *The LITTLE PRINCE* (1943), was commissioned by an American publisher and is one of the great masterpiece's of children's literature. In this philosophical work, the Little Prince's relationship with his rose inspires a touching exploration of love and responsibility. Poetic characters such as the fox and the snake offer simple yet deep reflections on love, friendship, life, and death.

In 1943 Saint-Exupéry left for Algeria, where he volunteered once more for the French air force. He subsequently disappeared on his ninth reconnaissance mission in 1944. He left behind an unfinished work, *Citadel,* published posthumously in 1948. Part fiction and part autobiography, in this last work a desert prince learns a lesson in wisdom from his father's parables. In this work that reflects the author's generosity of spirit, sincerity, and idealism, Saint-Exupéry again evokes the recurring themes of humanity's need for both a collective spiritual community and the possibility of personal accomplishment.

Pilots figure prominently in all Saint-Exupéry's works. Yet the figure of the pilot represents humankind in general. JEAN-PAUL SARTRE once wrote that Saint-Exupéry teaches us that the world and man are revealed in activity, while LÉON WERTH said that Saint-Exupéry turned flying into poetry.

FURTHER READING

Cate, Curtis. *Antoine de Saint-Exupéry: His Life and Times.* New York: Paragon House, 1990.

Master, Brian. *A Student's Guide to Saint-Exupéry*. London: Heinemann Educational, 1972.

Mooney, Philip. *Belonging Always: Reflections on Uniqueness*. Chicago: Loyola University Press, 1987.

SAINT-RÉAL, CÉSAR VICHARD DE

(1639–1692)   Historian and novelist, Saint-Réal was born in Savoy and educated by the Jesuits in Paris. He wrote historical novels in an easy style and his works were popular despite their mediocrity. Historical fiction was not his only genre; Saint-Réal also wrote a treatise, *On Criticism* (1691), challenging André de Boisregard's *Reflexions on the French Language,* and *The Spanish Plot Against the Republic of Venice in 1618* (1674). His most famous work is *Don Carlos* (1673). Drawn from history, this work recounts the tragic tale of Don Carlos, prince of Asurias, son of Philip II of Spain. The story is full of drama and intrigue. In 1559, Don Carlos was engaged to Elizabeth, the daughter of Henry II of France. Instead, Don Carlos's father married the young woman intended to be his son's wife. Don Carlos, showing signs of insanity, contemplates patricide, is imprisoned by his father, then mysteriously dies. The striking elements of a love triangle, incest, and patricide make the story an engaging one. The novel was well received. Along with the works of CATHERINE DESJARDINS and MADAME DE LAFAYETTE, *Don Carlos* contributed to the transformation of prose narrative in its use of a more or less contemporary historical setting to comment on human behavior.

SALAMMBÔ GUSTAVE FLAUBERT (1862)

Flaubert first conceived of the idea for this novel on a journey he made with his friend Maxime du Camp in 1849–51. Distraught by the legal proceedings over *MADAME BOVARY,* Flaubert apparently thought it best to turn to the past for *Salammbô,* a rich, violent epic set in the period after the First Punic War (264–241 BCE). Polybius's account of the war of the mercenaries provides much of the material for this work. Flaubert also did an immense amount of research to make this story from the history of Carthage as accurate as possible. He began his research and reading in 1857, then decided that he needed to see Carthage. So he left France once again in the spring of 1858. He returned feeling that nothing he had written thus far was of any worth. At the end of his travel notes, Flaubert wrote, "all the energy I inhaled may penetrate me and be exhaled in my book."

Flaubert was inspired both by his reading on ancient civilizations and his travels to the Orient. He also came across a young woman in the streets of Rome who, he said, resembled Salammbô, further fueling his interest in the story. Later, a conversation with THÉOPHILE GAUTIER finally led him to take up his pen.

Writing did not come easily to Flaubert and he struggled for years on his manuscript, living in isolation and sleeping little. Alone with his work, he wrote painfully slowly. From time to time he would pause and return to his research. He was occasionally tempted to abandon his project. "Carthage will make me burst with rage."

The manuscript was finally ready for publication in 1862. It was immediately successful with the reading public. Unfortunately, the press was not as receptive. Flaubert was accused of historical inaccuracies. After the novel's publication, an archaeologist also unsuccessfully challenged Flaubert's work. Flaubert refuted his points, first to SAINTE-BEUVE, who devoted three articles to *Salammbô* in the *Constitutionnel,* referring to specific historical documents he had consulted. Subsequent archaeological finds have supported Flaubert's account. Flaubert was also accused of obscenity. Nonetheless, the novel remained popular and influenced women's fashions.

Salammbô, the novel's heroine, bears one of the Phoenician names for Venus. According to the plot, Carthage has failed to remunerate the mercenaries who fought for it. Led by the Libyan Mâtho, a Greek slave named Spendius, and a Numidian named Narr' Havas, the Barbarian mercenaries attack Carthage. There, accompanied by Spendius, Mâtho secretly enters the temple of Tânit, the moon goddess who protects the city. Salammbô, a virgin priestess, guards Tânit's sacred veil. Mâtho is already bewitched by Salammbô, who is also the Carthaginian leader Hamilcar Barca's daughter, and has fallen in love with her. Mâtho steals the veil and after showing it to Salammbô, leaves the city.

Hamilcar commands the troops who try to defend the city but without success. With the veil gone, the war turns in favor of the Barbarians. Schahabarim, the high priest, holds Salammbô responsible for allowing Mâtho to take the veil out of Carthage. He instructs her that she must, like Judith, enter the enemy camp, take back the veil, and murder Mâtho, but Salammbô unexpectedly falls as passionately in love with Mâtho as he has with her. She gives in to his desires. Salammbô does take the veil back to Carthage but is unable to murder her lover.

Despite the return of the sacred talisman, besieged Carthage continues to suffer. The enemies have sabotaged the aqueduct and there is no water. Only after the sacrifice of male children does rain begin to fall, and the tide of war begins to turn in their favor under the leadership of Hamilcar. Narr' Havas, who has joined Hamilcar to defend Carthage and is now engaged to Salammbô, traps the mercenaries in a gorge, where they die a brutal death from hunger. To make this powerful episode as accurate as possible, Flaubert studied Savigny's *The Effects of Hunger and Thirst* (1812). Savigny was a naval officer who survived a 13 day ordeal on a raft following the infamous shipwreck of the *Medusa* in 1816. Hamilcar then leaves the city via the port and the mercenaries are caught between two armies. Their leaders are captured. Mâtho is horrifically tortured before Salammbô's eyes and she dies witnessing her lover's painful death.

Flaubert seems to have deliberately chosen a period and people with which most of his contemporaries were not familiar. He was thus able to underscore the differences with contemporary society at the same time as he pointed to the ways in which human desire and its impact on our lives is unchanging. For this reason, one may compare *Salammbô* with *Madame Bovary*. Flaubert, too, writes with passion. His attempts at restoring a past civilization to life may at times be stilted, but the text exudes a violent passion nonetheless. Flaubert's rich style influenced the SYMBOLISTS. In its depiction of passion in an exotic setting, *Salammbô* also stands as one of Flaubert's romantic works (see ROMANTICISM).

FURTHER READING

Brombert, Victor. *The Novels of Flaubert*. Princeton, N.J.: Princeton University Press, 1973.

Constable, E. L. "Critical Departures: *Salammbô's* Orientalism," *MLN* 111, no. 4 (1996): 625–646.

Orr, Mary. *Flaubert Writing the Masculine*. Oxford: Oxford University Press, 2000.

Porter, Laurence M., ed. *Critical Essays on Gustave Flaubert*. Boston: G. K. Hall, 1986.

SAND, GEORGE (AMANDINE-AURORE-LUCILE DUPIN, BARONNE DUDEVANT) (1804–1876)

"This hermaphrodite genius united the vigor of a man with the grace of a woman, like the Sphinx of Antiquity, a lively and mysterious enigma, she crouched down at the extreme limits of art with the face of a woman, the claws of a lion, and the wings of an eagle." With these words ALEXANDRE DUMAS described the writer Georges Sand, whose love affairs with ALFRED DE MUSSET and Frédéric Chopin, the wearing of men's clothes, and smoking a pipe, as much as her lyrical prose, make her a mythical figure, admired by many of her contemporaries such as HONORÉ DE BALZAC and the Russian writer Fyodor Dostoyevsky.

When Sand died in 1876, GUSTAVE FLAUBERT praised "what there was of the feminine in this great man." Nineteenth-century Europeans had a fairly clear idea of what constitutes the feminine, and Sand transgressed its limits in a number of ways. Some critics have argued that Sand is one of the first modern women writers, not solely for her defense of women against the constraints of society, but because she also wrote *as* a woman. In the tradition of her contemporary the English writer George Eliot and later, COLETTE, Sand drew on female experience to portray the world of human relations. Concerned with defending women against oppressive bourgeois society, Sand promoted passion and love over marriage. Still other critics have argued that Sand stands apart from other contemporary writers not only for her voice as a woman but for her androgynous mind, to use the British writer Virginia Woolf's words.

Sand's father was an officer in Napoleon's Grande Armée. Born Aurore Dupin, Sand was four years old when her father died in 1808, leaving her to be raised by her grandmother, an important figure in her life, at the family estate of Nohant. At age 13, Sand went to study at a Parisian convent school. At first she was in despair; later she rebelled. Ultimately, she experienced some sort of spiritual crisis and supposedly even contemplated entering religious life. But in 1820 Sand returned to Nohant and in 1822 married the baron Dudevant. The marriage was not a happy one, and by 1831 the couple had separated. Sand left for Paris with their two children.

Many contemporaries viewed her subsequent bohemian lifestyle in the capital as scandalous. But their reaction did not seem to affect her as she continued to dress in men's clothing, smoke, and carry on love affairs. Many of Sand's writings reflect her passionate life in which lyrical confessions appear almost as prose poems. Sand took her pen name from one of her lovers, Jules Sandeau, with whom she wrote *Rose et Blanche* (1831). The first novel she wrote on her own, *INDIANA* (1832), published under the name George Sand, was an instant success. *Indiana, Valentine* (1832), *LÉLIA* (1833), *Jacques* (1834), and *Mauprat* (1837) are on some level autobiographical works that reveal the passionate nature of the author's own life. In them, Sand celebrates sensual passion and idealism. Her passionate spirit has for a long time served as the prism through which critics have analyzed her work. Recent scholarship, however, has begun to reexamine Sand's contribution to the history of French literature.

Sand's liberty of spirit and morals is evident from the way she lived. She had several lovers after Sandeau, including Musset, Pietro Pagello, and political theorists Michel de Bourges, and Pierre Leroux. Contemporaries were particularly interested in her turbulent affair with Alfred de Musset (which both writers made public in memoirs) and the pianist Frédéric Chopin, with whom she shared life for nearly 10 years.

After meeting Musset in 1833, Sand traveled to Italy with him. Once there, Musset fell seriously ill and Sand subsequently fell in love with Pagello, the doctor who was treating him. Musset naturally perceived this as a betrayal. The details of this painful affair became the stuff of literature. Sand wrote of this agonizing period in *Her and Him* (*Elle et lui*) (1859). Musset drew on their affair in his *CONFESSION OF A CHILD OF THE CENTURY*. Musset's brother, too, responded publicly to Sand's account in *Him and Her* (*Lui et elle*).

Sand is principally remembered for her *"romans champêtres,"* pastoral novels of love idealizing rural life and its people, inspired by her native province of Berry. Sand's rich experience as a child growing up in the countryside provided her with much of the material for her writing, particularly the tradition of the *veillée,* evening gatherings for songs and storytelling at the home of a peasant. These country novels have sometimes been criticized for exaggerating the positive aspects of peasant life and for their naive, childlike tone. Nonetheless, they remain some of Sand's most popular novels. Many of these works such as *The DEVIL'S POOL* (1846), *PETITE FADETTE* (1849), and *FRANÇOIS THE WAIF* (1850) challenge the restraints imposed by society. François, for example, marries a wealthy peasant woman despite his obscure origins.

As of 1836, Sand was increasingly interested in politics and began to associate with democrats and utopian socialists. She was first introduced into leftist political circles by Michel de Bourges. A number of her novels reflect the inspiration Sand found in the humanitarian socialism of Pierre Leroux, the Christian socialism of the defrocked priest Robert de Lamennais, and the utopian socialism of the Saint-Simonists, followers of Henri de Saint-Simon. Lamennais was for Sand the prophet of a new religion of humanity. Sand celebrates ordinary people in such novels as *Horace* (1841) and *The Miller of Angibault* (1845).

Another significant influence on Sand's thought was the writing of JEAN-JACQUES ROUSSEAU, particularly his *Social Contract* and *JULIE, OR THE NEW HELOISE.* Sand once said that from her youth she was taken with "the beauty of his language and the power of his logic." Similar to Rousseau, in *The JOURNEYMAN JOINER,* Sand suggests that society and its institutions are the cause of human suffering. Only love is capable of overcoming social barriers.

Along with other contemporary intellectuals, Sand greeted the Revolution of 1848 with enthusiasm. She dove into the fray, establishing a journal whose title later inspired JEAN-PAUL SARTRE's *La Cause du people* (The People's Cause) in 1970. Sand also worked for the minister of the interior, editing official reports. Like VICTOR HUGO, she was inspired in her romantic political views by a love of the people, whether peasants or laborers. "I am attached to the people by blood as much as by the heart."

Disappointed by Louis-Napoleon Bonaparte's coup d'état of 1851, Sand retired to Nohant where she worked on her autobiography, *Story of my Life,* as well as a series of novels. In the preface to *Petite Fadette* Sand wrote that she was no longer interested in political events. Rather, she wanted "to distract her imagination in turning to an ideal of calm, innocence and reverie." In her country home, Sand brought together thinkers and writers such as SAINTE-BEUVE, Jules Michelet, and THÉOPHILE GAUTIER. She also exchanged ideas with EUGÈNE FROMENTIN, ALEXANDRE DUMAS, FILS, and GUSTAVE FLAUBERT, all the while participating actively in country life. She took care of her garden, played with her grandchildren, and was involved in the lives of local workers whose children she taught to read. Sand organized village fetes and distributed alms. Finally, Sand wrote numerous plays to be performed in her private theater. Some critics have suggested that she introduced valuable innovations into performance techniques of the period.

Sand was troubled by the Franco-Prussian War (1870–71) and the violence of the PARIS COMMUNE. Like other romantics, she struggled against institutions associated with modern bourgeois life that constrain the human spirit. Political life only leads to disillusionment. Concerned equally with love as a guiding principle in life and with social inequality, Sand offers a vision of true equality and fraternity in the conditions of country life.

Certain themes and moral principles permeate Sand's writings. She used fiction to express her concern with women's rights in a world of hypocrisy. Above all, Sand was the romantic writer (see ROMANTICISM) par excellence in art and in life, as she experienced and then unveiled the tension between absolute passion and the constraints imposed by society on the individual. Her assertion that "the mission of art is one of sentiment and love" is the statement of a woman who herself needed to love and who believed that love offers the possibility of moral rejuvenation; love equals life. Sand thus celebrates sensuality and passion. For her, love is more than happiness; it is a duty and a right. Almost anything done in the name of love is legitimate as long as it is sincere. Sand repeatedly depicts love between people of two different social conditions. In this she may have been inspired by her parents. Sand's father was an aristocrat, her mother the child of a fowler. The discrepancy in her parents' backgrounds may explain in part Sand's political engagement in favor of worker and peasant rights. MADAME DE GENLIS was also an influence on Sand, particularly in her examination of the dynamics of property, class, and political power.

The link between art and life is strong in Sand's novels as she makes song, theater, pictorial art, or dance central themes. Whether in Paris or at Nohant, Sand drew together some of the most talented romantic musicians and writers of her day. An idealist, Sand wrote novels that serve as a counterpoint to the REALISM of contemporary writers such as Balzac, EUGÈNE SUE, and Flaubert.

FURTHER READING

Barry, Joseph Amber. *Infamous Woman: The Life of George Sand.* Garden City, N.Y.: Doubleday, 1977.

Crecelius, Kathryn J. *Family Romances: George Sand's Early Novels.* Bloomington: Indiana University Press, 1987.

Dickenson, Donna. *George Sand: A Brave Man, the Most Womanly Woman.* Oxford, New York: Berg, 1988.

Glasgow, Janis, ed. *George Sand: Collected Essays.* Troy, N.Y.: Whitston, 1985.

Harlan, Elizabeth, *George Sand.* New Haven, Conn.: Yale University Press, 2004.

Hofstadter, Dan. *The Love Affair as a Work of Art.* New York: Farrar, Straus and Giroux, 1996.

Jack, Belinda. *George Sand: A Woman's Life Writ Large.* New York: Knopf, 2000.

Manifold, Gay. *George Sand's Theater Career.* Ann Arbor, Mich.: UMI Research Press, 1985.

Maurois, André. *Lélia: The Life of George Sand.* Translated by Gerard Hopkins. New York: Penguin Books, 1977.

Naginski, Isabelle Hoog. *George Sand: Writing for her Life.* New Brunswick, N.J.: Rutgers University Press, 1991.

Peebles, Catherine. *The Psyche of Feminism: Sand, Colette, Sarraute.* West Lafayette, Ind.: Purdue University Press, 2003.

Powell, David A. *George Sand.* Boston: Twayne, 1990.

Sand, George. *My Life.* Translated by Dan Hofstadter. New York: Harper and Row, 1979.

Schor, Naomi. *George Sand and Idealism.* New York: Columbia University Press, 1993.

Vitaglione, Daniel. *George Eliot and George Sand.* New York: Peter Lang, 1993.

Walton, Whitney. "Writing the 1848 Revolution: Politics, Gender and Feminism in the Works of French Women of Letters," *French Historical Studies* 18, no. 4 (Autumn 1994): 1,001–1,024.

West, Anthony. *Mortal Wounds.* London: Robson Books, 1975.

SAND CHILD, THE (L'ENFANT DE SABLE) TAHAR BEN JELLOUN (1985)

Sand Child recounts the birth and childhood of Hadj's supposed son. Ahmed/Zahra is an androgynous character forced to live the first 20 years of his/her life as a male because of Hadj's desperate desire for a son. In writing this story Ben Jelloun draws from the North African oral tradition. At the novel's opening, for example, the use of the second-person plural indicates that he is addressing the story to the reader. Moreover, various characters, storytellers in the marketplace, narrate their perspective on Zahra's life, raising questions about truth and illusion. For each narrator, their version is the truth. In *The SACRED NIGHT,* Zahra takes up her own story.

At the birth of Ahmed/Zahra, all of Hadj's extended family is present. Hadj has called them together to witness the birth of his first son after a series of daughters. It is unusual for family members to be present during labor but Hadj wants them there. Regardless of the real sex of the infant, he will announce the birth of a son as, according to Muslim tradition, it is better to have sons than daughters. Daughters cannot inherit their father's property.

The only people who know the truth are Hadj, his wife, and the midwife. The girl subsequently grows up with a masculine identity and education. As her body begins to develop, her torso is tightly bound so that her breasts cannot be seen. Ahmed/Zahra suffers internally whereas externally she benefits from the power afforded males in this patriarchal society, even to the point of lording it cruelly over her sisters. She thus collaborates in the suppression of her own identity. Ahmed/Zahra goes so far as to wed a crippled and deformed cousin who dies not long after their marriage. One day, however, Ahmed/Zahra agrees to perform with a group of actors in the role of Zhora. This chance event stirs Ahmed/Zahra's soul in unanticipated ways as he/she experiences a sudden sense of liberation after years of being divided by his/her male social identity and female biological identity. At the age of 25 he/she "feels that his/her age is at least half a century. Two lives with two perceptions and two faces but the same dreams and the same profound solitude."

Some critics have accused Ben Jelloun of depicting Muslim society with Western biases. Scholars are further divided in their assessment of Ben Jelloun's fiction. For some, his works draw from postmodernist (see POSTMODERNISM) or *NOUVEAU ROMAN* trends. For others, his inspiration is derived from Arab traditions. Truly bicultural, Ben Jelloun draws deliberately from both Arab and Western traditions.

FURTHER READING

Cazenave, Odile. "Gender, Age, and Narrative Transformations in by Tahar Ben Jelloun," *French Review* 64, no. 3 (February 1991): 437–450.

Fayad, Marie. "Borges in Tahar Ben Jelloun's *L'Enfant du sable:* Beyond Intertextuality," *French Review* 67, no. 2 (December 1993): 291–299.

Marrouchi, Mustapha. "Breaking Up/Down/Out of the Boundaries: Tahar Ben Jelloun," *Research in African Literatures* 21, no. 4 (Winter 1990): 71–83.

Zahiri, Mohammed, and Rachid Ameziane-Hassani. "The Father Figure in Tahar Ben Jelloun: *La Nuit Sacrée, Jour de Silence à Tanger,* and *Les Yeux baissés,*" *Callaloo* 15, no. 4 (Autumn 1992): 1,105–1,109.

SARDONIC TALES (CONTES CREULS) AUGUSTE, COMTE DE VILLIERS DE L'ISLE-ADAM (1883)

Although not a novel, Villiers de l'Isle d'Adam's collection of tales had an impact on the development of the SYMBOLIST movement in 19th-century French literature. His writings are thus associated with the works of JORIS-KARL HUYSMANS, such as *The DAMNED* and *EN ROUTE.* Like Huysmans, Villiers manifests his fascination with the occult. A number of critics have noted the influence of German romantic thought (see ROMANTICISM), and the philosopher Georg Wilhelm Friedrich Hegel in particular. Nonetheless, Villiers's works remain unique in French literature, with their blend of morbidity, dream states, and mysterious otherworldly communications.

In "Vera," dreams are more real than death as Villiers plays with the concept of an uncertain reality. At the opening of the tale, Count d'Athol and his wife, Vera, form a perfect couple. Then, Vera dies and the count buries her in the family tomb. For a year, he continues to live in the spiritual presence of his wife. The count's imaginary world even overcomes the power of the other world. On the anniversary of Vera's death, count d'Athol reads aloud from her favorite book.

Vera's presence becomes increasingly intense until the count actually hears her voice calling him. Anticipating later developments in psychoanalysis, Villiers has the count cry out, "You are dead!" and Vera disappears. By speaking out, the count is "cured."

Villiers seeks to surprise, astonish, and horrify his readers with a series of macabre events. A jealous husband disfigures his mistress with a razor, an accident victim wakes up in the morgue, and a sadistic lord enjoys replacing the executioner on the scaffold. Certain stories reflect Villiers's desire to reveal the emptiness of existence. He is particularly critical of materialism, POSITIVISM, and REALISM. According to Villiers, the writer's purpose is to "awaken intense, unknown, and sublime impressions" that lead one to a transcendent reality. Villiers is fascinated with the relationship between humankind and that other world, of which we are not always aware. Bourgeois values deter humankind from an interest in the absolute. The cruelty in Villiers's *Sardonic Tales* lies less in the stories themselves than in the values he opposes.

FURTHER READING

Conroy, William Thomas. *Villiers de l'Isle d'Adam.* Boston: Twayne, 1978.

Lathers, Marie. *The Aesthetics of Artifice: Villiers' l'Ève future.* Chapel Hill: University of North Carolina Department of Romance Languages, Distributed by the University of North Carolina Press, 1996.

Raitt, A. W. *The Life of Villiers de l'Isle d'Adam.* Oxford: Clarendon Press; New York: Oxford University Press, 1981.

SARRAUTE, NATHALIE (1900–1999)

After her parents separated in 1902, Sarraute lived part of the time in Russia, where she was born, and part in Frence, where she eventually settled permanently. Trained as a lawyer, she exercised that profession until 1940, when she turned literary critic and writer. In 1939 Sarraute published *Tropismes*. Not a novel per se, in this work Sarraute introduces the word *tropismes* that is the key to all of her writing. In a blend of narrative and prose poems, frequently focusing on a hostile, urban world, Sarraute evokes a sense of the nonverbal "movements that exist on the edge of consciousness." JEAN-PAUL SARTRE and the poet Max Jacob both praised this work but it received little attention from the reading public at the time of its publication. *Tropismes* was republished in 1957.

A Jew, Sarraute was forced to go into hiding during World War II. Under the name Nathalie Sauvage, she posed as her children's teacher in a boarding school. Gradually, she began to conceive of her next major project, *Age of Suspicion* (1956). In this theoretical work, Sarraute acknowledges her debt to MARCEL PROUST, the English writer Virginia Woolf, and the Russian writer Fyodor Dostoyevsky and offers reflections on the art of the novel. Her goal is to downplay the importance of plot and characters. In this respect, Sarraute is similar to other contemporary writers such as ALAIN ROBBE-GRILLET and CLAUDE SIMON.

In Sarraute's *Portrait of a Stranger* (1948), a distant, cold, yet cultivated first-person narrator observes a woman who both loves and hates her father. To escape him she marries a wealthy suitor. The narrator is connected to the woman because she once politely refused his offer of marriage. The narrator of *Martereau* (1953) is an indecisive esthete who lives with an aunt and uncle who shower him with a combination of affection and scorn. The couple commission Martereau to purchase a house in the country for them but he betrays their confidence by taking their money. In *The PLANETARIUM*, an omniscient narrator recounts the story of Alain Guimier, newly married and poor, who tries to convince his aunt to turn over a large apartment to him so that he can overcome his in-laws' derision. Alain has also written a thesis and wishes to launch a literary career, so he seeks guidance from an established writer. In this novel, Sarraute thus introduces the problem of artistic production and reception.

Sarraute differs from contemporary writers in these three novels in the sense that the objects (a country house, an apartment, works of art) that play a part in her stories are not simply enumerated in the manner typical of NOUVEAU ROMAN novels; rather, they signify the instinct for accumulation and a parallel fear of death.

Narrative and dialogue alternate in these works, whereas in Sarraute's later novels, dialogue predominates. In her autobiographical *Childhood* (1983), Sarraute recalls how her father lent her a book. When she was reading it, she skipped over long descriptive passages to get to the dialogue. In her own works, dialogue, real or internal (between different parts of the self) dominates, yet the delineation between the two is obscure. At the same time, one could argue that her characters express themselves less by words than by intonation and gesture.

The reader senses the characters' anxiety that the people who surround them have somehow detected their secret fears. Aware of their vulnerability, Sarraute's characters wear a mask. They never seek solace in being alone, however, as solitude is unbearable. In subsequent works, Sarraute's characters become increasingly less solid and identifiable. Sarraute is famous for creating characters identified solely by the pronouns "he," "she," or "they." Her characters are thus anonymous because unnamed. They exist, moreover, in a constant state of change.

Her notion of the self made Sarraute a natural critic of the traditional novel. Like other writers associated with the NOUVEAU ROMAN, Sarraute denied the traditional 19th-century novel's capacity to represent reality. For Sarraute, traditional novels fail to reveal the complexity of the self and reality. Sarraute believed that a psychological approach surpasses reality but only in recognizing *"tropismes,"* those things that are experienced but not expressed. Sarraute thus shares with James Joyce an emphasis on internal monologue and a parallel exploration of the self found in the writings of American author Henry James, Marcel Proust, ANDRÉ GIDE, and Czech writer Franz Kafka. Sarraute defined the "I" of the NOUVEAU ROMAN as "a being without contours, indefinable and invisible, who is nothing and who is most often a reflection of the author him- or herself."

Solitude is an important theme in Sarraute's work as it is necessary, for example, for reading or for the contemplation of a work of art, as is evident in *Portrait of a Stranger*. Introspection and reflection, however, may not be good for the work of art itself. In *Between Life and Death* (1968), Sarraute introduces a writer whose life she follows from childhood. She describes with irony the writer's mother and teachers, who believe that he shows signs of genius even at a young age. Later, his words seem to whither as the writer fusses too much over them.

Golden Fruit (1963) is centered on a discussion about a best-selling novel of the same title that has provoked much debate but is only an expression of intellectual snobbery. The reader learns nothing of the novel's content, only that its aesthetic vision has become obsolete. Comments on the novel reveal instead what the speaker thinks of him- or herself. The novel exists as a labyrinth, a world of illusions from which there is no escape until it is destroyed from within by its inherent falsehood.

In the 1960s Sarraute began writing for theater. Her plays are similar to her fiction in the sense that they evoke feelings, desires, and aggressions that one usually tries to suppress. In a novel written in 1972, for example, *Do You Hear Them?*, Sarraute focuses on intergenerational conflict, culture and counterculture. In *Fools Say* (1976), a terrorist's message forces those who oppose it into silence.

The problem of language is central to Sarraute's thinking as is evident, too, in *Use and the Word* (1980), in which she explores the way in which words are expressed. The origin of this work lies in 10 random sentences that then become the foundation for 10 separate texts that together make up this novel. Prevailing themes are death, love, friendship, family, and, perhaps most important, misunderstanding. Through these themes, Sarraute explores the unexpected depth and consequences of the language we use, as what appear to be insignificant words can provoke unforeseen actions and responses.

Sarraute's novels are marked by minute psychological analysis and descriptions of the way in which an individual moves from one feeling to another. Because she viewed the self as unstable and ever-shifting, her narrative frequently shifts its points of view, moving from third-person to dialogue and back again. Her novels consistently focus on an intimate group of people, family, or friends, emphasizing the dramatic nature of internal debates. In *You Do Not Love Yourself* (1989), a highly abstract and experimental novel, the voice that makes the accusation in the title is never identified. The obvious questions—Who is the subject? What is the object? What are the obstacles to love?—all remain obscure.

In addition to her novels and plays, Sarraute wrote works of literary criticism. In all her works, she seeks to evoke both sensual experience and the power of the spoken language. Sharp, innovative, and original, Sarraute's writing is difficult and yet she has sparked the interest of readers the world over, having been translated into over 20 languages. Readers have perhaps been attracted by Sarraute's fascination with "that bit of reality as yet unknown" as much as by her graceful use of language.

Inspired by Dostoyevsky, Proust, and Joyce, Sarraute believed that the truth of the human psyche is revealed not in the individual but in the exchange between individuals, hence her focus on dialogue. Consequently, her interest in the human psyche does not lie at the level of individuals but with humanity as a whole. Yet what fascinated her most was not human interaction itself, but what precedes it, the movement that takes place within, before the psyche settles into individual expression. As she wrote in *Tropismes,* Sarraute sought to capture "the indefinable moments that glide rapidly to the limits of our consciousness. They are the origin of our gestures, our words, the feelings that we express, that we believe we experience and that are impossible to define. It seems to me that they constitute the secret source of our experience."

Sarraute's novels are inherently psychological but not in any usual way as she seeks to reveal the impulse of consciousness rather than to analyze a character's actions or feelings. This is possible only through the "under-conversations" that lie hidden beneath a word or gesture. Conversation is thus the materialization of internal movements of the psyche. Sarraute received the National Grand Prize for Literature in 1982.

FURTHER READING

Barbour, Sarah. *Nathalie Sarraute and the Feminist Reader: Identities in Process.* Lewisburg, Pa.: Bucknell University Press; London: Associated University Presses, 1993.

Besser, Gretchen. *Nathalie Sarraute.* Boston: Twayne, 1979.

Jefferson, Ann. *Nathalie Sarraute, Fiction and Theory: Questions of Difference.* Cambridge, New York: Cambridge University Press, 2000.

Minogue, Valerie. *Nathalie Sarraute and the War of Words: A Study of Five Novels.* Edinburgh: Edinburgh University Press, 1981.

O'Beirne, Emer. *Reading Nathalie Sarraute: Dialogue and Difference.* Oxford, New York: Clarendon Press, 1999.

Ramsay, Raylene L. *The French New Autobiographies: Sarraute, Duras, and Robbe-Grillet.* Gainesville: University of Florida Press, 1996.

Temple, Ruth. *Nathalie Sarraute.* New York: Columbia University Press, 1968.

Watson-Williams, Helen. *The Novels of Nathalie Sarraute, Towards an Aesthetic.* Amsterdam: Rodopi, 1981.

SARRAZIN, ALBERTINE (1937–1967)

Born and orphaned in Algiers, Sarrazin was first raised on public assistance and later brought up by a fairly wealthy family in France. A talented student, as an adolescent, Sarrazin nonetheless frequently ran away from home and committed a series of minor crimes that led to her incarceration. When she left prison for the last time, Sarrazin had with her the manuscripts she had written while in prison.

Sarrazin's novel *The Runaway* (1965) was extremely successful. Unfortunately, she died in 1967 from complications after an operation. In her writing, Sarrazin drew from her own experience. In this novel, Sarrazin unveils the peculiar world of a women's prison and the strange beings who inhabit it. The two principal characters are Anne, who clearly resembles the author, and Julien who is not entirely honest but seductive and sweet nonetheless. He is modeled on Sarrazin's husband, Julien Sarrazin, whom the author married in 1959.

A later novel, *Astragal* (1966), focuses on an earlier period in Anne's life. In this work, Anne, age 19, escapes from a juvenile detention center but in the process breaks a bone in her foot, the astragal of the novel's title. Julien finds and protects her and love blooms. As she moves from one hiding place to the next, Anne's foot slowly heals. Sarrazin also wrote *The Crossing* (1966), some short stories, poems, journals, and correspondence.

SARTRE, JEAN-PAUL (1905–1980)

As a child Sartre dreamed of becoming famous. He achieved his goal but, ironically, in part by challenging the myth of "great men." One might argue that the two greatest figures of the postwar era in France were president Charles de Gaulle and Sartre, and the conflict between them marked the spirit and struggle of an age. Later in life, when a government minister proposed to arrest Sartre for inciting young people over the war in Algeria, Sartre's nemesis, de Gaulle, reportedly responded, "One does not imprison Voltaire."

Sartre's father died when his son was only 15 months old. His mother remarried in 1917, and the family moved to La Rochelle, a difficult adjustment for Sartre, who did not get along with his stepfather or his new classmates. Life improved when Sartre returned to Paris for high school, where he met Paul Nizan. The two friends went on to study philosophy at the prestigious École Normale Supérieure. There Sartre encountered fellow-student SIMONE DE BEAUVOIR who became his lifelong companion. They were destined to become a legendary couple.

During his years as a philosophy student, Sartre began to develop his own vision of the human condition, drawing on the thought of philosophers Edmund Husserl and René Descartes and first articulated in *The Imagination* (1940), a critique of the traditional concept of the image and its role in human consciousness. Sartre's first success as a writer came with the publication of *NAUSEA* (1938) and a collection of short stories, *The Wall* (1939). *Nausea* is as much a work of philosophy as fiction in its exploration of the existential crisis of Antoine Roquentin, the novel's principal character. Drafted in 1939, Sartre was taken prisoner in 1940 and freed in 1941. Throughout the war Sartre continued to write, working on *The Age of Reason* (1945) and his *War Diaries: Notebooks from a Phony War*.

During the German Occupation, Sartre worked on what is arguably his most famous philosophical work, *Being and Nothingness* (1943), which begins with the essential element of existential philosophy (see EXISTENTIALISM), the notion that man is defined by his existence, not his essence. Through action, man determines his own reality but only through constant questioning. Sartre suggests that man is free only when he is capable of putting objects at a distance, in order to bring them into nothingness by focusing on the relationship between the consciousness and the objective world. We are free, but only in "situation,"; that is to say, the possibility of action is constrained by the circumstances in which we find ourselves. We always have the capacity to alter situations, to escape. The danger is being imprisoned by others who define us as an object. We can be judged solely on the basis of our actions and they are irreversible. Reliance on any moral system that comes from outside of ourselves only leads to inauthenticity and bad faith.

The blurred boundaries of Sartre's thinking are manifest in this work that offers philosophical analysis but reads like literature. A novelist and philosopher, Sartre also wrote extensively as a literary critic. The first of 10 volumes of *Situations* was published in 1947. Later volumes include Sartre's commentary on the writings of NATHALIE SARRAUTE and ANDRÉ GIDE, among others. Sartre also wrote for the theater, producing such monumental plays as *The Flies* (1943), *No Exit* (1944), and *Dirty Hands* (1948). Sartre's plays as well as his unfinished trilogy *Paths of Liberty* (1945–49) are firmly situated in the social, political, and historical context of the period 1938–40. All of Sartre's writings place man squarely at the center of a philosophical enquiry marked by a synthesis of Marxism and existentialism. Sartre's humanist vision is equally apparent in his studies of JEAN GENET and GUSTAVE FLAUBERT.

In 1944 Sartre left teaching and, along with intellectuals Raymond Aron, Simone de Beauvoir, Michel Leiris, Maurice Merleau-Ponty, Albert Olivier, and Jean Paulhan, established the review *Modern Times* with its mixture of journalism, literature, and philosophy. Its collaborators articulated their theory of the writer's political "engagement." For the next 50 years that journal played a central role in French intellectual life. By 1945 Sartre had become a fashion. The traumatic experience of the war led many French intellectuals to embrace existentialism. Sartre's plays became the means to spread existentialist philosophy to a broader public.

After 1960 Sartre focused more and more on the burning political questions of his day. His own interests became increasingly politicized as he turned to Marxism. By 1946, however, his relations with the Communist Party were turning sour, particularly after the publication of an article in which Sartre defended existentialism from attacks by dogmatic communist intellectuals. Sartre renewed his relations with the party in 1952 only to break with it again after the Soviet occupation of Hungary in 1956. He openly supported liberation movements in the Third World, traveling to China, Cuba, Brazil, and Egypt.

His political occupations did not prevent Sartre from continuing an impressive flow of literary production. He published the third volume of *Paths of Liberty* (1949), *What Is Literature?* (1947), *Troubled Sleep* (1949), a series of essays, *Baudelaire* (1947), *Mallarmé* (1948), and *Saint Genet: Actor and Martyr* (1952). Then in 1964, Sartre published his autobiography, *Words*.

In this work Sartre recounts his childhood and explains how literature and art at first provided him with the means of escape from the constraints of bourgeois life. He describes himself thus: "Between the two wars he advanced pretty far in his studies, yet he lived only with an utter misunderstanding of the meaning of life. He was the victim of a hoax until one morning he found out that one can be the victim of circumstance: a morning in 1939, when on his shoulders fell a uniform, a registration number and the duty of fulfilling a 'commitment' that others had accepted on his behalf. From then on he will decide to commit himself on his own." Applying a Marxist psychoanalytical method to himself, Sartre seeks to explain why he writes.

In 1964 Sartre won the Nobel Prize, but in accordance with his principle that one should reject all honors, he refused to accept it. In 1971 he founded the famous leftist Parisian daily *Liberation*, and in 1971–72, he published a monumental study of Flaubert, *The Family Idiot*.

Throughout his life Sartre wrote several hours each day. Only when he had succumbed to blindness did he turn to a tape recorder, a device with which he was never entirely comfortable. Sartre produced a remarkably diverse oeuvre, all of which manifests his rejection of bourgeois values and the idealization of art. Each of his characters confronts the problem of existence. Through them, Sartre reflects on the themes of anguish, responsibility (personal, public, and political), loss of freedom, and inauthenticity. In Sartre's view the writer bears an even greater burden of responsibility than ordinary people. He cannot simply be an observer, rather, his work must promote the humanist cause. In consequence, in his commitment to political engagement, Sartre did not hesitate to grapple with the most pressing issues of his day such as racism (*The Respectable Prostitute,* 1945), social and political issues of the interwar period (*Reprieve,* 1945), anti-Semitism (*Portrait of an Anti-Semite,* 1946), and anticommunism (*Nekrassov,* 1955). Sartre's oeuvre is marked by the-

matic continuity within change. After 1945 he rejected the notion of the isolated individual epitomized by Roquentin for one who bears responsibility in public life and thought.

Sartre's funeral in 1980 recalls the death of Hugo a century earlier. Over 50,000 people came to mark the occasion of his death and the contribution of his life. He died along with the utopian visions of the revolutionary movement of 1968; perhaps this is what the crowd mourned as much as the loss of the man himself. With his demise, the Left lost its greatest voice and the last great intellectual of a generation. Sartre's image was later tarnished by Gilbert Joseph's book depicting him as an opportunist during the war, even though his clandestine *French Letters* are an eloquent defense against Joseph's accusations. Despite the debate over Sartre's character, he remains an important literary and cultural figure. A number of unfinished works recovered after his death reveal a powerful mind engaged in a struggle to discover the mystery of the human condition during a period when traditional humanist values had been called into question.

Some critics view Sartre's works as nothing more than a vulgarization of the philosophies of Hegel, Husserl, and Heidegger. But such a characterization fails to recognize Sartre's own contribution to a philosophy of freedom. His works of fiction and drama have become classics, and his analysis of Flaubert and Genet, among others, even if not as well known to the reading public, constitutes a valuable contribution to the history of literary criticism.

FURTHER READING

Brée, Germaine. *Camus and Sartre: Crisis and Commitment.* London: Calder and Boyars, 1974.

Glynn, Simon, ed. *Sartre: An Investigation of Some Major Themes.* Aldershot, England: Avebury; Brookfield, Vt.: Gower, 1987.

Howells, Christina. *Sartre: The Necessity of Freedom.* Cambridge, New York: Cambridge University Press, 1988.

Jackson, Tommie Lee. *The Existential Fiction of Ayi Kwei Arma, Albert Camus and Jean-Paul Sartre.* Lanham, Md.: University Press of America, 1997.

Kern, Edith. *Existential Thought and Fictional Technique: Kierkegaard, Sartre, Beckett.* New Haven, Conn.: Yale University Press, 1970.

McBride, William L. *Existentialist Literature and Aesthetics.* New York: Garland, 1997.

Thody, Philip Malcolm Waller. New York: St. Martin's Press, 1992.

Wilcocks, Robert. *Critical Essays on Jean-Paul Sartre.* Boston: G. K. Hall, 1988.

SASSINE, WILLIAMS (1944–1997)

Born in Guinea, Sassine was of mixed heritage. His father was a Lebanese Maronite and his mother a Muslim from Guinea. Sassine was introduced to French culture at school. From a young age he was aware of his difference: "I am a half-breed and they made me feel this very early." Sassine's sense of alienation was only augmented later by 30 years of exile.

In 1961, still in high school, Sassine participated in a strike against the repressive regime of Sékou Tourné. A number of his friends were arrested and imprisoned, an experience he recalls in *Young Man of the Sand* (1979), an unsettling work evoking the themes of adultery, ritual murder, and an unjust political regime.

In this story of Oumarou, Sassine blends first- and third-person narrative, combining Oumarou's subjective and unstable vision of the world with that of an omniscient narrator. Oumarou's narrative is both hallucinatory and obsessional. In his nightmarish visions strange figures appear, one of whom at least the reader later learns is dead. Oumarou often repeats the phrase "The school is right next to the mountain of stones," and it is unclear at first why he is fixated on the school. Only later, through the other narrative voice, the reader discovers Oumarou has been thrown out of school. In another scene Oumarou raises a toast to his former teacher who "will be freed tomorrow." Only the next day, Tahirou dies. Oumarou is arrested and he, too, dies.

After participating in a strike that led to numerous arrests of 1961, Sassine went into voluntary exile. He eventually became a teacher of mathematics, living in several African countries before returning to Guinea in the 1980s. He earned his living as a teacher but he was in his heart an intellectual and a writer. He published four novels that include *Saint Monsieur Baly* (1973), *Wirriyamu* (1976), and *Zéhéros Is Not Just Anyone* (1985). His characters tend to be marginalized in a heartless society. They are also messianic figures who prophesy a new future for Africa. Sassine also wrote tales for children, short stories, and two plays.

SAVARD, FÉLIX-ANTOINE (1896–1982)

Born in Quebec, Savard was ordained as a priest in 1922 and for many years worked as a missionary in Abitibi, Quebec province, an experience he later recalls in his writings. Savard was also a professor of literature at the University of Laval in Quebec. His best-known novel, *MASTER OF THE RIVER* (1937), depicts the problem of colonization while bringing to life the image of a strong people set against a background of nature that is both beautiful and savage.

One of the most significant French-Canadian novels, *Master of the River* is set in rural Quebec. On the surface it is the story of Menaud and his daughter Marie. In fact, the novel tells the story of the Quebecois people and their chances for survival in an ever-changing world. Quotations from LOUIS HÉMON's novel *MARIA CHAPDELAINE* are interspersed throughout this work like a call to battle for the Quebecois people, "that race that does not know how to die."

Savard loved the Quebecois countryside. Like his compatriots, he was suspicious of industrialization and modernization promoted by the English that threatened their traditional way of life. For Savard it is the land and tradition that are important. Yet Savard's message is not overly simple. He does not merely extol the virtues of agricultural life. Menaud, for example, may work the land but he craves something else. It was his wife who convinced Menaud to turn to agriculture. What he really desires is to return to his days of freedom in the wilds.

Menaud worked for an Anglophone timber company as a log driver and he regrets this decision, wishing he had spoken out when he had the chance, even if through an interpreter. Menaud may need a translator to speak with the English engineer but not with the natural world. He so desires to return to the mountains that he will even agree to work for an English company. Over time, however, the once strong and proud Menaud sinks into weakness and dementia and thus seems to represent the questionable future of his people.

Marie, meanwhile, sits weaving, reminding the reader of the centrality of female characters to many Quebecois novels. Marie's domestic work and calm presence signify both the comfort and security of domestic life and the Quebecois people's struggle to survive. She is torn between two suitors, one of whom would bring her to the United States, the other who supports English industrialists.

Many rich sounds of the mountains, the forest, the river flow through the narrative, serving as the background for Menaud's and Marie's reflections. The presence of nature marks all of Savard's writings. The bond between father and daughter is threatened by outsiders just as their traditional way of life is. The two contrasting themes of silence and speech mark the tension they feel.

Savard's works made a significant contribution to Quebecois regional literature. With its celebration of tradition, *Master of the River,* inspired an entire generation of writers and won the David Prize. When Savard published his second novel, *Midnight* (1948), he was already a well-known writer. His works reflect his fears that the excessive individualism associated with the rise of modern society will break down the bonds among humankind. *Master of the River* and *Midnight* reveal Savard's love for his country and the Christian principles that inspire his vision.

SCARRON, PAUL (1607–1701)
Despite a debilitating illness that left him a grotesque parody of a human being, this poet and dramatist remained throughout his days a spirited wit. Born in Paris to a family of magistrates, Scarron was a wayward youth until he turned to an ecclesiastical career as secretary to Charles de Levardin, bishop of Mans. He spent eight years in Mans, socializing with the local aristocracy. This experience may have provided him with much of the material for his COMICAL ROMANCE.

Paralyzed by an illness in 1638, he returned to Paris, poor but indomitable, to make his living by his pen. Occasionally his opinions caused him more harm than good. In 1651 he supported the aristocratic opposition to the Crown, the Fronde, writing a "Mazarinade" against the much hated first minister, Cardinal Mazarin. In 1652, he married the orphan Françoise

d'Aubigné, (granddaughter of the Protestant poet Agrippa d'Aubigné), the future Madame de Maintenon, morganatic wife of Louis XIV.

Cared for tirelessly by his young and talented wife, Scarron ended his days surrounded by brilliant society. Inspired by the Italian BURLESQUE, he introduced that genre into France with his parody of Virgil's *Aeneid, Virgil Travesty* (1648–52), and his *Comical Romance* (1651–57). In reaction to the excesses of the *précieuse* novel (see PRECIOSITY), the burlesque promoted the joyful and amusing in the tradition of RABELAIS, as opposed to the austere and grand. A writer, Scarron was also interested in the theater. He wrote nine plays, some of which entered the repertory of the Opéra Comique and a number of other fictional works.

FURTHER READING
Phelps, Naomi Forsythe. *The Queen's Invalid; A Biography of Paul Scarron.* Baltimore: Johns Hopkins Press, 1951.
Armas, Frederick A. de. *Paul Scarron.* New York: Twayne, 1972.

SCHWARZ-BART, SIMONE (1938–)
Born in Guadeloupe, Schwarz-Bart cowrote her first novel, *Pork with Green Bananas* (1967), with her husband André. In this novel, Martiotte, an old woman from the Antilles, ends her days reflecting painfully on her past in a Parisian retirement home that she refers to as "the hole." The theme of exile is central to this novel. The Schwarz-Barts also wrote together the seven-volume *In Praise of Black Women.*

Schwarz-Bart's second novel, The BRIDGE BEYOND (1972), written on her own, followed by *Between Two Worlds* (1979), mark her as a leading Caribbean writer. In the latter, the sky and sea dominate the mythical story of Ti-Jean. A monster has swallowed the sun and so Ti-Jean goes in search of it. Fantastic and magical, this novel translates a traditional Caribbean myth into modern times while evoking both the lush beauty of the Caribbean islands and the lives of poor blacks living in conditions not much better than when they were slaves.

Poetic and rich in symbolism and imagery, Schwarz-Bart's novels also offer powerful portraits of the strong women of the Antilles. Schwarz-Bart once said, "I write for my people, I write for myself." Her writings express both Creole and female identity. The rhythm of Creole, its expressions and character, penetrate Schwarz-Bart's French. Her language, infused with elements of Creole folklore and oral traditions, recalls the traditional "griot," or African storyteller. Life and death are intertwined in stories that evoke strange metamorphoses and dream worlds.

Some critics have accused Schwarz-Bart of not being sufficiently political or feminist, charges that are not entirely justified. As she puts it, "For me [writing] is a political act, but not with a seal, a political mark." Schwarz-Bart is concerned with expressing "a complete Creole universe." She focuses on female characters of depth and capable of great love. They are the heart and soul of the Caribbean people.

FURTHER READING

McKinney, Kitzie. "Memory, Voice and Metaphor in the Works of Simone Schwarz-Bart." In Mary Jean Green, Karen Gould, Micheline Rice-Maximien, Keith Walker, and Jack Yeager, eds. *Postcolonial Subjects: Francophone Women Writers.* Minneapolis: Minneapolis University Press, 1996.

Ormerod, Beverley. *An Introduction to the French Caribbean Novel.* London: Heinemann, 1985.

Wallace, Karen Smyley. "The Female and the Self in Schwarz-Bart's *Pluie et vent sur Télumée miracle,*" *French Review* 59, no. 3 (February 1986): 428–436.

Wilson, Elizabeth. "History and Memory in *Un Plat de porc aux bananes vertes* and *Pluie et vent sur Télumée Miracle,*" *Callaloo* 15, no. 1, The Literature of Guadeloupe and Martinique (Winter 1992): 179–189.

SCUDÉRY, MADELEINE DE (1607–1701)

An orphan from a poor noble family, Madeleine de Scudéry was raised by an uncle who provided her with an extraordinary education for a woman of her time. Her talents as a writer and leader of the movement referred to as PRECIOSITY were such that, even as a woman, she was considered for, although not admitted to, the Académie Française.

Meeting in her home on Saturdays beginning in 1652, Madeleine de Scudéry led one of the most important salons of the second half of the 17th century. Surrounded by brilliant figures such as La Rochefoucauld, MADAME DE LAFAYETTE, and the famous

correspondent Madame de Sévigné, her circle included minister of finance Nicolas Fouquet, whom the group did not abandon even after his fall from the king's graces after being accused of embezzlement. Madeleine de Scudéry, or Sapho as she was known by her friends, was the center of the *précieuse* movement. The primary subjects of discussion in her salon were love, marriage, and literature. The clearest articulation of the *précieuse* concept of love is found in the famous "Map of the Land of Tenderness" (*Carte de Tendre*) in CLÉLIA.

Her first works were written with her brother Georges, whom she later surpassed with her two lengthy and immediately popular novels ARTAMÈNE, OR THE GREAT CYRUS (1649–53) and CLELIA (1645–60). She also wrote some shorter stories and "moral conversations." But it is *The Great Cyrus* and *Clelia* that left her name to posterity. While the novels she collaborated on with her brother fall under the category heroic, *The Great Cyrus* and *Clelia* introduce a new genre that defines the code of values and behavior associated with the *précieuses*. These *romans fleuves,* a sort of serial novel, were published over several years. These multivolume, extremely lengthy works were peculiar to the 17th-century literary tradition.

The setting for the novels is antiquity, either Persian or Roman, but the novels are *romans-à-clef,* that is to say, the characters depicted are well-known and recognizable contemporary figures. Artamène is the famous leader of the Fronde revolt, the Grand Condé; Mandane is the illustrious court intriguer Madame de Longueville; and Sapho is Madeleine de Scudéry herself. These thinly disguised characters were fascinating to contemporary readers, who recognized in the novels their own world.

The *précieuse* code of values outlined in Madeleine de Scudéry's novels was concerned above all with love and glory. Conversations in *Clelia* in particular reproduce those that took place in Madeleine de Scudéry's salon, the focus of which was an elaborate discourse on the nature of love. The Neoplatonist spiritual love of the *précieuses* emphasized respect for women. It is thus a sort of protofeminist literary movement. Madeleine de Scudéry's concern for the role of women in society permeates her depiction of an ideal world of gallantry and sophistication. It can also be seen in her piece published in *Illustri-*

ous Women in 1642, "Sapho to Érinne," in which she promotes women's education.

The exaggerated, sophisticated, and hyperbolic language of the *précieuses* took on a negative connotation with Molière's play, *Les précieuses ridicules* (1659). Despite this parody of *précieuse* society, Madeleine de Scudéry's writing is renowned for its discriminating and refined analysis of an endless array of emotions subtly distinguished and defined. Her works influenced moralists of the second half of the 17th century such as La Bruyère and Madame de Lafayette, whose analysis of love takes on a new subjective and highly psychological form in *The PRINCESS OF CLÈVES*.

FURTHER READING

Aronson, Nicole. *Mademoiselle de Scudéry.* Translated by Stuart R. Aronson. Boston: Twayne: 1978.

Davis, Joanne. *Mademoiselle de Scudéry and the Looking Glass.* New York: P. Lang, 1993.

Harth, Erica. *Cartesian Women: Versions and Subversions of Discourse in the Old Regime.* Ithaca, N.Y.: Cornell University Press, 1992.

McDougall, Dorothy. *Mademoiselle de Scudéry: Her Romantic Life and Death.* New York: B. Blom, 1972.

SEASON IN THE LIFE OF EMMANUEL, A (UNE SAISON DANS LA VIE D'EMMANUEL) MARIE-CLAIRE BLAIS (1966)

This story of one family's winter is told in part through the eyes of an infant, Emmanuel, the 16th child of a poor Quebecois family. The dominant figure in the family is the grandmother, Antoinette. The character of Jean the Thin, a child poet, adds an element of the mythical to this tragic family whose collective life is full of misery, degradation, and morbid sexuality.

In this work, Blais explores the themes of rural life and Catholicism as she draws from and subverts the traditional rural novel associated with other Canadian writers such as LOUIS HÉMON. The novel moves from third-person narrative to the first person in the voice of the young poet Jean the Thin, who is writing his autobiography from a tuberculosis ward. Jean recounts the story of his birth as a writer. The awareness of his vocation first came to him as he sat on a shared toilet seat with one of his siblings, hardly the typical beginning for a poet.

In the traditional rural novels of French Canada, the family and the church together represent community and survival in a harsh environment. In Blais's novel, however, these two social institutions appear dubious. If the figure of the grandmother dominates this work, the parents are weak. The mother, overcome with hard work and suffering, is no longer capable of distinguishing her living children from the dead. The only children she addresses are those who are gone—Gemma, who died unexpectedly on the day of her first communion; the infant Olive, whose head was crushed under her father's plow; and Leopold, the young seminarian who hung himself. The father, an illiterate patriarch, deals harshly with his wife and children. To become a writer is Jean's means of escape. Héloïse, in contrast, finds peace and comfort in a brothel.

With the exception of the mother, other members of the family appear to accept tragedy with resignation or cold indifference. When his brothers discover Leopold's body, for example, they simply sling it over their shoulders like the game they have caught hunting. It is not accidental that a number of the children's deaths are connected in some way to religion. The presence of the church runs like a current through the novel but not necessarily as a source of solace. Brother Théodule, for instance, is a pederast.

In this cruel and cynical look at rural life, Blais attacks without mercy traditional social institutions. While young intellectuals in the 1960s such as Blais often promoted regional identity and language, they did not hesitate to portray the grimness of rural life. Her writing is thus part of a reaction in French Canadian literature against the myth of Hémon's *MARIA CHAPDELAINE*. This may explain why her works are more warmly received in France than in Canada. *A Season in the Life of Emmanuel* won the Médicis Prize in 1966.

FURTHER READING

Green, Mary Jean Matthews. *Marie-Claire Blais.* New York: Twayne; London: Prentice Hall International, 1995.

Stratford, Philip. *Marie-Claire Blais.* Toronto: Coles, 1974.

SEA WALL, THE (BARRAGE CONTRE LE PACIFIQUE) MARGUERITE DURAS (1950)

This autobiographical novel tells the story of Duras's family. Attracted by stories of success in the colonies, a young teacher and her husband move to Siam (Thailand). The husband dies, leaving the woman to raise her two children, Suzanne and Joseph, in poverty. After many years of hard work, she amasses enough savings to buy land on which to grow rice, only to struggle in vain against a corrupt administration and the floods that inundate her fields. The only desire of her children is to escape the battle for life that their mother engages in. When Mr. Jo appears, as vile and offensive as he is rich and powerful, personal relations become increasingly complicated. Through the figures of the mother and the lover the recurring themes of love and death rise to the surface.

Love, death, and life in Indochina are the currents that flow through the works of Duras, as life and art merge into one. With its themes of colonialism, politics, and female oppression, this work reflects Duras's militant communism and sets the stage for later postcolonial and feminist writings (see FEMINISM). *Sea Wall* bears a certain resemblance to contemporary American novels of the "lost generation" that Duras admired. With the publication of *The Ravishing of Lol V. Stein,* Duras's writing began to move in a new direction even as she continued to draw from her wealth of personal experience.

FURTHER READING

O'Neill, Kevin C. "Structures of Power in Duras's 'Un Barrage contre le Pacifique," *Rocky Mountain Review of Language and Literature* 45, Mp 1/2 (1991): 47–60.

SECOND EMPIRE
The Second Empire was inaugurated on December 2, 1851, following Napoleon III's coup d'état after which he declared himself emperor, thus ending the Second Republic. The Second Empire was the golden age of wealthy businessmen who became the new aristocracy. Napoleon III's authoritarian regime was marked by censorship, suppression of political opposition, and manipulation of the electoral process. His regime drew support from the conservative bourgeoisie who sought above all social and political order. The centralization of political and economic power thus marked this regime.

The Second Empire witnessed the rebuilding of Paris under Baron Georges Haussmann, who promoted rationalization, modernization, and improved sanita-

tion in the city. This was also the age of POSITIVISM in philosophy and the rise of impressionism in the arts. In literature, the Second Empire gave birth to NATURALISM and REALISM. ÉMILE ZOLA's 20-volume ROUGON-MACQUART novels are entitled the "Natural and Social History of a Family under the Second Empire." Together these works such as GERMINAL, NANA, L'ASSOMMOIR, and *The BELLY OF PARIS* reveal the many and varied aspects of Second Empire society.

In this period of industrialization and economic growth, the Second Empire met with opposition from workers who advocated either republicanism or democratic socialism. The Second Empire ended with France's defeat by the Prussians at Sedan in 1871.

SEMBÈNE, OUSMANE (1923–)
An multifaceted and talented man, Sembène began his life in a small fishing village in Senegal and was later sent to live with an uncle in Dakar to go to school. Thrown out for causing trouble, Sembène subsequently engaged in manual labor until he was drafted in World War II. Sembène fought in Italy and Germany. When the war ended, he became a docker in Marseille. This experience revealed to him the problems of social injustice and the plight of workers.

Sembène joined the Communist Party, and in a labor union library he began reading the great French authors of the 19th century, such as HONORÉ DE BALZAC, GUY DE MAUPASSANT, and ÉMILE ZOLA. An autodidact, unlike other African writers Sembène had little formal schooling. However, he wrote several novels, all of which reflect his Marxist vision, including *Black Docker* (1956), *O My Beautiful People* (1957), *GOD'S BITS OF WOOD* (1960), and *Xala* (1981), along with several collections of short stories. Sembène's SOCIALIST REALISM reflects his concern with the future of the collective over that of the individual. Sembène once said, "so far as I am concerned, writing, which is now my job, is a social necessity, like the jobs of the mason, the carpenter, or the iron worker." A pioneer of African cinema, Sembène has adapted a number of his novels to film.

In all his works, Sembène denounces both pre- and postcolonial systems that continue to oppress the African people, attacking institutions that have contributed, in his view, to social alienation. Sembène considers, too, alienation and modernization. A militant Marxist, Sembène calls for freedom that can be attained only when the people gain political consciousness. Sembène is also a great defender of the ethics of traditional African society.

The notion of the "griot," or traditional African storyteller, is central to an understanding of Sembène's works. According to him, the griot is like the medieval troubadour, "a man of learning, a historian, a storyteller, the living memory and conscience of his people." This is also the role that Sembène envisions for himself. "I will try to the maximum," he has said, "to be of my time, to be not only Senegalais or African, but in the measure of the possible, universal."

FURTHER READING

Aire, Victor O. "Didactic Realism in Ousmane Sembène's Les Bouts de bois de Dieu." Canadian Journal of African Studies 11, no. 2 (1977): 283–294.

Gadjigo, Samba, et al., eds. Ousmane Sembène: Dialogues with Critics and Writers. Amherst: University of Massachusetts Press, 1993.

Murphy, David. Sembène: Imagining Alternatives in Film and Fiction. Oxford: J. Curry; Trenton, N.J.: Africa World Press, 2001.

Smith, Craig. "The Stereography of Class, Race, and Nation in God's Bits of Wood," Research in African Literatures 24, no. 1 (1993): 51–56.

Tsabedze, Clara. African Independence from Francophone and Anglophone Voices: A Comparative Study of the Post-Independence Novels by Ngugi and Sembène. New York: P. Lang, 1994.

SEMPRUN, JORGE (1923–) Born in Madrid, Semprun lived in both his native land and in France. His father was a lawyer and professor of philosophy and law at the University of Madrid. When general Francisco Franco's troops occupied that city in 1936, the Semprun family fled. After wandering from Holland then to Switzerland, the family settled in Paris.

Semprun was preparing for the university entrance exam when World War II broke out and at age 19, he joined the Resistance. Arrested in September 1943, Semprun was tortured and deported to Buchenwald as prisoner number 44904. His knowledge of German (Semprun's mother was German) and the support of communists within the camp assured his assignment to the Arbeitstatistik, where he registered new prisoners. Because of this, Semprun was able to learn of the arrival of former colleagues from the Resistance.

Liberated by American troops in 1945, Semprun returned to Paris, where he worked as a journalist and translator. He subsequently returned in secret to Madrid and joined the communists in Spain. Living under the name Frederico Sanchez, Semprun explored the city he had known as a child. A major theme in his works is the notion of man existing as a stranger to his city, his time, his very life. During this period, Semprun wrote The Long Journey (1963), largely in French.

In this work, Semprun relives the horrors of the concentration camp. The long journey of the title is Semprun's journey to Buchenwald in a closed wagon with 20 other prisoners. In contrast to MARCEL PROUST, who savors "lost time," Semprun is terrified by his memories. He recalls a conversation with one of the other prisoners, who dies standing up at the end of the journey. Later, he recounts the final words of a fellow Resistance fighter who passes his brother's cell on his way to execution calling out, "It's over, Philippe. I'm going. It's over."

As he travels along unable to see outside the car, Semprun imagines the landscape through which they pass, the valley of the Moselle. The first time he tastes Moselle wine after the Liberation, Semprun recollects showing the crematorium to a group of social workers and is overcome with the image of the charred bodies of his comrades.

In a similar instance of "involuntary memory," one day after the war, the taste of black bread (a far cry from Proust's experience with the madeleine pastry) makes him think of the hunger he experienced in the camps. He is at a dinner party. When his hosts ask why he has suddenly become so pensive, he finds that he cannot explain that he is "dying of hunger, far from them." More than a series of recollections, The Long Journey also considers the moral and philosophical implications of the camps. To ease his recollection, Semprun moves back and forth from memories before and after the war, abandoning any sense of linear time.

In 1962, Semprun was forced to leave Spain once again and so returned to France. In 1964 he broke with the Communist Party when he disagreed with the party line. *The Second Death of Ramon Mercador* appeared in 1969. This spy novel pitting agents of the CIA against the KGB won the Femina Prize. In all his writings, Semprun turned his sharp eye to the problems of contemporary history, Nazism, Stalinism, and the Spanish civil war. Semprun treated these burning issues with brutal honesty. With the return of democracy to Spain in 1975, Semprun was appointed minister of culture under the socialist government of Felipe González, serving his country in that position from 1988 to 1991.

SENANCOUR, ÉTIENNE PIVERT DE
(1770–1846)   Senancour was born in Paris. As a youth he preferred to spend time alone, often reading. From a young age Senancour was taken with the works of JEAN-JACQUES ROUSSEAU, and many of the themes associated with Rousseau's fiction and philosophy wend their way into Senancour's later works. Rousseau's influence remained strong throughout Senancour's life. His need for solitude resembles the great master, who spent so many hours of reverie walking in nature, away from society. Rousseau's philosophy seemed to legitimize Senancour's natural inclinations. First and foremost, Senancour was inspired by nature's beauty.

When his father pushed him to enter the priesthood against his will, Senancour ran away to Switzerland. There he met Marie François Daguet, a young woman who convinced him to marry her in 1790. The union was unfortunate for both of them.

In 1795, Senancour left his wife for Paris, where he oversaw the publication of his first work of fiction, *Aldomen, or Happiness in Obscurity*. Having been placed on the list of émigrés during the FRENCH REVOLUTION, Senancour was in danger of imprisonment. Moreover, his family had lost their fortune. Still, he continued to write, producing his *Reveries on the Primitive Nature of Man* (1799). This work went largely unnoticed by the public. Nonetheless, both *Aldomen* and *Reveries* lay the foundation for *Obermann*, Senancour's undisputed masterpiece. When Senancour wrote these earlier works he had already begun to turn his Rousseauesque vision of the world in a more pessimistic direction, as we see in his novel *Obermann*.

In 1802, Senancour's wife announced that she was pregnant, and he returned to Switzerland to avert a scandal. Shortly thereafter he secured a separation from her. Bitter and disillusioned, Senancour retired to the mountains to work on *Obermann*. Similar to *Aldomen*, in this novel a young man frustrated with the world searches for happiness and fulfillment. But whereas Aldomen ultimately found a sense of purpose in the simple pleasures of conjugal life in the country, Oberman was to remain frustrated in his attempts at fulfillment.

In 1805 Senancour published *On Love*, a defense of divorce, and in 1807 a play, *Valombré*. However, Senancour's richest period as a writer began as of 1814, when he turned his energy toward political philosophy, producing over the next 15 years *Simple Observations on the Congress of Vienna, On Napoleon, Simple Meditations of an Unknown Solitary Man*, and *A Resume of the History of the Moral and Religious Traditions of All Peoples*. Senancour almost went to prison for this last work in which he described Jesus as simply a young wise man (*un jeune sage*).

Senancour's disillusionment with life, revolution, and failed marriage moved him to his greatest work. Published two years after CHATEAUBRIAND's *RENÉ*, *Obermann* articulates even more eloquently the romantic disease or *"maladie du siècle"* (see ROMANTICISM). *René*, *Obermann*, and CONSTANT's *ADOLPHE* are romantic heroes who suffer from a tragic and despairing vision of the world. Unable to discern life's meaning, Senancour describes the romantic's "ennui" as resulting from the conflict between life as one wishes it to be and life as it is. Obermann's "slow agony of the heart" is another expression of the romantic disease. Only nature seems to offer the potential for solace. Consequently, Obermann attempts to escape from a world he disdains into nature's sublime beauty. Unfortunately, every moment of hope is followed by a moment of despair, his heart "wilted and dried up."

Both Aldomen and Obermann engaged in a search for a place to live both literally and figuratively, a place of spiritual and emotional fulfillment. If one novel is optimistic in its conclusion and the other pessimistic, the core themes remain the same. "Modern" urban society distorts human nature, diverting one's attention away from the natural order, in nature and in love. To live happily, one must love and live in nature in the harmonious order and simplicity that mirrors the divine order. Obermann reflects the author's sense of happiness and fulfillment as ultimately unattainable.

By the time *Obermann* was republished in 1833, Senancour was 63 years old and no longer suffered from the malaise of his youth. He had largely forgotten this earlier work when SAINTE-BEUVE's preface to the 1833 edition finally brought Senancour's work to the public's attention. It has subsequently come to hold its place in the literary history of France as one of the first romantic novels. Obermann's strain of the romantic disease leads the reader in the direction of EXISTENTIAL-ISM. Senancour describes a metaphysical malaise that inevitably develops as one becomes conscious of oneself. The resulting turn inward is both incurable and irreversible.

FURTHER READING

Brooks, Van Wyck. *The Malady of the Ideal: Obermann, Maurice de Guérin and Amiel.* Folcroft, Pa.: Folcroft Library Editions, 1973.

Call, Michael J. *Back to the Garden: Chateaubriand, Senancour, and Constant.* Saratoga, Calif.: Anma Libri, 1988.

Heck, Francis S. *Spiritual Isolation in French Literature from Benjamin Constant and Senancour.* Madrid: Dos Continentes, 1971.

SENSUAL MAN, THE (VOLUPTÉ) CHARLES AUGUSTIN SAINTE-BEUVE (1834)

In the introduction to *The Sensual Man,* Sainte-Beuve writes, "Sensuality has seized your flesh, it floats in your blood, winds through your veins, sparkles and swims in your eyes; a glance exchanged in which sensuality is mixed is enough to foil the most austere promises." In this work, the great 19th-century literary critic's only novel, the priest Amaury travels to America. Along the way he tells the story of his life to a young man as a lesson on passion. His story is one of three love affairs that ultimately led him to enter the priesthood.

Orphaned at a young age, Amaury, an aristocrat, is raised in Brittany by his uncle. He first falls in love with the charming and innocent, Amélie de Liniers, but Amaury is a romantic (see ROMANTICISM) who seeks more from life. He hesitates to form an attachment despite, or perhaps because of, the calm happiness he shares with Amélie.

On a hunting party, Amaury meets M. de Couaën. Set during the period of the consulate 1799–1804, Couaën is the head of a group of royalists who takes Amaury under his wing. This time the young man falls in love with Couaën's wife. Although she is attached to Amaury, she keeps him at a distance, maintaining a Platonic affair. When Couaën is arrested, Amaury follows Madame de Couaën to Paris, where her husband has been detained. Increasingly frustrated by her refusal to make their relationship more intimate, Amaury turns to debauchery, only to find that this, too, is unsatisfying. Disappointment leads to the demise of their relationship, at which point Amaury takes up with a coquette, thus beginning his third and last love affair.

Principally occupied with improving her position in society, Madame R. teases the romantic hero, compelling him to wave to her each night at midnight from under her windows, but nothing more. Having failed at love three times, Amaury enters the priesthood and is able to confess Madame de Couaën on her deathbed.

Amaury's turn to religion is not as surprising as at first glance. There is a certain logic to Sainte-Beuve's plot. If love is an impossible dream, it will necessarily wear itself out; only religion can replace it. Sainte-Beuve's idealization of a woman as a maternal lover translates in Catholicism into an adoration of the Virgin Mary.

Amaury experiences the moral uncertainty that CHATEAUBRIAND described as a "wave of passions," and thus reflects characteristics of romantic thought. While it is partly autobiographical, the novel is principally one of apprenticeship in which a young man learns about life and love through a woman who remains nonetheless faithful to her husband in a manner recalling ROUSSEAU's *JULIE.* The novel likewise echoes CONSTANT's *ADOLPHE.*

This novel is one of confession, in which the exploration of character in the form of autobiography allows for digressions on literature, philosophy, and morality. Written in the midst of his affair with Adèle, the wife of VICTOR HUGO, Sainte-Beuve idealizes love's beginning, pure and full of grace, despite the fact that theirs was anything but a Platonic relationship. Sainte-Beuve's desire for the lost purity of first love reflects the romantic (see ROMANTICISM) yearning for the unattainable. His confessional tone inspires BALZAC's *LILY OF THE VALLEY* (1835). Now principally read by scholars, Sainte-Beuve's novel is written in an awkward style and the plot sometimes drags. Yet, the novel is marked by the acute psychological observation for which Sainte-Beuve is known.

FURTHER READING

Call, Michael J. *Back to the Garden: Chateaubriand, Senancour and Constant.* Saratoga, Calif.: Anma Libri, 1988.
Chadbourne, Richard McClain. *Charles-Augustin Sainte-Beuve.* Boston: Twayne, 1977.
Proust, Marcel. *Against Sainte-Beuve and Other Essays.* London, New York: Penguin Books, 1988.

SENTIMENTAL EDUCATION (L'ÉDUCATION SENTIMENTALE) GUSTAVE FLAUBERT (1869)

Flaubert wrote two novels of the same title. He began the first as a young man in 1843, finishing it in 1845; the second he wrote between 1864 and 1869, when he was a mature writer. What is most remarkable in comparing the two is the way Flaubert transformed the underlying values of the novel in his second version. This work has been characterized as both a novel of apprenticeship and a novel of failure. Frédéric Moreau and Deslauriers, friends since childhood, ultimately fail in their dreams of love and ambition. This work is the story of the generation that experienced the JULY MONARCHY and the Revolution of 1848 and a romantic novel of one man's search for the unattainable (see ROMANTICISM). It is a novel about society and a personal confession.

As in a number of his other works, Flaubert draws in part from his own experience in writing *Sentimental Education.* As a young man, Flaubert fell in love with Élisa Schlésinger, an older married woman. This encounter inspired the story of Frédéric's love for Madame Arnoux in the novel. Two earlier works also lay the foundation for *Sentimental Education,* both of which also draw on Flaubert's love for Schlésinger, *Memoirs of a Madman* (1836) and *November* (1841). A number of the novel's principal characters are subtly modeled on real persons. Not only is Madame Arnoux

modeled on Madame Schlésinger but Monsieur Arnoux draws on her real-life husband. Frédéric is a composite of Flaubert and his friend Maxime du Camp. Madame Dambreuse has been associated with Madame Delessert (a friend of PROSPER MÉRIMÉE).

The novel opens in 1840. Frédéric is an 18-year old student, impressionable, sensual, and weak. Traveling by boat to his mother in the country, he encounters and is fascinated by Madame Arnoux. When he returns to Paris, Frédéric tries to find her. His social life in Paris revolves around Deslauriers, a wealthy family named Dambreuse whose patronage he seeks, and various friends who finally introduce him into the Arnoux circle. Frédéric is occasionally moved by sudden surges of energy that then recede; he is equally inclined to cowardly compromises.

When he finds himself in financial difficulties, Frédéric is obliged to return to his mother in the country for two years. There he becomes reacquainted with a neighbor's daughter, Louise, who has loved him since childhood. In 1845, an unanticipated inheritance allows Frédéric to leave both the country and Louise and return to Paris. There he develops an intensely passionate but platonic relationship with Madame Arnoux. One day Madame Arnoux admits that she loves him and promises a meeting. Frédéric waits for hours at the appointed place. Enervated, disappointed, and with his pride wounded, he feels as if his love has disappeared "like leaves carried away by a hurricane." And so he sobs out his pain in the courtesan Rosanette's arms. He later learns that the only reason Madame Arnoux failed to meet him was because her son was ill.

Together Frédéric and Rosanette witness the revolutionary events of 1848. Despite the fact that his friends are involved, Frédéric cannot compel himself to take an active stand. Moreover, his love life has become extremely complicated. Rosanette is expecting his child, yet Frédéric has taken up with Madame Dambreuse, whom he agrees to marry when she is widowed. But on discovering that the Arnoux family has gone bankrupt, Frédéric is determined to help and tries to borrow money from Madame Dambreuse to aid his true love. Madame Dambreuse is naturally offended. Rosanette's child dies and Frédéric breaks with his two lovers. He returns to the countryside thinking that he can pick up with his childhood sweetheart, but she has married someone else.

Years later, in March 1867, as night is falling, Frédéric is alone in his room when a woman enters. It is Madame Arnoux and together they recall their love. Suddenly Madame Arnoux cries out "Farewell. . . . I will never see you again. This was my last act as a woman." Before leaving she removes her comb, letting her gray hair fall. She violently pulls out a lock from her head saying, "Keep it. Farewell. . . . " The novel ends in the winter of 1868–69 as Deslauriers and Frédéric talk over their failed ambitions.

From the beginning the reader witnesses Frédéric's development from adolescence into adulthood. The women in his life are varied in character; each represents a different possibility. Madame Arnoux is the unattainable ideal against whom all other women are measured. Madame Dambreuse represents wealthy society and the opportunity for advancement. Rosanette is the typical kept woman, coarse and materialist but essentially loving. Louise Rocque is the independent woman. Madame Arnoux is the only woman Frédéric ever truly desires to possess but she is inaccessible. When he breaks with Madame Dambreuse Frédéric destroys his social ambitions and Rosanette can no longer offer him comfort. Even Louise has married Frédéric's friend. Frédéric is a failure, a spectator of his own life. His personal disappointment echoes those of his generation.

Flaubert thus simultaneously weaves the story of a romantic (see ROMANTICISM) antihero with social commentary on bourgeois values and materialism. Drawing on his own recollections of 1848, Flaubert sensitively evokes the tumult of those dramatic events. With his scrupulous attention to detail, Flaubert also did research into political and economic events in 1847 and 1848. The result is a carefully documented portrait of Parisian life and society in the 1840s. In a manner particular to Flaubert, he retained his characteristic distance as the objective and minute observer. In *Sentimental Education* Flaubert makes use of the device that marks his contribution to the development of the modern novel, the *style indirect libre* (represented discourse), blurring the lines between narrator and characters.

The novel was at first only a moderate success although, the naturalists (see NATURALISM) admired it right away and the novel subsequently influenced a whole generation of literary heroes. Critics continue to take note of Flaubert's inimitable capacity to place his characters in a historical context from which they remain strangely detached. Some critics have viewed this tension between internal feelings and external events as Flaubert's statement about the relationship between art and society.

FURTHER READING

Brombert, Victor. *The Novels of Flaubert.* Princeton, N.J.: Princeton University Press, 1973.
Culler, Jonathan. *Flaubert and the Uses of Uncertainty.* Ithaca, N.Y.: Cornell University Press, 1974.
Orr, Mary. *Flaubert Writing the Masculine.* Oxford: Oxford University Press, 2000.
Porter, Laurence M., ed. *Critical Essays on Gustave Flaubert.* Boston: G. K. Hall, 1986.

SENTIMENTAL NOVEL (C. 1740–1780)

The sentimental novel's exploration of feeling offers a window onto 18th-century ideas about the novel, art, and beauty. It is frequently associated with, but not limited to, the EPISTOLARY NOVEL. It is a genre of literature concerned with the relationship between the individual and society in a period of socioeconomic transition. Not surprisingly, the emphasis on human emotion in the sentimental novel draws on the legacy of sensationist theory that asserts the predominance of experience and that is associated with such thinkers as the English philosopher John Locke and, in France, Étienne Bonnot de Condillac.

The foremost writer of sentimental novels was the Englishman Samuel Richardson, whose sensitive heroines, Pamela and Clarissa, had an enormous impact on the French novel of the 18th century. DIDEROT, for example, an admirer of Richardson, wrote an elegy in praise of Richardson in the year of that author's death. *The NUN* echoes some of the themes in *Pamela,* in its first-person narrative and pathos. In writing *The Nun,* Diderot wished to imitate Richardson in producing a work of fiction that is believable, moving, and morally useful.

The sentimental novel created a space in which authors could work out the paradoxes so apparent to

18th-century Frenchmen and -women. Morally didactic, sentimental novels tend to emphasize the contrast between virtue and vice. In a period of socioeconomic and political transition that led to the collapse of the OLD REGIME, the sentimental novel frequently portrayed male aristocratic characters as moral degenerates who tend to manipulate women in their own, usually sexual, interests. In contrast to aristocratic vice, female characters represent the Christian virtues, in particular, charity and selflessness. Given the centrality of feeling and emotion to these texts, love and marriage are predominant themes. The sentimental novel was particularly attractive to a female audience. Literary critics tended to view it as a "safe" form of secular reading for women who might otherwise succumb to the negative influence of LIBERTINE NOVELS.

Some scholars have argued that the sentimental novel endorses essentially middle-class values, promoting a concept of virtue that corresponds to a discourse on political virtue that fed into the FRENCH REVOLUTION.

FURTHER READING

Denby, David. *Sentimental Narrative and the Social Order in France, 1760–1820*. Cambridge, New York: Cambridge University Press, 1994.

Miller, Nancy K. *French Dressing: Women, Men and Ancien Régime Fiction*. New York: Routledge, 1995.

Reddy, William. *The Navigation of Feeling: A Framework for the History of Emotions*. Cambridge, New York: Cambridge University Press, 2001.

SERAPHITA HONORÉ DE BALZAC (1835)

This fantastic story is set in Norway. Wilfred and Minna are seduced by an androgynous creature that appears to each of them as a being of the opposite sex. Seraphita/Seraphitus appears as an angel who brings them to the top of a mountain on the edge of the infinite. She/he offers to Wilfred and Minna the power to understand the divine. Thus the two characters begin to understand the interconnectedness of the material and spiritual worlds.

Seraphita reflects Balzac's fascination with contemporary trends in mysticism and philosophy, particularly the works of the Swedish theosopher Emanuel Swedenborg (1688–1772). In its emphasis on the invisible links between two separate realities that are connected to the divine, the novel also manifests elements of pantheism so prevalent in certain works of the romantic period (see ROMANTICISM).

FURTHER READING

Allen, James Smith. *Popular French Romanticism: Authors, Readers and Books in the Nineteenth Century*. Syracuse, N.Y.: Syracuse University Press, 1981.

Carrère, Jean. *Degeneration in the Great French Masters.* Translated by Joseph McCabe. Freeport, N.Y.: Books for Libraries Press, 1967.

Kanes, Martin, ed. *Critical Essays on Balzac*. Boston: G. K. Hall Co., 1990.

Smith, Edward C. III. "Honoré de Balzac and the 'Genius' of Walter Scott: Debt and Denial," *Comparative Literature Studies* 36, no. 3 (1999): 209–225.

SHE CAME TO STAY (L'INVITÉE) SIMONE DE BEAUVOIR (1943)

Written between 1935 and 1937, this novel explores the question of female jealousy, drawing from Beauvoir's experience with JEAN-PAUL SARTRE and one of her students, Olga Kosakievicz. It was published in 1943, the year Beauvoir was dismissed from teaching for having "corrupted" a female student.

The novel begins with a quote from the 19th-century German philosopher Hegel referring to the self's desire for the death of the other ("*Chaque conscience poursuit la mort de l'autre*"). Françoise, the principal character, wants to know what her rival is thinking. The equation knowledge = power reflects de Beauvoir's philosophy as well as her view of women. In the end, Françoise concludes that her only choice is to murder Xavière. De Beauvoir's analysis of the tension between the self and others is powerful and, in the case of Françoise, leads to an existential and emotional crisis until she realizes that her relationship with Pierre must be continually affirmed and *chosen* (see EXISTENTIALISM).

The character of Françoise thus reflects de Beauvoir's belief in the power of ideas and the notion that the mind, body, and will are one. She also articulates de Beauvoir's view of human freedom. Set in the period leading up to World War II, war, too, affects the relationships between individuals. In *The Blood of Others*, set during the war, the question of "the other" is treated differently, becoming a question of social responsibility.

FURTHER READING

Appignanesi, Lisa. *Simone de Beauvoir*. Harmondsworth, England: Penguin, 1988.

Arp, Kristana. *The Bonds of Freedom*. Chicago: Open Court Publishing, 2001.

Bair, Dierdre. *Simone de Beauvoir: A Biography*. New York: Summit Books, 1990.

Bauer, Nancy. *Simone de Beavoir, Philosophy and Feminism*. New York: Columbia University Press, 2001.

Evans, Mary. *Simone de Beauvoir: A Feminist Mandarin*. London: Tavistock, 1985.

Fallaize, Elizabeth. *The Novels of Simone de Beauvoir*. London: Routledge, 1988.

Keefe, T. *Simone de Beauvoir. A Study of her Writings*. Totowa, N.J.: Barnes and Noble, 1984.

Moi, Toril. *Feminist Theory and Simone de Beauvoir*. Oxford: Blackwell, 1990.

———. *Simone de Beauvoir*. Oxford: Blackwell, 1994.

SIEGE OF CALAIS, THE (LE SIÈGE DE CALAIS) CLAUDINE-ALEXANDRINE GUÉRIN, MADAME DE TENCIN (1739)

According to legend, madame de Tencin wrote this popular novel as a bet to prove that she could produce a decent novel beginning at the point where typical novels end (marriage). The context for the story is the Hundred Years' War and, like the MEMOIRS OF THE COUNT OF COMMINGE, the novel is centered on the theme of thwarted love.

Madame de Granson is in a loveless marriage, struggling out of duty against her feelings for Monsieur de Canaple. One night he accidentally gets into her bed and she mistakes him for her husband. Their error is revealed in the morning light and leads to further complications in their relations. Interwoven into their interactions are the thwarted love stories of two other couples that together lead to misunderstandings, a convent, an abandoned child, and a secret marriage, all stock elements in 18th-century fiction. The story ends with the English taking the city of Calais. Edward II demands the execution of six citizens (the burghers of Calais). Canaple and his friend Châlons hide their noble origins to sacrifice themselves. Madame de Granson, now a widow and lately convinced of Canaple's love, dresses as a man and tries to replace

him in line for execution. The queen, touched by this sign of devotion, intervenes and all are pardoned. Marriages follow.

The novel is reminiscent of 17th-century historical romances yet, typically for Tencin, she adds a new twist. A famous event in medieval history becomes a story of female strength. Similarly, Adelaïde in *Comminges* manifests a superior character. Other recurring themes in Tencin's works include the tension between love and duty, the cult of suffering by virtuous heroines, and a critique of social oppression.

FURTHER READING

Jones, S. "Madame de Tencin: An Eighteenth-Century Woman Novelist." In *Woman and Society in Eighteenth-Century France*. Edited by E. Jacobs, W. H. Barber et al. London: Athlone Press, 1979.

Stewart, Philip, *Imitation and Illusion in the Memoir-Novel, 1700–1750: The Art of Make-Believe*. New Haven, Conn.: Yale University Press, 1969.

SILENCE OF THE SEA (SILENCE DE LA MER) VERCORS (1942)

An old man and his niece are obliged to take a German officer into their home during the Occupation of France. Their unwelcome guest tries to break their silence that represents patriotic resistance. The style is simple and sober. A highly successful novel, *Silence of the Sea* was adapted to film in 1949 by Jean-Pierre Melville.

A strange relationship develops between the German officer and the French family. It is the winter of 1940. Each evening the three gather in the living room where the officer delivers a monologue since the old man and his niece refuse to respond to him. The officer reveals himself to be cultured and refined. He loves France and is sickened by what he has been obliged to participate in. He is equally disturbed by Nazism in his own land. The officer is a pacifist at heart.

The officer speaks to the couple about his country, music, his love for France, and his hopes. Although he speaks only to their silence, a sense of mutual, if unspoken, respect develops around this daily ritual. The officer is almost happy with the situation in which he finds himself, charging it with a deeper meaning. "I am happy to have found here a dignified old man. And a silent girl. I must conquer the silence of France. That pleases me."

With his lengthy monologues, the officer slowly draws his hosts out of their indifference; they were never hostile. Although they still refuse to speak, they are at least listening. They even begin to admire the officer's passion and persistence. After a leave in Paris, however, the officer stops coming down to them in the evening. For six months he remains distant until one evening he comes downstairs once more crying out, "They will put out the flame entirely. Europe will no longer be illuminated by this light." Seeing what the German army had done to Paris was too much for the officer's romantic soul. He is almost prepared to encourage his hosts to rebel. Instead, he chooses to return to battle. At the end of the novel the officer prepares to leave. Only at that moment does the young woman break the silence, bringing some comfort to the departing officer. A simple yet moving story, *Silence of the Sea* is full of both pain and hope.

Silence appeared in 1942 and was the first of a series of clandestine works published during the German Occupation of France during World War II in which writers such as FRANÇOIS MAURIAC and LOUIS ARAGON were published under pseudonyms. Vercors later told the story of clandestine publishing in *Battle of Silence* (1992). Vercors was one of the founders of the Éditions de Minuit. Enormously successful, *Silence* was republished 72 times and translated into 40 languages. This novel received far more attention than Vercors's other works, a rich oeuvre written in a variety of genres that includes history, theater, and aesthetics.

SIMENON, GEORGES (1903–1989)   The caricaturist Ralph Soupault once called Simenon "the Citroën of literature," a Citroën being a famous make of French cars. Born in Belgium, Simenon wrote some 380 novels, hundreds of short stories, and more than 20 autobiographical works.

Simenon began work as a journalist at the age of 16. In 1922 he left Belgium for Paris, where he began earning his living as a writer. Simenon was a extremely popular novelist. He traveled widely in Europe, Africa, North America, and the Pacific, and his experiences furnished much of the material for his novels. He is particularly noted for his detective fiction featuring the character Maigret.

During the Occupation Simenon collaborated on Vichy publications (see VICHY FRANCE), and this led to an investigation after the Liberation. After the war, Simenon left France for the United States, where he traveled across the country.

Simenon sought to portray "naked man"—modern man torn from within, alienated from his environment and haunted by emptiness. He was equally concerned with the problems of the modern market economy, the rise of the middle class, mass culture, and the dehumanization associated with modern society generally. At the same time, Simenon was capable of evoking joy, camaraderie, and the innocence of childhood. His writing is marked by juxtapositions such as human nature and civilization, tradition and progress, good and evil. Simenon was as interested in the discomfort felt by modern man as other contemporary writers such as JULIEN GREEN and JEAN-PAUL SARTRE, but he ignored specific historical conflicts. More than one literary critic has compared Simenon to BALZAC. Although ANDRÉ GIDE was an admirer of Simenon, by and large the literary establishment failed to recognize Simenon as a serious writer.

SIMON, CLAUDE (1913–)   Born in Madagascar, Simon grew up in the southern French city of Perpignan. He never knew his father, who died at the front in 1914. His mother died in 1924 when Simon was only nine years old. In 1939 Simon joined other international volunteers fighting in Spain and learned firsthand of the absurdity and horror of war when he was sent out on horseback to confront German tanks. Simon's wartime experience provided much of the material for his subsequent novels. From Spain Simon traveled to England, Germany, and the USSR.

Mobilized in 1939, Simon was taken prisoner in 1940. He escaped that same year. After the war Simon divided his time between Paris and the southern Roussillon region, where he owned vineyards inherited from his family. He also began to write. Simon wrote 14 novels that form a coherent whole in the sense that they all draw from his own life experience or that of his family members.

Between 1945 and 1957 Simon produced five novels: *Trickster* (1945), *Tightrope* (1947), *Gulliver* (1952), *Rite of Spring* (1954), and *Wind* (1957). Unlike a traditional novel, *Tightrope* consists of an autobiographical meditation that is close to poetry. The influence of the American writer William Faulkner, whom Simon greatly admired, is evident in these works. So too are the themes that mark Simon's later novels: war, death, and memory. The strength of Simon's writing lies not in dialogue but in description, particularly in his allusions to painting. His early novels have a stronger sense of narrative than his later works, while at the same time laying the foundation for future developments in his writing.

Simon acquired notoriety with the publication of *Wind* (1957) and *Flanders Road* (1960). Through them, Simon came to be associated with the NOUVEAU ROMAN. His long descriptions play a similar role to the "under conversations" in NATHALIE SARRAUTE's works while recalling techniques used by ALAIN ROBBE-GRILLET and MICHEL BUTOR.

Grass (1958) introduces a new cycle of novels that focus on the author's family. This series includes *Flanders Road* (1960), *Palace* (1962), and *History* (1967). In these novels Simon no longer tries to create traditional fiction or characters, admitting that he had no imagination. Hence the influence of Faulkner gives way to MARCEL PROUST as Simon, too, seeks to recapture the past in words and through lost sensations. Characters reappear from one novel to the next. The dominant theme is time and history.

Flanders Road, one of Simon's most famous novels, draws on the author's experience in the Second World War. The character of Georges, who first appeared in *Grass,* reappears in this work, fighting in Belgium. Georges witnesses the death of his commander in an ambush and wonders if it was not in fact suicide, as the commander's wife, Corinne, was unfaithful to her husband. The novel not only condemns war but also deals with other questions of the human condition: fantasy, desire, and the question of reality. The identity of the narrator seems to dissolve over the course of the novel, his voice becoming increasingly ambiguous and unclear. As dreams and reality overlap, the reader increasingly wonders who is speaking. *Palace,*

in turn, focuses on the author's experience in the Spanish civil war and introduces the idea that the individual is capable of altering history. For Simon such a notion is a disastrous illusion. Man must rather submit to the forces of history.

In *History* (the title has an ambiguous meaning in French), for example, the characters in the novel have no story, or is it history? This work, which won the Médicis Prize, recounts a day in the life of an anonymous narrator. The events are banal yet they recall to the narrator memories of his mother's death, of his uncle Charles, his cousin Corinne, and the Spanish civil war. The narrator attempts to reconstruct his parents' lives from a series of postcards his father once sent to his mother before their marriage. Typical of Simon's works, the narrative is repeatedly interrupted by description and is marked by the sense of the disorder inherent in memory.

Simon's novels can be disconcerting to the reader as he deemphasizes the importance of chronology associated with the traditional novel. Simon's rejection of linear time reflects a philosophical stance as he was convinced of the impossibility of giving coherence to events that in the real world have none. His narrative is thus nonlinear. Past, present, and future are intermingled.

Words and images, not time, have power. In the preface to his essay *Blind Orion* (1970), Simon wrote, "One after another the words burst like Roman candles, showering their sparks in all directions. They are like intersections where several roads meet." Pictorial elements in his writing are strong. A painting, an altarpiece, or a postcard may trigger writing, leading to what some critics have characterized as a proliferation of words, phrases, and images in page after page of a verbal stream full of repetitions and parentheses that give rise to unexpected relations. Simon called this form of writing "magma." It is, in its complexity baroque.

Simon's *Battle of Pharsalus* (1969) marks a transition in his oeuvre, as the tone changes even as familiar characters appear. This work contains numerous intertextual references to Proust as well as various Greek and Latin authors in a sort of literary collage. The novel also reveals Simon's fascination with visual imagery in his descriptions of paintings by the artists Nicolas Poussin, Albricht Dürer, and Pieter Breughel. The visual element in Simon's works is also evident in *Women* (1966; republished in 1983 as *Berenice's Hair*), in which he depicts the feelings evoked by the Spanish artist Joan Miró's paintings, while *Conducting Bodies* explores the geometric structure of New York architecture. The first 60 pages of this work were also published separately as *Blind Orion.*

In *Conducting Bodies* (1971), *Triptych* (1973), and *The World About Us* (1975) Simon plays with form and structure in collagelike writing. While the autobiographical element in these works remains strong, Simon is no longer seeking to recapture the past. Writing thus becomes a reflection of what the writer feels at the moment of writing. Simon refers to *The Life of Henry Brulard,* for example, by saying that STENDHAL "realized all of a sudden that he does not describe what he has experienced but an engraving of the event that he has looked at since and which, he says, has taken the place of reality."

Reality is nothing more than what memory makes of it. Hence the "reality" of what is written is problematic as is the narrator's stance in relation to what is recounted. The least object or image has the potential to release a torrent of associated signs that writing both produces and controls. Our perception of the world exists in memory but is fragmented and disordered.

In *Tryptich* and *The World About Us,* Simon creates fiction out of description. In the latter novel, a room gives birth to three different stories. These are highly cinematographic works. Simon's innovative writing reaches its height with GEORGICS (1981) and *Acacia* (1989).

Acacia blends images of the two World Wars, a trip across Europe in 1937, and the life of Simon's parents. Simon's father was the son of peasants who became an army officer thanks to his sisters, who sacrificed everything to support their brother's career. His mother was from a wealthy bourgeois family. She married Simon's father despite her family's disapproval. They were united after a four-year engagement. Simon once said, "What's the point of inventing things when reality is better than fiction?"

Georgics refers to earlier themes of war and death, time and forgetfulness. The three parallel stories that make up this work are almost musical in composition, recalling the structure of a fugue. They are set in three different historical periods, during the Napoleonic Wars, the Spanish civil war, and World War II. Simon makes use of family documents and draws from his own experience to bring these three historical moments to life. In the background, an old woman sits at home, powerless against the world's struggles.

What readers most appreciate in Simon's works is his sumptuous writing. Critics are generally fascinated with his writing process. Yet Simon is not overly intellectual; he explores through writing a very concrete and real world. His writing is fragmented and disjointed because he sees the world in a state of decomposition, victim of the absurd jolts of history. War, a recurring theme, Simon sees as impossible to avoid. Whether he considers the Napoleonic Wars, civil war in Spain, or the two world wars, the consequences for humanity are the same. History repeats itself. What Simon offers then, is a strong sense of the disorder of the world. Ironically, the soldier who attacks the earth with his weapons finds his parallel in the farmer who labors in the fields, engaged in his own battle against the elements, victim of the cycles of nature as much as the soldier is victim of the cycles of history. Simon won the Nobel Prize in 1985.

FURTHER READING

Britton, Celia. *Claude Simon: Writing the Visible.* Cambridge: Cambridge University Press, 1987.
———, ed., *Claude Simon.* London, New York: Longman, 1993.
Duncan, Alistair B. *Claude Simon: Adventure in Words.* Manchester, England: Manchester University Press, 2003.
———. *Claude Simon, New Directions: Collected Papers.* Edinburgh: Scottish Academic Press, 1985.
Evans, Michael. *Claude Simon and the Transgressions of Modern Art.* New York: St. Martin's Press, 1988.
Gould, Karen. *Claude Simon's Mythic Muse.* Columbia, S.C.: French Literature Publications, 1979.

SIMPLE HEART, A (*UN COEUR SIMPLE*)

GUSTAVE FLAUBERT (1877)   The story depicts the life of a simple servant, intellectually limited but great in heart and entirely devoted to her mistress and her family. In developing the character of Felicity, Flaubert drew from Julie, a woman who had entered the Flaubert household as a servant in 1825 and who remained there until Flaubert's death in 1880. She died three years later.

Felicity suffered tragedy as a young woman when her lover abandoned her, so she entered into service in Madame Aubain's household. Madame Aubain is not a particularly agreeable person; she is haughty and cold. Felicity's principal quality is, in contrast, her devotion—to Madame Aubain, to Madame Aubain's daughter who dies while away at school, to her nephew who dies in the colonies, to the parrot that dies and that she has stuffed. After Madame Aubain's death, Felicity begins her own demise, expiring in poverty on a religious holiday, her stuffed parrot placed on a ceremonial altar and strangely recalling the image of the Holy Spirit in a stained-glass window of the church.

Felicity is no more an ideal heroine than Emma in MADAME BOVARY, but she is infinitely more touching. Felicity's joys and pains, faith and actions reflect a humble simplicity that evokes sympathy. Unconscious virtue is the natural product of Felicity's character; it is simple, as the title implies. Felicity is not even aware that she is good; her character would perhaps be less appealing if she were.

Like *Madame Bovary* and SENTIMENTAL EDUCATION, *A Simple Heart* falls into the category of Flaubert's works that examine contemporary society reflecting both NATURALISM and REALISM. Flaubert seeks to depict human life the way it really is. In this instance, his honest portrayal of a lowly servant shows how even the simplest of persons may be sublime.

FURTHER READING

Brombert, Victor. *The Novels of Flaubert*. Princeton, N.J.: Princeton University Press, 1973.

Chambers, Ross. "An Invitation to Love: Simplicity of Heart and Textual Duplicity in 'Un Coeur simple.'" In *Story and Situation: Narrative Seduction and the Power of Fiction*. Minneapolis: University of Minnesota Press, 1984.

Culler, Jonathan. *Flaubert and the Uses of Uncertainty*. Ithaca, N.Y.: Cornell University Press, 1974.

Porter, Laurence M., ed. *Critical Essays on Gustave Flaubert*. Boston: G. K. Hall, 1986.

SIMPLE PASSION (PASSION SIMPLE)

ANNIE ERNAUX (1991) In *Simple Passion* Ernaux moves away from her experience growing up to reflect on the power of passion to alter one's life, if temporarily. In this first-person narrative, a woman recounts her affair with a married East European businessman whom she refers to as *A.* It is an intense, physical affair and the narrator's passion for *A.* overwhelms her and permeates her life. For two years she exists only for him, always waiting, anticipating a meeting, or fearing that he will not return. Eventually, the affair ends when *A.* leaves France. When the two meet again later, the passion is gone. In this powerful work, Ernaux translates intense, erotic, and sexual passion into words.

FURTHER READING

McIlvanney, Siobhán. *Annie Ernaux: The Return to Origins*. Liverpool, England: Liverpool University Press, 2001.

Thomas, Lyn. *Annie Ernaux: An Introduction to the Writer and Her Audience*. Oxford, New York: Berg, 1999.

SIMPLE PAST, THE (LE PASSÉ SIMPLE)

DRISS CHRAÏBI (1954) This story of a son who rebels against his father is set in Morocco in the 1930s. At the time, Morocco was still a French protectorate and the narrator opposes his father and colonial power. The novel is full of the violence that permeates this society within and outside of the family. Narrated in the first person, the protagonist, like the author, is named Driss. Like the author, he leaves for France in the end.

Recalling his past, Driss the narrator powerfully evokes the absolute power his father holds over the family that also includes his mother and his brothers. The father is referred to as lord, the mother as wife. Theirs is a master-slave relationship. Driss's mother has born seven children and has lived her entire life confined within the home, first her father's then her husband's. Her body is hidden by her voluminous attire. She dreams of death as liberation, either her husband's death or her own; it does not seem to matter which. In praying for death, this Muslim woman ironically invokes the saints of the Greeks and Russians. The father is brutal and violent yet the entire family must submit in total obedience to his will. The mother is nothing but an object to satisfy her husband's needs, sexual and otherwise. He need only snap his fingers and she instantly responds.

Driss dreams of murdering his father to liberate his mother and brothers from the violent and cruel treatment to which they are constantly subjected. In one poignant scene, he fingers the sharp knife in his pocket, one that has cut the neck of chicken and sheep and even his mother's belly in childbirth. Almost ready to plunge the knife into his father, something holds him back. The father's power is so great that rebellion is impossible. Driss's only means of escape from tyrannical authority is to leave his country.

Tradition and religion permeate the atmosphere of this novel, but there is no comfort in it for the family. The style of writing is nervous, abrupt, violent, and occasionally obscene. Chraïbi once said, "The hero is called Driss Ferdi. Perhaps it is I. At any rate, his despair is mine. Despair in a faith, Islam, in which I believed, and which talked of equality, of God's part in each individual of the creation, of tolerance, of liberty and of love." This work caused such a scandal in a period of heightened nationalism that Chraïbi felt obliged to denounce his own work, which he later regretted.

FURTHER READING

Joyaux, Georges J., Albert Memmi, and Jules Roy. "Driss Chraïbi, Mohammed Dib, Kateb Yacine and Indigenous North African Literature," Yale French Studies, no. 24, Midnight Novelists (1959): 30–40.

Yetiv, Isaac. "Iconoclasts in Maghrebian Literature," French Review 50, no. 6 (May 1977): 858–864.

SISTER TO SCHEHERAZADE, A (OMBRE SULTANE) ASSIA DJEBAR (1987)

This novel begins with the French conquest of Algeria in 1830 then leaps to the Algerian war of independence ending in 1962. It also tells the story of two women whose lives are linked through their marriage to the same man.

Isma is a modern woman, independent and emancipated, while Hajila lives a traditional life, confined within the home and beneath the veil. When Isma leaves her husband, he marries Hajila and the two women come together by chance at a public bath where they begin to form a friendship. Djebar thus explores the notion of space and the way in which it is delineated as male or female, public or private, as well as the many meanings of confinement.

Hajila slowly begins to taste the independence that Isma has always demanded for herself by going out secretly into the city without her veil. Having found freedom, she cannot return to the prison of marriage. Hajila begins to speak of the brutal treatment she has received at the hands of her husband. Ultimately, the two women, who complement each other, join forces. At the same time, as is her want, Djebar explores mother-daughter relationships, essentially criticizing the older generation that contributed to the confinement and suppression of women in contemporary society. Finally, Djebar suggests that Algerian independence as a nation should mean independence for women as well.

FURTHER READING

Donadey, Anne. Recasting Postcolonialism: Women Writing Between Worlds. Portsmouth, N.H.: Heinemann, 2001.

Elia, Nada. Trances, Dances and Vociferations: Agency and Resistance in Africana Women's Narratives. New York: Garland, 2001.

Erickson, John. "Women's Space and Enabling Dialogue in Assia Djebar's L'Amour, la fantasie." In Post-Colonial Subjects: francophone Women Writers. Edited by Mary Green et al. Minneapolis: University of Minnesota Press, 1996.

Merini, Rafika. Two Major francophone Women Writers, Assia Djebar and Leila Sebbar: A Thematic Study of their Works. New York: P. Lang, 1999.

SOCIALIST REALISM

Socialist realism rejects bourgeois art and values. In the Soviet leader Joseph Stalin's words, "the artist must give first priority to the truthful representation of life, and if he truly portrays our life, then he cannot but note, cannot but show, that it leads to Socialism. This will be Socialist art. This will be Socialist Realism."

Socialist realism was adopted by the Soviet Union of Writers in 1934. It is an aesthetic vision that finds its origins in the writings of the Russian author Maksim Gorky, whose work Mother is generally considered the first example of socialist realist literature. The Hungarian writer Georg Lukacs developed the most sophisticated definition of the socialist realist aesthetic, calling it a "reflection of reality." The purpose of socialist realist art is to contribute to the building of a socialist and, ultimately, communist society. A certain tension results from the fact that socialist realist writers have two parallel goals, to describe society as it is and as they think it should be.

Both artists and writers of Marxist orientation such as LOUIS ARAGON, whose "Real World" cycle of novels reflects his Marxist interpretation of history, and ELSA TRIOLET, expressed themselves in this form (see MARXISM). Socialist realism is obviously charged with political meaning. With socialist realism, art and literature become propaganda.

Like 19th-century NATURALISTS and REALISTS such as ÉMILE ZOLA, socialist realist writers seek to depict reality accurately but for a didactic purpose. The movement first arose in France in 1932 and is also associated with the works of PAUL NIZAN. After World War II, communist writers again promoted socialist realist literature in contrast to writers such as JEAN-PAUL SARTRE, ALBERT CAMUS, and Roland Barthes, who argued in favor of "committed literature."

Socialist realism focuses on the conditions of the working class and the poor, and serves as a means by which to offer a critique of existing bourgeois social institutions and structures.

SOLLERS, PHILIPPE (1936–) Sollers is the pseudonym for Philippe Joyaux. Born in the Bordeaux region, Sollers was 20 years old when he embarked on a literary career. His first work, a short story entitled "The Challenge" (1957) that was published in the journal *Écrire,* won the Feneon Prize. FRANÇOIS MAURIAC gave it a positive critique. The next year LOUIS ARAGON praised *A Curious Solitude* (1958), Sollers's first full novel. An immediate success, this work tries to capture the sense and sound of multiple conversations overheard as they drift down into the courtyard of an apartment building. This real experience marks a turning point in Sollers's life and defines his project as a writer. "Suddenly I felt that it was there that I must labor, to express all my life this unexpected sentiment vis-à-vis the world and the body, this sudden assurance of a harmony and happiness, incommunicable certainly, but which for me would become perfect in my effort to

retell them." These early works draw from the tradition of the psychological novel at the same time as Sollers begins to develop his own style.

Sympathetic to innovations associated with the NOUVEAU ROMAN, Sollers established his own literary journal in 1960. *Tel Quel* quickly became one of the most dynamic reviews of the avant-garde literary world. Founded in a period of crisis (it was the middle of the Algerian war), in this journal Sollers and his collaborators openly supported victims of injustice. The journal became a center of protest as well as theorizing about literature. The *Tel Quel* group sought to establish a theory based on literary games and the text as a mode of production. Structuralist and Marxist elements are evident in their thinking.

The Parc (1961) won the Médicis Prize and brought Sollers to the attention of a broader reading public. Four characters identified only by the pronouns "I," "he," or "she" all participate in writing the novel with the color of the print distinguishing one voice from another, yet identity and color overlap. In fact, unity in multiplicity is the dominant theme of this novel. Readers immediately connected Sollers's writing with the NOUVEAU ROMAN style, while ALAIN ROBBE-GRILLET and the philosopher Michel Foucault, among others, took note of Sollers's originality in exploring the limits of consciousness in dreams, memories, and imagination.

Drama (1965) and *Numbers* (1968) clearly marked Sollers as a leader of the literary avant-garde and drew the attention of critics and literary theorists such as Roland Barthes, Jacques Derrida, and Julia Kristeva. *Drama* articulates Sollers's vision of the relationship between subject and language, a central theme in all his works, and is structured on the pattern of a chessboard. Similarly, *Numbers* reproduces the configuration of Chinese magic squares and is based on the mathematical formula $(1 + 2 + 3 + 4)^2 = 100$. The novel is divided into 100 parts, subdivided into 25 smaller parts each containing four sections. All parts of the novel are numbered. Each section, representing a thought or state of consciousness, concludes with a dash. It could continue, but the author chooses not to pursue it further. Sollers's stream-of-consciousness style echoes the writings of the Irish novelist James Joyce, to whom the author acknowledges his debt.

Linear time has no meaning; rather, past and present, memory and dreams flow into each other. The reader's time and the time when the author wrote the novel are all different. Sollers's works thus manifest an unusual blend of formalism with a deliberate exploration of the act of writing. Above all, Sollers is concerned with the creative act.

Between 1965 and 1972, Sollers's style continued to evolve in dramatic ways as he focused increasingly on the writer as a producer of texts. He was interested, too, in literature's potential to encourage social and political change. The text becomes a situation in which to explore the conflict between the individual and the collective. For a time Sollers was associated with the Communist Party; he later turned to Maoism. Like *Drama* and *Numbers, Laws* (1972) makes use of geometrical formulas but is more explicitly political as it explores historical, political, and social conditions. In this work Sollers deliberately breaks down and then reconstructs language.

As of 1974, Sollers moved away from Marxism and Maoism while working on two of his most significant novels, *Paradise* (1981) and *H* (1973). In these works Sollers abandons all traditional grammar and punctuation. There are no capital letters, no paragraphs, no chapters. *H* consists of one long phrase. In these works, writing resembles music, as polyphonic voices bring to life the rhythm and sound of words that flow in an unending stream. The musicality of the texts is particularly pronounced when they are read aloud. In *Paradise* (1981), Sollers also completely rejects traditional narrative forms. The writing flows in a continuous, unpunctuated stream. Moreover, the subject "I" is both active and passive, actor and observer. Sollers's style in this work is poetic and lyrical. He describes his writing as magma. Again, when read aloud, its rhythm and musicality are evident.

Tel Quel was dissolved in 1982, and in 1983 Sollers established another journal, *L'Infini,* and published a novel, *Women,* a 600-page work in which he offers a portrait of Parisian intellectual and literary circles of the 1980s. Readers recognized such figures as Roland Barthes, Jacques Lacan, Louis Althusser, and the author, among others, in Sollers's supposedly fictional characters. The narrator is an American journalist whose perceptions differ from those of another writer, his friend S., who ends up editing the American's memoirs. Numerous sexual encounters become the means to explore both sexuality and its representation. At the heart of this world are women. "The World belongs to women," Sollers writes. "That is to say to death. Everyone lies about that. Come closer reader, this book is sharp. You will not get bored along the way . . . I am writing the memoirs of a navigator without precedent, an unveiler of errors, the temple of errors, of illusions, of tensions, the buried murderer, the end of things." *Women* stands apart from Sollers's other works and perhaps best reflects the author's role in the 1980s as a media personality.

Portrait of a Gambler (1984) is Sollers's autobiography, recalling his childhood in the Bordeaux region, his bourgeois upbringing and family, his turn to Marxism, and various other stages he passed through in his focus on eroticism, love, and prayer. The reader is often struck by an unusual blend of libertinism and Catholicism. In this work Sollers introduces a series of themes that mark his subsequent writings, as he brings together psychological and linguistic analysis in a somewhat pessimistic vision of the world.

Sollers also wrote essays on literary theory and aesthetics in which he explores the tradition of art and literature in the West while bringing to life such diverse figures the 14th century Italian poet Dante Alighieri, the painters Jean-Antoine Watteau and Jean-Honoré Fragonard and Homer. He also wrote on SADE, sculptor Auguste Rodin, belle époque photography, and painter Willem de Kooning. One of the most significant French intellectual figures in the second half of the 20th century, Sollers won the grand prize of the Académie Française in 1992.

FURTHER READING

Barthes, Roland. *Writer Sollers.* Translated by Philip Thody. Minneapolis: University of Minnesota Press, 1987.
Champagne, Roland A. *Philippe Sollers.* Amsterdam, Atlanta: Rodopi, 1996.
Clark, Hilary. *The Fictional Encyclopedia: Joyce, Pound, Sollers.* New York: Garland, 1990.

SOMEONE (QUELQU'UN) ROBERT PINGET (1965)

The narrator of this novel has lost an essential paper for the manuscript he is writing as an amateur botanist. In an attempt to recall how the paper was lost, he undertakes an exhaustive account of his day, occasionally including rather sordid details in a small boardinghouse tended by feebleminded maidservant named Fonfon. At the same time, the narrator makes a pathetic attempt to construct an acceptable image of his life. As is the case with other characters created by Pinget, he often forgets things. The lost sheet of paper seems to represent something more substantial, even elemental, than at first glance. Perhaps the narrator's soul?

The question of identity lies at the heart of this novel as the character, in searching for his lost scrap of paper, seems to be searching for himself. The themes of absence, loss, and forgetting, frequent in Pinget's works, provide the pretext for writing. Although inspired by the Spanish writer Miguel de Cervantes, Pinget's character is the opposite of Don Quixote as he cannot escape reality, much as he would like to.

Like Pinget's other novels, this work takes a mocking view of the absurdity of daily life. Its connection to the NOUVEAU ROMAN lies in its expression of the fundamentally subjective nature of reality. Although this novel was accepted favorably by literary critics, it was never popular with the reading public. The narrative returns seven times to the beginning, to the moment when the piece of paper was lost, creating a sense of uncertainty. In doing so, Pinget eradicates any coherent sense of time. In the end, the piece of paper that is central to the text is significant not for what it says, but simply because it is lost.

FURTHER READING

Henkels, Robert M. *Robert Pinget: The Novel as Quest.* Tuscaloosa: University of Alabama Press, 1979.

Reid, Martin. "Robert Pinget," *Yale French Studies,* Special Issue: After the Age of Suspicion: The French Novel Today (1988): 97–100.

Rosmarin, Léonard. *Robert Pinget.* New York: Twayne, London: Prentice Hall, 1995.

SONG OF ROLAND, THE (CHANSON DE ROLAND) (C. 1098–1100) The *Song of Roland* is one of the finest examples of an epic poem (CHANSON DE GESTE) written in medieval French, expressing the loyalty of vassal and Christian to his earthly and heavenly lords.

The setting of the poem is northern Spain in the late 8th century. Charlemagne, ruler of the Franks, (r. 768–814), was engaged in a confrontation with the Muslims in Spain. On their return to France, Charlemagne's rearguard was attacked in the Pyrenees by Basques. Roland, the principal character of the epic poem, was present at the time although he did not lead the troops. In the *Song of Roland,* written some 300 years after the original events, the story is altered. Roland is the leader of the French troops ambushed in the mountain pass. The account is written in the shadow of the First Crusade (1096–99) and Charlemagne's enemy is Muslim. The conflict is transformed into the Christian struggle against Islam. For this reason, and because the poem recounts important events in the great unifying reign of Charlemagne, the *Song of Roland* plays an important role in French nationalist ideology.

As for the poem's author, we know only what the last line tells us: "Here ends the story which Turoldus relates." Turoldus may have been the original author or a later copyist. He was certainly a talented poet and a learned man, a member of the clergy who knew something about military affairs.

Roland is Charlemagne's hotheaded nephew and his right-hand man. Betrayed by his stepfather Ganelon, Roland dies on the battlefield, the epitome of the true knight, supported by his loyal friend Oliver. Brave knights both, neither hero is idealized. Roland's soul is taken up heaven by the archangels, reflecting the traditional mix of Christian and chivalric elements in the *chansons de geste.* The depiction of Charlemagne and his 12 peers echoes Christ and the 12 apostles, both leaders ultimately betrayed by one of his own.

The poem illustrates the values of a male-dominated and rigidly hierarchical feudal society and lays the foundation for the medieval ROMANCES, a literary tradition that inspired a number of 16th- and 17th-century novels including HÉLISENNE DE CRENNE's *The DISORDERS OF LOVE.*

FURTHER READING

Ailes, Marianne. *The Song of Roland, on Absolutes and Relative Values.* Lewiston, N.Y.: Mellen Press, 2002.

Ashby-Beach, Genette. *The Song of Roland: A Generative Study of the Formulaic Language in the Single Combat.* Amsterdam: Rodophi, 1985.

Haidu, Peter. *The Subject of Violence: The Song of Roland and the Birth of the State.* Bloomington: Indiana University Press, 1993.

Jones, George Fenwick. *The Ethos of the Song of Roland.* Baltimore: Johns Hopkins University Press, 1963.

SOREL, CHARLES (C. 1597–1674)

We know little about Charles Sorel's life except that he was historiographer of France in 1635. Born in Paris, Sorel wrote in a variety of genres and on many subjects including science, history, and religion. In 1615 he wrote a panegyric to Louis XIII. Some of his earlier works are marked by the sentimental style that he later rejected, yet they display innovation. Despite the exaggerated emotions, passions, and duels that punctuate Sorel's early works, they take place in contemporary France, not some imaginary time or place in the distant past, as is common in the pastoral novel.

Sorel is best known for his two novels, *The Comical History of Francion* and *The Extravagant Shepherd.* In these adventure stories, Sorel challenges the reigning pastoral novel, especially mocking HONORÉ D'URFÉ'S *L'ASTRÉE.* By the time he wrote *Francion,* Sorel had fallen under the influence of libertine circles (see LIBERTINISM). Their iconoclasm is manifest in *Francion,* in which social satire blends with a critique of the pastoral and sentimental novel in a manner that recalls RABELAIS.

The Extravagant Shepherd is Sorel's strongest statement against the pastoral tradition. He intended for it to be the "tomb of novels," an antinovel. A sort of French *Don Quixote* (Sorel was influenced by the Spanish picaresque), *The Extravagant Shepherd* is a BURLESQUE novel and is thus similar to the works of his contemporary PAUL SCARRON. In this story, the main character, Lysis, has read so many novels that he can no longer distinguish between fact and fiction (something we see again in GUSTAVE FLAUBERT'S *MADAME BOVARY*). Lysis believes that he is the hero of one of the novels he has read. Through him, Sorel condemns heroic and sentimental novels for disregarding reality. The question of verisimilitude in 17th-century literature was an important point of debate. In one scene Lysis struggles to write a poem to his mistress but cannot come up with the right words. He turns to Clarimond, a sensible character who mocks Lysis by suggesting the most ridiculous words possible. Lysis, unaware that he is a dupe, accepts them all. Sorel combines fantasy with realism, all the while poking fun at the extravagant language of contemporary literary styles associated with the *précieuses.*

FURTHER READING
Hinds, Leonard. *Narrative Transformations from L'Astrée to Le Berger Extravagant.* West Lafayette, Ind.: Purdue University Press, 2002.

Howells, R. J. *Carnival to Classicism: The Comic Novels of Charles Sorel.* Paris, Seattle, Tübingen Germany: *Biblio* 17, 1989.

STAËL-HOLSTEIN, ANNE-LOUISE GERMAINE NECKER, BARONNE DE (1766–1817)

A French writer of Swiss origin, Germaine de Staël was a intellectual, essayist, and novelist. She was one of the foremost figures in articulating theories on romantic literature (see ROMANTICISM) and in putting those theories into practice in her own fictional works, such as *DELPHINE* and *CORINNE, OR ITALY.* She is one of the founders of comparative literature, and her writings on the relationship between art and society had a significant impact on 19th-century thought. It has been said that her greatest novel was her life. Because she wove elements of her own life into her works, the boundary between fiction and reality is blurred, reflecting Staël's process of self-realization through writing.

The daughter of Louis XVI's finance minister, Jacques Necker, Staël was brought up in a highly cultured environment. Her mother, Suzanne Necker, hosted one of the most brilliant salons in Paris, gathering important leaders of French ENLIGHTENMENT thought such as the Baron Grimm, Marmontel, and Buffon. Her daughter thrived in the company of such illustrious men.

In 1786, Germaine was married to baron de Staël-Holstein, the Swedish ambassador to Paris. He was older than she by 17 years, and theirs was not a happy marriage. Nonetheless, the young bride was dazzling in society, holding her own successful salon much as her mother had done.

Much of her adult life was spent in exile. Despite her initial enthusiasm for the Revolution, as political conditions in Paris worsened Staël was obliged to flee France with her husband in 1792. After traveling to Sweden, Staël settled down with her father at Coppet, Switzerland. There she gathered a cosmopolitan group of intellectuals and writers whose number included, over the years Jean-Charles Léonard de Sismondi, August Wilhelm von Schlegel, prince Auguste of Prussia, Madame Récamier, and BENJAMIN CONSTANT. The Coppet group shared Staël's political views. Influenced by Enlightenment thought, Staël greeted the Revolution of 1789 (see FRENCH REVOLUTION) with enthusiasm and the Reign of Terror of 1793 with horror.

It is perhaps surprising that Staël placed so much emphasis on eloquence, given her rejection of CLASSICISM. The question of language was important to Staël, however, particularly in relation to politics, and she believed that the French revolutionaries had abused language and, in consequence, the very concept of liberty. Literature, she felt, should contribute to the betterment of humanity.

In 1794, when the political climate in France had calmed, Staël returned to Paris. She was a great supporter of liberalism, and her salon attracted opposition figures of whom the government was increasingly suspicious. Staël's *The Influence of Literature upon Society* was published in 1800 and drew negative attention from the censors. Staël's friendship with CHATEAUBRIAND dates from this period when he came to her defense. Staël precedes him in celebrating Christianity's contribution to culture.

In *The Influence of Literature,* Staël makes an argument concerning aesthetic relativism. Perhaps the first major work of comparative literature, *The Influence of Literature* rejects the notion that modern literature should be judged by the standards of antiquity (see CLASSICISM). Drawing on MONTESQUIEU, Staël believed instead that literature should reflect the political, social, and cultural institutions of the nation that gave it birth. She thus draws a distinction between the literatures of northern and southern Europe. By arguing that there is no objective definition of beauty, Staël suggests that the value of art lies in its capacity to reflect culture.

As a romantic, she also believes that literature should express feeling.

The year 1802 marked her husband's death and the publication of her popular novel, *Delphine.* Despite this success, Staël's situation vis-à-vis the government was again tenuous. She was presumed to have collaborated with her father on *Recent Views on Politics and Science,* which resulted in her exile from Paris. Thus begin her famous travels.

Constant, with whom she carried on a turbulent affair for many years, traveled with her to Germany and Italy. These journeys provided much of the material for her subsequent writings. In 1804 Staël was invited to the Prussian court when the death of her father called her back to Coppet. There she led the voice of opposition to Napoleon while continuing her literary pursuits. Staël published *Corinne or Italy* in 1807, a work that inspired a generation of romantics.

Staël traveled to France incognito to oversee the publication of *On Germany,* a work that analyzes German values, characteristics, and philosophy in relation to developments in literature and the arts. Unfortunately, censors seized and destroyed the 2,000 copies that had been printed. Once again, Staël went into exile. *On Germany,* perhaps her greatest theoretical work on the romantic movement in German literature, was published three years later in London. In this text Staël articulates ideas that circulated earlier in her salon at Coppet. It is thus in a sense a collaborative work by a group of intellectuals who together defined romanticism.

In Coppet Staël lived through difficult times. Certain of her friends suffered because of their association with her. The arm of Napoleon was long and it took a woman like Germaine de Staël to challenge him. Napoleon is reputed to have said, "I detest that woman." Bitter and afraid of growing old, Staël married a young Swiss officer in 1811, but this did not mean settling down. Staël traveled to Russia, Sweden, and England, in each instance inciting Napoleon's enemies outside of France. In London, Staël met the future Louis XVIII, who rekindled her hopes for a constitutional monarchy. In 1816 she traveled to Pisa with M. Rocca, her husband, and fell ill. She returned to Paris, where she died in 1817.

A cosmopolitan intellectual, Germaine de Staël made a mark on the literary world of 19th-century Europe. Like her female characters, she was conflicted by her desire to follow both her mind and her heart. It is not surprising that she is one of the most significant figures to bridge the gap between the Enlightenment and the romantic movement. Moreover, Staël introduced a form of romantic feminism that would come to fruition in the works of GEORGE SAND. For both Staël and Sand, woman is the embodiment of the romantic individual because of her passionate nature. At the same time, she is a victim of society and of her own heart.

Staël's concern with a woman's place in society can be linked to the writing of her lover Benjamin Constant and to ISABELLE DE CHARRIÈRE. As a young woman Charrière corresponded with a Swiss officer, baron Auguste Constant d'Hermenches, whose nephew, Benjamin Constant, she later met. Charrière was opposed to Constant's liaison with Staël. In her turn, Staël was somewhat irritated with Charrière. Nevertheless, not only were the three connected personally, but there are also overlapping themes in their fiction. Staël's character Oswald chooses to marry the woman his father has destined for him rather than Corinne, whom he loves. Charrière's William is unable to overcome his family's disapproval and social expectations to marry Caliste. Constant's ADOLPHE, in an interesting turn, is incapable not of marrying his lover but of leaving her. In each instance woman is the victim of a combination of male weakness and repressive social institutions.

Staël was concerned with the recognition of the intellectual equality of women through cultural self-representation. The writing of fiction permits this. Despite her professed admiration for JEAN-JACQUES ROUSSEAU (Staël's first publication was *Letters on the Writing and Character of J. J. Rousseau, 1788*), her one bone of contention with Rousseau concerned his belief that women should not engage in intellectual life.

FURTHER READING

Christopher-Herold, J. *Mistress to an Age: A Life of Mme de Staël*. New York: Bobbs-Merrill, 1958.

Gutwirth, Madelyn. *Madame de Staël, Novelist: The Emergence of the Artist as a Woman*. Urbana: University of Illinois Press, 1978.

Hess, Carla. *The Other Enlightenment: How French Women Became Modern*. Princeton, N.J., Oxford: Princeton University Press, 2001.

Hogsett, Charlotte. *The Literary Existence of Germaine de Staël*. Carbondale: Southern Illinois University Press, 1987.

Smith, Bonnie G. "History and Genius: The Narcotic, Erotic, and Baroque Life of Germaine de Staël," *French Historical Studies* 19, no. 4 (Autumn 1996): 1,059–1,081.

Trouille, Mary Seidman. *Sexual Politics in the Enlightenment*. Albany: State University of New York Press, 1997.

STATES AND EMPIRES OF THE MOON AND SUN, THE (LES ÉTATS ET EMPIRES DE LA LUNE ET DU SOLEIL) SAVINIEN CYRANO DE BERGERAC (1657, 1662)

In describing these two fantastic journeys to the moon and sun, Cyrano de Bergerac ridicules the traditional view that humanity is at the center of the universe. In these tales, Cyrano travels to space by a rocket outfitted with firecrackers; according to Arthur C. Clarke, this is the first literary depiction of a rocket journey to space. When he arrives on the moon, its inhabitants think he is a bird, since he has two legs. On the second trip he is tried by a court of birds for crimes against humanity. Cyrano defends himself by arguing that he is an ape, not a man. In his journey to the sun, Cyrano explains why its heat does not burn. There he meets Tommaso Campanella, author of another fantastic journey, the utopian *City of the Sun*. He also shows his opposition to the philosopher René Descartes's view that animals are without souls.

As a 17th-century libertine (see LIBERTINISM), Cyrano espoused humanism, skepticism, and naturalism. Most important, he attacked religious dogmatism. In these two works, also known collectively as *The Other World*, Cyrano rejects God in favor of reason. A visionary, Cyrano makes use of his fantastic voyages to show a world turned upside down. He challenges traditional power structures by playing with the relationship between signs and symbols. A double relativity is apparent in his encounter with the lunar people, who view human beings as apes of themselves. By exploiting language, Cyrano distorts the patriarchal order so imbedded in his own society. On the moon the sons have authority over their fathers. While Cyrano's subversion of the political and social order may reflect in part his strained relationship with his father, it also reveals the problem of a new generation of intellectuals who found it difficult to define their social identity in a fairly rigid social order. Libertinism, with its hedonistic challenge to authority in search of freedom, raised the problem of identity. More pessimistic than fellow libertine CHARLES SOREL, Cyrano de Bergerac questions the possibility of a meaningful reality.

The States and Empires of the Moon and Sun were both published posthumously by Cyrano's lifelong friend Henri Le Bret, who edited the more heretical parts. Even with this censorship, the works reveal Cyrano's continuation of the Rabelaisian tradition of satire (see RABELAIS) and the influence of the Roman satirist Lucian, from whose *A True Story* he drew inspiration. He supposedly wrote a third part, *The History of the Stars,* but this text was either lost or destroyed. Cyrano de Bergerac has a significant place in the genre of science fiction. While his works were not appreciated in their own time, they influenced later works such as Jonathan Swift's *Gulliver's Travels* and VOLTAIRE's *MICROMÉGAS.*

FURTHER READING

De Jean, Joan. *Libertine Strategies: Freedom and the Novel in Seventeenth-Century France.* Columbus: Ohio State University Press, 1981.

Harth, Erica. *Cyrano de Bergerac and the Polemics of Modernity.* New York: Columbia University Press, 1970.

Lanius, Edward. *Cyrano de Bergerac and the Universe of the Imagination.* Geneva: Droz, 1967.

STENDHAL (HENRI BEYLE) (1783–1842)

Henri Beyle, who wrote under the pseudonym Stendhal, was one of the greatest French writers of the 19th century. Like GUSTAVE FLAUBERT, he bridged ROMANTICISM and REALISM. Stendhal's writings blend romantic sensibility with a sharply critical attitude about society that reveals the author's hatred of hypocrisy and his desire for authenticity in the modern world.

Born in Grenoble to a wealthy bourgeois family, Stendhal did not have a happy childhood. His mother whom he adored, died when he was only seven years old. From that time on, Stendhal's lonely childhood was dominated by a conservative, staunchly royalist father and aunt, whose views may have driven Stendhal to liberal republicanism. Stendhal's only real joy came from contact with his grandfather and his sister Pauline.

Stendhal's autobiography, *The Life of Henry Brulard* (posthumous, 1890), retraces the author's childhood fraught with tension between tender feelings and hatred, familial constraints, and ambition. In contrast to his royalist father, Stendhal was from early on a convinced republican, a patriot who agreed with the execution of the king that had taken place in 1793. He was even pleased with his father's brief arrest. Moreover, one of Stendhal's teachers succeeded in turning him away from the church. Stendhal thus rejected all traditional authority.

In 1799, Stendhal won a prize in mathematics. Thinking that this might offer the means to escape from the mediocrity of provincial life, Stendhal left for Paris. After falling ill, however, he quickly abandoned his studies. A relative helped him find a position in the Ministry of War and in 1800 Stendhal joined Napoleon's Italian campaign. For most of his adult life Stendhal went back and forth between France and Italy, his spiritual home.

But military life did not appeal to him and in 1801 he returned to France. Having fallen in love with the actress Melanie Guilbert, Stendhal followed her to Marseille. When the relationship ended in 1806, Stendhal returned to Paris and, with the support of his family, found another position in the military. By 1806 Stendhal was thus once again with the army on campaign in Germany.

The year 1810 found Stendhal back in Paris. It was a time of success. Appointed to the Council of State, Stendhal also enjoyed a life of pleasure: love affairs, evenings at the theater, and the company at some of the best salons in Paris. In his own words, Stendhal focused his life on the pursuit of pleasure (*la chasse au bonheur*). Mistress succeeded mistress. Still Stendhal was not only ambitious in love; he also sought recognition in society and as a writer. To understand himself better, he began to focus on his diary.

For some time, Stendhal wandered across Europe following his hero Napoleon, who would figure largely in the background of his novels. These and other travels afforded him much material for his fiction. He witnessed, for example, the battle of Jena and Napoleon's entry into Berlin. In 1812 Stendhal accompanied Napoleon's army into Russia.

In 1814, Stendhal left Paris for Milan, where he would spend the best part of the next seven years. This was probably the happiest time in Stendhal's life, despite his disappointment over the fall of Napoleon in 1815 and the vagaries of his own personal life. Italy provided compensation. The fall of Napoleon in 1814 hampered Stendhal's political ambitions but it also allowed him to return to Italy, where he began to focus on writing in earnest. Throughout this period Stendhal wrote at first under various pseudonyms, *The Lives of Haydn, Mozart, and Métastase* (1814), *The History of Painting in Italy* (1817) and, under the name Stendhal (the name of a small German town), *Rome, Naples and Florence.*

In 1818 Stendhal fell in love with the viscontini Mathilde Dembowski but she did not return his affections. Stendhal's love for Mathilde inspired one of his most significant works, *Love* (1822), "a detailed and minute description of all the feelings that compose the passion named love." In this work Stendhal introduces his theory of crystallization, a process by which the spirit, fashioning reality after its own desires, ascribes to the beloved the characteristics of perfection. Here Stendhal distinguishes between different types of love according to temperament, political systems, climate, and mores. The crystallization theory is apparent in Stendhal's other fictional works such as *The Red and the Black* and *The Charterhouse of Parma.*

From the outset of his adult life, we see the ways in which Stendhal's own experience and desires fueled his writing. Each of his principal characters, Julien Sorel in *The RED AND THE BLACK,* Fabrice del Dongo in *The CHARTERHOUSE OF PARMA,* and LUCIEN LEUWEN resemble their creator. Stendhal's principal characters all manifest his ideal of passion, energy, and egotism.

Stendhal was obliged to leave Milan in 1821, as Austrian authorities suspected him of sympathizing with the Carbonari, who sought to free Italy from foreign rule. After a brief stint in London, Stendhal returned to Paris and the life of a dandy. Still writing nonetheless, in 1823 he published the first part of his romantic

manifesto *Racine and Shakespeare.* In this work Stendhal defines romanticism as "the art of presenting literary works to people that . . . are likely to give them the greatest possible pleasure. Classicism, in contrast, presents to them a literature that gave the greatest pleasure to their great grandfathers." The second part was published in 1825. This work did not receive much attention. Stendhal also published a series of articles on painting and on Italian opera.

In May 1826 Stendhal broke with his current mistress, the countess Curial, and traveled to England, where he began work on his first novel, *Armance,* published in 1827, a story of love defeated by impotency. This work, too, received little notice, and Stendhal set off once again for Italy, but the Italian police sent him back to France.

In 1828 again in Paris, Stendhal worried about his financial situation as he was not earning enough from articles published in English journals. In 1829 he produced *Promenades in Rome* and then, during a journey through the south of France, he was struck with the idea of "Julien" and began writing his first masterpiece, published in 1830 as *The Red and the Black.* This novel offers a sharp critique of French society under the BOURBON RESTORATION. In this story of ambition and class struggle, a poor provincial boy rises in society through the seduction of women. The title represents the two principal avenues of social mobility in the first half of the 19th century, the army and the church, a theme that Stendhal picks up again in *The Charterhouse of Parma.*

Stendhal was appointed consul in Civitavecchia in 1830, but this administrative position bored him, and in 1831–32 he spent far more time working in Rome on the manuscripts that would eventually become *Italian Chronicles* than he did fulfilling his professional obligations. He also worked on *Souvenirs of Egotism,* outlining what later critics referred to as "Beylism," his sharply critical unfinished novel *Lucien Leuwen,* and began work on his autobiography, *The Life of Henry Brulard.*

In 1837–38, Stendhal was once again enjoying the pleasures of Parisian society, all the while continuing to write. His travels through the French countryside led, for example, to *Memoirs of a Tourist* (1838). He was then struck with the idea for his second masterpiece, *The Charterhouse of Parma*, written in a burst of inspiration in two months and published in 1839. This is perhaps his greatest work in that Stendhal reveals himself completely. At the height of his talent as a writer, in this novel Stendhal offers all of his dreams, passions, his love of adventure, and his love of Italy. While the novel did not meet with enthusiasm from the public, Balzac praised it: "M. Beyle has produced a book in which the sublime bursts forth from chapter to chapter."

Stendhal returned to Civitavecchia in August 1839, where he worked on *Lamiel*, but he was increasingly bored. He also fell in with a young Roman woman but this was to be his last love affair. Stendhal's health was failing and in March 1841 he had an attack of apoplexy. By the time he arrived in France in November, he was exhausted and in March 1842 suffered another attack of apoplexy in the street. He died the next day and was buried in the cemetery of Montmartre. A number of Stendhal's works were published posthumously: *Lucien Leuwen, The Life of Henry Brulard, Souvenirs of Egotism, Lamiel*, his *Journal* (1801–23), and his *Correspondence*.

What is most striking today is Stendhal's rehabilitation as an author since the late 19th century. Aware that his contemporaries could not appreciate his writing, he said that his time would come in 1935. Hence, it was only after his death that Stendhal came to be appreciated as one of the greatest figures in French literary history.

Stendhal's character is unusual in its combination of romantic sensibility and sharp intellect. Both a romantic and a realist, Stendhal possessed a passion for authenticity and a hatred of hypocrisy. For Stendhal, the principle purpose of life is the search for happiness, and this is reflected in his concept of egotism and the cult of the self, found in all of his heroes. Stendhal's own personality permeates his works. Julien Sorel, Fabrice del Dongo, and Lucien Leuwen all possess traits associated with the author. Stendhal was nonetheless a capable observer of society who sought to write in a style possessing the clarity of the civil code, marking his writing as a precursor to realism.

FURTHER READING

Alter, Robert in collaboration with Carol Cosman. *A Lion for Love: A Critical Biography of Stendhal*. New York: Basic Books, 1979.

Auerbach, Erich. *Mimesis: The Representation of Reality in Western Literature*. Translated by Willard R. Trask. Princeton, N.J.: Princeton University Press, 1953.

Fineshriber, William. H. *Stendhal the Romantic Rationalist*. Philadelphia: R. West, 1977.

Girard, René. *Deceit, Desire and the Novel: Self and Other in Literary Structure*. Translated by Yvonne Freccero. Baltimore, London: Johns Hopkins University Press, 1976.

Green, Frederick Charles. *Stendhal*. New York: Russell and Russell, 1970.

Haig, Stirling. *Stendhal: The Red and the Black*. Cambridge: Cambridge University Press, 1989.

Haig, Stirling and De la Motte, Dean, eds. *Approaches to Teaching Stendhal's* The Red and the Black. New York: MLA, 1999.

Hemmings, F. W. J. *Stendhal: A Study of His Novels*. Oxford: Clarendon Press, 1964.

Jefferson, Ann. *Reading Realism in Stendhal*. Cambridge: Cambridge University Press, 1988.

Keates, Jonathan. *Stendhal*. New York: Carroll and Graf, 1997.

May, Gita. *Stendhal and the Age of Napoleon*. New York: Columbia University Press, 1977.

Pearson, Roger. *Stendhal's Violin: A Novelist and His Reader*. Oxford: Clarendon Press, 1988.

———, ed. *Stendhal: The Red and the Black and the Charterhouse of Parma*. London: Longman, 1994.

Stendhal. *The Life of Henry Brulard*. Translated by Jean Stewart and B. C. J. G. Knight. Chicago: University of Chicago Press, 1986.

———. *Memoirs of an Egotist*. Translated by David Ellis. New York: Horizon Press, 1975.

Talbot, Emile. *Stendhal and Romantic Esthetics*. Lexington, Ky.: French Forum, 1985.

———. *Stendhal Revisited*. New York: Twayne, 1993.

Wakefield, David. *Stendhal: The Promise of Happiness*. Bedford, England: Newstead Press, 1984.

STORY OF A CHILD, THE (*LE ROMAN D'UN ENFANT*) Pierre Loti (1890)

"It is with a sort of fear that I approach the enigma of my impressions from the beginning of life." Loti was 40 years old when he wrote this autobiographical novel depicting his childhood in Rochefort-sur-Mer. With nostalgia for a gentle past, Loti evokes the beauty of childhood where, surrounded by the loving affection of his mother and three old aunts, he dreams of adventure. Evenings in the red salon, afternoons playing in the countryside, and water, waves, and sand make up the world of his youth that Loti so powerfully suggests.

FURTHER READING

Blanch, Lesley. *Pierre Loti: Portrait of an Escapist.* London: Collins, 1983.

———. *Pierre Loti: the Legendary Romantic.* San Diego: Harcourt Brace Jovanovich, 1983.

Hartman, Elwood. *Three Nineteenth-Century French Writers/ Artists and the Maghreb: The Literary and Artistic Depictions of North Africa by Théophile Gautier, Eugène Fromentin and Pierre Loti.* Tübingen, Germany: Narr, 1994.

Hughes, Edward J. *Writing Marginality in Modern French Literature: From Loti to Genet.* Cambridge, New York: Cambridge University Press, 2001.

Lerner, Michael. *Pierre Loti's Dramatic Works.* Lewiston, Me.: E. Mellen Press, 1998.

STORY OF THE GRAIL, THE (PERCEVAL)

CHRÉTIEN DE TROYES (12TH CENTURY) Chrétien wrote only the first 9,000 lines of this 32,000-line ROMANCE depicting the adventures of Perceval as he gradually develops from an innocent country lad into the perfect knight. Written under the patronage of Philip of Alsace, count of Flanders, either his patron's death or his own marked the end of Chrétien's composition. It was later continued or adapted by several writers including Wauchier de Denain, Gerbert de Montreuil, Manessier, and Robert de Boron. The romance is divided into two parts. Somewhat inexplicably, the first describes Perceval's introduction to knighthood and the second describes Gawain's quests (King Arthur's nephew). It remains a subject of debate among scholars today whether the romance should be read as an allegory. If so, it is a Christian allegory introducing into literature the search for the Holy Grail. A number of 16th- and 17th-century novels such as HÉLISENNE DE CRENNE's *The* TORMENTS OF LOVE draw from the tradition of the medieval romance such as are found in the works of de Troyes.

FURTHER READING

Frappier, Jean. *Chrétien de Troyes: The Man and His Work.* Translated by Robert J. Cormier. Athens: Ohio University Press, 1982.

Lacy, Norris. *The Craft of Chrétien de Troyes: An Essay on Narrative Art.* Leiden, Netherlands: Brill, 1980.

Troyes, Chrétien de. *Arthurian Romances.* Translated by William W. Kibler. London: Penguin, 1991.

STRAIT IS THE GATE (LA PORTE ÉTROITE) ANDRÉ GIDE (1909)

Jerome, who is being raised by his mother, grows up with his cousins Juliette and Alissa Bucolin. The family's calm is disrupted when Madame Bucolin runs away and Alissa's response is to engage in an increasingly intense spiritual quest.

Although Jerome loves her, Alissa refuses to marry him for any number of pretexts. Jerome understands Alissa's motivation of self-sacrifice yet is unable to dissuade her. In the end Alissa dies from her internal torment, leaving behind a journal in which she reveals her love for Jerome and the conflict between her sensual and spiritual nature. Gide paints a portrait of Alissa as heroic, even sublime, and yet cruel and misguided. As for Jerome, he can neither equal his cousin's greatness nor turn her away from her superhuman ideal.

This dramatic story about the excesses of spirituality and personal freedom reflects an underlying tension in many of Gide's works born of the author's own experience. The story of Jerome and Alissa draws on Gide's relationship with his wife, Madeleine. Like the real-life couple, Jerome and Alissa have loved each other since childhood, and their love exists only on a spiritual level. Drawing on Christian symbolism, the novel portrays Alissa's choice as one of sacrifice, as it is through her effort alone that their relationship attains its mystical height. This is despite her very real sensual desire, another major theme in Gide's works. Alissa represents Madeleine Gide, who married her cousin despite his homosexuality and who accepted an ambiguous conjugal life with a man whom she loved.

In Gide's own words, *Strait is the Gate,* whose title is taken from a parable in the Gospel of Luke, is an expression of the spirit of Protestantism that marked Gide's own puritanical upbringing. His exploration of the dynamic between Jerome and Alissa, as well as the question of the individual's freedom and its consequences, are a continuation of themes found in *The Immoralist*.

FURTHER READING

Bettinson, Christopher D. *Gide: A Study*. London: Heinemann; Totowa, N.J.: Rowman and Littlefield, 1977.

O'Brien, Justin. *Portrait of André Gide: A Critical Biography*. New York: Octagon Books, 1977; 1953.

O'Keefe, Charles. *Void and Voice: Questioning Narrative Conventions in André Gide's Major First-Person Narratives*. Chapel Hill: Dept. of Romance Languages, University of North Carolina, 1996.

Sheridan, Alan. *André Gide: A Life in the Present*. Cambridge, Mass.: Harvard University Press, 1999.

Stoltzfus, Ben. "André Gide and the Voices of Rebellion," *Contemporary Literature* 19, no. 1 (Winter 1978): 80–98.

Walker, David, ed. *André Gide*. London, New York: Longman, 1996.

STRANGER, THE (*L'ÉTRANGER*) ALBERT CAMUS (1942)

One of the most important works of 20th-century French literature, *The Stranger* is famous for its opening line: "Mama died today. Or perhaps yesterday. I don't know."

Camus's first published novel, *The Stranger* was written in six weeks in 1940 and published at the same time as *The Myth of Sisyphus,* a companion philosophical essay in which Camus expresses his version of existentialist thought (see EXISTENTIALISM). *The Stranger* is essentially divided into two parts. The first three chapters precede the murder, while the last three chapters follow it.

At the opening of the novel, Meursault, the principal character, is living a completely ordinary, monotonous life in Algiers. He goes to work and to the beach. Then his mother dies and, to the dismay of all, Meursault feels nothing. He refuses to look at her dead body. He cannot even cry at her funeral as if he were a stranger. Moreover, Meursault refuses to conform to a social code that, in his mind, demands an excess of false words. He speaks in simple phrases about his feelings, sensations, boredom, and indifference. "It's all the same to me." Meursault describes his mother's funeral with the same detachment as his encounter with a woman or a day at work. Ultimately, however, the "strangeness" of his character comes from his passion for the truth, despite his apparent amorality. In the end, the honesty of his responses causes the judge to condemn Meursault to death.

The day after his mother's funeral, Meursault runs into Marie at the beach. They have sex. Afterward when they are dressing, Marie is surprised to discover that Meursault is in mourning and that his mother's funeral took place only the day before. Meursault continues his affair with Marie although he does not love her. When she asks him, Meursault's only response is "that doesn't mean anything, but it seems to me, no."

Meursault's neighbors include old Salamano, who beats his dog, and, Raymond Sintès, who is suspected of being a pimp. One day after a fight, Raymond asks Meursault for help in seeking revenge against his attacker, the brother of one of his clients.

The second part of the novel opens when Meursault goes with Raymond to the beach for a picnic. When a fight breaks out on the beach with the client's brother and his friends, one of whom has a knife, Meursault, his eyes blinded by sweat and overcome by the heat and the glare of the sun, takes Raymond's revolver and shoots one of the Arabs "like four brief knocks on the door of misery." Meursault is subsequently arrested and interrogated, not just about the murder but also the feelings he had for his mother. Meursault remains silent, expressing no regret for his crime.

From his cell, Meursault can see the water. He misses the sea, a woman, cigarettes. Slowly, however, he grows accustomed to his imprisonment. He mulls over past memories and sleeps. During his trial, Meursault is again required to speak of his mother's death as well as of the murder. The court learns that Meursault did not cry at her funeral. Marie testifies that their affair began the day after his mother was buried. That evening they even went to see a comic film. Meursault is deemed a monster, proven by his indifference to his mother's death. Finally, he decides to speak in his own defense, explaining that he never intended to murder the Arab; the sun caused the crime. At this, the courtroom breaks into laughter. Meursault too realizes the absurdity of his explanation. He is ostensibly condemned to death for murder; his head will be cut off "in a public square in the name of the French people." In fact, his sentence may have more to do with his attitude at his mother's death than for the murder itself. "Society needs more people who cry at their mother's funeral."

While in prison and awaiting his execution, a priest comes to offer Meursault comfort but, in a moment of revolt, Meursault rebels against God and the absurdity of his own death. Then calm returns and he falls asleep. When he awakens, Meursault is lucid and at peace as he contemplates the stars and recognizes the world's "tender indifference." At the moment of his death, Meursault is capable of accepting his own strangeness.

Camus's style is simple and austere. Sentences are short and there is no complicated syntax. The very structure of the novel invites the reader first to consider Meursault's guilt then later to recognize the absurd logic of events. "One is never condemned for the crime one ought to be. I can still see ten other possible conclusions."

Meursault recognizes that one's gestures and expressions are essentially meaningless to others. He is thus passive, does not react, and does not even appear to recognize cause and effect. He feels that he is persecuted but he is weak and therefore an unsettling character to readers. Meursault's approach to life is inadequate.

In *The Myth of Sisyphus,* Camus wrote, "In a Universe suddenly deprived of illusions and enlightenment, man feels himself a stranger. This exile is without remedy since he is deprived of memories of a lost country or of hope for a promised land." Meursault is just such as man. Despite his crime he is not a criminal. Meursault's experience reveals Camus's notion of the absurd, that is to say, the irrational nature of life derived from man's essential alienation from himself and from the world. The recognition of the absurdity of existence may lead man to rebel. Meursault, however, makes no attempt to change the condition of his life.

FURTHER READING

Brée, Germaine. *Camus.* New Brunswick, N.J.: Rutgers University Press, 1972.

Brombert, Victor. "Camus and the Novel of the 'Absurd,'" *Yale French Studies,* no. 1, Existentialism (1948): 119–123.

Brosman, Catharine Savage. *Albert Camus.* Detroit: Gale Group, 2001.

Cruickshank, John. *Albert Camus and the Literature of Revolt.* New York: Oxford University Press, 1960.

STRUCTURALISM

In a structuralist approach to literature, meaning is derived from a system of signs that consist of a signifier (word) and signified (concept). Structuralism is thus related to semiotics. One sign's meaning does not exist in isolation; it is related to others signs sharing the same cultural context. The sign system consists of binary opposites that are then reflected in literature.

This theory thus rests on the supposition that the world is structured by binary opposites that, in turn, structure meaning. The different fields of culture consist of binary sets such as male/female, good/evil, and light/dark. Structuralists examine the relations between different signs by exploring, among other things, metonymy and metaphor.

Structuralism shares with formalism a belief that literature is encoded with meaning, but for the structuralist that meaning is derived from a cultural context. Cultural codes provide the context for signs. If signs have a very general meaning in a broader cultural context, they are considered myths.

Rather than focusing on the individual, structuralists emphasize the subject in such a way that even things that the individual experiences are formed by culture and are thus, on some level, collective. The self is socially constructed just like everything else. Consequently, structuralists are also interested in the subconscious as reflecting repressed signs prevalent in culture. Even reality is structured by codes and conventions that are made up of signs. Hence, structuralists refer to the social construction of reality. Whether one considers the individual, the subconscious, or society, all are structured by the same signs.

For structuralists anything can be read as a text; one simply needs to explore signs and their meaning. Consequently, structuralism is closely linked to cultural anthropology, particularly the works of Claude Lévi-Strauss.

When literature imitates reality, it does so through the use of codes perceived by the reader. The reader thus has a role to play in a structuralist approach to literature. Some poststructuralists go so far as to suggest that without the reader there is no text (see POST-STRUCTURALISM).

In France, structuralism is particularly associated with the linguistic theories of Ferdinand de Saussure, who sought a scientific approach to language and literature. Structuralism has been criticized for neglecting history. The inadequacies of structuralist theory led to deconstruction, poststructuralism, FEMINISM, and late versions of MARXISM.

SUE, EUGÈNE (1804–1857)
Born in Paris in 1804 to a family of surgeons, Sue first followed in the family tradition. At the age of 20 he joined the navy as a surgical assistant and traveled to the Mediterranean and to the Antilles. Upon his father's death, Sue inherited a fortune that allowed him to leave the navy and turn full-time to writing. One of the first serial novelists of the 19th-century, Sue wrote novels that were highly successful. Over the course of his career he produced more than 100 volumes.

Sue first wrote novels about men at sea and on historical subjects, but he gained notoriety with his serial novels, especially The MYSTERIES OF PARIS and The WANDERING JEW. Already fairly successful and certainly prolific, Sue became a household word in 19th-century France with the publication of The Mysteries in the Journal des débats, 1842–43. This novel recounting the adventures and misadventures of Fleur-de-Marie appealed to readers of all social classes. People lined up in the streets for the latest installment. Legend has it that Sue was supposed to be sent to prison for missing his watch in the National Guard when he was pardoned by the minister of war himself, an avid follower of The Mysteries, who wanted to prevent any delay in publication. THÉOPHILE GAUTIER once said, "the dying waited to expire until the end of The Mysteries." Parisian journals competed with one another for the right to publish Sue's novels by offering him fantastic sums.

Sue created a remarkable blend of various literary genres, including the gothic novel and adventure stories, allowing him to reach out to a broad reading public. Making skillful use of the serial novel form, Sue kept his readers eager for the next installment. Colorful street language contributes to Sue's ability to bring to life the suffering of the urban poor, the corruption of

the wealthy, and the need for social reform. An influence on VICTOR HUGO's LES MISÉRABLES, Sue's novels reflect a similar Manichean dualism to that of the great master. At the same time, generosity, optimism, and a powerful imagination allow Sue to blend entertainment with social justice. Leading into REALISM, Sue's socialist undertones echoed the sentiments of many readers in the period before the Revolution of 1848. His popularity as a writer undoubtedly contributed to his success in running for political office. Like Hugo, Sue was forced into exile by Louis-Napoléon Bonaparte's coup d'état of 1851. He died in Savoy.

SUNS OF INDEPENDENCE, THE (LES SOLEILS DES INDÉPENDENCES) AHMADOU KOUROUMA (1968)
One of the most significant works in the history of African fiction, this novel of deception and disillusionment tells the story of Fama, a disinherited African prince who struggles valiantly against colonialism only to be cast aside once independence is attained, left with nothing but an identity card and membership in the one political party that now governs his land.

Fama is disillusioned by the new regime in the "République des Ébenes," a thinly disguised Ivory Coast. In Malinke, Fama means "chief." In another time Fama would have inherited leadership of his people but this is no longer possible. The novel opens with a funeral that Fama has left angrily because he has been derided for his performance as a professional mourner. He subsequently wanders irritably through the streets of his city, bearing witness to the monumental change that has accompanied colonization and decolonization. The marketplace inspires him to consider questions of trade and commerce in relation to colonialism.

The avenue of the city that Fama traverses is a metaphor for his life. It leads to the cemetery and lagoon, in other words, death and stagnation. Although Fama struggled valiantly against the French colonial system, he finds himself equally disenfranchised in the new regime. There is no place for him. He is a comical character whose literal sterility has deep symbolic meaning as well, representing the impotence of the Malinke people, whose traditional occupations of war and commerce are now denied them. At the end of the novel,

Fama is killed by a crocodile on the border between two lands that represent Mali and the Ivory Coast. The novel's symmetry lies in its beginning and ending with death.

Despite the rise of a new system, the country remains racially divided. The whites are still the haves and the blacks the have-nots. Even though Fama represents the elite of the former social order, Kourouma is not using his character to view the past nostalgically. The former hierarchical order appears as no more rational than the new, oppressive, one-party regime.

Sharply critical of both colonial and postcolonial society, this novel is written in an unusual style that grafts traditional Malinke proverbs and expressions onto the French language in ways that are not always immediately clear to the reader. Drawing from oral traditions, Kourouma has the gift of the traditional "griot," or storyteller. The narrative is full of repetitions and digressions that include songs, proverbs, and stories within stories. At times the reader has the sense of being addressed directly by the narrator, whose voice alternates between the second and third person, mimicking the audience participation of a traditional storyteller's performance. Chapter headings sound like the titles of African fables. Kourouma's linking of oral and written traditions adds to the narrative's sense of immediacy. Furthermore, the use of onomatopoeia heightens the sense of sound and rhythm in the narrative.

FURTHER READING

Schikora, Rosemary G. "Narrative Voice in Kourouma's *Les Soleils des Independences*," *French Review* 55, no. 6, Literature and Civilization of Black Francophone Africa (May 1982): 811–817.

Sellin, Eric. *"Les Soleils des Independences."* Review Article, *French Review* 44, no. 3 (February 1971): 641–642.

SUPERMALE (LE SURMÂLE) ALFRED JARRY (1902)

One night, at a gathering of friends in the castle of Lurance, André Marcueil announces that "the act of love is of no significance because one can do it indefinitely." To prove his virility, he trains for a 10-thousand-mile race that pits cyclists against a steam engine. André, of course, proves his superiority to the athletes trained by William Elson and returns to expend his sexual energy on William's daughter. When he sees that the "supermale" is more than a machine, Elson, along with the engineer Arthur Gough, is inspired to develop another machine that will inspire love. When they do so, the machine itself falls in love with André and kills him.

The novel is set in 1920, hence in the future given that it was published in 1902. It is one of Jarry's best-known works, similar in theme to other novels and plays in which Jarry plays with the notion of "pataphysics," a science of excess. Jarry's works influenced later surrealists (see SURREALISM).

FURTHER READING

Beaumont, Keith. *Alfred Jarry: A Critical and Biographical Study.* St. Martin's Press, 1984.

Fell, Jill. *Alfred Jarry, an Imaginary Revolt.* Madison, N.J.: Farleigh Dickinson University Press, 2005.

LaBelle, Maurice Marc. *Alfred Jarry, Nihilism, and the Theater of the Absurd.* New York: New York University Press, 1980.

Lennon, Nigey. *Alfred Jarry: The Man with the Axe.* Los Angeles: Panjandrum Books, 1984.

Murphy, Patrice. "Rabelais and Jarry," *French Review* 51, no. 1 (October 1977): 29–36.

Shattuck, Roger. *The Banquet Years: The Arts in France, 1885–1918: Alfred Jarry, Henri Rousseau, Erik Satie, Guillaume Apollinaire.* New York: Harcourt Brace, 1958.

SURPRISE OF LIVING, THE (LA SURPRISE DE VIVRE) JEANNE GALZY (1969)

Written when the author was almost 80 years old, *The Surprise of Living* is a remarkably sensual novel. MARGUERITE YOURCENAR once described it as "containing so many summer days, warm nights along the river, burning siestas. I did not expect such a feverish idyll. The love of two women is described with not a word too many, nor too few."

Vibrant and flowing, this novel is the story of a woman torn between what society expects of her and what she desires. Eva, the principal character, is a woman like Galzy, born into a conventional Protestant family in Montpellier. Set in the period before World War I, her love affair with another woman develops gradually in this novel about choice.

Eva, a wealthy heiress whose family possesses much land, is married off to David, the son of a banker in

Montpellier. Both families are strict, traditional, and Protestant. Eva is barely 20 years old when she finds herself living with her husband's family. Both David and her mother-in-law pressure her to conform to social expectations. They are dismayed that she is so wild, riding horseback and swimming in an immodest bathing suit (one that does not cover her calves). Eva suffers at the realization of what her future life will be like within such strict moral confines. Shortly thereafter, David dies and Eva is subsequently torn between duty to her family and her love for a woman named Hilda. In the end, Eva chooses to rebel.

Galzy has been recognized for her sensual and flowing style as well as for her contribution to lesbian literature and her exploration of the female condition and female sexuality, themes that mark much contemporary feminist literature (see FEMINISM).

FURTHER READING
Garreta, Anne F., and Josyane Savigneau. "Same Sex/Different Text? Gay and Lesbian Writing in French," *Yale French Studies,* no. 90 (1996): 214–234.

SURREALISM Although the term *surrealism* was coined in 1917 by the poet Guillaume Apollinaire to describe the realm of poetry, it now refers to a broader literary and artistic movement that developed in France and spread across Europe and the Americas after World War I.

ANDRÉ BRETON is the central figure of the French surrealist movement, having articulated its program in *The Surrealist Manifesto* (1924). According to Breton, men are dreamers by nature but are no longer able to give rein to their imagination. He was joined by other innovative writers such as LOUIS ARAGON and Philippe Soupault who sought a new means of expression in the wake of Dadaism (see DADA). These three writers established the journal *Literature* to promote their revolutionary ideas for the transformation of literature.

It is in a spirit of rebellion that Breton and Soupault offered the first definition of surrealism as "pure psychic automatism by which we propose to express [ourselves], verbally or in writing, or by some other means, the real function of thought, dictated by thought, in the absence of all control exercised by reason, outside of all aesthetic or moral preoccupations." They drew on and renewed interest in certain writers such as the poets Arthur Rimbaud, the comte de Lautréamont, ALFRED JARRY, romantic writers like Novalis (see ROMANTICISM), the marquis de SADE, gothic novels, JORIS-KARL HUYSMANS, and the symbolists (see SYMBOLISM).

In a broader context, the surrealists were reacting against events associated with World War I, leading them to reject traditional values such as humanism and rationalism. Other surrealist writers are Robert Desnos, René Crevel, and Paul Éluard. Together they engaged in innovative experiments with language intended to reinvent literature and life along new lines, and to provoke new means of inspiration. They believed that poetic language is capable of liberating the human spirit and reconciling humankind with the world.

Heirs to romanticism, the surrealists continued the romantic quest to escape the limitations of rationalism. Seeking a new understanding of the human condition, they explored the world of the subconscious, imagination, and dreams. Developments in the field of psychoanalysis associated with Sigmund Freud and others served as a strong influence, as the surrealists were fascinated by the power of the subconscious to reveal an alternate reality. To attain that reality, the surrealists engaged in "automatic writing," a process that would allow for the expression of the subconscious liberated from the constraints of reason. Their ultimate goal was to reach the level of the surreal, a superior and transcendent reality present in the material world. Poetry held a special place in this quest. As a result, surrealist novels tend to give greater weight to the poetic rather than the narrative function, as in Aragon's *PARIS PEASANT* and Breton's *NADJA*.

Surrealism spread from literature to other art forms such as theater (Sergey Diaghilev), painting (Max Ernst and Salvador Dalí), and film (Luis Buñuel). As was the case with many intellectual and cultural movements in the interwar period, after 1925 the surrealists were associated with Marxist theory and, consequently, with the Communist Party. Literature and politics came together as Marx's call to "transform the world" merged with Rimbaud's exhortation to "change life." Breton wrote of a way of living "the true life." Because the surrealists envisioned this new way of life as a revolution, it is not surprising that they made the leap to leftist politics. Often sharing ideas with the communists, they took a stand against colonialism and the French wars in Indochina and Algeria. But politics led to tensions within the group. By the early 1930s, it was clear to most surrealists (except Aragon) that adherence to the Communist Party would deny their creative independence as writers.

Breton's *Second Surrealist Manifesto* (1930) goes beyond language to engage the surrealist project specifically in a revolt against the family, the nation, religion—in essence all traditional institutions—in an attempt to revolutionize the human condition toward a surrealist totality (a *Gesamkunstwerk*). Not surprisingly, the movement became increasingly esoteric and occultist.

During World War II, most of the surrealists left France for New York, where the surrealist movement was particularly strong among such artists as Max Ernst, Roberto Matta, and Arshile Gorky, who left a lasting impression on postwar painting in America. In 1952 Breton published his history of the surrealist movement. In the postwar period, surrealism expanded into new areas of enquiry such as ancient civilizations, the art of the insane, Trotskyism, anarchism, liberation movements, and feminism. Over time the group slowly began to dissolve, ending definitively with Breton's death in 1966.

FURTHER READING

Ades, Dawn. *Dada and Surrealism*. London: Thames and Hudson, 1974.

Alquié, Ferdinand. *The Philosophy of Surrealism*. Translated by Bernard Waldrop. Ann Arbor: University of Michigan Press, 1965.

Bataille, Georges. *The Absence of Myth: Writings on Surrealism*. Translated by Michael Richardson. London, New York: Verso, 1994.

Bohn, Willard. *The Rise of Surrealism: Cubism, Dada and the Pursuit of the Marvelous*. Albany: State University of New York Press, 2002.

Carrouges, Michel. *André Breton and the Basic Concepts of Surrealism*. Translated by Maura Prendergast. Tuscaloosa: University of Alabama Press, 1974.

Choucha, Nadia. *Surrealism and the Occult*. Oxford: Mandrake, 1991.

Hedges, Inez. *Languages of Revolt: Dada and Surrealist Literature and Film*. Durham, N.C.: Duke University Press, 1983.

Lomas, David. *The Haunted Self: Surrealism, Psychoanalysis, Subjectivity*. New Haven, Conn.: Yale University Press, 2000.

"SYLVIE" GERARD DE NERVAL (1854) *Sylvie* is a collection of seven short stories and novellas published together, of which "Sylvie" is the most famous. In this autobiographical work, the narrator is in love with an actress but is afraid to reveal his feelings. He attends the theater every night just to see her perform. One night Gerard learns that Aurelia has a lover.

This information is a catalyst to Gerard's memory and he begins to dream of a young woman he knew growing up in his native village whose name is Sylvie. Gerard decides to leave at that moment and return to the village, for it is the evening of a traditional dance and he knows he will find her again. As he travels along, Gerard's memories of the past merge with dreams. He recalls not only Sylvie, the pretty, simple, gay brunette from his village, but also Adrienne, the blond aristocrat with an otherworldly beauty. He recalls her voice in a song. All Gerard knows is that Adrienne entered a convent.

When Gerard meets Sylvie again she has changed. Now she is sensible, earning her own living. She also has an admirer. Nonetheless, Sylvie and Gerard tenderly recall their past and visit the château where Gerard had once seen and heard Adrienne. While they are there, Gerard simultaneously recalls both Adrienne and Aurelia while contemplating Sylvie. He even thinks that perhaps he will marry her. Gerard hopes that Sylvie will draw him out of his confused dreams into reality, only this is not possible. The story ends several years later when Gerard is visiting Sylvie, now married with children, and he learns that Adrienne died long before in the convent.

Together the three women who dominate Gerard's imagination exist as one eternal and mythical feminine in the narrator's confused mind. The theme of the eternal feminine is recurring in Nerval's works. In each instance the author draws from particular women who played a significant role in his own life even as he blends a world of dreams and reality, until they are no longer distinguishable from one another. This essentially romantic quality (see ROMANTICISM) led to Nerval's influence on subsequent surrealist writers (see SURREALISM).

FURTHER READING

Gilbert, Claire, *Nerval's Double: A Structural Study.* Jackson: University of Mississippi: Romance Monographs, 1979.

Jones, Robert Emmet. *Gérard de Nerval.* New York: Twayne, 1974.

Knapp, Bettina Liebowitz, *Gérard de Nerval: The Mystic's Dilemma.* Tuscaloosa, Ala.: University of Alabama Press, 1980.

MacLennan, George. *Lucid Interval: Subjective Writing and Madness in History.* Rutherford, N.J.: Fairleigh Dickinson University Press, 1992.

Miller, David. *There and Here: A Meditation on Gérard de Nerval.* Frome, Somerset, England: Bran's Head Books, 1982.

Prendergast, Christopher. *The Order of Mimesis: Balzac, Stendhal, Nerval, Flaubert.* Cambridge: Cambridge University Press, 1986.

Strauss, Jonathan. *Subjects of Terror: Nerval, Hegel and the Modern Self.* Palo Alto, Calif.: Stanford University Press, 1998.

SYMBOLISM Jean Moréas first coined the term *symbolism* in an article in *Le Figaro* in 1886. It is generally associated with such poets as Charles Baudelaire, Paul Verlaine, and Stéphane Mallarmé, but the symbolist movement also included painters and musicians such as Gabriel Fauré, Maurice Ravel, and Claude Debussy, the latter of whom put Mallarmé's poetry to music in *The Afternoon of a Fawn.* Moréas's article signals the return of IDEALISM and spiritual values to literature despite the amorphous nature of the movement. The most obvious manifestations of symbolist novels are JORIS-KARL HUYSMAN's *AGAINST THE GRAIN* along with the works of ANDRÉ GIDE and MARCEL PROUST. Through the power of image symbolists sought to reveal the hidden reality behind appearances. The resulting ambiguity leads to multiple interpretations of symbolist literature.

Diverging directions in the work of individual artists makes it difficult to discern a coherent definition of symbolism. But some common elements link symbolist works such as a desire to break with scientific POSITIVISM and materialism. The bywords of symbolism are idealism, free verse, and musicality.

The symbolists' general crisis of conscience led to an innovative exploration of the "poetic function of language," in the words of Mallarmé. Accordingly, words have two purposes, one utilitarian, and another poetic. Symbolists chose to emphasize the poetic and the ephemeral. They believed that language can be suggestive through its musicality. Symbolist works are also marked by a desire to be innovative in the use of language. Critics often note the development of the internal monologue, as exemplified by Huysmans, as a distinctive symbolist trend.

The symbolists sought an autonomy in literature that some critics view as a reaction against the contemporary sociopolitical situation. The development of a mass press contributed to the symbolists' desire to distinguish themselves from the crowd. Unlike the naturalists (see NATURALISM), symbolists desired to create a completely different, exclusive literary movement open only to a few initiates. Symbolism was thus not a popular movement in literature.

Symbolism grew out of the naturalist movement in literature. Naturalism draws principally from science. Symbolists attempted to bring literature back to itself by rejecting realist representations in favor of allusion or suggestion that parallel developments in the visual arts associated with impressionism and postimpressionism. Symbolists wished to renew a more sensitive approach to reality that emphasizes the subconscious in a way that also reflects new movements in philosophy and psychology.

Symbolists preferred suggestion and allusion to description. Drawing from diverse sources such as mythology, hermeticism, and Wagnerian music, symbolists often sought to evoke the mysterious, hidden connections beneath the surface of life. Influenced by the German philosopher Arthur Schopenhauer, later symbolists manifest a pessimism typical of late 19th-century thinkers. Symbolism influenced a number of new movements in modern literature as is evident in the works of PAUL VALÉRY and much 20th-century poetry.

T

TALLEMANT DES RÉAUX, GÉDÉON (1619–1690)

Born in La Rochelle to a wealthy Huguenot family, Tallemant added "des Réaux" to his name when he purchased property in 1650. Although he had studied law and took a position in parliament, a legal career was not to his liking. Tallemant des Réaux's marriage to Elisabeth de Rambouillet brought him into contact with the famous salon at the Hôtel de Rambouillet in Paris. Here he found ample material for his writing, as revealed in his *Love Tales from Tallemant*. His sometimes unkind but accurate portraits of contemporary literary and social figures such as Voiture, Malesherbes, Jean de La Fontaine, and Ninon de Lenclos provide a rich source in the literary history of France.

FURTHER READING

Gosse, Edmund. *Tallemant des Réaux, or The Art of Miniature Biography*. Oxford: Clarendon, 1925.

Wortley, W. Victor. *Tallemant des Réaux: The Man Through His Style*. The Hague: Mouton, 1969.

TARTARIN DE TARASCON ALPHONSE DAUDET (1872)

Along with his *LETTERS FROM MY MILL*, *TARTARIN DE TARASCON* is one of Daudet's most famous works. Composed of short chapters, the novel offers easy and agreeable reading. Its unforgettable hero, Tartarin, is a vibrant character leaning toward the obese. Tartarin lives peacefully in his Provençal village of Tarascon in a little house where he reads the American author Fennimore Cooper. In his garden is a famous baobab that refuses to grow tall.

Blessed with an active imagination, Tartarin dreams of adventures. He has already earned a reputation as an adventurer by recounting his journey to Shanghai, a voyage that took place solely in his mind. As Daudet wrote, "No one in the south really tells lies, although everybody makes statements contrary to fact."

Like most of his compatriots, Tartarin is a great hunter and one day, frustrated by the lack of game in Tarascon, decides to go to Africa to hunt lions. Tartarin disguises himself as an Arab and travels to Algeria. It is too civilized by far for Tartarin. There he falls for a veiled woman, causing him some difficulties. Moreover, he befriends a prince who only cheats him. Then he sets off on his hunting expedition and succeeds in killing a blind old lion. His achievement only leads him into legal straits, however, as an old beggar had trained the lion to appear in the public square. Preceded by the lion's skin (ensuring his fame), Tartarin finally returns to Tarascon followed by a camel who refuses to leave his side.

In this very popular novel, Daudet reveals his talent and sympathy for his native Provence. Tartarin's adventures continue in *Tartarin in the Alps* and *Port Tartarin,* in which the reader likewise discovers Daudet's joyful fantasy and joie de vivre typical of the Midi (south of France).

FURTHER READING

Dobie, Vera G. *Alphonse Daudet.* Folcroft, Pa.: Folcroft Library Editions, 1974.

Roche, Alphonse. *Alphonse Daudet.* Boston: Twayne, 1976.

Sachs, Murray. *The Career of Alphonse Daudet. A Critical Study.* Cambridge, Mass.: Harvard University Press, 1965.

TELEVISION (LA TÉLÉVISION) Jean-Philippe Toussaint (1997)

The opening line of this novel is simply "I stopped watching television." It is the story of a young academic who has come to Berlin from Paris to research and write a book on the Italian painter Titian. His companion and child leave him to work in peace while they go on vacation to Italy. Once alone, however, the scholar discovers that he has writer's block. He spends too much time watching television and decides that he must stop and focus on writing. The narrator also has the sense that he is cutting himself off from life.

Unfortunately, he still cannot write. He goes to the swimming pool, telling himself that "not writing is at least as important as writing." When he goes to water the plants in a neighbor's apartment, he finds himself watching their television. The same thing occurs when he is invited to the home of a friend's student. Even walking down the street he encounters a bank of television monitors in a store window. There seems to be no escape. The narrator's struggle to avoid television causes him to reflect on the relationship among that medium, the individual, and society. There is no grand denouement; this is rather a simple reflection on modern life. "I spent most afternoons at home, watching television three or four hours at a stretch, half-reclining on the couch, taking it easy . . . my feet bare, my hand cradling my privates. Just being myself in other words."

TEMPTATION OF SAINT ANTHONY, THE (LA TENTATION DE SAINT ANTOINE) Gustave Flaubert (1874)

The novel opens with the hermit Saint Anthony suffering in solitude and doubt as he contemplates what his life might have been like had he lived otherwise, even as he recognizes the sin of pride that lay at the heart of all his desires. For guidance, Anthony turns to *The Lives of the Saints* and discovers that God has often looked favorably on those who have dominated others. Anthony is subsequently transported into a nightmarish hallucination in which he encounters the seven deadly sins. The sin of pride, however, is ever-present as Anthony contemplates the power he might have over others through a given sin. He meets with the major heresies of the early Christian Church as well as the gods of antiquity. He also witnesses bizarre and bloody rites and is tormented by a vision of his former disciple Hilarion, who is transformed into the devil. Finally, the Sphinx and the Chimera melt into the sand and the devil carries Anthony away on his wing, ultimately challenging Anthony's vision of God by revealing the infinite nature of matter. Anthony becomes deliriously passionate, desiring to descend into the depths of matter, to *be* matter.

Flaubert's novel is troubling to the senses, and difficult to read and to assimilate. Perhaps this is why his friends advised him to throw the manuscript into the fire. The flow of words seems to possess a life force of its own and reveals Flaubert's mastery of language. The novel offers a confusing succession of images that bring the reader as close as possible to the experience of Saint Anthony that Flaubert seeks to depict.

In that overwhelming flow of images Flaubert offers a view of the world's religions as grounded in their specific historical contexts. Hence Christianity is necessary to Anthony; it is his path to understanding. Flaubert's vast knowledge reveals the length and breadth of human thought over the course of centuries. Anthony's journeys reflect humankind's varied understanding of the world around us. Anthony asks, "What is the point of all that?" The devil responds, "There is no point," and goes on to explain that everything humanity perceives is filtered through the mind and spirit.

Because of the limitations of human thought, it is impossible to know God. Nor can we comprehend the infinite. We are necessarily subsumed in a world of matter, hence Anthony's desire to descend into matter. His is a mysticism that leads to materialism and signifies on some level the demise of reason. Flaubert seems to suggest that in contemplating the rich tapestry of *this* world we may find satisfaction. It is at least within our reach, whereas the metaphysical world is but a shadow. Drawing on the philosophy of Baruch Spinoza, Flaubert offers the notion that creator and creation exist as one in a pantheistic vision connected to ROMANTICISM. *The Temptation of Saint Anthony* finds its echo in Flaubert's last work, BOUVARD AND PÉCUCHET, in which human intelligence is revealed once more to be but a tiny part of the infinite.

FURTHER READING

Davenport, Nancy. "Between Carnival and Dream: St. Anthony, Gustave Flaubert and the Arts in Fin-de-Siècle Europe," *Religion and the Arts* 6, no. 3 (September 2002): 291–357.

Zants, Emily. "Flaubert's Temptation: An Escape from Power over Others," *French Review* 52, no. 4 (March 1979): 604–610.

TENCIN, CLAUDINE-ALEXANDRINE GUÉRIN, MADAME DE (1682–1749)

Born in Grenoble, Madame de Tencin was educated in a convent school as were many aristocratic women of her time. Her father later forced her to take her vows. Madame de Tencin thus serves as an example of practices DIDEROT so eloquently attacked in *The NUN*. Unlike Diderot's character Suzanne, however, Madame de Tencin was finally freed from convent life in 1712.

Released from her vows, Madame de Tencin profited from Parisian social life. She is known to have had several lovers. Her illegitimate son by the chevalier Destouches was the celebrated mathematician and coeditor of the ENCYCLOPEDIA, Jean le Rond d'Alembert.

Madame de Tencin led a brilliant salon, frequented by such literary figures as MARIVAUX, MONTESQUIEU (whose *Spirit of the Laws* she actively promoted), and DUCLOS. She flippantly referred to her circle as her "beasts" or her "menagerie." These friends nonetheless drew sympathetic portraits of Madame de Tencin. Marivaux praised her salon and its good company through the character of Madame Dorsin in *The LIFE OF MARIANNE*. Duclos also created a character modeled on Madame de Tencin.

A born intriguer, Tencin first used her salon to promote energetically her brother's ecclesiastical career. She was an outspoken advocate for the papal bull Unigenitus, condemning the branch of Catholic thought termed Jansenism. Tencin was also connected to the economic reformer John Law, who was instrumental in making her fortune.

After a scandal arose in 1726 when her former lover, Charles de la Fresnaye, committed suicide in her salon, Madame de Tencin chose to lead a somewhat calmer life focused on literary pursuits. The MEMOIRS OF THE COUNT OF COMMINGE (1735) marks Madame de Tencin's first success as a novelist. This work of pseudomemoirs, an extremely popular genre in the 18th century, is unusual in that a female author chooses to write with a male voice, thus subverting the patriarchal social order. Madame de Tencin wrote four other novels as well, *The SIEGE OF CALAIS* (1739), *The Misfortunes of Love* (1747), *Anecdotes of the Court and Reign of Edward II, King of England* (1766), and *The Story of a Nun Written by Herself* (1786). The latter two works were published posthumously. Tencin's novels are typically characterized as SENTIMENTAL in the tradition of ROUSSEAU's NEW HELOISE.

FURTHER READING

Jones, S. "Madame de Tencin: An Eighteenth-Century Woman Novelist." In *Woman and Society in Eighteenth-Century France. Edited by E. Jacobs, W. H. Barber, et al.* London: Athlone Press, 1979.

Stewart, Philip, *Imitation and Illusion in the Memoir-Novel, 1700–1750: The Art of Make-Believe,* New Haven, Conn.: Yale University Press, 1969.

TERROR ON THE MOUNTAIN (LA GRANDE PEUR DANS LA MONTAGNE) CHARLES-FERDINAND RAMUZ (1926)

In this novel, the inhabitants of a mountain village, desperate to improve their economic situation, decide to investigate some high pastures. Older residents resist, recalling a series of disasters that occurred 20 years before. Younger villagers, however, reject their superstitious fears. After visiting the site, the village councilors decide that the farmers should make use of the land, and six men along with a younger volunteer ascend the mountain with their animals. As they go, one of the men tells the story of the terrible events that took place the last time there was an attempt to use the pastures.

Soon afterward, the curse on the land again takes effect. The youngest of the group is overcome with fear and runs away mad, the mule falls into a ravine, and the animals are decimated by an unknown disease. One of the men is wounded and dies of an infection. Victorine, the fiancée of Joseph, dies while bringing the men food. Her lover then runs away also to die on the mountain. One by one the men disappear until, finally, an avalanche crushes the remaining animals and then rushes down onto the village. The novel ends on the word *death*.

"There are only two interesting things," Ramuz once wrote, "love and death." In this richly poetic work, Ramuz explores the problem of evil and thus exceeds the limits of the traditional regional novel to focus on universal questions. We dare not challenge or provoke the powerful and inexplicable force of nature or the consequences will be disastrous.

THÉRAME, VICTORIA (1937–)

Born in Marseille, Thérame began writing when she was about 14 years old. The first works she produced were short stories followed by three novels, all of which were rejected by publishers. Thérame's fourth novel, *Morbidezza,* was accepted for publication in 1960. Her four subsequent novels were again rejected. Then in 1974 Éditions des Femmes published Thérame's most famous work, *Hosto-Blues.*

This novel, situated squarely in its time, it recounts the strikes by French nursing students and hospital employees that took place in 1974. This book is by no means, however, a cold, sociological study of contemporary events. The reader cannot help but feel that Thérame's engagement with politics, injustice, and oppression is visceral. In fact, it is intended to incite revolt.

Hosto-Blues tells the story of one woman's rebellion against an oppressive, hierarchical system. The novel depicts in minute detail 12 hours in this nurse's life, interspersed with recollections from her nine years of professional experience. The novel cries out against the injustice of keeping women in ignorance in order to safeguard a system in which the gendered division of labor is obvious. Thérame also denounces a health care system that victimizes the poor and the sick. The body itself comes to life in Thérame's writing, even though diseased, filthy, and putrid. Her style draws from pop-

ular language, rendering the novel even more convincing. *Hosto-Blues* is a call to action, speaking the truth of our lives and our struggles.

THÉRÈSE DESQUEYROUX François Mauriac (1927)

The narrative of this tragic tale is structured in such a way as to turn back on itself. In the prologue, Thérèse Desqueyroux leaves the courthouse in Bordeaux where she has just been acquitted of attempting to poison her husband. She then enters the train that will bear her home to the man she tried to murder. While she is traveling, Thérèse goes back over the journey of her life, trying to understand what led her to this point. She recalls how she married Bernard, a neighbor's son, principally to join the two families' properties. Yet certain questions remain unanswered. Why did Thérèse *really* marry Bernard? Was it to conform to social expectations? Was it the result of greed? Certainly family interests dominate over personal need or desire, and Thérèse is incapable of taking an independent stance. Nor does she really understand herself.

Thérèse and Bernard are never able to form a solid relationship. In the course of her inner monologue, a technique typical of Mauriac's works, Thérèse describes the stifling atmosphere and isolation of bourgeois respectability that caused her hatred for Bernard to grow. At the same time, Thérèse feels within herself a potential for love and passion that is never fulfilled. Thérèse is perhaps most alone when she is pregnant, as Bernard and his family only care for her for the sake of the child she bears. This becomes the sole reason for her existence.

At first she turns to Bernard's sister Anne, then to her notion of Jean Azevedo, Anne's former lover, knowing that she must seek some release from the tension building up within her. When she breaks, Thérèse tries to poison Bernard yet it is his testimony that ensures her release. As Thérèse approaches her train stop, she imagines that once home, she might confess to Bernard and begin life anew. Once she arrives, however, it is clear that confession is not possible. Bernard and his family have judged and sentenced her themselves. She will live as a prisoner in their home. As her internment grows increasingly intolerable, Thérèse begins to consider suicide, imagining that God might accept the monster that she has become. Even the thought of her own daughter is of no comfort. Thérèse withers both morally and physically, until Bernard finally brings her to Paris and, in a final scene at a café, sets her free. Mauriac picked up Thérèse's story at this point in a sequel entitled *The End of the Night* (1935).

Mauriac depicts a soul starving for love and purity in a conflict between grace and sin, recalling Louis's struggle in VIPERS' NEST. From the beginning Thérèse's father, Bernard, and his family are only concerned with avoiding scandal. It is as if Thérèse has ceased to exist in her own right. JEAN-PAUL SARTRE commented on Thérèse's total lack of freedom. She appears only as a shadow of her true self. Certain critics have also noted in this novel the beginning of a current of dehumanization that marks the psychological novel and leads into the works of writers such as MICHEL BUTOR and MARGUERITE DURAS. But one might also interpret Mauriac's novels as offering an innovative approach in which a spiritual or metaphysical questioning of the human condition becomes central to the novel.

In the sequel, *The End of the Night,* Thérèse has aged. When her future son-in-law shows an interest in her, Thérèse struggles to suppress her own passionate nature but exhausts herself in doing so. She feels no joy at having done the right thing. While Thérèse is glad that her daughter has found love, she suffers at the same time from the recognition of the void in her own life. She fears her own cold heart. The end of the night for Thérèse can only be death. While Mauriac hints that Thérèse may be capable of attaining grace, like Louis in *Vipers' Nest,* the reader never knows for sure if she ultimately finds peace.

FURTHER READING

Bessent, Edna. "Solitude in the Novels of François Mauriac," *French Review* 8, no. 2 (December 1934): 129–134.

Garaudy, Roger. *Literature of the Graveyard: Jean-Paul Sartre, François Mauriac, André Malraux, Arthur Koestler.* Translated by Joseph M. Bernstein. New York: International Publishers, 1948.

Penn, Dorothy. "Three French Writers of Contemporary Catholic Realism: The Inner Consciousness Studied by Georges Bernanos, Henri Ghéon, and François Mauriac," *French Review* 12, no. 2 (December 1938): 128–137.

Speaight, Robert. *François Mauriac: A Study of the Writer and the Man.* London: Chatto and Windus, 1976.

THÉRÈSE PHILOSOPHE, OR THE HISTORY OF FATHER DIRRAG AND MADEMOISELLE ÉRADICE (THÉRÈSE PHILOSOPHE, OU MEMOIRES POUR SERVIR A L'HISTOIRE DE P. DIRRAG ET DE MLLE. ÉRADICE) JEAN-BAPTISTE DE BOYER, MARQUIS D'ARGENS (1748)

In 1731 there was a great scandal in France when a young woman named Cadière accused her spiritual advisor, Girard, of using magic to seduce and impregnate her, after which he forced her to have an abortion. Since Girard was a Jesuit and Cadière's second advisor a Jansenist, the scandal fed into the already acrimonious religious and political conflict between the Jesuits (supporters of absolutism) and the Jansenists (proponents of the traditional rights of parliament and the Gallican church). Boyer drew from this recent episode for his novel: Dirrag and Éradice are anagrams of Girard and Cadière.

The novel is divided into three parts unified by the presence in each of the main character, Thérèse. As narrator, Thérèse describes her education in eroticism first by a pair of penitents (part one), then by the libertine Madame de Bois-Laurier (part two) (see LIBERTINISM). In the third part, she goes to live with a count in his château. There, unlike the poor Cadière, she can freely enjoy the pleasures of the flesh without fear of pregnancy as her lover practices withdrawal.

The marquis de SADE described *Thérèse Philosophe* as a charming book. There are parallels between the two writers' works. *Thérèse* prefigures the libertine philosophy of Sade in its blending of sex and philosophy. Like other 18th-century libertine novels, *Thérèse* draws a link between sensuality and metaphysics. For so long, religion had made people ashamed of natural desires. These desires or instincts are given priority in the libertine novel. Similar to the novels of DIDEROT, *Thérèse* adheres to a determinist view that our passions are beyond the control of reason. Passion and desire motivate us. Boyer, however, does not take the argument as far as SADE. For Boyer the pursuit of pleasure is checked in the end by the need to maintain social order. In this respect he promotes certain ideas inherent in ENLIGHTENMENT philosophy. Good and evil are for him social constructs, not absolute truth. Virtue is what is useful to maintain society; vice is what is harmful. At the same time, sexual desire is a human need just like hunger or thirst. Boyer argued that sensation determines one's will. Reason can only enlighten us; it does not direct us. In the third part of the novel, when Thérèse unites with her count, Boyer promotes the idea that sensuality and philosophy together make human beings happy.

The innovation of *Thérèse* lies in its assertion of a woman's independence. Thérèse has the same right to pleasure as a man, without becoming a wife and mother. Such are the constraints on a woman's independence that female authors of the 18th century such as ISABELLE DE CHARRIÈRE cried out against.

FURTHER READING

Bush, Newell Richard. *The Marquis d'Argens and His Philosophical Correspondence: A Critical Study of d'Argens' Lettres juives, Lettres cabalistiques, Lettres chinoises.* New York: Diss., Columbia, University, 1953.

THIBAULTS, THE (LES THIBAULT), 8 VOLUMES ROGER MARTIN DU GARD (1922–1940)

This cycle of novels focuses on the story of two brothers. Antoine becomes a successful doctor. Jacques, who might have become a famous writer, is instead compelled by his inner sense of justice to join a group of pacifist revolutionaries in Geneva. The first six volumes, rich in style and language, subtly evoke the emotions and personalities of the various characters.

Volume 1, *The Gray Notebook* (1922), introduces the principal characters of this massive work while hinting at their destiny. Oscar is the patriarchal head of the Thibault household. While Antoine is preparing to become a doctor, Jacques runs away with his friend Daniel de Fontanin after school administrators accuse the boys of an indecent relationship. After a series of adventures, Jacques returns to Paris only to have his father put him away in a reform school of which he is the patron.

Volume 2, *The Penitentiary* (1922), describes Jacques's miserable experience in the reformatory. In volume 3, *The Beautiful Season* (1923), Jacques

is finally released five years later with Antoine's aid, and goes on to taste the pleasures of friendship and love. Meanwhile, Antoine has begun to establish a brilliant career as a doctor, but he is troubled by his conscience, the subject of volume 4, *The Consultation* (1928). When Oscar falls seriously ill, Jacques has run away again and no one knows where he is. In volume 5, *Sorellina* (1928), Antoine recognizes his brother's style in a Swiss journal article and manages to track him down, just in time to bring him back to their father's deathbed.

Jacques has been living in Lausanne with a group of radicals. Volume 6, *Father's Death* (1929), recounts Oscar's suffering as well as the reactions of those around him when confronted with death. Antoine reflects on hidden aspects of his father's character while Jacques, who feels like a stranger, can only think of going back to his friends.

In part 7, *Summer, 1914,* Oscar has died. Jacques, a militant pacifist, witnesses the assassination of Jean Jaurès and decides to return to Switzerland to take action. He and his friend Meynestrel fly to the front to drop pacifist pamphlets to the French and German troops. In a dramatic scene, their plane is shot down and Meynestrel is burned alive. Jacques, however, is captured as a spy and executed. He dies not knowing that Jenny, Daniel's sister, is carrying his child. In the *Epilogue,* the reader learns that Antoine has been gassed while fighting in the trenches in 1917 and there is no hope of recovery. When his suffering becomes intolerable, he commits suicide by an injection, one week after the armistice, having left his journal to his nephew. Despite their differences, both Antoine and Jacques sought to discover a new system of values in a world torn apart by violence. One of the greatest cycle of novels in French literary history, *The Thibaults* was even more popular than ROMAIN ROLLAND's *JEAN-CHRISTOPHE,* the first volume of which appeared in 1904.

FURTHER READING

Barbert, Gene J. "Roger Martin du Gard: Recent Criticism," *French Review* 41, no. 1 (October 1967): 60–69.

Boak, Denis. *Roger Martin du Gard.* Oxford: Clarendon Press, 1963.

Gibson, Robert. *Roger Martin du Gard.* New York: Hillary House, 1961.

Hall, Thomas White. "A Note on the So-Called Change in Technique in Les Thibault of Roger Martin du Gard," *French Review* 27, no. 2 (December 1953): 108–113.

Jouejati, R. *The Quest for Total Peace: The Political Thought of Roger Martin du Gard.* London, Totowa, N.J.: F. Cass, 1977.

O'Nan, Martha. *Roger Martin du Gard Centennial, 1881–1981.* Brockport, N.Y.: Department of Foreign Languages, State University of New York College, 1981.

Ru, Yi-Ling, *The Family Novel: Toward a Generic Definition.* New York: P. Lang, 1992.

Savage, Catharine H. *Roger Martin du Gard.* New York: Twayne, 1968.

Schalk, David L. *Roger Martin du Gard: The Novelist and History.* Ithaca, N.Y.: Cornell University Press, 1967.

Taylor, Michael John. *Martin du Gard-Jean Barois.* London: Edward Arnold, 1974.

THINGS, A STORY OF THE SIXTIES (LES CHOSES) GEORGES PEREC (1965)

The novel begins in a Parisian apartment in the conditional tense, then shifts to the past. It is the story of Jerome and Sylvie, who have come to Paris with the dream of possessing all the luxurious objects the world has to offer. Unfortunately, they resist the hard work and stable professional life necessary to ensure them. Jerome and Sylvie's obsession with wealth ultimately renders life in the capital impossible so they set off for Tunisia, where they settle in the town of Sfax. However, their dream of a new life falls apart when Sylvie begins taking courses at a local technical university while Jerome becomes increasingly idle. The novel ends as Jerome and Sylvie (now in the future) return to France and take on the management of an advertising agency in Bordeaux.

Perec's first novel, *Things*, won the Renaudot Prize. One might almost characterize this work as a study in sociology. Perec offers trenchant criticism of consumer society in its enumeration of objects and in its focus on the banal details of everyday life. The themes of proliferation and accumulation are found in a number of Perec's writings. The novel is marked by Perec's own particular style of writing that involves a manipulation of grammar associated with RAYMOND QUENEAU and the "Workroom of Potential Literature" or OuLiPo, an avant-garde literary movement in which Perec participated during the 1960s. The novel also contains numerous literary allusions to GUSTAVE FLAUBERT'S *SENTIMENTAL EDUCATION*.

FURTHER READING

Andrews, Chris. "Puzzles and Lists: Georges Perec's *Un homme qui dort*," *MLN* 111, no. 4 (1996): 775–796.

Bellos, David. *Georges Perec: A Life in Words.* Boston: Godine, 1993.

Motte, Warren F. Jr. "Georges Perec on the Grid," *French Review* 57, no. 6 (May, 1984): 820–832.

———, ed. *Oulipo: A Primer of Potential Literature.* Lincoln: University of Nebraska Press, 1986.

Schwartz, Paul. *Georges Perec, Traces of his Passage.* Birmingham, Ala.: Summa, 1988.

THIRD REPUBLIC The Third Republic witnessed the rise of nationalism after the French defeat at the hands of the Prussians in 1871. Most French people desired a republic, as was evident in elections to the National Assembly, even though the assembly was dominated by monarchists.

By the 1880s the Chamber of Deputies, elected through universal manhood suffrage, came to dominate French politics. The Third Republic was a period of educational reform and secularization. France also witnessed the rise of conservative nationalism and anti-Semitism that is particularly associated with the Dreyfus affair in which a Jewish officer was falsely accused and convicted of treason in 1894. Many of ÉMILE ZOLA'S works reflect the atmosphere of the Third Republic. Although one frequently associates the Third Republic with 19th-century literature, as a political entity it lasted until 1940. LOUIS ARAGON'S *The Bells of Basel* and ANATOLE FRANCE'S *PENGUIN ISLAND* also evoke the atmosphere and tensions of the Third Republic.

THOMAS THE OBSCURE (THOMAS L'OBSCUR) MAURICE BLANCHOT (1941)

Thomas meets with nothingness. Alone on a beach, he confronts the endless chain of waves as he swims. He faces the anguish of the arrival of night. When he returns to his hotel, Thomas sees Anne but does not respond when she calls him. Instead, he goes to his room where, while reading, he has the strange impression of being himself read by his book. He digs his own grave and has a vision of Anne as a spider.

Thomas and Anne fall in love with each other but they cannot communicate or understand each other. Anne winds up in a state of silent sleepiness, full of anguish before Thomas, who reflects on absence and the absurd. Thomas walks toward the sea, across a town falling into nothingness, and disappears into the waves. There is little action. Characters are but shadows that weave in and out of the text until they dissolve into death or the sea, as writing disappears into the nothingness that it has created. Thomas says, "I have made myself a creator against the act of creation."

Central themes to this and other novels by Blanchot are absence, disappearance, and dissolution. Throughout his career Blanchot focused on the problems of language, emptiness, and death. In his view literature must confront these things even if language is unintelligible. "Language is obscure because it says too much, opaque because it says nothing: ambiguity is everywhere."

This unsettling book is in part about the experience of reading. Thomas represents all of human history. He emerges from the sea, then becomes a caveman, then a savage, subject to the forces of nature. He subsequently discovers his own power and experiments with love. Nonetheless, Thomas remains obscure because he belongs to the night, to infinity. He represents all that language is incapable of revealing.

FURTHER READING

Foucault, Michel. *Maurice Blanchot: The Thought from the Outside.* Translated by Brian Massumi. New York: Zone Books, 1987.

Gregg, John. *Maurice Blanchot and the Literature of Transgression.* Princeton, N.J.: Princeton University Press, 1994.

Hill, Leslie. *Bataille, Klossowski, Blanchot: Writing at the Limit.* Oxford, New York: Oxford University Press, 2001.

Holland, Michael, ed. *The Blanchot Reader.* Oxford, Cambridge, Mass.: Blackwell, 1995.

Iyer, Lars. *Blanchot's Vigilance: Literature, Phenomenology, and the Ethical.* New York: Palgrave Macmillan, 2005.

Shaviro, Steven. *Passions and Excess: Blanchot, Bataille, and Literary Theory.* Tallahassee: Florida State University Press, 1990.

Smock, Ann. *What Is There to Say?* Lincoln: University of Nebraska Press, 2003.

THREE MUSKETEERS, THE (*LES TROIS MOUSQUETAIRES*) ALEXANDRE DUMAS (1844)

Dumas's great rival was BALZAC, who chose to reveal the corrupt nature of contemporary society. In contrast, Dumas, the romantic, turned to the past (see ROMANTICISM). *The Three Musketeers* is set in 1625. Europe is ravaged by the Thirty Years' War and France troubled by domestic conflict. Set in a historical context of disorder and violence, Dumas offers a novel that is about loyalty and honor. It first appeared in serial form in the journal *Le Siècle.*

Dumas's serial novel competed successfully with EUGÈNE SUE's enormously popular MYSTERIES OF PARIS. The rise of the popular press in the mid-19th century triggered a corresponding rise in serialized novels (*ROMAN FEUILLETON*). Dumas's romances also coincided with a renewal of French historical studies. Overflowing with imagination, Dumas wrote with ease and vigor. This work stands out as a masterpiece among his many volumes. In this exciting historical novel, the first in the d'Artagnan trilogy, Dumas presents four heroes, who are musketeers under Louis XIII and inseparable friends (their motto: one for all and all for one!).

The proud and noble Athos, who is actually the comte de la Fère, is broken by a tragic marriage to an adventures's and murderer, from whom he is separated. But in a surprising twist, she turns out to be pivotal to the story. Despair has led him to join the musketeers. Athos is the most romantic of the four. Porthos possesses almost superhuman physical strength. He is simple and vain, but loyal and full of love for life's pleasures. His real name is Vallon. Aramis, the chevalier d'Herblay, was torn from his religious vocation by a love affair. He wavers between a vague sort of mysticism, Jesuitical intrigues, and secret love affairs. He is brave, clever, and daring.

Then there is d'Artagnan, the young Gascon who arrives in Paris penniless but full of bravado to become a musketeer. He is the hero of the story. As soon as he arrives in Paris, d'Artagnan meets Athos, Portos, and Aramis by challenging each to a separate duel on the same day. The triple duel ends with the four joining forces to defeat a group of Cardinal Richelieu's guards, traditional enemies of the king's musketeers. From that moment on, one of the greatest illustrations of male friendship in literature is formed.

By chance d'Artagnan later encounters Milady, who is none other than Athos's former wife. A spy and dangerous manipulator, Milady is equally wicked and beautiful. A series of events that involve her in the musketeers' affairs leads her to seek vengeance on them. In the meantime, d'Artagnan has fallen in love with Constance Bonacieux, Queen Anne of Austria's maid. This leads to the musketeers' involvement in royal affairs.

One of the most significant episodes of the novel occurs because the queen has given her lover, Lord Buckingham, a present of 12 diamonds that had been a gift from the king. Cardinal Richelieu, the king's first minister and the queen's sworn enemy, advises the king to ask Anne to wear her diamonds to a court ball, knowing that she no longer has them. Consequently, the four faithful musketeers, with Constance's assistance, undertake a perilous voyage to England to bring back the queen's diamonds in time. The Cardinal has placed numerous obstacles in their path, including the dangerous Milady.

Athos, Porthos, and Aramis are all put out of commission, leaving only d'Artagnan to complete the mission. Again he meets up with the terrible Milady, whose shadow hangs over all of the musketeers' recent adventures. Over the course of the novel she tries to poison the musketeers, has a follower stab Buckingham, and succeeds in poisoning Constance. The four companions finally overtake her, along with Lord Winter, brother of Milady's second husband whom she murdered. Together they condemn her to death and execute her in one of the most powerful passages of the novel.

The novel has been an astounding success. The combination of diverse characters, adventures, intrigue, passion, murder, and suspense appeal to many readers. Dumas was inspired by his discovery of Courtilz de Sandras's *The Memoirs of d'Artagnan* (1700), and he was accused of plagiarizing from this earlier work. In reality, Dumas transformed a story that would otherwise have remained in obscurity. *The Three Musketeers* was an instant success, inspiring Dumas to continue the musketeers' adventures. His skill in creating an atmosphere of suspense and his fertile imagination guarantee that this novel will remain one of the most popular works in French literature.

Dumas quickly followed the novel with the next volume in the series, *Twenty Years After,* published the next year. As the title suggests, 20 years have passed since the musketeers were together. The powerful ministry of Cardinal Richelieu has succeeded that of Mazarin, who is in need of loyal men. D'Artagnan has remained a musketeer and hopes to reunite with his three friends, all of whom have since gone their separate ways. Only Porthos, however, is willing to join him in Mazarin's service. Aramis continues his various intrigues both amorous and political, while Athos, who has taken up again his name of count de la Fère, has retired to his country estate to bring up his illegitimate son Raoul. D'Artagnan and Porthos subsequently find themselves in the opposite camp from Aramis and Athos, who are both linked to the aristocratic opposition of the Fronde.

Circumstances lead all four to England. D'Artagnan and Porthos have been sent by Mazarin as emissaries to the radical parliamentarian leader Oliver Cromwell, while Athos and Aramis seek to rescue King Charles I from the ravages of civil war. All are threatened by the vengeance of Mordaunt, Milady's son, who seeks to punish the men who murdered his mother. Friendship proves stronger than party politics and the four musketeers join forces to save the king. They are sadly unsuccessful and a dramatic passage finds Athos beneath the scaffold to receive the king's last words before his head falls. On their return to France, Mordaunt nearly succeeds in blowing up their ship. In a life-and-death struggle, Athos succeeds, against his inclination, in plunging a dagger into the evil Mordaunt's heart.

Dumas completed the trilogy between 1848 and 1850 with *The Vicomte de Bragelonne.* This time the novel is set in the early reign of Louis XIV. D'Artagnan, now a mature man and captain of the king's guards, is still the hero. D'Artagnan is determined to restore the Stuart kings to the throne of England and so captures General Monk, whom he persuades to facilitate Charles II's accession to the throne. As Charles is linked to the French crown, d'Artagnan's star rises at the court of Louis XIV. Moreover, his loyalty and intrepid character make him a valuable ally.

The novel recounts the fantastic love affairs and intrigues of Louis XIV's court. But such adventures are nothing next to Aramis's plot to replace Louis XIV with his long-imprisoned twin brother, the "man in the iron mask." Again, d'Artagnan saves the day, ensuring the continued reign of Louis XIV and the eternal imprisonment of the poor twin whose virtuous soul and tragic fate move him deeply.

In a parallel story line, Dumas recounts the troubled love and life of Raoul, whose childhood sweetheart becomes mistress to the king. In the depths of despair, Raoul goes off to war seeking a noble death. His demise in battle breaks his father's heart and Athos, too, succumbs. Porthos, deceived by Aramis, has followed his longtime friend in his dreadful machinations. He, too, dies, having saved his comrade from certain death. D'Artagnan, having attained the rank of marshal of France, dies on the battlefield. Only Aramis survives.

Readers who have followed the dramatic adventures and misadventures of the four brave friends witness their end with great sadness. Dumas himself is said to have wept over the pages that recount the valiant Porthos's death. The remarkable trilogy that begins with *The Three Musketeers* remains one of the most popular works in the history of French literature and ensures Dumas's legendary status as one of the great authors of the 19th century.

FURTHER READING

Hemming, F. W. J. *Alexandre Dumas. The King of Romance.* New York: Scribner, 1979.

Ross, Michael. *Alexandre Dumas.* Newton Abbot, Devon, England; North Pomfret, Vt.: David and Charles, 1981.

TIN FLUTE, THE (*BONHEUR D'OCCASION*) GABRIELLE ROY (1945)

In this powerful novel, Rose-Anna Lacasse has given birth to 12 children. She thus represents the image of the mother of a large family that is so much a part of the Quebecois literary tradition. The need to preserve French culture combines with Roman Catholic doctrine to promote large families. At the same time, sex is associated with sin and shame. Hence, Roy once more evokes the inner tension that marks human existence, a recurring theme in many of her works.

Roy skillfully draws the reader into her character's consciousness, as in the episode leading up to the birth of Rose-Anna's 12th child. Roy evokes Rose-Anna's confusion so effectively as she goes into labor that the reader does not even realize what is taking place until the infant is born. In her mind, Rose-Anna looks back to the death of her son Daniel, the night before she went into labor. She wanders still further back, to her childhood and her mother, who, like Rose-Anna, never let out a sound in childbirth. Life and death are intertwined.

Just as Rose-Anna sustains her labor without complaint, so too does she submit to the difficulties of life and poverty. Yet she suffers from shame and humiliation. Rose-Anna does not want to rely on others for help, even at this moment. Nor does she want strangers to know of her penury. Only briefly does she think she might like the struggle of life to end, but motherhood brings back a sense of purpose. Roy's depiction of the mother in this work thus stands in stark contrast to that of MARIE-CLAIRE BLAIS in *A SEASON IN THE LIFE OF EMMANUEL,* where pain and poverty have reduced the mother to madness.

The Tin Flute was an instant success, winning the prestigious Femina Prize. This innovative work is one of the first Quebecois novels to be set in an urban environment, in contrast to the traditional rural novel. A highly psychological tale, it explores human destiny with equal sensitivity to joy and suffering, thus manifesting the dualism that marks all of Roy's writings.

FURTHER READING

Clemente, Linda M. *Gabrielle Roy: Creation and Memory.* Toronto: ECW Press, 1997.

Lewis, Paula Gilbert. "The Incessant Call of the Open Road: Gabrielle Roy's Incorrigible Nomads," *French Review* 53, no. 6, Numéro Spécial sur Le Québec (May 1980): 816–825.

Ricard, François. *Gabrielle Roy: A Life.* Translated by Patricia Claxton. Toronto: M & S, 1999.

Roy, Gabrielle. *The Fragile Lights of Earth: Articles and Memories, 1942–1970.* Translated by Alan Brown. Toronto: McClelland and Stewart, 1982.

TOILERS OF THE SEA, THE (*LES TRAVAILLEURS DE LA MER*) VICTOR HUGO (1866)

Living in exile on the island of Guernesey provided Hugo with much of the material for this novel that opens with the steamship *Durande* running from Saint-Malo to Guernesey. The backdrop for the novel then is the Industrial Revolution. Most local sailors were skeptical of steam power as they feared that it might reduce their income. One sailor, Captain Clubine, causes the ship to sink. In a literary device that recalls a fairy tale, the ship's owner, Lethierry, who wants to put the boat back into service, will marry off his niece, Déruchette, to anyone able to recover at least the ship's engines. The only one willing to try is Goliatt, because he is in love with Déruchette. Risking his life many times over, Goliatt finally succeeds, but not before he has undergone a struggle with a giant octopus. But upon his return Goliatt discovers that Déruchette is in love with Ebenezer, a young minister. Goliatt sacrifices his own love and helps the couple to run away, going off to a rock on the edge of the sea to die at the same spot where he had once rescued Ebenezer from drowning.

At first glance the novel is an epic work on progress, revealing Hugo's belief in the victory of man and machine over nature. On a deeper level, Hugo again manifests his deep sympathy for working people. The theme of man's powerlessness before destiny (*ananké*) recurs in Hugo's novels. Goliatt's generous renunciation is not unlike that of Jean Valjean in LES MISÉRABLES. Goliatt defeats the obstacles the ocean places before him. Symbolizing humanity, Goliatt overcomes the octopus, or evil, but is in the end defeated by moral and spiritual obstacles in the form of his love for a woman. As in HERNANI, Hugo the romantic once again proffers a heroic defeat before impossible love.

FURTHER READING

Brombert, Victor. *Victor Hugo and the Visionary Novel.* Cambridge, Mass.: Harvard University Press, 1984.

Evans, David O. *Social Romanticism in France: 1830–1848.* New York: Octagon, 1969.

Hudson, William Henry. *Victor Hugo and His Poetry.* London: Harrap, 1918.

Maurois, André. *Victor Hugo and His World.* Translated by Oliver Bernard. New York: Viking, 1966.

Peyre, Henri. *Victor Hugo: Philosophy and Poetry.* Translated by Roda P. Roberts. Tuscaloosa: University of Alabama Press, 1980.

Richardson, Joanna. *Victor Hugo.* London: Weidenfeld and Nicolson, 1976.

TOMORROW'S EVE (*L'EVE FUTURE*)
JEAN-MARIE VILLIERS DE L'ISLE D'ADAM (1886)   In this science fiction novel, the American scientist and inventor Thomas Edison receives his friend, the young English lord Ewald, who confesses that he is considering suicide. Ewald is in love with a beautiful singer, Alicia Clary, whose body fits neither her mind nor her voice. She is vulgar and lacking in intellect, as if her body has been possessed by a foreign being, a recurring theme in Villiers's work. The duality of body and soul are central themes in romantic thought (see ROMANTICISM), an influence on Villiers and gothic literature generally. Mary Shelley's *Frankenstein,* for example, offers another illustration of themes present in Villiers's writings.

In effect, it is not Alicia who is possessed but Ewald. Edison then introduces Ewald to his female robot, Hadaly, suggesting that he will cure Ewald by giving the robot Alicia's physical appearance. As for the robot's mind, two golden phonograph records, like lungs, will speak the words of great poets, writers, and philosophers. The theme of disembodied voices is central to Villiers's works, which also anticipate developments in psychoanalysis.

Villiers was an important contributor to the development of the symbolist movement in 19th-century French literature (see SYMBOLISM). There are thematic and stylistic links between his writing and that of E. T. A. Hoffmann, THÉOPHILE GAUTIER, JULES VERNE, and Edgar Allan Poe, whom he admired greatly. Expanding on gothic, fantastic, and science fiction literature, Villiers's symbolist works were intended to illustrate the power of ideas to transcend everyday reality.

FURTHER READING

Conroy, William Thomas. *Villiers de l'Isle d'Adam.* Boston: Twayne, 1978.

Lathers, Marie. *The Aesthetics of Artifice: Villiers' l'Éve future.* Chapel Hill: University of North Carolina Department of Romance Languages: Distributed by the University of North Carolina Press, 1996.

Raitt, A. W. *The Life of Villiers de l'Isle d'Adam.* Oxford: Clarendon Press; New York: Oxford University Press, 1981.

TORMENTS OF LOVE, THE (*LES ANGOISSES DOULEUREUSES QUI PROCÈDENT D'AMOURS*) Hélisenne de Crenne (1538)

This tremendously popular semi-autobiographical novel was written by an author now considered to be one of the most important early French women writers. The first of two parts tells the story of a married woman's passionate love for a young man whom she sees from her window.

Surprised that love could take her unawares, especially since she is married, Hélisenne tries to ward off her desire for Guenelic. The character Hélisenne was married at the age of 11 to a man who, in the course of the novel, treats her brutally. When the correspondence she shares with her young lover is discovered, her husband imprisons her in a tower. There she writes of her love, hoping that Guenelic will rescue her.

The second part draws on the medieval ROMANCE tradition. The narration continues in the first person, but this time it is the voice of Guenelic speaking. He describes his rescue of Hélisenne from the tower and their subsequent travels, marking this portion of the work a *roman d'aventure*. The novel ends with Guenelic's companion Quézinstra's narrative of the lovers' death.

The Torments of Love is modeled on the Italian writer Giovanni Boccaccio's *Elegia di Madonna Fiammetta* (1343–44). This tale too, supposedly autobiographical but written by a man, recounts a young married woman's tragic love. Fiammetta is more self-involved than Hélisenne, who desires to warn other women of the dangers love poses to their virtue and happiness. Unlike Fiammetta, Hélisenne remains chaste, and this leads to her frustrated lover's departure. Echoing CHRISTINE DE PIZAN, Hélisenne shows how adulterous love should be avoided.

The first part of the novel is the best known. Its learned Latinate style is far less inviting to modern readers than it was to its audience in the 16th century. Its greatest appeal lies in its realistic portrayal of the tormented woman's psychological state. As such, this portion of the novel presages the rise of both the psychological novel (most often associated with Madame de Lafayette's PRINCESSE DE CLÈVES, 1678) and the later SENTIMENTAL NOVEL.

FURTHER READING

Crenne, Hélisenne de [Marguerite Briet]. *The Torments of Love*. Edited and translated by Lisa Neal. Minneapolis: University of Minnesota Press, 1996.

Nash, Jerry C. "Constructing Hélisenne de Crenne: Reception and Identity." In *Por le soie amisté: Essays in Honor of Norris J. Lacy*. Edited by Keith Busby and Catherine M. Jones. (Faux Titre; no. 183), Amsterdam, Atlanta: Rodophi, 2000.

Randall, Catherine. "Positioning Herself: A Renaissance-Reformation Diptych." In *Attending to Early Modern Women*. Edited by Susan D. Amussen and Adele Seeff. Newark: University of Delaware Press; London; Cranberry, N.J.: Associated University Presses, 1998.

Wood, Diane S. *Hélisenne de Crenne: At the Crossroads of Renaissance Humanism and Feminism*. Madison, N.J.: Fairleigh Dickinson University Press; London; Cranberry, N.J.: Associated University Presses, 2000.

TO THE FRIEND WHO DID NOT SAVE MY LIFE (*À L'AMI QUI NE M'A PAS SAUVÉ LA VIE*) Hervé Guibert (1990)

In this autobiographical novel Guibert recounts his life, beginning with the moment he discovers he has AIDS. In a period when the discussion of AIDS was still taboo, Guibert writes that he became aware of his illness on the day that his friend returned from the United States, "the friend who did not save my life."

Nothing is hidden in Guibert's depiction of the world of homosexual artists and intellectuals. While there is a playful side to his writing, he is principally concerned with exploring these men's feelings about an incurable illness. The rest of their lives will be altered because of AIDS. "This Misery, once one had plunged into it, was far more livable than its anticipation, much less cruel, in fact, than one would have believed." Still, Guibert recounts sad sexual encounters in which each partner is aware of the presence of the disease and the frustrating search for a cure. Guibert writes in clear, everyday language that brings the reader into intimate contact with his experience. "AIDS is not really an illness . . . it's a state of weakness and abandon that opens the caged beast that is contained within oneself, to whom I am constrained to give the power to devour me, whom I permit to do to my living body what it is preparing to do to my cadaver, in order to make it disintegrate." Yet this work is about life as much as it is about death.

FURTHER READING

Apter, E. "Fantom Images: Hervé Guibert and the Writing of 'sida' in France." In T. F. Murphy and S. Poirier, eds. *Writing AIDS: Gay Literature, Language, and Analysis.* New York: Columbia University Press, 1993.

Sarkonak, Ralph Williams. *Angelic Echoes: Hervé Guibert and Company.* Toronto, Buffalo: University of Toronto Press, 2000.

Schehr, Lawrence R. "Thanatopsis: Writing and Witnessing in the Age of AIDS." Review Essay. *Modern Fiction Studies* 48, no. 3 (2002): 746–750.

Stambolian, G., and E. Marks, eds. *Homosexualities and French Literature.* Ithaca, N.Y.; London: Cornell University Press, 1979.

Orban, Clara. "Writing, Time and AIDS in the Works of Hervé Guibert," *Literature and Medicine.* 18, no. 1 (1999): 132–150.

TOUR DE FRANCE, THE G. BRUNO (1877)

This popular work, with its 212 engravings and 19 maps, was often used as a text in French elementary schools into the 20th century. It is the story of two orphans, Julien and André, forced to flee their native village after it has been captured by the Germans in the Franco-Prussian War (1870–71). The novel's subtitle, "Duty and the Fatherland," gives some indication of the author's purpose in providing a patriotic education to simple folk.

Julien and André travel through France describing the topography of various regions and the mines, forges, and other manufactories they encounter. Not only does Bruno wish to revive the French spirit after the defeat of 1870, she also reveals the context of the Industrial Revolution and the rise of modern manufacturing processes.

The *Tour de France* is a pedagogical work written in defense of secular republican values and bourgeois life. One chapter, for example, describes iron production at Le Creusot, "the biggest factory in Europe." Bruno's message is didactic without subtlety: "The power of industry and its machines is so great as to terrify at first glance, but it is a beneficial power that works for humanity." The text provides diagrams of the furnace at Le Creusot and its function, as well as an engrav-

ing of the village citing its "fast-growing" population. Readers are introduced to the notion of child labor and steam power. The *Tour de France* offers an interesting combination of history and geography while serving as an example of a moral and practical guide.

TOURNIER, MICHEL (1924–　)

Tournier was born in Paris to a fairly well-off, cultured, Catholic family. As a child he suffered from poor health. As a student, Tournier was interested in philosophy and law, intending to pursue a career in teaching. He began to associate with a group of intellectuals and writers such as MICHEL BUTOR, Gilles Deleuze, and François Châtelet. Along with structural anthropologist Claude Lévi-Strauss, Tournier studied in Tübingen, Germany, and earned a certificate in ethnography. Upon his return to France, Tournier failed to attain his degree in philosophy.

From that point on, Tournier worked in a variety of positions, as a journalist, a radio announcer, translator, and on the editorial board at Plon publishers. Nonetheless, in certain respects Tournier never completely abandoned his career as a philosopher; he simply changed its means of expression. The novel ultimately became the vehicle for the transmission of his ideas about philosophy. Tournier almost always either drew from an existing myth or legend or created a new one. For example, the principal character of *FRIDAY* (1967) is Robinson Crusoe. This novel was an instant success and won the grand prize of the Académie Française. Translated into numerous languages, *Friday* was also adapted to the stage by Antoine Vitez. It was followed by *The ERL-KING,* which won the Goncourt Prize in 1970. After these successes, Tournier was able to devote himself entirely to writing.

In 1971 Tournier published an edition of *Friday* rewritten for children. He went on to publish *GEMINI* (1975) and *Wind Spirit,* his intellectual autobiography (1977). In this work, Tournier explains, "My purpose is not to be innovative in form, but to pass on, in a form as traditional, preserved and reassuring as possible, material that has none of these qualities." In referring to the metaphysical dimension of his novels, Tournier makes clear that he sought to express the "comic cosmic," "the laughter of God," and the abyss that is the world. He rejected innovations associated with the NOUVEAU ROMAN, preferring instead a traditional narrative form, but only so as to infuse it with philosophical questioning while exploring the sensually rich terrain of the imagination.

Tournier's early works are more or less novels of apprenticeship in which characters are subject to exile, shipwreck, or war and through these experiences eventually arrive at some greater understanding of themselves and the world. Female characters are frequently marginalized. In each novel the freedom of the sky plays an important role, both literally and figuratively. In *Friday* the character who gives his name to the title teaches Robinson to attain the ecstasy of the sun. In *The Erl-King,* the flight of pigeons invokes the open sky, while the very title of *Gemini* gives significance to spaces beyond this world. A unique combination of a powerful imagination and systematic reasoning mark Tournier's early works, what the author refers to as "hyperrationalization." The function of the narrative is to reveal this rationalism and, ultimately, to reflect a metaphysical order.

What drives Tournier's narrative is a character's gradual realization of his calling. Nonconformist by nature, Tournier's characters also engage in philosophical reflection on the world around them. His works are philosophical novels in this sense alone. Unlike other novels of that genre, Tournier develops neither a philosophical system nor a utopian vision. He is concerned solely with the transformation of an individual character. Marvelous and fantastic stories thus serve as the backdrop for philosophical pursuits. A hint of JEAN-PAUL SARTRE's existential philosophy (see EXISTENTIALISM) is apparent in Tournier's focus on the construction of the self.

Other novels include *The Four Wise Men* (1980), *Gilles et Jeanne* (1983), and *Golden Droplet* (1985). In *Golden Droplet* a North African boy named Idriss is 15 years old when a couple of French tourists take his picture. They promise to send it to him but never do. Partly driven by Muslims' discomfort with visual representations, Idriss sets off in search of the photograph. In France he suffers indignities because of his identity and eventually goes mad. Tournier's essays on art offer a more theoretical discussion of the image as

sign that renders more comprehensible his handling of this theme in fiction.

In his last three novels, Tournier combines partly autobiographical narrative with photographs and drawings, reflecting a long-held interest in image and representation. Even *The Four Wise Men,* nominally a novel, is in reality a collection of tales in which history merges with philosophy in a manner that recalls GUSTAVE FLAUBERT's *SALAMMBÔ.* These later works also cast a more generous light on women.

Tournier unites myths and legends with reality. Reflecting his dualist vision of the world, Tournier argues that God reveals himself in the real and even in the sordid. This occasioned accusations of blasphemy and sacrilege from hostile readers. He is provocative and the response to his works among critics is consequently varied. Over and over the literature on Tournier refers to him as a storyteller. Yet he plays with myths and legends to raise metaphysical questions. Tournier constantly raises doubts about the ideas to which we generally ascribe certainty. This challenge to the established order makes his writings troubling to some readers. Moreover, as a highly contentious media persona on radio, television, and in the press, Tournier has frequently offended readers and critics, either for his style or his content.

FURTHER READING

Anderson, Christopher. *Michel Tournier's Children: Myth, Intertext, Initiation.* New York: P. Lang, 1998.

Cloonan, William J. *Michel Tournier.* Boston: Twayne, 1985.

Davis, Colin. *Michel Tournier, Philosophy and Fiction.* Oxford: Clarendon Press; New York: Oxford University Press, 1988.

Edwards, Rachel. *Myth and the Fiction of Michel Tournier and Patrick Grainville.* Lewiston, N.Y.: E. Mellen Press, 1999.

Petit, Susan. *Michel Tournier's Metaphysical Fictions.* Amsterdam, Philadelphia: J. Benjamins, 1991.

Platten, David. *Michel Tournier and the Metaphor of Fiction.* New York: St. Martin's Press, 1999.

Worton, Michael, ed. *Michel Tournier.* London; New York: Longman, 1995.

TOUSSAINT, JEAN-PHILIPPE (1957–   )

Toussaint was born in Belgium but grew up in Paris, where he studied history and politics. After completing his studies, he went to Algeria to teach from 1982 to 1984. That is where he wrote his first novel, *Bathroom* (1985), published by the Éditions de Minuit, the publishing house associated with the NOUVEAU ROMAN movement in literature.

Some critics have characterized Toussaint's work as the NOUVEAU NOUVEAU ROMAN. He is by all accounts a minimalist, in the sense that his works retain only the most essential elements of the narrative. Toussaint's novels, devoid of action or plot, focus instead on the minutiae of daily life in detailed descriptions. One critic has described his works as "an epic of trivia." *Bathroom,* for example, is about a man who lives in this one room, while TELEVISION (1997) is the story of an academic living for a year in Berlin who tries to break himself of the habit of watching television.

Equally passive and detached, characters in *Monsieur* (1991) and *The Camera* (1989) separate themselves from life's complications. In *Making Love* (2004), a French couple traveling to Japan is forced to confront their otherness as well as their previously unperceived estrangement from each other. Toussaint has also published an autobiographical *Self-Portrait* (2000).

"Just as my books are devoid of sociology and politics, philosophy and metaphysics are always apparent, even if not explicitly named. They are always a reflection of time and death." Toussaint sensitively evokes the feeling of a generation experiencing the end of history while exploring the problem of identity in postmodern society (see POSTMODERNISM). Irony, sober reflection, and gentle humor mark Toussaint's style. Direct and honest, above all he never takes himself too seriously.

TRIOLET, ELSA (1896–1970)   Born in Moscow, Triolet grew up amid Russia's progressive Jewish intelligentsia, and the Russian writer Maksim Gorky was the first to encourage Triolet to write. In 1919 she married André Triolet, a Frenchman with whom she traveled to Berlin and Tahiti. This experience provided the material for her first novel, *To Tahiti* (1926). The couple separated two years later.

In 1924 Triolet settled in Paris in the bohemian neighborhood of Montparnasse. At first she wrote in Russian. *Wild Strawberry* (1926) is a bittersweet recollection of her childhood, while *Camouflage* evokes

Triolet's sense of solitude and isolation. In 1928 she met LOUIS ARAGON and from then on the two writers' lives were inextricably connected as Triolet became both Aragon's companion and his muse. Although Triolet was never a member of the Communist Party, she shared with Aragon a devotion to its principles. Together they traveled to the Soviet Union and supported antifascist movements in England and Spain.

Triolet's criticism of Stalin meant that Soviet publishers were sure to refuse her works. After they rejected her fourth novel, *Necklaces* in 1933, Triolet was compelled to write in French. Her first novel in French, *Good Night, Theresa,* was published in 1938. It evokes the rise of the extreme Right in Paris during the 1930s. Despite praise from JEAN-PAUL SARTRE, this work received little attention on the eve of World War II. A series of short stories published under the title *A Thousand Regrets* (1942) portrays the Occupation. This work was acclaimed by such contemporaries as ROGER MARTIN DU GARD, ALBERT CAMUS, and the poet Max Jacob. In contrast to *Good Night, Theresa,* this work was also a success with the reading public.

During the war Triolet and Aragon fled to the southern (unoccupied at the time) zone, where they participated in the Resistance along with other writers. Triolet continued to write fiction; *White Charger* (1943) focuses on the elusive nature of happiness. Despite the violence of human history, love is the only force capable of transcending the pain of existence. *The Lovers of Avignon* (1943), published under the pseudonym Laurent Daniel, re-creates the experience of the Resistance. Published a year later with *Yvette* under the title *Fine of 200 Francs,* this work won the Goncourt Prize in 1944.

In the tense political climate after the Liberation and during the Cold War, Triolet expressed her disillusionment in *No One Loves Me* (1946) and *Armed Phantoms* (1947), but these are weaker than her earlier works. Some critics went so far as to call them incomprehensible. Such harsh criticism led Triolet to consider publishing her next novel, *Inspector of Ruins* (1948), under the pen name Antonin Blond. In the end, she signed the work with her own name. Almost hallucinatory, this somber account of survivors of the war recalls German romantic works (see ROMANTICISM). It was followed by *Red Horse* (1953), in which Triolet anticipates the horror of an atomic war. *The Monument* (1957), in contrast, analyzes the failure of Stalinist art.

Collectively, Triolet's works offer a portrait of her time from the perspective of a Russian woman transplanted into France, as is evident in *Rendez-vous of Stangers* (1959), a book about exile, homesickness, patriotism, nationalism and internationalism. *The Great Never* (1965) evokes the mystery of the human condition, as Triolet reflects on history, time, and death and finds its echo in Aragon's *Mise à Mort.* In her cycle of novels *Roses on Credit* (1959), *Luna Park* (1959), and *Soul* (1963), together known as *The Nylon Age,* Triolet writes in a socialist realist style (see SOCIALIST REALISM), which she defines not as a literary style but as a certain perspective on the world while evoking the failure of humanist ideals. *Roses on Credit* is the sad story of Martine Donnelle, who becomes a victim of consumer society. She rises above poverty only to reduce herself to penury after accumulating possessions and debt while simultaneously driving away her husband. *Luna Park* is composed of fictional letters written by her lovers to a female aviator, Blanche Hauteville, who disappeared in the Sahara. Aragon responded to this novel in *Elsa, Poem* (1959) and *Blanche, or Forgetting* (1967). In *Soul,* Triolet suggests that science and technology are incapable of replacing human creativity. *The Nightingale Becomes Quiet at Dawn* (1970) combines a dream narrative written in red with fragments of dialogue written in black.

Triolet's works did not always receive the warmest reception. All her life she suffered in some degree the fate of a writer in exile. Her close relationship both personally and professionally with Aragon meant that her writings were not always considered in their own right. She has also been accused of pushing Aragon toward militant leftist politics. Finally, some of Triolet's later works lack the narrative power of her earlier novels. That, too, may have contributed to a negative assessment of her contribution to literature. Triolet also translated a number of Russian authors into French.

In her own way Triolet was a politically "engaged" writer. She certainly believed that it is the writer's duty to deal directly with the time in which he or she lives. Triolet herself wrote honestly and directly about the problems we face in the modern world and suggested how we might improve life for ourselves and for others. If there is mystery, love, and death, there is also the possibility of happiness. One must have hope, even when one's search for happiness is painful and ridden with doubt. As she once wrote, "Right feelings do not always make good books, I know that in my heart, but right feelings don't necessarily make bad ones."

FURTHER READING
Bieber, Konrad. "Ups and Downs in Elsa Triolet's Prose," *Yale French Studies,* no. 27, Women Writers (1961): 81–85.

Mackinnon, Lachlan. *The Lives of Elsa Triolet.* London: Chatto and Windus, 1992.

Pflaum-Vallin, Marie-Monique, and Joseph H. McMahon. "Elsa Triolet and Aragon: Back to Lilith," *Yale French Studies,* no. 27, Women Writers (1961): 86–89.

TRISTAN L'HERMITE (1601–1655)

Tristan l'Hermite is the pseudonym for the playwright, novelist, and poet François l'Hermite. Tristan wrote a number of successful plays. His BURLESQUE novel, *The Disgraced Page,* draws from his adventures as a youth. As a page to the court of Henry II, Tristan was forced to flee France after killing his opponent in a duel. He returned to France in 1620 and served as poet to Gaston d'Orléans, the duchesse de Chaulnes, and the duc de Guise.

FURTHER READING
Abraham, Claude Kurt. *Tristan l'Hermite.* Boston: Twayne, 1980.

———. *The Strangers. The Tragic World of Tristan l'Hermite.* Gainesville: University of Florida Press, 1966.

Gude, Mary Louise. *Le Page disgracié: The Text as Confession.* University, Miss.: Romance Monographs, 1979.

TROJAN HORSE (CHEVAL DE TROIE)

PAUL NIZAN (1925)   Central to this work, as well as to Nizan's *ANTOINE BLOYÉ,* is the theme of nothingness, a concept drawn from the German philosopher Martin Heidegger. To avoid the sense of nothingness that so troubled his father, in this novel Pierre Bloyé turns to political activism.

At the high school where he teaches philosophy, Pierre has a colleague named Lange. JEAN-PAUL SARTRE later recognized himself in this character. Lange and Bloyé have opposing philosophical points of view as each deals in his own way with the malaise and, as Bloyé puts it, the idea of death that is in the air. For Bloyé, the sense of nothingness is the product of a failed capitalist society and what is needed is political activism to end social injustice. "It's difficult to imagine a more disgraceful world than that in which we are now unfortunate enough to live." In contrast to Bloyé, Lange serves as the sort of academic philosopher who ignores reality that Nizan later attacked in his pamphlet "Watchdogs" (1932).

The Trojan Horse is set in a small industrial town in 1934–35, a period of economic depression. Nizan was inspired by a real event that took place in February 1934, in which fascists ignited street riots in an attempt to overthrow the THIRD REPUBLIC. As workers became increasingly radical due to economic hardship, the middle class responded by turning toward fascism.

Bloyé is leading the workers. Like the author, he is a graduate of the prestigious École Normale Supérieure and teaches philosophy at a local high school. He helps workers publish a newspaper and paint revolutionary slogans around town. Slowly the workers begin to develop a sense of their own power, and "Bloyé dreamed about the time when men like them, exiting the Trojan Horse of factories and workers' streets, would take over cities in the night."

During the riots one worker is killed in a confrontation with fascists, among whom is Lange. Bloyé subsequently plays an important role in giving symbolic meaning to Paul's death; it becomes a sacrifice that gives the others a reason to live and continue the struggle, even if they may also die: "It's hard to die. But there are some deaths that mean nothing and others that one can understand." Paul's death helps the workers confront the inevitability of their own mortality.

Choosing death can give meaning to one's life, especially for a worker whose life denies him all dignity. Lange, in contrast, has begun to consider the possibility of a new social system that might allow us to escape from isolation and meaninglessness, that is to say, he has begun to consider fascism as a possible solution. In a literally surreal moment (see SURREALISM), Lange blindly fires a revolver into a crowd, igniting the fascist attack that ends in Paul's death.

The Trojan Horse reflects Nizan's commitment to a Marxist revolutionary movement. In contrast to intellectuals like Lange, Nizan was convinced that intellectuals and writers have an obligation to transform society. In one form or another, all of his novels address this point and yet retain a literary quality rare in polemical works of this nature.

FURTHER READING

McCarthy, Patrick. "Sartre, Nizan, and the Dilemmas of Political Commitment," *Yale French Studies,* no. 68, Sartre after Sartre (1985): 191–205.

Redfern, W. D. *Paul Nizan: Committed Literature in a Conspiratorial World.* Princeton, N.J.: Princeton University Press, 1972.

Schalk, David L. "Professors as Watchdogs: Paul Nizan's Theory of the Intellectual and Politics," *Journal of the History of Ideas* 34, no. 1 (January–March 1973): 79–96.

Scriven, Michael. *Paul Nizan: Communist Novelist.* New York: St. Martin's Press, 1988.

Stoekl, Allan. "Nizan, Drieu, and the Question of Death," *Representations,* no. 21 (Winter 1988): 117–145.

Suleiman, Susan Rubin. "The Structure of Confrontation: Nizan, Barrès, Malraux," *MLN* 95, no. 4, French Issue (May 1980): 938–967.

Wasson, Richard. "'The True Possession of Time:' Paul Nizan, Marxism and Modernism," *Boundary* 5, no. 2 (Winter 1977): 395–410.

TROYES, CHRÉTIEN DE (12TH CENTURY)

Chrétien de Troyes is probably the best-known writer of medieval ROMANCES. His Aurthurian legends are the oldest extant manuscripts we have recounting the adventures of King Arthur and his brave Knights of the Round Table.

Chrétien was probably born in Troyes, in Champagne, where he lived and wrote during the third quarter of the 12th century. His first literary patron was countess Marie of Champagne, the daughter of Louis VII and Eleanor of Aquitaine. His patron in later life was Philip of Alsace, count of Flanders. He may also have spent time at the English court of Henry II.

The world of the 12th-century aristocracy and its values come alive in Chrétien's tales of the exploits of Erec and Enide, Cligés, Lancelot, Yvain, and Perceval.

The knights errant must prove themselves by courage, self-sacrifice, and generosity. Beauty equals nobility in these adventure stories in which love and valor are continually put to the test. While Chrétien's plots are action-based, the psychological element of self-reflection is strong. Lovers carefully explore their psychological and emotional states through inner dialogue and with one another, offering a picture of the courtly love ideal promoted by Marie de Champagne. Chrétien's particular contribution to posterity lies in his vivid descriptions of clothing, gestures, ceremonies, and rituals, bringing to life the material culture of the 12th-century aristocracy.

Chrétien clearly drew from a variety of sources: Breton and Celtic legends, Geoffrey of Monmouth's *History of the Kings of England* (c. 1136–37), the literature of classical antiquity (Homer, Virgil, and Ovid in particular), and contemporary tales told by the *jongleurs*. Chrétien acknowledges a number of these sources. His prologues gave him the opportunity to articulate his view of himself as a writer and to acknowledge his patrons.

Chrétien holds an important position in the 12th-century literary transition from Latin to the vernacular. This movement brought contemporary literature to a broader audience. MARIE DE FRANCE makes explicit reference to this development in the prologue to her *LAYS*. The shift away from Latin sources is reflected in a variety of genres associated with the troubadours: CHANSONS DE GESTE, epic poems, and courtly lyrics. These literary forms traveled north with Marie de Champagne. A versatile poet, Chrétien was the first writer to play with the rhythm of the standard octosyllabic rhyming couplet.

From 1190 to 1240, the influence of Chrétien's Arthurian legends dominated the literary world in France. By the end of the 12th century his romances had been translated into German. JEAN RENART attempted to compete with Chrétien's idealized world of King Arthur's court by turning to "realism." His legacy rests on the promotion of the possibility of COURTLY LOVE *within* marriage, in the story of Lancelot's passion for Guinevere, and in the first tale of the Holy Grail. The tradition of the Arthurian legends, originating with Chrétien's romances, inspired a number of 16th-

and 17th-century novels and continues to live on in literature, poetry, and film.

FURTHER READING

Frappier, Jean. *Chrétien de Troyes: The Man and His Work.* Translated by Robert J. Cormier. Athens: Ohio University Press, 1982.
Lacy, Norris. *The Craft of Chrétien de Troyes: An Essay on Narrative Art.* Leiden, Netherlands: Brill, 1980.
Troyes, Chrétien de. *Arthurian Romances.* Translated by William W. Kibler. London: Penguin, 1991.

TWENTY-THOUSAND LEAGUES UNDER THE SEA (VINGT MILLE LIEUES SOUS LES MERS) JULES VERNE (1870)

In this popular novel Verne draws once more on the theme of castaways. Set in 1866, the novel opens with a strange occurrence, as several ships are mysteriously damaged by an unknown object. Some believe it is a sea monster. An American frigate, *Abraham Lincoln,* sets out on an exploration to discover the source of the attacks. On board is Captain Faragutt; Ned Land, a great Canadian harpooner; Aronnax, a French professor and naturalist; and his servant, Conseil (which in French means "advice"). One day Ned spies a submerged monster but it promptly disappears. At night, while the beast is asleep, the frigate slowly approaches. Ned tries to harpoon the animal only to discover that its body is hard. Suddenly two water spouts throw Ned and Aronnax onto the monster's back. Aronnax's servant, always faithful, jumps on after them. Suddenly they discover that this is not a monster but a machine.

The ship's captain, Nemo, takes them prisoner. Nemo is particularly interested in talking to the knowledgeable professor Aronnax. He shows his prisoners/guests his extraordinary submarine containing a library with 12,000 volumes, a museum, and all sorts of navigational devices. Aronnax, too, is fascinated by Nemo's explanation of the *Nautilus* and how it works. Nemo is an amazing if enigmatic engineer and scientist.

For 10 months they travel along the bottom of the sea, passing under the isthmus of Suez (the canal had not yet been dug) and then under the South Pole. They see the mysterious Atlantis, battle against cannibals and a giant squid, discover an enormous pearl, travel through underwater forests, and witness a burial in a cemetery of coral.

Aronnax realizes that Nemo's purpose is not simply scientific investigation but revenge, particularly when Nemo attacks a ship, sending it to the bottom of the sea. Eventually they discover Nemo's true identity. He is an Indian prince defeated by the English. "I am the oppressed and there is the oppressor who has destroyed everything that I loved—my fatherland, wife, children, father and mother. I saw them all perish." Fearful of the cold, self-possessed Nemo yet overcome with homesickness, the prisoners manage to escape. They are miraculously saved after being torn from the ship in a storm and return to France.

Verne's fascination with cartography permeates this adventure novel. As his characters explore unknown and mysterious worlds, Verne's descriptions give those fantastic landscapes color and contour. Verne manifests his didactic purpose as well. As in the other novels that make up Verne's "Extraordinary Adventures," the purpose of this journey is the acquisition of knowledge. Hence Verne displays his usual combination of fairy-talelike adventure with serious themes. Famous for his ability of popularize developments in science and technology, Verne continues to anticipate future inventions such as the submarine.

Beyond themes of science and technology, Verne also delves into the tradition of myths and literature. Captain Nemo resembles a modern Ulysses. He is also a heroic avenger of injustice, appearing again in Verne's *MYSTERIOUS ISLAND*. Finally, Nemo represents man's rebellion as well as his connection to the forces of evil as he seeks to use science and technology willfully to pursue his own aims. Exploring the undersea world on the edge of continents, Nemo's journey also plunges to the depths of the human psyche and the unknown force at work on humankind and the universe.

FURTHER READING

Born, Franz. *Jules Verne, the Man who Invented the Future.* Translated by Juliana Biro. Englewood Cliffs, N.J.: Prentice Hall, 1964.

Butcher, William. *Verne's Journey to the Center of the Self: Space and Time in the "Voyages Extraordinaires."* New York: St. Martin's Press; London: Macmillan, 1990.

Costello, Peter. *Jules Verne: The Inventor of Science Fiction.* London: Hodder and Stoughton, 1978.

Evans, I. O. *Jules Verne and His Work.* Mattituck, N.Y.: Aeonian Press, 1976.

Freedman, Russell. *Jules Verne, Portrait of a Prophet.* New York: Holiday House, 1965.

Lottman, Herbert R. *Jules Verne: An Exploratory Biography.* New York: St. Martin's Press, 1996.

TWENTY YEARS AFTER (VINGT ANS APRÈS) ALEXANDRE DUMAS (1845)

As the title of this novel indicates, the four heroes of *The THREE MUSKETEERS* join forces again 20 years later. If the villain of the first volume was France's first minister, Cardinal Richelieu, now it is Mazarin, who informs d'Artagnan, the only one of the four heroes who remained a musketeer, that he will need loyal men to carry out his plans, challenged by the aristocratic Frondeurs, who oppose royal policy under this latest powerful minister.

D'Artagnan is at first unsuccessful in bringing the four friends together again. Only Porthos, now the wealthy baron du Vallon de Bracieux de Pierrefonds agrees to join him. Despite his great wealth, Porthos is bored on his country estates and welcomes d'Artagnan's invitation.

Aramis has entered religious life but is also occupied in political and amorous intrigues with Madame de Longueville. Athos, using his real name now (the comte de la Fère), has retired to his country estate, where he is raising his natural son Raoul, vicomte de Bragelonne, whose mother is Madame de Chevreuse. Aramis and Athos both support the Fronde.

By a strange twist of fate, our four friends encounter one another in England where Mazarin has sent d'Artagnan and Porthos to the radical parliamentarian leader Oliver Cromwell while Aramis and Athos are on a mission to save Charles I. All four find themselves in difficulty, particularly as Mordaunt, one of Cromwell's minions and the son of Milady, seeks vengeance for his mother's death at the hands of the Musketeers in the first volume of the trilogy. The four friends, united again, fail to rescue the English king. The most dramatic scene depicts Charles I's death by beheading.

On their return voyage to France, Mordaunt is almost successful in blowing up the musketeers' ship, but the four heros manage to escape. Mordaunt continues his pursuit until he is overcome by Athos, who prevails over his spiritual crisis after the death of Charles, stirred into action by the memory of Raoul.

With this novel, Dumas produces another riveting adventure drawing on dramatic events in English and French history. The narrative treats five separate historical events: the opposition to Mazarin in January 1648, Beaufort's escape from the Vincennes prison, unrest in Paris in August 1648, the execution of Charles I in January 1649, and the end of the first Fronde in April 1649. The fact that Dumas's novel is not always historically accurate does not detract from the power of this work, in which the reader detects again Dumas's theatrical gifts. The aristocratic opposition to the crown in France (the Fronde) and the English civil war both challenged absolutist monarchies, but the circumstances were very different, as was the outcome. Nonetheless, in this dramatic adventure friendship wins out over political differences in the end.

Like *The Three Musketeers, Twenty Years After* was also published in serial form (see ROMAN FEUILLETON). The first installments began to appear before Dumas had even finished the novel. There are parallels in the structure of these first two novels in the d'Artagnan trilogy. Richelieu's counterpart in the second work is Mazarin, Anne of Austria's role is replaced by Charles I, Madame de Chevreuse becomes Madame de Longueville, and the villainous Milady is replaced by her son Mordaunt. In this story Dumas again pits good against evil. Although he makes the source of Mordaunt's anger and resentment understandable, Mordaunt's evil nature, inherited from his mother, is in the end unforgivable. Mordaunt differs from Edmond Dantès in *The COUNT OF MONTE CRISTO,* who, despite his desire for revenge, is at heart a moral man.

At the end Aramis returns to Madame de Longueville, Porthos to his estates, and Athos to his son. D'Artagnan, captain of the musketeers, remains close to the king, awaiting the next series of adventures in *The VICOMTE DE BRAGELONNE.*

FURTHER READING

Bell, David F. *Real Time: Accelerating Narrative from Balzac to Zola.* Urbana: University of Illinois Press, 2004.

Hemming, F. W. J. *Alexandre Dumas: The King of Romance.* New York: Scribner, 1979.

Maurois, André. *Three Musketeers. A Study of the Dumas Family.* Translated by Gerard Hopkins. London: Cape, 1957.

Ross, Michael. *Alexandre Dumas.* Newton Abbot, Devon, England; North Pomfret, Vt.: David and Charles, 1981.

Schopp, Claude. *Alexandre Dumas: Genius of Life.* New York: Franklin and Watts, 1988.

Stowe, Richard. *Dumas.* Boston: Twayne, 1976.

U

UNDER FIRE (LE FEU) Henri Barbusse
(1916) This powerful novel, drawing on the author's
experience in the trenches of World War I, is one of
the most remarkable examples of combat literature.
The Great War witnessed the construction of lines of
trenches across northern France. The combination of
mass mobilization and the introduction of new technology resulted in enormous casualties with over a
million and a half dead in France alone.

The trauma of the war called into question basic values and instilled a spirit of revolt among many intellectuals in the postwar period. It also engendered a genre
of combat literature that offered a new perspective on
war in which heroism is absent. In one particularly
powerful scene in *Under Fire,* a group of journalists
question soldiers about their experience but the soldiers are unable to find the words to describe what
they have endured. The individual soldier has no sense
of perspective, no understanding of a larger meaning
of the events he witnesses. These are simply ordinary
men in extraordinary circumstances. The novel is thus
subtitled "Journal of a Squad."

In a first-person narrative, Bertrand, the squad
leader, describes the first two years of the war through
the eyes of an ordinary infantryman, evoking the gruesome reality of the trenches marked by nights of fear,
horror, mud, and death. Most important, perhaps, Barbusse emphasizes the collective experience of trench
soldiers. His concern is for the suffering of humanity;
he blames those individuals responsible for the war,

leaders who through their actions have slowed the
progress of humanity. The underlying message of the
novel and its critique of the society that led to war
indicates the author's subsequent turn toward leftist
politics and pacifism.

In his greatest novel Barbusse holds nothing back
yet manages, even in his depiction of violence, fear,
and death, to do so with a lyricism that both shocks
and attracts the reader. Along with Dorgelès's *Wooden
Crosses* and Duhamel's *Life of Martyrs, Under Fire* is one
of the most compelling testimonies of the war, winning
the prestigious Goncourt Prize in 1917.

FURTHER READING

Field, Frank. *Three French Writers and the Great War.* Cam-
bridge: Cambridge University Press, 1975.
Green, M. J. *Fiction in the Historical Present: French Writers
in the Thirties.* Hanover, N.H.: University Press of New
England, 1986.
Klein, Holger, ed. *The First World War in Fiction.* London:
Macmillan, 1976.

UNDER SATAN'S SUN (SOUS LE SOLEIL DE SATAN) Georges Bernanos (1926) One
of Bernanos's most original works, *Under Satan's Sun*
expresses a spirituality and violence that takes the
reader by surprise. There is a fundamental ambiguity
in this novel in which the priest, abbé Donissan, offers
his soul to save a young woman named Mouchette. In
its most famous passage, Donissan, lost in the dark of
night, encounters a horse trader whom he later realizes

is Satan. When he looks the Devil in the eye, he sees his own reflection.

Mouchette has murdered her lover and is consequently haunted by her secret. The day after his encounter with Satan, Donissan compels Mouchette to reveal her story. Once liberated by her confession, Mouchette commits suicide. Donissan, the "Saint of Lumbres," has committed the sin of pride in offering his soul in exchange for the salvation of sinners. In the end, however, he is linked with Mouchette in the "communion of saints," a recurring theme in Bernanos's works.

In Bernanos's first novel the character of Donissan paves the way for the saintly priest in DIARY OF A COUNTRY PRIEST. It is an unusual novel, particularly in the modern world, as the author depicts evil as a distinct physical entity. Written in a simple, sober style, *Under Satan's Sun* offers a compelling spiritual message in troubled times.

FURTHER READING

Balthasar, Hans Urs von. *Bernanos: An Ecclesial Existence.* San Francisco: Ignatius Press, 1996.
Blumenthal, Gerda. *The Poetic Imagination of Georges Bernanos.* Baltimore: Johns Hopkins University Press, 1965.

UNMARRIED GIRLS (LES JEUNES FILLES) HENRI DE MONTHERLANT (1936)

This cycle of novels includes four volumes: *Unmarried Girls* (1936), *Pity for Women* (1936), *The Demon of Good* (1937), and *The Lepers* (1939). Together they tell the story of Pierre Costals, a brilliant young writer who bears certain traits of Montherlant himself. Passionate about his work and attentive to his illegitimate son, Brunet, Pierre has only one other occupation: to satisfy his pleasure with women. Determined to remain independent and unattached, Pierre goes from one woman to another, caught between his desire to conquer and to do good. Andrée Hacquebaut, the principal female character of the first volume, is a young intellectual, whereas Thérèse Pantevin is an unattractive and unstable young woman who suffers from hysteria. Along with Solange Dandillot, the epitome of the young unmarried woman, these women suffer the most from Pierre's manipulation.

In the first volume, Montherlant introduces Pierre as a libertine who carries on a correspondence with Andrée (see LIBERTINISM). After four years of intellectual friendship, Andrée hopes for a more substantial relationship with Pierre. Their situation becomes complicated when Pierre decides to withdraw slowly from Andrée, rather than hurt this woman for whom he has a certain respect. Andrée, however, convinces herself that Pierre actually loves her but is too shy to say so. Their connection weaves in and out of the subsequent volumes, unresolved for most of the time. Thérèse, in contrast, has never met Pierre. Their relationship exists solely in letters. Volume one ends with Thérèse's first nervous crisis.

One day, Pierre encounters Solange Dandillot. When he unexpectedly sees her a second time, he decides to set his sights on her. Solange, of course, falls immediately in love with Pierre, and as they become closer, she decides to marry him. In *Pity for Women,* Solange introduces Pierre to her parents. Solange's mother is a bourgeoise of the worst sort while her father, pleasant enough, is dying. Pierre grows uncomfortable as marriage seems increasingly unavoidable. Finally, he runs away to Toulouse, where he learns of Monsieur Dandillot's death.

In *Demon of Good,* Pierre returns to Solange, who does everything in her power to keep him. For a time he considers "doing good" by marrying Solange. The couple goes on a trip to Italy where Solange hopes to resolve their future together. But the trip only creates distance between them. In the end, Pierre decides not to marry her.

In *The Lepers,* Pierre leaves for North Africa, where he has an affair with a young Moroccan woman, Rhadidya, only to discover that she has leprosy. He takes her to a doctor then leaves. When he notices a spot develop on his fist, he thinks he must have caught the terrible disease and returns to Paris, where he consults a number of specialists who inform him that he does not, in fact, have leprosy. In this stressful period, Pierre suddenly decides to contact Solange and ask her if she would be willing to marry a leper. When she says yes, Pierre decides never to see her again. He then arranges to meet Andrée in Paris but, due to a misunderstanding, they miss each other and Pierre decides to break with her as well. Solange, meanwhile, marries another man but proposes a few months later that she become Pierre's mistress, an offer that he rejects completely.

Each time he parts from these women, Pierre ends with the words, "all is well that ends well."

The appendix, supposedly notes written by Pierre, offers his view of women as morally and physically inferior to men. Moreover, they are in need of protection, which makes men wish to do good though women are unreliable, unstable, and emotional. Translated into several languages, *Unmarried Girls* was Montherlant's most popular book for its merciless depiction of men and women both. This is a pitiless work whose language is hard, subtle, and ironic.

FURTHER READING
Becker, Lucille Frackman. *Henry de Montherlant: A Critical Biography.* Carbondale: Southern Illinois University Press, 1970.
Gerrard, Charlotte Frankel. *Montherlant and Suicide.* Madrid: J. Porrúa Turanzas, 1977.
Johnson, Robert Brown. *Henry de Montherlant.* New York: Twayne, 1968.

UNNAMEABLE, THE (L'INNOMABLE)

SAMUEL BECKETT (1953) This novel opens with three mysterious, unsettling questions: Where now? When now? And Who now? Thus begins a long monologue lost in time and space and devoid of meaning. The narrator is not identified and one has the sense of incorporeality. There is only an indecisive and uncertain voice trying in vain to communicate the incommunicable. Words build up but the sequences are fragmented and disjointed. They bear no meaning in relation to one another. Scraps of narrative succeed one another with no logic. The result is that, in the end, there is no outside world, no subject, simply the decay of language itself.

This is the last novel in Beckett's trilogy, which includes *MOLLOY* and *MALONE DIES*. In all three, Beckett's characters are weak, wounded, decaying and decayed antiheroes incapable of coherence in thought or speech. In this trilogy the very concept of the novel falls apart. *Molloy* retains some form of traditional narrative, however broken and disjointed. In *Malone Dies* there is no longer a "story" but a series of heterogeneous passages. In *The Unnameable,* there is nothing but the flow of words. "I speak but have nothing to say, nothing but the words of others."

The Unnameable reflects movements in contemporary philosophy that challenge the notion that it is possible to find justification or meaning in life outside of oneself. Reality is no longer certain and the project of the novel as traditionally conceived is no longer valid.

FURTHER READING
Bair, Dierdre. *Samuel Beckett: A Biography.* New York: Summit Books, 1990.
Cronin, Anthony. *Samuel Beckett: The Last Modernist.* New York: Harper Collins, 1997.
Dukes, Gerry. *Samuel Beckett.* London: Penguin, 2001.
Gordon, Lois. *The World of Samuel Beckett, 1906–1946.* New Haven, Conn.: Yale University Press, 1996.
Pattie, David. *The Complete Critical Guide to Samuel Beckett.* London, New York: Routledge, 2000.
McCarthy, Patrick A. *Critical Essays on Samuel Beckett.* Boston: G. K. Hall, 1986.
Rathjen, Friedhelm, ed. *In Principle, Beckett Is Joyce.* Edinburgh: Split Pea Press, 1994.

UPROOTED, THE (LES DÉRACINÉS)

MAURICE BARRÈS (1897) In this novel, seven young men from Lorraine, inspired by their philosophy professor, Paul Bouteiller, follow him to Paris in search of a political and social ideal. The novel is set in the years 1882–85. Uprooted from their native province, they are soon disillusioned and the story ends in disaster. They do not understand the rules of the Parisian social game. Two of them, Racadot and Mauchefrin, turn to crime. One escapes the guillotine but the other is executed.

The novel bears the influence of Arthur Schopenhauer's pessimistic philosophy on Barrès's thinking as well as the French defeat by the Prussians in 1870. This was an important turning point for Barrès. Moreover, Barrès directs his critique against a sterile form of empiricism in his depiction of the world of journalism and politics in the 1880s.

The Uprooted is the first volume in Barrès's trilogy, *A Novel of National Energy.* It is followed by *Call to a Soldier* (1900) and *Their Faces* (1902). LOUIS ARAGON considered it to be the first modern, political novel. The novel's central themes fit into Barrès's conservatism as well as his concept of the cult of the self as the author criticizes a system of education that takes no account of the individual, a system that draws young people away from their homes to Paris, without showing them how to develop their own unique energy.

FURTHER READING

Curtis, Michael. *Three Against the Third Republic: Sorel, Barrès, and Maurras.* Westport, Conn.: Greenwood Press, 1976; 1959.

Doty, Charles Stewart. *From Cultural Rebellion to Counter-revolution: The Politics of Maurice Barrès.* Athens: Ohio University Press, 1976.

Field, Trevor. *Maurice Barrès: A Selective Critical Biography (1848–1979).* London: Grant and Cutler, 1982.

Guérard, Albert Léon. *Five Masters of French Romance: Anatole France, Pierre Loti, Paul Bourget, Maurice Barrès, Romain Rolland.* New York: Scribner, 1916.

UPSTART PEASANT (LE PAYSAN PARVENU) Pierre Carlet de Marivaux (1734–1735)

The Upstart Peasant is an unfinished novel in five parts, plus a continuation by another, anonymous author. It falls in the tradition of the pseudomemoir, a genre particularly popular in the 18th century that lends authenticity to the narrative.

Jacob, the upstart peasant of the novel's title, comes from Champagne. He is attractive and perceptive, particularly in his dealings with the older women he meets on his way to Paris and thereafter. Like Lesage's novel *The Adventures of Gil Blas de Santillane*, *The Upstart Peasant* is a novel of upward mobility and self-fashioning. Jacob moves up in the world through various social milieux, those of the world of finance, the bourgeoisie, the aristocracy, to the point of becoming M. de la Vallée.

When he arrives in Paris, Jacob is taken on as a servant in the household of Mademoiselle Habert, a pious woman of about 50 who lives with her sister and a servant, Catherine. Jacob marries Mademoiselle Habert, who loves him passionately. For Jacob, she is an excellent choice in a wife according to 18th-century standards. She is in love with her husband and therefore likely to remain faithful. More important, she brings him status and financial security with few limits to his (sexual) freedom. Marivaux's focus on male sensuality and freedom makes this novel a complement to *The Life of Marianne*. Together, the two novels reveal the distinctly gendered spheres that marked 18th-century French society.

FURTHER READING

Haac, Oscar A. *Marivaux.* New York: Twayne, 1974.

Jamieson, Ruth. *Marivaux: A Study in Sensibility.* New York: Octagon Books, 1969.

Marshall, David. *The Surprising Effects of Sympathy: Marivaux, Diderot, Rousseau, and Mary Shelley.* Chicago: University of Chicago Press, 1988.

Rosbottom, Ronald. *Marivaux's Novels: Theme and Function in Early Eighteenth-Century Narrative.* Madison, N.J.: Farleigh Dickinson University Press, 1974.

V

VALÉRY, PAUL (1871–1945) A poet and essayist, from early on Valéry displayed a broad range of intellectual interests. As a youth he avidly read VICTOR HUGO, ÉMILE ZOLA, THÉOPHILE GAUTIER, J.-K. HUYSMANS, Charles Baudelaire, and STÉPHANE MALLARMÉ. Mallarmé was a particularly influential figure in Valéry's life. While he is principally remembered today as a one of the great poets of the 20th century, Valéry also wrote a work of fiction, *Mr. Teste,* in which this singular character expresses Valéry's views on intellectual life.

Valéry fought for a long time against his natural inclination to pursue a literary career. He studied law and in 1897 took a position in the Ministry of War, where he remained for three years. Then in 1890 Valéry wrote to Mallarmé offering him two poems and the master responded. In this earlier period Valéry moved in literary circles, associating with figures such as the writer Pierre Louÿs and ANDRÉ GIDE. In 1891 he appeared on Mallarmé's doorstep and from that time on participated in Mallarmé's salon on Tuesdays.

In 1892 Valéry gave the first in a series of lectures on VILLIERS DE L'ISLE D'ADAM. In that same year he suffered an intellectual and spiritual crisis during the famous "night at Gênes," after which he decided to give up literature completely in favor of mathematics and philosophy. In his journal he described that night saying, "I am between me and myself . . . I want to scorn everything that passes between my temples." He became increasingly preoccupied with the function of the intellect. For the next 50 years he devoted his early-morning hours to an exploration of thought although he remained distant from contemporary literary and intellectual movements such as SURREALISM, MARXISM, cubism, and psychoanalysis. Two hundred sixty-one notebooks document these musings.

In 1896 Valéry published "An Evening with Mr. Teste," in the journal *Centaur,* although the collection of writings that *Mr. Teste* comprises were published together only in 1946. Mr. Teste, who appears to be modeled roughly on Valéry after the "night at Gênes," detests the banality of everyday life. Following his strict internal discipline, Mr. Teste avoids everything that does not nourish the spirit, giving up reading and writing. Intellect must exist purely for its own sake. Mr. Teste avoids all petty emotions and material concerns that might distract him from his cerebral endeavors. At the opera he even turns his back on the stage to observe audience response. He follows an essentially Cartesian formula; it is sufficient for Mr. Teste to think as thinking and being are one and the same. In Gide's opinion, one can't help but read this work in one sitting; it is "incomparable." Although he continued to write, Valéry did not publish again until 1917, under pressure from friends.

The year 1898 marked Mallarmé's death, a painful event for Valéry. However, in 1900 Valéry started life anew, marrying Jeannie Gobillard, the painter Berthe Morisot's niece, and accepting a position as private secretary to Édouard Lebey, director of the Havas news agency where he remained until 1922 when he began again to earn a living by his pen. In 1927 Valéry was elected to the Académie Française and in 1936 he became a professor at the Collège de France. Although Valéry was fascinated with the intellectual aspects of poetry, his writings are far from arid; rather, he was able to blend word and spirit magically. Valéry's views on the relationship between author and text are decidedly modern, anticipating subsequent poststructuralist literary movements (see POSTSTRUCTURALISM). He once wrote: "There is no true sense of a text. No author's authority. Regardless of what he *wanted to say,* he wrote what he wrote. Once published, a text is like an apparatus that each may use in his own fashion." He died in 1945 and was honored with a national funeral.

FURTHER READING

Bosanquet, Theodora. *Paul Valéry.* New York: Haskell House, 1974.

Crow, Christine. *Paul Valéry: Consciousness and Nature.* Cambridge: Cambridge University Press, 1972.

Ince, W. N. *The Poetic Theory of Paul Valéry, Inspiration and Technique.* Leicester, England: Leicester University Press, 1961.

Lawler, James R. *The Poet as Analyst: Essays on Paul Valéry.* Berkeley: University of California Press, 1974.

Putnam, Walter C. *Paul Valéry Revisited.* New York: Twayne; Toronto: Maxwell Macmillan Canada; New York: Maxwell Macmillan International, 1995.

Suckling, Norman. *Paul Valéry and the Civilized Mind.* Westport, Conn.: Greenwood Press, 1978.

VALLÈS, JULES (1832–1885)

Principally remembered for his political activism as a radical journalist and participant in the revolt of the PARIS COMMUNE in 1871, Jules Vallès also wrote an autobiographical trilogy collectively called *JACQUES VINGTRAS.*

Raised by narrow-minded, unaffectionate parents, Vallès had an unhappy childhood. His father, a professor, was withdrawn and cold; his mother limited and authoritarian. As a family, they never fit well into the constrained world of petit bourgeois society. Vallès began to rebel while still living in Nantes by participating in the tumultous events of 1848. Only escape to Paris appeared to offer the possibility of rebirth.

Although he had ostensibly moved to the capital to continue his studies, Vallès was soon caught up in the agitated atmosphere that reigned after the failure of the 1848 revolution. He participated in a plot to abduct the president, for which he was imprisoned for a time. Struggling to make his way, Vallès engaged in a variety of pursuits as journalist, teacher, and employee in the mayor's office. He lived a bohemian existence focused on literature and politics, while he wrote poems and the outlines for novels and plays. In 1860, however, the publication in *The Figaro* of his article "Sunday for a Poor Young Man" opened up new possibilities.

From 1861 to 1865 Vallès wrote numerous articles for a series of Parisian newspapers. His major articles were published together in *The Recalcitrants* in 1866. Inspired by his love for the people, Vallès was far from a barren theoretician. Even when his own material conditions had improved, he continued to observe and document carefully, with remarkable sensitivity, ordinary peoples' lives. Vallès established his own journal, *The Street (La Rue),* in 1867, but his writings were censured and he went to prison again.

Once released, in 1871 Vallès founded yet another revolutionary journal, *Le Cri du people* (The Cry of the People), recalling anarchist Pierre-Joseph Proudhon's *The Voice of the People (La Voix du Peuple).* That same year, due to his popularity and his reputation as a revolutionary, Vallès was chosen a delegate of the Paris Commune. While in the Assembly, Vallès argued for peace and understanding between the social classes. Such a message did not decrease his anger against injustice and the current regime. Vallès was one of the last fighters to leave the barricades of the Commune in 1871. With its violent suppression Vallès escaped into exile, having been condemned to death in absentia.

In England Vallès served as a correspondent for several Parisian newspapers, writing under the pseudonym John of the Street (Jean de la Rue). He also began writing the trilogy of *Jacques Vingtras,* which includes *Child* (1879), *Bachelor* (1881), and *The Insurrectionist* (1886).

Frequently described as "cruel," "lucid" and "virulent," as well as "lyrical" and "humorous," this story of alienation and disenfranchisement begins with Jacques's childhood and traces his development as a revolutionary, as he rebels first against the petit bourgeois values of his parents, much as the author did.

As he matures politically, Jacques inveighs against the coup d'état of 1851, social ranking, and bourgeois values. *The Insurrectionist* is dedicated to "all those who, victims of social injustice, take up arms against a world badly made."

After the amnesty of 1880, Vallès returned to Paris in 1883 and started up *The Cry of the People* once more, again with a violent and revolutionary tone. Although he sought to restore a sense of solidarity and to break down institutions that perpetuate social injustice, he was not a socialist. Writing principally in the first person, as both journalist and novelist Vallès consistently voiced his sympathy for sufferings of the man in the street. Generations of young people grew up reading Vallès's works. Despite the violence of his writings, Vallès remains a sympathetic figure on the basis of his REALISM and authenticity.

FURTHER READING

Bouvier, Luke. *Writing, Voice, and the Proper: Jules Vallès and the Politics of Orality*. Amsterdam, Atlanta: Rodolpi, 1998.
Langford, Rachael. *Jules Vallès and the Narration of History: Contesting the French Third Republic in the Jacques Vingtras Trilogy*. Bern, New York: P. Lang, 1999.
Long, Robin McArthur. *Self, Language and the Social in the Writings of Jules Vallès (1832–1885): The Jacques Vingtras Trilogy*. Lewiston, N.Y.: E. Mellen Press, 2004.

VATARD SISTERS, THE (LES SOEURS VATARD) Joris-Karl Huysmans (1879)

In this novel from Huysmans's naturalist phase (see NATURALISM), the author depicts 19th-century working-class life through two sisters, Céline and Désirée, who are seamstresses in a small atelier. Céline has a series of worthless lovers. Désirée, more reserved, chooses to take care of their ailing mother.

Céline eventually meets Cyprien Tibaille, a painter fascinated with working-class life. They have an affair but Tibaille soon tires of Céline's vulgar ways, while she is disgusted with Tibaille's elitist aestheticism. Céline leaves him for Anatole, a thug who beats her. Désirée has a liaison with an honest worker named Auguste but decides to follow her father's advice and marry a foreman.

Tibaille is a precursor to Huysmans's famous character des Esseintes from *AGAINST THE GRAIN*. Like des Esseintes, Tibaille seeks new and strange sensations and experiences, although he chooses the sordidness of working-class life rather than a refined DECADENCE. Tibaille also shares des Esseintes's elitist aesthetic sensibility.

Huysmans inherited a seamstress's small atelier and so was able to write from experience. Following the naturalist doctrine, his knowledge of the inner workings of the atelier allowed him to document his subject matter. Huysmans was also inspired by Raphaello Raphaëlli's paintings of factories and working-class neighborhoods. Critics have often noted the close connection between Huysmans's writing and contemporary trends in the visual arts.

Gustave Flaubert and Edmond de Goncourt both admired the novel despite its flaws. Goncourt suggested that Huysmans choose a "superior sphere" of life for his next literary endeavor. Flaubert felt that the novel was badly constructed. Nonetheless, *The Vatard Sisters*, for all the scandal it caused, was a successful novel. For its psychological analysis of Céline and Désirée, the character of Tibaille as a prototype for des Esseintes, and its naturalist characteristics, *The Vatard Sisters* constitutes an important work in Huysmans's oeuvre.

FURTHER READING

Banks, Brian. *The Image of Huysmans*. New York: AMS Press, 1990.
Gilman, Richard. *Decadence: The Strange Life of an Epithet*. New York: Farrar, Straus and Giroux, 1979.
Nalbantian, Suzanne. *Seeds of Decadence in the Late Nineteenth-Century Novel*. New York: St. Martin's Press, 1983.
Praz, Mario. *The Romantic Agony*. Translated by Angus Davidson. New York: Oxford University Press, 1970.

VENUS OF THE COUNTING HOUSE (LA CURÉE) Émile Zola (1872)

In this second novel in the ROUGON-MACQUART series, Aristide Rougon, operating under the name Saccard, builds an enormous fortune in real estate. The Rougon-Macquart series traces the history of a family during the SECOND EMPIRE, a period of rapid industrialization and modernization that had a significant impact on socioeconomic conditions in France. The particular context for Saccard's success is the city planner Baron Georges Eugène Haussman's program for Parisian urbanization.

Sidonie, Aristide's sister, arranges a marriage for him to a wealthy heiress, Renée Béraud du Chatel. To make free use of her money, Aristide turns a blind eye to her behavior and whims, including her affair with his son from a first marriage, Maxime. Maxime, in turn, marries a consumptive young woman for her dowry. Renée, who is both their accomplice and their victim, dies of meningitis.

Zola's pessimism, for which contemporaries criticized him, reflects his own rejection of bourgeois decadence in this period. Here, Zola focuses on the moral weakness of the bourgeoisie. In subsequent novels he examines with equal care workers and peasants. He appears to be fascinated by financial speculation and sensuality, in other words, desire. The theme of desire for food and sex parallels a desire for wealth and power. Anticipating Freud, Zola seems to argue that all appetites are ultimately connected with the death instinct.

FURTHER READING

Bell, David. *Real Time: Accelerating Narrative from Balzac to Zola.* Urbana: University of Illinois Press, 2004.

Berg, William J., and Laurey K. Martin. *Émile Zola Revisited.* New York: Twayne; Toronto: Maxwell Macmillan Canada; New York: Maxwell Macmillan International: 1992.

Bloom, Harold, ed. *Émile Zola.* Philadelphia: Chelsea House. 2004.

Bowlby, Rachel. *Just Looking: Consumer Culture in Dreiser, Gissing and Zola.* New York: Methuen, 1985.

Brown, Frederick. *Zola: A Life.* Baltimore: Johns Hopkins University Press, 1996.

Chessid, Ilona. *Thresholds of Desire: Authority and Transgression in the Rougon-Macquart.* New York: P. Lang, 1993.

Gallois, William. *Zola: The History of Capitalism.* Oxford, New York: P. Lang, 2000.

Lethbridge, Robert, and Terry Keefe, eds. *Zola and the Craft of Fiction.* Leicester, England; New York: Leicester University Press, 1990.

Lukács, Georg. *Studies in European Realism.* Translated by Edith Bone. New York: Grosset and Dunlop, 1964.

Petrey, Sandy. *Realism and Revolution: Balzac, Stendhal, Zola and the Performance of History.* Ithaca, N.Y.: Cornell University Press, 1988.

VERCORS (1902–1991)

After earning a degree in electrical engineering, Vercors, the pseudonym for Jean Bruller, turned to the visual arts. In 1928 he published a series of drawings entitled *21 Delightful Ways of Committing Suicide.* An active member of the Resistance, in 1941, along with the journalist Pierre de Lescure, he founded the then clandestine Éditions de Minuit publishing house. Later in life, Vercors told the story of clandestine publishing during the war in *Battle of Silence* (1992). In 1942 Vercors earned recognition as a writer for SILENCE OF THE SEA, his most famous novel. In this work a German officer lodges with a French family during the Occupation; this reflects Vercors's concern with war and its consequences for humanity.

Vercors was both an existentialist (see EXISTENTIALISM) and a communist, although he broke with the Communist Party in 1956. Influenced by these two movements, Vercors engaged in a philosophical questioning of the human condition. *Guiding Star* (1943) accuses collaborators of betraying France by denying its very nature and character, a theme present in other works by Vercors. In this novel, Thomas Muriz, a young Czech subject of the Austro-Hungarian Empire, dreams of France and freedom. He leaves his family and walks to Paris.

At first life appears to offer everything that Muriz had hoped for. But when his son dies in 1914, Muriz's only solace is in knowing that now he is French. Then, in 1942, although he is an old man, the French authorities hand Muriz over to the Germans because his mother was Jewish. Muriz dies sobbing not from fear but despair.

After the war, Vercors took an even harsher stance in *Sand of Time* (1948), the year he traveled to Germany to give a series of public lectures in which he announced, "I have come to say hard things to you." The tragedy of war and the Occupation is at the center of Vercors's works, leading him to elaborate upon his humanist vision in *More or Less Man* (1950) and *You Shall Know Them* (1952).

In the latter work Vercors suggests that the difference between man and beast is that man rebels against nature. "Humanity is not a state to submit to, it is a dignity to conquer." The main character, Douglas Templemore, is put on trial after murdering the offspring of a female "Paranthropus erectus" whom he had artificially inseminated with his own sperm. Templemore's purpose is to create a situation that would require a court to determine exactly what a human is. The story also raises questions of racial discrimination but is lighter in tone than other satirical works such as VOLTAIRE'S CANDIDE and ANATOLE FRANCE'S PENGUIN ISLAND, which share similar concerns. This novel was later adapted to the stage in *Zoo, or the Philanthropic Assassin* (1963). A similar theme marks a subsequent essay, *Questions on Life to Messieurs the Biologists* (1973), in which the author suggests that political engagement is the only means of escape from our tragic condition, and *What I Believe* (1975). In *Sylva* (1961), Vercors uses the female fox as an allegorical figure in a novel about the education of humanity.

VERNE, JULES (1828–1905)

The son of a Nantes attorney, Jules Verne even as a child dreamed of traveling to distant exotic lands such as he describes in his fantastic novels. When he was 11 years old, he signed on as cabin boy on a ship headed to India, but his father stopped him at the last moment. Verne supposedly responded, "I will voyage no more except in my dreams." Later he realized those dreams of adventure in his writing.

In 1848 Verne left for Paris, ostensibly to study law although he was initially more interested in the theater. He attended various literary salons and became acquainted with ALEXANDRE DUMAS, who was at that time running his famous "historical theater." Verne began to write plays, and Dumas agreed to put on Verne's *Broken Straws,* which opened in 1850. It was a moderate success. Meanwhile, passionately interested in the sciences, Verne avidly read about recent scientific discoveries in the national library. A whole new world seemed to open up to him and Verne was captivated by the beauty of the potential of scientific and technological progress to improve the world. Verne also met a blind former explorer who shared with him the story of his travels, further fueling Verne's imagination.

Verne took a position as secretary in a theater and continued to write, at first short stories, and later, a historical novel, while continuing his intellectual pursuits. He began to work seriously at developing the vocabulary necessary to write his "novel of science" in 65 volumes, of which the most famous are *Five Weeks in a Balloon* (1862), VOYAGE TO THE CENTER OF THE EARTH, TWENTY THOUSAND LEAGUES UNDER THE SEA, AROUND THE WORLD IN EIGHTY DAYS, and MYSTERIOUS ISLAND.

In 1857 Verne married a young widow and, in need of steady income, began working as a stockbroker. He rose at 5:00 a.m. and wrote until 10:00, when he left for work. Verne's reputation as a writer was ensured with the publication of *Five Weeks in a Balloon.* His publisher was so excited that he signed Verne on for a contract by which Verne was to produce two volumes a year for 20 years. The novel, an instant success, was translated immediately into a number of European languages. For the next 40 years Verne went on to produce 80 novels and 15 plays. His other major works include *The Adventures of Captain Hatteras* (1864), *From the Earth to the Moon* (1865), *Captain Grant's Children* (1867–68), *Around the Moon* (1870) and *The CASTLE OF THE CARPATHIANS* (1892). Verne quickly became one of the wealthiest and most famous authors of his day.

By far her greatest success was *Around the world in Eighty Days,* first published in serial form in 1872. Profits from the novel's adaptation to theater allowed Verne to purchase a luxurious yacht that he sailed regularly until 1886. He then settled in Amiens, where he continued to write.

The extraordinary popularity of Verne's novels reflects the 19th-century reader's fascination with the exotic and with new forms of knowledge. Verne skillfully combined both in his writing. His heroes might be men of learning or adventurers. In each case their journey, one that nearly always ends at the point of departure, is one of education. Verne popularizes recent developments in all the natural sciences, bringing together an encyclopedic knowledge of geography, geology, physics, and astronomy. Consequently, despite the fantastic nature of these explorations (under the sea, to the center of the earth, and in outer space), they seem realistic. Verne even foresaw future inventions, such as the submarine.

Although certain earlier works such as CYRANO DE BERGERAC'S *The STATES AND EMPIRES OF THE SUN AND MOON* or VOLTAIRE'S *MICROMÉGAS* share characteristics with Verne's works, Verne is considered to be the father of modern science fiction. His contemporary and rival in this budding genre was the British writer H. G. Wells.

Like other great novelists of his time, Verne creates another world for his readers. While he looked to the future, Verne also included elements of traditional mythology that reflect his nostalgia for a lost golden age. Verne was a visionary with a sense of poetry evident in his descriptions of the landscapes and animals that fill his fantastic journeys. In the 20th century the surrealists (see SURREALISM) rediscovered Verne's writings.

These novels also provided Verne with the opportunity to engage in social criticism concerning, for example, the abuses of European colonization, whales as an endangered species, fossil fuel pollution, and slaughtering elephants for ivory. It is not surprising that critics have called Verne a prophet.

Verne's writing also reflects certain biases of the time. He can be simplistic in his descriptions of national or cultural differences. Long hopeful for technological progress, toward the end of his life Verne expressed anxiety and pessimism over contemporary events such as colonial rivalry among European nations, threats of war, and the potential dangers of scientific discoveries. Verne ended by fearing for humankind's future.

FURTHER READING

Born, Franz. *Jules Verne: The Man who Invented the Future.* Translated by Juliana Biro. Englewood Cliffs, N.J.: Prentice Hall, 1964.

Butcher, William. *Verne's Journey to the Center of the Self: Space and Time in the "Voyages Extraordinaires."* New York: St. Martin's Press; London: Macmillan, 1990.

Costello, Peter. *Jules Verne: The Inventor of Science Fiction.* London: Hodder and Stoughton, 1978.

Evans, I. O. *Jules Verne and His Work.* Mattituck, N.Y.: Aeonian Press, 1976.

Freedman, Russell. *Jules Verne: Portrait of a Prophet.* New York: Holiday House, 1965.

Lottman, Herbert R. *Jules Verne: An Exploratory Biography.* New York: St. Martin's Press, 1996.

VIAN, BORIS (1920–1959)

Vian studied philosophy but earned a degree in engineering in 1942. He suffered from poor health and heart disease all his life, which may explain his overwhelming drive to live life to its fullest. After the World War II Vian was a well-known figure in the Parisian neighborhood of Saint-Germain-des-Prés, where he played jazz all night and associated with existentialists (see EXISTENTIALISM) and avant-garde literary figures such as RAYMOND QUENEAU. The versatile Vian produced surrealist paintings (see SURREALISM), played the trumpet, and was a music critic, artistic director, singer, actor, translator, playwright, and novelist.

Vian's first novel, *I Spit on Your Graves* (1946), denounces racism in America. Published under the pseudonym Vernon Sullivan, this novel caused offense to many readers with its violent, overtly sexual content mitigated only by Vian's humor. The narrator, Lee Anderson, has left home and family to seek revenge for the death of his brother, the victim of a hate crime. Lee has blond hair and fair skin, but he is partly black. The novel ends in blood, as Lee takes revenge on the social class he deems responsible for his brother's death by sadistically murdering two white girls in a manner that recalls the writings of SADE. The last chapter ends with a description of Lee's punishment and closes with the image of his hanging corpse. The novel shares with Vian's other works a sense of despair. Vian died at the age of 39 while working on a film version of this novel. *I spit on Your Graves* is a harsher work than Vian's subsequent novels, which are gentler in tone, more lyrical, and full of humor. Vian also published short stories, poetry, plays, and an opera, *Fiesta* (1958).

In *Red Grass* (1950) the principal character is, like Vian, an engineer who builds a time machine that subsequently traps him in the past. In this work, Vian pokes fun at psychoanalysis, love, and intellectual life. The only means of escaping the absurdity of life is to turn it into a game, which Vian does by skillfully playing with language. The power of odors is strong in Vian's writing, as scent elicits deeper meaning. Every description of a woman, for example, evokes a scent.

Vian's interest in the relationship between words and objects is particularly evident in his greatest work, *FROTH ON THE DAY DREAM* (1947). In it, Vian explores the cruelty of life, the inhumanity of humankind and its institutions, the problems of alienation, ideology, illness, and the fear of death that plagues us all. Vian's vision is not entirely bleak, as his characters are tender and gentle. Vian is remarkable in his ability to transform the horror of life into a love song.

In Vian's last novel, *Heartsnatcher* (1953), Jacquemont, a psychoanalyst, is married to Clementine, who rejects him to live in a metaphorical "golden cage," where she pretends to protect her children. The plot gradually gives way to a series of nightmarish visions of which the crucifixion of a horse is but one example. Jacquemont is a victim of his own indifference, Clementine of her blind passion for her children. Jacquemont, who is disgusted by the villagers around him, analyzes them to the point of robbing them of their souls. In this work, language is thus revealed to be a trap that distorts reality.

Many of Vian's principal characters do not attain adulthood either because of death or a refusal to accept social constraints. For Vian, the adult world destroys dreams, imagination, and creativity. He rejects a society that he sees as undermining the individual and expresses concern over the power of modern states and armies to subvert humanity. He argues in favor of the rights of workers, environmentalism, and, above all, the right to live happily and creatively, not in servile submission to an inhumane system.

Not well known during his lifetime, after his death Vian became a legendary figure for his passionate approach to life. Discovered by the public in the 1960s, Vian's works were particularly popular among the young.

FURTHER READING

Jones, Christopher M. *Boris Vian Transatlantic: Sources, Myths and Dreams.* New York: P. Lang, 1998.

VICHY FRANCE

France suffered such losses in World War I that the country was unprepared for the next world war. Defeated again in 1940 by Germany, France was divided into an Occupied Zone and a smaller Free Zone that was allowed nominal independence. The capital of the Free Zone was Vichy, a small town in central France.

The right-wing, anti-Semitic Vichy regime was headed by Philippe Pétain. Supported by conservative Roman Catholics, Pétain dissolved the Chamber of Deputies and banned divorce. Vichy France was the only European country whose government deported Jews to the German concentration camps voluntarily:

Opposition to the Vichy regime consisted of an internal Resistance movement and General Charles de Gaulle's London-based government-in-exile. The period of the Occupation and the Vichy regime witnessed the publication of a number of troubling works associated with the fascist movement by Drieu la Rochelle, Céline, and Robert Brasillach.

VICOMTE DE BRAGELONNE Alexandre Dumas (1848–1850)

This last volume of Dumas's d'Artagnan trilogy, which began with The Three Musketeers, is usually published in English in three separate volumes: *The Vicomte de Bragelonne, Louise de la Vallière,* and *The Man in the Iron Mask.* In this work the author has matured, like his four heros, d'Artagnan, Athos, Portos, and Aramis. *The Vicomte de Bragelonne* is longer than the first two novels, consisting of four volumes rather than two. Of all the novels in the trilogy, *The Vicomte de Bragelonne* is also the most faithful to the atmosphere of the historical period it depicts.

The Three Musketeers was set in the period of France's prime minister Cardinal Richelieu and Twenty Years After during the Fronde's opposition to prime minister Mazarin. This last work is set in the early years of Louis XIV's reign. A much older and wiser d'Artagnan is now captain of the king's musketeers and a trusted right-hand man to Louis XIV. Again drawing on as well as altering historical events, Dumas's novel depicts the king's love affairs, the fall of finance minster Fouquet, and the rise of the powerful Colbert. Most important to the narrative is the discovery of the king's twin brother, "The Man in the Iron Mask." According to historical sources, there was an unknown masked prisoner in the Bastille who died in 1703, the subject of much rumor.

Aramis, now the general of the Jesuits, replaces Louis XIV with his twin brother, of whose existence no one knows as he has been locked away as a secret state prisoner for most of his life. In the end, d'Artagnan, of course, saves the day.

Meanwhile, Athos's son Raoul, the vicomte de Bragelonne, has troubles of his own. Raised with Mademoiselle Louise de la Vallière, Raoul has fallen hopelessly in love with his childhood companion. But Louise abandons Raoul to become the king's mistress.

In despair, Raoul determines to die heroically in battle. Athos, who for years has lived only for his son, follows Raoul to the grave.

Porthos, ever loyal to his friends, also dies in combat. For the first time his Herculean strength does not suffice, although he manages to save Aramis from their pursuers. D'Artagnan receives the marshal's baton from the crown only to die himself in battle. Only Aramis survives.

The reader witnesses the end of these four heros' lives with great sadness. Dumas's son, found his father crying over his desk on the day he wrote Porthos's death scene. The d'Artagnan trilogy is one of literature's greatest examples of heroic male friendship.

FURTHER READING

Bell, David F. *Real Time: Accelerating Narrative from Balzac to Zola.* Urbana: University of Illinois Press, 2004.

Hemming, F. W. J. *Alexandre Dumas. The King of Romance.* New York: Scribner, 1979.

Maurois, André. *Three Musketeers. A Study of the Dumas Family.* Translated by Gerard Hopkins. London: Cape, 1957.

Ross, Michael. *Alexandre Dumas.* Newton Abbot, Devon, England; North Pomfret, Vt.: David and Charles, 1981.

Schopp, Claude. *Alexandre Dumas: Genius of Life.* New York: Franklin and Watts, 1988.

Stowe, Richard. *Dumas.* Boston: Twayne, 1976.

VIGNY, ALFRED DE (1797–1863) Poet,

novelist, and dramatist Alfred de Vigny was proud of his family's noble lineage. Ruined by the FRENCH REVO-LUTION, the family had little left but its pride. Following in the family tradition of military careers, Vigny's father had fought in the Seven Years' War. Wounded and infirm, he was 60 years old when his wife, 30 years younger, gave birth to their son Alfred. Three of their children died young.

In 1799 the family moved from the provinces to Paris. After completing his secondary education, Vigny began his own military career in 1814. Bored by the monotony of military life, by 1816 he was writing his first poems. Vigny's character was not suited to military life; nonetheless he stuck to it until 1827 when he decided to devote himself entirely to literature. Vigny's meeting with VICTOR HUGO, then editor

of a literary journal, was propitious. Vigny began to contribute articles to Hugo's journal. In 1822 he published his first volume of poetry. Vigny frequented literary salons, becoming friends with SAINTE-BEUVE, among others.

Stationed in Pau, Vigny met and married a wealthy young English woman, Lydia Bunburry. Despite the couple's affection for each other, the marriage was not a happy one. Lydia had a difficult time adjusting to life in France. She was childless and suffered from poor health that, by the end of her life in 1862, had left her completely debilitated. She was also unsympathetic to her husband's literary endeavors.

Although he is principally remembered for his poetry, Vigny published *Cinq-Mars,* a historical novel, in 1826. It was a success, as the public appreciated his blending of French history with romantic dreams and visions.

Although Vigny's translations of Shakespeare were not particularly successful, his play *Chatterton* marked Vigny as one of the major romantic writers (see ROMANTICISM). Vigny's dramatic works brought him into contact with the actress Marie Dorval, who became his mistress. Their tumultuous affair lasted until 1838. Affected by the death of his mother, his wife's illness, and the breakup with his mistress, he led an increasingly isolated life. In 1845, with the support of Hugo and the poet Alphonse de Lamartine, Vigny was elected to the Académie Française. Although he continued to write, he published only sporadically from then on. His collection of poems, *Destinies,* appeared posthumously.

Vigny was a moralist and a pessimist, like many of his contemporaries disillusioned by the materialism of modern life. The world's rejection of the spiritual discouraged him. At the same time, Vigny continued to express hope in humankind's ability to regenerate itself. Vigny manifests a situation typical of his generation, caught between a romantic nostalgia for a lost world and hope for the future.

FURTHER READING

Kelly, Linda. *The Young Romantics: Victor Hugo, Sainte-Beuve, Vigny, Dumas, Musset, and George Sand and Their Friendships, Feuds and Loves in the French Romantic Revolution.* New York: Random House, 1976.

Shwimer, Elaine K. *The Novels of Alfred de Vigny: a Study of their Form and Composition.* New York: Garland Publishers, 1991.

VILLIERS DE L'ISLE-ADAM, AUGUSTE, COMTE DE (1838–1889)

Born into one of the most illustrious noble families of France that was ruined by the FRENCH REVOLUTION, Jean-Marie-Mathias-Philippe-Auguste, comte de Villiers de l'Isle-Adam grew up believing that he was destined for glory. His literary ambitions manifested themselves early, and in 1855 his family moved to Paris where he could pursue his dreams. There he moved in literary and artistic circles, meeting the poets Charles Baudelaire and Stéphane Mallarmé. He also corresponded with GUSTAVE FLAUBERT and associated with painters such as Claude Monet and Gustave Courbet.

Villiers's first attempts at writing poetry drew little attention. His stated purpose was to create "a series of works where dreams would be based on logic, a philosophical literature that would renew ideas." Slowly he began to establish a reputation, exciting admiration in symbolist and decadent circles (see DECADENTISM and SYMBOLISM). Villiers continued to write for 25 years but died in poverty, his friends paying for a decent burial.

In 1862 Villiers produced his first novel, *Isis,* drawing on his experience as an adolescent. It was intended as the first part of a larger series blending philosophy and fiction, a project he never completed. In 1872 he published the first part of *Axël;* the completed text appeared in 1885–86 and an edited version appeared posthumously. This play was considered unperformable because of its style deemed too poetic for the stage. Nonetheless, it is a masterpiece of symbolist literature that had a significant impact on developments in theater at the end of the century.

In 1883, the publication of *SARDONIC TALES* brought Villiers the fame he deserved. Although it is not a novel per se, *Sardonic Tales* was also an important influence on the development of the symbolist movement. In this collection Villiers describes a universe in which dreams simultaneously serve as the expression of suffering, revolt, and an ideal.

In 1886 *TOMORROW'S EVE* appeared, featuring the American scientist Thomas Edison as a principal character. In 1887 Villiers published *Tribulat Bonohomet,* another collection of tales, and in 1888, *Strange Stories* and *New Sardonic Tales,* in which he continued to speak out against contemporary intellectual trends. Villiers's writings are marked by a disdain for modern life and its values. Through his character of Tribulat Bonhomet, for example, he castigated materialism and petit bourgeois culture in particular. In his *Sardonic Tales,* Villiers expressed with dark humor his disillusionment and despair.

Villiers rejected REALISM, characterizing realists as "eternal provincials of the human spirit." Influenced by German and French ROMANTICISM, the works of the philosopher Hegel, in particular, Villiers sought a superior, transcendent reality. Villiers held an idealist conception of art (see IDEALISM). The artist's purpose is to "awaken intense, unknown, and sublime impressions." Not surprisingly, he was attracted to the mysterious, the supernatural, and the occult, as he explored the spiritual nature of the universe. A fascination with states of mind, the unconscious, and the world of dreams and imagination mark 19th-century thought. By this time, Villiers was associated with JORIS-KARL HUYSMANS, whose writings, particularly *The DAMNED* and *EN ROUTE,* reflect similar interests.

For Villiers, art is life. Drawing on the composer Richard Wagner's aesthetics, Villiers promoted the notion that love is greater even than death. Interested in metaphysical questions, Villiers was one of the most important contributors to the symbolist movement. Recurring themes in his writings are hauntings, phantoms, the return of the dead, and disembodied voices.

FURTHER READING

Conroy, William Thomas. *Villiers de l'Isle d'Adam.* Boston: Twayne, 1978.
Lathers, Marie. *The Aesthetics of Artifice: Villiers' l'Ève future.* Chapel Hill: University of North Carolina Department of Romance Languages: Distributed by the University of North Carolina Press, 1996.
Raitt, A. W. *The Life of Villiers de l'Isle d'Adam.* Oxford: Clarendon Press; New York: Oxford University Press, 1981.

VIPER IN HAND (VIPÈRE AU POING)

HERVÉ BAZIN (1948) This novel recounts the difficult childhood experience of two brothers, Ferdinand

and Jean. The story begins in 1922, when, like the legendary Hercules, Jean strangles a viper. Twenty-five years later he narrates the story of his life with his brother in their grandmother's home. At first their experience is like that of most children, with days full of typical games and misadventures. The boys' grandmother gives them a traditional upbringing. When she dies, the boys' parents return with their younger brother, Marcel, from China, and everything in their lives changes.

The boys' father has no authority over his cruel and abusive wife, whose only desire is to crush her sons. As a result, the boys detest their mother, whom they call Folcoche (a combination of the French words for "crazy" and "pig"). From this point on, their upbringing is rough and violent. Only by banding together can the brothers survive. In an act of desperation, Jean runs away to his maternal grandparents' home. For a time the gravity of this action eases the situation and then the boys are sent away to school. Jean, nonetheless, ends up marginalized, rebellious, incapable of trusting others and, most important, disdainful of bourgeois society.

Bazin's novels, *Viper in Hand, Head Against the Wall,* and *Death of a Pony,* together make up the first period in Bazin's career as a writer. Each of these novels draws from Bazin's own unhappy childhood experience. The public viewed the novels as scandalous for their harsh description of family life, as well as for the author's implicit approval of rebellion and nonconformism among the young.

FURTHER READING

Brosman, Catherine Savage. *French Novelists Since 1960.* Detroit: Gale Research, 1989.

VIPERS' NEST (LE NOEUD DE VIPÈRES)

FRANÇOIS MAURIAC (1932)   Tormented by 40 years of hatred, Louis decides to take revenge on his family before his death. Once a successful lawyer, Louis is rich and his beneficiaries are anxious to reap the rewards of his labor. In a last will and testament, Louis reflects on his life and family and decides to disinherit his children in favor of his illegitimate son, Hubert. Not that Louis loves Hubert; he is simply the means of vengeance. Louis also resents his wife, Isa, who once

revealed to him that she had agreed to marry him only in order not to remain single. There is no love in this vipers' nest of a family. As he considers his past, Louis realizes that only a few people have ever touched his now cold heart. They are his granddaughter Marie, his nephew Luc, and the abbé Ardouin.

When Isa unexpectedly dies, Louis begins to develop a closer relationship with another granddaughter, Jeanne, who is suffering from a broken heart. In the end, Louis finds saving grace and dies in peace. Less pessimistic than Mauriac's THÉRÈSE DESQUEYROUX, *Vipers' Nest* recalls the works of GEORGES BERNANOS and JULIEN GREEN. Mauriac's concern over isolation when alienated from God, as well as his critique of bourgeois society, are recurring themes in his works.

FURTHER READING

Bessent, Edna. "Solitude in the Novels of François Mauriac," *French Review* 8, no. 2 (December 1934): 129–134.

Garaudy, Roger. *Literature of the Graveyard: Jean-Paul Sartre, François Mauriac, André Malraux, Arthur Koestler.* Translated by Joseph M. Bernstein. New York: International Publishers, 1948.

Penn, Dorothy. "Three French Writers of Contemporary Catholic Realism: The Inner Consciousness Studied by Georges Bernanos, Henré Ghéon, and François Mauriac," *French Review* 12, no. 2 (December 1938): 128–137.

Speaight, Robert. *François Mauriac: A Study of the Writer and the Man.* London: Chatto and Windus, 1976.

VOLTAIRE (FRANÇOIS-MARIE-AROUET)

(1694–1778)   Born in Paris to a bourgeois family (his father was a notary), Voltaire became one of the greatest voices of the French ENLIGHTENMENT. Voltaire was educated by the Jesuits at the famous college of Louis-le-Grand, where he received an excellent education in literature while developing a taste for history and theater that would continue throughout his life. Although his father wanted him to study law, Voltaire turned to writing. As a young man he traveled in libertine circles (see LIBERTINISM) and began his literary career with satirical poems directed against the regency. This resulted in 11 months in the Bastille. Upon his release from prison Voltaire adopted his pseudonym.

Voltaire's first literary success was the tragedy *Oedipus,* bringing him praise as the successor to the great

17th-century dramatists Corneille and Racine. His near duel with a famous courtier led to another brief imprisonment. Voltaire was released on the condition that he leave for England. Once there, Voltaire was fascinated by contemporary intellectual circles as well as the English system of government. His experience in England remained an important influence on his thinking.

In 1728 Voltaire returned to France but was soon in trouble again. Subject to arrest after the publication of his *Philosophical Letters,* Voltaire took refuge at Cirey in 1734, the home of Émilie du Châtelet, a thinker, writer, and Voltaire's companion until her death in 1749. For most of the next 10 years (1734–44) Voltaire lived and worked at the Châtelet home producing some of his great historical works. He also began his correspondence with Frederick II of Prussia, whose reign Voltaire initially viewed as the model of royal absolutism. In 1744, with the patronage of Madame de Pompadour, mistress to Louis XV, Voltaire had the opportunity again to pursue a career at court (Versailles). But his propensity to get into trouble meant that he was disgraced by 1747 and again forced into exile, though he had been accepted into the Académie Française in 1746. This time Voltaire's refuge was the home of the duchesse du Maine. There he wrote his first philosophical tale (*conte philosophique*), ZADIG (1748).

Madame du Châtelet's death in 1749 came as a terrible blow to Voltaire despite the stormy periods in their relationship. Suffering from his loss, Voltaire accepted Frederick II's invitation to Berlin. Disillusioned that the great Prussian monarch did not live up to his expectations as an enlightened despot, Voltaire left under yet another cloud in 1755. This time he sought refuge near Geneva. Despite the vagaries of his career, Voltaire had succeeded in making a fortune. From his property at Ferney, where he spent the next 18 years, he continued to produce some of his greatest works, including his *Essay on Morals* (1756), in which he discussed the development of civilization emphasizing the modern concept of cultural relativity, CANDIDE (1759), and his *Treaty on Intolerance* (1763). During this period Voltaire also contributed to the ENCYCLOPEDIA, edited by DIDEROT and the mathematician Jean le Roud d'Alembert. In 1778 Voltaire felt the urge to return once more to Paris. He died in that city later in the same year. In 1792 revolutionaries buried his ashes in the Pantheon in Paris, in recognition of his contribution as a father of the FRENCH REVOLUTION.

All Voltaire's works, fiction and nonfiction, are permeated with a consistent set of philosophical ideas. He speaks out against injustice, war, tyranny, intolerance, and religious fanaticism, ideas that correspond to the principal themes of Enlightenment thought. Voltaire rejected orthodox religion in favor of a deism that fed into his concern with human happiness in *this* life. His concept of happiness is based on a belief that moral values and material well-being will ultimately lead toward peace and progress in all spheres of human endeavor including science, technology, and the arts. In this respect Voltaire's philosophy resembles that of his collaborator Diderot. These views define the project of the Enlightenment.

Voltaire had long admired the English parliamentary system and its protection of individual liberties. English society clearly benefited from commerce and hard work, so different from the French aristocracy. Since Voltaire felt that the English system of government could not work everywhere, he promoted the concept of enlightened absolutism for continental European states. Unlike ROUSSEAU, Voltaire did not offer innovative works of political theory but struggled to combat injustices of OLD REGIME society when he encountered them. Voltaire's gift to the Enlightenment lies in his contribution to the rise of a new mentality in preparation for reforms. He made Enlightenment ideas accessible to a broad readership through fictional works like *Candide,* which uses irony and humor to promote philosophical principles. In doing so Voltaire created an entirely new genre, the *conte philosophique,* or philosophical tale. These works combined fantasy and philosophy to reveal social injustices. Gifted at satire, Voltaire wrote in a wide variety of genres (history, poetry, drama, novels, and philosophy) in a clear and elegant style.

FURTHER READING

Bonneville, Douglas A. *Voltaire and the Form of the Novel.* Oxford: Voltaire Foundation, 1976.

Bottiglia, William F. *Voltaire's "Candide": Analysis of a Classic.* Geneva: Institut et musée Voltaire, 1964.

Cutler, Maxine G., ed. *Voltaire, the Enlightenment, and the Comic Mode: Essays in Honor of Jean Sareil.* New York: P. Lang, 1990.

Sherman, Carol. *Reading Voltaire's Contes: A Semiotics of Philosophical Narration.* Chapel Hill: University of North Carolina. Department of Romance Languages: Distributed by University of North Carolina Press, 1985.

Wade, Ira O. *Voltaire and "Candide."* Princeton, N.J.: Princeton University Press, 1959.

WANDERER, THE (LE GRAND MEAULNES) ALAIN-FOURNIER (1913)

This still popular novel, Alain-Fournier's one famous work, preserves the beauty and simplicity of childhood. Fournier captures the adolescent's desire for complete happiness while evoking the mystical and magical. As the story opens, Augustin Meaulnes arrives at boarding school. The village and the school reflect the unchanging nature of provincial life, calm and tranquil. A larger-than-life figure from the beginning, Augustin begins a friendship with the schoolmaster's son, the narrator of the novel.

One night Augustin accidentally loses his way in and stumbles onto a mysterious château celebrating the lord's marriage to a stranger, a young woman whom no one has yet seen or met, but she never arrives and the wedding does not take place. The groom, Frantz de Galais, is in despair. Augustin returns to his village and school but is obsessed with a young woman he met on that wondrous night, Frantz's sister, Yvonne.

Augustine's adventure has given him a touch of the mysterious. He has changed and his friends have noticed. With the exception of the narrator, Augustin's schoolmates distance themselves from him. As for Augustin, he only desires to see Yvonne and tries to find the château again but fails.

One day a new student arrives at school who turns out to be Frantz de Galais. Before disappearing, Frantz informs Augustin that his sister Yvonne is in Paris and then asks, in parting, that Augustin and the narrator respond to him if ever he is in need of help. Augustin leaves for Paris but cannot find Yvonne, who has returned to the château. In the interim, Augustin has an amorous encounter with Valentine, who, it turns out later, is Frantz's fiancée.

One day the narrator discovers the château and meets Yvonne, who is moved at the mere mention of Augustin's name. Eventually the couple marries but on the night of the wedding there is a wild cry of despair from Frantz, who demands that Augustin help him to find his lost love. Augustin answers his friend's call, leaving the next day. In his absence Yvonne dies. Augustin returns to discover his loss. He and the child Yvonne bore him subsequently leave, never to be heard from again.

Fournier's particular gift as a writer is skillfully to blend richness of detail and mystery into a tension between dreams and reality. There is no strong character analysis. Fournier rather fosters a sense of the spiritual. The novel reminds the reader that once a moment of happiness is past it can never be recaptured. Augustin is driven by a dream of happiness, an absolute desire that allows him no peace or contentment and that separates him from others. A novel of adolescent torment and passion, the novel remains a favorite among young people today.

FURTHER READING

Arkell, David. *Alain-Fournier: A Brief Life (1886–1914)*. Manchester, New York: Carcanet, 1986.

Ford, Edward. *Alain-Fournier and Les grand Meaulnes (The Wanderer)*. Lewiston, N.Y.: E. Mellen Press, 1999.

Gurney, Stephen. *Alain-Fournier*. Boston: Twayne, 1987.

WANDERING JEW, THE (LE JUIF ERRANT) EUGÈNE SUE (1844–1845)

This popular serial novel by the author of *The MYSTERIES OF PARIS* opens in 1832 as members of the Rennepont family, representing various social strata, meet to inherit the fortune left them by a persecuted Huguenot (French Protestant). The collective inheritors meet with opposition from the Society of Jesus, which wants Gabriel de Rennepont, a Jesuit missionary, to be the sole legatee so that he can turn over the inheritance to the order.

An unavoidable delay makes it impossible to distribute the inheritance immediately. Father Rodin makes use of the time to sow discord within the family and provoke their deaths. As the story unwinds, Gabriel destroys the box holding the inheritance and Father Rodin meets his demise when he is poisoned by the Secret Society of Indian Stranglers. Meanwhile, the Wandering Jew and his wife mysteriously and quietly assist the family members.

More ambitious than *The Mysteries of Paris, The Wandering Jew* is stronger in its call for social reform. The Wandering Jew and his wife, representing the oppressed proletariat, call the reader to reconsider contemporary social prejudices. It is significant that Sue chose to publish this novel in the *Constitutionnel,* whose petit bourgeois readers were more likely to respond to the author's views than the more conservative readers of the *Journal des débats,* the publisher of *The Mysteries*. Because of its strongly anticlerical stance, the novel was placed on the Roman Catholic Church's Index of Banned Books.

WAYWARD HEAD AND HEART, THE (LES ÉGAREMENTS DU COEUR ET DE L'ESPRIT) CLAUDE-PROSPER JOLYOT DE CRÉBILLON, FILS (1736)

The Wayward Head and Heart tells the story of a naive young man's apprenticeship in the ways of the world, juxtaposing the ideal of an education based on a concept of virtue and the reality of a society in which this same concept of virtue defines social behavior, but only in theory. It is a world of hypocrisy.

The first two parts of the novel depict Meilcour as a young man full of false ideas who is corrupted by others. For a time Meilcour confuses his senses and his heart, convincing himself that he is in love with his libertine mentor, Madame de Lursay (see LIBERTINISM) because of the passion she inspires in him. In the end, he chooses a virtuous young woman, Hortense de Théville, who brings him back to the straight and narrow. Before this happy ending, however, Meilcour has been both the lover of Madame de Lursay and the disciple of the cynical Versac. They introduce him to a world of sensuality in which the moment of seduction is emphasized and where there is as much subtlety in the physical aspects of love as in the metaphysical.

At first Meilcour is blinded by vanity but he eventually feels that something is missing, "without knowing what was missing, I felt an emptiness in my soul." This recognition causes him to recall Hortense, although it takes some time for him to withdraw from his dissolute life. In an earlier period, Christian morality and/or reason would have brought Meilcour to his senses, rather than love.

Other libertine novels put forth a philosophical argument that favors the senses over reason. With Crébillon, the heart is drawn along the wrong path by the senses, and Meilcour's situation can be corrected only when he chooses the love of a virtuous woman over the immediate satisfaction of the senses in a dissolute society. Crébillon, thus lives up to his preface in which he states his intention to censure and ridicule vice in a manner comparable to LACLOS in *DANGEROUS LIAISONS*. The theme of redemption of love appears, too, in DUCLOS's *Confessions of the count of ****. Like MARIVAUX or PRÉVOST, Crébillon envisioned a perfect passion that unifies heart and mind.

The novel depicts a narrow world of aristocratic society where love or rather seduction is the central theme. Public opinion is everything; each individual's existence is defined by others. The novel reveals the manners of high society alone. No other social classes are represented. But this aristocratic society has already lost its function. Its only resources are diversion, conversation, and affairs of the heart. In the end, however, libertinism is not satisfying. One yearns for something more authentic. This world in which appearance is more important than reality is precisely what ROUSSEAU attacks. At the same time, the lesson Meilcour learns cannot be universally applied. It is his experience, his lesson.

FURTHER READING
Conroy, P.-V. Jr, *Crébillon fils: Techniques of the Novel.* Oxford: Voltaire Foundation, 1972.

WE'LL TO THE WOODS NO MORE (*LES LAURIERS SONT COUPÉS*) ÉDOUARD DUJARDIN (1887)

We'll to the Woods no More is the story of a young lover in Paris who recounts, almost as a confession, every detail of a few happy moments he knows he can never relive. In Dujardin's own words, "It is simply the story of six hours in the life of a young man in love with a young woman—six hours during which *nothing* happens." The young man is Daniel Prince, a student who meets up with a friend, dines alone in a restaurant, goes home to dress, then joins an actress with whom he is taken. She is a flirt.

The entire story takes place in Daniel's head, making *We'll to the Woods no More* the first example of an interior monologue. The novel is not well known today but was an important influence on the Irish novelist James Joyce's *Ulysses*. Dujardin likewise influenced the English writer Virginia Woolf, ANDRÉ GIDE, SAMUEL BECKETT, and NATHALIE SARROUTE, among others.

Dujardin defined the interior monologue, or stream of consciousness, as "an unspoken discourse by which a character expresses his most intimate thought, closest to the unconscious, prior to any logical organization and in its nascent state, by means of phrases reduced to a syntactical minimum." Dujardin's use of stream of consciousness marks him as part of an innovative group of writers exploring the possibilities of subjective narrative through the SYMBOLIST and DECADENT movements.

FURTHER READING
Genova, Pamela Antonia. *Symbolist Journals: A Culture of Correspondence.* Aldershot, England; Burlington, Vt.: Ashgate, 2002.
McKilligan, Kathleen M. *Édouard Dujardin, Les Lauriers sont coupés and the Interior Monologue.* Hull, England: University of Hull, 1977.

WERTH, LÉON (1878–1955)

Werth attended secondary school in Lyon, where he won first place in philosophy and subsequently earned a degree in literature. In the course of his career, he served as secretary to Octave Mirabeau and wrote articles published in a number of Parisian journals. A defender of the impressionists, Werth was also interested in art criticism. His first major publication was a translation of the Russian writer Fydor Dostoyevsky's *The Double*.

Werth's first novel, *The White House,* was published in 1913 with a preface by Mirabeau. It is the story of the trials in the hospital of a victim of a brain tumor. The novel was considered for but did not win the Goncourt Prize, that went instead to ALAIN-FOURNIER for *The WANDERER*.

Despite his pacifist views, Werth fought in World War I. This experience provided him with the material for *Soldier Clavel,* published in 1919. After the war, Werth worked as a journalist, art critic, and sports announcer. He also commented on literature and film. A Jew, he was forced into hiding during World War II.

In 1943 ANTOINE DE SAINT-ÉXUPERY dedicated *The LITTLE PRINCE* to Werth. "I ask the children to forgive me for dedicating this book to a grown-up. I have a serious excuse: this grown-up is my best friend in the world. I have another excuse: this grown-up can understand everything, even books for children. I have a third excuse: this grown-up is living in France which is hungry and cold and in need of solace. If all these excuses are insufficient, then I wish to dedicate this book to the child this grown-up used to be. All grown-ups were once children (but few of them remember). I correct my dedication: To Léon Werth when he was a little boy." Werth died in Paris in 1955.

WIESEL, ELIE (1928–)

Romanian-born Wiesel was deported to the German concentration camp of Auschwitz along with his family during World War II when he was only 16 years old. Wiesel's father, mother, and sister all died. At the end of the war, Wiesel was one of 400 adolescents who refused to return to their homeland after the liberation of the camps. He arrived in Paris in 1945, where he resumed his studies.

Wiesel wrote for a number of Isreali, French, and American journals. He eventually moved to the United States, where he held a chair in social sciences at Boston University. Wiesel was awarded the Nobel Peace Prize in 1986. He has written some 30 books, many in French, which include novels, plays, and essays. All his works are written in memory of the Holocaust, serving as witness and testimony, calling on humankind to fight against injustice. "The important thing is to combat silence with the word or with another form of silence." He once said, "this is what characterizes our generation, the obsession to avoid silence. People are afraid of silence. As for myself I believe in silence."

In NIGHT (1958), Wiesel's first novel, he tells the story of what happened to the Jews of his birthplace. Having refused to believe in the destiny fate had in store for them, they ended up in Germany, exterminated. Night powerfully evokes the sense of having been abandoned by both man and God. It also reveals the pain evoked by having survived one's father. This experience led to Wiesel's life purpose of serving as witness and keeping memory alive.

All of Wiesel's subsequent works, including Dawn (1960), The Accident (1961), Town Beyond the Wall (1961), and Gates of the Forest (1964), explore the question whether it is possible to believe in God and humanity after the Holocaust. In his essays Wiesel struggles against man's indifference, having once said that "literature is the antithesis of indifference." Jews of Silence (1966) exposes the situation of Jews in the Soviet Union, while Jew Today (1977), Words of a Stranger (1982), and Signs of Exodus (1985) evoke the suffering of oppressed peoples in labor camps, in Cambodia, Lebanon, and elsewhere. Wiesel continued to write novels, including Beggar in Jerusalem, which won the Médicis Prize in 1968, The Testament (1980), Fifth Son (1983), and Twilight (1987). All expose the inherent tension between death and hope. In 1994 Wiesel published his memoirs, All Rivers Flow to the Sea. In 1995, a series of conversations between Wiesel and the Jacques Chirac president of France were published covering a wide range of topics. Wiesel continues to advocate on behalf of international humanitarian issues.

WILL O' THE WISP (LE FEU FOLLET)

PIERRE DRIEU LA ROCHELLE (1931)   The central character of this novel, Alain, is weak, irresolute, and unstable. He has mistresses but is never drawn to them by real desire. He has no truly sensual nature and remains strangely distant from life. Nonetheless, he lives off of women. Disturbed by his own indifference, Alain turns first to drugs, then to writing as a means of salvation. He is more successful at this endeavor than he is in human relations. But incapable of finding meaning in his life and convinced of his own uselessness, Alain commits suicide.

Will o' the Wisp is one of Drieu's first novels, the principal character of which was inspired by the poet Jacques Rigaud, who also put an end to his life. The novel is arguably autobiographical in that the author himself was equally solitary and unstable.

The figure of Alain is also symbolic of man's confusion and uncertainty in modern life, with its culture devoid of shared values and meaning. The novel reflects the uncertainty and instability of the interwar period. Drieu was opposed to the decadence of bourgeois society that produces weak men like Alain. While other contemporary writers such as ANDRÉ MALRAUX and LOUIS ARAGON found purpose in leftist political movements, Drieu, increasingly isolated, turned toward fascism only to recognize his error at the end of his life. He committed suicide in 1945.

FURTHER READING
Cadwallader, Barrie. Crisis of the European Mind: A Study of André Malraux and Drieu La Rochelle. Cardiff: University of Wales Press, 1981.

Green, M. J. Fiction in the Historical Present: French Writers and the Thirties. Hanover, N.H.: University Press of New England, 1986.

Kaplan, Alice Y. Reproductions of Banality: Fascism, Literature, and French Intellectual Life. Minneapolis: University of Minnesota Press, 1986.

Klein, Holger, ed. The First World War in Fiction. London: Macmillan, 1976.

Leal, Robert Barry. Drieu La Rochelle. Boston: Twayne, 1982.

Reck, Rima Drell. Drieu La Rochelle and the Picture Gallery Novel: French Modernism in the Inter-war Years. Baton Rouge: Louisiana State Press, 1990.

Soucy, R. *A Fascist Intellectual: Drieu La Rochelle.* Berkeley;
    Los Angeles, London: University of California Press,
    1979.
Zelden, Theodore. *France 1848–1945*, Vol. 5, "Anxiety and
    Hypocrisy." Oxford: Oxford University Press, 1979.

WIND, SAND AND STARS (TERRE DES HOMMES) Antoine de Saint-Exupéry (1939)

Like Saint-Exupéry's other novels, *Wind, Sand and Stars* is based on the author's experience as a pilot. Saint-Exupéry and his friend Guillemet are the heroes of this work. Guillemet has an accident in the Andes and survives only because of his will. "What I did, I swear, no beast would have done."

The novel focuses on the pilots' experiences but also reflects Saint-Exupéry's vision of humanity. In his thinking he is generous, even aristocratic in outlook, passionate about the nature and character of men of action like himself. An idealist, too, Saint-Exupéry reveals the professional identity of men whose courage and heroism are the qualities the author most admires. In *Wind, Sand and Stars, The* Little Prince, *and other works, Saint-Exupéry promotes the idea of a human community in which each individual would act in the service of others. Implicit in this and other works is Saint-Exupéry's critique of contemporary society marred by egotism, materialism, and selfishness. In contrast, Saint-Exupéry espouses the beauty, virtue, and greatness of soul of which humankind is capable. The courage to act saves man from isolation for "Man in the presence of man," he writes, "is as solitary as in the face of a wide winter sky in which there sweeps, never to be tamed, a flight of trumpeting geese." *Wind, Sand and Stars* won the national book award.

FURTHER READING

Cate, Curtis. *Antoine de Saint-Exupéry: His Life and Times.*
    New York: Paragon House, 1990.
Master, Brian. *A Student's Guide to Saint-Exupéry.* London:
    Heinemann Educational, 1972.
Mooney, Philip. *Belonging Always: Reflections on Uniqueness.*
    Chicago: Loyola University Press, 1987.

WITCH GRASS (LE CHIENDENT) Raymond Queneau (1933)

In this experimental novel, Queneau links theory with practice, thus laying the foundation for innovative ideas about the novel articulated later by OuLiPo, the avant-garde "Workroom for Potential Literature," established in 1960. Drawing from the philosophy of René Descartes, *Witch Grass* also reflects Queneau's interest in mathematics, as various combinations of mathematical principles give structure to the work. The novel consists of 91 sections, the product of the primary numbers 7×13. Moreover, $9 + 1 = 10$, 1 being significant because the last section of each series of 13 is placed outside the chapter and printed in italic. The proportions of the novel's content are also determined mathematically. The formula $7 \times 13 =$ the death of a character, while 1 signifies his or her return to existence.

This cyclical narrative is set alternately in Paris, the suburbs, and by the Normen seaside. It is in essence a treasure hunt. A series of catastrophic events are related to a strange door that a sleazy antique dealer named Taupe refuses to sell. With the help of her nephew, Madame Coche sets off in search of a treasure that eventually other characters come to believe in. As the story unfolds there are more mysterious accidents; some characters are wounded, others die, and the treasure disappears. Finally, war breaks out with the Etruscans. Years later, Madame Cloche turns out to be the queen.

There is no real ending to the novel, only another beginning as full of illusions as the first. The work concludes with the same sentence with which it began. Characters include Peter the Great, the observer, Étienne Marcel, Madame Coche, and her brother, Saturnin. The treasure hidden behind the door is a bearded dwarf, Bébé Toutout. Queneau wrote the novel when he was in Greece, where, in the novel, Peter the Great and his friend Catherine take refuge until war breaks out. Eventually they wind up in Gaul.

When it was first published, the novel did not receive much attention. However, along with André Gide's *The* Counterfeiters, this work prepared the way for future innovations in the novel. It also presages elements found in Queneau's later works. OuLiPo and the Nouveau roman are both heirs of Queneau's novel form.

FURTHER READING

Bastin, Nina. *Queneau's Fictional Worlds.* Oxford, New York:
    P. Lang, 2002.

Guicharnaud, Jacques. *Raymond Queneau.* New York: Columbia University Press, 1965.

Hale, Jane Alison. *The Lyric Encyclopedia of Raymond Queneau.* Ann Arbor: University of Michigan Press, 1989.

Shorley, Christopher. *Queneau's Fiction: An Introductory Study.* Cambridge, New York: Cambridge University Press, 1985.

Stump, Jordan. *Naming and Unnaming: On Raymond Queneau.* Lincoln: University of Nebraska Press, 1998.

Thiher, Allen. *Raymond Queneau.* Boston: Twayne, 1985.

Velguth, Madeleine. *The Representation of Women in the Autobiographical Novels of Raymond Queneau.* New York: P. Lang, 1990.

WITTIG, MONIQUE (1935–2003) Wittig contributes in a unique way to the contemporary literary movement of *"écriture féminine,"* or female writing. Since the cannon of Western literature is, by and large, male, Wittig proposes to start again. She will invent a new literary genre that suits the female word. Wittig thus takes up the traditional literary forms of the epic poem and the CHANSONS DE GESTE but gives them an entirely new purpose. Rather than a single, male hero, Wittig substitutes a collective female protagonist, a group that will open itself up to women of all races and nations.

One of her most famous and striking works is *Guérillères* (1969). This novel is unusual in form, having no chapters, no single protagonist, no unifying plot. The narrative is interspersed with poetry and lists of female names. Wittig's purpose is to create women's language and narrative in such a way that multiple women's voices dominate her text.

The title in French is derived from the masculine for "warrior." In Wittig's view, the term she invents, *guérillères,* is inferior, "colonized," and recalls the guerrilla wars that have marked Third World independence movements. Wittig links this notion with women's war. Her writing is highly political, as she seeks to prove that women can and must produce their own words to describe their own condition and their own hopes. In Wittig's view, women have long been controlled and constrained by men's words and they must now seek in solidarity to overcome those forces that have colonized, exploited, and oppressed them. "One must understand," she writes, "that men are not born

with a faculty for the universal and that women are not reduced by birth to the particular. The universal has been, and is continually, at every moment, appropriated by men. It does not happen by magic. . . . It is an act, a criminal act, perpetrated by one class against another. It is an act carried out at the level of concepts, philosophy, and politics."

What emerges from her text is a series of legends, myths, fables, and fairy tales reinterpreted by women narrators/warriors who demonstrate the way in which traditional mythology has consistently devalued women. Her goal of liberating women is through altering masculine discourse and the literary heritage of the Western world. She seeks to put an end to women's silence by inventing a new vocabulary that allows women to tell their story differently. Wittig thus feminizes male names, sometimes in a shocking manner, as in "Christa, the much-crucified." Equally disturbing to some readers is her reinterpretation of the story of Genesis in which Eve's companion is not Adam but her lover Lilith.

A recurring theme in her works is a vision of the phoenix rising from the ashes, representing the triumph of women. Another unusual device that Wittig repeatedly uses is the symbolic meaning of the letter *O.* This letter evokes the notion of revolution and the circle, hence a woman's genitalia, marked by the absence of the phallus. The nothingness of the hole associated with women will give rise to a new order that signifies inclusion and totality, the whole rather than the part.

In a poststructuralist (see POSTSTRUCTURALISM) understanding of the world, gender is located in language. Wittig reflects this vision in a series of works that includes not only *Guérillères* but also *The Opoponax* (1969) and *Lesbian Body* (1973). Together her writings create a new nonphallocentric discourse that counteracts the traditional heterosexual and patriarchal narrative. Through "lesbian language," she seeks to destroy notions of gender and sex. One way in which Wittig attempts to do this is through her unusual use of pronouns, preferring "we" or "one" to "I," certainly not "he" or "she."

Wittig's "lesbianization of language" differs, for example, from the bisexuality of HÉLÈNE CIXOUS. Wittig's embracing of the lesbian stands in opposition to the power structure of heterosexual, bourgeois capitalism. For her, lesbianism exists apart from traditional political, social, and linguistic structures. Since time immemorial women have been defined by their reproductive function; only the lesbian can escape. "Lesbian is the only concept I know of," she writes, "which is beyond the categories of sex (woman and man), because the designated subject (lesbian) is *not* a woman, either economically, or politically, or ideologically." Some scholars have argued that Wittig goes so far as to try and destroy the very notion of woman.

Despite, or perhaps because of, her radical approach to women's writing, Wittig has often not received the attention that her works deserve. She approaches women's writing from a Marxist perspective while trying to create a new culture in which the individual is not defined by gender or sexuality. She thus differs significantly from other proponents of women's writing who seek to celebrate women's difference through "writing the body." At the same time, Wittig does not deny the body but glorifies, in love, all its parts.

FURTHER READING

Crowder, Diane Griffin. "Amazons and Mothers? Monique Wittig, Hélène Cixous and Theories of Women's Writing," *Contemporary Literature* 24, no. 2 (Summer 1983): 116–144.
Duffy, Jean. "Women and Language in *Les Guérillères* by Monique Wittig," *Stanford French Review* 7, no. 3 (Winter 1983): 399–414.
Ostrovsky, Erika. *A Constant Journey: The Fiction of Monique Wittig.* Carbondale: Southern Illinois University Press, 1992.
Porter, Lawrence. "Writing Feminism: Myth, Epic and Utopia in Monique Wittig's *Les Guérillères,*" *L'Esprit Créateur* 29, no. 3 (Fall 1989): 92–99.
Shaktini, Namascar. *On Monique Wittig: Theoretical, Political, and Literary Essays.* Urbana and Chicago: University of Illinois Press, 2004.
Spraggins, Mary P. "Myth and Ms: Entrapment and Liberation in Monique Wittig's *Les Guérillères,*" *International Fiction Review* 3, no. 1 (1976): 47–51.
Thiébaux, Marcelle. "A Mythology for Women: Monique Wittig's *Les Guérillères.*" In Randolph Pope, ed. *The Analysis of Literary Texts.* Ypsilanti, Mich.: Bilingual Press, 1980, 88–99.
Wenzel, Hélène Vivienne. "The Text as Body/Politics: An Appreciation of Monique Wittig's Writings in Context," *Feminist Studies* 7, no. 2 (Summer 1981): 264–287.
Zerelli, Linda. "The Trojan Horse of Universalism: Language as a 'War Machine' in the Writings of Monique Wittig," *Social Text,* no. 25/26 (1990): 146–170.

WOMAN'S STORY, A (UNE FEMME) ANNIE ERNAUX (1987)

In *A Woman's Story* Ernaux continues her autobiographical exploration of social identity and the female condition, this time telling the story of her relationship with her mother. The novel thus contributes to themes explored in contemporary feminist literature (see FEMINISM). After her mother's death, Ernaux seeks to give birth to her mother in words. Through the act of retelling her mother's life she legitimizes and validates her mother's experience as a woman from the lower classes. Ernaux thus grapples with her own social origins and reveals her commitment to give voice to the voiceless through literature.

FURTHER READING

McIlvanney, Siobhán. *Annie Ernaux: The Return to Origins.* Liverpool, England: Liverpool University Press, 2001.
Thomas, Lyn. *Annie Ernaux: An Introduction to the Writer and Her Audience.* Oxford, New York: Berg, 1999.

WOMAN WHO WAS POOR, THE (LA FEMME PAUVRE) LÉON BLOY (1897)

In this semiautobiographical novel, Clotilde Maréchal comes to Gacougnol's studio to work as a model. She is so miserable and poor that Gacougnol first takes her for a beggar. Moved by her suffering, Gacougnol decides to save her but dies tragically, leaving Clotilde with no support.

Léopold, a friend of Gacougnol, finds Clotilde wandering the streets of Paris. Léopold thinks he has found in her a woman who can understand him. The two marry but unhappy events ensue. Only their faith can support the couple. Bloy's depiction of the misery of poverty is derived from his own experience. A Roman Catholic writer, Bloy also uses the story to promote his vision of Christianity in a world of suffering.

FURTHER READING

Brady, Sister Mary Rosalie. *Thought and Style in the Works of Léon Bloy.* New York: AMS Press, 1969, c. 1946.

Polimeni, Emmanuela. Léon Bloy, *The Pauper Prophet, 1846–1917*. New York: Philosophical Library, 1951.

WOODEN CROSSES (LES CROIX DE BOIS) ROLAND DORGELÈS (1919)

A powerful work depicting the horror of everyday life in the trenches of World War I, *Wooden Crosses* won the Femina Prize and came close to winning the Goncourt Prize but that prize went to MARCEL PROUST.

Dorgelès writes of the "divine wave" that inspires courage among men, yet eschews all idealism to reveal the truth of the Great War, with its mud, trenches, and death. The real battle is fought not against the enemy but against one's own misery and fear. Constantly confronted with death, the common soldier is a moving figure. "In order to tell of your long misery, I wanted also to laugh, laugh your life. All alone in a taciturn dream, I put on my backpack and with no travel companion, I followed in a dream your regiment of ghosts."

The shock of war inspired a body of realist combat novels reflecting the need of writers to articulate their experience during the war and to give a voice to the soldier in the trenches. Writers like Dorgelès, HENRI BARBUSSE, and LOUIS-FERDINAND CÉLINE served as witnesses, preserving the memory of fallen comrades.

The rhythm of life in the trenches is slow. Soldiers are concerned with eating, sleeping, dealing with mud and lice, and staying alive. Abstract concepts of patriotism and heroism are absent. Dorgelès's language is simple, straightforward, and often crude. Like prolonged trench warfare, there is no climax nor a sense of larger meaning: "There will always be wars, always, always." The narrative of life in the trenches is in itself an indictment of the society that led to war.

World War I inaugurated a new kind of war, driven by technology that denied the individual soldier in the trenches the possibility of grand heroic gestures. Dorgelès sought to debunk the myth of war promoted in propaganda. He opens the novel with the pronoun "we." Like Barbusse, whose novel *UNDER FIRE* was subtitled "Journal of a Squad," Dorgelès focused on the collective. Today we are accustomed to literature and film that focuses on the platoon, but this was new in the combat literature that emerged out of World War I.

FURTHER READING

Field, Frank. *Three French Writers and the Great War*. Cambridge: Cambridge University Press, 1975.
Klein, Holger, ed. *The First World War in Fiction*. London: Macmillan, 1976.
Wohl, Robert. *The Generation of 1914*. Cambridge, Mass.: Harvard University Press, 1979.

WORDS TO SAY IT, THE (LES MOTS POUR LE DIRE) MARIE CARDINAL (1975)

"So it was on that day that I foresaw what was going to happen to me. However, I had never yet seen anyone 'cured' by psychiatry. Since then I have seen a few: inoffensive, cautious, stuffed versions of themselves, humans with moist hands and a look in their eyes that moves between the flame and the ashes, the flame and the ashes. . . . I believe that the Thing no longer made them suffer but that it remained alive in them. It is still the Thing which is the driving force in them."

The Words to Say It is the story of one woman's experience with Freudian psychoanalysis. In a first-person narrative, she recounts a difficult childhood, being placed in an asylum, her escape, and her subsequent experience with an analyst who helps her overcome the Thing, an ailment that is both physiological and psychological. Ultimately, Cardinal recognizes the power of words that may destroy or cure. Words can also be a rich source for expressing the female condition.

The narrator's problems are associated with an abnormal menstrual cycle. She speaks of bleeding. "I keep close watch on the Thing, but it doesn't stir. I installed myself on the bidet to watch the blood flow. Since I am here it is a favorite activity. It makes me think of the sea and the waves lapping against the shore with a sigh. I think of the planets spinning in their orbits."

The Thing is like a living force. It is the source of her madness and something that takes over her body. Beyond her physiological problems, the narrator also suffers from her past. She grew up in a troubled Catholic family in colonial Algeria. She is thus repressed by social and cultural values as well as by being separated from her own body.

At the heart of the novel are questions of identity and the implication that the language of male-dominated culture is a barrier to the narrator's self-expression. As the novel progresses, the narrator begins to reconstruct her life as she tells it to her psychoanalyst. An important theme, thus, is the function of storytelling in the creation of identity. The narrator's physical suffering is only a symptom. The problem is one of translation. How does she translate the experience of her body into words? Cardinal's emphasis on the relationship between the word and the body recalls the works of HÉLÈNE CIXOUS and the concept of writing the body that is associated with contemporary feminist literature (see FEMINISM).

The narrator's abnormal menstrual bleeding is a reaction to the violent impact of her environment on her body. In a central passage, the narrator's mother admits to having tried to abort her daughter. Hence, the daughter's continual bleeding is a repetition of her mother's desire to terminate her pregnancy. Only through psychoanalysis and, ultimately through writing, is the narrator able to overcome this traumatic revelation. In a Freudian sense, she becomes an agent, rather than a being that is simply acted upon.

The theme of the absent father is recurring in Cardinal's works. The narrator's parents are divorced. While she does have some contact with her father, she sees him through the lens of her mother's hatred. The problem of the absent father is then repeated through her husband.

Parallel to the absent father is the omnipresent mother. In *The Words to Say It,* the mother-daughter relationship is one of love and hatred. The mother, resentful of her daughter's birth, tries to suppress the child's personality through a set of repressive values (colonial, Catholic, bourgeois) that becomes the source of her daughter's madness. The narrator is able to defeat the Thing and her madness only by destroying the identity her mother created for her. Once the mother dies, literally and figuratively, the daughter is liberated and can be reconciled with the memory of her mother.

The story of the narrator's body and her life is complex and overlapping. There is tension between the story her family (her mother in particular) tells and her own experience, which she is only just learning to voice. Eventually the narrator recovers her own iden-

tity. Her liberation is both personal and political, as she makes broader reference to the revolutionary events of May 1968.

Eight years later Cardinal wrote a sequel, *Le Passé empiété* (not translated), which makes use of a metaphor for writing drawn from embroidery and refers to a stitch that passes over itself several times. In this work, too, there are multiple layers, as the narrator tells the story of her father's life, her own life, and the life of Clytemnestra, the wife of Agamemnon who, like the narrator, was separated from her father, Zeus. Telling these stories becomes the means to affect change and recalls the works of ANNIE ERNAUX, with whom Cardinal sometimes collaborated.

FURTHER READING

Durham, Carolyn A. "Feminism and Formalism: Dialectical Structures in Marie Cardinal's *Une Vie pour Deux,*" *Tulsa Studies in Women's Literature* 4, no. 1 (Spring 1985): 83–99, and "Patterns of Influence: Simone de Beauvoir and Marie Cardinal," *French Review* 60, no. 3 (February 1987): 341–348.

Stephens, Sonya, ed. *A History of Women's Writing in France.* Cambridge: Cambridge University Press, 2000.

WORLD AS IT IS, THE (LE MONDE COMME IL VA) VOLTAIRE (1759)

This satirical work on the meaninglessness of war is more of a parable than Voltaire's usual philosophical tale. Drawing again on the popular 18th-century theme of Orientalism, the story begins with the angel Ituriel, who approaches Babouc and sends him on a mission to observe the City of Persepoles whose inhabitants have annoyed the gods, to decide whether they should be chastised or destroyed. Babouc discovers that the Persians are at war with the Indians, although no one, from the lowliest soldier to the highest general, appears to know why.

Following a rumor that peace is about to be concluded, the war becomes even more violent and brutal. Babouc wonders whether these are men or ferocious beasts and concludes that the Persians, at all events, should be destroyed. He then decides to observe the Indians, who turn out to be just as bad.

When Babouc begins to look more closely at society, he realizes to his pleasure that in the midst of violence and cruelty there are also acts of generosity and grandeur. Babouc is led to ponder the inexplicable and paradoxical in human nature, much as the reader of Voltaire's CANDIDE is encouraged to do. Peace, in the end, is declared.

Arriving at a large, dirty, crowded city, Babouc is shocked to discover that according to custom, the dead are buried in the temple where people come to pray, though this leads to epidemics and disease. Babouc is perplexed. Like Voltaire's other works, the outsider satirically observes society, offering a critique of social values that reflect the major themes of ENLIGHTENMENT thought.

FURTHER READING

Bonneville, Douglas A. *Voltaire and the Form of the Novel.* Oxford: Voltaire Foundation, 1976.

Bottiglia, William F. *Voltaire's "Candide": Analysis of a Classic.* Geneva: Institut et Musée Voltaire, 1964.

Cutler, Maxine G., ed. *Voltaire, the Enlightenment, and the Comic Mode: Essays in Honor of Jean Sareil.* New York: P. Lang, 1990.

Sherman, Carol. *Reading Voltaire's Contes: A Semiotics of Philosophical Narration.* Chapel Hill: University of North Carolina, Department of Romance Languages: Distributed by University of North Carolina Press, 1985.

Wade, Ira O. *Voltaire and "Candide."* Princeton, N.J.: Princeton University Press, 1959.

Y

YACINE, KATEB (1929–1989)

An Algerian writer, Yacine played a significant role in the development of 20th-century North African literature through his exploration of the tension between traditional African culture and the forces of history. The relationship between the individual and history is thus a central theme in his writing. Do men shape history? Or does history destroy men? His answers to these fundamental questions are not entirely clear.

Much like CAMARA LAYE, Yacine first studied in an Islamic school before attending a French school. In 1945 he joined in a demonstration in Setif against the injustice of the colonial system that was brutally suppressed by French authorities. Like many others, Yacine was arrested, beaten, and imprisoned. Once released, he was not allowed back in school. From this experience, Yacine said he learned that the two most important things for him were poetry and revolution. Close to a group of nationalists and communists, for a time Yacine worked as a journalist for the newspaper *Alger républicain,* the same paper for which ALBERT CAMUS wrote.

Yacine's father died in 1950, leaving him the responsibility of providing for the family. Yacine gave up journalism to become a dock worker in Algiers. When he lost his job, he left for France, where he was willing to do almost anything to earn money, working as a day laborer, mason, and electrician's assistant. After 1952, with the financial support of friends, Yacine could devote more time to writing and developing his interest in theater. Remembered principally as a playwright, Yacine actually began his literary career with the publication of a collection of poetry in 1946. His novel NEDJMA appeared 10 years later. In this work, the female character of Nedjma serves as an allegory for Algeria. Yacine returned to Algeria in 1972.

FURTHER READING

Aresu, Bernard. *Counter-hegemonic Discourse from the Maghreb: The Poetics of Kateb's Fiction.* Tübingen, Germany: G. Narr, 1993.

Joyaux, Georges J., Albert Memmi, and Jules Roy. "Driss Chraïbi, Mohammed Dib, Kateb Yacine, and Indigenous North African Literature," *Yale French Studies,* no. 24, Midnight Novelists (1959): 30–40.

Salhi, Kamal. *The Politics and Aesthetics of Kateb Yacine: From Francophone Literature to Popular Theater in Algeria and Outside.* Lewiston, N.Y.: E. Mellen Press, 1999.

Tcheho, Isaac Celestin. *The Novel and Identity in Algeria: A Study of the Works of Mohammed Dib, Mouloud Feraoun, and Kateb Yacine, 1950–1966.* Thesis. University of Yaoundé s.n., Cameroon, 1980.

YOURCENAR, MARGUERITE (1903–1987)

Yourcenar is an anagram of the author's real name, Marguerite Crayencour. The anagram, devised by her father, became her legal name when Yourcenar became an American citizen in 1947. Yourcenar's father was French and her mother Belgian. She spent much of her childhood in the north of France near Lille. Her father was a gambler but he was also concerned that his daughter receive a solid, private education and encouraged her to study classical languages and literature. Her knowledge of the classics was to be a major influence on her later works.

Yourcenar's father also fostered her taste for travel. She traveled with him to Italy, Switzerland, and Greece. Although she had no regular schooling, Yourcenar obtained her baccalaureate at the age of 16 in Aix-en-Provence. Not long afterward, she conceived of the idea for her two works on the Roman emperor Hadrian and a Renaissance physician Zeno. The idea for these works, born in her youth, matured in her mind for some time. Even when the novels were theoretically completed, Yourcenar continued to revise them.

Yourcenar's first novel, *Alexis,* was published in 1929. This work takes the form of a long letter from a husband explaining why he abandons his wife and clearly bears the influence of ANDRÉ GIDE, as does *New Eurydice* (1931). A translation of the greek poet Pindarus appeared in 1932. *A Coin in Nine Hands* (1934) is set in Mussolini's Italy. History, ancient and modern, figures prominently in Yourcenar's writings. Recurring themes are the relationship between the human and the divine, death, homosexuality, love, passion, and eroticism.

In 1934 the character of Zeno first appeared in a short story. In 1936 Yourcenar published *Fires,* a collection of meditations and prose poetry on the passions in a style that recalls JEAN COCTEAU. From there Yourcenar went on to write a series of short stories and essays. *Coup de Grâce* (1939), evokes the pain of unreciprocated love. Like *Alexis,* this novel focuses on the theme of an ill-suited couple. It is set in the tense climate of the Baltic nations, struggle against the Russian Bolsheviks after World War I. At the same time, Yourcenar completed her first version of *Hadrian.*

Yourcenar made her first trip to the United States in 1932–38. She subsequently returned after the German invasion of France, later dividing her time between America and France. The pessimism of the war years gives the tone to a number of Yourcenar's plays that draw bitterly from Greek mythology. In the United States she taught at Sarah Laurence college before settling on Mount Desert Island in Maine in 1950. She lived there with her partner, leaving less and less frequently as the years passed.

Published in 1951, *The* MEMOIRS OF HADRIAN was an instant success. It is, arguably, Yourcenar's greatest work. Written in the first person, it recounts the life and thoughts of the second-century Roman emperor. As he approaches death, Hadrian reflects on his life, political power, and the memory of Antinous, the young man whom he once loved and who sacrificed himself for Hadrian's sake. Yourcenar's fame only increased after the appearance of ABYSS (1968). *Abyss,* another historical novel, whose French title refers to an alchemical process, is a third-person narrative set in 16th-century Flanders. It traces the life of a besieged intellectual, Zeno, through war, pestilence, and persecution.

Yourcenar's originality lies in her ability to create a balance between historical accuracy and fictional characters. She draws from her rich knowledge of other cultures to create an oeuvre that is unified in its humanist vision, a humanism that is both classical and modern. Concerned with the relationship between body and spirit, Yourcenar's works are also philosophical.

By the late 1960s, Yourcenar had become a renowned writer. She was elected to the Belgian Royal Academy of French Language and Literature in 1971, and in 1980 she was the first woman to be elected to the Académie Française since its creation in 1635. The Pléiade edition of her works was published during Yourcenar's lifetime. Her writing is complex, which may explain why her work has received little attention from the general reading public. Furthermore, she has been accused of being a misogynist and an anti-Semite. Independent, erudite, and original, Yourcenar has also aroused suspicion due to her distance from contemporary literary movements such as the NOUVEAU ROMAN. Hers is definitely not *"écriture feminine"* (female writing). For some feminist scholars, this explains why Yourcenar, of all women, was admitted to the Académie Française. SIMONE DE BEAUVOIR called Yourcenar's acceptance into this august body a "non-event."

In the last period of her career as a writer, Yourcenar turned to her family's past. *Labyrinth of the World* was intended to consist of three volumes. *Dear Departed* appeared in 1973 and *How Many Years* in 1977. In these works, too, Yourcenar manifests her skill as a historian. Perhaps more important, Yourcenar's chronicle of her family allows her to reflect on the human condition. The last volume, *What? Eternity* was published posthumously in 1988; just before leaving for France to attend the filming of *Abyss,* Yourcenar died in her home in 1987. Two other posthumous works appeared later, *A Pilgrim Abroad* (1989) and *Prison Tower* (1991).

In her autobiographical writings, Yourcenar refers to "the being I call me." The first volume opens with Yourcenar's birth and her mother's death 10 days later, before reaching into the more distant past of her matrilineal line. In the second volume, Youcenar gives symmetry to the work by beginning in the past and then tracing her father's family into the present. Together these works blur the boundary between history and fiction. Some scholars have argued that her mother's death from complications in childbirth plays a central, if not readily apparent, role in Yourcenar's thought. On the surface, there is no evidence of the emotions one usually associates with the loss of a parent. However, these scholars view the subsequent focus in all Yourcenar's works on male figures as symbolic of the author's reaction to the absence of her mother in her life.

FURTHER READING

Farrell, C. Frederick. *Marguerite Yourcenar in Counterpoint.* Lanham, Md.: University Press of America, 1983.

Horn, Pierre L. *Marguerite Yourcenar.* Boston: Twayne, 1985.

Howard, Joan E. *From Violence to Vision: Sacrifice in the Works of Marguerite Yourcenar.* Carbondale: Southern Illinois University Press, 1992.

Sarnecki, Judith Holland, and Ingeborg Majer O'Sickey, eds. *Subversive Subjects: Reading Marguerite Yourcenar.* Madison, N.J.: Fairleigh Dickinson University Press, 2004.

Savigneau, Josyane. *Marguerite Yourcenar: Inventing a Life.* Translated by Joan E. Howard. Chicago: University of Chicago Press, 1993.

Shurr, Georgia Hooks. *Marguerite Yourcenar: A Reader's Guide.* Lanham, Md.: University Press of America, 1987.

Z

ZADIG Voltaire (1748)   While living with his companion, Madame du Châtelet, Voltaire attended parties given by the duchesse du Maine, another of his patrons. She and her intellectual guests conceived of a parlor game that was something like a letter lottery. The letter you received indicated the genre of literature you were meant to produce. In this case, C is for *conte* (tale) and *Zadig* is the result of the game. This tale, drawing on the popular 18th-century theme of Orientalism, was a great success. Later editions included additional chapters.

The preface states that the tale was supposedly translated from ancient Chaldean into Arabic, and it competed in popularity with the *Thousand and One Nights*. It is the story of Zadig, a handsome young man of good character who, through a series of misadventures, acquires wisdom and happiness.

Zadig lives in Babylon and is on the verge of marrying the beautiful Sémire when a rival tries to kidnap her. In the ensuing fight, Zadig is left blind in one eye. Sémire then no longer wants to marry him. This is not the only occasion in the novel when a woman proves to be fickle and faithless.

The loss of his fiancée is only the first of many difficulties Zadig encounters. He is forced to leave Babylon when he falls in love with queen Astarté (whom he later rescues). He is sold into slavery after helping a battered woman on the way to Egypt. Ultimately, his travails render Zadig undisputedly the wisest and most valiant of men and he is chosen to marry Astarté (then a widow) and to rule over Babylon.

Critics accused Voltaire of simply piecing together stories borrowed from Oriental tales and travel accounts. In fact, the many episodes of Zadig's life hold together well. On his long, arduous journey toward wisdom (the classical philosophical journey), Zadig is admired by some and hated by others, but he always manages to extricate himself from difficult situations with good grace. Echoing themes in Voltaire's other works, Zadig attacks unjust rulers, clerical abuse, tyranny, and frivolous, inconstant women. Zadig thus makes for agreeable reading even if it is not the masterpiece of *CANDIDE* (1758).

FURTHER READING

Bonneville, Douglas A. *Voltaire and the Form of the Novel.* Oxford: Voltaire Foundation, 1976.

Cutler, Maxine G., ed. *Voltaire, the Enlightenment, and the Comic Mode: Essays in Honor of Jean Sareil.* New York: P. Lang, 1990.

Sherman, Carol. *Reading Voltaire's Contes: A Semiotics of Philosophical Narration.* Chapel Hill: University of North Carolina Department of Romance Languages: Distributed by University of North Carolina Press, 1985.

ZAZIE IN THE METRO (ZAZIE DANS LE MÉTRO) Raymond Queneau (1959)   This novel is the story of Zazie Lalochère's two-day sojourn in Paris. Twelve years old, she goes to visit her uncle Gabriel, who works as a dancer in a caba-

ret in Montmartre. Zazie's greatest wish is to see the subway. Unfortunately, it is closed due to a strike, which Zazie takes as a personal affront. She is thus obliged to explore the capital on foot or in her friend Charles's taxi. During her adventures Zazie meets several extraordinary characters who include the widow Mouaque, gentle Marceline, and the parrot Laverdure, whose famous line is "you talk and talk; that's all you know how to do."

Queneau's most successful novel, *Zazie* includes a moral lesson on the fragility and uncertainty of the human condition. Zazie's life has not always been easy. Nonetheless, she still has a lot to learn about life and is anxious to do so. She explores the Eiffel Tower, the Invalides, the flea market, and Sacré Coeur. Zazie is, moreover, fascinated to find out whether her uncle is homosexual or, as she puts it, "hormosessuel." When she returns to the provinces, her mother asks her, "So, what did you do?" and Zazie responds, "I grew up."

Zazie has adventures while in Paris. She is also exposed to a sometimes sad and hard world. Queneau's style is simple, his language inventive and humorous. Inspired by the popular language of the streets, the novel still retains a sense of the poetic. *Zazie* was an immediate success, but readers often fail to appreciate its depth. "Being or nothingness, that's the problem. Going up, coming down, going, coming, that's what man does until eventually he disappears."

FURTHER READING

Bastin, Nina. *Queneau's Fictional Worlds*. Oxford, New York: P. Lang, 2002.

Guicharnaud, Jacques. *Raymond Queneau*. New York: Columbia University Press, 1965.

Hale, Jane Alison. *The Lyric Encyclopedia of Raymond Queneau*. Ann Arbor: University of Michigan Press, 1989.

Shorley, Christopher. *Queneau's Fiction: An Introductory Study*. Cambridge, New York: Cambridge University Press, 1985.

Stump, Jordan. *Naming and Unnaming: On Raymond Queneau*. Lincoln: University of Nebraska Press, 1998.

Thiher, Allen. *Raymond Queneau*. Boston: Twayne, 1985.

Velguth, Madeleine. *The Representation of Women in the Autobiographical Novels of Raymond Queneau*. New York: P. Lang, 1990.

ZEMGANNO BROTHERS, THE (LES FRÈRES ZEMGANNO) EDMOND HUOT DE GONCOURT (1879)

This is the story of two brothers, Gianni and Nello, who are circus performers. After losing their parents, Gianni and Nello work for a time in provincial circuses. Then they return to Paris, where they develop a famous act. Unfortunately, a horsewoman whom Nello had jilted causes him to fall in a rehearsal. Both his legs are broken, and he is forced to give up the circus life. Loyal to the end, Gianni leaves with his brother and they take up a career as fiddlers. As in a number of other works by the Goncourt brothers, a woman plays a pivotal role but not a positive one. She is destructive, bringing disorder to the brothers' lives, yet is also somehow fascinating of them.

Although Edmond and Jules de Goncourt conceived of the plot together, Edmond wrote the novel alone after his brother's death. The narrative serves as an analogy for the brothers' life together, except the pair in the novel are clowns, not writers. In essence, Edmond bids farewell to the collaborative life he led with his brother. He also reaffirms his adherence to the doctrine of REALISM, asserting that his only subjects as a novelist will be the vice and corruption of contemporary society. In this novel Edmond continues in the tradition of the brothers' earlier works in his exploration of the brutal, seamy side of life albeit in an elegant style.

FURTHER READING

Billy, André. *The Goncourt Brothers*. New York: Horizon Press, 1960.

Goncourt, E. *The Goncourt Journals, 1851–1870*. New York: Greenwood Press, 1968.

Grant, Richard B. *The Goncourt Brothers*. New York: Twayne, 1972.

ZOLA, ÉMILE (1840–1902)

Zola's father, François, was an engineer of Italian origin who, for professional reasons, moved his family from Paris to Aix-en-Provence in 1843. In Provence, Zola was a happy, successful student, and became friends with the future painter Paul Cézanne and with Jean-Baptiste Baille, who became an astronomer. With these childhood friends Zola lost himself in nature and in books, discovering the great romantic writers such as Alphonse de Lamartine, VICTOR, HUGO, and ALFRED DE MUSSET (see ROMANTICISM), writing plays and poems, and dreaming of becoming a writer. When Zola's father died he left his family in debt, and Zola's mother decided to return to Paris with her parents and children. Zola was eight years old. His father left behind the image of a champion of progress who may have inspired some of Zola's later characters, such as Octave Mouret in *The LADIES' PARADISE.*

The transition was a difficult, as life in Paris was hard and the family was very poor. Between 1858 and 1862, they moved some seven times. This experience may have contributed to Zola's later ideas about money and its role in society and one's own life, some of which shocked his contemporaries. "To be poor in Paris is to be poor twice over," he wrote in *The Kill.*

Harboring dreams of glory, Zola decided to give up his studies and look for work. The period 1860–61 was particularly trying financially yet Zola was not entirely unhappy. He discovered the historian Jules Michelet and GEORGE SAND. His friend Cézanne, also in Paris, introduced him to other painters, among them Camille Pissarro, Edouard Manet, Claude Monet, Auguste Renoir, and Alfred Sisley. Zola thus began to associate with a group of young, innovative painters, many of whom would become the future impressionists.

In 1862 Zola accepted a position at the publishing house Hachette, soon becoming head of publicity. He remained with Hachette for four years and his professional life brought him into contact with such writers as SAINTE-BEUVE. The years at Hachette were rich and active as Zola explored various intellectual and cultural movements such as POSITIVISM, LIBERALISM, and anticlericalism. His growing circle of literary acquaintances and his intellectual pursuits all came to bear on his writing.

By 1864 Zola had turned from poetry to prose with his first collection of stories, *Ninon's Tales,* and a novel drawing on his love affair with a woman named Berthe entitled *Claude's Confession.* That year Zola began living with Alexandrine Meley, whom he later married. In 1866 Zola left Hachette to make his living by his pen, regularly writing articles on literary and art criticism for a number of Parisian newspapers.

Zola was one of the few critics who praised GUSTAVE FLAUBERT's *SENTIMENTAL EDUCATION.* His defense of Manet's painting in the salon of 1866, in particular, brought him notoriety; it also caused him difficulties. Newspaper publishers were anxious about airing Zola's innovative views on literature and painting. As a result 1867 was an extremely difficult year financially but also a productive one. Zola wrote and published a serial novel (ROMAN FEUILLETON). The title of *The Mysteries of Marseille,* a love story about a republican and the daughter of a wealthy and influential aristocrat set against the backdrop of the Revolution of 1848, refers to EUGÈNE SUE's extraordinarily successful serial novel *The MYSTERIES OF PARIS.* Zola's equally successful *Thérèse Raquin* was also published in this period.

In 1868 Zola conceived of his great literary project, becoming the author we think of today, the father of NATURALISM and creator of the ROUGON-MACQUART series of 20 novels on "the Natural and Social History of a Second Empire family." The SECOND EMPIRE was the period following Louis Napoléon Bonaparte's coup d'état in 1851, after which he declared himself emperor. Bonaparte's regime witnessed the rise of wealthy businessmen who dominated the economy and politics.

Zola's purpose was to trace inherited traits through several generations. Adelaide Fouque transmits her madness first through her marriage to the industrialist Rougon and second through her affair with the alcoholic Macquart. The consequences are such that Gervaise Macquart also falls prey to alcoholism (*L'ASSOMMOIR*); her son Jacques Lantier murders his mistress (*LA BÊTE HUMAINE*); and Aristide Rougon murders his wife and his son commits incest (*The Kill*). In contrast, Étienne Latier serves as the symbol of hope to the miners of GERMINAL. Ultimately, it is possible to trace the movement in Zola's oeuvre from pessimism to messianism.

Zola adhered to the naturalist doctrine, drawing on recent developments in the sciences, especially discoveries about the role of heredity in determining character. This became the foundation for Zola's somewhat scandalous representation of contemporary moral and social values. His vision is determinist. Heredity is like destiny. Zola's parallel evocation of the individual and the multitude reveals them to be equally subject to external forces. The central metaphor within each novel, be it the still, the train, or the mine, represents an anthropomorphized force that dominates society.

Like HONORÉ DE BALZAC's COMÉDIE HUMAINE, Zola also offered extensive analysis of contemporary society in his evocation of the many and varied characteristics of Second Empire economic and political life. The rise of the Rougon family, for example, symbolizes the dominance of wealthy merchants and businessmen in the reign of Napoleon III, a period of socioeconomic transition. Yet Zola's history of a family is equally a history of society and a reflection on the human condition that reveals the author's socialist humanism.

In 1870 Zola married Alexandrine. When the Franco-Prussian War broke out in 1870, he moved with her and his mother, first to Marseille and later to Bordeaux, where he covered the National Assembly's meetings, an experience that provided him with material of a political nature for future novels. As a correspondent Zola wrote more than 800 articles covering parliament. In 1871 Zola and his family returned to Paris. The following year he signed a contract with the publisher Georges Charpentier, guaranteeing financial stability in the form of a salary 500 francs a month.

Zola's career as a writer took off as he produced a novel a year, hundreds of articles on art, literature, and theater, and two unsuccessful plays, all the while continuing to work as a journalist. Zola associated with other members of the literary world, becoming friends with Flaubert, the GONCOURT brothers, ALPHONSE DAUDUET, and Ivan Turgenev. Still relatively unknown at the publication of L'Assommoir (1877), an astonishing success, Zola became famous with the publication of NANA in 1880.

Young writers began to gravitate around Zola, who by this time had purchased a country house in Médan, outside Paris. The literary circle that met there included Paul Alexis, Henry Céard, JORIS-KARL HUYSMANS, Léon Hennique, and GUY DE MAUPASSANT. Under Zola's leadership, these men founded the naturalist school, publishing the famous Médan Evenings in 1880, a collection of naturalist novellas in which the authors reacted against the patriotic literature that flourished in the period following the Franco-Prussian

War (1870–71). They chose, in contrast, to depict the horrors of the battlefield. Their goal was demystification or demythologization by challenging a number of taboo subjects.

Over his mantelpiece Zola had written "Nulla dies sine linea" (not a day without a line). He continued to write prolifically, producing The Experimental Novel (1880), his manifesto of naturalism, and in 1881 The Naturalist Novelists, Naturalism in Theater, Our Dramatic Authors, and Literary Documents. Zola's theoretical works on the novel drew on the physiologist Claude Bernard's Introduction to Experimental Medicine (1865) to articulate the role of observation and experimentation in naturalist literature. Zola again emphasized the role of heredity in determining human behavior. The response to this approach was not entirely positive; critics accused the naturalists of pessimism and immorality in their sometimes brutal depiction of society.

Zola published a number of masterpieces of fiction: L'Assommoir (1878), Page of Love (1878), Nana (1880), Piping Hot; Ladies' Paradise (1883), Germinal (1885), and The MASTERPIECE (1886), a novel that caused his break with Cézanne. These novels were soon translated into all major European languages; Zola became famous and wealthy. More important, his naturalist school dominating European fiction of the period. In 1883 Zola wrote to an acquaintance, "All you have to write on the envelope is Émile Zola, France, for the letter to arrive." Not surprisingly, Zola's success excited the jealousy of other writers. Goncourt, Daudet, and the Médan group were vehemently critical of EARTH (1887). The famous Manifesto of the Five, written by his former collaborators, attacked Zola.

In 1888 Zola fell in love with Jeanne Rozerot, a young laundress hired by his wife. She bore him two children whom his wife generously accepted as legitimate. There is undoubtedly some influence of this experience on his writing as the Rougon-Macquart series ends on a hopeful note, closing with the image of a woman suckling her child. "I found myself feeling like I was twenty years old again, when I wanted to devour mountains."

Toward the end of his life, Zola set off in a new direction with Three Cities: Lourdes (1894), Rome (1896) and Paris (1898) and The Four Gospels: Fruit-

fulness (1899), *Labor* (1901), *Justice,* and *Truth* (1903). This last productive period is also remembered for the strong position Zola took in the Dreyfus affair (in which a Jewish officer was wrongly accused of treason and convicted in 1894), publishing his famous letter to the president of the Republic, *"J'Accuse,"* in 1898. Zola was subsequently fined 3,000 francs and sentenced to a year in prison but he left for the safety of England, returning to France the next year. He died in 1902, a great writer yet never admitted to the Académie Française. Zola's passion for truth and justice resonates throughout his works and continues to attract readers today.

FURTHER READING

Barbusse, Henri. *Zola.* Translated by Mary Balairdie Green and Frederick C. Green. New York: E. P. Dutton, 1933.

Bell, David. *Real Time: Accelerating Narrative from Balzac to Zola.* Urbana: University of Illinois Press, 2004.

Berg, William J., and Laurey K. Martin. *Émile Zola Revisited.* New York: Twayne; Toronto: Maxwell Macmillan Canada; New York: Maxwell Macmillan International: 1992.

Bloom, Harold, ed. *Émile Zola.* Philadelphia: Chelsea House. 2004.

Bowlby, Rachel. *Just Looking: Consumer Culture in Dreiser, Gissing and Zola.* New York: Methuen, 1985.

Brown, Frederick. *Zola: A Life.* Baltimore: Johns Hopkins University Press, 1996.

Chessid, Ilona. *Thresholds of Desire: Authority and Transgression in the Rougon-Macquart.* New York: P. Lang, 1993.

Friedman, Lee M. *Zola and the Dreyfus Case: His Defense of Liberty and Its Enduring Significance.* Boston: Beacon Press, 1937.

Gallois, William. *Zola: The History of Capitalism.* Oxford, New York: P. Lang, 2000.

Hemmings, F. W. J. *Émile Zola.* Oxford: Clarendon Press, 1966.

———. *The Life and Times of Émile Zola.* New York: Scribner, 1977.

Lapp, John C. *Zola Before the Rougon-Macquart.* Toronto: University of Toronto Press, 1964.

Lethbridge, Robert, and Terry Keefe, eds. *Zola and the Craft of Fiction.* Leicester, New York: Leicester University Press, 1990.

Lukács, Georg. *Studies in European Realism.* Translated by Edith Bone. New York: Grosset and Dunlop, 1964.

Petrey, Sandy. *Realism and Revolution: Balzac, Stendhal, Zola and the Performance of History.* Ithaca, N.Y.: Cornell University Press, 1988.

Schom, Alan. *Émile Zola: A Bourgeois Rebel.* London: Queen Anne Press, 1987.

Walker, Philip. *Zola.* London: Routledge and Kegan Paul, 1985.

LIST OF TITLES IN FRENCH

In the body of this book, entries on novels are listed in alphabetical order according to the standard published English translation of the French title. To assist readers who may be familiar only with the French title or with a variant of the standard English title, we have listed below, in alphabetical order, the French titles of novels with entries in this book and their corresponding standard English translations, under which the entry can be found. Only those novels whose French title is substantially different from the English version have been included here. For example, Flaubert's *Madame Bovary*, which is always given in English as *Madame Bovary*, is not included; however, his *Un coeur simple*, usually translated in English as *A Simple Heart*, is included.

FRENCH TITLE

120 journées de Sodome, Les
Adventures de Jerome Bardini
Aline et Valcour
L'Amant
À l'Ami qui ne m'a pas sauvé la vie
L'Amour fou
Angoisses douleureuses qui procèdent d'amours, Les
L'Argent
Armoires vides, Les
Artamène, ou le grand Cyrus
L'Astrée
Atala, ou les amours de deux sauvages dans le désert
L'Atlantide
Au Bonheur des dames
Au Château d'Argol
Aventures de Télémaque, fils d'Ulysse, Les
Baiser au lépreux, Le
Bal du comte d'Orgel, La
Balcon en forêt, Un
Barrage contre le Pacifique

ENGLISH TITLE

One Hundred Twenty Days of Sodom
Adventures of Jerome Bardini, The
Crimes of Love
Lover, The
To the Friend Who Did Not Save My Life
Mad Love
Torments of Love, The
Money
Cleaned Out
Artamène, Or the Great Cyrus
Astrea
Atala, or the Love of Two Savages in the Desert
Atlantida
Ladies' Paradise, The
Castle of Argol, The
Adventures of Telemachus, The
Kiss for the Leper, A
Count d'Orgel's Ball
Balcony in the Forest, A
Sea Wall, The

Beau ténébreux, Un	*Beautiful Tenebrous*
Beaux Quartiers, Les	*Residential Quarter*
Bijoux indiscrets, Les	*Indiscrete Jewels, The*
Blanche ou l'oubli	*Blanche or Forgetting*
Blé en herbe, Le	*Ripening Seed, The*
Bleu du ciel, Le	*Blue of Noon*
Bonheur d'occasion	*Tin Flute, The*
Bouts de bois de Dieu, Les	*God's Bits of Wood*
Caves du Vatican, Les	*Lafcadio's Adventures*
Chanson de Roland	*Song of Roland, The*
Chaque Homme dans sa nuit	*Each Man in his Night*
Chartreuse de Parme, La	*Charterhouse of Parma, The*
Château des Carpathes, Le	*Castle of the Carpathians, The*
Cheval de Troie	*Trojan Horse*
Chiendent, Le	*Witch Grass*
Choses, Les	*Things, A Story of the Sixties*
Chroniques maritales	*Marital Chronicles*
Chute, La	*Fall, The*
Cinq semaines en ballon	*Around the World in Eighty Days*
Claudine à l'école	*Claudine at School*
Claudine à Paris	*Claudine in Paris*
Clélie	*Clelia*
Coeur simple, Un	*Simple Heart, A*
Colline inspirée, La	*Sacred Hill, The*
Comédie humaine, La	*Human Comedy, The*
Companion du Tour de France, Le	*Journeyman Joiner or Companion of the Tour de France*
Comte de Monte Cristo, Le	*Count of Monte Cristo, The*
Condition humaine, La	*Man's Fate*
Confession d'un enfant du siècle, La	*Confessions of a Child of the Century, The*
*Confessions de Comte de ***, Les*	*Confessions of Count ***, The*
Conquérants, Les	*Conquerors, The*
Conspiration, La	*Conspiracy, The*
Contes cruels	*Sardonic Tales*
Corinne, ou l'Italie	*Corinne, or Italy*
La Cousine Bette	*Cousin Bette*
Crime de Sylvestre Bonnard, Le	*Crime of Sylvester Bonnard, The*
Croix de bois, Les	*Wooden Crosses*
Curée, La	*Venus of the Counting House*
Dame aux camélias, La	*Camille*
Débâcle, La	*Downfall, The*
Dedans	*Inside*
Déracinés, Les	*Uprooted, The*
Désordres de l'amour, Les	*Disorders of Love, The*
Diable au corps, Le	*Devil in the Flesh, The*
Diable boiteux, Le	*Devil Upon Two Sticks, The*

Dieux ont soif, Les	*Gods Will Have Blood, The*
Docteur Pascal, Le	*Doctor Pascal*
L'Écume des jours	*Froth on the Day Dream*
L'Éducation sentimentale	*Sentimental Education*
Égarements du coeur et de l'esprit, Les	*Wayward Head and Heart, The*
L'Emploi du temps	*Passing Time*
Encyclopédie	*Encyclopedia*
L'Enfant de sable	*Sand Child, The*
L'Enfant noir	*Dark Child*
Enfants terribles, Les	*Holy Terrors, The*
Erec et Enide	*Erec and Enide*
L'Espoir	*Hope*
États et empires de la lune et du soleil, Les	*States and Empires of the Moon and Sun, The*
L'Étranger	*Stranger, The*
L'Eve future	*Tomorrow's Eve*
Faux monnayeurs, Les	*Counterfeiters, The*
Femme gelée, La	*Frozen Woman, A*
Femme pauvre, La	*Woman Who Was Poor, The*
Femme, Une	*Woman's Story, A*
Feu follet, Le	*Will o' the Wisp*
Feu, Le	*Under Fire*
Fille aux yeux d'or, La	*Girl with the Golden Eyes, The*
Fous de Bassan, Les	*In the Shadow of the Wind*
François le champi	*François the Waif*
Frères Zemganno, Les	*Zemganno Brothers, The*
Gaspard des montagnes	*Gaspard of the Mountains*
Génie du Christianisme, Le	*Genius of Christianity, The*
Géorgiques, Les	*Georgics, The*
Gestes et opinions du Docteur Faustroll, pataphysicien	*Doctor Faustroll*
Gil Blas de Santillane	*Adventures of Gil Blas de Santillane, The*
Grand Meaulnes, Le	*Wanderer, The*
Grande Maison, La	*Big House, The (Algeria Trilogy)*
Grande peur dans la montagne, La	*Terror on the Mountain*
Guillaume de Dole	*Romance of the Rose, The or Guillaume de Dole*
Histoire contemporaine	*Contemporary History*
Histoire de Madame de Luz	*History of Madame de Luz, The*
L'Homme qui dort	*Man Who Sleeps, The*
L'Homme qui rit	*Man Who Laughs, The*
Hommes de bonne volonté, Les	*Men of Good Will*
Hussard sur le toit, Le	*Hussar on the Roof, The*
L'Île des pengouins	*Penguin Island*
L'Île mystérieuse	*Mysterious Island, The*
Illusions perdues, Les	*Lost Illusions*
L'Immoraliste	*Immoralist, The*
L'Incendie	*Fire (Algeria Trilogy)*

L'Innommable	Unnameable, The
L'Inquisitoire	Inquisitory, The
L'Invitée	She Came to Stay
Jacqou le croquant	Jack the Rebel
Jacques le Fataliste	Jack the Fatalist and His Master
Jalousie, La	Jealousy
Jeunes filles, Les	Unmarried Girls
Journal d'un curé de campagne	Diary of a Country Priest, The
Juif errant, Le	Wandering Jew, The
Justine, ou les malheurs de la vertu	Justine, Or the Misfortunes of Virtue
La Maison de Claudine	Claudine's Home
Là-Bas	Damned, The
Lac, Le	Lake, The
Lauriers sont coupés, Les	We'll to the Woods No More
Lettres d'une Péruvienne	Letters of a Peruvian Princess
Lettres de Mistriss Fanni Butlerd	Letters of Mistress Fanny Butlerd, The
Lettres de mon moulin	Letters from My Mill
Lettres de Mistriss Henley publiées par son ami	Letters of Mistress Henley
Lettres écrites de Lausanne and Caliste ou suite des lettre écrites de Lausanne	Letters Written from Lausanne
Lettres persanes, Les	Persian Letters, The
Liaisons dangéreuses, Les	Dangerous Liaisons
Livre de la cité des dames, Le	Book of the City of Ladies, The
Lois de l'hospitalité, Les	Laws of Hospitality, The
Lys dans la vallée, Le	Lily of the Valley
Madame Chrysanthème	Madame Chrysanthemum
Maîtres sonneurs, Les	Bagpipers, The
Malone meurt	Malone Dies
Mandarins, Les	Mandarins, The
Mare au diable, La	Devil's Pool, The
Mémoires d'Hadrien, Les	Memoirs of Hadrian, The
Mémoires du comte de Comminge, Les	Memoirs of the Count of Comminge, The
Météores, Les	Gemini
Métier à Tisser, Le	Tunisian Loom (Algeria Trilogy)
Monde comme il va, Le	World as It Is, The
Mont Analogue, Le	Mount Analogue
Mort à crédit	Death on the Installment Plan
Mots pour le dire, Les	Words to Say It, The
Mystères de Paris, Les	Mysteries of Paris, The
Naissance du jour, La	Break of Day
Nausée, La	Nausea
Neveu de Rameau, Le	Rameau's Nephew
Noeud de vipères, Le	Viper's Nest
Notre-Dame de Paris	Hunchback of Notre Dame, The
Notre Dame des Fleurs	Our Lady of the Flowers

Nourritures terrestres, Les	*Fruits of the Earth*
Nouvelle Héloïse, La	*Julie, or the New Héloïse*
Nuit	*Night*
Nuit sacrée, La	*Sacred Night, The*
Ombre sultane	*Sister to Scheherazade, The*
L'Œuvre	*Masterpiece, The*
L'Œuvre au noir	*Abyss*
Passé simple, Le	*Simple Past, The*
Passion simple	*Simple Passion*
Paul et Virginie	*Paul and Virginia*
Paysan de Paris, Le	*Paris Peasant*
Paysan parvenu, Le	*Upstart Peasant, The*
Peau de chagrin, La	*Magic Skin, The*
Pêcheur d'Islande	*Iceland Fisherman, An*
Père Goriot, Le	*Father Goriot*
Particules élémentaires, Les	*Elementary Particles, The*
Peste, La	*Plague, The*
Petit Prince, Le	*Little Prince, The*
Philosophie dans le boudoir, La	*Bedroom Philosophers, The*
Pierre et Jean	*Pierre and Jean*
Place, La	*Man's Place*
Planétarium, La	*Planetarium, The*
Pluie et vent sur Télumée Miracle	*Bridge Beyond, The*
Porte étroite, La	*Strait Is the Gate*
Princesse de Clèves, La	*Princess of Cleves, The*
Quart Livre de Pantagruel	*Book Four*
Quatre-vingt treize	*Ninety-Three*
Quelqu'un	*Someone*
Ravissement de Lol v. Stein, Le	*Ravishing of Lol v. Stein, The*
À Rebours	*Against the Grain*
À la Recherche du temps perdu	*Remembrance of Things Past*
Regain	*Renewal*
reine Margot, La	*Queen Margot*
Religieuse, La	*Nun, The*
Rivage des Syrtes, Le	*Opposing Shore, The*
Roi des aulnes, Le	*Erl-King, The*
Roi miraculé, Le	*King Lazarus*
Roman bourgeois	*Bourgeois Novel*
Roman d'un enfant, Le	*Story of a Child, The*
Rouge et le noir, Le	*Red and the Black, The*
Saison dans la vie d'Emmanuel, Une	*Season in the Life of Emmanuel, A*
Sang noir, Le	*Bitter Victory*
Sans famille	*Foundling, The*
Semaine de bonté, Une	*Kindness Week*
Siècle des Lumières, Le	*Enlightenment*

Siège de Calais, Le	*Siege of Calais, The*
Siegfried et le Limousin	*My Friend from Limousin*
Silence de la mer	*Silence of the Sea*
Soeurs Vatard, Les	*Vatard Sisters, The*
Soleils des indépendances, Les	*Suns of Independence, The*
Sous le Soleil de satan	*Under Satan's Sun*
Surmâle, Le	*Supermale*
Surprise de vivre, La	*Surprise of Living, The*
Symphonie pastorale, La	*Pastoral Symphony, The*
Télévision, La	*Television*
Tentation de saint Antoine	*Temptation of Saint Anthony, The*
Terre des hommes	*Wind, Sand and Stars*
Terre, La	*Earth*
Thérèse Philosophe, ou Mémoires pour servir a l'histoire de P. Dirrag et de Mlle Éradice.	*Thérèse Philosophe, Or the History of Father Dirrag and Mademoiselle Éradice*
Thibault, Les	*Thibaults, The*
Thomas l'Obscur	*Thomas the Obscure*
Tiers Livre des faits et dits héroïques du noble Pantagruel	*Book Three*
Travailleurs de la mer, Les	*Toilers of the Sea, The*
Traversée de la mangrove	*Crossing the Mangrove*
Trois Mousquetaires, Les	*Three Musketeers, The*
Vendredi ou les limbes du Pacifique	*Friday*
Ventre de Paris, Le	*Belly of Paris, The*
Vie de Marianne, La	*Life of Marianne, The*
Vie mode d'emploi, La	*Life, A User's Manual*
Vie sur Epsilon, La	*Life on Epsilon*
Vingt Ans après	*Twenty Years After*
Vingt mille Lieues sous les mers	*Twenty Thousand Leagues under the Sea*
Vipère au poing	*Viper in Hand*
Voie royale, La	*Royal Way, The*
Vol de nuit	*Night Flight*
Volupté	*Sensual Man, The*
Voyage au bout de la nuit	*Journey to the End of the Night*
Voyage au centre de la terre	*Journey to the Center of the Earth*
Zazie dans le métro	*Zazie in the Metro*

SELECTED BIBLIOGRAPHY

Adereth, M. *Commitment in Modern French Literature: Politics and Society in Péguy, Aragon and Sartre.* New York: Schocken, 1968.

Alter, R. *Partial Magic: The Novel as a Self-Conscious Genre.* Berkeley: University of California Press, 1975.

Atack, M. *Literature and the French Resistance.* Manchester, England: Manchester University Press, 1989.

Atack, M., and P. Powrie, eds. *Contemporary French Fiction by Women: Feminist Perspectives.* Manchester, England: Manchester University Press, 1990.

Auerbach, E. *Mimesis: The Representation of Reality in Western Literature.* Princeton, N.J.: Princeton University Press, 1968.

Badran, M., and M. Cooke, eds. *Opening the Gates: A Century of Arab Feminist Writing.* London: Virago, 1990.

Baguley, D. *Naturalist Fiction. The Entropic Vision.* Cambridge: Cambridge University Press, 1990.

Bal, M. *Narratology: Introduction to the Theory of Narrative.* Toronto, London: University of Toronto Press, 1985.

Balakian, Anna, ed. *The Symbolist Movement in the Literature of the European Languages.* Budapest: Akadémiai Kiadó, 1982.

Barnes, H. E. *Humanistic Existentialism: The Literature of Possibility.* Lincoln: University of Nebraska Press, 1959.

Benjamin, A., ed. *The Lyotard Reader.* Oxford: Blackwell, 1989.

Bennington, G. *Lyotard. Writing the Event.* Manchester, England: Manchester University Press, 1988.

———. *Sententiousness and the Novel: Laying Down the Law in Eighteenth-Century Fiction.* Cambridge: Cambridge University Press, 1991.

Bersani, L. *Balzac to Beckett: Center and Circumference in French Fiction.* New York: Oxford University Press, 1970.

Birkett, J. *The Sins of the Fathers: Decadence in France, 1870–1914.* London: Quartet Books, 1986.

Blair, D. S. *African Literature in French.* Cambridge: Cambridge University Press, 1976.

Booth, W. C. *The Rhetoric of Fiction.* Chicago: University of Chicago Press, 1983.

Brée, G., and M. Guitton. *An Age of Fiction: The French Novel from Gide to Camus.* London: Chatto and Windus, 1958.

Britton, C. *The Nouveau Roman: Fiction, Theory and Politics.* Basingstoke, England: Macmillan, 1992.

Brombert, V. *The Intellectual Hero: Studies in the French Novel, 1880–1955.* Chicago: University of Chicago Press, 1964.

———. *The Romantic Prison.* Princeton, N.J.: Princeton University Press, 1978.

Brooks, P. *The Novel of Worldliness: Crébillon, Marivaux, Laclos, Stendhal.* Princeton, N.J.: Princeton University Press, 1969.

———. *Reading for the Plot: Design and Intention in Narrative.* New York: Knopf, 1984.

Butler, J. *Gender Trouble: Feminism and the Subversion of Identity.* London, New York: Routledge, 1990.

Calinescu, M. *The Five Faces of Modernity: Modernism, Avant-Garde, Decadence, Kitsch, Postmodernism.* Durham, N.C.: Duke University Press, 1987.

Carter, A. E. *The Idea of Decadence in French Literature.* Toronto: University of Toronto Press, 1958.

Cassirer, E. *The Philosophy of the Enlightenment.* Translated by Fritz C. A. Koelln and James P. Pettegrove. Princeton, N.J.: Princeton University Press, 1951.

Chambers, I. *Border Dialogues: Journeys in Postmodernity.* London: Routledge, 1990.

Chambers, R. *Story and Situation: Narrative Seduction and the Power of Fiction.* Manchester, England: Manchester University Press, 1984.

Charlton, D. G., ed. *The French Romantics,* 2 Vols. Cambridge: Cambridge University Press, 1984.

———. *Positivist Thought in France (1872–1870).* Oxford: Clarendon Press, 1959.

Cheal Pugh, A., ed. *France 1940: Literary and Historical Reaction to Defeat.* Durham, N.C.: University of Durham, 1991.

Compagnon, A., and J. Lough. *Writer and Public in France.* Oxford: Clarendon Press, 1978.

Cook. M. *Fictional France: Social Reality in the French Novel, 1775–1800.* Providence, Oxford: Berg, 1993.

Cruickshank, J., ed. *The Novelist as Philosopher: Studies in French Fiction 1935–1960.* London: Oxford University Press, 1962.

———. *Variations on Catastrophe: Some French Responses to the Great War.* Oxford: Oxford University Press, 1982.

Cryle, P. M. *The Thematics of Commitment.* Princeton, N.J.: Princeton University Press, 1985.

DeJean, J. *Tender Geographies: Women and the Origins of the Novel in France.* New York, Oxford: Columbia University Press, 1991.

DeJean, J., and N. K. Miller, eds. *Displacements: Women, Tradition, Literatures in French.* Baltimore, London: Johns Hopkins University Press, 1991.

Duchen, C. *Feminism in France from May '68 to Mitterrand.* London: Routledge and Kegan Paul, 1986.

Ellmann, M., ed. and intro., 1991. *Psychoanalytic Literary Criticism.* London, New York: Longman, 1994.

Engleton, M., ed. *Feminist Literary Criticism.* London: Longman, 1991.

Fallaize, E. *French Women's Writing: Recent Fiction.* London: Macmillan, 1993.

Field, F. *Three French Writers and the Great War.* Cambridge: Cambridge University Press, 1975.

Flower, J. *Linguistics and the Novel.* London, New York: Methuen, 1977.

———. *Literature and the Left in France.* London: Methuen, 1985.

———. *Writers and Politics in Modern France.* London: Hodder and Stoughton, 1977.

France, P., ed. *The New Oxford Companion to Literature in French.* Oxford: Oxford University Press, 1995.

Gallop, J. *The Daughter's Seduction: Feminism and Psychoanalysis.* Ithaca, N.Y.: Cornell University Press, 1982.

Green, G., and C. Kahn, eds. *Making a Difference: Feminist Literary Criticism.* London: Methuen, 1985.

Green, M. J. *Fiction in the Historical Present: French Writers and the Thirties.* Hanover, N.H.; London: University Press of New England, 1986.

Greenberg, Mitchell. *Subjectivity and Subjugation in Seventeenth-Century Drama and Prose: The Family Romance of French Classicism.* Cambridge: Cambridge University Press, 1992.

Griffiths, R. *The Reactionary Revolution: The Catholic Revival in French Literature, 1870–1914.* London: Constable, 1966.

Harasym, S., ed. *The Post-Colonial Critic: Interviews, Strategies, Dialogues.* London: Routledge, 1990.

Hargreaves, A. G. *Voices from the North African Immigrant Community in France: Immigration and Identity in Beur Fiction.* New York, Oxford: Berg, 1991.

Hargreaves, A. G., and M. J. Heffernen. *French and Algerian Identities from Colonial Times to the Present: A Century of Interaction.* Lewiston, N.Y.: Mellen Press, 1993.

Harris, F. J. *Encounters with Darkness: French and German Writers on World War II.* New York: Oxford University Press, 1983.

Hawkes, T. *Structuralism and Semiotics.* London: Methuen, 1977.

Heath, S. *The Nouveau Roman: A Study in the Practice of Writing.* London: Elek, 1970.

Hewitt, N. *'Les Maladies du Siècle': The Image of Malaise in French Fiction and Thought in the Inter-War Years.* Hull, England: Hull University Press, 1988.

———. *Literature and the Right in Post-War France. The Story of the 'Hussards'.* New York, Oxford: Berg, 1996.

Hinde Stewart, J. *Gynographs: French Novels by Women of the Late Eighteenth Century.* Lincoln, London: University of Nebraska Press, 1993.

Hollier, D., and R. H. Block, eds. *A New History of French Literature.* Cambridge, Mass.: Harvard University Press, 1989.

Hughes, A., and K. Ince, eds. *French Erotic Fiction: Women's Desiring Writing.* Washington D.C.: Berg, 1996.

Hunt, L., ed. *Eroticism and the Body Politic.* Baltimore: Johns Hopkins University Press, 1991.

Hutcheon, L. *A Poetics of Postmodernism: History, Theory, Fiction.* London: Routledge: 1988.

Jefferson, A. *The Nouveau Roman and the Poetics of Fiction.* Cambridge: Cambridge University Press, 1980.

Kadish, D. *Politicizing Gender: Narrative Strategies in the Aftermath of the French Revolution.* New Brunswick: Rutgers University Press, 1991; *Surrealism and the Novel.* Ann Arbor: Michigan University Press, 1966.

King, A. *French Women Novelists: Defining a Female Style.* London: Macmillan, 1989.

Klein, H., ed. *The First World War in Fiction.* London: Macmillan, 1976.

Laubier, C., ed. *The Condition of Women in France: 1945 to the Present.* London, New York: Routledge, 1990.

Lionnet, F. *Autobiographical Voices: Race, Gender, Self-Portraiture.* Ithaca, N.Y.: Cornell University Press, 1989.

———. *Postcolonial Representations: Women, Literature, Identity.* Ithaca, N.Y.: Cornell University Press, 1995.

Lukacs, G. *The Historical Novel.* London: Merlin Press, 1962.

———. *Studies in European Realism.* London: Merlin Press, 1972.

———. *The Theory of the Novel.* London: Merlin, 1971.

Macey, D. *Lacan in Contexts.* London, New York: Verso, 1988.

Magraw, R. *France 1815–1914:* The Bourgeois Century. London: Fontana, 1983.

Marks, E., and I. De Coutivron. *New French Feminisms: An Anthology.* Brighton, England: Harvester, 1981.

Matthews, J. H. *The Imagery of Surrealism.* Syracuse, N.Y.: Syracuse University Press, 1977.

McFarlane, I. D. *A Literary History of France. Vol. II: Renaissance France 1470–1589.* London: E. Benn, 1974.

Miller, C. *Blank Darkness: Africanist Discourse in French.* Chicago: University of Chicago Press, 1985.

———. *Theories of Africans: Francophone Literature and Anthropology in Africa.* Chicago: University of Chicago Press, 1990.

Miller, N. *Subject to Change: Reading Feminist Writing.* New York: Columbia University Press, 1988.

Moi, T., ed. *French Feminist Thought: A Reader.* Oxford: Basil Blackwell, 1987.

———. *Sexual/Textual Politics.* London, New York: Methuen, 1985.

Mortimer, M. *Journeys through the French African Novel.* Portsmouth, N.H.; London: Heinemann Educational Books and James Currey, 1990.

Motte, W. F., ed. *Oulipo: A Primer of Potential Literature.* Lincoln: University of Nebraska Press, 1986.

Mulhearn, F., ed. and intro. *Contemporary Marxist Literary Criticism.* London, New York: Longman, 1992.

Mylne, V. *The Eighteenth-Century French Novel: Techniques of Illusion.* Cambridge: Cambridge University Press, 1981.

Nelson, B., ed. *Naturalism in the European Novel. New Critical Perspectives.* New York, Oxford: Berg, 1992.

New, W. H. *A History of Canadian Literature.* London: Macmillan, 1989.

Newton, J., and D. Rosenfelt, eds. *Feminist Criticism and Social Change: Sex, Class and Race in Literature and Culture.* London: Methuen, 1985.

Ngaté, J. *Francophone African Fiction: Reading a Literary Tradition.* Trenton, N.J.: Africa World Press, 1988.

Paul, H. W. *From Knowledge to Power: The Rise of the Science Empire in France.* Cambridge: Cambridge University Press, 1985.

Peyre, H. *French Novelists Today.* Oxford: Oxford University Press, 1967.

Poster, M. *Existential Marxism in Postwar France, from Sartre to Althusser.* Princeton, N.J.: Princeton University Press, 1977.

———, ed. and intro. *Jean Beaudrillard: Selected Writings.* Cambridge: Polity Press, 1988.

Praz, M. *The Romantic Agony.* London: Oxford University Press, 1970.

Prendergast, C. *The Order of Mimesis.* Cambridge: Cambridge University Press, 1986.

Prince, G. *Narratology: The Form and Functioning of Narrative.* Berlin; New York, Amsterdam: Mouton, 1982.

Ray, W. *Story and History: Narrative Authority and Social Identity in the Eighteenth-Century French and English Novel.* Cambridge, Mass.; Oxford: Basil Blackwell, 1990.

Reader, K. *The May 1968 Events in France: Reproductions and Interpretations.* London: Macmillan, 1993.

Rigby, B., ed. *French Literature, Thought and Culture in the Nineteenth Century: A Material World: Essays in Honor of D. G. Charlton.* London: Macmillan, 1993.

Robinson, C. *Scandal in the Ink: Male and Female Homosexuality in Twentieth-Century French Literature.* London: Cassell, 1995.

Rose, A. *Surrealism and Communism. The Early Years.* New York: Peter Lang, 1991.

Saïd, E. *Orientalism.* London: Routledge and Kegan Paul, 1978.

Scott, M. *The Struggle for the Soul of the French Novel: French Catholic and Realist Novelists 1850–1970.* London: Macmillan, 1989.

Selden, R., and P. Widdowson. *A Reader's Guide to Contemporary Literary Theory.* Hemel Hempstead, U.K.: Harvester Wheatsheaf, 1993.

Sellers, S., ed. *Writing Differences: Readings from the Seminar of Hélène Cixous.* Milton Keynes: Open University Press, 1988.

Shattuck, R. *The Banquet Years: Origins of the Avant-Garde in France, 1885 to World War I.* New York: Vintage Books, 1968.

Shek, B.-Z. *Social Realism in the French-Canadian Novel.* Montreal: Harvest House, 1977.

Smith Allen, J. *Popular French Romanticism: Authors, Readers and Books in the Nineteenth Century.* Syracuse, N.Y.: Syracuse University Press, 1981.

Smyth, E. J., ed. *Postmodernism and Contemporary Fiction.* London: Batsford, 1991.

Spivak, G. C. *In Other Worlds: Essays in Cultural Politics.* London: Methuen, 1987.

Still, J., and M. Worton. *Textuality and Sexuality: Reading Theories and Practices.* Manchester, England: Manchester University Press, 1993.

Stambolian, G. and E. Marks, eds. *Homosexualities and French Literature.* Ithaca, N.Y.; London: Cornell University Press, 1979.

Suleiman, S. R. *Authoritarian Fictions: The Ideological Novel as a Literary Genre.* Princeton, N.J.: Princeton University Press, 1993.

Tanner, T. *Adultery in the Novel.* Baltimore: Johns Hopkins University Press, 1979.

Teich, M., and R. Porter, eds. *Fin de siècle and Its Legacy.* Cambridge: Cambridge University Press, 1990.

Tilby, M., ed. *Beyond the Nouveau Roman.* London, New York: Berg, 1990.

Todd, C. *A Century of Best-Sellers (1890–1990).* Lewiston, N.Y.; Queenston; Lampeter: E. Mellen, 1994.

Uitti, K. D. *The Concept of the Self in the Symbolist Novel.* The Hague, Paris: Mouton, 1961.

Waller, M. *The Male Malady: Fictions of Impotence in the French Romantic Novel.* New Brunswick, N.J.: Rutgers University Press, 1993.

Welleck, R., and A. Warren. *Theory of Literature.* New York: Harcourt, 1956.

Woodhill, W. *Transfigurations of the Maghreb: Feminism, Decolonization and Literatures.* Minneapolis: University of Minnesota Press, 1993.

Yager Kaplan, A. *Reproductions of Banality: Fascism, Literature and the French Intellectual Left.* Minneapolis: University of Minnesota Press, 1986.

INDEX

Boldface page numbers denote extensive treatment of a topic.